Communications
in Computer and Information Science 203

Dhinaharan Nagamalai Eric Renault
Murugan Dhanuskodi (Eds.)

Advances in Parallel, Distributed Computing

First International Conference on Parallel, Distributed Computing Technologies and Applications, PDCTA 2011
Tirunelveli, Tamil Nadu, India, September 23-25, 2011
Proceedings

Springer

Volume Editors

Dhinaharan Nagamalai
Wireilla Net Solutions PTY Ltd
Melbourne, VIC, Australia
E-mail: dhinthia@yahoo.com

Eric Renault
Institut Telecom/Telecom SudParis (ex. GET-INT)
Departement Reseaux et Services Multimedia Mobiles (RS2M)
Samovar UMR INT-CNRS 5157
9, rue Charles Fourier, 91011 Evry Cedex, France
E-mail: eric.renault@it-sudparis.eu

Murugan Dhanuskodi
Manonmaniam Sundaranar University
Department of Computer Science and Engineering
Tirunelveli, Tamil Nadu, India
E-mail: dhanushkodim@yahoo.com

ISSN 1865-0929
ISSN 1865-0937 (eBook)
ISBN 978-3-642-24036-2
ISBN 978-3-642-24037-9 (eBook)
DOI 10.1007/978-3-642-24037-9
Springer Heidelberg Dordrecht London New York

Library of Congress Control Number: Applied for

CR Subject Classification (1998): C.2, H.4, I.2, H.3, D.2, H.5

Typesetting: Camera-ready by author, data conversion by Scientific Publishing Services, Chennai, India

Printed on acid-free paper

Springer is part of Springer Science+Business Media (www.springer.com)

Preface

The First International Conference on Computer Science, Engineering and Information Technology (CCSEIT-2011), The First International Conference on Parallel, Distributed Computing Technologies and Applications (PDCTA-2011), and The First International Conference on Digital Image Processing and Pattern Recognition (DPPR-2011) were held in Tirunelveli - Tamil Nadu, India, during September 23–25, 2011. The events attracted many local and international delegates, presenting a balanced mixture of intellects from all over the world. The goal of this conference series is to bring together researchers and practitioners from academia and industry to focus on understanding parallel, distributed computing technologies, digital image processing and pattern recognition and all areas of computer science, information technology, and to establish new collaborations in these areas.

The CCSEIT 2011, PDCTA 2011 and DPPR 2011 committees invited original submissions from researchers, scientists, engineers, and students that illustrate research results, projects, survey works, and industrial experiences describing significant advances in the areas related to the relevant themes and tracks of the conferences. This effort guaranteed submissions from an unparalleled number of internationally recognized top-level researchers. All the submissions underwent a strenuous peer-review process which comprised expert reviewers. Besides the members of the Technical Program Committee, external reviewers were invited on the basis of their specialization and expertise. The papers were reviewed based on their technical content, originality, and clarity. The entire process, which includes the submission, review, and acceptance processes, was done electronically. All these efforts undertaken by the Organizing and Technical Program Committees led to an exciting, rich, and high-quality technical conference program, which featured high-impact presentations for all attendees to enjoy and to expand their expertise in the latest developments in this field.

There were a total 1,256 submissions to the conference, and the Technical Program Committee selected 185 papers for presentation at the conference and subsequent publication in the proceedings. This small introduction would be incomplete without expressing our gratitude and thanks to the General and Program Chairs, members of the Technical Program Committees, and external reviewers for their excellent and diligent work. Thanks to Springer for the strong support. Finally, we thank all the authors who contributed to the success of the conference. We also sincerely wish that all attendees benefited academically from the conference and wish them every success in their research.

Dhinaharan Nagamalai
Eric Renault
Murugan Dhanushkodi

Organization

General Chairs

David C. Wyld	Southeastern Louisiana University, USA
Michal Wozniak	Wroclaw University of Technology, Poland

Steering Committee Chairs

Murugan Dhanuskodi	Manonmaniam Sundaranar University, India
Jan Zizka	SoNet/DI, FBE, Mendel University in Brno, Czech Republic
John Karamitsos	University of the Aegean, Samos, Greece
Khoa N. Le	University of Western Sydney, Australia
Nabendu Chaki	University of Calcutta, India
Salah S. Al-Majeed	University of Essex, UK
Dhinaharan Nagamalai	Wireilla Net Solutions, Australia

Publicity Chairs

Roberts Masillamani	Hindustan University, India
Chih-Lin Hu	National Central University, Taiwan

Program Committee

A. Arokiasamy	Eastern Mediterranean University, Cyprus
A.P. Sathish Kumar	PSG Institute of Advanced Studies, India
Abdul Aziz	University of Central Punjab, Pakistan
Abdul Kadir Ozcan	The American University, Cyprus
Al-Sakib Khan Pathan	Kyung Hee University, South Korea
Andreas Riener	Johannes Kepler University Linz, Austria
Andy Seddon	Asia Pacific Institute of Information Technology, Malaysia
Antelin Vijila	Manonmaniam Sundaranar University, India
Arvinth Kumar	M.S. University, India
Athanasios Vasilakos	University of Western Macedonia, Greece
Atilla Elci	Eastern Mediterranean University, Cyprus
B. Srinivasan	Monash University, Australia

Balasubramaniam	Manonmaniam Sundaranar University, India
Bong-Han Kim	Chongju University , South Korea
Boo-Hyung Lee	KongJu National University, South Korea
Brajesh Kumar Kaushik	Indian Institute of Technology, India
Charalampos Z. Patrikakis	National Technical University of Athens, Greece
Chih-Lin Hu	National Central University, Taiwan
Chin-Chih Chang	Chung Hua University, Taiwan
Cho Han Jin	Far East University, South Korea
Cynthia Dhinakaran	Hannam University, South Korea
Danda B. Rawat	Old Dominion University, USA
David W. Deeds	Shingu College, South Korea
Debasis Giri	Haldia Institute of Technology, India
Deepak Garg	Thapar University, India
Dhinaharan Nagamalai	Wireilla Net Solutions Pty Ltd., Australia
Dimitris Kotzinos	Technical Educational Institution of Serres, Greece
Dong Seong Kim	Duke University, USA
Emmanuel Bouix	iKlax Media, France
Eric Renault	Institut Telecom – Telecom SudParis, France
Farhat Anwar	International Islamic University , Malaysia
Firkhan Ali Bin Hamid Ali	Universiti Tun Hussein Onn Malaysia, Malaysia
Ford Lumban Gaol	University of Indonesia
Geuk Lee	Hannam University, South Korea
Girija Chetty	University of Canberra, Australia
H.V. Ramakrishnan	Dr. MGR University, India
Henrique Joao Lopes Domingos	University of Lisbon, Portugal
Ho Dac Tu	Waseda University, Japan
Hoang, Huu Hanh	Hue University, Vietnam
Hwangjun Song	Pohang University of Science and Technology, South Korea
J.Arunadevi	Thiagarajar College, Madurai, India
Jacques Demerjian	Communication & Systems, Homeland Security, France
Jae Kwang Lee	Hannam University, South Korea
Jan Zizka	SoNet/DI, FBE, Mendel University in Brno, Czech Republic
Jansirani	Manonmaniam Sundaranar University, India
Jeong-Hyun Park	Electronics Telecommunication Research Institute, South Korea
Jivesh Govil	Cisco Systems Inc. - CA, USA
Johann Groschd	University of Bristol, UK

John Karamitsos	University of the Aegean, Samos, Greece
Johnson Kuruvila	Dalhousie University, Halifax, Canada
Jose Enrique Armendariz-Inigo	Universidad Publica de Navarra, Spain
Jung-Gil Song	Hannam University, South Korea
Jungwook Song	Konkuk University, South Korea
K.P. Thooyamani	Bharath University, India
Kamaljit I Lakhtaria	Atmiya Institute of Technology & Science, India
Kannan	Anna University, Chennai, India
Khamish Malhotra	University of Glamorgan, UK
Khoa N. Le	Griffith University, Australia
Krzysztof Walkowiak	Wroclaw University of Technology, Poland
L. Ganesan	Alagappa University, India
Lu S. Veiga	Technical University of Lisbon, Portugal
Lu Yan	University of Hertfordshire, UK
Maode Ma	Nanyang Technological University, Singapore
Marco Roccetti	Universty of Bologna, Italy
Michael Peterson	University of Hawaii at Hilo, USA
Michal Wozniak	Wroclaw University of Technology, Poland
Mohsen Sharifi	Iran University of Science and Technology, Iran
Murugan D.	Manonmaniam Sundaranar University, India
Murugeswari	M.S. University, India
Muthulakshmi	M.S. University, India
N. Krishnan	Manonmaniam Sundaranar University, India
Nabendu Chaki	University of Calcutta, India
Natarajan Meghanathan	Jackson State University, USA
Neerajkumar	Madha Vaisnavi Devi University, India
Nicolas Sklavos	Technological Educational Institute of Patras, Greece
Nidaa Abdual Muhsin Abbas	University of Babylon, Iraq
Paul D. Manuel	Kuwait University, Kuwait
Phan Cong Vinh	London South Bank University, UK
Ponpit Wongthongtham	Curtin University of Technology, Australia
Prabu Dorairaj	NetApp Inc., India
Rajalakshmi	Manonmaniam Sundaranar University, India
Rajendra Akerkar	Technomathematics Research Foundation, India
Rajesh Kumar P.	The Best International, Australia
Rajesh	Manonmaniam Sundaranar University, India
Rajesh Bawa	Punjabi University, India

Rajkumar Kannan	Bishop Heber College, India
Rakhesh Singh Kshetrimayum	Indian Institute of Technology-Guwahati, India
Ramayah Thurasamy	Universiti Sains Malaysia, Malaysia
Rituparna Chaki	West Bengal University of Technology, India
Roberts Masillamani	Hindustan University, India
S. Arumugam	Nandha Engineering College, India
S. Hariharan	B.S.Abdur Rahman University, India
Sadasivam	Manonmaniam Sundaranar University, India
Sagarmay Deb	Central Queensland University, Australia
Sajid Hussain	Acadia University, Canada
Sajid Hussain	Fisk University, USA
Salah S. Al-Majeed	University of Essex, UK
Sanguthevar Rajasekaran	University of Connecticut, USA
Sarmistha Neogy	Jadavpur University, India
Sattar B. Sadkhan	University of Babylon, Iraq
Seemabawa	Thapar University, India
Sergio Ilarri	University of Zaragoza, Spain
Serguei A. Mokhov	Concordia University, Canada
Seungmin Rho	Carnegie Mellon University, USA
Shivan Haran	Arizona State University, USA
Somitra Sanadhya	IIT-Delhi, India
Soodamani, ramalingam	Uuniversity of Hertfordshire,UK
Sriman Narayana Iyengar	VIT University, India
Subha	M.S. University, India
Sudip Misra	Indian Institute of Technology-Kharagpur, India
Sundarapandian Viadyanathan	Vel Tech Dr.RR & Dr.SR Technical University, India
Sundaresan	Manonmaniam Sundaranar University, India
SunYoung Han	Konkuk University, South Korea
Suruliandi	Manonmaniam Sundaranar University, India
Susana Sargento	University of Aveiro, Portugal
Syed Rahman	University of Hawaii-Hilo, USA
Syed Rizvi	University of Bridgeport, USA
Taruna S.	Banasthali University, India
Thamaraiselvi	Madras Institute of Technology,India
Thambidurai	Pondicherry University, India
Velmurugan Ayyadurai	Center for Communication Systems, UK
Vishal Sharma	Metanoia Inc., USA
Wei Jie	University of Manchester, UK

Yan Luo	University of Massachusetts Lowell, USA
Yannick Le Moullec	Aalborg University, Denmark
Yao-Nan Lien	National Chengchi University, Taiwan
Yeong Deok Kim	Woosong University, South Korea
Yuh-Shyan Chen	National Taipei University, Taiwan
Yung-Fa Huang	Chaoyang University of Technology, Taiwan

External Reviewers

Alejandro Regalado Mendez	Universidad del Mar, Mexico
Alireza Mahini	Islamic Azad University-Gorgan, Iran
Amandeep Singh Thethi	Guru Nanak Dev University Amritsar, India
Ashok Kumar Sharma	YMCA Institute of Engineering, India
Ayman Khalil	Institute of Electronics and Telecommunications of Rennes (IETR), France
Buket Barkana	University of Bridgeport, USA
Christos Politis	Kingston University, UK
Hao Shi	Victoria University, Australia
Indrajit Bhattacharya	Kalyani Government Engineering College, India
Jyotirmay Gadewadikar	Alcorn State University, USA
Khoa N. Le	University of Western Sydney, Australia
Laiali Almazaydeh	University of Bridgeport, USA
Lakshmi Rajamani	Osmania University, India
Michel Owayjan	American University of Science & Technology - AUST, Lebanon
Mohamed Hassan	American University of Sharjah, UAE
Monika Verma	Punjab Technical University, India
N.K. Choudhari	Bhagwati Chaturvedi College of Engineering, India
Nitiket N. Mhala	B.D. College of Engineering - Sewagram, India
Nour Eldin Elmadany	Arab Acadmy for Science and Technology, Egypt
Premanand K. Kadbe	Vidya Pratishthan's College of Engineering, India
R. Murali	Dr. Ambedkar Institute of Technology, Bangalore, India
Raman Maini	Punjabi University, India
Rushed Kanawati	LIPN - Université Paris 13, France
S.A.V. Satyamurty	Indira Gandhi Centre for Atomic Research, India
Shrikant K. Bodhe	Bosh Technologies, India

Sridharan	CEG Campus - Anna University, India
Utpal Biswas	University of Kalyani, India
Wichian Sittiprapaporn	Mahasarakham University, Thailand

Technically Supported By

Networks & Communications Community (NCC)
Digital Signal & Image Processing Community (DSIPC)
Computer Science & Information Technology Community (CSITC)

Organized By

ACADEMY & INDUSTRY RESEARCH COLLABORATION CENTER (AIRCC)

Table of Contents

Parallel, Distributed Computing Technologies and Applications

An Energy Efficient Clustering Protocol Using Minimum Spanning Tree for Wireless Sensor Networks

B. Baranidharan and B. Shanthi

SASTRA University, School of Computing, Thanjavur, India
baranidharan@it.sastra.edu, shanthi@cse.sastra.edu

Abstract. Energy efficiency in wireless sensor network [WSN] is the highly sorted area for the researchers. Number of protocols has been suggested for energy efficient information gathering for sensor networks. These protocols come under two broad categories called tree based approach and clustering techniques. In these techniques clustering is more suitable for real time applications and has much more scalability factor when compared with its previous counterpart. This paper presents the importance and factors affecting the clustering. Also this paper surveyed the different clustering algorithms with its extensions till date and proposed the clustering technique using Minimum Spanning Tree [MST] concept with its strength and limitations.

Keywords: Clustering, Energy efficiency, MST.

1 Introduction

The advancement in wireless technologies and miniaturized hardware has led to the development of the new area called pervasive computing. The base concept behind this pervasive computing is 'anywhere' and 'anytime' computing. Wireless sensor network is one of the pervasive networks which sense our environment through various parameters like heat, temperature, pressure, etc… For battle field surveillance in military applications, habitat monitoring, industrial applications wireless sensor network is an essential one nowadays. A wireless sensor network is built of thousands of sensor nodes. A sensor node has embedded low power processor, limited memory and battery. In WSN , devices are battery operated and unrechargeable, to meet out this challenges, an energy efficient operation of the WSN is the need of the hour for some critical applications like military surveillance, remote patient monitoring. For energy efficient data gathering in the sensor networks we have been following two approaches,

- Tree based approach
- Clustering based approach

When compared with tree based approaches clustering of sensor nodes have more advantages like scalability, avoiding redundant data, latency.

D. Nagamalai, E. Renault, and M. Dhanushkodi (Eds.): PDCTA 2011, CCIS 203, pp. 1–11, 2011.

On studying the clustering algorithms proposed for ad hoc networks their main goal was node reach ability and stability. These protocols are not suitable for the WSN since coverage area is an important factor in WSN. The section 2 in this paper gives a brief idea about importance and objectives of clustering suitable for WSN. The section 3 analyzes the existing clustering algorithms in WSN. A new energy efficient clustering scheme has been proposed in section 4 and in section 5 concludes with the future direction.

2 Importance and Objectives of Clustering

Clustering is the process of dividing the sensor nodes into groups based on some attributes. Generally based upon geographical location and remaining residual energy value clusters are formed. A Cluster Head would be selected for each cluster which is having more responsibilities than cluster members. Clustering sensor network and electing the cluster heads can be in distributed or in centralized way. In distributed mechanism each sensor nodes will broadcast its location and energy level to its one hop neighbors and the node which is having higher energy level and connectivity will be elected as cluster head. In centralized mechanism all the nodes have to transmit their location and residual energy to the base station and base station will form the new clusters with the cluster head and broadcast it to the nodes.

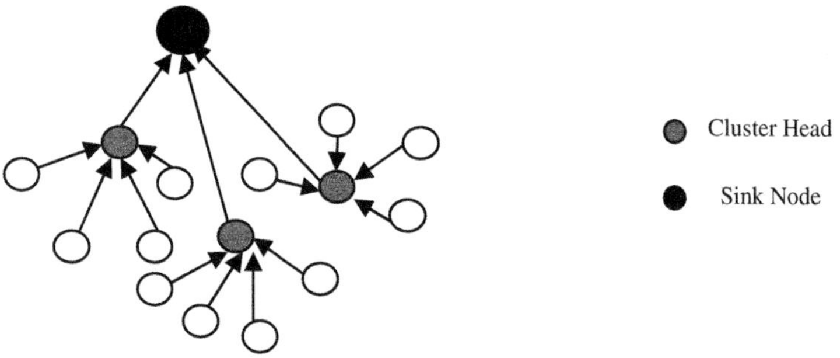

Fig. 1. Clustering Architectural Diagram

In case of homogenous sensor network the cluster heads are selected from the available nodes. The cluster head nodes are relieved from other sensor activities like monitoring the environment to conserve its energy for data aggregation and communication with base station. In case of heterogeneous sensor network, the node which is having more energy than other nodes is selected as cluster head or co-coordinators.

For ad hoc networks clustering is used for improving the reach ability of the nodes. But for wireless sensor networks clustering is an energy efficient scheme which concentrates on network longevity and better coverage. Also scalability is a major challenge in clustering for WSN. For different applications, objectives of the clustering also varies like load balancing, fault tolerance, improved coverage. Based upon the objective of the applications appropriate clustering algorithms are used.

3 Existing Clustering Algorithms

Since wireless communication always consumes higher percentage of energy than wired the number of message transmitted should be reduced. But when we reduce the number of message transmission in the network there may be the chances of reduced performance of the network. To make a tradeoff between performance and energy efficiency we are going for the clustering algorithms. Based upon its cluster formation we are having two categories of clusters,

- Geographical area based clusters.
- Clustering based on residual energy level.

3.1 Based on Residual Energy Level

3.1.1 LEACH

Low energy adaptive clustering hierarchy [13] is a distributed clustering protocol to distribute the energy consumption all over its network. Here, based on data collection, network is divided into Clusters and Cluster heads are elected randomly. The cluster head collects the information from the nodes which are coming under its cluster. The phases involved in each round in the LEACH protocol as follows,

Advertisement phase: This is the starting phase in LEACH protocol. The eligible cluster head nodes will be sending a request to its nearby nodes to join in its cluster. The non-CH node will be joining with the cluster head which offers higher Received Signal Strength (RSS).

Cluster set-up phase: In this step the nodes with its new cluster head form a new cluster.

Schedule creation: After cluster set-up phase, the cluster head have to generate a TDMA scheme and pass it to its cluster members to intimate them when they have to send their data to it.

Data transmission: The data sensed by the individual sensors will be forwarded to its cluster head during its TDMA time interval.

Here in the LEACH protocol multi cluster interference problem was solved by using unique CDMA codes for each cluster.

It helps to prevent energy drain for the same sensor nodes which has been elected as the cluster leader, using randomization for each time cluster head would be changed. The cluster head nodes collect data from its cluster members and aggregate it. Finally each cluster head will be forwarding the aggregated data to the base station. When compared with LEACH, it have shown a better improved lifetime, in terms of number of data gathering rounds.

LEACH-Centralized [13] works in the same way as LEACH. It follows the centralized mechanism. All the nodes have to transmit their current location and residual energy to the base station. Then the base station forms the new cluster with a cluster head for each of it. The newly formed clusters with its cluster head IDs is transmitted to the nodes. If the nodes receive the message with its own ID as cluster

ID it assumes the cluster head role. The steady state phase is same to both LEACH and LEACH-C.

LEACH-F [13] is another variant of LEACH protocol. The cluster formed in the setup phase is fixed. The energy wasted due to new cluster formation in each data collection round is reduced by maintain fixed clusters. But the major drawback in this scheme is the newly arriving nodes cannot be included in the fixed clusters.

3.1.2 HEED

Though the LEACH protocol is much more energy efficient when compared with its predecessors like Direct Transmission (DT), the main drawbacks in LEACH is the random selection of cluster head. In the worst case the CH nodes may not be evenly distributed among the nodes and it will have its effect on the data gathering rounds. To avoid the random selection of CHs a new algorithm called HEED [12] was developed which selects the CHs based on both residual energy level and communication cost. The HEED protocol works in three subsequent phases,

Initialization phase: During this phase the initial CHs nodes percentage will be given to the nodes. It is represented by the variable C_{prob}. Each sensor node compute its probability to become CH by the formula, $CH_{prob}=C_{prob} * E_{residual}/E_{max}$ where $E_{residual}$ to residual energy level of the concerned node, E_{max} corresponds to maximum battery energy. Since HEED supports heterogeneous sensor nodes E_{max} may vary for different nodes according to its functionality and capacity.

Repetition phase: Until the CH node was found with the least transmission cost, this phase was iterated. If the node cannot find the appropriate CH, then the concerned node itself was selected as the CH.

Finalization phase: The selection of CH is finalized here. The tentative CH now becomes the final CH node.

3.1.3 DECA

DECA is an acronym for **D**istributed **E**fficient **C**lustering **A**pproach [9]. DECA differs from HEED in deciding and arriving at the score computation. The phases involved in DECA operations are:

Start Clustering: In the initial phase all the nodes will compute its score with the help of the function $score=w_1E+w_2C+w_3I$. E refers to residual energy, C to node connectivity, and I to node identifier and 'w' to weight which is equal to unity. After some delay the score value will be given to the neighboring nodes with the node ID and cluster ID if the computed score is of a higher value.

Receive Clustering Message: When the node is receiving the score value more than its own value and if it is not attached to any cluster it accepts the sender node as its CH.

Actual announcement: After the previous phase, the new nodes with the already existing nodes from some other previous cluster which are intended to form a new cluster with a new head, the CHs ID, cluster ID and score value would be broadcasted.

Finalize Clustering: In this last step the CH nodes with its Cluster Members forms the new clusters.

points, that these nodes are having shortest path to its neighboring nodes. The energy wastage due to inter cluster communication is reduced using GESC.

3.2 Geographical Area Based Clustering

In Geographical area based clustering approach the nodes coming under particular geographical area are combined to form a cluster. Some of the protocols coming under this category are GAF, SPAN, and PANEL.

3.2.1 GAF

The geographical regions in which the sensor nodes are fixed are divided into equal sized grids [16]. The nodes coming under the particular geographical range will be associated with a particular grid. The communication cost of nodes coming under the same grid will be same. During the routing decision any one node from the particular grid will wake up and takes part in routing and all other nodes in the same grid will go to the sleeping state to avoid unnecessary energy depletion.

3.2.2 SPAN

SPAN [14] is similar to GAF protocol. In SPAN for every node if its neighbors are not directly or indirectly connected with each other it is elected as the coordinator node. And in any situation if the neighboring nodes can be connected without it assistance it can withdrawn from its coordinator responsibilities. The nodes nearby the coordinator node will be in sleeping state unless when it has to send or receive any data. All the routing activities will be carried over by the coordinator nodes. The major advantage of SPAN is that the nodes can integrates with 802.11 power saving mode easily. The limitation in this method is the coordinator node will drain its energy quickly since it follows geographical based clustering.

3.2.3 PANEL

PANEL, Position based aggregator node election [7] is also one of the distributed clustering algorithm. Here, in this protocol the sensor deployed area is divided into fixed equal sized rectangular area. For each data gathering round, the sensor nodes in each clusters computes the reference points for its cluster. The node coming near to the reference point is selected as the aggregator node for that round. The nodes learn the shortest path to the aggregator node at the end of aggregator election procedure which is useful for intra cluster communication. For inter cluster communication any position based routing protocols can be used.

4 Proposed Algorithm

To improve the efficiency in clustering protocol, this paper suggests few modifications in the existing clustering techniques. On analyzing the existing clustering algorithms it can be categorized as follows,

- Partitioning
- Hierarchical
- Graph theoretic

- Density based
- Grid based

Every clustering method has its own strengths and limitations. The proper hard and fast rules are not needed in this network topology. Because according to the application and size of data user can define the methodology.

Here this paper tailors the methods to suit the limited energy of the network and also it considers the scalability factor. MST, Minimum Spanning Tree approach is followed in our proposed scheme for Cluster and Super Cluster formation. In the previously mentioned algorithms the energy wastage in data transmission from distance cluster head node to the sink node is not considered. In our proposed scheme the energy wastage in distance CH node transmission to the sink node is reduced by having multi hop communication between cluster head node to the sink node and having Super cluster head nodes, which aggregates the information from different cluster heads and transmits it to the sink node. The Proposed algorithm has three phases:

1. Cluster Formation.
2. Cluster head selection.
3. Data transmission using shortest path.

Cluster Formation

Unlike previous algorithms, cluster formation precedes before cluster head selection. This is based on Minimum Spanning Tree (MST) concept. A tree is a connected graph without cycles. The spanning tree is 'minimal' when the total length of the edges is the minimum necessary to connect all the vertices in the graph. MST may be constructed using kruskal's (or) Prim's algorithm. In [5] Wenyu, used MST technique in the intra cluster topology control. But in our proposed algorithm MST is used in the initial cluster formation phase and in super cluster formation phase. The steps involved in cluster formation phases are as follows,

- Generate a matrix 'M' based on RSS (Received Signal Strength) values of each node.
- Calculate a threshold value based on the Mean of RSS values.
- In order to reduce the size of matrix (if it is big), remove the elements from the matrix which is lesser than the threshold value.
- Draw the graph for this adjacency matrix and apply suitable algorithm to generate MST.
- Decide the number of clusters 'k' and remove 'k-1' number of edges from that MST (remove from highest value edges).

Cluster Head Selection

In the newly formed clusters, the node with the highest energy level is selected as the cluster head and the next higher energy level node is selected as the next CH node. To maintain the stability within the clusters, next CH nodes were selected. Once the cluster head are selected, it generates the TDMA schedule for its cluster members and broadcasts to its cluster members.

Data Transmission Using Shortest Path

In order to reduce further energy wastage due to data transmission between the long distanced Cluster head and sink node, multi-hop data transmission takes place. The data from the nearby cluster heads to the sink node will be directly transmitted to the sink node whereas the data from the distanced cluster head will be transmitted through the shortest multi-hop path. The steps involved in transmission as follows,

- Preparing proximity matrix using distance metric; distance between CH and sink and between CH's.
- Constructing MST to form a super cluster.
- Find shortest path between each CH to sink.
- Find the predominant node [node in maximum number of path].
- Select that node as super cluster head node and aggregation takes place at this node.
- Forward aggregated information to the sink node.

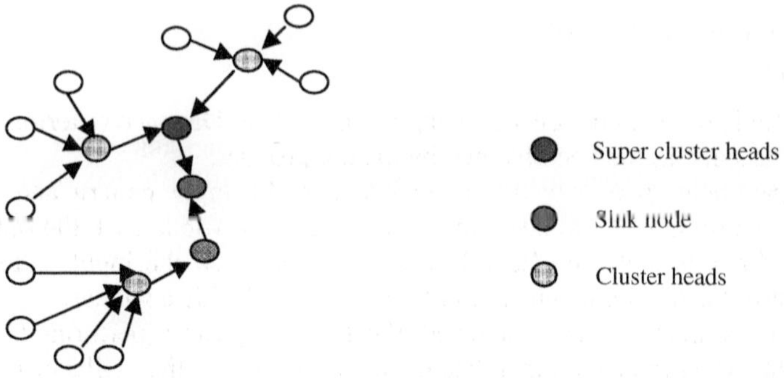

Fig. 3. Architectural diagram of proposed scheme

Strengths of the proposed algorithms are,

- Scalability is addressed by performing cluster formation twice.
- To avoid fault tolerance, node leader is selected.
- All nodes are taken into account by MST technique.
- Delay is avoided by sending packets through, shortest path.
- Aggregation reduces the redundancy.

Limitations:

- Cluster formation is based on certain parameters like RSS and distance; On changing the cluster formation parameters, cluster efficiency may be improved.
- Cluster efficiency also changes.
- Mobility is not considered.
- This algorithm based on the assumption that the network is static.

5 Conclusions

In this paper, the detailed study about existing clustering algorithms in the wireless sensor networks have been presented and a new algorithm which focuses on energy efficient data transmission between the cluster heads and the sink node is proposed. Using MST mechanism we proposed to find clusters and shortest path for the data transmission. Our future work concentrates on the following,

- Simulating the proposed algorithm using a suitable node level simulator.
- Studying all possible parameters for each sensor node and find rule to merge and create matrix for graph.
- Study the dynamic graph algorithm and use it in cluster formation, for addressing the mobility and node discard due to its energy exhausted.
- Finding the optimum number of CH node selection which leads to prolong the lifetime of the network.
- Applying new techniques to reduce energy consumption within intra-cluster communication.

References

1. Bajaber, F., Awan, I.: Adaptive decentralized re-clustering protocol for wireless sensor networks. Journal of computer and Systems sciences, doi:10.1016/j.jcss.2010.01.007
2. Zhu, Y.-h., Wu, W.-d., Pan, J., Tang, Y.-p.: An energy efficient data gathering algorithm to prolong lifetime of wireless sensor networks. Computer Communications 33, 639–647 (2010)
3. Bajaber, F., Awan, I.: Energy efficient clustering protocol to enhance lifetime of wireless sensor network. Journal of Ambient Intelligence and Human Computing 1, 239–248 (2010)
4. Dimokas, N., Katsaros, D., Manolopoulos, Y.: Energy-efficient distributed clustering in wireless sensor networks. Journal of Parallel and Distributed Computing 70, 371–383 (2010)
5. Cai, W., Zhang, M.: MST-based Clustering topology control algorithm for wireless sensor networks. Journal of Electronics 27(3), 352–362 (2010)
6. Bajaber, F., Awan, I.: Centralized dynamic clustering for wireless sensor network. In: International Conference on Advanced Information Networking and Applications Workshops, pp. 193–198 (2009)
7. Buttyan, L., Schaffer, P.: PANEL: Position-based Aggregator Node Election in Wireless Sensor Networks. In: Proceedings of the IEEE International Conference on Mobile Ad hoc and Sensor Systems, MASS, pp. 1–9 (2007)
8. Abbasi, A.A., Younis, M.: A Survey on Clustering Algorithms for Wireless Sensor Networks. Computer Communications 30, 2826–2841 (2007)
9. Yu, M., Li, J.H., Levy, R.: Mobility Resistant Clustering in Multi-Hop Wireless Networks. Journal of Networks 1(1), 12–19 (2006)
10. Youssef, M., Younis, M., Youssef, A., Agrawala, A.: Distributed formation of overlapping multi-hop clusters in wireless sensor networks. In: Proceedings of the 49th Annual IEEE Global Communication Conference (Globecom 2006), San Francisco, CA, pp. 1–6 (2006)

11. Akkaya, K., Younis, M.: A Survey on routing protocols for Wireless Sensor Networks. Ad Hoc Networks 3, 325–349 (2005)
12. Younis, O., Fahmy, S.: HEED: A Hybrid,Energy-Efficient, Distributed clustering approach for Ad Hoc sensor networks. IEEETransactions on Mobile Computing 3(4), 366–379 (2004)
13. Heinzelman, W.B., Chandrakasan, A.P., Balakrishnan, H.: Application specific protocol architecture for wireless microsensornetworks. IEEE Transactions on Wireless Communication 1(4), 660–670 (2002)
14. Chen, B., Jamieson, K., Balakrishnan, H., Morris, R.: SPAN: An energy efficient coordination algorithm for topology maintenance in ad hoc networks. ACM/Kluwer Wireless Networks 8(5), 481–494 (2002)
15. Manjeshwar, A., Agarwal, D.: APTEEN: a hybrid protocol for efficient routing and comprehensive information retrieval in wireless sensor networks. In: Proceedings of the 16th International Parallel and Distributed Processing Symposium, pp. 195–202 (2002)
16. Xu, Y., Heidemann, J., Estrin, D.: Geography-informed Energy Conservation for Ad-hoc Routing. In: Proceedings of the Seventh Annual ACM/IEEE International Conference on Mobile Computing and Networking, pp. 70–84 (2001)
17. Yu, Y., Estrin, D., Govindan, R.: Geographical and Energy-Aware Routing: A Recursive Data Dissemination Protocol for Wireless Sensor Networks, UCLA Computer Science Department Technical Report, UCLA-CSD TR-01-0023 (2001)
18. Manjeshwar, A., Agarwal, D.P.: TEEN: a routing protocol for enhanced efficiency in wireless sensor networks. In: 15th International Parallel and Distributed Processing Symposium (IPDPS 2001), vol. 3, pp. 2009–2015 (2001)

DOA Estimation for Rectangular Linear Array Antenna in Frequency Non Selective Slow Fading MIMO Channels

A.V. Meenakshi[1], V. Punitham[1], and T. Gowri[2]

[1] Department of ECE, Periyar Maniammai University, Thanjavur
meenu_gow@yahoo.com, puniwell@yahoo.co.in
[2] PSNA College of Engineering and Technology, Dindigul
gowri.badra@rediffmail.com

Abstract. This paper presents a tool for the analysis, and simulation of direction-of-arrival (DOA) estimation in wireless mobile communication systems utilizing adaptive antenna arrays and evaluates the performance of a number of DOA estimation algorithms in frequency non-selective and slow fading multipath for multi input multi output (MIMO) system. It reviews six methods of Direction of arrival (DOA) estimation, all of which can be derived from the parametric based and subspace based methods. The parametric based method results from the application of the Maximum Likelihood principle to the statistics of the observed raw data. Second, the standard Multiple Signal Classification (MUSIC) can be obtained from the subspace based methods. In improved MUSIC procedure called Cyclic MUSIC, it can automatically classify the signals as desired and undesired based on the known spectral correlation property and estimate only the desired signal's DOA. The next method is an extension of the Cyclic MUSIC algorithm called Extended Cyclic MUSIC by using an extended array data vector. By exploiting cyclostationarity, the signal's DOA estimation can be significantly improved. Finally, Estimation of signal parameter via rotational invariance techniques called ESPRIT algorithm is developed. In this paper, in addition with two different types of data model viz received signal with coherent frequency non selective slow fading channel and received signal with non coherent non selective slow fading channel are used for which estimates the DOA of narrow band signals. This paper provides a fairly complete image of the performance and statistical efficiency of each of above four methods with QPSK and exponential pulse signal (FM).

Keywords: MUSIC, QPSK, MIMO, RMSE, SNR, MLM, ULA, ESPRIT.

1 Introduction

Adaptive signal processing sensor arrays, known also as smart antennas, have been widely adopted in third-generation (3G) mobile systems because of their ability to locate mobile users with the use of DOA estimation techniques. Adaptive antenna

D. Nagamalai, E. Renault, and M. Dhanushkodi (Eds.): PDCTA 2011, CCIS 203, pp. 12–24, 2011.

arrays also improve the performance of cellular systems by providing robustness against fading channels and reduced Channel interference [1]. The goal of direction-of-arrival (DOA) estimation is to use the data received on the downlink at the base-station sensor array to estimate the directions of the signals from the desired mobile users as well as the directions of interference signals. The results of DOA estimation are then used by to adjust the weights of the adaptive beamformer so that the radiated power is maximized towards the desired users, and radiation nulls are placed in the directions of interference signals. Hence, a successful design of an adaptive array depends highly on the choice of the DOA estimation algorithm which should be highly accurate and robust. Array signal processing has found important applications in diverse fields such as Radar, Sonar, Communications and Seismic explorations[20]. A proper central to array signal processing is the estimation of the DOA of the signals. The problem of estimating the DOA of narrow band signals using antenna arrays has been analyzed intensively over fast few years.[1]-[9]. Several methods have been proposed that operate on the sample covariance matrix of the observed outputs (the "data") to produce estimates of the DOA's. The goal of this paper is to present four DOA methods, which might be thought of as being basically different, under the parametric and subspace based methods. This statistical property of signal and noise subspace estimates for uncorrelated FM signals and correlated QPSK signals over the observation period are delineated. The comparative analysis has been conducted for Root Mean Squared Error (RMSE) Vs SNR for multi path fading channel. The results from such a comparison can then be used to indicate solutions for different levels of applications, **e.g.** for measurement systems with the capability to provide spatial information, for cellular base stations with the capability to improve range-capacity-service quality erc., for user positioning systems, and many more.

This paper is organized as follows. Section II presents the signal model by exponential pulse, QPSK source signals. In section III the above mentioned data model is extended to multi path fading channel. Here we describe two-channel models namely coherent frequency non selective wave front slow fading and non-coherent frequency non selective slow fading channel. Section IV briefly describes the algorithms we have used. Section IV.a. Reviews the so called deterministic or conditional Maximum Likelihood Model (MLM) [1] and presents the main results of its statistical performance. Section IV.b and section IV.c deal with MUSIC and Cyclic MUSIC algorithms. MUSIC procedures are computationally much simpler than the MLM but they provide less accurate estimate [2]. The popular methods of Direction finding such as MUSIC suffer from various drawbacks such as 1.The total number of signals impinges on the antenna array is less than the total number of receiving antenna array. 2. Inability to resolve the closely spaced signals 3. Need for the knowledge of the existing characteristics such as noise characteristics. Cyclic MUSIC algorithm overcomes the above drawbacks. It exhibits cyclostationarity, which improves the DOA estimation. Extended Cyclic MUSIC shows dramatic improvements than the Cyclic MUSIC of its extended data vector. IV.e section exploits the ESPRIT algorithm. Finally Section V describes the simulation results and performance comparison. Section VI concludes the paper.

2 Signal Model

The algorithm starts by constructing a real-life signal model. Consider a number of plane waves from M narrow-band sources impinging from different angles θ_i, $i = 1, 2, \ldots, M$, impinging into a uniform linear array (ULA) of N equi-spaced sensors, as shown in Figure 1.

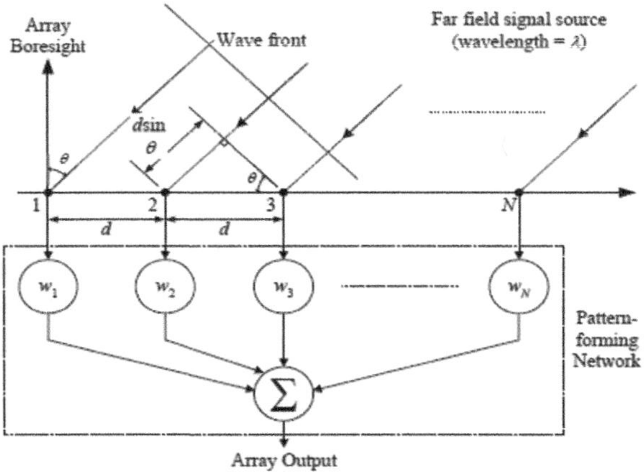

Fig. 1. A Plane wave incident on a uniform linear array antenna

In narrowband array processing, when n signals arrive at an m-element array, the linear data model

$$y(t)=A(\Phi)x(t)+n(t) \quad (1)$$

is commonly used, where the m*n spatial matrix $A=[a_1, a_2, \ldots\ldots\ldots a_n]$ represents the mixing matrix or the steering matrix. In direction finding problems, we require A to have a known structure, and each column of A corresponds to a single arrival and carries a clear bearing. $\mathbf{a}(\Phi)$ is an $N\times1$ vector referred to as the array response to that source or array steering vector for that direction. It is given by:

$$\mathbf{a}(\Phi) = {}_{.}1 e^{-j\tilde{\phi}.} e^{-j(N-1)\phi.} T \quad (2)$$

where T is the transposition operator, and φ represents the electrical phase shift from element to element along the array. This can be defined by:

$$\phi = \tilde{\pi}\ \lambda\,.d\,\theta \quad (3)$$

where d is the element spacing and λ is the wavelength of the received signal.

Due to the mixture of the signals at each antenna, the elements of the m×1 data vector y(t) are multicomponent signals. Whereas each source signal x(t) of the n×1 signal vector, x(t) is often a monocomponent signal. n(t) is an additive noise vector whose elements are modeled as stationary, spatially and temporally white, zero mean complex random processes that are independent of the source signals. That is

$$E[n\,(t+\Gamma)\,n^H(t)]=\sigma\delta(\tau)I$$

$$E[n\,(t+\Gamma)\,n^T(t)]=0, \quad \text{for any } \tau \tag{4}$$

Where $\delta(\tau)$ is the delta function, I denotes the identity matrix, σ is the noise power at each antenna element, superscripts H and T, respectively, denote conjugate transpose and transpose and E(.) is the statistical expectation operator.

In (1), it is assumed that the number of receiving antenna element is larger than the number of sources, i.e., m>n. Further, matrix A is full column rank, which implies that the steering vectors corresponding to n different angles of arrival are linearly independent. We further assume that the correlation matrix

$$R_{yy} = E\lfloor y(t)\,y^H(t)\rfloor \tag{5}$$

is nonsingular and that the observation period consists of N snapshots with N>m. Under the above assumptions, the correlation matrix is given by

$$R_{yy} = E[(y(t)y^H(t))] = AR_{xx}A^H + \sigma I \tag{6}$$

Where $R_{xx} = E[(x(t)x^H(t))]$ is the source correlation matrix.

Let $\lambda_1 > \lambda_2 > \lambda_3 \ldots\ldots\ldots\ \lambda_n = \lambda_{n+1} = \ldots.\ \lambda_m = \sigma$ denote the eigen values of $R_{yy.}$ It is assumed that $\Lambda_{i,}$ i=1, 2, 3…….n are distinct. The unit norm Eigen vectors associated with the columns of matrix S= [s_1 s_2 …..s_n], and those corresponding to $\lambda_{n+1} \ldots.\lambda_m$ make up matrix G=[g_1 …….g_{m-n}] . Since the columns of matrix **A** and **S** span the same subspace, then $A^HG=0$;

In practice R_{yy} is unknown and, therefore, should be estimated from the available data samples y(i), i= 1 2 3………N. The estimated correlation matrix is given by

$$R_{yy} = 1/N \sum_{n=1}^{N} (y(t)\,y^H(t)) \tag{7}$$

Let { $s_{1,}$ $s_{2,}$ ………… $s_{n,}$ ……..g_{m-n} } denote the unit norm eigen vectors of R_{yy} that are arranged in descending order of the associated eigen values respectively. The statistical properties of the eigen vectors of the sample covariance matrix R_{yy} for the signals modeled as independent processes with additive white Gaussian noise are given in [9].

3 Proposed Signal Model

The received signal data model that is used is given by

$$y_l(t) = \sum_{k=1}^{K} \alpha_l(k)\, x_{mk}(t) + n_l(t) \tag{8}$$

Where $\alpha_l(k) = \alpha(k) a_k(\Phi)$; $a_k(\Phi)$ is the antenna response vector. Where $x_{mk}(t)$ is the signal transmitted by k^{th} user of mth signal , $\alpha_l(k)$ is the fading coefficient for the path connecting user k to the lth antenna, $n_l(t)$ is circularly symmetric complex Gaussian noise. Here we examine two basic channel models [4]. In the first case, fading process for each user is assumed to be constant across the face of the antenna array and we can associate a DOA to the signal. This is called coherent wave front fading[3]. In coherent wave front fading channel the fading parameters for each user is modeled as $\alpha_l(k) = \alpha(k) a_k(\Phi)$, where $\alpha(k)$ is a constant complex fading parameter across the array , Φ_k is the DOA of the kth user's signal relative to the array geometry, and $a_k(\Phi)$ is the response of the lth antenna element to a narrow band signal arriving from Φ_k. The signal model is represented in vector form as

$$y_l = \sum_{k=1}^{K} \alpha_l(k)\, g_{mk}(k) + n_l \tag{9}$$

Here g_{mk} is a vector containing the kth user's $m_k{}^{th}$ signal.

The second model we consider is non-coherent element- to- element fading channel on which each antenna receives a copy of the transmitted signal with a different fading parameter. In this case, the dependency of the array response on the DOA for each user cannot be separated from the fading process, so that no DOA can be exploited for conventional beam forming.

4 Algorithms

a. Maximum Likelihood Method (MLM)

The likelihood function is the probability density function of all the observations given the unknown parameters. The likelihood function is obtained as

$$L(\phi, x(t), \sigma^2) = 1/(\pi\sigma^2)^L \times e^{-\|y(t)-Ax(t)\|^2} / \sigma^2 \tag{10}$$

As indicated above, the unknown parameters in the likelihood function are the signal parametersθ, the signal waveforms x(t) and the noise variance σ^2. The ML estimates of these unknowns are calculated as the maximizing arguments of $L(\Phi,x(t),\sigma^2)$, the rationale being that these values make the probability of the observations as large as possible. For convenience, the ML[5][6] estimates are alternatively defined as the minimizing arguments of the negative log likelihood function log $L(\Phi,x(t),\sigma^2)$. Normalizing by N and ignoring the parameter – independent Llog π- term, we get

$$L(\phi, x(t),\sigma^2) = L\log\sigma^2 + 1/(\pi\sigma^2)^L \times e^{\|Y(t)-Ax(t)\|^2} / \sigma^2 \quad (11)$$

Whose minimizing arguments are the maximum likelihood estimate the ML signal parameter is estimated.

Under the assumptions made above, the likelihood functions of the observations {y(1)…..y(N)} can easily be derived. After concentration with respect to {x(t) and σ, the negative log likelihood function is given by [1]

$$F_{ML}(\phi) = \mathrm{tr}\left[I - A(A^*A)^{-1}A^*\right]\hat{R} \quad (12)$$

The ML estimate of Φ is obtained as the minimized of (10). The function $F_{ML}(\Phi)$ is highly nonlinear and multimodal. The computational complexity of the MLM is high and the fact that this method is not statistically efficient.

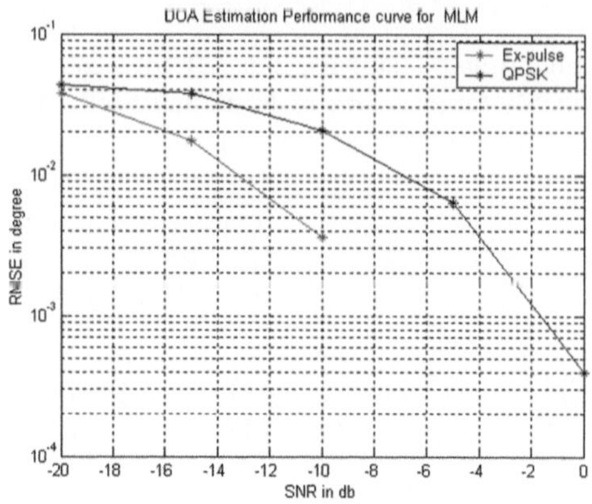

Fig. 1. Performance comparison of ML Method

b. MUSIC

MUSIC is a method for estimating the individual frequencies of multiple times – harmonic signals. MUSIC is now applied to estimate the arrival angle of the particular user [1],[2].

The structure of the exact covariance matrix with the spatial white noise assumption implies that its spectral decomposition is expressed as

$$R = APA^H = U_S A U^H{}_S + \sigma^2 U_n U^H{}_n \quad (13)$$

Where assuming APA^H to be the full rank, the diagonal matrix Us contains the M largest Eigen values. Since the Eigen vectors in Un (the noise Eigen vectors) are orthogonal to A.

$$U_n a(\phi) = 0, \text{ where } \phi \in \{\varphi_1, \phi_2, \ldots \phi_m\} \quad (14)$$

To allow for unique DOA estimates, the array is usually assumed to be unambiguous; that is, any collection of N steering vectors corresponding to distinct DOAs Φm forms a linearly independent set { $a_{\Phi 1}$,.....$a_{\Phi m}$ } .If a(.) satisfies these conditions and P has full rank, then APA^H is also full rank. The above equation is very helpful to locate the DOAs in accurate manner.

Let {s_1 ....s_n, g_1....g_{m-n}} denote a unit norm eigenvectors of R, arranged in the descending order of the associated eigen values, and let $\check{S}$ and $\hat{G}$ denote the matrices S and G made of {s_I} and {g_I} respectively. The eigen vectors are separated in to the signal and noise eigen vectors. The orthogonal projector onto the noise subspace is estimated. And the MUSIC 'spatial spectrum' is then defined as

$$f(\phi) = \left\lfloor a^*(\phi)\hat{G}\hat{G}^* a(\phi) \right\rfloor \quad (15)$$

$$f(\phi) = \left\lfloor a^*(\phi) \left\lfloor I - S\check{S}^* \right\rfloor a(\phi) \right\rfloor \quad (16)$$

The MUSIC estimates of {Φ_i} are obtained by picking the n values of Φ for which f(Φ) is minimized.

To conclude, for uncorrelated signals, the MUSIC estimator has an excellent performance for reasonably large values of N, m and SNR. If the signals are highly correlated, then the MUSIC estimator may be very inefficient even for large values of N, m, and SNR.

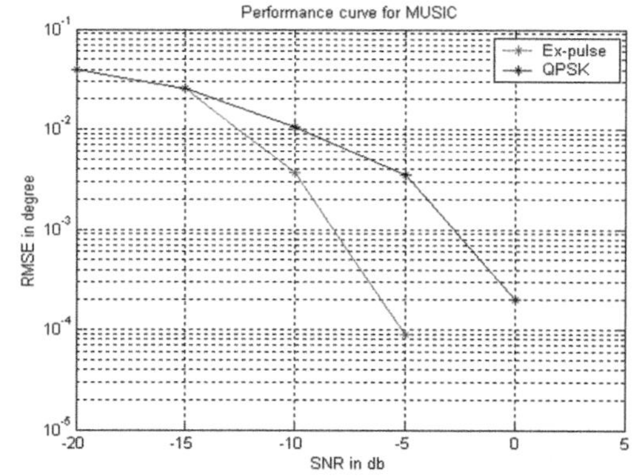

Fig. 2. Performance comparison of MUSIC

c. Cyclic MUSIC

We assume that m_α sources emit cyclostationary signals with cycle frequency α ($m_\alpha \leq m$). In the following , we consider that x(t) contains only the m_α signals that exhibit cycle frequency α, and all of the remaining m-m_α signals that have not the cycle frequency α.

Cyclic autocorrelation matrix and cyclic conjugate autocorrelation matrix at cycle frequency α for some lag parameter τ are then nonzero and can be estimated by

$$Ryy\alpha(\tau) = \sum_{n=1}^{N} y(tn+\tau/2)y^{H}(tn-\tau/2)e^{-j2\pi\alpha t_n} \quad (17)$$

$$Ryy^{*}\alpha(\tau) = \sum_{n=1}^{N} y(tn+\tau/2)\,y^{T}(tn-\tau/2)e^{-j2\pi\alpha t_n} \quad (18)$$

where N is the number of samples.

Contrary to the covariance matrix exploited by the MUSIC algorithm [1], the Cyclic MUSIC method [8] is generally not hermitian. Then, instead of using the eigenvalue decomposition (EVD), Cyclic MUSIC [15] uses the singular value decomposition (SVD) of the cyclic correlation matrix. For finite number of time samples, the algorithm can be implemented as follows:

- Estimate the matrix $R_{yy}^{\alpha}(\tau)$ by using (15) or $R_{yy*}^{\alpha}(\tau)$ by using (16).
- Compute SVD

$$[\,U_s \;\; U_n\,]\begin{bmatrix}\Sigma_s & 0\\ 0 & \Sigma_n\end{bmatrix}[\,V_s \;\; V_n\,]^{H} \quad (19)$$

Where [Us Un] and [Vs Vn] are unitary, and the diagonal elements of the diagonal matrices $\sum s$ and $\sum n$ are arranged in the decreasing order. $\sum n$ tends to zero as the number of time samples becomes large.

- Find the minima of $\| Un^{H}a(\Phi) \|^{2}$ or the max of $\| Us^{H}a(\Phi) \|^{2}$

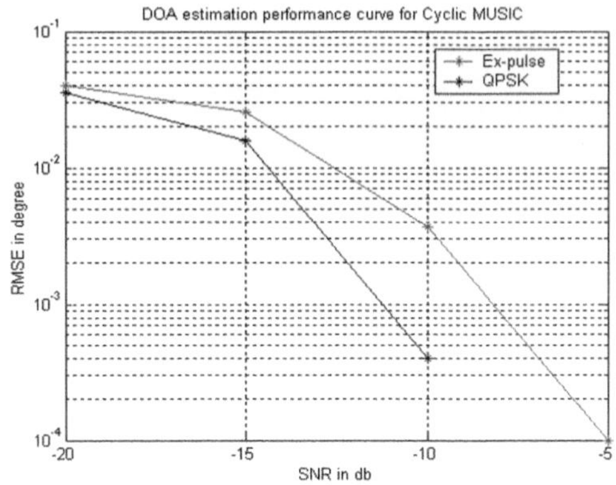

Fig. 3. Performance comparison of Cyclic MUSIC

d. Extended Cyclic MUSIC

Here we give an extension of the conventional model in order to exploit the cyclostationarity of the incoming signals. We form the following extended data vector

$$Yce(t)=[\ y(t);\ y^{*}t]];$$

We can estimate the cyclic correlation matrix for the extended data model as

$$R_{ce} = \sum_{n=1}^{N} I^{\alpha}{}_{2m}(t_n) Y_{ce}(tn+\tau/2)\, Y_{ce}{}^{H}(tn-\tau/2) \tag{20}$$

where the time dependent matrix

$$I_{2m}(t)= [\ I_M e^{-j2\Pi t} \quad 0; \quad 0 \quad I_M e{+}^{j2\Pi t}\ ];$$

Im is the M-dimensional identity matrix.

By computing the SVD of R_{ce} similarly to the Cyclic MUSIC algorithm, the spatial spectrum of the Extended Cyclic MUSIC method is given by

$$p(\phi) = \frac{1}{a^{H}(\phi)U_n a(\phi) - \left\| a^{T}(\phi)U_n a(\phi) \right\|} \tag{21}$$

But this method is dedicated to cyclostationary signals that have no particular limitation.

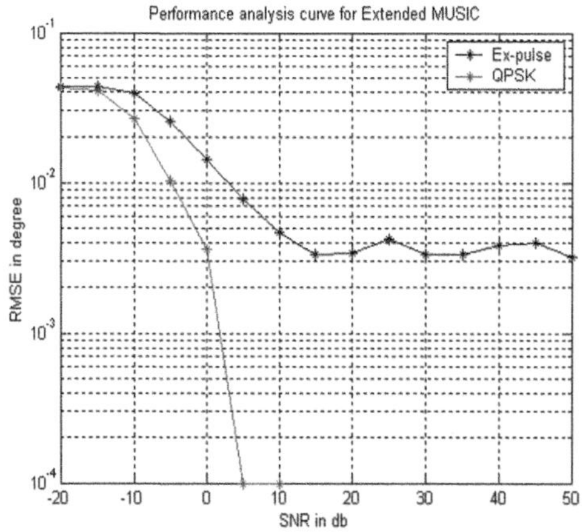

Fig. 4. Performance comparison of Extended Cyclic MUSIC

e. ESPRIT

The significant computational advantage of ESPRIT becomes even more pronounced on multidimensional parameter estimation where the computational grows linearly with dimension in ESPRIT, while that of MUSIC [8] grows exponentially [4]. The idea behind Unitary ESPRIT is to perform a forward backward averaging of the signal matrix so that the signal poles are constrained to the unit circle [5]. Also, the forward backward averaging results in improved estimation accuracy. In addition to this, for complex signals, the algorithm has a lower computational complexity than standard ESPRIT because the special structure of the signal matrix employed can be exploited. For real signals, the computational complexity of ESPRIT and Unitary ESPRIT is the same. ESPRIT [5] is a computationally efficient and robust method for estimating DOA which was developed in order to overcome the disadvantages of MUSIC. Other versions of ESPRIT have been developed to improve the technique, e.g. Least Squares (LS-ESPRIT), Total Least Squares (TLS-ESPRIT) [6], Unitary-ESPRIT [7]. Unitary-ESPRIT further reduces the computational complexity of the standard ESPRIT algorithm [21] by using real-valued computations from start to finish. It not only estimates the DOA but it can be used to estimate the number of sources present. It also it incorporates Forward-backward averaging which overcomes the problem of coherent signal sources. In this paper, the standard version of ESPRIT and Unitary-ESPRIT are also tested.

5 Simulation and Performance Comparison

Data Specification

Signal specification:

Data Model: QPSK

Input bit duration	T	= 0.5μsec
Sampling interval	t	= T/10;

Antenna Array Model:

Type: Uniform Linear array antenna

No. of array Elements	N	= 16
Free space velocity	c	= $3*10^8$
Centre frequency	fc	= 2.4GHz
Wavelength	λ	= c / fc
Inter element Spacing	d	= λ/2
Angle of arrival in degrees	θ	= -5 to 20 degree

In this section, we present some simulation results, to show the behavior of the four methods and to compare the performance with the analytically obtained Root Mean Squared Error (RMSE). We consider here a linear uniformly spaced array with 16-antenna elements spaced λ/2 apart.

It is evident that using more elements improves there solution of the algorithm in detecting the incoming signals. This is achieved, however, at the expense of computational efficiency and hardware complexity of the sensor array. Incoming QPSK cyclostationary signals are generated with additive white Gaussian noise with signal to noise ratio 10dB, the bit rate of the QPSK signal of interest is 2Mb/s and other QPSK modulated signals with data rate 1Mb/s are considered as interference. Maximum Likelihood Method and MUSIC are simulated using the specified parameters. The Cyclic MUSIC and Extended Cyclic MUSIC algorithms are also simulated with some cyclic frequency of 4MHz and some lag parameter of 2. One QPSK signals arrived at 20 degree and an interferer at 5 degree DOA .The Extended Cyclic MUSIC method allows perfect selection of the Signal of Interests and ignores the interference signal. RMSE Vs SNR plots for proposed four methods as shown in fig.1, fig.2, fig. 3 and fig.4. This section presents Mont Carlo computer simulation results to illustrate the performance of the proposed algorithms for synchronous system. Each Monte Carlo experiment involved a total of 500 runs, and each estimation algorithm is presented with exactly the same data intern. It is interesting to note that QPSK signal performs better than Exponential signal. So that bandwidth requirement is as low as possible for QPSK signals as exponential signals. In fig 5.it is interesting to note that the conventional MUSIC would require more data samples than Cyclic MUSIC to achieve the same RMSE. Extended Cyclic MUSIC shows the dramatic improvements than the Cyclic MUSIC. The error performance of MLM is not as good as Extended MUSIC and Cyclic MUSIC algorithms in severe fading environment. It is concluded that MLM does not provide consistent solution in multi path fading environment some residual error will always be present.

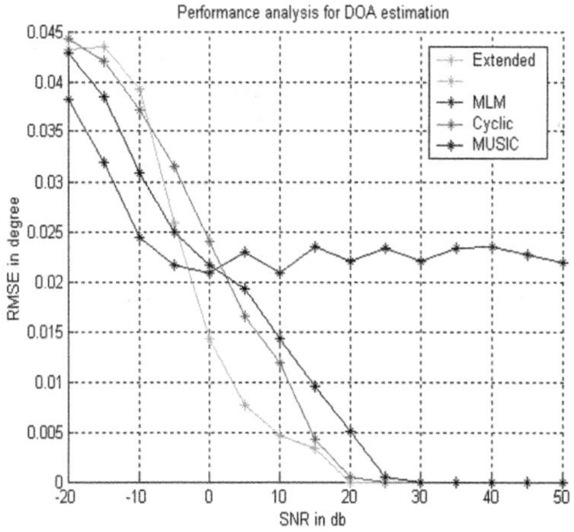

Fig. 5. Performance comparison Of all Methods with fading channel

6 Conclusion

It has been shown that for signals such as QPSK, smaller estimation errors in the signal and noise subspaces can be achieved than Exponential signals. Unlike MUSIC, Cyclic and Extended Cyclic does not suffer from the drawback of requiring a higher number of antenna elements than sources. Good signal selective capability and high resolution is achieved in extended Cyclic MUSIC algorithm than Cyclic MUSIC algorithm. This algorithm exploits cyclostationarity, which improves the signal Direction of Arrival estimation. The DOA estimation error produced by the Unitary-ESPRIT Algorithm showed that this algorithm is more sensitive to the SNR changes than the other algorithms. In addition, for complex signals and rectangular array unitary TLS-ESPRIT algorithm has a lower computational complexity and minimum error than standard ESPRIT, unitary ESPRIT and MUSIC algorithms.

References

[1] Lee, A., Stoica, P.: Maximum likelihood methods in radar signal processing (February 1998)

[2] Krim, A., Viberg, M.: Two decades of array signal processing Research. IEEE Signal Processing Magazine (July 1996)

[3] McCloud, M.L., Varanasi, K.: Beamforming, Diversity,and Interference Rejection for Multiuser communication over fading channels with a receive antenna array. IEEE Trans. on Comm. 51 (January 2003)

[4] Kumaresan, R., Tufts, D.W.: Estimating the angles arrival of multiple plane waves. IEEE Trans. Aerosp., Electron. Syst. AES -19 (January 1983)

[5] Sharman, K.C., Durrani, T.S.: Maximum Likelihood parameter estimation by simulated anneling. In: Proc. IEEE Int. Conf. Acoust. Speech Processing (April 1988)

[6] Miller, M., Fuhrmann, D.: Maximum Likelihood Direction of Arrival Estimation for multiple narrow band signals in noise. In: Proc. 1987 Conf. Inform. Sciences, Syst., pp. 710–712 (March 1987)

[7] Schell, S.V.: Performance analysis of the Cyclic MUSIC method of Direction Estimation for Cyclostationary Signals. Trans. on (November 1994)

[8] Stoica, P., Sharman, K.C.: A novel eigenanalysis method for direction estimation. In: Proc. Inst. Elec. Eng., pt (Febraury 1990)

[9] Zoltowski, M.D., Wong, K.T.: Closed-form eigenstructure-based direction finding using arbitrary but identical subarrays on a sparse uniform Cartesian array grid. IEEE Trans. Signal Processing 48, 2205–2210

[10] Athley, Engdahl, C.: Direction-of-arrival estimation using separated subarrays. In: Proc. 34th Asilomar Conf. zignals, Syst., Comput., Pacific Groove, CA, vol. 1, pp. 585–589 (November 2000)

[11] Swindlehurst, A.L., Stoica, P., Jansson, M.: Exploiting arrays with multiple invariance using MUSIC and MODE. IEEE Trans. Signal Processing 49, 2511–2521 (2001)

[12] Pesavento, M., Gershman, A.B., Wong, K.M.: Direction of arrival estimation in partly calibrated time- varying sensor arrays. In: Proc. ICASSP, Salt Lake City, UT, pp. 3005–3008 (May 2001)

[13] Pesavento, Gershman, A.B., Wong, K.M.: Direction finding in partly-calibrated sensor arrays composed of multiple subarrays. IEEE Trans. Signal Processing 50, 2103–2115 (2002)

[14] See, C.M.S., Gershman, A.B.: Subspace-based direction finding in partly calibrated arrays of arbitrary geometry. In: Proc. ICASSP, Orlando, FL, pp. 3013–3016 (April 2002)

[15] Pesavento, M., Gershman, A.B., Wong, K.M.: On uniqueness of direction of arrival estimates using rank reduction estimator (RARE). In: Proc. ICASSP, Orlando, FL, pp. 3021–3024 (April 2002)

[16] Pesavento, M., Gershman, A.B., Wong, K.M., Böhme, J.F.: Direction finding in partly calibrated arrays composed of nonidentical subarrays: A computationally efficient algorithm for the RARE estimator. In: Proc. IEEE Statist. Signal Process. Workshop, Singapore, pp. 536–539 (August 2001)

[17] Xiao, Y., Lee, M.H.: MIMO multiuser detection for CDMA systems. IEEE Signal Processing 1 (February 2006)

[18] Boubaker, N., Letief, K.B., Much, R.D.: Performance of BLAST over frequency-selective wireless Communication Channels. IEEE Trans. on communications 50(2), 196–199 (2002)

[19] Choi, J.: Beamforming for the multiuser detection with decorrelator in synchronous CDMA systems:Approaches and performance analysis. IEEE Signal Processing 60, 195–211 (1997)

[20] Yang, W., Li, S., Tan, Z.: A two dimensional DOA Estimation algorithm for CDMA system with plane antenna array. In: IEEE ISCAS, pp. 341–344 (2004)

[21] Miao, H., Juntti, M., Yy, K.: 2-D unitary ESPRIT base Joint AOA and AOD estimation for MIMO System. Personal, Indoor and Mobile Radio Communications, 5 (September 2006)

AGRO-ELECTRONICS

M. Mithra Kiran[1] and Bondili Kohitha Bai[2]

[1] Department of Electronics and Communication Engineering, SBIT, JNTUH, India
[2] Department of Electronics and Communication Engineering, ASET, AUUP, India
harshamithra@gmail.com, kohitha@gmail.com

Abstract. Electronics has been reaching to new fronts. Even Agriculture has benefited from this, keeping in the view the basic needs of farmers, horticulture, several advancements have been proposed that could use the electronics exhaustively. The complete thesis is prepared on the basis of analog circuitry. We have used analog circuitry purposefully, as the farmer could relax with this "once and for all" installation. Auto irrigation is the method of application of precise amount of water automatically as per crop requirement through saving resources like water, power, and fertilizer. Also, we have shown how the basic electronic devices can be made to work in horticulture. Some devices like photo transistor, IR LED have been used, which are robust, and very cheap. Going for analog circuitry has another reason. It is extremely cost effective.

1 Introduction

The rapid advances in electronics and its successful use in developing auto irrigation system has made it possible to practice efficient irrigation system and various other applications of technology in agriculture. Auto irrigation is done based on volume, time, and sensor and so on.

The sensor based systems are also called as real time feed back systems, because these are directly related to the plant response to the surrounding environment and different parameters related to plant stress and yield produced. This system is based on the actual dynamic demands of plants for inputs like water fertilizer temperature, various sensors to sense temperature, humidity, rainfall, soil moisture contents soil moisture stress, pH, etc are developed and being in use in well-developed countries. Out of these sensors, soil moisture sensor, based on nichrome [1] rods is a robust method and a very cost effective one.

The import of the automatic systems is very costly and also they may need some critical modifications to suit for our soil and environmental conditions. Hence it is a need to develop indigenous devices for automation and also their cost should be in the economic range of small and marginal farmer too.

As the power in rural areas may not be available throughout the day and it may be during night times mostly. The available power may not have constant voltage and as

D. Nagamalai, E. Renault, and M. Dhanushkodi (Eds.): PDCTA 2011, CCIS 203, pp. 25–30, 2011.

a result, the motor may get damaged. A solar panel powered motor is a better option which can be operated according to the convenience of the farmer anytime during the day time. The excess voltage can be stored in a rechargeable battery that may be used for lighting systems at the field or to the plants (in horticulture) during night time.

The conventional fencing systems used in the fields by the farmers is power lines which cause a huge loss of animals and the farmers themselves when entered without proper care. This can be prevented by the usage of an IR fencing system which generates an IR frequency along the perimeter of the field and when crisscrossed by animals and trespassers, an alarm can be driven.

2 Architecture

2.1 Pump Section

Commonly available nichrome [1] rods are used to sense the moisture content of the soil. The tuning of the preset provided in the circuit enables to detect the level of moisture in the soil.

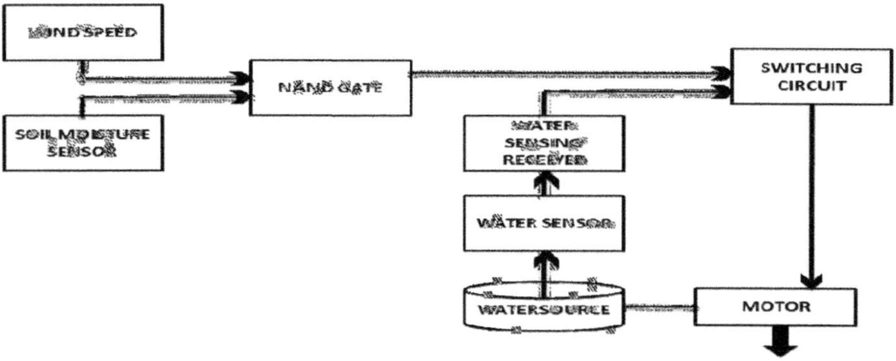

Fig. 1. Pump section

The wind speed also shows an impact in the evaporation of the moisture content in the open fields. Greater the speed of wind, greater is the evaporation of water in the soil. Both the wind section [2] and the moisture sensor section may drive the switching circuit, if the water is not available in the water source, then the motor coils may be blown away. To prevent this hazard, a water sensing circuit is designed which senses the water content in the water source and then turns on the power circuit. The water source may be a well, bore well, near by canal, storage tank, etc.

The water sensing circuit comprises of a mercury enabled switch which is gravity dependent. When water present in the water source, the mercury closes the circuit which falls on the wires by gravity. And when the water source is empty or dry, then the mercury falls back in the bottle, thereby opening the circuit and cutting off the power supply to the pump section.

2.2 IR Fencing System

The conventional electric fencing may harm the farmer itself when he goes around the field during night times for switching on the motor or something else. Instead of this conventional technique, an Optical based Security System can be used where, a Beam transmitter is used, that transmits Infrared Beams, and a receiver that senses these IR signals, also known as Photo Eyes. These sensors detect the presence of a person or object that interrupts the Infrared beam by passing through its path. Light beams use a transmitter/receiver system to send an invisible or infrared light beam through the air along a desired path. When the beam is interrupted, a signal is sent to the internal relay, which is wired into the device controls. An alarm output is attached or is placed where it is needed, to alarm the farmer that someone or something has crossed the fencing of the field. This eliminates the usage of electrical fencing system thereby saving the lives of farmer itself.

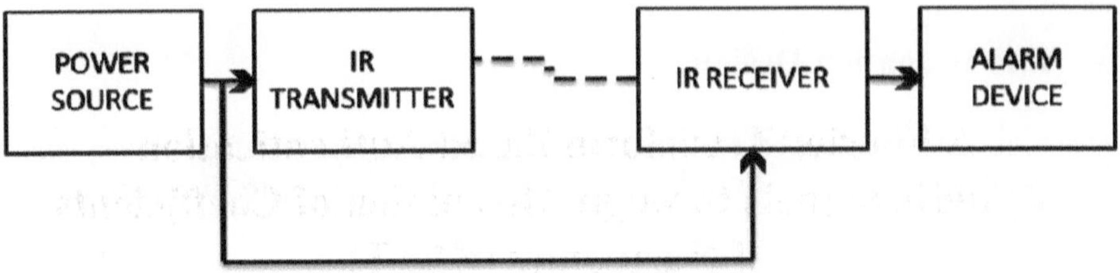

Fig. 2. IR fencing system

2.3 Artificial Lighting System

As the final production depends upon the light intensity there is a need to supply the excess amount of light when there is no sufficient light available. In enclosed or limited area farming, a dispersive reflector can be installed. Where the minimum light received by the mirror gets reflected and also dispersed. This job can be accomplished with the usage of a convex mirror. The motion of this reflector is controlled by a small motor which rotates in the direction of the light-source. The light is sensed with the usage of photo detectors [3] like high power photo transistors, etc. Hence, when there is sufficient lighting available, there is no need for the usage of these reflectors. And when there is dim light, the reflectors will do their job.

In odd seasons like rainy seasons or winter season or whenever the weather is cloudy, a panel of pre-arranged lighting system gets turned on. Whenever the light intensity decreases from a predetermined level, it can be given to an inverter circuit (NOT GATE) that turns on the light array. These light arrays may comprise of LEDs. This will be particularly helpful in the horticultural [4] fields and in ornamental flowers/fruits development centers.

Fig. 3. Artificial lightning system

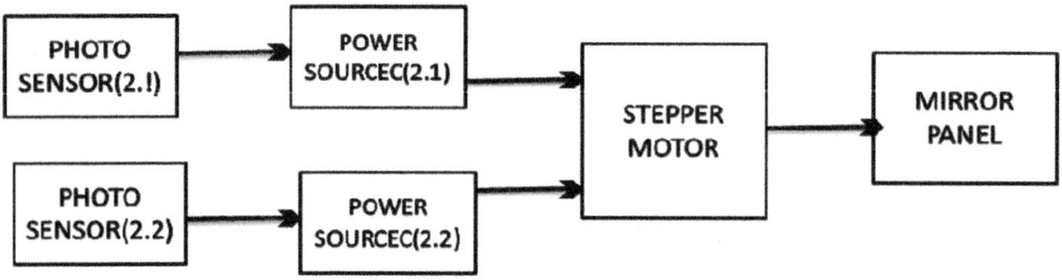

Fig. 4. Artificial lightning system

3 Auto Irrigation Design

In auto-irrigation, sensor based systems are also called as real time feed back systems, because these are directly related to the plant response to the surrounding environment and different parameters related to plant stress and yield produced. This system is based on the actual dynamic demands of plants for inputs like water fertilizer temperature, various sensors to sense temperature, humidity, rainfall, soil moisture contents soil moisture stress, pH, etc are developed and being in use in well-developed countries. Out of these sensors, soil moisture sensor, based on Nichrome rods is a robust method and a very cost effective one.

The import of the automatic systems is very costly and also they may need some critical modifications to suit for our soil and environmental conditions. Hence it is needed to develop indigenous devices for automation and also their cost should be in the economic range of small and marginal farmer too.

As the power in rural areas may not be available throughout the day and it may be during night times mostly. The available power may not have constant voltage and as a result, the motor may get damaged. A solar panel powered motor is a better option which can be operated according to the convenience of the farmer anytime during the day time. The excess voltage can be stored in a rechargeable battery that may be used for lighting systems at the field or to the plants (in horticulture) during night time.

The conventional fencing systems used in the fields by the farmers is power lines which cause a huge loss of animals and the farmers themselves when entered without proper care. This can be prevented by the usage of an IR fencing system which generates an IR frequency along the perimeter of the field and when crisscrossed by animal and trespassers, an alarm can be driven.

4 Circuit Photographs

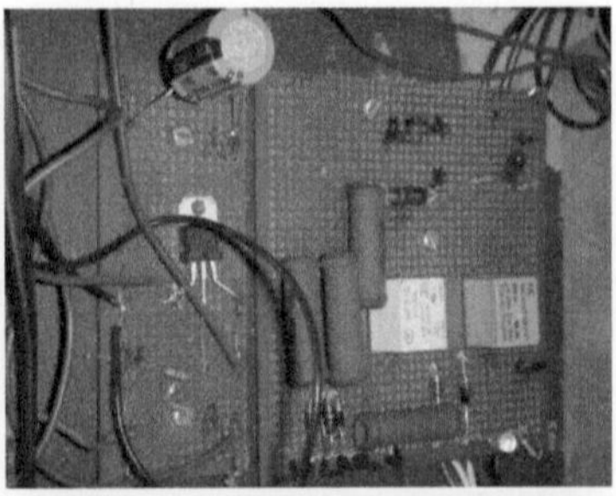
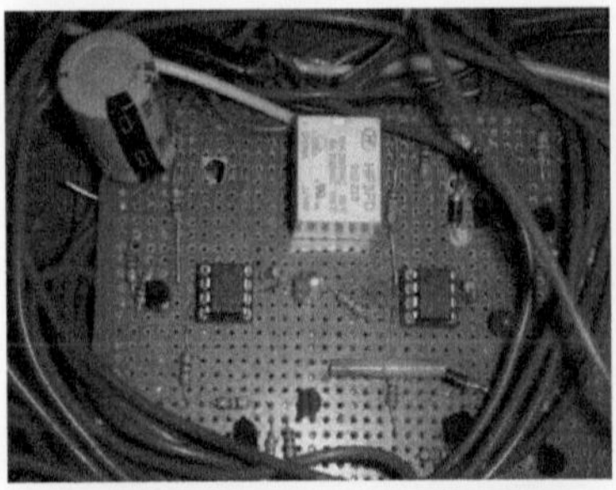

5 Conclusions

Excessive watering to the crop may result in a variety of problems like water logging, development of microbes that may affect the plant growth. Several weeds may grow due to the presence of excess of water and with it, the nutrients also. Such incidents could be avoided by the use of electronic gadgets suggested in the preceding paragraphs. It would not only avoid the losses, but also improve the yield while saving the unnecessary expenditure also.

And a method has been suggested to improve the overall production especially in the limited area farming and in horticulture by the double layer stacked version farming, which is almost a new technique of its kind.

References

1. Zhou, J., Ohno, T.R., Wolden, C.A.: High-temperature stability of nichrome inreactive environments. Journal of Vacuum Science & Technology A: Vacuum, Surfaces, and Films
2. Shen, Qin, G.P., Dong, M., Huang, Z.Q.: An intelligent wind sensor system with auto-zero function (June 21-25, 2009), doi:10.1109/ sensor.2009.5285514
3. Sawhney, A.K.: Electronics measurement and Instrumentation
4. Kumar, H.: Thesis on Tensiometer, Bapatla Agricultural Engineering College, Bapatla, Andhra Pradesh
5. Electronics for You 42(2) (February 2010)

Vector Quantization Based Face Recognition Using Integrated Adaptive Fuzzy Clustering

Elizabeth B. Varghese and M. Wilscy

Department Of Computer Science, University Of Kerala
Kariavattom, Thiruvananthapuram-695581, Kerala, India
{eliza.b.varghese,wilsyphilipose}@gmail.com

Abstract. A face recognition system is a computer application for automatically identifying or verifying a person from a digital image or a video frame. In this paper, an improved codebook design method is proposed for Vector Quantization (VQ)-based face recognition which improves recognition accuracy. A codebook is created by combining a systematically organized codebook based on the classification of code patterns and another codebook created by Integrated Adaptive Fuzzy Clustering (IAFC) method. IAFC is a fuzzy neural network which incorporates a fuzzy learning rule into a neural network. The performance of proposed algorithm is demonstrated by using publicly available AT&T database and Yale database. The evaluation has been done using two methodologies; first with no rejection criteria, and then with rejection criteria By applying the rejection criteria an equal error rate of 3.5 % is obtained for AT & T database and 6 % is obtained for Yale database Experimental results also show the face recognition using the proposed codebook with no rejection criteria is more efficient yielding a rate of 99.25% for AT & T and 98.18% for Yale which is higher than most of the existing methods.

Keywords: Face Recognition, Vector Quantization, Codebook, Integrated Adaptive Fuzzy Clustering, Self Organization Map.

1 Introduction

In most situations face recognition is an effortless task for humans. Machine Recognition of faces from still and video images is emerging as an active research area spanning several disciplines such as image processing, pattern recognition, computer vision, neural networks etc [1]. Face recognition technology has numerous commercial and law enforcement applications [1]. Applications range from static matching of controlled format photographs such as passports, credit cards, photo IDs, driver‘s licenses to real time matching of surveillance video images [1].

A lot of algorithms have been proposed for solving face recognition problem [2]. Among these Principal Component Analysis (PCA) is the most common one. PCA [3] is used to represent a face in terms of an optimal coordinate system which contains the most significant eigenfaces where the mean square error is minimal. Fisherfaces

D. Nagamalai, E. Renault, and M. Dhanushkodi (Eds.): PDCTA 2011, CCIS 203, pp. 31–43, 2011.

[4] which use Linear Discriminant Analysis (LDA); Bayesian methods[5], which use a probabilistic distance metric; and SVM methods [6], which use a support vector machine as the classifier, are also present. Being able to offer potentially greater generalization through learning, neural networks have also been applied to face recognition [7]. Feature-based approach [8] uses the relationship between facial features, such as the locations of eye, mouth and nose. Local Feature Analysis (LFA) [9], local autocorrelations and multiscale integration technique [10], etc are some of the methods.

Kotani et al. [11] have proposed a very simple yet highly reliable VQ-based face recognition method called VQ histogram method by using a systematically organized codebook for 4x4 blocks with 33 codevectors. Chen et al [12] proposed another face recognition system based on an optimized codebook which consists of a systematically organized codebook and a codebook created by Kohonen's Self Organizing Maps (SOM) [16].

VQ algorithm [13] is well known in the field of image compression. A codebook is very important since it directly affects the quality of VQ processing. In [12] an optimized codebook is created based on classification of code patterns and SOM. The Kohonen self-organizing feature map has to assume the number of clusters a priori and to initialize the cluster centroids. SOM guarantee convergence of weights by ensuring decrease in learning rates with time. Such learning rates, however, do not consider the similarity of the input pattern to the prototype of the corresponding cluster [17].

In this paper an improved codebook design method for VQ-based face recognition is proposed. At first a systematically organized codebook is created based on the distribution of code patterns [12], and then another codebook with the same size is created using Integrated Adaptive Fuzzy Clustering Method (IAFC) [17]. IAFC addresses the problems associated with SOM. In IAFC a fuzzy membership value is incorporated in the learning rule. This fuzzy membership value of the input pattern provides additional information for correct categorization of the input patterns. Moreover IAFC does not assume the number of clusters in the data set a priori, but updates it during processing of data [17].

The two codebooks are combined to form a single codebook which consists of 2x2 codevectors. By applying VQ the dimensionality of the faces are reduced. The histograms of the training images are created from the codevectors. This is considered as the personal identification information. It can represent the features of the facial images more adequately. The system was tested using publicly available AT & T database and Yale database. A recognition rate of 99.25% and 98.18% are obtained for AT & T and Yale respectively without rejection. By applying the rejection criteria an equal error rate of 3.5 % is obtained for AT & T database and 6 % is obtained for Yale database.

The rest of the paper is organized as follows: Proposed face recognition system based on systematically organized codebook and IAFC is explained in section 2. Proposed Adaptive Codebook design is discussed in section 3. Experimental results are presented and discussed in section 4. Conclusions are given in section 5.

2 Design of the Proposed Face Recognition System

The proposed method starts with the pre-processing step. Preprocessing is explained in detail in section 2.1.During pre-processing each face image in the training set is processed to get the intensity variation vectors. Vector Quantization (VQ) is then applied to these vectors by using the proposed codebook which is a combination of two codebooks. The first codebook is developed by code classification [12]. The second codebook is created using IAFC [17]. During VQ the most similar codevector to each input block is selected.

After performing VQ, matched frequencies for each codevector are counted and histogram is saved in the database as Personal Identification Information. This histogram becomes the feature vector of the human face. Thus histogram is a very effective personal feature for discriminating between persons.

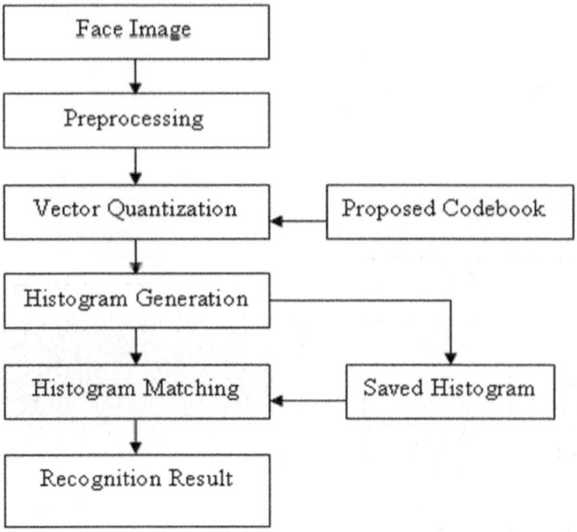

Fig. 1. Proposed Face Recognition System without rejection

In the recognition procedure, the histogram made from an input test image is compared with registered individual histograms and the best match is output as the recognition result. Manhattan distance between the histograms is used as the matching measure. Figure 1 shows the block diagram of the proposed method without rejection

For practical applications of face recognition, not a simple recognition rate but a False Accept Rate (FAR) and a False Reject Rate (FRR) are more important [11]. To calculate FAR and FRR rejection rate is also needed. The simplest way to add rejection ability is to set a threshold on the minimum Manhattan distance, which is denoted by *Th* and to reject a face if *Th,* exceeds this threshold. Based on this rejection criteria the image is either recognized (classified as a known person) or rejected (classified as unknown person).Figure 2 shows the block diagram of the proposed method with rejection.

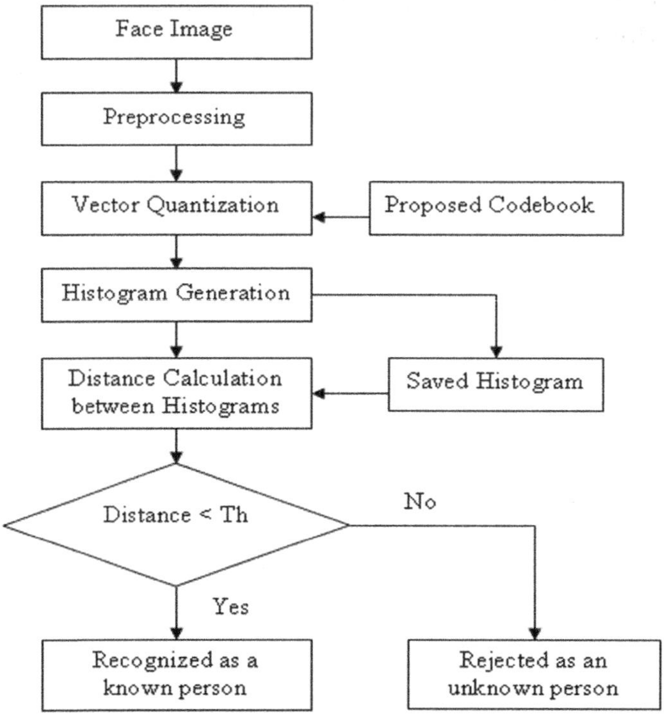

Fig. 2. Proposed Face Recognition System with rejection

Codebook which consists of typical feature patterns for representing the features of the face image is important. The proposed codebook design is explained in section 3.2

2.1 Preprocessing

During preprocessing initially a low pass filtering is carried out using a simple 2D mean filter [11]. A low pass filtering is effective for eliminating the noise component. By applying the filter, detailed facial features degrading recognition performance such as wrinkles and local hairstyle, are excluded. Only the important personal features, such as the rough shape of facial parts can be extracted.

The image is then divided into 2x2 overlapping blocks. Minimum intensity of the individual block is subtracted from each pixel in the block. Minimum intensity subtraction effectively excludes dc and vary low frequency component, such as shade variations due to small variations in lighting conditions and retains only the relevant information for distinguishing images. The preprocessing steps are explained in figure 3.

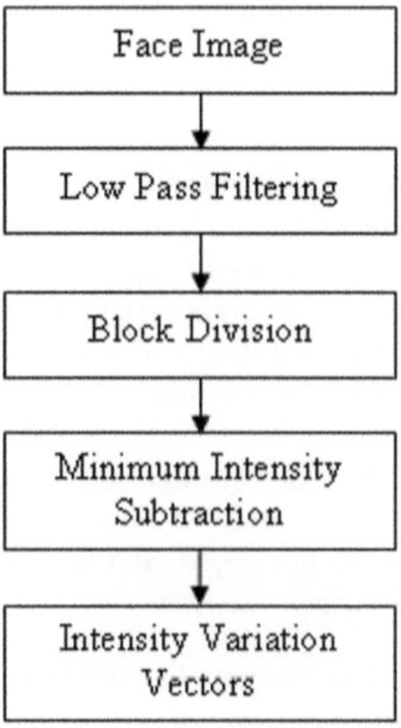

Fig. 3. Preprocessing Steps

3 The Proposed Adaptive Codebook Design

The proposed codebook for VQ is obtained from two codebooks. One codebook with size N is obtained by code classification [12] which is explained in section 3.1. This codebook is created by the variation in the intensity of the code patterns. It does not consider the intensity variations of the face images. So it cannot represent the facial features efficiently. So a second codebook is needed from the facial images to represent the facial features more efficiently.

In [12] a second codebook is created using Kohonen‘s SOM [16]. The self-organizing feature map self-organizes its weights by incremental adjustments in proportion to the difference between the current weight and the input pattern. In real applications, it is often difficult to assume the number of clusters present in many real data sets. And, different initial conditions result in different results. This neural network also requires considerable time to train [17]. In the proposed method the second codebook is created using IAFC [17] of the same size N. In IAFC a fuzzy membership value is incorporated in the learning rule. This fuzzy membership value helps in the correct categorization of the input patterns. Also IAFC does not assume the number of clusters in the data set a priori, but updates it during processing of data [17].

Thus a codebook of size 2N is obtained. To reduce the size of the codebook from 2N to N, the face images in the training set is preprocessed to get the intensity variation vectors. Then VQ is applied to these intensity variation vectors, matched frequencies of each codevector are counted and histogram of each face image is generated. Then the average histogram of all images is calculated. Next, the frequencies of individual codevectors are sorted. From this sorted 2N codevectors, only the high frequency N codevectors are selected. Thus, the final codebook consisting of 2x2 codevectors is generated.

3.1 Codebook Generated by Code Classification

Nakayama et al [14] have developed complete classification method for 2x2 codebook design in image compression. Figure 3 shows all categories for the 2x2 image block patterns without considering the location of pixels. In a 2x2 block, pixel intensities are marked by alphabet 'a', 'b', 'c', 'd', and a > b > c > d is prescribed. In ref. [14], it was found that the number of typical patterns for all 2x2 image block is only 11. The number of varieties in pixel arrangement of each 2x2 typical pattern is also shown in figure 4. That means the total number of image patterns for 2x2 pixel blocks is theoretically only 75.By the similar consideration, Chen et al [15] classified and analyzed the code patterns in the face images. They found that in all filter size, the number of code patterns belong to categories 7, 10, and 11 are very few. It means such code patterns are almost not used in face images. Based on this result, a new codebook for 2x2 code patterns is created, and the rules of codebook creation are as follows.

- Change the intensity difference among the blocks to from 1 to 10.
- Create very small intensity variation codes. The total number of patterns is 16
- Create code patterns of category no: 2,3,4,5,6,8 and 9
- Add one code pattern having no intensity variation

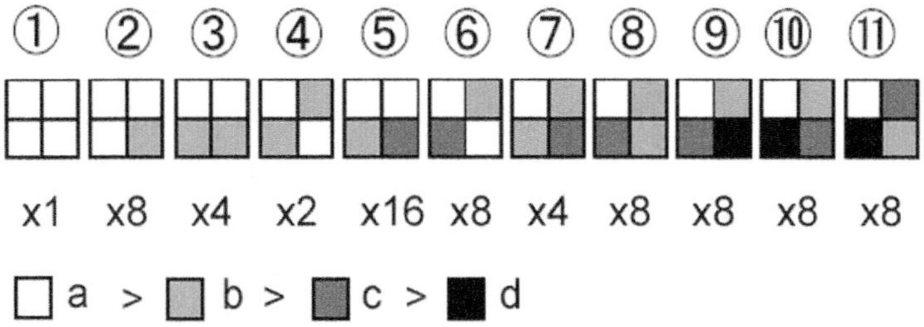

Fig. 4. Categories of 2x2 code patterns

3.2 Codebook Design Using IAFC

The IAFC model is a fuzzy neural network which incorporates a fuzzy learning rule into a neural network [17]. The learning rule, developed in IAFC, incorporates a fuzzy membership value (μ_i), an intracluster membership value (π), and a function of the number of iterations (f (l)) into a Kohonen-type learning rule. The number of clusters in IAFC is updated dynamically. An intracluster membership value (π) is decided by the distance between the input pattern and the centroid of the chosen cluster. The combination of the π-function and a function of the number of iterations guarantee weights to converge. The IAFC model incorporates a similarity measure that includes a fuzzy membership value into the Euclidean distance. The similarity measure considers not only the distance between the input data point and the centroid of a winning cluster but also the relative location of the input point to the existing cluster centroids as the degree of similarity. Thus, it gives more flexibility to the shape of clusters formed [17].

IAFC consists of three major procedures: deciding a winning cluster, performing the vigilance test, and updating the centroid of a winning cluster. The input pattern X is normalized prior to presentation to the fuzzy neural network and this normalized input pattern is fed to the fuzzy neural network in parallel to the input pattern. A dot-product operation used to find the winner is shown below

$$I \bullet b_i = \frac{X \bullet v_i}{\|X\| \bullet \|v_i\|} \tag{1}$$

Where *bi* is the normalized weights from the input neurons to the ith output cluster, and v_i is the ith cluster centroid. The output neuron that receives the largest value for the equation (1) wins the competition. In this process, the winner is decided by the angle between the input pattern and the centroids of clusters. This can cause misclassifications because a cluster of which the direction of the centroid vector has the smallest angle with the input vector wins the competition even though its centroid is located farther from the input pattern than other cluster centroids. In such a case, Euclidean distance can be used as a better similarity measure to determine a winner. However, cluster centroids cannot approach appropriate locations during the early stage of learning, thus causing poor performance of clustering algorithms. To prevent both problems, the IAFC algorithm uses a combined similarity measure to decide a winner.

After deciding a winner by the dot product, the IAFC algorithm compares the fuzzy membership value, μ_i of the input pattern in the winning cluster with the parameter σ that user can decide as a threshold of the fuzzy membership value. If the fuzzy membership value is less than the value of the parameter σ, the angle between the input pattern and the cluster centroid is the dominant similarity measure to decide a winner. On the other hand, if the parameter σ is high, the Euclidean distance between the input pattern and the cluster centroid is the dominant similarity measure to decide a winner. After selecting a winning cluster, IAFC performs the vigilance test according to the criterion:

$$e^{-\gamma\mu_i}\|X - v_i\| <= \tau \tag{2}$$

Where γ is a multiplicative factor that controls the shape of clusters, X is the input pattern, v_i is the centroid of the ith winning cluster, τ is the vigilance parameter and the value of γ is normally chosen to be 1[17]. The fuzzy membership value μ_i, is calculated as follows:

$$\mu_i = \frac{\left(\frac{1}{\|X - v_i\|^2}\right)^{1/m-1}}{\sum_{j=1}^{n}\left(\frac{1}{\|X - v_j\|^2}\right)^{1/m-1}} \tag{3}$$

Where m is a weight exponent which is experimentally set to 2 [17] and n is the number of clusters. If a winning cluster satisfies the vigilance criterion, the centroid of a winning cluster is updated as follows:

$$v_i^{new} = v_i^{old} + \lambda_{fuzzy}\left(X - v_i^{old}\right) \tag{4}$$

Where λ_{fuzzy} is $[f(l).\ \pi(X;\ v_i^{(old)};\ \tau).\ \mu_i^2].f(l)$ is a function of number of iterations, l being the number of iterations, and π decides the intra-cluster membership value of the input pattern X in the ith cluster as:

$$\pi(X;\ v_i^{(old)};\ \tau)=\begin{cases} 1-2\left(\dfrac{\left\|X-v_i^{old}\right\|}{\tau}\right)^2, 0\le\left\|X-v_i^{old}\right\|\le\tau/2 \\ 2\left(1-\dfrac{\left\|X-v_i^{old}\right\|}{\tau}\right)^2, \tau/2\le\left\|X-v_i^{old}\right\|\le\tau \\ 0, \left\|X-v_i^{old}\right\|\ge\tau \end{cases} \tag{5}$$

And

$$f(l)=\frac{1}{k(l-1)+1} \tag{6}$$

Where k is a constant

IAFC algorithm for the codebook design can be summarized by the following steps:

1. Initialize parameters τ and σ.
2. Transform the facial images in dataset to intensity variation vectors, and combine all vectors together into one training set.
3. Initialize the weight vectors with the intensity variation vectors.
4. Select a new input pattern from the training set.
5. Decide a winning cluster (best matching codevector) using the combined similarity measure.

   5(a) Calculate the dot product between the normalized input pattern and the normalized weight vector using equation (1).

   5(b) Calculate the Euclidean distance between the input pattern and the weight vector.

6. Calculate the fuzzy membership value, μ_i of the input pattern in the winning cluster using equation (3).

6(a) If $\mu_i < \sigma$,
 the winner neuron is selected from 5(a)
 else
 the winner neuron is selected from 5(b)

7. Perform the vigilance test using equation (2). If the criterion is satisfied then update the weights using equation (4).
8. If all the input patterns are processed go to step 9 else go to step 4.
9. Stop.

4 Experimental Results and Discussions

Publicly available AT & T database [18] and Yale database [19] are used for recognition experiments. The AT & T database contains 400 images in pgm format of 40 persons. There are 10 different images of each of 40 distinct subjects. The images were taken at different times, varying the lighting, facial expressions (open / closed eyes, smiling / not smiling) and facial details (glasses / no glasses) [18]. The Yale Face Database contains 165 grayscale images in GIF format of 15 individuals. There are 11 images per subject, one per different facial expression or configuration: center-light, with glasses, happy, left-light, without glasses, normal, right-light, sad, sleepy, surprised, and wink [19]. Initially, the system has been tested with no rejection criteria. Then, a rejection criterion has been imposed into the system. The results without rejection and with rejection are explained in section 4.1 and 4.2 respectively.

4.1 Experiments with No Rejection Criteria

Five images were selected from each person's 10 images (in the case of AT & T) and from 11 images (in the case of Yale) for training purpose. The remaining images are used for testing. So 200 images from AT & T are used for training and the remaining 200 is used for testing. But in the case of Yale 75 images are used for training and 90 images are used for testing.

It is necessary to choose a suitable size for the codebook. As the codebook size is large, number of codevectors increases, the resolution of histogram may become so sensitive that noise corrupted codevectors may distort the histogram. On the contrary, if the number of codevectors is small, the histogram cannot sufficiently discriminate between faces. Recognition rate was observed for the codebook sizes 50, 60, 70, 80, 90, 100 and 110. It is clear from the figures 5 and 6 that the best performance is obtained with a codebook of size 80 for AT & T and with sizes 70 and 80 for Yale. With that size a recognition rate of 99.25% is obtained for AT & T and 98.18 % is obtained for Yale.

Figures 5 and 6 also show a comparison between the proposed approach and the existing method with SOM [16]. It is clear from the figures that in all the cases the proposed method yields a better recognition result than the existing method. It can be said that the proposed codebook is more efficient in representing the facial features than the existing method using systematically organized codebook and SOM [12].

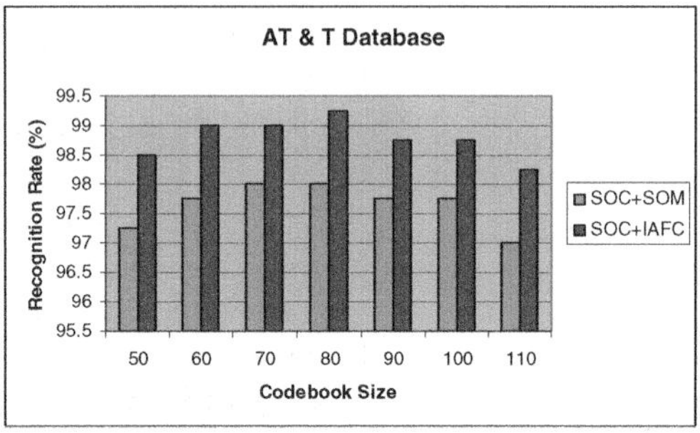

Fig. 5. Comparison of the recognition rate using AT & T database

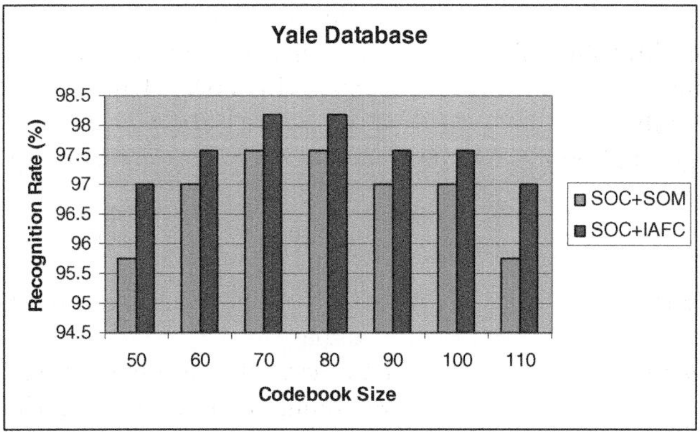

Fig. 6. Comparison of the recognition rate using Yale Face database

Experiments are also done by varying the values for the vigilance parameter, τ .The results are shown in figure 7. It is clear from the figure that for the value, $\tau = 2$, a higher recognition rate is achieved. In all the cases the codebook size is 80 and the value for σ is 0.5.

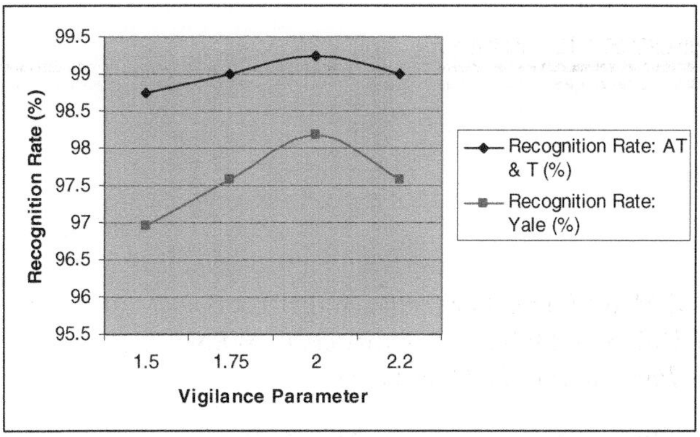

Fig. 7. Recognition rate for different values of τ

4.2 Experiments with Rejection Criteria

In complete absence of a rejection mechanism, all images presented to the recognition system, including images of unknown persons and background are mapped to the closest known face [10]. Reliably recognizing known persons while rejecting unknown persons is found to be a much more challenging task. Rejecting unknown faces means that the system has not only to accept wide variations in facial expression, head rotation, and so on, but also to reject patterns which lie quite close in the pattern space.

For the evaluation of the rejection performance of the system the databases are divided into two parts containing known faces and unknown faces. In the case of AT & T database, the 40 persons are divided into two parts containing 20 known faces and 20 unknown faces. So training is done with 100 images of the known 20 faces. The recognition and rejection performance of the system is then tested on all the 400 images of the database.

For verification a threshold was placed on the minimum distance between the histogram of the test face and the saved histograms in the database. Figure 8 shows False Acceptance Rate (FAR) and False Rejection Rate (FRR) plots for the verification experiment. An Equal Error Rate (ERR) of 3.5 % is achieved. In all these cases the codebook size is 80 and the value for the vigilance parameter, τ is 2.

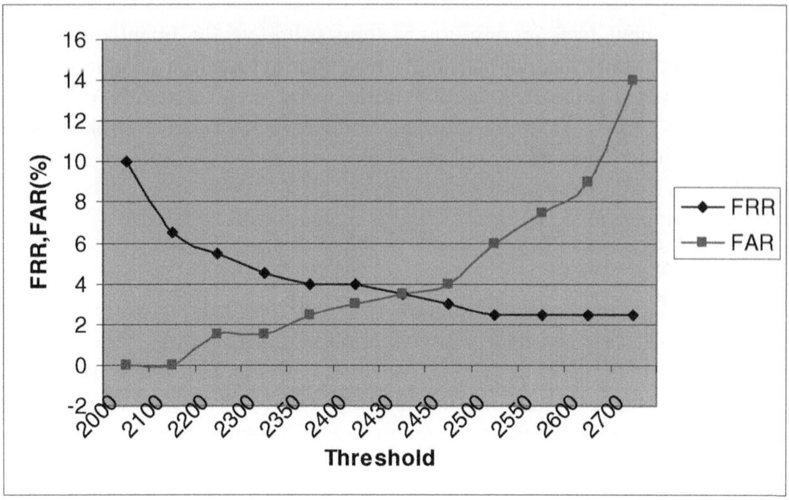

Fig. 8. False Acceptance Rate and False Rejection Rate (%) for AT & T database

Experiments are also done with the Yale database. In this case, 15 persons are divided into 8 known faces and 7 unknown faces. Training is done with 40 face images and testing is done with the all the 165 images in the database. Figure 9 shows False Acceptance Rate (FAR) and False Rejection Rate (FRR) plots for the verification experiment. An Equal Error Rate (ERR) of 6 % is achieved. In all these cases the codebook size is 80 and the value for the vigilance parameter, τ is 2.

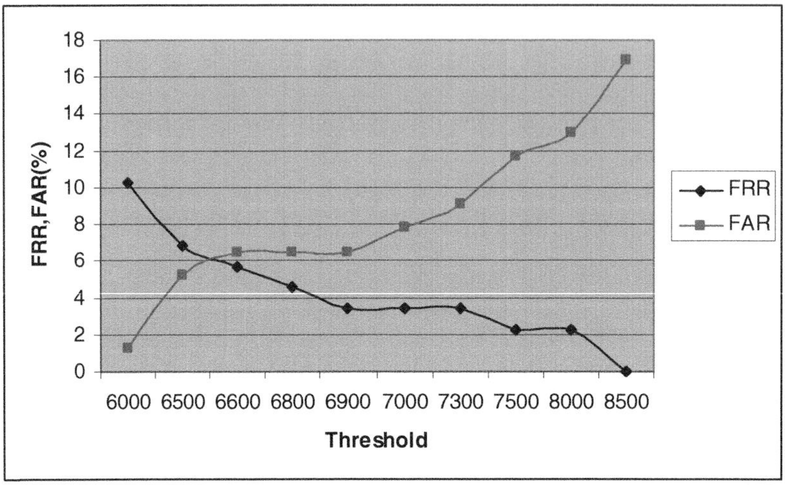

Fig. 9. False Acceptance Rate and False Rejection Rate (%) for Yale database

5 Conclusion

In this paper, a new face recognition system using vector quantization based on Integrated Adaptive Fuzzy Clustering (IAFC) is developed. A simple and efficient codebook design algorithm for face recognition using vector quantization is proposed. The codebook is created from two different codebooks. One codebook is created by code classification. The other codebook is created from the face images using Integrated Adaptive Fuzzy Clustering (IAFC). To create the codebook, the face images are divided into 2x2 blocks with a fixed codebook size. A good initial codebook is created from these blocks by code classification. The resultant initial codebook is combined with the codebook which is created by IAFC to become the final codebook. Utilizing such a codebook of size 80, a recognition rate of 99.25% is obtained for the AT & T database. For codebook sizes 70 and 80, a recognition rate of 98.18 % is obtained for Yale database. The results are more efficient than the existing method which consists of an optimized codebook with systematically organized codebook and Kohonen's SOM. For practical applications of face recognition, not a simple recognition rate but a False Acceptance Rate (FAR) and a False Rejection Rate (FRR) are more important. Rejection rate is calculated for obtaining the FAR and FRR. An Equal Error Rate (ERR) of 3.5 % and 6 % is obtained for AT & T and Yale database respectively.

References

1. Chellappa, R., Wilson, C.L., Sirohey, S.: Human and machine recognition of faces: a survey. Proc. IEEE 83(5), 705–740 (1995)
2. Li, S.Z., Jain, A.K.: Handbook of Face Recognition. Springer, New York (2005)

3. Turk, M., Pentland, A.: Eigenfaces for recognition. Journal of Cognitive Neuroscience 3(1), 71–86 (1991)
4. Belhumeur, P.N., Hespanh, J.P., Kriegman, D.J.: Eigenfaces vs Fisherfaces. Recognition using class specific linear projection. IEEE Trans. Pattern Anal. Machine Intell. 19, 711–720 (1997)
5. Moghaddam, B., Nastar, C., Pentland, A.: A Bayesian similarity measure for direct image matching. In: Proceedings International Conference on Pattern Recognition (1996)
6. Phillips, P.J.: Support vector machines applied to face fecognition. Advanced Neural Information Processing Systems 11, 803–809 (1998)
7. Zhao, W., Chellappa, R., Phillips, P.J., Rosenfeld, A.: Face Recognition: A Literature Survey. ACM Computing Surveys 35(4), 399–458 (2003)
8. Brunelli, R., Poggio, T.: Face recognition: features versus templates. IEEE Transactions on Pattern Analysis and Machine Intelligence 15(10), 1042–1052 (1993)
9. Penev, P.S., Atick, J.J.: Local Feature Analysis: A general statistical theory for object representation. Network: Computation in Neural Systems 7(3), 477–500 (1996)
10. Goudail, F., Lange, E., Iwamoto, T., Kyuma, K., Otsu, N.: Face recognition system using local autocorrelations and multiscale integration. IEEE Transaction on Pattern Analysis and Machine Intelligence 18(10), 1024–1028 (1996)
11. Kotani, K., Chen, Q., Ohmi, T.: Face recognition using vector quantization histogram method. In: Proceedings of the 2002 Int. Conf. on Image Processing, vol. II of III, pp. II-105–II-108 (2002)
12. Chen, Q., Kotani, K., Lee, F.F., Ohmi, T.: A VQ based fast face recognition algorithmn using optimized codebook. In: Proceedings of the 2008 Int. Conf. on Wavelet Analysis and Pattern Recognition (2008)
13. Sayood, K.: Introduction to Data Compression. Morgan Kaufmann, San Francisco (2000)
14. Nakayama, T., Konda, M., Takeuchi, K., Kotani, K., Ohmi, T.: Still image compression with adaptive resolution vector quantization technique. Int. Journal of Intelligent Automation and Soft Computing 10(2), 155–166 (2004)
15. Chen, Q., Kotani, K., Lee, F.F., Ohmi, T.: Face recognition using codebook designed by code classification. In: IEEE Int. Conf. on Signal and Image Processing, pp. 397–401 (2006)
16. Kohonen, T.: The Self-Organizing Maps. Proceedings of the IEEE 78(9) (September 1990)
17. Kim, Y.S., Mitra, S.: An adaptive integrated fuzzy clustering model for pattern recognition. Journal Fuzzy Sets and Systems (65), 297–310 (1994)
18. AT & T. The Database of Faces, `http://www.cl.cam.ac.uk/research/dtg/attarchive/facedatabase.html`
19. Yale Face Database, `http://cvc.yale.edu/projects/yalefaces/yalefaces.html`

Transformation of Active Reference Graph into Passive Reference Graph for Distributed Garbage Collection

B. Seetha Lakshmi, C.D. Balapriya, and R. Soniya

KLN College of Information Technology, Pottapalayam, Sivagangai District, Tamil Nadu, India

Abstract. With the increasing use of active object systems, agents and concurrent object oriented languages like Java, the problem of garbage collection of unused resources has become more complicated. Since Active objects are standalone computational agents identifying garbage in active objects system cannot be based on reachability from a root set (which we use for passive objects). We have to go for separate algorithm to collect garbage on system which uses active objects. For the systems which use both active and passive objects we have to use 2 separate methods for collecting garbage. To avoid this we can use a transformation algorithm that can transfer active object reference graph into passive object reference graph, after which we can apply the passive object algorithm to collect garbage from the entire system. An attempt is made to travel through the transformation algorithms.

Keywords: Active Objects, Garbage Collection, Passive Objects, Distributed Garbage Collection, Transformation Algorithm.

1 Introduction

Automatic Storage Reclamation or Garbage collection is the process of automatically freeing objects that are no longer referenced by the program. When an object is no longer referenced by a program, the heap space it occupies can be recycled so that the space is made available for subsequent new objects. If there is no automatic storage reclamation then the programmer has to manually find the objects which are unused and has to collect them, which may be error prone. If there is automatic storage reclamation then the programmer can be relieved from the burden of memory management and hence the programs may be shorter.

Outline of the Paper

This paper is divided into 4 sections. In the first section the fundamentals of Actor System and Traditional Passive objects were introduced. In the second section Transformation Algorithm given by Vardhan et al. and in the third section Transformation algorithm given by Wei-Jen Wang et.al were discussed. In the section 4 conclusions were presented.

D. Nagamalai, E. Renault, and M. Dhanushkodi (Eds.): PDCTA 2011, CCIS 203, pp. 44–52, 2011.

1.1 Features and Terminology of the Actor Model

The principle features and terminology of the actor model which relate to the garbage collection problem are these:

Passive Object: A passive object is one that only speaks when spoken to. i.e., only responds and calls other functions on other objects, when one of its own functions is called. In essence, a traditional programming object.

Active Object: An active object has a mind and life of its own. It owns its own thread of control, notionally associated with its own mini address space.

Actor: A concurrently active object. There are no passive entities. Each actor is uniquely identified by the address of its single mail queue.

Acquaintance: Actor B is an acquaintance of actor A if B's mail queue address is known to actor A.

Inverse acquaintance: If actor A is an acquaintance of actor B, then actor B is an inverse acquaintance of A.

Acquaintance list: A set of mail queue addresses including any mail queue address contained in a message on the actors mail queue or in transit to the mail queue. This accounts for delays in message processing.

Blocked actor: All behaviors are blocked.

Active actor: An actor with at least one active behavior.

Root actors: An actor designated as being "always useful." Examples of root actors are those which have the ability to directly affect real-world through sensors, actuators, I/O devices, users, etc.

1.2 Distributed Garbage Collection

Detecting garbage in systems of active objects was first addressed in the framework of Actor-based languages, and detailed later by Kafura *et. al.* Intuitively, an object is garbage if 1) its absence from the system cannot be detected through external observation, excluding memory and processor resource consumption 2) it cannot potentially call a root object, nor be called by a root object; in other terms, 3) it cannot potentially interact with a root object. Actual detection of garbage relies on the introduction of root objects, depicted by triangles in the following figure; these objects are always needed, as they have the ability to directly interact with the external world. In Fig. 1, Object H embeds a reference to the root object G and is running, and thus it may call G; therefore, H is not garbage. Similarly, C is not garbage, since it may call the root object A. Objects I, J and F are garbage's, as they are insulated from the rest of the object graph. K is inactive and cannot be activated in the future because no object embeds a reference to it; thus, K is garbage. Objects B, D and E are not garbage, because they may be activated and then call a method on a root object. For example, in the case of object B, if C calls a method on B and gives it a reference to A as a parameter, B may then call the root object A, and thus is not garbage. Note that an object that cannot call a root object at a given time (either because it is inactive or does not contain a reference to a root object) may do so later since it may get a reference to a root object from another object through parameter passing (e.g., see object B in Fig.1). Therefore, there exists a set of transformations that changes the graph of objects from a representation of what can currently happen to what can potentially happen. Note also that a key property of garbage objects is that they cannot subsequently become non-garbage (stability property). This is because an object becomes garbage only if there is no possibility of interaction between it and a root object. Therefore, once an object is garbage, there is no sequence of transformation which could cause it to become non-garbage. It is significantly more difficult to detect garbage objects in systems of active objects as both the state and activity of objects have to be considered. Both the traditional mark and sweep and reference counting techniques that are based on reachability from root objects are not suited to systems of active objects. If mark and sweep were used for the system depicted in Fig.1 all the non-root objects would be incorrectly marked as garbage, because they are not reachable from a root object. Similarly, if reference counting were used, objects E and H would be wrongly considered as garbage, as their reference count is zero.

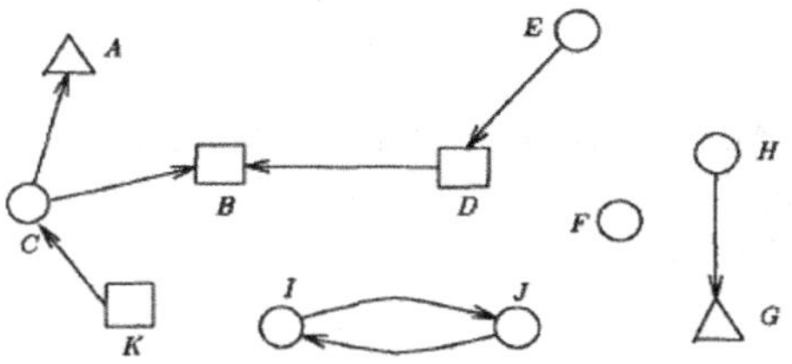

Fig. 1.

When a system contains both active and passive object garbage then we have to use active object garbage collection algorithm to collect actor garbage and use passive object garbage collection algorithm to collect passive object garbage. Instead of using two algorithms we can use transformation algorithm to transform active object graph into passive object graph. In the following sections let us discuss about 2 transformation algorithms. They are

1. Transformation Algorithm by Vardhan and Agha.
2. Transformation algorithm by Wei-Jen Wang et al.

2 Transformation Algorithm by Vardhan and Agha

The method proposed by Vardhan and Agha performs transformation of the actor reference graph which captures all the information necessary for actor GC, and makes it possible to apply a garbage collection algorithm for passive objects to the transformed graph in order to collect garbage actors. References between nodes in the transformed graph are derived using rules which depend not only on the actors to which know a particular actor, but also on which actors it knows; and whether or not that actor has messages pending in its mail queue.

2.1 Definition: Identifying Live Actors

1. A root actor is live.
2. If an actor 'a' is live, a forward acquaintance of 'a' is live.
3. If an actor 'a' is live, an inverse acquaintance of 'a' which is not permanently blocked is live.

2.2 Garbage Collection Framework

Without loss of generality Algorithm assumes that there is a single root actor r in the actor-reference graph: if there are more than one root actors, algorithm can add a hypothetical root actor which has references to the actual roots. Again without loss of generality algorithm assume that the root actor is always unblocked. This is because whether or not the root is unblocked is only important for deciding aliveness for an actor b which has the root in the recursive closure of the inverse acquaintance relation (by application of Rule 3 for identifying live actors as in Definition 1). Thus, we might decide that b is not permanently blocked when in fact it might have been considered permanently blocked if the root was blocked. The concern would then be that b should not be incorrectly classified as live. However, b must be in the recursive closure of the forward acquaintance relation from the root and hence by successive applications of Rule 2, will be considered live regardless of the application of Rule 3. Therefore, it makes no difference to the garbage status of any actor whether the root is blocked or unblocked.

Given the actor reference graph $G = (V,E)$ and a root actor $\rho \in V$, we define a transformation function $\tau : (G, \rho) \rightarrow (G', \rho')$ where $G' = (V',E')$ is another graph and $\rho' \in V'$. The nodes and edges of G' are constructed from the following rules:

2.3 Rules

Transformation $\tau : (G, \rho) \rightarrow (G', \rho')$ Let α and μ be bijective functions from actor names to labels such that $\text{Range}(\alpha) \cap \text{Range}(\mu) = \varnothing$.

1. The root object ρ' in G' is given by $\rho' = \mu(\rho)$.
2. For every actor named a in V, there are two corresponding nodes: $\alpha(a) \in A'$ and $\mu(a) \in M'$. $V'=A' \in M'$.
3. If an actor a is unblocked, there is an edge from $\mu(a)$ to $\alpha(a)$ in G'.
4. If an actor a has a reference to an actor b, there is an edge from $\alpha(a)$ to both $\alpha(b)$ and $\mu(b)$; and an edge from $\mu(b)$ to $\mu(a)$. The following figure illustrates this:

2.4 Algorithm

1. Obtain a snapshot $G = (V,E)$ of the actor reference graph. This can be done by any of the standard techniques for obtaining distributed snapshots.

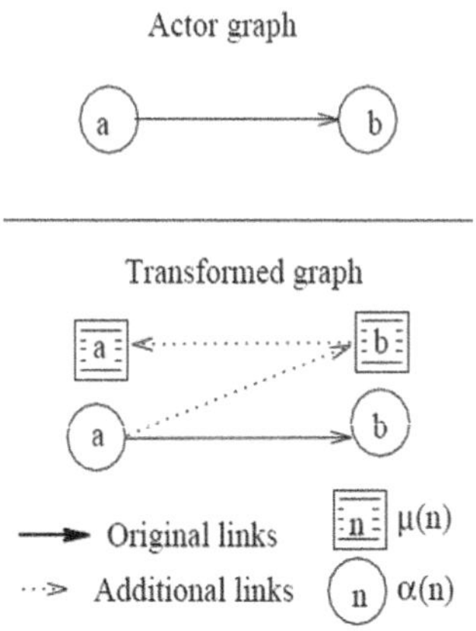

Fig. 2.

2. Apply the transformation to obtain (G', ρ') = τ (G, ρ) with G' = (V ',E') and V ' = A' ∪ M'.
3. Run any passive object garbage collection on G' with V' as the objects; E' as the edges defining the references; and root object ρ'. Let $V'_g \subset V'$ be the objects found as garbage on G'.
4. For all v' ∈ (V'_g ∩ A'), actor α^{-1}(v') is declared as garbage.

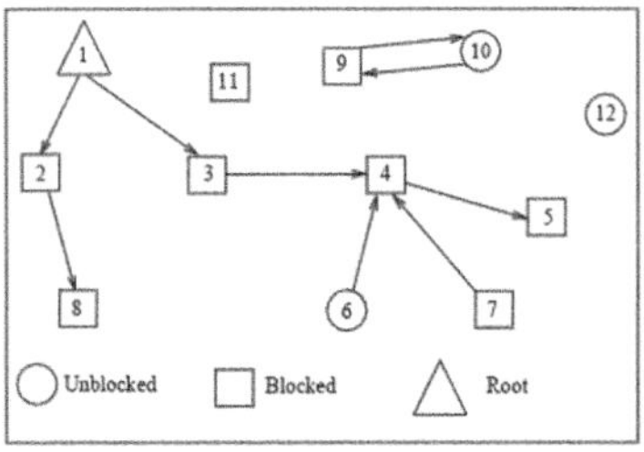

Fig. 3. Original Actor Reference Graph

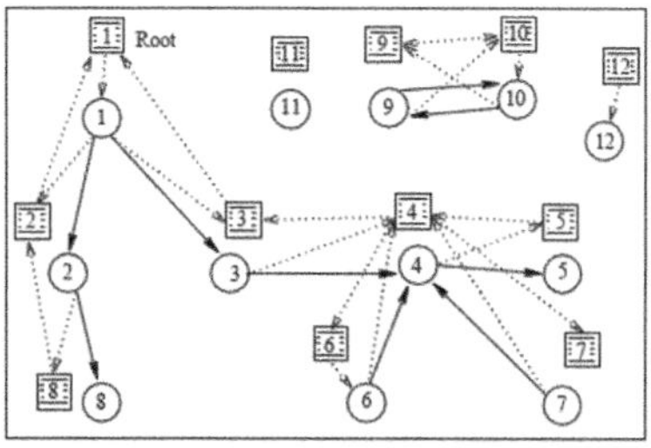

Fig. 4. Transformed Object Graph

In the above figure for actor names i = {1, 6, 10, 12} which are unblocked, there is an edge from μ(i) to α(i). Looking at this graph we can see that a garbage collector for passive objects would regard α(1), α(2), α(3), α(4), α(5), α(6) and α(8) as live and all others objects in A' as garbage. A look at the original actor-reference graph shows that it is exactly actors 1, 2, 3, 4, 5, 6 and 8 that are live. Of special interest is α(6) in the transformed graph. Because α(6) has a reference from μ(6) which is reachable from μ(1) (the root), it is correctly identified as being live. The reader can also note that, although μ(7) is reachable in the transformed graph, α(7) is not. By step 4 of Algorithm 1, it is α(7) that is used for deciding garbage status of actor 7 and hence 7 is correctly identified as garbage.

3 Transformation Algorithm by Wei-Jen Wang et al.

3.1 Garbage in Passive Object Systems

The essential concept of passive object garbage lies in the idea of the possibility of object manipulation. Objects that can be manipulated by the thread of control of the application are live; otherwise they are garbage. Root objects are those which can be directly accessed by the thread of control, while transitively live objects are those transitively reachable from the root objects by following references. The problem of passive object garbage collection can be represented as a graph problem. To concisely describe the problem, the algorithm introduces transitive reachability $\rightsquigarrow$. The transitive reach ability relation is reflective ($a \rightsquigarrow a$) and transitive ($((a \rightsquigarrow b) \wedge (b \rightsquigarrow c) \Rightarrow (a \rightsquigarrow c))$). Then the algorithm uses it to define the passive object garbage collection problem.

3.2 Definition: Transitive Reachability

Entity (object or actor) o_q is transitively reachable from o_p, denoted by $o_p \rightsquigarrow o_q$, if and only if $o_p = o_q \vee (\exists o_u : o_p o_u \wedge o_u \rightsquigarrow o_q)$ 2. Otherwise, we say $o_p \rightsquigarrow o_q$.

3.3 Definition: Live Passive Objects

Given a passive object reference graph G = <V,E>, where V represents objects and E represents references, let R represent roots such that $R \subseteq V$: The problem of passive object garbage collection is to find the set of live objects, Liveobject(G,R), where

$$\text{Liveobject}(G,R) \equiv \{o_{live} \mid \exists o_{root} : (o_{root} \in R \wedge o_{live} \in V \wedge o_{root} \rightsquigarrow o_{live})\}$$

3.4 Garbage in Actor Systems

The definition of actor garbage is related to the idea of whether an actor is doing meaningful computation, which is defined as having the ability to communicate with any of the root actors, where root actors are I/O services or public services such as web services and databases. Algorithm assumes that every actor/object has a reference to itself, which is not necessarily true in the actor model. The widely used definition of live actors is based on the possibility of message reception from or message delivery to the root actors — a live actor is one which can either receive messages from the root actors or send messages to the root actors.

3.5 Definition: Potential Message Delivery from a_p to a_q.

Let the current system state be S. Potential message delivery from Actor a_p to Actor a_q (or message reception of a_q from a_p) is defined as:

$$\exists S_{future} : a_p \text{ is unblocked and } a_p \rightsquigarrow a_q \text{ at } S_{future}, S \rightarrow^* S_{future}.$$

Now, consider two actors, a_p and a_q. If they are both transitively reachable from an unblocked actor or a root actor, namely a_{mid}, message delivery from Actor a_p to Actor a_q (or from a_q to a_p) is possible. The reason is that there exists a sequence of state transitions such that a_{mid} transitively makes a_p unblocked and transitively creates a directional path to a_q. As a result, $a_p \rightsquigarrow a_q$ is possible. The relationship of a_p and a_q can be expressed by the may-talk-to relation, defined as $\leftrightsquigarrow$ (Definition 3.6). It is also possible that a message can be delivered from a_p to another new actor a_r if ($a_p \leftrightsquigarrow a_q \wedge a_q \leftrightsquigarrow a_r$) because the unblocked actors can create a path to connect a_p and a_r. The generalized idea of the may-transitively-talk-to relation, $\leftrightsquigarrow^*$, is shown in Definition 3.7 to represent potential message delivery.

3.6 Definition: May-talk-to $\leftrightsquigarrow$

Given an actor reference graph G = <V,E> and $\{a_p, a_q\} \subseteq V$, where V represents actors and E represents references, let R represent roots and U represent unblocked actors such that $R, U \subseteq V$, then:

$$a_p \leftrightsquigarrow a_q \Longleftrightarrow \exists a_u : a_u \in (U \cup R) \wedge a_u \rightsquigarrow a_p \wedge a_u \rightsquigarrow a_q.$$

We call $\leftrightsquigarrow$ the may-talk-to relation.

3.7 Definition: May-Transitively-talk-to $\leftrightsquigarrow^*$

Following Definition 3.6,

$$a_p \leftrightsquigarrow^* a_q \Longleftrightarrow \exists a_{mid} : a_p \leftrightsquigarrow a_q \vee (a_p \leftrightsquigarrow a_{mid} \wedge a_{mid} \leftrightsquigarrow^* a_q).$$

We call $\leftrightsquigarrow^*$ the may-transitively-talk-to relation.

The definition of the set of live actors can then be concisely rewritten by using the $\leftrightsquigarrow^*$ relation:

3.8 Definition: Live Actors

Given an actor reference graph G = <V,E>, where V represents actors and E represents references, let R represent roots and U represent unblocked actors such that $R, U \subseteq V$. The problem of actor garbage collection is to find the set of live actors Liveactor(G,R, U), where

$$\text{Liveactor}(G,R,U) \equiv \{a_{live} \mid \exists a_{root} : (a_{root} \in R \wedge a_{live} \in V \wedge a_{root} \leftrightsquigarrow^* \text{alive})\}$$

3.9 Transformation

3.9.1 Transformation by Direct Back Pointers to Unblocked Actors

This is a much easier approach to transform actor garbage collection into passive object garbage collection, by making $E' = E \cup \{a_q a_u \mid a_u \in (U \cup R) \wedge a_u \rightsquigarrow a_q\}$.

For example, in the above Fig.5, Actors 2 and 3 have back pointers to Unblocked Actor 1 because they are reachable from Actor 1. Actor 11 has a back pointer to Root Actor 9 and another one to Unblocked Actor 13 for the same reason. Actor 3 does not have a back pointer to Actor 5 because Actor 5 is neither a root nor an unblocked actor. Notice the use of term back pointers to describe the newly added references is to avoid ambiguity with the term in-verse references.

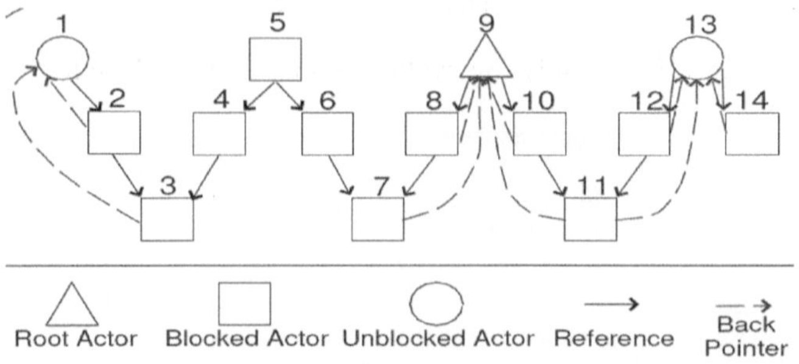

Fig. 5.

3.9.2 Transformation by Indirect Back Pointers to Unblocked Actors

This is an another similar approach to transform actor garbage collection into passive object garbage collection,

$$E' = E \cup \{a_q a_p \mid a_u \in (U \cup R) \wedge a_p a_q \in E \wedge a_u \rightsquigarrow a_p\}.$$

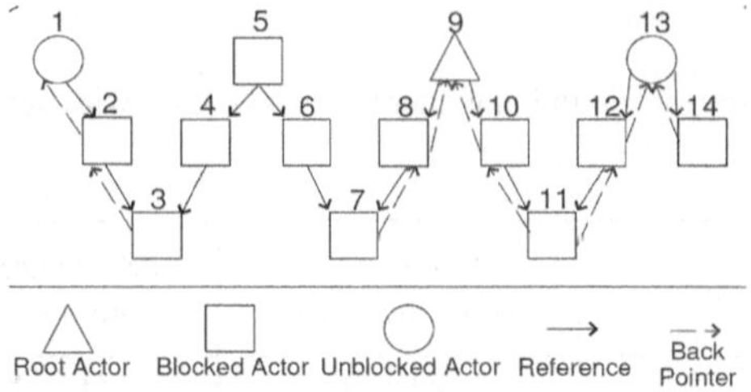

Fig. 6.

For example, in the above Fig.6, Actor 2 has back pointers to Unblocked Actor 1 and Actor 3 has back pointers to Actor 2 because they are reachable from Actor 1. The newly added back pointers will create a corresponding counter-directional path of a path from an unblocked/root actor to another actor which is reachable from the unblocked/root actor. Similarly, Actor 11 has a new counter-directional path to Root Actor 9 and another one to Unblocked Actor 13.

4 Conclusions

Both Passive object garbage collection and actor garbage collection can be represented as graph problems. The traditional root reachability condition that determines live objects in passive garbage collection does not correctly detect live actors in an actor graph. Hence developing transformation methods from actor to passive object graph is beneficial for actor programming language implementation. In this paper we have presented the transformation methods given by Vardhan et al. and Wei-Jen-Wang et al.

References

Kafura, D., Washabaugh, D., Nelson, J.: Garbage collection of actors. In: OOPSLA 1990 ACM Conference on Object-Oriented Systems, Languages and Applications. ACM Press, New York (1990)

Vardhan, A., Agha, G.: Using passive object garbage collection algorithms for garbage collection of active objects. In: ISMM 2002. ACM SIGPLAN Notices. ACM Press, Berlin (2002)

Wang, W.-J., Varela, C., Hsu, F.-H., Tang, C.-H.: Actor Garbage Collection Using Vertex-Preserving Actor-to-Object Graph Transformations. CiteseerXbeta

Agha, G.: Actors: A Model of Concurrent Computation in Distributed Systems. MIT Press, Cambridge (1986)

Abdullahi, S.E., Ringwood, A.: Garbage collecting the internet: A survey of distributed garbage collection. ACM Computing Surveys 30(3), 330–373 (1998)

Wang, V.: Distributed garbage collection for mobile actor systems: The pseudo root approach

Dickman: Incremental, Distributed Orphan Detection and Actor Garbage Collection using graph partitioning and Euler cycles submitted for publication

Washabaugh: Real-time garbage collection of actors in a distributed system

Cormen, T.H., Leiserson, C.E., Rivest, R.L., Stein, C.: Introduction to Algorithms, ch. 21, 2nd edn., pp. 498–522. MIT Press/McGraw-Hill (2001)

Nelson, J.: Automatic, incremental, on-the-fly garbage collection of actors. Master's thesis, Virginia Tech, Blacksburg, VA (February 1989)

Face Recognition Using Fuzzy Neural Network Classifier

Dhanya S. Pankaj and M. Wilscy

Department Of Computer Science, University Of Kerala
Kariavattom, Thiruvananthapuram-695581, Kerala, India
{dhanyaspankaj,wilsyphilipose}@gmail.com

Abstract. Given a still image or a video, a face recognition application identifies or verifies face images using a stored database of faces. In this paper a method for face recognition using a fuzzy neural network classifier based on the Integrated Adaptive Fuzzy Clustering (IAFC) method has been proposed. IAFC forms the cluster boundaries by a combined similarity measure and by integrating the advantages of the fuzzy c-means (FCM), the adaptive resonance theory, and a fuzzified Kohonen-type learning rule. The proposed system achieved a recognition rate of 98.75% and 99.39% for the AT & T and Yale databases respectively, which is better compared to the Back Propagation Neural Network (BPNN) system. Considering the rejection rate for the non-registrants, the system achieved an equal error rate of 3.7 % and 1.3% for the AT & T and the Yale databases respectively which is better compared to most of the existing systems.

Keywords: Face Recognition, PCA, LDA, Integrated Adaptive Fuzzy Clustering, Fuzzy Neural Network.

1 Introduction

Face Recognition has been an active research area due to both its scientific challenges and wide range of potential applications such as biometric identity authentication, human-computer interaction, and video surveillance [1]. Given a still image or a video, a face recognition application identifies or verifies one or more persons in the scene using a stored database of faces.

Various appearance-based approaches to face recognition have been proposed in literature [2]. The appearance based methods extract features that optimally represent the faces belonging to a class and separate faces from different classes [3]. A class of face recognition algorithms employ various classifiers such as probabilistic [4], hidden Markov models (HMMs) [5], neural networks (NNs) [6], and support vector machine (SVM) [7] and feature extraction methods like Principal Component Analysis (PCA)[16], Linear Discriminant Analysis (LDA)[8], Discrete Cosine Transform (DCT)[9].

Most of the face recognition algorithms are designed as classifiers. The automatic classification of human faces is still a challenging problem due to two main factors - large intra-subject variations due to change in pose, illumination, facial expression, aging, occlusion etc and small inter-subject variations due to the similarity of

D. Nagamalai, E. Renault, and M. Dhanushkodi (Eds.): PDCTA 2011, CCIS 203, pp. 53–62, 2011.

individual appearances. Hence, forming well defined class boundaries is a major challenge for the existing face recognition algorithms based on classifiers.

A number of neuro-fuzzy clustering algorithms have been proposed in literature [11-15]. However, all of these algorithms developed suffer from restrictions in identifying the exact decision boundaries of the clusters in proximity [10]. The integrated adaptive fuzzy clustering (IAFC) developed by Y.S.Kim and S.Mitra[10] addresses this issue and forms better decision boundaries in the case of closely located clusters. A new similarity measure for the vigilance criterion and a new learning rule based on fuzzification of Kohonen- learning rule is used in IAFC.

The face recognition classifiers often face the problem of forming class boundaries in the case of similar face images. This paper proposes a new architecture for the classification of faces for the face recognition task based on the IAFC model [10] to address this challenge. The face images are pre-processed, dimensionality reduction is performed using PCA [16], feature extraction is performed using LDA [8] and then classified using the fuzzy neural network based on IAFC.

A practical face recognition system should identify a known individual as well as reject an unknown individual accurately. This is a challenging task since the system has to deal with the large intra-class variations and the small inter-class variations. The proposed system effectively rejects an unknown person by adaptively forming a new class for the unknown person.

The proposed system has been tested using the publicly available AT&T and Yale Face databases. A recognition rate of 98.75% and 99.39% was achieved for the AT&T and Yale databases respectively, which is better compared to the Back Propagation Neural Network (BPNN) system. The system achieved an equal error rate of 3.7 % and 1.3% for the AT & T and the Yale databases respectively.

The details of the face recognition system are discussed in the remainder of this paper. Section 2 covers the Proposed Face Recognition system. The design of the fuzzy neural network classifier is explained in section 3. In Section4, experimental results of evaluating the developed techniques and discussions are presented. Finally, conclusions are summarized in Section 5.

2 Proposed Face Recognition System

In the proposed face recognition system, the face images are first preprocessed to compensate for the intensity variations. PCA is applied to reduce the dimensionality of the face images and LDA is performed for extracting the features. The feature vectors obtained are then given to the neural network. The neural network classifies the input vector into one of the existing classes if some criteria are met or into a new class, otherwise. Thus, if the person in the input image is present in the database used for training (registrant), the person is identified as one of the persons in the database. If the person in the input image is a non-registrant (not present in the training database) then the person is rejected and classified into a new class by the neural network classifier.

2.1 Preprocessing

The face images are preprocessed by histogram equalization to account for the intensity variations in the face images. The two-dimensional face image of size p x q is converted into a vector of size m (m = p x q).

2.2 Feature Extraction

The face images are represented by a feature vector which helps the classifier to efficiently classify the face images. The PCA [16] is the most widely used feature for representing face images. However, PCA maximizes the intra class as well as the inter class scatter while performing the dimensionality reduction. For efficient classification, a feature like LDA [8] which maximizes the inter class scatter and minimizes the inter class scatter is more efficient. However the performance of LDA is affected by the Small Sample Size (SSS) problem and to deal with this, often PCA and LDA are combined. In this paper, the face images are represented by a feature vector obtained by combining PCA and LDA.

Principal Component Analysis (PCA)

The face images represented as vectors are subject to dimensionality reduction to reduce computational complexity. Principal Component Analysis (PCA) [16] is used for dimensionality reduction. Let the database of n training images be represented by n vectors $Z = (Z_1, Z_2, \ldots, Z_n)$ of size m each. The mean vector $\overline{Z}$ and the covariance matrix are calculated as in (1-2).

$$\overline{Z} = \frac{1}{n}\sum_{i=1}^{n} Z_i \tag{1}$$

$$\Gamma = \frac{1}{n}\sum_{i=1}^{n}\left(Z_i - \overline{Z}\right)\left(Z_i - \overline{Z}\right)^T = \phi\phi^T \tag{2}$$

The eigen values and eigen vectors of the covariance matrix Γ are calculated. Let $E = (E_1, E_2, \ldots, E_t)$ be the t eigen vectors corresponding to the t largest eigen values. For the n patterns Z, their corresponding eigen face-based features X can be obtained by projecting Z into the eigen space as follows:

$$X = E^T Z \tag{3}$$

Thus the patterns of dimension m (m=p x q) is reduced to the dimension t. (t < m, t is taken to be (No of classes * No of training patterns per class) - No of classes.)

Linear Discriminant Analysis (LDA)

The objective of Linear Discriminant Analysis (LDA) is to perform dimensionality reduction while preserving as much of the class discriminatory information as possible. It is also more capable of distinguishing image variation due to identity from variation due to other sources such as illumination and expression. Two scatter matrices are calculated as in (4-5).

$$S_W = \sum_{j=1}^{R} \sum_{i=1}^{M_j} (x_i^j - \mu_j)(x_i^j - \mu_j)^T \tag{4}$$

$$S_b = \sum_{j=1}^{R} (\mu_j - \mu)(\mu_j - \mu)^T \tag{5}$$

Where S_w is called the within-class scatter matrix while S_b is called the between lass scatter matrix. j denotes the class while i denotes the image number. μ_j is the mean of class j while μ is the mean of all classes. M_j is the number of images in class j and R is the number of classes. LDA computes a transformation that maximizes the between-class scatter while minimizing the within-class scatter.

$$\text{maximize } |S_b| / |S_W| \tag{6}$$

The linear transformation is given by a matrix U whose columns are the eigenvectors of $S_W^{-1} S_b$ (called Fisherfaces). There are at most R - 1 non-zero generalized eigenvectors. However, in practice, S_w is often singular since the data are image vectors with large dimensionality while the size of the data set is much smaller. To alleviate this problem, PCA is first applied to the data set to reduce its dimensionality.

3 Proposed Fuzzy Neural Network Classifier

The design of the proposed fuzzy neural network classifier is explained in this section. The IAFC clustering algorithm based on which the proposed network is built is explained in section 3.1. The proposed network is explained in section 3.2.

3.1 Integrated Adaptive Fuzzy Clustering(IAFC)[10]

The IAFC [10] model is a fuzzy neural network similar to ART-1 that finds the cluster structure embedded in data sets. IAFC finds the actual decision boundaries of closely located clusters by incorporating a new similarity measure for the vigilance criterion and a new learning rule into a neural network.

The new learning rule, developed in IAFC, incorporates a fuzzy membership value μ_i, an intra-cluster membership value π, and a function of the number of iterations f(l)) into a Kohonen-type learning rule. The fuzzy membership value used in IAFC is based on the FCM model. The use of an intra-cluster membership value guarantees the fast convergence of the weights [10]. IAFC consists of three major procedures: deciding a winning cluster, performing the vigilance test, and updating the centroid of a winning cluster [10].The IAFC algorithm is explained in Fig.1.

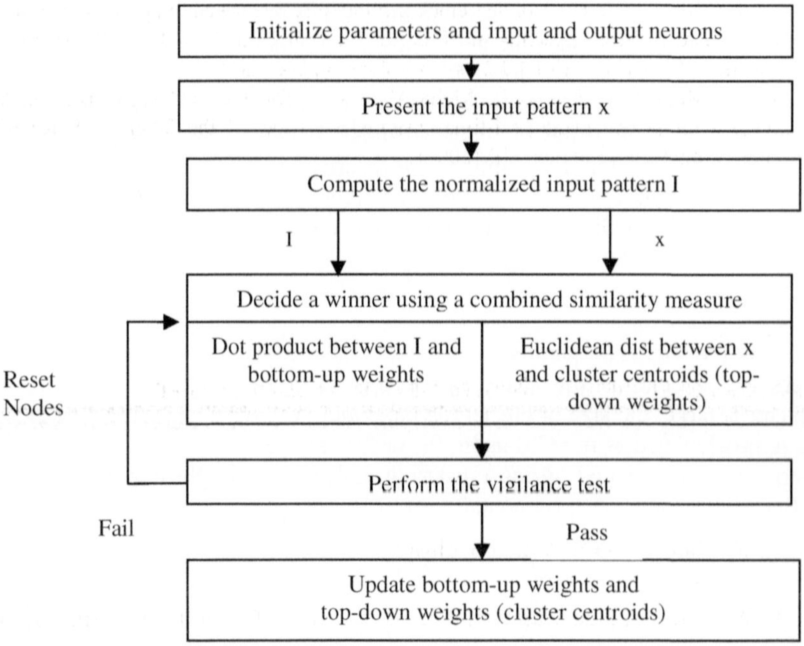

Fig. 1. The IAFC Algorithm

The input pattern and the normalized input pattern are presented to the fuzzy neural network in parallel. The dot product between the normalized input pattern and the bottom up weights is performed as in the equation

$$I \bullet b_i = \frac{x \bullet v_i}{\|x\| \bullet \|v_i\|} \tag{7}$$

where b_i is the bottom-up weight, which is the normalized version of the ith cluster centroid (v_i) , from the input neurons to the ith output neuron (cluster).

The output neuron that receives the largest value for the dot product in (7) wins the competition. Here, the winner is decided by the angle between the input pattern and the cluster centroids. This may lead to misclassifications because a cluster of which the direction of the centroid vector has the smallest angle with the input vector wins the competition regardless of its location with respect to the cluster centroids. In such a case, Euclidean distance can be used as a better similarity measure to determine a winner. However, cluster centroids cannot approach appropriate locations during the early stage of learning, thus causing poor performance of clustering algorithms. To prevent both problems, the IAFC algorithm uses a combined similarity measure to decide a winner.

In the IAFC algorithm, the winner is first decided by dot product as in (7). If the fuzzy membership value of the input pattern in the winning cluster is less than the value of the parameter σ, a threshold of the fuzzy membership value, the IAFC algorithm finds the winning cluster using the Euclidean Distance criterion. Otherwise the winner is same as the one obtained by the dot product.

If the parameter σ is low the angle between the input pattern and the cluster centroid is the dominant similarity measure to decide a winner. On the other hand, if the parameter σ is high, the Euclidean distance between the input pattern and the cluster centroid is the dominant similarity measure to decide a winner.

Once the winning cluster is selected, the IAFC algorithm performs the vigilance test using the un-normalized input data pattern according to the vigilance criterion.

$$e^{-\gamma\mu_i}\left\|x - v_i\right\| <= \tau \tag{8}$$

where τ is the vigilance parameter and the γ is a constant . τ controls the size of clusters and γ controls the shape of clusters [10]. If the value of the vigilance parameter is large, the size of clusters is large and vice versa. The fuzzy membership value μ_i is calculated as in FCM as in (9). In (9), n is the number of currently existing clusters which is updated during clustering and m is a weight exponent called the fuzzifier whose value is experimentally set to 2[10].

$$\mu_i = \left(\frac{1}{\left\|x - v_i\right\|^2}\right)^{1/m-1} \Bigg/ \sum_{j=1}^{n}\left(\frac{1}{\left\|x - v_j\right\|^2}\right)^{1/m-1} \tag{9}$$

If the winning cluster satisfies the vigilance test, its centroid is updated as in (10).

$$v_i^{new} = v_i^{old} + \lambda_{fuzzy}(x - v_i^{old}) \tag{10}$$

where λ_{fuzzy} is [f(l). π(x; v_i(old); τ). μ_i^2]. f(l) is a function of the number of iterations l, and π(x; v_i(old); τ) decides the intra-cluster membership value of the input pattern x in the ith winning cluster. f(l) and π are calculated as in [10].

The centroid of each cluster is used as the top down weight related with each cluster. If the vigilance test is not satisfied, the winning output neuron is temporarily reset and the similarity test is performed using the remaining neurons. If all committed output neurons are reset, the first uncommitted output neuron is activated to form a new cluster.

3.2 Proposed Neural Network Classifier Based on IAFC

In this paper, a face recognition system based on IAFC is proposed. The training face images are clustered using IAFC and the trained network is then used for classifying the test face images. In the proposed system, an initial direction for the convergence of the weights and cluster centroids is provided by initializing the cluster centroids using the training face patterns. As a result of this, convergence of the algorithm is faster and classification accuracy is improved. This aids in a better classification of the face images.

The proposed system can be explained as follows:

1. In the training phase, the average training face patterns are used to initialize the weights and the centroids of the clusters. The number of classes is initialized to the number of persons in the database.
2. The network is then trained using the training face patterns. The refinement of the weights and the centroids is performed using the equation (10) as in IAFC.
3. Once the clustering is performed, the training of the network is completed.
4. The test face patterns are given as input to the trained network. The weights and the cluster centroids are not updated in the testing phase. The winner is computed using the combined similarity measure and the vigilance test is performed to find the class of the input pattern.

If the vigilance test is satisfied for any of the existing classes, the input pattern is classified into one of the classes in the database. Otherwise, a new class is adaptively formed which indicates that the input pattern is not present among the training classes. In the first case, the input pattern is a registrant (person in the database) and in the second case the pattern is a non-registrant (not present in the database).

4 Experimental Results and Discussion

Experiments have been carried out using the publicly available AT & T [17] and Yale [18] databases. The AT & T database also known as the ORL database of faces contains ten different images of each of 40 distinct subjects. The Yale Face Database contains 165 grayscale images in GIF format of 15 individuals. There are 11 images per subject.

4.1 Results

Recognition rate is considered for the registrants (i.e. the persons in the training classes) and the rejection rate is considered for the non-registrants (i.e. the persons not present in the training database.)[16]. Recognition Rate (for registrants) is the ratio of the number of patterns correctly classified to the total number of patterns tested multiplied by 100. Rejection Rate (for non-registrants) is the ratio of the Number of rejected patterns to the total number of patterns tested multiplied by 100.

From the AT & T database, 20 persons were selected as registrants and 20 persons as non-registrants. From the 10 patterns of each individual, 5 patterns were used for training the network and all the 10 patterns were used for testing the network. Hence 200 images from the database were used for training and all the 400 images were used for testing.

From the Yale Face Database of 15 persons, 7 persons were considered as registrants and 8 persons as non-registrants. Out of the 11 patterns of each person, 6 patterns were used for training and all the 11 patterns were used for testing the network. Hence 42 patterns were used for training and 165 patterns were used for testing the system.

The Fig. 2 shows the rejection rate and recognition rate obtained by the system for different values of the vigilance parameter for the 2 databases.

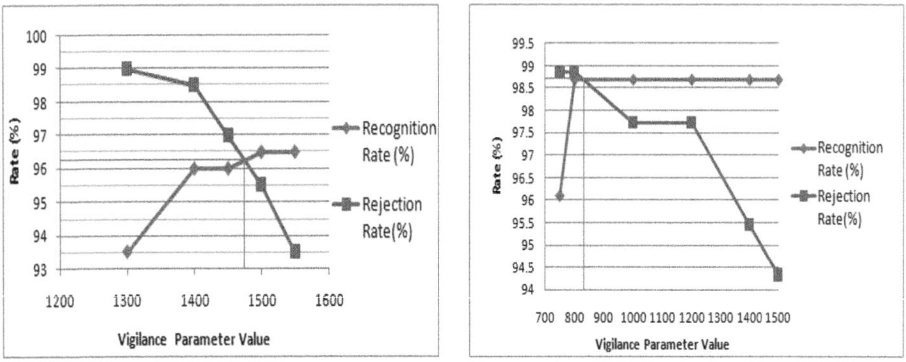

Fig. 2. Recognition and Rejection Rates for different values of τ for AT&T and Yale Databases

For the AT & T database, the system achieved a False Acceptance Rate (FAR) of 4% and False Rejection Rate (FRR) of 1.5 % for the vigilance parameter value of 1400 and the gamma value of 1.3. An Equal Error Rate (ERR) of 3.7 % is achieved. The proposed system achieved an FAR of 1.3% and FRR of 1.14 % for the vigilance parameter value of 800 and the gamma value of 1.3 for the Yale Face database. An Equal Error Rate (ERR) of 1.3 % is achieved.

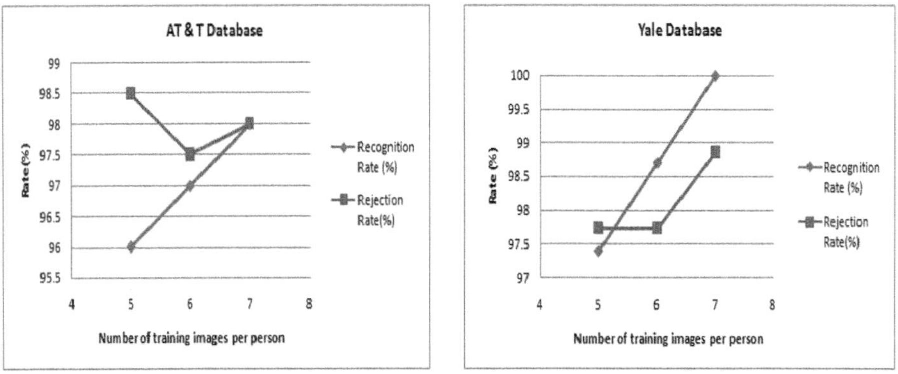

Fig. 3. Recognition and Rejection Rates for different number of training images per subject

The Fig.3 shows the performance achieved by the system when the number of training images is varied. The results were obtained on the AT & T and the Yale Face Databases.

The proposed face recognition system has been compared with the recognition results obtained by a face recognition system with Back Propagation Neural Network (BPNN) as the classifier and PCA+LDA as the feature extractor. The BPNN maps the face patterns of a non-registrant to the closest match in the database and hence the entire database has been considered as registrants for testing. The proposed system has also been tested considering all the persons in the database as registrants. The Fig. 4 shows the performance comparison of the proposed system and the BPNN system. The results show that the proposed system achieves better recognition rates compared to the BPNN system.

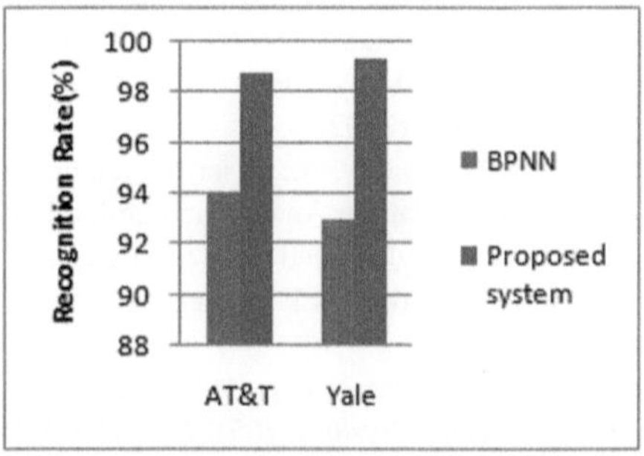

Fig. 4. Comparison of Recognition Rates for BPNN and proposed system

5 Conclusion

In this paper, a face recognition system using a fuzzy neural network classifier based on IAFC is proposed. The IAFC integrates the advantages of the fuzzy optimization constraint in fuzzy c-means (FCM), the control structure of adaptive resonance theory and a fuzzified Kohonen type learning rule. The decision boundaries for the classes are obtained by a combined similarity measure and a vigilance criterion. The face features are extracted using a combination of PCA and LDA. LDA maximises the between class to within class scatter ratio and provides good discrimination information required for face recognition. The face features are given as input to the fuzzy neural network classifier. The network classifies the input face image as a registrant or a non-registrant in the database. The proposed system achieves better recognition rates compared to the BPNN system. A recognition rate of 98.75% and 99.39% is obtained by the proposed system for the AT & T and Yale databases respectively. The system achieved an equal error rate of 3.7 % and 1.3% for the AT & T and the Yale databases respectively, considering the rejection rate for non-registrants also. Practical applications of face recognition often require the rejection of non-registrants as well as the recognition of registrants reliably and the proposed system performs better in this respect compared to many of the existing systems.

References

1. Su, Y., Shan, S., Chen, X., Gao, W.: Hierarchical Ensemble of Global and Local Classifiers for Face Recognition. IEEE Transactions on Image Processing 18(8) (2009)
2. Zhao, W., Chellappa, R., Rosenfeld, A., Phillips, P.J.: Face Recognition: A Literature Survey. ACM Computing Surveys, 399–458 (2003)
3. Sahoolizadeh, H., Ghassabeh, Y.A.: Face recognition using eigen-faces, fisher-faces and neural networks. In: 7th IEEE International Conference on Cybernetic Intelligent Systems, pp. 1–6 (2008)

4. Moghaddam, B.: Principal manifolds and probabilistic subspaces for visual recognition. IEEE Trans. pattern Anal. Machine Intel. 24(6), 780–788 (2002)
5. Othman, H., Aboulnasr, T.: A separable low complexity 2D HMM with application to face recognition. IEEE Trans. Pattern. Anal. Machine Intel. 25(10), 1229–1238 (2003)
6. Er, M., Wu, S., Lu, J., Toh, L.H.: Face recognition with radial basis function (RBF) neural networks. IEEE Trans. Neural Networks 13(3), 697–710 (1999)
7. Lee, K., Chung, Y., Byun, H.: SVM based face verification with feature set of small size. Electronic Letters 38(15), 787–789 (2002)
8. Zhao, W., Chellappa, R., Krishnaswamy, A.: Discriminant analysis of principal component for face recognition. IEEE Trans. Pattern Anal. Machine Intel. 8 (1997)
9. Er, M.J., Chen, W., Wu, S.: High speed face recognition based on discrete cosine transform and RBF neural network. IEEE Trans. on Neural Network 16(3), 679–691 (2005)
10. Kim, Y.S., Mitra, S.: An adaptive integrated fuzzy clustering model for pattern recognition. Journal Fuzzy Sets and Systems (65), 297–310 (1994)
11. Huntsbergerd, T.L., Ajjimarangsee, P.: Parallel selforganizing feature maps for unsupervised pattern recognition. Int. J. General Systems 16(4), 357–372 (1990)
12. Carpenter, G.A., Grossberg, S., Rosen, D.: Fuzzy ART: Fast stable learning and categorization of analog patterns by an adaptive resonance system. Neural Networks 4, 759–771 (1991)
13. Simpson, P.K.: Fuzzy min-max neural networks Part 2: clustering. IEEE Trans. on Fuzzy systems 1(1), 32–45 (1993)
14. Newton, S.C., Mitra, S.: Self-organizing leader clustering in a neural network using a fuzzy learning rule. In: SPIE Proc., vol. 1565, pp. 331–337 (1991)
15. Newton, S.C., Pemmaraju, S., Mitra, S.: Adaptive fuzzy leader clustering of complex data sets in pattern recognition. IEEE Trans. on Neural Networks 3(5), 794–800 (1992)
16. Lu, J., Yuan, X., Yahagi, T.: A Method of Face Recognition Based on Fuzzy c-Means Clustering and Associated Sub-NNs. IEEE Transactions on Neural Networks 18(1) (2007)
17. AT & T. The Database of Faces, `http://www.cl.cam.ac.uk/research/dtg/attarchive/facedatabase.html`
18. Yale Face Database, `http://cvc.yale.edu/projects/yalefaces/yalefaces.html`

Impulse Noise Removal from Grayscale Images Using Fuzzy Genetic Algorithm

K.K. Anisha and M. Wilscy

Department of Computer Science
University of Kerala, Kariavattom, Thiruvananthapuram 695 581, Kerala, India
anisha.kelamkumarath@gmail.com, wilsyphilipose@hotmail.com

Abstract. Many practical applications require analysis of digital images. An accurate analysis is possible only from an image free of noise. Image denoising with multiple image filters might produce better results than a single filter, but it is difficult to find a set of appropriate filters and the order in which the filters are to be applied. In this paper, we propose a Fuzzy Genetic Algorithm to find the optimal filter sets for removing all types of impulse noise from grayscale images. Here, a Fuzzy Rule Base is used to adaptively change the crossover probability of the Genetic Algorithm used to determine the optimal filter sets. The results of simulations performed on a set of standard test images for a wide range of noise corruption levels shows that the proposed method outperforms standard procedures for impulse noise removal.

Keywords: Adaptive Genetic Algorithm, Fuzzy Genetic Algorithm (FGA), Fuzzy Rule Base (FRB), Genetic Algorithm (GA), Image filters, Impulse noise.

1 Introduction

Digital image processing plays a key role in medical imaging, satellite imaging, underwater imaging, robot vision and many such applications. Since images can be deteriorated during acquisition, storage and transmission, image denoising is a primary precursor for almost all image analysis tasks. Conventional smoothening filters and median filters are the most popular filters for noise reduction in digital images [1]. But, a single smoothening or median filter is not enough for completely removing the noise, especially when the noise level is high. Also, it may not preserve image details such as edges during filtering. Hence, many methods have been proposed for noise removal. While some of these methods use complicated formulations, some other methods require deep knowledge about image noise factors. Hence, a simple noise reduction method that removes noise well and preserves image details without relying on image noise factors is desirable.

Applying a set of denoising and enhancement filters successively on a noisy image may remove noise and preserve image details much more efficiently than a single median or smoothening filter. Such a set of standard filters is called a composite filter. The type of the filters in the composite filter, as well as the order in which the filters are applied must be appropriately chosen for good results. Jin Hyuk Hong, Sung Bae Cho and Ung Keun Cho proposed a method that used Genetic Algorithm (GA) [2] to

D. Nagamalai, E. Renault, and M. Dhanushkodi (Eds.): PDCTA 2011, CCIS 203, pp. 63–75, 2011.

determine composite filters that remove different levels of impulse noise from an image [3].They have extended this method to determine composite filters that performs local and global image enhancement [4]. In these methods, the GA considers a set of possible filter combinations of a particular length, selects the best combinations among them according to a fitness value assigned to each combination based on a fitness function, and applies genetic operators such as crossover and mutation [2] on the selected combinations to create the next generation of composite filters. This process is repeated, enabling GA to find the optimal composite filters. In this method, GA parameters, which affect the quality of the solutions produced, are kept fixed. If these parameters are not assigned with suitable values, GA may converge to a sub optimal solution, or it may take a long time to converge to the optimal solution. However, choosing the best parameter values is difficult because the parameter values are problem dependent.

The performance of GA can be improved by adaptively varying its parameters instead of keeping them fixed. Fuzzy logic [7] based techniques have been used for adaptively selecting GA parameters [5] [8-10]. In Fuzzy Genetic Algorithm (FGA) [5], [8-10], a Fuzzy Rule Base (FRB) [7] is used to adapt any of the GA parameters.

The proposed method is an extension of the method in [3]. Here, an FGA is used to determine the optimal filters that can remove different levels of impulse noise from grayscale images. From a pool of standard filters, the GA part of FGA selects several filters and constructs a composite filter. GA analyses such a set of composite filters and determine the optimal filters for removing different levels of impulse noise. The crossover probability [2] of GA, which determines the number of selected solutions that undergo crossover operation, is adapted by the fuzzy part of FGA, where an FRB is used to determine the amount of variation that should be undergone by the crossover probability value in order to improve the quality of the solutions produced. This method does not rely on deep knowledge about the type of image noise factors. Hence, this method can be used to remove almost all types of impulse noise [11] from images. The method has been tested on benchmark images and its performance has been evaluated using performance metrics such as PSNR value, Tenengrad measure and IQI [6] value. These evaluations clearly show the superiority of the proposed method over standard procedures for impulse noise removal.

The rest of the paper is organized as follows. Section 2 explains the different types of impulse noise. Section 3 gives a detailed account of the proposed method, where the design and working of the FGA is explained. Section 4 discusses the experimental results. Section 5 provides conclusions.

2 Impulse Noise Models

There are four different types or models of impulse noise [11]. They are as follows:

Noise Model 1: Noise is modeled as salt-and-pepper impulse noise. Here, pixels are randomly corrupted by two fixed extreme values, 0 and 255 (for gray level image), generated with the same probability. That is, if P is the noise density, then the noise density of salt (P_1) and pepper (P_2) is P/2.

Noise Model 2: This is similar to Noise Model 1, but here each pixel might be corrupted by either pepper noise or salt noise with unequal probabilities. That is $P_1 \neq P_2$.

Noise Model 3: Instead of two fixed values, impulse noise could be more realistically modeled by two fixed ranges that appear at both ends with a length of m each, respectively. That is, [0, m] denotes salt and [255-m, 255] denotes pepper. Here for noise density P, $P_1=P_2=P/2$. *This noise is also known as random impulse noise or uniform noise.*

Noise Model 4: This is similar to Noise Model 3 but here probability densities of low intensity impulse noise and high intensity impulse noise are different. That is, $P_1 \neq P_2$.

Many techniques have been proposed for impulse noise removal from grayscale images. Some of these methods work only for either low density noised images or high density noised images. Some other techniques are specifically designed for certain noise models. Some techniques use complicated formulations or require deep knowledge about the image noise factors. The proposed method, which is explained in section 3, is a method which removes any level of impulse noise, is applicable for almost all noise models, does not use complicated formulations and does not require deep knowledge on image noise factors.

3 The Proposed Method Using Fuzzy Genetic Algorithm

The proposed method for impulse noise removal consists of two parts: A GA part and a Fuzzy part. The GA part selects several filters and constructs a composite filter. GA analyses such a set of composite filters and determine the optimal filters for removing different levels of impulse noise. The crossover probability [2] of GA, which determines the number of selected solutions that undergo crossover operation, is adapted by the fuzzy part of FGA, where an FRB is used to determines the amount of variation that should be undergone by the crossover probability value in order to improve the quality of the solutions produced. The following subsections explain about these two parts of the proposed method.

3.1 The GA Part

When there are **m** filters in the filter pool, optimal composite filters containing **l** standard filters are to be determined from a total of $\mathbf{(m+1)^l}$ filter combinations, where **m+1** includes the case of not using any filter on the image. Trying all cases to find out the best one is practically impossible, especially when m is large. In this paper, GA is used to find the optimal composite filter, in which the proper type and order of filters are determined [3]. In GA [2], each solution to the problem to be solved is called an individual or a chromosome. GA starts by randomly initializing a set or a population of individuals. This is the first generation of individuals. Each individual is assigned a fitness value based on a fitness function. GA selects those individuals with a good fitness value and applies operations such as crossover and mutation on them to create the next generation of individuals. This process is repeated until GA satisfies a predefined termination criterion such as the number of generations created, upon which GA is expected to have produced very good individuals.

Table 1 shows the filter pool used in this paper which contains 23 image filters, each indexed by a value from 1 - 23. Value 0 represents the case where no filtering operation is performed. The first 3 filters are histogram brightness measures that adjust the value of the pixel p in the image according to equation (1) for a given scale (-100 <= s <=100).

$$v_{new(p)} = v_{old(p)} + \frac{v_{old}(p) * s}{100} \quad (1)$$

Filters 4 – 7 are histogram contrast measures that adjusts the value of the pixel p for a given scale (-127 <=s <=127) as shown in equation (2).

$$v_{new}(p) = v_{old}(p) + \frac{v_{old}(p) - 128 * s}{128} \quad (2)$$

Filter 8 performs contrast stretching by spanning the range of intensity values in an image, [c, d], to a desired range of values [a, b]. It scales each image pixel p according to equation (3).

$$v_{new}(p) = v_{old}(p) - c * \left(\frac{b-a}{d-c}\right) + a \quad (3)$$

Filter 9 equalizes the histogram of the image, thereby improving the image contrast. Filters 10 – 13 are edge enhancement filters of different types. Filters 14 – 22 are standard median filters of different sizes and shapes. Filter 23 is an adaptive median filter with a maximum window size of 7 [1].

Table 1. Description of image filters used in this paper

Filter	Type	Index
Brightness	3 values	1~3
Contrast	4 values	4~7
Stretch	-	8
Equalize	-	9
Sharpening	4 masks	10~13
Median, Adaptive Median	10 masks	14~23
None		0

Each composite filter is represented by a string of **l** real numbers corresponding to the filter index, where **l** is the number of standard filters in the composite filter.

The following procedure describes how GA determines the optimal standard filters [3]. At first, GA randomly initializes a population of composite filters. Then, the fitness of each composite filter is evaluated using the fitness function given in equation (4). Here, the objective of GA is to find the optimal composite filter that can remove impulse noise from all the training images in a given training set. The training images are created by artificially corrupting an image with different levels of impulse noise. In equation (4), n is the number of training images used, MAE_i is the mean absolute error (MAE) of the output image obtained after applying the composite filter x on the ith training image, and MAE_{max} is the maximum MAE; it would be 255 for 8-bit grayscale images. The fitness value f(x) is assigned to x. From equation (4), it is clear that the composite filter x receives a high fitness value if it can considerably remove the noise from all the training images (thereby producing low MAE_i values).

$$f(x) = \frac{1}{n}\sum_{i=1}^{n} 1-(MAE_i/MAE_{max}) \qquad (4)$$

GA then selects the composite filters with high fitness value using Roulette Wheel selection strategy [2], where selection is based on the probability assigned to each composite filter proportional to its fitness value. Then, genetic operators such as crossover and mutation are applied on the selected individuals, to produce the next generation. Elitist-strategy [2] that keeps the best individuals of the previous generation in the current generation is also used. From this generation, GA produces the next generation using the above procedure. This process is repeated until a predefined termination criterion is satisfied. Here, the termination criteria is the maximum number of generations created by GA.

When GA parameter values are kept fixed for solving a problem, it must be ensured that the parameter values suit the problem. Otherwise, the convergence of GA may be to a sub optimal solution. Even if GA converges to the optimal solution, it may take a large amount of time to do so. The occurrence of these problems can be avoided by adaptively varying the GA parameters. In the proposed method, the fuzzy part adapts the crossover probability of the GA using an FRB. The fuzzy part is explained in detail in the next subsection.

3.2 The Fuzzy Part

An FGA [5], [8 – 10] is an adaptive GA in which an FRB is used to adapt one or more of the GA parameters so as to increase the quality of the solutions produced by GA. In FGA, the fuzzy part accepts one or more measures, which indicate the quality of the outputs produced by GA, as inputs. These values are fuzzified [7] using the corresponding membership functions [7]. From these fuzzified input values, one or more fuzzy outputs are determined using a FRB [7]. These outputs are then defuzzified [7] using the output membership functions. The defuzzified outputs enable the adaptive variation of one or more GA parameters. Thus, the fuzzy part enables GA to converge to the most optimal solution. It also results in an increase in the speed of convergence of the GA to the best solution.

In the proposed method, an FRB is used to adapt the crossover probability of GA. The fuzzy part accepts Genotypic diversity (GD) and Phenotypic diversity (PD) as inputs [5]. GD and PD are two measures that depict the quality of the composite filters produced by GA.

GD represents the genetic diversity of the population and it is evaluated as shown in equation (5).

$$GD = (d - d_{min}) / (d_{max} - d_{min}) \tag{5}$$

Where d, d_{max} and d_{min} are the average, maximum and minimum distances of the chromosomes in the population from the composite filter with the highest fitness value.

PD, as shown in equation (6), is the ratio of average fitness of the population, f_{avg}, to the best fitness f_{best}.

$$PD = f_{avg} / f_{best} \tag{6}$$

Figures 1(a) and (b) shows the membership functions of GD and PD respectively for fuzzifying it to enable the fuzzy part to use it.

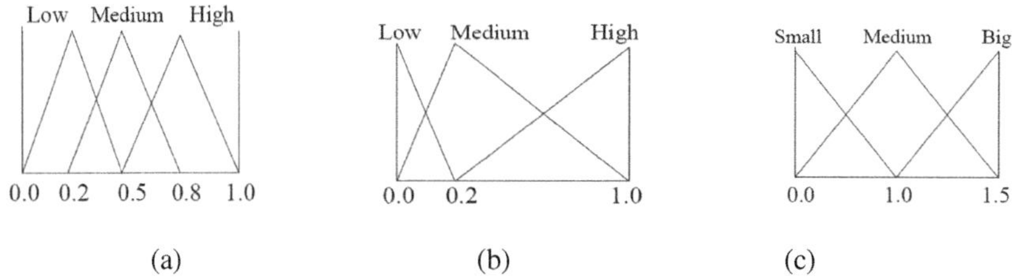

Fig. 1. Membership function of (a) GD (b) PD (c) δp_c

Table 2 shows the FRB which is used to determine the fuzzy output value, which is defuzzified using the membership function shown in figure 1(c) to obtain the crisp output value δp_c ,from GD and PD values. GD and PD values range from Low to High, for which the change in δp_c , which ranges from Small to Big, is given in the respective cells. When GD and PD values are 'Low', the population is diverse, even if it has not converged to the best solution. In this case, a low crossover probability is desired to prevent loss of this diversity due to crossover. Hence, δp_c is given a 'Small' value, to allow as little crossover operations as possible. Similar arguments follow for all the conditions specified in the rule base.

δp_c, which ranges from [0, 1.5], determines the degree to which the current p_c value, which is kept within the range [0.25, 0.75], should vary. The variation is carried out by multiplying the δp_c value with the current p_c.

Table 2. The Fuzzy Rule Base

GD	**PD**		
	Low	***Medium***	***High***
Low	Small	Small	Medium
Medium	Big	Big	Medium
High	Big	Big	Medium

In the proposed method, GA creates the first generation of composite filters using a randomly initialized p_c value. The GD and PD values for this generation are fed into the fuzzy part of FGA, which calculates the value of δp_c, which is multiplied with the current p_c value. This adapted p_c value is given to the GA, which uses it to create the next generation to produce a better population of composite filters. The entire process is repeated until GA satisfies its termination criterion.

4 Results and Discussion

The proposed method was implemented and tested using the following GA parameters: population size = 50, number of generations = 50, number of filters in the composite filter = 5, mutation probability = 0.05 and selection rate = 0.9. The initial value assigned to p_c is 0.7. The adapted p_c value obtained after 50 iterations is 0.75.

The well-known Lena, Elaine, Peppers and Baboon images, all of size 512 × 512, were used as benchmark images. These images are shown in figures 2 (a), (b), (c) and (d) respectively. The Lena image is artificially corrupted by each impulse noise model with corruption rates of 10%, 30%, 50%, 70% and 90%. The range of impulse noise intensities for noise model 3 and noise model 4 is 4. The resulting 20 corrupted images (5 images for each noise model) are used as training images. The training images, as well as benchmark images such as Elaine, Baboon and Peppers images corrupted with various noise levels are used for testing the proposed method.

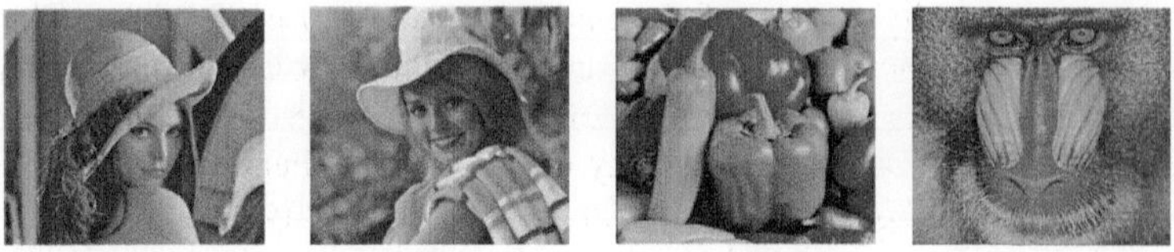

(a) (b) (c) (d)

Fig. 2. Benchmark images – (a) Lena, (b) Elaine, (c) Peppers, (d) Baboon

Table 3 shows the composite filters created by the proposed method for different impulse noise levels by using the Lena training images. From now on, we call these composite filters as FGA filters (FGA-F).

Here, the same composite filter, made up of relatively simple standard filters, can be used to remove upto 50% model 1 and 3 impulse noises and 30% model 2 and 4 impulse noises. For higher noise levels, separate composite filters are evolved, which are composed of standard filters that either uses the information of larger neighbourhoods or perform further enhancements. It can also be observed that the filters evolved for noise models 1 and 3, and noise models 2 and 4 are the same. This may indicate the fact that the noise models 1 and 3 have similar characteristics. The same goes for noise models 2 and 4.

Table 3. Composite filters evolved by FGA for the training images

Noise Model	*Impulse Noise Level (%)*	**FGA filter (in the order of application)**
1	**10**	Adaptive median, Adaptive median, Adaptive median
1	**30**	Adaptive median, Adaptive median, Adaptive median
1	**50**	Adaptive median, Adaptive median, Adaptive median
1	**70**	Adaptive median, Adaptive median, Adaptive median, 3x1 vertical median
1	**90**	Adaptive median, Adaptive median, Adaptive median, 3x1 vertical median, Adaptive median
2	**10**	Adaptive median, Adaptive median, Adaptive median
2	**30**	Adaptive median, Adaptive median, Adaptive median
2	**50**	Adaptive median, Adaptive median, Adaptive median
2	**70**	Adaptive median, Adaptive median, Adaptive median, 3x1 vertical median, Adaptive median
2	**90**	Adaptive median, Radius 5 diamond median, contrast control with s= -100, 5x5 median
3	**10**	Adaptive median, Adaptive median, Adaptive median
3	**30**	Adaptive median, Adaptive median, Adaptive median
3	**50**	Adaptive median, Adaptive median, Adaptive median
3	**70**	Adaptive median, Adaptive median, Adaptive median, 3x1 vertical median
3	**90**	Adaptive median, Adaptive median, Adaptive median, 3x1 vertical median, Adaptive median
4	**10**	Adaptive median, Adaptive median, Adaptive median
4	**30**	Adaptive median, Adaptive median, Adaptive median
4	**50**	Adaptive median, Adaptive median, Adaptive median
4	**70**	Adaptive median, Adaptive median, Adaptive median, 3x1 vertical median, Adaptive median
4	**90**	Adaptive median, Radius 5 diamond median, contrast control with s= -100, 5x5 median

4.1 Performance Evaluation

The performance of FGA-F was compared with a single 5 × 5 median filter since a median filter (MF) is conventionally used for impulse noise removal [1]. FGA-F was also compared with variations of MF such as a 5 × 5 Weighted MF (WMF) [12] with a weight of [1 1 1 1 1;1 2 2 2 1;1 2 3 2 1; 1 2 2 2 1;1 1 1 1 1], a 5 × 5 Center Weighted MF (CWMF) [12] with a center weight of 3 and an Adaptive MF (AMF) [1] with a maximum window size of 7. All of these filters are standard methods for impulse noise removal.

Following are the metrics used for performance evaluation:

Peak Signal to Noise Ratio (PSNR)

PSNR value of a denoised image with respect to the original image is calculated as shown in equation (7). This value, represented in dB, denotes the closeness of the denoised image to the original image. A high PSNR value for the denoised image shows its closeness to the original image.

$$PSNR = 10 * \log 10(255^2 / MSE) \tag{7}$$

where MSE is the mean squared error.

Tenengrad Measure

Tenengrad measure indicates the amount of edge details present in an image. Higher the value, the more edge details present in the image. Tenengrad method is based on obtaining the gradient magnitude from the Sobel operator. It is calculated as shown in equation (8).

$$TEN = \sum_{x=2}^{M-1} \sum_{y=2}^{N-1} (\nabla S(x,y))^2 \text{ for } \nabla \text{S(x, y)} > \text{T} \tag{8}$$

Where T is a discrimination threshold value and $\nabla S(x, y)$ is the Sobel gradient magnitude value. Here, T is taken to be zero. When the TEN for the denoised image R is close to the original image O, it shows that the denoising process preserves the edge details in the image. TEN of R is less than TEN of O when the denoising process results in loss of edge details. TEN of R is greater than TEN of O when the denoising process creates false edge details.

Image Quality Index (IQI)

IQI [6] is designed by modelling any image distortion as a combination of three factors: loss of correlation, luminance distortion and contrast distortion. It is calculated as shown in equation (9). The value of IQI ranges from [-1, 1]. A denoised image, which is much similar to the original image, and hence of high quality, has an IQI value close to one.

$$IQI = Corr(O,R) * Lum(O,R) * Cont(O,R) \tag{9}$$

4.2 Experimental Analysis

Table 4, 5, 6 and 7 shows the values of different metrics obtained for the Lena training images corrupted by noise model 1, 2, 3 and 4 respectively, denoised by FGA-F in table 3, MF, WMF, CWMF and AMF for the respective impulse noise levels. From the four tables, it can be seen that FGA-F performs equally well for all types of impulse noise, except for high level model 2, and medium level and high level model 4 impulse noises. This result shows that the proposed method can be used to remove all levels of models 1 and 3 impulse noise, low and medium level model 2 noises and low level model 4 impulse noise from grayscale images.

Tables 4 ~ 7 shows that for all noise models, using composite filters produced by FGA for impulse noise removal yields better results than using a single MF, especially for high noise levels. The difference between the PSNR values of the denoised images created by the single MF and composite filter becomes larger as the noise level in the input image increases. The quality of the denoised image produced by the median filter is less than that of the denoised image produced by the composite filters, as shown by their IQI values. The Tenengrad value for the original Lena image is 22034. For MF, Tenengrad value is smaller than that for the composite filters for low noise levels, which indicates that loss of edge detail is more when using single filters. For high noise levels, this value is much higher than 22034 and the TEN values for the composite filters, which indicates that MF creates more false edge details than composite filters. Altogether, composite filter is better than a single MF for impulse noise removal with edge preservation.

Table 4. Compairing PSNR, Tenengrad measure and IQI obtained for Lena training images corrupted with 10%, 30%, 50%, 70% and 90% model 1 impulse noise

Filters	*PSNR(dB)*					*IQI*					*TEN*				
	10	*30*	*50*	*70*	*90*	*10*	*30*	*50*	*70*	*90*	*10*	*30*	*50*	*70*	*90*
MF	30.5285	27.1045	22.9126	14.0837	7.5496	0.65	0.6245	0.5187	0.1495	0.0136	5157	50688	27580	222462	2820290
WMF	29.6927	27.7033	24.32	19.9758	14.3556	0.6102	0.5448	0.4299	0.2672	0.0692	9927	157422	537702	593024	132108
CWMF	29.7019	27.9361	24.886	20.6605	14.758	0.6151	0.5554	0.4476	0.2884	0.0769	16830	27607	428542	581744	597647
AMF	38.2187	33.7991	30.2533	22.0065	10.3722	0.8956	0.8635	0.7797	0.5467	0.0567	16993	34850	41245	22982	450028
FGA-F	35.6546	32.9135	30.4875	27.7668	18.4924	0.7809	0.7483	0.694	0.6015	0.3338	13423	21752	44055	25280	60552

Table 5. Compairing PSNR, Tenengrad measure and IQI obtained for Lena training images corrupted with 10%, 30%, 50%, 70% and 90% model 2 impulse noise

Filters	*PSNR(dB)*					*IQI*					*TEN*				
	10	*30*	*50*	*70*	*90*	*10*	*30*	*50*	*70*	*90*	*10*	*30*	*50*	*70*	*90*
MF	30.2113	27.3407	20.2326	9.8384	5.6583	0.6508	0.6256	0.4374	0.0627	-0.0066	15103	14257	97643	568666	0
WMF	29.6986	27.6925	23.2366	13.1258	5.657	0.6113	0.5442	0.4149	0.1163	-0.0027	13986	244719	844263	52316	0
CWMF	29.7289	27.9719	23.6966	13.7259	5.657	0.6172	0.5558	0.4312	0.1334	-0.0015	13707	10682	738087	43164	0
AMF	38.0592	33.9589	27.9893	13.3566	5.7434	0.8933	0.8642	0.7575	0.7575	-0.0472	21297	12197	63082	63082	0
FGA-F	35.5918	32.9615	29.9758	21.6476	13.5538	0.7805	0.7491	0.6868	0.4783	-0.0044	21297	12197	62996	215288	270000

Table 6. Compairing PSNR, Tenengrad measure and IQI obtained for Lena training images corrupted with 10%, 30%, 50%, 70% and 90% model 3 impulse noise

Filters	*PSNR(dB)*					*IQI*					*TEN*				
	10	*30*	*50*	*70*	*90*	*10*	*30*	*50*	*70*	*90*	*10*	*30*	*50*	*70*	*90*
MF	30.3897	27.1525	22.924	14.154	7.5931	0.651	0.6233	0.517	0.1527	0.0128	9708	28576	9018	113525	6331253
WMF	29.828	27.6254	24.4861	19.9874	14.2524	0.6116	0.5434	0.429	0.2734	0.0668	4863	15951	510281	393912	610508
CWMF	29.8139	27.8739	24.922	20.4492	14.3358	0.6169	0.5523	0.4444	0.2911	0.0717	6598	15662	519791	446663	563850
AMF	38.0144	33.8203	30.1644	21.9719	10.3488	0.8951	0.864	0.7798	0.5438	0.0543	20113	25764	7037	39692	2624504
FGA-F	35.5872	32.9447	30.3784	27.7634	18.3689	0.7815	0.7494	0.6952	0.6011	0.3348	20113	22498	5606	33137	115404

Table 7. Compairing PSNR, Tenengrad measure and IQI obtained for Lena training images corrupted with 10%, 30%, 50%, 70% and 90% model 4 impulse noise

Filters	*PSNR(dB)*					*IQI*					*TEN*				
	10	*30*	*50*	*70*	*90*	*10*	*30*	*50*	*70*	*90*	*10*	*30*	*50*	*70*	*90*
MF	30.3142	27.3641	12.0008	11.1374	5.8413	0.6502	0.6232	0.1139	0.0866	0.005	12061	36779	475793	579517	243
WMF	29.6615	27.5901	16.1394	15.4544	5.8413	0.6112	0.5413	0.2572	0.1713	0	12141	182897	979335	146211	243
CWMF	29.6808	27.8971	16.6251	16.1094	5.8413	0.6154	0.5521	0.2689	0.1934	0	11966	84163	877878	81675	243
AMF	38.0285	33.7159	16.9826	15.4291	5.8466	0.8944	0.8621	0.4248	0.3069	-0.023	22096	14705	84861	57471	243
FGA-F	35.5445	32.8724	24.8092	24.4028	13.7651	0.7812	0.7477	0.6012	0.5237	-0.005	22096	12847	83245	10693	286443

For all types of impulse noise and for all noise levels, FGA-F performs noise removal with detail preservation much better than WMF and CWMF as shown by the results in tables 4 to 7. For all noise models, AMF performs better than FGA-F for low noise levels. But, as the noise level increases, FGA-F outperforms AMF. All in all, the performance of FGA-F is much superior to the standard impulse noise removal procedures.

The proposed method has been tested on Baboon, Peppers and Elaine images. Figure 3 shows examples of outputs produced by MF, WMF, CWMF, AMF and FGA-F for Baboon image corrupted with 10% model 1 noise, Peppers with 30% model 2 noise, Elaine with 50% model 3 noise with an intensity range of 4 and Lena with 70% model 4 noise with an impulse noise intensity range of 4. While some amount of impulse noise is present in the outputs of the median filters (MF, WMF, CWMF and AMF) especially for high noise levels, noise is almost completely removed by the FGA filters. In particular, it is hard for MF and AMF to remove noise from 70% noise model 4 Lena image. WMF and CWMF produce images with a smeared appearance. But, FGA-F almost restores the original view of the image. Even though the quality of this image is not so good, the result can be used for further processing that does not require any high precision analysis. It can also be seen that FGA-F works equally well on images other than the Lena training images. Here too, for low noise levels, AMF performs better than FGA-F. But, considering the fact that FGA-F was not trained using these images, this fact is not a shortcoming of the proposed method. However, for high noise levels, FGA-F outperforms AMF for these test images as well, which shows that altogether, the proposed method is better.

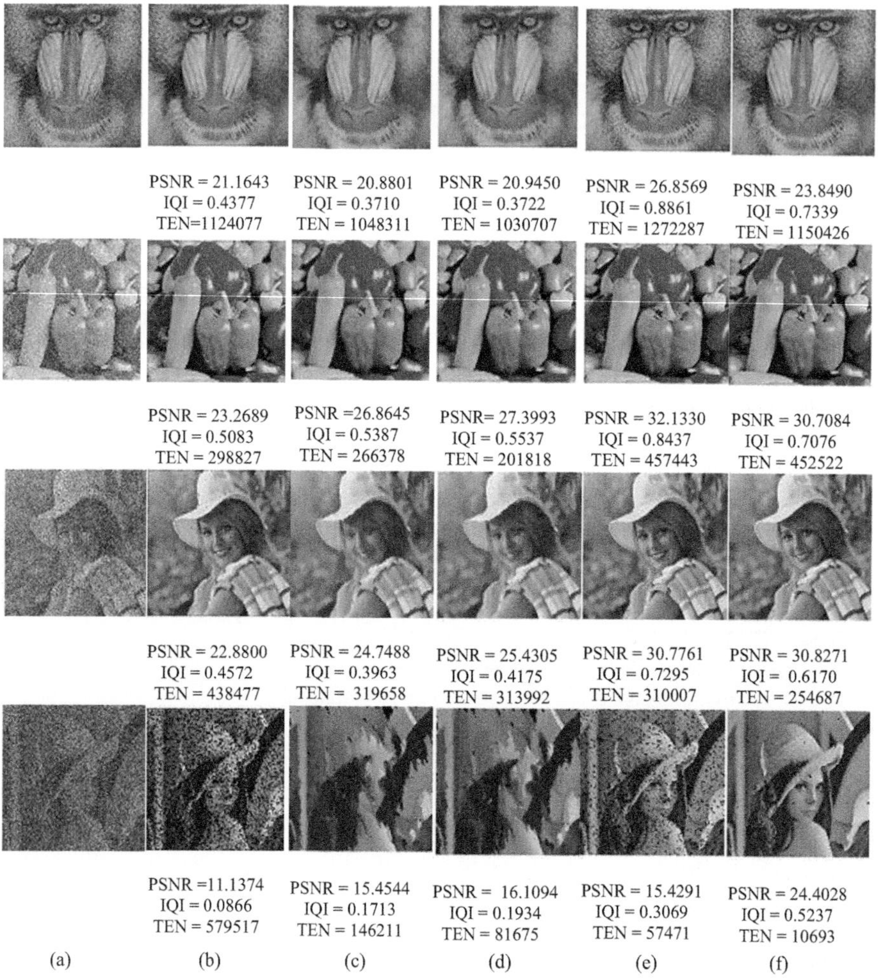

Fig. 3. Column (a): Baboon with 10% model 1impulse noise, Peppers with 30 % model 2 impulse noise, Elaine with 50% model 3 impulse noise with noise intensity interval of 4 and Lena with 70% model 4 impulse noise with noise intensity interval 4. Column (b), (c), (d), (e) and (f): Outputs produced by MF, WMF, CWMF, AMF and FGA filter respectively.

5 Conclusion

Median filters are commonly used for impulse noise removal. But, they result in loss of image details. Also, for high noise levels, they are not sufficient in completely removing the noise. In this paper, a FGA is used to determine the optimal composite filters for removal of different impulse noise levels without using deep knowledge about noise factors. Here, an FRB is used to adaptively change the crossover probability of GA. Experiments on benchmark images shows the superiority of the proposed method. This method can be used to remove any type of low density impulse noise, and performs considerably well for very high density model 1 and 3 impulse noises. As future work, the proposed method can be used for impulse noise removal in colour images and can be used in applications such as impulse noise removal in medical and satellite images.

References

1. Gonzalez, R., Woods, R.: Digital Image Processing. Addison Wesley, Reading (1992)
2. Goldberg, D.: Genetic Algorithm in Search, Optimization and Machine Learning. Addison-Wesley, Reading (1989)
3. Hong, J.H., Cho, S.B., Cho, U.K.: A Novel Evolutionary Method to Image Enhancement Filter Design: Method and Applications. IEEE Transactions on Systems, Man and Cybernetics – Part B, Cybernetics 39(6), 1446–1457 (2009)
4. Hong, J.H., Cho, S.B., Cho, U.K.: Evolutionary Image Enhancement for Impulsive Noise Reduction. In: Huang, D.S., Li, K., Irwin, G.W. (eds.) ICIC 2006. LNCS, vol. 4113, pp. 678–683. Springer, Heidelberg (2006)
5. Herrera, F., Lozano, M.: Adaptive Genetic Algorithms based on Fuzzy Techniques. In: Proceedings of the Sixth International Conference on Information Processing and Management Uncertainty in Knowledge Based Systems, pp. 775–780. IEEE, Los Alamitos (1996)
6. Wang, Z., Bovik, A.C.: A universal image quality index. IEEE Transactions on Signal Processing Letters 9(3), 81–84 (2002)
7. Ross, T.J.: Fuzzy Logic with Engineering Applications. McGraw Hill, New York (1995)
8. Herrera, F., Lozano, M.: Adaptive Genetic Operators Based on Coevolution with Fuzzy Behaviours. IEEE Transactions on Evolutionary Computation 5(2), 149–165 (2001)
9. Lee, M.A., Takagi, H.: Dynamic Control of Genetic Algorithms using Fuzzy Logic Techniques. In: Proceedings of Fifth International Conference on Genetic Algorithms, Urbana – Champaign, IL, pp. 76–83 (1993)
10. Cordon, O., Herrera, F., Hoffmann, F., Magdalena, L.: Genetic Fuzzy Systems - Evolutionary Tuning and Learning of Fuzzy Knowledge Bases. In: Advances in Fuzzy Systems — Applications and Theory, vol. 19, World Scientific Publishing Co. Pte. Ltd., Singapore (2001)
11. Nair, M.S., Raju, G.: A new fuzzy-based decision algorithm for high-density impulse noise removal. Signal Image and Video Processing (2010), doi:10.1007/s11760-010-0186-4
12. Ko, S.J., Lee, Y.H.: Center Weighted Median Filters and their application to Image Enhancement. IEEE Transactions on Circuits and Systems 38(9) (1991)

A Fourier Transform Based Authentication of Audio Signals through Alternation of Coefficients of Harmonics (FTAT)

Uttam Kr. Mondal[1] and J.K. Mandal[2]

[1] Dept. of CSE & IT,
College of Engg. & Management, Kolaghat ,
Midnapur (W.B), India
[2] Dept. of CSE,
University of Kalyani,
Nadia (W.B), India
uttam_ku_82@yahoo.co.in, jkm.cse@gmail.com

Abstract. With commercial growth of digital processing of audio signals like song, voice, speech etc the intention to make piracy of originality of the same is increasing day by day. It is a real problem of intellectual property right (IPR) for providing security over audio signal without changing its quality. In this paper, an approach has been made to provide security of digital song with embedding some authenticating secret code through coefficient alternation of harmonics over some specific region of the song without affecting its audible quality. Decomposing constituent frequency components of signal using Fourier transform followed by alternating coefficients of specific harmonics generates a secret code and this unique code is utilized to detect the originality of the song. A comparative study has been made with similar existing techniques and experimental results are also supported with mathematical formula based on Microsoft WAVE (".wav") stereo sound file.

Keywords: Average absolute difference (AD), maximum difference (MD), mean square error (MSE), normalized average absolute difference (NAD), normalized mean square error (NMSE), song authentication.

1 Introduction

Digitizing of audio signals revolutionize the world and people are now entertained with more enriched quality audio medium like song, voice, speech etc. It explores a new kind of era for million of people to create good songs for commercial purpose. Creating a quality song involved a number of factors like singer quality, compositions, lyrics, rhythms, etc. [4]. Lots of investment is needed to produce good quality songs. A kind of people is making piracy version of original songs and capturing market with lower price. Therefore, it is a big challenge for business persons, computer professionals or concerned people to ensure the security to retain the originality of songs [1, 2] and to protect from releasing the duplicate versions.

D. Nagamalai, E. Renault, and M. Dhanushkodi (Eds.): PDCTA 2011, CCIS 203, pp. 76–85, 2011.

In this paper, a framework for identifying a particular song with the help of unique secret code obtained through coefficient alternation of harmonics over the song without affecting its quality has been presented. Proposed technique is evolved by decomposing frequency components of the signal and alternating coefficients of specified near harmonics by generating a secret code. Embedded song signals with secrete code can easily distinguish the original from similar available songs. It is experimentally observed that alternating coefficients of harmonics will not affect the song quality but provide a level of security to protect the piracy of song signal.

Organization of the paper is as follows. Embedding secret key and coefficient alternation are presented in section 2.1 and 2.2 respectively. The authentication procedure has been depicted in section 2.3 that of extraction in section 2.4. The separation of embedding message is performed in section 2.5. Experimental results are given in section 3. Conclusions are drawn in section 4. References are given at end.

2 The Technique

The scheme fabricates the secret key followed by alteration of some of the coefficients. Algorithms namely FTAT-ESK and FTAT-CAL are proposed as double security measure, the details of which are given in section 2.1 and section 2.2 respectively.

2.1 Embedding Secret Key (FTAT - ESK)

Embedding a secret key in the specific positions of signal is computed through a hash function. The procedure of embedding secret key is depicted in the algorithm.

Algorithm

Input: Original song signal, text message.
Output: Modified song signal with embedded message.
Method: Embedding a secret key in the lower frequency areas to avoid distortion of the quality of songs as follows

Step 1: Find all frequency components which are less than 300 Hz using Fast Fourier Transform (FFT).

Step 2: Take a secret key less than 150/4 or, 37 characters [using steps 3 to 6 , each character will embed within a set of four frequency components (in sequence) which are less than 300Hz (step 1). Therefore, half of the range of frequency components (1-150 Hz) will be used to embed at most 37 characters].

Step 3: Choose a song identification message (secret key) and find its equivalent ASCII bit pattern. Suppose, the secret message is "Indrani", Its equivalent ASCII bit sequence in binary is 01001001, 01101110, 00110010, 01110010, 01100001, 01101110, 01101001 respectively, i.e., a stream of 56 bits.

Step 4: Divide the bit sequence of secret key into small bit patterns of size two i.e. total number of small bit patterns is 56/2=28. To append 28 bit pairs in the song signal, need at least 28 rows in sampled data set.

Step 5: Represent each bit pair into equivalent lower magnitude value in sequence. (00 will be represented by 0, 01 by 0.0001,10 by 0.0010, and 11 by 0.0011).

Step 6: Put the lower magnitude values over the sampled data of the signal using the following rules.

i. *Choose position starting from first position upto 300 Hz frequency range [if message size is less than half of frequency range (1-150Hz) then, find suitable gap between appended positions]. Here, message size 28 (after taking 2 bit units), therefore, require gap is 150/28 or, 5 positions .i.e. each value of message should add at 1st, 6st, 11st ,... position and make frequency component zero at all these specified positions of two columns of sampled data set .*

i. *Append the magnitude values (in sequence) in specified positions of song signal by the following method.*
*i^{th} position value(ival) of message should add at k^{th} position of x, i.e., x(k,1)=ival and x(i+1,2)= ival, where k = (i-1)*5 + 1. If i^{th} position is the last position then , x(k,1)=ival and x(i+1,2)= ival.*

iii. *Stop when all magnitude values are assigned to their respective positions over the specified frequency range of the signal.*

Step 7: Apply inverse FFT to get back the sampled values of modified song signal.

Therefore, if any value altered in processing, it will create a difference with the assigned magnitude values which present throughout the signal and changing one position will change the content of embedded message.

2.2 Coefficient Alternation (FTAT - CAL)

Let, x(n,2) is set of total sampled data of a song, Fourier series of a function $f(x)$ can be written as

$$f(x) = \frac{1}{2}a_0 + \sum_{n=1}^{\infty} a_n \cos(nx) + \sum_{n=1}^{\infty} b_n \sin(nx),$$

Where,

$$a_0 = \frac{1}{\pi}\int_{-\pi}^{\pi} f(x)\,dx$$

$$a_n = \frac{1}{\pi}\int_{-\pi}^{\pi} f(x)\cos(nx)\,dx$$

$$b_n = \frac{1}{\pi}\int_{-\pi}^{\pi} f(x)\cos(nx)\,dx \qquad \text{and n=1,2,3.....}$$

The Fourier coefficients (a_n,b_n)en commonly expressed using the formulae which is given in equation (1).

$$c_n = \frac{1}{2\pi}\int_{-\pi}^{\pi} f(x)e^{-inx}\,dx. \tag{1}$$

The Fourier coefficients a_n,b_n, c_n are related via

$$a_n = c_n + c_{-n} \text{ for } n = 0, 1, 2, \ldots,$$

and

$$b_n = i(c_n - c_{-n}) \text{ for } n = 1, 2, \ldots$$

We can also use Euler's formula,

$$e^{inx} = \cos(nx) + i\sin(nx),$$

where *i* is the imaginary unit, to give a more concise formula:

$$f(x) = \sum_{n=-\infty}^{\infty} c_n e^{inx}.$$

The notion of a Fourier series can also be extended to a customize form by modifying f, such as F or $\hat{f}$, and functional notation often replaces subscripting, which is given in equation (2).

$$\begin{aligned} f(x) &= \sum_{n=-\infty}^{\infty} \hat{f}(n)\cdot e^{inx} \\ &= \sum_{n=-\infty}^{\infty} F[n]\cdot e^{inx} \end{aligned} \tag{2}$$

Particularly when the variable x represents time, the coefficient sequence is a frequency domain representation (discrete).

It has been experimentally observed the alternation of the coefficients of closely harmonics of song signal is not affecting the audio quality of song. Therefore, finding coefficient values of closely specified harmonics and interchanging those coefficients, we can derived another song signal which will carry some authenticate information with the modified song signal without affecting its audible quality. C_n of equation (1) can be represented by equation (3).

$$C_n = \sum_{k=0}^{N-1} f(x)e^{-i2\pi nk/N} \tag{3}$$

i.e., $\mathbf{C_n}$ will be interchanged with $\mathbf{C_{n-p}}$ coefficient. The value of p is determined based on quality of song.

The proposed encoding technique has been outlined in subsection 2.3 that of decoding is in subsection 2.4 and 2.5.

2.3 Authentication

The proposed authentication technique is embodied here as algorithm

Algorithm

Input: Song signal with embedded message.
Output: Song signal with interchanged coefficients of specified harmonics along with untouched embedded message.
Method: Extraction of coefficient values and altering of the same using a hash function without affecting the quality of signal.
Step 1: Apply FFT over the signal (song) x(n,2) to find the magnitude values of frequencies of the signal and put into an array s(i) , 1<=i<=n. Obtain the coefficients(C_i) using equation (III) of some specified harmonics. The selected harmonic number i is calculated by using the formula i = k*(1000-p), where k=1, 2, 3,... , p=0 or 10 and i<=n.
Step 2: Interchange the values of coefficients (for each k) between two values of p, where i=1, 2, 3, ... and i<=n [using equation (III) and step 2].
Step 3: Apply IFFT over the modified values of s(i), 1<=i<=n to modify authenticated song signal with embedded unaltered message.

2.4 Extraction

The decoding is performed using similar mathematical calculations. The same is outlined as an algorithm.

Algorithm

Input: Modified song signal with interchanged coefficients of specified harmonics.
Output: Modified song signal with embedded message.
Method: Extraction of coefficients and reallocating them in their original positions.

Step 1: Apply FFT over embedded signal (song) x(n,2) to get the magnitude values of frequency and put into s(i) , 1<=i<=n. Find the coefficients(C_i) using equation (III) of specified of harmonics. The selected harmonic number i is calculated by similar way as used in authentication algorithm.
Step 2: Interchange the value of coefficients (each k) between two values of p, where i=1, 2, 3,... and i<=n as done in authentication algorithm.

Step 3: Apply IFFT over the output values s(i) , 1<=i<=n of step 2 to get the sampled values of original song signal with embedding secret message.

2.5 Emb-Extraction

The separation of embedded message is performed using simple techniques which is described in the algorithm.

Algorithm

Input: Modified song signal with embedded message
Output: Original song with separated embedded message
Method: Extracting sampled values and authenticating codes of original song
Step 1: Find FFT of output of extracted sample values and search the specified positions where the messages are inserted.
Step 2: Collect all non-zero magnitudes values on above 300 Hz.
Step 3: Represent the collected magnitude value into equivalent small bit sequence as value 0 by 00, 0.0001 by 01, 0.0010 by 10, and 0.0011 by 11 respectively. Therefore, the ASCII bit sequence of input message is the sequence of all small bit sequence putting side by side. After obtaining the ASCII bit sequence, respective ASCII character are regenerated by taking bits in sequence of size 8.

3 Experimental Results

Encoding and decoding techniques have been applied over 1 minute recorded songs, which is represented by complete procedure along with results in each intermediate step has been outlined in subsections 3.1.1 to 3.1.4. The results are discussed in section 3.1 and 3.2 out of which 3.1 deals with result associated with FTAT and that of 3.2 gives a comparison with existing recent techniques.

3.1 Results

For experimental observation, strip of 10 seconds classical song ('100 Miles from Memphis', sang by Sheryl Crow) has been taken. The sampled value of the song is given in table 1 as a two dimensional matrix. Figure 1 shows amplitude-time graph of the original signal. FTAT is applied on this signal and as a first step of the procedure FFT is performed over input song signal. The output generated in the process is shown in figure 2 (number of sampled values is 2646000). Selected coefficient values are shown in figure 3. The intermediate output corresponding of interchanged coefficients is given in figure 4. Figure 5 shows the difference of frequency ratio of original and interchanged coefficients of selected harmonics. From figure 5 it is seen that the deviation is very less and will not affect the quality of the song at all.

3.1.1 Original Recorded Song Signal (10 Seconds)

The values for sampled data array x(n,2) from the original song is given in table 1. The graphical representation of the original song, considering all rows (2646000) of x(n,2) is given in the figure 1.

Table 1. Sampled data array x(n,2)

Sl no	x(k,1)	x(k,2)
…	…	…
	0	0.0001
	0.0000	0.0000
	-0.0009	-0.0009
	-0.0006	-0.0007
	-0.0012	-0.0012
	-0.0014	-0.0014
	-0.0016	-0.0017
	-0.0023	-0.0022
	-0.0027	-0.0027
	-0.0022	-0.0021
…	…	…

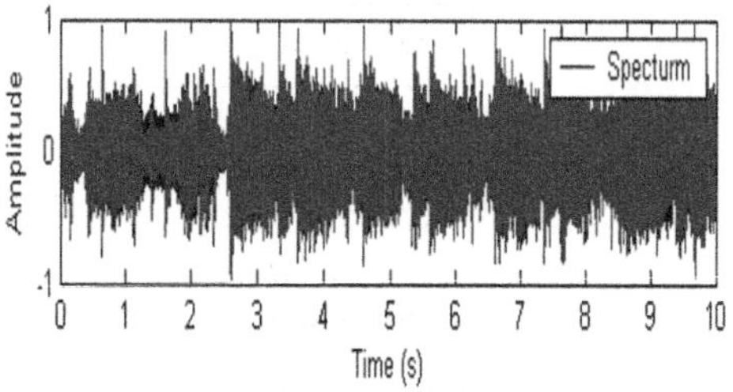

Fig. 1. Original song ('100 Miles from Memphis', sang by Sheryl Crow)

3.1.2 Coefficient Values of Selected Harmonics for Each k

The graphical representation of the selected harmonics is shown in the figure 2.

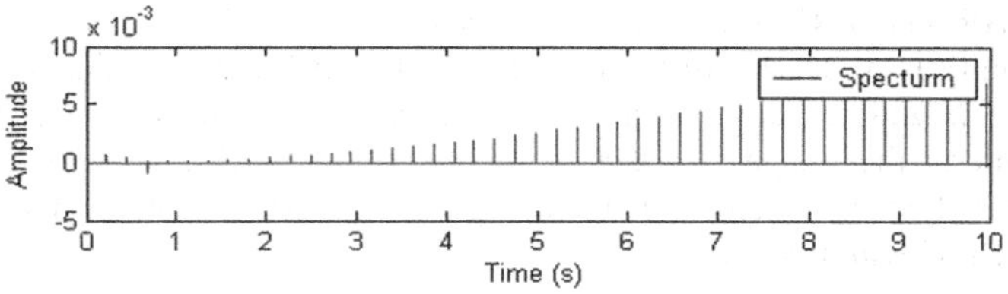

Fig. 2. Selected coefficient values

3.1.3 Modified Song after Alternating Coefficient Values and Embedding Secret Key (10 Seconds)

The graphical representation of the modified song signal is shown in the figure 3.

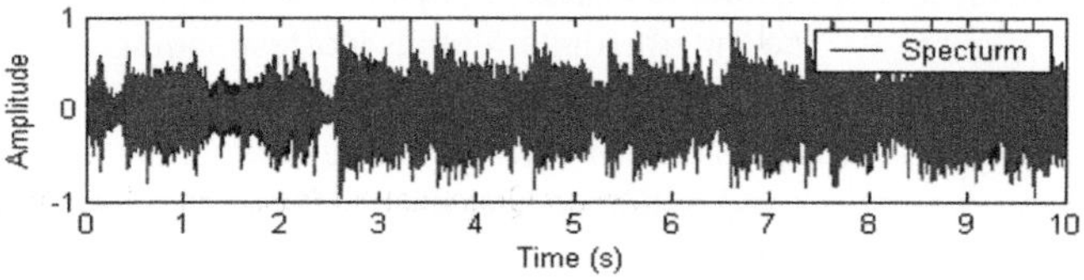

Fig. 3. Modified song after alternating coefficient values and embedding secret key

3.1.4 The Difference of Magnitude Values between Original Signal and Modified Signal

The graphical representation of the magnitude differences of original and modified songs is shown in the figure 4.

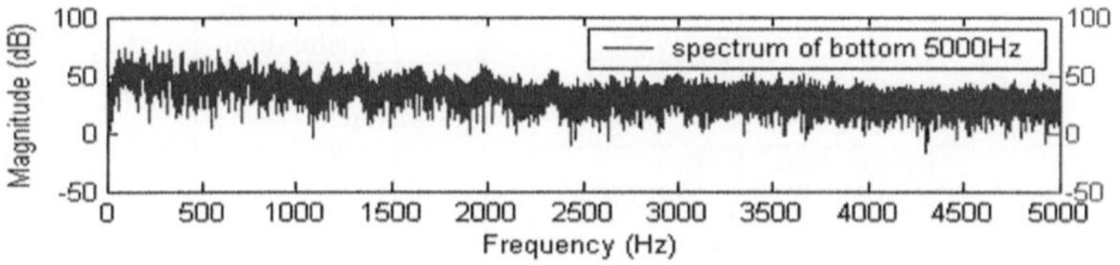

Fig. 4. The magnitude values difference between signal figure 1 and figure 3

3.2 Comparison with Existing Systems

Various algorithms [5] are available for embedding information with audio signals. They usually do not care about the quality of audio but the proposed scheme enforced authentication technique without changing the quality of song. A comparative study of properties of proposed method with data hiding via phase manipulation of audio signals(DHPMA)[3] before and after embedding secret message/modifying parts of signal (16-bit stereo audio signals sampled at 44.1 kHz.) is given in table 2, table 3 and table 4. Average absolute difference (AD) is used as the dissimilarity measurement between original song and modified song to justify the modified song. A lower value of AD signifies lesser error in the modified song. Normalized average absolute difference (NAD) called quantization error which is used to measure normalized distance between 0 and 1. Mean square error (MSE) is the cumulative squared error between the embedded and original song. A lower value of MSE signifies lesser error in the embedded song. The SNR is used to measure how much a signal has been tainted by noise. It represents embedding errors between original song and modified song and calculated as the ratio of signal power (original song) to the noise power corrupting the signal. A ratio higher than 1:1 indicates more signal than noise. The PSNR is often used to assess the quality measurement between the original and a modified song. The higher the PSNR represents the better the quality of the modified song. Thus from our experimental results of benchmarking parameters (NAD, MSE, NMSE, SNR and PSNR) in proposed method obtain better performances without affecting the audio quality of song.

Table 3 gives the experimental results in terms of SNR (Signal to Noise Ratio) and PSNR (Peak Signal to Noise Ratio). Table 4 represents comparative values of Normalized Cross-Correlation (NC) and Correlation Quality (QC) of proposed algorithm with DHPMA. Table 5 shows PSNR, SNR, BER (Bit Error Rate) and MOS (Mean Opinion Score) values for the proposed algorithm. Here all the BER values are 0. The figure 5 summarizes the results of this experimental test. It shows that the performances of the algorithm are stable for different types of audio signals.

Table 2. Metric for different distortions

Sl No	Statistical parameters for Differential distorstion	Value using FTAT	Value using DHPMA
1	MD	0.4456	3.6621e-004
2	AD	2.5590e-005	2.0886e-005
3	NAD	1.7576e-004	0.0063
4	MSE	5.8431e-006	1.4671e-009
5	NMSE	6.1743e+003	8.4137e-005

Table 3. SNR and PSNR

Sl No	Statistical parameters for Differential distorstion	Value using FTAT	Value using DHPMA
1	Signal to Noise Ratio (SNR)	37.9059	40.7501
2	Peak Signal to Noise Ratio (PSNR)	52.2330	45.4226

Table 4. NC and QC

Sl No	Statistical parameters for Corelation distorstion	Value using FTAT	Value using DHPMA
1	Normalised Cross-Correlation(NC)	1	1
2	Correlation Quality (QC)	-0.0803	-0.5038

Table 5. SNR, PSNR BER, MOS

Audio (1s)	SNR	PSNR	BER	MOS
Song1	38.6410	53.3922	0	5
Song2	37.3916	46.8229	0	5
Song3	36.7033	50.7415	0	5
Song4	37.9059	52.2330	0	5
Song5	36.6881	49.9851	0	5

The figure 6 shows the changes of SNR and PSNR for considering different values of **p** of $\mathbf{C_{n-p}}$ [equation (3)]. This quality rating (Mean opinion score) is computed by using equation (4).

$$Quality = \frac{5}{1 + N * SNR} \tag{4}$$

where N is a normalization constant and SNR is the measured signal to noise ratio. The ITU-R Rec. 500 quality rating is perfectly suited for this task, as it gives a quality rating on a scale of 1 to 5 [6]. Table 6 shows the rating scale, along with the quality level being represented.

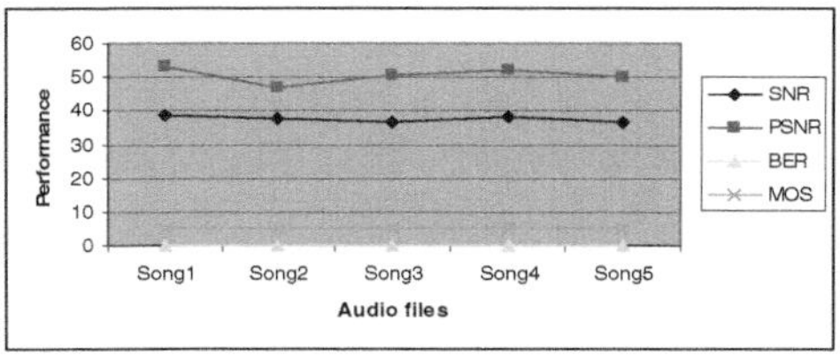

Fig. 5. Performance for different audio signals

Table 6. Quality Rating Scale

Rating	Impairment	Quality
5	Imperceptible	Excellent
4	Perceptible, not annoying	Good
3	Slightly annoying	Fair
2	Annoying	Poor
1	Very annoying	Bad

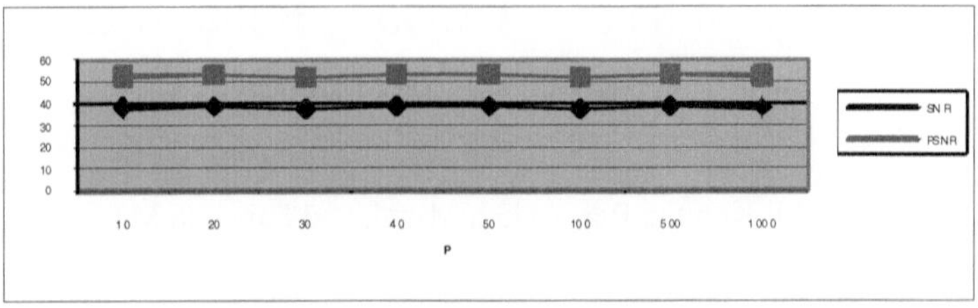

Fig. 6. SNR and PSNR for different values of P

4 Conclusion and Future Work

In this paper, an algorithm for alternating closely coefficients of lower harmonics with embedding secret key over song signal has been proposed which will not affect the quality of songs but it will ensure to detect the characteristics of distortion of song signal by intruder. Additionally, the proposed algorithm is very easy to implement.

This technique is developed based on the observation of characteristics of different songs but the mathematical model for representing the variation of those characteristics after modification may be formulated in future. It also can be extended to embed an image into an audio signal instead of text and audio. The perfect estimation of percentage of threshold numbers of sample data of song that can be allowed to change for a normal conditions will be done in future with all possibilities of errors.

References

1. Mondal, U.K., Mandal, J.K.: A Practical Approach of Embedding Secret Key to Authenticate Tagore Songs(ESKATS). In: Proceedings of Wireless Information Networks & Business Information System (WINBIS 2010), vol. 6(1), pp. 67–74. Organized by Rural Nepal Technical Academy (Pvt.) Ltd., Nepal (2010) ISSN 2091-0266
2. Mondal, U.K., Mandal, J.K.: A Novel Technique to Protect Piracy of Quality Songs through Amplitude Manipulation (PPAM). In: International Symposium on Electronic System Design (ISED 2010), pp. 246–250 (2010) ISBN 978-0-7695-4294-2
3. Dong, X., Bocko, M.F., Ignjatovic, Z.: Data Hiding Via Phase Manipulation of Audio Signals. In: IEEE International Conference on Acoustics, Speech, and Signal Processing (ICASSP 2004), vol. 5, pp. 377–380 (2004) ISBN 0-7803-8484-9
4. Erten, G., Salam, F.: Voice Output Extraction by Signal Separation. In: ISCAS 1998, vol. 3, pp. 5–8 (1998) ISBN 07803-4455-3
5. Katzenbeisser, S., Petitcolas, F.A.P.: Information Hiding Techniques for Steganography and Digital Watermarking. Artech House, Norwood (2000) ISBN 978-1-58053-035-4
6. Arnold, M.: Audio watermarking: Features, applications and algorithms. In: IEEE International Conference on Multimedia and Expo, New York, vol. 2, pp. 1013–1016 (2000)

Infrared Source Tracking Robot with Computer Interface

Bondili Kohitha Bai, Ankita Mittal, and Sanchita Mittal

Department of Electronics and Communication Engineering, ASET, AUUP, India
{kohitha,mittal.ankita4}@gmail.com,
mittal_sanchita2@rediffmail.com

Abstract. In this infrared source tracking robot system, a target has a light emitting section with a high light emitting directivity, for emitting a light beam modulated into pulses. A tracking robot has a tracking sensor section for monitoring a light beam by a pair of light receiving elements, for processing signals from the received light beam, and for generating and supplying drive control signals to a travel control section. In response to drive control signals the travel control section generates and supplies drive signals to a driver section. The driver section drives the tracking robot so that the robot advances while turning to the right when the output level of the right side light receiving element is higher than that of the left side light receiving element, and to the left when the latter is higher than the former. There are basically two modes, the first being the one in which the robot transmits the path sequence to the computer while tracking the source. In the second mode, the computer transmits the remembered path sequence to the robot which travels along the path guided by the computer signals, without any infrared source assistance.

1 Introduction

A robot is a virtual or mechanical artificial agent. In practice, it is usually an electro-mechanical system which, by its appearance or movements, conveys a sense that it has intent or agency of its own.

People have a generally positive perception of the robots they actually encounter. Domestic robots for cleaning and maintenance are increasingly common in and around homes. There is anxiety, however, over the economic effect of automation and the threat of robotic weaponry, anxiety which is not helped by the depiction of many villainous, intelligent, acrobatic robots in popular entertainment. Compared with their fictional counterparts, real robots are still benign, dim-witted, and clumsy.

An infrared tracker robot is designed implementation is described. In this robot a group of receivers can detect the beams source and a controller, which is based on classic control, leads it to the source of beams. In this design a commonplace CPU is used to implement all intelligent parts such as a controller. Designing of IO part, detectors, and all interfacing circuits is also mentioned. This inexpensive robot has a high movement precision and can be used in many applications including, searching for living persons and rescuing them.

D. Nagamalai, E. Renault, and M. Dhanushkodi (Eds.): PDCTA 2011, CCIS 203, pp. 86–90, 2011.

2 Archirecture

Implementation of the "Infrared source tracking with computer interface" here is done by a digital logic circuit. If data input is given through the computer there no need of infrared sources i.e., data sources can be in any one of the form. The other is, robot simply follows the infrared source without any communication with a computer.

A. *using infrared as source*: Infrared source tracking with computer interface has three sections, namely, sensor, controller and driver.

Fig. 1. System architecture using sensor

The sensing section detects the 38 kHz infrared radiation. The output of the sensors is fed to the monostable multi-vibrator [1], which serves as the input to the logic gate circuit. Depending on the input sequence obtained the logic gate performs sequential operations and gives out its decision, which is a sequence of bits to drive DC motors [2]. The logic controller section processes the information from the sensor and provides input to the driver section, which has DC motors for driving the robot. The camera that is placed on the robot starts capturing the actions around and displays it using television or computer (as required).

B. using computer as source: The instructions are given through the computer to the robot using the interaction Radio signal transmitter and receiver. Transmitter and receiver is fitted with both computer and the robot respectively

In the first mode, the receiver part (RWS-434N) of the robot is switched off and the logic circuit and the transmitter part (TWS-434) are switched on. The robot constantly sends the signals to the computer about both the motors (which are the wheels of robot), whether they are moving or not. '1' is transmitted for motor 'on' and '0' is sent for motor 'off'. Both signals are sent simultaneously.

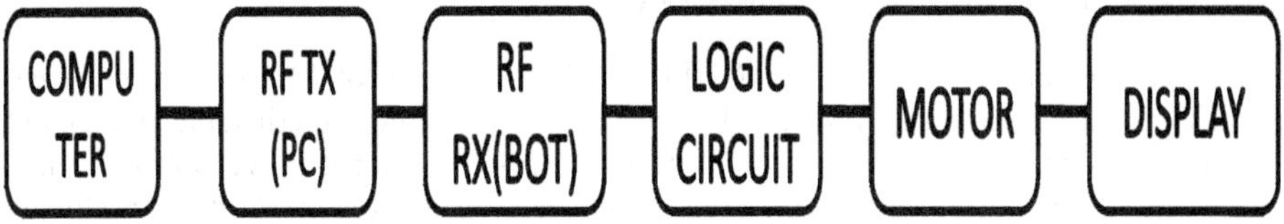

Fig. 2. System architecture using computer

The signal is received by the receiver of the computer. The receiver sends the signals into the computer by the parallel port (DB25 connector). The signal is received by the port and processed by the VB program.

In the second mode, the computer sends the information ('1' or '0') to the robot by its transmitter. The transmitter and logic part of the robot is switched off and only the receiver part of the robot is switched on and power supply is given to the motors to act according to the received signals.

The main logic is that the robot sends the signals about whether the motors are moving or not. The computer saves the time for which each motor moves and later sends the same signals to the motors for the same time. We assume that if the motors help the robot move a distance of 1 meter in 10 seconds, then later on when they are switched on, the robot will again travel a distance of 1 meter given the same conditions.

3 Logic Implementation

The inputs from the sensors (Left, Centre and Right) are fed into the logic design as shown in the figure. The circuit is implemented according to the truth table shown. '1' received indicates high or positive result from that sensor. E.g. If 'L' or left sensor indicates that the sensor is receiving an infrared signal from the transmitter, it indicates this to the logic, which thereafter, performs the action of turning the robot left. The left motor is switched off and the right motor remains on (high), due to which the robot turns left.

The digital logic is implemented according to the truth table shown. The solutions are obtained for Left and Right Motors separately. The minimized equations are obtained by SOP (Sum of Products) usage. The equations are solved/implemented using the logic gates as shown in the figure. The ICs are used for practical working of the circuit.

Table 1. Digital logic implementation

left	centre	right	actions
0	0	0	Rotate left
0	0	1	right
0	1	0	straight
0	1	1	right
1	0	0	left
1	0	1	stop
1	1	0	left

4 Design Model

Fig. 3. Top view of IR source tracking robot

5 Applications

This robot primarily has two applications: Heat-seeking missile and fire extinguisher.

5.1 As a Heat-Seeking Missile

The heat seeking missile is a special kind of missile that not only reaches the target emitting heat radiations (aircraft, ship or boat) but also tracks it. As the target moves, it follows the target and finally hits it. The missile is based on the concept of detecting and following the heat radiating source. The robot, designed for 2-dimensional motions, performs the task of a heat-seeking missile as it tracks heat-radiating objects.

5.2 As a Fire Extinguisher

The robot can be used as a highly sophisticated fire extinguisher. The fire extinguisher, when it detects fire, will move towards fire, deviating away from any signed for this carrier frequency.

5.3 As a Payload Robot

The robot may also be used to take things from one place to another. If the motors with higher power can be included, they can be used to make the robot carry payloads along a remembered path.

5.4 For Navigation Purposes

Since IR is invisible to human eyes, it will not disturb humans if used in devices that project the light out. If a device needs light to measure a large distance for navigation purpose, IR can be used without attracting attention or disturbing anyone.

6 Future Trends

a. If a microcontroller based IR source tracking robot is made then it can be reprogrammed to increase speed, sensitivity.

b. For use as a fire extinguisher, a temperature sensor can be added to the robot. Once the temperature reaches a predetermined value, an interrupt is activated .This will bring the robot to a safe distance from fire and put out and operate the extinguisher.

c. Better path remembrance algorithms can be included along with obstacle avoidance for better functioning of robot.

7 Conclusions

In this project robot basically tracks the IR source[3] and moves accordingly. Automated systems like robots carry out specific tasks. These systems are usually employed in environments where conditions keep changing. The robot described here senses the 38 kHz infrared radiation and moves towards that direction. In doing so, it sends the path traversed to a nearby computer by wireless communication through the parallel port of computer, where after, the computer remembers the path. The computer can later guide the robot to travel along the remembered path without any source assistance.

There are basically two modes, the first being the one in which the robot transmits the path sequence to the computer while tracking the source. In the second mode, the computer transmits the remembered path sequence to the robot which travels along the path guided by the computer signals, without any infrared source assistance.

References

1. A monostable multivibrator circuit using complementary transistors, Solid-State Circuits Conference, Digest of Technical Papers 1957 IEEE International, vol. 0.2 (February 1957)
2. Bird, J.: Electrical and Electronic Principles and Technology, 3rd edn., The catalogue of this book is available from British library and library of congress
3. Gerlach, G., Budzier, H.: Thermal infrared sensors: Theory, optimisation and practice

An Evolutionary Algorithm Based Performance Analysis of Multiprocessor Computers through Energy and Schedule Length Model

Paulraj Ranjith Kumar[1] and Sankaran Palani[2]

[1] ECE Department, K.S. Rangasamy College of Technology, Tiruchengode, Tamilnadu, India
p_ranjith_kumar@rediffmail.com
[2] ECE Department, Sudharsan Engineering College, Tamilnadu, India
keeranur_palani@yahoo.com

Abstract. Multiprocessors have emerged as a powerful computing means for running real-time applications, especially where a uniprocessor system would not be sufficient enough to execute all the tasks. The high performance and reliability of multiprocessors have made them a powerful computing resource. Such computing environment requires an efficient algorithm to determine when and on which processor a given task should be executed. In multiprocessor systems, an efficient scheduling of parallel tasks onto the processors is known to be NP- Hard problem. With growing of applications of the embedded system technology, energy efficiency and timing requirement are becoming important issues for designing real time embedded systems. This paper focuses the combinational optimization problem, namely, the problem of minimizing schedule length with energy consumption constraint and the problem of minimizing energy consumption with schedule length constraint for independent parallel tasks on multiprocessor computers. These problems emphasize the tradeoff between power and performance and are defined such that the power-performance product is optimized by fixing one factor and minimizing the other and vice versa. The performance of the proposed algorithm with optimal solution is validated analytically and compared with Particle Swarm Optimization (PSO) and Genetic Algorithm (GA).

Keywords: Dynamic voltage scaling, Evolutionary Algorithm, Energy optimization, Scheduling and Multiprocessor.

1 Introduction

In recent years, processor performance has increased at the expense of drastically increased power consumption. On the one hand, such increased power consumption decreases the lifetime of battery operated systems, such as hand-held mobile systems or remote solar explorers. On the other hand, increased power consumption generates more heat, which causes heat dissipation a problem which requires more expensive packaging and cooling technology. Further this problem decreases reliability of the

D. Nagamalai, E. Renault, and M. Dhanushkodi (Eds.): PDCTA 2011, CCIS 203, pp. 91–101, 2011.

systems that have many processors. To reduce processor power consumption, many hardware techniques have been proposed, such as shutting down unused parts or reducing the power level of non fully utilized functional units [1]. Now a day's most of the processors have multiple supply voltages which have chosen by the operating frequency of the processor. Using this feature, several software techniques have been proposed to adjust the supply voltage, especially for mobile or uniprocessor systems [2], [3]. The Dynamic Voltage Scaling (DVS) technique [3] is recognized as the basis of numerous energy management solutions. DVS exploits the fact that the dynamic power consumption is a strictly convex function of the CPU speed, and attempts to save energy by reducing the supply voltage and frequency at run-time. Many of today's advanced processors, such as AMD and Intel, have this technology. The CPU power consumed per cycle in a CMOS processor can be expressed as [4]

$$P = C_L f V_{DD}^2 \tag{1}$$

where C_L is the total capacitance of wires and gates, V_{DD} is the supply voltage and f is the clock frequency. It is obvious that a lower voltage level leads to lower power consumption. The price to pay for lowering the voltage level is that it also leads to a lower clock frequency and thus slows down the execution of a task. The relation between the clock frequency and the supply voltage is expressed as [4]

$$f = (K * (V_{DD} - V_{TH})^2) / V_{DD} \tag{2}$$

where K is a constant which depends on gate size and capacitance, and V_{TH} is a Threshold voltage of the CMOS processor

This paper is organized as follows: Section 2 discusses background and related work. The problem statement and the proposed energy and schedule length models are discussed in Section 3. Section 4 presents the results and analysis of simulation. The conclusions and future work are stated in Section 5.

2 Related Research Work

This section introduces a genetic-based approach that performs task mapping and scheduling, using voltage scaling inside the inner energy optimization loop. The approach is described in detail in [8,9]. In the genetic task mapping approach, solution candidates are encoded into mapping strings, each gene in these strings describes a candidate mapping of a task to a processor. The genetic scheduling algorithm finds for a given mapping, energy efficient schedule that respects all the task deadlines. In [10], the Power Variation (PV) DVS algorithm provides a portion of slack time to the task of maximum energy saving. But PV-DVS is a greedy strategy that might generate local optimal result which is based on the unrealistic assumption of continuous voltage mode. In [13] Mir Masoud Rahmani et al. proposed the elitism stepping technique for the task scheduling problem in multiprocessor systems, with the objective to reduce the schedule length within an acceptable computation time. Recently, a parallel genetic algorithm for scheduling has been proposed in [14]. Bita Gorjiara et al.[15] have proposed an Adaptive Stochastic Gradient Voltage-and-Task Scheduling (ASG-VTS), which combines slack distribution and iterative adjustment of task ordering. Through cycles of slack recovery and distribution, the algorithm quickly converges to high quality solutions. In [17],the author studied the problems of minimizing the expected execution time given a hard energy budget and minimizing the expected energy expenditure given a hard execution deadline for a single task with randomized execution requirement. Dan Ding [18] et al. have proposed that fine and coarse grained voltage selection for energy efficient system through ant colony based optimization.

3 Problem Statement

Power dissipation and circuit delays in CMOS can be accurately modeled by simple equations, even for complex microprocessor circuits. CMOS circuits have both static and dynamic power dissipations; however, the dominant component is dynamic power consumption, which is given as $P \alpha fV^2$, where f is the clock frequency and V is the supply voltage. Since $f \alpha V$ and $s \alpha f$, power consumption of the CMOS processor is $P \alpha s^3$, where s is the processor speed [21]. For high supply voltages occurring when carrier velocity saturates, the frequency $f \alpha V^\gamma$ with $0 < \gamma < 1$, which implies that voltage is directly proportional to $f^{1/\gamma}$ and power consumption P is directly proportional to f and is also directly proportional to s^α, where α is the variation factor of the processor and has the constraint that $1+2/\gamma \geq 3$.

Assume that we are given n independent parallel tasks to be executed on m identical processors. Task i requires π_i processors to execute where $1 \leq i \leq n$, and any π_i of the m processors can be allocated to task i. We call π_i as the size of task i. It is possible that in executing task i, the π_i processors may have different execution requirements (i.e., the numbers of CPU cycles or the numbers of instructions executed on the processors). Let r_i represent the maximum execution requirement on the π_i processors executing task i. We use p_i to represent the power supplied to execute task i. Further, we assume that p_i is simply s_i^α , where $s_i = p_i^{1/\alpha}$ is the execution speed of task i. The execution time of task i is $t_i = r_i/s_i = r_i/ p_i^{1/\alpha}$. Note that all the π_i processors allocated to task i have the same speed s_i for duration t_i, although some of the π_i processors may be idle for some time. The energy consumed to execute task i is $e_i = \pi_i p_i t_i = \pi_i r_i p_i^{1-(1/\alpha)} = \pi_i r_i s_i^{\alpha-1}$.

3.1 Problem 1: Minimizing Schedule Length

Given n independent parallel tasks with task sizes $\pi_1, \pi_2, \ldots, \pi_n$ and task execution requirements $r_1, r_2, \ldots, r_n$, the problem of minimizing schedule length with energy consumption constraint E on a multiprocessor is to find the power supplies $p_1, p_2, \ldots, p_n$ and a nonpreemptive schedule of the n parallel tasks on the m processors such that the schedule length is minimized and the total energy consumed does not exceed E. The scheduling problems contain three nontrivial subproblems, namely, task decomposition, task scheduling, and power supplying. Scheduling the tasks is essentially to partition the n tasks into m groups such that each processor executes one group of tasks. We first consider the case when the n tasks have to be scheduled sequentially. This may happen when $\pi_i > m/2$ for all $1 \le i \le n$ .In this case, the m processors are treated as one unit, called a cluster, to be allocated to one task. Of course, for each particular task i only π_i of the m allocated processors are actually used and consume energy. It is clear that the problem of minimizing schedule length with energy consumption constraint E is simply to find the power supplies $p_1, p_2, \ldots, p_n$, such that the schedule length is minimized and the total energy consumed $E_1 + E_2 + \ldots\ldots\ldots E_n$ does not exceed E, i.e.

$$\pi_1 r_1 p_1^{1-\frac{1}{\alpha}} + \pi_2 r_2 p_2^{1-\frac{1}{\alpha}} + \pi_3 r_3 p_3^{1-\frac{1}{\alpha}} + \ldots\ldots\ldots + \pi_n r_n p_n^{1-\frac{1}{\alpha}} \le E \tag{3}$$

$$T = \frac{r_1}{p_1^{1/\alpha}} + \frac{r_2}{p_2^{1/\alpha}} + \frac{r_3}{p_3^{1/\alpha}} \ldots\ldots\ldots + \frac{r_n}{p_n^{1/\alpha}} \tag{4}$$

$$M = \pi_1^{1/\alpha} r_1 + \pi_2^{1/\alpha} r_2 + \pi_3^{1/\alpha} r_3 + \ldots\ldots\ldots + \pi_n^{1/\alpha} r_n \tag{5}$$

Theorem 1

When the n tasks are scheduled sequentially, the schedule length is minimized when task i is supplied with power $p_i = (E/M)^{\alpha/(\alpha-1)} / \pi_i$ *, where* $1 \le i \le n$ *.The optimal schedule length is* $T = M^{\alpha/(\alpha-1)} / E^{1/(\alpha-1)}$

Proof

We can minimize *T* by using the Lagrange multiplier method. Since

$$\nabla T(p_1, p_2, p_3 \ldots\ldots p_n) = \lambda \nabla F(p_1, p_2, p_3 \ldots\ldots p_n) \tag{6}$$

where T is viewed as function of $p_1, p_2, \ldots, p_n$ and λ is a Lagrange multiplier and F is the constraint

$$\pi_1 r_1 p_1^{1-\frac{1}{\alpha}} + \pi_2 r_2 p_2^{1-\frac{1}{\alpha}} + \pi_3 r_3 p_3^{1-\frac{1}{\alpha}} + \ldots\ldots\ldots + \pi_n r_n p_n^{1-\frac{1}{\alpha}} - E = 0$$

differentiating equation (4), we get

$$p_i = \frac{1}{\lambda(1-\alpha)\pi_i} \tag{7}$$

which, implies that

$$p_i = (E/M)^{\alpha/(\alpha-1)} / \pi_i \tag{8}$$

for all, $1 \le i \le n$, Consequently, we get the optimal schedule length.

$$T=\sum_{i=1}^{n}\frac{r_i}{p_i^{1/\alpha}}=\sum_{i=1}^{n}\pi_i^{1/\alpha}r_i\left(\frac{M}{E}\right)^{1/(\alpha-1)}=M\left(\frac{M}{E}\right)^{1/(\alpha-1)}=\frac{M^{\alpha/(\alpha-1)}}{E^{1/(\alpha-1)}} \tag{9}$$

Let M_k denote the total $\pi_i^{1/\alpha}r_i$ of the tasks in group k. For a given partition of the n tasks into j groups, we are seeking power supplies that minimize the schedule length. Let E_k be the energy consumed by all the tasks in group k. The following result characterizes the optimal power supplies.

Theorem 2
For a given partition $M_1, M_2, \ldots, M_j$ of the n tasks into j groups on a multiprocessor computer partitioned into j clusters, the schedule length is minimized when task i in group k is supplied with power $p_i = (E_k / M_k)^{\alpha/(\alpha-1)} / \pi_i$ where

$$E_k=\left(\frac{M_k^{\alpha}}{M_1^{\alpha}+M_2^{\alpha}+M_3^{\alpha}+\ldots\ldots\ldots+M_m^{\alpha}}\right)E \tag{10}$$

$$T=\left(\frac{M_1^{\alpha}+M_2^{\alpha}+M_3^{\alpha}+\ldots\ldots\ldots+M_m^{\alpha}}{E}\right)^{1/(\alpha-1)} \tag{11}$$

3.2 Problem 2: Minimizing Energy Consumption

Given n independent parallel tasks with task sizes $\pi_1, \pi_2, \ldots, \pi_n$ and task execution requirements $r_1, r_2, \ldots, r_n$, the problem of minimizing energy consumption with schedule length constraint T on a multiprocessor computer with m processors is to find the power supplies $p_1, p_2, \ldots, p_n$ and a nonpreemptive schedule of the n parallel tasks on the m processors such that the total energy consumption is minimized and the schedule length does not exceed T. The problem of minimizing energy consumption with schedule length constraint is simply to find the power supplies $p_1, p_2, \ldots, p_n$, such that the total energy consumption

$$E=\pi_1 r_1 p_1^{1-\frac{1}{\alpha}}+\pi_2 r_2 p_2^{1-\frac{1}{\alpha}}+\pi_3 r_3 p_3^{1-\frac{1}{\alpha}}+\ldots\ldots\ldots+\pi_n r_n p_n^{1-\frac{1}{\alpha}} \tag{12}$$

is minimized and the schedule length $T_1+T_2+T_3\ldots\ldots+T_n$ does not exceed T, i.e.,

$$\frac{r_1}{p_1^{1/\alpha}}+\frac{r_2}{p_2^{1/\alpha}}+\frac{r_3}{p_3^{1/\alpha}}\ldots\ldots\ldots+\frac{r_n}{p_n^{1/\alpha}}\le T \tag{13}$$

Theorem 3
When the n tasks are scheduled sequentially, the total energy consumption is minimized when task i is supplied with $p_i = (M / T)^{\alpha} / \pi_i$, where $1 \le i \le n$. The minimum energy consumption is $E = M^{\alpha} / T^{(\alpha-1)}$

Proof
We can minimize E by using the Lagrange multiplier system

$$\nabla E(p_1, p_2, p_3 \ldots. p_n) = \lambda \nabla f(p_1, p_2, p_3 \ldots. p_n) \tag{14}$$

where E is viewed as function of $p_1, p_2, \ldots, p_n$ and λ is a Lagrange multiplier and F is the constraint

$$\frac{\partial E}{\partial p_i} = \lambda \frac{\partial F}{\partial p_i}$$

differentiating equation (13), we get

$$p_i = \frac{1}{\lambda(1-\alpha)\pi_i} \tag{15}$$

which, implies that

$$\frac{(1-\alpha)}{\lambda} = (T / M)^{\alpha}$$

$$p_i = (M / T)^{\alpha} / \pi_i \tag{16}$$

for all, $1 \le i \le n$, Consequently, we get the optimal energy consumption

$$E = \sum_{i=1}^{n} \pi_i r_i p_i^{1-(1/\alpha)} = \sum_{i=1}^{n} \pi_i r_i \frac{1}{\pi_i^{1-(1/\alpha)}} \left(\frac{M}{T}\right)^{(\alpha-1)} = M \left(\frac{M}{T}\right)^{(\alpha-1)} = \frac{M^{\alpha}}{T^{(\alpha-1)}} \tag{17}$$

Theorem 4
For a given partition $M_1, M_2, \ldots, M_j$ of the n tasks into j groups on a multiprocessor computer partitioned into j clusters, the total energy consumption is minimized when task i in group k is executed with power $p_i = (M_k / T)^{\alpha} / \pi_i$, where $1 \le k \le j$. The minimum energy consumption is

$$E = \left(\frac{M_1^{\alpha} + M_2^{\alpha} + M_3^{\alpha} + \ldots\ldots\ldots. + M_j^{\alpha}}{T^{\alpha-1}} \right) \tag{18}$$

4 Simulation Results

The proposed algorithms were tested through a series of simulation on the multiprocessor environment. The experimental parameter settings of PSO and GA algorithms are described in Table 1. It is to be noted that for a given heuristic algorithm, the expected Normalized Schedule Length (NSL) and the expected Normalized Energy Consumption (NEC) are determined by m, n , α, the probability distributions of the π_i 's and r_i's. For our convenience, the r_i's are treated as independent and identically distributed (i.i.d.) continuous random variables. The π_i 's are i.i.d. discrete random variables. where $1 \le r_i \le 100$ and $1 \le \pi_i \le 5$. We considered a finite number of processors in our multiprocessor environment and assumed that the processing speed of each processor and the cost time of each task are known. Each experiment has been done with different speed factor (α). We recorded the optimal values of the best solutions throughout the optimization iterations and all tasks are scheduled in different processors.

Fig.1 shows the plot of objective function (10, 11) vs. iteration for four different values of speed factor α=3, 4, 6and 10.The objective function comprises the problem of minimizing schedule length with energy consumption constraint. Further it is observed that the objective function decreases as their iteration increases. Furthermore it is minimized as the speed factor α is decreased and reaches the optimum solution. In each case all the tasks use the different power supply $p_1, p_2, p_3 \ldots \ldots p_n$. In fig.2 the energy consumption of the processor vs number of iteration are plotted. In about 200 iterations of search, the optimal solution is obtained. In this case, the energy consumption of the processors is equal and all the processors utilize the same energy. Fig.3 shows the plot of objective function (17) vs. iteration for four different values of speed factor α=3, 4, 6 and 10. The objective function comprises the problem of minimizing energy consumption with schedule length constraint. Further it is observed that objective function decreases as their iteration increases. Furthermore it is minimized as the speed factor α is decreased and reaches the optimum solution. In each case all the tasks use the different power supply $p_1, p_2, p_3 \ldots \ldots p_n$. In fig.4 the schedule length of the processor vs number of iteration are plotted. In about 200 iteration of search, the optimal solution is obtained. In this case, the schedule length of the processors is equal and all the processors complete the tasks with same time. Table (2) shows the best result of GA and PSO algorithm for four different types speed level. It is to be noted that PSO usually spent as shorter time to accomplish the various task scheduling tasks and has the better results compared with GA algorithm.

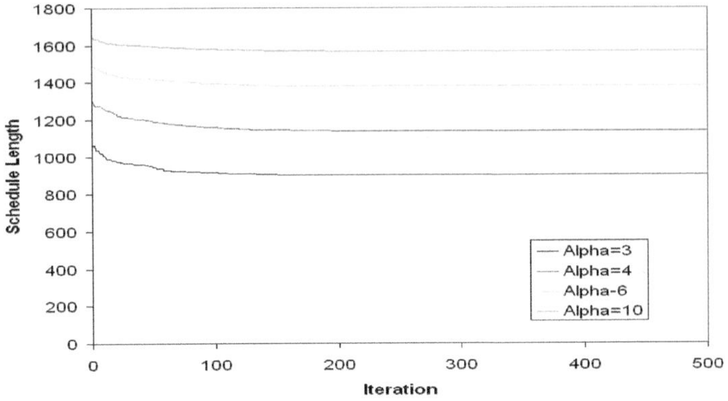

Fig. 1. Schedule length minimization of m processors with expected energy 20000J

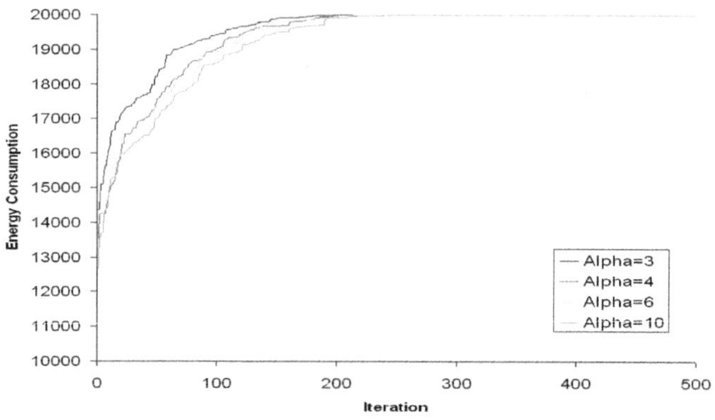

Fig. 2. Achieving Expected energy consumption

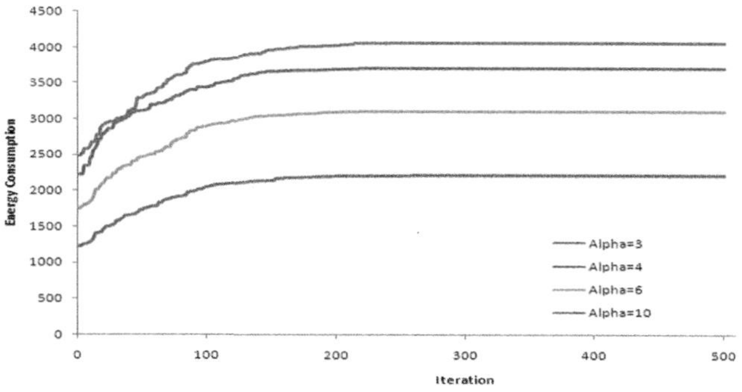

Fig. 3. Energy Consumption minimization of m processors with expected schedule length 2000

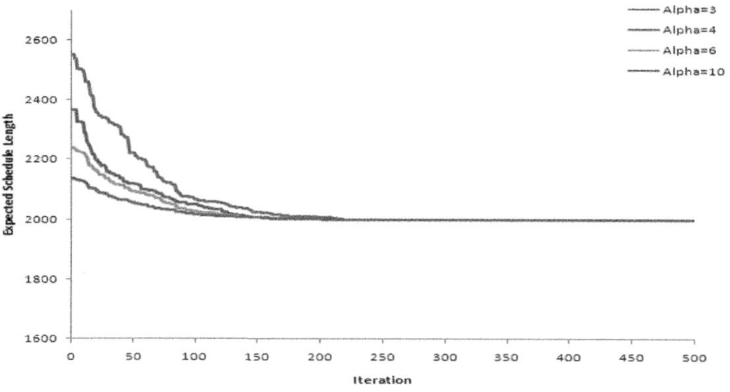

Fig. 4. Achieving Expected schedule length 2000

It shows that as the value of α increases (speed decreases) the expected energy consumption is achieved by increasing the schedule length. It is also noticed that as speed of the multiprocessor decreases, the deadline of the tasks are increased to attain the expected energy level. Table (3) shows that as the value of α increases (speed decreases), the expected schedule length is achieved by increasing the energy consumption. It is also noticed that as speed of the multiprocessor increases, the energy consumption of the processors decreases to attain the expected schedule length.

Table 1. Simulation parameters of GA and PSO

Sl. No.	Genetic Algorithm		PSO Algorithm	
	Parameters	Value	Parameters	Value
1.	Population size	50	Size of the swarm	50
2.	Crossover type	Single point	Dimension of the problem	40
3.	Crossover rate	0.8	PSO parameter C1 and C2	2 and 2
4.	Mutation rate	0.001	Inertia factor	0.01
5.	Selection method	Tournament	Velocity minimum and Maximum	-4 and +4
6.	Generation	500	Maximum number of birds steps	500

Table 2. Simulation result of minimizing schedule length with energy consumption constraint for parallel tasks

Expected Energy consumption (J)	(α)	GA schedule length	PSO schedule length	PSO and GA energy consumption (J)
10000	3	1274.34	1275	10000
	4	1435.85	1436	10000
	6	1583	1583	10000
	10	1692	1692.32	10000
20000	3	901.09	902	20000
	4	1139.63	1139.63	20000
	6	1378.14	1378.14	20000
	10	1556.58	1558	20000
25000	3	805.96	806	25000
	4	1058	1058	25000
	6	1318	1318	25000
	10	1528.22	1528	25000

Table 3. Simulation result of minimizing energy consumption with schedule length constraint for parallel tasks

Expected schedule length	(α)	GA energy consumption(J)	PSO energy consumption(J)	PSO and GA schedule length
1500	3	7217.58	7217.58	1500
	4	8771.22	8771.22	1500
	6	13093	13093	1500
	10	29566	29566	1500
2000	3	4060	4060	2000
	4	3700	3700	2000
	6	3107	3107	2000
	10	2219	2219	2000
2500	3	2598	2598	2500
	4	1894	1894	2500
	6	1018	1018	2500
	10	298	298	2500

5 Conclusion

In this paper, we have proposed an energy efficient dynamic voltage scaling with different power supply and varying speed factor on multiprocessor system. We defined the problem of minimizing schedule length with energy consumption constraint and the problem of minimizing energy consumption with schedule length constraint on multiprocessor systems. We argued that each heuristic algorithm should solve three nontrivial subproblems efficiently, namely, task partitioning, task scheduling and power supply. The evolutionary algorithm calculates the objective function according to the schedule and adjusts the power supply of the processor while meeting the constraints. It is found that the PSO requires less iteration than GA. The simulation results emphasize the tradeoff between power and performance and are defined such that the power-performance product is optimized by fixing one factor and minimizing the other in DVS enabled multiprocessor systems. Furthermore it can be extended to energy-aware heterogeneous embedded multiprocessor system with task precedence graphs.

References

1. Burd, T.D., Brodersen, R.W.: Energy efficient cmos microprocessor design. In: Proc. of The HICSS Conference, Maui, Hawaii, pp. 288–297 (1995)
2. Krishna, C.M., Lee, Y.H.: Voltage clock scaling adaptive scheduling techniques for low power in hard real-time systems. In: Proc. of The 6th IEEE Real-Time Technology and Applications Symposium (RTAS 2000), Washington D.C (2000)
3. Aydin, H., Melhem, R., Mossé, D., Mejia-Alvarez, P.: Dynamic and aggressive scheduling techniques for power-aware real-time systems. In: Proc. of the 22nd IEEE Real-Time Systems Symposium, London, UK (2001)

4. Trescases, O., Ng, W.T.: Variable Output, Soft-Switching DC/DC Converter for VLSI Dynamic Voltage Scaling Power Supply Applications. In: 35th Annual IEEE Power Electronics Specialists Conference, pp. 4149–4155 (2004)
5. Benten, T., Sait, M.: Genetic Scheduling of Task Graphs. International Electron Journal 77(4), 401–415 (1994)
6. Ahmad, I., Dhodhi, K.: Multiprocessor Scheduling in a Genetic Paradigm. IEEE Parallel Computing 22, 395–406 (1996)
7. Hou, H., Ansari, N., Ren, H.: A Genetic Algorithm form Multiprocessor Scheduling. IEEE Transaction of Parallel and Distributed Systems 5(2), 113–120 (1997)
8. Andrei, A., Eles, P., Peng, Z., Schmitz, M., Al-Hashimi, B.M.: Voltage selection for time-constrained multiprocessor systems on chip (in Press)
9. Henkel, J., Parameswaran, S.: Designing Embedded Processors: A Low Power Perspective, pp. 259–282. Springer, Heidelberg (2007)
10. Schmitz, M.T., Al-Hashimi, B., Eles, P.: Considering Power Variation of DVS Processing Elements for Energy-Minimization in Distributed Systems. In: Proc. ISSS (2001)
11. Schmitz, M.T., Al-Hashimi, B., Eles, P.: System Level Design Techniques for Energy-Efficient Embedded Systems. Kluwer Academic Publishers, Dordrecht (2004)
12. Bohler, M., Moore, F., Pan, Y.: Improved Multiprocessor Task Scheduling Using Genetic Algorithms. In: Proceedings of the Twelfth International FLAIRS Conference (1999)
13. Rahmani, A.M., Vahedi, M.A.: A novel Task Scheduling in Multiprocessor Systems with Genetic Algorithm by using Elitism stepping method (in press)
14. Kwok, K., Ahmad, I.: Efficient Scheduling of Arbitrary Task Graphs to Multiprocessors Using a Parallel Genetic Algorithm. Parallel and Distributed Computing Journal 47, 58–71 (2006)
15. Gorjiara, B., Bagherzadeh, N.: Ultra-Fast and Efficient Algorithm for Energy Optimization by Gradient-Based Stochastic Voltage and Task Scheduling. ACM Transactions on Design Automation of Electronic Systems 12(4), article 39 (2007)
16. Zhang, L., Chen, Y., Sun, R., Jing, S., Yang, B.: A Task Scheduling Algorithm Based on PSO for Grid Computing. International Journal of Computational Intelligence Research 4(1), 37–43 (2008)
17. Barnett, J.A.: Dynamic Task-Level Voltage Scheduling Optimizations. IEEE Trans. Computers 54(5), 508–520 (2005)
18. Ding, D., Zhang, L., Wei, Z.: A Novel Voltage Scaling Algorithm through Ant Colony Optimization for Embedded Distributed Systems. In: Proceedings of the 2007 IEEE International Conference on Integration Technology, Shenzhen, China, March 20-24, pp. 547–552 (2007)
19. Bunde, D.P.: Power-Aware Scheduling for Makespan and Flow. In: Proc. 18th ACM Symp. Parallelism in Algorithms and Architectures (SPAA 2006), pp. 190–196 (2006)
20. Rusu, Melhem, R., Mossé, D.: Maximizing the System Value While Satisfying Time and energy Constraints. In: Proc. 23rd IEEE Real-Time Systems Symp. (RTSS 2002), pp. 256–265 (2002)
21. Gara, et al.: Overview of the Blue Gene/L System Architecture. IBM J. Research and Development 49(2/3), 195–212 (2005)
22. Graham, R.L.: Bounds on Multiprocessing Timing Anomalies. SIAM J. Applied Math. 2, 416–429 (1969)
23. Li, K.: Performance Analysis of Power-Aware Task Scheduling Algorithms on Multiprocessor Computers with Dynamic Voltage and Speed. IEEE Transactions On Parallel and Distributed Systems 19(11), 1484–1497 (2008)
24. Zhang, L., Chen, Y., Sun, R., Jing, S., Yang, B.: A Task Scheduling Algorithm Based on PSO for Grid Computing. International Journal of Computational Intelligence Research 4(1), 37–43 (2008)

A Novel Technique for Removal of Random Valued Impulse Noise Using All Neighbor Directional Weighted Pixels (ANDWP)

J.K. Mandal and Somnath Mukhopadhyay

Department of Computer Science and Engineering,
Kalyani University, Kalyani,
West Bengal, India, 741235
jkm.cse@gmail.com, som.cse@live.com
http://jkmandal.com, http://www.klyuniv.ac.in

Abstract. In this paper an All Neighbor Directional Weighted Pixels (ANDWP) based filter has been proposed for removal of highly random valued impulse noise (RVIN). The proposed approach works in two phases. The first phase detects the contaminated pixels by making the differences between the test pixel and its all neighbor pixels aligned in four main directions in the 5 x 5 window. The second phase filters only the noisy pixels based on minimum variance of the four directional pixels. Extensive simulations show that the proposed filter not only provide better performance of de noising RVIN but can preserve more fine detail features even thin lines.

Keywords: All neighbor directional weighted pixels, de noising, miss and false, random valued impulse noise, sensitivity, specificity.

1 Introduction

The nonlinear characteristics of noise affect the performance of linear filters. Median Filter is effectively used for such purposes[10]. The main drawback of the median filter is that it performs satisfactory for salt and pepper noise but not for images corrupted highly with RVIN and another thing is it also modifies the noise free pixels and blurs the images by removing the fine details. For performance enhancement, many filters with an impulse detector has been proposed, such as signal-dependent rank order mean (SD-ROM)[1] filter, adaptive center-weighted median (ACWM) [4] filter, (Med)[2] filter, multi state median (MSM)[5] filter and the pixel-wise MAD (PWMAD)[6] filter. These filters usually perform well but when the noise level is more than 30%, they do not give satisfactory performances even they cannot remove some black patches on the reconstructed images as well.

To deal with RVIN, a directional weighted median (DWM)[7] filter were proposed, which uses minimum of 8 to 10 iterations and a total of 16 neighbor pixels. The number of iterations used in detection and filtering of noisy image

D. Nagamalai, E. Renault, and M. Dhanushkodi (Eds.): PDCTA 2011, CCIS 203, pp. 102–111, 2011.

using median filter is very important, because not only it increases the complexity but also blurred the reconstructed image as the idea of applying the median filter recursively has been examined [10] and produced highly correlated image with increased blurring. The recent method of sa, dash and majhi[11] uses second order difference based noise suppression method, where all the neighborhood pixels in the 3 x 3 window are taken for such purpose. This method does not work well for highly corrupted images but it has very low computational cost.

The primary objective of the proposed work is to de noise the highly corrupted image as well as to preserve the quality of the reconstructed image. Proposed method uses all the neighborhood pixels for noise detection as well as for noise filtering in the 5 x 5 window.

The organization of the paper is as follows. Proposed impulse detector and filtering method are given in section 2 and 3 respectively. Experimental results and discussions are demonstrated in section 4. Conclusions are given in section 5.

2 Impulse Detector

There are two types of impulse noises; fixed and random valued impulses. In a gray scale image the fixed valued impulse, known as salt and pepper noise[9] occurs where pixel value converted to either 0 or 255 with equal probability, while the random valued impulses is uniformly distributed over the range of [0,255].

The proposed scheme applied on 5 x 5 window of the image in row major order to detect the noisy pixels, focuses on the pixels aligned in the four main directions along with two end pixels in each direction, shown in Fig 1. The proposed impulse detection is given in Algorithm 1.

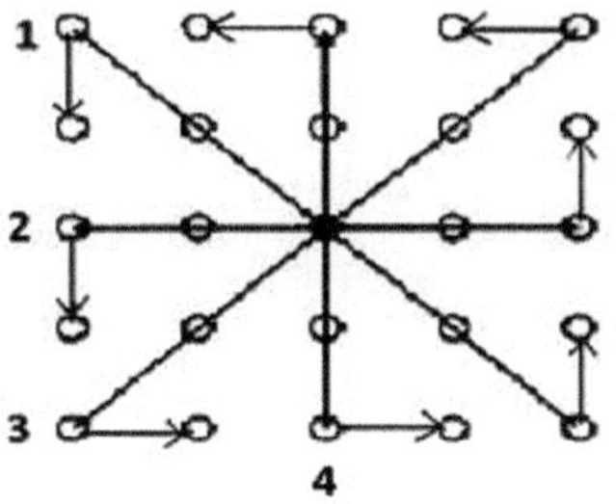

Fig. 1. Four Directional Weighted Pixels in the 5 x 5 Window

3 Impulse Filter

Most median based filters simply replace the noisy pixels by median values in the window. But when the objective is to de noise the images with highly random valued impulses, we cannot use conventional median filter because in that case most of the pixels were changed randomly in the noisy images. In this paper

Algorithm 1. Impulse detector

1: Let S_k (k=1 to 4) denotes a set of seven pixels aligned in the kth direction centered at (0, 0), i.e.,
$S_1 = \{(-1,-2), (-2,-2), (-1,-1), (0, 0), (1, 1), (2, 2), (1, 2)\}$
$S_2 = \{(1,-2), (0,-2), (0,-1), (0, 0), (0, 1), (0, 2), (-1, 2)\}$
$S_3 = \{(2,-1), (2,-2), (1,-1), (0, 0), (-1, 1), (-2, 2), (-2, 1)\}$
$S_4 = \{(-2,-1), (-2, 0), (-1, 0), (0, 0), (1, 0), (2, 0), (2,1)\}$.
Then let $S_k^0 = S_k/(0,0)$, $\forall$ k =1 to 4.

2: In each direction of the 5 x 5 window centered at (i,j), define $d_{i,j}^{(k)}$ as the sum of all absolute differences of gray values between $y_{i+s,j+t}$ and $y_{i,j}$ with (s,t)$\in S_k^0$ (k= 1 to 4), given in eqn. 1.

3: In each direction, weigh the absolute differences between two closest pixels from the center pixel with a large ω_m, weigh the the absolute differences between the center pixel and the corner pixels by ω_n and that of absolute differences between two end pixels from the center pixel with a small ω_o. Assign ω_m =2, ω_n=1 and ω_o=0.5.
Thus define

$$d_{i,j}^{(k)} = (\sum_{(s,t)\in S_k^0} \omega_{s,t}|y_{i+s,j+t} - y_{i,j}|, 1 \le k \le 4) \tag{1}$$

where

$$\omega_{s,t} = \begin{cases} \omega_m & : (s,t) \in \Omega^3 \\ \omega_o & : (s,t) \in \Omega^2 \\ \omega_n & : \text{otherwise} \end{cases} \tag{2}$$

where

$$\Omega^3 = \{(s,t) : -1 \le s,t \le 1\}, and \tag{3}$$

where

$$\Omega^2 = \{(s,t) : (s,t) = \pm\{(-2,-1),(-1,-2),(1,-2),(2,-1)\}\}. \tag{4}$$

4: $d_{i,j}^{(K)}$ is termed as direction index. The minimum of these four direction indices are used for impulse detection, which is denoted as

$$r_{i,j} = min\{d_{i,j}^{(k)} : 1 \le k \le 4\} \tag{5}$$

Three assumptions may be made depending on the values of $r_{i,j}$.

1. $r_{i,j}$ is small when the current pixel is on a noise free flat region.
2. $r_{i,j}$ is small when the current pixel is on the edge.
3. $r_{i,j}$ is large when the current pixel is noisy .

5: From the definition of $r_{i,j}$, a noisy pixel is identified efficiently from the window of noise free pixels by employing a threshold(T).
Define the impulse detector as

$$y_{i,j} = \begin{cases} NoisyPixel & : r_{i,j} > T \\ NoiseFreePixel & : r_{i,j} \le T \end{cases} \tag{6}$$

a new scheme has been introduced based on minimum variance of all the four directional pixels. Starting with a noisy image and a threshold value (T), in row major order it scans each 5 x 5 window in the noisy image. If any pixel is detected as noisy, the filtering scheme restores it to a pixel which is most suitable in the 5 x 5 window. The technique has been depicted in algorithm 2.

Algorithm 2. Impulse filter

1: Calculate the standard deviations $\sigma_{i,j}^{(k)}$ of gray values of all $y_{i+s,j+t}$ with (s,t) $\in S_k^0$ (k= 1 to 4).

2: Find the minimum of $\sigma_{i,j}^{(k)}$, where k= 1 to 4, as

$$l_{i,j} = \min_k\{\sigma_{i,j}^{(k)} : k = 1 \textit{ to } 4\} \tag{7}$$

3: Select the set of seven pixels in the $l_{i,j}$ direction.

4: Replace the middle pixel of the set of pixels by a variable x to construct the set given in eqn. 8).

$$S = \{a, b, c, x, d, e, f\}. \tag{8}$$

5: Form a quadratic equation f(x) by calculating the variance (σ^2) of the step 4, as given in eqn. 9.

$$\begin{aligned} f(x) = (a - mean)^2 + (b - mean)^2 + (c - mean)^2 \\ + (x - mean)^2 + (d - mean)^2 + (e - mean)^2 + (f - mean)^2 \end{aligned} \tag{9}$$

where

$$mean = (a + b + c + x + d + e + f)/7. \tag{10}$$

6: Compute first order and second order derivatives (f' (x)) and (f"(x)) respectively of f(x).

7: f"(x) is always positive for any value of x, where x ∈ [0, 255]. So by solving the equation f'(x) =0, get an x, where x ∈ [0,255], for which f(x) is minimum.

8: Replace $y_{i,j}$ by x.

Methods of detection and filtering of noisy pixels work with three important user parameters, viz., Number of Iterations (I), Threshold Value (T) and Decreasing Rate(R) of Threshold Value in each iteration. These parameters are tuned to obtain much better results and described in Section 4.4.

4 Results and Discussions

Experiment has been performed on various benchmark images and comparisons are made with various available algorithms. Image restoration results are quantitatively measured in terms of Mean Squared Error(MSE), Peak Signal to Noise

Ratio(PSNR) and Image Fidelity(IF). So we give all results in terms of these three parameters.

4.1 Results

Table 1 gives the restoration results in terms of MSE and IF on three bench mark images for 50% and 60% corrupted images. It is seen from these results that the proposed ANDWP filter performs very good in objective(MSE) evaluation and also preserves the fidelity of the enhanced image.

Table 1. Restoration Results for *Lena*, *Boat* and *Bridge* images using ANDWP Filter

Filter	*Lena*		*Boat*		*Bridge*	
	50%	60%	50%	60%	50%	60%
MSE	57.94	96.29	87.27	131.21	182.79	269.61
IF	0.996699	0.994514	0.995407	0.993095	0.988573	0.983093

4.2 Comparisons

To evaluate the performance of the proposed algorithm with the existing algorithms, proposed filter has been compared with various existing techniques and the results of comparison on 512 x 512 *Lena* image corrupted with various degree of noises are given Table 2. It is seen from this table that the performances of the MED[3] operator is very poor. PSM[12] is much better than the MED[3] in restoring only 20% corrupted images. Performance of ACWM[4], MSM[5], SD-ROM[1] and Iterative Median[8] are almost similar. Among them, SD-ROM[1] performs best in restoring 40% to 60% noise densities. PWMAD[6] performs better than the second order[11] filter in all cases except 60% case. DWM[7] operator outperforms than any existing filter in all cases. But the proposed filter performs significantly better than any existing filter in restoring 40% or more corrupted images.

On close observation of table 3 and table 4 it is seen that for *Bridge* and *Boat* images DWM[7] filter performs better than any existing filters in terms *PSNR(dB)*. But ANDWP performs better than any existing filter in restoring 40% or more corrupted images.

Fig. 2 shows the comparative results of restoration between the existing filters and ANDWP on 60% noisy *Lena* image. It is seen from the figure that the output image using MSM[5] contains maximum noisy patches and performs worst. SD-ROM[1] and PWMAD[6] performs better than MSM[5] but not so good as it contains noises in the reconstructed image. Though DWM[7] performs satisfactory as it removes the impulses but still can not remove some black patches on the enhanced image. From the figure it is clear that the ANDWP obtains best restoration results. Considering very high noise density and fine details of the images, the performance of the proposed filter is very good.

Table 2. Comparison of restoration results in terms of PSNR for *Lena* Image

Filter	20% Noisy	30% Noisy	40% Noisy	50% Noisy	60% Noisy
Med[3]	30.37	30	27.64	24.28	21.58
PSM[12]	35.09	30.85	28.92	26.12	22.06
ACWM[4]	36.07	32.59	28.79	25.19	21.19
MSM[5]	35.44	31.67	29.26	26.11	22.14
SD-ROM[1]	35.72	30.77	29.85	26.80	23.41
Iterative Median[8]	36.90	31.76	30.25	24.76	22.96
2nd Order[11]	34.35	32.53	30.90	28.22	24.84
PWMAD[6]	36.50	33.44	31.41	28.50	24.30
DWM Filter[7]	37.15	34.87	32.62	30.26	26.74
ANDWP	34.42	33.01	32.65	30.50	28.29

Table 3. Comparison of restoration results in terms of PSNR (dB) for *Bridge* image

Filter	40% Noisy	50% Noisy	60% Noisy
ACWM[4]	23.23	21.32	19.17
MSM[5]	23.55	22.03	20.07
SD-ROM[1]	23.80	22.42	20.66
2nd Order[11]	23.73	22.14	20.04
PWMAD[6]	23.83	22.20	20.83
DWM Filter[7]	24.28	23..04	21.56
ANDWP	26.38	25.51	23.42

Table 4. Comparison of restoration results in terms of PSNR (dB) for *Boat* image

Filter	40% Noisy	50% Noisy	60% Noisy
ACWM[4]	26.17	23.92	21.37
MSM[5]	25.56	24.27	22.21
SD-ROM[1]	26.45	24.83	22.59
PWMAD[6]	26.56	24.85	22.32
DWM Filter[7]	27.03	25.75	24.01
ANDWP	29.23	28.72	26.95

4.3 Comparison of *Sensitivity* and *Specificity* Values

Prior to applying the filtering operator on any corrupted image, noise detection is very important. Number of noisy pixels those are not identified by the process is known as *miss* value and number of noise free pixels those are identified as noisy pixels by the technique is known as *false* value. Both of these values are required to be minimized.

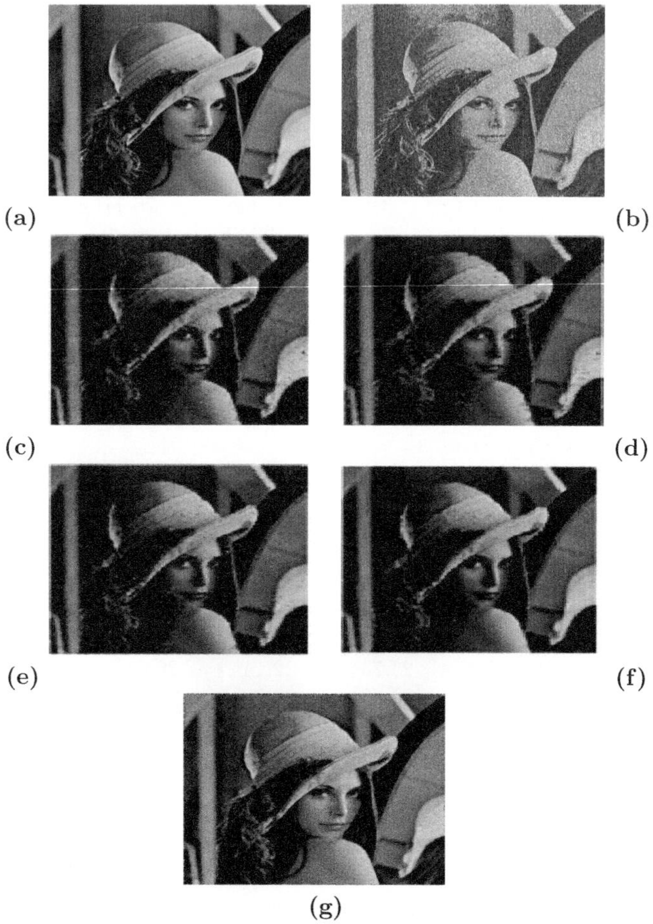

Fig. 2. Results of different filters in restoring 60% corrupted image Lena, (a) Original image (b)Noisy Image (c) (SD-ROM)[1] (d)(MSM)[5] (e)(PWMAD)[6] (f)(DWM)[7] (g)Proposed Filter

From table 5 it is seen that SD-ROM[1] and ACWM[4] filter give very good *false* values when it applied on 40% corrupted *lena* image but it performs very poor to identify the noisy pixels and generate noticeable patches on the reconstructed image. But ANDWP filter can identify the noisy pixels as well as it can ignore the noise free pixels with a remarkable difference compared to all other existing filters, by obtaining optimal *miss* and *false* values.

Two other statistical performance evaluation tools of noise detection algorithm are sensitivity and specificity. Sensitivity measures the percentage of noisy pixels which are correctly identified as having the condition. Specificity measures the percentage of noise free pixels which are correctly identified as not having the condition.

Table 5. Comparison of *miss* and *false* Results for *Lena* image

Filter	40% Noisy		50% Noisy		60% Noisy	
	Miss	False	Miss	False	Miss	False
SDROM[1]	22842	411	32566	998	45365	2651
MSM[5]	16582	7258	20857	10288	26169	15778
ACWM[4]	16052	1759	23683	2895	32712	7644
PWMAD[6]	11817	9928	14490	15003	17760	19577
DWM[7]	9512	7761	9514	11373	12676	12351
ANDWP	7852	6018	8260	7512	8812	9304

Table 6. Comparison of *Sensitivity* and *Specificity* Results for *Lena* image

Filter	40% Noisy		50% Noisy		60% Noisy	
	Sensitivity	Specificity	Sensitivity	Specificity	Sensitivity	Specificity
SDROM[1]	78%	99%	72%	99%	71%	98%
MSM[5]	84%	97%	84%	92%	83%	89%
ACWM[4]	84%	98%	81%	97%	79%	95%
PWMAD[6]	88%	90%	88%	88%	88%	87%
DWM[7]	90%	92%	92%	91%	91%	92%
ANDWP	93%	94%	94%	94%	94%	94%

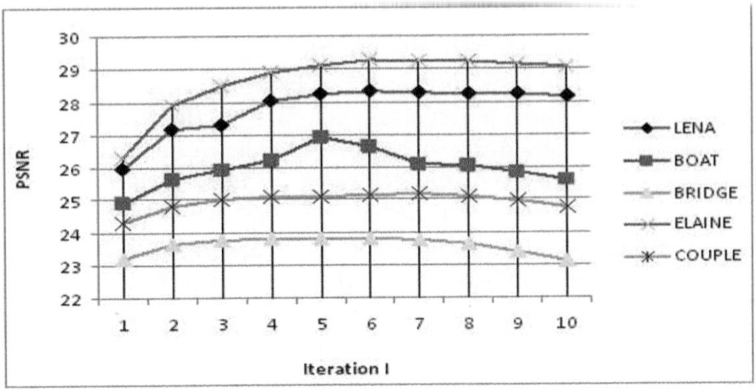

Fig. 3. Comparison of *PSNR* against *iteration* on various benchmark images

Sensitivity and specificity obtains from various filters for for 40% to 60% noisy *Lena* images are given in table 6. Proposed ANDWP performs better than any existing filters as it is most sensitive to detect true positives and also most specific to detect the true negatives.

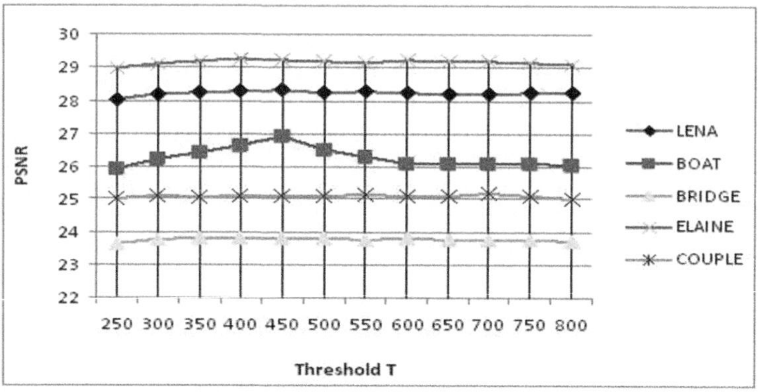

Fig. 4. Comparison of *PSNR* against *threshold* on various benchmark images

4.4 Threshold Value (T), no. of Iterations (I) and Decreasing Rate(R) of Threshold Value in Each Iteration

In this paper, the proposed scheme uses three user parameters viz., I, T and R in the following ranges to show the contributions of these three parameters. These are maximum number of iterations(I)$\in$ [5, 6], threshold value(T) $\in$ [300, 500] and decreasing rate of threshold value in each iteration (R) $\in$ [0.7, 0.9].

From fig. 3 and 4, we can see the restoration results using the proposed filter in terms of PSNR(dB) for 60% corrupted five bench mark images for the various ranges of values of the three parameters. Fig. 3 gives the relationship of PSNR against I and that of fig. 4 gives the correspondence of PSNR against T. In these two charts, the maximum PSNR values are plotted. In fig. 3, the PSNR at I=5 is obtained by varying T from 250 to 800 with an increment of 50 and R from 0.7 to 0.9 with an increment of 0.05 (I=5, T $\in$ [250, 800], R $\in$ [0.7, 0.9]) and then the maximum PSNR is plotted in the chart. In the same way in fig. 4, the PSNR at T=500 is obtained by varying I from 1 to 10 with an increment of 1 and R from of 0.7 to 0.9 with an increment 0.05 (T=500, I $\in$ [1, 10], R $\in$ [0.7, 0.9]) and then the maximum PSNR is plotted in the chart.

From these two figures it is seen that, by varying the parameters in a wide range we can obtain optimal restoration results for different images.

5 Conclusion

In this paper, a variance based filter has been proposed for removing high random valued impulse noise from digital images. In the proposed algorithm, all the 24 neighbors of the center pixel in the 5 x 5 window are included and used for noise detection. As a result it gives very less miss and false values compared to other filters. It obtains best sensitivity and specificity results too. The fundamental superiority of the proposed operator over most other operators is that it efficiently removes impulse noises from highly corrupted images while successfully preserves the thin lines, edges and fine details in the enhanced image.

Acknowledgments. Authors express deep sense of gratitude towards the Dept of CSE, University of Kalyani and the IIPC Project, AICTE, (Govt. of India), of the department where the computational recourses are used for the work.

References

1. Abreu, E., Lightstone, M., Mitra, S.K., Arakawa, K.: A new efficient approach for the removal of impulse noise from highly corrupted images. IEEE Transactions on Image Processing 5(6), 1012–1025 (1996)
2. Bovik, A., Hang, T., Munson, D.: A generalization of median filtering using linear combinations of orders statistics. IEEE Transactions, Acoust., Speech, Signal Processing ASSP-31, 1342–1350 (1983)
3. Brownrigg, D.: The weighted median filter. Communication Association Computer 27, 807–818 (1984)
4. Chen, T., Wu, H.R.: Adaptive impulse detection using center weighted median filters. IEEE Signal Processing Letters 8(1), 1–3 (2001)
5. Chen, T., Wu, H.R.: Space variant median filters for the restoration of impulse noise corrupted images. IEEE Transactions on Circuits and Systems-II: Analog and Digital Signal Processing 48(8), 784–789 (2001)
6. Crnojevic, V., Senk, V., Trpovski, Z.: Advanced impulse detection based on pixelwise mad. IEEE Signal Processing Letters 11(7), 589–592 (2004)
7. Dong, Y., Xu, S.: A new directional weighted median filter for removal of random - valued impulse noise. IEEE Signal Processing Letters 14(3), 193–196 (2007)
8. Forouzan, A.R., Araabi, B.: Iterative median filtering for restoration of images with impulsive noise. Electronics, Circuits and Systems 1, 232–235 (2003)
9. Gonzalez, R.C.: Woods: Digital image processing, 2nd edn. Pearson, Prentice-Hall (2002)
10. Nodes, T., Gallagher, N.: Median filters: some modifications and their properties. IEEE Trans. Acoust. Speech, Signal Process ASSP 30(5), 739–746 (1982)
11. Sa, P.K., Dash, R., Majhi, B.: Second order difference based detection and directional weighted median filter for removal of random valued impulsive noise. IEEE Signal Processing Letters pp. 362–364 (December 2009)
12. Wang, Z., Zhang, D.: Progressive switching median filter for the removal of impulse noise from highly corrupted images. IEEE Transactions on Circuits and Systems 46(1), 78–80 (1999)

Critical Aware Community Based Parallel Service Composition Model for Pervasive Computing Environment

P. Kumaran and R. Shriram

Department of Computer Science and Engineering,
B.S. Abdur Rahman University, Chennai, Tamil Nadu, India
p_kumaran@hotmail.com,
shriram@bsauniv.ac.in

Abstract. Service composition in pervasive computing environments is needed to provide best quality of service. Services need to be discovered at run time and composed together for best possible user scenarios. The need for identifying the best services among the service nodes is essential in pervasive computing systems as the environment of operation can change rapidly. Pervasive computing demands systems that are scalable, adaptive, fault tolerant and can work in heterogeneous environments. Hence an adaptive method that takes into account the environment is the need of the hour. In this work, a dynamic parallel composition model to compose the best matched services is proposed for the pervasive computing environment exhibiting the quality of service and contingency management properties. The model ensures that the highest quality of service conditions is fulfilled. Facilities for contingency management ensure efficient fault tolerance and failure recovery. The proposed model uses the community framework for grouping the service nodes and composing the services provided by the nodes. This ensures that resultant composition mechanism is dynamic in nature to adapt to the service nodes failure without compromising the quality of service with better fault error recovery time. The model has been validated experimentally and the results show considerable promise. The work is unique in its extensive mechanisms for modeling the pervasive computing environment, failure handling, fault tolerance and best quality of service parameters.

Keywords: Community Manager, Fault Recovery, Pervasive Computing, Service Composition, Service Evaluation.

1 Introduction

Pervasive Computing is a vision of the world where the computing happens anywhere and at any time. Service Composition is the process of composing the unit services into an integrated service to provide end user requirement. Service oriented architecture relies on interaction between autonomic loosely couple services which can be composed together for delivery of goals by the users. These services can be expressed in a middleware system. The middleware system composes the services

D. Nagamalai, E. Renault, and M. Dhanushkodi (Eds.): PDCTA 2011, CCIS 203, pp. 112–121, 2011.

dynamically for accomplishing the goals. Service Composition in the pervasive environment is a challenging research problem due to the unpredictable dynamic behavior of the pervasive environment. The biggest challenge is in developing the middleware [2] for the pervasive environment. The services residing in the nodes need to be composed in parallel in the absence of a centralized entity as the environment needs services dynamically. The key objectives of this work are a) to propose a critical ware service composition model to improve the quality of service, b) to optimize the metrics for improved quality of service and c) to demonstrate the experimental prototype that validates our architecture.

The rest of the paper is organized as follows. In section 2, we discuss the related work carried out supporting our service composition model. In section 3, we describe our composition middleware. In section 4, we give the experimental results and analysis. Finally, section 5 concludes our work and gives research directions to the service composition problem.

2 Related Study

There have been many studies on Service composition in Pervasive Computing. In [8], the user preference is integrated with the system preference to evaluate the service model. The proposed work considers the services residing in the node are of equal priority and based on the utility function value, the higher utility value node in the ordered list is selected. We classified the services residing in the node as critical and non-critical service.

In PICO model [11], mobile and static delegents representing camileuns in communities try to use resources as effectively as possible. The challenges due to mobility and heterogeneity in the pervasive environment are addressed by providing transparent, autonomous and continual middleware services. We have adopted the community formation methodologies used in the PICO model to address the node mobility and heterogeneity. The mobile community network [4] is proposed for the interaction of middleware client installed in the mobile devices. The middleware client request contains device profile, network status, personal profile and requested service data.

In [5], graph based service composition mechanism is proposed. The inputs and the outputs of the services are represented as nodes in the graph and the dependencies of each service are represented as edges. The services' input and output are considered as single parameter which is not the practical and adaptive as the real time services have multiple parameters.

In [3], service composition for mobile environments is achieved through the Dynamic Broker selection and Distributed Broker selection based protocols and suggested to incorporate the parallel broker arbitration to handle parallel service flows. Our earlier work [6] focused on parallel service composition middleware model to addresses the pervasive attribute issues.

In [2], survey on Service composition middleware in pervasive environments discussed on the attributes such as Context Awareness, Interoperability, Discoverability, Adaptability, QoS management, Spontaneous Management, Managing Contingencies,

Leveraging Heterogeneous Devices and Security Mechanisms. These are the key design rationale in designing the middleware for the pervasive computing environments. Our work addresses the design rationale such as QoS management, Spontaneous management and managing contingencies effectively.

We incorporated the parallel composition model in this critical aware model to improve the quality of service by reducing the fault recovery time and service composition length. Our work uniquely differs from the existing service composition middleware for pervasive computing in classifying the services as critical and non-critical dynamically based on the community, evaluating the service nodes based on the service value, activating the critical service execution in parallel and handling the fault recovery. Our experimental result shows the better improvement in the fault recovery time and service composition length compared to the existing works.

3 Service Composition Model

The architecture of the proposed critical aware service composition model is shown in Fig 1.

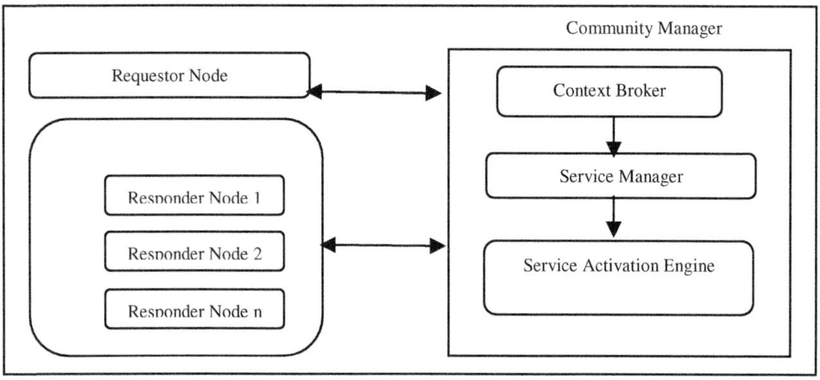

Fig. 1. Service Composition Architecture Model

The Requestor Node is the consumer of the service. Any node in the network can make a request. The Responder nodes are the set of the nodes which receives the service initialize request message sent by the requestor node. The Community manager is responsible for the execution of the service and sent back the required service to the requestor node.

The Community contains the set of nodes actively participating in the service execution. The service manager is responsible for the task coordination. The data communication includes the service initialize request, Community manager response messages and the data transfer between the responder nodes & community manager. The process steps involved in the model are explained in the following sections.

3.1 Service Request Initialization

The requestor node initiates the service request by sending the broadcast message. The responder nodes having the exact composite, abstract service or the service link sends back the response to the requestor node.

Responder Node Service Response
M(Id,Sn,La,Oc,Ts,Pc,Sp)

The reply message format of the responder node contains the Service Identifier(Id) to uniquely identify the service, Service Name(Sn) to describe the service, Abstract Level service definition (La) to represent the exact composite (0) or Service abstract(1) or service link(2), Child Object (Oc) to know whether the service requires to complete any pre-requisite services, Terminating Service(Ts) to represent whether the service is the end service, PreCondition for executing the service (Pc), Service Parameters(Sp) containing the list of service level parameter such as failure rates, trust binding values and the task decomposition.

3.2 Community Manager Selection

The service initialize request message contains the Service Identifier(Id) to uniquely identify the service, Service Name(Sn) to describe the service, Intermediate results (Ir), user preferences(Pr) containing the list of user preferences which helps the community manager to maintain the service quality as requested by the requestor node, community manager identifier (Cm) to uniquely identify the community manager, context broker identifier (Cb) to identify the context broker to handle the user inputs and the reply messages(Rm) sent by the responder nodes which contains the list of the information along with the service level information in each responder nodes which can be used as the results of the service discovery.

Service Initialize Request Message
M(Id,Sn,Ir,Cm,Cb,Pr,Rm)

The Pr contains the list of user preferences which includes the quality of service parameters, task decomposition values, service level agreement between the community manager and requestor node. The requestor node simply acknowledges the message sent by the community manager.

Service Response Message
M(Id,Ir,Cm,Tm,C)

The service response message sent by the community manager contains the service identification(Id) to uniquely identify the service, Intermediate results (Ir), community manager identifier (Cm) to uniquely identify the community manager, timeout (Tm) in milliseconds to denote the validity of the intermediate results sent by the community manager and the criticality flag (C) specifying the completion of the task. The last response message has the value true set in the flag.

3.3 Critical and Non-critical Service Identification

The proposed service composition model classifies the entire services as critical and non-critical based on the service level parameters. The critical services are those services whose providers are very less in number (N), higher failure rates and low trust binding values. The value of N is either system preferences or the user preferences. The requestor node sent the value for N as part of the user preference parameter Pr. If not specified, the system preferences is chosen.

The community manager forms the community using the Rm updated as part of the service initialize request message. It might not be necessary that all the nodes available in the Rm to be part of the community. The Service Evaluation model shown in Figure 2 is used to identify the nodes which are actively participating in the community by the community manager. The Service Evaluation model used in our work is the enhancement of the work proposed in [3]. We have enhanced the evaluation model to incorporate the identification of service criticality.

3.4 Service Evaluation Model and Community Formation

The parameter C is introduced for representing the criticality of the service and its value is decided based on the integration function of system and user preference.

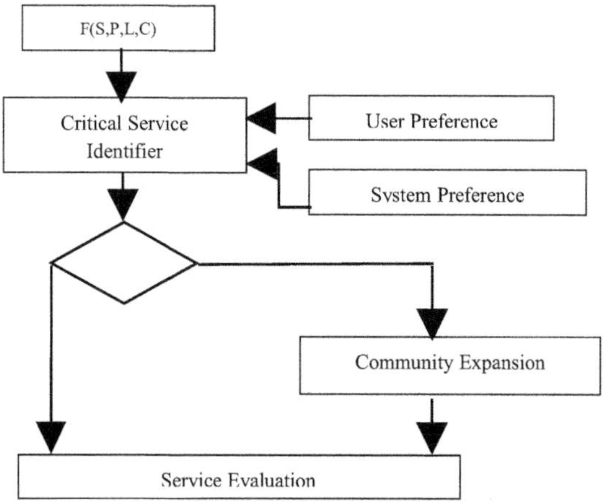

Fig. 2. Service Evaluation Model

If the C takes the value R, then Cs(No of critical service) is checked. Based on the value of Cs, the community manager decides to proceed for the dynamic community expansion or not. If the value of Cs is 1, then the community manager will go for the dynamic expansion of the community (Figure 3).

Once the service evaluation model is constructed, there may be more than one qualified node for a service. The objective of the service evaluation is to evaluate the service value for each node in the list L, and then sorts in the descending order. We are calculating the service value by taking into account the parameters such as quality of service, time taken for completion and past trust rating. After the service evaluation nodes are ranked, the community manager identifies the top ranked nodes in the list for forming the community. Though only one service node is chosen for the non-critical service, two top ranked service nodes for critical services in the list is considered for forming the community. Hence the community manager constructs the community with the nodes providing both the critical and non-critical services.

Service Evaluation Function
F(S,P,L,C)

The community manager sends the message containing the information related to the community to the requestor node and the participating nodes in the community. The requestor node updates this message as part of the intermediate results(Ir) and sends back the responds to the community manager. The timeout for the next message will also be sent along with this message. The Intermediate result(Ir) format sent by the community manager for the community formation contains the number of nodes (N) to denote the set of nodes in the community, objective of the community (M) to represent the set of community goals or missions, define the community characteristics (Cp) such as community identity, number of nodes, community coordination manager, and community resources needed.

Intermediate Result Message
M(N,M,Cp)

3.5 Service Activation

In the service activation phase, the critical services are given priority and are executed using the parallel service composition model. The two top ranked service nodes in the service evaluation model ordered list (L) are executed in parallel. If either of the service faulted, the next ranked node providing the critical service is executed. If not available, the service discovery for critical service is initiated by the community manager. The parallel composition model we proposed in our earlier work [4] is used to execute the critical services in parallel to achieve better quality of service. We briefly have given below the service activation using our parallel composition model.

The composition task is implemented with two major components: a) the service manager, b) service activation engine. The service manager works for parallel composition by dividing the overall task into a set of independent set of service tasks that can be executed in parallel. The task is now split by the service manager into two independent threads. The threads are executed in the service activation engine.

After the execution of the critical services, the results are sent back to the requestor node with the next timeout period mentioned. The requestor Node acknowledges the message. The service nodes providing the critical services can be released by the community manager from the community. After all the critical services are executed the non-critical services are executed.

3.6 Fault Management

We have incorporated the fault handling mechanism for achieving the better quality of service. We have identified three fault origination points which includes Service Node failure, Community manager failure and the Requestor node failure. The service node failure happens when either the service node leaves the community, move away from the network or due to the any kind of network failure. If the service node was not able to activate the service due to any of the reasons mentioned above, the next ranked node in the list (L) providing the similar service is activated.

There might be the scenario where the community manager can itself get faulted due to network instability. The community manager updates the requestor node with the intermediate results and the timeout for the arrival of the next message. If the community manager itself faulted and not able to communicate to the requestor node, the requestor node will wait till the timeout period lastly updated by the community manager along with the intermediate result. After the timeout period, it recognizes that the community manager is not reachable and initiates the new service initialize request for the new community manager selection and the intermediate results are sent to the new community manager for further processing.

If the community manager does not get the acknowledgement from the requestor node after sending the intermediate results, then it considers the requestor node gets faulted. If the user preference parameter for erred acknowledgement is false, then it stops the service execution and stores the intermediate results to the PSNR with a timeout period above which the data are deleted. If the requestor node had a chance to acknowledge with the delay or trying to initialize the same service initiate request, then the community manager shares the data from the PSNR. If the user preference parameter for erred acknowledgement is true, then the community manager continues the service activation till the end and stores the service results in the PSNR.

4 Experimental Setup and Results

The middleware was implemented in J2ME with an Apache Server backend working as the community network server. The community network server in turn contacts the various service providers and gets the jobs executed. The faults are injected at the service nodes at runtime. If any service node faults, the community manager selects another service node from the ordered list and the service execution proceeds. This is done till the job is completed. At any point of time, for the critical service two alternative parallel services by service nodes are always executing.

We have conducted ten experiments with different number of mobile nodes forming different communities. For experiment purpose, currently QoS and Service Execution Time for each mobile node are taken for the evaluation. The two top ranked service nodes in the ordered list are executed in parallel. The failure nodes and their failure times are defined at runtime during the service execution. The Service reconfiguration is done when the node gets faulted, the next service node in the ordered list is chosen and the time taken for reconfiguration is noted. The Service Composition Time and the fault recovery time are calculated at the completion of task. For the experimental purpose, we have considered the independent service tasks.

In the service initialize request message the nodes that provide the required tasks are identified by the community manager. Based on the service response messages which contains the failure rates and trust binding values the requestor node selects the community manager. We used N0 as the community manager.

Table1. Experimental Datasets and Results

DATASET	NO OF MOBILE NODES	PARALLEL COMPOSITION			CRITICAL AWARE COMPOSITION		
		TOTAL TIME TAKEN	RECOV ERY TIME	QOS	TOTAL TIME TAKEN	RECOV ERY TIME	QOS
1	6	16	0	35	10	0	42
2	5	11	0	26	7	0	35
3	5	37	19	23	20	10	31
4	6	69	38	65	45	16	72
5	6	51	9	18	32	6	29
6	5	37	18	47	18	10	60
7	5	39	0	18	19	0	23
8	4	40	16	22	20	10	30
9	4	49	14	30	24	9	40
10	6	38	20	19	17	11	34

In the service evaluation phase, we identified the critical and non-critical services. We then execute the function to rank the service nodes. The ordered list is updated based on the function. The QoS values are updated as part of the ordered list. We injected the fault he node dynamically into the service node. In our model, the top two ranked service value threads are executed in parallel and based on the rankings, the clusters are formed with the given set of nodes. In the service activation phase, the top ranking nodes are executed in parallel to accomplish the task. If any error occurs during the activation phase, the faulted sub tasks need not be re-executed as the same is done in parallel with the another set of nodes which leads to the minimal composition length. The same pattern is followed for the entire cluster in the execution phase till the task is completed. In our proposed work, instead of the rankings based on the QoS parameter, we have used the function to construct the list of service nodes for parallel execution which improves the performance of the overall system.

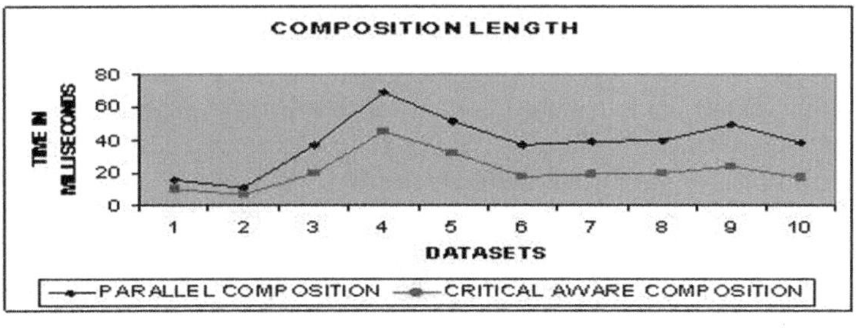

Fig. 3. Results of Critical Aware Service Composition Models – Composition time

The result graphs in the Figure 4 shows that the critical service composition model gives better results compared to the parallel composition model for the data sets.

The Figure 5 infers that for a set of independent subtasks taken, the failure recovery time is comparatively less in our model compared to the traditional model.

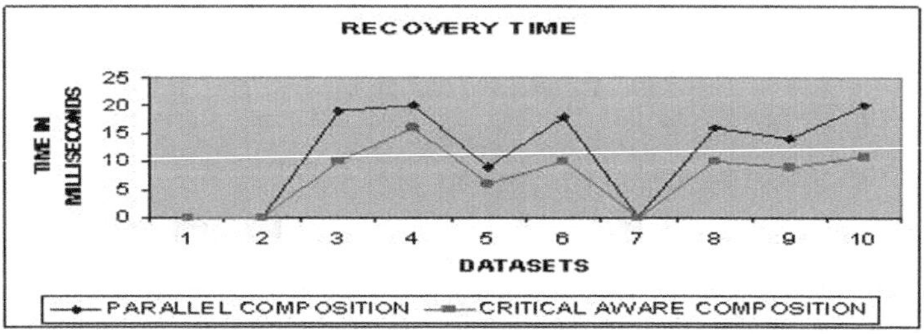

Fig. 4. Results of Critical Aware Service Composition Models – Recovery time

The Figure 6 shows that the critical aware service composition model shows better quality of service than the parallel model for the set of independent sub tasks services.

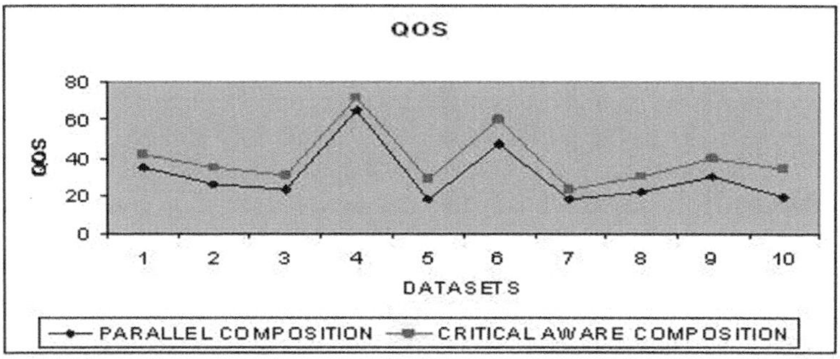

Fig. 5. Results of Critical Aware Service Composition Models – QoS

5 Conclusion and Future Work

We introduced a novel approach to study the service composition problem for pervasive composition environments. The services have been classified as critical and non-critical based on the service parameters. We modeled the systems operation for various eventualities and designed a fault tolerant critical aware parallel service composition model using an ad-hoc community network. The system was tested experimentally. The proposed critical aware composition model gives better performance in the fault situation as the recovery time is comparatively less. In future, the work will be tested in a large scale with over 100 nodes for more parameters and the operation of the overall system improved. Our work is unique and different from the existing systems in that the work combines the best of a parallel, critical task aware community based architecture for the pervasive computing system.

References

1. Brønsted, J., Hansen, K.M., Ingstrup, M.: Service Composition Issues in Pervasive Computing. IEEE Journal of Pervasive Computing 9(1), 62–70 (2010)
2. Ibrahim, N., Mouël, F.L.: A Survey on Service Composition Middleware in Pervasive Environments. IJCSI International Journal of Computer Science Issues 1 (2009)
3. Chakraborty, D., Joshi, A., Finin, T., Yesha, Y.: Service Composition for Mobile Environments. Journal on Mobile Networking and Applications, Special Issue on Mobile Services 10(4), 435–451 (2005)
4. Shriram, R., Sugumaran, V., Vivekanandan, K.: A middleware for information processing in mobile computing platforms. International Journal of Mobile Communications 6(5), 646–666 (2008)
5. Kalasapur, S., Kumar, M., Shirazi, B.: Dynamic Service Composition in Pervasive Computing. IEEE Transactions on Parallel and Distributed Systems 18(7), 907–918 (2007)
6. Kumaran, P., Shriram, R.: Service Composition Middleware for Pervasive Computing. In: 3rd International Conference on Network and Computer Science, vol. 6, pp. 26–28 (2011)
7. Chang, S.-C., Liao, C.-F., Liu, Y.-C., Fu, L.-C., Wang, C.-Y.: A spontaneous Preference Aware Service Composition Framework for Message-Oriented Pervasive Systems. In: 4th International Conference on Pervasive and Computing Applications (2009)
8. Chang, H.-C., Liao, C.-F., Fu, L.-C.: Unification of Multiple Preferences and Avoidance of Service Interference for Service Composition in Context-Aware Pervasive Systems. In: 7th ACM International Conference on Pervasive Services (2010)
9. Qian, Z., Wang, Z., Xu, T., Lu, S.: A dynamic service composition schema for pervasive computing. J. Intell. Manuf. (2010)
10. Kumar, M., Shirazi, B.A., Das, S.K., Sung, B.Y., Levine, D., Singhal, M.: PICO: A middleware framework for Pervasive Computing. IEEE Pervasive Computing 2(3), 72–79 (2003)

Staggered Checkpointing and Recovery in Cluster Based Mobile Ad Hoc Networks

Parmeet Kaur Jaggi[1] and Awadhesh Kumar Singh[2]

[1] Department of Computer Science, Jaypee Institute of Information Technology, NOIDA, UP, India
parmeet.kaur@jiit.ac.in
[2] Department of Computer Engineering, National Institute of Technology, Kurukshetra, Haryana, India
aksinreck@rediffmail.com

Abstract. Checkpointing uses stable storage available in the distributed system for saving the consistent states of processes to which they can rollback at the time of recovery. But the checkpointing techniques for wired and cellular mobile systems are not trivially applicable to ad hoc networks as these networks have limited stable storage and wireless links are of low bandwidth. Moreover if synchronous checkpointing is employed, the processes contend for these limited resources at the time of checkpointing. This paper addresses the application of checkpointing to ad hoc networks and proposes a staggered approach to avoid simultaneous contention for resources. The staggering causes events, which would normally happen at the same time, to start or happen at different times. The proposed protocol does not need FIFO channels and logs minimum number of messages. It supports concurrent checkpoint initiation and successfully handles the overlapping failures in ad hoc networks.

Keywords: Checkpointing, Staggering, Concurrent initiators, Recovery, ad hoc networks.

1 Introduction

A mobile ad hoc network (MANET) is an autonomous collection of mobile nodes that communicate over relatively bandwidth constrained wireless links. The network topology is dynamic and decentralized; where all network activity including discovering the topology and delivering messages must be executed by the nodes themselves. Since the nodes communicate over wireless links, they have to contend with the effects of radio communication, such as noise, fading, and interference. In addition, the links typically have less bandwidth than in a wired network. The nodes have limited storage capabilities and typically no stable storage. The lifetime of a node may be determined by the battery life, thereby requiring the minimization of energy expenditure.

In such a scenario, the failure probability of the computing process increases greatly along with enlarging scale of the system. If a failure occurs in a computing process and there is not an appropriate method to protect it, more cost will be wasted

D. Nagamalai, E. Renault, and M. Dhanushkodi (Eds.): PDCTA 2011, CCIS 203, pp. 122–134, 2011.

for restarting the program. This need for reliability leads to the requirement of some fault tolerance method specifically designed for such networks. A major class of distributed systems uses checkpointing along with rollback recovery for providing fault tolerance. The work presented in this paper aims to present checkpointing as a fault tolerance approach in mobile ad hoc networks. We consider clustered mobile ad hoc networks in which nodes are partitioned into a number of virtual and disjoint groups called clusters. Under the cluster structure, mobile nodes are assigned a different function, such as cluster head (CH) or cluster member. One node in each cluster is chosen as the cluster head based on some criteria and the other members of the cluster use the stable storage at the cluster head for saving their checkpoints.

Three types of checkpointing protocols have been proposed in the literature,: *synchronous checkpointing*, where each process checkpoints simultaneously with every other process [1], *quasi- synchronous checkpointing*, where the communication history is piggybacked on each message, and each process checkpoints independently based on that information [1], and *asynchronous checkpointing*, where each process checkpoints independently, but the end result may be an inconsistent global state [1]. However, none considers contention.

The stable storage contention may not be a problem for asynchronous checkpointing as the processes take their checkpoints independently. Hence, checkpoints are often spaced apart on time axis. However, the synchronous checkpointing does not have this advantage. Therefore, it is advantageous for the synchronous checkpointing to stagger the checkpoints in order to avoid stable storage contention. The staggered checkpoints improve performance because, as the number of processes taking their checkpoints simultaneously and the checkpoint size grow, there is more contention present during synchronous checkpointing and thus more room for improvement when checkpoints are staggered [2]. When processes in a mobile ad hoc network's cluster contend for storage over limited bandwidth, staggering will bring a huge benefit to system performance.

Therefore the approach described in this paper uses a staggered checkpointing scheme adapted to the cluster based ad hoc environment. We aim to demonstrate that checkpointing can be a useful fault tolerance approach in ad hoc networks and staggering the checkpoints will give a boost to the performance. The next section discusses the work done in the area of checkpointing in MANETs. Further we put forth our system model. Subsequently, we describe our algorithm and its working. Then we present the recovery protocol. Lastly we conclude the presentation.

2 Related Work

Research on fault tolerance for the distributed systems has received tremendous interests in recent years. But these schemes can not be applied directly in ad hoc wireless networks due to the reason that there is no support of any static centralized administration and there are no fixed stable hosts or Mobile Support Stations.

2.1 Checkpointing MANETs

The work in [15] presents a cluster based checkpointing and rollback recovery scheme for ad-hoc wireless networks based on processes checkpointing and the cluster-based multi-channel management protocol (CMMP).The network of mobile hosts is partitioned into several clusters. The mobile nodes act as cluster heads, gateways or ordinary members. Quasi synchronous checkpointing algorithm is employed along with pessimistic logging. Mobile hosts take checkpoints periodically managed by the local cluster head and log their output/input and messages related to the gateway.

The migratory services [16] model supports continuous and stateful client-service interactions in highly volatile ad hoc networks. The scheme uses context aware checkpointing to extend the primary backup approach for fault tolerance.

A checkpoint protocol for ad hoc networks has been proposed in [17]. Here, a checkpoint request message is delivered by flooding. State information of a mobile computer is carried by this message and stored into neighbor mobile computers. In the model of [18] the MANET is geographically partitioned into several disjoint and equal sized cluster regions. Each cluster is assigned a unique cluster id and has only one manager which is the one that can directly communicate with the adjacent managers For the recovery algorithm each manager must keep an ($n_{total\ h}$ * $n_{cluster\ h}$) dependency matrix where $n_{total\ h}$ is the total number of mobile hosts in the system and $n_{cluster\ h}$ is the total number of mobile hosts in its cluster

None of the above approaches addresses the problem of simultaneous access to stable storage and wireless channels by the checkpointing nodes.

2.2 Staggered Checkpointing

Staggered checkpointing has been proposed in literature for wired distributed systems. Chandy-Lamport algorithm [3] can stagger checkpoints when marker messages are forwarded, by the coordinator, to its neighbors only, which further forward the marker to their neighbors. However, the staggering vanishes in a completely connected topology where the coordinator directly forwards marker simultaneously to all processes. Based on Chandy-Lamport algorithm, two protocols, [4] and [5] have considered contention. Both allow processes to stagger their checkpoints and use either message logging or some form of additional synchronous checkpoints to guarantee a consistent state. A topology dependent algorithm to stagger a limited number of checkpoints is proposed in [4]. The work in [5] proposed an approach that could stagger all checkpoints. All three schemes work with single initiator and require FIFO message delivery.

The authors of [6] pointed out that the approach in [5] suffers from a major limitation. All messages must be logged in order to ensure global consistency. Hence, when the number of checkpointing processes in the system increases, the size of message log also increases dramatically. A heavy message log causes traffic for the stable storage leading to overall performance degradation. A solution to the problem has been put forth in [6]. As, processes contend for the stable storage; the availability of stable storage has been increased by using concurrent disks through a distributed RAID system [7].Since increasing the size of stable storage is not feasible in MANETs, we present an approach that can reduce the size of message log while staggering checkpoints.

Our algorithm is designed to work in MANETs with limited storage and non-FIFO channels. There can be concurrent initiators of the checkpointing process which will speed up the process. The issue of concurrent initiations has been handled in literature. Most of the checkpointing algorithms[9][10][11][12], have assumed that the channels to be FIFO and have not considered the issue of contention.

We have used an approach similar to [10] to handle multiple initiations but our proposed protocol handles contention and does not need FIFO guarantee. Recently, two staggered quasi-synchronous checkpointing algorithms, as [13] and [14], have been presented. However, our checkpointing protocol is a staggered synchronous one.

3 System Model

Clustering approaches have been found suitable for large scale and high-density ad hoc network applications. A special node such as the cluster head can coordinate the message transmission and checkpointing of nodes in its cluster. We therefore apply our checkpointing algorithm to a cluster based network as in Fig 1. The nodes of the mobile ad hoc network are divided into clusters and one node is chosen as the Cluster Head (CH) in each cluster. For instance a node N identifies itself as a cluster head when it recognizes that it meets some predefined qualifying criteria. This criterion could be that a node having the lowest node ID within its one-hop neighborhood will become a CH. A CH and all its neighbors thus form a cluster.

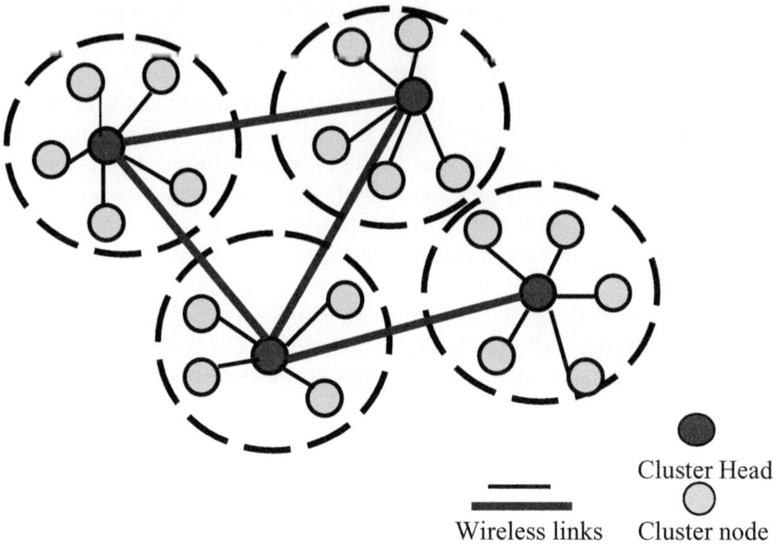

Fig. 1. System Model

The nodes which are chosen as the cluster heads, can then take part in the inter-cluster communication with the other CHs in their communication range. Ordinary nodes in each cluster can talk only within the cluster. The topology is such that any node can communicate with any other node in the cluster either directly or via the

CH. The CHs are assumed to have enough stable storage for saving the checkpoints of nodes in their cluster.

The processes in the system are fail-stop. The processes communicate with each other only by exchanging messages through an asynchronous and reliable channel with unpredictable but finite transmission delays. No message will be lost in the channel. The channel is non-FIFO and each message has a unique sequence number.

4 The Algorithm Concept

We present a staggering based synchronous checkpointing scheme adapted for handling the limited storage and bandwidth problems of MANETs. Controlled sender-based message logging is used, where only those messages are recorded in the message log that have been sent and yet not received at their respective destinations. We call them *in-channel* messages because these are the messages presently in the channel. If we could delay the recording of a local snapshot, the *in-channel* messages would get more propagation time and most of them would reach their respective destinations. Hence, the global snapshot collected by our approach represents a much more recent state of the system than what is collected without the proposed approach. In addition, the number of *in-channel* messages would be drastically reduced, which requires the small-sized message log to be maintained at sender. The messages are given sequence numbers to maintain consistency at the time of recovery.

Each CH has a distinct identifier (or id) and the hosts on joining a cluster also get an id. Each CH keeps a list, LOCAL of the active nodes in its cluster. The nodes in a cluster use the stable storage at the CH to save their most recent checkpoints.

Any CH may initiate the checkpointing and there can be multiple initiators of the checkpoint process. The initiator CHs are called leaders. The checkpoints are assumed to be sequenced so that all checkpoints with the same sequence number form a consistent state of the system. The further discussion of the algorithm describes the checkpointing process for a given checkpoint sequence number.

A leader CH after taking its own checkpoint sends a *take_chkpt* message, containing its own id, to other CHs in its transmission range and then initiates the checkpoint in its cluster. All the clusters which take a checkpoint in response to the message from the same leader form a group. Thus there will be as many groups formed in the system as there are concurrent leaders. Any CH on receiving the *take_chkpt* message for the first time saves the sender's id as its PARENT and the initiator's id as its LEADER. Every CH keeps a record of the recipients of its *take_chkpt* message by a 2D array, GLOBAL

A CH on receiving a *take_chkpt* message another time, sends a DENY message to the sender. It however keeps track of any concurrent leaders by a boundary-set data structure. If the initiator's id in any subsequent *take_chkpt* message is different from that saved in the LEADER variable at the CH, then the receiver CH saves this initiator's id in its boundary-set after sending a DENY message to the sender CH.

Thus the CHs form a forest of spanning trees in the system. Each leader is the root of a spanning tree and all CHs which take a checkpoint due to it belong to its spanning tree. A CH which sends a *take_chkpt* message to another for the first time is its parent in the spanning tree. The receiver of this *take_chkpt* message is its child node. Within a cluster, a CH, after taking its own checkpoint, initiates the checkpoint by sending the *take_chkpt* message to its cluster nodes one by one in increasing order of their ids. This procedure continues till the last member of the cluster. Hence the nodes of the cluster take checkpoints at the CH in a staggered fashion.

When a leaf CH in the spanning tree has completed a checkpoint in its cluster, it sends an *ACK* message along with the boundary set to its parent in the spanning tree. This boundary-set is merged with the parent's boundary-set. After an intermediate CH in a spanning tree has received such *ACK* messages from its entire set of child CHs and has completed the checkpoint in its cluster, it sends an *ACK* message along with the boundary-set to its parent in the spanning tree

When the leader receives the acknowledgement of all its children CHs, it also knows the identifiers of other initiators in the system using boundary-set information it receives from the child CHs. The initiator then sends the *chkpt_taken* message to other initiators. When it has received similar messages from all concurrent initiators, it propagates a *chkpt_taken* message in the group formed by its child nodes to complete the checkpointing process for a given sequence number.

Thus our checkpointing protocol initiates the cluster heads at each level of a spanning tree in parallel. However, the nodes in a cluster are initiated sequentially. This approach has a two fold benefit. Firstly it removes the contention for CH storage and the wireless bandwidth as the checkpointing within each group is ordered sequentially for the nodes in the cluster while the checkpointing of different clusters can take place in parallel. Secondly, by delaying the checkpointing of some nodes, due to the sequence imposed upon them, some *in-channel* messages can reach their destinations, thereby reducing the size of message log.

5 The Working of Algorithm

The following messages have been used in the algorithm:

***take_chkpt<initiator CH id >*:** a CH sends this message to other CHs to take checkpoint, a CH also passes information about the initiator.

***ACK<boundary-set>*:** a CH sends this message to its PARENT after taking a checkpoint in its cluster carrying along with it the information it has about other concurrent leaders

***DENY*:** a CH which has already taken a checkpoint, on receiving a subsequent *take_chkpt* message sends *DENY* to sender

***chkpt_taken*:** a leader sends this message to other leaders after completing the checkpointing in its group

Any CH may initiate the checkpointing process by sending the *take_chkpt* message to the CHs in its transmission range. This message carries with it the sender's id so that any process receiving the *take_chkpt* message for the first time is included in the group of this initiator or leader. Since there can be multiple concurrent initiations, a CH receiving the *take_chkpt* message more than once replies to any subsequent senders with a *DENY* message. A CH which is not the leader replies with an *ACK* message to its PARENT after completing the checkpointing in its cluster. The *ACK* message is appended with the information, if any, of other concurrent initiators.

For accomplishing the above, the algorithm uses the following data structures:

$GLOBAL_i$< CH id, flag>: is a 2D vector where each row denotes the recipients of the *take_chkpt* message; flag is 0 till the time an *ACK/DENY* is received back from the corresponding CH.

$LOCAL_i$: the set of active nodes in a cluster C_i // for simplicity assume nodes in a cluster are numbered 0,1,2…so on

PARENT: the CH which has sent the first *take_chkpt* message to CH_i

$LEADER_i$: the initiator CH due to which CH_i takes a checkpoint

Boundary-set$_i$: list of known concurrent initiators other than the LEADER

time_out: Boolean flag which denotes whether the waiting time for *ACK/DENY* messages has expired or not

Cluster_time_out: Boolean flag which denotes whether the waiting time for checkpoint of a node in the cluster has expired or not. If a node has not taken a checkpoint in this interval, CH can remove it from active nodes list.

Some member nodes may voluntarily or involuntarily disconnect from the MANET but we assume that a CH will not disconnect from the MANET. Every CH therefore maintains the status of each recipient CH of its *take_chkpt* message by the GLOBAL array .The flag bit in each row of the array is set to 1 only after receiving the *ACK/DENY* message from the corresponding CH. The recipients of the *take_chkpt* message keep a record of the sender by the PARENT identifier and the initiator by the LEADER identifier. If a CH does not respond within the *time_out* interval, its parent will again initiate that cluster to take the checkpoint. Since a CH does not disconnect, ultimately the flag bit for this CH at its parent will be set to 1. Within a cluster, some nodes may disconnect. Therefore a CH removes an inactive node from its current nodes list, $LOCAL_i$ if it does not take a checkpoint within a *cluster_time_out* interval.

6 The Algorithm

6.1 Pseudo Code

a) Initialization

for all b=0 to m-1,
  $GLOBAL_b$=NULL
  $LEADER_b$= NULL
  $PARENT_b$ =NULL
  boundary-set$_b$ = NULL

Let CH_m, CH_n,… be various concurrent initiators

b) **PROCEDURE leader_chkpt(i) {**
//Each leader CH_i executes leader_chkpt(i)
(i) CH_i sends *take_chkpt(i)* to all CH_x in transmission range of CH_i
(ii) CH_i adds a record < CH_x, 0> to $GLOBAL_i$

(iii) CH_i calls Cluster_chkpt(i)
(iii) if(chk_global(i) ==TRUE) then send *chkpt_taken* message to boundary initiators
(iv)Wait for *chkpt_taken* message from other leaders
(v) If CH_i has has received *chkpt_taken* message from all members of its boundary-set, propagate *chkpt_taken* message in own group
}

PROCEDURE Cluster_chkpt(j) {
//Within a cluster j
(i) CH_j takes its checkpoint;
(ii) m=1
(iii) While there exists more elements in $LOCAL_j$
{ s=$LOCAL_j$[m] // member node of the cluster//
(iv) CHj sends *take_chkpt* to node s;
(v) If Node s takes checkpoint then
{m++
Goto(iii)
}
else
{ if (cluster_time_out=1) then
{remove node s from $LOCAL_j$
goto (iii)
}
}
}
}

Procedure CH_checkpoint(i,j,k) {
//Each CH_k, which is not a leader, on receiving the *take_chkpt*(i) message from CH_j executes CH_checkpoint()
(i)If $LEADER_k$ <> NULL then
{send *DENY* to CH_j;
if $LEADER_k$ <>i then add i to < boundary-set_k >
}
else
{ Set $LEADER_k$ = i
Set $PARENT_k$ = j
CH_k sends *take_chkpt(i)* to all CH_y // *y<>j*
Add a record < CH_y, 0> to $GLOBAL_k$
}
(ii) CH_k calls Cluster_chkpt(k)
(iii)if chk_global(k) is TRUE then
Send *ACK*<$boundary_k$> message to $PARENT_k$
}

PROCEDURE chk_GLOBAL(p) {
// A CH calls chk_GLOBAL to check if all child nodes have replied
While each flag(GLOBAL$_p$)<> 1
{
if (time_out=0)
then
{ wait for *ACK* and *DENY* messages from CHs in GLOBAL$_p$
If CH$_p$ receives a *DENY* message from CH$_y$, then set GLOBAL$_p$< CH$_y$, 1>
If CH$_p$ receives an *ACK*<boundary-set> message from CH$_y$, then set GLOBAL$_p$< CH$_y$,1>, merge <boundary-set>$_y$ with <boundary-set>$_p$
}
}
if each flag(GLOBAL$_p$)== 1 , // *all CHs for which CH$_i$ was the PARENT have replied back//*
Return TRUE }

6.2 Proof of Correctness

Theorem 1. The checkpointing algorithm converges.

Proof: We prove this by contradiction. Suppose the checkpointing algorithm does not converge. Hence, there exists at least one cluster, say C$_i$ that never finalizes its checkpoint. Now, there could be the following possibility: cluster C$_i$ takes checkpoint under group leader, say C$_{l,}$ as it receives *take_chkpt* message from another CH, say CH$_j$. Thus, if C$_i$ is the last i.e. a leaf cluster of its group then it will send an *ACK* message to its parent CH$_j$; otherwise, it will send *take_chkpt* message to the next cluster of its group after taking its own checkpoint. The next process proceeds similarly and the last member i.e. leaf of the group sends an *ACK* message to its parent. Every parent ensures that each group member under its group has taken a checkpoint by checking the GLOBAL vector present with it. If some bit in the GLOBAL vector is zero corresponding to any particular cluster and *time_out* timer has expired then that parent will again initiate that cluster to take the checkpoint and corresponding messages will be replayed. Moreover within a cluster, a CH removes an inactive node from its current nodes list if it does not take a checkpoint within a cluster_time_out interval. Eventually, the checkpoint for the group is finalized. Therefore, there does not remain any cluster C$_i$ which is not able to finalize its checkpoint. It is a contradiction. Thus, the checkpointing algorithm converges.

Theorem 2. No orphan messages can be generated in the system.

Proof: The algorithm requires controlled sender based message logging. Every message is logged at the sender at the time of sending. It is logged from the time it is sent till the time it is known to have been received at its destination. Thus the recording of the receipt of a message is preceded by the logging of its sending. Any message that is received has its determinant i.e. sending event logged at the sender. So, orphan messages cannot be generated by the system.

7 The Recovery Procedure

7.1 Data Structures Used

Let a process P_i be running on a node i
The following data structures are used for the recovery of process P_i :

SentSet$_i$: Every process maintains the set of all those processes to whom it has only sent messages to since the last checkpoint

RcdSet$_i$: Every process maintains the set of all those processes from which it has received messages since the last checkpoint

Countrcd$_i$: It keeps the count of messages P_i has received from any other processes P_j since the last checkpoint

nCountrcd$_i$: It keeps the count of messages P_i receives from other processes P_j during the recovery

rollback_status: Boolean variable (value 1 indicates that process is running recovery thread and value 0 indicates that process has completed the recovery successfully)

7.2 On Cluster Node Failure and Subsequent Recovery

We are using controlled sender based message logging. Only the *in-channel* messages are logged at the sender. Fig. 2 shows a failure at process P_i after it has sent messages m & m' to process P_k and received the message m" from P_j since its last checkpoint i2. Once the process P_i needs to recover after the failure, it rollbacks to its latest checkpoint, here i2, and replays the logged messages.

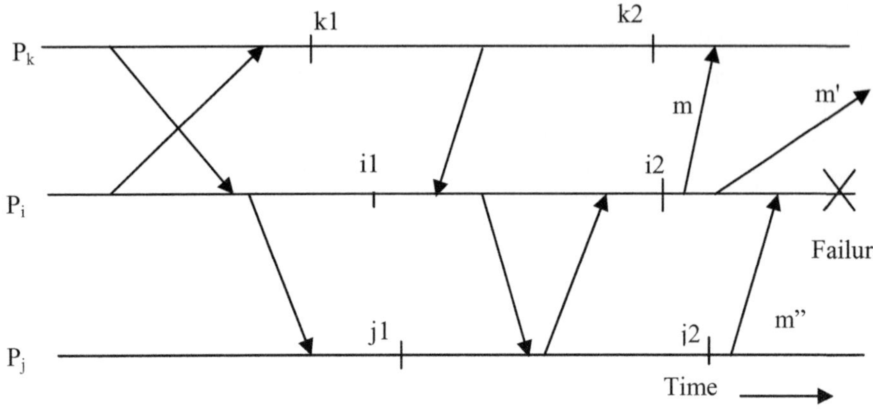

Fig. 2. Recovery of processes

Hence any process P_k that has received messages from P_i before P_i's failure need not rollback as it has either already received the message m from P_i before P_i's failure or will receive the in-channel message m' at the time of P_i's recovery. However, if a process P_j has also sent messages to P_i then P_j needs to rollback to the last checkpoint

, here j2, so that it can re-send any message m" earlier sent by P_j but un-received due to the rollback by P_i.

To avoid inconsistency in the system due to the recovery process, two approaches are possible. A non-blocking approach would allow processes like P_k to continue normal operation during recovery of any other process P_i to which no messages were sent during the last checkpoint interval. In such a case, all checkpoints of the same sequence number would form a consistent state of the system. A second blocking approach for recovery can require a recovering process P_i to send a RECOVERING message to all processes in $SentSet_i$ so that they do not advance their checkpoint till P_i has recovered. This will prevent orphan messages in the system. Upon the completion of recovery process, P_i can send a RECOVERED message to $SentSet_i$.

We assume the non-blocking approach described above for achieving consistent state in the system. No process is restarted from a state that has recorded the receipt of a message that no other process has recorded as received. If a process P_k has recorded the receipt of a message m between its checkpoint k2 and a later checkpoint k3, the sending of m shall be recorded by P_i between its checkpoint i2 and a later checkpoint i3.The recovery procedure never leads to an inconsistent state in the system.

Thus our algorithm provides an optimization by not requiring all processes in the system to roll back at the time of recovery. Only the processes in the $RcdSet_i$ are required to rollback to their latest checkpoint.

7.3 The Recovery Algorithm

Step1: upon restart after failure

(i) read $RcdSet_i$ from stable storage,
(ii) rollback to latest checkpoint
(iii) *Status* =Recovering;
(iv) *Rollback_status*=1;
(v) Send recover request to all processes those are in $RcdSet_i$

Step 2: if P_j receives a recovery request from P_i then

(i) P_j rollbacks to its latest checkpoint
(ii) P_j forwards the recovery request to all members of $RcdSet_j$;

Step 3: if multiple failure then

repeat step1 through step2 at each failed node P_k;
Step 4: P_i and each P_j replay the logged in-channel messages;
Step 5: if ($ncountrcdset_i$ = =$countrcdset_i$) then
$Status_i$= normal;
Rollback_status=0;
else initiate recovery again;

7.4 Proof of Consistent Recovery

Theorem 3. Recovery is consistent assuming reliable CHs and channels.

Proof: Upon recovery after failure, a process rollbacks to its latest checkpoint and resends any in-channel messages which are logged with it. Thus the messages to be sent by the process are eventually sent assuming reliable channels. Also the process sends a recovery request to processes in its *RecdSet* i.e. those processes from which it had received messages in the interval between its last checkpoint and failure. These processes rollback too and replay their messages. At any destination, messages can be placed in sequence and duplicates removed by using sequence numbers of the messages. Hence the recovery of nodes is consistent assuming reliable CHs and channels.

Theorem 4. The algorithm handles multiple failures.

Proof: Let, during the recovery of some failed process P_i at a node i some other process P_j has also failed at node j. When the failed process P_i initiates its recovery, it rolls back to its last checkpoint and then it sends the recovery request to all those processes from which it had received messages. On receiving the recovery request these processes will also roll back to their last checkpoints. Meanwhile, if some other process P_j fails, then P_j will also send the recovery request to the processes listed in its *RcdSetj*. Thus, same procedure would be executed by P_j as for P_i .The two recovery threads would run concurrently. Thus, the protocol can successfully handle multiple failures.

8 Conclusions and the Scope of Future Work

Many researchers have concluded that, due to heavy message logging, the staggering should be discouraged in communication-intensive applications. Our technique subverts this inherent disadvantage of staggering. The small-sized message log makes our staggered approach a suitable candidate to checkpoint the communication-intensive applications too. Also, the more recent global snapshot collected by the proposed staggered protocol, jointly with the small-sized message log, eliminate any possibility of occurrence of the missing message problem. The algorithm will also scale up even when number of nodes is increased, since nodes are organized in a cluster based hierarchy. As the clusters can be initiated in parallel, the performance of the system does not degrade when new clusters are added to the system. The algorithm uses concurrent initiation and handles overlapping failures. Moreover, it does not need the channels to be FIFO. The rollback distance is limited to last checkpoint, even if frequency of application messages are less and processes are running in isolation. However, the algorithm has a scope for further improvement. We propose to utilize the inherent spatial and message redundancy present in the MANETs for better results in our future work.

References

1. Elnozahi, E.N., Alvisi, L., Wang, Y.M., Johnson, D.B.: A survey of rollback-recovery protocols in message-passing systems. ACM Computing Surveys 34(3), 375–408 (2002)
2. Norman, A.N., Choi, S.E., Lin,C.: Compiler-generated staggered checkpointing. In: Proc. 7th ACM Workshop on Languages, Compilers, and Run-time Support for Scalable Systems LCR 2004, pp. 1–8 (2004)

3. Chandy, K.M., Lamport, L.: Distributed snapshots: determining global states of distributed systems. ACM Transactions on Computer Systems 3(1), 63–75 (1985)
4. Plank, J.S.: Efficient checkpointing on MIMD architectures, Ph.D. dissertation, Dept. of Computer Science, Princeton Univ. (1993)
5. Vaidya, N.H.: Staggered consistent checkpointing. IEEE Transactions on Parallel and distributed Systems 10(7), 694–702 (1999)
6. Jin, H., Hwang, K.: Distributed checkpointing on clusters with dynamic striping and staggering. In: Jean-Marie, A. (ed.) ASIAN 2002. LNCS, vol. 2550, pp. 19–33. Springer, Heidelberg (2002)
7. Hwang, K., Jin, H., Ho, R., Ro, W.: Reliable cluster computing with a new checkpointing RAID-x architecture. In: Proc. 9th Workshop on Heterogeneous Computing HCW 2000, Cancun, Mexico, pp. 171–184 (2000)
8. Ahn, J.: An efficient algorithm for removing useless logged messages in SBML protocols. In: Chakraborty, G. (ed.) ICDCIT 2005. LNCS, vol. 3816, pp. 166–171. Springer, Heidelberg (2005)
9. Koo, R., Toueg, S.: Checkpointing and rollback-recovery for distributed systems. IEEE Transactions on Software Engineering SE-13(1), 23–31 (1987)
10. Spezialetti, M., Kearns, P.: Efficient distributed snapshots. In: Proc. 6th IEEE International Conference on Distributed Computing Systems, pp. 382–388 (1986)
11. Prakash, R., Singhal, M.: Maximal global snapshot with concurrent initiators. In: Proc. 6th IEEE Symposium on Parallel and Distributed Processing, pp. 344–351 (1994)
12. Mandal, P.S., Mukhopadhyay, K.: Concurrent checkpoint initiation and recovery algorithms on asynchronous ring networks. Journal of Parallel and Distributed Computing 64(5), 649–661 (2004)
13. Manivannan, D., Jiang, Q., Yang, J., Persson, K.E., Singhal, M.: An asynchronous recovery algorithm based on a staggered quasi-synchronous checkpointing algorithm. In: Pal, A., Kshemkalyani, A.D., Kumar, R., Gupta, A. (eds.) IWDC 2005. LNCS, vol. 3741, pp. 117–128. Springer, Heidelberg (2005)
14. Jiang, Q., Manivannan, D.: An optimistic checkpointing and selective message logging approach for consistent global checkpoint collection in distributed systems. In: Proc. IEEE International Parallel and Distributed Processing Symposium, pp. 1–10 (2007)
15. Men, C., Xu, Z., Li, X.: An Efficient Checkpointing and Rollback Recovery Scheme for Cluster-Based Multi-channel Ad Hoc Wireless Networks. In: Proc. of the 2008 IEEE International Symposium on Parallel and Distributed Processing with Applications (ISPA 2008), pp. 371–378. IEEE Computer Society, Washington, DC, USA (2008)
16. Riva, O., Nzouonta, J., Borcea, C.: Context-aware fault tolerance in migratory services. In: Proceedings of the 5th Annual International Conference on Mobile and Ubiquitous Systems: Computing, Networking, and Services (Mobiquitous 2008). ICST (Institute for Computer Sciences, Social-Informatics and Telecommunications Engineering), ICST, Brussels, article 22 (2008)
17. Ono, M., Higaki, H.: Consistent Checkpoint Protocol for Wireless Ad-hoc Networks. In: The 2007 International Conference on Parallel and Distributed Processing Techniques and Applications, Las Vegas, Nevada, USA, pp. 1041–1046 (2007)
18. Juang, T.T., Liu, M.C.: An Efficient Asynchronous Recovery Algorithm In Wireless Mobile Ad Hoc Networks. J. of Internet Technology 4, 143–152 (2002)

An O(1/n) Protocol for Supporting Distributed Mutual Exclusion in Vehicular Ad Hoc Networks

Bharti Sharma[1], Ravinder Singh Bhatia[2], and Awadhesh Kumar Singh[2]

[1] DIMT Kurukshetra India
bharti_kanhiya@yahoo.co.in
[2] NIT Kurukshetra India
rsibhatia@yahoo.co.in, aksinreck@rediffmail.com

Abstract. The article proposes a token based algorithm to ensure mutual exclusion in clustered vehicular ad hoc networks (VANETs). Since our scheme is dual token based, it handles the token passing among the processes at the inter-cluster level and intra-cluster level in separate manners, which makes the approach suitable for strategic VANET environment. In the interest of efficiency, we implement a centralized scheme at intra-cluster level. The centralized schemes are inherently failure prone, thus, we also attempt to make the intra-cluster token passing fault tolerant. In order to enhance reliability, we have applied a distributed scheme at inter-cluster level. More importantly, the message complexity turns out not only to be independent of *N*, the total number of nodes in the system; rather, under heavy load, it is inversely proportional to *n*, the (average) number of nodes per each cluster. We also present the complexity analysis and correctness proof of the protocol.

Keywords: VANET, Inter-Cluster, Intra-Cluster, Mutual Exclusion, Token Ring.

1 Introduction

The mutual exclusion is a classical coordination problem in distributed computing systems. The purpose of mutual exclusion protocols is to guarantee exclusive access to the critical resource. The processes competing for the shared resource cycle through entry, critical section, exit, and remainder states. Fundamentally, designing protocol for mutual exclusion is to design entry and exit protocols. It is one of the highly researched problems in computing community. Thus, a number of protocols applying various approaches have been proposed in the literature. A good classification of mutual exclusion protocols is given in [1, 2]. However, the last two decades have witnessed tremendous development in the communication technology that resulted in the emergence of various types of networks, e.g. static distributed networks, cellular mobile networks, mobile ad hoc networks, and sensor networks. The change in networking technology has greatly altered the way of distributed computing. Unfortunately, the protocols developed for one type of network either fails to work at all or fail to work with matching performance, in other types of networks. Thus, every change in networking technology virtually triggers the computing scientists to develop new protocols for the new environment. A survey of

D. Nagamalai, E. Renault, and M. Dhanushkodi (Eds.): PDCTA 2011, CCIS 203, pp. 135–147, 2011.

mutual exclusion protocols for static distributed systems is given in [2, 3]. A two-tier principle for adapting protocols for mutual exclusion in cellular mobile networks is given in [4] and a method to restructure, distributed algorithms for mobile computing, is presented in [5].

The ad hoc networks are formed for special purpose on temporary basis. Moreover, the constituting component nodes have various limitations, e.g., constrained battery backup, thin storage, small computing power and, thus, susceptible to failures. Nevertheless, the ad hoc networks are easy to set up and can operate without any pre-existing infrastructure. They do not need base station and each host acts a router. They try to provide connectivity beyond the range of fixed and cellular infrastructure. The mobile ad hoc networks (MANETs) use wireless communication between nodes and have three-dimensional movement of network nodes. Hence, the patterns of movement may be unpredictable. There are many well-understood MANET algorithms. An overview of mutual exclusion protocols for mobile ad hoc networks is given in [6, 7].

2 The Vehicular Ad Hoc Network

The vehicular ad hoc network (VANET) [8, 9] is a variant of MANET where each vehicle is a wireless network enabled node that has somewhat predictable movement pattern. In a sense, the nodes have constrained three-dimensional movement that may, optimistically, approximate as one-dimensional, e.g., the movement along highway. Although, for mutual exclusion, the VANET may use existing MANET algorithms, there is sufficient room for performance enhancement by deriving the advantage from the restricted traffic movement pattern. The vehicle-specific algorithms may provide better results; however, their implementation is costly. In clustering algorithms, the nodes are grouped into clusters to reduce communication overhead. One node from each cluster acts as cluster head. All inter-cluster communication relays through the cluster head. The following figure 1 represents the schematic view of assumed VANET environment. The dotted thick directed edges represent the wireless links that connect the cluster heads. They jointly form the dynamic ring that is computed on-the-fly.

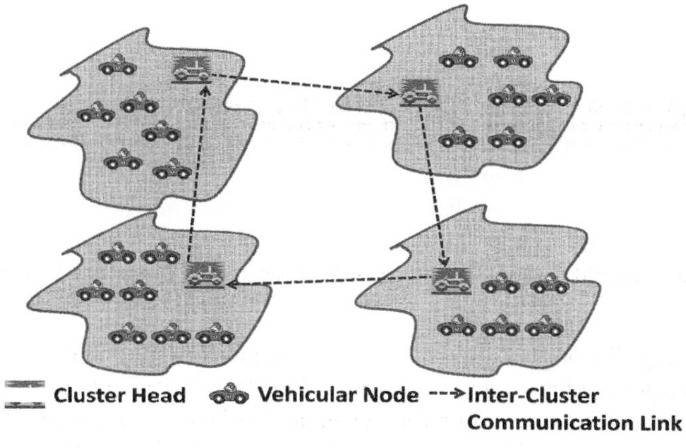

Fig. 1. The Schematic View

Many algorithms exist for clustering and head selection. In VANETs, most traffic flow involves movement on roads. The vehicles know movement components, like velocity, acceleration, position, etc. Thus, it is possible to create clustering algorithms based on traffic movement components. In many existing clustering algorithms for MANETs, each node chooses its cluster head by selecting that with the lowest random id value. The network infrastructure is assumed fairly stable for a long time period. The clusters are formed quickly. The id distribution leads to smaller clusters overall. In some other algorithms, the node which can connect with the highest number of nodes is chosen. The most-connected node is given highest priority. They use larger clusters relative to lowest-id approach. They assume relatively unstable clusters where nodes frequently change to different cluster heads.

In VANET algorithms, it is preferable to choose node with position closest to the average position of all reachable nodes. The vehicles tend to travel in packs. The algorithms suffer overhead of vehicle state information passing and require some location awareness. They, preferably, choose node with velocity closest to the average velocity of all the reachable nodes. The vehicles tend to travel in packs based on velocity. Hence, it is possible to predict which vehicles are likely to remain together. Therefore, in order to take advantage of multiple clustering algorithms, it is advisable to go for a clustering scheme that combines the lowest-id or highest-degree logic and the traffic-specific information.

The VANETs are widely applicable in scenario, like military and rescue. In such environments, due to strategic needs, the nodes move in well coordinated clusters; hence, the clusters are comparatively stable. However, the movement of individual cluster is unpredictable to a large extent because the clusters move autonomously in order to execute their assigned task, though, each cluster is assigned individual task that is decided jointly by all the cluster heads as per strategic needs. The clusters share the critical resources that may be needed time and again. Some of them are to be accessed in a mutually exclusive way. To the best of our knowledge, the paper presents first mutual exclusion algorithm that has been designed, keeping in view the particular requirements of the VANETs.

3 The System Model

As explained above, the nodes are arranged in clusters. Each node is assigned a unique id. Each cluster has a cluster head. Informally, in military applications, a strategic unit (e.g., company, battalion, or brigade) may be constituted of various types of vehicles modeled as nodes. These strategic units can be modeled as clusters and their individual commanders as cluster heads. Although, the nodes of a cluster may not always (or may not always need to) be in the communication range of each other, they remain connected always with the cluster head, in order to guarantee better control and coordination, till they are active/alive. However, a cluster head may not always remain connected with other cluster heads due to its autonomous and strategic movement.

4 The Algorithm Concept

The proposed protocol is token based and has two types of tokens; a unique global token which circulates among the cluster heads and a number of local tokens, each belongs uniquely to one cluster. In other words, the number of surviving local tokens is equal to the number of clusters in the system. Hence, each cluster has one local token which is private to that cluster. The proposed algorithm uses both, token circulation as well as token asking schemes.

The strategic networks execute the applications that have heavy contention for critical resources; thus few nodes of every cluster, always, have outstanding request. Hence, the cluster heads remain, mostly, ready to welcome global token. It is well established that the token ring is very efficient under heavy contention; but inefficient under light contention. Hence, we use token circulation scheme, among the cluster heads, in dynamic ring that is computed on-the-fly. Moreover, the token asking schemes incur delay when used in some logical structure.

However, it is unlikely that every node of a cluster has outstanding request; therefore, we use token asking scheme within the nodes of a cluster. As a result, our protocol has two components; the inter-cluster component and the intra-cluster component. The former is executed among the cluster heads and the later is executed locally among the nodes of each cluster. Unlike [10, 11, 12], our protocol does not have a ring coordinator. Despite having some advantages, the existence of coordinator injects centralized character in the protocol that results in reduced reliability. Although, in above three papers, the protocols rotate the coordinator, every change in coordinator results in flow of large number of message to inform every node about the new coordinator. Moreover, especially in VANET, during some time interval, a cluster head may not be in the communication range of any other cluster head. Thus, the centralized coordination can't work effectively in the assumed VANET environment. Hence, no cluster head has been elected or nominated as ring coordinator. We have used fully distributed approach to pass global token among cluster heads. However, our clusters are more reliable with robust cluster heads and, thus, in order to have better message efficiency, we have applied a centralized protocol, to pass local token, within the nodes of a cluster. Nevertheless, in order to compensate for the loss due to use of centralized scheme, the scheme has been made fault tolerant. Now, we will discuss the working of both the components one by one.

4.1 The Inter-cluster Component

The cluster heads are assumed to be in a dynamic ring and the ring is computed on-the-fly. In order to forward the global token, the holder of global token finds the neighbor cluster heads with the help of routing layer. Out of these neighbors it forwards the global token to the cluster head that is yet to receive the global token. However if there is no such cluster head, then it forwards the global token to the cluster head that did not have any pending requests from its cluster members when it received the global token last time. However, when the global token holder observes that each cluster head has received the global token once, in the current round, the current global token holder starts new round. For this purpose, it resets (like initialization) the information contained in the global token as if no cluster head has received the global token yet.

4.2 The Intra-cluster Component

The cluster head of each cluster acts as coordinator for the cluster. Each hungry node of a cluster requests to its cluster head, for the local token, in order to enter in critical section. The cluster head collects the requests sent by the hungry nodes and serves them with the help of local token once it receives the global token. When all the requests received, before the reception of global token, get served the global token is forwarded to the next cluster head according to some pre defined priority scheme. It is done to avoid starvation. In case, the cluster head had not received any request from its cluster members, before it received the global token, it forwards the global token to the next cluster head. However the request received from the hungry nodes, after the reception of global token, are kept pending till the global token is received by the cluster head next time.

5 Data Structures, Message Types and Process Behavior

The protocol uses the following data structures and messages types:

5.1 At Intra-cluster Component

5.1.1 Data Structure Maintained at Each Cluster Node P_i

i. *Try*: A boolean variable which is set to true when node wants to enter CS
ii. *In*: A boolean variable which is set to true when node is in its critical section
iii. *co*: Identifier of cluster head
iv. *seqno*: It is round no of localtokenmsg stored at each cluster node
v. *type*: It is a variable. It may assume any of the following values depending upon the type of message to be sent by cluster node to cluster head:
   a. *req*: Request to cluster head when the node is hungry
   b. *over*: To inform cluster head on exit CS.
   c. *over&out*: To return local token back to cluster head when there is no pending request entry in local token
vi. *tokenholder*: It is Boolean variable which turns true after receiving local token
vii. *tokenvalue*: It is an integer to store value for the number of token at site
viii. *requestmsg*: It is a request for CS to cluster head. It has the form <identifier of cluster node, type as req, identifier of cluster head >.

5.1.2 Messages

A node communicates with other node with in a cluster by the following messages.

i. *Localtokenmsg<localtoken, roundno>*: It has two fields, first is queue of all requesting nodes of the cluster, and second is sequence number of the localtokenmsg and indicates how many times it has completed its round in cluster. Its initial value is zero. Localtokenmsg is used to grant privilege for accessing critical section. It is sent, initially, by the cluster head to the requesting node entered at index 0, which on exit CS, deletes its entry from the localtokenmsg and forwards the localtokenmsg to next hungry node by looking the entry in local token. When there is no entry left unserved in the localtokenmsg, the site, which executed CS last, would return it to the cluster head.

ii. *msg_to_ch*: *<Id, type, co>* The nodes of cluster use it to send various types of messages to their cluster heads. It has three variables. First is identifier of the sender node, second is type of message, and third is the ID of cluster head. If destination for sending request message is far away to reach a message, process will wait for a finite amount of time and then try to transmit the message again until it succeeds.

5.1.3 Behavior of a Process at Cluster Node

Each hungry node sends a request to its cluster head by executing a procedure named *requestingCS*. After getting *localtokenmsg*, it matches its *seqno* with *roundno*. If it is less than round no then it enters in its critical section. On exit CS, the node sets its *seqno* equal to the *roundno* in *localtokenmsg*. Further, it sends *'over'* message to its cluster head and forwards the *localtokenmsg* to next hungry node. However, if next hungry node is not in its communication range, the node returns l*ocaltokenmsg* back to its cluster head that forwards the *localtokenmsg* to next hungry node. Nevertheless, if the *localtokenmsg* has no unserved request, the node sends *'over&out'* message to its cluster head and returns the *localtokenmsg* back to its cluster head.

A. Request message by cluster node *i*:
Site *i* sends a request message to the cluster head by running procedure requestingCS(); cluster head collects the request in its local pending request queue(*LQ*)

Procedure *requestingCS*( )

1. *Try* ← TRUE;
2. Send *requestmsg*<i, req, co> to cluster head
3. Wait for *localtokenmsg*;

B. Execution of Critical Section by Cluster Node: requesting site gets permission in the form of *localtokenmsg* either from cluster head or from a neighbor. Only on receiving *localtokenmsg* the cluster node can execute its critical section.

Procedure executingCS( )

4. *TRY* ← True;
5. *Tokenholder* ← TRUE;

// Case I: when single *localtokenmsg* is at a cluster node

```
6.  IF Tokenvalue == 1 THEN
7.      IF seqno < roundno THEN
8.          In ←TRUE; // in CS
            On exit CS execute STEPS 25-28;
9.      ELSE
10.         execute STEPS 25-28;
```

//Case II: Simultaneously two *localtokenmsg* (T_1 and T_2) are at a cluster node

```
11. IF (Tokenvalue == 2) THEN
12.     IF seqno ≥ roundno
13.         Discard one localtokenmsg arbitrarily;
14.         Send over message to cluster head and execute STEPS 25-28
15.             ELSE IF (seqno < roundno ) THEN
16.                 Execute critical section with greater round number
17.                 Execute STEPS 25-28; Discard another localtokenmsg
```

C. Exiting CS by cluster node: Cluster node after exiting from critical section run procedure exitCS().

Procedure exitCS( )

```
18. In ← false;
19. seqno ← roundno;
20. Dequeue node i from localtoken;
21. IF localtoken[] == ϕ THEN
22.     Send 'over &out' message;
23.     Send localtoken  to cluster head;
    ELSE
24.     Send over message to cluster head;
25. IF localtoken[head] ≠ neighbor of cluster node THEN
26.     Send localtokenmsg to cluster head;
27. ELSE
28.     Send localtokenmsg to next hungry node;
```

5.2 At Inter-cluster Component

5.2.1 Data Structure Maintained at Each Cluster Head P_i

i. *Co*: Id of cluster head.

ii. *globalvalue:*It is an integer ;initially its value is zero. It is incremented at each circulation of *globaltokenmsg*

iii. *LQ*: It is N×2 matrix of the pending requests that stores the request according to their sequence of occurrence at cluster head. In *LQ*[color[0….N-1], fill[0…..N-1]], the first component color will be set to blue for those hungry nodes of cluster whose request has arrived at cluster head, initially color will be green for each node of cluster. Second component fill, whose initial value is 0, will be set to 1 after arrival of over or over&out message. *LQ* is used to generate local token. After receiving global token, it is copied into the *localtokenmsg* by the cluster head before forwarding the *localtokenmsg* to the requesting node entered at index 0.

iv. *N-LIST*$_i$: It is the list of cluster heads that are current neighbors of cluster head i. Initially, it is empty.

v. *Hold*$_i$: It is a Boolean variable whose value is false, initially, and set to true when cluster head i receives the global token

vi. *Hungry*: Boolean variable that is set true when some node within the cluster is hungry.

vii. *globaltoken*: It is N×2 matrix that stores the status of cluster head. In *globaltoken* [color[0…N-1], fill[0..1]], the entries could be of the following:

   a. (w, 0) signifies that the corresponding cluster head is yet to receive the global token.

   b. (w, 1) signifies that the corresponding cluster head did not have any hungry node in its cluster when it received the global token last time, and

   c. (R, 1) signifies that the corresponding cluster head has received the global token and used it to serve the requests from its cluster.

viii. *NLQ*: It is queue of pending requests after receiving the *globaltoken*

5.2.2 Behavior of a Process at Cluster Head

In the beginning, randomly, one cluster head will be the holder of global token. If it has some pending request from its cluster then it will use *globaltoken* to generate *localtokenmsg* and circulate it in its cluster. After serving its cluster, it makes its entry in *globaltoken* (R, 1). However, if it does not have any pending request from its cluster, it makes its entry in *globaltoken* (w, 1). Afterwards, the cluster head that is nearest (in terms of hop distance) among the cluster heads that are in the communication range, is chosen as next successor. However, the *global token* is forwarded to the next successor cluster head whose entry in the *globaltoken* is (W, 0). The new recipient of global token also uses it as mentioned above. However, if all entries in the *globaltoken* are (R, 1), it resets them as (W, 0) and starts new round.

Request message handler at cluster head P$_i$: The request sent by hungry site is saved at cluster head site by entering it in the pending request queue. Now, the cluster head handles it as follows:

```
// execution of code after STEPS 1, 2, and 3 of Intra-Cluster Communication
IF type == req THEN
        IF globaltoken is not received yet THEN
                Enter i in LQ[0….N];
        Else
                Enter i in NLQ[0…N]
        END IF
END IF
```

Cluster head *i* with *globaltoken*

```
Hold← TRUE;
IF Hungry == FALSE THEN
     globaltoken[i] ← (w, 1);
     Forward globaltoken to next successor cluster head in N-LIST_i
ELSE
      Increment globalvalue;
      roundno←globalvalue;
      IF (∃j: color[j] = blue) THEN
            Localtoken[] ← j; \\ generation localtoken
            Process ← Localtoken[head];
            Send localtokenmsg<localtoken, roundno> to Process;
      END IF
      IF received message (from cluster node x) == over
        || received message (from x) == over&out THEN
        Update LQ[color[],fill[x]] ← 1;
       ELSE
        wait for selected timeout value to get 'over' or 'over&out' message;
       ENDIF
       IF timeout == true for 'over' or 'over&out' message THEN
              Generate new localtokenmsg with roundno of lost localtokenmsg
       ENDIF

       IF localtoken[] == ϕ OR over&out message is receivedTHEN
            ∃i globaltoken[i] ← (R,1);
             IF {∃j: globaltoken[color[0…N-1], fill[0..1]] == (W,0) THEN
                 IF j ∈ N-LIST_i}THEN
                   Send globaltoken randomly to a cluster head that has entry (W, 0);
                 ELSE
                   Send token randomly to some neighbor;
                    Hold ← FALSE;
                   Hungry ← FALSE | TRUE; //depends upon NLQ
                  ENDIF
             ELSE
             ∀j: globaltoken[color[j], fill[j]] ← (W, 0); \\ making red token as white
             Send token randomly to some neighbor;
             ENDIF
        ENDIF
```

6 The Correctness Proof

In this section, we show that the algorithm achieves mutual exclusion and is free from deadlock and starvation.

6.1 Mutual Exclusion

The proof of mutual exclusion is trivial in token based protocols. However, in our protocol, there is the provision of more than one type of tokens, namely global token and local token. Hence, in order to show that it ensures mutual exclusion, we need to prove that at most one site holds the privilege to execute in CS. In our protocol, only the local token message is used to grant privilege to enter CS. Moreover, the local token message is generated by a cluster head only after receiving the global token and the local token remains in circulation within its cluster till the cluster head holds the global token. In addition, to generate the local token message, the global token is the only privilege among cluster heads. Initially, only one cluster head holds the global token, say site S. There are three situations where site S sends the global token to another cluster head: (1) All the hungry sites, within the cluster of S that have requested before the receipt of global token, have finished the execution of CS and the site that executed CS last, has returned local token back to S, or (2) No site, within the cluster of S, was hungry before the receipt of global token, or (3) Site S has already received the global token once in the current round and therefore, it is prohibited to generate the local token message again, in the current round. In either case, site S sends the global token to only one of the reachable cluster heads that is yet to receive the global token in the current round. The new holder of the global token also uses it in the above explained manner before sending it out. Therefore, at most one site holds the privilege to execute in CS.

6.2 Freedom from Starvation

The starvation occurs when a few sites repeatedly execute the CS while other sites wait indefinitely for their turns to do so. In the algorithm, the local token queue (LTQ) is a FCFS (First-Come-First-Serve) queue, which is used to contain all the requests that have been received, at the cluster head, before the cluster head itself received the global token. Moreover, the local token is passed around according to the order of requests in LTQ. After a site Y, whose request is in front of site X's request in LTQ, has finished execution of the CS, its subsequent request will never be added to current LTQ after site X's request. Moreover, the number of hungry nodes within the cluster being finite, the length of LTQ is also finite. Hence, site X will get the local token because any of the sites, whose requests are in front of site X's request in LTQ, will be able to make subsequent request and, therefore, get the local token again only in the next LTQ round. Consequently, the algorithm is free from starvation.

7 The Complexity Analysis

Message Complexity

Assume there are n nodes in each cluster and there are m cluster heads. However, each cluster may not have the same number of nodes; in that case n is the average number of nodes per each cluster. The cluster heads has been identified as m_0, m_1, .. , $m_{m\text{-}1}$. The global token is assumed to traverse clockwise in the dynamic ring that is computed on-the-fly. Now, we will analyze the performance of the protocol under both, heavy load and light load conditions.

(i) *Heavily Loaded System*
Under heavy load condition, every node in all clusters is assumed to be hungry. Therefore, the total number of requesting node will be $m \times n$, which will generate $m \times n$ request messages. In order to serve these requests, the total number of global token messages generated will be m and the total number of local token messages generated will be $m \times n$. Therefore, total number of all types of messages will amount to $(m \times n) + m + (m \times n)$. Hence, the number of messages required to fulfill one request will be equal to $\{2(m \times n)+m\}/(m \times n)$ that is $(2+1/n)$. Hence, the message complexity under heavy load conditions would be $O(1/n)$. It is obvious that the message complexity is independent of m, the number of cluster heads. Here, it is worth noting that n is the (average) number of nodes per each cluster, not the total number of nodes in the system.

(ii) *Lightly Loaded System*
Under light load condition, it is assumed that no request is pending. For a newly generated request, the worst case situation occurs when the request is from cluster head m_1 and the global token is at cluster head m_2. In order to fulfill this request, the algorithm would generate one local token request message, one local token message and $(m\text{-}1)$ global token messages. Hence, in order to fulfill the request, the total number of required messages amounts to $(1+m)$. Thus, the message complexity under light load conditions would be $O(m)$. It is worth mentioning that, in strategic networks, the number of cluster heads $m << N$, where N is the total number of nodes in the system. Usually, in clustered VANETs, $m \leq \sqrt{N}$.

Synchronization Delay
After a site leaves the CS, it is the time required and before the next site enters the CS. It is a performance metric that has significance under high load condition. It is obvious from the message complexity analysis that there is a delay of only one message from a CS exit to next CS entry. Therefore, the synchronization delay would be T, where T is the propagation time of single message.

Response Time
The response time is important only for lightly loaded systems. It is the time interval a request waits for its CS execution to be over after its request messages have been sent out. The message complexity analysis show that the response time would be $(m + 1)T$, where m is the number of clusters and T is the propagation time of single message. Although, the value of m is constant, the response time depends on the current position of the global token because we have used token forwarding, rather than token asking, among the cluster heads. Thus, it is noteworthy that response time would amount to $(m + 1)T$ only in the worst case. In the best case, when the global token is received at the requesting node's cluster head immediately after receiving the CS request, the response time would boil down to $2T$ (*i.e.*, 1 request message + 1 local token message). Therefore, if we represent the response time as R, the following relation holds: $2T \leq R \leq (m + 1)T$.

8 The Fault Tolerance

The protocol provides limited fault tolerance within the cluster using over and over-out messages as follows. On exit CS, each node sends an over message to cluster head and forwards the local token LTQ to next hungry node. When cluster head receives over message from a node it makes entry, in the copy of LTQ that remains with the cluster head, corresponding to that node as 'served'. If local token is detected as lost in transit, the cluster head can regenerate it using this copy. As over message is the record of 'served' nodes, the newly generated local token would be made available only to nodes that are yet to be 'served' in the current round. However, this mechanism may lead to simultaneous availability of more than one local token within a cluster, thus, violating the mutual exclusion (safety). Nevertheless, the protocol has the provision to combat this situation as follows. Assume a cluster C that has cluster head CH. Now, say node N1, on exit CS, sends over message to CH and passes LTQ to N2. Afterwards, say LTQ message suffered excess delay and, thus, CH got timed out while waiting for the next over message. Hence, CH suspects the loss of LTQ and generates new local token, say LTQ'. However, it might so happen that LTQ is not lost and only it got delayed excessively. Now, there are three possible cases:

(i) LTQ' reached at N2 first. N2 will enter CS and, on exit CS discards LTQ received subsequently, if it bears the same round number as LTQ'.

(ii) LTQ and LTQ' both reached at N2 at the same time. N2 discards LTQ if it bears the same round number as LTQ' and subsequently enters CS.

(i) LTQ reached at N2 first. N2 will enter CS and, on exit CS discards LTQ' if it bears the same round number as LTQ.

9 Conclusion

To the best of our knowledge, the paper proposes first protocol to solve the problem of mutual exclusion in vehicular ad hoc networks (VANETs). In order to have advantage of both worlds, the protocol uses both, centralized and distributed schemes, at different levels. The centralized algorithms are efficient but fault prone. Therefore, the intra-cluster component, which uses centralized scheme, has been made fault tolerant. It improves robustness and makes it suitable for comparatively long running applications. The message complexity of the protocol is remarkable under heavy load as well as under light load conditions. The token asking schemes suffer synchronization delay when they are used in logical structures. Nevertheless, this loss has been largely compensated by our dual token based approach. The comparative analysis and experimental evaluation is part of our future work and it is being postponed for full paper.

References

1. Raynal, M.: A simple taxonomy for distributed mutual exclusion algorithms. ACM SIGOPS Operating Systems Review 25(2), 47–50 (1991)
2. Singhal, M.: A taxonomy for distributed mutual exclusion. Journal of Parallel and Distributed Computing 18, 94–101 (1993)

3. Saxena, P.C., Rai, J.: A survey of permission-based mutual exclusion algorithms. Journal of Computer Standards and Interface 25(2), 159–181 (2003)
4. Badrinath, B.R., Acharya, A., Imielinski, T.: Designing distributed algorithms for mobile computing networks. Computer Communications 19, 309–320 (1996)
5. Ghosh, R.K., Mohanty, H.: On restructuring distributed algorithms for mobile computing. In: Das, S.K., Bhattacharya, S. (eds.) IWDC 2002. LNCS, vol. 2571, pp. 224–233. Springer, Heidelberg (2002)
6. Benchaiba, M., et al.: Distributed mutual exclusion algorithms in mobile ad hoc networks: an overview. ACM SIGOPS Operating Systems Review 38(1), 74–89 (2004)
7. Sharma, B., et al.: DMX in MANETs: Major Research Trends Since 2004. In: Int. Conf. on Advances in Computing and Artificial Intelligence, ACAI 2011 (to appear, 2011)
8. Hartenstein, H., Laberteaux, K.P.: A tutorial survey on vehicular ad hoc networks. IEEE Communications Magazine, 164–171 (June 2008)
9. Nekoui, M., Pishro-Nik, H.: Fundamental tradeoffs in vehicular ad hoc networks. In: 7th ACM International Workshop on Vehicular Internetworking, VANET 2010, pp. 91–96 (2010)
10. Kumar, V., Place, J., Yang, G.-C.: An efficient algorithm for mutual exclusion using queue migration in computer networks. IEEE Trans. Knowledge and Data Engineering 3(3), 380–384 (1991)
11. Chaudhury, P., Edward, T.: An O(√n) distributed mutual exclusion algorithm using queue migration. Journal of Universal Computer Science 12(2), 142–159 (2006)
12. Baldoni, R., Virgillito, A., Petrassi, R.: A distributed mutual exclusion algorithm for mobile ad hoc networks. In: 7th IEEE Symposium on Computer and Communications (ISCC 2002), pp. 539–545 (July 2002)

Reliability Estimation of Mobile Agents for Service Discovery in MANET

Roshni Neogy, Chandreyee Chowdhury, and Sarmistha Neogy*

Jadavpur University
sarmisthaneogy@gmail.com

Abstract. Recently mobile agents are used to discover services in mobile ad-hoc network (MANET where agents travel through the network, collecting the dynamically changing service information. But no work addresses how reliable the agents are for this application. However reliability issues are needed to be addressed before mobile agents can be used for a broad range of commercial applications (including service discovery) in MANET. In this paper, we propose an algorithm for estimating the task route reliability of mobile agent systems (MAS), (deployed for discovering services) which are based on the conditions of the underlying wireless network and shows that reliability is almost independent of network size if the MANET provides sufficient bandwidth to support an appreciable no. of agents. Here we also estimate the optimum value of network bandwidth (needed to support the agents) for our application. However the reliability of MAS is highly dependent on link failure probability.

Keywords: Reliability, Mobile agents, Monte Carlo simulation, Mobile ad-hoc network.

1 Introduction

A mobile agent is a combination of software program and data which migrates from a site to another site to perform tasks assigned by a user according to a static or dynamic route [1]. It can be viewed as a distributed abstraction layer that provides the concepts and mechanisms for mobility and communication [2]. An agent consists of three components: the program which implements it, the execution state of the program and the data. An agent may migrate in two ways, namely, weak migration and strong migration [3]. The platform is the environment of execution. The platform makes it possible to create mobile agents; it offers the necessary elements required by them to perform their tasks such as execution, migration towards other platforms and so on.

Typical benefits of using mobile agents include bandwidth conservation, reduced latency, load balancing etc. The route of the mobile agent can be decided by its owner or it can decide its next hop destination on the fly. Here, we assume the underlying network to be a Mobile Ad Hoc Network (MANET) that typically undergoes constant

* Correponding author.

D. Nagamalai, E. Renault, and M. Dhanushkodi (Eds.): PDCTA 2011, CCIS 203, pp. 148–157, 2011.

topology changes, which disrupt the flow of information over the existing paths. Mobile agents are nowadays used in MANETs for various purposes like service discovery [4], network discovery, automatic network reconfiguration etc. But before mobile agent based applications become commercially available for MANET, reliability estimation of them is very essential. Because of motion and location independence [1], this environment itself introduces new aspects to reliability (in terms of continuity of correct service).

In [1, 5] we tried to address this issue. Here we have considered service discovery [4] agents and explored their reliability. Then we propose few modifications to the basic mechanism [4] in order to reflect the dynamicity of the underlying environment.

In the following section we discuss about the service discovery process using mobile agents in MANET. Then in section 3 state of art regarding this topic is mentioned. In section 4 our model is introduced that is designed to estimate reliability of the mobile agent based system (MAS). The next section (5) gives the experimental results followed by concluding remarks in section 6.

2 The Process of Service Discovery

A service can be regarded as any hard- or software resource, which can be used by other clients. Service discovery is the process of locating services in a network. The following methods are used to discover and maintain service data [6]:

- service providers flood the network with service advertisements;
- clients flood the network with discovery messages;
- nodes cache the service advertisements;
- nodes overhear in the network traffic and cache the interesting data.

The first one corresponds to passive discovery (push model) whereas the next one describes active discovery (pull model). The other two methods mentioned above are the consequences of the first two. While the push mechanism is quite expensive in terms of network bandwidth (in the context of MANET), the pull mechanism suffers from poor performance (longer response times). Moreover there are other factors to be taken into account such as the size of the network (no. of nodes), availability of a service (how frequently services appear and disappear in the network), and the rate of service requests. Traditionally static service brokers are used for sharing service information which is not suitable for MANET due to its inherent dynamic nature. So as in [4] mobile agents can be deployed for this purpose (looking for services offered) as the agents can migrate independently [7], behave intelligently [8] and can negotiate with other agents according to a well defined asynchronous protocol [9].

The service discovery protocol presented in [4] is taken to be the basis here. We first estimate the reliability of MAS where the agents are roaming around the underlying MANET, discovering various services provided by the nodes in MANET. To do this the algorithm [4] uses two types of agents – a static Stationery Agent (SA) and mobile Travel Agent (TA). The SAs are deployed on per node basis. On the contrary the TAs are deployed dynamically to collect and spread service information among the nodes in MANET. A TA prefers those nodes on its route which it has not yet visited but which are reachable via nodes it already knows. In order to enforce this

TA Route algorithm is proposed in [4] that determines the next target migration site of a TA. The SAs are responsible for controlling the no. of TAs roaming around the network. Thus depending on the incoming agent frequency (that is, no. of agents TA visiting a node is said to be incoming agent frequency) of TA, an SA can either create or terminate a TA.

3 Related Works

Reliability analysis of MAS in MANET is a complicated problem for which little attention has been paid. As pointed out in [10], features like scalability/reliability becomes critical in challenging environment with wireless networks. However these issues have been highlighted in [11] although the work does not focus on MANET and also does not take into account the specific task for which the agents are deployed. But this is very much important as route of an agent primarily depends on the purpose for which it is deployed. However, we could not find any work that considers estimation of reliability of service discovery agents for MANET but we found the following.

There are already some approaches for service discovery in MANETs. In [6] some device and service discovery protocols are discussed along with the issues in MANET. However the work does not provide a detailed concrete solution to the problem of service discovery though it suggests possible use of mobile agents in discovering services. In [12] an overlay structure is used to distribute service information. Here the network is divided into groups of nodes and nodes share service information among the group members. But in highly dynamic scenario this group formation can become an overhead. To reduce such overhead in [4] mobile agents are used. But this work does not take into consideration the movement of nodes before an agent finishes its job. Moreover this algorithm expects the network to retain the same connectivity pattern while an agent is roaming around.

Little attention has been given to the reliability analysis of MAS. In [13], two algorithms have been proposed for estimating the task route reliability of MAS. A third algorithm is also stated that is based on random walk generation. However, in both the works the agents are assumed to be independent and the planning strategy seemed to be static. So this work does not address the scenario where agents can change their routes dynamically. Moreover, it does not address the issue of node mobility in between agent migrations. In [1] a preliminary work has been done on estimating reliability of independent mobile agents roaming around the nodes of a MANET. The protocol considers independent agents only. Node and link failure due to mobility or other factors is predicted according to NHPP. An agent is allowed to migrate to any node with equal probability. This may not be realistic as some nodes may provide richer information for a particular agent deployed by some application. In [5] the MAS are assumed to be consisting of a no. of agent groups demanding for a minimum link capacity. In this scenario the reliability calculation shows that even with large no. of heterogeneous agent groups with differing demands of link capacity, the MAS gradually reached a steady state. Since the task given to an agent primarily controls its routes, it is an important aspect and must be considered while estimating reliability. But the nature of the task and hence the agent's movement pattern is not considered in any of these works.

4 Our Model

Though mobile agents (MA) are recently used in many applications of MANET including service discovery, dependability analysis of such applications is not much explored. In the present work agents used for service discovery are presented. So the agents will tend to migrate towards the crowded portion of MANET to collect and fast spread service information.

4.1 Problem Definition

In this paper, we assume that our MAS (S) at a time instant has m(t) independent agents (Travel Agents in [4]) that may move in the underlying MANET. Here m(t) indicates the fact that the no. of TAs varies with time as an SA can kill TAs [4]. The reliability of (S) is defined as the probability that (S) is operational during a period of time [2]. Later we define reliability of an individual agent in this context.

We model the underlying network as an undirected graph G= (V,E) where V is the set of mobile nodes and E is the set of edges among them. Let the network consist of N nodes, thus |V|=N that may or may not be connected via bidirectional links (e).

Depending on a given probability a link may either exist or not at a particular point of time. The node mobility can be simulated using non homogeneous Poisson distribution (NHPP) [25]. So, the link failure probability is calculated using NHPP. In NHPP the fixed rate parameter of Poisson distribution becomes a function of time. So the mean rate of node movement itself varies with time reflecting the dynamicity of MANET. Initial configuration would be assumed. Afterwards due to mobility few links may fail and still a few may be revived also according to NHPP considering the transient nature of the faults.

In this scenario we can think of an agent as a token visiting one node to another in the network (if the nodes are connected) based on the strategy listed as TA Route Algorithm in [4]. But node mobility in between agents' journey was not considered in [4]. So we have made necessary modifications to make the service discovery process more suited to the dynamics of MANET. A TA starts its journey from an owner (where it is created by SA) and moves from one node to another according to the TA route Algorithm [4]. But this movement is successful if the two nodes are connected and there is no simultaneous transmission in the neighborhood of the intended destination (taken care of by the MAC protocol). So, we associate a probability with the movement to indicate transient characteristics of the environment, since, for example, the routing table may not be updated properly or the link quality may have degraded so much (due to increased noise level) that the agents are unable to migrate. Thus, if an agent residing at node A decides to move to node B (connected to A) then the agent successfully moves to B with probability p_t. Here p_t denotes the problem of unpredictability mentioned above. For example, noise level may increase due to heavy rainfall. If at any time an agent finds all unvisited nodes to be unreachable, the agent waits and then retries. This step tolerates the transient faults (temporary link failure) as an agent retries after some delay and hence improves system performance. This is not considered in [4] but to make the service discovery process more suitable to the MANET dynamicity, transient fault tolerance becomes a necessity.

In this scenario we study the reliability of MAS (consisting of the TAs) with respect to the network status and its conditions (for example connectivity of the links, path loss probability etc.). Each agent is expected to visit all operating nodes in MANET in order to collect and spread service information. We have taken the failure probability (P) of the mobile nodes (P_{Node}) to be a variable of Weibull distribution [5].

Now reliability of MAS (R_s) can be defined as

$$R_s = \{R_{MAS} | R_{MANET}\} \tag{1}$$

Here reliability of MANET (R_{MANET}) can be treated as an accumulative factor of (1-P_{Node}) and P_{Link}. P_{Link} can be treated as a combination of P (p_r is at an acceptable level)and the mobility model. Here p_r denotes the received power at node j after traversing distance d_{ij} from sender node i. Here we calculate individual agent reliability on the underlying MANET as follows:

If an agent can successfully visit M nodes out of N(desired) then it has accomplished M/N portion of its task. Thus reliability in this case will be M/N.

But if the application requires all N nodes to be visited to complete the task and in all other cases the task will not be considered to be done, the calculation will be modified as:

If an agent can successfully visit all N nodes desired then it has accomplished its task. Thus reliability in this case will be 1. In all other cases it will be 0.

Above definitions of agent reliability works only if there is no software failure of the agent (assumed to follow Weibull distribution [5]).

Now, the probability that the MAS is operational i.e., reliability of MAS (R_{MAS}) can be calculated as the mean of reliability of all its components, that is, the agents in this system. Clearly it is function (m(t)) of time as the total no. of TAs present varies with time

$$R_{MAS}(t) = \frac{\sum\{AgentReliabilities\}}{m(t)} \tag{2}$$

Finally to calculate R_s in equation 1 an algorithm is proposed in the next section.

4.2 Detailed Steps of Reliability Estimation

1) Input parameters: M (initial no. of TAs in the system), the initial state of the network (node position, location, speed of the nodes)

2) Detailed Steps:

The TA determines its next target according to the following algorithm.

TA_Route_Mod()

1 First the travel agent tries to find yet unvisited nodes, which are common neighbors of previously visited nodes. These common neighbor nodes have highest priority because their services can be used directly by more than one node.

2 If all such common neighbors have been visited then the agents will next visit the nodes not visited yet. If there are more than one unvisited neighbors, the mobile agent can choose to visit any one of them.

3 If there are no unvisited nodes in direct range of a mobile agent then a node with unvisited neighbors is revisited. If there are two such potential nodes, the node with the lowest RSN is chosen.
4 If the first three conditions fail, the node with the lowest RSN becomes the node visited next.

Node mobility is considered here and is detailed in the following algorithm. As such the agent's decision in choosing the next destination depends on the currently reachable set of nodes. Here we are hoping that at short time intervals the network topology will not show huge changes so as to render the common neighboring nodes absolutely disconnected or be reduced to a node with very few neighbors (less than the number of nodes which influence the MA's decision to grant it the highest priority).

Reliability_Calculation()

1. Initialize n (that is the no. of mobile nodes successfully visited by an agent) to 0 and a source for the mobile agent.
2. Input network configuration (V, E) in the form of an edge list.
3. i. To simulate the effect of node mobility create E', a subset of VXV with the same V using NHPP (or uniform distribution can also be used) distribution. Likewise a probability p_i is associated with each link e_i. This probability is calculated using NHPP. If this falls within the range [p,1] for $0<p<1$ then e_i is assumed to be operating. Otherwise it will be deleted from E assuming e_i to be failed.
   ii. Some nodes may also fail because of software/hardware failure or become disconnected from the network according to another NHPP (or uniform) distribution. Node failure can be simulated by deleting the edges e from E' further that are incident on the failed node $v \in V$.
4. According to Weibull distribution we find individual software reliability r_i for an agent i.
5. BFS is used unless all connected subgraphs are assigned a proper cluster id. Thus, an isolated node is also a cluster.
6. The agents perform their job on this modified graph according to *TA_Route_Mod()*.
7. Repeat step 6 for all agents (m(t)) in the system.
8. Repeat steps 3 to 7 until all nodes are visited or the new destination falls in a different cluster.
9. Calculate $\lambda_i(t) = \dfrac{n}{N}$ (3)

   Here the value of n depends heavily on the conditions of the underlying network.
10. Reset the value of n.
11. Calculate $\lambda(t) = \dfrac{1}{k}\sum_{i=1}^{k} \lambda_i(t) r_i$ (4)
12. Repeat steps 3 to 11 Q (simulation steps) times.
13. Calculate node reliability $\dfrac{1}{Q}\sum_{q=1}^{Q} \lambda(q,t)$ (5)

It is to be noted that step 3 is repeated for every move of the agent to take care of network dynamicity. If an agent fails to move because of background noise level, then it may retry depending on the amount of delay that the respective application can tolerate.

5 Results

The simulation is carried out in java and can run in any platform. The initial positions of MAs and the initial network configuration are read from a file. The default values of parameters are listed in table-1. Unless otherwise stated, the parameters always take these default values. First we site an example and show the data generated by our simulation program and then the detailed analysis of simulation results are shown.

Table 1. Default values for simulation parameters

Parameter Name	Value	Parameter Name	Value
Number of nodes(N)	25	Maximum Agent Frequency tolerated	20
Number of agents(M)	20	Link Failure Probability	0.1
Number of simulations(Q)	100	Time for each simulation run	750min

In our example five nodes are taken to form a network. Every ($\Delta t =$) 3 seconds the positions of the nodes and hence the connectivity graph is updated according to NHPP. Five mobile agents are deployed by the five different owners (nodes) and they start their journey from their owners. Thus agents 0, 1, 2, 3 and 4 start their journey from nodes MN_0, MN_1, MN_2, MN_3 and MN_4 respectively and roam around the network to accomplish its task. Our job is to find the no. of nodes that are successfully visited by these agents which indicates how many services the agent discovers and how far it spreads discovered service information in the MANET and consequently the reliability of the agents will be calculated. Average reliability of all agents taken over a certain time period for a no. of simulations represents the reliability of the MAS despite the uncertainties of MANET. Our migration policy is adopted from [4] indicating the fact that all reachable destinations may not be equally likely. As shown in figure 1(a), at time instant $t=t_0$ agents 0, 1 and 3 are stuck at their owners however agents 2 and 4 move to their respective neighbors. Thus after Δt time interval, agents 2 and 4 can be found at MN_4 and MN_2 respectively. In the next time instant agents 0, 1 and 2 discover services provided by MN_1 and MN_0 (figure 1(b)). But agent 2 and agent 4 do not migrate as they have already visited MN_2 and MN_4 respectively. In the next time instant the connectivity graph changes (figure 1(c)) significantly enabling the agents discover more services. In the next time instant the nodes become sparse. Only agent 3 makes a successful migration. Thus as the simulation ends, only agent 3 is found to visit 4 nodes successfully thus covering (4/5) portion of its task. All other agents seem to have completed only (3/5) of their task. Thus the resulting reliability comes out to be $[(3/5)*4 + (4/5)]/5=0.64$. So it can be concluded that in a MANET where the link failure probability is as high as 0.4 and the nodes can accept maximum 5 service discovery agents within a specified time (that is, incoming frequency), an agent on an average is able to cover 64% of the network.

In reality network dynamicity affects agent migration and hence the reliability of MAS is found to depend heavily on its size (no. of agents) particularly for bigger MANETs. This fact is shown in figure 2. This graph is taken for two different scenarios. In one of them, each node can receive maximum (maximum tolerated frequency) 20 agents (white columns), additional agents would get killed resulting in a drop in agent reliability. For the other one, the maximum tolerated frequency is kept at 15. For M (<=15) as far as the underlying MANET remains connected, all agents will be able to complete their job if there is no software failure in them as shown in figure. But if M is increased any further, then agent reliability drops as it exceeds the maximum tolerated agent frequency. Higher the no. of agents tolerated in the network greater will be the overall agent reliability. This justifies the left side of the graph in figure 2.

Every MANET has a bandwidth limitation that in turn restricts the maximum value of M during a period. Thus, we observe that there is a maximum incoming agent frequency supported by a node (figure 3). Higher value of this indicates greater bandwidth provided by MANET. So as expected, with higher bandwidth our MAS become more reliable. But it can be observed that with M=20 when the incoming agent frequency reaches above 16, the MAS reaches an almost steady state with overall reliability of (around) 0.98. This gives the optimum value of bandwidth to be provided by MANET for this scenario.

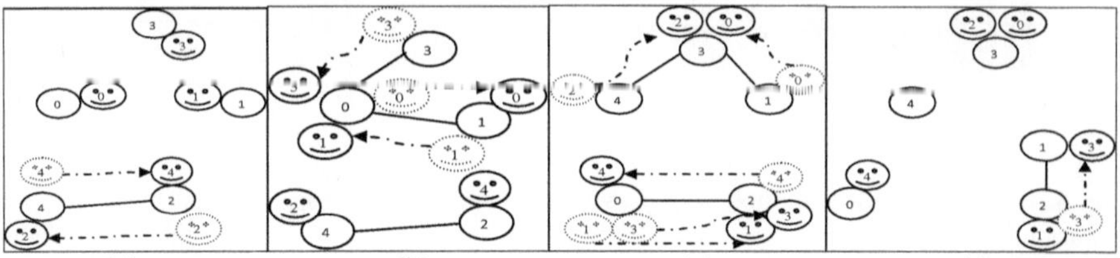

(a) (b) (c) (d)

Fig. 1. (a) MANET configuration along with agent migration route at $t=t_0$
(b)MANET configuration along with agent migration route at $t=(t+\Delta t)$
(c) MANET configuration along with agent migration route at $t=(t+2\Delta t)$
(d) MANET configuration along with agent migration route at $t=(t+3\Delta t)$

Now if N is increased, the overall reliability does not change appreciably as long as M (<=30) is comparable to the agent frequency (=20) supported by the nodes (see figure 4). Thus our approach is found to be scalable for MANETs as big as 40 nodes. But for large M (>30), nodes may kill some agents resulting in a drop in reliability for N>32. But this result indicates the scalability of the service discovery approach for crowded MANET as change in network size does not appreciably affect the reliability of MAS.

Now stability of the solution is studied. As time increases, more agents will be able to tolerate transient link failures and thus the chance to discover and spread service information is higher resulting in improvement of reliability. But the graph in figure 5 also indicates an optimum point (=750 min onwards) after which the system reaches a steady state for our configuration (table I). This figure also indicates that in absence of software fault at the agents MAS reliability may approach the ideal case (=1).

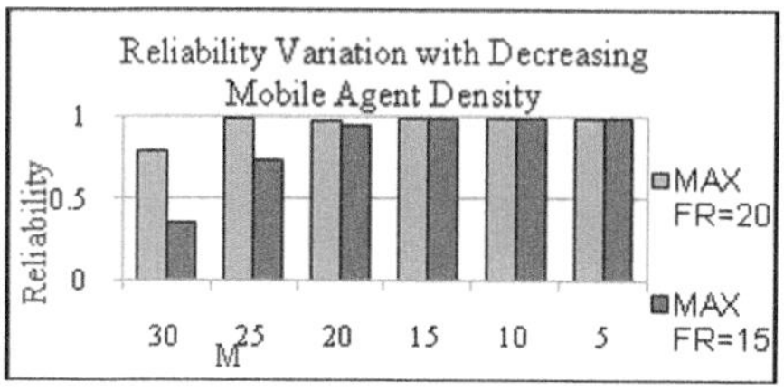

Fig. 2. Reliability variation with no. of agents(M)

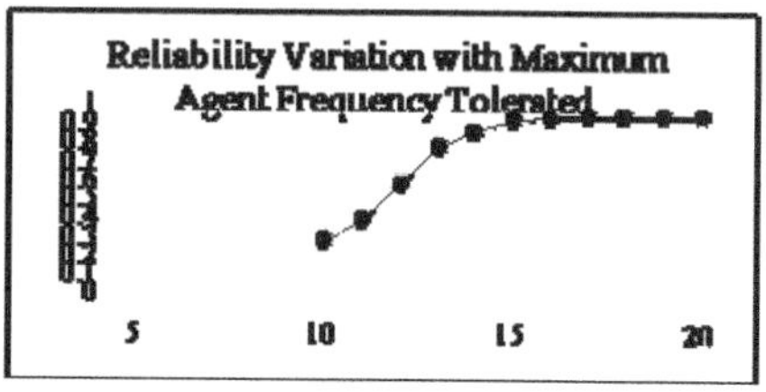

Fig. 3. Reliability variation with varying tolerance limit on accepted agent frequency

The link failure probability also affects reliability of the agents. As more links fail, the network becomes partitioned resulting in a sharp fall in MAS reliability (see figure 6). It can be observed that when the link failure probability reaches above 0.5, the network graph loses connectivity as some agents may never reach the nodes residing in another component of the network.

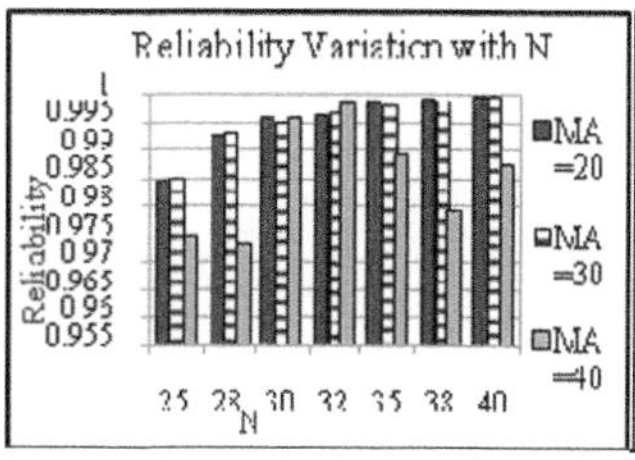

Fig. 4. Reliability with Variation of varying no. of nodes

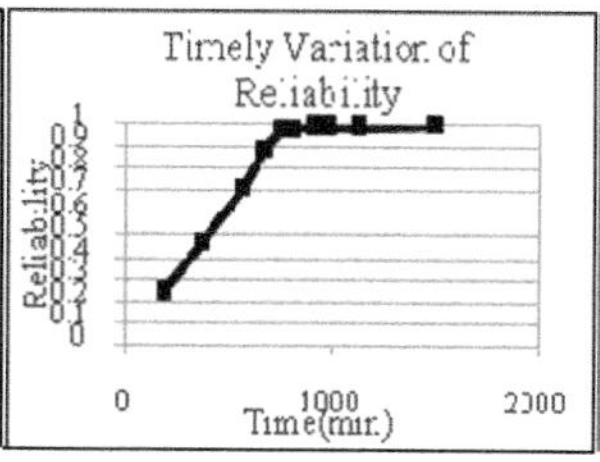

Fig. 5. Variation of reliability with time

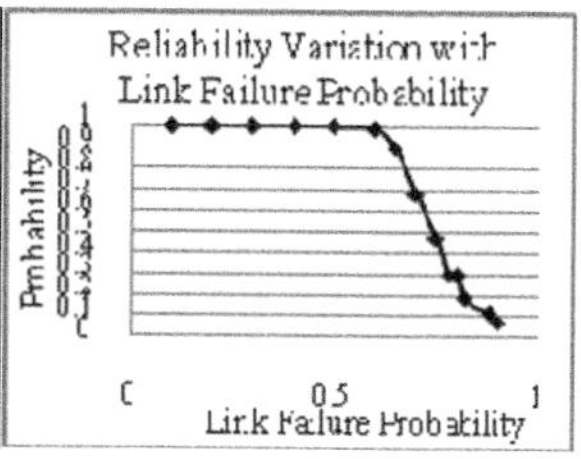

Fig. 6. Reliability variation with varying link failure probability

6 Conclusion

In this paper, a scalable approach to estimate the reliability of MAS for MANET is presented. The agents are deployed for collecting and spreading service information in the network. The reliability is found to depend heavily on MANET dynamics and supported network bandwidth. However our approach is found to be scalable for bigger MANETs too. The agents choose their destination on route according to a service discovery algorithm based on [4]. During the time an agent is visiting a node, the underlying network may change according to NHPP.

The protocol is validated and results are shown in section 5. As can be seen, reliability improves heavily if the network supports higher no. of agents. Moreover if the agents are allowed to roam around the network for sufficient amount of time, reliability improves in spite of node mobility. Hence as per expectation, this modified model works well in an efficient manner regardless of the changes in the network topology. The results of the simulation also corroborated our expectation. Our future work may include multiagent communication to make the process of service discovery even more reliable and efficient.

References

[1] Chowdhury, C., Neogy, S.: Estimating Reliability of Mobile Agent System for Mobile Ad hoc Networks. In: Proc. 3rd International Conference on Dependability, pp. 45–50 (2010)

[2] Cao, J., Feng, X., Lu, J., Das, S.K.: Mailbox-Based Scheme for Designing Mobile Agent Communications. Computer 35(9), 54–60 (2002)

[3] Migas, N., Buchanan, W.J., McArtney, K.: Migration of mobile agents in ad-hoc, Wireless Networks. In: Proc.11th IEEE International Conference and Workshop on the Engineering of Computer-Based Systems, pp. 530–535 (2004)

[4] Meier, R.T., Dunkel, J., Kakuda, Y., Ohta, T.: Mobile agents for service discovery in ad hoc networks. In: Proc. 22nd International Conference on Advanced Information Networking and Applications, pp. 114–121 (2008)

[5] Chowdhury, C., Neogy, S.: Reliability Estimate of Mobile Agent Based System for QoS MANET Applications. In: The Annual Reliability and Availability Symposium, pp. 1–6 (2011)

[6] Albert, J., Chaumette, S.: Device and Service Discovery in Mobile Ad-hoc Networks, Technical report, Master 2 SDRP, Université, Bordeaux 1 (January 16, 2007)

[7] Wooldridge, M., Jennings, N.R.: Intelligent agents - theory and practice. Knowledge Engineering Review 10(2), 115–152 (1995)

[8] Ossowski, S., Omicini, A.: Coordination Knowledge Engineering. Knowledge Engineering Review 10(2), 115–152 (2002)

[9] Dunkel, J., Bruns, R.: Software Architecture of Advisory Systems Using Agent and Semantic Web Technologies. In: Proceedings of the IEEE/ACM International Conference on Web Intelligence, Compiégne, France, pp. 418–421. IEEE Computer Society, Los Alamitos (2005)

[10] Urra, O., Ilarri, S., Mena, E.: Agents jumping in the air:dream or reality. In: Cabestany, J., Sandoval, F., Prieto, A., Corchado, J.M. (eds.) IWANN 2009. LNCS, vol. 5517, pp. 627–634. Springer, Heidelberg (2009)

[11] Ilarri, S., Trillo, R., Mena, E.: SPRINGS: A scalable platform for highly mobile agents in distributed computing environments. In: 4th International WoWMoM 2006 Workshop on Mobile Distributed Computing (MDC 2006), pp. 633–637. IEEE, Los Alamitos (2006)

[12] Klein, M., Konig-Ries, B., Obreiter, P.: Lanes – A Lightweight Overlay for Service Discovery in Mobile Ad Hoc Networks. In: Proc. of the 3rd IEEE Workshop on Applications and Services in Wireless Networks, ASWN 2003 (2003)

[13] Daoud, M., Mahmoud, Q.H.: Monte Carlo simulation-based algorithms for estimating the reliability of mobile agent-based systems. Journal of Network and Computer Applications, 19–31 (2008)

Mobile Agent Security in MANET Using Reputation

Chandreyee Chowdhury and Sarmistha Neogy

Dept. of Computer Science and Engineering
Jadavpur University
sarmisthaneogy@gmail.com

Abstract. The emerging trend of using mobile agents for mobile adhoc network (MANET) applications intensifies the need for protecting them. Here we propose a distributed trust based framework to protect both the agents and the host platforms (running at the nodes). This paper develops a distributed reputation model of MANET using concepts from Dempster-Shafer theory. The agents and the host platforms work together so that each trusted node may form a consistent trust view of MANET. An agent may share its view of the network with a visited host. To speed up convergence, a node broadcasts information regarding a suspected node. Thus an inactive node, without deploying agents may also get a partial view of the network. The agents use combination of encryption and digital signature to provide privacy and authentication services. Node mobility and the effect of environmental noise are considered. The results show the robustness of our proposed scheme.

Keywords: Mobile Agent, Security, Digital Signature, Trust, Mobility Model, Dempster–Shafer Belief Theory.

1 Introduction

Nowadays mobile agents are used for various kinds of networked applications like service discovery, network discovery, automatic network reconfiguration etc. where the agents roam in the network and consequently get the task done. But securing agents is a big concern particularly when the underlying network is (Mobile AdHoc Network) MANET that typically undergoes continuous topology changes. Applying cryptographic functions [1] are not sufficient rather if we can prevent an agent from visiting a malicious node most of the risk factors are covered. To enforce, we use the concept of trust that has received considerable attention in information security literature. In a way, trust and security are two sides of the same coin, because if a system is secure, it is trusted, and if it is trusted, then it must be secure and vice-versa [2].

This observation leads us to consider security as a property of a system in a given environment, and trust as a subjective belief resulting from assessing a system and its environment. As in [1] we define trust as a subjective quantified predictor of the expected future behavior of a trustee according to a specific agreement elicited from the outcomes of the previous interactions, both from direct experiences and indirect experiences. Reputation of an individual host refers to certain characteristics related to its trustworthiness. In a mobile agent system reputation can be obtained from

D. Nagamalai, E. Renault, and M. Dhanushkodi (Eds.): PDCTA 2011, CCIS 203, pp. 158–168, 2011.

agent's interaction feedbacks about a visited host's performance in fulfilling its obligations. Indirect experiences can also be considered which is gathered from other trustworthy nodes. Thus agents are encouraged to behave in a cooperative manner so that from their feedbacks, the malicious hosts can be easily and efficiently identified.

In this paper we describe a trust based framework for mobile agent based system(MAS) in a dynamic and hostile MANET environment. This paper shows how the agents' feedbacks (direct experiences) and node dynamicity help the hosts to converge to a consistent view of the trustworthy nodes in the network. This point onwards, the terms node and host are used interchangeably unless otherwise stated.

Additionally, in order to speed up convergence, once the node/s identified a host to be malicious (via the agent/s deployed by it/them), it will broadcast this information (indirect experience) to others. But a receiver will respond to this message promptly if it knows quite well without any uncertainty the sender to be trusted. Thus our definition of trust may range from complete belief to complete disbelief to full uncertainty as well. The following section (2) describes the design of our reputation system. In section 3, state of the art regarding this area of research is elaborated. The next section illustrates the way we model MAS on MANET detect a malicious agent and/or platform (depending on trust level defined later) in a distributed way (using the reputation system designed in section 2). Section 5 gives the experimental results to show the robustness of our scheme followed by concluding remarks (in section 6).

2 Trust Model

A reputation system [3] represents a promising method for fostering trust among complete strangers and for helping each individual to adjust or update its degree of trust towards its corresponding interaction partner and thereby reduce uncertainty. In general, threats found in a reputation system are Strategic rater [4], Strategically malicious visited host [3] that can be addressed by taking opinions from the agents and peers.

Due to the inherent distributed nature of MANET nodes can only have imperfect knowledge about others. Thus it is impossible to know with certainty whether a host is malicious or not; but we can only have an opinion about it, which translates into degrees of belief (how much the host is trustworthy) or disbelief (how much the host is suspicious) as well as uncertainty in case both belief and disbelief are lacking. We express this mathematically [5] as:

$$b+d+u=1 \tag{1}$$

Here b, d, u designate belief, disbelief and uncertainty respectively.

The design of our reputation system is shown in figure 1. It focuses on how to exploit the collected information to quantify the reputation of a node so that an agent can be prevented from migrating to a malicious node. The parameters (b, d and u) are updated from direct and indirect observations. Additionally an aging factor is added for the indirect observation part as dynamicity of MANET may reduce the significance of a message broadcast with time (figure 1).

2.1 Direct Observation

A portion of agent code is meant for computing hashcode(i.e., hashcode computation algorithm) of itself along with data. This part is signed by the agent's owner since the algorithm for hashcode computation is not expected to be changed en-route. Moreover this is also encrypted using public key cryptography in order to hide it in transit. Thus each agent carries the following

$ENCRYPT_{public\_key}$[$SIGNATURE_{owner}$(code for hashcode computation + private key of agent)] + application code + data

We encrypt the private key of the agent so that the agent can detect any attempt to break this ciphertext even if the encryption technique is not foolproof. Here application code refers to the purpose for which it is deployed by its owner. Upon reaching a host site an agent takes its own hash code to check if it is attacked in transit or by the current site. Once authenticated it executes the application code and updates the results in its data. Then takes a new hashcode and replaces the old one. If in the mean time the agent finds anything suspicious, it marks that and returns back to its owner. Otherwise the agent moves to a new host site according to the task given. In the end, every agent shares its experience with the owner. Thus we assume that an agent eventually finds its owner whenever it needs. Here we take Beta(α,β) distribution as in [5].α_{ij} represents the no. of good transactions between the agents deployed by $owner_i$and $node_j$. Thus for each positive feedback from agents, $\alpha_{ij}$is incremented. Otherwise β_{ij} is incremented. But β_{ij} may not reflect the exact scenario as an agent may be attacked in transit but it will be able to detect it only when it reaches at a host site and checks its own hash code. Also a node may act as a good host site for an agent (for some time) and behave maliciously to others (later on). Thus there is an uncertainty associated with the agent's observation. To deal with such issue, an approach proposed in [5], leveraging on the Dempster–Shafer Belief Theory [6] is adopted here to quantify the uncertainty of some random variables. Thus the uncertainty in predicting the nature of $node_j$ by $node_i$ is [7]:

$$u_{ij} = \frac{12 * \alpha_{ij} * \beta_{ij}}{(\alpha_{ij} + \beta_{ij})^2 * (1 + \alpha_{ij} + \beta_{ij})} \tag{2}$$

Now if $agent_k$'s observation about $node_j$ is $p_j^{k,}$ then α_{ij} is updated as follows

$$\alpha_{ij(new)} = \omega * \alpha_{ij(old)} + (1 - \omega) * p_j^k \tag{3}$$

Here weighted average is taken, where ω (0<ω<1) represents our absolute trust on each agent's observation as this observation may change from time to time taking care of network dynamicity. Also a malicious host may behave rationally for some time to gain trust from its peers. To tackle this part ω should be close to 1. Again ω behaves as the aging factor for values to close to 0. However if an $agent_k$ deployed by $owner_i$ retracts because it has visited a suspicious host site ($node_j$) then $\beta_{ij}$is updated in a similar way as

$$\beta_{ij(new)} = \omega * \beta_{ij(old)} + (1 - \omega) * p_j^k \tag{4}$$

An agent while visiting a host site may also share is experience with the host. This will also be considered as direct experience. However lesser importance will be given to this agent's observation (p_j^k) so as to protect the host from misleading observations given by suspicious agents. In essence, (1-ω) should be small, for visiting agents.

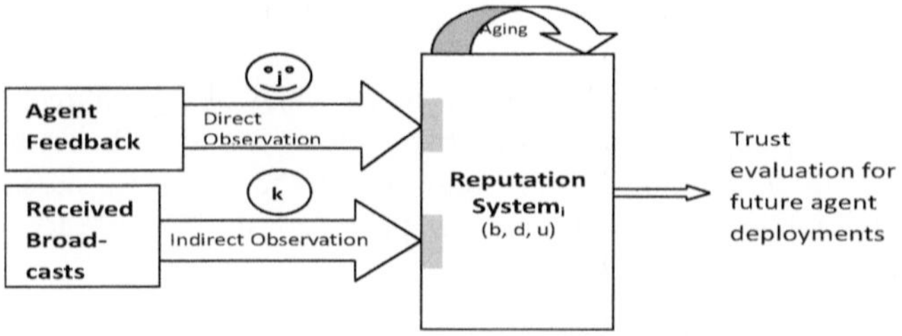

Fig. 1. Trust evaluation framework at hosts taking direct feedbacks from agent$_j$ and indirect observation from node$_k$

Now these values of α_{ij} and β_{ij} are fed to the reputation system that maps these to a tuple (b_{ij}, d_{ij}, u_{ij}). Here u_{ij} is calculated using eqn 2. Consequently following eqn 1, the total certainty (= ($1-u_{ij}$)) is divided into b_{ij} and d_{ij} according to their proportion of supporting evidence as follows [5]:

$$b_{ij} = \frac{\propto_{ij}}{\propto_{ij}+\beta_{ij}}\left(1 - u_{ij}\right) \tag{5}$$

$$d_{ij} = \frac{\beta_{ij}}{\propto_{ij}+\beta_{ij}}\left(1 - u_{ij}\right) \tag{6}$$

Here b_{ij} gives node$_i$'s belief in node$_j$'s behavior as safe host site for agents deployed by node$_i$. Similarly d_{ij} indicates node$_i$'s disbelief and u_{ij} reflects node$_i$'s uncertainty of predicting node$_j$ as a safe host site for its agents.

In this way with the help of Dempster–Shafer Belief Theory [6] uncertainty can be significantly reduced even though perfect accuracy could not be achieved.

2.2 Indirect Observation

For faster convergence of trust the nodes share information among each other. Upon finding a node to be suspicious, each node broadcasts a message to all nodes in the network to inform about that (suspicious) node. A node is suspected if its $b<u<d$. This information indirectly influences a node's view of the network. The influence is indirect as the sender of the broadcast message may not be a trusted node at all. Thus to prevent a malicious node from influencing others through malicious broadcasts, receivers update their views depending on their belief on sender of the received broadcast massage. The broadcast message has the following format (shown in figure 2). Here (b,d,u) is the tuple obtained from final observation of the sender about the suspicious node. Obviously b will be closer to 0 and d and/or u will be close to 1. The duration field stops this message from hopping in the network infinitely, by making it invalid once duration elapses. This second-hand information helps a node to cope with long delays and frequent network partitions.

Sender id	Code indicating message broadcast	(b,d,u) of the sender about the suspicious node	Duration

Fig. 2. Format of broadcast message

Let $b_l^{i:j}$ represents belief (b) of $node_i$ on $node_l$ while taking indirect observation from $node_j$. So this parameter depends on two factors-(i) $node_i$'s belief on $node_j$ and (ii) $node_j$'s final observation on $node_l$ as indicated in the broadcast message received by $node_i$. Thus following the approaches proposed in [5] ($b_l^{i:j}$,$d_l^{i:j}$,$u_l^{i:j}$) can be formulated as

$$b_l^{i:j} = b_j^i \times b_l^j \tag{7}$$

$$d_l^{i:j} = b_j^i \times d_l^j \tag{8}$$

$$u_l^{i:j} = b_j^i \times u_l^j + d_j^i + u_j^i \tag{9}$$

It can be noted that $node_i$'s disbelief in $node_j$'s observation becomes an uncertainty for predicting $node_l$. Also $node_i$'s uncertainty on $node_j$ amounts to the uncertainty of $node_i$ in predicting $node_l$'s future behavior. Thus a node predicts about the future behavior of a node taking indirect feedbacks from all broadcasts that it has received in the last time interval (Δt) and updates its view (b, d, u) as follows [5]

$$b_{i:l} = \sum_{k\in S} \frac{b_l^{i:k}}{|S|} \tag{10}$$

$$d_{i:l} = \sum_{k\in S} \frac{d_l^{i:k}}{|S|} \tag{11}$$

$$u_{i:l} = \sum_{k\in S} \frac{b_k^i \times u_l^k + d_k^i + u_k^i}{|S|} \tag{12}$$

Here $b_{i:l}$ represents the indirect belief of $node_i$ about $node_k$. S denotes the set of nodes that sent message broadcasts (that $node_i$ received) in the last time interval.

2.3 Combining Direct and Indirect Observation

After collecting first-hand information from the agents and second-hand information from broadcast messages, a node attempts to integrate them all to come to a unified conclusion about future behavior of the nodes. Thus the comprehensive belief ($b_j^{i(f)}$), disbelief ($d_j^{i(f)}$) and uncertainty ($u_j^{i(f)}$) of $node_i$ on $node_j$ are derived from the following eqns, as in [5]

$$b_j^{i(f)} = \varphi_1 \times b_{ij} + \varphi_2 \times b_{i:j} \tag{13}$$

$$d_j^{i(f)} = \varphi_1 \times d_{ij} + \varphi_2 \times d_{i:j} \tag{14}$$

$$u_j^{i(f)} = 1 - b_j^{i(f)} - d_j^{i(f)} \tag{15}$$

Where

$$\varphi_1 = \frac{\gamma \times u_{i:j}}{(1-\gamma)\times u_{ij}+\gamma\times u_{i:j}-0.5\times u_{ij}\times u_{i:j}} \quad (16)$$

$$\varphi_2 = \frac{(1-\gamma)\times u_{ij}}{(1-\gamma)\times u_{ij}+\gamma\times u_{i:j}-0.5\times u_{ij}\times u_{i:j}} \quad (17)$$

Here γ ($0<\gamma<1$) indicates a node's confidence on the agents it deployed. Larger values of γ (>0.5) means a node tends to trust its agents whereas smaller values (<0.5) indicates that a node tends to trustothers' recommendations. Now trust can be quantified from the comprehensive belief, disbelief and uncertainty as [2][7]

$$T_{ij} = b_j^{i(f)} + \sigma \times u_j^{i(f)} \quad (18)$$

Here σ gives relative atomicity based on the principle of indifference. Here the possibility that an agent's visit to a host will be safe or unsafe indicates two mutually exclusive and collectively exhaustive states. The principle of indifference states that if all (say n) possibilities are indistinguishable except for their names, then each possibility should be assigned a probability equal to 1/n. Thus here σ could be 0.5. Among the total uncertainty associated with an agent's visit, there is a 50% chance that the agent will be safe. But we can tune this parameter more accurately in a sense that for higher values of disbelief, there is a possibility that $\sigma<0.5$ and vice versa.

Consequently depending on the trust values calculated from eqn 18 and the safety requirement of the applications (running at the nodes) that deploys agents, an owner decides an agent's task route or asks it to avoid suspicious host sites.

3 Related Works

This section summarizes the literature related to trust management schemes in MANETs and mobile agent based systems.

Trust-based data routing has been extensively studied in wireless networks including MANETs [5], [7]. The basic framework of a Trust Management System (TMS) includes a Reputation System (RS) and a Watchdog like the one in figure 1. The watchdogs normally monitor the event of data forwarding and counts the arrival of ACKs corresponding to data sent out/forwarded. To cope with mobility, in [7] multiple feedbacks are compressed together. But using mobile agents for this purpose will yield far better results as agents are designed to cope with frequent disconnections and limited bandwidth that characterizes MANET especially delay tolerant networks [7]. In [5] it is shown that mobility increases the chance of direct interaction with a node.

Trust management system for mobile agents is also well studied [1] in literature. In [8] a distributed reputation management model is proposed that is based on Dempster-Shafer theory of evidence. A trust model is described in [9] for MAS that considers the information provided from several sources (interaction trust, witness reputation, role based trust and certified reputation). It also uses Dempster-Shafer theory of evidence. In [1] a reputation-based trust model is proposed for mobile agents. Bayesian Network based trust computing is used for strategically malicious trustee prevention.

But these works are not focused on MANET and so the effect of dynamic topology changes, noisy environments, and more importantly mobility are not considered in these works. Thus, securing mobile agents and nodes in MANET by using the notion of trust is a comparatively new research paradigm.

4 Our Work

In this paper, we define our MAS (S) to be consisting of M independent agents deployed by k owners that may move in the underlying MANET. To describe our model we will take help of the following abstraction of an Ad hoc network. Here we try to protect mobile agents and prevent trusted nodes from sending agents to malicious ones. We assume the compromised nodes can send malicious agents to mislead a node about its trust level.

In our previous works [10] we have described our model of MANET, which is also adopted here. The mobility of nodes in MANET can be simulated using smooth random mobility model (SRMM) [11]. (x_i,y_i) represent location of $node_i$ at an instant according to SRMM. Now the average received power (p_r) is a function of the distance between the transmitter and the receiver. Here we take the two-ray model for radio propagation in order to show how the transmitted signal with power (p_t) suffers from multipath propagation while reaching the receiving end.

In this scenario we can think of a mobile agent as a token visiting one node to another in the network (if the nodes are connected) based on some strategy as needed by the underlying applications to accomplish its task. Mobile agents are deployed for various purposes like service discovery [12]. Thus an agent starts its journey from a given owner and moves from one node to another depending on a *Priority list* as explained below.

The following data structures are needed Priority_list of agent j: node_id and trust_level(unvisited 0; suspected -1; trusted +1)

(α, β): positive integers to be kept at node Default trust level : TS (> k)

Trust level view at $node_i$:(Trust $level_1$, Trust $level_2$, Trust $level_3$,...................$)_I$ where trust $level_1$ represents the trust value assigned to node id=1 by $node_i$ according to eqn 18.

Initially the priority lists (PL) of all agents have 0 trust level for all nodes. Accordingly $node_i$'s view of the network will be $(TS,TS,......)_i$.

The workflow can be divided into two parts: (i) Computation/Action in mobile node and (ii) functions of the agents. Algorithm I gives the function of the agents that helps to collect first hand information. Then algorithm II running at the nodes takes its input from algorithm I and any broadcast message received by the node to update the distributed trust model and hence the node's trust level view of the network. Steps followed by each agent

Algorithm – I: *Agent_code()*

1. While task given to the agent is not completed
   1.1. Move to an agent site (MN) (unvisited) according to the PL provided.

1.2. If that destination falls in the same cluster as it is now residing, the agent moves to the new destination with probability p
1.3. Before processing, take hashcode of the agent's own code and data.
1.4. If the hashcode matches with the one stored in a *secured way*(see section 2.1) in the agent's data, then
1.4.1. Gather information needed by the application that deployed this agent.
1.4.2. Update the computed results.
1.4.3. Compute hashcode of the code and data and store it in a secured way.
1.4.4. Share status of the PL with this trusted node.
1.5. Go to step 2.//inference: most likely agent's visit was not safe
2. Retract back to the owner.
3. Stop.

Steps followed by every mobile node (host platform)

Algorithm – II: *MN_code()*

1. Input network configurations.
2. For $t=t_0$ to T repeat the following.
2.1. Some nodes may also fail because of software/hardware failure according to Weibull distribution. If a node fails then go to step 3.
2.2. Nodes move according to SRMM and received signal power(P_r) is calculated according to Two ray propagation model as in [10]
2.3. If an agent comes to this site/node (MN_j)
2.3.1. If the agent is found to be suspected (authentication fails) then it is killed.
2.3.2. Otherwise allow computation at this node.
2.3.2.1. Update direct observation of this node according to the agent's shared experience
2.3.2.1.1. If a node is found to be trusted,α is incremented using to eqn 3.
2.3.2.1.2. Otherwise β is updated according to eqn 4.
2.3.2.1.3. Using eqns 2, 5 and 6 update yield values of b_{ij}, d_{ij} and u_{ij} for all j visited by the agent
2.4. If an agent owned by this node comes back containing at most one suspected node in its PL then
2.4.1. Update the results.
2.4.2. Update direct observation of this node.
2.4.2.1. If a node is found to be trusted α is incremented according to eqn 3.
2.4.2.2. Otherwise β is updated according to eqn 4.
2.4.2.2.1. Also *learn* to avoid the existing route followed by the agents towards this node
2.4.2.3. Using eqns 2, 5 and 6 update yield values of b_{ij}, d_{ij} and u_{ij} for all j visited by the agent
2.4.3. Kill the agent (Algorithm – I, steps 1.4 and 1.5).
2.5. Whenever a message regarding suspected node id is received from a trusted node, then update the indirect observation according to eqns 10 through 12.

2.6. Hence update comprehensive (b,d,u) for visited nodes using eqn 13 through 17.
2.7. Compute the trust of this node for other nodes in the network following eqn 18.
2.8. If the resulting trust level of any node falls below Trust_thresholddemanded by the deployer application then advertise the node id to be a suspected one to the rest of the nodes.
2.9. The owners create PL for each agent containing trusted nodes ids.
2.10. Deploy the agents.

3. Stop.

In step1.4 of algorithm I if the current host platform (where the agent currently resides) is found to be malicious, then most likely the data part of the agent is changed(corrupted PL), not the code. So to save network bandwidth the agent can be asked to move back to its owner (so that the owner may update its trust level accordingly). Here we assume some means to authenticate an agent at a host site so that a host eventually detects a malicious agent. Agents in our system work as watchdogs [7]; they migrate and collect feedback about the trustworthiness of the nodes they visit. The reputation system at the nodes updates its view of the network based on the first hand and second hand information and accordingly guides (providing PL) the agents it deploys.

5 Experimental Results

The simulation is carried out in java and can run on any platform. MANET environment is simulated according to section 4. For simplicity, in our simulation the PL tells the agents which nodes to visit. The agent moves back to its owner at the end of its journey. We have done a series of experiments to show the robustness of our proposed algorithm. The default values for the experiments are shown in table-I. We will explicitly mention any change in these values for individual experiments. By step 1.5 of algorithm I, whenever an agent finds a suspected node, it comes back to its owner immediately. This strategy saves bandwidth but makes detection of other malicious nodes in the network a time consuming task. Hence the sharp slope of the curve (in figure 3) indicates that as more nodes in the network become compromised, the time to detect all of them increases even further. But if the agents are expected to visit more nodes (longer PLs) the probability of discovering a suspicious node increases. As more and more nodes gets visited, the direct experience becomes richer-which also improves the indirect and hence the overall trust convergence process (see figure 3). Thus for a more or less connected network, MANET becomes more secured with longer trails for the agents. Now the effect of direct and indirect observation on the reputation system is shown in figure 4. Initially indirect observation is not significant. But with increasing time (54 sec onwards) the difference became more apt. This explains the detection of suspicious nodes first from direct experience (by some nodes which), then broadcasting messages to others so that indirect experience can prove to be helpful to the rest. But in both cases the system eventually reaches a steady state.

Now we introduce a metric called the ratio of agents passed that is defined as follows

$$Ratio\ of AgentsPassed(t) = \frac{No.of agents going through malicious nodes till time t}{Total no.of agents deployed till time t} \tag{19}$$

We take a case (see figure 5) where MN_3 behaved maliciously from the beginning of simulation but MN_{10} was compromised during the simulation. In the beginning performance varies as MN_{10} become malicious at different time instants. But it can be observed that eventually the ratio of agents passed becomes almost independent of the point when a node is compromised. This explains the robustness of our protocol.

Table 1. Default values of our configuration

Parameter	Default Values	Parameter	Default Values
M	20	Trust View default(b,d,u)	(0,0,1)
N	25	Trust_threshold	0.499
Length of priority list	0.5N	Minimum required P_r	18 dBm

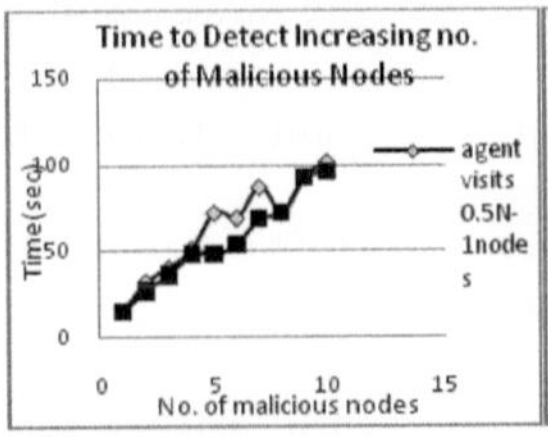

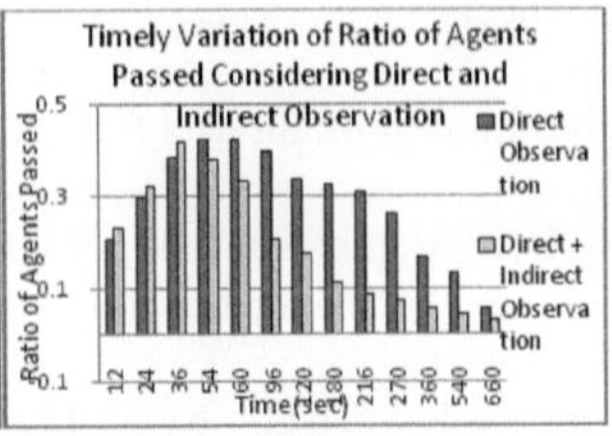

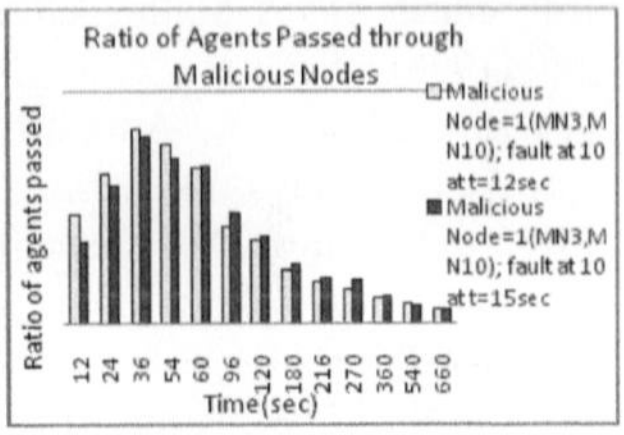

Fig. 3. System performance as threat to the agents increases

Fig. 4. Effect of direct and indirect observation in ratio of agents attracted

Fig. 5. Ratio of agents passed where MN_{10} is compromised in run time

6 Conclusions

This paper provides a trust based framework for securing the hosts and preventing the agents from visiting or passing through a compromised node in MANET. Possible modification in data is detected by taking hash code of an agent's data and code. Our model establishes trust among the nodes in a totally distributed manner and does not assume any central coordinator (for example a trusted third party). But the agent owners (nodes) are given the responsibility of killing malicious agents and creating new agents. If any node is found to be malicious, its entry gets removed from the PL of agents that are further deployed. The scheme enables an agent to share information about the network with the nodes it trusts. Trust is quantified using a tuple (b,d,u). For faster convergence of trust (consistent (b,d,u)s), the nodes share indirect information through broadcasts. This proves to be beneficial for nodes waiting for an agent response or particularly nodes which have not deployed agents at all. Also, to protect from malicious broadcasts, the nodes only listen to (and update trust level) broadcast messages from the senders they trust. SRMM is used to simulate the movement of the nodes. The protocol is validated and results are shown in section 5. It can be observed that for a larger MANET longer time will be necessary to detect all compromised nodes. In run time whenever a node becomes malicious, it is detected eventually and the system always reaches a steady state.

References

[1] Songsiri, S.: MTrust: A Reputation-Based Trust Model for a Mobile Agent System. In: Yang, L.T., Jin, H., Ma, J., Ungerer, T. (eds.) ATC 2006. LNCS, vol. 4158, pp. 374–385. Springer, Heidelberg (2006)

[2] Jøsang, A.: Trust-Based Decision Making for Electronic Transactions. In: Yngström, L., Svensson, T. (eds.) Proc. of the 4th Nordic Workshop on Secure Computer Systems (1999)

[3] Whitby, A., Jøsang, A., Indulka, J.: Filtering out unfair Ratings in Bayesian Reputation Systems. The Icfain Journal of Management Research 4(2), 48–64 (2005)

[4] Luke Teacy, W.T., Patel, J., Jennings, N.R., Luck, M.: Coping with Inaccurate reputation Sources: Experimental Analysis of a Probabilistic Trust Model. In: AAMAS 2005 (2005)

[5] Li, F., Wu, J.: Mobility reduces uncertainty in MANETs. In: Proc. of INFOCOM 2007, pp. 1946–1954 (2007)

[6] Shafer, G.: A Mathematical Theory of Evidence. Princeton University Press, Princeton (1976)

[7] Li, N., Das, S.K.: A trust-based framework for data forwarding in opportunistic networks. Ad Hoc Networks (in press)

[8] Yu, B., Singh, M.: Detecting Deception in Reputation Management. In: Proc. of the 2nd International Joint Conf. on Autonomous Agents and Multi Agent Systems, pp. 73–80 (2003)

[9] Lu, P., Li, B., Xing, M.L., Li, L.: D-S Theory-based Trust Model FIRE in Multi-agent Systems. In: The Proc of the 8th ACIS International Conference on Software Engineering, Artificial Intelligence, Networking, and Parallel/Distributed Computing, pp. 255–260 (2007)

[10] Chowdhury, C., Neogy, S.: Reliability Estimate of Mobile Agent Based System for QoS MANET Applications. In: The Annual Reliability and Availability Symposium, pp. 1–6 (2011)

[11] Bettstetter, C.: Smooth is better than sharp: a random mobility model for simulation of wireless networks. In: The Proc. of the Fourth ACM International Workshop on Modeling, Analysis and Simulation of Wireless and Mobile Systems, pp. 19–25 (2001)

[12] Meier, R.T., Dunkel, J., Kakuda, Y., Ohta, T.: Mobile agents for service discovery in ad hoc networks. In: Proc. 22nd International Conference on Advanced Information Networking and Applications, pp. 114–121 (2008)

A State-of-the-Art Survey on IDS for Mobile Ad-Hoc Networks and Wireless Mesh Networks

Novarun Deb, Manali Chakraborty, and Nabendu Chaki

Department of Computer Science & Engineering, University of Calcutta, India
92 APC Road, Kolkata 700009, India
novarun.db@gmail.com, manali4mkolkata@gmail.com,
nabendu@ieee.org

Abstract. An Intrusion Detection System (IDS) detects malicious and selfish nodes in a network. Ad hoc networks are often secured by using either intrusion detection or by secure routing. Designing efficient IDS for wireless ad-hoc networks that would not affect the performance of the network significantly is indeed a challenging task. Arguably, the most common thing in a review paper in the domain of wireless networks is to compare the performances of different solutions using simulation results. However, variance in multiple configuration aspects including that due to different underlying routing protocols, makes the task of simulation based comparative evaluation of IDS solutions somewhat unrealistic. In stead, the authors have followed an analytic approach to identify the gaps in the existing IDS solutions for MANETs and wireless mesh networks. The paper aims to ease the job of a new researcher by exposing him to the state of the art research issues on IDS. Nearly 80% of the works cited in this paper are published with in last 3 to 4 years.

Keywords: Intrusion, Intrusion detection systems, trust, MANET, wireless mesh network.

1 Introduction

An intrusion may be defined as any action that attempt to compromise the integrity, confidentiality or availability of a resource or that goes against the security goals of a resource. This can be something as severe as stealing confidential data or misusing the email system for spam. External intrusion attempts are targeted to cause congestion, propagate incorrect routing information, prevent services from working properly or shutdown them completely. The internal intrusions could be a lot more damaging since malicious insider already belongs to the network as an authorized party. Since prevention of intrusions is not always possible, supportive intrusion detection techniques are required. Intrusion detection systems (IDSs) are not to prevent or deter attacks. Instead, the purpose is to alert the users about possible attacks, ideally in time to stop the attack or mitigate the damage [1].

Detecting Intrusion is difficult, particularly in the wireless domain. IDS often attempts to differentiate abnormal activities from the normal ones. Unfortunately, normal activities can be varied, and an attack may have resemblance to normal

D. Nagamalai, E. Renault, and M. Dhanushkodi (Eds.): PDCTA 2011, CCIS 203, pp. 169–179, 2011.

activities. Also, consistency of data in the time domain can detect unusual behavior but unusual behavior is not necessarily malicious. An IDS reaches perfection if it accurately detects majority of attacks and hardly makes any false or phantom detection. One basic assumption while designing any IDS should be that the attacker is intelligent and that the attacker has no shortage of resources.

An IDS essentially consists of three functions. First, the IDS must monitor some event and maintain the history of data related to that event. Second, the IDS must be equipped with an analysis engine that processes the collected data. It detects unusual or malicious signs in the data by measuring the consistency of data in the time domain. Currently there are two basic approaches to analysis: misuse detection and anomaly-based detection. Third, the IDS must generate a response, which is typically an alert to system administrators. It is up to the system administrator, how he wants to scrutinize the system after receiving an alert.

1.1 Why IDS Solutions Need to Be Different for MANET and WMN?

In MANETs, mobile nodes communicate with each other without the assistance of any infrastructure. The communication between nodes, not directly in transmission range, is performed via multiple hops, i.e., nodes cooperate and forward packets for other nodes. In addition to that, in WMN some nodes are stationary forming a kind of backbone and possibly functioning as gateway to further networks like the Internet. Thus from the architectural point of view, a MANET is necessarily a infrastructure-less or ad-hoc network, whereas a mesh networks uses a backbone.

Due to this basic difference in architecture, security issues, as considered for MANETs, are often quite different compared to that for WMNs. Some of these at times are in favor of the attacker and some in favor of protecting the network from intrusion. As for instance, let's consider that an attacker wants to launch a wormhole attack in both types of networks. When the mobility of the nodes is high in a MANET, it becomes practically impossible for the attacker to establish the "tunnel" through which packets are routed to another point in the network. The scenario is different in case of WMNs as the backbone routers are static and if such nodes are compromised, "tunnels" can be easily built through them. On the other hand, in case of a WMN, one may deploy more robust IDS solutions that uses the backbone of the mesh network. Thus, even if some of the protocols do well towards securing both MANET and WMNs, tailor-made solutions are required keeping in mind the differences of the two types of wireless networks. The study in this paper reveals that many gaps still exist for detecting intrusions, particularly in case of mesh networks, that has been relatively new and deployed more recently.

1.2 Organization of the Paper

In this paper, we have studied most recent works for IDS for MANETs and wireless mesh networks. In section 2 of this paper, we have reported and analyzed seven different IDS approaches for MANET out of which four has been published in last 4 years. In section 3, 100% of the six reported IDS approaches on wireless mesh networks have been proposed in last 2 years. Each of the sections 2 and 3 ends with separate tables highlighting the basic features and limitations of the existing IDS solutions.

Survey papers like this one often include simulation results to compare different approaches. However, here the authors have carefully avoided simulation for performance evaluation for a couple of reasons. Firstly, different approaches for intrusion detection assume different configurations in the network. Even the underlying routing protocols are not the same. Some of the approaches claim to be compatible with multiple existing routing protocols. However, there would be significant impact in the simulation results for such variance. This in turn would spoil the entire purpose of the simulation. Besides, the paper covers a total of 13 IDS solutions, most of which have been published very recently. Usually simulation based graphs are good for comparing a small number of alternate solutions. Thus, in stead of simulations, the authors have followed a careful analytic approach to compare the works referred.

2 IDS for Mobile Ad-Hoc Networks

A Mobile Ad hoc Network (MANET) can be defined as a collection of mobile nodes that are geographically distributed and communicate with one another over a wireless medium. Ideally, in a MANET, each node is assumed to be a friendly node and participates willingly in relaying messages to their ultimate destinations. A mobile ad hoc network is built on ad-hoc demand and consists of some wireless nodes moving within a geographically distributed area. These nodes can join or leave the network at any time. MANET does not use fixed infrastructure and does not have a centralized administration. The nodes communicate on a peer-to-peer basis. The networks are built on the basis of mutual cooperation and trust. This leads to an inherent weakness of security.

Security in mobile wireless ad hoc networks was particularly difficult to achieve, notably because of the vulnerability of the links, the limited physical protection of each of the nodes, the sporadic nature of connectivity, the dynamically changing topology, the absence of a certification authority, and the lack of a centralized monitoring or management point [11]. This, in effect, underscored the need for intrusion detection, prevention, and related countermeasures. Like any other research area, one needs to do a systematic re-search of the existing works in the area of intrusion detection too. In a very recent paper [4], a number of IDS methods have been described for MANET. Although the compilation is good, no serious attempt has been initiated to identify the gaps in the works cited. Survey papers on IDSs for Wireless Mesh Networks are very few in numbers. In [2], contrary to the promise of the title of the paper, the methods referred are mostly applicable for wireless ad-hoc networks and MANETs.

Before one attempts to detect an intrusion, it is important to understand the nature and variation of attacks. The work by Martin Antonio [5] provides a fairly good analysis of MANET specific attacks and risk analysis by identifying assets, vulnerabilities and threats, usable for future MANET deployments and security work. Consequently, security solutions with static configuration would not suffice, and the assumption that all nodes can be bootstrapped with the credentials of all other nodes would be unrealistic for a wide range of MANET applications [3]. In practice, it is not possible to build a completely secure MANET system in spite of using the most complex cryptographic technique or so-called secured routing protocols. Some of the IDS algorithms that have been developed for MANETs are explained below. A comparative study is provided at the end of this section.

IDSX [1] was a cluster-based solution which used an extended architecture. The proposed solution acted as a second line of defense. Individual nodes could implement any IDS solution. IDSX was compatible with any IDS solution acting as the first line of defense. Simulation results show that the IDSX solution hardly produced any false positives. This was because it formed a consensus of the responses from different individual IDS solutions implemented in the nodes. Anomaly-based intrusion detection schemes could be deployed as the first line of defense. The proposed approach in [1] works within preset boundaries. In general, these are quite feasible and practical enough considering the nature of ad hoc networks. However, some of these may also be considered as the limiting constraints. IDSX has not been compared with any of the existing IDS solutions. Also, the proposed two-step approach would make the task of intrusion detection expensive in terms of energy and resource consumption.

In another innovative approach in [7], a solution is proposed using the concept of unsupervised learning in Artificial Neural Networks using Self-Organizing Maps. The technique named eSOM used a data structure called U-matrix which was used to represent data classes. Those regions which represented malicious information were watermarked using the Block-Wise method. Regions representing the benign data class was marked using the Lattice method. When a new attack is launched it causes changes in the pixel values. eSOM and the Watermarking technique can together identify if any pixel has been modified. This makes it very sensitive towards detecting intrusions. The authors claim that the solution is 80% efficient and remains consistent even with variations in mobility. Mentioned below are some of the drawbacks of this work [7]. The IDS employing eSOM would be trained in regular time periods. This results in additional overhead and takes a toll on the energy efficiency of the algorithm. However, the proposed intrusion detection engine has not been employed on various routing protocols for the detection of various types of attacks.

A leader election model for IDS in MANET based on the Vicky, Clarke and Groves (VCG) model was suggested in [8]. This requires every node to be as honest as possible. Leaders are elected in a manner which results in optimal resource utilization. Leaders are positively rewarded for participating honestly in the election process. By balancing the resource consumption amongst the nodes, a higher effective lifetime of the nodes was achieved. Experimental results indicate that the VCG model performs well during leader election by producing a higher percentage of alive nodes. However, the simulation results indicate that the normal nodes will carry out more duty of intrusion detection and die faster when there are more selfish nodes. Besides, as selfish nodes do not exhaust energy to run the IDS service, the percentage of packet analysis decreases with time. This is a severe security concern. In the case of static scenarios, the model elects the same node as leader repeatedly. This causes the normal nodes to die very fast.

CONFIDANT, another approach, similar to Watchdog and Path-rater scheme, has been proposed to overcome the drawbacks of the Watchdog and Path-rater by ignoring misbehaving nodes in the routing process [9]. Every node identifies its neighbors as friends and enemies, based on trust. Friends are informed of enemies. CONFIDANT claims that the packet delivery ratio is very high (97% and above). A couple of the issues that still leaves a gap in [9] are mentioned below. However, CONFIDANT keeps the packet delivery ratio high even in a very hostile environment, with the assumption that enough redundant paths are available to reach the destination node, bypassing the malicious ones. This assumption may not always hold. Also, in comparing the throughput of clients and servers, the CONFIDANT fortified network performs very poorly in contrast to the benign network.

SCAN [10] is based on two central ideas. First, each node monitors its neighbors for routing or packet forwarding misbehavior, independently. Second, every node observes its neighbors by cross validating the overhead traffic with other nodes. Nodes are declared malicious by a majority decision. This assumes that the network density is sufficiently high. However, in SCAN the network services are temporarily halted during intrusion detection. The lack of mobility reduces the detection efficiency. The assumption that network density is high may not always hold. Increase in mobility results in higher false positives. Besides, the packet delivery ratio can be heavily affected in the interval during which an attack is launched and when it is detected. Also, the communication overhead for SCAN grows with increase in the percentage of malicious nodes and with mobility.

In HIDS [3], another approach to the IDS has been proposed. HIDS is based on trust or reputation or honesty values of the mobile nodes. The trust value of a node is dynamically increased or decreased depending on its behavior. When a node behaves normally, it is positively rewarded; malicious activity results in negative rewards for that node. The trust on a node is recomputed based on its current honesty rate, and the rewards that it has earned. A comparative study between SCAN and HIDS shows that the latter involves lower storage and communicational overhead than SCAN. HIDS is inherently protected against false positives. However, maintaining up-to-date tables at different nodes, as required by HIDS, may not be an energy-efficient strategy. Also the proposed HIDS offers only a generic architecture for secure route detection. More detailed testing is required before it can be used for secure routing in MANET applications.

In [16] OCEAN was proposed as another extension to the DSR protocol. OCEAN also uses a monitoring system and a reputation system. The proposed solution exchanges second-hand reputation messages. OCEAN implements a stand-alone architecture to avoid phantom intrusion detections. Depending on whether a node participates in the route discovery process, OCEAN can detect misbehaving nodes and selfish nodes. However, the detection efficiency of OCEAN rapidly decreases with increase in the density of misbehaving nodes. Simulation results show that at high threshold values, other second hand protocols perform better with high mobility of the nodes. Also, the mobility model simulated for OCEAN is not very realistic. At high mobility, OCEAN is very sensitive to change of the threshold parameter, while second hand protocols are more consistent over varying threshold limits. OCEAN is not quite effective in penalizing misleading nodes.

A hybrid solution, proposed in [17], combines the Watchdog and Path-Raters scheme proposed by Marti et al. and SCAN[10]. However, neither SCAN nor Watchdog and Path-raters address the mobility issue that well. As a result, this hybrid solution also suffers from the same problems. Besides, there are no fixed nodes which can behave as umpires. There must be some kind of a leader election model which runs in every node to select the Umpire nodes. This results in an increased overhead and energy consumption. The authors did mention the scenario where Umpire nodes themselves can become malicious. However, it still remains as a drawback of the method. In order to detect DoS attacks like flooding, the criteria for attack detection cannot be so rigid. Also, the history of a node that had being behaving normal, should be taken in to consideration before writing it off as malicious as soon as it deviates from normal behavior.

Table 1. Summary on Comparison for Different IDS for Mobile Ad-hoc Networks

IDS Reference	Under-lying Routing Protocol	Architecture	Types of attacks addressed	Comments
IDSX [1] (2007).	Compatible with any routing protocol	Extended Hierarchical Architecture	Routing misbehavior - dirty packet forwarding.	1. The solution talks about a two-step approach. This leads to making the intrusion detection approach quite expensive in terms of energy and resource consumption.
Neural Networks and Watermarking Technique [7] (2007)	AODV	Self Organizing Maps (Neural Networks)	Routing behavior attack and Resource utilization attack.	1. The IDS using eSOM needs to be trained in regular interval. This additional overhead affects the energy efficiency of the algorithm. 2. The proposed intrusion detection engine has not been employed for various routing protocols for detection of different attacks.
CONFIDANT [9] (2002)	DSR	Distributed and Cooperative.	Packet drop attack.	1. CONFIDANT assumes that there are enough nodes to provide harmless alternate partial paths around malicious nodes. This may not always hold. 2. A CONFIDANT fortified network with one third malicious nodes does not provide any additional benefits over a regular benign DSR network without malicious nodes.
HIDS [3] (2008)	Compatible with reactive And proactive routing protocols.	Distributed and Collaborative	Packet drops, black-hole attack, Resource utilization attacks	1. Maintenance of tables at different nodes affects energy efficiency and communication overhead. 2. Detailed testing is required before it can be used for secure routing in MANET applications.
Leader Election Model [8] (2008)	Not specified.	Based on the Vickey, Clarke, and Groves (VCG) model by which truth-telling is the dominant strategy for each node.	Resource utilization attack-selfish nodes.	1. Simulation results indicate that normal nodes will work more to detect intrusion and die faster in presence of selfish nodes. 2. As selfish nodes do not exhaust energy to run the IDS service, the percentage of packet analysis decreases with time. 3. In the case of static scenarios, the model elects the same node as leader repeatedly. This causes the normal nodes to die very fast.
SCAN [10] (2006)	AODV	Distributed and Collaborative	Routing misbehavior and packet forwarding misbehavior	1. Network services are temporarily halted during intrusion detection. 2. Lack of mobility reduces the detection efficiency. 3. The assumption that network density is high may not always hold. Increase in mobility results in higher false positives. 4. Packet delivery ratio can be heavily affected in the interval between an attack is launched and when it is detected. 5. The communication overhead steadily increases with increase in the percentage of malicious nodes and with mobility.

Table 1. (*Continued*)

OCEAN [16] (2003)	Not identified	Stand - alone IDS	Routing behavior attack, resource utilization attack, rushing attack.	1. At high faulty thresholds, approaches like SEC-HAND protocols are able to perform better than OCEAN at high mobility. 2. At lower numbers of misbehaving nodes, the performance of OCEAN falls drastically. 3. OCEAN is not very effective in thwarting the throughput of the misleading nodes.
A System of Umpires [17] (2010)	Not identified	Stand - alone IDS for single user; Collaborative IDS for double and triple Users	Routing misbehavior attack and Packet Dropping attack.	1. Umpires are not static. Some kind of leader election is required. This may require additional energy. 2. Attack detection criteria are very rigid. 3. Nodes are not rewarded for normal behavior.

3 IDS for Wireless Mesh Networks

The proposed methodology successfully detects any moving object maintaining low computational complexity and low memory requirements.

Although mobility of nodes was removed and a certain infrastructure was established for Sensor Networks, yet these remained vulnerable to security threats. Researchers realized that mobility is a feature which cannot be compromised with as it provides tremendous flexibility to end users. Yet, retaining an infrastructure would definitely be helpful. All these underlying observations led to the conclusion that a different type of network must be designed which incorporates both the mobility of clients and a basic infrastructure. This had been a major driving factor behind the inception of Wireless Mesh Networks.

Wireless mesh networks (WMNs) consist of mesh routers and mesh clients, where mesh routers have minimal mobility and form the backbone of WMNs [2]. They provide network access for both mesh and conventional clients. The integration of WMNs with other networks such as the Internet, cellular, IEEE 802.11, IEEE 802.15, IEEE 802.16, sensor networks, etc., can be accomplished through the gateway and bridging functions in the mesh routers. WMNs include mesh routers forming an infrastructure for clients that connect to them. The WMN infrastructure/backbone can be built using various types of radio technologies.

The client meshing provides peer-to-peer networks among client devices. In this type of architecture, client nodes constitute the actual network to perform routing and configuration functionalities as well as providing end user applications to customers. Hence, a mesh router is not required for these types of networks. In Client WMNs, a packet destined to a node in the network hops through multiple nodes to reach the destination. Client WMNs are usually formed using one type of radios on devices. Moreover, the requirements on end-user devices is increased when compared to infrastructure meshing, since, in Client WMNs, the end-users must perform additional functions such as routing and self-configuration.

Mesh clients can access the network through mesh routers as well as directly meshing with other mesh clients. While the infrastructure provides connectivity to other networks such as the Internet, Wi-Fi, WiMAX, cellular, and sensor networks;

the routing capabilities of clients provide improved connectivity and coverage inside the WMN. The hybrid architecture will be the most applicable case in our opinion.

The redundancy and self-healing capabilities of WMNs provide for less downtime, with messages continuing to be delivered even when paths are blocked or broken. The self-configuring, self-tuning, self-healing, and self-monitoring capabilities of mesh can help to reduce the management burden for system administrators. Besides, the advanced mesh networking protocols coordinate the network so that nodes can go into sleep mode while inactive and then synchronize quickly for sending, receiving, and forwarding messages. This ability provides greatly extended battery life.

A mesh network can be deliberately *over-provisioned* simply by adding extra devices, so that each device has two or more paths for sending data. This is a much simpler and less expensive way of obtaining redundancy than is possible in most other types of networks. In comparison to the cost of point-to-point copper wiring and conduit required for traditional wired networks, wireless mesh networks are typically much less expensive. The protocols that have been developed so far for WMNs are described briefly. A comparative study is provided at the end of this section.

A technique was devised based on the communication history between two communicating clients through a common set of routers in [15]. Individual trust relationships are evaluated for both clients sharing the common set of routers. Malicious clients are detected based on threshold values. The algorithm performs well when the density of malicious nodes is low. Routers in the path have to perform $O(N^2)$ operations to cooperatively reach a conclusion. It is found that false positives are reduced to a great extent but not eliminated. The algorithm performs better only when the percentage of misbehaving clients is smaller. Performance degrades as malicious activity within the network increases.

RADAR [12] introduces a general concept of reputation. Highly detailed evaluation metrics are used to measure the behavior of mesh nodes. This allows RADAR to better classify / distinguish normal behavior from anomalous activity. RADAR takes into consideration the spatio-temporal behavior of nodes before declaring them as malicious. Simulation results show that RADAR detects routing loops with higher false alarms. The algorithm is resilient to malicious collectives for subverting reputations; but involves a relatively high latency for detection of DoS attacks. The Detection Overhead Ratio (DOR) is directly proportional to the number of anomaly detectors and the size of detection window implemented in the algorithm.

Although developed initially for wired networks, Principal Component Analysis (PCA) based method [11] could also be implemented for wireless networks. The threshold value used in [11] for detecting malicious nodes assumes that network traffic follows the normal distribution. Tuning the threshold also reduces the number of phantom intrusion detections considerably. The proposed solution is energy-efficient. However, despite the promises, the PCA based method in [11] is not consistent to variations in normal network traffic due to unrealistic assumptions in the method. Anomalies such as node outages cannot be detected as this method [11] looks for spurious traffic generation. A statistical analysis of how the behavior varies with changing threshold values is yet to be performed.

In [14] a solution to defend against selective forwarding attacks based on AODV routing protocol is presented. The algorithm works in two phases – detecting malicious activities in the network and identifying the attacker, respectively. However, the proposed methodology of [14] suffers from some serious limitations. The proposed scheme fails to detect attackers when the threshold value is less than the throughput. Even in the absence of an attacker, the throughput is low when the detection threshold is higher than throughput of the path. Performance overhead of the system increases with increase in the density of malicious nodes.

Table 2. Summary on Comparison for Different IDS for Wireless Mesh Networks

IDS Reference	Under-lying Routing Protocol	Architecture	Types of attacks addressed	Comments
Trust based approach I [14] (2008).	AODV	Distributed System	Gray hole attacks.	1. The overhead of the system increases with the number of attackers. 2. When detection threshold is less than the throughput of a path, attacks will not be detected and network throughput will suffer. 3. On the contrary, when the detection threshold is higher than throughput of the path, the throughput would suffer even if there is no attacker.
Trust based approach II [15] (2008)	Not specified.	Distributed Systems	Misbehavior of a node	1. The detection efficiency decreases and false positive rate increases with the increase of percentage of malicious clients. 2. False positives are reduced to a great extent but not eliminated.
Principal Component Analysis (PCA) [11] (2008).	Not specified	Distributed Systems	DoS, port scan, jamming etc.	1. Anomalies such as node outages are not detected as the method looks for spurious traffic generation. 2. Analysis on performance evaluation with changing threshold values is yet to be performed. 3. The method is not consistent due to unrealistic assumptions on network traffic.
RADAR [12] (2008).	DSR	Distributed Systems	Malicious behavior of a node, DOS Attack, Routing Loop Attack.	1. Higher false alarms. 2. Resilient to malicious collectives for subverting reputations. 3. High latency for detection of DoS attacks. 4. The Detection Overhead Ratio (DOR) is a linear overhead.
OpenLIDS [13] (2009).	Not specified	Distributed Systems	Resource starvation attacks, mass mailing of internet worms, IP spoofing.	1. Higher false positives as OpenLIDS is unable to distinguish between RTP stream and a UDP DoS flood with fixed source and destination ports. 2. Not as efficient for new connections. 3. It is not possible to arbitrarily adjust timeout values.
Reputation systems and self-organizing maps. [6] (2010).	Not specified.	Distributed agent based Systems	Routing misbehavior and resource utilization attacks.	1. It is assumed that the confidentiality and integrity cannot be preserved for any node. 2. The reputation system identifies the attacked node immediately. However, it is not fast enough to prevent the neighbor nodes from being affected

OpenLIDS [13] analyzes the ability of mesh nodes to perform intrusion detection. Due to the resource constraints of mesh nodes, detailed traffic analysis is not feasible in WMNs. An energy – efficient scheme was proposed in OpenLIDS. Results show that performance improved for detecting malicious behavior in mesh nodes. OpenLIDS is an improvement over other signature-based approaches both in terms of memory requirements and packet delivery ratio. However, simulation results show that OpenLIDS is unable to distinguish an RTP stream from a UDP DoS flood with fixed source and destination ports. For new connections, this approach is not as efficient as expected as generating and receiving connection tracking events is costly.

In [6], a framework has been proposed that is based on a reputation system. This isolates ill-behaved nodes by rating their reputation as low, and distributed agents based on unsupervised learning algorithms, that are able to detect deviations from the normal behavior. The solution is very effective in detecting novel intrusions. This algorithm had already been deployed for WSNs. Experimental results show that even though redundancy reduces drastically in WMNs the proposed method works efficiently. However, the approach is not fast enough to prevent the neighbor nodes from being affected by an attack. Also, initially the solution [6] cannot exactly determine the source of the anomaly. Therefore, the system reduces the reputation of all the nodes within the malicious region.

4 Conclusion

The thirst of flexibility in operations and application requirements for wider access has triggered the evolution of ad-hoc networks. The infrastructure-less ad-hoc networks offer even greater flexibility when the nodes are mobile. This flexibility is however two-fold. Just the way, a greater number of applications are made possible in ad-hoc networks, especially for MANETs, the lack of centralized control, dedicated security infrastructure, non-standard topology, etc. offers additional "flexibility" to the intruder as well. Designing efficient IDS that would not affect the performance of the network is in fact an uphill task due to the vulnerability of the links, the limited physical protection of the nodes, the irregularity and dynamic changes in topology, and the lack of a centralized authority and monitoring. In spite of this, recent works propose adept IDS methodologies that extract the advantages of base station in sensor networks and the backbone in wireless mesh networks. In section 1 of the paper, the reasons for avoiding simulation have been explained. Instead, critical analytic comparisons are done for 13 different IDS solutions. The findings are summarized in tables I to II. An IDS needs a scalable architecture to collect sufficient evidences to detect those attacks effectively. Researchers are now being motivated to design a new IDS architecture that involves cross layer design to efficiently detect the abnormalities in the wireless networks. The selection of correct combination of layers in the design of cross layer IDS is very critical to detect attacks targeted at or sourced from any layers rapidly. It is optimal to incorporate MAC layer in the cross layer design for IDS to detect DoS attacks. This cross layer technique incorporating IDS leads to an escalating detection rate in the number of malicious behavior of nodes increasing the true positive and reducing false positives in the MANET. The current study may be extended to review recent works on cross-layer IDS architecture.

References

1. Chaki, R., Chaki, N.: IDSX: A Cluster Based Collaborative Intrusion Detection Algorithm for Mobile Ad-Hoc Network. In: Proceedings of the IEEE International Conference on Computer Information Systems and Industrial Management Applications, CISIM (2007)
2. Chen, T.M., Kuo, G.-S., Li, Z.-P., Zhu, G.-M.: Intrusion Detection in Wireless Mesh Networks. In: Security in Wireless Mesh Networks. CRC Press, Boca Raton (2007)
3. Sil, P., Chaki, R., Chaki, N.: HIDS: Honesty-rate based collaborative Intrusion Detection System for Mobile Ad-Hoc Networks. In: Proc. of 7th IEEE International Conference on Computer Information Systems and Industrial Management Applications, CISIM (2008)
4. Sahu, S., Shandilya, S.K.: A Comprehensive Survey on Intrusion Detection in MANET. Int'l J. of Information Technology and Knowledge Mgmt. 2(2), 305–310 (2010)
5. Martin, A.: A Platform Independent Risk Analysis for Mobile Ad hoc Networks. In: Proc. of the Boston Univ. Conference on Information Assurance and Cyber Security (2006)
6. Bankovic, Z., et al.: Improving security in WMNs with reputation systems and self-organizing maps. Journal of Network and Computer Applications (2010) ISSN 1084-8045
7. Mitrokotsa, A., Komninos, N., Douligeris, C.: Intrusion Detection with Neural Networks and Watermarking Techniques for MANET. In: IEEE International Conference on Pervasive Services, pp. 118–127 (2007)
8. Mohammed, N., Otrok, H., Wang, L., Debbabi, M., Bhattacharya, P.: Mechanism Design-Based Secure Leader Election Model for Intrusion Detection in MANET. IEEE Transactions on Dependable and Secure Computing 99(1) (2008)
9. Buchegger, S., Le Boudec, J.: Performance Analysis of the CONFIDANT Protocol (Cooperation Of Nodes - Fairness In Dynamic Ad-hoc NeTworks). In: Proceedings of the 3rd ACM International Symposium on Mobile Ad Hoc Networking and Computing (MobiHoc 2002), pp. 226–336 (2002)
10. Yang, H., Shu, J., Meng, X., Lu, S.: SCAN: self-organized network-layer security in mobile ad hoc networks. IEEE J. on Sel. Areas in Communications 24, 261–273 (2006)
11. Zaidi, Z.R., Hakami, S., Landfeldt, B., Moors, T.: Detection and identification of anomalies in wireless mesh networks using Principal Component Analysis (PCA). World Scientific Journal of Interconnection Networks, JOIN (2008)
12. Zhang, Z., Naït-Abdesselam, F., Ho, P.-H., Lin, X.: RADAR: A ReputAtion-Based Scheme for Detecting Anomalous Nodes in WiReless Mesh Networks. In: IEEE Wireless Communications & Networking Conference, pp. 2621–2626. IEEE, Los Alamitos (2008)
13. Hugelshofer, F., Smith, P., Hutchison, D., Race, N.J.P.: OpenLIDS: A Lightweight Intrusion Detection System for Wireless Mesh Networks. In: MobiCom 2009, Beijing, China (September 20-25, 2009)
14. Shila, D.M., Anjali, T.: Defending Selective Forwarding Attacks in WMNs. In: Proc. of IEEE Int'l. Conference on Electro/Information Technology, USA, pp. 96–101 (2008)
15. Hamid, A., Islam, S., Hong, C.S.: Misbehavior Detection in Wireless Mesh Networks. In: ICACT 2008, pp. 1167–1169 (2008)
16. Bansal, S., Baker, M.: Observation-Based Cooperation Enforcement in Ad hoc Networks, Research Report cs.NI/0307012, Stanford University (2003)
17. Kathirvel, A.: Enhanced Triple Umpiring System for Security and Performance Improvement in Wireless MANETS. International Journal of Communication Networks and Information Security (IJCNIS) 2(2) (2010)

LPC VOCODER Using Instants of Significant Excitation and Pole Focusing

A. Saranya and N. Sripriya

Department of Information Technology, Sri Sivasubramania Nadar College of Engineering, Kalavakkam, Chennai 603 110
saran.anbalagan@gmail.com, sripriyan@ssn.edu.in

Abstract. Vocoders are designed/used to reduce the bit rate requirement for speech signal transmission without significant degradation in the quality of the resultant speech. In most of the speech coding techniques, the system and the source parameters are coded separately. The system is generally coded using a codebook which demands only less number of bits compared to source coding. Coding of the source parameters requires significant computational complexity and memory to preserve the identity and naturalness of the speaker. In this work, a LPC vocoder is designed which uses the instants of significant excitation estimated from the speech signal to code the source information. Traditional pitch excited LPC vocoders produce intelligible speech at a bit rate of 2400 bps, but they are often synthetic. Hence source is coded by identifying the locations of instants of significant excitation and the corresponding strength at those instants. Thus the bit rate requirement is reduced significantly in the order of 1.6Kbps when a code book of size 1024 is used. The number of bits used for coding the system is further reduced by using the codebook of reduced size, namely 64. But the quality of resynthesized signal decreases as the poles representing the system are defocused due to high averaging. Hence, pole focusing, increasing the radius of the poles is done. This causes the increment in the gain/magnitude of the corresponding frequency component in the spectrum thereby improving the signal quality. Finally, the bit rate requirement is further reduced in the order of 1.3kbps. The performance analysis shows that the resultant synthesized speech is intelligible and quite natural preserving the identity of the speaker.

Keywords: VOCODER, LPC, Instants of significant excitation, pole focusing.

1 Introduction

In speech coding techniques, the major motive is to reduce the number of bits required to represent the speech signal without significant degradation in the resultant speech quality. Two major applications of speech coding are mobile phones and internet phones. VOCODER is used for speech coding that preserves the spectral properties of speech in the encoded signal and produce intelligible speech at the receiver end at much lower bit rates.

D. Nagamalai, E. Renault, and M. Dhanushkodi (Eds.): PDCTA 2011, CCIS 203, pp. 180–190, 2011.

In most of the speech coding techniques, the system and the source information are coded separately, interleaved and then transmitted to the receiver. To code the system, relatively fewer bits are required as the system information is responsible for intelligibility alone. Source coding forms the major part of the vocoder as it requires larger number of bits to code them in order to have better quality of the resultant signal.

From the literature, it is found that vocoders are classified in to low-rate and medium/ high-rate vocoders [1]. Some of the low rate vocoders are channel vocoder [2][3], LPC vocoder [4] and cepstral vocoder. All of them employ different ways to represent the system parameters. But the source parameters are represented in a similar fashion requiring only a few bits to code them which are explained as follows. It needs a voicing detector and pitch detector. The voicing detector gives one bit information about whether a segment is voiced or unvoiced. It uses train of pulses as the excitation source for a voiced segment and a noise generator for unvoiced segment. The pitch period with which the train of pulses are generated is dictated by the pitch detector. Different algorithms are proposed in the literature for pitch detection.

This low-rate vocoders, codes speech at rates below 2400bps, with an expected sacrifice in sound quality. The resultant speech signal is only intelligible and the speaker's identity, emotional state, and prosodic nuances are totally missing and sound synthetic. The medium/high rate coders operate at bit rates greater than 24000bps (typically 16000-48000 bps) and they can deliver more robust and higher quality speech. In these systems, efforts are taken to improve the vocoder quality understanding that poor representation of the excitation function plays an important role in quality deterioration.

In voice-excited systems, a spectrally flattened version of the original sound is used as a suitable excitation signal [5]. In voice-excited channel vocoder, the speech is low-pass filtered to create a base-band signal and is transmitted by some waveform coding technique. At the receiver, the base-band signal is decoded, spectrally flattened, applied as excitation to vocode for frequencies higher than the baseband, and also added to the vocoded speech to produce the output.

Magill and Un [6] invented a residual excited LPC (RELP) vocoder that was able to operate at 9600bps. It relies on the fact that exciting the LPC synthesizer with the complete residual error signal produces the input speech, and so the problem is to find a compressed version of the error signal that can be conditioned to act as an appropriate excitation. Voice-excited linear prediction (VELP) vocoder [7] uses the LPC error-signal concept to perform spectral flattening.

Though the previous versions of LPC vocoders show better performances, the application of vector quantization techniques to the problem of coding the excitation signal improves the performance further at less bandwidth requirement. The resultant technique is called Code Excited Linear Prediction vocoder (CELP). In conventional CELP [8][14], the difference in excitation from frame to frame is not characterized by a few pulses, but rather as one of a fixed number of sequences in the codebook. This CELP vocoder has the problem of choosing the code book sequence that will produce the least distortion. It operates at 4.8 kbps.

Multi-band CELP wideband speech coder implements a pitch prediction using an adaptive codebook [9]. Mixed excitation LPC vocoder model uses mixed excitation pulses to excite the system [10].Periodic pulses for the unvoiced sound and aperiodic pulses for the voiced and jittery voiced sounds. Voicing decisions is based on the strength of the pitch periodicity. The pitch is estimated from a search of the normalized correlation coefficients of the low-pass filtered LPC residual signal, with an explicit check for possible pitch doubling. It achieves a bit rate of 2400 bits/s.

Variable rate CELP based on sub-band flatness maintains a separate codebook for excitation patterns. The codebook contains 256 centre clipped Gaussian vectors. This coder produces good quality encoded speech at an average rate of around 2 kbps. It employs a variable rate, variable dimension, lag-driven scheme for quantizing pitch filter co-efficient vectors. [11]

Some use adaptive codebook which contains the past history of the excitation signal itself and is an implementation of a pitch period. Once the parameter of the two synthesis filter is found the excitation is determined. [12]

It is observed from the literature that a serious trade-off exists between the performance of the resultant speech signal and the bit rate requirement in the design of vocoders. The very successfully used CELP vocoders also operate in the range 2.4 to 4.8kbps to yield acceptable performance. In this paper, we have proposed to design a LPC vocoder which uses the instants of significant excitation and their strengths in the speech signal as excitation parameters. It is found to operate at the bit rate of 1.6kbps and the quality of the resynthesised speech is found to be very high and sounds very natural. This bit rate requirement is further decreased by reducing the size of the code book used for system coding. Usage of smaller sized codebook actually reduces the signal quality which is compensated by focusing the poles at the receiver side.

2 The Approach

This research work involves the design of a LPC VOCODER system with reduced bit rate enabling resynthesis of high quality speech signal. Generally, system coding and source coding are done separately. In the design of the vocoders, the source coding is generally complicated as it requires lot of bits to represent the speaker information. In this work, the source coding is done using the instants of significant excitation that has greatly reduced the bit rate requirement and also has produced natural sounding speech at the receiver. A brief description of the technique used to estimate the instants of significant excitation in the speech signal presented in [13] is discussed below.

Voiced speech is produced by excitation of the vocal tract system with the quasi-periodic vibrations of the vocal folds at the glottis. These excitations have become significantly stronger when the vocal folds are fully opened or about to be closed. This, in turn, is reflected in the speech signal as a high energy region within a pitch period known as the instant of significant excitation.

These instants of significant excitation are estimated directly from the speech signal using the temporal phase periodicity present in it. Assuming the quasi-periodic vibrations of the vocal folds as a slowly varying sinusoid, the phase of this signal is computed using the phase of the fundamental frequency component of the discrete Fourier transform. At the peaks of the speech signal, i.e., at the locations of significant instants, the phase of this component is expected to be zero.

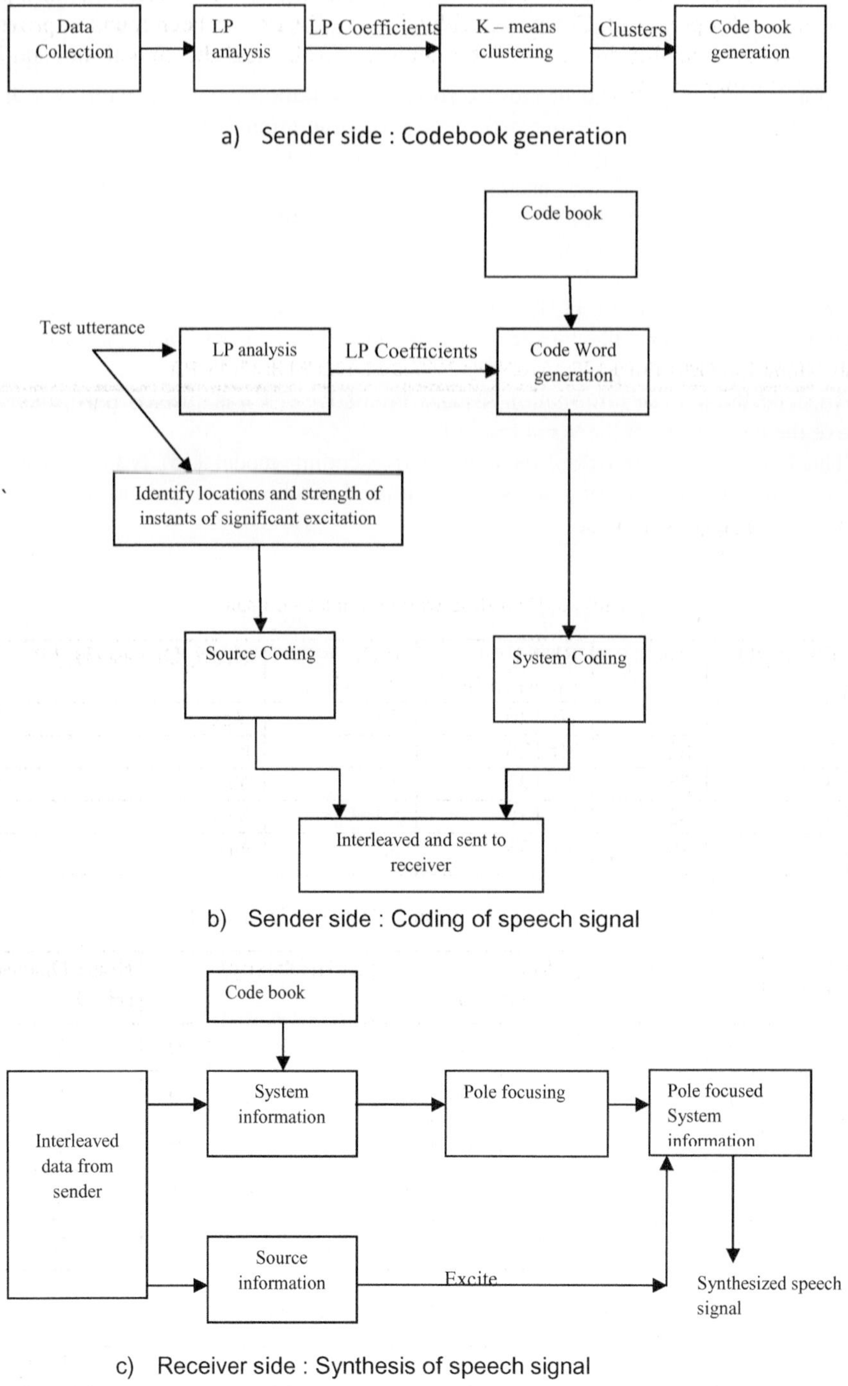

Fig. 1. Block diagram of the overall project

Temporal phase of the signal is the change in phase with respect to time. Temporal phase function is computed by calculating the phase of the signal at the first frequency bin using DFT by moving the analysis window sample by sample. Temporal phase is expected to cross zero at the excitation point and wrap at valley points (Phase is pi). Considering two successive wrap-arounds in the temporal phase function and picking the speech sample with highest amplitude that lies between these two wrap-arounds yields the instants of significant excitation. Figure 2 shows the significant instants estimated from a male speech signal of the TIMIT corpus using the above discussed technique.

The step-by-step procedure used for the estimating the instants of significant excitation is discussed in [13] .To code the source information, the frames are examined to determine the location and strength the of excitation points using the above-mentioned technique.

To code the system information, Linear Predictive (LP) analysis is performed to derive the parameters of the vocal tract filter.

The basic idea behind the Linear predictive coding model [15] is that given a speech sample at time n, s(n), can be approximated as a linear combination of the past p speech samples such that

$$s(n) = \sum_{k=1}^{p} a_k\, s(n-k) + G\, u(n) \tag{1}$$

In equation (1), ak‘s are the predictor coefficients which are assumed to be constant over the speech analysis frame, u(n) is the normalized excitation and G is the gain of the excitation.

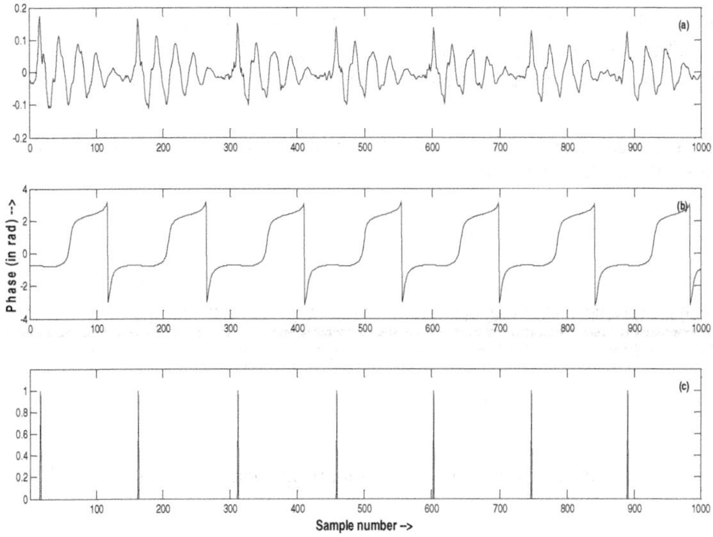

Fig 2. Estimation of instants of significant excitation. a)Speech signal corresponding to a male speaker, b) the temporal phase function and c) the significant instants (window size = 8 ms).

The predictor coefficients, {ak} have to be determined from the speech signal so that the spectral properties of the digital filter match those of the speech waveform. Since the spectral characteristics of speech vary over time, the predictor coefficients at a given time, n, must be estimated from a short segment of speech signal occurring around time n. Thus the basic approach is to find the set of predictor coefficients that minimize the mean-squared prediction error over a short segment of speech waveform. The mean-squared prediction error at instant n is given by

$$E_n = \sum_{m=1}^{p} [\, s_m(m) - \sum_{k=1} a_k \, s_n(m-k)]^2)] \tag{2}$$

The LP analysis is applied to each frame and the LP coefficients are obtained which act as the feature vectors. These feature vectors are given to the K-means algorithm to generate the code book. This algorithm generates the clusters and returns a set of feature vectors comprising the LPC coefficients which are nothing but the cluster centroids. These cluster centroids forms the codebook. In this work, the k-means algorithm uses the Itakura-Saito (I-S) distance measure for calculating the distance between two feature vectors.

Itakura-Saito distance measure is defined as

$$E_{IS} = \frac{1}{N} \sum_{m=1}^{N} \frac{P(\omega m)}{\hat{P}(\omega m)} - \ln \frac{P(\omega m)}{\hat{P}(\omega m)} - 1 \tag{3}$$

where P(w) is the given discrete spectrum defined at N frequency points ωm ϵ Ω, and $\hat{P}(\omega_m)$ is the all-pole model spectrum [16].During testing, the test utterance is converted in to a set of frames and the feature vectors are extracted using LP analysis. The same Itakura-Saito distance measure is used to find the closest match for each feature vector in the test utterance from the codebook. The index position of the codeword that matched feature vector is to be communicated to the receiver. This codeword provides the necessary system information in that frame. The receiver receives the address of the codeword and retrieves the corresponding feature from the codebook. Now the system can be built with these coefficients and has to be excited by the source for resynthesis. The locations of the instants and their strength which are transmitted by the source coder are used to excite the system to synthesize the speech signal back.

The code words obtained from the code book of size 64 seem to be defocused. Hence we move to pole focusing the LP coefficients obtained from the code book. Consider a signal, s(n), with sampling period T. Let us presently assume that an all-pole transfer function of s(n) be S(Z). Consider a complex pole a_k. Let the radius and angle of a_k in z-domain be r_k and θ_k . Further, the relation between r_k and 3-dB bandwidth $\boldsymbol{B}_k$, of the corresponding frequency component in the spectrum can be written as $r_k = e^{B_k T}$. That is, greater the radius of a pole, narrower the bandwidth (increased gain) of the corresponding resonant frequency in the spectrum. If r_k is increased without changing θ_k, in other words, pushing the pole towards the unit circle (polefocusing), causes the increment in the gain (magnitude) of the corresponding frequency component in the spectrum [18]. Thus the poles of LP coefficient are obtained and the radius is increased nearing to the unit circle without changing the angle. Thus by pushing the poles close to radius of the unit circle, the signal does not die down quickly and the poles are also focused. Hence the signal quality is improved. These are illustrated in the figures 3, 4, 5.

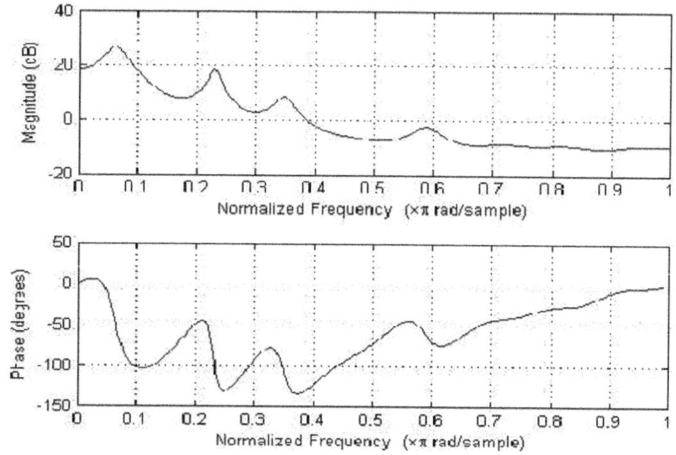

Fig. 3. LP spectrum of the original codeword

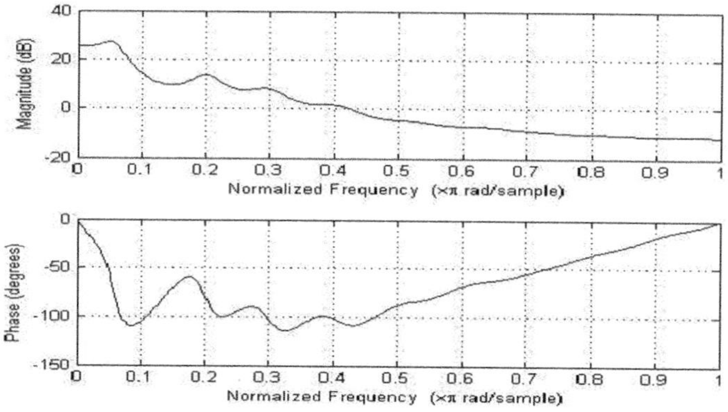

Fig. 4. LP spectrum of the codeword obtained from the codebook which seems to be defocused

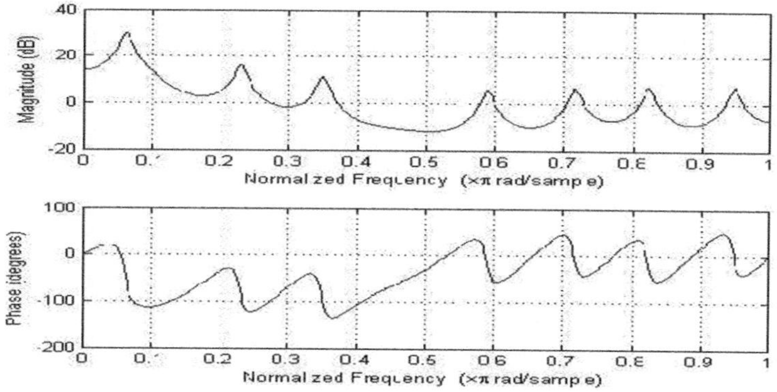

Fig. 5. LP spectrum of the codeword after pole focusing

3 Experimental Setup

For code book generation, 15 minutes of speech data of a female speaker is collected/recorded. The frame size and frame shift chosen for short time analysis of the speech data is 20ms and 20ms respectively. LP analysis is performed to obtain the LP coefficients for which the order is set as 20. These extracted features are given to K-means algorithm to generate a code book of sizes 64 and 1024. Also, 15 minutes of speech data of 5 different speakers are collected to generate multi-speaker codebook to perform comparative analysis. In the process of extraction of instants of significant excitation, the window size is chosen as 5ms for a female speaker and 10ms for a male speaker. Though instants estimation algorithm is less sensitive to variations in window size, it was observed that choosing the window size close to the pitch period of the speaker better estimates the instants. Also, the temporal phase function is computed only for the first frequency bin and is used for instants estimation.

4 Performance Analysis

In system coding, the distance between two feature vectors can be calculated in different ways using different distance metrics. Analysis is carried out to find the metric that performs better than all the other metrics in this task. The Itakura distance, Itakura-Saito distance, Cosh spectral distance metrics are used to calculate the distance between two sets of autoregressive (AR) / LP coefficients.

Table 1. Performance Analysis For The Distance Metric

Scores / Distance	Poor	Fair	Average	Good	Excellent
Euclidean Distance	✓				
Itakura –Saito Distance					✓
Itakura Distance			✓		
Cosh Spectral Distance			✓		

The speech signal was synthesized with codebooks generated using various distance metrics mentioned above. Perceptual analysis was carried out with 10 listeners. They were asked to give the scores according to the intelligibility, naturalness and preservation of the identity of the speaker. The scale of evaluation was specified as 1.Poor, 2.Fair, 3.Average, 4.Good, and 5.Excellent. The average scores of the listeners are tabulated in Table I. Comparatively Itakura – Saito distance measure is found to be better than others. The other method is to convert the LP coefficients (LPC) in to LP cepstral coefficients (LPCC) and use the Euclidean squared distance measure to find the distance between them. It is observed that using the Itakura-Saito distance metric yields better results as it gives the minimum intra cluster distance and maximum inter cluster distance compared to all the other metrics.

The qualities of the resynthesized speech signal using code books of different sizes are analyzed. Code books of different sizes (64, 128, 256, and, 1024) are generated and used for testing the performance. It is observed that

1024 sized codebook yield better performance which gives a conclusion that larger codebooks required to give good performance.

The code books generated using single speaker data and multiple data are used to code speech utterances of different speakers and the performance of the resynthesized signal are analyzed. It is interesting to observe that the resultant speech is intelligible and also natural preserving the identity of the speaker. This proves that the source coding done using the instants of significant excitation retains the actual source information i.e. the identity of the speaker.

The bit rate requirement for the designed vocoder is calculated and found to be around 1.6Kbps when the system was encoded using a code book of size 1024. In this, 10 bits are used to encode the system information for each frame. There are 50 frames per second (according to the sampling rate of 16 KHz and frame size of 20ms chosen), 500 bits/sec are used for coding the system. To reduce the number of bits further, the code book size is reduced to 64 and the deterioration in the performance is compensated by pole focusing. Finally, only 300 bits are required for system coding.

Our experiments carried out on TIMIT speech corpus have shown that the performance of the algorithm is quite promising. Further, we observed that it is less sensitive to wide range of windows sizes, gender, and variations in the strength of the signal. Figure 6 and 7 shows that the algorithm is less sensitive to gender, variations in window size and variations in signal strength.

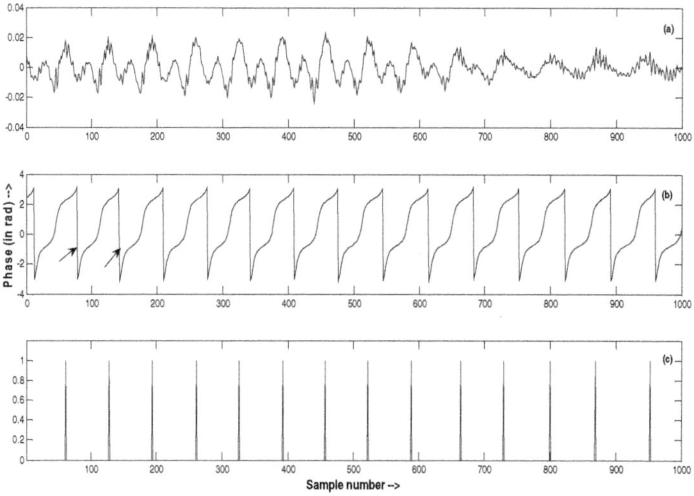

Fig. 6. Speech signal corresponding to a female speaker, the temporal phase function and the significant instants (window size = 8 ms)

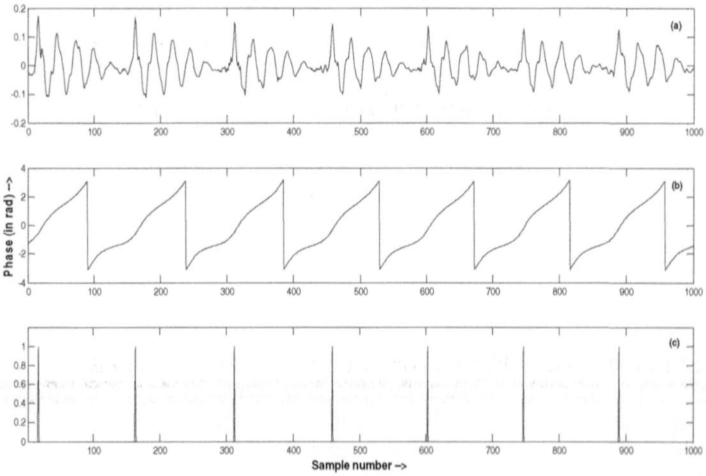

Fig. 7. Speech signal corresponding to a male speaker, the temporal phase function and the significant instants (window size = 4 ms)

There are around 150 excitation instants per second (if the pitch period is 5ms). The location of the instants and the strength of the excitation at those instant are used for coding for source. Two bits are used to encode the strength of the instants as four-level quantization is sufficient. To code the instant location, instead of the using sample numbers directly, the location of the next instant is specified relative to the previous instant. Also, we have used 5 bit quantization to encode the instant location. Hence, a total of 7 bits are utilized to encode an instant leading to 1050 bits/sec (150*7).

The system required 300 bits/sec and the source required 1050 bits/sec as mentioned above resulting in a bit rate of 1350 bits/sec (1.3kbs approx.).

5 Conclusion and Future Work

In this paper, we have proposed a new technique for source coding using the instants of significant excitation in a LPC vocoder. Using the locations of the instants and their strengths to code the source information, it is shown that the bit rate requirement is reduced significantly. Also, the resultant synthesized speech is intelligible and quite natural; preserving the identity of the speaker.The system is coded using a codebook that is generated using the LP coefficients. During code book generation, it has been proven that 1024 sized code book yield better performance than 64 sized one. But, using 64 size code book reduces the bit rate requirement for system coding. However, the performance compensation is done using a novel technique called pole focusing. The performance can be further improved by performing selective pole focusing than focusing all the poles. Also, it is shown that using the Itakura-Saito distance metric to calculate the distance between two feature vectors is relatively better than other metrics to do the same.

References

[1] Gold, B., Morgan, N.: Speech and Audio Signal Processing: Processing and Perception of Speech and Music. John Wiley & Sons, Inc., New York (1999)

[2] Gold, B., Rader, C.M.: The Channel Vocoder. IEEE Transactions on Audio and Electro Acoustics AU-15(4) (December 1967)

[3] Davie, M.C.: Channel vocoder based on c.c.d. discrete-fourier transform Processors. IEEE Proc. 127, pt. F(2) (April 1980)

[4] Martins, J.A., Violaro, F.: Low bit rate LPC vocoders using vector quantization and interpolation, pp. 597–600. IEEE, Los Alamitos (1991)

[5] David, E.E., Schroeder, M.R., Logan, B.F., Prestigiacoma, A.J.: Voice-excited vocoders for practical speech bandwidth reduction. Presented at the Speech Communication Seminar, Stockholm (1963)

[6] Magil, D.T., Un, C.K.: Residual-excited linear predictive coder. JASA 55, Suplement abstract NN3 in the April 24-26 87th meeting of the Acoustical Society, 581

[7] Weinstein, C.J.: A linear prediction vocoder with voice excitation. In: Proc. Eascon 1975, Washington, D.C, pp. 30A-30G (1975)

[8] Schroeder, M., Atal, B.: Code-excited linear prediction: high-quality speech coding at very low bit rates. In: Proc. ICASSP 1985, Tampa, pp. 937–940 (1985)

[9] Ubale, A., Gersho, A.: A multi-band CELP wideband speech coder. In: IEEE Proc. ICASSP 1997, pp. 1367–1370 (April 1997)

[10] McCree, A.V., Barnwell, T.P.: A Mixed Excitation LPC Vocoder Model for Low Bit Rate Speech Coding. IEEE Transactions on Speech and Audio Processing 3, 4 (1995)

[11] McCkllan, S.A., Gibson, J.D.: Variable Rate CELP Based On Subband Flatness. IEEE Transactions on Speech and Audio Processing 5(2) (March 1997)

[12] Park, Y., Yang, J., Sohn, S., Bae, M.: On a time reduction of pitch searching by the regular pulse search technique in the CELP vocoder. IEEE, Los Alamitos (1997)

[13] Sripriya, N., Vijayalakshmi, P., Arun Kumar, C., Nagarajan, T.: Estimation of Instants of Significant Excitation from Speech Signal using Temporal Phase Periodicity. In: IEEE TENCON 2009 (2009)

[14] Yang, G., Leich, H.: A Robust and Fast DP-CELP (Double-Pulse CELP) Vocoder at the Bit Rate of 4 kbh. In: International Symposium on Speech, Image Processing and Neural Networks (April 13-16, 1994)

[15] Rabiner, L., Juang, B.-H., Yegnanarayana, B.: Fundamentals of Speech Recognition. Pearson Education, London (1993)

[16] Wei, B., Gibson, J.D.: Comparison of distance measures in discrete spectral modeling. In: Proc. 9th DSP Workshop & 1st Signal Processing Education Workshop (2000)

[17] Rabiner, L.R., Schafer, R.W.: Digital Processing of Speech Signals. Prentice-Hall, Inc., Englewood Cliffs (1978)

[18] Abraham, A., Vijayalakshmi, P., Nagarajan, T.: Pole-focused linear prediction-based spectrogram for coarticulation analysis. In: IEEE TechSym, pp. 94–97 (2010)

An Enhanced DSR Caching Scheme Based on Cross Layer Information

Gaurav Bhatia and Vivek Kumar

Department of Computer Science,
Gurukul Kangri Vishwavidyalya,
Haridwar-249404, India
gbhatia13@gmail.com, vivekdcg@gkvharidwar.org

Abstract. Dynamic Source Routing (DSR) is an efficient reactive routing protocol for mobile ad hoc networks, in which only needed routes are found and maintained. Route caching is employed to avoid the need for discovering a route before each data packet is sent. DSR employs caching of routes to increase the protocol efficiency. However, the absence of any opportune mechanism to remove cache entry causes cache to contain stale information, also the aggressive use of cache cause dissemination of stale route information, which leads to delay and increases loss rate in high mobility scenario. In this paper, we propose a dynamic mechanism which computes Expected Link Expiration Time (ELET) using cross layer parameter which timely removes the stale cache entry from route cache, also an updated route reply method is used to prevent dissemination of stale routes. Simulation results in NS2 show that enhanced DSR (EDSR) cache scheme can swiftly adapt to scenario changes and can perform better than the existing caching scheme.

Keywords: DSR, RSSI, Route Cache, Cross Layer Information, MANET.

1 Introduction

Dynamic Source Routing (DSR) is an on-demand protocol that uses source routing and makes aggressive use of route caches. The current specification of DSR lacks a mechanism to determine the validity of routes in the route caches. DSR uses fixed time interval for cache invalidation, i.e., entry in cache appoints a fixed time and removed when time expired. This mechanism is not efficient as waiting too long to invalidate route introduces stale route cache and its dissemination. Also not waiting long enough removes the routes from cache which are still valid and causes unnecessary retransmission of route request and route reply. The weakness of this scheme is that it cannot adapt to the change of the network topology. Because of these, setting the timeout close to the expected link expiration time is considered to improve the performance. Since the actual lifetime of a link highly depends on node mobility, to achieve good performance, dynamic caching schemes are desired. Our goal is to develop and analyze enhanced cache strategies for reducing number of stale route entries and their dissemination. The basic idea of the scheme is to use the *Expected Link Expiration Time* (ELET) as its cache timeout and preventing the distribution of stale

D. Nagamalai, E. Renault, and M. Dhanushkodi (Eds.): PDCTA 2011, CCIS 203, pp. 191–203, 2011.

information by updated route reply. The ELET is a measure of time duration in which a node will become out of transmission range of another node. ELET is determined dynamically by the *Enhanced DSR* (EDSR) when it receives RREQ from nearby node using the cross layer information. Cross layer design [1] refers to protocol stack that intercommunicate the useful information to collectively achieve the desired optimization goal by allowing the different protocols to share information related to the network status. In this paper, we propose a cross layer based cache mechanism in which DSR computes timeout value of individual links by utilizing received signal strength from physical layer. This method uses locally available network information and does not require any external support.

This paper has been structured as follows. Section 2 gives an overview of DSR protocol and its cache structure. Section 3 describes the problem statement. In section 4, we discuss related work. Section 5 describes proposed work and EDSR cache mechanism, it explains how the cross layer information is collected and how it is used to predict the link expiration time which is further used in cache invalidation. Section 6 presents simulation and result analysis, and finally, in section 7 we present our conclusions and future work.

2 Dynamic Source Routing (DSR) Overview [2]

DSR is a reactive and efficient routing protocol designed specifically for use in multi-hop wireless ad hoc networks of mobile nodes. It allows the network to be completely self-organizing and self-configuring, without the need for any existing network infrastructure or administration. The operation of DSR is based on source routing, in which the sender of a packet determines the complete sequence of hops to be used as the route for that packet to its destination. The source route, the complete sequence of hops through which the packet passes, is represented in the header of each packet. DSR protocol operates entirely on-demand and lacks periodic activity of any kind at any layer within the network. This allows the network overhead caused by DSR to minimum only to that needed to react to changes in the currently using routes. DSR protocol consists of following mechanisms:

2.1 Route Discovery

When a source node originates a new packet addressed to a destination node, it will search its Route Cache for a source route. If no route is found in the cache, the sender initializes Route Discovery by broadcasting a *Route Request* (RREQ) packet (Fig. 1), containing destination node address, unique request identification, and an initial empty list which together uniquely identify this Route Discovery.

A node receiving the RREQ, if it is not the intended destination, appends its address to the node list and forwards the packet. However, first it checks whether it has recently seen another RREQ from the same source node with the same request identification and target address, or whether its own address has already presented in the traveled node list of this RREQ. If either check is true, the node silently drops this packet. When the RREQ packet reaches the destination node, this node returns a *Route Reply* (RREP) to the source node (Fig. 2) with a copy of the node list from the RREQ.

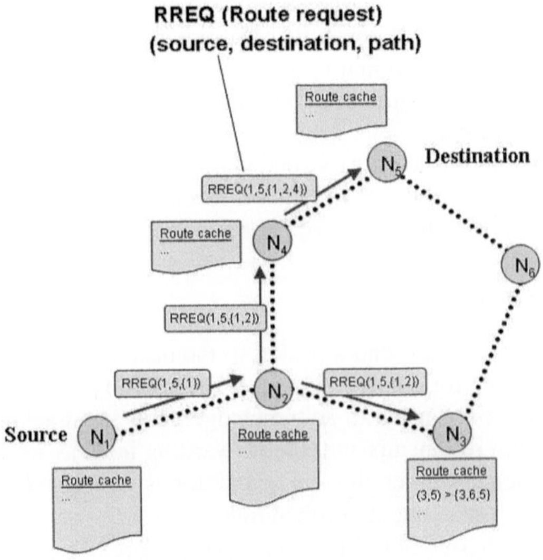

Fig. 1. Node N_1 sends RREQ

If an intermediate node receiving the RREQ contains the route to the destination in its Route Cache then this node returns a RREP to the source node from its own route cache (Fig. 2) rather than forwarding the route request. If the destination node receives the multiple RREQ propagated from different routes, it replies to all RREQ by RREP. As a result of single route discovery to a destination node leads to multiple

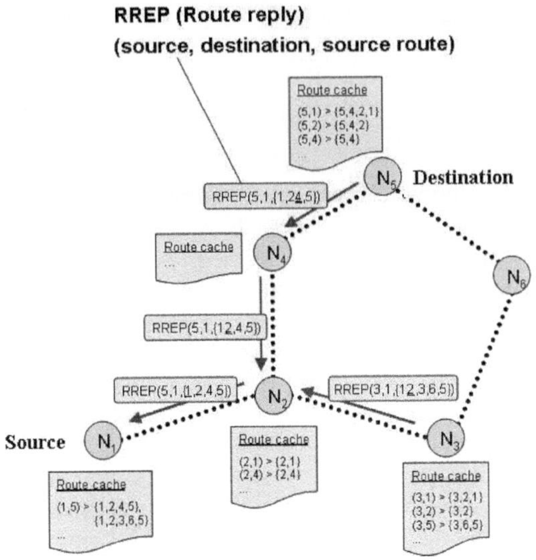

Fig. 2. Nodes N_5, N_3 sends RREP

routes for it. The RREP can be delivered to the initiator by simply reversing the node list, by using a route to the initiator in its own cache, or "piggybacking" the packet on a new Route Request to the original initiator. When the initiator receives the RREP, it adds the source route in its route cache for use in sending subsequent packets to the destination and for future use.

An additional method to learn new routes information is to allow nodes in DSR to add all usable routing information to its own Route Cache by overhearing the source routes on packets sent by other nodes or packets forwarded by it.

2.2 Route Maintenance

While using a source route to send a packet to the destination, each node transmitting the packet is responsible for confirming that it successfully reaches the next hop in the route. The node can confirm by an acknowledgement. If no acknowledgement is received after maximum retransmission, the forwarding node assumes that the next-hop destination is unreachable over this link, and sends a *Route Error* (RERR) to the source of the packet, indicating the broken link.

An additional feature of Route Maintenance is packet salvaging. When an intermediate node forwarding a packet determines the next hop is unreachable over the link, in addition to sending back RERR, it replaces the original route with an alternate route, if it finds any other route to the destination, from its route cache then it forwards the packet to the next hop along with the new route. A node, either source or intermediate, receiving a RERR removes that link from its route cache.

2.3 Route Cache

DSR protocol maintains a Route Cache, containing routing information needed by the node. A node adds information to its Route Cache as it learns new links between nodes in the ad hoc network, for example, a node may learn new links when it receives a packet carrying a Route Request, Route Reply or DSR source route. Likewise, a node removes information from its Route Cache as it learns that existing links in the ad hoc network have broken. The Route Cache can be implemented either in two types of organization [3]:

Path Cache. A path is complete sequence of links leading to the destination node from source node (Fig. 3). By caching each of these paths separately, a path cache organization for the Route Cache can be formed. A path cache is very simple to implement and easily guarantees that all routes are loop-free, since each individual route from a Route Reply or Route Request used in a packet is loop-free. To search for a route in a path cache data structure, the sending node can simply search its Route Cache for any path (or prefix of a path) that leads to the intended destination node.

Link Cache. Each individual link in the routes returned in Route Reply packets (or otherwise learned) is decomposed into individual links and added to a unified graph data structure of this node's current view of the network topology (Fig. 4). To search for a route in link cache, the sending node use a graph search algorithm, such as the well-known Dijkstra's shortest-path algorithm or the breath-first-search (BFS) shortest path algorithm, to find the current best path through the graph to the destination node.

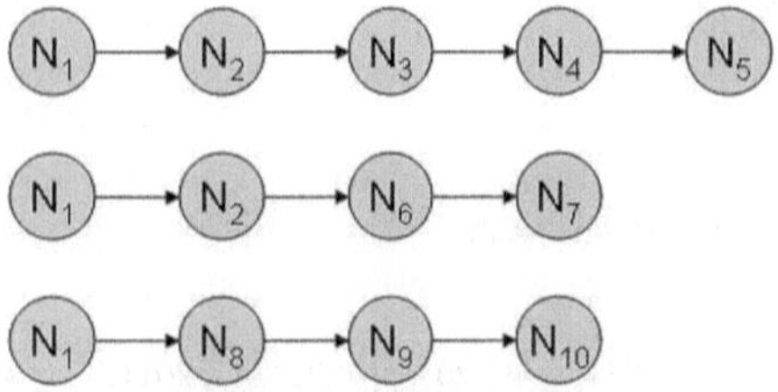

Fig. 3. Path Based Organization

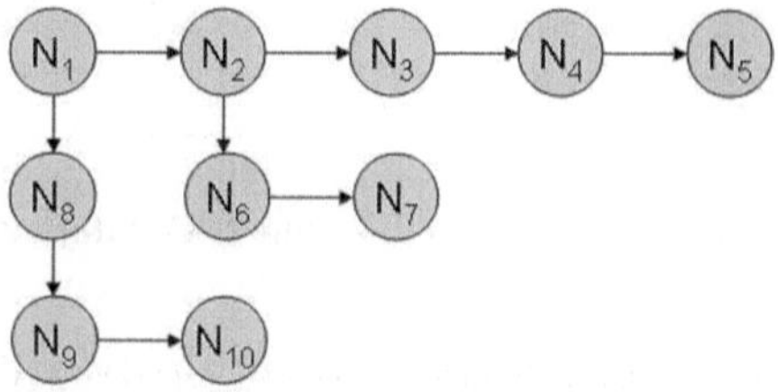

Fig. 4. Link Based Cache Organization

3 Problem Definition

DSR makes very aggressive use of route caching. It adds source route information in route cache when it receives route reply in response to a route request and when it overhears any packet's transmission nearby it. Also, it learns the routes when it forwards any packet. This route cache information is used in sending packets to the destination, sending route reply to another node and for packet salvaging.

DSR protocol uses route cache to avoid the need to rediscover route for each individual packet. If route cache contains stale information, this may degrade performance of DSR rather than improve it.

3.1 Stale Cache Information

The route cache may contain the stale information [3-5] containing links that are no longer exists. When node mobility is high, entries in route caches quickly become invalid as node becomes unreachable when it goes out of transmission range of its nearby nodes. A stale route cache entry is noticed by a node when it sends a packet and receives the route error message by intermediate node. The sender or any other node receiving route error message removes that link from its route cache. This is inefficient error notification as, when a link breaks, route errors are not propagated to all caches that have an entry with the broken link. Instead, the route error is unicast only to the source whose data packet is responsible for identifying the link breakage. Thus only a limited number of caches are cleaned. The failure information is, however, propagated by piggybacking it onto the subsequent route requests from the source. But as the route requests may not be propagated network-wide (because of replies from caches), many caches may remain uncleaned. Thus this is an inefficient method of stale route cache cleaning.

DSR has static timeout mechanisms associated with each entry in the Route Cache to allow that entry to be deleted after a fixed interval of time (RouteCache-Timeout). This leads to stay the stale source route entry for a longer time in route cache when the link becomes invalid. DSR lacks of any timely stale route cache invalidate mechanism. When a stale route is used to send data packets it takes significant time to detect a broken link, which causes data packets to suffer unnecessary longer delays.

3.2 Dissemination of Stale Cache Information

The stale route cache entry can easily spread widely into the network [4], as the DSR has a mechanism through which a node can reply the route request message from its own route cache. However, DSR does not ensure the validity of route which it replies from its cache. Thus a node may reply a route which is stale. When a node uses information from its route cache, the cache staleness problem is compounded, since stale information could circulate in the network indefinitely. For example, one node may use some stale information to route a packet that it sends, allowing a number of nodes to overhear that packet and to cache that stale routing information. If any node that overheard the use of the route does not subsequently overhear the corresponding route breakage notification, that node will be left with a stale link in its route cache, which it may later use in routing its own packets. This may cause a node, which has actually learned that a link no longer exists, to again add the stale route information in its cache.

Thus, DSR protocol has inefficient method of stale route cache cleaning and lacks of any timely stale route cache invalidate algorithm. Also the use of route cache in route reply spread the stale route information in the network. This leads to higher delay latency and reduced throughput.

4 Related Work

Some earlier work [3-5] proposed adaptive timeout for route cache to address the stale cache problem. In [3], author proposed Link-MaxLife timeout mechanism for link cache based on observed link usage and breakages. In [4], Marina and Das use average lifetime of route and time since last link is broken for calculation of timeout value. They multiply average life time of route by some factor then apply MAX function on both values. They also proposed wider error notification and use of negative cache to reduce the distribution of stale cache information. In [5], author proposed adaptive lifetime estimation scheme that adaptively estimate the link lifetime based on the moving average of the previous collected lifetime statistics. These mechanisms predict the timeout of a route cache using pre determined parameters. However, predetermined value of timeout may work for certain scenarios but may not work well for all.

In [6], authors proposed a distributed adaptive algorithm to proactively distribute the broken link information to the nodes that have broken link in their cache. They defined a cache table structure, kept by each node, to maintain the local information necessary for cache updates. Based on it, the proposed algorithm notifies all reachable nodes that have cached the link in a distributed manner. In this work, timeout for route cache entry is not used, thus if nodes become unreachable in some cases then they will not remove the stale route from their caches. In [7], Huang, Chan developed a RERR-Enhance mechanism by transmitting RERR to all nodes that have cached the broken link, they also propose a hierarchical link cache structure, accompanied with a link stability measurement mechanism to determine the stability of a link based on the historical statistic of successful data packets transmission. Ashish Shukla [8] presented a cross-layer approach for predicting the route cache lifetime. The author assigns timeouts of individual links in route cache by utilizing RSSI values received from physical layer. This scheme requires RSSI thresholds for link timeout on every node of the ad hoc network. In this method the timeout value directly depends on thresholds value selected. In [9], authors proposed an algorithm which performs distributed cache updating by using the local information kept by each node. When a node receives information about a link failure, it checks the field NeighboursToBeInformed and sends a notification to these neighbors. When a neighbor receives a notification, it uses the same algorithm to notify its selected neighbors and so on which quickly propagate broken link information to all reachable nodes whose caches contain that link. The timeout for link cache is also used which is based on Link-Adapt [3] timeout strategy. In [10], a smart packet is generated periodically which travels through the network, collects topology information, and the nodes update their route caches. Route entries then contain new routes reflecting the most recent topology changes. The algorithms [9][10], seem to be effective but they increase the overhead of DSR as they required extra control packets generation.

In this paper, we propose a route cache invalidation mechanism using cross layer parameter. It uses locally available network parameter and does not require any extra control packet generation to get topology information. Our method not only timely removes the stale route cache entry, it also helps in prevention of its dissemination. The novelty of the proposed method is that it is suitable to work with both the cache structures, path and link caches.

5 Proposed Work

An *Enhanced DSR* (EDSR) Route Cache Scheme has been developed to invalidate the route cache entry and updated route reply from route cache. Our approach is to find *Expected Link Expiration Time* (ELET) in between two communicating nodes in the route. Whenever a node adds its link in route request it also adds ELET with respect to nearby requesting node. So that ELET will be used as timeout value for EDSR route cache. When ELET expires, EDSR drops the cache entry to maintain the cache freshness. Also, when a node replies a route request from its cache, it first validates the route by updating the expected link expiration time by subtracting the time spent in the route cache, i.e., the time for which a route stays in the cache, and if it is found that the route is expired or going to be expired it does not reply from cache and further propagate the route request after adding its own information into the source route.

To reduce the problem of stale caching, a route cache invalidation scheme is introduced based on path time out in path cache and link time out in link cache. For path cache, the timeout of source route is considered as minimum of all ELET (from all links in a route). Since if any of links in path fails, it will invalidate the whole route. For link cache, each link is treated individually and path is decided by combining different links, thus, each link is individually invalidated according to its ELET. Also, each time when a node receives the RREP containing already learned link, it updates the cache information from the newer one. So, any link that has not been updated within the ELET period from the time of its addition to the cache is discarded being stale.

For the computation of ELET, each node uses two received signal strength values, one in the table called as neighbor table and other one it gets from the received packet (RREQ). These are used to compute two distances that further predict the relative velocity and the direction of the movement of the nearby nodes.

5.1 Estimation of the Expected Distance to Be Traveled for Separation

When a node receives or overhears a packet from a nearby node at the physical layer, it measures the *receive signal strength indicator* (RSSI). In order to determine link timeout, each node keeps a record of the RSSI of nearby nodes with timestamp.

Assuming a free space path loss model, we have

$$P_i = P_t G_t G_r \left(\frac{\lambda}{4\pi d} \right)^2 \tag{1}$$

where, Pi is the RSSI from node i and P_t is the default transmission strength, G_t and G_r are the antenna gains of the transmitter and the receiver respectively, d is the separation distance in meter and λ is the wavelength in meters.

Thus,
$$P_i = \frac{K}{\mathrm{d}_\mathrm{i}^2} \tag{2}$$

and
$$d_i^2 = \frac{K}{P_i} \Rightarrow d_i = \sqrt{\frac{K}{P_i}} \tag{3}$$

where, K denotes a constant that depends on the transmission power, antenna gains of the two nodes and the wavelength of the transmission.

The distance d to the transmitter of a packet can be calculated using (3). For simplicity, we assume that nodes of a given link have the same transmission range, which is a maximum communication distance d_{max} (Fig. 5). The distance between the two nearby nodes is approximated by d $(d \le d_{max})$. Let d_{pre} be the previous distance of nearby node estimated using the RSSI, P_{pre}, at time t_{pre}, (stored in neighbor table) and the d_{cur} is the current distance measured when the route request is received from that node. We need to compute the distance, d_{break}, that two nodes need to be traveled mutually to be out of transmission range.

Case 1 : Nodes are Moving Closer. If $d_{cur} < d_{pre}$, the nodes are moving close together and thus distance traveled to break the link, d_{break}, is

$$d_{break} = (d_{\max} + d_{cur}) \tag{4}$$

Case 2 : Nodes are Moving Apart. If $d_{cur} > d_{pre}$, the nodes are moving far away and their link will be broken after traveling distance d_{break} , where

$$d_{break} = (d_{\max} - d_{cur}) \tag{5}$$

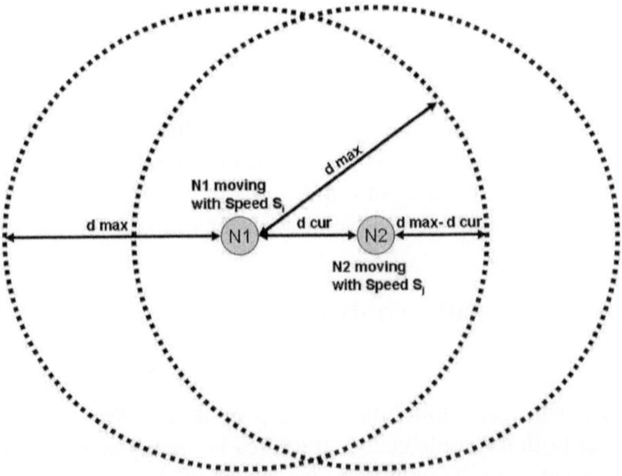

Fig. 5. Two successive nodes constituting a path

5.2 Prediction of Relative Velocity between Two Nodes

We assume that nodes are moving in a straight direction, without any pause and with a constant speed. Using (3), their relative velocity V_{rel} can be predicted as follows:

$$\left|d_{cur} - d_{pre}\right| = \left|\sqrt{\frac{K}{P_{cur}}} - \sqrt{\frac{K}{P_{pre}}}\right| \tag{6}$$

$$V_{rel} = \frac{\sqrt{K}}{t_{cur} - t_{pre}} \left|\left(\frac{1}{\sqrt{P_{cur}}} - \frac{1}{\sqrt{P_{pre}}}\right)\right| \tag{7}$$

where $|(d_{cur} - d_{pre})|$ is the distance traveled by two nodes mutually with in a time duration $(t_{cur} - t_{pre})$. V_{rel} in (7) allows us to compute the relative velocity. The P_{cur}, P_{pre} are the RSSI measured in between two nearby nodes at time t_{cur} and t_{pre} respectively.

5.3 Expected Link Expiration Time

We estimate the expected link expiration time (τ) as follows:

$$\tau = \left(d_{break} / V_{rel}\right) \tag{8}$$

5.4 Path Expiration Time

Since a route becomes stale as soon as one of its links is broken, thus the *Path Expiration Time* (Γ) for path cache is given by:

$$\Gamma = \min_{i=1}^{N}\left(\tau_i\right) \tag{9}$$

where, a path is composed of N links and τ_i represent the expected link expiration time of node i. Only nodes that are in the route from the source to destination are considered in the analysis of path time out duration. If the neighbor table does not have an entry for nearby node then the default value for time out is used.

6 Simulation and Result Analysis

For performance analysis of the proposed scheme, ns-2 [11] simulation tool has been employed. We perform the simulation of the proposed EDSR caching schemes with DSR. We consider both the route cache structures i.e. path cache and link cache.

The scenario consists of 50 mobile nodes which move in an area of 1000×1000 m according to the random way point model. In this model, a node starts in a random position and moves towards in a straight line with a constant velocity and pauses for a specified pause time. We used 0 s as pause time for all scenarios. The nodes move continuously with speed range set to 4, 8, 12, 16, 20 and 24 m/s for different simulation runs. The link layer model is the Distributed Coordinated Function (DCF) of the IEEE 802.11 wireless LAN standard. The default transmission range is 300 meters and channel capacity is 2 Mbits/sec. We considered 15 CBR connections with 4 packets per second and packet size of 512 bytes. Each simulation last for 500 s.

In this simulation, the following performance metrics have been considered for performance evaluation of routing protocol and caching scheme:

- Total Route Error: the total number of route errors generated in the network.
- Stale Cache Ratio: the ratio of stale links present in cache to the total number of links present in the cache.
- End to End Delay: the delay from when a data packet is sent by the source until it is received by the destination.
- Packet Delivery Ratio: the ratio of data packet delivered to the destination and the number of packets generated by the source.

The first two metrics measure the effectiveness of the proposed enhanced DSR caching scheme and the remaining metrics measure the overall performance i.e. latency and loss rate.

6.1 Total Route Errors

Fig.6. shows the total route error generated in network using DSR and EDSR. For both cache structures the total route error for DSR in comparison to EDSR is very high, the reason behind this difference is that the DSR cache structures contain stale routes, which leads to route errors. This is due to the fact that our scheme not only keeps the routes in cache validated but also replies only the valid routes from cache, reducing the possibility of route errors.

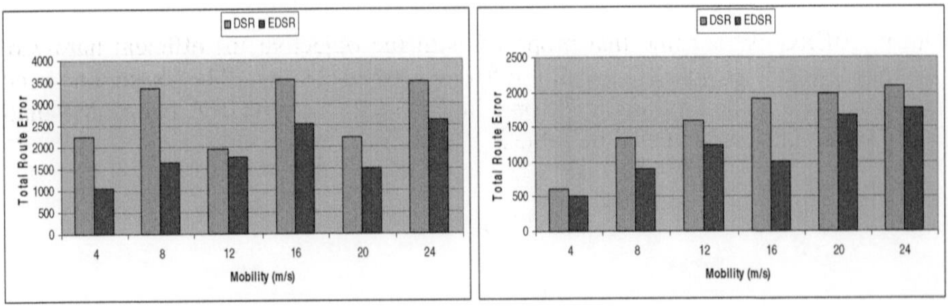

(a) Path Route Cache

(b) Link Route Cache

Fig.6. Total Route Errors

6.2 Stale Cache Ratio

Fig.7. shows the stale route cache ratio in path cache and link cache. For EDSR it is much smaller than DSR, this is due to the fact that EDSR timely invalidates the stale route information and does not disseminate it. Such significant improvement shows that EDSR efficiently removes stale routes as the topology changes.

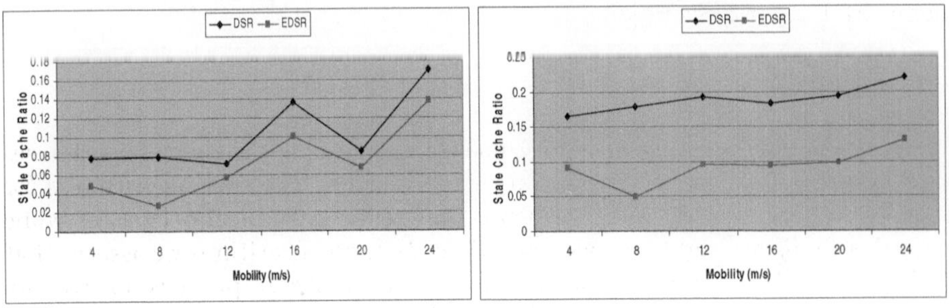

(a) Path Route Cache

(b) Link Route Cache

Fig.7. Stale Cache Ratio

6.3 End to End Delay

Fig.8. shows the performance comparison of end-to-end delay for DSR and EDSR protocol. In both path and link cache the end-to-end delay is lower in EDSR as compared to DSR. This is because the time required to recover from broken link due to stale route is very large. It includes the time for a packet travel along the route to the node immediately before the broken link, the time for that node to detect the broken link and the time for a route error message to travel from that node back to the source node. Therefore, we observe that EDSR results in low end to end delay, as delay caused by broken routes are minimized.

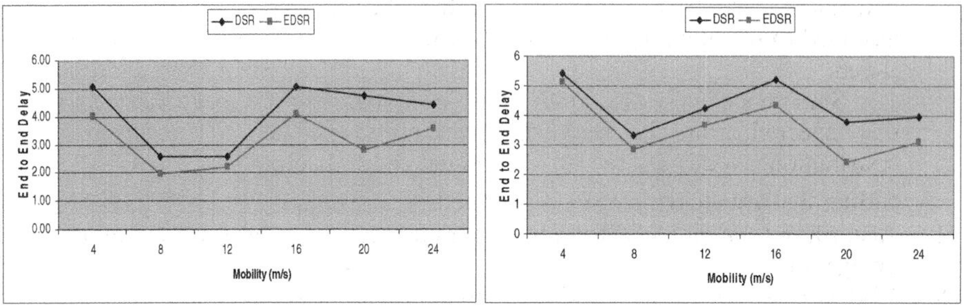

(a) Path Route Cache (b) Link Route Cache

Fig. 8. End to End Delay

6.4 Packet Delivery Ratio

Fig.9. shows that in both cache structures the packet delivery ratio of EDSR is better than DSR. As discussed in section 6.1, DSR reports more route error as compared to EDSR (Fig. 6). DSR drops the data packet due to stale route cache entry which leads to decreased packet delivery ratio for it.

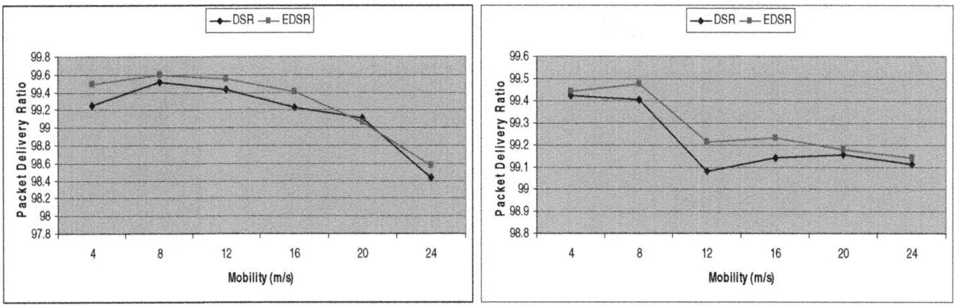

(a) Path Route Cache (b) Link Route Cache

Fig. 9. Packet Delivery Ratio

7 Conclusion and Future Work

In this paper, we present an Enhanced DSR (EDSR) caching scheme for mobile adhoc networks. Towards this, we propose an Expected Link Expiration Time (ELET) that helps in timely removal of stale cache entry. This scheme is based on cross layer information which is gathered at the physical layer (RSSI) and used in DSR to determine the route lifetime.

Our objective is to reduce the stale cache information and its dissemination. With our extension, the Enhanced DSR caching scheme dynamically computes the ELET and adds this value when a route is discovered by source node. The ELET is stored by node in route cache and used to clean the cache entry after its expiration. If a node replies a route request from its cache then it first updates the ELET value of route by subtracting the time which is spent by route in cache to prevent the stale information dissemination. The simulation results show that Enhanced DSR caching scheme can considerably improve the performance. It reduces the route error which causes lower end to end delay and higher packet delivery ratio. Future work includes implementing the proposed scheme in selection of more stable route for DSR.

References

1. Srivastava, V., Motani, M.: Cross-layer design: a survey and the road ahead. IEEE Communication Magazine 43(12), 1112–1119 (2005)
2. Johnson, D., Maltz, D., Hu, Y.-C.: The Dynamic Source Routing for mobile ad hoc networks. IETF Internet Draft (2004), `http://www.ietf.org/internet-drafts/draft-ietf-manet-dsr-10.txt`
3. Hu, Y., Johnson, D.: Caching Strategies in On-Demand Routing Protocols for Wireless Ad Hoc Networks. In: Sixth Annual International Conference on Mobile Computing and Networking, Boston, MA, USA (2000)
4. Marina, M., Das, S.: Performance of Route Caching Strategies in Dynamic Source Routing, pp. 425–432. IEEE Computer Society, Washington, DC, USA (2001)
5. Lou, W., Fang, Y.: Predictive Caching Strategy for On-Demand Routing Protocols in Wireless Ad Hoc Networks. Wireless Networks 8(6), 671–679 (2002)
6. Yu, X., Kedem, Z.: A distributed adaptive cache update algorithm for the dynamic source routing protocol. In: IEEE INFOCOM 2005, Miami, Florida, USA, vol. 1, pp. 730–739 (2005)
7. Huang, T., Chan, C.: Caching Strategies for Dynamic Source Routing in Mobile Ad Hoc Networks. In: Wireless Communication and Networking Conference (WCNC), pp. 4239–4243 (2007)
8. Shukla, A.: Ensuring Cache Freshness in On-demand Routing Protocols for Mobile Ad Hoc Network: A Cross-layer Framework. In: 4th IEEE Conference of Consumer Communication and Networking, pp. 264–268 (2007)
9. Garrido, J., Marandin, D.: A Linkcache Invalidation Mechanism for Dynamic Source Routing (DSR) in Ad Hoc Networks. In: 18th IEEE International Symposium on Personal, Indoor and Mobile Radio Communications, pp. 3–7 (2007)
10. Ashokraj, N., Arun, C., Murugan, K.: Route Cache Optimization Mechanism Using Smart Packets for On-demand Routing Protocol in MANET. In: International Conference on Information Technology (ICIT), pp. 141–146 (2008)
11. The Network Simulator – ns-2, `http://www.isi.edu/nsnam/ns/`

The Design and Performance of a Checkpointing Scheme for Mobile Ad Hoc Networks

Ruchi Tuli[1] and Parveen Kumar[2]

[1] Singhania University, Pacheri Bari (Rajasthan) India
[2] Meerut Institute of Engineering & Technology, Meerut, India

Abstract. The mobile ad hoc network architecture consists of a set of mobile hosts that can communicate with each other without the assistance of a base station. This has brought a revolution in mobile computing environment as well as several challenges. Fault-tolerance is an important design issue in building a reliable mobile computing system. This paper considers checkpointing recovery services for a mobile computing system based on the mobile ad-hoc network environment. In this paper we propose a new minimum process checkpointing scheme in ad hoc networks for the Cluster Based Routing Protocol (CBRP) which belongs to a class of Hierarchical Reactive routing protocols. The protocol proposed by us is non-blocking coordinated checkpointing algorithm suitable for ad hoc environments. It produces a consistent set of checkpoints; the algorithm makes sure that only minimum number of nodes in the cluster are required to take checkpoints; it uses very few control messages. Performance analysis shows that our algorithm outperforms the existing related works and is a novel idea in the field.

Keywords: Ad hoc routing, checkpointing, fault tolerance, mobile computing, clusterheads, clustering routing protocol.

1 Introduction

Ad hoc networks have recently been considered as an attractive research field. In some case, such as emergency, disaster relief or battlefield operations, when a wire line is not available, an ad hoc network can be set for the communication. Clustering of MH provides a convenient framework for resource management. The main advantage of clustering is reducing the number of messages sent to each BS from each node, channel access, power control and bandwidth control. In cluster based architecture, whole network is divided into several clusters and in each cluster network elects one node to be called as cluster head. Hence, clustered ad hoc network consists of three kinds of nodes – cluster heads, gateways and ordinary nodes. Clusterheads are the nodes that are given the responsibility for routing the messages within the cluster and performing the data aggregation. The communication between two adjacent clusters are conducted through the gateway nodes. All nodes other that gateway and clusterheads are called ordinary nodes. Both gateways and ordinary nodes are managed by their clusterheads. There is no physical backbone architecture available in ad hoc

D. Nagamalai, E. Renault, and M. Dhanushkodi (Eds.): PDCTA 2011, CCIS 203, pp. 204–212, 2011.

wireless networks. For routing of the message, a node depends on other nodes to relay packets if they do not have direct links. Wireless backbone architecture can be used to support efficient communications between nodes [1], [2], [3], [4],[5].

Designing an ad hoc network poses some new challenges. In ad hoc networks, the communication cost is much higher than the operation cost. The algorithms that are based on clustering routing protocols must be designed to reduce the number of messages sent to the BS from each node. In this paper, we propose a minimum process checkpointing algorithm for cluster based architectures in which a MH first takes a tentative checkpoint and later on when it receives commit request from the initiator, MH converts its tentative checkpoint into permanent checkpoint. A cluster head sends routing and collected data information to BS, which periodically save the state of cluster head. If a cluster head fails or some fault is detected, then BS detects the cluster head failure and some new node in the cluster is assigned the responsibility of the cluster head. Using checkpointing the cluster can quickly recover from a transient fault of cluster head.

In this section we briefly introduce prior studies related to our work. In [6], a cluster takes two types of checkpoints – processes inside the cluster take synchronous checkpoints and a cluster takes a communication induced checkpoint whenever it receives an inter-cluster application message. Each cluster mainitains a sequence number (SN). SN is incremented each time a cluster level message is committed.

In [7], authors proposed a simple non-blocking roll-forward checkpointing/recovery mechanism for cluster federation. The main feature of their algorithm is that a processs receiving a message does not need to worry whether the received message may become orphan or not. It is the responsibility of the sender of the message to make it non-orphan.

In [17], the authors proposed a integrated independent and coordinated checkpointing schemes for the applications running in hybrid distributed environments. They stated that independent checkpoint subsystem takes a new coordinated checkpoint set if it sends an intercluster application message.

1.1 Problem Formulation

The mobile ad hoc network distinguishes itself from traditional wireless networks by its dynamic changing topology, no base station support and the need of multihop communication MANET, a mobile host (MH) is free to move around and may communicate with others at anytime. Clustering an ad hoc network means partitioning its nodes into clusters CLs, each one with a clusterhead (CH) and possibly some ordinary nodes. The clusterhead which acts as a local coordinator of transmissions within the cluster. Each cluster is represented by the ID of its clusterhead. For example, Figure 1 shows a cluster based distributed mobile computing systems and there are four clusters CL1, CL2, CL3 and CL4. A MH can communicate with other MHs in different cluster or in the same cluster only through its own CH. A clustered architecture is characterized by two types of messages – inter-cluster messages and intra-cluster message. The main aim of clustering routing protocols is to efficiently maintain energy consumption of nodes by involving them in multi-hop communication within a particular cluster and by performing data aggregation in order to decrease the number of messages transmitted to MSS.

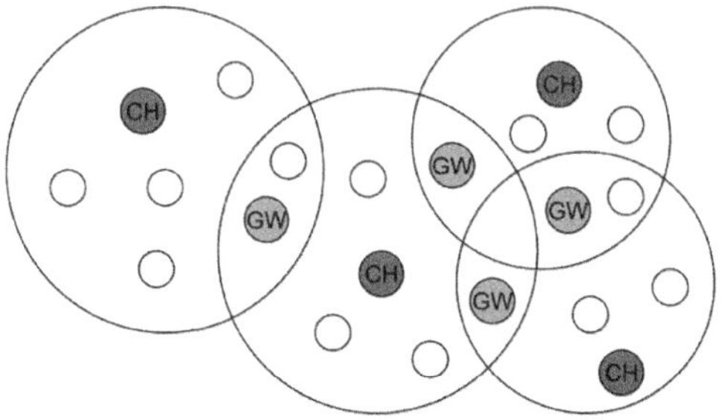

Fig. 1. The concept of a clustering routing protocol

During the cluster head election setup, our scheme elects the cluster head that has more weight function [18]. Then we have proposed a non-blocking coordinated checkpointing algorithm in which MHs take a tentative checkpoint and then on receiving a commit message from the initiator, the MHs convert their tentative checkpoint into permanent. Also whenever a MH is busy, the process takes a checkpoint after completing the current procedure. The proposed algorithm requires fewer control messages and hence fewer number of interrupts. Also, our algorithm requires only minimum number of MHs in a cluster to take checkpoints, it makes our algorithm suitable for cluster based protocols in ad hoc networks.

2 Checkpointing Algorithm

An ad hoc network does not have any predefined set up or structure. Nodes may always be moving and there may be frequent link failures. Each node acts as a router to pass the message. When a node fails, all other nodes learn the failure in finite time. We assume that the checkpointing algorithm operates both intra-cluster and inter-cluster. Nodes are referred to as process. Consider a cluster having a set of n nodes { N1, N2……N_i} involved in the execution of the algorithm. Each node N_i maintains a dependency vector Dv_i of size n which is initially empty and an entry $Dv_i[j]$ is set to 1 when N_i receives since its last checkpoint at least one message from N_j. It is reset to 0 again when Node N_i takes a checkpoint. Each node N_i maintains a checkpoint sequence number csn_i. This csn_i actually represents the current checkpointing interval of node N_i. The ith checkpoint interval of a process denotes all the computation performed between its ith and $(i+1)^{th}$ checkpoint, including the ith checkpoint but not the $(i+1)^{th}$ checkpoint. The csn_i is initially set to 1 and is incremented when node N_i takes a checkpoint. In this approach, we assume that only one node can initiate the chekpointing algorithm and that is the cluster head. This node is call as initiator node or cluster head. We define that process N_k is dependent on another process N_r, if process N_r since its last checkpoint has received at least one application message from process N_k. In our proposed scheme, we assume primary and secondary checkpoint request exchanges between cluster head and rest n-1 ordinary nodes. A permanent checkpoint request is denoted by $R_i(i=csni)$ where i is the current checkpoint sequence number of cluster head that initiates the checkpointing algorithm. It is sent by the initiator process N_j to all its dependent nodes asking them to take their repective checkpoints. A tentative checkpoint request denoted by R_{si} is sent from process N_m to process N_n which is dependent on N_m to take a checkpoint R_{si} means to its receiver process that i is the current checkpoint sequence number of the sender process. When P_i sends m to P_j, P_i piggybacks c-state$_i$, own_csn$_i$ alongwith m. c_state$_i$ A flag. Set to '1' on the receipt of the minimum set. Set to '0' on receiving *commit* or *abort*. *own*_csn is the csn of P_i at the time of sending m.

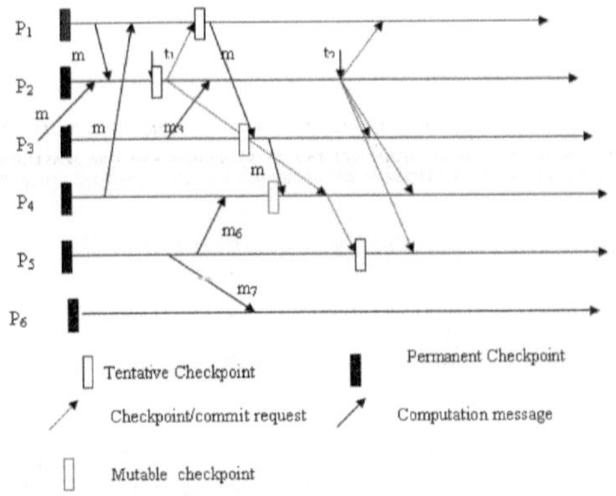

Fig. 2. An example showing the Execution of the Proposed Protocol

We explain our checkpointing algorithm with the help of an example. In Figure 4, at time t1, P2 initiates checkpointing process. Dv2[1]=1 due to m1; and Dv1[4]=1 due to m2. On the receipt of m0, P2 does not set Dv2 [3] =1, because, P3 has taken permanent checkpoint after sending m0. We assume that P1 and P2 are in the cell of the same Cluster, say Clusterin. Clusterin computes minset (subset of minimum set) on the basis of Dv vectors maintained at Clusterin, which in case of figure 3 is {P1, P2, P4}. Therefore, P2 sends checkpoint request to P1 and P4. After taking its tentative checkpoint, P1 sends m4 to P3. P3 takes mutable checkpoint before processing m4. Similarly, P4 takes mutable checkpoint before processing m5. When P4 receives the checkpoint request, it finds that it has already taken the mutable checkpoint; therefore, it converts its mutable checkpoint into tentative one. P4 also finds that it was dependent upon P5 before taking its mutable checkpoint and P5 is not in the minimum set. Therefore, P4 sends checkpoint request to P5. At time t2, P2 receives responses from all relevant processes and sends the commit request along with the minimum set [{P1, P2, P4, P5}] to all processes. When a process, in the minimum set, receives the commit message, converts its tentative checkpoint into permanent one. When a process, not in the minimum set, receives the commit message, it discards its mutable checkpoint, if any. For the sake of simplicity, we have explained our algorithm with two-phase scheme. When a process sends a computation message, it appends its own csn with it. When Pi receives m from Pj such that m. csn <=csn[j], the message is processed and no checkpoint is taken. Otherwise, it means that Pj has taken a checkpoint in the current initiation before sending m. Pi checks the following conditions:

1. Pj was in the checkpointing state before sending m
2. Pi has sent at least one message since last checkpoint
3. Pi is not in checkpointing state while receiving m

If all of these conditions are satisfied, Pi takes its induced checkpoint before processing *m*. If only conditions 1 and 3 are satisfied, P*i* updates its own *csn* before processing m. In other cases, message is processed. On the receipt of a message, D*v*[] of the receiver is updated.

2.1 Algorithm

We define the pseudo code here.

Initiator Node N_i (we call it as cluster head also)

1. Take a checkpoint, check the dependency vector $DV_i[]$;
2. when $DV_i[k]==1$ for 1<=k<=n
send primary request – Rn to node Nk;
/* checks dependency vector and sends checkpoint request */
3. increment the checkpoint sequence number csn_i;
4. continue normal computation;
if any tentative checkpoint checkpoint request is received
discard it and continue normal execution;
Any node N_j j!=I and 1<=j<=n
If N_j receives a Permanent checkpoint request from N_i
Take a checkpoint;
/* if N_j is busy with other high priority job, it takes checkpoint after completing the job; otherwise takes checkpoint immediately */
If DV*j*[ ]=null;
Increment csn_j;
Continue computation;
Else
send secondary checkpoint request to each of N_k such that $DV_j[k]=1$;
increment csn_j;
continue computation;
else if N_j receives a secondary checkpoint request
if N_j has already participated in the checkpoint algorithm
ignore the checkpoint request and continue computation;
else
take a checkpoint;
/* if N_j is busy with other high priority job, it takes checkpoint after completing the job;*/
if DV*j*[]=null;

increment csn_j;
continue computation;
else
send tentative checkpoint request to each N_k such that $DV_j[k]=1$;
increment csn_j;
continue computation;
else if N_j receives piggybacked application message
If N_j has already participated in the checkpointing algorithm
/* csn_j is greater than the received checkpoint sequence number */
process the message and continue computation
else
/* if N_j is busy with other high priority job, it takes checkpoint after completing the job; otherwise takes checkpoint immediately */
if $DV_j[]$=null;
increment csnj;
process the message;
continue computation;
else
send tentative checkpoint request to each N_k such that $DV_j[k]=1$;
increment csn_j;
process the message;
continue computation;

Consider the pseudo code for any node N_j. Node N_j makes sure that all processes from which it has received messages also take checkpoints so that there are no orphan messages that it has received. Also, the node N_j first takes its checkpoint if needed, then processes the received piggybacked application message. Thus, such messages cannot be an orphan. Hence, algorithm generates a consistent global state.

3 Performance Comparison

We compare our work with [6], [17], [8] and [9]. In [6], a cluster takes two types of checkpoints; processes inside a cluster take checkpoints synchronously and a cluster takes a communication induced checkpoint whenever it receives an intercluster application message. Each cluster maintains a sequence number (SN). SN is incremented each time a cluster level checkpoint is committed. Each cluster also maintains a Dv (Direct dependency vector) with a size equal to the number of clusters in the cluster federation. Whenever a cluster (i.e. a process in it) fails, after recovery it broadcasts an alert message with the SN of the failed cluster. This alert message triggers the next iteration of the algorithm. All other clusters, on receiving this alert message decide if they need to roll back by checking the corresponding entries in the Dv vectors. This algorithm has the following advantage; simultaneous execution of the algorithm by all participating clusters contributes to its speed of execution. However, the main drawback of the algorithm is that if we consider a particular message pattern where all the clusters have to roll back except the failed cluster, then all the clusters have to send alert messages to every other cluster. This results in a message storm. But in our approach when a process of a cluster fails it broadcasts just one control message for link failure.

In [17], the authors have addressed the need of integrating independent and coordinated checkpointing schemes for applications running in a hybrid distributed environment containing multiple heterogeneous subsystems. This algorithm mainly works as follows – Firstly, it states that, independent checkpoint subsystem takes a new coordinated checkpoint set if it sends an intercluster application message. Secondly, it states that, a process Pi of independent checkpointing subsystem takes a new independent checkpoint before processing an already received intercluster application message, if Pi has sent any intracluster application message after taking its last checkpoint. So, if the independent checkpointing subsystem has sent k number of intercluster application messages in a time period T, then it has to take k number of coordinated checkpoint sets besides the regular local checkpoints taken asynchronously by its processes. In our approach, if we consider the same situation, only the minimum number of processes takes checkpoints. So we reduce drastically the number of checkpoints to be taken by the cluster subsystem.

In [8] Cao-Singhal proposed a mutable checkpoint based non-blocking minimum-process coordinated checkpointing algorithm. This algorithm completes its processing in the following three steps. First initiator MSS sends tentative checkpoint request to minimum number of processes that need to take checkpoint. Secondly MSS gets the acknowledgement from all processes to whom it sent checkpoint request. At last MSS sends the commit request to convert its tentative checkpoint into permanent. Thus algorithm is non-blocking and minimum process but suffer from useless checkpoints.

In [9], P.Kumar et al. also proposed minimum process coordinated checkpoint algorithm for mobile system. The algorithm suffers from useless checkpoint.

Our proposed approach is quite different from all the above mentioned approaches. Firstly, our approach considers a cluster based protocols from the class of ad hoc networks whereas in the above mentioned three approaches general concept of mobile computing is considered. Secondly, our approach also explains the recovery process of the ordinary nodes and cluster head. Lastly, our proposed algorithm generates the consistent global state without using any useless checkpoint, it is non-blocking and it is applied on the ad hoc networks.

Table 1. Comparison with the related work

Parameters	Compariosn with [6]	Comparison with [17]	Comparison with [8]	Comparison with [9]	Our algorithm
Non-blocking	Yes	Yes	Yes	Yes	Yes
Minimum Process	No	No	Yes	Yes	Yes
Supports MANET's	Yes	Yes	No	No	Yes
Number of checkpoints	Less	More	Less	Less	Less
No. of control messages	More	More	Less	Less	Less

4 Conclusion

When designing an efficient ad hoc network application, we must consider the resource constraints and their scalability. Ad hoc network users concerned about information quality and user requirements for real-time features are also increasing. Moreover, ad hoc network applications are expanding into harsher and more dangerous environments. Therefore, checkpointing schemes have emerged as an important issues. Clustering routing protocols such as CBRP are designed to improve both energy efficiency and scalability. These protocols compose clusters and elect a cluster head in each cluster. The cluster heads aggregate data from its member nodes and reduces the amount of messages sent by member nodes to the BS directly. In clustering routing protocol, cluster head management is needed because the role of cluster head is more important than other member nodes.

In this paper, we have proposed a minimum process and non-blocking checkpointing scheme for clustering routing protocols. The main features of our algorithm are 1) it caters the needs of ad hoc environment ; 2) minimum number of processes take the checkpoint. Also, our scheme minimizes the number of control messages needed and also take no useless checkpoints. And finally, it reduces the energy consumption and recovery latency when a cluster head fails.

References

1. Baker, D.J., Ephremides, A.: The Architectural Organisation of a Mobile Radio Network via a Distributed algorithm. IEEE Trans. Commun. 29(11), 1694–1701 (1981)
2. Baker, D.J., Ephremides, A., Flynn, J.A.: The design and Simulation of a Mobile Radio Network with Distributed Control. IEEE J. Sel. Areas Commun., 226–237 (1984)
3. Das, B., Sivakumar, R., Bharghavan, V.: Routing in Ad-hoc networks using a Spine. In: Proc. Sixth International Conference (1997)
4. Das, B., Sivakumar, R., Bharghavan, V.: Routing in Ad-hoc networks using Minimum connected Dominating Sets. In: Proc. IEEE International Conference (1997)
5. Gerla, M., Pei, G., Lee, S.J.: Wireless Mobile Ad-hoc Network Routing. In: Proc. IEEE/ACM FOCUS 1999 (1999)
6. Monnet, S., Morin, C., Badrinath, R.: Hybrid checkpointing for parallel applica-tuions in cluster federation. In: 4th IEEE/ACM International Symposium on Cluster Computing and the Grid, Chicago, USA, pp. 773–782 (April 2004)
7. Gupta, B., Rahimi, S., Ahmad, R.: A New Roll-Forward Chekpointing/Recovery Mechanism for cluster federation. International Journal of Computer Science and Network Security 6(11) (November 2006)
8. Cao, G., Singhal, M.: Mutable checkpoints: A new checkpointing approach for mobile computing systems. IEEE Transactions on parallel and Distributed Sys-tems 12(2), 157–172 (2001)
9. Kumar, P., Kumar, L., Chauhan, R.K., Gupta, V.K.: A Non-intrusive Minimum process Synchronous Checkpointing Protocol for Mobile Distributed Systems. In: IEEE International Conference on Personal Wireless Communications, ICPWC 2005, New Delhi, pp. 491–495 (January 2005)

10. Prakash, R., Singhal, M.: Low-Cost Checkpointing and Failure Recovery in Mobile Computing Systems. IEEE Transaction on Parallel and Distributed Systems 7(10), 1035–1048 (1996)
11. Cao, G., Singhal, M.: On the Impossibility of Min-process Non-blocking Checkpointing and an Efficient Checkpointing Algorithm for Mobile Computing Systems. In: Proceedings of International Conference on Parallel Processing, August 1998, pp. 37–44 (1998)
12. Koo, R., Toueg, S.: Checkpointing and Roll-Back Recovery for Distributed Systems. IEEE Trans. on Software Engineering 13(1), 23–31 (1987)
13. Kumar, L., Misra, M., Joshi, R.C.: Low overhead optimal checkpointing for mo-bile distributed systems. In: Proceedings of 19th IEEE International Conference on Data Engineering, pp. 686–688 (2003)
14. Higaki, H., Takizawa, M.: Checkpoint-recovery Protocol for Reliable Mobile Systems. Trans. of Information Processing Japan 40(1), 236–244 (1999)
15. Kumar, P.: A Low-Cost Hybrid Coordinated Checkpointing Protocol for mobile distributed systems. To appear in Mobile Information Systems
16. Awasthi, L.K., Kumar, P.: A Synchronous Checkpointing Protocol for Mobile Distributed Systems: Probabilistic Approach. International Journal of Information and Computer Security 1(3), 298–314
17. Cao, J., Chen, Y., Zhang, K., He, Y.: Checkpointing in Hybrid Distributed Systems. In: Proc. of the 7th International Symposium on Parallel Architectures, Algorithms and Networks (ISPAN 2004), Hong Kong, China, pp. 136–141 (May 2004)
18. Dow, C., Lin, J., Hwang, S., Wen, Y.: An efficient distributed clustering scheme for ad hoc wireless networks. IEICE Trans. Commun. E-85-B(8) (August 2002)

A Reliable Distributed Grid Scheduler for Mixed Tasks

Ram Mohan Rao Kovvur[1], S. Ramachandram[2],
Vijayakumar Kadappa[3], and A. Govardhan[4]

[1] Department of Computer Science and Engineering,
Vasavi College of Engineering, Hyderabad, Andhra Pradesh, India
krmrao@staff.vce.ac.in
[2] Department of Computer Science and Engineering,
Osmania University, Hyderabad, Andhara Pradesh, India
schandram@gmail.com
[3] Department of MCA, East West Institute of Technology, Bangalore, Karnataka, India
kadappakumar@gmail.com
[4] Department of Computer Science and Engineering, JNTUH,
Karimnagar Dist, Andhara Pradesh, India
govardhan_cse@yahoo.co.in

Abstract. Scheduling of jobs is one of the crucial tasks in grid environment. We consider non-preemptive scheduling of mixed tasks in a computational grid. Recently, a general distributed scalable grid scheduler (GDS) was proposed, which prioritizes mission-critical tasks while maximizing the number of tasks meeting deadlines. However, the GDS scheduler did not consider the reliability factor, which may result in low successful schedule rates. In this paper, we propose a novel distributed grid scheduler which considers various parameters - Priority, Deadline, CCR and reliability of grid nodes. The proposed scheduler maintains the tasks allocated to deficient grid nodes in a queue. Further the queued tasks are rescheduled to the other nodes of the grid. It is observed that RDGS-MT scheduler shows a significant improvement in terms of successfully scheduled tasks (hard, firm, soft) as compared to a GDS-S (GDS without shuffle phase). The results of our exhaustive simulation experiments demonstrate the superiority of the proposed scheduler over the GDS-S scheduler.

Keywords: Grid Computing, Scheduling, Re-Scheduling, Distributed Scheduler, Reliability, Priority, Deadline.

1 Introduction

Grid computing and its technologies mainly emerged for fulfilling the mounting demand of the scientific computing community for more computing power. A Grid computing environment is comprised of geographically distributed computers connected to internet in a Grid-like way, are used to create virtual super computers of huge amount of computing capacity able to solve intricate problems. Thus Grid computing is able to provide an unlimited computing capacity, collaboration, and information access to every user associated to the grid [1] [2] [3].

D. Nagamalai, E. Renault, and M. Dhanushkodi (Eds.): PDCTA 2011, CCIS 203, pp. 213–223, 2011.

Grid scheduling is a process of mapping grid tasks to grid resources over multiple administrative domains. The grid scheduler has four phases, which consists of resource discovery, resource selection, job selection and job execution. The responsibility of a scheduler is selecting resources and scheduling tasks in such a way that the user and application constraints are satisfied, in terms of overall execution time and cost of the resources utilized [6].

Quality-of-Service (QoS) support in resource management and scheduling has been the focus of many research studies in the computational studies. Ali Afzal et al. [7] bring out a scheduling algorithm that minimizes the cost of execution of workflows while ensuring that their associated QoS constraints are satisfied. Cesar A.F.De Rose et al. [9] present an explicit allocation strategy, in which an adaptor automatically fits grid requests to the resource in order to decrease the turn-around time of application. Mustafizar et al. [8] propose an approach for decentralized and cooperative workflow scheduling in a dynamic and distributed grid resource-sharing environment. The participants in the system such as the workflow brokers, resources and users who belong to multiple control domains, work together to enable a single cooperative resource sharing environment. Peijie Huang et al. [10] propose a method, which combines of an off-line static strategy using time series prediction and an online dynamic adjustment using reinforcement learning. The superiority of this scheduling algorithm is that it shows better load balancing of the whole hierarchical grid and achieves higher success rate of the grid service request. Ruay-Shiung Chang et al. [11] propose a balanced ant colony optimization (BACO) algorithm for job scheduling in the grid environment. The BACO algorithm balances the entire system load while trying to minimize the makespan of a given set of jobs. In contrast to these methods, Cong Liu et al. [12] developed a general distributed scalable grid scheduler (GDS) for independent tasks with different priorities and deadlines. GDS has three phases, which consists of a multiple attribute ranking phase, a shuffling phase, and peer-to-peer dispatching phase.

However, the aforementioned methods do not consider the reliability factor, which is vital in the context of grid environment. There is no guarantee that the task will be scheduled successfully if the system is not reliable. In general, reliability is an ability of a system to perform and continue its functions in routine circumstances, as well as hostile or unexpected circumstances [14]. The reliability of a grid scheduling scheme depends upon the following three important factors:

- Task execution time: The time taken by the task to complete its execution.
- Communication time: The time consumed in communication in order to obtain the required resources from the various nodes of the grid.
- Rate of failure: The rate of failure of elements of grid computing system such as grid nodes, communication channels.

As given by Min Xie et al. [5], failure rate function $\lambda(t)$ is defined as the probability that a device of age *t* will fail in the small interval from t to t+dt and is given by

$$\lambda(t) = \lim_{\Delta t \to 0} \frac{R(t) - R(t + \Delta t)}{\Delta t R(t)}$$

The quantity *R (t)* represents the probability that system will be successfully operating without failure in the interval from time 0 to t.

We consider three kinds of tasks - hard, firm and soft. RDGS-MT uses such a task taxonomy which considers the consequence of missing deadlines and the importance of task property. A hard task cannot tolerate any deadline miss, since a single job that finishes after its deadline may collapse the entire system. A soft task can tolerate jobs that finish after their deadlines, whereas a firm task can tolerate only some job failures. Typically, a firm job should either finish before its deadline or not execute at all. In other words a soft job that misses its deadline can still do some useful work, while a firm job that misses its deadline is useless, though it does not jeopardize the system.[15]

Recently, we proposed a distributed Grid Scheduler with reliability factor with respect to failure of grid nodes for independent tasks without Priority and Deadline [16].

In this work, we propose a distributed grid scheduler for mixed tasks (Hard, firm, soft) which takes into account (RDGS-MT) reliability factor with respect to failure of grid nodes. The proposed scheduler also considers Communication to Computing Ratio (CCR) [12], which is useful to decide the appropriate grid site for scheduling tasks.

The rest of the paper is organized as follows. In section 2, we outline the grid model used in this work. Section 3 describes the proposed scheduling algorithm. Our experimental results are presented in section 4. Finally we conclude in section 5.

2 Grid Model

We consider the grid model as shown in Fig.1, for our investigation. The grid model consists of geographically distributed sites which are interconnected through WAN.

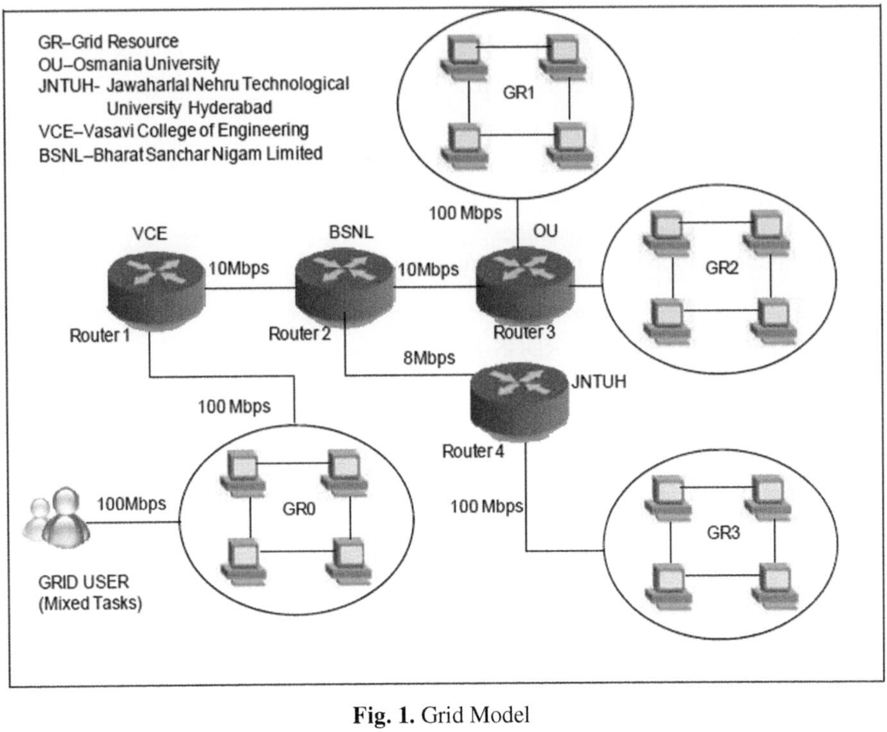

Fig. 1. Grid Model

At each site, there is a Grid Resource (GR) consisting of several machines of different processing capabilities and a grid user have many tasks to be scheduled by the grid scheduler. The communication within the site (intra-site) is fast Ethernet (100Mbps); where as the communication across the sites (inter-site) is Ethernet (10Mbps). Here we show a live model with well-known educational institutions in India (VCE-Vasavi College of Engineering, OU-Osmania University, Hyderabad, JNTUH- Jawaharlal Nehru Technological University, Hyderabad) and BSNL, an Internet Service Provider.

3 Reliable Distributed Grid Scheduler for Mixed Tasks

In this section, we propose our scheduling algorithm (RDGS-MT), which meets the following objectives:

- RDGS-MT assigns priorities as high, normal, and low to the tasks which corresponds to mission hard, firm and soft tasks and completes execution in the same order.
- RDGS-MT is based on Communication to Computing Ratio (CCR), which is used to decide local or remote site for task scheduling.
- RDGS-MT maximizes the total number of tasks completing execution and meeting their deadlines.
- RDGS-MT exploits reliability factor with respect to failure of nodes.
- RDGS-MT makes use of re-scheduling concept

3.1 Notation

The following notation is used in this paper.

T_i : ith Task
Q : Task Queue
U : Queue of tasks assigned to a failed node
S_i : ith site with a number of machines
$CCRi$: communication to computing ratio for task T_i
N_i : i th grid node

Now, we present our proposed RDGS-MT algorithm.

3.2 Proposed RDGS-MT Algorithm

The proposed algorithm (RDGS-MT) consists of two phases: In the first phase all incoming tasks at each site are classified based on priority, deadline and CCR value. Next in the second phase, scheduler assigns tasks to a specific resource on a site. Those tasks that are unable to execute due to Grid node failure are placed in a queue for rescheduling.

First Phase (Classification of Tasks Based on Priority, Deadline and CCR Value)

At each site, the users may submit a number of tasks with Priority, deadline and CCR values of ‘low’ and ‘high’. The scheduler at each site puts all the incoming into task queue *Q*. First, tasks are sorted by decreasing priority, then by decreasing CCR-type and then by increasing deadline. Sorting by decreasing priority allows us to execute the tasks in the order of hard, firm and soft tasks. Sorting by decreasing CCR value permits us to execute communication intensive tasks locally and to execute computational intensive tasks remotely.

Second Phase (Scheduling of Tasks on a Grid Node with Rescheduling)

To schedule a task T_i on a site S_i, the scheduler selects a node randomly to balance the load. If the status of the selected node is 'working', the task T_i is executed on the selected node. If the status of the selected node is 'failed', the grid scheduler makes a provision for Task T_i to put up in a queue *U*. Further the tasks in the queue, *U* are simultaneously re-scheduled to other available resources.

We present the algorithm in a more formal way as given below. A user submits tasks to be executed, which are maintained in a Task Queue, *Q*. For each task T_i in Queue, *Q* we use RDGS-MT() algorithm for scheduling.

```
Algorithm RDGS-MT(Q)
begin
1.   Sort the Task Queue Q
        (i) in descending order of priority followed by
        (ii) in increasing order of deadline.
2. For each unscheduled task Ti
   2.1 Call RDGS-Select(Ti, CCRi)
end
Algorithm RDGS-Select (Ti, CCRi)
begin
        1. If (CCR is 'low') then
            1.1 Ti is assigned to Remote Grid Site, Si
            1.2 Call RDGS-Execute (Ti, Si) for execution of Ti
        2. Else If (CCR is 'high') then
            2.1 Ti is assigned to Local Grid Site, Sj
            2.2 Call RDGS-Execute (Ti, Sj) for execution of Ti

end
Algorithm RDGS-Execute (Ti, Sk)
begin
        1. Select a node, Ni randomly at Grid Site, Sk
        2. Check the status of the node, Ni.
        3. If (Status of Ni is 'Failed')
              3.1 Insert Ti in Queue U.
              3.2 Re-schedule Ti by calling, once RDGS-Execute (Ti,
           Sk)
        4. Else (Status of Ni is 'Working') then
           4.1 Ti is scheduled to Node Ni
End
```

4 Experimental Results and Analysis

In this section, we present our experimental results and compare RDGS-MT and GDS-S schedulers.

4.1 Experimental Setup

We used the following parameters in our experimental study: Task ID, Task length, Task file size, and Task output size, Priority, Deadline and Communication to computational Ratio (CCR). We considered 'low', 'high' values for CCR.

We assumed the number grid of nodes as 10% of the tasks under consideration in our experiments. We varied number of failed nodes as 5%, 8%, 10%, 16%, 20% of nodes under consideration and obtained results. We computed Overall Successful Schedule Percentage (OSSP) using number of tasks successfully scheduled and total number of tasks and also Critical Successful Schedule Percentage (CSSP) using number of mission critical (hard) tasks successfully scheduled and total number of mission critical tasks.

We used GridSim [13] simulator for simulating Grid environment and the experimental results are shown in Figs. (2)-(5). We used Pentium-4 based system with CPU clock speed of 3GHz, 2.99 GB RAM running with Windows XP operating system.

4.2 Discussion of Results

4.2.1 Experiment 1 (Computing Overall Successful Schedule Percentage by Varying Number of Tasks with Fixed Number of Failed Nodes)

We plotted Figs. (2)(a)-(d) by computing Overall Successful Schedule Percentage (OSSP) with varying number of tasks. For each of these cases, we assumed fixed number of failed nodes (5%, 8%, 10%, and 16%,) as shown in Figs. (2)(a)-(2)(d). From the Figs. 2(a)-2(d), we observed that RDGS-MT scheduler shows improved OSSP as compared to GDS-S scheduler with varying number of tasks. With minimum node failure (i.e. 5%) RDGS-MT shows higher OSSP i.e. 98.75% (hence higher reliability) against 94.65% with GDS-S method. With maximum node failure (i.e. 16%), RDGS-MT shows significantly better OSSP (95.35%) as compared GDS-S method (82.6%). As the node failure rate increases RDGS-MT is able to achieve much better OSSP as compared to GDS-S scheduler, thus showing better reliability . Also note that GDS-S scheduler's reliability is worsened with increased node failure. In other words, RDGS-MT is able to cope-up well with failed grid nodes, where as GDS-S is lagging.

4.2.2 Experiment 2 (Computing Overall Successful Schedule Percentage by Varying Percentage of Failure Nodes with Fixed Number of Tasks)

We plotted Figs. (3)(a)-3(d) by computing OSSP with varying percentage of failure rate and fixed number of tasks. For each these cases, we assumed fixed number of tasks as 2000, 4000, 6000, 8000 in Figs. (3)(a)-3(d) respectively. From theFigs. 3(a)-(d), we observed that RDGS-MT scheduler shows improved and consistent OSSP as compared to GDS-S Scheduler. In other words, as the percentage of failed nodes increases (from 4% to 16%), fall in OSSP of RDGS-MT is not significant, where as

GDS-S shows wide variation in OSSP. For RDGS-MT, the difference minimum and maximum in OSSP is 6% and the corresponding difference in OSSPs for GDS-S is 12%. In other words, RDGS-MT is robust against failure in grid nodes.

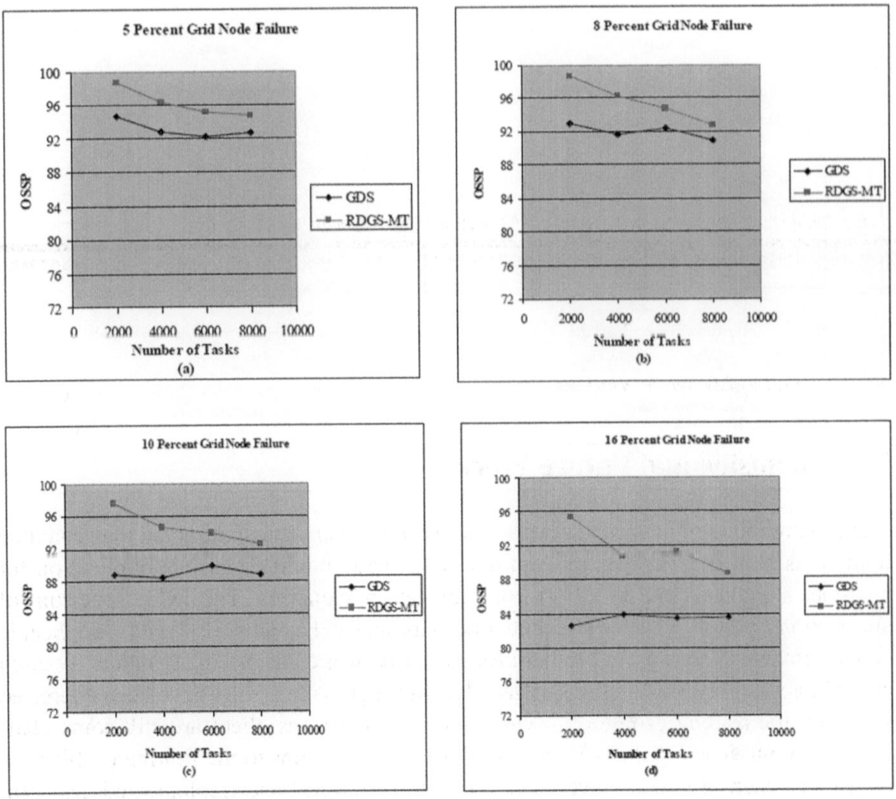

Fig. 2. Successful Schedule Percentage of RDGS-MT & GDS-S with varying number of tasks

4.2.3 Experiment 3 (Computing Critical Successful Schedule Percentage by Varying Number of Tasks with Fixed Number of Failed Nodes)

We plotted Figs. (4)(a)-(d) by computing Critical Successful Schedule Percentage (CSSP) with varying number of tasks. For each of these cases, we assumed fixed number of failed nodes (5%, 8%, 10%, and 16%,) as shown in Figs. (4)(a)-(4)(d).

From the Figs. 4(a)-4(d), we observed that RDGS-MT scheduler shows improved CSSP as compared to GDS-S scheduler with varying number of tasks. With minimum node failure (i.e. 5%) RDGS-MT shows higher CSSP i.e. 99.7% (hence higher reliability) against 95.2% with GDS-S method. With maximum node failure (i.e. 16%), RDGS-MT shows significantly better CSSP (94.9%) as compared GDS-S method (83.8%). As the node failure rate increases RDGS-MT is able to achieve much better

CSSP as compared to GDS-S scheduler, thus showing high reliability (4.8%). Also note that GDS-S scheduler's reliability is worsened (11.4%) with increased node failure. In other words, RDGS-MT is able to cope-up well with failed grid nodes, where as GDS-S is lagging.

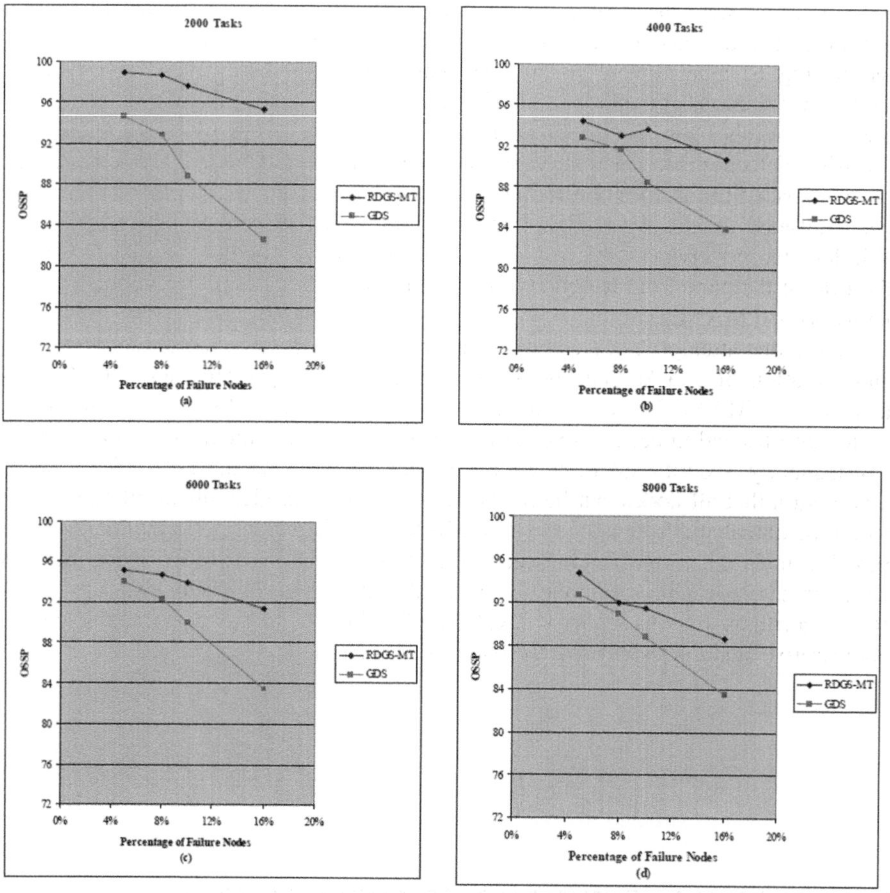

Fig. 3. Successful Schedule Percentage of RDGS-MT and GDS-S with varying number of failure nodes

4.2.4 Experiment 4 (Computing Critical Successful Schedule Percentage by Varying Percentage of Failure Nodes with Fixed Number of Tasks)

We plotted Figs. (5)(a)-5(d) by computing CSSP with varying percentage of failure rate and fixed number of tasks. For each these cases, we assumed fixed number of tasks as 2000, 4000, 6000, 8000 in Figs. (5)(a)-5(d) respectively. From the Figs. 5(a)-(d), we observed that RDGS-MT scheduler shows improved and consistent CSSP as compared to GDS-S Scheduler. In other words, as the percentage of failed nodes increases (from 4% to 16%), fall in CSSP of RDGS-MT is not significant, where as GDS-S shows wide variation in CSSP. For RDGS-MT, the difference maximum and minimum in CSSP is 7% and the corresponding difference in CSSPs for GDS-S is 13%. In other words, RDGS-MT is robust against failure in grid nodes.

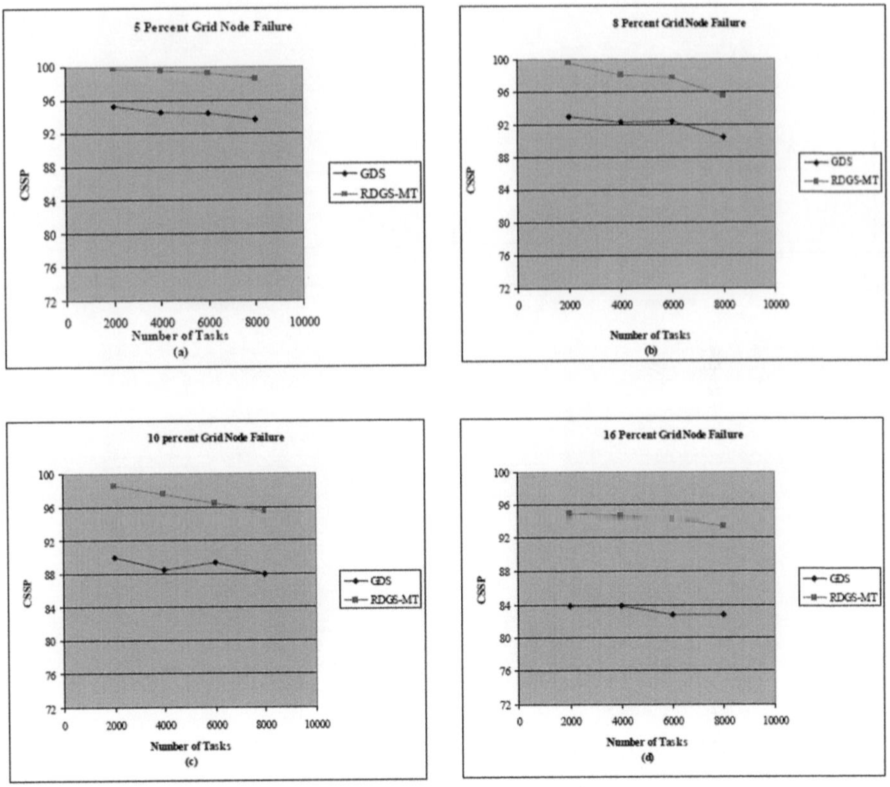

Fig. 4. Critical Successful Schedule Percentage of RDGS-MT & GD with varying number of task

4.2.5 Experiment 5 (Computational Requirements)

We analyze here the computational requirements of RDGS-MT and GDS-S schedulers by varying number of tasks from 2000 to 8000 (in steps of 2000) with 8% fixed grid node failure rate. We computed additional computational requirements for RDGS-MT to provide better reliability as compared to GDS-S scheduler (Shown in Table.1). From the Table it is evident that RDGS-MT provides better reliability (with respect to CSSP and OSSP) at the cost of an insignificant additional computational time (3.19% to 3.78%).

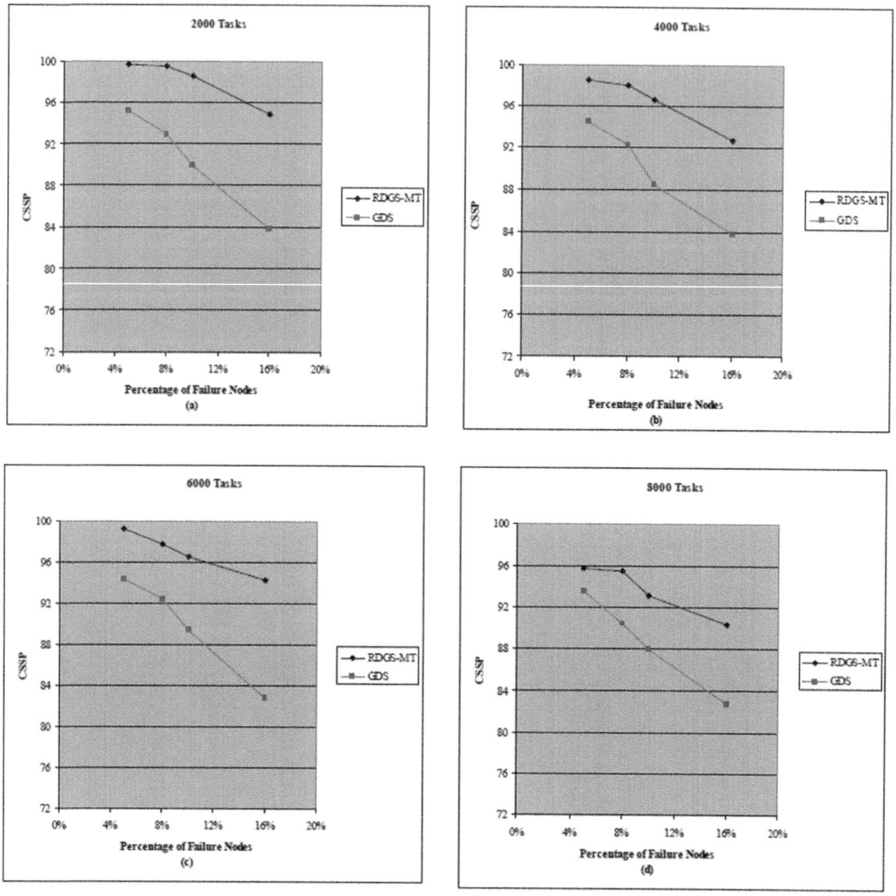

Fig. 5. Critical Successful Schedule Percentage of RDGS-MT and GDS-S with varying number of failure nodes

Table 1. Computational time requirements of RDGS-MT & GDS-S Schedulers

No. of tasks	No. of Nodes	Overall Successful Schedule Percentage (OSSP)		Critical Successful Schedule Percentage (CSSP)		Computational Time		Additional Comp. Time (2) - (1)
		GDS-S	RDGS-MT	GDS-S	RDGS-MT	GDS-S (1)	RDGS-MT (2)	
2000	200	92.90	98.70	92.95	99.55	16121	16477	3.56%
4000	400	91.65	92.30	92.28	98.00	38554	38873	3.19%
6000	600	92.30	94.72	92.40	97.70	57976	58328	3.52%
8000	800	90.96	91.68	90.44	95.40	77089	77467	3.78%

5 Conclusion

We proposed a reliable distributed grid scheduler for mixed tasks, which promised an improved successful schedule rate in spite of grid node failures. The proposed scheduler shows superior successful schedule percentage with respect to overall tasks and critical tasks at the cost of insignificant additional computational requirements. The proposed method is very useful in grid environment because there is a possibility for any node to get failed due to various factors. In future we improve the method by extending it by using resource discovery algorithms (instead of selecting the Grid node randomly) to find best node for given task.

References

[1] Xhafa, F., Abraham, A.: Computational models and heuristic methods for Grid scheduling problems. Future Generation Computer Systems (August 2009)

[2] Viswananathan, S., Veeravalli, B., Robertazzi, T.G.: Re-source-Aware Distributed Scheduling Strategies for Large-Scale Computational Cluster/Grid Systems, vol. 18(10) (October 2007)

[3] Minoli, D.: A Networking approach to grid computing. Wiley Interscience, A John Wiley & Sons, Inc., Hoboken, New Jersey (2005)

[4] Ryabinin, I.R.: Reliability of Engineering System Principles and Analysis. Mir Publishers, Moscow (1976)

[5] Xie, M., Dai, Y.S., Poh, K.L.: Computing System Reliability Models and Analysis. Kluwer Academic/Plenum Publishers, New York (2004)

[6] Li, M., Baker, M.: The Grid Core Technologies. A John Wiley & Sons, Inc., Chichester (2005)

[7] Afzal, A., Stephen McGough, A., Darlington, J.: Capacity planning and sched-uling in grid computing environments. Future Generation Computer Systems 24, 404–414 (2008)

[8] Rahman, M., Ranjan, R., Buyya, R.K.: Cooperative and decen-tralized workflow scheduling in global grids. Future Generation Computer Systems (2009)

[9] De Rose, C.A.F., Ferreto, T., Calheirros, R.N., Cirne, W., Costa, L.B., Fireman, D.: Allocation strategies for utilization of space-shared resources in Bag of Tasks grids. Future Generation Computer Systems 24, 331–341 (2008)

[10] Huang, P., Peng, H., Lin, P., Li, X.: Static strategy and dynamic Adjustment: An efficient method for grids task scheduling. Future Generation Computer Systems 25, 884–892 (2009)

[11] Chang, R.-S., Chang, J.-S., Lin, P.-S.: An Ant algorithm for balanced job scheduling in grids. Future Generation Computer Systems 25, 20–27 (2009)

[12] Liu, C., Baskiyar, S.: A general distributed scalable grid scheduler for independent tasks. J. Parallel Distrib. Comput. 69, 307–314 (2009)

[13] Buyya, R.K., Murshed, M., Anthony, S., de Marcos D.A., Agustin C.: GridSim Tool kit 4.1: A Grid simulation toolkit for resource modeling and application scheduling for parallel and distributed computing (2007)

[14] Wikipedia, Reliability, `http://en.wikipedia.org/wiki/Reliability` (visited February 2009)

[15] Abeni, L., Buttazzo, G.: QoS Guarantee using Probabilistic Deadlines. In: Proceedings of the IEEE Euromicro Conference on Real-Time Systems, York, UK (June 1999)

[16] Rao, K.R.M., Ramachandram, S., VijayaKumar, K., Govardhan, A.: A Reliable Distributed Grid Scheduler for Independent Tasks. IJCSI International Journal of Computer Science Issues 8(2) (March 2011)

Performance Evaluation of Weighted Associative Classifier in Health Care Data Mining and Building Fuzzy Weighted Associative Classifier

Sunita Soni[1] and O.P. Vyas[2]

[1] Department of Computer Applications, BIT, Durg, Chattisgarh India
Sunitasoni74@gmail.com
[2] Indian Institute of Information Technology, Allahabad- 211012 (U.P.), India
dropvyas@gmail.com

Abstract. In this paper we evaluate the performance of Weighted Associative Classifier and propose the theoretical concept of Fuzzy Weighted Associative Classifier (FWAC). Associative classifiers, the new classification approach is especially fit to applications where the model assists the domain (Medical diagnosis) experts in their decisions making. Weighted Associative Classifiers that takes advantage of weighted association rule mining is already being proposed [1]. The experiments on bench mark dataset reveals that WAC is a promising alternative in medical prediction with improved accuracy over the other associative classifiers and certainly deserves further attention. Further there is so-called a "sharp boundary" problem in association rules mining with quantitative attribute domains. To solve this problem we use fuzzy logic and partition the domains. The concept of Fuzzy Weighted Support and Fuzzy Weighted Confidence will be used to generate fuzzy weighted Classification Association Rules(CAR), which will ultimately used for prediction.

Keywords: Associative Classifiers, Weighted Associative Classifiers, Association Rule Mining, Classifiers, Prediction accuracy.

1 Introduction

Associative Classification is an integrated framework of Association Rule Mining (ARM) and Classification. A special subset of association rules whose right-hand-side is restricted to the classification class attribute is used for classification.

The traditional ARM was designed considering that items have same importance and in the database simply their presence or absence is mentioned. In several problem domains the attributes can't be assigned equal importance particularly in predictive modelling system where attributes have different prediction capability. The concept of Weighted Association Rule Mining is used to deal with the case where attributes are assigned a weights to reflect their importance. The authors have proposed a new Weighted Associative Classifier (WAC) that generates classification rules using Weighted Support and Confidence framework [1].

Another problem in the medical database as well as databases from other applications is that most of the attributes are associated with quantitative domains such as BMI, Age,

D. Nagamalai, E. Renault, and M. Dhanushkodi (Eds.): PDCTA 2011, CCIS 203, pp. 224–237, 2011.

Blood-Pressure, etc. Discretization technique are used for these domains before applying the Apriori-type method. Apart from domain Discretization, fuzzy logic is considered as suitable solution to deal with the "sharp boundary" problem. This gives rise to the notion of Fuzzy Association Rules (FAR). Building an associative classifier based upon fuzzy association rules provides two advantages: one is the need to mine large datasets with quantitative domains; the other is to generate classification rules with more general semantics and linguistic expressiveness [4].This paper proposes a new Fuzzy Weighted Associative Classifier (FWAC) that generates classification rules using Fuzzy Weighted Support and Confidence framework. We discussed the importance of Fuzzy Weighted Association rule in classification problem.

In section 2, we have discussed the concept of Weighted Association Rule Mining (WAC), Fuzzy Association Rule Mining and Fuzzy Weighted Association Rule Mining. In section 3 we described some formulae and given definitions for Weighted Associative Classifier (FWAC). In section 4 we have discussed the performance of Weighted Associative Classifiers in the field of medical prediction. In section 5 the formulae and definitions given in section 3 has been extended for Fuzzy Weighted Associative Classifier (FWAC). In section 6, Downward closure property for WAC and FWAC has been discussed. In section 7, conclusion and future work of this paper is given.

2 Related Work

2.1 Association Rule Mining

Let $I = \{i_1, i_2, \dots, i_n\}$ be a set of n distinct literals called *items*. D is a set of variable length transactions over I. Each transaction contains a set of items $i_1, i_2, \dots, i_k \in I$. A transaction has an associated unique identifier called *TID*. An *association rule* is an implication of the form $A \Rightarrow B$ (or written as $A \rightarrow B$), where $A, B \subseteq I$, and $A \cap B = \emptyset$. A is called the *antecedent* of the rule and B is called the *consequent* of the rule. The rule $X \Rightarrow Y$ has a *support s* in the transaction set D if $s\%$ of the transactions in D contain $X \cup Y$. In other words, the support of the rule is the probability that X and Y hold together among all the possible presented cases. It is said that the rule $X \Rightarrow Y$ holds in the transaction set D with *confidence c* if $c\%$ of transactions in D that contain X also contain Y. In other words, the confidence of the rule is the conditional probability that the consequent Y is true under the condition of the antecedent X. The problem of discovering all association rules from a set of transactions D consists of generating the rules that have a *support* and *confidence* greater than given thresholds. These rules are called *strong rules*, and the framework is known as the *support confidence framework* for association rule mining [21].

2.2 Weighted Association Rule Mining

A weighted association rule (WAR) is an implication $X \rightarrow Y$ where X and Y are two weighted items. A pair (i_j, w_j) is called a weighted item where $i_j \in I$ and $w_j \in W$ is the weight associated with the item i_j. A transaction is a set of weighted items where $0 < w_j <= 1$. Weight is used to show the importance of the item. In weighted association rule mining problem each item is allowed to have a weight. The goal of WAR is to steer the mining process to those significant relationships having items with significant weights rather than being flooded with insignificant relationships [12].

Wei Wang et al. proposed an efficient mining methodology for Weighted Association Rules (WAR) [15]. The authors have extended the traditional association rule-mining problem by allowing weights to be associated with each item to reflect the importance. In this paper WAR uses a two-fold approach where the frequent item sets are generated using standard association rule without considering the weight. Post processing is then applied in the frequent item sets during rule generation. This paper focuses on how weighted association rule can be generated using weighting factors of the items included in generated frequent item sets.

C.H.Cai et al have proposed a mining of association rules with Weighted Items [19]. Among the three parameters: weights of items, support of itemsets and the confidence factor, a weighted support, which is product of the total weight of items in the itemset and the support of the itemset is chosen in weighted association rule. The authors proposed, two new algorithms MINWAL (O) and MINWAL (W) to handle the problem Invalidation of Downward closure property . The proposed algorithm for mining weighted association rules is similar to the Apriori Gen Algorithm, but the detailed steps contain some differences. In the beginning large itemsets is generated with increasing sizes. However, since the subset of a large itemset may not be large, k-itemsets is not generated simply from the large (k -1) itemsets as in Apriori Gen. In order to extract such k-itemsets from the database, a new metric called the k-support bound has been used in the mining process. The algorithms MINWAL (O) is applicable to both normalized and unnormalized cases, and MINWAL (W) is applicable to the normalized case only.

In [5] the authors have identified the limitation of the traditional Association Rule Mining model. Weight can be integrated in the mining process to solve the problem. The authors have identified the problem of invalidation of downward closure property. A set of new concepts were proposed to adapt weighting in the new setting and "weighted downward closure property" is being proposed instead of "downward closure property". The authors have prove that if an itemset {AC} is not significant then its superset say {ACE} is impossible to be significant hence no need to calculate its weighted support A new algorithm called WARM (Weighted Association Rule Mining) has been proposed based on this improved weighted support framework. The algorithm is both scalable and efficient in discovering significant relationships in weighted settings.

2.3 Fuzzy Association Rule Mining (FARM)

In [4], the authors have has proposed a framework to integrate classification and fuzzy association rule mining. CFAR algorithm has also been proposed to build an accurate classifier. The experiments have been performed on benchmark dataset to evaluate the performance of CFAR. CFAR have been evaluated using three parameters i.e. accuracy, the impact of threshold *Minimum Support on* CFAR outcomes and number of rules produced. Compared with CBA the CFAR has been found to provide better understandability in terms of the number of rules and the smooth boundaries and satisfactory accuracy.

A data mining for Discovering Fuzzy Association Rules is proposed in [17]. The authors have given the technique to find Fuzz Association Rules without using the user supplied support values which are often hard to determine. The other unique feature of the work is that the conclusion of a fuzzy association rule can contain linguistic terms. The experimental result shows that the algorithm is capable to discover both positive and negative fuzzy association rules in an effective manner from real life database.

In [11] the authors have proposed a model to find the fuzzy association rules in fuzzy transaction database. The model is found to be useful technique to find the patterns in data in the presence of imprecision, either because data are fuzzy in nature or because we must improve their semantics. Authors have also discussed` some of the applications of the scheme, paying special attention to the discovery of fuzzy association rules in relational database.

2.4 Fuzzy Weighted Association Rule Mining

Fuzzy Weighted Association Rule Mining with Weighted Support and Confidence Framework is proposed in [3]. The authors have addressed the issue of invalidation of downward closure property (DCP) in weighted association rule mining where each item is assigned a weight according to their significance. Formulae for fuzzy weighted support and fuzzy weighted confidence for Boolean and quantitative items with weighted settings is proposed. The methodology follows an Apriori like approach and avoids the pre and post processing as opposed to most weighted ARM algorithm, thus eliminating the extra steps during rules generation.

A new algorithm which is applicable to Normalized and unnormalized case is proposed in [16]. The authors have introduced the problem of mining Weighted Quantitative Association rules based on Fuzzy approach. Using the fuzzy set concept, the discovered rules are more understandable to a human. Two different definition of weighted Support with and without normalization is proposed.

3 Problem Definition

The problem definition consists of the terms and basic concepts to define attribute weight, record weight, weighted support and weighted confidence for associative classifiers. Technique for Weighted Association Rule Mining is known as (WARM) and technique for associative classifiers is termed as Weighted Associative Classifier (WAC).

3.1 Associative Classifiers

Given a set of cases with class labels as a *training set*, *classification* is to build a model (called *classifier*) to predict future data objects for which the class label is unknown. Associative Classification is an integrated framework of Association Rule Mining (ARM) and Classification. A special subset of association rules whose right-hand-side is restricted to the classification class attribute is used for classification. This subset of rules is referred as the Class Association Rules (CARs). Since association rules explore highly confident associations among multiple variables, it may overcome some constraints introduced by a decision-tree induction method, which examines one variable at a time. Extensive performance studies show that association based classification have better accuracy in general [13-14].

3.2 Weighted Associative Classifiers

Weighted associative classifier consists of training dataset T= $\{r_1, r_2, r_3 \ldots r_i \ldots\}$ with set of weight associated with each {attribute, attribute value} pair. Each ith record r_i is a set of attribute value and a weight w_i attached to each attribute of r_i tuple / record. In a weighted framework each record is set of triple $\{a_i, v_i, w_i\}$ where attribute a_i is having value v_i and weight w_i, $0<w_j<=1$. Weight is used to show the importance of the item.

Definition 1. Attribute Weight: Attribute Weight is assigned depending upon the domain. For example item in supermarket can be assigned weight based on the profit on per unit sale of an item. In web mining visitor page dwelling time can be used to assign weigh. In medical domain symptoms can be assigned weight by expert doctor.

Example: Weight of different attribute in predicting the probability of Heart Disease is given in Table 1. A synthetic database is given in Table 2.

Table 1. Weight of symptoms for heart disease (attribute weight)

S.No.	Symptoms	Weights
1	Age<40	0.1
2	40<age<58	0.2
3	age>58	0.3
4	Smoking_habits=yes	0.8
5	Smoking_habits=no	0.7
6	Hypertension=yes	0.6
7	Hypertension=no	0.5
8	BMI<=25	0.1
9	26<=BMI<=30	0.3
10	31<=BMI<=40	0.5
11	BMI>=40	0.8

Definition 2. Attribute Set Weight: Weight of attribute set X is denoted by W(X) and is calculated as the average of weights of enclosing attribute. And is given by

$$W(X) \qquad \frac{\sum_{i=1}^{|X|} \text{Weight}(a_i)}{\text{Number of attributes in X}}$$

Example: Consider the 3 attribute set (Age , ">62"), (Smoking_habits, "yes") and (Hypertension, "yes") which may become the antecedent of a rule.

{(Age," >62"), (Smoking_habits, "yes"), (Hypertension, "yes")} = 0.3+0.8+0.6= 0.56

Table 2. Sample database for heart patient

R_ID	Age	Smoking_Habit	Hypertension	BMI	Heart_Disease
1	42	Yes	Yes	40	Yes
2	62	Yes	No	28	No
3	55	No	Yes	40	Yes
4	62	Yes	Yes	50	Yes
5	45	No	Yes	30	No

Definition 3. Record Weight/Tuple Weight: Consider the data in relational table, the tuple weight or record weight can be defined as type of attribute weight. It is average weight of attributes in the tuple. If the relational table is having n number of attribute then Record Weight is denoted by $W(r_k)$ and given by

$$W(r_k) = \frac{\sum_{i=1}^{|r_k|} weight(a_i)}{\text{Number of attributes in a record}}$$

Definition 4. Weighted Support: In associative classification rule mining, the association rules are not of the form $X \rightarrow Y$ rather they are subset of these rules where Y is the class label. Weighted Support (WSP) of rule X→Class_label, where X is set of non empty subsets of attribute-value set, is fraction of weight of the record that contain above attribute-value set relative to the weight of all transactions.

This can be given as

$$WSP(X\rightarrow Class\_label) = \frac{\sum_{i=1}^{|X|} weight(r_i)}{\sum_{k=1}^{|n|} weight(r_i)}$$

Here n is the total number of records.

Example: Consider a rule R, (Hypertension="yes") → Heart_Disease="yes" then Weighted Support of R is calculated as :

$$WSP(R) = \frac{\text{Sum of Record Weight having the condition Hypertension='yes' true and also given class label Heart\_Disease}}{\text{Sum of Weight of all transactions}}$$

$$WSP(R) = \frac{0.60+0.52+0.67+0.45}{0.60+0.42+0.52+0.67+0.45}$$

$$WSP(R) = 0.842$$

Table 3. Sample database with record weight

R_ID	Age	Smoking_habits	Hypertension	BMI	Record weight
1	42	Yes	Yes	40	(0.2+0.8+0.6+0.8)/4=0.60
2	62	Yes	No	28	(0.3+0.8+0.5+0.3)/4=0.42
3	55	No	Yes	40	(0.2+0.8+0.6+0.5)/4=0.52
4	62	Yes	Yes	28	(0.3+0.8+0.6+0.8)/4=0.67
5	45	No	Yes	30	(0.2+0.7+0.6+0.3)/4=0.45

Definition 5. Weighted Confidence: Weighted Confidence of a rule X→Y where Y represents the Class label can be defined as the ratio of Weighted Support of (X∪Y) and the Weighted Support of (X).

$$\text{Weighted Confidence} \quad \frac{\text{Weighted Support } (X \cup Y)}{\text{Weighted Support } (X)}$$

$$WC(R) = \frac{\text{Sum of Record Weight having the condition Hypertension='yes'' true and also the class label Heart\_Disease}}{\text{Sum of Record Weight having the condition Hypertension=''yes'' true}}$$

$$WC(R) = \frac{0.60+0.52+0.67+0.45}{0.60+0.52+0.67+0.45}$$

$$WC(R) = 1.0$$

4 Experimental Results

In order to evaluate the effectiveness of WAC, we used 3 benchmark Medical data set (UCI Machine learning dataset) i.e. heart.D53.N303.C5.num, breast.D20.N699.C2.num and hepatitis.D56.N155.C2.num and Java as front end and MS Access as backend tool. The dataset have been converted in Access databases. For training, entire record has been used and testing has been performed using entire dataset. The initial experimental result of Weighted Associative Classifier (WAC) yields following observations.

(1). From Table 4 it is clear that WAC outperforms as compare to three other associative Classifiers i.e. CBA, CMAR and CPAR in terms of average accuracy. The codes for these three Associative Classifiers have been downloaded from following side. http://www.csc.liv.ac.uk/~frans/KDD/Software/CBA/cba.html

(2). Increasing the high weight doesn't necessarily increase the amount of significant item sets; rather it always makes those item sets containing high weight items more likely to have a higher weighted support, hence holding more chances to become significant item sets containing no high weight items become relatively less likely to be significant.
(3). We noticed that the association rule classifier is sensitive to the unbalanced data. The heart.D53.N303.C5.num dataset is having almost 40% of cases with no heart disease and remaining 60% is further divided in to 4 types of heart disease hence the data is found to be suitable for predicting "No Heart disease". When the data set has been modified to incorporate only two class label one for "No Heart Disease" and others "Heart Disease" the accuracy is found to be 81.51% for WAC.
(4). The proposed concept has not been compared with other traditional tree based Classifiers as in [10-13] has already been proved that the Associative Classifiers are performing well than traditional classifiers.

Table 4. Accuracy Comparison of WAC, CBA, CMAR and WAC

S. No.	Data Set	WAC	CBA	CMAR	CPAR
1	heart	57.75	58.28	53.64	52.32
2	hepatitis	79.35	40.26	77.92	59.74
3	Cancer	90.41	93.7	88.82	92.84
Average Accuracy		**75.84**	64.08	73.46	68.3

5 Fuzzy Weighted Associative Classifiers

A fuzzy dataset consists of fuzzy relational database D={ r_1, r_2, r_3.... r_i...r_n} with a set of attributes I=(I_1, I_2, ...I_m}, each I_K can be associated with a set of linguistic labels L={l_1, l_2, ...l_L } for example L={young, Middle, Old}.Let each I_k is associated with fuzzy set F_k= {($I_{k,}l_{1)}$, ($I_{k,}l_{2)}$, ($I_{k,}l_{3)}$, ...($I_{k,}l_{L)}$}. So that a new Fuzzy Database D'' is defined as {($I_{1,}$ $l_{1)....}$ (I_1, $l_{L)}$ .... ($I_{k,}$ $l_{1)}$,...($I_{k,}$ $l_{L),...}$($I_{m,}$ $l_{1)}$...(I_m , $l_{L)}$ }. Each attribute I_i in a given transaction t_k is associated (to some degree) with Several fuzzy sets. The degree of association is given by a *membership degree* in the range [0..1]. t_k[μ(I_i, lj)] will denote the degree of membership for Fuzzy Attribute I_i to fuzzy set l_j in transaction t_k.

Table 5 shows the database D with continuous Domain of quantitative attribute. In Table 6 the transformed binary database (D') is shown that partition the quantitative attribute. Consider attribute *Age* in Table 5 again, three new attributes (e.g. *((Age,* young), (Age, middle) and *(Age old)* in place of *Age* may be used to constitute a new database (*D''*) with partial belongings of original attribute values to each of the new attributes. Table 7 illustrates an example of the new database obtained from the original database, given fuzzy sets {*Young, Middle, Old*} as characterized by membership functions shown in Figure 1.

Table 5. Data Base with continuous domain

(D) R_ID	Age	Blood Pressure (BP)	BMI (Obesity)	Heart_Disease(H_D)
1	42	90-130	40	Yes
2	62	80-120	28	No
3	55	82-122	40	Yes
4	62	92-135	50	Yes
5	45	95-135	30	No

Table 6. Transformed Binary Database D' from D

(D') R_ID	Age			Blood Pressure(BP)			BMI(Obesity)			Heart Disease (H_D)
1	0	1	0	1	0	0	0	1	0	Y
2	0	0	1	0	0	1	0	1	0	N
3	0	1	0	1	0	0	0	1	0	Y
4	0	0	1	1	0	0	0	0	1	Y
5	0	1	0	1	0	0	1	0	0	N

Table 7. Database D'' with Fuzzy Items

D''	Age			BP			BMI			H_D
	Young	Middle	Old	High	Low	Normal	Mild	Moderate	Severe	
1	0.2	0.7	0.1	0.4	0	0.6	0.6	0.3	0.1	Y
2	0.0	0.3	0.7	0.1	0.1	0.8	0.8	0.1	0.1	N
3	0.1	0.3	0.6	0.2	0.0	0.8	0.6	0.3	0.1	Y
4	0.0	0.3	0.7	0.5	0.0	0.5	0.1	0.2	0.7	Y
5	0.1	0.8	0.1	0.6	0.0	0.4	0.7	0.2	0.1	N

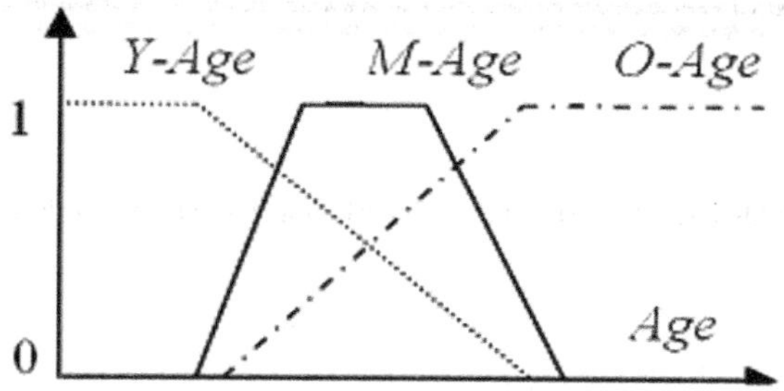

Fig. 1. Fuzzy Sets *Y-Age*, *M-Age* and *O-Age*

Here Fuzzy logic is incorporated to split the domain of quantitative attribute into intervals, and to define a set of meaningful linguistic labels represented by fuzzy sets and use them as a new domain. In this case it is possible that one item may appear with different label of same attribute. Hence he itemsets are needs to be restricted to contain at most one itemset per attribute because otherwise the rules of the form {(Age, Middle),(Age, old)….. ⇒ class_labels } have no meaning.

Definition 6. Fuzzy Attribute Weight: We assign a weight W, to each fuzzy Item (I_i, l_j) where($1 \leq i \leq n$), ($1 \leq j \leq L$) and ($0 \leq w \leq 1$). Table 8 shows the random weight assigned to different fuzzy attribute for heart disease.

Definition7. Fuzzy Attribute Set Transaction Weight: Weight of attribute set X a particular transaction t_k is denoted by t_k[FATW(X)] and is calculated as the product of membership degree of attribute in given fuzzy set in the transaction t_k and weight of fuzzy attribute; of all enclosing Fuzzy attribute in the set. And is given by

$$t_k[\text{FASTW}(X)] = \prod_{i=1}^{|X|} (\forall (I_i, l_j) \in X) \; [\, t_k[\mu (I_i, l_j)] \times W(I_i, l_j)]$$

Example: Consider the 2 attribute set (Age, old), (BP, high) **in transaction1**

$$\text{FASTW}((\text{Age, old}), (\text{BP, high})) = (0.1 \times 0.6)(0.4 \times 0.7) = 0.34$$

Table 8. Weight of symptoms for heart disease (attribute weight)

S.No.	Symptoms	Weights	S.No.	Symptoms	Weights
1	(Age, young)	0.1	5	(BP, Low)	0.2
2	(Age, middle)	0.2	6	(BP, High)	0.7
3	(Age, old)	0.6	7	(BMI, Mild)	0.3
4	(BP, Norma)l	0.3	8	(BMI, Moderate)	0.5
			9	(BMI, Severe)	0.7

Definition 8. Fuzzy Attribute Set Weight: Fuzzy Weight of attribute set X is calculated as sum of FASTW all transaction and is denoted by FASW(X). And is given by

$$\text{FASW}(X) = \sum_{k=1}^{|D''|} t_k[\text{FASTW}(X)]$$

$$\text{FSAW}(X) = \sum_{k=1}^{|D''|} \prod_{i=1}^{|X|} (\forall I_i, l_j \in X) \; [\, t_k[\mu (I_i, l_j)] \times W(I_i, l_j)]$$

Example: Consider the 2 attribute set (Age, old), (BP, high).

FASW ((Age, old), (BP, high)) = [(0.1×0.6)(0.4×0.7) + (0.7×0.6)(0.1×0.7) + (0.6×0.6)(0.2×0.7) + (0.7×0.6)(0.5×0.7) + (0.1×0.6)(0.6×0.7)] = 2.34

Definition 9. Fuzzy Weighted Support: In associative classification rule mining, the association rules are not of the form $X \rightarrow Y$ rather they are subset of these rules where Y is the class label.

Fuzzy Weighted support FWS of rule X→Class_label, where X is set of non empty subsets of fuzzy weighted attribute. Fuzzy Weighted Support FWS of a rule X→Class_label is calculated as sum of weight of all transaction in which the given class label is true, divided by total number of transaction, denoted by FWS(X→Class_label). And is given by

$$FWS(X \rightarrow Class\_label) = \frac{\sum_{\substack{\forall\ t_k \text{ having} \\ \text{Given} \\ \text{class\_label}}} t_k[FASTW(X)]}{\text{Number of records in } D''}$$

where t_k is all transaction for which the given class_label is true

$$FWS(X \rightarrow Class\_label) = \frac{\sum_{\substack{\forall\ t_k \text{ having} \\ \text{Given} \\ \text{class\_label}}} \prod_{i=1}^{|X|} \forall\ (I_i, l_j) \in X\ [\mu(I_i, l_j) \times W(I_i, l_j)]}{n}$$

Example: Consider the attribute set X= [(Age, old), (BP, high)] and a rule r = [(Age, old), (BP, high)→(Heart_disease= "yes") the Fuzzy Weighted Support of a rule is given by

FWS ((Age, old), (BP, high)→ (Heart_disease="yes"))

$$\frac{[(0.1\times0.6)(0.4\times0.7)+(0.6\times0.6)(0.2\times0.7)+(0.7\times0.6)(0.5\times0.7)]}{\mathbf{5}}$$

FWS(r) = 0.27 (27%)

Definition 10. Fuzzy Weighted Confidence: Fuzzy Weighted Confidence of a rule $X \rightarrow Y$ where Y represents the Class label can be defined as the ratio of Fuzzy Weighted Support of ($X \cup Y$) and Fuzzy Weighted Support of (X). And is given by

$$\text{Fuzzy Weighted Confidence} = \frac{\text{Fuzzy Weighted Support } (X \cup Y)}{\text{Fuzzy Weighted Support } (X)}$$

$$\mathrm{FWC}(X) = \frac{\sum_{\forall\, t_k \text{ having given class\_label}} \prod_{i=1}^{|X|} \forall\, (I_i, l_j) \in X\ [\mu(I_i, l_j) \times W(I_i, l_j)]}{\sum_{K=1}^{|D''|} \prod_{i=1}^{|X|} (\forall\, (I_i, l_j) \in X)\ [\mu(I_i, l_j) \times W(I_i, l_j)]}$$

Example: Consider the attribute set X= [(Age, old), (BP, high)] and a rule r = [(Age, old), (BP, high)→(Heart_disease= "yes"), the Fuzzy Weighted Confidence of a rule is given by

FWC [(Age, old), (BP, high)→ Heart_disease="yes")] =

$$\frac{[(0.1\times0.6)(0.4\times0.7)+(0.6\times0.6)(0.2\times0.7)+(0.7\times0.6)(0.5\times0.7)]}{[(0.1\times0.6)(0.4\times0.7)+(0.7\times0.6)(0.1\times0.7)+(0.6\times0.6)(0.2\times0.7)+(0.7\times0.6)(0.5\times0.7)+(0.1\times0.6)(0.6\times0.7)}$$

FWC(r) = 1.37/ 2.34

FWC(r) = 0.585(58%)

6 Fuzzy Weighted / Weighted Downward Closure Property

In a classical Apriori algorithm it is assumed that if the itemset is large, then all its subsets should also be large and is called Downward Closure Property (DCP). This helps algorithm to generate large itemsets of increasing size by adding items to itemsets that are already large. In the weighted ARM case where each item is assigned weight, the DCP does not hold. To solve the problem of invalidation of DCP, the new framework, "weighted support – significant" is designed. The authors have prove that if an itemset {AC} is not significant then its superset say {ACE} is impossible to be significant hence no need to calculate its weighted support

7 Conclusion and Future Work

This work presents a new foundational approach to Weighted Associative Classifiers where attributes are allowed to have weight depending upon their importance in predicting the class labels. The proposed concept has been implemented to evaluate the performance in terms of accuracy. Three benchmark Medical data set (UCI Machine learning dataset) have been used and the results reveal that by assigning weight to the attributes the prediction accuracy improves. To the best of our knowledge, the weighted concept has never been used in medical dataset. The result is found to be encouraging in medical prediction and needs further attention.

To deal with the sharp boundary problem associated with quantitative attribute domains a new foundational approach to Fuzzy Weighted Associative Classifiers where quantitative attributes are discritized to get transformed binary database.

In such data base each record fully belongs to only one fuzzy set. Such database will suffer the crisp boundary problem. By applying fuzzy logic the record will partially belonging to each fuzzy set. In future work the proposed concept needs to be implemented to evaluate the performance of FWAC in terms of average accuracy. Also we intend to further analyse the performance of WAC in terms of number of rule generating, impact of min. supp value and training time.

References

1. Soni, S., Pillai, J., Vyas, O.P.: An Associative Classifie Using Weighted Association Rule. In: Proceedings of International Symposium on Innovations in natural Computing published by 2009 World Congress on Nature & Biologically Inspired Computing, NaBIC 2009 (2009) 978-1-4244-5612-3/09/$26.00 c_2009 IEEE and IEEE-Xplore
2. Soni, S., Vyas, O.P.: Using Associative Classifiers for Predictive Analysis in Health Care Data Mining. International Journal of Computer Application (IJCA) 4(5), 821–1163 (2010)
3. Suleman Khan, M., Muyeba, M., Frans Coenen, M.: Fuzzy weighted Association Rule Minging with weighted Support and Confidence framework (2009)
4. Chen, Z., Chen, G.: Building an Associative Classifier Based on Fuzzy Association Rule. International Journal of Computational Intelligence Systems 1(3), 262–273 (2008)
5. Khan, M.S., Muyeba, M., Coenen, F.A.: Weighted Utility Framework for Mining Association Rules. In: Second UKSIM European on Symposium Computer Modeling and Simulation, EMS 2008, pp. 87–92 (2008)
6. Thabtah, F.: A review of associative classification mining. The Knowledge Engineering Review 22(1), 37–65 (2007)
7. Huang, M.-J., Chen, M.-Y., Lee, S.-C.: Integrating data mining with case-based reasoning for chronic diseases prognosis and diagnosis. Expert Systems with Applications 32, 856–867 (2007), Science Direct
8. Ordonez, C.: Association Rule Discovery with Train and Test approach for heart disease prediction. IEEE Transactions on Information Technology in Biomedicine 10(2) (April 2006)
9. Lu, S., Hu, H., Li, F.: Mining weighted association rules. Intelligent Data Analysis 5(3), 211–225 (2005)
10. Coenen, F., Leng, P., Ahmed, S.: Data Structures for association Rule Mining: T-trees and P-trees. IEEE Transactions on Data and Knowledge Engineering 16(6), 774–778 (2004)
11. Delgado, M., Marin, N., Sanchez, D., Vila, M.-A.: Fuzzy Association Rules: General Models and Applications. IEEE Transaction on Fuzzy System 11(2) (April 2003)
12. Tao, F., Murtagh, F., Farid, M.: Weighted Association Rule Mining using Weighted Support and Significance Framework. In: Proceedings of the Ninth ACM SIGKDD International Conference on Knowledge Discovery and Data Mining 2003, pp. 661–666 (2003)
13. Yin, X., Han, J.: CPAR: Classification based on predictive association rule. In: Proceedings of the SIAM International Conference on Data Mining, pp. 369–376. SIAM Press, San Francisco (2003)
14. Li, W., Han, J., Pei, J.: CMAR: Accurate and efficient classification based on multiple class-association rules. In: ICDM 2001, San Jose, CA, pp. 369–376 (November 2001)
15. Wang, W., Yang, J., Yu, P.: Efficient mining of weighted association rules (WAR). In: Proc. of the ACM SIGKDD Conf. on Knowledge Discovery and Data Mining, pp. 270–274 (2000)

16. Gyenesei, A.: Mining Weighted Association Rules for Fuzzy Quantitative Items. In: Zighed, D.A., Komorowski, J., Żytkow, J.M. (eds.) PKDD 2000. LNCS (LNAI), vol. 1910, pp. 416–423. Springer, Heidelberg (2000)
17. Au, W.-H., Chan, K.C.C.: FARM: A Data Mining System for Discovering Fuzzy Association Rules. In: Proc. of the 8th IEEE Int'l Conf. on Fuzzy Systems, Seoul, Korea (1999)
18. Liu, B., Hsu, W., Ma, Y.: Integrating classification and association rule mining. In: KDD 1998, New York, NY (August 1998)
19. Cai, C.H., Fu, A.W.C., Cheng, C.H., Kwong, W.W.: Mining Association Rules with Weighted Items, ideas. In: International Database Engineering and Applications Symposium, p. 68 (1998)
20. Ramkumar, G.D., Ranka, S., Tsur, S.: Weighted Association Rules: Model and Algorithm. In: KDD 1998 (1998)
21. Agrawal, R., Srikant, R.: Fast Algorithms for Mining Association Rules. In: Proceedings of 20th International Conference on Very Large Databases, Santiago, Chile, pp. 487–499 (1994)
22. Chan, K.C.C., Au, W.-H.: An Effective Algorithm For Mining Interesting Quantitative Association Rules. In: Proceedings of the 1997 ACM Symposium on Applied Computing, San Jose, California, United States, pp. 88–90 (1997)

A Parallel AES Encryption Algorithm Based on PCA

Debasis Das and Rajiv Misra

Department of Computer Science and Engineering,
Indian Institute of Technology, Patna
Patna-800013, Bihar, India
{ddas,rajivm}@iitp.ac.in

Abstract. Programmable Cellular Automata(PCA) employs some control signals on a Cellular Automata(CA) structure. Programmable Cellular Automata were successfully applied for simulation of biological systems, physical systems and recently to design parallel and distributed algorithms for solving task density and synchronization problems. In this paper PCA is applied to develop cryptography algorithms. This paper deals with the cryptography for a parallel AES encryption algorithm based on programmable cellular automata. This proposed algorithm based on symmetric key systems.

Keywords: CA, PCA, Cryptography, AES, Symmetric Key.

1 Introduction

A Cellular Automaton (CA)[1] is a computing model of complex system using simple rule. Researchers, scientists and practitioners from different fields have exploited the CA paradigm of local information, decentralized control and universal computation for modeling different applications. Wolfram [1] has investigated cellular automata using empirical observations and simulations. For 2-state 3-neighborhood CA, the evolution of the *ith* cell can be represented as a function of the present states of $(i\ 1)th$, $(i)th$, and $(i+1)th$ cells(shown in Fig 1) as: $x_i(t+1) = f(x_{i\ 1}(t), x_i(t), x_{i+1}(t))$ *where f*, represents the combinational logic. For a 2-state 3-neighborhood cellular automaton there are 2^3 =8distinct neighborhood configurations and 2^8=256 distinct mappings from all these neighborhood configurations to the next state, each mapping representing a CA rule.

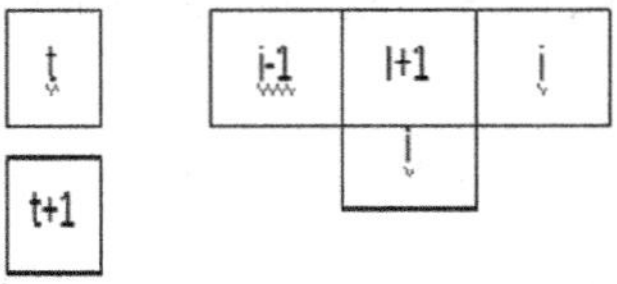

Fig. 1. One dimentional Cellular Automata

D. Nagamalai, E. Renault, and M. Dhanushkodi (Eds.): PDCTA 2011, CCIS 203, pp. 238–246, 2011.

The main aspect of cryptography and network security due to rapid development of information technology application. Cryptographic technique[2] based on two categories (1)symmetric key and (2)public key. CA based public cipher was proposed by guan[3].Stream CA based encryption algorithm was first proposed by wolfram[4]. Block encryption using hybrid additive cellular automata was proposed by Petre Anghelescu et. al[5].Cellular Automata computations and secret key cryptography was proposed by F. Seredynski et. al[6]. Block cipher based on reversible cellular automata was proposed by M. Seredynski and P. Bouvary[7].

1.1 Concept of Cellular Automata

Cellular Automata(CA)[1] is a collection of cells and each cell change in states by following a local rule that depends on the environment of the cell. The environment of a cell is usually taken to be a small number of neighboring cells. Fig 2 shows two typical neighborhood options (a) Von Neumann Neighborhood (b) Moore Neighborhood.

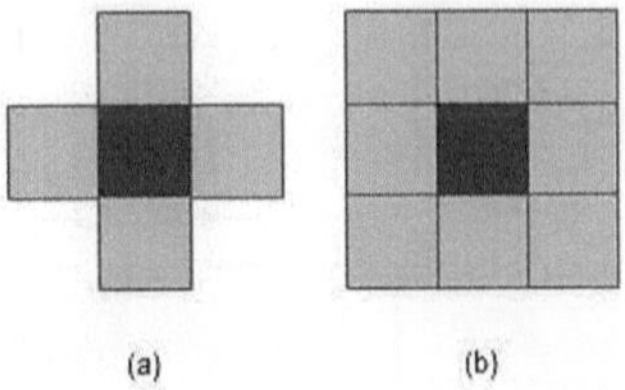

Fig. 2. (a) Von Neumann Neighborhood (b)Moore Neighborhood

1.2 Concept of Programmable Cellular Automata

In Programmable Cellular Automata (PCA)[1], the Combinational Logic (CL) of each cell is not fixed but controlled by a number of control signals. As the matter of fact, PCA are essentially a modified CA structure. It employs some control signals on a CA structure. By specifying certain values of control signals at run time, a PCA can implement various functions dynamically in terms of different rules. A huge flexibility into this programmable structure can be introduced via control signals in CL. For an n-cell CA structure can be used for implementing 2^n CA configurations. In Fig. 3 shows a 3-cell programmable CA structure and a PCA cell.

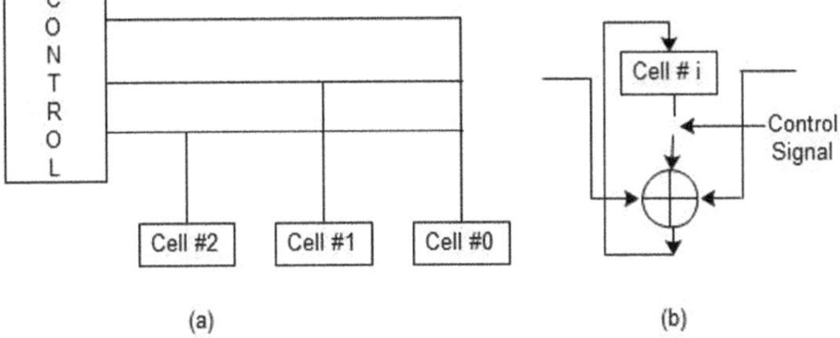

Fig. 3. (a) A 3-cell Programmable CA Structure (b) A PCA cell

1.3 AES Encryption Algorithm

The Advance Encryption Standard [2] is a block cipher that encrypts and decrypts a data block of 128 bits. It provides extra flexibility over that required of an AES candidate, in that both the key size and the block size may be chosen to be any of 128, 192, or 256 bits but for the Advanced Encryption Standard (AES) the only length allowed is 128. It uses 10, 12 or 14 rounds[2]. The key size, which can be 128, 192 or 256 bits[2], depends on the number of round.

1.3.1 General Design of AES Encryption

In Figure 4 [2] shows the general design for the encryption algorithm; the decryption algorithm[2] is similar, but round keys are applied in the reverse order. In this fig-4 Nr defines the number of rounds. There is a relationship between number of rounds and the key size, which means we can have different AES versions; they are AES-128, AES-192 and AES-256. The round keys, which are created by the key-expansion algorithm, are always 128 bits, the same size as the plaintext or cipher text block.

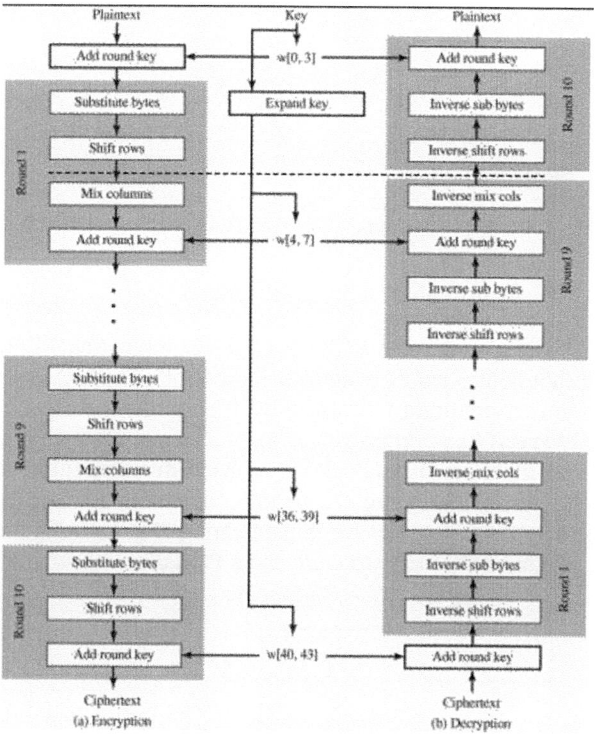

Fig. 4. AES Block Diagram

The above figure shows the structure of each round. Each round takes a state and creates another state to be used for the next transformation or the next round. The pre-round section uses only one transformation(AddRoundKey); the last round uses only three transformation(MixColumns transformation is missing).

To provide security, AES uses four types of transformations: substitution, permutation, mixing and key adding.

1.3.1.1 ***Substitution.*** The first transformation, SubBytes, is used at the encryption site. In the SubByte transformation, the state is treated as a 4x4 matrix of bytes. Transformation is done one byte at a time. The SubByte operation involves 16 independent byte-to-byte transformation. This transformation is non-linear byte transformation.

InvSubByte is the inverse of SubBytes. The transformation is used at decryption site.

1.3.1.2 ***Permutation.*** Next transformation in round is shifting, which permutes the bytes. Shifting is done at the byte level. In the encryption the transformation is called ShiftRows and the shifting is to the left. The number of shifts depends on the row number(0,1,2 or 3) of the state matrix.

In the decryption, the shifting is called InvShiftRows and the shifting is to the right.

1.3.1.3 ***Mixing.*** The mixing transformation changes the contents of each byte by taking four bytes at a time and combining them to recreate four new bytes. The mixing can be provided by matrix multiplication. The MixColumn transformation operates at the column level; it transforms each column of the state to a new column. The transformation is actually a matrix multiplication of a state column by a constant square matrix.

The InvMixColumn transformation is basically the same as the MixColumns transformation and it is used at the decryption site.

1.3.1.4 ***Key Adding.*** AddRoundKey also proceeds one column at a time. AddRoundKey adds a round key word with each state column matrix.

1.3.2 Analysis of AES

a. AES is more secure than DES due to the larger key size. For DES we need 2^{56} tests to find the keys; for AES we need 2^{128} tests to find the key.

b. The strong diffusion and confusion provided by the different transformation removes any frequency pattern in the plaintext.

c. The algorithms used in AES are so simple that they can be easily implemented using cheap processors and a minimum amount of memory.

2 Proposed AES Encryption Algorithm Based on PCA

2.1 Introduction

The Programmable Cellular Automata based on the elementary CA. proposed scheme is based on two CA one is elementary CA and the other is PCA. This PCA is used to provide real time keys for the block cipher. The block diagram of programmable cellular automata encryption systems is presented in Fig 5.

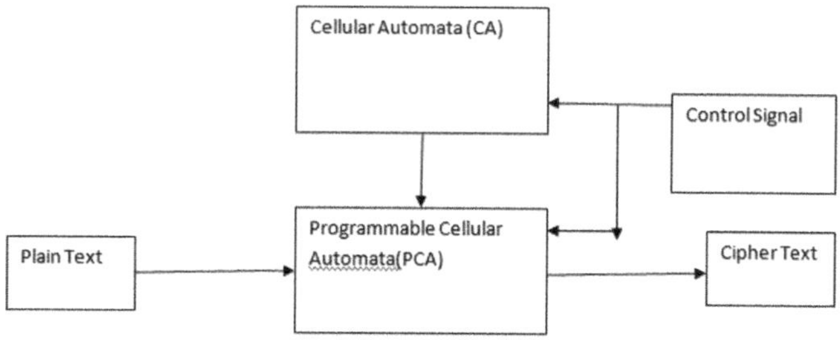

Fig. 5. Block Diagram of AES Encryption System Based on PCA

2.2 Proposed Algorithm

Algorithm: AES Enciphering and Deciphering Process Based on PCA

Input : Given Plain Text / Cipher Text
Output : Cipher Text / Plain Text
1: Enter the initial state of PCA, Convert decimal value to binary and store in an Array, A[ ],
2: for j=1 to 2^n
3: for i=1 to n
4: Apply the corresponding rule on the ith Cell, A[i].
5: Store the next state value, convert binary to decimal value
End of loop2 ,
End of loop1.
6: Create state transition diagram(or Rule Vector Graph(RVG)[8]: A Graph based on rule vector of PCA is called Rule Vector Graph. A node in RVG represents a set of RMTs(Rule Mean Time) while an edge between a pair of nodes represents the next state value (0 / 1) of a cell for specific RMTs.) of cycle length using Rule Vector (Rule Vector: The Sequence of rules< R_0, R_1,...R_i...,R_{n-1}> ,where ith cell is configure with rule R_i) and apply the corresponding rule.
7: Insert the value of plain text into original state of PCA.
8: If it is goes to its intermediate state after four cycles then
9: Plain Text is enciphered into cipher text.
10: Else after running another four cycle the intermediate state return back to its original state.
11: The cipher text is deciphered into plain text

2.3 Rules for PCA

The rules specify the evolution of the PCA from the neighborhood configuration to the next state and these are presented in Table 1. The corresponding combinational logic of rule 51, rule 195 and rule 153 for CA can be expressed as follows:

Rule 51: $a_i(t+1)$: NOT($a_i(t)$)
Rule 195 : $a_i(t+1)$: $a_{i-1}(t)$ XNOR $a_i(t)$
Rule 153 : $a_i(t+1)$: $a_i(t)$ XNOR $a_{i+1}(t)$

Table 1. The rules That Updated The next state of the CA cells

Rule	111	110	101	100	011	010	001	000
153	1	0	0	1	1	0	0	1
195	1	1	0	0	0	0	1	1
51	0	0	1	1	0	0	1	1

The operation of the simple PCA can be represented by the state transition graph. Each node of the transition graph represents one of the possible states of the PCA. The directed edges of the graph correspond to a single time step transition of the automata.

2.4 Procedure to Construct Transition Diagram

Considering the rule vector < 51,51,195,153> with length 4 so, the total number of states are $2^4 = 16$ states means 0000 to 1111. By using the rule vector if the start state is 0000 then next state is 1111 as shown in Figure 6.

1st bit= (NOT 0) =1
2nd bit= (NOT 0)=1
3rd bit = 0XNOR0 =1
4th bit=0 XNOR 0=1

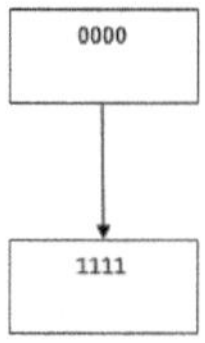

Fig. 6. State Changes from 0 to 15 using Rule Vector <51, 51,195, 153 >

If the start is 0001 then next state will be 1110 (shown in Fig 7) and continuing the process finally it returns back to state 0001 by completing a cycle. Initial state at time (t) : 0 0 0 1(left and right most cell connected to logic 0).

In Figure 8. the State Transition Diagram of PCA has four equal length cycles, each cycle has a cycle length 4. Considering this PCA as an enciphering function and defining a plain text as its original state it goes to its intermediate state after two cycles which is enciphering process. After running another four cycles, the intermediate state returns back to its original state which deciphers cipher text into plain text ensuring deciphering process.

1st bit= (NOT 0) =1
2nd bit= (NOT 0)=1
3rd bit = 0XNOR0 =1
4th bit=1XNOR 0=0

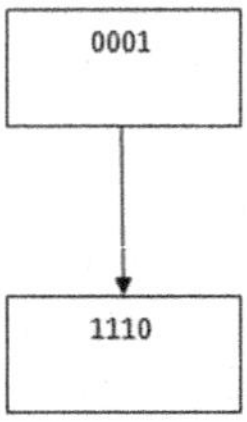

Fig. 7. State Changes from 1 to 14 using Rule Vector <51, 51, 195, 153>

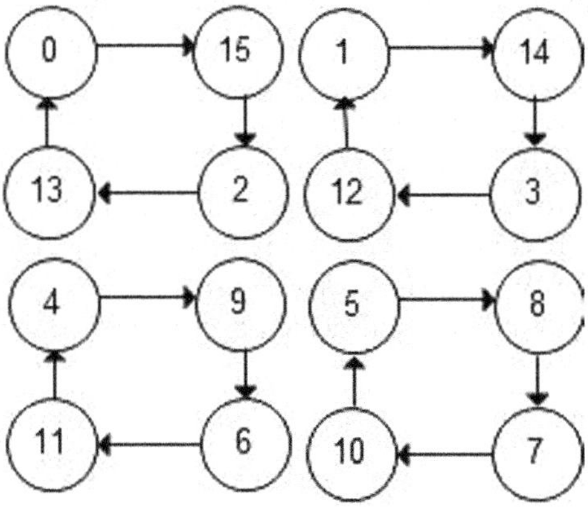

Fig. 8. State Transition Diagram of PCA

Table 2. Rule Selection Table

C1	C 2	Rule Applied
0	0	51
0	1	51
1	0	195
1	1	153

3 Performance Analysis

The ICEBERG [9] scheme that proposed with the objective for efficient hardware implementation was not efficient for software implementation. The execution speed of AES code and the proposed code on a Intel Core 2 Duo 2.0 GHZ, in openMP platform. The results are tabulated in Table 3.

Table 3. Execution Time for AES and Proposed Scheme

Key Size	AES	Proposed Scheme
128 bit	1.33 micro sec	1.05 micro sec
192 bit	1.57 micro sec	1.24 micro sec
256 bit	1.79 micro sec	1.44 micro sec

Implementation speed of our scheme was found to be faster than AES for all key sizes. This could be possible due to the inherited parallelism feature of PCA. Performance result of AES and Proposed Scheme shown in figure 9. The comparision result of AES and proposed scheme based on execution time(In micro second) and different key size(128 bit, 192 bit, 256 bit).

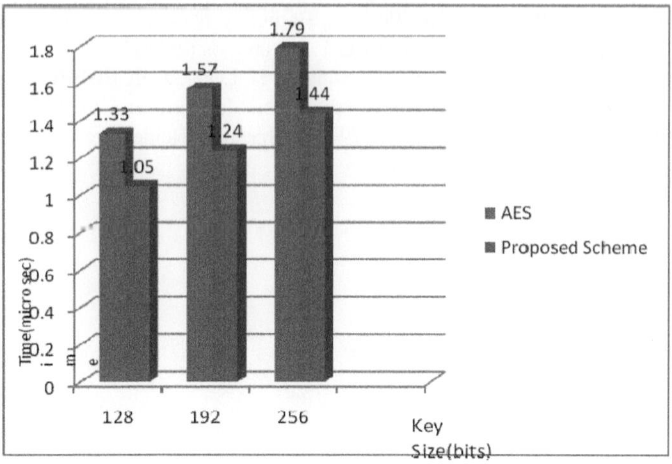

Fig. 9. Comparision result of AES and Proposed Scheme

4 Conclusion

The proposed model in this paper presents a parallel AES encryption algorithm which is based on Programmable Cellular Automata(PCA). PCA provides higher parallelism and simplification of software implementation. The AES Encryption algorithm is being implemented on a parallel platform (OpenMP) which ensures high encryption/decryption speed. The proposed model of this paper can be implemented on other parallel platform (other than OpenMP) which ensure more security with minimum processing time. Further development of a parallel AES encryption algorithm using two CA concepts PCA and Reversible Cellular Automata (RCA).

References

1. Wolfram, S.: A new kind of science Wolfram Media. Inc. (2002)
2. Stallings, W.: Cryptography and Network Security, 3rd edn. Prentice Hall, Englewood Cliffs (2003)
3. Guan, P.: Cellular Automaton Public Key Cryptosystem. Complex System 1, 51–56 (1987)
4. Wolfram, S.: Cryptography with cellular Automata, pp. 429–432. Springer, Heidelberg (1985)
5. Anghelescu, P., Ionita, S., Safron, E.: Block Encryption Using Hybrid Additive Cellular Automata. In: 7th International Conference on Hybrid Intelligent Systems. IEEE, Los Alamitos (2007)
6. Seredynski, F., Bouvry, P., Zomaya, A.Y.: Cellular Automata Computations and Secret Key Cryptography. Elsevier, Amsterdam (2004)
7. Seredynski, M., Bouvary, P.: Block Cipher Based On Reversible Cellular Automata. New Generation Computing, 245–258 (2005)
8. Kundu, A., Pal, A.R., Sarkar, T., Banarjee, M., Guha, S.K., Mukhopadhayay, D.: Comparative Study on Null Boundary and Periodic Boundary Neighbourhood Multiple Attractor Cellular Automata for Classification. IEEE, Los Alamitos (2008)
9. Standaert, F., Piret, G., Rouvroy, G., Quisquater, J., Legat, J.: ICEBERG: An involutional Cipher efficient for block encryption in reconfigurable Hardware. In: Roy, B., Meier, W. (eds.) FSE 2004. LNCS, vol. 3017, pp. 279–299. Springer, Heidelberg (2004)

Maintaining Shortest Path Tree in Dynamic Digraphs Having Negative Edge-Weights

Atul Kumar Rai and Suneeta Agarwal

Department of Computer Science & Engineering,
Motilal Nehru National Institute of Technology, Allahabad, India
atulkumarraijk@gmail.com,
suneeta@mnnit.ac.in

Abstract. Given a directed graph G, a source vertex s and shortest path tree (SPT), $T(s)$ rooted at s in G, the dynamic shortest path problem is to find the new SPT, $T'(s)$ in G from $T(s)$ when update(s) on edge weight(s) are performed. Previous works focus either on single edge weight update at a time or, process a set of updates together with the constraint that edge weights remain positive. In this paper we propose two semi-dynamic algorithms (one for increase only and the other for decrease only case) for maintaining SPT in a directed graph, even when some of edge weights assume negative values. Our algorithms process multiple edge weight updates simultaneously and also able to detect presence of negative weight cycle if introduced during update, to assert that no real SPT exists. From experiments conducted, we observe that dynamic algorithms perform better than the static algorithm when the percentage of updated edges is smaller than a certain threshold.

Keywords: Dynamic graphs, Dynamic shortest paths, Shortest path trees, Semi-dynamic algorithms, Fully-dynamic algorithms.

1 Introduction

The single source shortest path problem is a fundamental problem in graph theory. Finding and maintaining the shortest paths is primary problem in many application areas, such as communication network, transportation etc. Also, the solution to shortest path problem forms basis for the solution to many other problems in graph theory. This problem becomes more difficult when the changes on the graph are dynamically performed.

In this paper we present solution to the dynamic single source shortest path problem stated as: *Given a directed weighted graph $G = (V, E, W)$, where V is a finite set of vertices, E is set of edges and W is set of corresponding weights of the edges in G. Let source $s \in V$, and $T(s)$ be the shortest path tree (SPT) rooted at s in G . Let $G' = (V, E', W')$ be the new graph obtained by applying the update operation on G, then the dynamic single source shortest path problem is to obtain new SPT $T'(s)$ from $T(s)$.* The changes to the graph are applied by incremental updates due to a sequence of requests queries of the form: i)

D. Nagamalai, E. Renault, and M. Dhanushkodi (Eds.): PDCTA 2011, CCIS 203, pp. 247–257, 2011.

edge weight decrease ii) edge weight increase. An edge deletion can be treated as increasing the weight of that edge to infinity. Similarly, a new edge insertion can be treated as decreasing the weight of that edge from infinity to a finite value. There are two types of environment for dynamic shortest path problem : Semi-dynamic and Fully-dynamic. If either edge weight increase or, edge weight decrease operation is allowed on the graph then it's called Semi-dynamic. In fully dynamic shortest path problem arbitrary sequence of both of these operations are allowed.

Many dynamic shortest path algorithms have been proposed in the literature. But most of these algorithms are for the graphs having only positive edge weights [1,6,8]. There are some algorithms proposed for handling the graphs having negative edge weights as well, but they consider single update at a time [2,7]. To the best of our knowledge there is no work proposed in the literature for processing a whole set of edge weight update operations together for graphs having arbitrary edge weights. In this paper we propose two semi-dynamic algorithms for processing a set of edge weight update together to recompute the new SPT and detect the presence of negative weight cycle if one is introduced because of update(s) in the graph.

The rest of the paper is organized as follows: Section 2, defines some basic notation. In Sections 3, some of the works proposed previously on dynamic shortest path tree computation is presented. The proposed algorithms are described in section 4. In section 5, we present the experimental results and analysis. Finally, the paper is concluded in Section 6.

2 Preliminaries

2.1 Basic Notations

Let $G = (V, E, W)$ be a directed graph, where V is a finite set of vertices, E is the set of edges, and W be the set of real numbers corresponding to the edges in the graph called edge-weights. An edge $e : u \rightarrow v$ in G, is represented by $e = (u, v)$. Here u is called the tail of e denoted by Tail(e) and v is called head of e denoted by Head(e). The weight of an edge $(u, v) \in E$, is denoted as $w(u, v)$. For each vertex $u \in V$ in G, we denote OUT(u) as the set of edges emerging from u in G.

A path from u to v in G denoted as $P(u, v)$, is the sequence of vertices $(u = v_1, v_2, v_3 \ldots v_{n-1}, v_n = v)$ such that $(v_i, v_{i+1}) \in E, \forall i = 1, 2, 3, ..., n-1$. The length of a path is the sum of weights of all edges on the path. A vertex v is reachable from vertex u in G iff $\exists$ a path from u to v in G. For $u, v \in V$, a shortest path from u to v, denoted by $SP(u, v)$ in G, is a path such that there is no other path $P_1(u, v)$ of shorter length in G. A cycle is a path $(v_1, v_2, \ldots v_{n-1}, v_n, v_1)$ such that $(v_i, v_{i+1}) \in E, i = 1, 2, 3, ..., n-1$ and $(v_n, v_1) \in E$. A negative weight cycle is one for which the sum of weights of the edges contained in the cycle is negative.

Given a weighted digraph G, a shortest path tree (SPT) rooted at source vertex s, denoted as $T(s)$, is an acyclic subgraph of G constructed so that the distance between the root node and all other nodes is minimal i.e. $\forall v \in V$, if v is reachable from s, $T(s)$ contains a shortest path from s to v.

2.2 Data Structure Used

Other than standard representation of the graph, we use the following data structure in this paper. Each vertex $v \in V$ is unique and $\forall v \in V$, arrays Distance(v) and Predecessor(v) store shortest distance of v from s and parent of v in $T(s)$ respectively. Let Q be a min-based priority queue with element structure as: $\langle v, p, key \rangle$, where $v \in V$, p stores some useful information about v and key determines the priority of the entry. The priority queue supports some basic operations, like Enqueue(Q, $\langle v, p, key \rangle$) and Dequeue($Q$). Enqueue operation inserts an element $\langle v, p, key \rangle$ into the queue, but if an element with same v, is already present in the queue the element is replaced by new one providing new key is smaller, otherwise the element is discarded. The Dequeue operation extracts an element with lowest key value and removes it's entry from the queue.

3 Previous Work

Frigioni et al.[2] proposed two semi-dynamic algorithms to update SPT. One of these two algorithm handles edge weight increase and the other one handles edge weight decrease case. These algorithms can be applied to any directed graph with real valued edge weights, but can only handle single edge weight update at a time. If a set of updates is given, then the algorithm can handle them as a series of single edge weight updates, which makes it inefficient.

Narvez et al.[6] proposed dynamic SPT algorithm to handle multiple edge weight updates based on a ball-and-string model. This model illustrates how affected balls re-arrange themselves in a natural way into their optimal positions when the length of a string is increased or decreased. The dynamic SPT algorithm simulates the dynamics of the balls in this model, and processes affected vertices. It always consolidates the vertex of least distance increase (in the case of edge weight increases) or most distance decrease (in the case of edge weight decreases). But this ball-string model requires the edge weights to be positive only and hence this algorithm can not be applied on the graphs having negative edge weight. Also Chan & Yang [8] claimed that this algorithm is wrong for a certain case of multiple edge weight increases and they proposed a corrected version of the algorithm proposed in [6].

Chan & Yang [8] also proposed two semi-dynamic algorithm to process a set of edge weight updates together. These algorithms are dynamic version of Dijkstra's algorithm. The basic idea is to first recognize the affected vertices due the update(s) and process only these affected vertices to compute the new SPT. Just like Dijkstra's algorithm, these semi-dynamic algorithms use distance as priority to consolidate any vertex and hence the constraint that all the edge weights will always remain non-negative is applied here also.

In the proposed algorithms we have removed the constraints of edge weights to remain non-negative. Our algorithms work on directed graphs having positive as well as negative edge weights. We process a set of edge weight updates simultaneously to construct new SPT. If a negative weight cycle is formed during update, our algorithm is able to detect its presence. We have also conducted experiments to measure the performance of our algorithms and compared the results against the well known Dijkstra's algorithm and previously proposed dynamic SPT algorithms in [8].

4 Algorithm

In this section we present two algorithms for maintaining the shortest path trees of a graph $G = (V, E)$ with arbitrary edge weights. The first algorithm is for maintaining shortest path trees when edge weights have been decreased, while the other for edge weight increase operations. In these algorithms we assume that before the update operations have been performed, the graph does not contain any negative weight cycle and SPT of graph G is given.

4.1 Decreasing the Edge Weights

Here we show how to compute the new shortest path tree from an existing one, weights of set of some edges are decreased. Let the weight of edge (u, v) be decreased by $\delta(> 0)$ then shortest distance of any vertex in G will change only if $Distance(u) + w(u, v) - \delta < Distance(v)$. It is obvious that, if decreasing the weight of an edge (u, v) in G, introduces a negative weight cycle then the cycle must contain edge (u, v). This means while updating the shortest distance of vertices in G, if the shortest distance of vertex $u(tailofedge(u, v))$ is also decreased, then the presence of negative weight cycle is detected.

Algorithm 1. DSPDecrease $\langle s,\ T(s),\ G,\ E_{DEC}\rangle$
Input: E_{DEC}: set of edges whose weights are to be increased by δ (> 0), graph G, source vertex s, SPT $T(s)$ of G
Output: The new SPT $T'(s)$ of the updated graph G'

$Q \leftarrow \phi$
/ Step-1:Apply edge-weight update to G and enqueue affected vertices's to Q */*
for each edge $e_i \in E_{DEC}$ **do**
  $w(e_i) \leftarrow w(e_i) - \delta_i$
  $t \leftarrow$ Tail$(e_i), h \leftarrow$ Head(e_i)
  if Predecessor$(t) \neq Null$ and Distance$(h) >$ Distance$(t) + w(e_i)$ **then**
    $d_h \leftarrow$ Distance$(t) + w(e_i)-$Distance(h)
    for each vertex $v_i \in T(h)$ **do** *// Delete sub-tree rooted at h*
      Predecessor$(v_i) \leftarrow Null$
    end for
    if Predecessor$(t) = Null$ **then**
      Negative length cycle found
      return
    end if
    Enqueue$(Q, \langle h, t, d_h\rangle)$
  end if
end for
/ Step-2: Consolidate queued vertices's */*

```
while Q ≠ φ do
   ⟨y, x, d_y⟩ ← Dequeue(Q)
   Predecessor(y) ← x
   Distance(y) ←Distance(x) + w(x, y)
   for each edge (y, y_i) ∈ OUT(y) do
      if Distance(y_i) >Distance(y) + w(y, y_i) then
         if Predecessor(y_i) ≠ Null then
            for each edge v_i ∈ T(y_i) do          // Delete sub-tree rooted at y_i
               Predecessor(v_i) ← Null
            end for
            if Predecessor(y) = Null then
               Negative length cycle found
               return
            end if
         end if
         Enqueue(Q, ⟨y_i, y, d_{y_i}⟩)
      end if
   end for
end while
return T(s)
```

The algorithm DSPDecrease shown in Algorithm[1] updates the shortest path tree $T(s)$ in G to become $T'(s)$ in G' if there is no negative weight cycle formed after update operation. Otherwise the algorithm detects the presence of negative weight cycle. The description of the algorithm is as follows:

In step-1, the algorithm starts by performing the edge weight decrease operations on the graph. For each updated edge e_i, the algorithm checks if $Head(e_i)$ (say h), is affected by the update, *i.e.* if shortest distance of h is to be changed. If h is affected then dh is calculated as $dh = Distance(Tail(e_i)) + w(e_i) - Distance(h)$. The sub-tree $T(h)$ rooted at h is deleted from SPT $T(s)$. While deleting the sub-tree rooted at h, if $Tail(e_i)$ (say t), also gets deleted from SPT then presence of negative weight cycle is detected (since t will be deleted only if it belongs to the sub-tree $T(h)$ *i.e.* t is a successor of h in the SPT and decreasing the weight of edge e_i introduces a negative weight cycle). If no negative weight cycle is found then $\langle h, t, dh \rangle$ is queued in priority queue Q.

In step-2 vertices queued in Q are dequeued one by one according to their priority. Let $\langle v, u, dv \rangle$ is dequeued from Q. Here vertex v gets consolidated *i.e.* u is assigned as predecessor of v in SPT, $Distance(u) + w(u, v)$ as shortest distance of v from s and edge (u, v) is inserted in SPT. Now, $\forall v_i \in OUT(v)$, if a shorter path from s to v_i going through v is found then v_i is queued in priority queue Q as $\langle v_i, v, dv_i \rangle$ where $dv_i = Distance(v) + w(v, v_i) - Distance(v_i)$. The iteration in step-2 continues until Q becomes empty. At last the algorithm returns the new SPT and terminates. Following example shows how DSPDecrease algorithm works.

Example: In [Fig. 1a], let the weights of edges (s, e) and (a, g) are decreased by 7 and 5 unit respectively. In step-1 the DSPDecrease algorithm first removes e, g

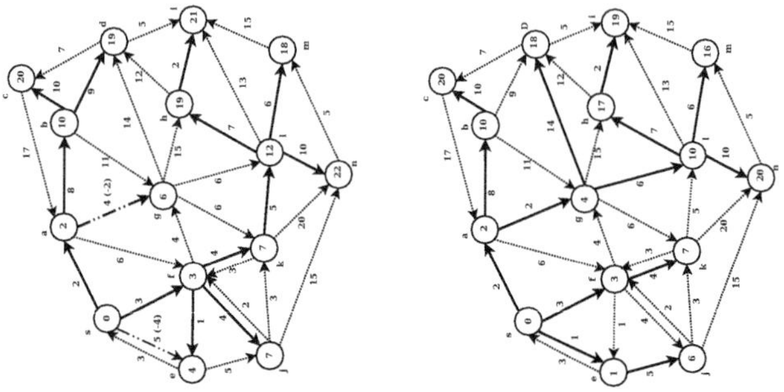

(a) Graph G & SPT $T(s)$ (b) Graph G' & SPT $T'(s)$

Fig. 1. Original and updated digraph & SPT

and their descendant vertices (if any), from SPT and queue e and g to priority queue Q as $\langle e, s, -6\rangle$ and $\langle g, a, -4\rangle$ respectively. In step-2 $\langle e, s, -6\rangle$ (element with minimum key) is dequeued from Q. Here vertex e gets consolidated and edge (s, e) is added to $T(s)$.Then $\langle j, e, -4\rangle$ is queued in Q. Similarly rest of the iterations in step-2 are carried out and Step-2 ends when Q becomes empty. At last algorithm returns $T(s)$ shown in [Fig. 1b] and terminates.

4.2 Increasing the Edge-Weights : DSPIncrease Algorithm

In this section we will compute the new shortest path tree $T'(s)$ from $T(s)$, when set of edge weight increase operations have been performed on the graph G. But first we state following observations:

- If weight increase operation is performed on an edge (u, v) then it will not introduce any negative weight cycle in G.
- If weight of an edge $(u, v) \in G$, is increased and $(u, v) \notin T(s)$ then it will have no effect on shortest path of any vertex in G.
- If weight of an edge $(u, v) \in G$, is increased and $(u, v) \in T(s)$ then for each vertex $x \notin T(v)$, shortest distance and predecessor of x is preserved in $T'(s)$.

The algorithm DSPIncrease shown in Algorithm[2] works in three steps. The description of the algorithm is as follows:

In step-1, the algorithm begins by applying the updates to the graph. If the updated edge belongs to the SPT then the edge gets deleted from SPT and all the vertices in subtree $T(h)$ are queued in V_1, where h is the head of the updated edge.This operation removes all the vertices in sub-tree $T(h)$ from $T(s)$.

In step-2, vertices are dequeued from V_1 and their current minimum possible distance from s is calculated. If vertex dequeued from V_1 (say v), is a boundary vertex i.e. directly reachable from set of nodes remaining in $T(s)$, then current possible shortest distance from s (say $dist$), is calculated and the vertex preceding v (say u), in this path is assigned as candidate predecessor of v in the SPT. Now, "$d_v = dist - Distance(v)$" is calculated and $\langle v, u, d_v\rangle$, is queued in the min-based

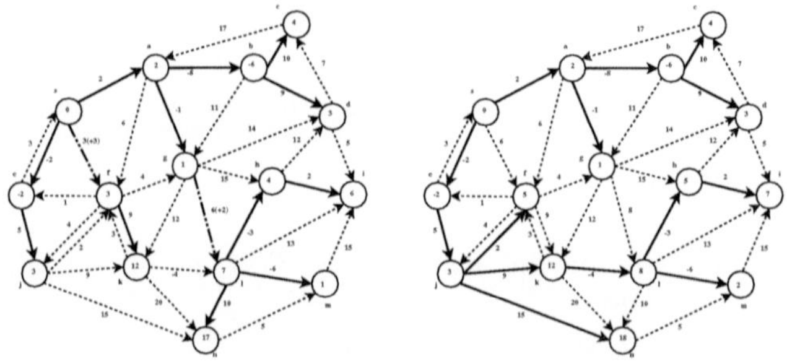

(a) Graph G & SPT $T(s)$ (b) Graph G' & SPT $T'(s)$

Fig. 2. Original and updated digraph & SPT

priority queue Q. If dequeued vertex is not a boundary vertex then it's shortest distance is assigned to ∞ and will be updated later. Step-2 is repeated until V_1 becomes empty.

In step-3, an element $\langle v, u, d_v \rangle$ with minimum key is dequeued from the priority queue Q. Here vertex v is consolidated i.e. u is assigned as predecessor of v in SPT, Distance$(u) + w(u, v)$ becomes shortest distance of v from source s and edge (u, v) is inserted in SPT. Now for each edge e_i from OUT(v), let h be the Head(e_i). If a shorter path to h going through v is found then, $\langle h, v, d_h \rangle$ is queued in the priority queue where $d_h = Distance(v) + w(v, h) - Distance(h)$. The iteration in step-3 is ended when Q becomes empty and we get new SPT of updated graph. To understand how algorithm works we will take a look on the following example.

Algorithm 2. DSPIncrease $\langle s,\ T(s),\ G,\ E_{INC} \rangle$
Input: E_{INC}: set of edges whose weights are to be increased by δ (a positive real number), graph G, source vertex s, $T(s)$: shortest path tree of G
Output: $T'(s)$ the new SPT of the updated graph G'

```
V_1 ← φ          //Simple queue of vertices
for each v ∈ V do
   Distance'(v) ← Distance(v) //Distance' holds temporary distances of vertices
end for
Q ← φ
/*Step-1:Apply edge weight increase operations on G and find affected vertices*/
for each edge e_i ∈ E_INC do
   w(e_i) ← w(e_i) + δ_i
   if e_i ∈ T(s) then
      remove edge e_i from T(s)
      h ← Head(e_i)
      for each vertex v_i ∈ T(h) do      // Add all the affected vertices to V_1
         Enqueue(V_1, ⟨v_i⟩)
      end for
```

```
    end if
end for
/*Step-2: Enqueue vertices to priority queue Q, such that edge (u,v) ∈ E
where u ∈ T(s) and v ∈ V1, with their current minimum possible distance*/

while V1 ≠ φ do
    v ← Dequeue(V1)
    dist ← min[{Distance(u) + w(u,v) | u ∈ T(s) and (u,v) ∈ E} ∪ {∞}]
    if (dist ≠ ∞) then
        parent ← u // where u is the predecessor of v for which Distance(u) +
        w(u,v) is minimized
        d_v ← dist − Distance(v)
        Enqueue(Q, ⟨v, parent, d_v⟩)
    end if
    Distance'(v) ← dist
end while
Step-3: Consolidate queued vertices's
while Q ≠ φ do
    ⟨v, u, d_v⟩ ← Dequeue(Q)
    add edge (u,v) to T(s)
    Distance(v) ← Distance(u) + w(u,v)
    for each e_i ∈ OUT(v) do
        h ← Head(e_i)
        if Distance'(h) > Distance(v) + w(v,h) then
            d_h ← Distance(v) + w(v,h)- Distance(h)
            Distance'(h) ← Distance(v) + w(v,h)
            Enqueue(Q, ⟨h, v, d_h⟩)
        end if
    end for
end while
return T(s)
```

Example: In [Fig. 2a], let the weights of edges (g, l) and (s, f) are increased by 2 and 3 unit respectively. The DSPIncrease algorithm first removes these two edges from SPT and affected vertices f, h, i, k, l, m, n are queued in V_1. In step-2 candidate shortest distances, change in shortest distance and candidate predecessor of boundary vertices f, h, i, k, l, n are calculated. One entry for each of these boundary vertices is queued in priority queue Q. Distance of the non boundary vertex m is changed to ∞. In step-3 a vertex with minimum key is dequeued from Q and consolidated. Also, all the vertices reachable from the consolidated vertex, are searched for finding shorter distances and if one found then it is queued in Q. The iterations in step-3 ends when Q becomes empty. At the end of step-3 DSPIncrease algorithm returns $T(s)$, the new SPT [Fig. 2b] and terminates.

5 Experiments

5.1 Experimental Setup

We performed our experiments on a PC with a Pentium IV 3.2 GHz processor and 1.5 GB of main memory, running Ubuntu 10.04. We have implemented all the programs using C-language. We use randomly generated graphs. We generate directed graphs, given the number of vertices, graph sparsity in percentage, and a range of edge weights. The weight of an edge is randomly selected from the input range. For each graph G, we randomly select a set of edges whose weights are updated.

Since most of the literature available on dynamic SPT computation focus only on graphs having positive edge weights. We have implemented the static and dynamic[8] Dijkstra algorithms for graphs with positive edge weights only and compare the running time of these algorithms with our algorithms. For graphs having both positive and negative edge weights, we have implemented the well known Bellman-Ford Algorithm for computing SPT and compare the results with our algorithms. As our algorithms are based on procedure similar to Dijkstra's algorithm, they outdo Bellman-Ford algorithm in most of the cases and therefore we use Bellman-Ford algorithm only for verifying the correctness of our algorithms on graphs having both positive and negative edge weights.

We have conducted our experiments based on three varying factors: *i*) Number of vertices in the graph (Graph-size), *ii*) Graph-density and *iii*) Percentage of edges updated (peu).

5.2 Experimental Results

The comparison of running time of dynamic and static algorithms while the graph-size, graph-density and peu are varied for decrease and increase case are shown in Figure[3] and [4] respectively. Although the figures include only few plots but the results on other test data sets are similar, and therefore are not included.

All dynamic algorithms outperform Dijkstra when peu is small, but as peu increases the performance gap between a dynamic algorithms and Dijkstra narrows and finally vanishes at some peu threshold value. Above this threshold value the Dijkstra's algorithm performs better compared to the dynamic algorithms. This behavior of the dynamic algorithm is expected as the running time of the dynamic algorithm also consists of the time taken for applying updates to the graph in addition to the time taken in performing algorithm iterations. Also it can be observed from the figures that increase in graph-size or, graph-density or, both lowers the dynamic algorithms peu-threshold value.

In decrease case, it is observed from the [Fig. 3] that DynDijkDec algorithm performs better than DSPDecrease algorithm. As the DSPDecrease algorithm works for general directed graphs having both positive and negative edge weights, so it always performs a check for the presence of any negative weight cycle before a vertex is queued in the priority queue for consolidation resulting in slight

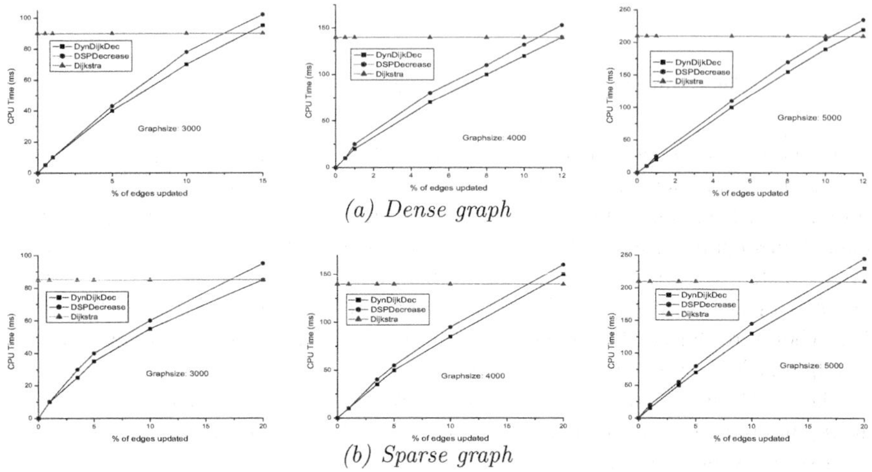

(a) Dense graph

(b) Sparse graph

Fig. 3. Comparison of algorithms while decreasing Edge weights

decrease in performance. This justifies the performance difference between the two algorithms.

As shown in [Fig. 4], in increase case, the average running time for DynDijkInc and DSPIncrease algorithms has negligible difference and performance curve of these two algorithms almost overlaps. This is due to the fact that both of these algorithms perform similar operations while recomputing the new SPT.

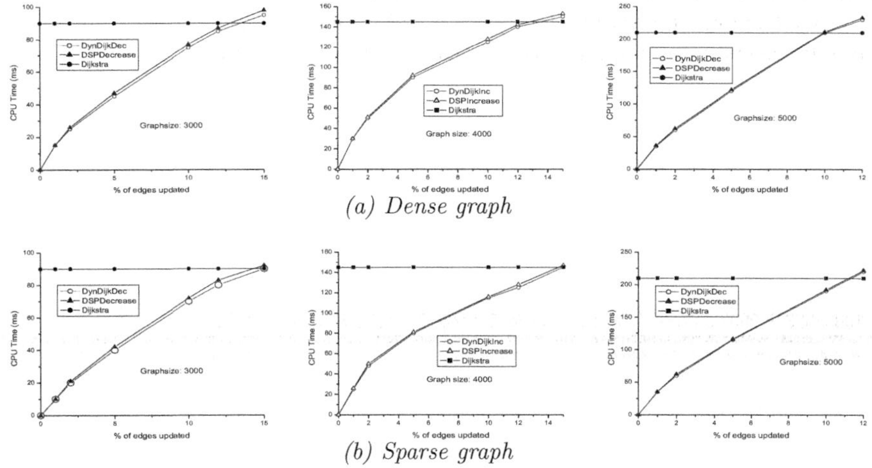

(a) Dense graph

(b) Sparse graph

Fig. 4. Comparison of algorithms while Increasing Edge weights

6 Conclusion

In this paper we proposed two semi-dynamic algorithms for dynamic SPT computation on directed graphs having both positive and negative weighted edges.

We conducted experiments to evaluate their performance, in terms of CPU running time and compared them with the well-known static algorithm Dijkstra and dynamic algorithms proposed by Chan and yang[8]. We verified the correctness of these algorithms experimentally.

From experiments conducted we came to the conclusion that, dynamic algorithms perform better than the static algorithm when the percentage of updated edges is smaller than certain threshold. When the threshold is reached it is better to compute SPT from scratch by using some static algorithm. The threshold value varies with the graph-size and graph-density. However, DSPDecrease algorithm performs slightly worse than DynDijkDce when edge weights are decreased, but in case of edge weight increase, both DSPIncrease and DynDijkInc algorithms take approximately same execution time. Unlike the DynDijk algorithms which require the edge weights of the graph to always remain positive, our algorithms allows the edge weights to assume both negative and positive values and therefore can be applied on a wide range of graphs. So the slight difference in performance when edge weights are decreased, may be overlooked.

References

1. Ramalingam, G., Reps, T.W.: An Incremental Algorithm for a Generalization of the Shortest-Path Problem. Journal of Algorithms 21(2), 267–305 (1996)
2. Frigioni, D., Marchetti-Spaccamela, A., Nanni, U.: Fully Dynamic Shortest Path and Negative Cycle Detection on Digraphs with Arbitrary Arc Weights. In: Proceedings of the 6th Annual European Symposium on Algorithms. Springer, London (1998)
3. King, V.: Fully dynamic algorithms for maintaining all-pairs shortest paths and transitive closure in digraphs. In: 40th Annual Symposium on Foundations of Computer Science, pp. 81–89 (1999)
4. Cherkassky, B., Goldberg, A.V.: Negative cycle detection algorithms. Mathematical Programming 85(2), 277–311 (1999)
5. Frigioni, D., Marchetti-Spaccamela, A., Nanni, U.: Fully Dynamic Algorithms for Maintaining Shortest Paths Trees. Journal of Algorithms 34(2), 251–281 (2000)
6. Narvez, P., Siu, K., Tzeng, H.: New Dynamic SPT Algorithm Based on a Ball-and-String Model. ACM Transactions on Networking 9(6), 706–718 (2001)
7. Demetrescu, C., Frigioni, D., Marchetti-Spaccamela, A., Nanni, U.: Maintaining Shortest Paths in Digraphs with Arbitrary Arc Weights: An Experimental Study. In: Proceedings of Fourth International Workshop on Algorithm Engineering, pp. 218–229 (2001)
8. Chan, E.P.F., Yang, Y.: Shortest Path Tree Computation in Dynamic Graphs. IEEE Transactions on Computers 58(4), 541–557 (2009)
9. Bauer, R., Wagner, D.: Batch Dynamic Single-Source Shortest-Path Algorithms: An Experimental Study. In: Vahrenhold, J. (ed.) SEA 2009. LNCS, vol. 5526, pp. 51–62. Springer, Heidelberg (2009)

Comparison of MAC Layer Performance of Reactive and Proactive Protocols for Different Mobility Conditions in WSN

Manjusha Pandey and Shekhar Verma

Indian Institute of Information Technology Allahabad, India
{rs58,sverma}@iiita.ac.in

Abstract. Wireless sensor networks are the most challenging networks for communication because of its resource constrained nature and the dynamical nature of network topographic anatomy. A lot of research is being going on in the diverse parts of the world for optimum utilization of communication resources in these special types of ad hoc networks. The utility and application domain of sensor networks ranges from commercial, public safety applications and military sector to be the most important ones. The magnificent challenges to the routing algorithms employed in such type of networks are due to the mercurial size of the network and its expandable topology that is quite dynamic in nature. The present paper offers a comparison and analysis of the packet drop at the MAC layer for different routing protocols under an experimental setup having different mobility condition based scenarios of the wireless sensor network application. The comparative study may have also an impact on the improvement of MAC layer performance for different simulation times of the experimental setup considering two of reactive as well as proactive protocols that are most widely used routing protocol in wireless sensor networks. Wireless sensor network application under consideration for the experimental is the battle field monitoring wireless sensor network and the comparative study has been performed for four different mobility patterns described as four different scenarios in the considered experimental application of wireless sensor networks.

The sensor network simulative electronic deception architecture used is for the battle field monitoring application of wireless sensor networks. The application provides support for sensing capabilities within the network nodes called as UGS (Unattended Ground Sensors).Mobile nodes gather data from battle field and direct it to the base station via mobile UGV (Unmanned Ground Vehicles).The performance of the MAC Layer varies with the different average jitter values for different simulation times in the network. Power usage model has been used to reliably represent an actual sensor hardware and sensor network oriented traffic pattern.

Keywords: Sensor networks, Packet drop, MAC Layer, Routing Protocols: AODV, OLSR, DYMO, LANMAR.

1 Introduction

Generally, the network are fractioned into two types counting on the operational mode they follow namely infrastructure and infrastructure less. The first type that is

D. Nagamalai, E. Renault, and M. Dhanushkodi (Eds.): PDCTA 2011, CCIS 203, pp. 258–269, 2011.

infrastructure network may be defined as a network with fixed and wired gateways. This type of network has fixed network topographic anatomy that comprises of nodes and base stations. The bridges present in the network are called as base stations. Any mobile unit in the network connects to the nearest base station for communication. In the infrastructure network, communication among the nodes takes place by shifting from one base station to some other base station. The fundamental difference between fixed networks and infrastructure less networks or adhoc networks is the nodes in an adhoc network may possibly be mobile. Because of the mobility of nodes, there are certain characteristics that are only applicable to adhoc networks. Some of these key characteristics are bandwidth constrained links, dynamic network topologies, and energy constrained operations. In the real-time applications, and real-time data, the ad hoc networks allow for Quality of Service (QoS) in terms of delay, bandwidth, as well as packet loss. This network does not have defined routers and routes. All nodes have capability of moving, may work as routers, and can be connected in an arbitrary manner. Functioning as routers, these nodes discover as well as maintain routes to other node within the network. The nodes move around randomly, thus making the network topology dynamic in nature. So it is important for the routing protocols to be adaptive and have the ability to maintain routes in spite of dynamic network topology. These networks have drew in a lot of attention throughout the past several years because of increased demand for ubiquitous connectivity and emergence of new communication scenarios such as sensor networks Some critical areas of applications of these networks are in the fields of military and civilian application such as communication in the battle field, disaster management, vehicular movement or communication in traffic management and scientific exploration etc. In all these applications, group communication is more important.

In the paper we present the sensor network simulator architecture that furnishes support for sensing potentialities in network nodes, existent sensor hardware and sensor network orienting traffic model. We have contemplated sensor network models in the various circumstance of network simulation and this is the exclusive work to our cognition that compares the routing mechanisms for detailed models on the operation of sensor networks [2]. The following four scenarios illustrate the comparative analysis of using accurate and representative ad hoc network models.

2 Wireless Sensor Networks Routing: Design Challenges

The generally design aim of any routing protocol is always been to increase the throughput while minimizing the packet loss ratio at the same architectural design considerations of the application network. In the wireless sensor networks the nodes are not static the mobility may define as changing of physical locations of the nodes with respect to time. This results in frequent alterations in the topology of the network. Hence the routing algorithms need to consider the ever changing dynamic topology of the network that may also be because of the summation of new nodes to the network or dying of the surviving nodes. Dying of nodes may be due to numerous reasons including physical tampering or malfunctioning due to being unattended or fading up of nodes because of energy constraints. Another important issue is link quality which is effects the routing of packets a lot. The factors affecting the link quality involve fading and high error rate within the wireless medium. Thus the effective handling of packet failures or packet drops has a major influence on the performance of wireless routing protocols.

In wireless ad hoc networks [9] out of numerous views to be taken into thoughtfulness one of the most significant is that of the effective energy management with the additional goal of prolonged connectivity of the network and increased lifetime of the network. These constraints are particularly true of sensor networks. In these networks the nodes are usually battery powered and left unattended after deployment. The routing algorithms designed for these networks need to monitor the energy of nodes and route packets accordingly. Ad hoc networks in general and wireless sensor networks in specific have the limitations in terms of bandwidth, memory and computation power. Many routing techniques have been proposed but few comparisons for different mobility conditions implemented as various application scenarios between different protocols have been done. Considering the work done in the field of comparison and analysis, the analysis has been done between the routing protocols evaluated based on quantitative and qualitative metrics [14]. But the analysis of a protocols performance for exhaustive variations in simulation time of the same network and for different application scenarios has not been proposed and performed yet. A great deal of research in the domain of routing protocols in ad hoc networks has been done; AODV, DYMO, OLSR, LANMAR to mentioned a few.

OLSR [3] is a variation of traditional link state routing, modified for improved operation in ad hoc networks. The key feature of OLSR protocol is that it uses multipoint relays (MPRs) to reduce the overhead of network floods and size of link state updates. Each node sustains a route to every node in the network. This technique importantly cuts down the numerous retransmissions in a flooding or broadcast routine. The OLSR protocol executes the hop by hop routing i.e. each node uses it's most recent information to route a packet. States involved in the same are as neighbor sensing, multipoint relay station, MPR information declaration, routing table calculation.

LANMAR [12] aggregates the characteristics of Fisheye State Routing (FSR) [13] and Landmark routing. The fundamental novel characteristic is the role of landmarks for each set of nodes that move like a group (e.g., a team of co-workers at a convening or a tank battalion in the battleground) in order to subdue routing update operating expense. Like in FSR, nodes exchange link state with their neighbors only. Routes amongst Fisheye scope are precise, while routes to distant groups of nodes are "summed up" by the representing landmarks. A packet addressed to a distant destination initially targets at the Landmark; as it gets nearer to destination it finally switches to the accurate route furnished by Fisheye. On the other hand, On-demand routing protocols like AODV [5], DYMO [8] etc. are more dynamic. Instead of periodically updating the routing information, these protocols update routing information whenever a routing is required. This type of routing produces routes only when in demand by the source node and therefore, in general, the signaling overhead is reduced compared to proactive approaches of routing.

DYMO is meant for use by moving nodes in wireless, multi-hop networks. DYMO determines unicast amongst DYMO routers in the network in an on-demand manner, offering bettered convergence in dynamic topologies. The introductory procedures of the DYMO protocol are route finding (by route request and route reply) and route maintenance. It is an improvement to AODV and more comfortable to implement. In networks with a prominent number of routers, it is best suited for sparse traffic scenarios. In each DYMO router, minimal state routing is preserved and therefore it is relevant to memory constrained devices. In this protocol only routing information proportional to active sources and destinations is retained. The routing algorithm in DYMO may be worked at layers rather than the network layer, using layer-approved addresses. For operation at other layers only adjustment of the packet/message format is needed. To ensure inevitable control overhead, DYMO router's rate of packet/message propagation should be bounded. The protocol is suitable for scalability. However, it is yet to be explored for its functionality.

3 Application Scenarios

This scenario demonstrates data collection from ground sensors using mobile vehicles. Sensors are randomly deployed in an observation region. The sensors constantly monitor any phenomena of interest in the area. The sensory information observed by each sensor is stored locally at the sensor. The mobile vehicles are moving inside the area where sensors are deployed. The vehicles have short range communication to sensors and long distance communication to a remote site which is called fusion centre in this scenario. The sensors send their locally stored data packets to the vehicles which at any time are within their radio range. The vehicles then relay sensory data packets to fusion centre using long distance communication to that centre. Node types in this scenario are: a) Unattended Ground Sensors (UGS) which refers to ground sensors. b) Unmanned Ground Vehicles (UGV) which refers to mobile vehicles c) Fusion centre refers to remote site. UGS and UGV are both battery-powered devices. Short rage communication between UGSs and UGVs has been configured as ZigBee. PHY and MAC protocol is 802.15.4 and the four protocols mentioned as the paper follows are used Long distance communication between UGVs and fusion centre is configured as WiFi (802.11a) also different protocols have been used for this communication as defined by the two communicating interfaces for the UGVs and all the four routing protocols have been used in both the interfaces. The scenario consists of: 100 UGS nodes (nodes from 1 through 100) with linear battery model and micaZ radio energy model .5 UGV (nodes from 100 through 105) with random way point mobility initially inside the area where sensors are deployed (velocity range 0.1-0.4 damp). Linear Battery model and micaZ radio energy model are configured for UGSs and UGVs. Fusion centre is node 121.When the scenario is run, it shows that UGVs moving inside the area. The UGVs communicate with the UGVs which are inside their ZigBee communication range. The sensors which have CBR flows to fusion centre then are able to send their sensory data to the centre. The four different conditions for the scenario taken as mentioned above may be described as follows:

a. All nodes of the network are static. The UGS (unattended ground sensors) as well as the UGV (Unmanned ground station) are static while the fusion centre remains static in each and every condition in which the scenario has been implemented.
b. In the second condition of scenario implementation the UGS (unattended ground stations) are static while the UGV (unmanned ground station) are mobile.
c. The third condition of scenario says the implementation of the UGS (unattended ground stations) is mobile while the UGV (unmanned ground station) are static.
d. The last condition of scenario implementation refers to situation when the UGS (unattended ground stations) are mobile as well as the UGV (unmanned ground station) are also mobile.

4 Methodology

The overall goal of our experiments was to compare and analyze the packets dropped ratio of the two considered reactive and proactive protocols for various application scenarios considered for the experimental simulations. Also the analysis has been done for routing protocol during the variations in the simulation time for the experimental setup. The protocols were carefully implemented according to its specifications. During the process of implementation of the AODV routing protocol and analyzing the results for each simulation runs, we discovered some modifications in the average jitter of the network for each simulation interval the network varied its performance, while carrying on to succeed to deliver data packets to their destinations. To measure these variations, our basic methodology was to apply to a simulated network a variety of, simulation intervals and different application scenarios implementing various mobility conditions that affect the routing protocols performance, and it's testing with each data packet originated by some sender whether the routing protocol can at that time route to the destination of that packet. We were not attempting to measure the protocols' performance on a particular workload taken from real life, but rather to measure the protocols' performance under a range of conditions.

5 Simulation Parameters

NUMBER OF NODES

UGS	*100*
UGV	*05*
Ground station	*01*

MAC

UGS	*IEEE802.15.4*
UGV	*IEEE802.11*
Ground station	*IEEE802.11*

TRAFFIC

UGV	*CBR*
Data Payload	*1024 bytes/packet*
Path Loss Model	*Two Ray Model*
Mobility Model	*Random Waypoint*
Interface queue type	*Priority queue/drop tail*

OTHER NETWORK PARAMETERS

Antenna	*Omni directional*
Simulation time	*30 sec*
Transmission range	*35 meter*
Transmission Power(dbm)	*3.0dbm*
Temperature	*290.0*
Node speed (mobility)	*Min: 0m/sec Max: 10m/sec*
Area	*500x500 meters*
Energy Model	*MICAZ*
Battery Model	*Simple Linear, 1200 mAhr*

6 Results Analysis

The average delivery ratio decrements as channel error rate gains due to the increased packet loss error rate and this begins, reflecting the packet loss obtained both by increased congestion and due to packet loss at the MAC Layer. The packet loss rate at the MAC layer (between two routers, or between a router and a host) must be made very small in order to achieve better network routing protocol performance .It is the job of the MAC layer to achieve this condition of optimized data packet control.

6.1 AODV (Adhoc on Demand Distance Vector Routing)

AODV routing protocol with the increase in the simulation time represents a steep variation from a high rate of packet loss for the highest simulation time having the highest average of 2700 packets lost to a low of 100 packets lost during the lowest simulation interval for which the application was implemented Though for the lesser variation in the simulation time the net packet loss at the MAC layer does not varies much.

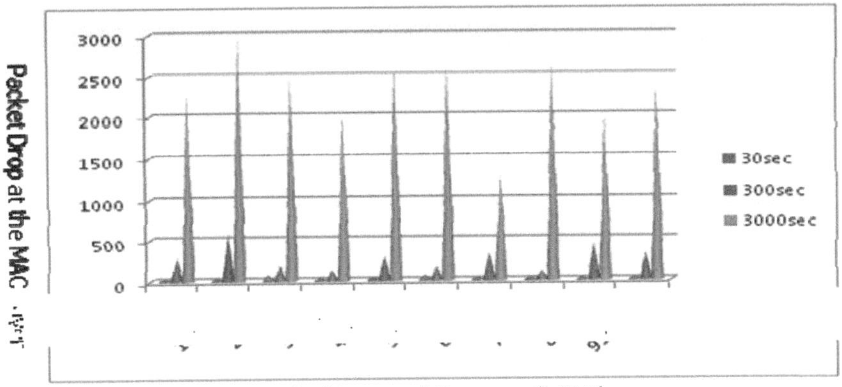

Fig. 1. Packet Drop at MAC layer for AODV

6.2 DYMO (Dynamic MANET on Demand Routing Protocol)

DYMO being an on demand reactive routing protocol like AODV still performs best for higher simulation time while the net packet loss presenting a minimum value of less than 100 packets loosed for the highest simulation time though with decrease in the simulation time the packet drop rate has increased thus making DYMO a suitable choice for longer period of simulation or network utilization in case of real life applications.

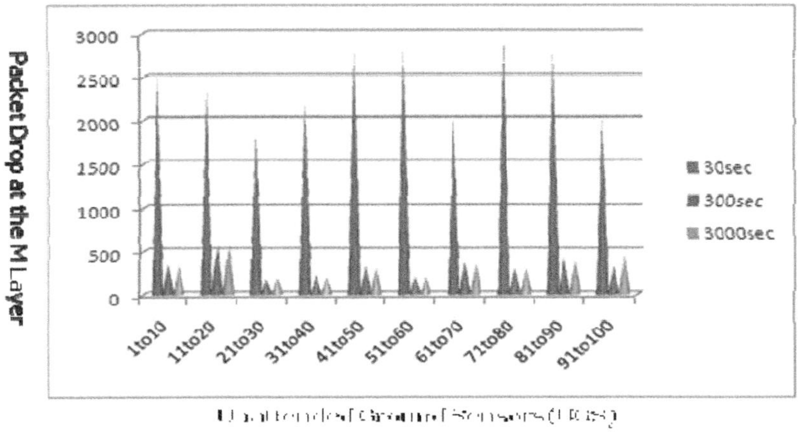

Fig. 2. Packet Drop at MAC layer for DYMO

6.3 OLSR (Optimized Link State Routing Protocol)

OLSR uses the proactive methodology of routing techniques depending on the link states of the network. The results being analyzed show that this routing protocol produces best MAC layer performance in the case of smallest simulation time interval with the lowest number of packets dropped in that case being lesser than 50 packets dropped and the maximum packet drop was visible for the largest simulation time the highest value of packet dropped being 4500.

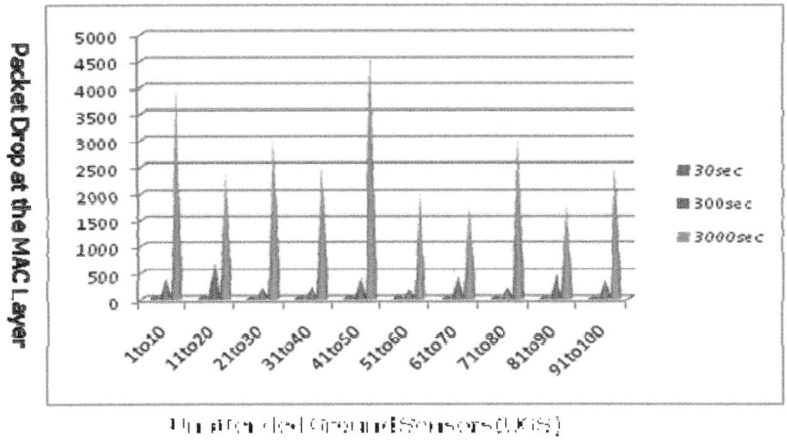

Fig. 3. Packet Drop at MAC layer for OLSR

6.4 LANMAR (Land Mark Routing Protocol)

LANMAR that is also a proactive routing protocol depicts the similar results as the earlier proactive routing protocol and of performs best in the case of smallest simulation time that is taken to be 3000 seconds. The highest packet drop witnessed at the MAC layer in this case of routing is about 3500 packets and the lowest being above 50 packets.

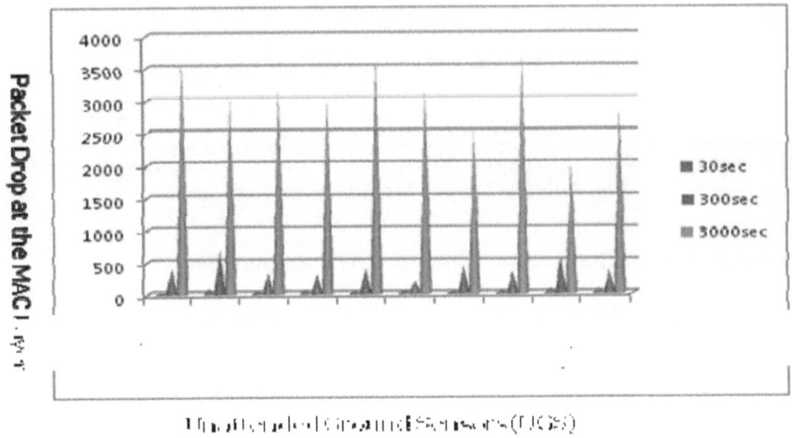

Fig. 4. Packet Drop at MAC layer for LANMAR

Recent swerves in sensor network simulation can be categorized between less flexible but precise simulation based advance and more generic but less elaborated network simulator models. Simulator which furnishes a rich suite of following models: sensing stack to model wave and diffusion anchored sensor channels, a precise battery model, processor power use model, energy usage model and sensor network based traffic pattern. We also introduce our study on the effects of elaborated modeling on the functioning of higher layer protocols. We describe the affect of using precise models for battery, processor power usage and tracking models on the network layer stats as network lifetime and accessibility, throughput and routing operating cost. Our results show that comparative MAC layer packet drops at various time durations of simulation. Next section discusses the results for packets dropped at the MAC Layer when the two reactive and proactive protocols were implemented for various mobility condition based scenarios.

Scenario 1: Both the UGS as well as the UGV are static

For the first scenario having the UGSs as well as the UGVs static the OLSR performs the best with the lowest number of packets dropped at the MAC layer and having the least high packet dropped value of 2900, and LANMAR being the least performing routing protocol with the highest packet drop rate of more than 5000.

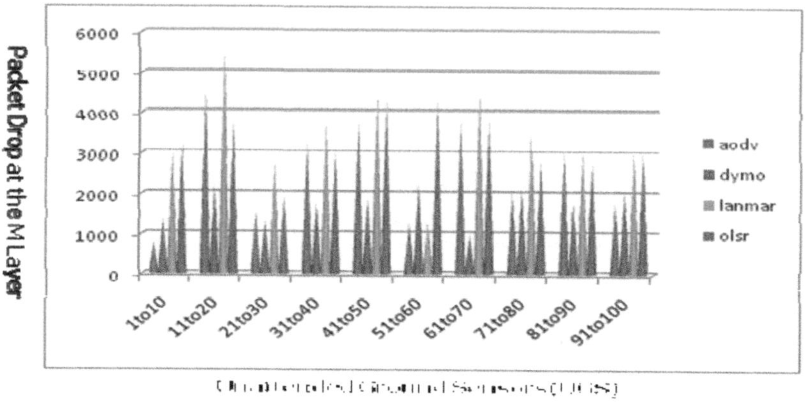

Fig. 5. Packet Drop at MAC layer for First Scenario

Scenario 2: The UGS are static while the UGV are mobile

In the case of second scenario having the UGSs as Static and UGVs mobile the total number of packets dropped is highest for the OLSR routing protocol having the packet drop rate more than 2900 and the best MAC Layer performance is depicted by the AODV having the lowest packet drop rate as below as 500 packets.

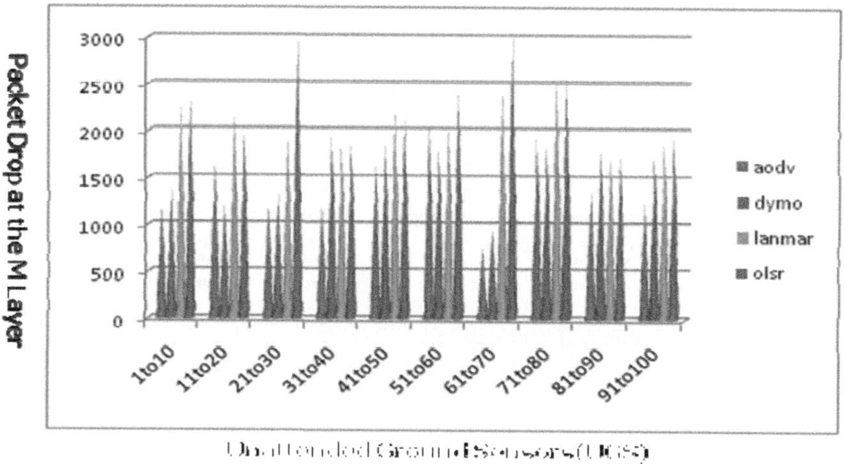

Fig. 6. Packet Drop at MAC layer for Second Scenario

Scenario 3: The UGS are mobile while the UGV are static

For the third scenario having the UGSs as mobile and UGVs static the lowest packet drop rate has been depicted by the AODV protocol having average packet as low as 800 packets. While the highest packet drop rate has been witnessed in the case of OLSR having the highest packet drop rate of more than 2900 packets being dropped.

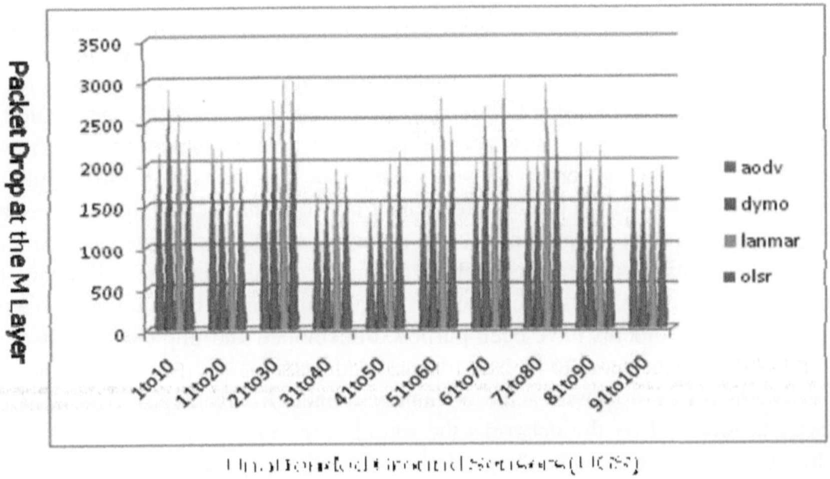

Fig. 7. Packet Drop at MAC layer for Third Scenario

Scenario 4: Both the UGS as well as the UGV mobile

In the case of fourth scenario having both the UGSs as well as UGVs are mobile the AODV depicts the best performance with the lowest number of packets being dropped having the lowest packet drop value of 700 packets. While the worst performance is being depicted by the DYMO routing protocol in this scenario having the highest packet dropped value of 1700.

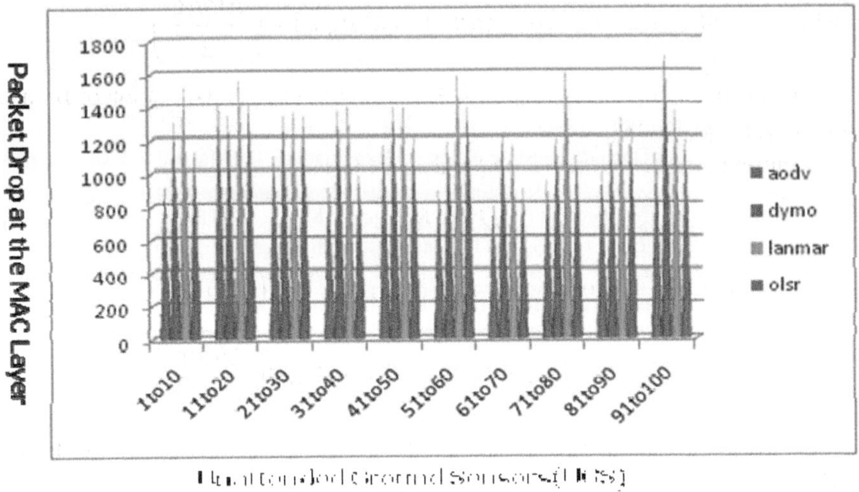

Fig. 8. Packet Drop at MAC layer for Fourth Scenario

7 Conclusion and Future Work

The research area of ad hoc and sensor network has very much attracted the academic domain as well as the industry both due to its wide-ranging possible application for anytime, anywhere, and any how communication scenarios. This wide spectrum of applications possible for sensor networks has made the network vividly applicable and acceptable. The routing protocol for sensor networks has been a dynamic research area altogether through the present decade. Although wide efforts have been exercised so far on the routing problem in wireless communications, there are still some challenges via multicasting that still confront effective solutions to the routing problem. A number of such protocols have been purposed developed and implemented also. But no protocol has been found to be best for the wide domain of sensor network applications. Each protocol possess its advantages and disadvantages. Counting the constraints followed by the networks the routing algorithms have been updated and modified time to time to make the routing more and more efficient and accurate. The present work proposes to find out the effect of different patterns of node mobility within the network. The results though don't present a steep comparative orientation of the results towards a specific routing protocol but the comparative study leads towards some interesting results.

Further research is needed to find most suitable protocol for each and every scenario condition so that an optimized routing protocol could be suggested for various real life applications have concurrency to the mentioned scenarios of the simulated wireless network environment.

References

1. Toh, C.K., Royer, E.M.: A review of current routing protocols for ad hoc mobile wireless network, vol. 15, pp. 46–55 (April 1999)
2. Akyildiz, I.F., Su, W., Sankarasubramaniam, Y., Cayirci, E.: A survey on sensor networks, vol. 40, pp. 102–1148 (November 2002)
3. Santivanez, C., McDonald, B., Stavrakakis, I., Ramanathan, R.: Making link state routing scale for ad hoc network, doi:10.1145/501417.501420
4. Basagni, S., Conti, M., Giordano, S., Stojmenovic, I.: Mobile Ad Hoc Networking (2004)
5. Perkins, C., Royer, E.B., Das, S.: Ad hoc on-demand distance vector (AODV) routing, RFC 3561 (2003)
6. Chakeres, I., Perkins, C.: Dynamic MANET On-demand (DYMO) Routing, 12 (2008)
7. Qualnet, http://www.scalablenetworks.com
8. Heinzeelman, W.B., Chandra Kasan, A., Bala Krishnan, H.: Energy-Efficient communication protocol for wireless micro-sensor networks, pp. 3005–3014 (2000)
9. Siva Rama Murthy, C., Manoj, B.S.: Ad hoc Wireless Networks: Architecture and protocols, 2nd edn. Prentice Hall, Englewood Cliffs
10. Mohanty, S., Patra, S.K.: Performance Analysis of Quality of Service Parameters for IEEE 802.15.4 Star Topology using MANET routing, ACM 978-1-60558-812-4 (2010)
11. Varshney, M., Bagrodia, R.: Detailed models of sensor networks simulations and their impact on network performance (2004)

12. Tsuchiya, P.F.: The Landmark Hierarchy: a new hierarchy for routing in very large networks, vol. 18, pp. 35–42 (1988)
13. Ren, H., Meng, M.Q.-H., Chen, X.: Investigating network optimization approaches in wireless sensor networks, pp. 2015–2021(2006)
14. Das, S.R., Castaneda, R., Yan, J., Sengupta, R.: Comparative performance evaluation of routing protocols for mobile ad hoc networks, pp. 153–161(1998)

Manipulating Objects through Hand Gesture Recognition in Virtual Environment

Siddharth S. Rautaray and Anupam Agrawal

Indian Institute of Information Technology Allahabad, India
sr.rgpv@gmail.com, rs54@iiita.ac.in

Abstract. Virtual environments have always been considered as a means for more visceral and efficient human computer interaction by a diversified range of applications. The spectrum of applications includes analysis of complex scientific data, medical training, military simulation, phobia therapy and virtual prototyping. Evolution of ubiquitous computing, current user interaction approaches with keyboard, mouse and pen are not sufficient for the still widening spectrum of Human computer interaction. Gloves and sensor based trackers are unwieldy, constraining and uncomfortable to use. Due to the limitation of these devices the useable command set based diligences is also limited. Direct use of hands as an input device is an innovative method for providing natural Human Computer Interaction which has its inheritance from text-based interfaces through 2D graphical-based interfaces, multimedia-supported interfaces, to full-fledged multi-participant Virtual Environment (VE) systems. Conceiving a future era of human-computer interaction with the implementations of 3D application where the user may be able to move and rotate objects simply by moving and rotating his hand - all without help of any input device.

This paper centralizes on the efforts of implementing an application that employs computer vision algorithms and gesture recognition techniques which in turn results in developing a low cost interface device for interacting with objects in virtual environment using hand gestures. The prototype architecture of the application comprises of a central computational module that applies the camshift technique for tracking of hands and its gestures. Haar like technique has been utilized as a classifier that is creditworthy for locating hand position and classifying gesture. The patterning of gestures has been done for recognition by mapping the number of defects that is formed in the hand with the assigned gestures. The virtual objects are produced using Open GL library. This hand gesture recognition technique aims to substitute the use of mouse for interaction with the virtual objects. This will be useful to promote controlling applications like virtual games, browsing images etc in virtual environment using hand gestures.

Keywords: Hand gesture, virtual objects, virtual environment, tracking, recognition.

1 Introduction

The impendent of virtual environments brings in a whole new set of problems for user interfaces. The unveiling of 3D objects and worlds in which the user is engrossed allows

D. Nagamalai, E. Renault, and M. Dhanushkodi (Eds.): PDCTA 2011, CCIS 203, pp. 270–281, 2011.

such people as scientists, engineers, doctors and architects to envision composite structures and systems with eminent degrees of quality and naturalism. Shutter glasses furnish a stereo or 3D view of the scene, which is no longer confined to a desktop monitor, but may be a large table, projection screen or room. The limiting component in these systems currently is the fundamental interaction. Virtual environments seek to produce a world where the interaction experiences are real. Current mechanical, acoustic and magnetic input devices track the user and provide control of movement, selection and manipulation of objects in virtual scenes. Several tools are purported and used so far to make such interaction more and more prompt and effortless. Touch screens are the most widely used example: though the ramification of the underlying system is hidden from the user, and makes it possible for a user to point to the choices as he could do in real life. The cost associated to it is the major limitations of the aforesaid technology other limitations may be size, requirement of a physical location, and other intrinsic limitation to 2D. Other more innovative devices proposed for virtual reality include gloves or wearable tools such as mechanical sensors, actuators and micro cameras [1]. They are capable to handle 3D worlds, making it natural and realistic, and also provide in some implementations tactile sensations. Regrettably, their cost is usually very high, and thus the user acceptance confined, hence making them more desirable for professional applications such as a flight simulator or remote surgery equipment. However these interactions are often limited and non rational, while the devices are awkward, unmanageable and prone to distortion from the physical environment. We are interested in formulating an alternative, natural interface that more intimately models the way we interact with the real world. The user should be able to reach out, grab, point and move 3D objects just as we do with real objects.

These challenges open a new direction for human-computer interaction which combined with computer vision techniques and it is possible to build an advanced input devices. The computer vision devices can be implemented and upgrade to the new input devices in the future. It gives the input command to the computer rather than just a function of taking photo or record video. We can do more implementation to transform the computer vision devices to become an input command device to reach the function as keyboard or mouse. One of the ways to give signal to computer vision devices is by using hand gesture. More specifically hand gesture is used as the signal or input modality to the computer. Certain signal can be recognized by computer as an input of what computer should do. These will benefits the entire user without using a direct device and can do what they want as long as the computer vision device can sense it. These make computer user easier than using the keyboard or mouse. The future computer or laptop may eliminate the use of keyboard and mouse by substituting with a vision-based interpretation devices.

Interaction between humans comes from different sensory modes like gesture, speech, facial and body expressions [2]. The main advantage of using hand gestures is to interact with computer as a non-contact human computer input modality. The state of art of human computer interaction presents the facts that for controlling the computer processes gestures of various types of hand movements have been used .The present research effort defines an environment where a number of challenges have been considered for obtaining the hand gesture recognition techniques in the virtual environment. Being an interesting part of the Human computer interaction hand gesture recognition needs to be robust for real life applications, but complex structure of human hand presents a series of challenges for being tracked and interpreted. Other than the gesture complexities like variability and flexibility of structure of hand other challenges include the shape of gestures, real time application issues, presence of background noise and variations in illumination conditions. The specifications also involve accuracy of detection and recognition for real life applications [3].

The present research effort has a goal of developing an application using vision based hand gestures for manipulation of objects in virtual environment. Our application presents a more effective and user friendly methods of human computer interaction intelligently with the usage of hand gestures. Functions of mouse like controlling of movement of virtual object have been replaced by hand gestures. The complexity involved is with the detection and recognition phases of the simulated virtual application. The challenges encountered are noisy environment which creates a big impingement on the detection and recognition performance of human hand gestures. The application has been designed to be cost effective and uses low cost input tools like webcam for capturing hand as input. Manipulation of virtual objects has been done through modeling of some predefined command based hand gestures. The rest of the paper has been organized under following sections: section 2 deals with the state of art. Section 3 introduces the application architecture design. Section 4 presents the experimental setup and the functioning of the application. Application results and analysis of the generated results have been highlighted in section 5. The effort ends in Conclusion that is in the section 6.The scope of present work and future work is discussed in section 7. References used by the application are summarized in section 8.

2 State of Art

In earlier days hand gesture detection was done using mechanical devices to obtain information of the hand gesture [4]. One of the most widely used and accepted examples for hand gestures recognition is data glove. Evolution of computer hardware improved a lot of in present scenario this also effects the performance of computing. Enhancements of gesture recognition has replaced the role of data gloves to non wearable devices due to its naturalness without using any device this is quite user friendly in human computer interaction. One of the major drawbacks of data glove is that it is cumbersome with the limitation of hand movement. Also vision is one of the major six physical senses that computer must be instantiated perceptibly when communicated to humans [1].So vision based approaches are preferred more than wearable devices in hand gesture recognition. Generally there are three stages in most of the gesture recognition systems. The three stages may be enumerated as image pre – processing tracking and recognition stage [16] as shown in Figure 1.

In tracking, there are several researchers who have done the similar research like Viola-Jones based cascade classifier, commonly used for face tracking in rapidly image processing [5]. Cascade classifiers are currently considered more robust pattern detection against the noises and lighting conditions as well [6].

For tracking Viola-Jones and several other researchers have developed algorithms used for face tracking in rapid image processing like HAAR cascade classifier. This is presently one of the robust detection techniques under different constraints like noise [6].Gesture as input of human computer interaction based applications is an emerging field in which many researchers have worked and proposed different practical techniques. Jain [7] implemented a vision based hand gesture pose estimation based

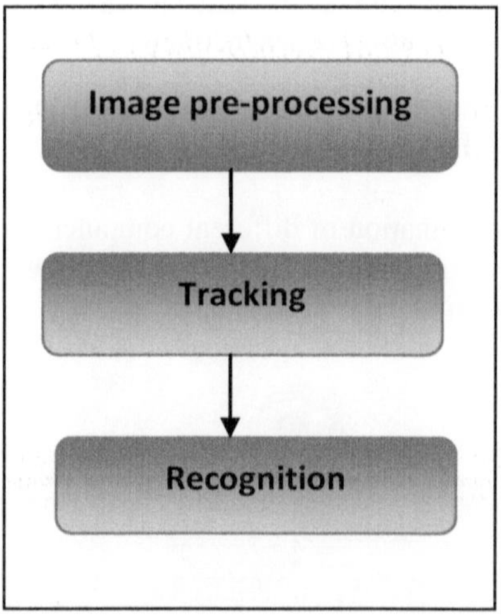

Fig. 1. Three common stages of gesture recognition systems

application for mobile devices. Pavlovic et al. [8] accomplished in their work that the gestures of users must be explained logically for developing a good human computer interaction based system. Though the present technologies of gesture recognition are not feasible in providing the logical explanations to the human gestures. Some of the major challenges evolved in due course of time are the complexness and robustness of human gestures. Another hand gesture recognition method based on input-output Hidden Markov Models of tracking skin color blobs was proposed by Marcel et al. [9]. Controlling VLC media player using hand gesture recognition is done in real time environment using vision based techniques [10]. The sign language tutoring tool studied by Aran et al. [11] which their research designed to teaching the fundamental of the sign language in interactive way.

Liu and Lovell [12] implemented a technique for real time tracking of hand capturing gestures with the use of a web camera, personal computer and image processing algorithms making it more users friendly. Chen et al. [13] implemented hidden Markov model technique for training the hand gesture for recognizing the hand postures. Nevertheless, this model is more complicated in training the hand gesture equated with Cascade classifiers. Lee et al. [14] developed a Virtual Office Environment System (VOES), in which avatar is used navigate and interact with other participants.

Contemporary works in hand gesture recognition by many researchers show that hand gesture system can also be practically implemented into several type of application systems and various environment. Ahn et al. developed an interactive way of slide show presentation system in the virtual environment [15]. Research in hands, gestures and movement helps in developing models of the human body. This makes it possible to solve the challenges from mathematical viewpoint. How so ever, these techniques proposed are excessively complex and sophisticated for typical application scenarios. Generally, pattern recognition methodologies are capable of solving the problem with humbler hardware and computation necessities. In the present research effort, we will consider these aspects by taking it as a reference to a smart interaction environment of virtual object manipulation and control. Here the user can execute different actions that translate into a command in an intelligent system and further execute the user requirements into practical actions.

3 Application Architecture Design

The application uses a combination of different computer vision techniques for hand gesture recognition. It recognizes static hand gestures. Figure 2 shows the application architecture design for manipulating virtual objects using hand gestures.

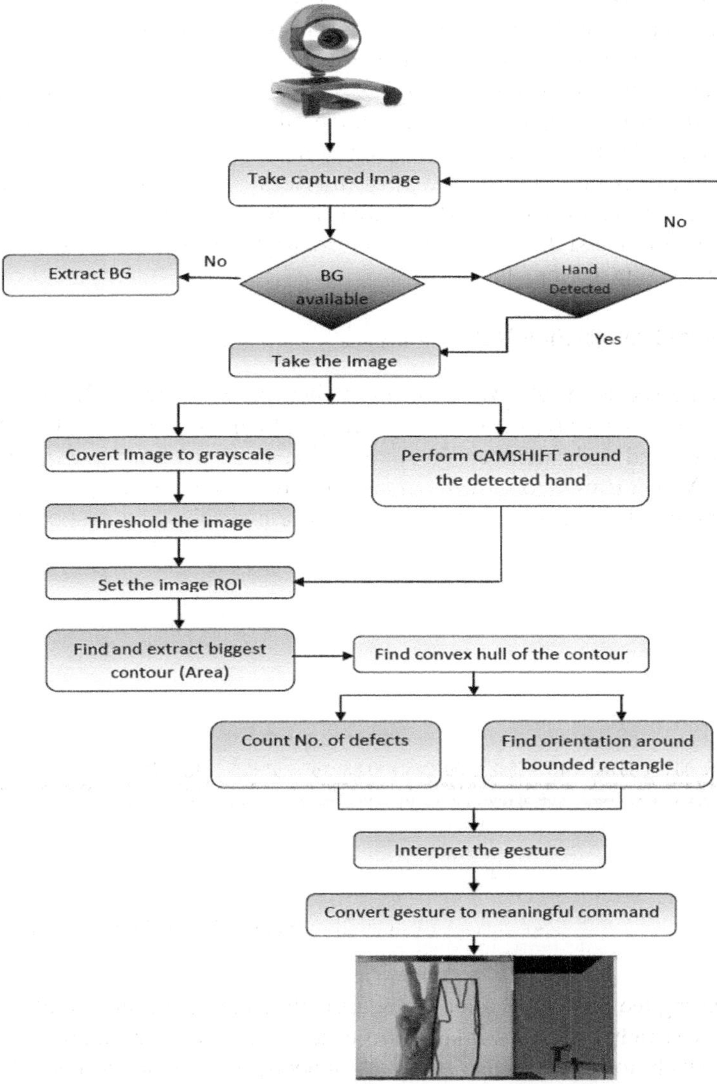

Fig. 2. Application architecture design

Images are captured from camera and passed through following phases/techniques. Starting with the acquisition phase that is the first phase. Since a standard input peripheral (keyboard, pointing device) will be unacceptable in this application context. So we have focused on possible alternatives by considering smart interfaces that have been inspired by natural behavior of the users in real-world actions. The choice of the capturing device is being done in accordance with the idea of spreading the installation in homes, labs, play stations etc, hence maintaining the resulting costs low. For this reason, special care has been taken to ensure good performance even in the presence of low-cost cameras. The camera is supposed to be fixed, and illumination slowly varying. Real-time constraints are being imposed for a careful design of the processing system. To this purpose, the unnecessary information is first removed.

In particular, a background suppression procedure has been performed in the HSV color space, in which the scene can be modeled discarding illumination variations. Thus focusing the attention on areas corresponding to human skin color. The next section deals with the computer vision techniques/algorithms used for hand tracking and recognition.

4 Experiments

The computer vision techniques used in the application for manipulation of objects in virtual environment have been implemented in C++ with the use of OpenCV Library. The virtual objects (front end) have been designed using OpenGL library. The hardware requirements of the application to be implemented include computer with 1.99 GHz processor. The web cam used in the experimental setup captures image sequences at the resolution of 320x240. Practical experiments show that our application is implemented well in environments with little noises (i.e., existence of objects whose color is similar to human skin) and with the balanced lightning condition.

First, the user places his hand in front of the webcam. The webcam then detects the user's hand by creating a rectangle around it as shown in figure 3.

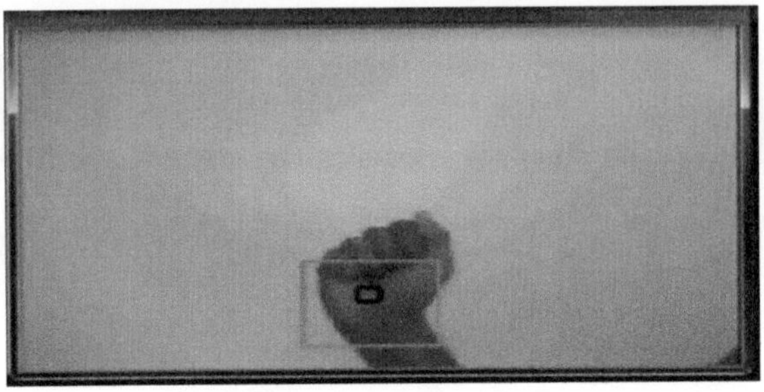

Fig. 3. Hand Detected

Once the hand has been detected the application further tracks different gestures of the user performed by his hand and generates contour around it.

The application uses seven hand gestures defined within the application for manipulation with objects in virtual environment. Figure 4 shows the different gestures along with their assigned commands (functions) to manipulate the objects in virtual environment.

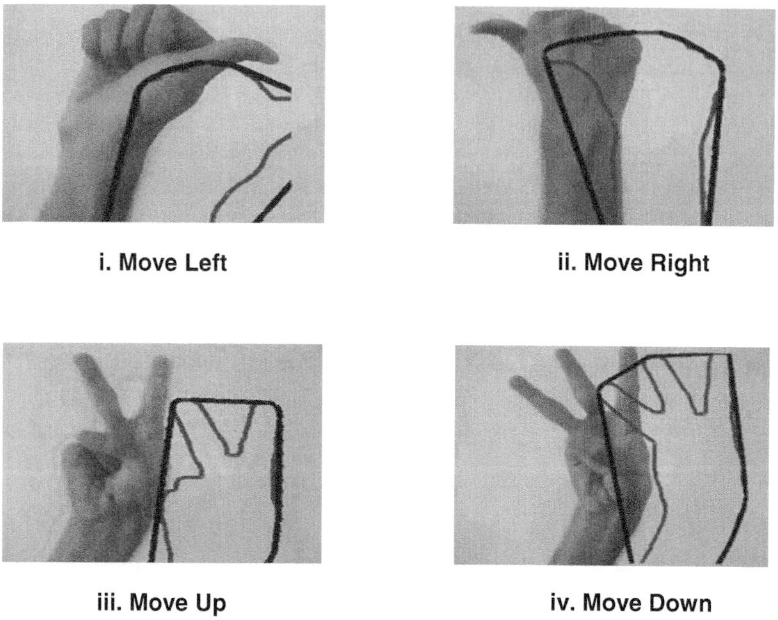

Fig. 4. Gestures for manipulating objects in virtual environment

5 Results

Following figures shows the results obtained from different gestures used for manipulating objects in virtual environment.

- Depicting the objects in virtual environments where different objects are manipulated by hand gestures. The red stick having a red ball is moving left direction as shown in the following figure 5.

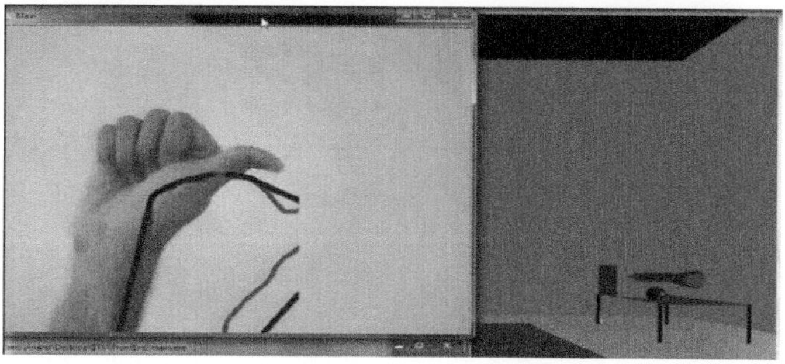

Fig. 5. Gesture for moving left

- Depicting the objects in virtual environments where different objects are manipulated by hand gestures. The red stick having a red ball is moving right direction (away from blue ball) as represented in figure 6.

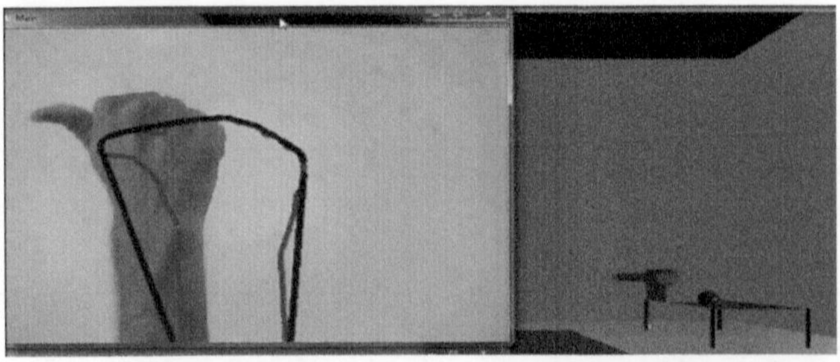

Fig. 6. Gesture for moving right

- Depicting the gesture of moving up for manipulating the object in virtual environment in up direction as shown in figure 7.

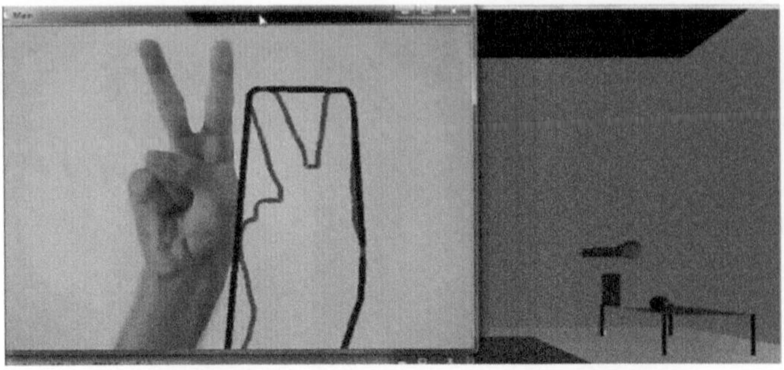

Fig. 7. Gesture for moving up

- Depicting the gesture of moving down for manipulating the object in virtual environment in down direction shown in figure 8.

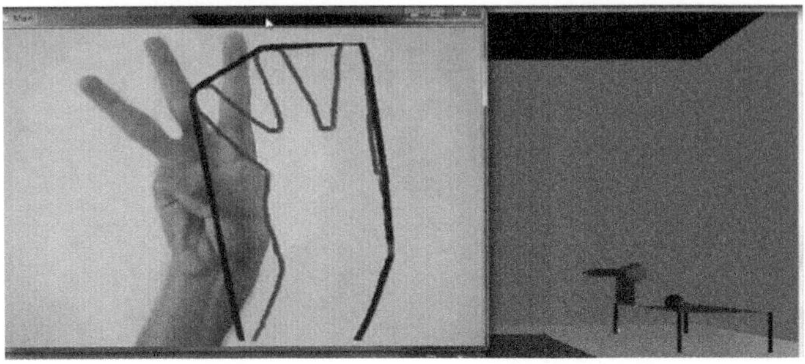

Fig. 8. Gesture for moving down

6 Testing and Analysis

In order to find out the performance and viability of the application in the experimental setup we have manipulated objects in virtual environment.

Table 1. Hand gesture recognition results

S.No.	Gesture	No. of diff. users played	No. of hits	No. of misses	Recognition rate (%)
1	Move Left	20	12	8	60
2	Move Right	20	14	6	70
3	Move Up	20	11	9	55
4	Move Down	20	15	5	75

We have tested the performance of the application by interacting with the virtual game through 20 different users. Table 1 show the number of hits and misses occur during interaction with virtual game by different users through different gestures.

The performance have been further tested for the application in different environmental condition based variations in parameters like lighting changes, number of different users etc.

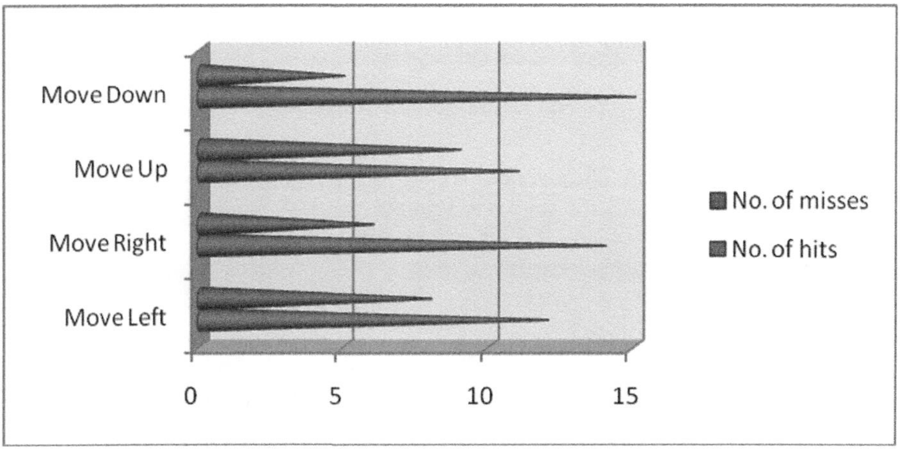

Fig. 9. Comparison of Number of hits versus misses of gestures recognition rate

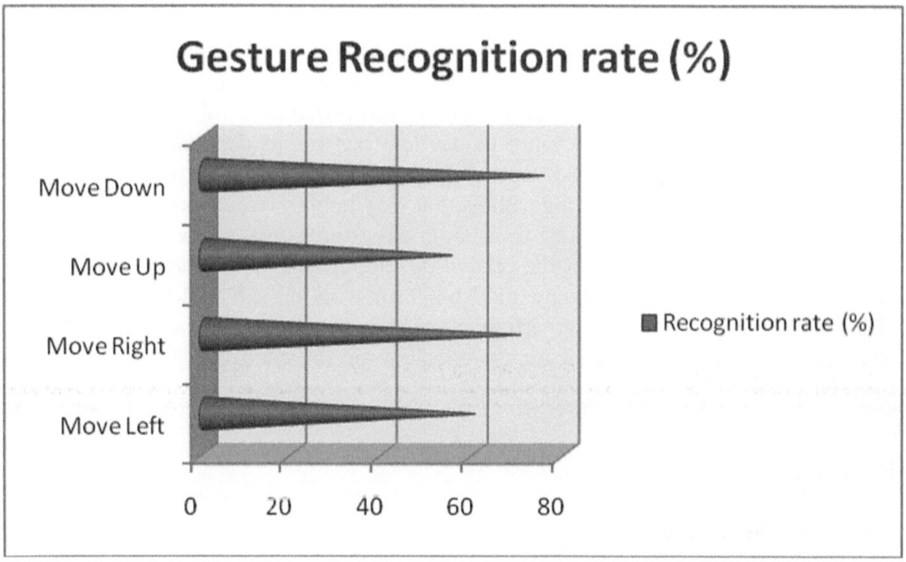

Fig. 10. Comparison of different gestures recognition rate

Also the application has been implemented for different gestures that could be associated with different possible commands for the manipulating of objects the virtual environment. The graph in figure 9 presents a comparative analysis of number of hits versus number of misses for the hand gesture recognition in the virtual environment. While the graph in figure10 presents the rate of recognition of gestures in percentage. These results though do not present a steep orientation towards some standard gesture recognition but do depict a basic vocabulary development statistics that could be further enhanced for real life applications of gesture recognition.

7 Conclusion

In present environment a number of facilities and various modes for providing input to any application are available. It is though unfortunate that with the ever increasing smart environments and corresponding input technologies still not many applications are available which are controlled using current and smart facility of providing input which is by hand gesture. The most important advantage of the usage of hand gesture based input modes is that using this method the user can interact with the application from a distance without using the keyboard or mouse. The application of manipulating objects through hand gestures in virtual environment is being proposed and implemented in the present paper provides a suitable efficient and user friendly human computer interface. With the help of this application the user can interact with the virtual objects using hand gesture instead of any other physical input devices. As the application provides the flexibility to the users and specifically physically challenged users to define the gesture according to their feasibility and ease of use.

8 Future Work

The present application though seems to be feasible and more user friendly in comparison to the traditional input modes but is somewhat less robust in recognition phase. An attempt to make the input modes less constraints dependent for the users hand gestures has been preferred. But robustness of the application may be increased by applying some more robust algorithms that may help to reduce noise and blur motion in order to have more accurate translation of gestures into commands.

Another important aspect for the related development could be design of an independent gesture vocabulary framework. This framework though could be independent of the application domain. Also the framework may be useful for controlling different types of games and other applications dependent on the controlled through user defined gestures.

References

1. Conic, N., Cerseato, P., De Natale, F.G.B.: Natural Human- Machine Interface using an Interactive Virtual Blackboard. In: Proceeding of ICIP 2007, pp. 181–184 (2007)
2. Ismail, N.A., O'Brien, A.: Enabling Multimodal Interaction in Web-Based Personal Digital Photo Browsing. In: Proceedings of the International Conference on Computer and Communication Engineering 2008, Kuala Lumpur, Malaysia, May 13-15, pp. 907–910 (2008)
3. Pang, Y.Y., Ismail, N.A., Gilbert, P.L.S.: A Real Time Vision-Based Hand Gesture Interaction. In: Fourth Asia International Conference on Mathematical Analytical Modelling and Computer Simulation, pp. 237–242 (2010)
4. Kortum, P.: HCI Beyond the GUI: Design for Haptic, Speech, Olfactory, and Other Nontraditional Interfaces, pp. 75–106. Morgan Kaufmann Publishers, San Francisco (2008)
5. Viola, Jones: Rapid object detection using boosted cascade of simple features. In: Proceedings of Computer Vision and Pattern Recognition, pp. I-511–I-518 (2001)
6. Chen, Q., Coredea, M.D., Petriu, E.M., Varkony, A.R., Koczy, I., Whalen, T.E.: Human Computer Interaction for Smart Applications Using Hand Gesture and Facial Expressions. International Journal of Advanced Media and Communication 3c(1/2), 95–109 (2009)
7. Jain, G.: Vision-Based Hand Gesture Pose Estimation for Mobile Devices. University of Toronto (2009)
8. Pavlovic, V., Sharma, R., Huang, T.S.: Visual interpretation of hand gestures for human-computer interaction: A review. IEEE Trans. on Pattern Analysis and Machine Intelligence (PAMI) 7(19), 677–695 (1997)
9. Marcel, S., Bernier, O., Viallet, J.E., Collobert, D.: Hand Gesture Recognition using Input-Output Hidden Markov Models. In: Proc. of the FG 2000 Conference on Automatic Face and Gesture Recognition (2000)
10. Rautaray, S.S., Agrawal, A.: A Novel Human Computer Interface Based On Hand Gesture Recognition Using Computer Vision Techniques. In: Proceedings of ACM IITM 2010, pp. 292–296 (2010)
11. Aran, O., Ari, I., Benoit, F., Campr, A., Carrillo, A.H., Fanard, Akarun, L., Caplier, A., Rombaut, M., Sankuru, B.: Sign Language Tutoring Tool. In: The Summer Workshop on Multimodal Interfaces, eNTERFACE 2006, Croatia (2006)

12. Liu, N., Lovell, B.: Mmx-accelerated realtime hand tracking system. In: Proceedings of IVCNZ (2001)
13. Chen, F., Fu, C., Huang, C.: Hand gesture recognition using a real-time tracking method and hidden Markov models. In: Image and Vision Computing, pp. 745–758 (2003)
14. Lee, C.S., Ghyme, S.W., Park, C.J., Wohn, K.: The Control of avatar motion using hand gesture. In: Proceeding of Virtual Reality Software and Technology (VRST), pp. 59–65 (1998)
15. Ahn, S.C., Lee, T.S., Kim, I.J., Kwon, Y.M., Kim, H.G.: Computer Vision-Based Interactive Presentation System. In: Proceedings of Asian Conference for Computer Vision (2004)
16. Moeslund, T.B., Norgaard, L.: A brief overview of hand gestures used in wearable human computer interfaces, Technical report, Aalborg University, Denmark (2002)

Greedy Heuristic Based Energy Efficient Routing in Wireless Sensor Network

Sourabh Jain[1], Praveen Kaushik[1], and Jyoti Singhai[2]

[1] Department of Computer Sciene and Engineering,
Maulana Azad National Institute of Technology, Bhopal
Sourabh52@gmail.com, kaushikp@manit.ac.in
[2] Department of Electronic and Communication,
Maulana Azad National Institute of Technology, Bhopal
j.singhai@gmail.com

Abstract. Most routing algorithm in wireless sensor networks uses the energy efficient path that consumes less energy. A single best path puts extra load to a specific node causing lower lifetime. If all the traffic is routed through minimum energy path, nodes of that path will depleted their battery power quickly. So instead of using single minimum cost path after some amount of transmission redirect the flow through alternate path. This paper proposes an energy efficient maximum lifetime routing algorithm. It is based on a greedy heuristic technique to maximize lifetime of the system. For achieving maximum system lifetime proposed algorithm uses the energy cost of links for constructing energy efficient path. Simulation results show that EEMLR algorithm balanced the energy for entire network as well as increases the lifetime of the network and gives the better result than AODV routing algorithm.

Keywords: battery power, energy cost, routing algorithm, wireless sensor netweork.

1 Introduction

Wireless sensor networks (WSN's) have attracted a great deal of research attention due to their wide-range of potential applications. Applications of WSN include battlefield surveillance, biological detection, medical monitoring, home security and inventory tracking. This type of network consists of a group of nodes and each node has limited battery power. There may be many possible routes available between two nodes over which data can flow. Assume that each node generated some information and this information needs to be delivered to a destination node. Any node in the network can easily transmit their data packet to a distance node, if it has enough battery power. If any node is far from its neighbor node then large amount of transmission energy is required to transmit the data to distance node. After every transmission, remaining energy of this node decreases and some amounts of data transmission this node will be eliminated from the network because of empty battery power and

D. Nagamalai, E. Renault, and M. Dhanushkodi (Eds.): PDCTA 2011, CCIS 203, pp. 282–292, 2011.

in similar situation there will be a condition that no node is available for data transmission and overall lifetime of network will decreases. Whereas network lifetime is define as the time until the first node in the network dies. For maximizing the network lifetime, data should be routed such that energy expenditure is fair among the nodes in proportion to their energy reserved, instead of routing the data to a path that minimize consumed power.

In this paper, we propose greedy heuristic based routing algorithm to maximize network lifetime in terms of first node death. Proposed approach generates an energy efficient routing path that spans all the sensor nodes. Nodes transmit some amount of data in that path and then energy efficient path is recalculated.

The organization of the rest of the paper is as follows. Section 2 discusses about related work. Section 3 describes the some assumptions. In section 4, we define energy efficient maximum lifetime routing algorithm. Next, in section 5, we describe performance evaluation. Finally in section 6, some concluding remarks are made.

2 Related Work

Most of the earlier works on energy efficient routing in wireless sensor network uses the minimum total energy (MTE) routing for data transmission approach in this work to minimize the energy consumption to reach the destination was by sending the traffic to same path but if all the traffic follows the same path then all the nodes of that path will depleted their energy quickly [1]. Instead of trying to minimize the consumed energy the main objective is to maximize the lifetime of the system [2]. As in [2] the maximum lifetime problem is a linear programming problem and solvable in polynomial time. In this works Chang and Tassiulas proposed energy efficient routing algorithms such as flow redirection and maximum residual energy path routing. Flow redirection is the redirection based algorithm where some amount of flow is redirected from smallest longest length path to largest longest length path. Where largest longest length path is the path in which has largest capacity in terms of battery power and have less energy consumption per bit transmission. MREP algorithm augments the flow on the path whose minimum residual energy after the flow augmentation will be longest. In this work considers the single destination version of the problem.

As in [3] lifetime maximization problem is extended to multicommodity case, where each commodity has their own set of destination. Chang and Tassiulas [3] proposed flow augmentation and flow redirection algorithms for the set of origin and destination nodes and formulated the routing problem with the objective of maximizing the system lifetime. [2],[3] proposed maximizing the lifetime of a network when message rate is known but Q. Li, J. Aslam and D. Ras proposed max-min zPmin and zone based routing algorithms. These are the online, hierarchical and scalable algorithms that do not rely on knowing the message rate and optimize the lifetime of network. max-min zPmin algorithm combines the benefit of selecting the path with the minimum energy consumption and the path that maximize the minimal residual power of the node in the network. Scalability of this algorithm is provided in zone based routing. In zone based routing it's systematize the network structurally in geographical zones, and hierarchically to control routing across the zones [4].

Routing algorithms [2]-[4] consider energy consumption on sender side only, but in [5] the maximum lifetime routing problem is extended to include the energy consumption at the receive. Author used flow redirection algorithm as in [5] and the objective of this algorithm is to find the best link cost function which will lead to the maximization of the system lifetime and also consider the energy expenditure for unit data transmission at receiver end also.

The relation of maximizing the minimum lifetime of the nodes to minimizing the energy cost per packet was defined as in [2]-[5] but this relation take one step further to provide a delay guarantee in the time the packets reach their destination, while maximizing network lifetime [6]. Routing algorithms used as in [6] aims to give delay guarantee on the arrival of packets at the Access Point (AP) while generating energy efficient path.

C. Pandana and R. Liu proposed keep connect routing algorithm for network capacity maximization in energy constrained ad hoc network. Keep connect algorithm finds the weight of node based on how many components are connected with this node. Weight of the node can be thought as the importance of the node. Most important node is the node that results in large number of disconnected component as it dies. The proposed KC algorithm along with flow augmentation or with Minimum Total Energy algorithm provide the best result such as these combine algorithm provide maximum connectivity of the network as well as maximize the lifetime of network [7].

K. Kar, M Codialam, T. V. Lakshman and L. Tassiulas provided routing algorithm for network capacity maximization in energy constrained ad hoc network [8]. G. Anastasi, M. Conti, M. D. Francesco and A. passarella discussed various energy conservation schemes in wireless sensor network. To reduce power consumption in wireless sensor network, they identified three main enabling techniques, namely, duty cycling, data-driven approach and mobility [9].

Distributed energy balanced routing is proposed as in [10]. This routing algorithm uses the energy balance path for data transmission. It firstly calculates the total energy cost of all the paths from source node to base station and then select energy efficient path for data transmission. But distributed energy balanced routing algorithm considers a network scenario where few nodes can communicate with base station. For large network DEBR algorithm is not works properly, a more precise routing algorithm and problem definition is required for this class of scenario.

3 Assumptions

- Network is static.
- Energy consumption at the receiver and energy consumption at the unintended receiver nodes that overhear the transmission is not included.
- Consider a directed graph G (V, A) where V is the set of all nodes and A is the set of all directed links (m, n) where m, n Є A.
- Let P_m be the set of nodes that can be reached by node m with a certain power level in its dynamic range, where link (m, n) exists, if n Є S_m.

- Let each node m have the initial battery energy E_m
- Let g_m be the rate at which information is generated at node m.
- The transmission energy required for node m to transmit a bit to its neighboring node n is e_{mn},
- The rate at which information transmitted from node m to node n is called the flow f_{mn}
- $\tilde{E}_m$ and $\tilde{E}_n$ are the residual energy of node m and node n respectively.

4 Energy Efficient Maximum Lifetime Routing Algorithm

The proposed routing algorithm uses shortest energy cost path that maintained the energy balance for entire network. For energy efficiency algorithm uses greedy heuristic path. For energy efficient greedy heuristic optimal path algorithm calculate the energy cost of each and every link in the network. This means it finds a subset of the links that forms an optimal path that includes every node, where total cost of all the links in that path is minimized.

The information of energy available in the nodes is used to compute greedy heuristic path, and to balance the energy consumption across all nodes. Node that has minimum battery power will drain out their battery power quickly and would be the first one to die. So node with less energy can be added later in greedy heuristic optimal path because energy cost for a transmission from this node will be the maximum.

When network is setup each node can broadcast their residual energy information. All the nodes in network know the residual energy of neighboring nodes. Initially we assume that base station is in greedy heuristic optimal path. Algorithm can calculate greedy heuristic path using the energy cost function defined in equation (1). The node of the network added to the optimal path at each point is that node adjacent to a node of the optimal path by the link of minimum energy cost. The link of the minimum cost becomes in a path are connecting the new node to the path.

When all the nodes of the network have been added to the optimal path, a greedy heuristic route is constructed for a network. All the nodes of this greedy heuristic network can transmit their data on energy efficient path. After transmitting the 'θ' amount of data flow on that path new routing path is computed. After every transmission, residual energy $\tilde{E}_m$ of node m changes, so after 'θ' amount of transmission energy cost of each node is recalculated. With the updated energy costs the greedy heuristic path is recalculated and procedure is repeated until any node drain out its residual energy power.

4.1 Energy Cost Function

The objective is to find out best energy efficient algorithm that will lead to the maximization of system lifetime. The energy cost for a transmission from node m to node n is calculated by

$$EC_{(m,n)} = (e_{mn})\tilde{E}_m^{-1} + (e_{nm})\tilde{E}_n^{-1} \; ; \qquad (1)$$

Where, $EC_{(m,n)}$ is the energy cost for transmitting a packet from node m to node n.

4.2 Energy Cost Model

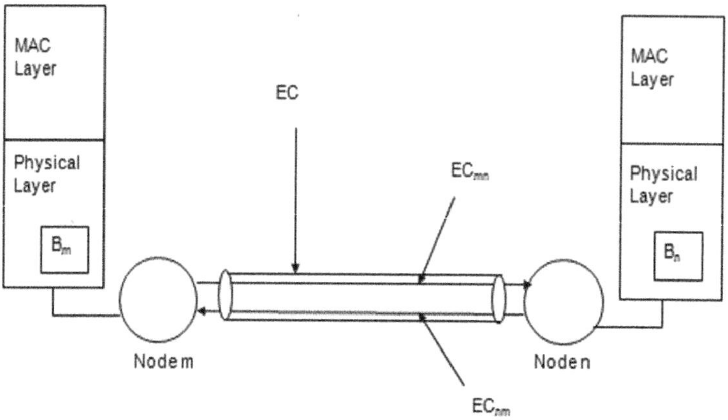

4.3 Steps for Creating Energy Efficient Optimal Path

The routing path is computed variant of prim's MST algorithm [11]. The idea behind the algorithm is that every new node added to the greedy heuristic optimal path has the minimum cost to reach the base station. The algorithm works as follows:

Step (1): Initially we assume that base station is in optimal path. Base station can add any node if energy cost for a transmission from base station to one of its neighbor node is minimum, and suppose this neighbor node is i then create a link between base station and node i. Then node i is also included in optimal path.

Step (2): The next link (i, j) to be added is such that i is a node already included in a optimal path, j is a node not yet included, and the energy cost of (i, j) is minimum among all links (p, q) such that node p is in the optimal path and node q is not in the optimal path.

Step (3): If any link (i, l) has minimum energy cost and energy cost of this link is also minimum among all links (p, q) where node p is in the optimal path and node q is not in optimal path then link (i, l) is added in path but after adding this link if create a cycle in optimal path then this link is not included in a path (fig. 1(a)).

Step (4): Select another link (BS, k) where BS is a node already included in a optimal path, and k is a node not yet included and energy cost is greater than link (i, l) but minimum among all links (p, q) such that node p is in path and node q is not in path.

Step (5): Repeat this procedure until all nodes of the graph have been added to the optimal path, a greedy heuristic path is constructed for the network.

Step (6): After transmitting θ amount of data in greedy heuristic path, the new optimal path is computed. Because after transmitting the data, residual energy of all the nodes are decreases and energy cost increase.

Step (7): Suppose in network 1(b) all the nodes can transmits the data packets and let energy cost of all the links will increases by 0.5. So after θ amount of transmission minimum energy cost path will be recalculated shown in fig. 2(b). All the traffic flow should follow this new minimum energy cost path.

Step (8): Repeat these steps until the first node in the network dies.

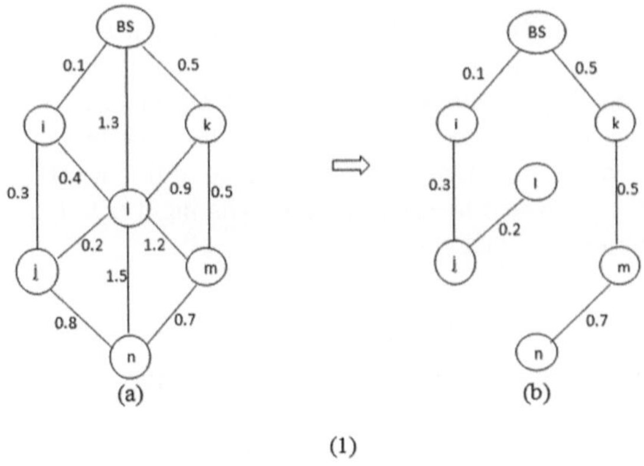

Fig. 1. minimum energy cost path

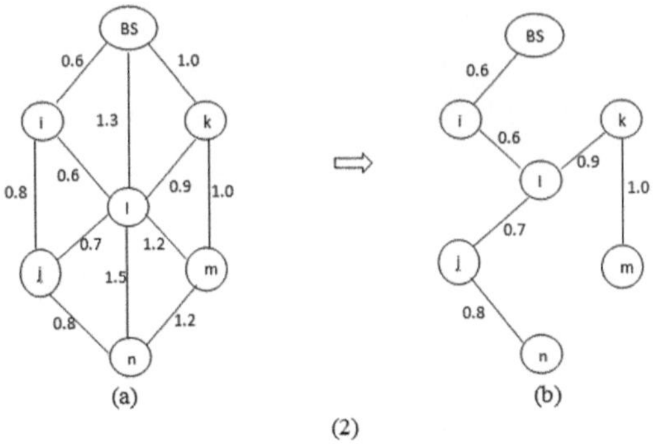

Fig. 2. Minimum energy cost path after θ amount of transmission

5 Performance Evaluations

We have carried out extensive simulation studies of the proposed algorithm to evaluate its performance, and compared its performance with Ad-hoc on Demand Distance Vector routing algorithm (AODV). The AODV protocol is one of the reactive routing protocols that can construct the route when data transmission is required. In this protocol, a source node broadcasts the route request (RREQ) packet to the entire network, and all the nodes rebroadcast the received RREQ packet immediately.

Therefore, we use the AODV protocol as the basic protocol since its operation is quite simple. In order to observe the affect of static parameter on AODV we have consider the platform's based simulation on Qualnet version 5.0 which is a standard tool set used sensor networks standards.

5.1 Simulation Model

In our simulation, we have varied the number of nodes from 10 to 50, which are randomly deployed using uniform distribution in different parts of deployment area with a fixed density. Assume that transmission range of each node is limited by 10 meter. The packet size was kept at 80 Bytes. We used Constant Bit Rate (CBR) as traffic source with average packet rate 0.5 packets /sec. Each node has initial energy E_i = 100 J. By experiment, we find that the suitable value of θ to be 10 packet and we have set the duration of each round to 1000 seconds. The input data is generated randomly in every second duration at each node.

Table 1. Configuration Table

Simulation Time	1000 Seconds
Terrain Area	500 x 500
Number of Nodes (Sensors)	10 to 50
Remote Site (Access Point)	1 (Base Station)
Channel Frequency	2.4 GHz
Traffic Type	UDP
Mobility	NONE
Application Type	CBR

5.2 Simulation Result

5.2.1 Node Energy

The remaining node energy of all sensors at the end of simulation has been plotted in fig. 1. The graph shows that EEMLR has distributed overall energy over the entire network in a more balanced way. In EEMLR algorithm after θ amount of transmission new routing path is constructed so this algorithm balanced the energy for entire network. Therefore, EEMLR routing algorithm should consider not only energy efficiency, but also the amount of energy available in each sensor. For example, EEMLR uses different path after every θ amount of transmission. Excessively energy consumption of one path (node 1 and node 3) has been shared by another path (node 8 and node 9). From the results, the remaining battery capacity of nodes in AODV decreases very early. This is because the sensor nodes near the sink nodes consume a large amount of battery power to forward data packets from a sensor node which is located far from the sink node. Therefore, the sensor nodes far from the sink nodes cannot find the route to the sink node. If the route is not found, each sensor node tries to find it again. As results, many sensor nodes consume a large amount of battery power to find the route to the sink nodes

5.2.2 Network Lifetime

We compare the performance of algorithm over 16 trails with respect to lifetime of the network where network lifetime is define as the time until the first node in the network dies or the number of accepted message until the first rejection. Fig (2) shows the lifetime of both algorithms and algorithm EEMLR outperforms the AODV algorithm. For AODV

Effect of θ

Note that θ = 10 packet means that new routing path is computed after every 10 packets transmission. We could observe that as the size of θ became larger, the performance deteriorated. This phenomenon is natural and was expected because larger θ means all the data traffic should follow the minimum energy routing path for long time.

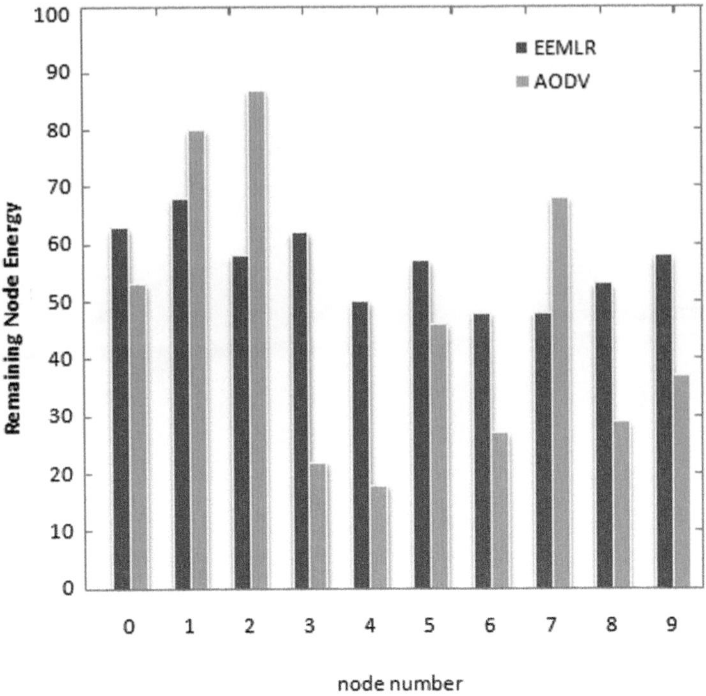

Fig. 3. Remaining Energy of Nodes after simulation

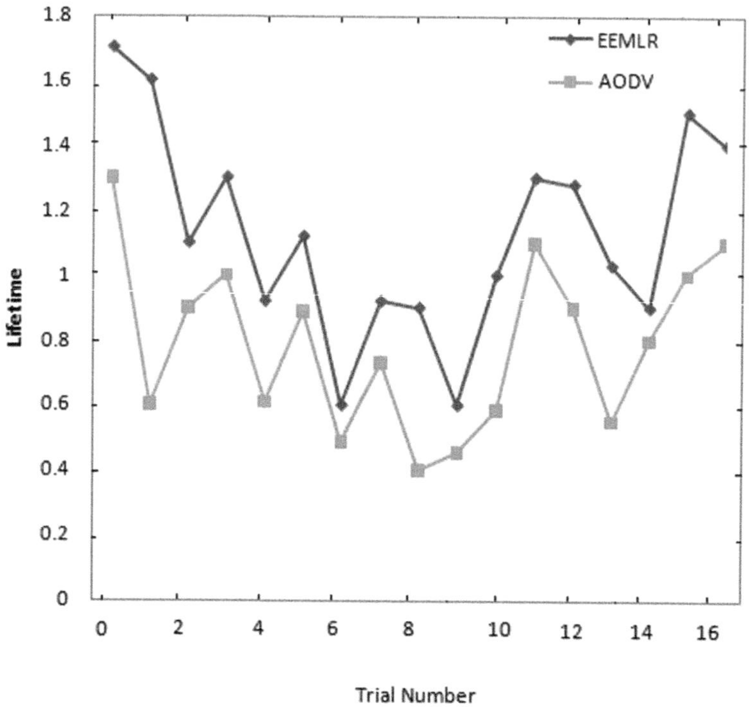

Fig. 4. Lifetime of the network

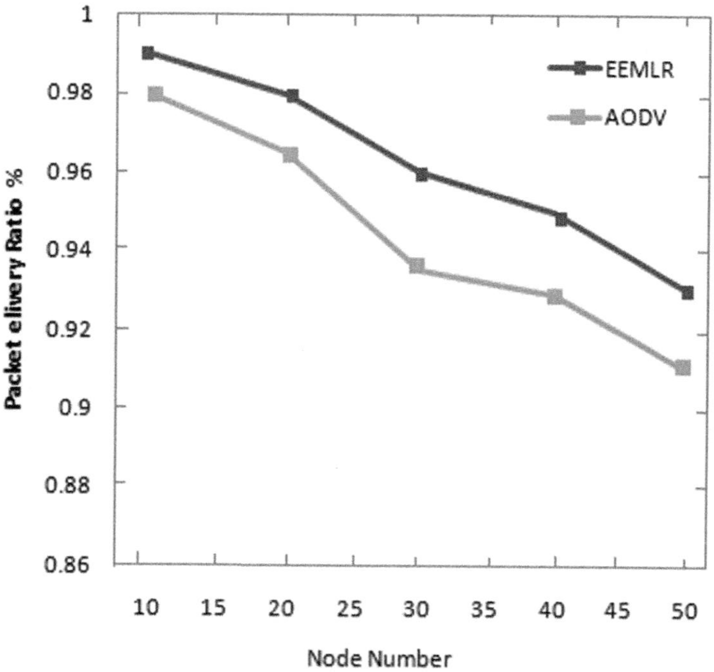

Fig. 5. Packet Delivery Ratio for varying number of nodes

5.2.3 Packet Delivery Ratio

Figure 3 gives percentage packets delivered in each round using EEMLR and AODV approach for WSNs. It is to be noted that EEMLR algorithm consistently gives higher percentage of packets delivered in comparison to AODV algorithm. As shown in fig. (3), EEMLR outperforms the AODV because of limited congestion due to less routing overhead. It is to be noted that percentage of packets delivered in EEMLR routing is slightly more than that in AODV routing. The ratio of data packets delivered to the destination and the data packets generated by the CBR sources are taken packet delivery ratio in our study.

6 Conclusions

In wireless sensor network, the battery energy is the most important resource, so route the traffic through the minimum energy path to the destination is fatal for the network because all the nodes in that path will drain out their battery power rapidly. Therefore it's not a feasible solution and instead of this solution forwards the traffic such that energy expenditure is balanced among the nodes. Most of the energy aware routing algorithm only concerned energy efficiency of the nodes but proposed energy efficient maximum lifetime routing algorithm present the heuristic measure, called energy cost, to balance the energy consumption rates among the nodes in proportion to their energy reserved. We have evaluated the performance of our protocol through simulation studies for different number of nodes. Simulation results show that lifetime of the network is increases and data packet delivery in our EEMLR routing is more than that using AODV routing, and energy consumption of nodes is also balanced.

References

[1] Singh, S., Woo, M., Raghavendra, C.S.: Power-aware routing in mobile ad hoc networks. In: 4th Annual IEEE/ACM Int. Conf. Mobile Computing and Networking, Dallas, TX, pp. 181–190 (1998)

[2] Chang, J.-H., Tassiulas, L.: Routing for maximum system lifetime in wireless ad hoc networks. In: 37th Annual Allerton Conf. Communication, Control, and Computing, Monticello, IL (1999)

[3] Chang, J.-H., Tassiulas, L.: Energy conserving routing in wireless ad hoc networks. In: Proc. IEEE INFOCOM, Tel Aviv, Israel, pp. 22–31 (2000)

[4] Li, Q., Aslam, J., Rus, D.: Online power-aware routing in wireless ad hoc networks. In: IEEE/ACM Int. Conf. Mobile Computing and Networking (MobiCom 2001), Rome, Italy (2001)

[5] Chang, J.-H., Tassiulas, L.: Maximum Lifetime Routing in Wireless Sensor Networks. IEEE/ACM Transactions on Networking 12(4) (August 2004)

[6] Ergen, S.C., Varaiya, P.: Energy Efficient Routing with Delay Guarantee for Sensor Networks. Wireless Networks 13(5), 679–690 (2007)

[7] Pandana, C., Ray Liu, K.J.: Maximum Connectivity and Maximum Lifetime Energy-aware Routing for Wireless Sensor Network. In: IEEE GLOBOCOM (2005)

[8] Kar, K., Kodialam, M., Lakshman, T.V., Tassiulas, L.: Routing for Network Capacity Maximization in Energy-constained Network. In: IEEE INFOCOM (2003)
[9] Anastasi, G., Conti, M., Francesco, M.D., Passarella, A.: Energy conservation in wireless sensor networks: A survey. Ad Hoc Networks 7(3), 537–568 (2009)
[10] Ok, C.-S., Lee, S., Mitra, P., Kumara, S.: Distributed Energy Balanced Routing for Wireless Sensor Networks. Computer & Industrial Engineering 57(1), 125–135 (2009)
[11] Horowitz, E., Sahni, S., Rajasekharan, S.: Fundamentals of Computer Algorithms, 2nd edn. Silicon Press (2008)

Algorithms for Efficient Web Service Selection with Different Constraints

Kavya Johny and Theresa Jose

Department of Computer Science,
Viswajyothi College of Engineering & Technology, Vazhakulam,
Kerala-686670, India
{kavyajovita,theresajos}@gmail.com

Abstract. Web Services are gained much popularity in business applications. There are many web services that can handle same requests. So to select better service from them is an important issue. In this paper, we study different selection algorithms that consider various constraints for better service selection, thereby provide better web service composition.

Keywords: Web services, web service selection, end-to-end constraints, implementation constraints, QoS.

1 Introduction

Web Services enable systematic application-to-application interaction on the Web. A customer gives the request of the service. Based upon the request a workflow will be generated. The workflow contains many activities which are served by special web services that are intended for such operations. As there are number of web services that serve particular requests, web service selection are done. An example for workflow has shown in Fig.1.

Web service selection can be done considering certain constraints for better service selection. With the increasing number of available web services, maintaining these services and searching for the ones that satisfy a given requirement has become an important problem. Several algorithms consider QoS, transactional properties or both as their constraints while some other consider some implementation constraints. Mainly the service selection algorithms for web service composition on QoS perform locally or globally. Local service selection consider QoS locally i.e., they consider QoS of each web services for the composition. In global service selection they consider the QoS factors of the entire work flow together to provide better service composition. The service selections are performed in composite web service selection to provide better efficiency in which services from different providers that give more performance can be integrated regardless of their locations and platforms.

1.1 Local Web Service Selection

The work flow for Web service composition consists of many activities. The service selection for each activity is done from a set of services. When they are performed

D. Nagamalai, E. Renault, and M. Dhanushkodi (Eds.): PDCTA 2011, CCIS 203, pp. 293–300, 2011.

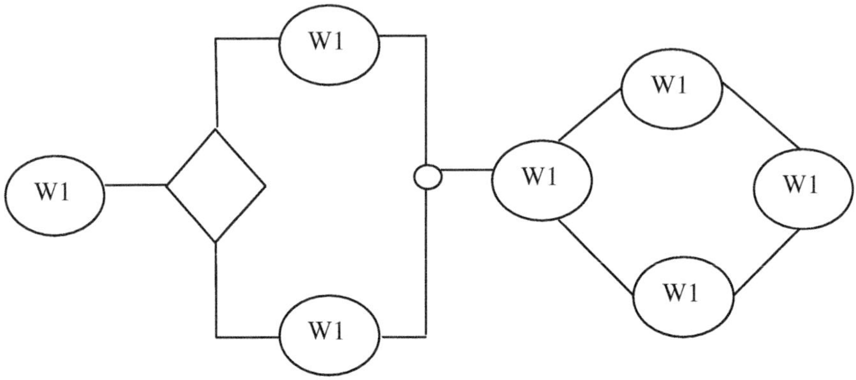

Fig. 1. An example for workflow

locally they consider the QoS factors for web services for each activity. The Web service with best QoS will be selected for each activity.

The QoS factors mainly consider are Response Time, Availability, Throughput, Latency, Cost etc [1].

1 Response Time refers to the time interval between the given input and output obtained.
2 Availability refers whether the services are available or not.
3 Throughput is the invocation of services per second.
4 Latency is the execution duration.
5 Cost is the price for invoking each web services.

1.2 Global Service Selection

When the service selection is done globally, they consider end-to-end constraints [2]. When consider the cost of entire web service composition, the global approach is used. The web service with best QoS for each activity in the workflow sometimes may not gain better end-to-end QoS. The service selection considering the end-to-end QoS constraints can be done using combinatorial approach and Graph approach. Both of them consider only sequential workflow. The selection of algorithms depends on the problem size, network structure and other factors.

2 Combinatorial Approach

Combinatorial approach can be used to find the execution path in a composite service that is structured in directed acyclic graph. We need to run the algorithm several times to get an optimal solution. Transmission overheads are considered for the problem formulation. Transmission overhead includes the delay and cost between two services.

The problem is modelled as multiple choice knapsack problem. MCKP select one item from each class of web service in order to place them in knapsack with a fixed capacity such that maximum profit should be obtained.

Different algorithms are used to model problem as MKCP:

Exhaustive Search Algorithm: This is also known as generate and test method, backtracking and brute force method. Exhaustive searches are all about trying every possible method to find a solution. It is conceptually simple and often effective but such an approach to problem solving is sometimes considered inelegant. This is time consuming and requires a large amount of memory.

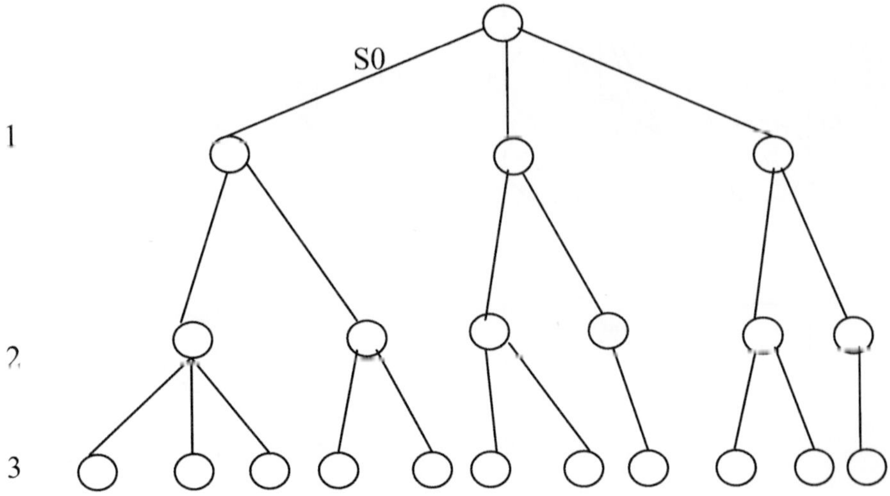

Fig. 2. Tree Structure

The search is said to be **exhaustive** because it is guaranteed to generate all reachable states before it terminates with failure. By generating the all of the nodes at a particular level before proceeding to the next level of the tree this strategy guarantees that the space of possible moves will be systematically examined. In Fig2. S0 represents root node. All the nodes in the third level are called leaf nodes.

Dynamic Programming: Dynamic programming is a very powerful method in which problems are solved by combining solutions to sub problems. Steps in Dynamic programming is:

1. Characterize structure of an optimal solution.
2. Define value of optimal solution recursively.
3. Compute optimal solution values either top-down with caching or bottom-up in a table.
4. Construct an optimal solution from computed values.

3 Graph Approach

Graph approach can also be used to handle different composite services. They only need to be run once in order to get an optimal solution. They are most commonly used. This approach uses shortest path algorithm to get the best solution. In Fig.3 S1 represents source node, S8 represents sink node, L_{ij} are intermediate services in each intermediate node where i=1, 2, .. 8 and j= 1, 2, 3.

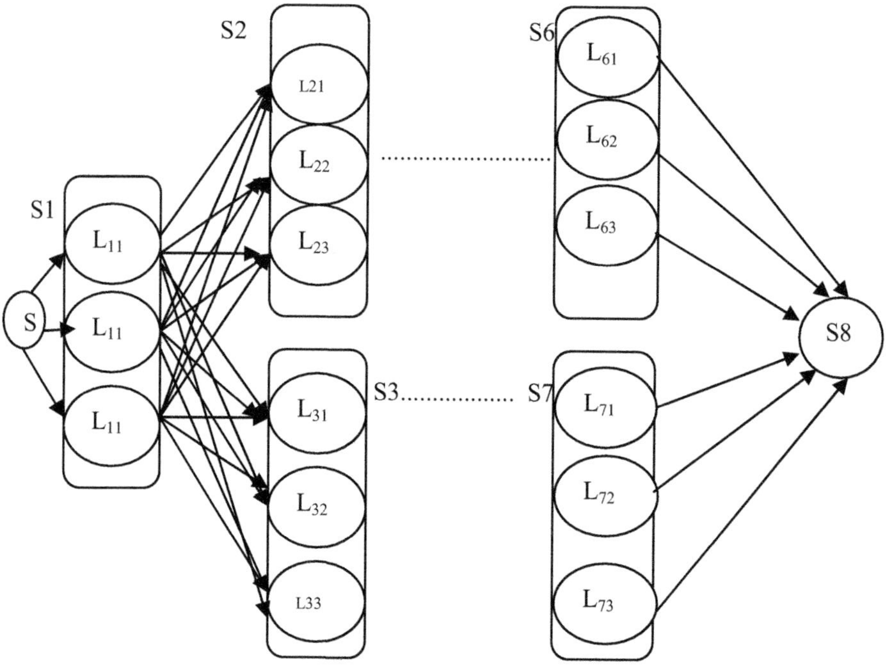

Fig. 3. Constructed DAG

Some of the shortest path algorithms:

Constrained Bellman-Ford Algorithm: Generally, Bellman-Ford algorithm solves the single-source shortest-paths in a weighted graph. The algorithm uses a breadth-first search to find the highest utility path between source and destination. Detailed description of CBF can be found in [3].The running time of CBF grows exponentially.

Constrained shortest path algorithm: CSPF is an extension of shortest path algorithms in which the path computed is a shortest path fulfilling a set of constraints. It prunes those links that violate a given set of constraints. The breadth-first approach is used. Since the composite service graph is a DAG, the classical DAG shortest path algorithm is modified to a more efficient constrained shortest path algorithm to solve the problem. First topological sort of all nodes in the graph is performed and later they are visited.

4 Genetic Algorithms

The genetic algorithm [4] provides an optimal web service selection by solving mutual constraints between some web service implementations. Fig.4 gives a better idea of how the genome is made. The abstract service S can be performed using any of the concrete web services (CS). The mutual constraints are dependency constraints and conflict constraints. In the web service selection, both dependency constraints and conflict constraints must be considered [5].

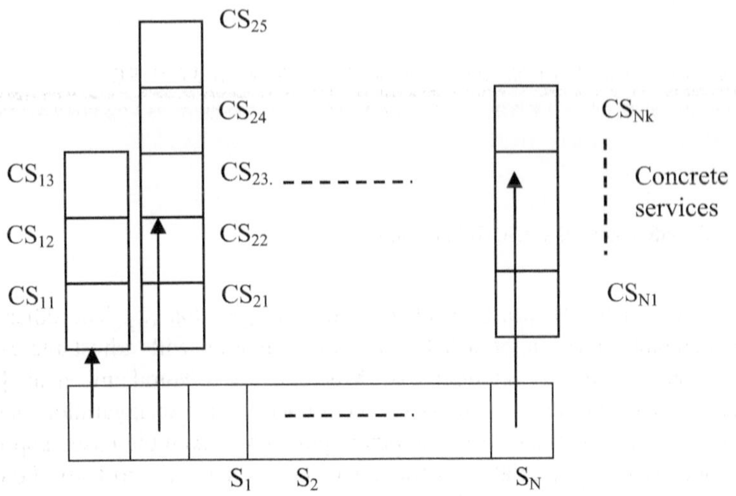

Fig. 4. Genetic Encoding

Dependency Constraint: For a web service, if an implementation is selected, then a different implementation must be selected for another web service. For instance, a travel booking web service can be built by aggregating a flight booking web service, a car rental web service, a travel insurance web service, an accommodation booking web service, a payment web service, and an itinerary planning Web service. When building a travel booking web service, if we select a particular travel insurance web service that only accepts payments made by Master cards, then we must select a payment web service that accepts Master cards. This kind of constraints is called dependency constraint.

Conflict Constraint: The conflict constraint is, sometimes when an implementation for one web service is selected, a set of implementations for another web service must be excluded in the web services composition. When building a travel booking web service, if we select a particular flight booking web service implementation that does not accept deposits made by Master cards, then we must not select an implementation for the payment web service that supports Master cards. This type of constraints is called conflict constraint.

The genetic algorithms solve the above implementation constraints along with the QoS issues and provide better web service composition. The algorithm can be given as follows:

```
Begin
    Initialize population with random candidate solutions;
    Evaluate each candidate;
    Repeat
        Select parents from the population;
        Crossover is performed by randomly selecting
    the atomic services without any constraints and
    generates a child with those atomic services of
    parents.
        Mutate the resulting children by selecting a
    web service and replace with another one.
        Evaluate children;
        Select individuals for the next generation
    Until termination-condition is satisfied
End
```

Crossover: There are two types of crossover operators: one-point crossover and combining crossovers [8].

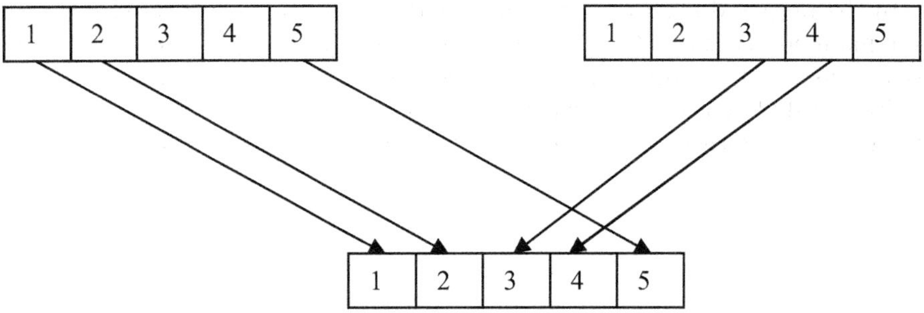

Fig. 5. Crossover Operation

The one-point crossover works in the same way as binary one-point crossover except the cross point is always generated on the boundary of the blocks. This ensures that always the whole centers are exchanged between individuals.

The combining crossover combines the two solutions as shown in Fig 5. It builds the new offspring centre by centre. For each centre from the parent individual it finds the nearest centres from the second parent and generates two new centres randomly on the line joining the two parent centres.

Mutation: Mutation is the process of randomly selecting one web service and replacing it with an alternative as shown in Fig 6.

There are five kinds of mutation operators.

The first two of them- one-point mutation and biased one-point mutation change the value of a centre randomly picked. In the former, the selected centre is replaced by point chosen at random. The latter moves slightly the centre in random direction. The third operator- K-means mutation performs several steps of k-means algorithm. The other two operators- cluster addition and cluster removal- modify the number of clusters. The cluster addition adds one centre chosen randomly from the data set S, the cluster removal deletes one centre chosen at random.

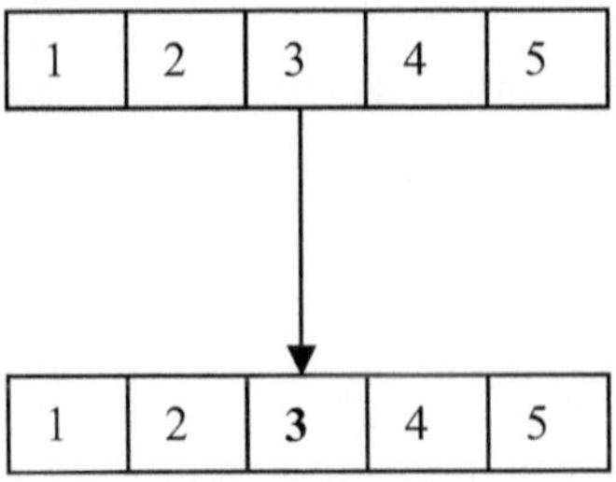

Fig. 6. Mutation Operation

5 TQoS Algorithm

Most of the algorithms only consider QoS factors for the web service selection. The TQoS Algorithm considers both quality and transactional properties for the web service composition thereby provide a better web service composition. The transactional properties are pivot, compensatable and retriable [6].

Pivot WS: A pivot WS is one which is neither compensatable nor retriable. On one hand, there is no guarantee that this type of web service can be executed successfully. On the other hand, a committed pivot web service cannot be rolled back.

Compensatable WS: A WS is compensatable if it is able to offer compensation policies to semantically undo the original activity. For example, a web service that reserves a seat in an airline reservation system can be compensated for by a transaction that cancels the reservation.

Retriable WS: A web service is retriable if it is able to offer forward recovery. In other words, activities with this property can guarantee a successfully termination after a finite number of invocations. Cancellation of a seat in an airline reservation system, or crediting a bank account, is examples of Retriable transaction.

Based upon these three transactional properties, web service selection is done. TQoS works on either of the two assumptions. On one hand it assumes the system guarantees that if the execution is successful, the obtained results can be compensated by the user. On the other hand, it assumes the system does not guarantee that the result can be compensated by the user in case of successful execution. The algorithm considers both sequential and parallel workflow of activities [7].

6 Conclusions

"Web services" is an effort to build a distributed computing platform for the Web. For providing efficient services to the customer appropriate web services have to be selected. In this paper, we study different algorithms for composite business processes that consider various constraints for better web service selection. This study extends the service selection problem to multiple QoS constraints. This paper helps to study the pros and cons between different algorithms and thereby helps to determine the new advancements that can overcome the existing disadvantages. We have presented service selection algorithms that consider QoS end-to-end constraints, implementation constraints and transactional constraints. The objective of the algorithms is to maximize efficiency while meeting better performance constraints.

References

1. Zeng, L., Benatallah, B., Ngu, A., Dumas, M., Kalagnanam, J., Chang, H.: QoS-aware middleware for web services composition. IEEE Transactions on Software Engineering 30(5), 311–327 (2004)
2. Yu, T., Zhang, Y., Lin, K.-J.: Efficient algorithms for web services selection with end-to-end QoS constraints. ACM Trans. on Web 1(1), 6 (2007)
3. Yang, W.-L.: A comparison of two optimal approaches for the MCOP problem. Elsevier Ltd., Amsterdam, doi:10.1016/j.jnca.2003.10.003
4. Canfora, G., Di Penta, M., Esposito, R., Villani, M.L.: An Approach for QoS aware Service Composition based on Genetic Algorithms. In: ACM GECCO 2005 (June 25-29, 2005)
5. Tang, M., Ai, L.: A Hybrid Genetic Algorithm for the Optimal Constrained Web Service Selection Problem in Web Service Composition. In: 2010 IEEE Congress Evolutionary Computation, CEC (July 2010)
6. Li, L., Liu, C., Wang, J.: Deriving Transactional Properties of Composite Web Services. In: Proc. IEEE Int'l. Conf. Web Services (ICWS 2007), pp. 631–638 (July 2007)
7. El Haddad, J., Manouvrier, M., Rukoz, M.: TQoS: Transactional and QoS-Aware Selection Algorithm for Automatic Web Service Composition. IEEE Transactions on Services Computing 3(1) (January-March 2010)
8. Koduva, P.: Clustering Genetic Algorithm. In: 18th International Workshop on Database and Expert Systems Applications

Efficient ID-Based Signature Scheme from Bilinear Map

Rajeev Anand Sahu and Sahadeo Padhye

Department of Mathematics,
Motilal Nehru National Institute of Technology, Allahabad, India
{rajeevs.crypto,sahadeomathrsu}@gmail.com

Abstract. We propose an identity (ID)-based signature scheme from bilinear map. The scheme is proved secure against existential forgery on adaptively chosen message and given ID attack in random oracle model under the Computational Diffie-Hellman (CDH) assumption. The new scheme is simple and computationally more efficient than other existing schemes. Furthermore, since the building blocks for proposed ID-based signature is the BLS short signature, hence in communications of ID-based signatures over low band width channels, the proposed scheme will be more economic and applicable.

Keywords: ID-based signature scheme, Bilinear map, Computational efficiency.

1 Introduction

A digital signature provides source authentication in cryptography. In a signature scheme, the users are supposed to obtain their authenticated public key from certificate authority. But in a certificate-based system, the problem is to maintain certificates of users, storage space and large overhead to transfer the certificates, which leads to increase the associated cost significantly. ID-based setting simplifies the key management procedure and provides added security with comparison to certificate-based settings. In ID-based cryptosystem, the identity of users (as proxy, IP address) can be used to generate their public and private keys. In 1984, Shamir [11] introduced the concept of ID-based cryptosystem and signature scheme. Following the ID-based setting, many popular signature schemes [4,7,9,13] have been proposed and are still in use to design new signatures. The bilinear map provides ease of computation and makes system simple. Bilinear map shows the property of linearity in both components, hence it is very effective in terms of both efficiency and functionality. After the work of Boneh and Franklin [1], the bilinear maps are highly applicable to construct efficient ID-based signatures.

In message communication, the cost and process associated with the frequency and bandwidth of channels are significant computationally. Due to the huge size of signature, many signatures can not be sent over low frequency bands. To communicate the signature over low bandwidth channels Boneh, Lynn and Shacham

D. Nagamalai, E. Renault, and M. Dhanushkodi (Eds.): PDCTA 2011, CCIS 203, pp. 301–306, 2011.

(BLS) proposed the first practical and secure short digital signature [3]. Their scheme is secure in the random oracle model under the CDH assumption. Moreover, the signature size in their scheme is almost half of the digital signature generated by Digital Signature Algorithm (DSA) with the same level of security. Following the theme of Yi's signature [13] and Hess's signature [7], many ID-based short signature schemes have been proposed [5,12]. In [12], Wang and Chen has shorten the signature, folding the message part into signature in such a way that it is recoverable. Du and Wen have proposed an ID-based short signature scheme [6], based on k-CAA problem [8], their scheme is computationally efficient than [2,7]. Cha and Cheon [4] proposed the security notion for an ID-based signature scheme as existential forgery on Adaptively chosen message and given ID attack (EUF-ACMIA), which can be used as building blocks for security model of an ID-based signature scheme. In this paper, we have proposed a new ID-based signature scheme from bilinear map. We have proved that our scheme is existential forgery on Adaptively chosen message and given ID attack (EUF-ACMIA) in random oracle model under the CDH assumption. The new scheme is significantly more efficient in computational sense, than other existing schemes [5,7,9,12]. Moreover, the proposed scheme can be regarded as an ID-based version of BLS short signature scheme [3], hence in communications of ID-based signatures over low band width channels, the proposed scheme will be more economic and applicable.

The rest of this paper is organized as follows: In Section 2, we introduce some related mathematical problems. The proposed ID-based signature scheme is presented in Section 3. In Section 4, we prove the security of proposed scheme and compare the computational efficiency of the new scheme with others. Finally Section 5 gives a brief conclusion of the work.

2 Preliminaries

In this section, we briefly introduce some related mathematical problems.

2.1 Bilinear Map

Given a cyclic additive group G_1 of a prime order q, with generator P, and a cyclic multiplicative group G_2 of the same order q; a map $e : G_1 \times G_1 \to G_2$ satisfying the following properties is called bilinear map:

(a)Bilinearity: $e(aP, bQ) = e(P, Q)^{ab}$, $\forall a, b \in Z_q^*$ and $P, Q \in G_1$.
This can be stated in other way as: For $P, Q, R \in G_1$,
$e(P + Q, R) = e(P, R)e(Q, R)$ and $e(P, Q + R) = e(P, Q)e(P, R)$.

(b)Non-Degeneracy: There exists $P, Q \in G_1$such that $e(P, Q) \neq 1$.

(c)Computability: There exists an efficient algorithm to compute $e(P, Q) \in G_2$, $\forall P, Q \in G_1$.

Modified Weil pairing and Tate pairing are examples of cryptographic bilinear maps.

2.2 Computational Diffie-Hellman Problem(CDHP)

For given $P, aP, bP \in G_1$, to compute $abP \in G_1$. Where $a, b \in Z_q^*$,

2.3 CDH Assumption

If G_1 is a group of prime order q with a generator P, then a CDH assumption holds in G_1 if there is no algorithm which solves CDHP with a non-negligible advantage.

2.4 Elliptic Curve Discrete Logrithm Problem (ECDLP)

For given $P, Q \in G_1$, to find an integer $n \in Z_q^*$, such that $P = nQ$.

3 Proposed Scheme

The motivation behind the proposed scheme is BLS short signature scheme given by Boneh *et al.* [3], hence the scheme described below can be regarded as an ID-based version of BLS short signature scheme. The scheme is as follow:

Setup: For a given security parameter k, let G_1 be a cyclic additive group of prime order q, with generator P and G_2 be a cyclic multiplicative group of the same prime order q. Define a bilinear map $e : G_1 \times G_1 \rightarrow G_2$. PKG selects $s \in_R Z_q^*$, sets the public key $P_{pub} = sP$ and keeps the master key s secret. Define hash functions $H_1 : \{0,1\}^* \rightarrow G_1$ and $H_2 : \{0,1\}^* \rightarrow Z_q$. The system's public parameters *params* is $\{G_1, G_2, e, P, q, H_1, H_2\}$.

Extract: For a given identity ID, the PKG computes public key $Q_{ID} = H_1(ID)$ and private key $S_{ID} = sQ_{ID}$.

Sign: To sign a message m, the signer computes $h = H_2(m)$, then $\sigma = hS_{ID}$. The σ is signature on message m.

Verify: Given a message m and signature σ on it, the verifier accepts if the equality $e(P, \sigma) = e(P_{pub}, H_2(m)Q_{ID})$ holds.

4 Analysis of Proposed Scheme

In this section, we analyze the security notion of our ID-based signature scheme and compare its computational efficiency with others. The security notion is according to the *Security against existential forgery on Adaptively chosen message and given ID attack* , given by Cha and Cheon in [4].

4.1 Theorem 1

Our proposed scheme is secure against existential forgery on adaptively chosen message and given ID attack in the random oracle model if CDHP in G_1 is hard.

Proof: According to the security notion given in [4], we can state that, if there is a polynomial time algorithm A_0 for an adaptively chosen message and given ID

attack to our scheme, then there exists an algorithm A_1, with the same advantage for adaptively chosen message and given ID attack.

Suppose (Q_{ID}, S_{ID}) is public, private key pair for the given identity ID. Now using the Forking Lemma [10], we can obtain a result that, if there exists an efficient algorithm A_1 for an adaptively chosen message and given ID attack to our scheme, then there exists an efficient algorithm B_0 which can produce two valid signatures (m, h, σ) and (m, h', σ') such that $h \neq h'$. Now, using B_0, an algorithm B_1 can be constructed with the inputs P, P_{pub}, Q_{ID}. B_1 selects a message m and runs the algorithm B_0 to output two forgeries (m, h, σ) and (m, h', σ') such that $h \neq h'$, and $e(P, \sigma) = e(P_{pub}, hQ_{ID})$, $e(P, \sigma') = e(P_{pub}, h'Q_{ID})$. From left and right sides of these equalities, we can write $e(P, \sigma - \sigma') = e(P_{pub}, (h - h')Q_{ID})$ or $e(P, \sigma - \sigma') = e(P, (h - h')S_{ID})$. In other hand, we can write $e(P, (\sigma - \sigma') - (h - h')S_{ID}) = 1$. Now, since the bilinear map e is non-degenerate, so $(\sigma - \sigma') - (h - h')S_{ID} = \bigcirc$ or $S_{ID} = (\sigma - \sigma')(h - h')^{-1}$, where $\bigcirc$ is point at infinity on elliptic curve where the bilinear map is defined. The above equality shows that S_{ID} can be computed only with the help of σ, σ', h and h'. But the structure of $S_{ID} = sQ_{ID} = svP$ (for any $v \in Z_q^*$, such that $Q_{ID} = vP$). This implies that B_1 can solve any instance of CDHP in G_1, as $sP = P_{pub}$ and $vP = Q_{ID}$ are given. But, since CDHP in G_1 is assumed to be hard in our scheme, hence there is no efficient algorithm for an adaptively chosen message and given ID attack to our scheme. Therefore, our scheme is secure against *Existential forgery on Adaptively chosen message and given ID attack* .

In another way, if anyone wants to forge the proposed signature σ, he will have to compute the master secret key $s \in_R Z_q^*$ of PKG, since the signature $\sigma \in G_1$ is structured as $\sigma = hsQ_{ID}$ or $\sigma = shQ_{ID}$, where $hQ_{ID} \in G_1$ can be computed publicly. But finding $s \in_R Z_q^*$, to compute $\sigma = shQ_{ID}$, for given $\sigma, hQ_{ID} \in G_1$ is equivalent to solving the ECDLP in G_1 which is assumed to be intractable, as ECDLP in G_1 is polynomial time equivalent to CDHP in G_1. Hence by any way, existential forgery on Adaptively chosen message and given ID attack s is not possible in proposed scheme.

4.2 Efficiency Comparison

In this section, we compare the computational efficiency of our scheme with other ID-based signature schemes [5,7,9,12] and show that our scheme is comparably more efficient.

Signing phase:

Scheme	e	H	E	SM
Paterson's scheme (2002) [9]	0	2	0	4
Hess's scheme (2002) [7]	1	1	1	2
Cheng et al's scheme (2005) [5]	0	1	0	3
Wang and Chen's scheme* (2007) [12]	0	1	1	2
Our scheme	0	1	0	1

* Also 3 additional compression functions are required.

Verification phase:

Scheme	e	H	E	SM
Paterson's scheme (2002) [9]	3	2	2	0
Hess's scheme (2002) [7]	2	1	1	0
Cheng et al's scheme (2005) [5]	2	1	0	1
Wang and Chen's scheme* (2007) [12]	2	2	1	0
Our scheme	2	1	0	1

* Also 2 additional compression functions are required.

In the above tables e = no. of bilinear maps, H = no. of hash functions, E = no. of exponentiations and SM = no. of scalar multiplications in G_1.

4.3 Application and implementation

Since from the above tables it is clear that the proposed scheme is significantly more efficient in computational sense than other existing schemes [5,7,9,12], hence in communications of ID-based signatures over low band width channels, the proposed scheme will be more economic and applicable. Also the exact running time, signature size etc. can be computed and compared for the above schemes through open source cryptographic softwares like PBC Library (http://crypto.stanford.edu/pbc/), SAGE etc.

5 Conclusion

In this paper, we have proposed a new ID-based signature scheme from bilinear map. The scheme is proved existential forgery on adaptively chosen message and given ID attack (EUF-ACMIA) in random oracle model with the CDH assumption. We have compared the computational efficiency and showed that the proposed scheme is significantly more efficient in computational sense, than other existing schemes [5,7,9,12]. Furthermore, since the building blocks for proposed ID-based signature is the BLS short signature, hence in communications of ID-based signatures over low band width channels, the proposed scheme will be more economic and applicable.

References

1. Boneh, D., Franklin, M.: Identity based encryption from the Weil pairing. In: Kilian, J. (ed.) CRYPTO 2001. LNCS, vol. 2139, pp. 213–229. Springer, Heidelberg (2001)
2. Barreto, P.S.L.M., Libert, B., McCullagh, N., et al.: Efficient and provably-secure identity-based signature and signcryption from bilinear maps. In: Roy, B. (ed.) ASIACRYPT 2005. LNCS, vol. 3788, pp. 515–532. Springer, Heidelberg (2005)
3. Boneh, D., Lynn, B., Shacham, H.: Short signatures from the weil pairing. In: Boyd, C. (ed.) ASIACRYPT 2001. LNCS, vol. 2248, pp. 514–532. Springer, Heidelberg (2001)

4. Cha, J.C., Cheon, J.H.: An identity based signature from gap Diffie-Hellman groups. In: Desmedt, Y.G. (ed.) PKC 2003. LNCS, vol. 2567, pp. 18–30. Springer, Heidelberg (2002)
5. Cheng, X., Liu, J., Wang, X.: Identity-based aggregate and verifiably encrypted signatures from bilinear pairing. In: Gervasi, O., Gavrilova, M.L., Kumar, V., Laganá, A., Lee, H.P., Mun, Y., Taniar, D., Tan, C.J.K. (eds.) ICCSA 2005. LNCS, vol. 3483, pp. 1046–1054. Springer, Heidelberg (2005)
6. Du, H., Wen, Q.: An efficient identity-based short signature scheme from bilinear pairings. In: International Conference on Computational Intelligence and Security, IEEE Explore, pp. 725–729 (2007)
7. Hesss, F.: Efficient identity based signature scheme based on pairings. In: Nyberg, K., Heys, H.M. (eds.) SAC 2002. LNCS, vol. 2595, pp. 310–324. Springer, Heidelberg (2003)
8. Mitsunari, S., Sakai, R., Kasahara, M.: A new traitor tracing. IEICE Trans. E85-A(2), 481–484 (2002)
9. Paterson, K.G.: ID-based signatures from pairings on elliptic curves. IEEE Electronic Letters 38(18), 1025–1026 (2002)
10. Pointcheval, D., Stern, J.: Security arguments for digital signatures and blind signatures. Journal of Cryptology 13(3), 361–396 (2000)
11. Shamir, A.: Identity based cryptosystem and signature scheme. In: Blakely, G.R., Chaum, D. (eds.) CRYPTO 1984. LNCS, vol. 196, pp. 47–53. Springer, Heidelberg (1985)
12. Wang, Z., Chen, H.: A practical identity-based signature scheme from bilinear map. In: Denko, M.K., Shih, C.-s., Li, K.-C., Tsao, S.-L., Zeng, Q.-A., Park, S.H., Ko, Y.-B., Hung, S.-H., Park, J.-H. (eds.) EUC-WS 2007. LNCS, vol. 4809, pp. 704–715. Springer, Heidelberg (2007)
13. Yi, X.: An identity-based signature scheme from the Weil pairing. IEEE Communication Letters 7(2), 76–78 (2003)

Sleep Scheduler Protocol for Network Reliability in Wireless Sensor Networks

Harsh Kumar Singh and Jyoti Bharti

Department of Computer Science & Information Technology,
MANIT, Bhopal, India
{harshku4,jyoti2202}@gmail.com

Abstract. We have proposed to employ gossiping to place nodes in a sensor network in network reliability via a Gossip based sleep protocol [1]. With GSP and piggy backing we actually used a synchronous network to send data from sensor node to the sink node for any last network. So an percentage P' node will always there in network to send data while remaining node can go to sleep so as to maximize reward point and minimum delay from delivery point to the base station through wireless sensor network.

Keywords: sensor network, battery power, energy efficient routing, network reliability.

1 Introduction

Sensor network form a class of ad-hoc network, where the nodes are low-cost, limited computing power and that operates using batteries. They are deployed in a very huge numbers to collect data about the surroundings or any physical event like an aggregate the information, and communicate parameters of interest to monitor nodes either on demand or periodically. Typical scenarios of interest include seismic monitoring, power plant or nuclear reactor, traffic management, close-circuit camera in retail, military usage to sense the enemy territory. The nodes are organized into hierarchical cluster to reduce long range message transfer. To optimize power consumption message are short and bursty in nature, and spaced apart.

A good sensing coverage and connectivity at the same time can be provided in dense sensor nodes by keeping only necessary set of sensor nodes active to incerease lifetime of a network. While keeping other nodes in sleeping modes the scheme tries to not adversely affect the sensing coverage and connectivity.

For an each period the nodes which are having with lower remaining energy level are given higher priority that is done periodically for some selected sleep mode. So as to prolong the life time of the sensor nodes energy consumption load are more eventually distributed at the end of data transfer we find out that the energy level of nodes are distributed in randomly fashion as a result there is no single point of failure which eliminate exhaust condition from network.

D. Nagamalai, E. Renault, and M. Dhanushkodi (Eds.): PDCTA 2011, CCIS 203, pp. 307–311, 2011.

2 Related Works

For collecting and communication with some necessary nodes while keeping remaining modes into a sleep mode is the one way energy consumption. GAF [12] (Geographic adaptive fidelity). The networks are divided into grids. So nods are placed on the adjacent of a rectangular grid and each other nodes can successfully communicate information. Here in this at point time, only one node in each grid is active. GPS or other positioning system is required to gate the location information for grid formation.

SPAN [6] forms a multihop forwarding back bone to preserve the original capacity of the network. While remaining nodes can go to sleep mode so as to preserve energy. Back bone functionality is rotated amount the nodes to balance the energy consumption.

AFECA [5] define three operating states of nodes, sleeping, listening and active. Initially notes are in sleeping state. After Ts time period, it switches to the listening states, during the state that is listening state the radio turns on and listens for a message for a time period. If routing message is received during the period then node is active for routing. Here it change to the active stage if it decided to sent date or else as soon as time period T1 space elapsed it will go to the sleeping state. AFECA algorithm uses the advantage of interchanging activates among nodes in a dense network. As densely increase so as to increase the life time.

This approach causes less complexity and lower energy consumption [2], but it has some disadvantage: 1) Network reliability is hard to preserve: 2) Synchronization cannot be forward to base station; 3) Optimization can be more difficult. his is our challenging jobs that are needed to consider and this paper tells optimal solution for all above problem Wireless sensor network are tiny and in expansible sensor node which are having an small memory, computing power and work with batteries

3 Proposed Work

The objective of the proposed protocol is to improve overall network reliability by allowing nodes in the network to sleep for random time --proportional to their remaining battery life with a given gossip probability, with informing their neighbors or any control packet transmissions. A node tosses a coin to decide whether or not to forward a message. The probability p that a node forwards a message is called gossip probability. A node tosses a coin to decide whether or not to forward the message. The probability P' that a node forward a message is called the gossip probability. The piggybacking on acknowledgement scheme is explicitly designed for used in sensor network where data are usually follow form all the sensor to the monitor, which is a fixed node with greater computing and power resources.

On paper [1] if gossiping through randomly can make all the nodes receive a message, then the message passes through are connected at least by the path the nodes forwarding the message while using static network if above logic of receiving of message through every node is taken P' probability then if all the nodes go to sleep with probability P' = (1-P') almost all the awake nodes stay connected. So we can easily make P' nodes into a sleep mode which are actually uses a network reliability which used time to time a particular node.

But the problem arises while using and independent channel for transmission of control packet which increases routing overhead and to avoid the problem we uses an possibility of piggybacking synchronization which actually reduced an overhead of routing as a result delay is minimum. The effectiveness of piggyback depends upon the duration of queuing allowed to control packet. A small latency will not give the advantage of piggybacking while very large latency will delay synchronization of the network.

To solve problem here every node chooses uniformly decentralized time period termed as gossip period and after time is up, the node will choose another same period immediately. The node in the network toss the coin at the same time and all the node have some knowledge of other node through coin tossing time, even its own timing is same as the current period. We make the maximum time gossip period is much smaller than the lifetime of the network in other way we used maximumpiggybackwait for any data packet to be sent before it create its independent control packet and to relay the synchronization.

4 Results

4.1 Simulation Model

The proposed synchronization protocol was implemented on Qualnet simulation platform. To study the characteristic of GSP the distribution coordination function (DCF) of IEEE 802.11(b) for wireless LANs is used as the MAC/PHY layer. We have chosen a simulation area of 2000m * 300m with number of nodes ranging from 40 to 120. The Beacon Wait duration was taken 4*slot where the slot duration with each slot width is 40ms. Also, the MaximumPiggybackWait duration was taken in the range 1ms to 100ms. The packet size was kept at 100 bytes. We used constant bit rate (CBR) as traffic source with average packet rate 0.5 packet/sec. The receiver and transmitter power were kept at 0.3mW. The simulations were run for 300 sec for different source-destination traffic pair and various node positioning.

4.2 Performance Result

We compare the performance of our GSP+AODV protocol with it. We have take parameters of our GSP+AODV protocol with it. We have taken three performance metrics (i) routing overhead. (ii) Consumed node energy of all the nodes after simulation and (iii) Delay which include looping error .

1. Node Energy

The consumed node energy of all routers at the end of simulation in Fig1.The graph shows that GSP+AODV has distributed overall energy over the entire network in more balanced way. For example using election algorithm we can any node consumed the energy for that period and when period changes node changes while using we active only the necessary node and apart from this will go to sleep for a period.

2. Routing overhead for Piggyback

The total number of message is taken to synchronized base station or sink node is taken as routing overhead in our study. The routing overhead shown in Fig. 2 shows the characteristic of GSP+AODV and AODV with regard to routing overhead. On the average GSP+AODV reduces the routing overhead by 20 percent as compared to AODV. This is because while we send a message to synchronize we used a piggy-backing which uses a lower level for timestamp as a result overhead decreases.

3. Packet Network Delay

The ratio of data packets delivered to the destination and the data packets generated by the source are taken packet delay ratio. Because synchronized take place from top to bottom which reduces clock drift and guard band can't detect.

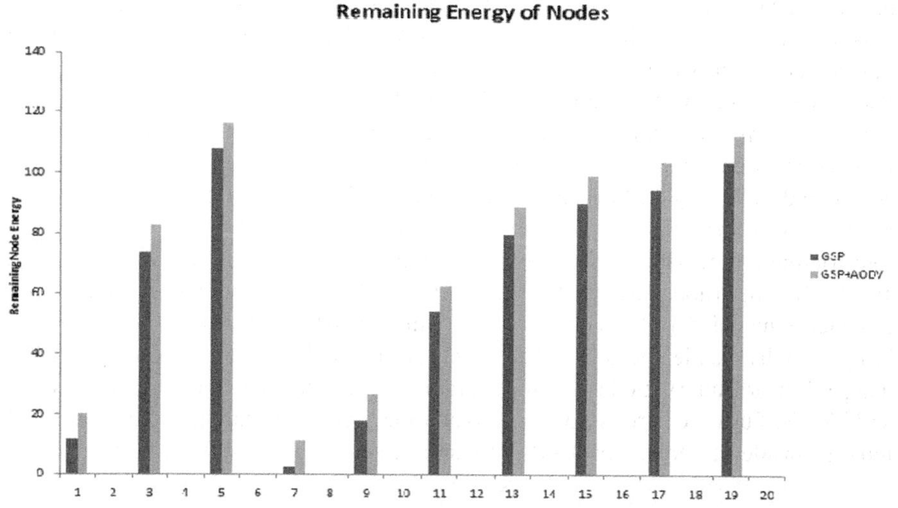

Fig. 1.

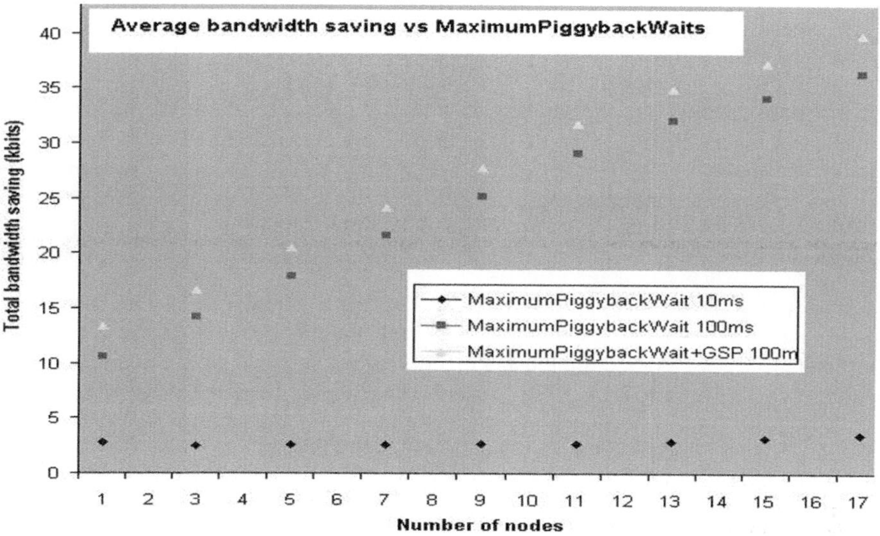

Fig. 2.

5 Conclusion and Future Work

Our research state due to this protocol ie GSP energy consumption is more evenly distributed in the entire network since the average energy of the network decrease because the traffic forwarding continuously via the same path can be avoided. To address various properties of GSP, e.g. With GSP using energy cosumption the network is fully reliable since entire nodes go to sleep in fully randomly fashion. So as a result there is no single point of failure or backbone infrastructure that can fail and therefore there is higher reliability. We are evaluating network lifetime improvement along with other standard metrics to find out effectiveness of the proposed scheme as compared to the existing ones. Deriving optimal values of protocol parameters for a given network configuration. Deriving optimal link of protocol parameters for given network configuration when both source and destination nodes is static so as to increase reliability is part of future work.

References

[1] Hou, X., Tipper, D.: Gossip-based sleep protocol (GSP) for energy efficient routing in wireless ad hoc networks. In: IEEE WCNC 2004, March 21-25, vol. 3, pp. 1305–1310 (2004)

[2] Bulut, E., Korpeoglu, I.: A Dynamic Sleep Scheduling Protocol for prolonging the Lifetime of Wireless Sensor Networks. In: 21st International Conference on AINAW 2007 (2007), 0-7695-2847-3/07

[3] Ye, F., Zhong, G., Lu, S., Zhang, L.: PEAS: A Robust Energy Conserving Protocol for Long-lived Sensor Networks. In: The 23rd International Conference on Distributed Computing Systems (2003)

[4] Ye, F., Lu, S., Zhang, L.: GRAdient Broadcast: A Robust, Long-lived Large Sensor Network (2001), http://irl.cs.ucla.edu/papers/grab-tech-report.ps

[5] Xu, Y., Heidemann, J., Estrin, D.: Adaptive Energy Conserving Routing for Multihop Ad Hoc Networks. USC/ISI Research Report 527 (2000)

[6] Chen, B., Jameison, K., Balakrishnan, H., Morris, R.: SPAN: An Energy Efficient Coordination Algorithm for Topology Maintenance in Ad Hoc Wireless Networks. In: Mobicom 2001 (2001)

[7] Tian, D., Georganas, N.: A Coverage-Preserving Node Scheduling Scheme for Large Wireless Sensor Networks. In: Proceedings of the 1st ACM International Workshop on Wireless Sensor Networks and Applications, Atlanta, Georgia, pp. 32–41 (2002)

[8] Heinzelman, W., Chandrakasan, A., Balakrishnan, H.: Energy-Efficient Communication Protocol for Wireless Sensor Networks. In: Proceedings of the Hawaii International Conference on System Sciences (2000)

[9] Kasten, O.: Energy consumption, http://www.inf.ethz.ch/kasten/research/bathtub/energyconsumption.html

[10] Ye, W., Heidemann, J., Estrin, D.: An Energy Efficient MAC Protocol for Wireless Sensor Networks. In: IEEE Infocom (2002)

[11] Akyildiz, I.F., Su, W., Sankarasubramaniam, Y., Cayirci, E.: Wireless Sensor Networks: A Survey. Computer Networks (2002)

[12] Xu, Y., Heidemann, J., Estrin, D.: Geography Informed Energy Conservation for Ad Hoc Routing. In: Mobicom (2001)

Mobility and Battery Power Prediction Based Job Scheduling in Mobile Grid Environment

S. Stephen Vaithiya and S. Mary Saira Bhanu

Department of Computer Science &Engineering,
National Institute of Technology, Tiruchirappalli, India
stephenvaithiya@gmail.com, msb@nitt.edu

Abstract. Over the past decade, the grid has emerged as an attractive platform to tackle various large-scale problems, especially in science and engineering. Recent advances in mobile communications and computing, and strong interest of the scientific community in the *Grid* have led to research into the *Mobile Grid*. However, mobile devices often have limited resources in terms of CPU, storage, battery power, and communication bandwidth. One primary issue associated with the efficient and effective utilization of mobile resources in a mobile grid is scheduling. Mobile grid scheduling involves a number of challenging issues, mainly due to the dynamic nature of the mobile grid. In this paper, a task scheduling algorithm is proposed based on the dynamic availability prediction of mobile resources. A just-in-time approach is employed in this paper where availability prediction of a mobile resource is evaluated as tasks are submitted, allowing the system to consider run-time parameters (mobility and battery power) prior to execution. The evaluation study employs a number of experiments with various simulation settings. The simulation results points to the efficacy of the proposed work.

Keywords: mobile grid, movement model, mapper, C-rate.

1 Introduction

Grid computing is based on the coordinated sharing of distributed and heterogeneous resources to solve large-scale problems in dynamic virtual organizations. With the advent of high bandwidth third-generation mobile networks and other wireless networks, grid computing has migrated from traditional parallel and distributed computing to pervasive and utility computing based on the wireless networks and mobile devices, which results in the emergence of a new computing paradigm named mobile grid.

Mobile grid integrates traditional wired grid through wireless channel to share grid resources to mobile users or provide resources to grid [1]. Mobile devices have advantages over fixed computing resources such as mobility, portability, and pervasiveness. These strengths allows mobile grid well-applied to location-restricted fields requiring supportive infrastructure in wildfire prevention, disaster management, and e-health system, etc [2]. The exploding number of mobile devices implies an immense potential of the new breed even if an individual mobile device still has limitations in terms of computing resources and network stability. While integrating grid with

D. Nagamalai, E. Renault, and M. Dhanushkodi (Eds.): PDCTA 2011, CCIS 203, pp. 312–322, 2011.

mobile devices, the devices can act as service/resource consumer from the grid which offers reliability, performance and quality of service or they can act both as consumer and provider to host grid management services instead of relying on fixed infrastructure.

The characteristics of mobile devices such as inferior computing power, low network bandwidth, volatility, battery power, mobility and heterogeneity should be taken into account, to utilize mobile devices as resources. In such a resource-constrained environment, job scheduling plays a crucial role in overall performance. The scheduler should allocate jobs to proper mobile devices, minimize uncertainty in job execution and strive to optimize scheduling objectives such as maximize throughput, response time and balance available resources. However, it is impractical to assume that perfect performance information on underlying resources in a mobile grid is readily available. Especially, since the mobile grid is much less stable than the wired environment, dynamism should be considered at the scheduling time. Job scheduling in mobile grids thus require a robust system model that can incorporate all these factors. In order to meet the dynamic and mobile nature of resources, the availability should be predicted.

In this paper a scheduling algorithm is proposed which take into account the availability prediction of resources. The availability is predicted for mobility and battery power of mobile resources. The proposed work analyzed mobility patterns to quantitatively measure the resource physical availability. The battery power prediction is based on the C- rate of the battery.

The rest of the paper is structured as follows. Section 2 discusses the related work. Section 3 presents the system model in mobile grid. Section 4 describes the proposed scheduling algorithm. Section 5 deals with experimental setup and the performance analysis of the proposed algorithm. Section 6 gives the conclusion of the paper.

2 Related Work

Several studies are going on in scheduling issues in mobile grid focusing on power efficiency, communication availability due to mobility, and job replication. Kasula et al. [3] proposes a layered system model to bridge the gap between mobile and grid computing world. The paper presents an efficient algorithm, which addresses the problem of scheduling in the presence of nodes disconnection. Ghosh et al. [4] proposed a game theoretic pricing strategy for efficient job allocation in mobile grids. They proposed a two-player, non-cooperative, alternating-offer bargaining game between the Wireless Access Point Server and the mobile devices to determine a fair pricing strategy, which is then used to effectively allocate jobs to the mobile devices with a goal to maximize the revenue for the grid users. Chang-Qin Huang et al. [5] presents power-Aware hierarchical scheduling in wireless Grids. The mobile node selection is targeted to minimize the energy consumed for communication and computation. Farooq et al. [6] devised a generic mobility model to predict a time duration for which a resource will remain in a specific domain. It is based on learning from the resource's behavior in the past and not by the random movement of mobile devices. JongHyuk Lee et al [7] presents a novel balanced scheduling algorithm in mobile grid, taking into account the mobility and availability in scheduling. This classifies the mobile devices into nine groups based on full availability and partial availability. The availability is calculated by considering the uptime and downtime.

From the above literature it has been observed that either the mobility or battery power of the resource is considered for scheduling tasks in the mobile grid environment. The proposed work quantitatively predicts resource availability dynamically by taking parameters of mobile resources such as the mobility and battery power. The mobility within the cell is considered for predicting resource physical availability. Battery availability considers energy consumed for communication and computation of mobile grid user in addition to the mobile user's current usage.

3 The Proposed System Model and Scheduler

Fig. 1 illustrates a mobile grid system. It is based on a wireless cellular network in which each cell consists of a number of mobile devices. Mobile devices residing in a cell of wireless networks are coordinated by a central entity that resides at the Access Point/ Base Station (BS). Mobile devices (M) can be used as both resource consumers (M_U) and resource providers (M_{RP}). In mobile grid, submitting jobs and receiving the results back are not straightforward, since power constraints and frequent disconnections are prevalent in wireless and mobile communications. The BS is used as a gateway to the grid.

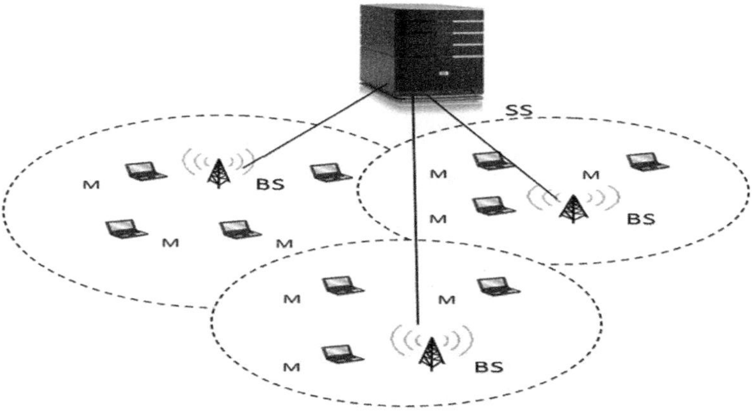

Fig. 1. Proposed mobile grid system

The BS in each cell acts as the scheduler, and undertakes the role of the mediator between the mobile device and the grid system, and try to hide the instability of the wireless/mobile environment by acting on behalf of the mobile resource. The mobile devices provide the description of their capabilities and the degree of their availability to the scheduler. The scheduler is then responsible for decomposing incoming request and scheduling the overall execution by providing specific tasks to each of the participating mobile devices. It is capable of hiding the heterogeneity of the participating devices from the requesting node, coordinating the overall execution of the submitted job and allowing the mobile device to appear to the rest of the network as an ordinary mobile resource. If BS cannot find a suitable resource provider in its region, it passes the request to the super scheduler (SS). The SS has the entire information about the grid community. Fig. 2 illustrates the proposed mobile grid scheduler.

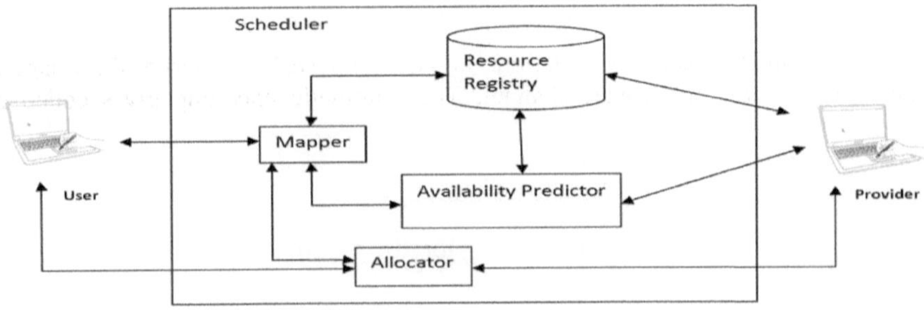

Fig. 2. Proposed mobile grid scheduler

The components of the mobile grid scheduler are Resource Registry (RR), Availability Predictor (AP), Mapper, and Allocator.

3.1 Resource Registry

The information about the registered resources is stored in the resource registry in the following format.

< *resource id,* system specification, *movement pattern, previous location of* M_{RP}, *current location of* M_{RP}, *battery info, Base Station info* >

resource id → A unique name for the particular resource.
system specification (S_{spec}) → processor and memory information
movement pattern → unknown or known with total duration
previous location of M_{RP} → geographical point at which the mobile resource stays previously.
current location of M_{RP} → geographical point at which the mobile resource stays at present.
battery info → capacity of the battery, C-rate and current battery power.
base station info → base station location.

3.2 Availability Predictor

The availability predictor predicts dynamic availability of the registered mobile resources.

Physical Availability Prediction. The physical availability is predicted based on movement type and movement model of the mobile resource.

Movement Type Prediction. The movement type is predicted based on the movement direction of mobile resource to the BS. There are two movement types namely movement towards BS and movement apart from BS. The movement type is predicted based on the concept of Markov chain process i.e. the mobile resource current location only depends on the previous location of the mobile resource. The locations of the mobile resources are found by the GPS which is part of the mobile devices. The distance between the mobile resource and the BS is found by using the Haversine formula [8]. The previous distance to the BS (D_β) is computed from,

$$D_\beta = R * c \tag{1}$$

where R is the radius of earth and $c = 2 * a\tan\left(2\left(\sqrt{a}, \sqrt{(1-a)}\right)\right)$

where $a = \sin^2(\Delta lat/2) + \cos(lat_\alpha)\cos(lat_\beta)\sin^2\left(\frac{\Delta long}{2}\right)$

where $\Delta lat = lat_\beta - lat_\alpha$, $\Delta long = long_\beta - long_\alpha$, α is location of BS and β is previous location of M_{RP}

The current distance to the BS (D_λ) is derived from,

$$D_\lambda = R * c \tag{2}$$

where R is the radius of earth and $c = 2 * a\tan\left(2\left(\sqrt{a}, \sqrt{(1-a)}\right)\right)$

where $a = \sin^2(\Delta lat/2) + \cos(lat_\alpha)\cos(lat_\lambda)\sin^2\left(\frac{\Delta long}{2}\right)$

where $\Delta lat = lat_\lambda - lat_\alpha$, $\Delta long = long_\lambda - long_\alpha$ and λ is current location of M_{RP}

From (1) and (2), if D_β is greater than D_λ then the movement type is towards BS otherwise movement type is apart from the BS.

Movement Model Prediction. The movement model prediction predicts the movement pattern of the mobile resource within the cell. The movement of the resource is predicted based on the movement model which can be a known movement model or unknown movement model.

The known movement model consists of identical movement patterns of each mobile device which represents the special behaviour of the movement of the mobile device within a defined period of time. There are two types known movement models namely movement circle (MC) and movement track (MT) models. The MC model is based on the assumption that wherever a user moves from a location, the user will eventually return or has returned back to the location. Thus, the movement behaviour of mobile users is modelled as different circle like patterns. The MT is a unidirectional itinerary which begins and ends with a stationary location or a boundary location. The MC/MT model assumes that the movement state has some regular patterns and the probability distributions for its future development depend very much on how and from where the process arrived in that location.

The physical availability of the known movement model can be computed by

$$Physical\ Availability = D_T - D_C \tag{3}$$

where D_T is the total life time of resource in a region and D_C is the current duration of the M_{RP} in the region.

The unknown movement model is the one whose movement pattern is random. The movement of a mobile user can be modeled by a discrete parameter and discrete state stochastic process if and only if it is assumed that the movement is random. Therefore, the Markov chain model is used to describe the behavior of the random parts of the user's movement. The Markov model assumes that location is random variable and the probability distributions for its future development depend only on the present location.

The physical availability of the unknown movement model can be computed by

$$Physical\ Availability = (BS\ \text{coverage area} - D_\lambda)/Mobility \tag{4}$$

where Mobility is the time taken by the M_{RP} to move from one location to another location and determined by

$$Mobility = (D_\beta - D_\lambda)/time\ \text{taken to reach from}\ \beta\ \text{to}\ \lambda$$

Battery Power Prediction. The battery availability is computed based on the battery capacity (C), C – rate and the current battery power usage. The C-rate is used to measure the charge and discharge current of a battery. On a new battery with a good load current characteristic or low internal resistance, the difference in the readings is only a few percentage points. On a battery exhibiting high internal resistance, the difference in capacity readings could swing plus/minus 10 percent or more. To compensate for the different readings at various discharge currents, error factor is included in battery availability prediction. Applying the error factor does not improve battery performance; it merely adjusts the availability calculation if discharged at a higher or lower C-rate than specified.

The available battery duration (B_{AD}) is determined by

$$B_{AD} = B_{TD} - B_{CD} - Error\ Factor \tag{5}$$

where the B_{TD} is the total battery duration and it is determined by

$$B_{TD} = C / C - rate$$

and B_{CD} is the current battery duration and it is determined by

$$B_{CD} = Current\ Battery\ Power\ in\ Percentage * B_{TD}$$

3.3 Mapper

The mapper performs following mapping process namely user identification, system specification and task requirement mapping. The user identification is done by mapping the user id in the RR, the system specification mapping is done by checking the system specification in the RR, and task requirement mapping is done by mapping the task requirement with the dynamically predicted resource availability. If the user requirements are met then these details about the resources are sent to the resource allocator.

3.4 Allocator

On receipt of resource details, the allocator checks priority of the resource to ascertain whether the task can execute on the available resources and meet the user-specified deadline. The resource allocator sets priority to registered resource based on availability factor (Physical Availability Factor (PAF), Battery Availability Factor (BAF) of the resource. If the availability of the resource is high, then the resource gets more priority than the other resources.

The PAF is determined by

$$PAF = \frac{PhysicalAvailability}{100}$$

if $PAF > 0.60$ then the priority is full
else if $PAF > 0.30 \&\& PAF <= 0.60$ then priority is high
else priority is low
BAF is determined by

$$BAF = \left(\frac{B_{AD}}{100}\right)$$

if $BAF > 0.60$ then the priority is full
else if $BAF > 0.30 \&\& BAF <= 0.60$ then priority is high
else priority is low

4 Proposed Algorithm

The factors that are taken into account when scheduling tasks on mobile grids are mobility and the battery power of mobile grid resources. In this section, a scheduling algorithm is presented, which incorporates mobility and battery power. Since the mobile grid resources fluctuate over time, the task requirements are organized dynamically during application runtime. In an attempt to efficiently deal with the dynamism of mobile grid resources, the algorithm adopts a resource prediction that is particularly helpful in avoiding serious schedule problems. The scheduler predicts the resource information based on mobility and battery power which is maintainable by the scheduler while scheduling the tasks. However, it is not assumed that the information is available for the next invocation of the application.

When a M_{RP} or M_U enters into a cell it register itself in the local scheduler by sending its id (M_{RP} id or M_U id), and the scheduler will authenticate M_{RP} or M_U by checking its id in the SS.

The table 1 gives the message format used by the resource as well as the consumer and table 2 gives the different types of flags used to differentiate data from control information. The proposed algorithm is given in the fig.3.

Table 1. Message format

2 bytes	2 bytes	2bits	6bytes
SRC	DEST	FLAG	Data/ACK

Table 2. Flag

FLAG	MEANING
00	DATA
01	ACK
10	NACK
11	SEND

5 Simulation Environment

Scheduling algorithm is evaluated using SimGrid toolkit [9]. A mobile grid environment is simulated with three cells, each with 2000 meters ×2000 meters. It is assumed that the tasks are independent and do not communicate among themselves or with other resources. The scheduler knows the internal task arrival rates and available bandwidth for all the resources. The immediate mode input model is used for the task distribution. The tasks are considered with uniform size. The available bandwidth is fixed and the same for each resource. It is assumed that once the resource is allotted for a task, it is available till the end of the task completion. The mobility and the battery power are considered for simulation.

Each mobile device in the simulated environment has a maximal radio range of 2000 m, and moves following a known or unknown mobility model. The speed of each mobile node is from 0 to 10 m/s. The mobile grid environment is dynamic and heterogeneous. The speeds of mobile devices have wide scope: some nodes are pedestrians, some nodes are vehicles. Mobile devices dynamically enter and leave the mobile grid. The movement pattern some of the resources is shown in the Fig.4.

Mobile device's battery capacity ([1.2KWPH, 4.4KWPH]) and current values of battery power are initialized with random values and current battery power changes dynamically with random values [0, 5]. Fig.5 shows the mobility pattern and battery power.

5.1 Experimental Results

The experiments were conducted using investigated effects of two factors (*i.e.* resource physical availability and battery power) on execution time.

Fig.6 shows the effect of resource's physical availability and battery power on average execution time when different number of jobs is executed. The effect of resource physical availability and battery power is experimented using PAF and BAF. As shown in the Fig.6, when the PAF >0.60 and BAF > 0.60 reports the shortest execution time this is due the higher priority of mobile resources. When PAF is 0.30<PAF<= 0.60 and BAF is 0.30<BAF<= 0.60 then the scheduler searchers for the other mobile resources with high priority within the cell and if it finds then sends the tasks to that resource. If it does not find any other resources then it checks the user requirement and if it is met then sends the job to that mobile resource. When the PAF and BAF is low the scheduler searches for higher priority mobile resources both within the cell and within other cells. If it finds the mobile devices with higher priority, then the scheduler sends the job to that mobile device. Otherwise it checks user requirement and sends the job to that resource. If the requirement is not met then the scheduler sends the job to the SS.

```
Algorithm:Job Scheduling in Mobile Grid Environment
Input: set of tasks
Output: a schedule on task onto mobile resources
begin
    send (source, destination, flag, data) // sending data
    begin while(1)
            begin send (source, destination, flag, data)
            end
    end
    int recv (source, destination, flag, data) // receiving data
    begin while(timer(5))
            begin flag =recv(source, destination, flag, data)
            end
    if (flag) return 0
    else return 1
    end
send (M_U, MP,11, M_Uid)                    //  M_U sends the M_Uid to the MP
if M_Uid is in RR then                      //  MP checks M_Uid in the RR
  flag ← recv ( MP,00,01,ACK)                 // receives ACK
if flag=0 send (M_U,MP,11, S_spec)          // M_U sends S_spec
else exit                                   // not member of grid
L1:if S_spec is in RR then                  // is S_spec in RR
     flag← recv (RR, M_U,01, ACK)                 // M_U receives ACK
else if S_spec is not met in current cell then
     send (M_U, AS, 11, S_spec)                   // M_U sends S_spec to AS
goto L1 else send (M_U, SS,11, S_spec)    // M_U sends S_spec to SS
goto L1
L2:if flag=0 send (M_U, MP, 11, TR)       // M_U sends TR to MP
     send (MP, AP, 11,request)                // MP sends request to AP
else goto L1
     L3: flag← recv (RR, AP, 00, static info of M_RP)
if flag=0 then L4: flag ← recv (M_RP, AP, 00, dynamic info of M_RP)
if flag = 0 then
   AP computes DA of M_RP         // computes physical and battery availability
else goto L4
else M_RP ++  goto L3
flag ← recv (AP, MP,00, DA of M_RP)   //MP receives DA of M_RP from AP
if flag = 0  then goto L5
else  goto L2
L5:if DA meets the TR then        // in current cell
     send (MP, JA, 11,M_RP info)        // MP sends M_RP info to JA
else if M_RP is not in current cell then
   send(MP , AS, 11, request) goto L2 // MP sends request to find DA in AS
else send (MP, SS,11, request) goto L2 // MP sends request to find DA in SS
if priority is met by M_RP then  // JA checks priority of M_RP
   send (JA, M_U, 11,M_RP id)      // JA sends M_RP id to M_U
   send (M_U, M_RP, 11,task)       // M_U sends task to M_RP
   M_RP executes the task
else goto L3
L6:if the task is done then
   send (M_RP , M_U , 11,output)       // M_RP sends output to M_U
else goto L3
   flag←recv(M_U, M_RP, 01,ACK)
if flag = 0  then              // checks ACK
destroy task
else goto L6
end
```

Fig. 3. Proposed algorithm

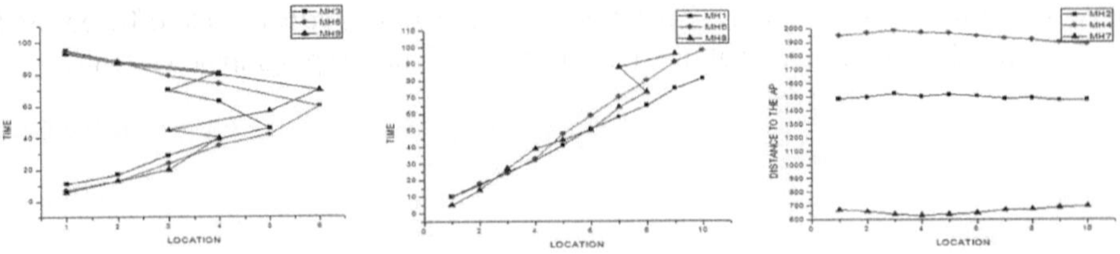

Fig. 4. Movement pattern of the mobile resources

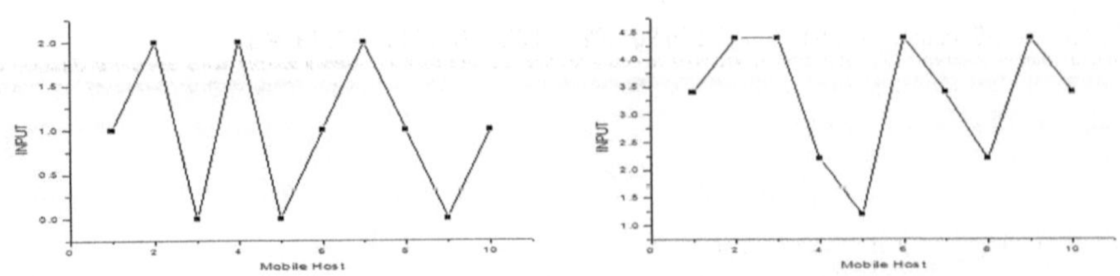

Fig. 5. Mobility Pattern and Battery Power

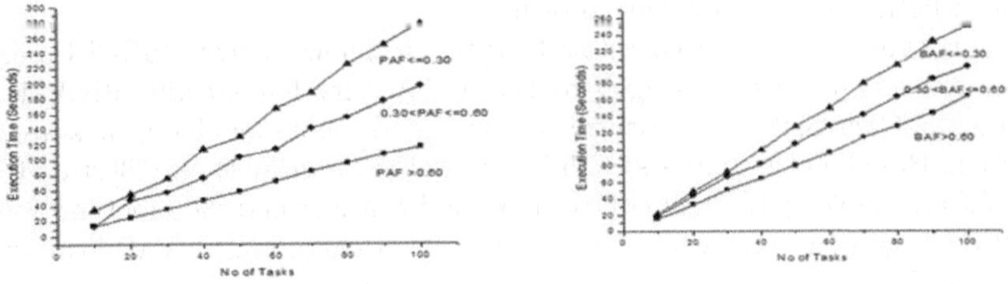

Fig. 6. A. Effect of Physical Availability and Battery Power on Execution Time

6 Conclusion

In this paper a task scheduling algorithm is presented for mobile grid environments based on dynamic availability prediction. The algorithm is carefully designed to incorporate the fundamental characteristics of the mobile grid (that is, mobility, dynamism and heterogeneity). A just-in-time approach is used for dynamic availability prediction. The simulation results point to the efficacy of proposed work and from these results, it is concluded that the PAF and BAF has an important role in the execution time as the difference in the execution time increases as the total number of tasks increases. The proposed work can be extended to include other dynamic parameters of mobile resources such as CPU and memory to increase the performance of the proposed system.

References

1. Otebolaku, A.M., Iyilade, J.S., Adigun, M.O.: CAAM: A context aware adaptation model for mobile grid service infrastructure. In: Proceedings of the 11th IEEE International Conference on Computational Science and Engineering, pp. 419–425 (2008)
2. Roy, N., Das, S.K.: Enhancing Availability of Grid Computational Services to Ubiquitous Computing Applications. IEEE Transactions on Parallel and Distributed Systems 20(7), 953–967 (2009)
3. Kiran, K.V.D.: Performance Analysis of Layered Architecture to Integrate Mobile Devices and Grid Computing with a Resource Scheduling Algorithm. In: Proceedings of the International Conference on Computational Intelligence and Multimedia Applications, vol. 4, pp. 352–356 (2007)
4. Preetam, G., Nirmalya, R., Das, S., Basu, K.: A Pricing Strategy for Job Allocation in Mobile Grids using a Non-Cooperative Bargaining Theory Framework. Special Issue on Design and Performance of Networks for Super-Cluster and Grid-Computing, pp. 1366–1383 (2005)
5. Huang, C.-Q., Zhu, Z.-T., Wu, Y.-H., Xiao, Z.-H.: Power-Aware Hierarchical Scheduling with Respect to Resource Intermittence in Wireless Grids. In: Proceedings of the Fifth International Conference on Machine Learning and Cybernetics, Dalian, pp. 693–698 (2006)
6. Farooq, U., Khalil, W.: A Generic Mobility Model for Resource Prediction in Mobile Grids. In: Proceedings of the International Symposium on Collaborative Technologies and Systems (2006)
7. Lee, J., Lee, H., Chung, K., Yu, H.: Balanced Scheduling Algorithm Considering Availability in Mobile Grid, pp. 212–222. Springer, Heidelberg (2009)
8. Yao, J.: Clustering in Ratemaking: with Application in Territories Clustering. Casualty Actuarial Society Discussion Paper Program Casualty Actuarial Society, Arlington, Virginia, pp. 170–192 (2008)
9. Casanova, H.: Simgrid: A Toolkit for the Simulation of Application Scheduling. In: Proceedings of 1st IEEE/ACM International Symposium on Cluster Computing and the Grid (2001)

Cell Range and Capability Analysis of WiMAX and LTE Network

Sandeep Singh Sengar and Neeraj Tyagi

Department of Computer Science & Engineering,
Motilal Nehru National Institute of Technology,
Allahabad, India-211004
sansen0911@gmail.com, neeraj@mnnit.ac.in

Abstract. WiMAX and LTE are the telecommunication technology standards. WiMAX and LTE both offer high data rate. Both are used to provide VOIP, online gaming, video conferencing, streaming media services to the users. In this paper we have done numerical analysis of WiMAX and LTE network in the form of maximum number of users supportable and minimum demand to all the users in a particular area based on different services provided by these networks and types of users. In this analysis we have found the actual bandwidth to transfer the data after reducing the overhead related to physical layer, MAC layer. In this paper analysis with matlab shows that LTE network performs better as compare to WiMAX network.

Keywords: WiMAX, LTE, Matlab, Overhead, Modulation, Coding, Downlink, Uplink.

1 Introduction

WiMAX (Worldwide Interoperability for Microwave Access) is a telecommunication technology that offers fixed and mobile internet access. WiMAX is a possible substitute candidate for cellular phone technologies such as GSM and CDMA, or can be used as an overlay to improve capacity. WiMAX not simply proposes high-speed broadband Internet access, but in addition VoIP (Voice over Internet Protocol) and IPTV (Internet Protocol Television) services to customers with comparative ease. This permits a WiMAX service to be a substitute for DSL, Cable and Telephony services [17]. Two standards WiMAX and LTE lead towards the next generation of mobile network standards. Mobile WiMAX exploits vigorous OFDMA physical layer with sub channelization allowing dynamic allotment of time and frequency resource to numerous users with non line of sight capability.

LTE is developed from 3G technology and identifies the long term evolution of the 3GPP UMTS/HSPA cellular technology. LTE uses OFDMA for DL and SC-FDMA (Single Carrier Frequency Division Multiple Access) for UL. LTE provides high mobility and high data rate up to 100 to 326.4 mbps for downlink and 50 to 86.4 mbps on the uplink depending on the antenna configurations and modulation technique [14].

D. Nagamalai, E. Renault, and M. Dhanushkodi (Eds.): PDCTA 2011, CCIS 203, pp. 323–333, 2011.

In this paper we have done overhead analysis of WiMAX and LTE network, and actual bandwidth to transfer only the data will be calculated after reducing the overhead related to physical layer and MAC layer. Physical layer overhead includes guard subcarrier, pilot sub carrier, DC sub carrier for multiplexing process, DL subframe, UL subframe overhead in frame structure and MAC layer overhead related to MAC PDU structure for both WiMAX and LTE network and in last we will compare the performance of both the LTE and WiMAX in shape of number of connected users and allocated bandwidth to each user, that performance will show LTE network can support more number of users with large bandwidth as comparison to the Mobile WiMAX.

2 Overview of Mobile WiMAX

WiMAX is a fast growing broadband wireless access technology, which is standardized by IEEE 802.16. The IEEE 802.16 standard identifies the MAC and Physical layers of the Open System Interconnection (OSI) model for WiMAX.

2.1 Physical Layer

Forward error correction coding, two way signal mapping, modulation and MIMO processing are carried out by Physical layer. Physical layer operations are given below.

2.1.1 Multiplexing Technique

WiMAX uses Orthogonal Frequency Division Multiplexing Access (OFDMA) for both Uplink (UL) and Downlink (DL) in physical layer. OFDMA is basically a hybrid of FDMA (Frequency Division Multiple Access) and TDMA (Time Division Multiple Access). Users are dynamically allocated subcarriers (using FDMA) in different time slots (using TDMA). UL part of physical layer uses scalable OFDMA i.e. bandwidth of the channel may depends on the number of users connected to it. OFDMA is used for performance modeling of Mobile WiMAX. Guard time between OFDM symbols is used for maintaining each OFDM symbol independent of the others after going through a wireless channel. OFDMA make use of several closely spaced sub-carriers, although the sub-carriers are partitioned into groups which are named a sub-channel. The sub-carriers that figure a sub-channel must not be adjacent. In the DL, a sub-channel may be anticipated for different recipients. Each OFDMA symbol contains data sub-carriers used for carry information, pilot sub-carriers as reference frequencies used for various synchronization and estimation purposes, DC sub-carrier like the center frequency, and guard sub-carriers for keeping the space between OFDMA signals [11] [8].

2.1.2 Channel Modulation and Coding

Mobile WiMAX uses BPSK, QPSK, 16-QAM, and 64-QAM Techniques for modulation purpose in UL and DL. QPSK, 16-QAM, 64-QAM is mandatory in DL but 64-QAM is optional in UL. Convolutional Coding and Convolutional Turbo Coding are used in Mobile WiMAX in which CC is the mandatory coding scheme. Table.1 shows the modulation and coding scheme in WIMAX [3] [15].

Table 1. Modulation Technique for WiMAX

Modulation Type	Coding Rate	Weight	K
BPSK	½	5%	1
QPSK	½	2.5%	2
QPSK	3/4	2.5%	2
16-QAM	½	5%	4
16-QAM	¾	5%	4
64-QAM	2/3	40%	6
64-QAM	3/4	40%	6

2.1.3 Frame Structure

Mobile WiMAX frame structure is divided into DL subframe and UL subframe. Both of two subframes are separated with a transmission gap. Mostly DL subframe occupies a higher ratio of the total frame. Preamble in the DL subframe is used for PHY layer procedures, like as initial channel estimation, time and frequency synchronization, and noise and interference estimation. Length and number of the bursts are specified by FCH (Frame Control Header). DL-MAP and UL-MAP contains the channel allocation information, Data burst includes the data for an individual user, and ranging in the UL is used for time and power synchronization purpose [9] [15] [3].

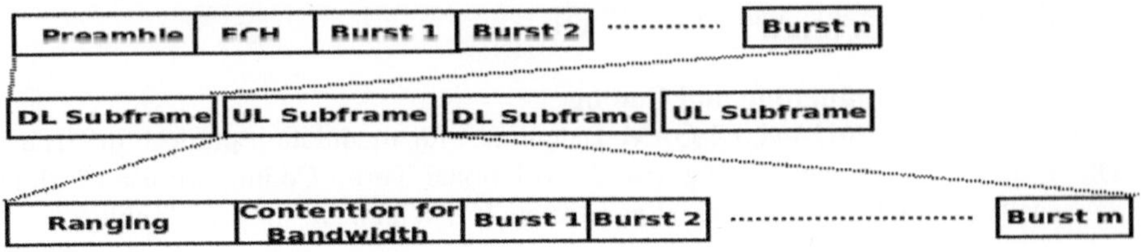

Fig. 1. WiMAX Frame Structure

2.2 MAC Layer

WiMAX MAC layer is divided in two parts MAC convergence sublayer (MCS) and MAC Common part sublayer (MCPS), MCS is used for classification and header suppression and MCPS for QoS, ARQ, Mobility Management, Security management, Connection management, Radio resource management [2]. MAC PDU structure for WiMAX is shown in Fig. 2.

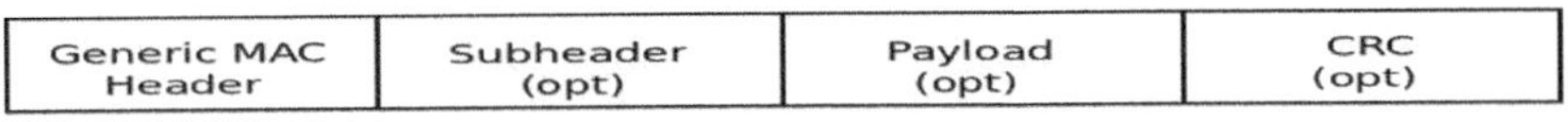

Fig. 2. MAC Protocol Data Unit Structure for WiMAX

3 Overview of Long Term Evolution

Long Term Evaluation (LTE) is the most recent standard in the telecommunication technology. It is standardized by 3GPP. LTE is the part of the GSM evolutionary path beyond 3G technology. The objective for LTE is to offer a tremendously high performance radio-access technology that provides full vehicular speed mobility and that can willingly coexist with HSPA and former networks.

3.1 Physical Layer

Physical layer in LTE includes the following parts.

3.1.1 Multiplexing Technique

OFDMA and SC-FDMA (Single Carrier Frequency Division Multiple Access) are used by LTE physical for DL and UL respectively. OFDMA symbol structure in LTE is same as WiMAX. SC-FDMA is also like as OFDMA, but numerous users can be assigned to a shared communication resource in SC-FDMA. SC-FDMA takes advantage of low peak to average power ratio (PAPR) as compared to S-OFDMA in WiMAX, which makes it appropriate for UL transmission user terminal. SC-FDMA covered the bandwidth is alike multi-carrier OFDMA. SC-FDMA is having advantage in the form of robust resistance to multipath without the problem of high PAPR. The area of SC-FDMA is limited to UL because the increased time-domain processing would be a considerable load on the BS [5].

3.1.2 Channel Modulation and Coding

LTE uses QPSK, 16-QAM, 64-QAM Techniques for modulation purpose in UL and DL. Both Convolutional Coding and Convolutional Turbo Coding are used in LTE same as WIMAX but with different parameters [6]. Which are shown in Table 2.

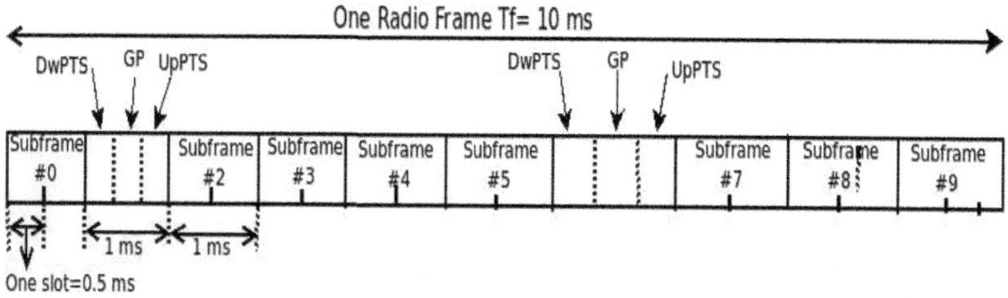

Fig. 3. LTE Frame Structure

3.1.3 Frame Structure

As shown in Fig. 3 Frame length of LTE is 10 ms and which is divided into 10 subframes of 1 ms each. Which are type of DL-subframe, UL-Subframe, and special subframe. DL-subframe and UL-subframe is further divided into two slots of .5 ms each. Special frame of 1 ms length contains three fields DwPTS (Downlink Pilot Timeslot), GP (Guard Period) and UpPTS (Uplink Pilot Timeslot) which are maintained by LTE TDD [12].

Table 2. Modulation Technique for LTE

Modulation Type	Coding Rate	Weight	K
QPSK	.076	2.6	2
QPSK	.117	2.6	2
QPSK	.188	2.6	2
QPSK	.301	2.6	2
QPSK	.438	2.6	2
QPSK	.588	2.6	2
16-QAM	.369	4	4
16-QAM	.479	4	4
16-QAM	.602	4	4
64-QAM	.455	12	6
64-QAM	.554	12	6
64-QAM	.650	12	6
64-QAM	.754	12	6
64-QAM	.853	12	6
64-QAM	.926	12	6

3.2 MAC Layer

MAC Layer in LTE provides the service to RLC layer by logical channel, error correction through HARQ, Control information is contained by MAC Control Element and MAC payload. MAC layer receives data from RLC layer in the form of MAC SDU. MAC PDU structure for LTE is shown in Fig. 4.

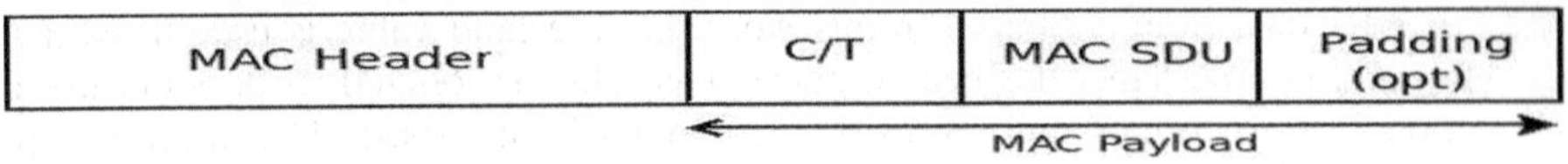

Fig. 4. MAC Protocol Data Unit Structure for LTE

3.3 RLC

The RLC (Radio Link Control) layer offers sequentially delivery of SDU to the upper layers and removes duplicate SDUs from being carried to the upper layers. The RLC layer is utilized to set-up and transport traffic among the UE and the eNB [7].

3.4 PDCP

The PDCP (Packet Data Control Protocol) layer is in charge for compressing/decompressing the headers of user plane IP packets using Robust Header Compression to permit efficient utilize of air interface bandwidth. This layer in addition executes ciphering of both user plane and control plane data [7].

3.5 RRC

The RRC (Radio Resource Control) layer in the eNB creates handover decisions based on neighbor cell measurements thrown by the UE, manages UE measurement reporting like as the periodicity of Channel Quality Information (CQI) reports, broadcasts system information and allots cell-level temporary identifiers to vigorous UEs. RRC in addition performs movement of UE context from the source eNB to the target eNB for the period of handover, and does integrity protection of RRC messages [14]. It is liable for the protection and setting up of radio bearers.

4 Overhead Analysis

In this paper we have done analysis of overhead in WiMAX and LTE network. After analysis we have reduced the overhead to find the actual bandwidth used in only transfer the data. So by using that we can find out how many maximum numbers of users can be connected to network and what will be the allocated bandwidth to the users.

4.1 Physical Layer Overhead

Physical layer overhead is divided into two parts

4.1.1 Downlink Overhead

In downlink subframe overhead consist of Guard and DC-subcarrier, preamble, FCH, DL-MAP, UL-MAP, burst used in DCD (Downlink Channel Descriptor) and UCD (Uplink Channel Descriptor). Here guard and DC-subcarrier (Transmission gap) is used to separate the DL/UL subframe and it is represented by cyclic prefix in OFDM symbol structure. FCH provides some properties of burst like duration and number of the bursts [7] [13]. Broadcasted Channel allocation information is provided by DL/UL MAP. DL and UL MAP information contains 8 and 11 bytes respectively for Header and 4 and 6 bytes respectively for Information Element. After listening the MAP information user can identify the subcarriers allocated to user in both DL and UL. DCD and UCD contain DL/UL burst profile information which occupied 9 and 4 bytes respectively.

4.1.2 Uplink Overhead

Useful bandwidth calculation procedure in UL is alike to the DL in numerous steps. BRH is used for bandwidth request allocation within the contention intervals that are periodically assigned in the UL subframe. But here in UL initial ranging and contention interval also used. The network administrator defines the size of initial ranging and contention interval. Initial and periodical ranging permits the BS and the MS to achieve time and power synchronization. Initial ranging take place once per connecting user and the periodical ranging should be done at least each 1.5 seconds in Wi-MAX and 2 seconds in LTE [11]. Ranging overhead in WiMAX may be calculated as

$$N_{Ranging} = (\text{Frame Length/Periodic Ranging Time}) \times (4/N_{S\text{-}UL}) \qquad (1)$$

Contention interval may be calculated as:

$$N_{Contention} = (\text{Frame Length/PPI}) \times (N\times(\text{BRH Size/MAU})+1)/ N_{S\text{-}UL} \quad (2)$$

Here $N_{S\text{-}UL}$ is the total number of symbols in UL subframe, PPI is the Periodic polling interval to send one BRH. N is the number of users connected. BRH size is the total size of Header and CRC, MAU is the Minimum Allocation Unit for user.

4.2 MAC Layer Overhead

MAC Protocol data unit (PDU) is the smallest unit in MAC for data transfer. WiMAX MAC PDU contains 6 bytes of generic header, optional payload of 0-2041bytes, 3 bytes for packing and fragmentation of sub header and 4bytes of CRC. It may also contain variable length optional sub headers for different purposes, which is shown in Fig. 2. MAC may also contain other types of bandwidth request PDU which only contains bandwidth request header with no payload and CRC field [3]. LTE MAC PDU format is different from WiMAX PDU which contains MAC Header, and MAC payload. MAC Header is divided into several sub headers for different purposes. MAC payload part contains 0 or more MAC control element, 0 or more MAC SDU (Service Data Unit) and optional padding field [6]. LTE MAC PDU contains 1.5 bytes for Packet Data Convergence Protocol header, .37 bytes of TCTF (target Channel Type Field), 4 Bytes for UE ID, .5 bytes for Control and transport, 3 bytes of CRC, 1byetes for Grant management. The size of MAC PDU in LTE is variable [5].

5 Configuration Parameters

We have used following application services provided by WiMAX and LTE Network. Table 3 shows the application datarate load [16].

Table 3. Application Data-Rate Load

Application	Data rate	Use
On Line Gaming	50kbps	22%
VoIP, Video Conf., Real Time Vedio	40kbps	12%
Streaming Media	135.73kbps	15.5%
Web Browsing + Email	Nominal	28%+4.5%
Media Content Downloading	BE	18%

WiMAX and LTE system parameters [13] [10] [8] used in analysis are given below in Table 4 and Table 5 respectively.

6 Simulation Result

To analyze the performance of WiMAX and LTE network, we build the simulation model developed using Matlab. We have used two different types of user urban class and suburban class for both WiMAX and LTE Network and analyzed the performance of WiMAX and LTE network in form of Demand and Capacity.

Table 4. WiMAX System Parameters

Parameters	Values		
Downlink			
System Bandwidth (MHZ)	5	10	20
FFT Size	512	1024	2048
Number of Data subcarriers	360	720	1440
Number of Null/guard subcarriers	92	184	368
Number of pilot subcarriers	60	120	240
Uplink			
Number of Data subcarriers	272	560	1130
Number of Null/guard subcarriers	103	183	367
Number of pilot subcarriers	137	281	551
Fixed Useful Symbol Duration (ms)	.0914		
Cyclic Prefix Rate	1/32, 1/16, 1/8, 1/4		
Frame Length (ms)	5		
Transmission gap duration (ms)	0.0114		

Table 5. LTE System Parameters

Parameters	Values				
System Bandwidth (MHZ)	2.5	5	10	15	20
FFT Size	256	512	1024	1536	2048
Number of Data subcarriers	151	301	601	901	1201
Number of Null/guard subcarriers	105	211	423	635	847
Number of Resource Blocks	12	25	50	75	100
Cyclic Prefix Rate	4.7, 16.7				
Frame Length (ms)	10				
Subframe Length (ms)	1				
Transmission gap duration (ms)	0.0057				
OFDM Symbols/Subframe	7/6				

We have taken 60% urban users and 40% sub urban users, require data rate for urban and sub urban class users are 1200 Kbps and 1000 Kbps respectively, Contention ratio is 30, 10 for urban and sub urban class users respectively. WiMAX and LTE

Table 6. Input Parameters of WiMAX and LTE

Parameters	Values (WiMAX)	Values (LTE)
Channel Bandwidth	5	10
DL/UL Frame Ratio	3/1	5/3
DL/UL Traffic Ratio	4	4
Cyclic Prefix Rate	8	16.7
Number of Connections per PDU	3	5
Number of PDUs per data burst	3	5

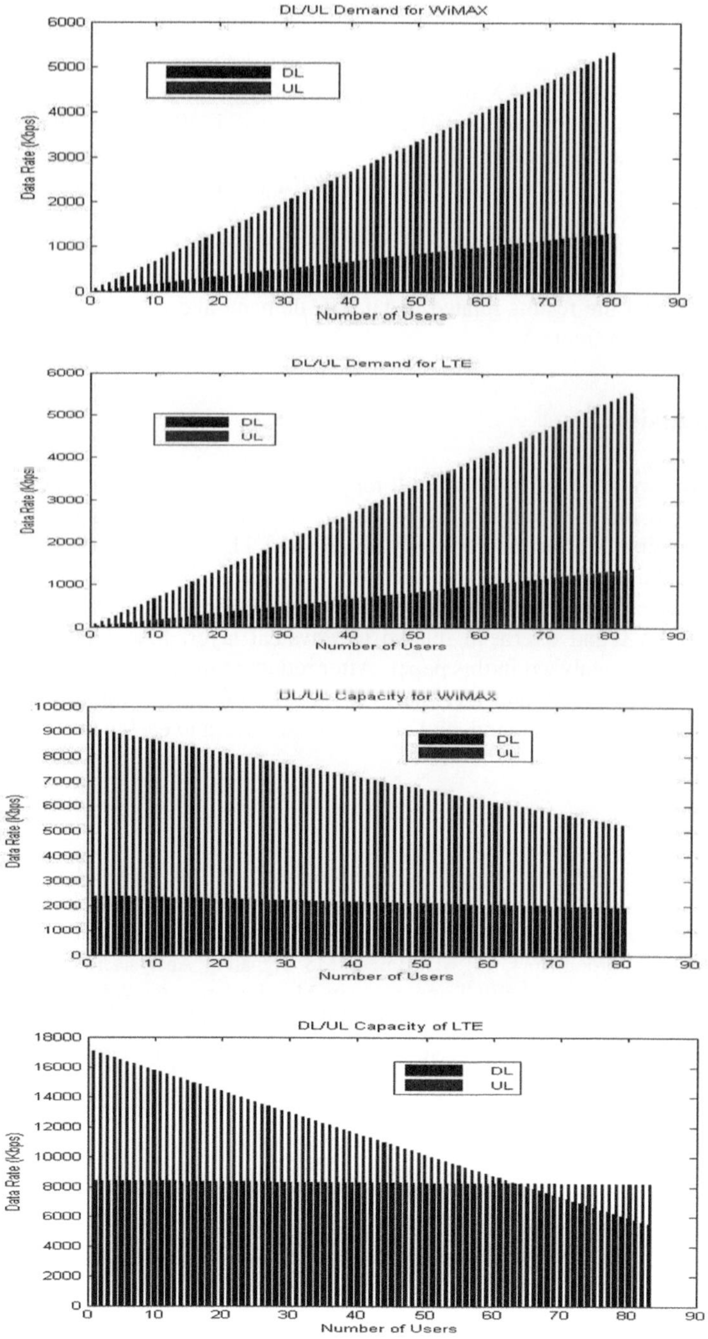

Fig. 5. DL/UL Demand and Capacity for WiMAX and LTE Network

system input parameters used in simulation are shown in Table 6. As can be examined, on the basis of input parameters, 80, 83 users can be simultaneously supported with the specified sector for WiMAX and LTE networks respectively. Peak offered data rate for WiMAX in DL is 9147.62 Kbps that decreases to 5288.26 Kbps as the numbers of users reach to 80 and for LTE it is 17196.2 Kbps that decreases to 5623.16 Kbps as the number of users reaches to 83. Minimum demand in DL for simultaneously connected 80, 83 users in WiMAX and LTE network are 5337.62 Kbps, 5537.78 Kbps.

Both the demand in WiMAX and LTE can be accomplished by available bandwidth. This result shows that LTE network is having best performance as comparison to WiMAX. All the results related to DL/UL demand and capacity for WiMAX and LTE are shown in figure 5.

7 Conclusion

In this paper we have analyzed the cell range, capability of Mobile WiMAX and LTE network by using different application data rate load, multiplexing and modulation techniques. First of all overview of WiMAX and LTE network are presented then we have found the maximum capacity and minimum demand for the network after reducing the overhead part. Overhead related to Physical layer (UL and DL), Mac layer in mobile WiMAX and overhead related to Physical layer, Mac Layer, RLC, PDCP, RRC in LTE are analyzed in this paper. After reducing the overhead we have done the comparison of WiMAX and LTE network in the form of maximum number of user supportable, minimum demand, and allocated bandwidth to each user.

References

1. Molteni, D., Nicoli, M., Spagnolin, U.: Performance of MIMO-OFDMA Systems in Correlated Fading Channels and Non-Stationary Interference. IEEE Transactions on Wireless Communications (99), 1–15 (2011)
2. Munir, A., Gordon-Ross, A.: SIP-Based IMS Signaling Analysis for WiMax-3G Interworking Architectures. IEEE Transactions on Mobile Computing 9(5) (2010)
3. So-In, C., Jain, R., Tamimi, A.K.: Capacity Evaluation for IEEE 802.16e Mobile WiMAX. J. Computer Systems, Networks, and Communications 2010 (2009), doi:10.1155/2010/279807
4. Banawan, K.A.S., Abdullah, M.S., El-Gharabawy, M.A.G.M.: Comparative study between Mobile WiMAX (IEEE802.16e based) and 3GPP LTE, `http://xa.yimg.com/kq/groups/20725580/2080579529/name/Comparative_study_between_Mobile_WiMAX_and_LTE_v3.pdf`
5. Hamza, A.: Long Term Evolution (LTE) - A Tutorial (2009)
6. WiMAX^{TM}, HSPA+, and LTE: A Comparative Analysis. WiMAX Forum (2009)
7. UMTS Long Term Evolution (LTE) Technology Introduction: Rohde & Schwarz Products (2009)
8. Bian, Y.Q., Nix, A.R.: Mobile WiMAX Multi-Cell Network Evaluation and Capacity Optimization. In: IEEE International Conference on Vehicular Technology Conference, ver. 2008, pp. 1276–1280 (2008), doi:10.1109/VETECS.2008.269

9. Ahmadzadeh, A.M.: Capacity and Cell-Range Estimation for Multitraffic Users in Mobile WiMAX. PhD thesis, University College of Bors (2008)
10. Mach, P., Bestak, R.: WiMAX performance evaluation. In: Sixth IEEE International Conference on Networking (ICN 2007) (2007), doi:0-7695-2805-8/07
11. Hasan, M.A.: Performance Evaluation of WiMAX/IEEE 802.16 OFDM Physical Layer. PhD thesis, Helsinki University of Technology (2007)
12. Zyren, J.: Overview of the 3GPP Long Term Evolution Physical Layer. White Paper (2007)
13. Mobile WiMAX – Part I: A Technical Overview and Performance Evaluation. WiMAX Forum (2006)
14. Long Term Evolution (LTE): A Technical Overview, Technical White Paper
15. WiMAX Capacity: Technical White Paper, SR Telecom
16. Wireless Communications Products/Services/Applications & Industries Site Map, http://wireless.agilent.com/
17. WiMAX Technology for Broadband Wireless Access, http://ylib.com/books/en/4.1.36.1.36/1/
18. WiMAX-OFDM Basics, http://www.tutorialspoint.com/wimax/index.htm

A Parallel Task Assignment Using Heuristic Graph Matching

R. Mohan[1] and Amitava Gupta[2]

[1] Dept. of Computer Science and Engineering,
National Institute of Technology,
Tiruchirapalli, Tamil Nadu 620015, India
rmohan@nitt.edu

[2] Dept. of Power Engineering, Jadavapur University,
Kolkata, West Bengal 700098, India
amitg@pe.jusl.ac.in

Abstract. Task assignment is one of the most challenging problems in distributed computing environment. An optimal task assignment guarantees minimum turnaround time for a given architecture. Using heuristic graph matching, it is often impossible to get optimal task assignment for practical test cases within an acceptable time limit. In this paper, the basic heuristic graph-matching algorithm of task assignment is parallelized which is suitable only for cases where processors and inter processor links are homogeneous. This proposal is a derivative of the basic task assignment methodology using heuristic graph matching. The results show that near optimal assignments (greater than ninety percentage) are obtained much faster than the sequential program with reasonable speed-up.

Keyword: task assignment, load balancing, graph partition, heuristic graph matching, symmetrical multi-processors.

1 Introduction

Load balancing is the process by which task modules constituting an application are assigned to processors, with the goals of maximizing the *processor utilization* and minimizing the *total turnaround time*. This can be viewed as a task assignment problem by which task modules are assigned to available processors in order to achieve the aforesaid two goals. Achievement of the above proposal is possible by a number of techniques viz. *graph partitioning, graph matching, hybrid methodology and mathemat- ical programming*. First, a survey of task assignment strategies is presented. Next, the heuristic graph matching based task assignment by methodology of Shen *et. al.* [3] is explained. Finally the parallel algorithm is presented and its performance is analyzed using several representative test cases.

1.1 Graph Partitioning Based Methodologies

Graph partitioning techniques view the task as a task graph where the vertices represent the task modules and edges represent the communication between those

D. Nagamalai, E. Renault, and M. Dhanushkodi (Eds.): PDCTA 2011, CCIS 203, pp. 334–343, 2011.

tasks. In load balancing, the graph partitioning methodologies are used to produce equal partitions of the task graph with the inter-node communication or the volume of such communication minimized. The number of partitions depends on the number of processing elements and their topology in the processor graph. Some factors are:

- Load balance The computational work of each processor should be balanced, so that no processor will be waiting for others to complete.
- Communication cost On a parallel computer, accumulating the contributions from nodes that are not on the current processor will incur communication cost which must be minimized.

The graph bisection problem has been studied by many authors (refer [4, 5, 6]) in the context of graph theory as well as VLSI circuit layout. Advances in parallel computing hardware and software have renewed interest in the problem. The graph bisection problem is a NP hard problem, so there are no known algorithms that can find the exact solution to the problem in polynomial time. Most of the graph bisection methods, therefore, seek a good approximation to the optimal partitioning that can be calculated efficiently. Some already proposed algorithms are:

- *Recursive graph bisection (RGB) algorithm* [6] attempts to partition the task graph recursively
- *Greedy algorithm* starts with a vertex with the smallest degree, and marks its neighbours, and then the neighbours' neighbours.
- K-L (*Kernighan-Lin) algorithm* ([4, 8, 9]) is an iterative algorithm. Starting from a load balanced initial bisection, it first calculates for each vertex the gain in the reduction of edge-cut that may result if that vertex is moved from one partition of the graph to the other. In each of inner iteration, it moves the unlocked vertex that has the highest gain, from the partition in surplus to the partition in deficit. This vertex is then locked and the gains updated. The procedure stops if the gain of the move is negative, and this negative move is undone which results with bisection with the smallest edge-cut in this iteration. Other iterations will continue until that time. If one iteration fails to result in reduction of edge-cut, the problem terminates.

1.1.1 Parallel Partitioning Algorithms

Although the multilevel approach of Kernighan-Lin Algorithm reduces the computing time significantly, it can prove to be memory intensive for a very large task graph - often exceeding the limits of single CPU memories. Furthermore as the ultimate purpose of partitioning is for the subsequent implementation of the application code on parallel machines, it makes sense to have a parallel partitioning code. Besides, a fast parallel partitioning algorithm can also be used for the purpose of dynamic load balancing. There have been a number of efforts in this area.

In [10, 11], the multilevel spectral bisection was parallelized specifically for the Cray architecture using the Cray SHMEM facility. The linear algebra algorithms are used to parallelize the tasks. Difficulties arose in the parallel graph coarsening, in particular, in the parallel generation of the maximal independent set. These were tackled by using a number of parallel graph theory algorithms. On a 256 processor

Cray T3D, the resulting algorithm PMRSB (Parallel multilevel recursive bisection algorithm) is able to partition a graph of 1/4 million vertices into 256 sub domains, which is 140 times faster than a workstation using an equivalent serial algorithm.

The parallel partitioning algorithms use a different refinement strategy. This algorithm is designed also for *dynamic load balancing*, the initial partitioning is assumed to be unbalanced. For any two neighbouring sub domains p and q, the flow (the amount of load to be migrated to achieve global load balance) is first calculated. The flow from p to q is denoted as $f(pq)$. Let $g(pq)$ denote the total weight of the vertices on the boundary of p which have a preference to migrate to q. Let $d = max(g(pq) \quad f(pq) + g(qp) \quad f(qp), 0)$, which represents the total weight of all boundary vertices with a positive gain after the flow is satisfied. Then the load has to be migrated from p to q. This allows the flow to be satisfied and at the same time an additional load of equal amount is exchanged between the two processors to optimize the edge-cut.

In other parallel graph partitioning algorithms, the parallel single level algorithm, combining inertia bisection with K-L refinement was implemented. Possible conflict during the refinement stage was avoided by the pairing of processors based on the edge coloring of the processor graph. The quality of the partition was not as good as multilevel algorithms. Then a spectral inertia bisection algorithm was introduced. The spectral set of eigenvectors for the coarsest graph was first calculated which serves as the spectral coordinates of the vertices. The graph was partitioned with the inertia bisection algorithm, based on these spectral coordinates. Part of the algorithm was parallelized. This algorithm is also suitable for dynamic load balancing on applications where the mesh is enriched by the refinement of the individual elements. In such a case, the refinement can be captured by updating the vertex weights of the dual graph of the mesh, without changing the graph itself. The mesh is repartitioned quickly after refinement, using the spectral information originally calculated for the top-level coarse mesh. Since the size of the dual graph does not change, the repartitioning time does not change with the increase of the mesh size, as the refinement steps are carried out.

1.2 Heuristic Graph Matching

This is a graph matching based method, which uses a *task-graph* and a *processor-graph*. While the task-graph denotes the dependency among the task modules, the *processor-graph* defines the topology of interconnection amongst the processors. A classical example of this is the work by Shen *et al.* [3] which uses the well-known A* algorithm to find the optimal task assignment.

A *mapping* implies assignment of any one or more of the n task modules to any one or more of the p processors with no task module assigned to more than one processor. This *branch and bound heuristics* based methods starts by an initial mapping and expands the state-space by generating other permissible mappings. Each mapping or state-space entry has a cost function associated which is denoted by f . In [3], this cost function is expressed in terms of a single entity viz. time may be considered to be composed of two parts viz. g which may be viewed as the cost of generation of the state-space entry and h, which may be viewed as the cost to generate the goal-state from the present state-space entry and is the heuristic weight associated with the state-space entry. Thus, for each mapping or state-space entry,

$$f = g + h \tag{1}$$

As long as there is an upper bound h_{max} for h, i.e. $h \leq h_{max}$, the A* algorithm guarantees that an optimal solution is found [14]. Thus with $g = 0$, the search becomes a purely heuristic search and with $h = 0$ it becomes a *best-first* search.

If n task modules are assigned to m processors, there can be m^n assignments theoretically possible. The method proposed by Shen *et. al.* has a typical complexity of $O(n^2)$ for $n \leq 20$ and this complexity approach $O(m^n n^2)$ as n becomes large. Therefore this algorithm is not suitable for large task graphs.

1.3 Hybrid Load Balancing Methodology for a Cluster of SMPs

A hybrid methodology to obtain an optimal task assignment across a cluster of SMPs was proposed by Gao *et. al.* in [1, 2]. Each processing element of a cluster is a node comprising a number of tightly coupled processors. The hybrid methodology graph partitioning first assigns the task modules across all nodes of the cluster so as to have equal load on all nodes with inter-node communication optimised. Next, modules constituting each of these sub-tasks are assigned to processors constituting respective nodes using this algorithm of heuristic graph matching. This algorithm works for a moderate number of modules (approximately 20) per node, but fails for large numbers. The intra-node task assignment algorithm proposed in [1] has been further modified by Gao *et. al.* in [2] where multi step algorithm has been proposed.

2 Parallel Graph Matching Algorithm

In this section, the original sequential algorithm proposed by Shen et. al. in [3] is first presented. This algorithm is then analyzed and the portions which can be parallelized are identified. Finally, the parallel graph-matching algorithm is presented and explained with an illustrative example.

2.1 Parallel Graph-Matching Algorithm

The basic methodology proposed by Shen *et. al.* is based on a generate and test mechanism. Genera- tion of state space nodes expand the state space and incurs computation time as successive nodes are generated and the associated costs are computed. The graph matching algorithm parallizes the gener- ate mechanism, thus dividing the state space into several smaller state-spaces. The basic parameters involved are as follows:

- Let N be the number of parallel graph matching tasks.
- Let $T = (VT , ET)$ represent the task graph
- $P = (V_P , E_P)$represent the processor graph
- Let $P_i = (V_{pi} , E_{pi})$ be a sub graph of P, which is used by the i^{th}task for mapping.

The number of sub graphs of P is assumed to be equal to the number of tasks. Each parallel graph- matching task is assumed to follow the steps listed below, also followed by the sequential algorithm. The only difference is that the node for expansion is the one with minimum value of f computed across all the parallel tasks. For this purpose, it is further assumed that the tasks send to each other the mapping corresponding to the entry with minimum value of f , once a fixed number of new entries are added to the state-space. This variable is defined as *node_count*.

Each parallel graph-matching task proceeds as follows:

It is clear that the value of *node_count* determines how frequently the parallel graph matching tasks communicate. If this value is small, the tasks communicate too often and this increases the turnaround time so far the task assignment problem is concerned. If this is too large, then the solution cannot find optimal solution, as many possibilities remain unexplored. The method is very useful in cases where processors and links are homogeneous.

3 Result and Discussion

A test case is presented in Fig. 1 representing task graph. In the figure, the vertices v_i , v_j represent task modules and the edge(e_{ij}) represent the connection between the vertices v_i and v_j . The number on the vertices represents the computation time of task module of that particular vertex. Similarly, the numbers on the edges represent the communication time involved in data transfer between two vertices v_i and v_j through edge *eij*. The computation and communication time are represented in m sec associated with the vertices and edges.

In Fig. 1, the number of nodes in the task graph is 12, which means that there are 12 modules defined by T = 0, 1, 2, 3. . . 11 which need to be mapped. The computation time associated with these modules defined by the set T P = 10.0, 15.0, 5.0, 20.0, 15.0, 10.0, 10.0, 5.0, 2.0, 1.0, 5.0, 10.0. The inter module communication is defined by the matrix C.

Algorithm 1.

---

1. Set Ki = /o on a list OP EN and set f (Ki) = 0 when f is the evaluation function. If Mglobal represents the global optimal mapping, i.e. the mapping with smallest value of f found by all graph matching tasks, then initialize this to Ki.
2. Set n = Mglobal
3. If n represents the state with no unmapped task, with the smallest value of f among all OP EN nodes, or the number of new additions to the state-space equals node_count then send this optimal mapping (Mlocal) to all parallel graph-matching tasks. Also wait for others to send in their Mlocal. Find the mapping with minimum value of Mlocal and set it to Mglobal . If Mglobal has no unmapped tasks, this is the desired optimal task. Otherwise set n = Mglobal and continue.
4. Remove from OP EN the node n with the smallest f value and put it on a list called C LOSED.
5. Expand the node n, using operators applicable to n and compute f (n′) = g(n′) + h(n′) for each successor n′ of n. It is to be noted that the ith graph matching task generates the successors by expanding the mapping corresponding to n by adding successive task modules to processors represented by the setVpi only. Go back to step 3.

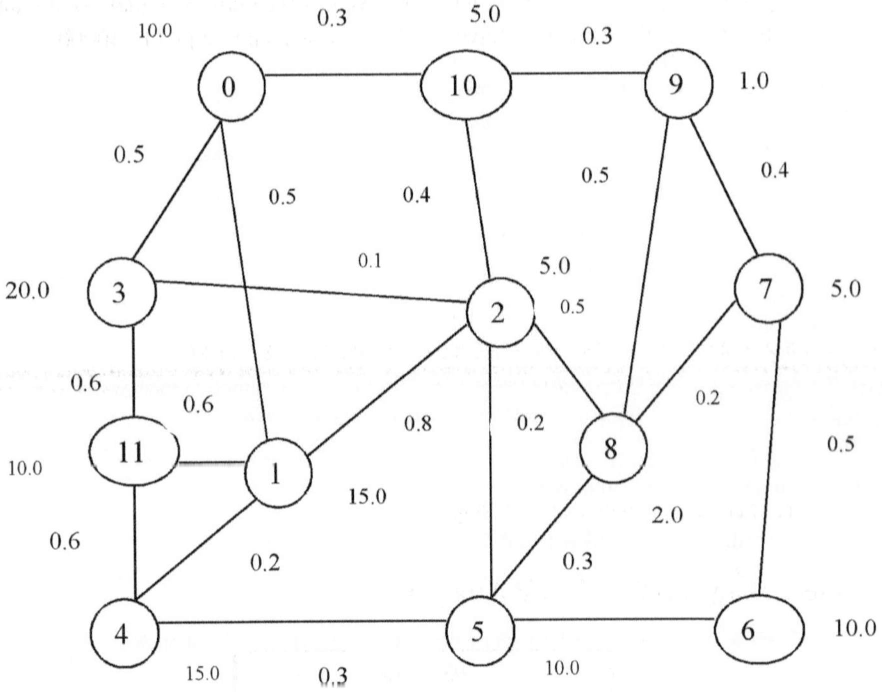

Fig. 1. A representative task graph with 12 nodes

Table 1. Results for a task graph with 12 task modules setting $h(n) = 0$

node_count	Optimal Mapping	Turnaround Time(msec)	No.of Nodes generated	No.of Nodes (Sequential)	Optimality index
2	0B 1A 2B 3B 4A 5A 6B 7B 8B 9B 10A 11A	74.199	1292	1292	0.841
3	0B 1B 2A 3A 4B 5A 6A 7B 8B 9B 10B 11A	62.500	84	1292	0.990
4	0B 1B 2B 3A 4A 5A 6B 7B 8B 9B 10B 11A	64.300	20	1292	0.970
6	0B 1B 2B 3B 4B 5A 6A 7A 8A 9A 10A 11A	72.699	13	1292	0.858
8	0B 1B 2B 3B 4B 5B 6B 7A 8A 9A 10A 11A	95.19	12	1292	0.655
10	0B 1B 2B 3B 4B 5B 6B 7B 8B 9A 10A 11A	104.80	12	1292	0.595

$$C = \begin{matrix} 0.0 & 0.5 & 0.0 & 0.5 & 0.0 & 0.0 & 0.0 & 0.0 & 0.0 & 0.0 & 0.3 & 0.0 \\ 0.5 & 0.0 & 0.8 & 0.0 & 0.2 & 0.0 & 0.0 & 0.0 & 0.0 & 0.0 & 0.0 & 0.6 \\ 0.0 & 0.8 & 0.0 & 0.1 & 0.0 & 0.2 & 0.0 & 0.0 & 0.5 & 0.0 & 0.4 & 0.0 \\ 0.5 & 0.0 & 0.1 & 0.0 & 0.0 & 0.0 & 0.0 & 0.0 & 0.0 & 0.0 & 0.0 & 0.6 \\ 0.0 & 0.2 & 0.0 & 0.0 & 0.0 & 0.3 & 0.0 & 0.0 & 0.0 & 0.0 & 0.0 & 0.6 \\ 0.0 & 0.0 & 0.2 & 0.0 & 0.3 & 0.0 & 0.6 & 0.0 & 0.3 & 0.0 & 0.0 & 0.0 \\ 0.0 & 0.0 & 0.0 & 0.0 & 0.0 & 0.6 & 0.0 & 0.5 & 0.0 & 0.0 & 0.0 & 0.0 \\ 0.0 & 0.0 & 0.0 & 0.0 & 0.0 & 0.0 & 0.5 & 0.0 & 0.2 & 0.4 & 0.0 & 0.0 \\ 0.0 & 0.0 & 0.5 & 0.0 & 0.0 & 0.3 & 0.0 & 0.2 & 0.0 & 0.5 & 0.0 & 0.0 \\ 0.0 & 0.0 & 0.0 & 0.0 & 0.0 & 0.0 & 0.0 & 0.4 & 0.5 & 0.0 & 0.3 & 0.0 \\ 0.3 & 0.0 & 0.4 & 0.0 & 0.0 & 0.0 & 0.0 & 0.0 & 0.0 & 0.3 & 0.0 & 0.0 \\ 0.0 & 0.6 & 0.0 & 0.6 & 0.6 & 0.0 & 0.0 & 0.0 & 0.0 & 0.0 & 0.0 & 0.0 \end{matrix}$$

The number of homogenous processors involved is assumed to be two to start with and the communication link speed is same between two modules of the application it maps. First the heuristic function $h(n)$ is assumed to be 0 for the state space based search algorithm. Next, the test is repeated with a non-zero $h(n)$. Each case is compared to corresponding sequential implementation.

An index called the optimality index denoted by μ is introduced to quantify the result.

$$\mu = \frac{Optimal\,turnaround\,time\,(Parallel)}{Optimal\,turnaround\,time\,(Sequential)} \tag{2}$$

Similarly, an index η is defined as

$$\eta = \frac{Number\,of\,nodes\,generated\,(Parallel)}{Number\,of\,nodes\,generated\,(Sequential)} \tag{3}$$

3.1 Discussions and Conclusions

The results presented in Tables 1 and 2 show that following:

1. As the value of node_count increases, the size of the search state-space reduces.

Table 2. Test case for task graph of Fig. 1 with 12 task modules with $h(n) = 0$

node_count	Optimal Mapping	Turnaround Time(msec)	No.of Nodes generated	No.of Nodes (Sequential)	Optimality index
2	0B 1A 2B 3B 4A 5A 6B 7B 8B 9B 10A 11A	62.70	1476	1052	1.0
3	0B 1B 2A 3A 4B 5A 6A 7B 8B 9B 10B 11A	63.200	100	1052	0.992
4	0B 1B 2B 3A 4A 5A 6B 7B 8B 9B 10B 11A	64.300	36	1052	0.975
6	0B 1B 2B 3B 4B 5A 6A 7A 8A 9A 10A 11A	70.69	12	1052	0.862
8	0B 1B 2B 3B 4B 5B 6B 7A 8A 9A 10A 11A	95.19	12	1052	0.658
10	0B 1B 2B 3B 4B 5B 6B 7B 8B 9A 10A 11A	104.80	12	1052	0.592

2. As the value of *node_count* is varied, optimality index also varies. It is maximum at a certain value of the ratio α, where

$$\alpha = \frac{node\_count}{nos\_nodes} \tag{4}$$

The variable *nos_nodes* represents the number of task modules. While μ defines the quality of solution reported by the parallel implementation, η defines the efficiency of the parallel implementation in terms of the time required to find optimal solution. From results, it is clear that higher the value of μ, lower the value of η because of the fact that to achieve a higher value of μ, the parallel graph matching tasks must communicate more often, thus reducing the value of η.

The variation of indices μ and η with the ratio α is plotted and the plots are represented in Fig. 2 and Fig. 3 (test case of Fig. 1 with $h(n) = 0$ and $h(n) \neq 0$) . The plots in solid line represent η and plots in dashed lines represent μ. The plots indicate that the variation of μ and η with α follows the same pattern for the 2 cases. From the plots it is seen that a mapping which is 90% optimal ($\mu \geq 0.9$) is obtained for $\alpha \leq 0.5$ in all cases. The corresponding values of η lies between 0.1 and 0.3. This means that a 90% optimal solution is obtained at roughly one-third time by the parallel implementation when compared to sequential implementation.

It is further seen that with h(n) ≠ 0, the value of η reduces much faster as α is increased which means that heuristic search further increases the efficiency of parallel graph matching algorithm. The theoretical value of α has to be matched against the actual value of α supported by the computation and communication speeds.

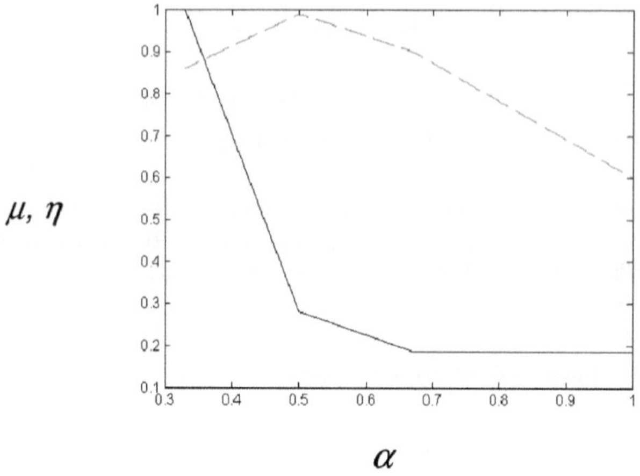

Fig. 2. Variation of μ,η with α,h(n) ≠ 0.$h(n)$ ≠ 0 for test case 2

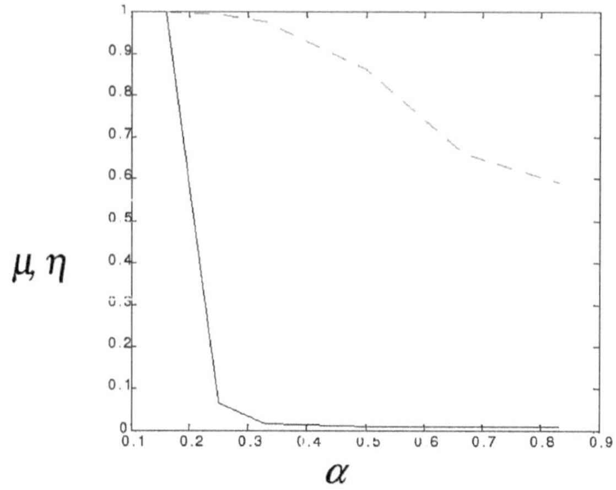

Fig. 3. Variation of μ,η with α, for test case 2

$$\beta = \frac{actual\,time\,(msec)\,for\,sequential\,implementation}{actual\,time\,(msec)\,for\,parallel\,implementation} \quad (5)$$

Then the actual value of β will depend upon the computation and communication speeds associated with parallel graph-matching tasks. The value of β is determined with $\alpha = 0.4$ for graph represented by Fig. 1 with $h(n) = 0$ and $h(n) \neq 0$ and the results are presented in Table 3.

Table 3. Actual speed up obtained

Test Case	β
Sequential	1.0
$h(n) = 0$	1.4
$h(n) \neq 0$	1.86

This represents the actual time taken from launch of the parallel job to its completion. Though the size of the state-space reduces drastically, the overheads incurred in communication over the network and mpirun to launch and terminate processes actually increase the turnaround time. This implies that the methodology shall be effective for cases with large number of task modules where the speed-up due to reduction is state-space size makes up for these overheads.

4 Conclusion

Results represent the actual time taken from launch of the parallel job to its completion. Though the size of the state-space reduces drastically, the overheads incurred in communication over the network and mpirun to launch and terminate processes actually increase the turnaround time. This implies that the methodology shall be effective for cases with large number of task modules where the speed-up due to reduction is state-space size meets these overheads.

5 Further Work

The following points are identified for further research:

- To investigate for hetrogeneous multiprocessor cases.
- To investigate behavior of the parallel implementation for large test cases.
- To investigate the use of a heuristic bound to eliminate expansion of 'non-promising' nodes in the state-space.

References

[1] Gao, H., Schmidt, A., Gupta, A., Luksch, P.: Load balancing for Spatial-Grid-Based Parallel Numeric Simulation on Clusters of SMPs. In: Proceeding of the Euromicro PDP 2003 Conference, Genoa, Italy, February 5-7, pp. 75–82. IEEE Computer Society Publications, Los Alamitos (2003)

[2] Gao, H., Schmidt, A., Gupta, A., Luksch, P.: A Graph-matching based Intra-node Load balancing Methodology for clusters of SMPs. In: Proceedings of the 7th World Multiconference on Systems, Cubernetics and Informatics (SCI 2003) (July 2003)

[3] Shen, C.-c., Tsai, W.-H.: A Graph Matching Approach to Optimal task as- signment in Distributed computing systems using a Minimax Criterion. IEEE Transactions on Computers C-34(3) (March 1985)

[4] Kernighan, B.W., Lin, S.: An efficient Heuristic procedure for partitioning graphs. Bell Systems Tech, J. 49, 291–308 (1970)

[5] Kernighan, B.W., Lin, S.: An efficient Heuristic procedure for partitioning graphs. Bell Systems Tech, J. 49, 291–308 (1970)

[6] Bui, T.N., Chaudhuri, S., Leighton, F.T., Sipser, M.: Graph Bisection Algorithms with good aver- age case behavior. Combinatorica 7, 171–191 (1987)

[7] Williams, R.D.: Performance of Dynamic load balancing algorithms for unstructured mesh calculations. Concurrency: Practice and Experience 3, 457–481 (1991)

[8] Farhat, C.: A simple and efficient automatic FEM domain decomposer. Computers and Structures 28, 579–602 (1988)

[9] Fiduccia, C.M., Mattheyses, R.M.: A liner-time heuristic for improve network partitions. In: ACM IEEE Nineteenth Design Automation Conference Proceedings, vol. 1982, ch.126, pp. 175–181 (1982)

[10] Sadayappan, P., Ercal, F., Ramanujam, J.: Cluster Partitioning approach to mapping parallel program onto a hypercube. Parallel Computing 13, 1–16 (1990)

[11] Barnard, S.T., Simon, H.D.: A parallel implementation of multilevel recursive spectral bisection for application to adaptive unstructured meshes. In: Bailey, D.H., Bjorstad, P.E., Gilbert, Jr., Mascagni, M.V., Schreiber, R.S., Simon, H.D., Torczon, V.J., Watson, J.T. (eds.). SIAM Proceedings Series, vol. 195, pp. 627–632. SIAM, Philadelphia (1995)

[12] Barnard, S.T.: PMRSB: parallel multilevel recursive spectral bisection (1996) (manuscript)

[13] Karypis, G., Kumar, V.: Parallel Multilevel k-way Partitioning Scheme for Irregular Graphs, Technical Report TR 96-036, Department of Computer Science, University of Minnesota (1996)

[14] Nilsson, N.J.: Artificial intelligence: a new synthesis (March 1998) ISBN: 1-55860-467-7

[15] Boman, E.G., Catalyurec, U.V., Chevalier, C.: Advances in Parallel Partitioning, Load Balancing and Matrix ordering for Scientific Computing. Journal of Physics: Conference Series, JPCS (2009)

[16] Dehne, F., Yogaratnam, K.: Exploring the Limits of GPUs with Parallel Graph Algorithms. Cornell University Library, Ithica (February 24, 2010)

[17] Zaslavskiy, M., Bach, F., Vert, J.-P.: Many-to-Many Graph Matching: A Continuous Relaxation Approach. In: Balcázar, J.L., Bonchi, F., Gionis, A., Sebag, M. (eds.) ECML PKDD 2010. LNCS, vol. 6323, pp. 515–530. Springer, Heidelberg (2010), doi:10.1007/978-3-642-15939-8_33

Automatic Caricature Generation Using Text Based Input

Kahkasha I. Siddavatam[1] and Irfan A. Siddavatam[2]

[1] Department of Electronic and Telecommunication, TPCT's Terna Engineering College, Nerul, Navi Mumbai-400706
[2] Department of Information Technology , K.J. Somaiya College of Engineering, Vidyavihar, Mumbai -400077
kahkasha_ks@yahoo.co.in, irfanasv@gmail.com

Abstract. In this paper we have discussed the developed automatic caricature generation system. System accomplishes face processing by converting 2-D face photo to caricature. The key feature of system is interface provided for the user to give input for the type of caricature generated. Once the input is provided by the user, the Text Search unit searches the keyword from the input and generates the Word Sequence, which is further provided for processing. Caricature generation unit process the input facial image to convert it into caricature. The method used to create caricatures involves exaggerating features that deviate from the prototype. The inputs provided to the units are the Word Sequence that describes type of deformation applied, Face Template that causes this deformation and the facial input to be processed.

Keywords: Exaggeration, Text Search, Word Sequence, Face Template, Caricature Generation.

1 Introduction

Caricatures have always been a funny way of creating drawings of people emphasizing the prominent features of the face. A caricature can be defined as an exaggeration likeness of a person made by emphasizing all of the features that make the person different from everyone else. The method used to create caricatures involves exaggerating features that deviate from the prototype, or average face. Somehow artists have the amazing ability to draw a caricature of someone's face. An artist is capable of capturing distinguished facial features that make his/her subject different from others, and then exaggerating these features. In order to generate an exaggeration, one has to make the following observations. Which of the subject's features are significantly different from others'? How can one define and measure the difference? How does one know which of the subject's features are larger, smaller, sharper, or rounder than other people's? [1]. There has been some previous work on how a caricature can reveal characteristics of a face. Based on psychological hypotheses, for example, Rhodes et al. reported on experiments where a caricature looks good. There have been a few attempts to interactively synthesize facial caricatures. Akleman et al

D. Nagamalai, E. Renault, and M. Dhanushkodi (Eds.): PDCTA 2011, CCIS 203, pp. 344–356, 2011.

developed a procedure to make caricatures using an interactive morphing tool. Brennan presented an interactive caricature generator. Tominaga et. Al developed the template-based facial caricature system PICASSO and Web-PICASSO. Many approaches have also been proposed to generate facial caricature.

Fig. 1. Albert Einstein's caricature created by A. Hughes with exaggerated hair, forehead and nose

We have developed system that will creates a caricature using field warping algorithm based on corresponding feature primitives for image warping for given input image. Nature of caricature generated will depend on the analysis of text input given by user.

Paper is organized in following sections. Section II discusses literature survey for automatic caricature generation. Section III explain framework for system. Section IV discusses results and section V concludes paper with future scope.

2 Literature Survey

For many years artists have entertained and profited by drawing caricatures of people. Every person's appearance is different. It is these differences that make each of us individuals and recognizable. Caricature artists take these differences and exaggerate them to produce a caricature. For example, a slightly large nose would be emphasized and drawn several times larger. Artists take all the visual characteristics of a person and blend them skillfully to produce the caricature. Alex Hughes describes a caricature as "the art of capturing the essence of someone's personality through an exaggerated likeness, to create a portrait that is ultimately more true to life than life itself". As with most portraits, caricatures are traditionally drawn in 2D only as the artist has to paint to a canvas or paper.

The basic definition of facial caricature is that it is the exaggeration for all the facial features which are found by comparing the impression features of the subject with the average face. The method used to create caricatures involves exaggerating features that deviate from the prototype, or average face. An ideal exaggeration algorithm should not only preserve the original features of the subject but also attain exaggeration effect. The first algorithm on caricatures generation belongs to Brennan who attempts development of computer-assisted caricature generation system by an interactive system for producing sketches with exaggeration [2]. The other method involves Template Based approach for caricature creation with adjustable exaggeration rate. The approach is attempted by Koshimize and Murakami et al. [3]. The drawback of this method is result is unrecognizable when exaggeration rate is too large as this method is line based. The other approach is example based approach [4, 5]. This approach uses partial least squares or neural networks to learn the drawing style of an artist and requires training set for exhibit some particular characteristics like nevus, beards. Chiang et al [6] analyzed facial features and warped the color caricature created by artist to the exaggerative style with analyzed result. However, the representation of result is limited by the prototype drawn by an artist. Another method for caricature generation is attempted by Akleman using morphing [7]. In this method preconstructed scheme is modified. A warping method to exaggerate the face is performed after that, regarding the changes done in the sketch. This method involves not only exaggerated facial features but also other particular characteristics. However, they also need a lot of manual works.

After analyzing various approaches for automatic caricature generation we adopt field warping algorithm based on corresponding feature primitives for image warping for given input image. The two image wrapping algorithms are analyzed here, Beier-Neely geometric warping and Mesh warping. Both algorithms are implemented in Matlab for their respective functions.

3 System Framework

Photo-realistic self-representation is now easier with the advent of multimedia computers equipped with digital cameras and peripherals such as scanners. The proposed system accomplishes face processing by converting 2-D face photo to caricature, a humorous photo-realistic self-representation and synthesis of facial expression. The framework of the system including text and images can be described as Figure 2. In the figure, the white block represents the data in the system, and the grey block represents data processing.

3.1 Text Processing

Basic purpose of this block is to provide interface for the user to give input, the type of caricature generated. It is not necessary for the user to provide or remember keyword to be punched, other than that user can explain in sentence what kind of caricature formation he wants. Once the input is provided by the user the Text Search block come into picture and searches the keyword from the input and generate the Word Sequence, which is further provided for processing.

Example:-

Input: - "Let the face have long nose"
Word Sequence: - long nose

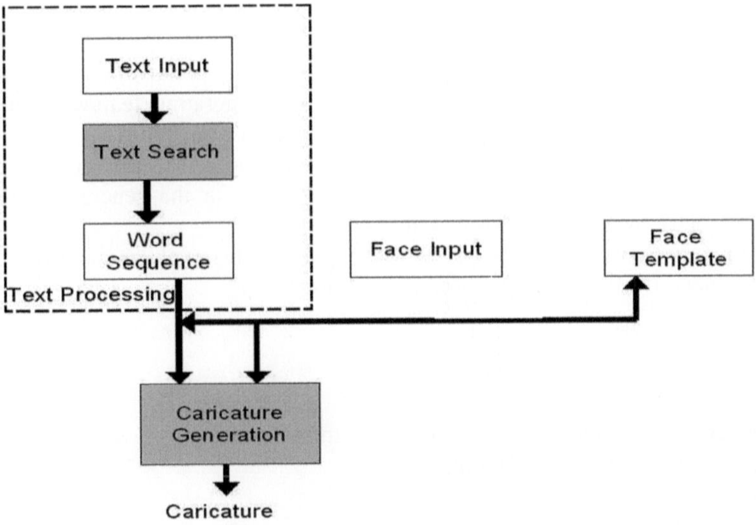

Fig. 2. System Architecture

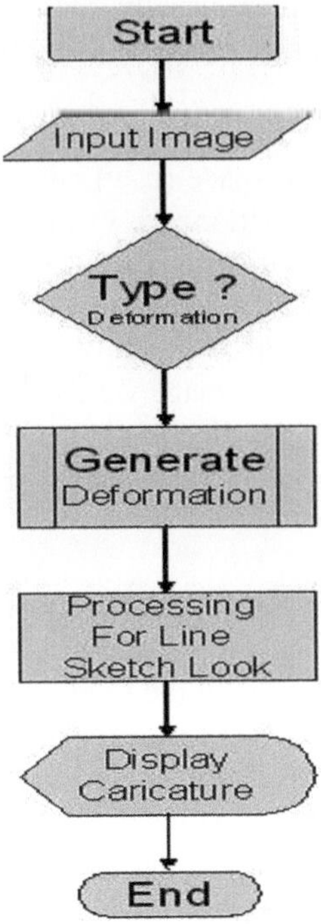

Fig. 3. Overall System Flow

3.2 Caricature Generation

Caricature generation unit process the input facial image to convert it into caricature. The method used to create caricatures involves exaggerating features that deviate from the prototype. The inputs provided to the units are the Word Sequence that describes type of deformation applied, Face Template that causes this deformation and the facial input to be processed. The algorithms used for the generation are Beier-Neely geometric warping and Mesh warping.

Here we try to explain overall flow of the system. This explains the progression of the input facial from simple neutral image to caricature.

4 Implementation and Result

For caricature generation steps involved are image wrapping, B-tone image generation, Edge detection and overlapping.

4.1 Image Wrapping

In image processing, we do image warping typically to remove the distortions from an image, while in computer graphics we are usually introducing one. Here in mentioned system we use image warping for exaggeration or distortion input facial image to create caricature.

Image warping is the act of distorting a source image into a destination image according to a mapping between source space (u, v) and destination space (x, y). The mapping is usually specified by the function x(u, v) and y(u, v). The general mapping function can be given in two forms, either as a forward mapping or an inverse mapping. Forward mapping consists of copying each input pixel onto the output image at positions determined by the mapping functions. Inverse mapping operates by projecting each output coordinate into the input image via the mapping transformations. The value of the pixel at that input point is copied onto the output pixel. The output pixels are centered on integer coordinate values, and are projected onto the input at real-valued positions.

4.1.1 Image Wrapping with Beier-Neely Algorithm

There are a few different techniques for feature-based inverse mapping warping, however the Beier-Neely algorithm is one of the most prominent [8]. The Beier-Neely technique for warping is based on fields of influence around two-dimensional control primitives, lines that delineate features.

Our objective is to discover the mathematics behind warping. Using linear algebra we will transform inaFace1 into inaFace2 the shown in Figure 4.

By applying the mathematics mentioned in Beier-Neely algorithm we were able to write code in Matlab to produce a program that can warp images with many lines drawn on them. Literature further explains the algorithms of the code developed along with the inputs provided and results obtained.

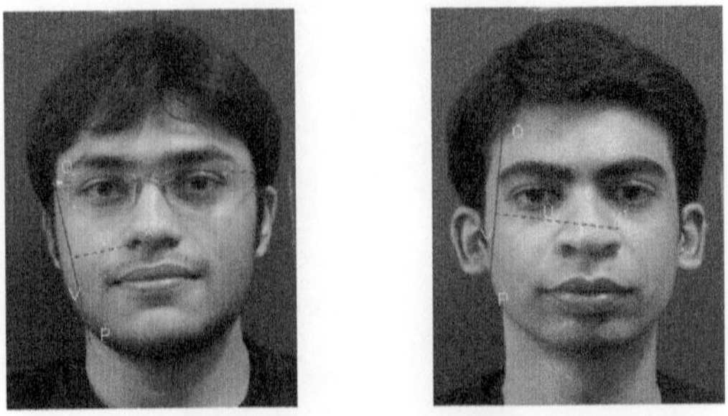

Fig. 4. Transformation Faces

Frame 1 and 2

Frame 3 and 4

Frame 5 and 6

Fig. 5. Result of Beier-Neely technique for warping

Frame 7

Fig. 5. (*Continued*)

4.1.2 Mesh Wrapping

The another wrapping technique considered for image wrapping is Mesh wrapping . Mesh warping was pioneered at Industrial Light & Magic (ILM) by D. Smythe for use in the movie Willow in 1988 (Smythe 1990). It has been successfully used in many subsequent motion pictures.

In this technique the features are identified simply by a series of corresponding points. Later techniques allow the user to select corresponding lines or even free-form shapes [9], the outline of a head for example, but it was felt these presented too many technical challenges to be feasible for this investigation.

One of the major benefits of the mesh warping technique is the simplicity of the interpolation stage. The objective of this stage is to create a mapping detailing the movement of every pixel from the initial to the final image. Since the features are identified as single points, this mapping can be generated by the process of scattered data interpolation, a very common computational process with a wealth of effective techniques available. The interpolation process used for the morphs presented in the report is 'biharmonic spline interpolation' (Sandwell 1987). This was chosen as it was observed to produce slightly better results than bicubic interpolation and is built in to the Matlab programming environment, used for this project.

Following figure shows result of mesh wrapping.

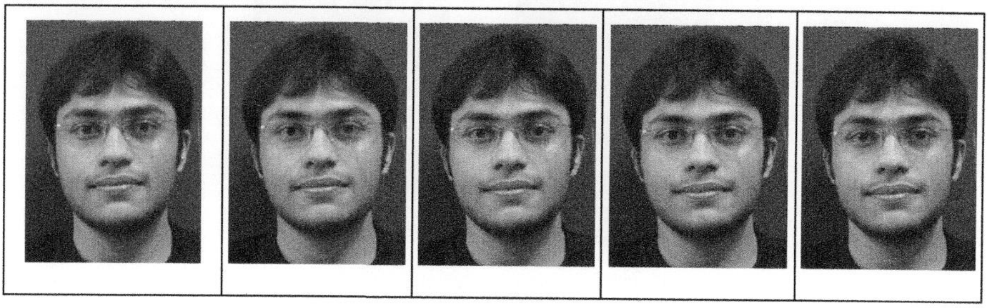

Fig. 6. Result of Mesh Wrapping

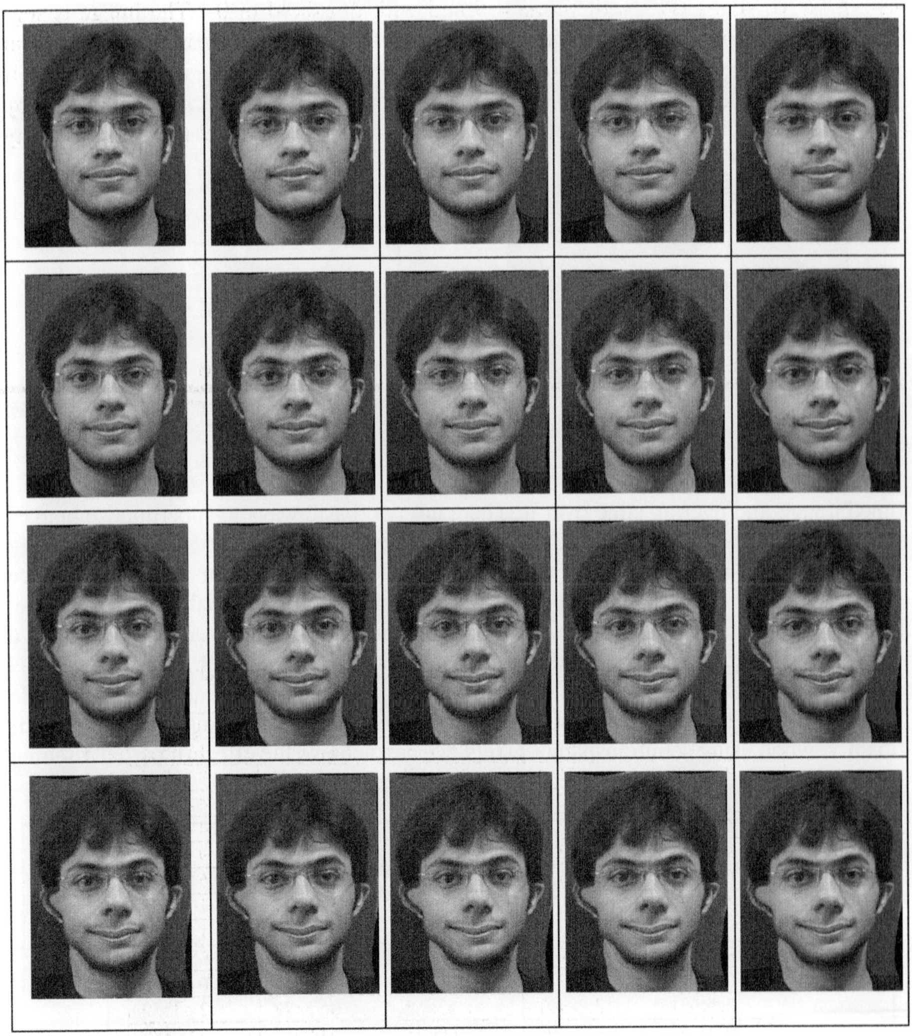

Fig. 6. (*Continued*)

After wrapping binary image is edges of images are found to give feel of hand drawn caricature. In the system we have use canny Edge detector. The Canny edge detector is widely considered to be the standard edge detection algorithm in the industry.

We use matlab's edge function with canny method, details are as follows:

BW = edge(I,'canny')

Specifies the Canny method. BW = edge(I,'canny',thresh)

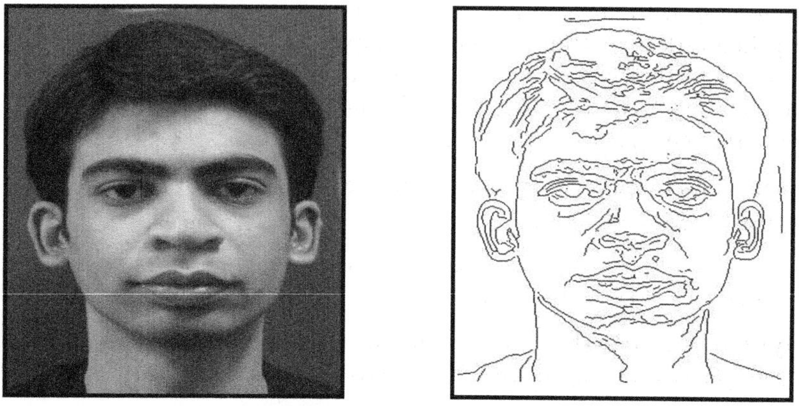

Fig. 7. Result of Edge Detection

As we try to get hand drawn caricature feel now the requirement is to overlap the bi-toned image and overlap edge over it. There are two basic ways to superimpose images in MATLAB. One involves using transparency for overlaying images objects that may not be exact rectangles, and the other involves indexing into the image data to replace pixels. We have an image with pixels that are transparent or partially transparent i.e. bitoned image, and we have another image that should serve as the background i.e. edge image. We want the first image to let the background show through wherever there is transparency. Note that, when using this method, we are actually dealing with multiple image objects. The superimposing is achieved by overlapping the image objects. Additionally, when using semitransparent pixels, we can achieve the effect of partially seeing through a pixel Rther than completely hiding the background.

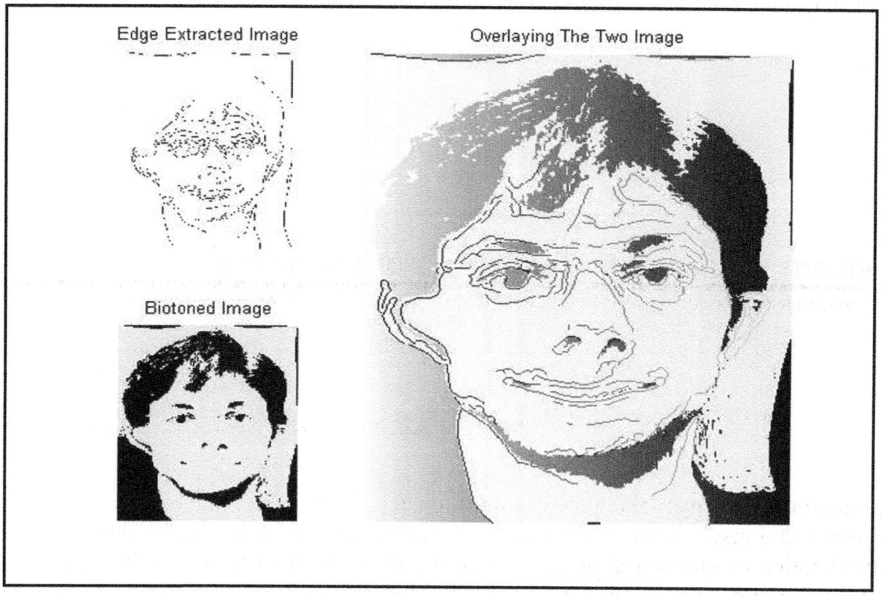

Fig. 8. Result of Overlapping

5 GUI for Automatic Caricature Generation Using Text Based Input

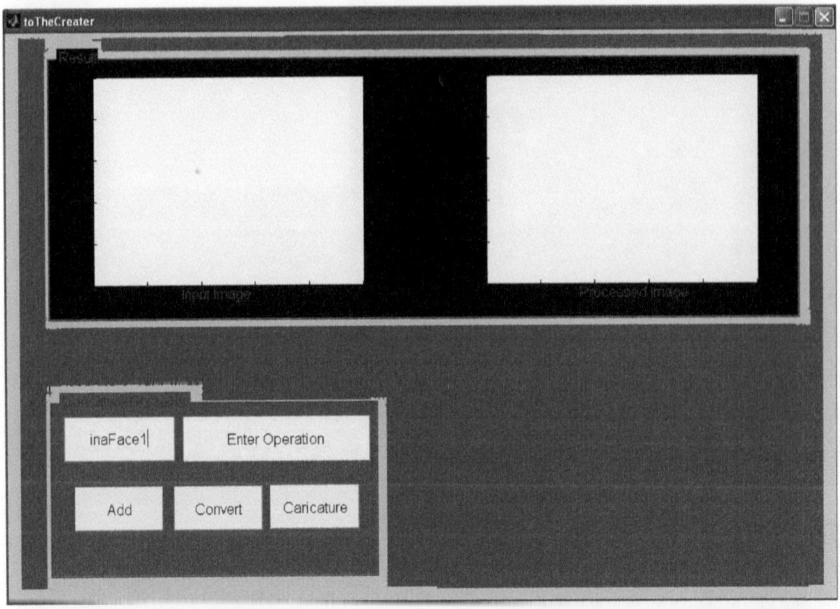

Fig. 7. User input to add input image

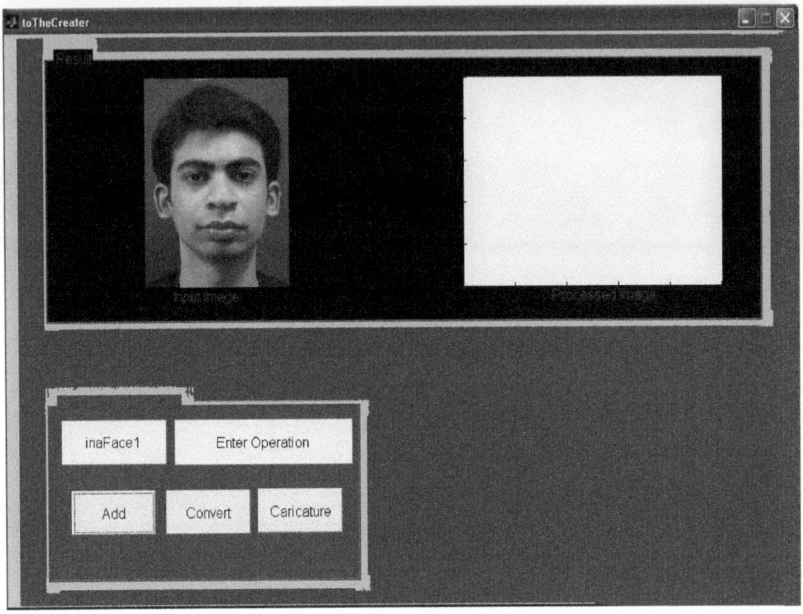

Fig. 8. Input image added

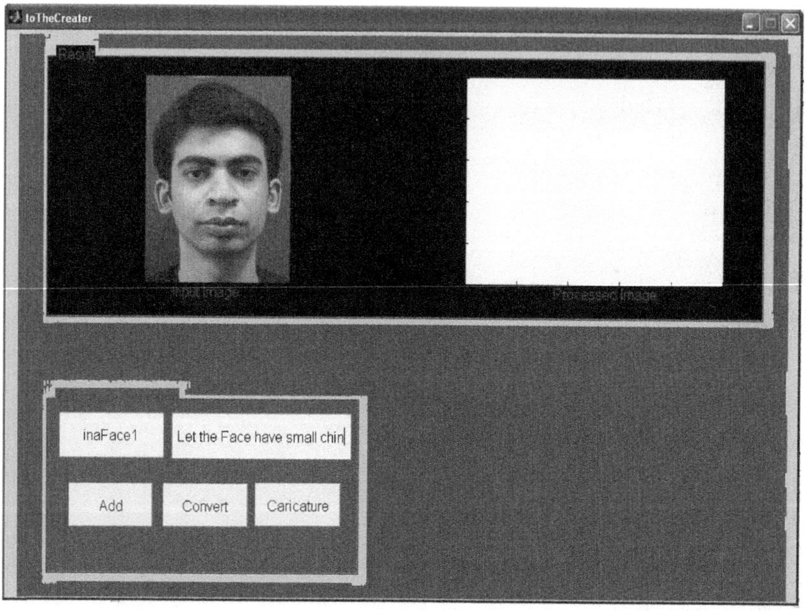

Fig. 9. Input String for caricature exaggeration

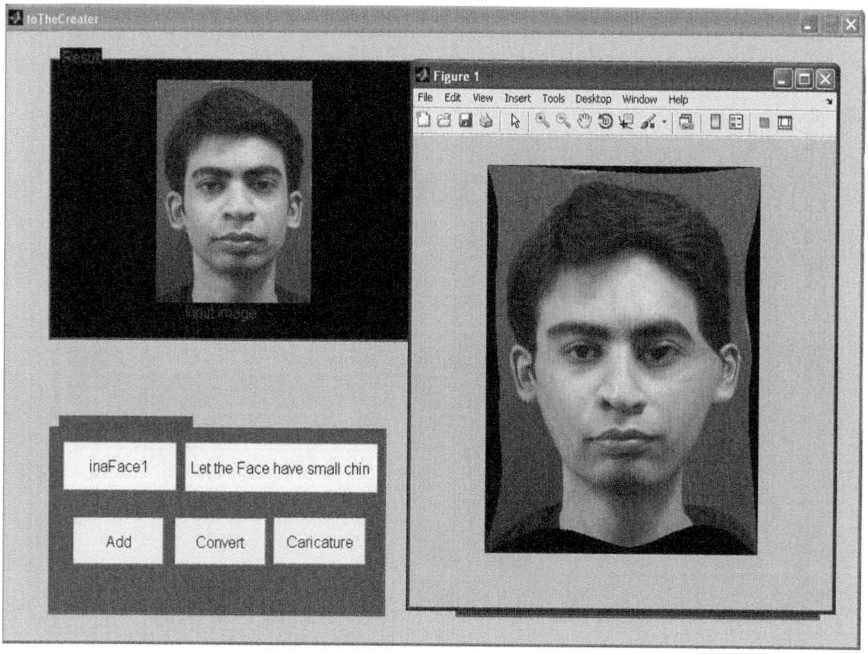

Fig. 10. Exaggeration as small chin

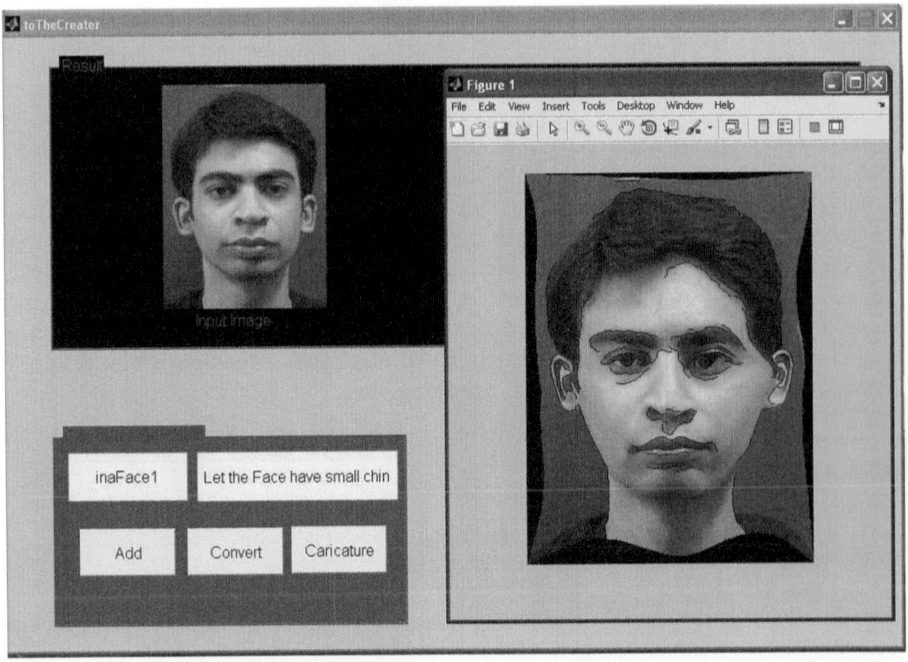

Fig. 11. Exaggeration as small chin place on GUI

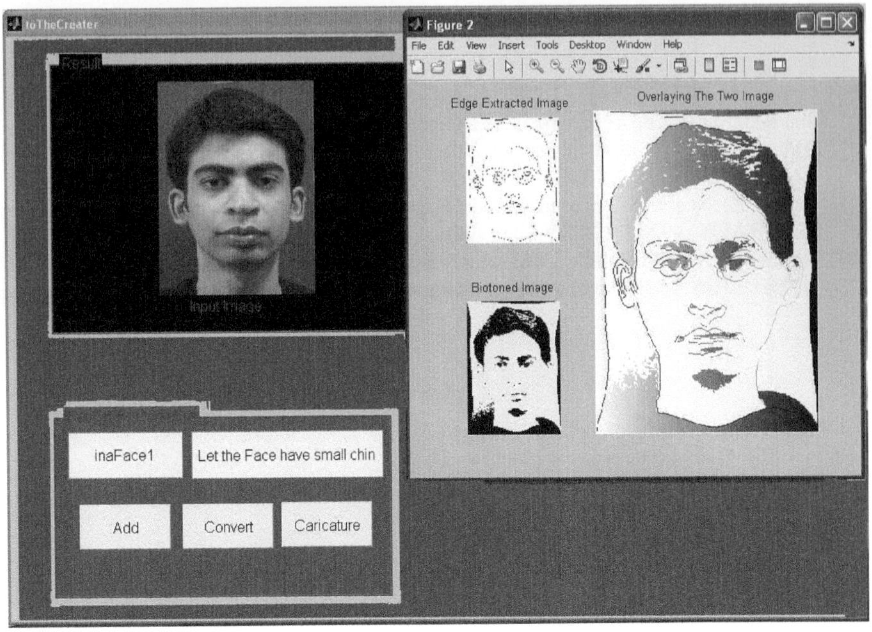

Fig. 12. Final caricatures with bi-tone edge overlap

6 Conclusion

The aim of this system was to develop system that transform people real photograph to caricature.

In automated caricature generation warping was carried out by mesh and Beier-Neely warping algorithm. The results indicate mesh warping give more smooth and controlled warping as compared to Beier- Neely warping. To get the feel of hand sketch caricature, warped image was converted to bi-toned image and edges were detected to form the sketch border. The best threshold found to bi-tone image lie in range of 60 to 75, similarly different edge detection algorithms were tried. Canny edge detection algorithm with threshold 0.2 to 0.3 was found best suited for getting edges of warped image. Overlapping bi-toned and canny edges gave best results in comparison to overlaying canny edge over gray image.

References

[1] Hughes, A.: Learn to draw caricatures. HarperCollins Publishers, London (1999)

[2] Brennan, S.: Caricature generator, Master's thesis, MIT, Cambridge (1982)

[3] Koshimizu, H., Tominaga, M., Fujiwara, T., Murakami, K.: On Kansei Facial Processing for Computerized Facial Caricaturing System Picasso. In: Proceedings of IEEE International Conference on Systems, Man, and Cybernetics, pp. 294–299 (1999)

[4] Lai, K.H., Edirisinghe, E.A., Chung, P.W.H.: A Facial Component based Hybrid Approach to Caricature Generation using Neural Networks. In: Proceedings of ACTA on Computational Intelligence (2006)

[5] Liang, L., Chen, H., Xu, Y.Q., Shum, H.Y.: Example-based Caricature Generation with Exaggeration. In: Proc. 10th Pacific Conf. on Computer Graphics and Applications (2002)

[6] Chiang, P.Y., Liao, W.H., Li, T.Y.: Automatic Caricature Generation by Analyzing Facial Features. In: Proceedings of Asia Conf. on Computer Vision (2004)

[7] Akleman, E.: Making caricatures with morphing. In: Proceedings of the Art and Interdisciplinary Programs of SIGGRAPH 1997. ACM Press, New York (1997)

[8] Beier, T., Neely, S.: Feature-based image metamorphosis. Computer Graphics (Proc. SIGGRAPH 1992) 26(2), 35–42 (1992)

[9] Wolberg: Image Morphing: A Survey. Visual Computer 14, 360–372 (1998)

[10] `http://en.wikipedia.org/wiki/Thresholding_(image_processing)`

A Novel and Efficient Technique to Generate Secured Biometric Key Using Cryptography

P.K. Mahesh and Anjan Gudigar

Department of Electronics and communication, M.I.T.E, Moodbidri, India
{mahesh24pk,anjangudigar83}@gmail.com

Abstract. This paper proposes a novel methodology to generate efficient and secured key by using cryptographic techniques for the shared data to be secure. Conventional techniques depend on biometric features like face, fingerprint, iris, signature, hand geometry, keystroke, voice and the like for the extraction of key information. If a Biometric Key is lost or stolen, it is lost forever and perhaps for every application where the biometric is used, because a biometric is enduringly linked with a user and cannot be changed. In this paper we propose a technique to produce secured and efficient key from fingerprint so as to surmount these problems. The exibility and dependability of cryptography is enhanced with the utilization of cancellable biometric features. There are several biometric systems in existence that deal with cryptography. We propose a new approach which uses the features of finger print and RSA-2 algorithm to generate Cryptographic Key.

Keywords: Biometric Key, Cryptographic key, Feature Matrix, Fingerprint, RSA-2.

1 Introduction

The measurement of biological data is known as BIOMETRICS. The term biometrics is commonly used today to refer to the authentication of a person by analyzing physical characteristics, such as fingerprints, handprints, eyes and voice, or behavioural characteristics, such as signatures. Fingerprints are one of many forms of Biometrics used to identify an individual and verify their identity.

There are two main types of features in a fingerprint:

(1) Local ridge and furrow minute details, and
(2) Global ridge and furrow structures which form special patterns in the central region of the fingerprint.

A fingerprint is classified based is uniquely identified based on the first type of features and on only the second type of features (ridge endings and bifurcations, also known as minutiae, see Fig .1).

Because of progress in communication technology a huge quantities of digital data are available in shared media this has necessitated the drastic development of

D. Nagamalai, E. Renault, and M. Dhanushkodi (Eds.): PDCTA 2011, CCIS 203, pp. 357–365, 2011.

cryptographic techniques. Building blocks of computer security are Cryptography. DES, AES [1, 2, and 4] and public key architectures such as RSA [17] is a notable few among the widely utilized cryptographic techniques. Cryptographic security is conditioned by an authentication step that characteristically depends on long pseudo-random keys (of at least 128 bits in symmetric encryption), which are nearly impossible to keep in mind. Moreover many people are intended towards using identical keys or password for a variety of applications and as a result breaching one system lead to the breaching of many others. This makes the work of an attacker simple by shockingly reducing the general security of the data being protected. It is possible to solve this in a variety of applications by producing powerful cryptographic keys from biometric data, possibly in combination with the entry of a password [10, 12, and 19].

Minutiae (○), Core (□), and Delta (△).

Fig. 1. Minutia, Core and Delta points

Cryptography is merged with biometrics in Biometric Cryptosystems, otherwise known as crypto-biometric systems [20]. The uniformity of biometric data over time is one of its huge merit and demerit at the same instant. In case of a missing credit card, it is possible to issue new one but it is impossible to substitute the biometric characteristics and it is fully evident since it is not feasible to provide a person with a fresh fingerprint when the old one is stolen. When the biometric information transmitted over the low bandwidth channel there is more chance of information hacked by the intruders. There is no security mechanism is provided by the sender to receive the information is receive by the receiver is not manipulated. The biometric information is most important information for human and some important operations such as military, new research; other security purpose. The low bandwidth channel is most unsecured channel where number of unauthorized users wants to access information. This problem is identified and solved through this paper. This paper provide solution of identified problems by authentication and confidentiality for the bio-metric data transmitted over the low bandwidth or covert channel with the enhancement of speed of encryption and decryption of plain text with RSA-2 Algorithm[1] and authentication code append with cipher text.

2 Related Work

In [13], arithmetic encoding technique is used with DES to encrypt the image and transmitted over the covert channel. The arithmetic encoding gives coded data values in between interval of 0 and 1. That gives security and compression over the input files[13,15].The Arithmetic Coding is extremely efficient, for providing both security and compression simultaneously is growing more important and is given the increasing ubiquity of compressed Bio-metric files in host applications of Defence, Internet and the common desire to provide security in association with these files. In [2,3] the RSA algorithm is used with some modifications which enhance the speed of RSA algorithm is called RSA-1 and the algorithm which provide security more than RSA algorithm is called RSA-2 algorithm which can enhance confidentiality to the sender. The problem of RSA algorithm is solved [2] through RSA-2 algorithm, it used the numbers instead of character in the plain text are represented by encoding scheme which can be able to represent special character. In case of character and number the intruder can easily know the cipher text and author can replaced it by the special symbols with the help of decimal value into their respective ASCII code character. The RSA-2 algorithm increased the speed of encryption and decryption with enhancement of security also due to special symbol.

In [7, 8], The Diffie-Hellmann key exchange was the first protocol to utilize public key cryptography. The Diffie-Hellmann protocol is used to exchange a secret key between two users over insecure channel without any previous information between them. The image is transferred with steganography technique and key is used for hiding image information is deliver to receiver with the help of Diffie-Hellmann exchange protocol [7]. The key used in RSA-2 algorithm is delivered to receiver with the help of Diffie-Hellmann algorithm [8-9].First proposed a remote password-based authentication scheme that could authenticate remote users over an insecure channel [20]. A lot of research has been carried out in the field of Authentication and Key Exchange protocols, which are based on passwords [17, 18]. In paper [7], image is transferred to the receiver by Steganography technique with secure key distribution technique. In [5, 6], it can provide a more secure authentication technique for sender and receiver with the help of ID and password mechanism. The user of system can register and gets an ID and Password. When any user send data it can encrypt data generate authentication code using receiver ID and password. These codes are appending with cipher text and send this message over the insecure channel.

3 Proposed Methodology

Recently, crypto-biometric systems have been studied for solving the key management problem of cryptographic systems and protecting templates in biometric systems at the same time. In general, the identity theft problem is drastically exacerbated for the biometric systems, since the biometric data and the corresponding feature vectors are non-renewable. To overcome this we generate a secured feature matrix from the fingerprint template and strengthened this by AES Encryption/Decryption algorithm. Besides that, this paper discusses how keys can be generated and demonstrates the technique using fingerprint images.

3.1 Key Generation from Fingerprint

This section confers the feature generation from finger-print biometric data. The stages are discussed below,

•Extracting minutiae points from Fingerprint.
•Secured Feature Matrix generation
•Key generation from Secured Feature Matrix (Sender and Receiver Prospects).

3.1.1 Extracting Minutiae Points from Fingerprint

For extracting minutiae points from fingerprint, a three level approach is broadly used by researchers. These levels are listed as follows,

•Pre-processing.
•ROI selection.
•Minutia extraction.

For the fingerprint image pre-processing, Histogram Equalization [20] and FFT are used to do image enhancement. Binarization is applied on the fingerprint image. Locally adaptive threshold method [13] is used for this process. Then Morphological operations [13, 18] are used to extract Region of Interest [ROI].

3.1.1.1 Pre-processing. Fingerprint Image enhancement is to make the image clearer for easy further operations. Since the fingerprint images acquired from sensors or other Medias are not assured with perfect quality, those enhancement methods, for increasing the contrast between ridges and furrows and for connecting the false broken points of ridges due to insufficient amount of ink, are very useful for keep a higher accuracy to fingerprint recognition. Two Methods are adopted in our fingerprint recognition system: the first one is Histogram Equalization; the next one is Fourier Transform.

Histogram equalization is to expand the pixel value distribution of an image so as to increase the perceptional information. The original histogram of a fingerprint image has the bimodal type, the histogram after the histogram equalization occupies all the range from 0 to 255 and the visualization effect is enhanced [Fig. 2(b)].Next, We divide the image into small processing blocks (32 by 32 pixels) and perform the Fourier transform according to:

$$F(u,v)=\sum_{x=0}^{M-1}\sum_{y=0}^{N-1} f(x,y)\times exp\left\{-j2\pi\times(\frac{ux}{M}+\frac{vy}{N})\right\} \tag{1}$$

For u = 0, 1, 2... 31 and v = 0, 1, 2... 31.

In order to enhance a specific block by its dominant frequencies, we multiply the FFT of the block by its magnitude a set of times. Where the magnitude of the original FFT = abs (F (u,v)) = |F(u,v)|.

Get the enhanced block according to

$$g(x,y)=F^{-1}\{F(u,v)\times|F(u,v)|^k\} \tag{2}$$

Where F^{-1}(F (u,v)) is done by:

$$F(u,v)=\frac{1}{MN}\sum_{x=0}^{M-1}\sum_{y=0}^{N-1} f(x,y)\times exp\left\{-j2\pi\times(\frac{ux}{M}+\frac{vy}{N})\right\} \tag{3}$$

For x = 0, 1, 2... 31 and y = 0, 1, 2... 31.

The k in formula (2) is an experimentally determined constant, which we choose k=0.45 to calculate. While having a higher "k" improves the appearance of the ridges, filling up small holes in ridges, having too high a "k" can result in false joining of ridges. Thus a termination might become a bifurcation. Fig.2(c) presents the image after FFT enhancement.

The enhanced image after FFT has the improvements to connect some falsely broken points on ridges and to remove some spurious connections between ridges. The side effect of each block is obvious but it has no harm to the further operations because as we find the image after consecutive binarization operation is pretty good as long as the side effect is not too severe.

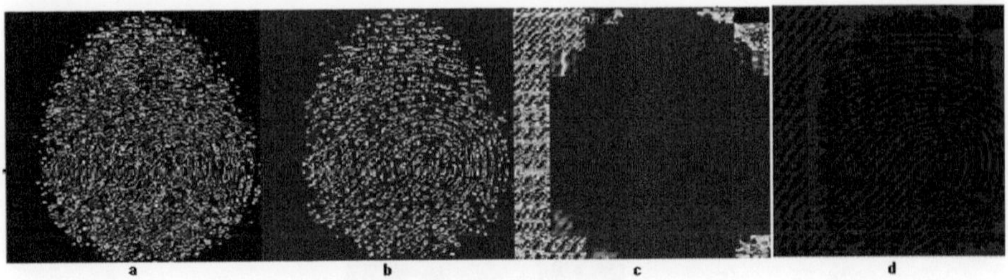

Fig. 2. a) Original image, b) Histogram Enhancement, c) Enhancement by FFT and d) Image after adaptive binarization

Fingerprint Image Binarization is to transform the 8-bit Gray fingerprint image to a 1-bit image with 0-value for ridges and 1-value for furrows. After the operation, ridges in the fingerprint are highlighted with black color while furrows are white. A locally adaptive binarization method is performed to binarize the fingerprint image. Such a named method comes from the mechanism of transforming a pixel value to 1 if the value is larger than the mean intensity value of the current block (16x16) to which the pixel belongs [Fig.2(d)].

3.1.1.2 ROI Selection. We perform morphological opening on the gray scale or binary image with the structuring element. We also performed morphological closing on the gray scale or binary image resulting in closed image. The structuring element is a single structuring element object, as opposed to an array of objects both open and close. Then as the result this approach throws away those leftmost, rightmost, uppermost and bottommost blocks out of the bound so as to get the tightly bounded region just containing the bound and inner area.

3.1.1.3 Minutiae Extraction. The last image enhancement step normally performed is thinning. Thinning is a morphological operation that successively erodes away the foreground pixels until they are one pixel wide. Ridge Thinning is to eliminate the redundant pixels of ridges till the ridges are just one pixel wide [16] uses a Ridge Thinning algorithm, which is used for Minutiae points' extraction in our approach shown in Fig.3. The image is divided into two distinct subfields in a checkerboard pattern. In the first sub-iteration, delete pixel p from the first subfield if and only if the conditions G1, G2, and G3 are all satisfied. In the second sub-iteration, delete pixel p from the second subfield if and only if the conditions G1, G2, and G3' are all satisfied.

Condition G1

$$X_H(P)=1.$$

Where,

$$X_H(P)=\sum_{i=1}^{4} b_i$$

$$b_i = \begin{cases} 1 & if\ x_{2i-1} = 0 \quad and \ = 1 \quad or \ \ x_{2i+1} = 1 \\ 0 & otherwise \end{cases} \tag{4}$$

Here, $x1$, $x2$,:::, $x8$, are the values of the eight neighbours of p, starting with the east neighbour and numbered in counter-clockwise order.

Fig. 3. Thinning and Minutiae points

Condition G2

$$2 \leq min\{n_1(p), n_2(p)\} \leq 3$$

Where,

$$n_1(p) = \sum_{k-1}^{4} X_{2k-1} \vee x_{2k},$$

$$n_2(p) = \sum_{k-1}^{4} X_{2k} \vee x_{2k+1}.$$

Condition G3

$$(x_2 \vee x_3 \vee \overline{x_8}) \wedge x_1 = 0.$$

Condition G3

$$(x_6 \vee x_7 \vee \overline{x}) \wedge x_5 = 0.$$

Two sub iterations together make up one iteration of thinning algorithm.

3.1.2 Secured Feature Matrix Generation

The steps involved in the generation of Secured Feature Matrix are discussed in this sub-section. We assume that the extracted minutiae point's co-ordinates are maintained in a vector. We proposed a security of Bio-metric information extracted minutia points using confidentiality and authentication mechanism when we transmit data over the low bandwidth and unreliable channel or covert channel.

3.1.3 Key Generation from Secured Feature Matrix (Sender and Receiver Prospects)

We have transfer the Bio-metric Information over the covert channel, In first step input the Bio-metric information from the User, store it in system and Register the user who uses this service and provide a unique ID and Password for authentication of users. In second step convert this Bio-metric information into integer format. These integer are compressed (encode) with help of arithmetic encoding scheme. Third step take compressed data as input and encrypted with the help of RSA algorithm. Fourth step generates the key for RSA algorithm. Fifth steps generate authentication code with the help of receiver ID and password. Sixth steps takes cipher text from encryption and appends it with message authentication code generated in sixth step. After that, this block send this append message over the covert channel. The receiver receives this message [See Fig.4 (a)].

The Cipher Text is receiving at receiver node. Detach the message authentication code form the cipher text and calculates own message authentication code with the help of own ID and password provided at time of registration and compared it with received cipher text authentication code, if it is same then he receive the cipher text otherwise discard it. In,second step accept this cipher text and decrypt with RSA algorithm. After decryption take this result and apply arithmetic decoding technique and decode. Receive key from the sender with and generate the Key for decryption of cipher text. The key is generated send to the RSA algorithm. In fourth steps take the integer result from arithmetic decoding and converted into Bio-metric information. After that original Bio-metric information is used [see Fig.4 (b)].

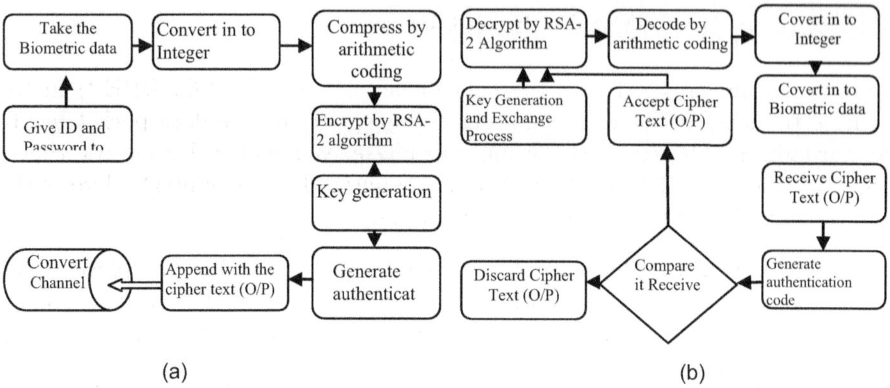

Fig. 4. a) Sender Prospects and b) Receiver Prospects

4 Experimental Results

The experimental analysis of our proposed approach is presented in this section. Our approach is programmed in Mat lab. We have tested our proposed an approach with different fingerprint images. The minutiae points are extracted from the fingerprint images using the three level approaches. Initially, in the pre-processing stage, histogram equalization and Fourier Transform are performed on the fingerprint images to enhance them.

Secondly, the binarization is applied on the fingerprint images and then the region of interest is determined. Subsequently minutiae points are extracted. Later, the secured feature matrix is generated based on the co-ordinates of minutiae points. Eventually, the 1024-bit key is generated from the secured feature matrix. The fingerprint images given in Fig.5 are depicted in Fig.6.

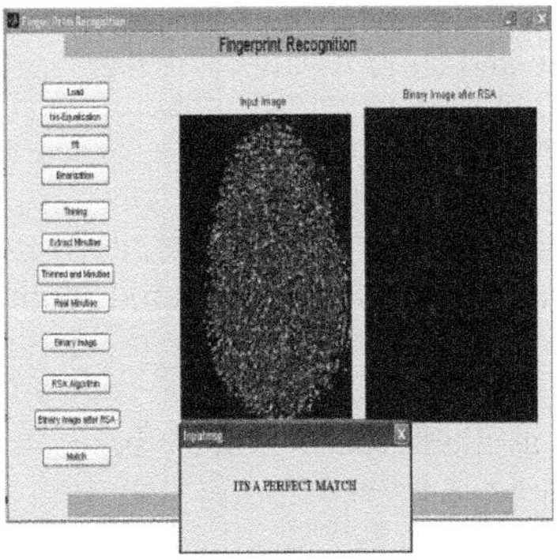

Fig. 5. After fingerprint match

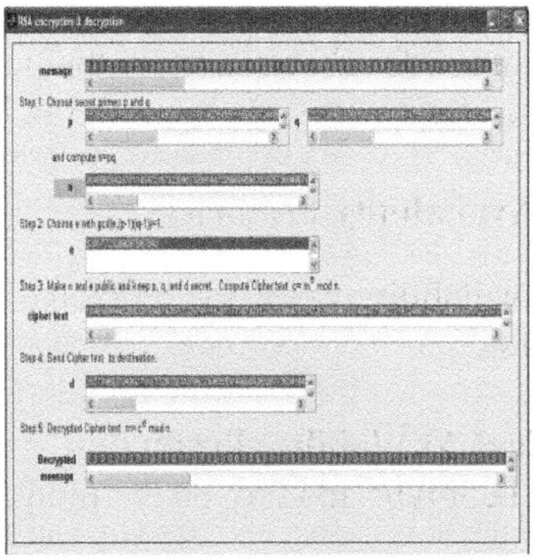

Fig. 6. Generated 1024 -bit key

5 Conclusion

Biometrics-based Key Generation outperforms traditional systems in usability domain. Precisely it is not possible for a person to lose his/her biometrics, and the biometric signal is intricate to falsify for steal. The proposed cancellable biometric Crypto System is an all-new technique for the authentication that yields the synergistic control of biometrics. The proposed system employs intentional distortion of fingerprint in a repeatable fashion and the fingerprint thus obtained is utilized in the cryptographic key generation. When the old finger print is "stolen" it is possible to obtain a "new" fingerprint just by altering the parameters of the distortion process. Subsequently, enhanced privacy for the user results as his true fingerprint is not utilized anywhere and diverse transformations for distortions can be utilized for a variety of accounts.

A notable enhancement in terms of decrease in the consumed time is attained with the elimination of more steps that are redundant with the mixture of the proposed methodology. Integration of the projected technique with the existing cryptographic methodologies is uncomplicated and as well decreases key-generation and key-release issues in a remarkable manner. This methodology can be further made efficient and sophisticated with the combination of any of the evolving cryptographic systems.

References

[1] AES Encrypt information, http://www.bitzipper.com/aes-encryption.html

[2] Ang, R., Safavi-Naini, R., McAven, L.: Cancellable key-based fingerprint templates. In: Boyd, C., González Nieto, J.M. (eds.) ACISP 2005. LNCS, vol. 3574, pp. 242–252. Springer, Heidelberg (2005)

[3] Announcing the Advanced Encryption Standard (AES), Federal Information, Processing Standards Publication 197 (November 26, 2001)

[4] Chang, Y.J., Wende, Z., Chen, T.: Biometrics- based cryptographic key generation. In: IEEE International Conference on Multimedia and Expo, vol. 3, pp. 2203–2206 (2004)

[5] Chen, B., Chandran, V.: Biometric Based Cryptographic Key Generation from Faces. In: Proceedings of the 9th Biennial Conference of the Australian Pattern Recognition Society on Digital Image Computing Techniques and Applications, pp. 394–401 (2007)

[6] Connie, T., Teoh, A., Goh, M., Ngo, D.: Palmhashing: A novel approach for cancellable biometrics. Information Processing Letters 93(1), 1–5 (2005)

[7] Feldmeier, D., Karn, P.: UNIX password security-Ten years later. In: Brassard, G. (ed.) CRYPTO 1989. LNCS, vol. 435, pp. 44–63. Springer, Heidelberg (1990)

[8] Feng, Y.C., Yuen, P.C., Jain, A.K.: A hybrid a Approach for face template protection. In: Proceedings of SPIE Conference of Biometric Technology for Human Identification, Orlando, USA, vol. 6944, p. ca.325 (2008)

[9] Santos, M.F., Aguilar, J.F., Garcia, J.O.: Cryptographic key generation using handwritten signature. In: Proceedings of SPIE, Orlando, Fla, USA, vol. 6202, pp. 225–231 (April 2006)

[10] GaborFilter, http://en.wikipedia.org/wiki/Gaborfilter

[11] Hao, F., Anderson, R., Daugman, J.: Combining crypto with biometrics effectively. IEEE Transactions on Computers 55, 1081–1088 (2006)

[12] Jain, L.C., Halici, U., Hayashi, I., Lee, S.B., Tsutsui, S.: Intelligent Biometric Techniques in Fingerprint and Face Recognition. CRC Press, Boca Raton (1999)

[13] Klein: Foiling the cracker: A survey of, and improvements to, password security. In: Proceedings of the 2nd USENIX Security Workshop, pp. 5–14 (August 1990)

[14] Lam, L., Lee, S.W., Suen, C.Y.: Thinning methodologies-A comprehensive survey. IEEE Transactions on Pattern Analysis and Machine Intelligence 14(9), 879 (1992)

[15] Menezes, A.J., Oorschot, P.C.V., Vanstone, S.A.: Handbook of Applied Cryptography, p. 180. CRC Press, Boca Raton (1997)

[16] Morris, R., Thompson, K.: Password security: A case history. Communications of the ACM 22(11), 594–597 (1979)

[17] Maio, D., Maltoni, D.: Direct gray-scale minutiae detection in fingerprints. IEEE Transactions on Pattern Analysis and Machine Intelligence 19(1), 27–40 (1997)

[18] Monrose, A., Reiter, M.K., Qi, L., Wetzel, S.: Cryptographic key generation from voice. In: Proceedings of IEEE Symposium on Security and Privacy, pp. 202–213 (2001)

[19] Uludag, U., Pankanti, S., Prabhakar, S., Jain, A.K.: Biometric cryptosystems: Issues and challenges. Proceedings of the IEEE 92, 948–960 (2004)

[20] Yeo, T., Tay, W.P., Tai, Y.Y.: Image Systems Engineering Program, Stanford University, Student project, http://scien.stanford.edu/class/ee368/projects2001/

Rootkit Detection Mechanism: A Survey

Jestin Joy[1], Anita John[1], and James Joy[2]

[1] Rajagiri School of Engineering & Technology, Kochi, Kerala
jestinjoy@acm.org, anitaj@rajagiritech.ac.in
[2] Tata Elxsi, Thiruvananthapuram, Kerala
jamesjoy@tataelxsi.co.in

Abstract. Rootkits are a set of software tools used by an attacker to gain unauthorized access into a system, thereby providing him with privilege to access sensitive data, conceal its own existence and allowing him to install other malicious software. An attacker needs administrative level privileges before he could install a rootkit. Rootkits are the most challenging malware to detect due to their elusive nature. Modern rootkit attacks mainly focus on modifying operating system kernel. This paper tries to provide a structured and comprehensive view of the research on rootkit detection/prevention.

1 Introduction

In recent years attackers employ a variety of sophisticated methods to gain access to the system. Kernel level rootkits are one of the most lethal attacking tool available with the intruders, because of the difficulty in detecting them and the considerable damage they cause to the system. Main goal of a rootkit is to conceal the evidence of intruder activities. Most rootkits need administrative level privileges to install it in the system. Usually attacker make use of some system vulnerabilities to get administrative level privileges. An ordinary user will find it difficult to detect the presence of rootkit, since he will not find any discrepancy in the behavior of the system, even if the system is infected by a rootkit. With the increasing use of operating system in smart phones and other embedded devices the threat posed by rootkits[4][27] are of great concern.

Rootkits first appeared in the end of 80's as method to hide log files and now they pose a serious threat to computer industry [6]. The first generation rootkits were easier to detect since they mainly aimed at modifying user level programs(logs, application binaries ...). Methods like checksum verification could easily detect these type of infections [15].Great deal of research is going on in the area of rootkit detection. In the past system administrators relied heavily on system utilities like ls, ps ... to find the presence of rootkits [15]. But new generation rootkits could easily hide their presence from these utilities.

Virtualization rootkits loads host OS as guest and can monitor all the host OS activities. BluePill, SubVirt etc are rootkits coming under this category. BluePill installs at the hypervisor level and controls the execution of the target OS. Kernel level rootkits modifies vital areas of an operating system like its kernel and

D. Nagamalai, E. Renault, and M. Dhanushkodi (Eds.): PDCTA 2011, CCIS 203, pp. 366–374, 2011.

the device drivers. Library level rootkits modifies or replaces standard system libraries with versions that help the attacker in hiding information. Difficulty in detecting kernel level rootkits arise out of the fact that they operate at the same security level as the kernel. Because of this, attackers now mainly rely on Kernel level rootkits. Our paper mainly focuses on kernel level rootkit detection mechanisms.

1.1 Kernel Level Rootkit

Unlike other rootkit types, kernel level rootkit modifies the kernel itself. Kernel being the lowest level of operating system makes it a good choice for the intruder to attack, since an attack on it is very difficult to detect. Also being at the kernel level provides the attacker with complete freedom to access all most all areas of an operating system.

First major attempt to categorize kernel level rootkits was done on the seminal paper[15] by Levine, Grizzard, Owen. They defined a framework for classifying rootkits. Their classification is based on the fact that along with the functionalities of a normal program, rootkit has some added functionalities that helps it to hide its activities.

In most cases rootkits finds its way into the kernel through Loadable Kernel Modules (LKM). LKM allows extending the functionality of the kernel, without recompiling the kernel. The code inserted using LKM provides same capability as a kernel code. Another important advantage of using LKM is that they can be added/removed on the fly. Though mainly aimed at debugging the kernel, */dev/mem* is also used by the intruders to attack the system [16]. In Linux based systems, modules can be inserted through the utilities *insmod* or *modprobe*.

Kernel level rootkits occur in different forms. They affect system call table [14], Virtual File System (VFS) (for example, by *adore − ng* rootkit), Interrupt Descriptor Table (IDT) [24] .... VFS can be thought of as a kernel subsystem which provides a unified API to user-space applications. There are certain other rootkits that employ a combination of these techniques (example *zk* rootkit [15]).

When a user level program access a system resource, it is accomplished through a system call. The user level application performs a system call, which passes the control to the kernel. The requested work is done by the kernel and result is passed back to the user level application. So system call is an important target for attackers. Kernel level rootkits attack System Call table by different mechanisms [15]. Three of them are listed below

1. System Call Table modification
   In this method, attacker replaces original system call with his own custom version. Mainly this is done by modifying the system call address by inserting malicious LKM's address. Knark [7] rootkit uses this approach.
2. System Call Target modification
   In this attack, legitimate code in the target address is modified. This type of attack does not modify system call table. It works by modifying the flow of control in a system call. Usually a jump instruction is used to pass the control to the malicious code.

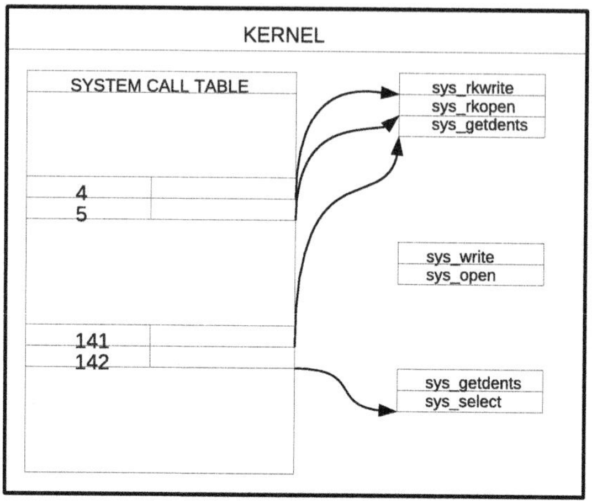

Fig. 1. System Call Redirection Example

3. System Call Table Redirection
   In this method attacker replaces the call to System Call Table with his own custom version. This is usually done by overwriting the memory where System Call Table address is stored. By comparing with *System.map* file this type of attacks of could easily be detected.

Fig.1 show the result of System Call redirection where, the system calls *sys_write*, *sys_open*, *sys_getdents* are replaced with modified ones; *sys_rkwrite*, *sys_rkopen*, *sys_rkgetdents*.

2 Detection Mechanism

Rootkit Detection mechanisms can be classified based on where the detection module resides. Early methods for detection relied mainly on archived copy of system files for detection [14]. But this method couldn't detect all type of attacks and also for the detection to work properly, the archived copy should be clean.

If kernel level rootkits are used, the method of using more than one application for detection doesn't work. For example we get information about the modules from both */proc/modules* and *lsmod* command. */proc* file-system is a special file-system that is used by the kernel to export information. Contents of this file-system are created when they are read. Many utilities get their information form */proc. lsmod* gets its information from */proc/modules*. If rootkit modifies */proc/modules* both *cat/proc/modules* and *lsmod* command gives same information. So gathering information relying solely on user space applications doesn't help.

This paper classifies detection mechanism into three (1) Host based (2) Virtualization based and (3) External observer based mechanisms. Another class; rootkit profilers helps to better understand rootkit attack strategies.

2.1 Host Based

Host based detection mechanism works from the infected system. Kern_check [14] is a utility that checks *System.map*, which stores symbols used by the kernel, against system call table of running kernel and warn about inconsistencies. Some other tools like CheckIDT, Chkrootkit [14], StMichael... are host based detection tools that make use of prior information for detection. StMichael is a LKM, that provides protection by monitoring various portions of the kernel, for modifications that may indicate the presence of a malicious kernel module. All the above tools rely heavily on prior information about the host system for detection.

Kruegel et al. [12] introduced a behavior based method for preventing rootkit modules from loading into the system. It uses static analysis to determine if a kernel module is malicious before the kernel module is loaded into the kernel and executed. Since this method is applied to the binary image of the module, it doesn't need source code for analysis. Detection is based on the following two major behavioral specifications

- Write operation to an illegal memory area
- Module contains instruction sequences that use forbidden kernel symbol reference to calculate an address in the kernels address space and a write operation based on this calculated address.

File integrity scanners like Tripwire [10], Samhain [26], AIDE [26] ... are powerful tools that aid system administrators in checking the trail of rootkits in the system. These tools generally use checksum based mechanism to take snapshot of the system, which is used for detecting modifications. Checksum based methods [15] fail when rootkits use dynamic directories to store rootkit related information. For example many rootkits rely on the */proc* directory(example *knark* rootkit) to store its contents. Strider Ghostbuster [3] identifies hidden files, processes ... by comparing two views of the system.

Another method of importance is using cryptographically signed kernel modules. This method prevents loading unauthorized modules into the kernel space. Greg Kroah-Hartman proposed a method based on this using RSA encryption to sign the modules [11].

Placing rootkit detection mechanism in the monitored host itself make it more visible, and could be modifiable by advanced rootkits. So the focus moved towards placing it in system other than the monitored host. The next two rootkit detection methods works based on this principle.

2.2 Virtualization Based

In virtual machine based rootkit detection, observer modules working in hypervisor mode aides in detection. They are designed based on the assumption that working on a layer higher than kernel helps the monitor module to efficiently track the host OS activities.

First major research in this direction was done by Tal Garfinkel and Mendel Rosenblum [8]. Their Livewire system used Virtual Machine Monitor (VMM) technique for detecting rootkits. Livewire implementation leverages on the isolation, inspection and interposition properties of a VMM. It consists of a policy engine, which interprets system state and events from the VMM interface and decides whether an attack occurred or not.

Petroni et al. [18] introduced a state based control flow integrity (SBCFI) based method for monitoring operating system kernel integrity dynamically. SBCFI is an extension of Control flow integrity where the monitor looks for change in state for detection. Based on the analysis of 25 Linux rootkits Petroni et al. [18] state that 96% of them employ persistent control-flow modifications and their method could detect them without having any false positives. In their approach VMM runs two virtual machines, one for the monitor and one for target.

SecVisor [23] is a hypervisor based mechanism to ensure code integrity for commodity OS kernels. It needs small modification to the host kernel to work. SecVisor prevents kernel code from unauthorized modification and execution, based on user specified approval policy.NICKLE [20] is a VMM based system that prevents unauthorized kernel code execution for unmodified commodity (guest) OSes. NICKLE uses VMM for restricting access to the kernel space. NICKLE works based on the technique of VMM based memory shadowing scheme. NICKLE module lies in the VMM layer and enforces that the guest OS kernel cannot access the shadow memory. At runtime, any instruction executed in the kernel space must be fetched from the shadow memory, which contains authenticated instructions.

VMwatcher [9] uses a technique called guest view casting for rootkit detection, based on systematically reconstructing internal semantic views of a VM from outside. One of the main challenge of moving monitoring out of the target OS is that there is a semantic gap between the view of VM from inside and outside. In VMwatcher guest view casting technique reconstruct the semantic-level view of the VM.

HookSafe [24] provides a hypervisor based system to protect kernel hooks from being attacked by rootkits. Hooking is an efficient technique employed by rootkits to evade detection. Hooking effectively modifies the flow of control and hides the presence of modification. HookSafe loads the target OS as Guest OS and monitors the possible hooks for modification. It provides a hook indirection layer to regulate access to hooks in the kernel. Only write access to hooks needs the control to transferred to the hypervisor.

Baliga et al. introduced Paladin [2] an automatic rootkit detection and contain technique by leveraging the virtual machine technology. File access control and memory access control policies are specified to protect memory areas that are targets of rootkit attack. Attack detection is based on the creation of dependency tree. Dependency tree lists process-file relationships. When access control policy is violated, based on the dependency tree, detection mechanism can stop malicious programs from cause further damages.

KernelGuard [19] offers a VMM based solution for preventing dynamic data rootkits. Dynamic data rootkits are difficult to detect since they didn't cause any change to kernel code. Since they do not execute any new code, they could easily

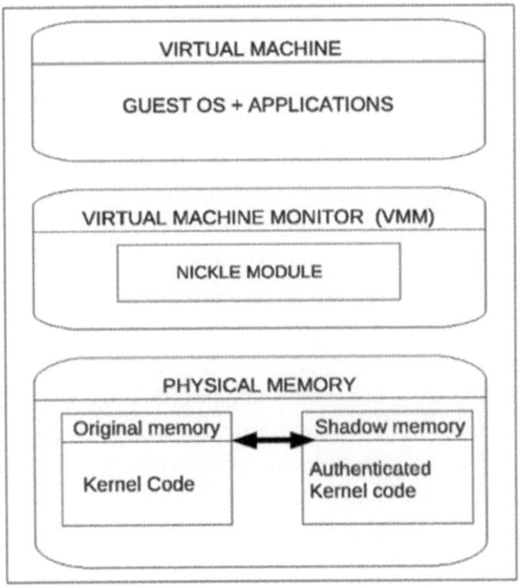

Fig. 2. NICKLE Architecture

elude detection efforts. KernelGuard works in Virtual machine environment and makes use of semantic information for validation.

Large number of research initiatives focus on using VMM based mechanism for rootkit detection, as compared to other two approaches. But Bratus, Locasto et al.in their paper [5] questions the viability of using VM technique for rootkit detection. They argue that many modern day applications couldnâĂŹt integrate VM technique as a detection mechanism. Moreover the VM complexity is increasing day by day and managing the VM becomes a major challenge.

2.3 External Observer Based

This method mainly use external observation mechanisms for detecting kernel level rootkits. Earlier work utilized Trusted Platform Modules (TPM) for defeating rootkits. Method proposed by Reiner Sailer et al [22]. need modification to the running kernel. It first takes measurements of uncompromised target. TPM is used to collect a sequence of hashes over target code. Validation is done on the basis of this hashed copy.

Petroni et al. [17] developed Copilot, a coprocessor based mechanism to check the integrity of kernel code. It uses a PCI-card to monitor the memory of the host system. Copilot first creates "known good hashes" of host kernels text, text of loaded LKM, and the contents of some of the host kernel's critical data structures. It then periodically checks for any changes.

Fig.3 depicts the copilot testbed architecture [17]. PCI add-in card contains the host monitor. Admin station is the machine from which an administrator can interact with the Copilot monitor.

Fig. 3. Copilot Testbed Architecture

Baliga, Ganapathy et al. [1] introduced a similar mechanism for detecting kernel level rootkits. Their detection tool Gibraltar focused on detecting both control and non-control data modification. Gibraltar uses an external PCI card to obtain information from target system. Gibraltar operates in inference mode and detection mode. During inference phase Gibraltar uses an uncompromised target to infer invariants. In detection mode it checks whether the data structures on the targets kernel satisfy the invariants inferred earlier.

This method couldn't find much interest from research community because of the need for having an external entity for monitoring. Some of these methods could also extended to VMM layer [1].

3 Rootkit Profiling

Profiling of rootkits is essential for better understanding their attack strategies and could help to contain the attacks. Profiling helps manual analysis easier for an expert. Riley et al. [21] introduced PoKeR, a profiler based on NICKLE [20]. PoKeR is deployed in scenarios which can tolerate high overheads. PoKeR (Profiler for Kernel Rootkits) is capable of producing rootkit profiles which include the revelation of rootkit hooking behavior, targeted kernel objects, user level impacts. It is also capable of extracting rootkit code.

HookFinder [28] helps to identify the hooking behavior of malicious code without relying on any prior knowledge of hooking mechanisms. HookMap [25] monitors normal kernel execution path to find kernel hooks that could be potentially hijacked for evasion. K-Tracer [13] dynamically analyze kernel code and extract malicious behavior from rootkits. It uses data flow analysis of kernel execution for profiling.

4 Conclusion

Rootkits are "Trojan horses" that resides in the operating system. Residing in kernel makes kernel level rootkits difficult to detect. Their self concealment behavior and administrative level privileges makes them the most difficult attack to detect. Researchers are looking for efficient methods, that needs less prior information, low overhead and high accuracy. Based on where the detection module lies, the detection mechanism can be classified into host based, virtualization based and external observer based mechanism. Virtualization based method is the most widely used detection method. But in terms of the area of application it has some limitations. Improved understanding of various detection mechanisms will help the researchers in not only improving the existing detection mechanisms but also to look for other efficient solutions.

References

1. Baliga, A., Ganapathy, V., Iftode, L.: Detecting kernel-level rootkits using data structure invariants. IEEE Transactions on Dependable and Secure Computing 99 (PrePrints) (2010)
2. Baliga, A., Iftode, L., Chen, X.: Automated containment of rootkits attacks. Computers and Security 27(7-8), 323–334 (2008), http://www.sciencedirect.com/science/article/B6V8G-4SYCPMR-1/2/0072c2079956faf503f8f683847fd3a2
3. Beck, D., Vo, B., Verbowski, C.: Detecting stealth software with strider ghostbuster. In: Proceedings of the 2005 International Conference on Dependable Systems and Networks, DSN 2005, pp. 368–377. IEEE Computer Society, Washington, DC, USA (2005), http://dx.doi.org/10.1109/DSN.2005.39
4. Bickford, J., O'Hare, R., Baliga, A., Ganapathy, V., Iftode, L.: Rootkits on smart phones: attacks, implications and opportunities. In: Proceedings of the Eleventh Workshop on Mobile Computing Systems & Applications, pp. 49–54. ACM, New York (2010)
5. Bratus, S., Locasto, M.E., Ramaswamy, A., Smith, S.W.: Vm-based security overkill: a lament for applied systems security research. In: Proceedings of the 2010 Workshop on New Security Paradigms, NSPW 2010, pp. 51–60. ACM, New York (2010), http://doi.acm.org/10.1145/1900546.1900554
6. Bunten, A.: Unix and linux based rootkits techniques and countermeasures (2004)
7. Clemens, J.: Intrusion Detection FAQ: Knark: Linux Kernel Subversion (2001)
8. Garfinkel, T., Rosenblum, M.: A virtual machine introspection based architecture for intrusion detection. In: Proc. Network and Distributed Systems Security Symposium, vol. 1, pp. 253–285. Citeseer (2003)
9. Jiang, X., Wang, X., Xu, D.: Stealthy malware detection through vmm-based out of the box semantic view reconstruction, pp. 128–138 (2007), http://doi.acm.org/10.1145/1315245.1315262
10. Kim, G.H., Spafford, E.H.: The design and implementation of tripwire: a file system integrity checker. In: Proceedings of the 2nd ACM Conference on Computer and Communications Security, CCS 1994, pp. 18–29. ACM, New York (1994), http://doi.acm.org/10.1145/191177.191183
11. Kroah-Hartman, G.: Signed kernel modules. Linux Journal (2004)
12. Kruegel, C., Robertson, W., Vigna, G.: Detecting kernel-level rootkits through binary analysis. In: Computer Security Applications Conference, Annual, pp. 91–100 (2004)
13. Lanzi, A., Sharif, M., Lee, W.: K-tracer: A system for extracting kernel malware behavior. In: Proceedings of the 16th Annual Network and Distributed System Security Symposium (2009)
14. Levine, J., Grizzard, J., Owen, H.: A methodology to detect and characterize kernel level rootkit exploits involving redirection of the system call table. In: Proceedings of Second IEEE International Information Assurance Workshop, pp. 107–125. IEEE, Los Alamitos (2005)

15. Levine, J.G., Grizzard, J.B., Owen, H.L.: Detecting and categorizing kernel-level rootkits to aid future detection. IEEE Security and Privacy 4, 24 (2006), http://portal.acm.org/citation.cfm?id=1115691.1115761
16. Lineberry, A.: Malicious Code Injection via/dev/mem. Black Hat Europe (2009), http://www.blackhat.com/presentations/bh-europe-09/Lineberry/BlackHat-Europe-2009-Lineberry-code-injection-via-dev-mem.pdf
17. Petroni Jr., N.L., Fraser, T., Molina, J., Arbaugh, W.A.: Copilot - a coprocessor-based kernel runtime integrity monitor. In: Proceedings of the 13th Conference on USENIX Security Symposium, SSYM 2004, vol. 13, pp. 13–13. USENIX Association, Berkeley (2004), http://portal.acm.org/citation.cfm?id=1251375.1251388
18. Petroni Jr., N.L., Hicks, M.: Automated detection of persistent kernel control-flow attacks. In: Proceedings of the 14th ACM Conference on Computer and Communications Security, CCS 2007, pp. 103–115. ACM, New York (2007), http://doi.acm.org/10.1145/1315245.1315260
19. Rhee, J., Riley, R., Xu, D., Jiang, X.: Defeating dynamic data kernel rootkit attacks via vmm-based guest-transparent monitoring. In: International Conference on Availability, Reliability and Security, pp. 74–81 (2009)
20. Riley, R., Jiang, X., Xu, D.: Guest-transparent prevention of kernel rootkits with vmm-based memory shadowing. In: Lippmann, R., Kirda, E., Trachtenberg, A. (eds.) RAID 2008. LNCS, vol. 5230, pp. 1–20. Springer, Heidelberg (2008)
21. Riley, R., Jiang, X., Xu, D.: Multi-aspect profiling of kernel rootkit behavior. In: Proceedings of the 4th ACM European Conference on Computer Systems, EuroSys 2009, pp. 47–60. ACM, New York (2009), http://doi.acm.org/10.1145/1519065.1519072
22. Sailer, R., Zhang, X., Jaeger, T., van Doorn, L.: Design and implementation of a tcg-based integrity measurement architecture. In: Proceedings of the 13th Conference on USENIX Security Symposium, SSYM 2004, vol. 13, p. 16. USENIX Association, Berkeley (2004), http://portal.acm.org/citation.cfm?id=1251375.1251391
23. Seshadri, A., Luk, M., Qu, N., Perrig, A.: Secvisor: A tiny hypervisor to provide lifetimekernel code integrity for commodity OSes. In: Proceedings of the 21st ACM Symposium on Operating Systems Principles (21st SOSP 2007), pp. 335–350. ACM SIGOPS, Stevenson (October 2007)
24. Wang, Z., Jiang, X., Cui, W., Ning, P.: Countering kernel rootkits with lightweight hook protection. In: Proceedings of the 16th ACM Conference on Computer and Communications Security, CCS 2009, pp. 545–554. ACM, New York (2009), http://doi.acm.org/10.1145/1653662.1653728
25. Wang, Z., Jiang, X., Cui, W., Wang, X.: Countering persistent kernel rootkits through systematic hook discovery. In: Lippmann, R., Kirda, E., Trachtenberg, A. (eds.) RAID 2008. LNCS, vol. 5230, pp. 21–38. Springer, Heidelberg (2008)
26. Wichmann, R.: A comparison of several host/file integrity monitoring programs (December 29, 2009), http://www.la-samhna.de/library/scanners.html
27. Yan, Q., Li, Y., Li, T., Deng, R.: Insights into Malware Detection and Prevention on Mobile Phones. In: Ślęzak, D., Kim, T.-h., Fang, W.-C., Arnett, K.P. (eds.) SecTech 2009. CCIS, vol. 58, pp. 242–249. Springer, Heidelberg (2009)
28. Yin, H., Liang, Z., Song, D.: Hookfinder: Identifying and understanding malware hooking behaviors. In: Proceedings of the 15th Annual Network and Distributed System Security Symposium (NDSS 2008). Citeseer (2008)

Efficiency Enhanced Association Rule Mining Technique

Abhishek Agrawal[1,*], Urjita Thakar[1], Rishi Soni[2], and Brijesh Kumar Chaurasia[2]

[1] SGSITS- Indore, India
[2] Institute of Technology and Management-Gwalior, India
Tel.: +91-8989248034, +91-9425117367
abhishek_abhiitm@yahoo.com, callrishisoni@rediffmail.com,
bkchaurasia_itm@gmail.com

Abstract. Data Mining has been widely used by business organizations and data analysts for extraction of implicit, previously unknown and potentially useful information from huge data sets. Out of the large number of data mining approaches, association rule mining is the most popular. In this paper, the conventional association rule mining technique has been improved to be able to extract better data from the large pool of data. A strategy has been proposed for selection of association rules that will result into extraction of more relevant and useful data from the data set. It is observed that the proposed method gives more precise results and thus is more efficient as compared to the commonly used rule mining technique. The method is more useful since more relevant information becomes available to the analysts and businesses.

Keywords: Data Warehouse; Data Mining; Association Rules.

1 Introduction

Data Mining is the process of discovering meaningful patterns and relationships that lie hidden within very large databases. The need of data mining originated from the emergence of data warehouse. According to W. H. Inmon [1], a leading architect in the construction of data warehouse systems, "A data warehouse is a subject- oriented, integrated, time variant and non volatile collection of data that supports management's decision making process". This short but comprehensive definition presents the major features of a data warehouse. Since methods for filtering/analyzing the data are required, a variety of data mining techniques have been developed for finding new knowledge by discovering hidden rules from huge amount of data.

Association rule mining [2] is a technique for discovering data dependencies and is one of the best known data mining techniques. For finding association rule, one of the oldest algorithms used is Apriori algorithm. It finds the association rules from the dataset. A typical example of association rule mining is the market basket analysis. Other than market basket analysis, association rules can also help in applications such as intrusion detection, heterogeneous genome data, mining remotely sensed data and product assortment decisions [2].

* Corresponding author.

D. Nagamalai, E. Renault, and M. Dhanushkodi (Eds.): PDCTA 2011, CCIS 203, pp. 375–384, 2011.

In past, many researchers have made their contributions towards improving the efficiency of data mining and association rule mining technique. All these works use a threshold value known as minimum confidence to find potentially useful information from huge data sets. The information with confidence value greater than this minimum confidence value is taken as useful information [3-9]. These approaches have been observed to have limitation that the data is not very much suited to the user's need.

In this paper, a critical review has been made on the conventional association rule mining technique to enhance its efficiency. A strategy has been proposed to be able to extract better data from database. In this work, no threshold value is used to extract the information. The paper has been organized as follows: Related work is discussed in section 2. In section 3, the requisite background is discussed. The proposed approach is discussed in section 4. In section 5, an example has been discussed. A discussion on the association rule mining method is proposed in section 6. The paper is concluded in section 7.

2 Related Work

Some work related to efficiency improvement of Apriori Algorithm for association rule mining has been done in the past. Sun *et al.* have proposed improved algorithm based on the combination of forward scan and reverse scan of a given database, which reduce the scanning times required for the discovery of candidate item-sets [3]. Xie *et al.* have proposed a new Apriori algorithm that can reduce the number of the times database is scanned to optimize the join procedure of frequent item-sets generated in order to reduce the size of the candidate item-sets [4].

An algorithm called Reduced Apriori Algorithm with Tag (RAAT), which reduces one redundant pruning operations of C2 has been discussed by Yu [5]. Qing *et al.* have introduced a method to improve the efficiency and quality of Apriori Algorithm [6].

Jing *et al.* have improved the Apriori algorithm by reducing the number of scans of the database and number of candidate item-set in advance [7]. Apriori algorithm has been enhanced based on the user interest by Ping [8]. Feng suggested that Apriori optimization association rule mining algorithm reduced the time complexity of the original algorithm, especially for large database [9].

3 Background

3.1 Data Mining

Data Mining [10] is the process of discovering meaningful patterns and relationships that lie hidden within very large databases. Browsing through tables and records rarely leads to discovery of useful pattern, data is typically analyzed by an automated process, commonly referred to data mining.

3.2 Apriori Algorithm

Apriori [2] is an algorithm to find frequent item-sets and association rule. The process of finding frequent item-sets involves two steps –frequent item-set generation and pruning.

3.3 Association Rule Mining

Association rule mining [2] has been proposed for finding correlation among different data attributes in a large set of data items. The relationships observed between data attributes are called association rules.

From the frequent item-sets generated by Apriori algorithm, the association rules that have confidence greater than a certain threshold called minimum confidence are generated.

Let $I = \{i_1, i_2, \dots \dots, i_n\}$ be a set of items. Given a set of transaction T is a set of items such that $T \subseteq I$, an association rule is an expression $X \Longrightarrow Y$ where $X \subseteq I$, $Y \subseteq I$ and $X \cap Y = \emptyset$. Then Support of $X \Longrightarrow Y$ is calculated as $|X \cup Y|/N$, and confidence of $X \Longrightarrow Y$ is calculated as $|X \cup Y|/|X|$, where N is total number of transactions. In other words, the confidence of a rule measures the degree of the correlation between itemsets, while the support of a rule measures the significance of the correlation between item-sets [11].

4 Proposed Approach

In the proposed approach, first of all, frequent item-sets are generated using Apriori algorithm. From these frequent item-sets, Association rules are mined without using minimum confidence as threshold. As per the user's input for number of association rules required, system will generate the Association rules with highest confidence. The architecture of the system is shown in Fig.1.

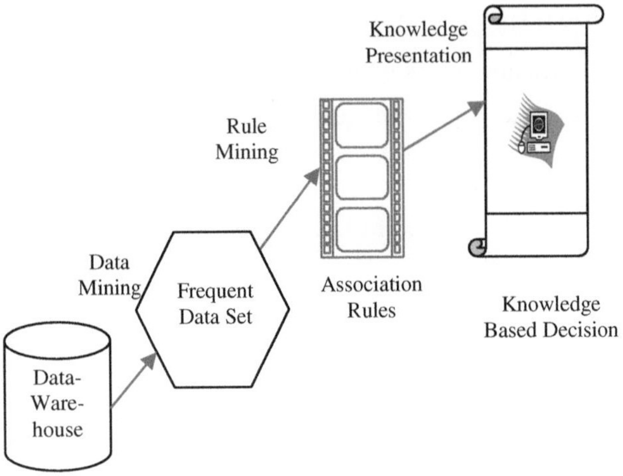

Fig. 1. Association Rule Mining Architecture

4.1 Frequent Item-Sets Generation

Frequent item-sets [2] are the item-set with support greater than a certain threshold, called minimum support. For generation of frequent item-sets from pool of data a basic algorithm Apriori, designed by Agrawal and others in 1993 is used [8]. Apriori uses the recursive method for generation of frequent item-sets. The core algorithm is:

Algorithm Apriori

Input: A database D, the minimum threshold of support minimum support
Output: the database of all the frequent item-sets

1) $L_1 = (Frequent\ 1 - Items)$;
2) for (k = 2; $L_k - 1$; k + +) do begin
3) C_k = apriori_gen ($L_k - 1$); / / After two-step connection and pruning operations generate a new candidate frequent itemsets
4) for all transactions $t \in D$ do begin
5) C_t= subset ($C_k - t$); / / In the database to scan t included in the candidate frequent item-sets C_k
6) for all candidates $c \in C_t$ do
7) $c.count++$;
8) end;
9) $L_k = (c \in C \mid c.count \geq minsupport)$
10) end;
11) $Answer = U_k L_k$;

The algorithm generates 1-frequent item-sets, 2-frequent item-sets,...., k -frequent itemsets. If C_k is empty for some k, the algorithm ends and gives the frequent item-sets. The steps for generating association rules are given in the next subsection.

4.2 Association Rules Generation

For generation of association rules following steps are performed.

Step1: Take all the frequent item-sets generated from previous subsection.
Step2: For each frequent item-set, generate all the possible association rules.
Step3: Calculate the confidence value of each association rules.

4.3 Selection of Association Rules

For selection of association rules following steps are performed.

Step1: Take all the association rules generated from previous subsection.
Step2: By applying selection sort, arrange all the association rules in descending order of their confidence value.
Step3: Based on the experience, the user selects few association rules with highest confidence value.

An Example has been discussed in the next section to clearly explain the working of the proposed approach.

5 Examples

A data set corresponding to tour planning has been taken as example to discuss the method proposed. The database consists of following fields. For each customer there is a id which is represented by CUSID, AGE field defines the age of corresponding customer, BUDGET field defines the budget of the customer for their tour, TRAVEL_MODE field shows that by which mode they travel, and PLACE field defines that place. Table 1 gives the sample database.

The data is preprocessed as given below. To create logical database it will convert age as $(AGE \leq 35{:}1; AGE > 35{:}2)$, budget as $(BUDGET \leq 40000{:}3;\ BUDGET > 40000{:}4)$, travel_mode as $(TRAVEL\_MODE = Plane{:}5;\ TRAVEL_{MODE} = Train{:}6)$, place as $(PLACE = Hill\ Station{:}7;\ PLACE = Spiritual\ Place{:}8)$. Table 2 shows the logical database which is corresponds with Table 1.

Table 1. Sample database

CUSID	AGE	BUDGET	TRAVEL _MODE	PLACE
100	25	50000	Plane	Hill Station
200	50	45000	Plane	Spiritual Place
300	30	25000	Train	Hill Station
400	60	20000	Train	Spiritual Place
500	28	40000	Train	Spiritual Place
600	35	70000	Plane	Hill Station
700	55	55000	Plane	Spiritual Place
800	31	18000	Train	Hill Station

Table 2. Logical database corresponds with the original database (preprocessed data)

CUSID	AGE		BUDGET		TRAVEL_ MODE		PLACE	
	1	2	3	4	5	6	7	8
100	1	0	0	1	1	0	1	0
200	0	1	0	1	1	0	0	1
300	1	0	1	0	0	1	1	0
400	0	1	1	0	0	1	0	1
500	1	0	1	0	0	1	0	1
600	1	0	0	1	1	0	1	0
700	0	1	0	1	1	0	0	1
800	1	0	1	0	0	1	1	0

Now the next task is to obtain the association between the different fields, like association between age and budget, budget and travel mode, travel mode and place, and so on. To find the association between these fields there is the need to convert these values in transaction. To do so corresponding to each customer a transaction is generated. In which there are two fields, first is RECID which is same as CUSID and for each RECID there is a ITEMS field which contains the information of age, budget, travel mode and place with value 1 as shown in Table 3.

Table 3. Value set of attribute items in database

RECID	ITEMS
100	1,4,5,7
200	2,4,5,8
300	1,3,6,7
400	2,3,6,8
500	1,3,6,8
600	1,4,5,7
700	2,4,5,8
800	1,3,6,7

5.1 Steps to Get Frequent Item-Sets

Assuming minimum support 0.33, namely $minsupport = 0.33$

(1) Generating $K = 1$ Larger Sets (i.e. contains only 1 item)

By scanning the database obtain the support of the items when the length $k = 1$. Then compare the obtained support with the minimum support 0.33, we get L1 (k=1 large sets). It is shown in Table 4.

Table 4. $K = 1$ Items and Corresponding Larger Sets

Item	Support	L_1
{1}	5/8=0.625	Y
{2}	3/8=0.375	Y
{3}	4/8=0.5	Y
{4}	4/8=0.5	Y
{5}	4/8=0.5	Y
{6}	4/8=0.5	Y
{7}	4/8=0.5	Y
{8}	4/8=0.5	Y

So corresponding larger sets when $k = 1$ are $L_1 = \{1,2,3,4,5,6,7,8\}$

(2) Generating $K = 2$ Larger Sets (i.e. contains 2 items)

The candidate sets are obtained when $K = 2\ by\ K = 1$ larger sets L_1, and calculating the support of 2 items to get larger sets L_2. It is shown in Table 5.

Table 5. K=2 Items and Corresponding Larger Sets

Items	Support	L_2
{1,2}	0/8=0	N
{1,3}	3/8=0.375	Y
{1,4}	2/8=0.25	N
{1,5}	2/8=0.25	N
{1,6}	3/8=0.375	Y
{1,7}	4/8=0.5	Y
{1,8}	1/8=0.125	N
{2,3}	1/8=0.125	N
{2,4}	2/8=0.25	N
{2,5}	2/8=0.25	N
{2,6}	1/8=0.125	N
{2,7}	0/8=0	N
{2,8}	3/8=0.375	Y
{3,4}	0/8=0	N
{3,5}	0/8=0	N
{3,6}	4/8=0.5	Y
{3,7}	2/8=0.25	N
{3,8}	2/8=0.25	N
{4,5}	4/8=0.5	Y
{4,6}	0/8=0	N
{4,7}	2/8=0.25	N
{4,8}	2/8=0.25	N
{5,6}	0/8=0	N
{5,7}	2/8=0.25	N
{5,8}	2/8=0.25	N
{6,7}	2/8=0.25	N
{6,8}	2/8=0.25	N
{7,8}	0/8=0	N

So corresponding larger sets when $k = 2$ are $L_2 = \{\{1,3\},\{1,6\},\{1,7\},\{2,8\},\{3,6\},\{4,5\}\}$

(3) Generating $K = 3$ Larger Sets (i.e. contains 3 items)

The candidate sets are obtained when K=3 by K=2 larger sets L_2, and calculating the support of 3 items to get larger sets L_3. It is shown in Table 6.

Table 6. K=3 Items and Corresponding Larger Sets

Items	Support	L_3
{1,3,6}	3/8=0.375	Y
{1,3,7}	2/8=0.25	N
{1,6,7}	2/8=0.25	N

So corresponding larger sets when $k = 3$ are $L_3 = \{\{1,3,6\}\}$

5.2 Steps to Get Association Rules

Assuming that user decides to have 2 association rules. Then, it will generate all the association rules for {1,3,6} item-sets from Table 6 and calculate the confidence of each of them. It is shown in Table 7.

Table 7. Association Rules Generation

Items	LHS	RHS	Confidence
{1,3,6}	1	3,6	3/5=0.6
{1,3,6}	3	1,6	3/4=0.75
{1,3,6}	6	1,3	3/4=0.75
{1,3,6}	1,3	6	3/3=1
{1,3,6}	1,6	3	3/3=1
{1,3,6}	3,6	1	3/4=0.75

So six association rules are generated for {1,3,6} item-set.

5.3 Steps to Select Association Rules

The association rules are sorted in the decreasing order of the confidence value as given in Table 8.

Table 8. Association Rules in Decreasing Order of Confidence Value

Items	LHS	RHS	Confidence
{1,3,6}	1,3	6	3/3=1
{1,3,6}	1,6	3	3/3=1
{1,3,6}	3	1,6	3/4=0.75
{1,3,6}	6	1,3	3/4=0.75
{1,3,6}	3,6	1	3/4=0.75
{1,3,6}	1	3,6	3/5=0.6

Next based on the experience, user decides to take 2 association rules with highest confidence value as given below:

Association Rules	Confidence
$I(1,3) \Rightarrow I(6)$	1
And $I(1,6) \Rightarrow I(3)$	1

These rules specify that:

1. $I(1,3) \Rightarrow I(6)$ means: Persons with AGE less than or equal to 35 and BUDGET less than or equal to 40000 will prefer to travel by train.
2. $I(1,6) \Rightarrow I(3)$ means: Persons with AGE less than or equal to 35 and TRAVEL_MODE by train have BUDGET less than or equal to 40000.

6 Discussion

In previous method, a threshold called minimum confidence is used to select association rules. If small value of minimum confidence is taken, then many association rules are generated, resulting in extraction of extra data not required by the user. In another condition of previous method, if value of minimum confidence is taken high then very less number of association rules are generate resulting in extraction of very few data. Such a method is also unable to fulfill user's need.

In the method proposed in this paper, the most relevant association rules are selected as per user's experience and judgment resulting in extraction of data more suitable to the user's need.

7 Conclusion

In this paper, efficiency enhanced association rule based data mining technique has been discussed. It has been observed that the presented approach enables extraction of most relevant data from the database. In this method, selection of association rules is performed using highest confidence value that is selected by the user as per his experience and judgment. The outcomes are more close to the user's need. The proposed method also helps in retraining better data along with the more useful for an experienced user since to decide association rules to be considered the user needs to be an expert. The future work is to device an automatic mechanism that will enable selection of optimized association rules using some AI techniques.

References

1. Chen, Y., Yang, M., Zhang, L.: General Data Mining Model System Based on Sample Data Division. In: The Second International Symposium on Knowledge Acquisition and Modeling, pp. 182–185 (2009)
2. Chi-Wing, W.R., Fu, A.W.-C.: Association Rule Mining and its Application to MPIS, `http://www.cse.ust.hk/~raywong/paper/dataWarehousing05-mpis.pdf`
3. Sun, D., Teng, S., Zhang, W., Zhu, H.: An Algorithm to Improve the Effectiveness of Apriori. In: The 6th IEEE Int. Conf. on Cognitive Informatics (ICCI 2007), pp. 385–390 (2007)
4. Xie, Y., Li, Y., Wang, C., Lu, M.: The Optimization and Improvement of the Apriori Algorithm. In: The International Workshop on Education Technology and Training & International Workshop on Geoscience and Remote Sensing, pp. 663–665 (2008)
5. Yu, W., Wang, X., Wang, F., Wang, E., Chen, B.: The Research of Improved Apriori Algorithm for Mining Association Rules. In: The 11th IEEE International Conference on Communication Technology Processing, pp. 513–516 (2008)
6. Yong-qing, W., Ren-hua, Y., Pei-yu, L.: An Improved Apriori Algorithm for Association Rules of Mining, pp. 942–946 (2009)
7. Jing, L., Yongquan, L., Jintao, W., Pengdong, G., Chu, Q., Hqipeng, J., Nan, L., Wenhua, Y.: An Improved Apriori Algorithm for Early Warning of Equipment Failue, pp. 450–452 (2009)

8. Ping, D., Yongping, G.: A New Improvement of Apriori Algorithm for Mining Association Rules. In: The International Conference on Computer Application and System Modeling (ICCASM 2010), pp. 529–532 (2010)
9. Lu-Feng, W.: Association Rule Mining Algorithm Study and Improvement. In: The 2nd International Conference on Software Technology and Engineering (ICSTE), pp. 362–364 (2010)
10. Han, J., Kamber, M.: Data Mining: Concepts and Techniques. Higher Education Press (2001)

An Improved Approach towards Network Forensic Investigation of HTTP and FTP Protocols

T. Manesh, B. Brijith, and Mahendra Prathap Singh

Dept. of Computer Engineering,
National Institute of Technology, Karnataka, Surathkal 575025, India
{maneshmon,brijithb,mahoo15}@gmail.com

Abstract. Network packet analysis and reconstruction of network sessions are more sophisticated processes in any network forensic and analysis system. Here we introduce an integrated technique which can be used for inspecting, reordering and reconstructing the contents of packets in a network session as part of forensic investigation. Network analysts should be able to observe the stored packet information when a suspicious activity is reported and should collect adequate supporting evidences from stored packet information by recreating the original data/files/messages sent/received by each user. Thus suspicious user activities can be found by monitoring the packets in offline. So we need an efficient method for reordering packets and reconstructing the files or documents to execute forensic investigation and to create necessary evidence against any network crime. The proposed technique can be used for content level analysis of packets passing through the network based on HTTP and FTP protocols and reports deceptive network activities in the enterprise for forensic analysis.

Keywords: Network Forensics, Packet Reordering and reconstruction, HTTP and FTP session reassembly, Pcap File.

1 Introduction

Network forensics is the process of capturing information that moves over a network and trying to make sense of it in some kind of forensics capacity. This method is based on reconstructive traffic analysis. It could be used for forensic analysis to read and analyze the contents of the Internet raw data in PCAP format for a particular session on the network. This technique also performs content level analysis and reconstruction of pre-captured internet or network raw data containing HTTP and FTP sessions and thus perform offline packet processing for creating more accurate forensic evidences. The aim of this work is to provide detailed overview of HTTP and FTP reconstruction process as part of network forensic investigation with help of a new improved network forensic investigation tool that we have developed.

Currently the development of the tool is in progress towards forensic investigation of P2P, HTTPS, VoIP protocols. This paper is organized as follows: Sections 2 and 3 gives an introduction about HTTP and FTP analysis respectively. The section 4 explains basic Idea behind the algorithm for packet reordering and reconstruction that we have developed. Sections 5 and 6 gives the flow diagram of our approach towards

D. Nagamalai, E. Renault, and M. Dhanushkodi (Eds.): PDCTA 2011, CCIS 203, pp. 385–392, 2011.

HTTP and FTP analysis for packet reconstruction respectively followed by explanation of each process involved in the analysis. Conclusions are given in the section 7 followed by acknowledgements and References.

2 Introduction to Http Analysis Process

This section deals with the digital forensic analysis of the HTTP traffic. This approach is used for analyzing the http traffic and often finds evidence that someone did or did not commit a crime. Thus we are interested in the message exchange sequence in the HTTP traffic. The proposed method includes capturing the Ethernet packets, filtering IP packets followed by the TCP packets and reconstruction of the http traffic after identifying the request, response messages included in a particular http network session and to produce necessary forensic information.

2.1 HTTP Headers

It forms the core of an HTTP request and response. The header specifies the details about the data which are transmitted in a that session which is crucial forensic information in the investigation of HTTP protocol. The management of these forensic information is well explained in the section 5.

3 Introduction to FTP Analysis Process

In FTP environment the clients and servers may interact with each other for the purpose of file transfer. FTP protocol can operate over network channels where packets move directly from source to destination.FTP is a TCP based connection services only. FTP does not use UDP content. FTP maintains two types of ports; one is known as the control port which is for maintaining connection details and second is data port used for maintaining original data transferred across TCP connection. The port numbers for these two connections are well defined. The control connection normally uses port number 21 and data connection normally uses port number 20. The port number for the data connection can be set by the FTP client also. Some valuable forensic information like source IP, destination IP, source and destination port number, name of the file transferred and time etc can be found by examining the control connection of FTP protocol. These forensic information will be extracted and processed to create the evidences in investigation.

3.1 Different Data Transfers in FTP Connection

There are basically two types of FTP data transfer. One is called "active " and second is called "passive". An FTP client program fixes the active mode by sending the "PORT" command to server to instruct it that it should connect back to a specified IP address and port number and then send the data, In FTP passive connection, a client program will fix passive mode by using the "PASV" command to ask that the server should tell the client an IP address and port number that the client can connect to and receive the data.

The PORT command is used when the server connects to the client, and PASV is used when client connects to the server. In the proposed methodology for handling FTP reassembly, the control connection of the FTP protocol will be processed first. All the TCP packets going through the port number 21 are filtered off to identify the type(active/passive) of connection. Once such connection is processed, the proposed method will find out the IPs and port numbers and name of the documents involved in a particular FTP session. After getting these information, the proposed algorithm can reconstruct the FTP stream effectively in network session.

4 Basic Idea Behind Proposed Algorithm for Packet Reordering and Reconstruction

4.1 Existing Methods

There exist many packet reordering methods developed for applications like packet sniffers, protocol analyzers and network forensic tools. We made an extensive study on various approaches towards packet reordering and found that most of the existing tools are not freeware and uses comparatively complex methods for reordering the packets and managing the retransmitted or duplicate packets. Here we have developed a new algorithm for TCP packet reordering separately for both HTTP and FTP analysis. This algorithm can efficiently identify, reorder and process retransmitted or duplicate packets for the purpose of reconstruction in forensic analysis. The logic behind the algorithm is well explained in the next session. This algorithm basically process a pcap file containing packets following HTTP and FTP protocol and have different phases to process, analyze and reorder packets based on the characteristics of above mentioned protocols. This algorithm can reconstruct any kind of data that are being transferred using HTTP and FTP protocol from the pre-captured pcap file of a particular network session.

4.2 Proposed Method

The basic idea of this algorithm is to organize or reorder packets based on sequence number of needed packets that follow a particular protocol with help of respective source, destination and port numbers. From the pcap file containing packets of a particular network session, the designed algorithm extracts all intended packets with HTTP and FTP protocols separately. Once packets are extracted, the HTTP analysis part will separate the header and body parts of such packets and regenerate the content from packets which are in order and stores all retransmitted packets which are not in order in a temporary pcap file. Similarly the FTP analysis part will extract all TCP packets containing FTP protocol and separates the body part of packets which are in order. It will also store all retransmitted packets in temporary pacp file. Then for further reconstruction, the body parts of packets (which are in correct order of sequence number) will be combined off by considering any missing packets if any from the temporarily stored pcap file in both the analysis. Thus algorithm identifies needed packets and fetches its contents and regenerates the original data as part its forensic activity with specific parameters.

5 Flow Diagram for HTTP Analysis

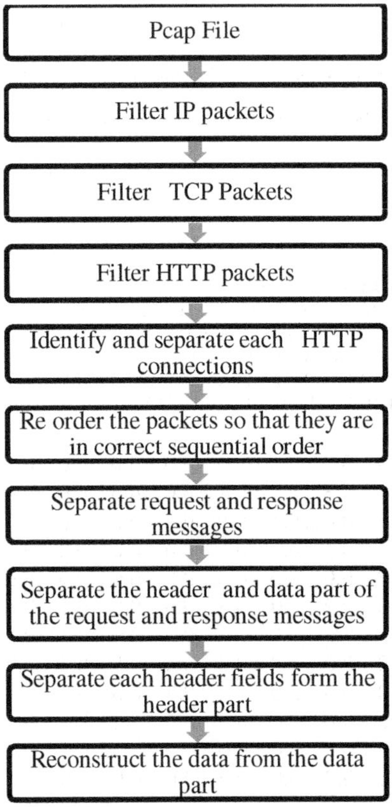

Fig. 1. Flow diagram for HTTP Analysis

5.1 Major Processes of HTTP Session Reconstruction and Analysis

Pcap File. This file consists of all the ethernet packets that have been captured from the ethernet card. This can be done by using the capture section in our software or using some other softwares like "Wireshark" that support pcap format. The analysis process is performed on this file. This analysis is performed after capturing the packets using some other software and then exporting that file to our software. If we need to get all the packets that are passing through the ethernet card, we must perform the capturing in the promiscuous mode.

Filtering IP Packets. The pcap file consists of different packets of different protocols in the network layer like ARP, DRARP, RARP, IP, MPLS etc, from this bunch of packets, the process will separate the IP packets to perform the further actvities.

Filtering TCP Packets. The IP packets separated in the previous layer consist of several transport layer protocols. From these bunches of transport layer protocols this process will separate the packets that follows TCP protocol.

Filtering HTTP Packets. This process will separate those packets that contain HTTP protocol. This is done by checking the source port and destination port of the TCP packet. If the source port or destination port is 80 or the port of the http proxy, then process will separate those packets from others and collects them for further investigations.

Separation of Connection. In order to perform the analysis, this process will separate each connection that is created for the http traffic. This can be done using the combination of the source port and the destination port.

Reordering the Packets. Managing the packets in the internet is a sophisticated mechanism as far as internet technology is concerned. This is mainly due to multipath routing or parallelism at the routers. i.e. For those packets which are in out of order, the TCP receiver sends a duplicate ACKS to enhance the fast retransmit algorithm in the sender side. As a result of this process the packets that we have collected in the pacp file will not be in correct sequence order. In order to perform the reconstruction of the original HTTP message this section will reorder packets in correct sequence number considering retransmitted and duplicate packets in an efficient manner explained below.

TCP Packet Reordering Algorithm for HTTP Analysis. This algorithm consists of two phases

PHASE 1

- Identifying all the retransmitted packets and collecting them in a temporary file for further processing
- This is done by comparing the sequence number of the current packet and the ACK number of the previous packet

PHASE 2

- This phase compares each packet's sequence number with its previous packets acknowledge number
- If a difference is found then we will search for the actual packet in the temporary file and insert them in correct position and reproduce the original file.

Separation of HTTP Request and Response Messages. This section will separate the request and the response messages in a single connection for the analysis process. This is accomplished by using the source and destination port combination. If we are filtering the connection with destination port 80(or proxy) and source port with the client port of the connection ,then we will get the request messages from that connection. On the other hand if we are filtering the connection with source port

80(or proxy) and destination port with the client port of the connection, then we will get the response messages for that connection.

Separation of the HTTP Header and Data Part. In the previous have separated the HTTP request and the response message. Now for the analysis purpose ,this section will separate the header part and the data part of the http message. The end of the header part is specified by "0d0a0d0a".So this section will parse the packet to get the header part. After separating the header part, the process will check the content length field in the header section. If the content length field is zero, then there is no data part. If there is a data part, then the content length will specify the size of the data that is followed by the http header. Using this content length, section can separate the data from the packets.

Separating the Header Fields in the Header Part. This section will separate each field in the header part of the HTTP message and use for the analysis process.

Reconstruction of the Files. This section will reconstruct the files from the data part that have already separated.

6 Flow Diagram for FTP Analysis

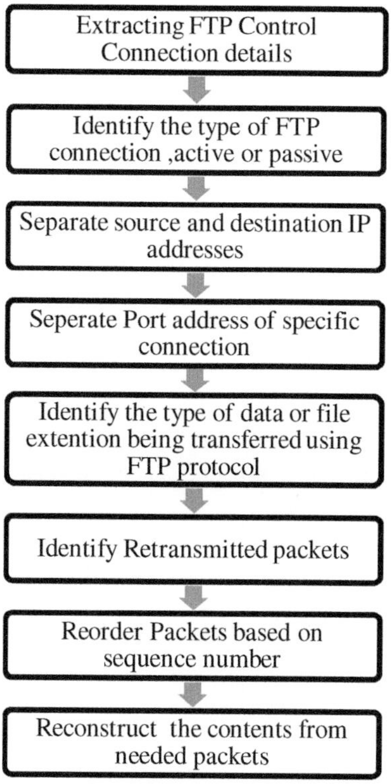

Fig. 2. Flow diagram for FTP Analysis

6.1 Major Processes in FTP Session Reconstruction and Analysis

Network Forensic Investigation Process. This process initially processes the pcap file and identify type of control connection details from the TCP packets that follow FTP protocol. Once such connection is identified, this process will extract available source and destination IP addresses and calculates respective data port addresses through which data transfer has been occurred.

Port Extractor Process. This process calculates respective port addresses form each connection and stores as an array of available port numbers.

IP Extractor Process. This process separates all source IP addresses from each control connection and maintains an array of IP addresses for all such connection. This also identifies destination IP addresses from respective packets of FTP connection.

File Reconstruction Process. This process play an important role in network investigation by reconstructing original data from the pre-captured pcap file based on the type of the data or extension of the file being transferred in the particular section.

TCP Packet Reordering Algorithm for FTP Analysis. This algorithm consists of three phases

PHASE 1

- Identify the control connection through port 21 and type of ftp connection(active or passive)
- Extract IP and Source port no. of specific data connection.

PHASE 2

- Read the pre-captured pcap file of transaction
- Identify the retransmitted packets and store it as another temporary pcap file by Filtering packets through source port number

PHASE 3

- Separate ftp data stream of each such packet.
- Use packet reorder algorithm to reconstruct the data based on sequence number of packets by using original pcap dump file and temporary pcap file containing retransmitted packets of specific session.

7 Conclusions

The concept of proposed method is conceived from the process of retrospective network analysis or network forensics. Two different algorithms have been developed for effective packet reordering and reconstruction of FTP and P2P traffic to know what had happened in a previous sessions. The proposed methodology is a strategic approach for the session recreation of HTTP and FTP traffic analysis as part of network forensic process and further related investigation. Once the source of such activity is traced along with the substantial regenerated content, it is possible to prosecute the malicious user involved in that session. This method or tool can be effectively used by network administrators, forensic investigators to identify any kind of network traffic breaches based on above mentioned protocol and to perform internet or network traffic content analysis.

Acknowledgements. We would like to express our sincere gratitude to our Guide Mr. Mahendra Prathap Singh, Assistant Professor, Department of Computer Engineering, National Institute of Technology Karnataka, Surathkal , Mr Bhadran V.K, Additional Director, Resource Centre for Cyber forensics, CDAC Trivandram for their insightful advice, motivating suggestions, invaluable guidance, help and support for doing this work. We also express our sincere gratitude to our project coordinator Mr. Alwyn Roshan Pais, Assistant Professor, Department of Computer Engineering, National Institute of Technology Karnataka, Surathkal for his continuous cooperation, providing critical information, help and support for doing this project work.

References

1. Almulhem, A.: Network Forensics: Notions and Challenges. In: IEEE International Symposium on Signal Processing and Information Technology, pp. 463–466 (February 2010)
2. Raphael, A.A., Phan, R.C.W., Parish, D.J.: Metrics for Network Forensics Conviction Evidence. In: International Conference for Internet Technology and Secured Transactions, pp. 1–8 (November 2009)
3. Ming, H.: A New System Design of Network Invasion Forensics. In: Second International Conference on Computer and Electrical Engineering, pp. 596–599 (December 2009)
4. Leung, K.-C., Yang, D.: An Overview of Packet Reordering in Transmission Control Protocol (TCP): Problems, Solutions and Challenges. IEEE Transactions on Parallel and Distributed Systems 18(4), 522–534 (2007)
5. Merkle, L.D.: Automated Network Forensics. Proceedings of ACM Workshop on Genetic and Evolutionary Computation Conference, pp. 131–137 (July 2008)
6. Slaviero, M., Granova, A., Olivier, M.: Active Traffic Capture for Network Forensics. IFIP AICT, vol. 222, pp. 215–221. Springer, US (May 2006)
7. Morariu, C., Stiller, B.: Distributed Packet Capturing architecture for high-speed network links. In: IEEE Conference on Local Computer Networks, pp. 168–175 (October 2008)

Indexing and Retrieval of Medical Images Using CBIR Approach

Ankita Chandrakar, A.S. Thoke, and Bikesh Kumar Singh

Dept. of Electrical Engineering, N.I.T Raipur, Raipur, India
ankitachandrakar007@gmail.com,
{asthoke,bikesh_020581}@yahoo.co.in

Abstract. Medical image indexing and storage is gaining increased importance. Indexing and retrieval of these images efficiently is becomes an essential task. Indexing of medical images using text or numbers is a cumbersome task, difficult to memorize and time consuming. Indexing and Retrieval of images can be done through query by text and query by image which is also known as content based image retrieval (CBIR). Different medical images possess different texture and shape features. This paper presents a novel and hybrid approach of managing a huge medical image database and retrieving a medical image from the database by fusion of shape and texture features. Image is retrieved by comparing the features of query image and images of database. We attach some document information with each medical image such as patient identity, diseases, age, and case history. It can be used for further diagnostic and analysis purpose. Further the proposed algorithm also updates the database automatically if new query is found. MATLAB ® 7.01 and its image processing toolbox have been used to implement the algorithm.

Keywords: content based medical image retrieval, medical image indexing, database, shape, texture.

1 Introduction

Content' based image retrieval (CBIR) systems uses the contents of a query image which is provided by the user to search for similar images in large database. Most common and advanced approaches are based on color, shape, textures or their combinations [1].

At present computer imaging and database techniques plays a vital role in medical field, which leads to the large amount of digital images generated at hospitals everyday such as Computer Assisted Tomography (CAT), Magnetic Resonance Imaging(MRI), X-ray and ultrasound, mammography etc. Developing efficient, effective and advanced techniques for medical imaging system is not an easy task. CBIR systems can greatly help us to retrieve useful information within enormous amount of medical images. There are several content based image retrieval systems that have emerged and provide satisfactory retrieval performance such as WebSEEk, QBIC, MIT's Photobook, etc.

In general, an image retrieval system uses image features such as color, texture, and shape. These features are properties of the image and can be extracted from the

D. Nagamalai, E. Renault, and M. Dhanushkodi (Eds.): PDCTA 2011, CCIS 203, pp. 393–403, 2011.

image itself with the help of digital image processing techniques. The efficiency and accuracy of retrieval of images depends on the method of feature extraction [2, 3].

The management and the retrieval of images using patient information such as patient id and patient number becomes a complex task. The retrieval based on visual features like color, shape and texture can be utilized to reduce the drawbacks of text based image retrieval system and extend retrieval technologies to medical domain [4].

In this paper, we address medical image indexing and retrieval problem by presenting an experimental design of Content-based Medical Image Retrieval (CBMIR) system by comparing the contents of images such as texture and shape of the image. Feature vector of each image present in the database are extracted and stored as mat format in MATLAB environment.

2 Overview of Feature Extraction

Generally, any CBMIR techniques use visual features of images, such as color, shape and texture yielding vectors with hundreds or even thousands of features. As many features are correlated to others it will bring extra knowledge and produces redundancies among them. Using a large number of features leads to the dimensional mismatch problem and is time consuming [5, 12]. In this paper we propose a new technique to retrieve the query image efficiently with accuracy by using two features namely texture and shape. Collectively all these features were combining to form a single vector which we call as feature vector.

2.1 Shape Analysis

An effective, working and efficient shape descriptor is a key component of content description for an image, since shape is a basic property of an object present in the image itself [6]. These shape descriptors are broadly categorized into two groups, i.e., contour-based shape descriptors and region based shape descriptors. Due to the fact that contour-based shape descriptors exploit only boundary information, they cannot capture the interior shape of the objects and also these methods cannot deal with disjoint shapes or the shape which is not closed where contour information is not available. In region based techniques, shape descriptors are derived using all the pixel information within a shape region. Region-based shape descriptors can be applied to general applications [7].

In this paper, a Fourier descriptor (FD) and moment invariants are used to extract shape feature. The proposed Fourier shape descriptor is derived by applying 2-D Fourier transformation on an image. This shape descriptor is application independent and robust. Their main advantages are that they are invariance to translation, rotation and scaling of the observed object. Thus shape description become independent of the relative position and size of the object in the input image [8, 9].

First the image is converted into the binary image and then filtered using a Gaussian mask of size 15x15 with sigma = 9 and with threshold of 0.7.The image is segmented and boundary of the object is determined. The boundary is presented as an array of complex numbers which correspond to the pixels of the object boundary if the image is placed in the complex plane. Fourier descriptors are now calculated by combining Fourier transform coefficients of the complex array. Let the complex array z0, z1, z2 … zN-1 represents the boundary belonging to the object whose shape needs to be described. The k-th Fourier transform Coefficient is calculated as [10]

$$z_n = \sum_{n=0}^{N-1} z_n e^{\frac{-2\pi kin}{N}} \quad k = 0,1,2, \dots\dots, N-1 \tag{1}$$

The Fourier descriptors are obtained from the sequence $z_k$by truncating elements z_1 andz_2, than by taking the absolute value of the remaining elements and dividing every element of thusly obtained array by $|z|$. To summarize, the Fourier descriptors

$$c_{k=2} = |z_k|/|z_1|, k = 2, \dots\dots, N-1 \tag{2}$$

$$\mathrm{s(x) = x(n) + jy(n)} \tag{3}$$

The Discrete Fourier Transform (DFT) of s (n) is

$$a(u) = \sum_{n=0}^{N-1} s(n)\, e^{\frac{-2jun}{N}}, \mathrm{u} = 0, 1, 2 \dots, \mathrm{N} - 1 \tag{4}$$

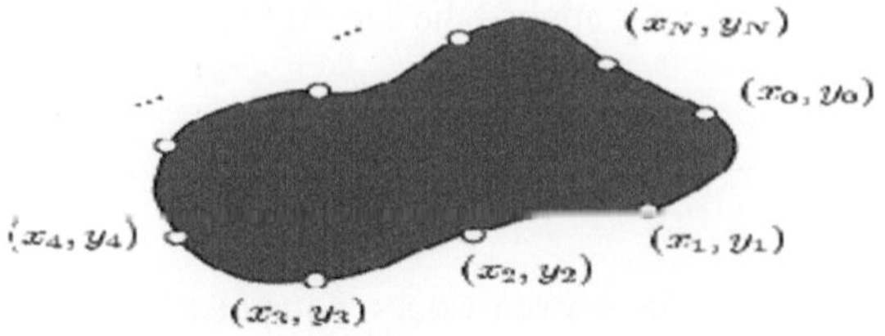

Fig. 1. N point digital boundary in x-y plane

The complex coefficients a(u) are known as Fourier descriptors of the boundary. The inverse Fourier transform of these coefficients restores s (n). Given by,

$$\mathrm{s(n)} = \frac{1}{\mathrm{N}} \sum_{\mathrm{u=0}}^{\mathrm{N-1}} \mathrm{a(u)e^{2\pi un/N}}, \mathrm{k} = 0,1,2 \dots, \mathrm{N} - 1 \tag{5}$$

Instead of using all the Fourier coefficients, only the first P coefficients are used. This is equivalent to setting a(u) = 0 for u > P-1 in the preceding equation for a(u). This result is the following approximation to s (n):

$$\hat{\mathrm{s}}(\mathrm{n}) = \frac{1}{\mathrm{P}} \sum_{\mathrm{u=0}}^{\mathrm{P-1}} \mathrm{a(u)\, e^{2\pi jun/N}}, \mathrm{n} = 0,1,2 \dots, \mathrm{N} - 1 \tag{6}$$

Although only P terms are used to obtain each component of ŝ (n), n still ranges from 0 to K-1. That is, the same number of points exists in the approximate boundary, but not so many terms are used in the reconstruction of each point. The high-frequency components account for fine detail, and low-frequency components determine global shape. Thus, loss of detail in the boundary increases as P decreases.

The second feature which is used for shape description is Moment Invariants. Regular moment invariants are one of the most popular, widely used contour-based shape descriptors and is a set of features derived by Hu(1962). Hu's moment invariants and extended Zernike moments were used as feature extractors.

A two-dimensional moment of a digitally sampled $M \times M$ image that has gray function $f(x, y = 0 \ldots\ldots M-1)$is given as [6, 10]:

$$m_{pq} = \sum_{x=0}^{M-1} \sum_{y=0}^{M-1} (x)^p (y)^q f(x,y), \ p,q = 0,1, \tag{7}$$

The moments $f(x, y)$ translated by an amount (a, b), are defined as

$$\mu_{pq} = \sum_x \sum_y (x+a)^p (Y+b)^q f(x,y) \tag{8}$$

Thus the central moments m'_{pq} or μ_{pq} can be computed from (2) on substituting $a = -x$ and $b = -y$ as,

$$\overline{x} = m_{10}/m_{00}, \bar{y} = m_{01}/m_{00} \tag{9}$$

$$\mu_{pq} = \sum_x \sum_y (x-\bar{x})^p (y-\bar{y})^q f(x,y) \tag{10}$$

When a scaling normalization is applied the central moments change as,

$$\eta_{pq} = \mu_{pq}/\mu_{00}^{\gamma} \tag{11}$$

$$\gamma = \left[\frac{p+q}{2}\right] + 1 \tag{12}$$

In particular, Hu (1962), defines seven values, computed by normalizing central moments through order three, that are invariant to object scale, position, and orientation. In terms of the central moments, the seven moments are given as,

$$M1 = (\eta_{20} + \eta_{02}) \tag{13}$$

$$M2 = (\eta_{20} - \eta_{02})^2 + 4\eta_{11}^2 \tag{14}$$

$$M3 = (\eta_{30} - 3\eta_{12})^2 + (3\eta_{12} - \eta_{03})^2 \tag{15}$$

$$M4 = (\eta_{30} + \eta_{12})^2 + (\eta_{21} + \eta_{03})^2 \tag{16}$$

$$M5 = (\eta_{30} - 3\eta_{12})(\eta_{30} + \eta_{12})\left[\left((\eta_{30} + \eta_{12})\right)^2 - 3\left((\eta_{21} + \eta_{03})\right)^2\right] (3\eta_{21} - \eta_{03})(\eta_{21} + \eta_{03})[3(\eta_{30} + \eta_{12})^2 - (\eta_{21} + \eta_{03})^2] \tag{17}$$

$$M6(\eta_{20} - \eta_{02})\left[\left((\eta_{30} + \eta_{12})\right)^2 - \left((\eta_{21} + \eta_{03})\right)^2\right] + [4\eta_{11}(\eta_{30} + \eta_{12})(\eta_{21} + \eta_{03} \tag{18}$$

$$M7 = (3\eta_{21} - \eta_{03})\left(\eta_{30} - \eta_{21}\right)[(\eta_{30} + \eta_{12})^2 - 3(\eta_{21} + \eta_{03})^2] - (\eta_{30} + \eta_{12})(\eta_{21} + \eta_{03})[3(\eta_{30} + \eta_{12})^2 - (\eta_{21} + \eta_{03})^2] \tag{19}$$

2.2 Texture

Another set of features which we used to describe a medical image is texture feature. Medical images possess different texture depending upon organs of human body considered for imaging. According to Smith and Chang [9, 13] texture refers to visual patterns which have properties of homogeneity and cannot result from the presence of only a single color or intensity. Texture property of an image has a very important aspect in the human visual system of recognition, interpretation and perception. Two main approaches concerning with texture analysis: statistical model-based and spectral measure.

Statistical approach is based on statistical properties of the intensity histogram the expression for the nth moment about the mean is given by

$$\mu_n = \sum_{i=0}^{L-1}(z_i - m)^n p(z_i) \tag{20}$$

Where z is a random variable indicating intensity, $p(z)$is the histogram of the intensity level in a region, L is the number of possible intensity level and m is the mean (average) intensity[10].

Gray Level Co occurrence matrix (GLCM)-Measure of texture is computed using the distribution of intensities and the relative positions of the pixels in an image. Let O be an operator that defines the position of two pixels relative to each other and an image $f(x, y)$ with L possible intensity levels. G is a matrix whose element g_{ij} is the number of times that a pixel pair with intensities z_i and z_j occur in f in the position specified by O, where $1 \leq i, j \leq L$ .This matrix is referred to as gray level co occur rence matrix [10]. In this paper we are using four properties of GLCM known contrast, correlation, energy and homogeneity.

Further we also use spectral features for texture analysis. Spectral measures of texture are based on Fourier spectrum, which is ideally suited for describing the directionality of period or almost periodic 2-D patterns in an image. The spectrum is expressed in polar coordinates to yield a function S(r, θ), where S is the spectrum function and r and θ are the variables in the coordinate system for each direction θ, S(r, θ) may be considered a 1-D function S_θ(r). Similarity for each frequency r, S_r(θ) is a 1-D function. Analyzing S_θ(r) for a fixed value of θ yields the behaviour of spectrum along a radial direction from the origin, whereas analyzing S_r(θ) for a fixed value of r yields a behaviour along a circle centred on the origin[14].

A global description is obtained by integrating these functions:

$$s(r) = \sum_{\theta=0}^{\pi} s_\theta (r) \tag{21}$$

and

$$s(\theta) = \sum_{r=1}^{r_0} s_r (\theta) \tag{22}$$

Where r_0 is the radius of the circle centred at origin [10, 14]. The result of these two equations constitutes a pair of value [S(r), S(θ)] for each pair of coordinate (r, θ). By varying this coordinates we can generate two 1-D functions, S(r) and S(θ) that constitute a spectral-energy description of texture for an entire image or region under consideration. Furthermore descriptors of these functions themselves can be computed in order to characterize their behaviour quantitatively. Descriptors typically used for these purpose are the location of the highest value, mean and variance of the amplitude and axial variations, the distance between the mean and the highest value of the function. Figure 2 and Figure 3 below shows spectral components (radial and angular respectively) of four different images from database.

3 Proposed Methodology

3.1 Development Environment

The functional code for our prototype system was implemented using MATLAB ® 7.0 on a Pentium dual core II, 2.40 GHz Windows-based PC. All of the code was written as MATLAB m-files.

3.2 Database Preparation

We used 2040 different medical images such as mammographic, MRI, X–rays, ultra sound collected from different hospitals and open source database. Figure (4) shows some example images from database. Candidate medical image terminology is used for the image which is already stored in the database.

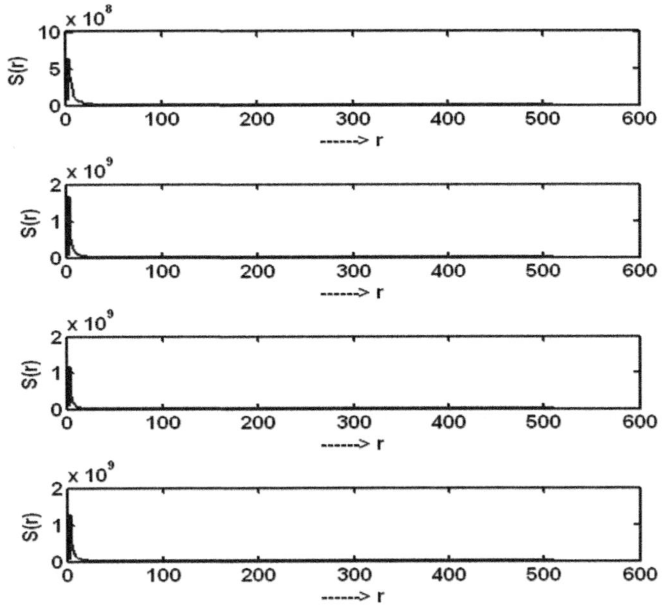

Fig. 2. Radial spectral components of four different mammographic images from database

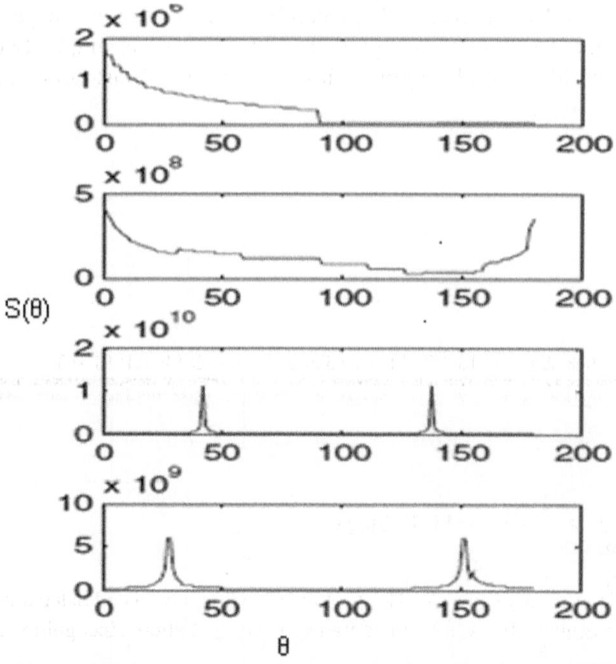

Fig. 3. Angular Spectral Components of four different x-ray images from database

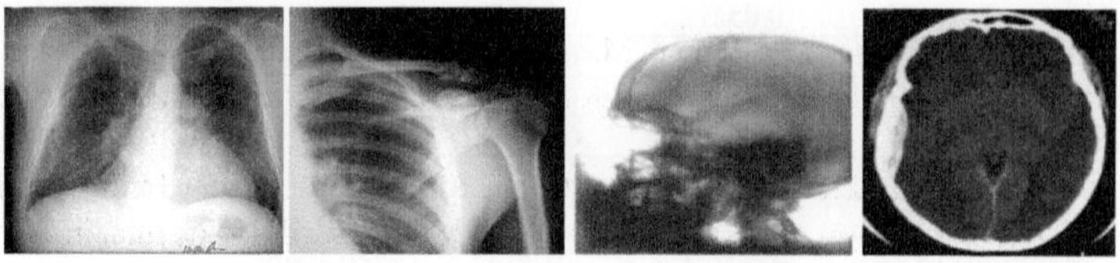

Fig. 4. Example images from database

We use two databases one for medical images and another for feature vector of these medical images. Query image terminology is used for image which is given or input to the CBMIR system and its feature vector is calculated at the run time. A excel file is associated with each medical image consisting of patient's identity, diseases, age etc, so it can be used for further diagnosis and analysis purpose.

3.3 Determining Feature Vector

Feature extraction is the main aspect of any CBMIR, CBIR and Computer Aided Diagnosis (CAD) system. We use selected feature of the images which is fruitful to replicate an exact image. Shape and texture properties can effectively represent medical image because medical image is highly textured image. Several medical images contain different organs of human body which have different shapes. We extracted texture and shape features. As discussed in section 2 features are extracted and represented in a single array called as feature vector.

Table 1. Feature vector of five different images from database

Image id_1	Image id_2	Image id_3	Image id_4	Image id_5
16.5171	17.5377	18.4016	17.6551	16.6621
32.4402	34.5141	36.2657	34.7484	32.7287
47.216	50.1924	52.7953	50.6052	47.6174
47.2056	50.1856	52.7922	50.6034	47.6152
94.4165	100.375	105.586	101.208	95.2314
63.5035	67.5158	70.9946	68.0501	64.0566
104.396	108.328	115.245	110.377	106.466
98.6112	149.327	156.13	132.253	115.253
90.0639	81.5447	69.4675	57.8084	68.8144
0.11091	0.09277	0.06909	0.04888	0.06788
2.34374	-3.98497	-2.43665	0.73178	2.63239
0.02992	0.00494	0.00665	0.00519	0.00886
6.80472	7.8246	7.52654	7.65068	7.28793
2.6416	2.43377	1.98515	1.90333	1.28247
2.65329	2.44207	1.57925	1.48251	0.37881
2.26794	0.83692	0.81902	2.44059	0.2488
2.43579	1.57734	1.663	2.52474	0.77811
2.69839	2.27452	1.3815	2.57093	0.94073
1.47446	2.45712	2.2132	3.12065	0.75887
1.39303	1.81109	1.95197	1.86623	0.79551
0.54668	2.51391	1.04716	3.32585	1.39473
1.228	2.15097	2.17142	2.3261	2.2037
1.91032	2.25028	2.67263	1.28649	1.80599
0.02273	0.05212	0.03771	0.03672	0.03773
0.99823	0.99508	0.99484	0.99317	0.99507
0.21893	0.1258	0.16679	0.15848	0.17387
0.98867	0.97394	0.98115	0.98164	0.98125
18.1653	18.0699	18.8502	18.6427	18.0349
20.5447	20.6741	21.2335	21.1462	20.655
20.1834	19.5751	20.5455	20.1648	19.79
19.7758	19.1287	19.8358	19.6301	19.5229
19.2434	18.7555	19.6318	19.4332	19.2751
18.9673	18.3921	19.4279	19.088	18.6031
18.6633	18.3697	19.3691	18.8072	18.616
18.4843	17.9963	19.1913	18.6147	18.3881
18.2098	17.8112	19.0889	18.5745	18.3395
18.0169	17.4772	18.7151	18.3243	17.9799
18.7575	18.5299	19.3201	19.059	18.5673
18.7602	18.4864	19.3023	19.0185	18.5313
18.755	18.4686	19.2792	18.9986	18.5154
18.7554	18.4593	19.2511	18.9874	18.5047
18.7605	18.462	19.2169	18.9702	18.4814
18.76	18.4629	19.2153	18.9508	18.4858
18.7634	18.4639	19.2149	18.9486	18.4789
18.7605	18.4812	19.2147	18.9317	18.4717
18.7636	18.4817	19.2084	18.9282	18.4712
18.7375	18.4834	19.2032	18.9226	18.4564

In our case the feature vector is a row of forty seven elements and composed of twenty six spectral texture features, four statistical texture features, ten Fourier Descriptor coefficients (First ten) and seven moment invariants. The feature vector of each image in the database is stored as .mat file. The feature vector of five different images from the database is shown in table 1.

3.4 Distance Calculation

The efficiency and accuracy of the image retrieval is significantly affected by the ability of the distance calculation techniques. Let $X = [X1, X2 \ldots\ldots\ldots\ldots\ldots\ldots Xn]$ be the feature vector of the candidate image and $Y = [Y1, Y2 \ldots\ldots\ldots\ldots\ldots Yn]$ be the feature vector of the query image. Euclidean distance between the candidate image feature vector and the query image feature vector is given by [11].

$$D = (\sum_{i=1}^{n} |X_i - Y_i| \,\hat{}\, 2)^{\frac{1}{2}} \tag{23}$$

The result of the distance calculation is used for retrieving or adding the image from/to database. Figure 4 shows the block diagram of proposed system.

4 Result and Conclusion

In this research, potential of CBIR techniques in indexing and retrieval of medical images is addressed. Experiments were conducted on 2040 medical images of various categories. 30 Statistical texture features and 17 shape features were used to determine the feature vector consisting of 47 values for each image in the database.

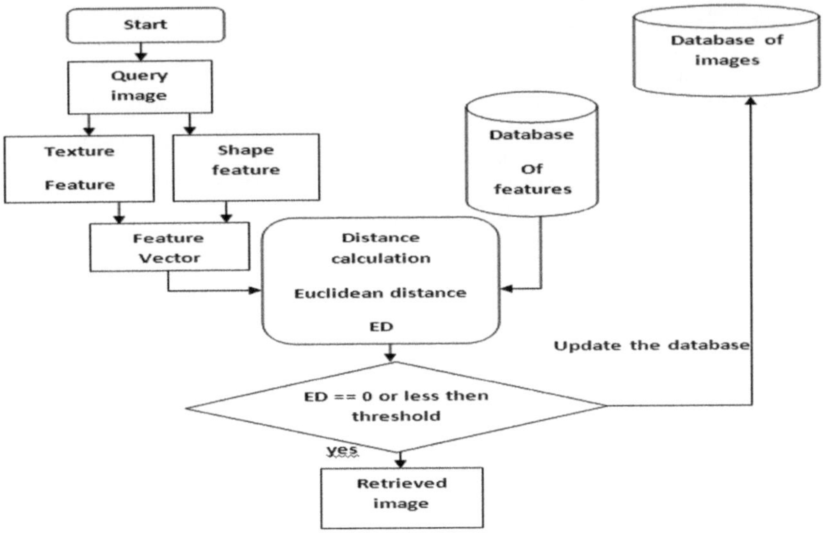

Fig. 5. Block Diagram of proposed system

When a query image is presented to the system, a vector consisting of similar features is generated and compared with feature vector of each image in the database using Euclidean distance. If the Euclidean distance between the feature vector of candidate image and the query image is zero or below threshold then the matched candidate image is shown at the output along with associated file or if the distance is not zero then the query image is added to the database thereby continuously updating the database. In our database of 2040 images 1813 images were retrieved correctly at threshold of 0.1 thereby giving 88.88% accuracy. The results show CBIR techniques may give satisfactory results in indexing and retrieval of medical images. The proposed work using CBIR approaches can be useful to assist Medical practitioners by making available a diagnostic tool to display relevant past cases with suitable proven information. Further it may help experienced Medical practitioners to refer their previously proven cases when making diagnosis and patient management decisions. Providing a computerized library can refresh the practitioner's mental memory with broad array of proven cases and concrete visualizations. The system may also be useful for new Medical practitioners while making diagnosis.

References

1. Wolf, C., Jolion, J.-M., Kropatsch, W., Bischof, H.: Content based Image Retrieval using Interest Points and Texture Features. In: Proceedings of IEEE International Conference on Pattern Recongnition, vol.4, pp. 234–237 (2000)
2. Rajakumar, K., Muttan, S.: Medical Image Retrieval using Energy Efficient Wavelet Transform. In: Second International conference on Computing, Communication and Networking Technologies, Department of Electronics and Communication Engineering College of Engineering, Guindy, Anna University, Chennai, India (2010)
3. Chen, K., Lin, J., Zou, Y., Yin, G.: Content-based Medical Ultrasound Image Retrieval Using a Hierarchical Method. In: Proceedings of IEEE 2nd International Congress on Image and Signal Processing, pp. 1–4 (2009)
4. Smeulders, A.W.M., Worring, M., Santini, S., Gupta, A., Jain, R.: Content-based image retrieval at the end of the early years. In: Proceedings of IEEE International conference on Pattern Analysis and Machine Intelligence, pp. 1349–1380 (December 2000)
5. Bugatti, P.H., Ponciano-Silva, M., Traina, A.J.M., Traina Jr., C., Marques, P.M.A.: Content-Based Retrieval of Medical Images: from Context to Perception. In: Proceedings of IEEE 22nd International Conference on Computer Based Medical System, pp. 1–8 (2009)
6. Mercimek, M., Gulez, K., Mumcu, T.V.: Real object recognition using moment invariants. Proceedings of Journal Sadhana 30, part-6, 765–775 (2005)
7. Singh, B.K., Wany, A.: Retrieval of M.R.I Images using Color & Spectral Features. In: Proceedings of National Conference Technologia 2010, MPCCET Bhilai (February 2010)
8. Petković, T., Krapac, J.: Tehnical Report on Shape description with Fourier descriptors
9. Prasad, B.G., Krishna, A.N.: Performance Evaluation of Statistical Texture Features for Medical Image Classification. In: Proceedings of the National Conference on Emerging Trends in Computing Science NCETCS (2011)
10. Gonzalez, R.C., Woods, R.E., Eddins, S.L.: Digital Image processing Using matlab, 2nd edn. McGraw-Hill, New York (2010)
11. Tao, Y., Lo, S.C.B., Freedman, M.T., Xaun, J.: A premilimary study of Content based mammographic masses retrieval. In: Proceedings of SPIE, Conference on Medical Imaging 2007: Computer-Aided Diagnosis (2007)

12. Malcok, M., Aslandogan, Y., Yesildirek, A.: Fractal dimension and similarity search in high-dimensional spatial databases. In: IEEE International Conference on Information Reuse and Integration, Waikoloa, Hawaii, USA, pp. 380–384 (2006)
13. Smith, J., Chang, S.: Automated Binary Texture Feature Sets for Image Retrieval. In: Proceedings of IEEE International Conference on Acoustics, Speech, and Signal Processing, vol. 4, pp. 2239–2242 (May 1996)
14. Singh, B.K., Sinha, G.R., Mazumdar, B., Khan, I.: Content Based Retrieval of X-ray Images Using Fusion of Spectral Texture and Shape Descriptors. In: Proceedings of IEEE International Conference on Advances in Recent Technologies in Communication and Computing, pp. 80–84 (2010)

Personalized Mobile Assistant Applications Using Cognitive Techniques

Rohan Sourav Saboo[1], Rakseh, Rohit Agarwal[1], Kiran Kumari Patil[1], and B.P. Vijaya Kumar[2]

[1] Department of Computer Science & Engineering, REVA Institute of Technology and Management,
[2] M.S. Ramaiah Institute of Technology, Bangalore, India
Kirankumari@revainstitution.org, vijaykbp@yahoo.co.in

Abstract. Developing a personalized, user-centric system to provide a peaceful and a better quality life is one of today's challenging issues. Cognition is the scientific term for "the process of thought". It refers to the processing of information, applying knowledge, and changing preferences. The paper discusses the development of a Cognition Based Personal Assistance Application, the idea of how we can use a smart phone to learn about the user's daily life pattern in a cognitive way and provide him assistance, making his/her life better and with less tension. In this paper we have presented our design and development of mobile application based on cognitive algorithm. The project is developed and tested at Nokia research lab, RITM, Bangalore, India.

Keywords: Cognitive, Nokia N900, Mobile Device, Maemo, adaptive.

1 Introduction

Recent years have seen lots of development in sector of mobile devices. Today mobile devices are not just a device which is used to make calls or send short messages but their usage is expanding day by day in a innovative way. They are being used to monitor health condition of patients in real time, replacing wallets with applications like e-wallet, with services like GPS providing user with all kind of maps and equipping with much more functionalities. The world is growing at a phenomenal rate and so is the competition in every sector. With more and more increase in competition the requirement of such applications which can be ported on mobile device, which is always with the user, are very help full. Cognitive based personal assistance application is a mobile application developed with an objective of making users life simple and less stressful by providing assistance in daily life by understanding user's life pattern in a cognitive and adaptive manner. Some of the functionalities that application can provide are predicting the time at which user wakes up, goes to office, time taken to reach office, wakening up at right time, finding and suggesting the best route to office with least traffic. Maintains record of user's recent visit to hospital and suggest health

D. Nagamalai, E. Renault, and M. Dhanushkodi (Eds.): PDCTA 2011, CCIS 203, pp. 404–409, 2011.

tips according to the requirement. It also maintains medical prescriptions and reports, which act as a medical profile when user visits doctor next time.

Rest of the paper is arranged accordingly; section 1.1 discusses on some of the related work. The hardware and software is described in section 1.2. Proposed System architecture is discussed in section 1.3. Section 2 discusses adaptive algorithm. Section 2.1 and section 2.2 contains the pseudo code and test sequence respectively. Concluding high lights are given in section 3, followed by acknowledgment and later the references.

1.1 Related Work

In recent years there has been a shift in the way all the big software and website companies design their services for the user. They are not focused on providing a simple and straight forward application which just do a specified task but are more focused on developing smarter software which uses cognitive and adaptive algorithms. One of such example is Google, one of the most famous and most used search engines. Till few years back, user, while typing his search query on Google, user was suppose to type it completely and no assistance was provided by the website. But Google today is smarter and better, now it knows what user wants to search before the complete query is entered. It does this by keeping track of users previous searches, understanding users search pattern and assisting in searches. It is now cognitive and adaptive about user's search.

1.2 Hardware and Software

Personal Assistant mobile application is being developed for Nokia N900. Nokia N900 is a mobile Internet device and Smart phone from Nokia that supersedes the N810. Based on the Maemo platform, it runs Maemo 5 Linux as its default operating system and is the first Nokia device based upon the TI OMAP3 microprocessor with the ARM Cortex-A8 core. Unlike the Internet Tablets preceding it, the Nokia N900 is the first Maemo device to include phone functionality (quad-band GSM and 3G UMTS). Its functional specifications are 5 mega pixel camera, a portable media player, and a mobile Internet device with email and full web browsing. Maemo is a software platform developed by the Maemo community for smart phones and Internet tablets. It is based on the Debian Linux distribution. The platform comprises the Maemo operating system and the Maemo SDK [4, 5]. Maemo is mostly based on open source code, and has been developed by Maemo Devices within Nokia in collaboration with many. Open source projects such as the Linux kernel, Debian, and GNOME. Maemo is based on Debian GNU/Linux and draws much of its Graphical User Interface (GUI), frameworks, and libraries from the GNOME project. It uses the Matchbox window manager, and the GTK-based Hildon as its GUI and application framework. The application is developed using Qt software [4], a cross-platform application and UI framework. It includes a cross-platform class library, integrated development tools and a cross platform IDE. Using Qt, we can write web-enabled applications once and deploy them across many desktop and embedded operating systems without rewriting the source code. SQLite database system is used. The source code for SQLite is in the public dominant implements most of the SQL standard.

In contrast to other databases, SQLite is not a separate process that is accessed from the client application, but is an integral part of it.

1.3 Proposed System Architecture

The proposed system architecture of the application is as shown in Figure 1. The User interacts with the application using GUI and various sensors of the device. The inputs are processed by the intelligent algorithm, and then the inputs and processed results are saved in the database. Based on the processed result, event is described and registered in the event queue, where events are sorted in the sequence of occurrence.

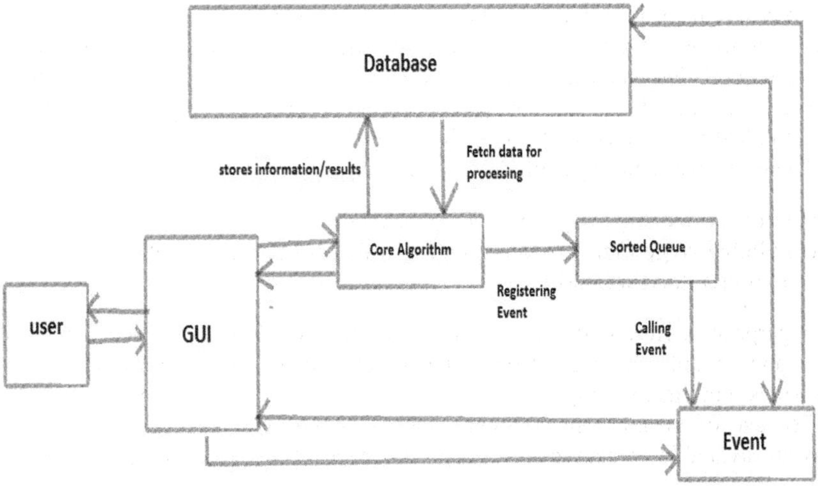

Fig. 1. Proposed System Architecture

When the timer exhaust, event fetches the data from the database and provide the required assistance to the user through Graphical User Interface (GUI) and also request user to response. Every input from the user and the processed results are stored into database. The same process is repeated till learning completes.

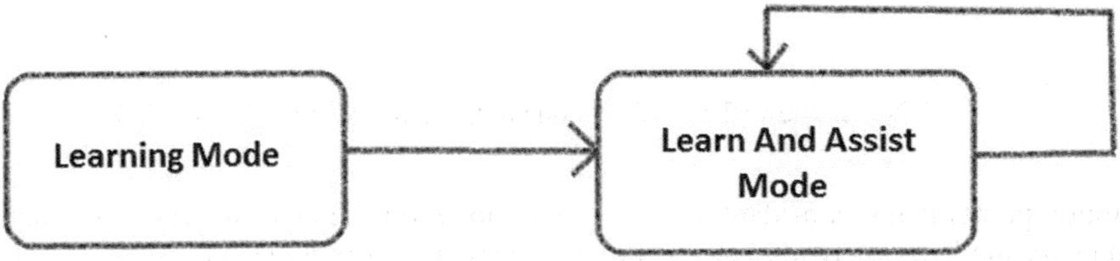

Fig. 2. Working Modes of the Proposed System

The proposed application works in two modes, learning mode and assist mode. In the learning mode application mainly learns about the user's pattern by user responses and provides a very low level of assistance. Over a period of usage for certain time, application gains accuracy about the user's pattern and it shifts to learn and assist mode where it provides assistance with accuracy and also observes the changes in the user's patterns. Figure 3, gives the over all flow chart of the application. When the user installs the application, few basic questions were asked about user, which helps in setting up the initial timers. When the timer exhaust user is alerted using ringing tone or flash message or vibration or by blinking lights depending on the current alert profile like silent, general, or loud etc. If the user does not respond for a specific period of time the alert will be repeated.

Once the user response the result is stored in database, processed by the adaptive algorithm and the future event is registered. Figure 4 presents the sequence diagram for the proposed system.

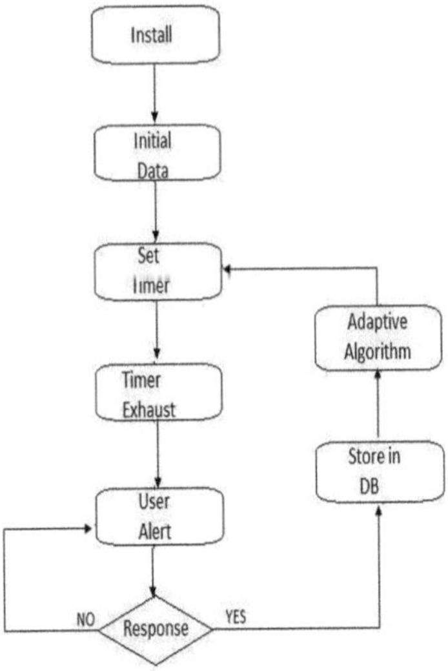

Fig. 3. Flow chart representation of proposed Application

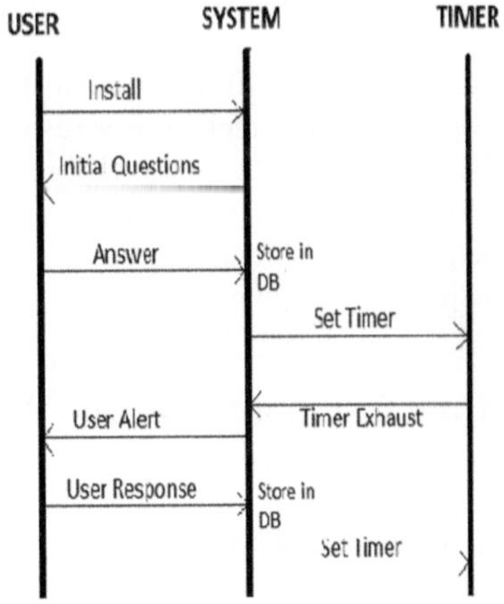

Fig. 4. Sequence diagram

2 Adaptive Algorithm

The adaptive algorithm used in the proposed application. Initial data stores data like users response for question like, at what time user does a specific task. Based on the initial data, timer is set. On receiving sufficient amount of response it is checked how many responses occurred before the time mentioned in the initial data and how many occurred after the time mentioned in the initial data. Suppose 5 responses occurred before the time mentioned in initial data and rest 2 occurred after that. Then the responses which occurred before are arranged in ascending order and the middle response in this ordered list is set as the adaptive data. Then same process is continued in recursive manner and the adaptive data gains more and more accuracy over time.

2.1 pseudo Code

```
Input    : Initial time for event
Action1  : Timer set for event
Action2  : Wait for timer exhaust
Event1   : Timer Exhaust
Action3  : User alert
Event2   : User response through GUI/sensors
Action4  : Store in database and set adaptive pattern
Action5  : Reset timer
Action 6 : Goto Action2
```

2.2 Test Sequence

Sequence1: initial time->timer set for event
Sequence2: timer set for event->wait for time exhaust
Sequence3: wait for time exhaust ->user alert
Sequence4: user alert-> user response (GUI/sensor)
Sequence5: user response->store in database
Sequence6: store in database->set adaptive pattern
Sequence7: set adaptive pattern->reset time
Sequence8: sequence2

3 Conclusion and Future Work

Cognition based application are the growing trend and this paper discusses about one of such application which is focused on understanding users daily patter and help user in making daily life peaceful by avoiding small tensions. The detailed design and implementation of the application is discussed. One of the algorithms for predicting the timings of various actions of user and assisting him/her in conducting those activities at right time in adaptive manner are discussed. This kind of application are never complete and there is always scope for future work as more and more algorithms can be added to it by understanding more specific needs of different kind of people.

Acknowledgment. We would like to thank Mr. Suresh chande from Nokia, Finland and Prof. Dr. T.N. Nagabhushan, JSS, Mysore, for their valuable guidance in this work.

References

1. International Journal of Computer Applications, `http://www.ijcaonline.org/journal/number1/pxc387110.pdf`
2. Konstantas, D., van Halteren, A., Bults, R., et al.: Mobile patient monitoring: the MobiHealth system. Stud. Health. Techno. Inform (2004) 103:30714.PMID: 15747935

3. The National Center for Biotechnology Information, http://www.ncbi.nlm.nih.gov/pmc/articles/PMC2232166/pdf/procamiasymp00005-0171.pdf
4. Forum Nokia, http://doc.qt.nokia.com/4.1/sql-driver.html
5. Forum Nokia, http://stackoverflow.com/questions/1429782/qt-and-sqliteexample

Intrusion Detection System for Detecting Malicious Nodes in Mobile Ad Hoc Networks

Yuvraj Singh and Sanjay Kumar Jena

Department of Computer Science and Engineering,
National Institute of Technology Rourkela, 769 008, Odisha, India
{yuvraj1510,skjenanitrkl}@gmail.com

Abstract. This paper proposes an intrusion detection system to detect the malicious nodes in MANETs. The proposed detection algorithm is divided into two phases: detection during route establishment and detection during data forwarding. The detection effectiveness of the proposed algorithm is more than 80% and for some cases detection effectiveness may reach to 100%. The silent feature of proposed scheme is its simplicity and effectiveness in detecting malicious nodes.

Keywords: MANET, security attacks, malicious nodes, wireless network.

1 Introduction

In the last few years, we have seen the rapid development of wireless communication technologies. Today wireless technologies are widely used across the globe to support the communication needs of a huge number of end users [1]. The cost of wireless devices and installing wireless networks in emerging market has significantly reduced and making them much more affordable to end users. A Mobile Ad hoc Network (MANET) is formed by a group of mobile wireless nodes often without the assistance of fixed network infrastructures. The mobile or portable devices are free to move at any direction and are part of the network only when they are within range [2]. Applications of Ad hoc network include military tactical operations, emergency services, instantaneous meeting room applications and sensor networks [3].

MANETs are highly vulnerable to attacks than wired networks due to the open medium, dynamically changing network topology, cooperative algorithms, lack of centralized monitoring and lack of a clear line of defense [4]. Most current ad hoc routing protocols cope well with the dynamically changing topology. However, they do not address the problems when misbehavior nodes present in the network [5]. A commonly observed misbehavior is packet dropping. These misbehaved nodes are very difficult to identify because we cannot tell that whether the packets are dropped intentionally by the misbehaved nodes or dropped due to the node having moved out of transmission range or other link error [6].

In this paper, we propose an intrusion detection mechanism that will operate in ad hoc network to detect the malicious nodes. The propose detection

D. Nagamalai, E. Renault, and M. Dhanushkodi (Eds.): PDCTA 2011, CCIS 203, pp. 410–419, 2011.

mechanism is divided into two phases: Detection during route establishment and Detection during data forwarding. In first phase, we use two timer Sense timer and Reward timer and a drop counter. In second phase, each node forwards the data packet to the next hop and ensures that next node handles the packet appropriately by receiving a certificate of packet received from the next hop.

2 Related Work

Many researchers have focused on developing efficient mechanism to secure the routing in MANETs. Various secure routing, intrusion detection and response mechanisms have been proposed. Zhang, Lee, and Huang proposed intrusion detection (ID) and response system [7, 8], each node is responsible for detecting signs of intrusion locally and independently, but neighboring nodes can collaboratively investigate in a broader range. Individual IDS agents are placed on each and every node. Kachirski and Guha proposed a multi-sensor intrusion detection system based on mobile agent technology [9]. The system can be divided into three main modules, each of which represents a mobile agent with certain functionality, i.e.: monitoring, decision-making and initiating a response. Sergio Marti [10] discusses two tools Watchdog and Pathrater for detecting and mitigating routing misbehavior. These two techniques improve the throughput of MANETs in presence of compromised nodes that agree to forward but failed to do so. Watchdog is used to detect and identify a malicious node, while the Pathrater performs the job of isolating that node. Every node in the network includes both a watchdog and a Pathrater.

3 Proposed Approach

In this section, we propose an algorithm for the detection of malicious nodes in the wireless ad hoc networks. The malicious node may be defined as a node which does not follow the exact behavior. Most of the attacks are accomplished by modifying a message or simply not to forward the message which it is supposed to forward [11]. While developing the algorithms we have taken some assumptions.

3.1 Assumptions

The assumptions are as follows:

- A malicious node either drops the packet, modify the packet or simply forward the packet.
- Each node is having a public and private key pairs.
- A key management system that helps each node to access the public key of other nodes.
- A key distribution algorithm exists.
- The availability of one way hash function H() that creates the digest of the input message.

3.2 Proposed Algorithm

This algorithm has been designed to keep the concept in the mind that malicious node may drop the packet or modify the packet. As we have seen that many routing protocol for ad hoc networks have been proposed. We mount our algorithm over the Ad hoc On-demand Distance Vector (AODV) routing protocol. The proposed algorithm is divided into two phases: Detection in route establishment phase and Detection in data forwarding phase.

Detection in Route Establishment Phase

AODV routing protocol uses the control packets (e.g. RREQ, RREP) in the route establishment. Once a route has been established the data packet has to forward via established route. During this phase, each node is having two timers (Sense Timer and Reward Timer) and a counter (Drop Counter). Here is the brief description of these timers and counters.

- **Drop Counter:** This is used as a counter and updated at two places when a packet received by the node and forwarded by the node. For each incoming RREQ packet, Drop Counter is increased by one and for each outgoing RREQ packet Drop Counter is decreased by one.
- **Sense Timer:** This timer used as a detection period for a wireless node to identify whether a node forwards the received RREQ packet during this detection period or not. If a node does not forward the RREQ packet and the sense timer expires, the value of Drop Counter is increased by one.
- **Reward Timer:** As we know the RREQ is having broadcast nature. So a node may receive duplicate RREQ. This timer is used to reward some time to a node in which node could drop the duplicate RREQ without being penalized. Reward timer is only initiated when a valid RREQ packet is forwarded during the period of Sense Timer.

The steps of the algorithm are shown in Algorithm 1. According to this algorithm, when a node receives a RREQ packet from its neighbor then we check whether this is a duplicate RREQ or not. If this is a duplicate RREQ and $Reward\_Timer$ is pending for that node then we will not penalize the node otherwise we increment the value of $Drop\_Counter$. If this is a fresh RREQ then first we initialize the both timers to $CURRENT\_TIME$ and start the $Sense\_Timer$. Then we increment the value of $Drop\_Counter$ and calculate the $Time\_To\_Send$ i. e. total time taken by the node to forward the packet. Now compare the value of $Time\_To\_Send$ with the $Sense\_Timer$. If the value of $Time\_To\_Send$ is greater than the $Sense\_Timer$ then we increment the value of $Drop\_Counter$ otherwise we start the $Reward\_Timer$ and decrease the $Drop\_Counter$. Finally, we compare the value of $Drop\_Counter$, if it is greater that a predetermined $Threshold\_Value$ then we mark node as a malicious node. Using this algorithm we can detect the nodes which are acting as maliciously during route establishment phase.

Algorithm 1 **Detection in Route Establishment Phase**

Require Notations
Boolean : *isduplicateRREQ* = FALSE
CURRENT_TIME : time in the system clock
Sense_Timer : the value of detection period for the node
Reward_Timer : the value of grace period for the node
SENSE_TIME : the duration of sense time
REWARD_TIME : the duration of reward time
Drop_Counter : 0
Time_To_Send : total time taken by the node to forward the packet
Threshold_Value : a predetermined threshold value for detection

```
INPUT: A RREQ packet to node
OUTPUT: Detection Status of Node
for all control packets to this node do
  if the packet is neither from nor to this node itself then
    if request is duplicate RREQ then
      isduplicateRREQ =TRUE
    end if
    Step 1
    if isDuplicateRREQ =TRUE AND Reward_Timer is pending then
      message "Not a New Request" and skip all the next steps
    else
      Drop_Counter = Drop_Counter + 1
    end if
    Step 2
    Set the timers
    Sense_Timer = CURRENT_TIME
    Reward_Timer = CURRENT_TIME
    Step 3
    Start the sense timer such that
    Sense_Timer = CURRENT_TIME + SENSE_TIME
    Drop_Counter = Drop_Counter + 1
    Calculate Time_To_Send for this packet
    if Time_To_Send > Sense_Timer then
      Drop_Counter = Drop_Counter + 1
    else
      Start the reward timer such that
      Reward_Timer = CURRENT_TIME + REWARD_TIME
      Drop_Counter = Drop_Counter - 1
    end if
  end if
  if Drop_Counter > Threshold_Value then
    "Mark the Node as Malicious" and stop
  end if
end for
```

Detection in Data Forwarding Phase

In AODV protocol, after the route establishment phase a route from sender to destination has been established. The sender has all the information about the path and hops which is followed by data packet. During this phase, when a node forwards the data packet to next hop then node will receive a certificate of packet received from its next hop. This certificate represents that the node has forwarded the data packet correctly. If a node in the path does not able to produce a valid certificate then node is detected as malicious. Here is the description of certificate of packet received.

- **Certificate of Packet Received:** When a node receives the data packet from its previous hop then it generate a certificate of packet received and send to previous hop. For example suppose node A forwards a message M to node B. Then B generates a certificate C_{AB} i. e. node A has sent the data packet to node B. This certificate is generated as:

$$C_{AB} = [H(M)]_{PR_B} \text{ where,}$$

C_{AB} = Certificate received by node A from node B
M = Data Packet
H () = One way hash function
PR_B = Private Key of node B
PU_A = Public Key of node A

The steps of the algorithm are shown in Algorithm 2. According to this algorithm, Let us consider a data transfer from node A to node B. When a route establishes between source and destination the data transfer takes place. When node B receives a data packet from node A then we initialize the *Sense_Timer* to *CURRENT_TIME*, start the *Sense_Timer* and increment the value of *Drop_Counter* for node B by 1. Now node B generates a certificate for node A such as $C_{AB} = [H(M)]_{PR_B}$ and send it to node A. After that node A will calculate the *Time_To_Receive* for this certificate and compare with the *Sense_Timer* of node B. If it is greater, then node A discards the certificate and increment the value of *Drop_Counter* for node B by 1. Otherwise node A verify the certificate with the help of node B's public key. If it is a valid certificate then we decrease the value of *Drop_Counter* for node B by 1 else increase the value of *Drop_Counter* for node B by 1. Finally, we compare the value of *Drop_Counter*, if it is greater that a predetermined threshold value then we mark node as a malicious node. Using this algorithm we can detect the nodes which are acting as maliciously during data forwarding phase.

4 Simulations

4.1 Simulation Scenario

We simulate our proposed algorithm using Network Simulator version 2.34. We modify the AODV protocol in ns-2 to enable some nodes to be configured as misbehaving. The misbehavior here is define as either drop the packets or not to forward the packet in the specified time interval. The following table shows the simulation parameters.

4.2 Performance Metrics

In this section, we discuss about the performance parameter which are used to measure the performance of the proposed algorithms. Some of them are as follows:

Algorithm 2 **Detection in Data Forwarding Phase**

Require Notations
$CURRENT\_TIME$: time in the system clock
$Sense\_Timer$: the value of detection period for the node
$SENSE\_TIME$: the duration of sense time
$Drop\_Counter$: 0
$Time\_To\_Receive$: total time to receive the certificate
$Threshold\_Value$: a predetermined threshold value for detection

INPUT: A DATA packet to node
OUTPUT: Detection Status of Node
for all all data packets to this node **do**
  if the packet is neither from nor to this node itself **then**
    Step 1
    $Sense\_Timer = CURRENT\_TIME$
    Step 2
    Start the sense timer such that
    $Sense\_Timer = CURRENT\_TIME + SENSE\_TIME$
    $Drop\_Counter = Drop\_Counter + 1$
    Step 3
    Generate a certificate for the previous hope consider to node A such that
    $C_{AB} = [H(M)]_{PR_B}$
    and send it to node A.
    Step 4
    A will calculate the $Time\_To\_Receive$ for this certificate
    if $Time\_To\_Receive > Sense\_Timer$ **then**
      "Discard the certificate" and
      $Drop\_Counter = Drop\_Counter + 1$
    else
      Node A will verify the certificate with node's public key
      if certificate is valid **then**
        $Drop\_Counter = Drop\_Counter - 1$
      else
        $Drop\_Counter = Drop\_Counter + 1$
      end if
    end if
  end if
  if $Drop\_Counter > Threshold\_Value$ **then**
    "Mark the Node as Malicious" and stop
  end if
end for

Table 1. Simulation Parameters

S. No.	Simulation Parameters	Values
1	Simulator Used	Network Simulator (version 2.34)
2	Number of Nodes	100
3	No. of malicious nodes	10, 20, 30, 40, 50
4	Routing Protocol	AODV
5	Area Size	1900m×1900m
6	MAC	802.11
7	Simulation Time	200Secs
8	Traffic Source	CBR
9	Packet Size	512
10	Propagation Model	Two ray ground model
11	Speed	10m/s
12	Pause Time	2sec

- **Detection Effectiveness:** This measures the performance of algorithm. This is measured as total number of detected nodes divided by the total number of malicious nodes in the network.

$$\text{Detection Effectiveness} = \frac{Detected\_nodes}{Total\_malicious\_nodes} \times 100$$

- **False Positive:** This is measured as total number of good behaving nodes but detected as malicious divided by the total number of good behaving nodes.

$$\text{False Positive} = \frac{Good\_behaving\_detected\_nodes}{Total\_good\_behaving\_nodes} \times 100$$

- **False Negative:** This is measured as total number of malicious nodes which are not detected divided by the total number of malicious nodes.

$$\text{False Negative} = \frac{Malicious\_Undetected\_nodes}{Total\_malicious\_nodes} \times 100$$

5 Results

In this section, we discuss about the results of simulation and evaluate the performance of the proposed algorithm. The descriptions of the results are as follows.

Detection Effectiveness: Table 2 and Figure 1 show the detection effectiveness of the proposed algorithm. In this table we have shown that the detection effectiveness is high if the network is highly connected. As number of malicious nodes increase then also the detecting effectiveness is around 70% for threshold value 20. If there are less number of malicious nodes in the network the detection effectiveness may reach to 100%.

False Positive: Table 3 and Figure 2 show the false positive of the proposed algorithm. In this table we have shown that we are reducing the false positive as the number of malicious nodes increase. As the number of malicious nodes increase and network is higly connected then the percentage of false positive is reaching to 0. After increase the threshold value the maximum percentage of false positive is 22 and minimum percentage reaches to 0. The following table and graphs describes the false positive of the proposed algorithm.

Table 2. Detection Effectiveness (%)

No. of Malicious Nodes	Maximum Connection=10		Maximum Connection=20	
	Threshold(20)	**Threshold(30)**	**Threshold(20)**	**Threshold(30)**
10	90	80	100	90
20	75	70	95	85
30	73.33	60	90	83.33
40	55	40	77.5	75
50	48	32	68	64

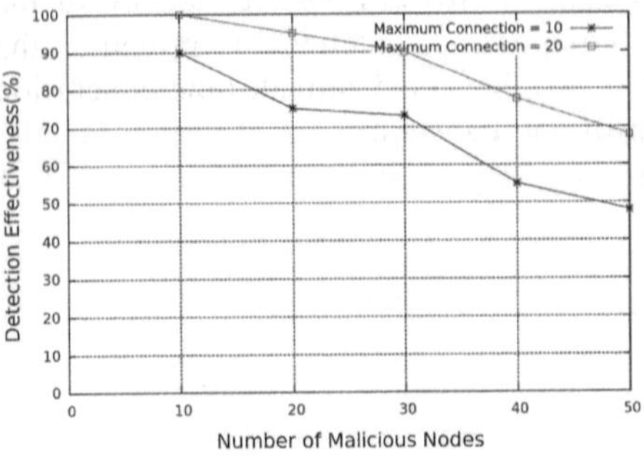

(a) Threshold=20, Max Nodes=100

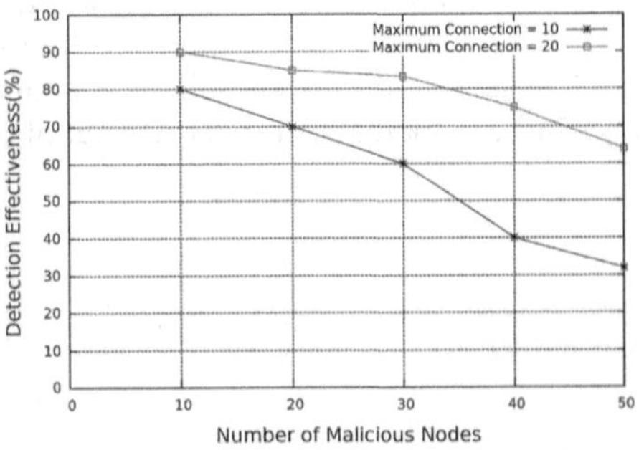

(b) Threshold=30, Max Nodes=100

Fig. 1. Detection Effectiveness vs Number of Malicious Nodes

Table 3. False Positive (%)

No. of Malicious Nodes	Maximum Connection=10		Maximum Connection=20	
	Threshold(3)	**Threshold(5)**	**Threshold(3)**	**Threshold(5)**
10	12.5	7.5	40	22.5
20	3.33	3.33	20	13.33
30	0	0	5	5
40	0	0	0	0
50	0	0	0	0

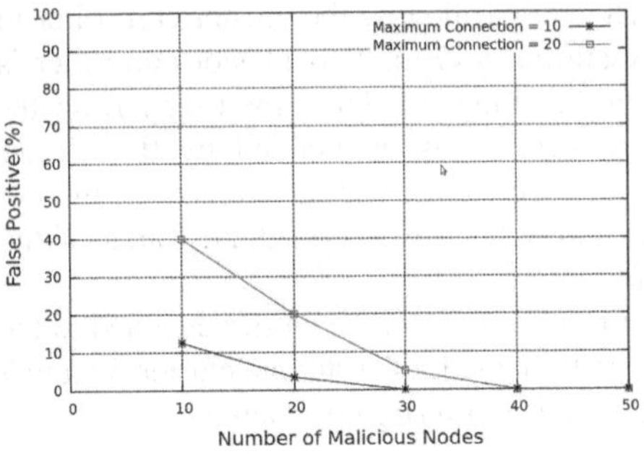

(a) Threshold=3, Max Nodes=100

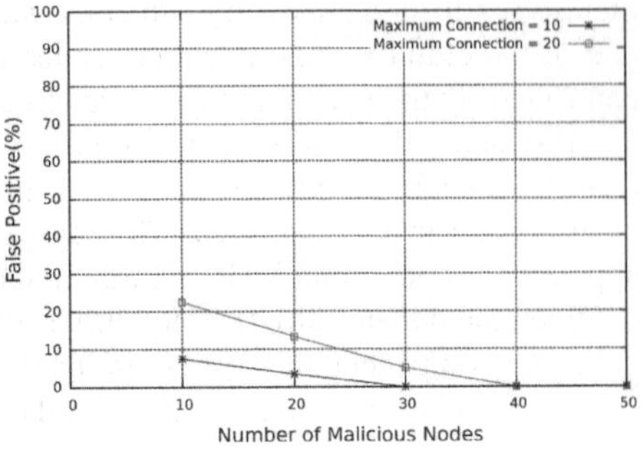

(b) Threshold=5, Max Nodes=100

Fig. 2. False Positive vs Number of Malicious Nodes

False Negative: Table 4 and Figure 3 show the false negative of the proposed algorithm. In this table we have shown that the percentage of false negative is below 30 for the higly connected network. As the number of malicious nodes increase and network is higly connected then the percentage of false negative is reaching to maximum 28. If the malcious nodes are less in the nework then the percentage of false negative may reach to 0. The following table and graphs describes the false positive of the proposed algorithm.

Table 4. False Negative (%)

No. of Malicious Nodes	Maximum Connection=10		Maximum Connection=20	
	Threshold(20)	**Threshold(30)**	**Threshold(20)**	**Threshold(30)**
10	10	20	0	0
20	25	30	5	5
30	26.66	40	10	10
40	45	60	22.5	22.5
50	52	68	28	24

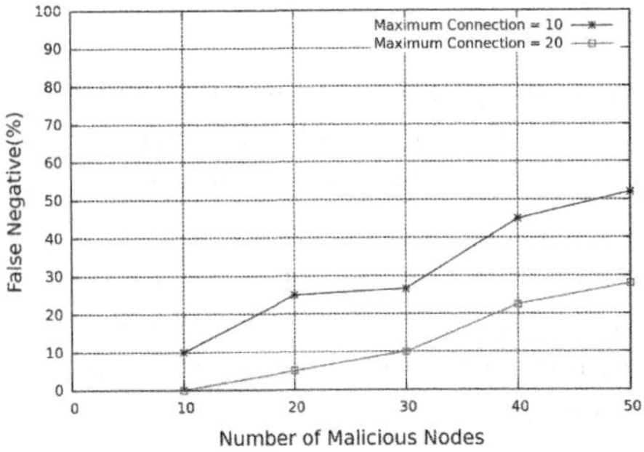

(a) Threshold=20, Max Nodes=100

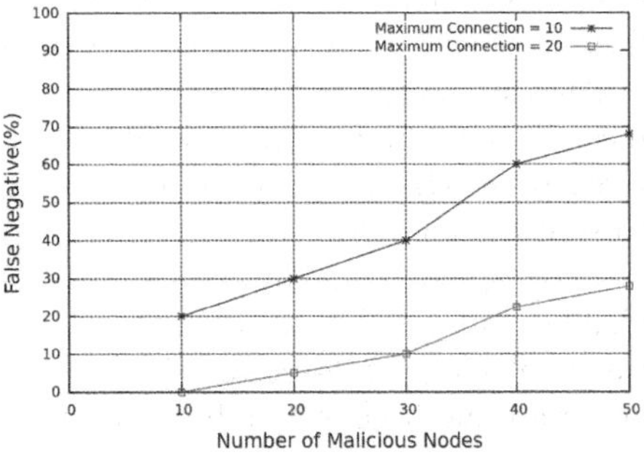

(b) Threshold=30, Max Nodes=100

Fig. 3. False Negative vs Number of Malicious Nodes

6 Conclusions

We implement packet dropping attack and an attack in which a node refuse to forward the packet within a specified interval with AODV routing protocol. The proposed algorithm has been analysed with different parameters such as connectivity of the networks and number of malicious nodes with different threshold values. The detection effectiveness of the proposed algorithm is more than 80% and for some cases detection effectiveness may reach to 100% and false positives are below 20% for different number of malicious nodes and threshold values. Thus, our experiment shows very predicting results on detecting malicious nodes. The silent feature of propose scheme is its simplicity and effectiveness in detecting malicious nodes. In the future, we would like to extend this scheme to detect other type of attacks such as application layer attack, denial of service, manipulation of network traffic and so on.

Acknowledgement. The authors would like to thank the Department of Information Technology, Ministry of Communication & Information Technology, Government of India for financial assistance in this research and development work.

References

1. Anjum, F., Mouchtaris, P.: Security for Wireless Ad Hoc Networks, 2nd edn. Wiley, Chichester (2007)
2. Murthy, C.S.R., Manoj, B.S.: Ad Hoc Wireless Networks: Architectures And Protocols. Pearson Education, India (2008)
3. Sterne, D.F., Balasubramanyam, P., Carman, D., Wilson, B., Talpade, R., Ko, C., Balupari, R., Tseng, C.Y., Bowen, T.F., Levitt, K.N., Rowe, J.: A general cooperative intrusion detection architecture for manets. In: IWIA, pp. 57–70 (2005)
4. Mandala, S., Ngadi, M.A., Abdullah, A.: A survey on manet intrusion detection. International Journal of Computer Science and Security 2(1), 417–432 (2007)
5. Marchang, N., Datta, R.: Collaborative techniques for intrusion detection in mobile ad-hoc networks. Ad Hoc Networks 6(4), 508–523 (2008), http://dx.doi.org/10.1016/j.adhoc.2007.04.003
6. Rajaram, A., Palaniswami, D.S.: Malicious node detection system for mobile ad hoc networks (IJCSIT) International Journal of Computer Science and Information Technologies 1(2), 77–85 (2010), http://dx.doi.org/10.1016/j.adhoc.2005.11.005
7. Zhang, Y., Lee, W.: Intrusion detection in wireless ad-hoc networks. In: Mobicom, pp. 275–283 (2000), http://doi.acm.org/10.1145/345910.345958
8. Huang, Y., Lee, W.: A cooperative intrusion detection system for ad hoc networks. In: SASN, pp. 135–147 (2003), http://doi.acm.org/10.1145/986858.986877
9. Kachirski, O., Guha, R.K.: Effective intrusion detection using multiple sensors in wireless ad hoc networks. In: HICSS, p. 57 (2003), http://computer.org/proceedings/hicss/1874/track2/187420057aabs.htm
10. Marti, S., Giuli, T.J., Lai, K., Baker, M.: Mitigating routing misbehavior in mobile ad hoc networks. In: Mobicom, pp. 255–265 (2000), http://doi.acm.org/10.1145/345910.345955
11. Komninos, N., Vergados, D., Douligeris, C.: Detecting unauthorized and compromised nodes in mobile ad hoc networks. Ad Hoc Networks 5(3), 289–298 (2007), http://dx.doi.org/10.1016/j.adhoc.2005.11.005

TDMA Based Low Energy Consuming MAC Protocol for Wireless Sensor Networks in Environmental Monitoring Applications

R. Rathna[1] and A. SivaSubramanian[2]

[1] Department of Information Technology, Sathyabama University, Jeppiaar Nagar, Rajiv Gandhi Road, Chennai-119, India
rathna08@yahoo.co.in
[2] Department of Electronics and Communication, St. Josephs' College of Engineering, Jeppiaar Nagar, Rajiv Gandhi Road, Chennai-119, India
shiva_31@yahoo.com

Abstract. Environmental monitoring applications need tiny sensor nodes randomly embedded in the target area. As the wireless Sensor Networks are made up of tiny energy hungry sensor nodes, it is a challenging process to retain the energy level of those nodes for a long period. They are equipped with limited computing and radio communication capabilities. This work is on the attempt to reduce the power consumption of nodes , by concentrating on the radio, which has four states of operations at various time intervals .

A proper sleep/wake up scheduling, when applied over these radios, can reduce the overall energy consumption of the Wireless Sensor Network minimally. The scheduling protocol used in this work is a TDMA based MAC protocol. When implemented in a simulated WSN, it reduces the energy consumption of the previously existing protocol and hence it proves to be efficient, when compared with other scheduling protocols.

Keywords: Wireless Sensor Network, Monitoring, Scheduling Protocol, TDMA, MAC, Energy consumption.

1 Introduction

Wireless Sensor Networks- the recent, powerful technology has important usage in environmental monitoring of particular phenomena. They are made up of tiny sensors which are used for monitoring or sensing data. Because of their small size, power supply is provided by a small battery, which, when deployed in a 'not-easily reachable' place, cannot be replaced or recharged frequently. Routing, Mobility (optional) and security are other functions taken care of by the node itself. These Wireless Sensor Networks are deployed in so many areas like vital signal monitoring in tele-homecare systems, ecology monitoring which are widely used for monitoring wildlife, rare-micro organisms, changes in the sea or lake water, soil after natural disasters like typhoon, tsunami, flood and soil erosion, monitoring climatic changes, structural

D. Nagamalai, E. Renault, and M. Dhanushkodi (Eds.): PDCTA 2011, CCIS 203, pp. 420–427, 2011.

monitoring for e.g. Monitoring the conditions of a bridge after its construction, monitoring the historic buildings and Surveillance in Defense organizations.

Storage mechanism is also very simple and can only provide limited space. So acquisition of precise data and immediate transfer of the data to sink node is very important. Data processing and data transfer require more power. When the data has to be transferred and when it needs to be stored depends on the state of the radio in the node. To conserve energy, we can switch the radio to sleep state when there is no data to send or receive. This method of making the radio to be in sleep state and making it active if any event is detected, is called as on-demand scheme or event-based scheme.

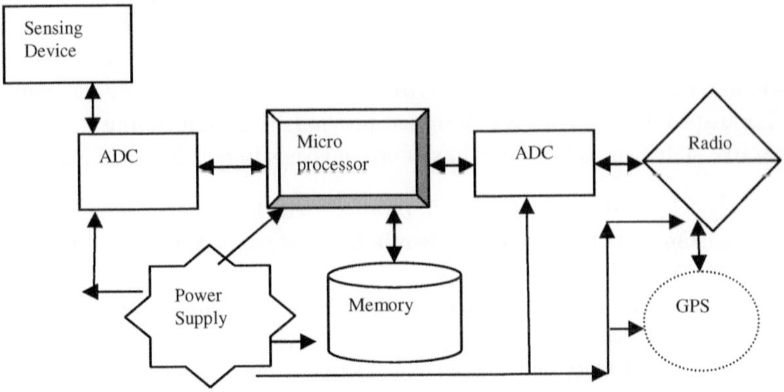

Fig. 1. Components of a Wireless Sensor Node

There is another method of scheduling i.e. on regular time interval all the nodes will be either in sleep mode or active mode. This is synchronous scheme. But the overhead of maintaining all the nodes in the synchronized state becomes complex. It is not necessary to keep all the nodes active at one time. WSN can follow a scheduling pattern, accordingly, at any instant, we can make only a limited number of nodes active. The work presented in this paper is based on this type of asynchronous mechanism.

2 MAC Protocols

The power supply unit should be very small and also it should support all its operations without degrading the performance. The communication protocol used should be light weight and it should not consume more energy. Hence, we are going for a good scheduling protocol and while applying it, power consumption is the one which should be kept in mind.

Any Scheduling protocol will keep only a subset of nodes to be in active state and keeping others in-active or in sleep state. A scheduling protocol will be the best if it keeps only a minimum number of nodes active at any instant. There are so many scheduling protocols available. For a WSN, a scheduling protocol should use narrow band modulation techniques. Low data transfer rate is enough for a WSN in Environmental monitoring applications.

The TDMA (Time Division Multiple Access) based scheduling protocols make the nodes to be in inactive mode, until their allocated time slots. The TDMA based protocols [1] are designed such that the shortest path for communication will be found out and only a particular link will be in wake up mode for a transmission.

Traffic adaptive MAC (TRAMA) and Node Activation Multiple Access (NAMA) are some of the TDMA based protocols. They use distributed election algorithms.

The S-MAC (self organizing Medium Access Control) protocol, one of the efficient MAC protocol, schedules the subset of nodes to be in active state by using very simple synchronization algorithms and low cost hardware mechanisms for timing control. It combines both the contention based and time scheduled protocols. By using S-MAC, all the nodes can be in active state more than once, a frame. By doing like this for all the nodes, they will not be having the same duty cycle. So automatically the life of a node will be short. This will reduce the overall power consumption.

Various protocols have been designed previously for scheduling the nodes in sleep and Active states and all of them have certain issues to be addressed [6].

- The B-MAC [12] is a MAC protocol which introduces the first Low power Listening (LPL) Protocols. But it does not support all types of Radio.
- The WiseMAC is an improved one, which reduces the length of the preamble by sending the data only to its neighbors. But this also faces the same problem of B-MAC.
- The SpeckMAC consists of SpeckMAC-B and SpeckMAC-D. It also aims at reducing the energy consumed for sending the data to active nodes by reducing the preamble size.
- The performance of X-MAC is similar to B-MAC, with the additional fixed length preamble using advertisement cycles for sending the data.
- The D-MAC protocol staggers or sends the 'send and receive' time slots for single packet exchange, to all the available paths to its neighbors.
- MIX-MAC protocol makes the WSN to adapt to different types of MAC protocols depending on the situations like packet size.
- Inverse Log Scheduling- centralized and distributed protocols[14] assigns long transmission times for those sensor nodes which face worse channel conditions.
- The centralized and de-centralized sensor scheduling protocols as given in [8] concentrate on both power conservation and coverage. They are designed for military surveillance purpose.
- Sift [12] is a MAC protocol which is designed on the basis of sending the important or high priority information first, with less delay and then sending the low priority information.

3 Sleep/Wake-Up Scheduling

Asynchronous type of sleep/wake-up scheduling necessitates only certain nodes have to periodically wake-up in order to send or receive. All the other nodes should be in sleep state. While going for a switch from active to sleep state, and then from sleep to active state, the condition to be checked is that the energy it consumes for the switch should be low when compared with the energy it consumes when it is always in the active state.

$$E_{\text{wasted in switching}} < E_{\text{Saved}}$$

This is depicted in the given figure fig.2. This scheduling protocol is designed based on the radio of the node.

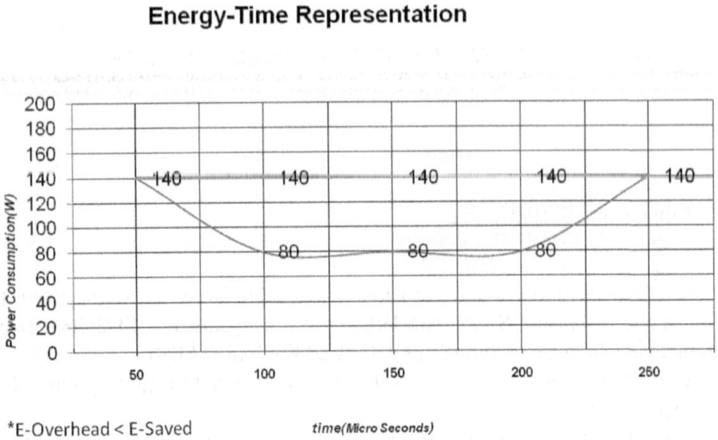

Fig. 2. Graph depicting change in power consumption by using a sleep/wake-up scheduling

This scheduling protocol is designed based on the radio of the node. So the node can be represented in sleep(rs) or active state. Active state is further classified into three states, namely transmitting state(rt), receiving state(rr) and listening state(rl). The energy conumed for the switch can be represented by E_{sl}(sleep to listen), E_{st}(sleep to transmit) and E_{sr}(sleep to receive).

For a time slot, say 't', if the node is in sending state, it will be denoted by $r_{t,t}$=1. If it is not in sending state, it will be denoted by $r_{t,t}$=0. So at a particular instant say t, a node can be in any one of the four states. So we can state the condition like this

$$r_{t,t}+ r_{r,t}+ r_{l,t}+ r_{s,t} =1$$

For the state switch from sleep state to listening state, the energy consumed can be calculated by $(r_{s,t}+ r_{l,t}+1)\, E_{sl}$.

During every cycle, the radio goes to all the four states. When the radio is either sending or receiving or simply listening, it is said to be active. If it goes to sleep, it is said to be in sleep state.

The Energy wasted in simply switching between states E_{wasted} in switching can be calculated by

$$E_{\text{wasted in switching}} = t_{s\text{-}a}\,(p_{\text{active}} + p_{\text{sleep}})/\,2$$

The Energy saved because of this switching can be calculated by

$$E_{Saved} = (t_a - t_s)\, p_{active} - (t_{a\text{-}s}(p_{active} + p_{sleep})/\, 2 + (t_a - t_s - t_{a\text{-}s})\, p_{sleep}$$

In this work, the basic scheduling is designed based on this first check i.e.

$$E_{wasted\ in\ switching} < E_{Saved}$$

Then only switching between active and sleep states will be beneficial. $E_{wasted\ in\ switching}$ and E_{Saved} can be calculated from the above derived equations. The same condition can be written like

$$(t_a - t_s) > ½(t_{a\text{-}s} + ((p_{active} + p_{sleep})/\, (p_{active} - p_{sleep}))\, t_{s\text{-}a})\ \text{this.}$$

The notations used in the above expressions are described in the Table 1.

Table 1. Notations used

Notations	Descriptions
r_s	Radio in sleep state
r_t	Radio in transmitting state
r_r	Radio in receiving state
r_l	Radio in listening state
E_{sl}	Energy consumption during the switch from sleep state to listen state
E_{st}	Energy consumption during the switch from sleep state to transmitting state
E_{sr}	Energy consumption during the switch from sleep state to receiving state
p_{active}	Power consumed in active state(r_t,r_r,r_l)
p_{sleep}	Power consumed in sleep state r_s.
$t_{s\text{-}a}$	Time taken for going to active state(r_t,r_r,r_l) from sleep state.
$t_{a\text{-}s}$	Time taken for going to sleep state from active state(r_t,r_r,r_l).
t_a	Time at which the radio becomes active as per the schedule to send or receive any data.
t_s	Time at which the radio decides to go to sleep state as per the schedule.

4 Cluster Based Sleep/Wake-Up Scheduling

A tree like arrangement of wireless sensor nodes is used in this work. All the nearby nodes are grouped to form different clusters. The tree is rooted at the sink. The tree is structured based on Shortest hop Path Tree algorithm. The data from each cluster is collected by a cluster head and this one in turn send the aggregated data to the active cluster head of the nearest cluster. While forming the clusters, the following rule should be followed- No two clusters should have one or more nodes in interference range. Interference range is that , the two nearest nodes in two different clusters should not be in either transmitting(r_t)or receiving state(r_r). This will cause interference and overhearing of packets and thereby wastage of energy.

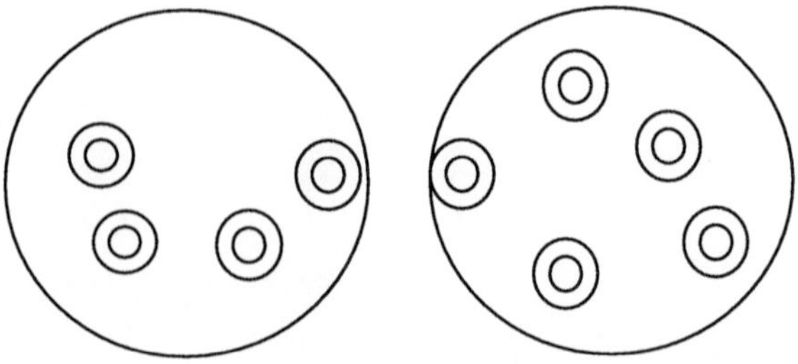

Fig. 3. Two clusters having two nodes in interference range

In the fig.3, the nodes c and f are said to be in interference range. For the two neighbouring clusters this rule should be followed. If a node 'c' at time slot 't' in a cluster say Ci is in active state (r c,t,a), then the node 'f' at the same time slot 't' in a neighbouring cluster say Cj should not be in active state

$$r_{c,t,a} + r_{f,t,a} = 1$$

For all the nodes in each cluster, certain weight(w) is added based on the data that is being sent to one of the node in that cluster along with the data, that each node senses on its own. All the nodes in each cluster will wake up based on the weight of the cluster. At that moment the nodes will either send or receive data to or from the other nodes respectively. This weight to the cluster is a group of time slots to all the nodes in that cluster.

So in a tree, there will be clusters with different weights. The cluster with greatest weight will be allotted the first available timeslot. Here weight is added based on the information received by the nodes from other nodes and environment. In a tree like structure, the nodes in the clusters will have to receive the data from its child nodes and have to send that data packet to the parent node (the node which is in the higher order of the sending node in the tree hierarchy). This weight is assigned in a decreasing order to the clusters in the tree structure. If this mechanism is followed for scheduling the nodes in a WSN for environmental monitoring applications, surely the overall energy consumption of the WSN can be reduced by a considerable range.

5 Simulation and Results

The above described method of Cluster based sleep/wake-up scheduling is tested in a simulated WSN and it proves to be efficient. Network Simulator-2(NS2) is used in this work for simulation.NS2 is one of the best simultion tools available for Wireless sensor Networks. We can easily implement the designed protocols either by using the otcl coding or by writing the C++ Program. In either way , the tool helps to prove our theory analytically. The graphical representation can be created by using the Xgraph tool.

When this scheduling algorithm is implemented it gives a good improvement in the reduction of time delay as well as the overall energy consumption.

Both the graphs are given below in Fig .4 and Fig.5

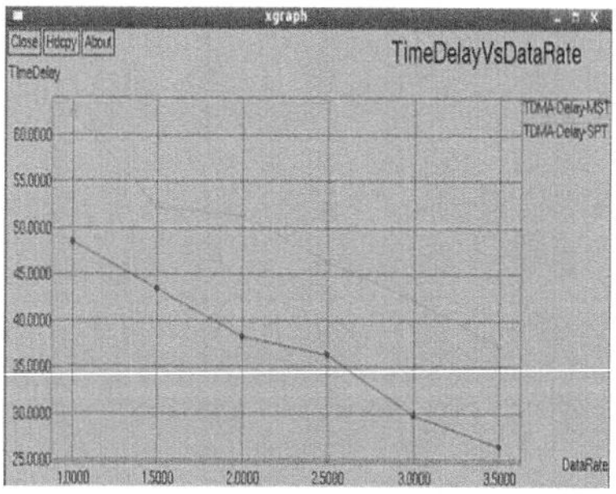

Fig. 4. Graph showing reduction in time delay

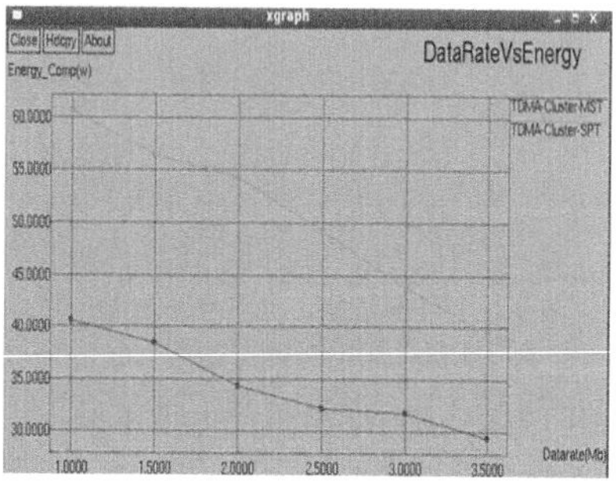

Fig. 5. Graph showing reduction in energy consumption

From the graphs, we can say that this algorithms efficiently reduced both the time delay and energy consumption.

6 Conclusion

The algorithm designed and implemented in this paper is completely TDMA based. It helps to reduce the energy consumption by reducing the number of times a node has to wake up during a time slot, to be in active mode. The data gathering and then transmitting according to the schedule dynamically created is based on the Shortest Hop Path Tree (SPT) which is better than any other type of tree structure. The same scheduling mechanism can be further enhanced by using a different type of tree structure. The underlying concept in this paper is efficient usage of energy. It has been proved also. The time delay is also reduced to a small extent. The future work can be done by combining both the TDMA and FDMA based slot allocation.

References

1. Merlin, C.J., Heinzelman, W.B.: Schedule Adaptation of Low-Power-Listening Protocols for Wireless Sensor Networks. IEEE Transactions on Mobile Computing 9(5), 672–685 (2010), doi:10.1109/TMC.2009.153.
2. Yao, Y., Giannakis, G.B.: Energy-Efficient Scheduling Protocols for Wireless Sensor Networks. IEEE Trans. on Commun. 51(8), 1389–1398 (2005)
3. Ghosh, S., Veeraraghavan, P., Singh, S., Zhang, L.: Performance of a Wireless Sensor Network MAC Protocol with a Global Sleep Schedule. International Journal of Multimedia and Ubiquitous Engineering 4(2) (April 2009)
4. Pantazis, N.A., Vergados, D.J., Vergados, D.D., Douligeris, C.: Energy efficiency in wireless sensor networks using sleep mode TDMA scheduling. Ad Hoc Networks 7(2), 322–343 (2009), Science Direct
5. Chamam, A., Pierre, S.: On the Planning of Wireless Sensor Networks: Energy-Efficient Clustering under the Joint Routing and Coverage Constraint. IEEE Transactions on Mobile Computing 8(8), 1077–1086 (2009)

6. He, T., Krishnamurthy, S., Luo, L., Yan, T., Gu, L., Stoleru, R., Zhou, G., Cao, Q., Vicaire, P., Stankovic, J.A., Abdelzaher, T.F., Hui, J., Krogh, B.: VigilNet: An Integrated Sensor Network System for Energy-Efficient Surveillance. ACM Transactions on Sensor Networks (TOSN) 2(1), 1–38 (2006) ISSN:1550-4859
7. Hadim, S., Mohamed, N.: Middleware Challenges and Approaches for Wireless Sensor Networks. IEEE Distributed Systems Online 7(3), art. no. 0603-o3001 (2006)
8. Jamieson, K., Balakrishnan, H., Tay, Y.C.: Sift: A MAC Protocol for Event-Driven Wireless Sensor Networks, MIT Laboratory for Computer Science, Tech. Rep. 894 (May 2003), http://www.lcs.mit.edu/publications/pubs/pdf/MIT-LCS-TR-894.pdf
9. Wu, Y., Li, X.-Y., Liu, Y., Lou, W.: Energy-Efficient Wake-Up Scheduling for Data Collection and Aggregation. IEEE Transactions on Parallel and Distributed Systems 21(2), 275–287 (2010), doi:10.1109/TPDS.2009.45
10. Gupta, A., Lin, X., Srikant, R.: Low-Complexity Distributed Scheduling Algorithms for Wireless Networks. In: Proceedings of IEEE Infocom, Anchorage, AK (May 2007)
11. Kotamäki, N., Thessler, S., Koskiaho, J., Hannukkala, A.O., Huitu, H., Huttula, T., Havento, J., Järvenpää, M.: Wireless in-situ Sensor Network for Agriculture and water Monitoring on a River Basin scale in southern Finland: Evaluation from a Data User's Perspective. In: Sensors 2009, vol. 9, pp. 2862–2883 (2009), doi:10.3390/s90402862
12. Lai, S., Cao, J., Zheng, Y.: PSWare: A publish / subscribe middleware supporting composite event in wireless sensor network, percom. In: 2009 IEEE International Conference on Pervasive Computing and Communications, pp. 1–6 (2009)

Extending Temporal and Event Based Data Modeling for RFID Databases

Sapna Tyagi[1], Abdul Quaiyum Ansari[2], and Mohammad Ayoub Khan[3]

[1]Institute of Management Studies,
Ghaziabad, UP, India
sapna.tyagi@imsgzb.com
[2] Department of Electrical Engineering,
Jamia Millia Islamia, New Delhi
aqansari@ieee.org
[3] Centre for Development of Advanced Computing,
(Ministry of Communications and IT), Noida, India
ayoub@ieee.org

Abstract. The Radio Frequency Identification System (RFID) uses radio waves to transfer data between readers and movable tagged objects. There are variety of applications where RFID data is time-dependent, dynamically changing, in large volumes, and carry implicit semantics. RFID application needs to effectively support such large scale temporal data created by RFID applications. These applications need an explicit temporal data model for RFID data to support tracking and monitoring queries. In addition, they need to have an automatic method to transform the primitive observations from RFID readers into derived data used in RFID-enabled applications. This paper propose an extended temporal and event based data model for such applications.

Keywords: RFID, Tags, Temporal, TT, AT, EPC.

1 Introduction

The Radio Frequency Identification (RFID) is a wireless technology that uses radio frequency waves as a career to transfer information between tagged objects and readers without line of sight (LOS). This creates tremendous opportunities in gathering information regarding people, goods and products in transit. This is also known as auto identification (Auto-ID) technology for identifying the object. An RFID system consists of tag and reader. The tag is Integrated Circuit (IC), which stores the information about the object to be identified. The Reader is a device that reads the information stored into the tag, whenever the tag comes into the vicinity of reader as shown in fig 1. The RFID technology has gained significant momentum in past few years, with several high profile adaptations (e.g. Wal-Mart, k-mart) [1]. RFID is automatic and fast, and does not require line of sight or contact between readers (or sensors) and tagged objects.

The amount of information that will be generated by radio frequency identification (RFID) tags is enormous. RFID data are time–dependent, dynamically changing, in large volumes, carry implicit semantics.That leaves us with questions like "What

D. Nagamalai, E. Renault, and M. Dhanushkodi (Eds.): PDCTA 2011, CCIS 203, pp. 428–438, 2011.

happens to data quality? What data should we capture, and how often should we capture it? What about 'white noise'?" While we can't address every issue regarding the coming data avalanche, we can highlight some of the more "front of mind" concerns surrounding RFID.

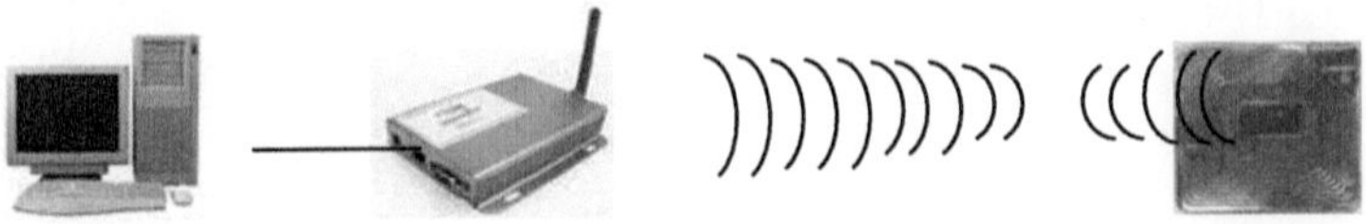

Fig. 1. RFID System

In the effort to address these many issues, adopters of RFID technology are overlooking various important aspects of RFID deployment like how back-end databases and business application can handle the massive amount of new data that RFID systems will produce.

As we have already discussed the amount of information that would be generated by RFID tags is on the verge of exploding. RFID observations contain redundant, missed and unreliable data because of the various parallel transponders. Generally these unreliable reading can be formalized in three typical undesired situations [2] False negative reading, false positive readings and duplicate readings explained. In false negative reading, RFID tags, which are in the vicinity of reader, might not be detected by reader. In false positive readings unexpected extra information are generated. Duplicate Reading which is very common in RFID application, in this RFID tags might be detected multiple times and every time reading is being stored .Thus it requires to manage the information flow which need a Complete Data Model capable of providing a complete implementation of RFID Application. It requires extensive preprocessing of the data so that it can be organized in more structured manner capable of extracting more meaningful information for Decision making process.

The paper is organized as follows: Section 2 Explores EPC architecture that consists of EPC code, EPC Architecture, EPCIS. This section also presents a survey on Data Models. The paper also presents Dynamic entity Relationship Model, Temporal Data Model, Extended Entity Relationship Model. The section 3 proposes two new models Extension of Temporal Data Model and Extension of Event Based Data Model. Finally, a conclusion is presented in the last section.

2 EPC Architecture

Electronic Product Code is a modern day replacement of the Universal Product Code. Each product tag has a unique embedded EPC number. The EPC protocol was developed at Developed at MIT's Auto-Lab in 2000. In this section, we present a detailed discussion on the EPC structure and the architecture.

2.1 EPC Structure

Electronic Product Code (EPC) is a unique number that identifies a specific item that will be stored on RFID tag's memory. These codes are generic and follow a universal numbering scheme for physical objects. The EPC is capable to identify every single, individual product item whereas the barcode only identifies the product. The structure of a 96-bit EPC code is as follows:

Table 1. 96 Bit EPC Format [3, 4]

Header	EPC Manager	Object Class	Serial Number
8 bit	28 bit	24 bit	36 bit

The first field in the header defines the coding schemes in operation with the remaining bits providing the actual product code. The Manager Field is responsible for identifying the product manufacturer. The object class defines the product class itself. The Serial number is unique for an individual product class. The length of EPC may be of 64, 96, 128,256,1K, 4K Bits [4]. 96-bit EPC belongs to Class I Generation that identifies 268 million manufactures (228) uniquely. Each manufacturer can have 16 million (224) unique object classes and 68 billion unique serial numbers (236) in each class.

2.2 EPC Architecture

Fig 2 represents a common architecture illustrating how an RFID application works. Each object is tagged with an RFID chip that contains a unique EPC. In layer 1 Data from these tags are collected periodically by RFID readers and sent to RFID Middleware in form of tuple <epc, Reader_id, time>. Instead of storing these massive, dirty, poor-semantic reads directly in repository, the RFID Middleware will filter (e.g., eliminate duplicate reads and missing reads) and correlate them with the business context to generate all clean and meaningful events. These events are then passed to EPCIS through Capture Interface and stored permanently in its repository or pushed to some applications interested in real-time information. The data can be queried from partners' accessing applications through Query Interface. Physical layer consist of Reader and RFID Middleware.

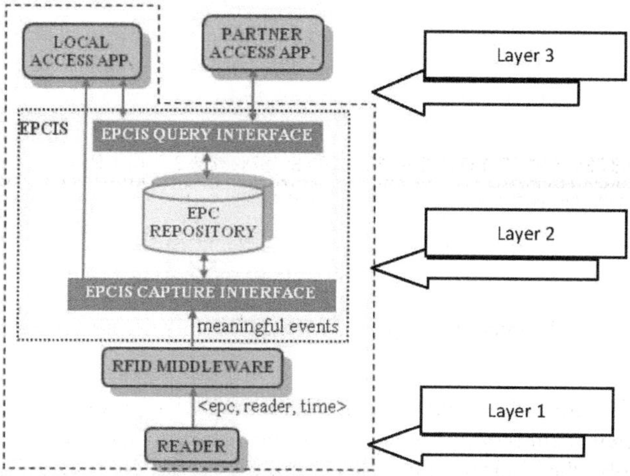

Fig. 2. EPC Architecture [5]

A brief overview of all the layers of EPC architecture is presented below in table 2.

Table 2. EPC Layer Description

Layer	Implementation	Description
1	Tags & Readers	EPC Data tagged on item is captured by the reader in the form of Hexadecimal number.
1	RFID Middleware	An Onsite software component that converts multiple readings to one read, adds information such as reader_id location_id, Timestamp.
2	EPCIS	It is responsible for capturing meaningful events, performs data modeling , maintains database and provide framework to execute query to obtain the information relevant to business context
3	Local object name services	Each of the industry partners maintain its own repository of product specific data. The local ONS provides a pointer to the local database.
4	Root ONS and Dictionary Services	The ONS identifies unique numbers for manufacturers and the discovery service points to a particular EPC-IS where detailed information can be obtained for specific item.
5	National Demonstrator project portal	The portal displays the data collected and stored in the system and to allow the queries on the movement of good through supply chain.

2.3 EPCIS

EPC Information Services (EPCIS) is a part of the EPCglobal Architecture Framework [1], an interrelated collection of hardware, software, data, and service standards towards a common goal of enhancing business flows, data flows and modeling and computer applications through the use of Electronic Product Codes (EPCs) [1]. EPC Information Services provides a common set of data elements, a common language for communication (Physical Markup Language, or PML), and a set of defined messages for storing, accessing, and communicating data about objects moving in the supply chain. The key to these information services is the EPC held in the RFID tag on each object. EPC-IS acts as the central nervous system of the EPCglobal Network. The EPC-IS manages and moves information in a way that does not overload existing corporate and public networks. EPCIS defines standard interfaces to capture and query on EPC data using a well-defined set of service operations and data standards [2]. Thus one of the major tasks which EPCIS has to do is to develop a data model which adds business context to EPC observational data. In this Paper we are going to present temporal data modeling for EPC data which is capable to support extensibility at multiple levels.

2.4 Related Work

The Siemens Corporate Research has presented a Dynamic Relationship ER Model for typical Supply chain environment. In this model they have emphasized on:

- RFID entities : static and are not altered in the business processes
- RFID relationships: dynamic and changes all the time

Thus they have proposed Dynamic Relationship ER Model– Simple extension of ER model. According to it there are two types of dynamic relationships (i) Event-based dynamic relationship in which a timestamp attribute added to represent the occurring time of the event. (ii) State-based dynamic relationship where tstart and tend attributes are added to represent the lifespan of a state. Below is the glimpse of table structures [5].

Table 3. Static and Dynamic Entity Relationship

Static Entity Tables	Dynamic Relationship Tables
Object (epc, name , description)	Transaction(Transaction_id, transaction_type, Timestamp)
Sensor(epc, name, description)	Observation(sensor_epc, value, timestamp Sensor-
Locations(Location_id, name, Owner)	Location(sensor_epc,location_id,position,tstart, tend)
	Transactionitem(transaction_id, epc, timestamp)

In paper [8], the authors have proposed temporal data models. In this, fundamental entities in RFID applications are EPC-tagged objects, readers, sensors, operators, locations and transactions. While these entities are static in general, the relationships among these entities can be either static or dynamic. Static relationships are similar to those in the traditional ER model explained in table 3 In addition to it this model extends ER model for modeling static entities and relationships with the following new features.

Temporal Relationships: There are two types of temporal relationships among RFID entities: relationships that generate events and relationships that generate state histories. For an event- based relationship, we use an attribute timestamp to represent the occurrence time of the event. For a state-based temporal relationship, we use attributes tstart and tend to represent the lifespan of the state.

Nested Relations: Nested relationship is a new characteristic in read- write RFID applications. For example, for an application with sensor-write tags, an onboard sensor records the temperature which will be stored in measurement history in the tag. Thus a reader observation contains both the EPC of the tag and the measurement history, i.e., a nested relation.

This model contains two state-based dynamic relations for a typical supply chain: OBJECTLOCATION and CONTAINMENT. OBJECTLOCATION preserves the location history of each object: the period [tstart, tend] during which an object stays in a location. CONTAINMENT records in what period [tstart, tend] an object is contained in its parent object. Besides state-based relations, there are also four event- based dynamic relations: OBSERVATION, SENSORMEASUREMENT, S-OBSERVATION and TRANSACTIONITEM. OBSERVATION records the raw reading data generated from readers and SENSORMEASURMENT records the measurement data generated from sensors. S-OBSERVATION represents a reader's observation of an object and its logged sensor measurement history. TRANSACTIO-NITEM records the event generated during the interaction between a transaction and an item.

In paper [5], authors have proposed an extended entity relationship diagram. As mentioned, data in EPCIS fall into two categories: master data (static data) and event data (dynamic data).Master data include (1) class-level Data describing properties for all objects of the same object class (product name, manufacturer, SKU, etc), (2) instance-level Data describing properties of each individual object (date of manufacture, lot number, etc), and (3) business context data providing necessary business context (business locations, transaction type, etc).Event data refer to things that happen at a specific time.

There are four kinds of events:

- Object Event which carries information about actual observations of or assertions about EPC-tagged objects (e.g., "EPC X was shipped from store Y at time Z").
- Aggregation Event which announces a specific group of EPC-tagged objects was contained in another one (e.g., "at time T, objects of EPCs A, B, C was aggregated to the case EPC X at factory L").
- Quantity Event which inventorially reports the number of instances of a specific object class (e.g., "at time T, there are 400 instances of object class X observed at location L").
- Transaction Event which describes the association of EPC-tagged objects with one or more business transactions (e.g., "at time T, the cases of EPC X, Y, Z were shipped for purchase order #123".

3 Proposed Temporal and Event Based Model

In this section, we propose extended temporal model and extended event model

3.1 Extended Temporal Data Model

The RFID data are time-dependent, dynamically changing, in large volumes, and carry implicit semantics. RFID application needs to effectively support such large scale temporal data created by RFID applications. These systems need to have an explicit temporal data model for RFID data to support tracking and monitoring queries. In addition, they need to have an automatic method to transform the primitive observations from RFID readers into derived data used in RFID-enabled applications. EPC data is a temporal data, usually as depicted in table 3 timestamp is attached by the RFID Middleware. Data in EPC repository fall into two categories as mentioned, data in EPCIS fall into two categories: Master data (static data) and Event data (dynamic data). Presently, we use EPC data as a tuple <EPC, Reader_id, Location_id, timestamp>. The timestamp is the time at which tagged item is captured by the reader.

In the proposed model, we have included validation time that denotes the time period during which a fact is true with respect to the real world. This is an important prospect of information captured for various type of items such as perishable food items, medicines etc. This model accounts more temporal dimension in order to evolve a better information system. The Transaction time (TT)/Timestamp is already on floor that denotes the time when transaction took place. In addition, Valid Time (VT) and Availability Time (AT) are the newly recognized temporal dimensions with respect to our RFID Application. The VT that records the time for which the given information is valid in the application data. The VT is usually provided by the users and TT is system generated. Let us assume that frozen food which is perishable food item must be consumed with 10 hrs. of its sale, or when this is taken out from freezer. So, here TT is when the food item is captured at the POS and its VT = 10+TT. So, VT is greater than TT. Even though VT and TT suffice for many database applications, they turned out to be inadequate to cope with the temporal requirements of complex organizations such as hospitals and public institutions. In these contexts, one often needs to model both the time at which someone/the information system becomes aware of a fact (availability time) and the time at which the fact is stored into the database. While the latter is captured by TT, the availability time AT. In many application domains, e.g., the medical field, decisions are taken on the basis of the available information, no matter whether it is stored in the database or not. AT captures this temporal dimension. Since there can be facts which are erroneously considered true by the information system, AT must be an interval: the starting point of AT is the time at which the fact becomes available to the information system, while its ending point is the time at which the information system realizes that the fact is not correct. As for TT, an ending point equal to uc (until changed) means that the fact is currently classified as correct.

Another Temporal dimension which can be useful for RFID Application is Event time. The event time (ET) of a fact is the occurrence time of a real-world event that either initiates or terminates the validity interval of the fact.

The relation PatTherapy stores information about patients attribute and prescribed therapies (attributes Therapy and Dosage), while the relation PatSymptom stores information about patients and detected symptoms (attributes Symptom and SevLevel). Both relations feature the four temporal dimensions VT, ETi , ETt, AT, TT. (Patid, Therapy) and (PatId, Symptom) are snapshot keys for the two relations, respectively as shown in tables 4 and 5 below. Relations which do not feature all the four temporal dimensions are preliminarily converted to complete relations according to the following rules (alternative rules can be defined to cope with specific application domains):

- If the relation has no (possibly implicitly defined) VT, the associated VT is the current timestamp, that is, the valid time is [now, now].
- If the relation has no (possibly implicitly defined) TT, we assume that information has been entered when the relation has been created and will last until it will be explicitly changed or deleted. Accordingly, TT is [c, uc), where c is the creation timestamp for the relation.
- Let R be a relation provided with VT and devoid of ET. For every tuple of the corresponding complete relation R the following properties hold:

  ETi = V Ts (the initiating event time is equal to the starting instant VTs of the valid time); ETt = V Te (the terminating event time is equal to the ending instant VTe of the valid time).

- Let R be a relation provided with TT and devoid of AT. For every tuple of the corresponding relation R the following properties hold:
  ATs = TTs (the starting instant of the availability time is equal to the starting instant of the transaction time);
  ATe = TTe (the ending instant of the availability time is equal to the ending instant of the transaction time).

Table 4. Database Instance for patient Therapy

Patient_id	Therapy	Dosage	VT	ETi	ETt	AT	TT
EPC_1	Paracetamol	Dose1	[2006-07-01, 2006-07-12]	2006-06-28	2006-06-28	[2006-06-28, 2006-09-06)	[2006-06-29, 2006-09-08)
EPC_2	Steptomycin	Dose3	[2006-05-08, 2006-11-15)	2006-05-05	2006-11-12	[2006-11-13, uc)	[2006-12-01, uc)
EPC_3	Paracetamol	Dose2	[2006-07-01, 2006-07-10)	2006-06-28	2006-07-10	[2006-09-07, uc)	[2006-09-08, uc)

Table 5. Database Instance for patient Symptoms

Patient_id	Symptom	Sev_Level	VT	ETi	ETt	AT	TT
EPC_1	Fever	1	[2006-06-25, now]	2006-06-23	null	[2006-06-27, 2006-07-11)	[2006-06-28, 2006-07-11)
EPC_2	Fever	2	[2006-06-25, 2006-07-11)	2006-06-23	2006-06-28	[2006-07-12, uc)	[2006-07-01, uc)
EPC_3	Fever & Dry Cough	4	[2006-05-01, 2006-10-21)	2006-03-23	2006-05-05	[2006-11-13, uc)	[2006-11-15, uc)

3.2 Extended Event Based Model

In an RFID system, a reader observation comprises of the reader EPC, the observed EPC value of an RFID tag, and the timestamp when the observation occurs. Usually Observations are in the form of <epc, Reader_id, Location_id, Timestamp>. RFID Systems generates vast amount of raw data at low level which contains duplicate readings, missed readings, noise readings due to the following reason:

"First, RFID readers cannot guarantee 100% accuracy of tag reading at the present because of interference, limited bandwidth, collision in the dense readers environment and high sensitivity by the surrounding environment."[7]
"Second, RFID reader is physically non-contact to communicate with tags and the number of RFID tag data flowed from a RFID reader ranges from 10s of tag data per second up to more than 100s a second. This leads to bring the big burden to the host system which is responsible to process all the data, so the appropriate scheme for data volume reduction is required."[7]

> "Third RFID reader can read multiple RFID tags simultaneously and, sometimes, tag are unintentionally sensed from an area beyond one intended to be monitored by the reader due to many reasons including the reflection of radio wave. Therefore, among the captured tag data, not all the data are required to the applications that consume RFID data, so the tag data in which the applications are not interested should be filtered out."[7]

In early RFID solutions, sensor readings are directly sent to applications and services, thus it is up to the applications to interpret the preliminary readings, and generate business logic data. This approach has much complexity on RFID data interpreting, and is not scalable and adaptable[6].Hence it is desirable to provide a data model at low level so that filtering and other transformation functions become easier and only relevant readings are stored for further processing and which can be easily modeled into business context. In this stage we will model the low-level data stream having the limited information to more manageable form suitable for application-level interactions. There are four stages for each tag – Unknown, Detected, Captured, Expired– and four different events – eventdetected, eventDisappered, eventCaptured and eventExpired, and the tag read can be passed to next stage only if the state transition between two adjacent states occurs in suitable situation. Initial state of a tag is 'Unknown' and, when a tag appears for the first time in the read range of any reader , the event 'eventdetected' is generated and the current tag state is moved onto the state 'Detected'. The event 'eventCaptured' is generated when the tag is seen for a certain period and its timestamp is attached and the event 'eventExpired' occurs if current state of the tag is 'detected' but has not been captured. The event 'eventDisappered' is generated when the tag hasn't seen for a time without subsequently generating 'eventCaptured' event.

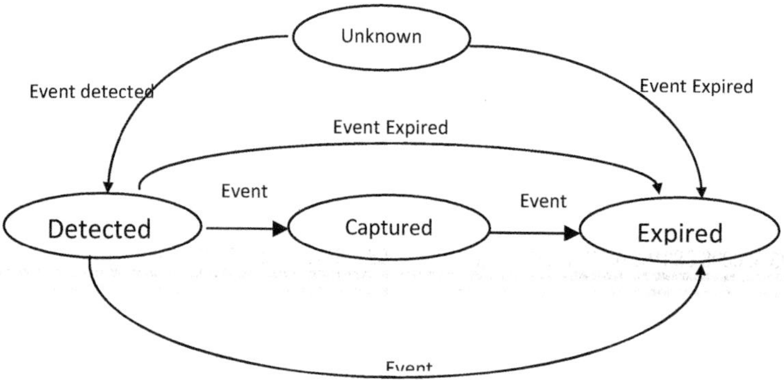

Fig. 3. Life-cycle of RFID Tag

We have devised following set of rules to determine which reader entries are treated as valid or not valid. Only valid entries will move to next stage. Non-valid entries will be discarded. Till now we are assuming our tuple as <epc, Reader_id,

Location_id, timestamp>, but now are adding more fields to our stream< epc, Reader_id, Location_id, Initial event, Event_stage, Final_Event, Timestamp> as presented in table 6.

Table 6. Database Instance for patient Symptoms

Rule	Initial Event	Event Stage	Final Event	Marking	Summary
1	Unknown	Event Detected	Detected	"Non-Valid"	Tag has been Detected but not captured
2	Detected	Event Captured	Captured	"Valid"	Tag has been detected and captured
3	Detected	Event Disappeared	Expired	"Non-Valid"	Tag has been detected but not captured and finally it expired
4	Captured	Event Expired	Expired	"Valid"	Tag has completed its life cycle.
5	Unknown	Event Expired	Expired	" Non-Valid"	Tag has not been even detected.
6	Detected	Event Expired	Expired	" Non-Valid"	Tag has initially detected but moved out of range immediately and hence not detected.

Let's consider the readings for one Reader R1, same Locations L1, for same item tagged with Epc1 code, usually multiple reading are added with one reader at same locations with same reader which generates duplicate readings. Now According to our model if tag don't follow the sequencing according to our rules specified in above table 6 , then tag entry will be considered as non-valid otherwise valid. The presented model is capable of eliminating duplicate entries at reader level. According to rules, there are 3 entries, in entry 1, tag is detected but not been captured, as Final_event is "Detected". Therefore, this entry will be regarded as "Non valid" and will be discarded, In Entry 2, as final_ stage is "captured" this entry will be considered as valid and accepted as shown in table 7.

Table 7. Event-sequence

Entry	EPC	Reader Id	Location Id	Initial event	Event stage	Final Event	Timestamp	Valid
1	Epc1	R1	L1	Unknown	Event Detected	Detected	2010-10-30 17:30:00.000	Non-Valid
2	Epc1	R1	L1	Detected	Event Captured	Captured	2010-10-30 17:36:00.000	Valid
3	Epc1	R1	L1	Detected	Event Disap-peared	Expired	2010-10-30 17:33:00.000	Non-Valid

These data carry implicit information, such as changes of states and business processes (e.g., change of locations), and further derived information such as aggregations (e.g., containment relationship among objects). Thus, a framework is needed to automatically transform observations into business logic data. Meanwhile, while the accuracy of current RFID readers is improving, in current RFID applications, there are still erroneous readings, such as duplicate readings or missing readings. Such erroneous data have to be semantically filtered.

4 Conclusion

This paper has discussed four stages for each tag – Unknown, Detected, Captured, Expired– and four different events – eventdetected, eventDisappered, eventCaptured and eventExpired. The tag read can be passed to next stage only if the state transition between two adjacent states occurs in suitable situation. We have also introduced additional attributes TT, AT and VT. This model accounts more temporal dimension in order to evolve a better information system. The model has used the existing Timestamp as Transaction time that denotes the time when transaction took place. The investigations and the results show that the proposed model is very useful in variety of applications where the tagged product has a requirement of time parameters.

References

1. Traub, K.R., et al.: EPCglobal Architecture Framework, EPCglobal technical document (September 2007), http://www.epcglobalinc.org/standards/architecture/architecture_1_2-framework-20070910.pdf (accessed on Date: 02/205/2011)
2. EPC Information Services (EPCIS) Version 1.0 Specification (April 2007), http://www.epcglobalinc.org/standards/epcis/epcis_1_0_1-standard-20070921.pdf
3. Khan, Ayoub, M., et al.: SHA–256 based n-Bit EPC generator for RFID Tracking Simulator. In: Proceeding of IEEE IACC, Patiala, Punjab (2009)
4. http://www.epcglobalinc.org (accessed on Date: 02/205/2011)
5. Nguyen, T., Lee, Y.-K., Huq, R., Jeong, B.-S., Lee, S.: A Data Model for EPC Information Services. In: DEWS 2007, Japan (2007)
6. Liu, P., Wang, F.: Simens Temporal Management of RFID Data. In: 31st International Conference on Very Large Databases, Integrated Data Systems Department Siemens Corporate Research Princeton, New Jersey (August 31, 2005)
7. Cheong, T.-S., Lee, Y.-J.: RFID Information Value Chain and ETRI RFID Ecosystem: Value-added Environment Linking Physical and Virtual Worlds. In: Turcu, C. (ed.) Development and Implementation of RFID Technology, ISBN: 978-3-902613-54-7, InTechIntegrated
8. Liu, S., et al.: Integrated RFID Data Modeling: An Approach for Querying Physical Objects in Pervasive Computing. In: CIKM 2006, Virginia, USA (2006)
9. Wang, F., Liu, P.: Integrated Data Systems, IBM Silicon Valley Lab San Jose, California, USA, Department Siemens Corporate Research Princeton, New Jersey, USA

Performance Analysis of Mammographic Image Enhancement Techniques for Early Detection of Breast Cancer

Shailaja Singh[1], Anamika Yadav[2], and Bikesh Kumar Singh[3]

[1] Dept. of Computer Science & Engineering, MPCCET, Bhilai
[2] Dept. of Electrical Engineering, N.I.T Raipur
[3] Dept. of Electrical Engineering, N.I.T Raipur, India
shailaja.singh2007@gmail.com,
{anamikajugnu04,bikesh_020581}@yahoo.co.in

Abstract. Mammogram breast cancer images have the ability to assist physician in detection of disease caused by cells normal growth. Developing algorithms and software to analyse these images may also assist physicians in their daily work. Micro calcifications are tiny calcium deposits in breast tissues. They appear as small bright spots on mammograms. Since micro calcifications are small and subtle abnormalities, they may be overlooked by an examining radiologist. Image Enhancement and Filtering is always the root process in many medical image processing applications. It is aimed at reducing noise in images. In this paper we have made comparison between several novel and hybrid enhancement techniques. The comparison is based on the basis of performance evaluation parameters (statistical parameter) such as PSNR, and CNR. These can be used for identifying breast nodule malignancy to provide better chance of a proper treatment. These methods are tested on digital mammograms present in mini-MIAS database.

Keywords: Mammograms, Image Enhancement, Spatial Filtering, Contrast to noise ratio (CNR), Signal to noise ratio (PSNR).

1 Introduction

Breast cancer is one of the most deadly diseases for middle-aged women. One out of eight women is prone to this disease in her lifetime [1]. The success of treatment depends on early detection. Breast cancer detection on mammograms (X-ray images of breasts) is currently carried out by radiologists who examine mammograms with a magnifying glass to find out tumors such as microcalcifications, masses, and stellate lesions [2]. As a matter of fact, the number of people having cancers has increased by time. And new kinds of cancers also appear with increasing level of harmfulness. Early cancer detection becomes a crucial matter when the recent medical achievement can cure more than 80% of all stage 1 cancers.

Diagnosing cancer tissues using digital mammograms is a time consuming task even for highly skilled radiologists because mammograms contain low signal to noise ratio (low contrast) and a complicated structured background. Therefore, in digital

D. Nagamalai, E. Renault, and M. Dhanushkodi (Eds.): PDCTA 2011, CCIS 203, pp. 439–448, 2011.

mammogram there is still a need to enhance imaging, where enhancement in medical imaging is the use of computers to make image clearer. This may aid interpretation by humans or computers. Mammography is one of the most promising cancer control strategies since the cause of cancer is still unknown. Radiologists turn to digital mammography as an alternative diagnostic method due to the problems created by conventional screening programs. A digital mammogram is created when a conventional mammogram is digitized, through the use of a specific mammogram digitizer or a camera, so it can be processed by the computer. Image enhancement techniques have been widely used in the field of radiology, where the subjective quality of images is important for human interpretation and diagnosis. Many algorithms for accomplishing enhancement have been developed and applied to medical images [3, 4].

Screening mammography can help early detection of breast cancer; however, this is dependent upon proper interpretation of the mammogram by a radiologist. Because of the subtleties and variations of the breast, errors can be common. There are two errors typical in examining mammograms. They are false positives and false negatives. False positives are instances where the radiologist identifies an area of the breast as cancerous when it is benign. False-negatives occur when an abnormality is not detected by the radiologist. False positives are the less severe of the two errors. They typically do not endanger the life of the patient, but they do have negative consequences. Additional mammogram and/or more invasive tests are required to determine the nature of the abnormality. False-negatives can be very serious. They directly delay or prevent early detection and can adversely affect the woman"s chances of surviving breast cancer. Tumors or signs of tumors that are not detected or misclassified as benign reduce the effectiveness of screening mammography.

(a) Objects in Mammogram Images

In addition to the basic anatomy of the breast, a variety of objects appear in mammogram images. These include masses, microcalcifications, and architectural distortions. A mass is a space-occupying lesion. If seen in only one projection it is referred to as a density. It is referred to as a mass only if viewed in both projections. There are several types of masses found in mammogram images. Masses are categorized by their shape, density, and margins. The shapes include: round, oval, lobular, and irregular. The margins include: speculated. The densities include: high density, low density, equal density, and fat containing.

These categories help radiologists to precisely describe masses found in mammograms and to classify masses as benign or potentially malignant. The term benign refers to a condition, tumor or growth that is not cancerous. This means that it does not spread to other parts of the body or invade and destroy nearby tissue. Benign tumors usually grow slowly. In general, benign tumor or condition is not harmful. However, this is not always the case. If a benign tumor is big enough, its size and weight can press on nearby blood vessels, nerves, organs or otherwise cause problems. Breast cancer, also known as carcinoma, is a malignant growth that begins in the tissues of the breast [5].

In this paper we have made comparison between several basic and hybrid enhancement techniques. The comparison is based on the basis of observations (we have taken consultation from radiologists to select best enhancement techniques) and performance evaluation parameters (statistical parameter) such as PSNR, and CNR

[6].These most common breast abnormalities that may indicate breast cancer are masses and calcifications. The challenge is to quickly and accurately overcome the development of breast cancer.

2 Overview, Implementation and Results of Enhancement Techniques

Enhancement is aimed at realizing improvement in the quality of a given image. Image enhancement can be defined as conversion of the image quality to a better and more understandable level [7]. The Applying contrast enhancement filters improve the readability of areas with subtle changes in contrast.

Image enhancement improves the quality (clarity) of images for human viewing. Removing blurring and noise, increasing contrast, and revealing details are examples of enhancement operations. For example, an image might be taken of an endothelial cell, which might be of low contrast and somewhat blurred. Reducing the noise and blurring and increasing the contrast range could enhance the image. The original image might have areas of very high and very low intensity, which mask details. An adaptive enhancement algorithm reveals these details. Adaptive algorithms adjust their operation based on the image information (pixels) being processed. In this case the mean intensity, contrast, and sharpness (amount of blur removal) could be adjusted based on the pixel intensity statistics in various areas of the image. Various Enhancement techniques implemented using MATLAB software for comparative analysis and evaluation are:

A. Contrast Stretching

One of the simplest piecewise linear functions is a Contrast Stretching transformation. Low contrast images can result from poor illumination, lack of dynamic range in the imaging sensor, or even wrong setting of a lens aperture during image acquisition. The idea behind Contrast Stretching is to increase the dynamic range of grey levels in the image being processed.

$$Y = \begin{cases} \alpha x & 0 \le x < a \\ \beta(x-a) + y_a & a \le x < b \\ \gamma(x-b) + y_b & b \le x < L \end{cases} \qquad (1)$$

Figure 1 shows the result of contrast stretching of mammographic image. Applying Contrast Stretching improve the readability of areas with subtle changes in contrast. How- ever, they will also destroy areas of the image where the intensity of the pixels is outside the range of intensities being enhanced.

B. Histogram Processing

Histogram of an image represents the relative frequency of occurrence of various grey levels in the image; apply a monotone transform resulting in an approximately uniform histogram.

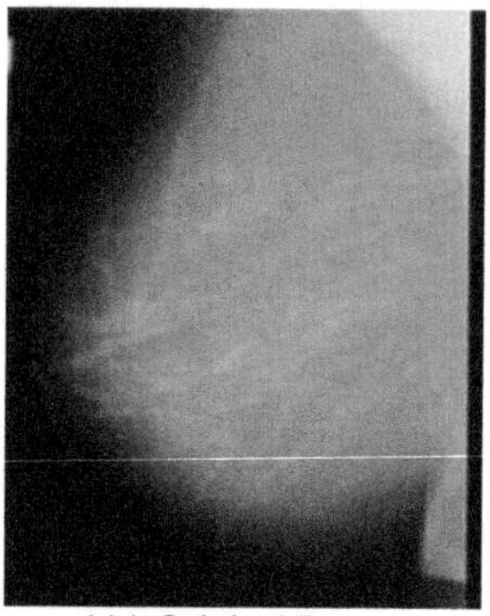

1(a):Original Image

1(b): Image after contrast stretching

Fig. 1. A mammographic image before and after contrast stretching

Histogram Equalization

In general, histogram equalization stretches/compresses an image such that, pixel values that occur frequently in image A occupy a bigger dynamic range in image B, i.e., get stretched and become more visible. And the pixel values that occur infrequently in A occupy a smaller dynamic range in image B, i.e., get compressed and become less visible. Normally, the image's histogram is dense in one side of the spectrum as shown in Figure 2. This will cause the image to be very dark or very bright, different parts of the image with different grey intensity will not be well detected by eyes. Spreading out the spectrum of the histogram (Figure 2) will enhance the contrast of the image. Normal eyes can now detect the full scale of the grey intensity easily.

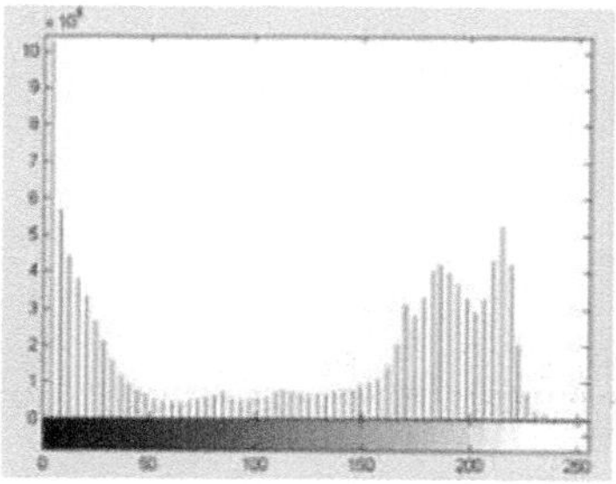

2(a):Original Image

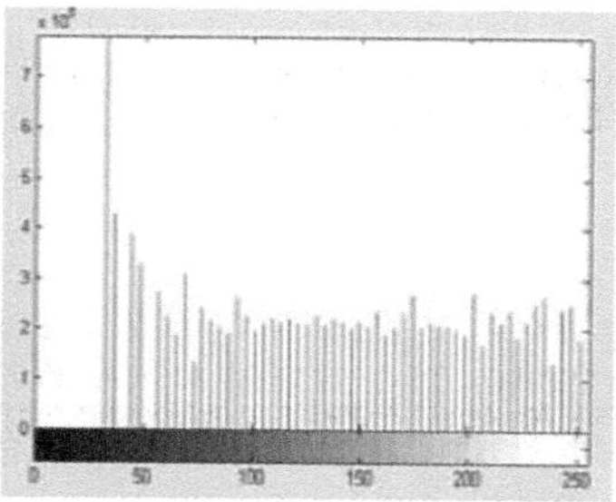

2(b): Histogram of Equalized Image

Fig. 2. Histogram before and after histogram equalization

Histogram equalization changes the mean brightness of input image to the middle level. One of the advantages of histogram based techniques is simplicity of implementation of the algorithm [8, 9]. Figure 3 shows the result of histogram equalization of mammographic image.

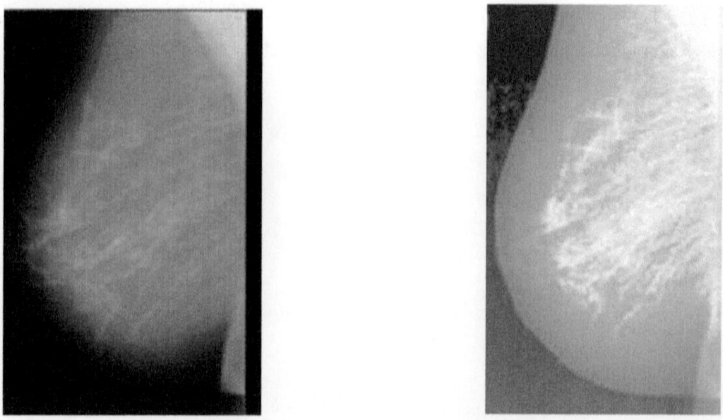

3(a):Original Image 3(b): Histogram Equalized Image

Fig. 3. Mammogram before and after histogram equalization

C. Spatial Filtering: We implemented two spatial filtering techniques:

1) Mean Filter

The Average (mean) filter smooths image data, thus eliminating noise. This filter performs spatial filtering on each individual pixel in an image using the grey level values in a square or rectangular window surrounding each pixel.

For example consider a 3 x 3 filter window

a1 a2 a3
a4 a5 a6
a7 a8 a9

The average filter computes the sum of all pixels in the filter window and then divides the sum by the number of pixels in the filter window:

$$\text{Filtered pixel} = (a1 + a2 + a3 + a4 \ldots + a9) / 9 \quad (2)$$

One of the simplest spatial filtering operations we can perform is a smoothing operation, simply average all of the pixels in a neighbourhood around a central value. Mean Filter especially useful in removing noise from images. It is also useful for highlighting gross detail.

2) Median Filter

The median filter is normally used to reduce noise in an image, somewhat like the mean filter. However, it often does a better job than the mean filter of preserving useful detail in the image.Like the mean filter, the median filter considers each pixel in the image in turn and looks at its nearby neighbors to decide whether or not it is representative of its surroundings. Instead of simply replacing the pixel value with the *mean* of neighboring pixel values, it replaces it with the median of those values. The median is calculated by first sorting all the pixel values from the surrounding neighborhood into numerical order and then replacing the pixel being considered with the middle pixel value. Figure 4 shows mean and median filtered mammographic image. The median of a set is more robust with respect to the presence of a noise.

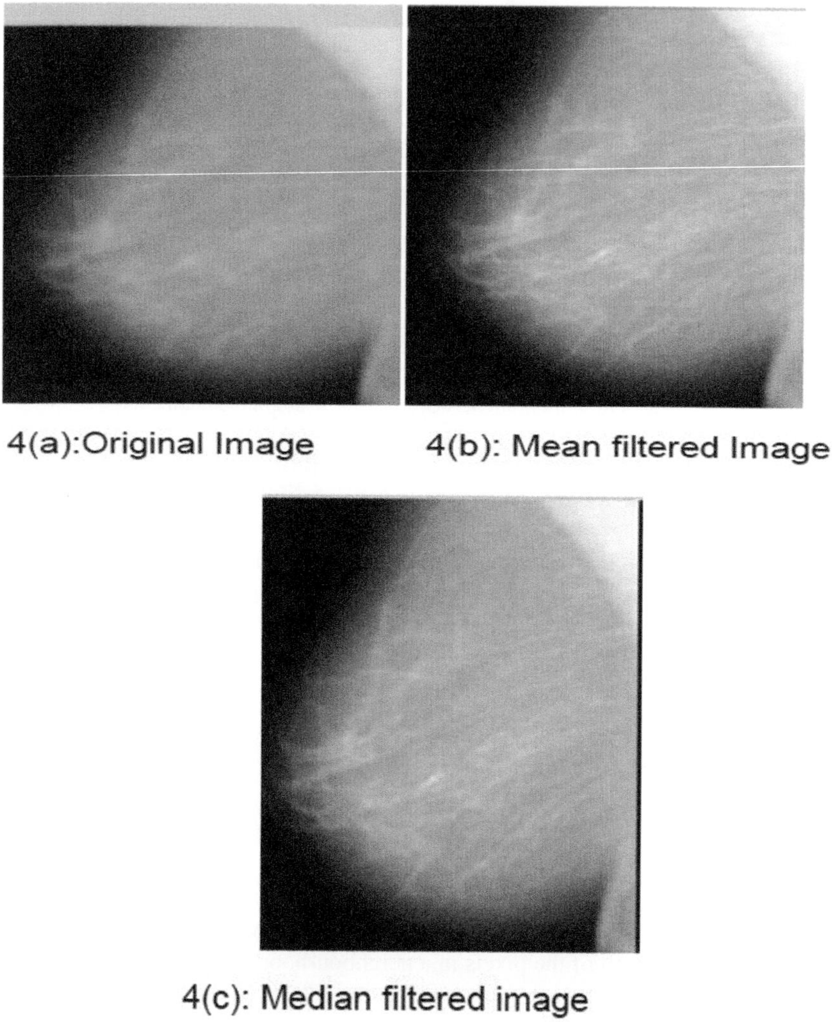

Fig. 4. Result of mean and median filtering of mammogram

D. Hybrid Technique for Enhancement

This method is designed [10] using basic operations performed on the original image using Tophat and Bottomhat filter.

1) Tophat Filter

Itop = imtophat(IM,SE),Tophat filtering computes the morphological opening of the image (using imopen) and then subtracts the result from the original image. imtophat uses the structuring element SE, where SE is returned by strel. SE must be a single structuring element object, not an array containing multiple structuring element objects.

2) Bottomhat Filter

Ibot = imbothat(IM,SE), performs morphological bottom-hat filtering on the grayscale or binary input image, IM, returning the filtered image, IM2. The argument SE is a structuring element returned by the strel function. SE must be a single structuring element object, not an array containing multiple structuring element objects.

$$\text{Ienhance=imsubtract(imadd(Itop,I),Ibot} \tag{3}$$

I=Original Image

Ienhance=Enhanced Image

Itop=Tophat Filtered Image

Ibot=Bottomhat Filtered Image

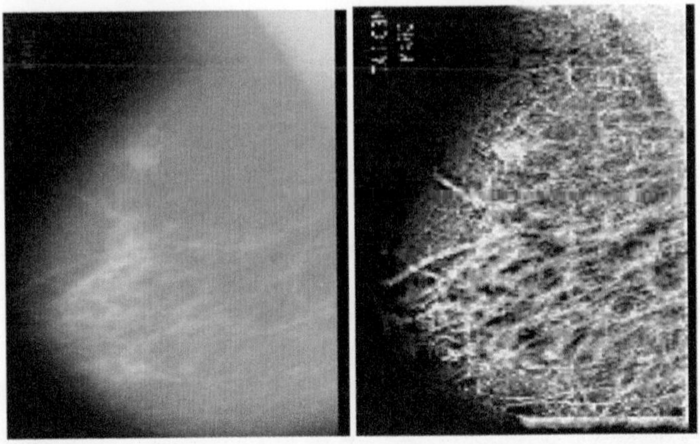

5(a):Original Image 5(b): Enhanced image

Fig. 5. Mammogram before and after enhancement using hybrid technique

E. Non Subsampled Contourlet Transform Filter

All existing methods of image enhancement decompose images in a separable fashion, and thus cannot use the geometric information in the transform domain to distinguish weak edges from noises. This method provides a shift invariant directional multi resolution image representation. The geometric information is gathered pixel by pixel from the Non Subsampled contourlet transform coefficients [11, 12]. The images are enhanced using nonsubsampled contourlet transform and a specific edge filter to enhance directional structures of the image in the contourlet domain. The inverse contourlet transform is applied to recover an approximation of the mammogram with the microcalcifications enhanced as shown in figure 6.

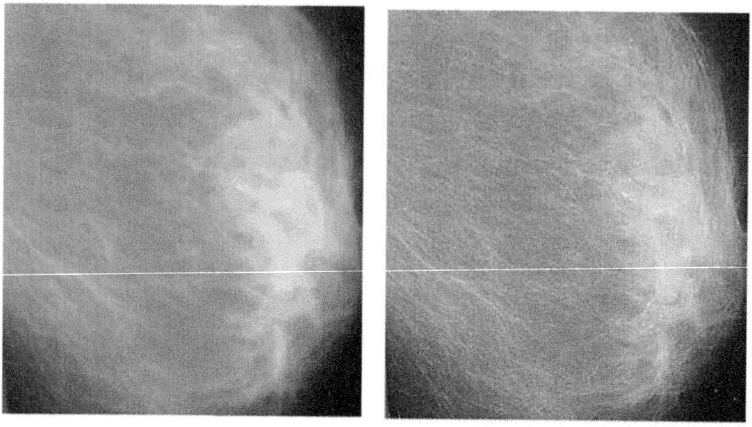

6(a):Original Image 6(b): Enhanced image

Fig. 6. Mammogram before and after enhancement using nonsubsampled contourlet transform filter

F. Steerable Filter

The steerable filters are synthesized by the interpolation of some ``basis functions" and ``steered" to arbitrary orientations. These filters measure the ``oriented energy" along certain orientations. When the oriented energy is minimized, the spectrum plane can be identified, for which the orientation indicates the velocity [14, 15, 16]. The result of mammographic image enhancement using steerable filter is shown in figure 7.

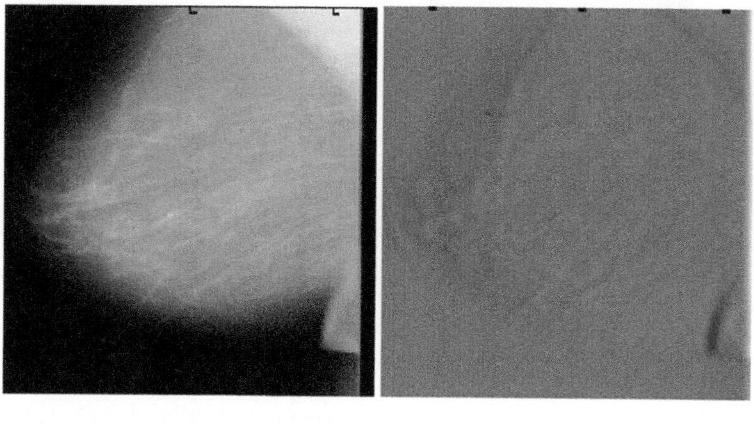

7(a):Original Image 7(b): Enhanced image

Fig. 7. Mammogram before and after enhancement using steerable filter

3 Evaluation Result

Two popular evaluation parameters are used for comparing performance of enhancement techniques. The first is PSNR (signal-to-noise-ratio) measure and the second measure is CNR (contrast-to-noise-ratio). The CNR and PSNR values for various enhancement techniques discussed in this paper are calculated and listed in table 1.

Tables 1. CNR and PSNR of various enhancement techniques

S.NO	Enhancement Technique	CNR (dB)	PSNR (dB)
1	*Contrast Stretching*	*0.0169*	*35.79*
2	*Histogram Equalization*	*0.0600*	*39.11*
3	*Mean Filter*	*0.0081*	*38.69*
4	*Median Filter*	*0.0221*	*19.92*
5	*Hybrid Technique*	*0.0229*	*20.98*
6	*Contourlet Transform Filter*	*0.0144*	*13.02*
7	*Steerable Filter*	*0.0716*	*50.81*

4 Conclusions

In this paper we implemented seven enhancement methods for enhancement of digital mammograms. The implementation of the method was done using MATLAB software. The results were evaluated using CNR and PSNR. The Experimental results show that the steerable filter yields maximum PSNR as well as CNR values and thus from statistical point of view this technique is superior among all. Further it also consumes less time compared to counterlet transform filtering. In future we plan to discuss these methods with some medical experts as comparison of image enhancement techniques for medical images using statistical evaluation parameters is not sufficient. Radiologist or Medical Expert openion will play a vital role on evaluation of these techniques.

References

1. Chan, H., Lo, S.B., Sahiner, B., Lam, K.L., Helvie, M.A.: Computer-aided detection of mammographic microcalcifications: Pattern Recognition with artificial neural network. Med. Phys. 22(10) (October 1995)
2. Gulsrud, T.O., Kjode, S.: Optimalfilter for detection of stellate lesions and circumscribed masses in mammograms. In: SPIE Visual Communications and Image Processing 1996, Orlando,Florida, March 17-20, vol. I, pp. 430–440 (1996)

3. Cheng, H.D., Cai, X., Chen, X., Hu, L., Lou, X.: Computer-aided detection and classification of microcalcfications in mammograms: a survey. Pattern Recognition 36, 2967–2991 (2003)
4. Thangavel, K., Karnan, M., Sivakumar, R., Kajamohideen, A.: Automatic detection of microcalcification in mammograms: a review. In: Graphics Vision and Image Processing (2008)
5. Subhash Chandra bose, J., Karnan, M., Sivakumar, R.: Detection of Masses in Digital Mammograms (IJCNS) International Journal of Computer and Network Security 2(2) (February 2010)
6. Jobson, D., Rahman, Z., Woodell, G.A.: Retinex image processing: Improved fidelity for direct visual observation. In: Proceedings of the IS&T Fourth Color Imaging Conference: Color Science, Systems, and Applications, pp. 124–126. IS&T (1996)
7. Hadhoud, M., Amin, M., Dabbour, W.: Detection of Breast Cancer Tumor Algorithm using Mathematical Morphology and Wavelet Analysis. In: GVIP 2005 Conference, December 19-21. CICC, Cairo (2005)
8. Yoon, H., Han, Y., Hahn, H.: Image Contrast Enhancement based Sub-histogram Equalization Technique without Over-equalization Noise. World Academy of Science, Engineering and Technology (2009)
9. Yeganeh, H., Ziaei, A., Rezaie, A.: A novel approach for contrast enhancement based on Histogram Equalization. In: ICCCE, Dept. of Electrical engg., Amikkabir Univ. of Technology, Tehran (2008)
10. Alhaddi, B., Zu'bi, M.H., Suleiman, H.N.: Mammogram Breast Cancer Image Detection Using Image Processing Function. Information Technology Journal 6(2), 217–221 (2007)
11. Muñoz, J.M.M., Domínguez, H.d.J.O., Villegas, O.O.V., Sánchez, V.G.C., Maynez, L.O.: The Nonsubsampled Contourlet Transform for Enhancement of Microcalcifications in Digital Mammograms. In: Aguirre, A.H., Borja, R.M., Garciá, C.A.R. (eds.) MICAI 2009. LNCS, vol. 5845, pp. 292–302. Springer, Heidelberg (2009), doi:10.1007/978-3-642-05258-3_26
12. Mumtaz, R., Iqbal, R., Khan, S.A.: Image Enhancement Using Nonsubsampled Contourlet Transform, vol. 228, pp. 391–400 (2007)
13. Singh, B.K., Parihar, J.S., Pal, P.R.: Wavelet Based information for Retrieval and Classification of Mammographic Images. In: Proceedings of the ACM International Conference on Communication, Computing & Security, pp. 365–370 (2011)
14. Huang, C.-L., Chen, Y.-T.: "Motion estimation method using a 3D steerable filter. Image and Vision Computing - IVC 13(1), 21–32 (1995)
15. Wu, Q., Schulze, M.A., Castleman, K.R.: Steerable Pyramid Filters For Selective Image Enhancement Applications. In: Proceedings of IEEE International Conference on Circuits and Systems, pp. 325–328 (1998)
16. Freeman, W.T., Adelson, E.H.: The Design and use of steerable filters. IEEE PAMI (1991)

Extremely Opportunistic Routing with Expected Transmission Count to Improve QoS in Hybrid Wireless Networks

S. Sumathy, R. Saravanan, M. Vijay Kumar, and C. Vinay Kumar

School of Information Technology and Engineering,
VIT University, Vellore 632014, Tamilnadu, India
ssumathy@vit.ac.in

Abstract. Dynamic nature of mobility in wireless networks has paved way for a new paradigm of communication in this era. Routing protocol design for hybrid wireless network is critical in order to improve the performance and reliability of the network. A good routing scheme increases the packet delivery ratio and the throughput of the network and thus improves the quality of service. Opportunistic Routing (OR) technique attempts to deal with unreliable transmissions by utilizing the broadcast nature and spatial diversity of the wireless medium, in an efficient manner [3].

OR scheme used in ad hoc networks gives lesser throughput than expected when minimum hop count metric is used. To combat the above limitations, an Extremely Opportunistic Routing (ExOR) scheme with ETX metric is proposed and implemented for a hybrid scenario. The simulation study reveals that this routing technique efficiently utilizes resources and increases the end-to-end throughput and the packet delivery ratio.

Keywords: ExOR, ETX, Throughput, Ad hoc networks, Hybrid networks.

1 Introduction

Wireless networks are group of nodes which communicate with each other over a wireless communication channel. Ad hoc networks are a category of wireless networks, whose decentralized nature, minimal configuration and quick deployment make them suitable for applications ranging from emergency situations like natural disasters, military sensing, disaster rescue, traffic monitoring, tracking, etc.

Hybrid wireless networks are integration of both 'ad hoc – infra structure less' and 'Wireless – Infra structure based' networks. Brust, Rothkugel define hybrid wireless networks as "multi-hop wireless networks combined with a backbone network" where the term "hybrid" stands in direct relation to the fact that different communication technologies are used to create such a network. Hybrid wireless network combine the advantages of ad-hoc networks and infrastructure based architecture as both paradigms are complementary. A hybrid network is formed by placing a sparse network of base stations in an ad hoc network. The use of base stations is to avoid overwhelming burden of relaying packets between source and

D. Nagamalai, E. Renault, and M. Dhanushkodi (Eds.): PDCTA 2011, CCIS 203, pp. 449–458, 2011.

destination by the mobile nodes. Also, incorporating base stations in infra structure less network overcomes the drawback of ad hoc networks and the existing routing protocols. Unlike traditional wireless routing protocols which use a single predetermined path, opportunistic routing explicitly takes advantage of the broadcast nature of wireless communications by using a set of relay nodes to opportunistically perform packet forwarding. Opportunistic routing is a technique chooses a path dynamically on per-transmission basis to forward a packet. Expected Transmission Count (ETX) is the routing metric used by OR to choose Candidate Relay Sets (CRS). It minimizes the expected total number of packet transmissions required to successfully deliver a packet to the destination [2].

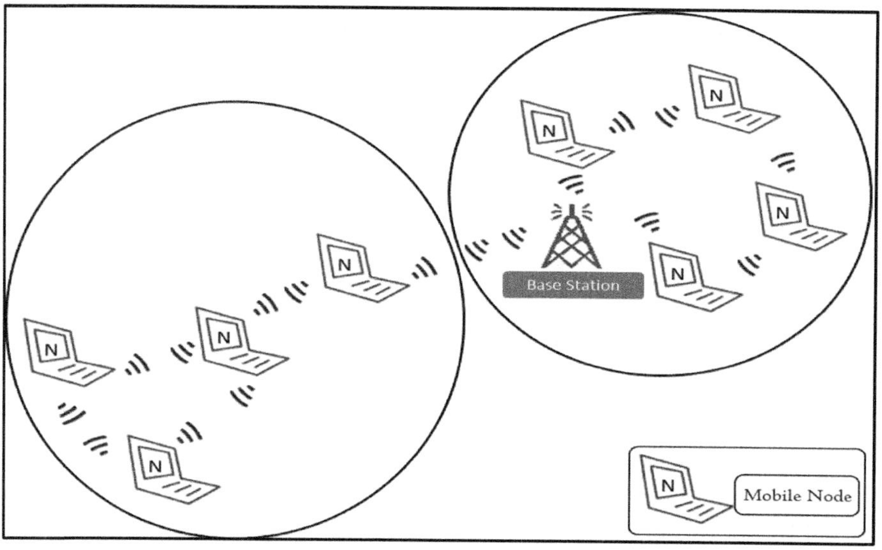

Fig. 1. Hybrid Wireless Network Scenario

In Hybrid wireless networks [Fig. 1], wireless nodes communicate with each other through multi hop ad hoc transmissions and nodes within the coverage range of a Base Station (BT), communicate with the BT using single-hop infrastructure mode. In Opportunistic Routing, nodes in the network are cooperative and forward each other's packets to their destinations [4].

Assumptions concerning the behavior of the nodes and base stations that participate in hybrid networks are as follows:

- Wireless nodes and Base stations are randomly located.
- Wireless nodes have the same set of transmission rates and equivalent ranges.
- Each wireless node could connect to at most one BT.
- Each node is identified by a unique ID within the network.

The proposed work is organized as follows, Section 2 explains the use of OR scheme in comparison with traditional routing protocols. Section 3 depicts ExOR protocol's design aspects. Section 4 describes the evaluation criteria of ExOR routing protocol in hybrid wireless networks. Section 5 gives the conclusion and discussion on implementation details of the proposed work.

2 Opportunistic Routing Technique

Benefits of OR over traditional Unicast Routing:

OR scheme extends the concept of Geographical routing [4]. As in geographical routing, OR uses the available node in the transmission range for the transmission of the packet. This node availability reduces the overhead of finding the node information in the network which is followed by traditional proactive routing schemes [5]. The performance of the network may go down because of routing loops and inconsistency.

Opportunistic routing scheme chooses each hop of a packet's route after the transmission for the present hop, to reflect on which intermediate node has actually received the transmission to make better progress [5]. This provides higher throughput than the traditional routing, since each transmission may have more independent chances of being received and forwarded [1][14]. Moreover loops are avoided with a tree structure of the participating nodes.

Traditional routing protocols follow the concept of routing similar to wired networks by abstracting the wireless links as wired links, and find the shortest, least cost, or highest throughput paths between a source and the destination [4]. When a packet is unicast to a specific next-hop node, all neighboring nodes in the communication range of the sender receives the packet and make use of the successful reception on the neighboring nodes instead of retransmitting the packet and saves the bandwidth [3]. In opportunistic routing protocols, all neighboring nodes that are closer to the destination may overhear a data packet, and may be a candidate to forward the packet to its destination.

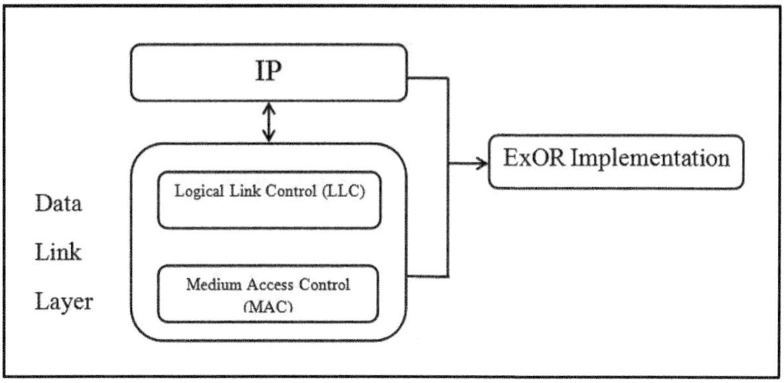

Fig.2. Layered Architecture of ExOR

ExOR and MORE (MAC independent Opportunistic Routing and Encoding) are few existing opportunistic routing protocols [6]. MORE protocol is independent of MAC and network layer. This protocol randomly mixes packets before forwarding, in order to ensure that routers that hear the same transmission do not forward the same packet. The other advantage is, it does not need any special scheduler to coordinate the routers and can run directly on top of 802.11 [8]. The proposed scheme (ExOR) with ETX for hybrid wireless network, which is an integration of MAC and network layer [5] choose the path dynamically on a per transmission basis.

3 System Design

- Routing Methodology in ExOR
- ExOR Protocol's design
- ETX Metric

3.1 Routing Methodology in ExOR

A source node S forwards a packet to a destination D. When the source broadcasts the packet, though a sub-set of the nodes receive the packet only the node closer to the destination rebroadcasts the packet. Further, the nodes that receive the second transmission broadcast the packet in turn to the nearest receiver. This procedure is followed until the packet reaches the destination node [3].

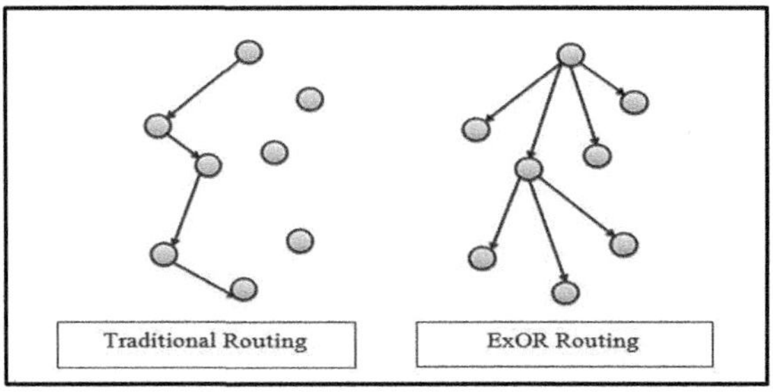

Fig. 3. Traditional Routing and ExOR Routing Methodologies

3.2 Extremely Opportunistic Routing (ExOR) Protocol's Design

Extremely Opportunistic Routing (ExOR) is a combination of routing protocol and media access control which follows a simple rule that, "Of all the nodes that were able to successfully decode the transmission, the one that is closest to the destination should forward it on". ExOR achieves high throughput in lossy wireless links and chooses paths dynamically on a per transmission basis.

3.2.1 Design Challenges

Although simple to define, the rule is quite difficult to implement in a Hybrid network. ExOR's design has the following challenges:

- The nodes should agree on which subset of them receives the packet. An agreement protocol should decide the candidate node that would forward the packet. i.e., the node closest to the ultimate destination that receives a packet should forward it.
- ExOR must have a Cost metric to move a packet from source to destination on per transmission basis.
- In a large dense network there is a penalty for using too many nodes as potential forwarders, since the costs of agreement grow with the number of participants. ExOR must choose only the most useful nodes as participants in large networks.
- ExOR must avoid simultaneous transmissions to minimize collisions.

The design is achieved with the following inclusions such that each node participating in ExOR routing uses the header format as given in Fig.4 [5].

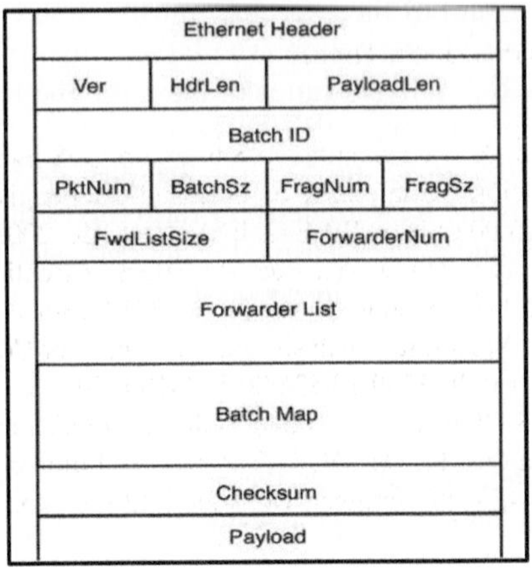

Fig. 4. ExOR packet Header format [5]

Batch Preparation

The source node chooses a unique batch ID and selects a Forwarder List for a batch of packets all destined to the same destination node. The source does this by adding an ExOR header to each packet of the batch, containing the batch ID and a forwarder list.

Forwarder List

The forwarder's list is specified by the source based on the expected cost and priority from each node in the list to the destination. The cost metric is calculated by counting both hops and retransmissions from the source to the destination. The cost metric ETX is used to find the path between the source and the destination with higher throughput.

Packet Reception

For every entry in the batch map of the packet, the node compares the corresponding entry with its local batch map, and replaces the later entry with highest priority.

Scheduling Transmissions

ExOR attempts to schedule high priority nodes to be sent first that helps avoid collision to forward one packet at a time from the subset of nodes.

3.3 ETX Metric Design

3.3.1 General

Expected transmission count (ETX) is a metric that finds high throughput paths on multi-hop wireless networks incorporating the effects of link loss ratios and interference among the successive links of a path. However, the minimum hop-count metric regardless of large differences in throughput, chooses different paths of same minimum length. This metric also account to issues like interference between successive hops among multi-hop paths.

3.3.2 Metric Calculation

The ETX of a route is a sum of the expected transmission count for each link in the route between the source and destination. The ETX of the link is calculated using the forward (d_f) and reverse (d_r) delivery ratios of the link. The forward delivery ratio (d_f) is the measured probability that a data packet successfully arrives at the recipient. The reverse delivery ratio (d_r) is the probability that the ACK packet is successfully received. ExOR uses only the forward delivery ratio (d_f) of the ETX metric.

The delivery ratios d_f and d_r are measured using dedicated link probe packets at an average period. Delivery ratio from the sender at any time t during the last w seconds is calculated as:

$$r(t) = \frac{\text{count}(t-w,t)}{w/\tau} \tag{1}$$

Count (t-w, t) is the determined with the number of probes received during the window w, and w/τ is the number of probes that should have been received.

4 Performance Evaluation

A well designed hybrid topology combines two or more network topologies together, and strengthens speed, reliability, efficiency, etc. This implementation would be applicable in mobile learning environment and in other cost effective applications like disaster management, group learning and so on. ExOR routing protocol with ETX metric is implemented using the network simulator by incorporating the protocol in hybrid scenario. The QoS parameters like packet delivery ratio and throughput for hybrid wireless networks using ExOR routing protocol is obtained and compared with that of the ad hoc wireless networks. It is observed that considerable improvement has been achieved and the same is shown in figures 6 and 8.

4.1 Methodology

This section covers the implementation of the proposed protocol design. The protocol is built in C++ implementation that is included in the NS2. The code has been implemented such that it corresponds well to the design aspects.

NS2 has many built-in routing protocols such as AODV, DSDV, and DSR etc. The routing protocol, ExOR is added to NS2. NS2 is open source and has a feature of adding new protocol. NS2 analyses the routing protocol and it is very useful to researches for discovering new protocols in the area of networks.

Network topologies are simulated and trace files generated are analysed using 'Awk' Script. AWK is a data driven programming language designed for processing text based data, either in files or data streams. Using Awk script, the data points for packet delivery ratio and throughput for wireless and hybrid networks has been calculated. The values thus computed are used to visualize the results graphically using 'Gnuplot', an interactive data plotting program mainly intended for depicting the scientific data.

4.2 Packet Delivery Ratio

The packet delivery ratio is the proportion of the number of packets received by the destination to the number of packets sent by the source.

$$\text{Packet Delivery Ratio} = \frac{\sum \text{Packets received by Destination}}{\sum \text{Packets sent by Source}} \quad (2)$$

4.2.1 Determining the Packet Delivery Ratio

The hybrid wireless networks are simulated using a network area of 200 m x 200 m with 4 wired nodes, 14 wireless ad hoc nodes and 2 base stations. The initial range for the nodes is assumed as 100 m. Movement of nodes and data transfer takes place according to the scenario and connection patterns dynamically due to ad hoc nature. By using this setting, packet delivery ratio with different simulation times of 30, 60, 90, 120, 150, 180 seconds is calculated as given in Table 1.

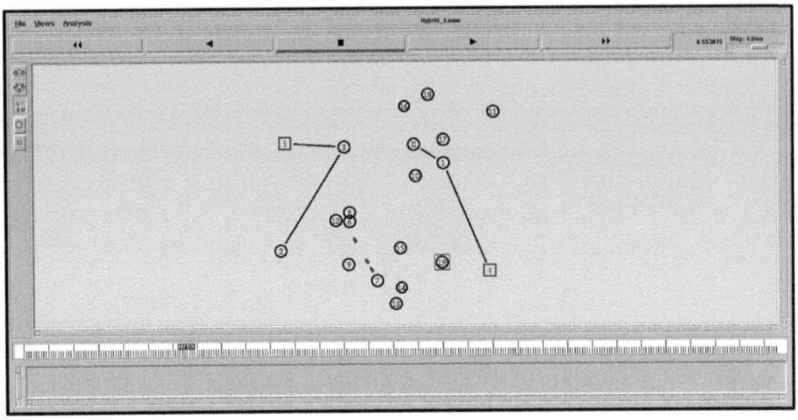

Fig. 5. Scenario for calculating Packet delivery ratio

Table 1. Data points for plotting Packet delivery ratio in Ad hoc and Hybrid Wireless Network

ExOR \ Time (Sec)	30	60	90	120	150	180
Ad Hoc	95.3714	97.4854	98.1968	98.5709	98.7386	98.9302
Hybrid	99.1089	99.395	99.4889	99.4837	99.4814	99.4863

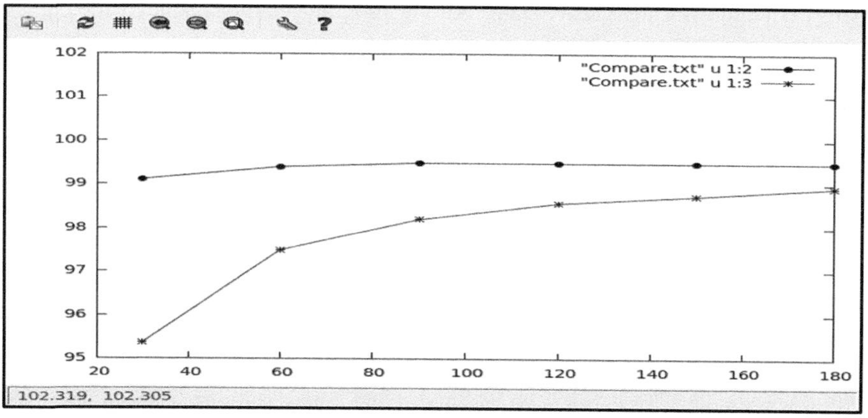

Fig. 6. Comparison of Packet Delivery Ratio for Ad hoc and Hybrid Wireless Networks using ExOR Routing Protocol

4.3 Throughput

Throughput refers to the total amount of bytes being transferred over a particular time.

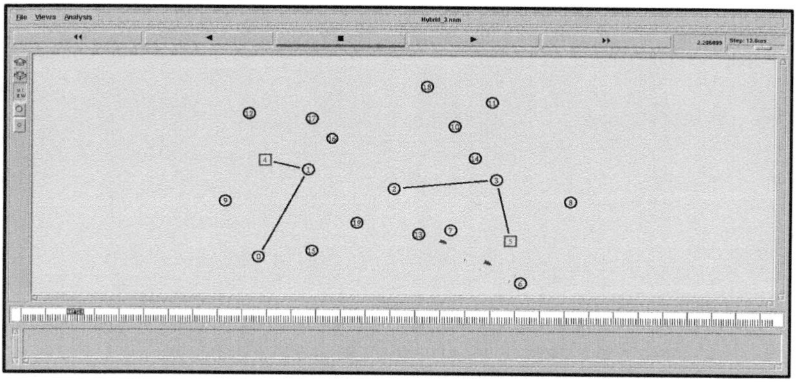

Fig. 7. Throughput calculation for Hybrid Scenario

4.3.1 Throughput Calculation

Hybrid wireless networks are simulated using a network area of 150 m x 150 m with 4 wired nodes, 14 wireless ad hoc nodes and 2 base stations. The initial range for the nodes is assumed as 100 m. Movement of nodes and data transfer takes according to the scenario and connection patterns. By using this setting, throughput with different simulation times of 30, 60, 90, 120, 150, 180 seconds is calculated as in Table 2.

Table 2. Data points for plotting throughput in Ad hoc and Hybrid Wireless Network

ExOR \ Time (Sec)	30	60	90	120	150	180
Ad Hoc	615.42	631.42	635.28	637.59	639.17	648.55
Hybrid	812.53	825.52	828.54	833.54	831.25	838.61

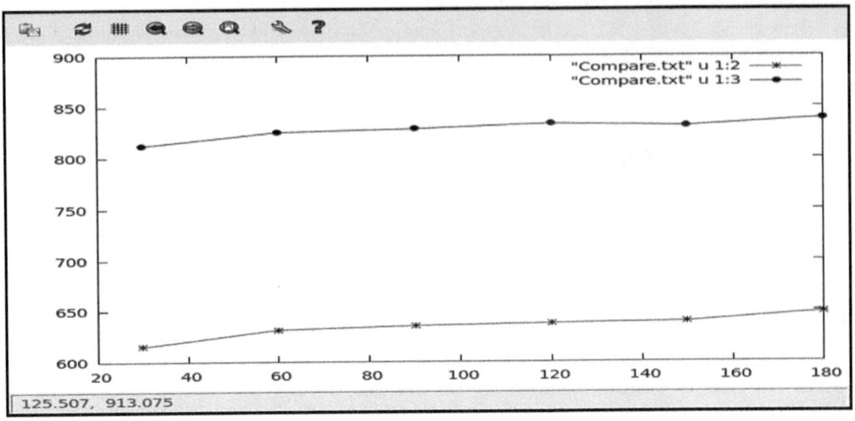

Fig. 8. Comparison of throughput for Ad hoc and Hybrid Wireless Network using ExOR Routing Protocol

5 Conclusion

Extremely Opportunistic Routing (ExOR), an integrated routing and MAC protocol for hybrid wireless networks, takes the advantage of long-distance but lossy links which is not addressed by the traditional routing protocols and increases the performance considerably. ExOR protocol is implemented using Expected Transmission Count (ETX) Metric that finds the optimal path with higher throughput in hybrid wireless networks. The packet delivery ratio and throughput calculated using different simulation times. There is a 20 to 30 % increase in packet delivery ratio and throughput taking into account the routing overhead in Hybrid wireless network when compared to that of ad hoc wireless networks. This implementation would be applicable in mobile learning applications and in other cost effective applications like disaster management, group learning/communication and so on. Further enhancement for this work would be to address the security aspects as it's an essential component for any wireless network.

References

1. Liu, B., Liu, Z., Towsley, D.: On the capacity of Hybrid Wireless Networks. In: IEEE Computer and Communication Societies (INFOCOM), vol. 2, pp. 1543–1552 (2003)
2. De Couto, D.S.J., Aguayo, D., Bicket, J., Morris, R.: A High Throughput Path Metric for Multi-Hop Wireless Routing. In: MobiCom 2003, San Diego, California, USA, pp. 134–146 (September 2003)
3. Zeng, K., Lou, W., Zhai, H.: On End – to – end throughput of Opportunistic routing in Multi rate and multi hop Wireless networks. In: INFOCOM 2008, Phoenix, Ariz, USA, pp. 1490–1498 (April 2008)
4. Shah, R.C., Wietholter, S., Wolisz, A.: When does Opportunistic Routing make sense? In: IEEE international Conference on Pervasive Computing & Communication Workshops (PerSens 2005), pp. 350–356 (March 2005)
5. Biswas, S., Morris, R.: ExOR: Opportunistic Multi-Hop Routing for Wireless Networks. In: SIGCOMM 2005, USA, August 21-26 (2005)
6. Chachulski, S.: Trading structure for Randomness in Wireless Opportunistic Routing. In: Proceedings of ACM SIGCOM Conference on Computer Communication, pp. 169–180 (2007)
7. Le, T., Liu, Y.: On the Capacity of Hybrid Wireless Networks with Opportunistic Routing. EURASIP Journal on Wireless Communication and Networking (2010)
8. Li, Y., Liu, Y.-a., Luo, P.: Link probability based opportunistic routing metric in wireless networks. In: International Conference on Communications and Mobile Computing, pp. 308–312 (2009)
9. Pei, Y., Modestino, J.W., Wang, X.: On the throughput capacity of hybrid wireless networks using an L-maximum hop routing strategy, pp. 2173–2176. IEEE, Los Alamitos (March 2003)
10. Li, F., Wang, Y., Li, X.-Y.: Gateway Placement for Throughput Optimization in Wireless Mesh Networks. In: Nusairat, A., Wu, Y. (eds.) ACM/Springer Mobile Networks and Applications (MONET), vol. 13(1/2), pp. 198–211 (April 2008)
11. Cao, L., Sharif, K., Dahlberg, T., Wang, Y.: Multiple-Metric Hybrid Anycast Protocol for Heterogeneous Access Networks. International Journal of Ad Hoc and Ubiquitous Computing, IJAHUC (2010)
12. Wang, Y., Wang, W., Dahlberg, T.A.: Truthful routing for Hybrid Networks. In: IEEE GLOBECOM, pp. 3461–3465 (2005)
13. Sun, Y., Belding-Royer, E.M.: Application oriented routing in hybrid wireless networks, pp. 502–506. IEEE, Los Alamitos (March 2003)
14. Sumathy, S., Saravanan, R., Vijay Kumar, M., Vinay Kumar, C.: Survey and Analysis of Various Routing Techniques and Metrics in Wireless Networks. IJCA 11(4), 17–22 (2010)
15. Marc Grei's Tutorial for the UCB/LBNL/VINT Network Simulator, `http://www.isi.edu/nsnam/ns/tutorial/index.html`

Integrating Grid Environment with Private Cloud and Storage Cluster and Provision for Dynamic Clustering and VO

Kailash Selvaraj[1] and Saswati Mukherjee[2]

[1] Centre for Development of Advanced Computing (CDAC), Chennai, India
[2] Dept of IST, College of Engineering, Guindy, Anna University, Chennai, India
kailashs@cdac.in, msaswati@cs.annauniv.edu

Abstract. Computational grids generally used for scientific applications are fully utilized only at certain times. During that period, shortage of grid resources occurs and causes delay in execution of jobs. In such situation the grid jobs can be migrated to private cloud for execution. On the other hand, the private cloud when reaches its peak load, can utilize the grid if the grid resources are idle thereby private cloud gain more resources dynamically. We propose architecture to integrate grid and private cloud using an integrator component along with a storage cluster, which is responsible for managing resources and execution of jobs over grid and private cloud when any of these lack resources. The architecture supports dynamic clustering over the virtual resources and formation of Virtual Organization in integrated environment

Keywords: Grid Cloud integration, Virtual Machine on grid, Grid Storage cluster, Grid Resource expansion, Cloud burst.

1 Introduction

Grid is generally referred to as computational grid for "coordinated resource sharing and problem solving in dynamic, multi-institutional virtual organizations". Because of its level of maturity added with the emergence of OGSA standards, Grid computing is widely accepted by the scientific community.

Although huge applications from various domains exploit the advantage of grid, its restrictions like preventing the root access to users, preventing users from deploying their custom software stack has a restriction that the complete control of the machines are not given to the users, lack dynamic provisioning of resources [2]. Because of this, users are restricted to adopt the existing runtime environment available with the grid. As a result, at times when the grid achieves its peak load and is running short of necessary resources, the application cannot be migrated due to non availability of runtime environment. This is the case even if various grids are interconnected.

During certain times a situation arises in grid where grid environment lacks the required resources and this forces other incoming jobs to wait in queue thereby

D. Nagamalai, E. Renault, and M. Dhanushkodi (Eds.): PDCTA 2011, CCIS 203, pp. 459–472, 2011.

causing delay in execution and hence poor performance. Since grid jobs are HPC jobs which need fast execution, it is unfair that the jobs wait in queue due to lack of resources. This may lead to far worse situation in case of commercial grid. Our research takes up this issue and proposes to migrate such grid jobs to private cloud, thereby not compromising on the security aspect of grid.

Cloud computing offers on demand service with rapid elasticity, on pay per use model, under ubiquitous network access and location independent resource pooling through different deployment models like Public cloud, Private cloud, Hybrid Cloud.

The public clouds are less secure and other issues such as availability, performance, latency, bottlenecks, common APIs, interoperability, management of resources, vendor lock-in etc exists. To solve some of these issues, many private clouds emerged. These private clouds largely display the quintessential properties of cloud. But these private clouds have restricted elasticity as this depends on the underlying limited physical resource capacity. These private clouds, as a result, are not able to accommodate the peak hour requirements of resources, popularly known as a cloud burst situation. To solve cloud burst, private clouds are interconnected with public cloud which may cause a security threat.

We propose to integrate grid and private cloud environment for mutual benefit of grid and cloud. We have considered the cloud burst situation where instead of private cloud fetching resources from public cloud, it approaches grid environment and grid, on turn, approaches private cloud when it faces lack of resources. The cloud virtual machines on which grid jobs are executed are not fully capable of processing large volume of datasets, which may be the need for many grid jobs. To handle this situation we introduce storage cluster with map-reduce to the integrated environment. Since data processing is not on VMs where jobs are executed, we believe that this approach can enhance the performance considerably.

In this paper, we propose architecture with Integrator component which is responsible for the integration for grid and cloud. Grid jobs, when waiting in queue for quite long period of time due to unavailability of execution nodes, are directed to cloud. When the number of grid instances increases, metascheduler queries the status of jobs, collect job state from all VMs. This may increase the network overhead in the environment and the workload of metascheduler. This is applicable to cloud also where the cloud controller should keep track of number of VMs deployed on Grid. To avoid the overhead of network, and to reduce the workload of cloud controller and metascheduler we introduce dynamic clustering approach within cloud instances over grid and grid instances over cloud. Grid generally requires multi-institutional VOs. Hence the design includes provision for forming a virtual organization across an integrated environment. As a result of this integration, resources locked under grid environment can be used to execute cloud instances when the private cloud needs additional resources.

Our work focus on both the grid and cloud computing owing to the usage of both in a rapidly increasing manner. The paper is organized as follows, Section 2 states the survey of literature related to the work, Section 3 provides the architecture of the integrated environment along with its components, Section 4 provides the implementation results and discussion, and finally Section 5 provides the conclusion and future work that can be carries out of this proposed work.

2 Literature Survey

The work proposed in [2] explains elastic site manager that directly interacts only with the cluster manager and extends the cluster resources with cloud. There is a restriction that monitoring is only at the cluster. Our approach focus on extending a level above the clusters

Private cloud would provide flexible load balancing, energy efficiency and addition of hybrid clouds will provide elasticity and thus integration provides flexibility. In Hybrid Grid and Cloud the issues arising are Multi-domain Communication, Multi-domain deployment, Support to dynamic resources Deployment of middleware encompasses the configuration of channels interconnecting the ProActive runtimes [3]. In [4] Single system image across multi cores for providing Ease of Administration, Transparent Sharing, Informed Optimizations, Consistency, Fault tolerance is proposed. In [1] Grid over VMs allows grid users to define an environment in terms of its requirements such as resource requirements and software configuration, control it, and then deploy the environment in the grid environment. The approach mentioned creates virtual machine for execution of grid jobs and executes them into grid resources. The number of virtual machines execution simultaneously depends on the capacity of grid and number of free resources. In [5], the authors explore the use of cloud computing for scientific workflows and their approach is to evaluate the tradeoffs between running tasks in a local environment, if such is available, and running in a virtual environment via remote, wide area network resource access. The work in [6] describes a scalable and lightweight computational workflow system for clouds which can run workflow jobs composed of multiple Hadoop MapReduce or legacy programs. But both works do not offer support for any other services.

Building a virtual grid over a local area network, deploying resources by pooling has been suggested in [7] but the capacity of grid is limited. The system uses one monitoring server to keep track of various parameters pertaining to the pooled resources and tasks deployed on the system which does not provide solution to single point of failure. In [8], a portable layer is proposed between different vendor clouds to avoid vendor lock-in, forming meta-cloud or cloud-of-clouds. It lacks framework for handling datasets.

Grid infrastructures do not isolate and partition the performance of the resources. The execution of application of one grid user may affect the execution of others. This limits the quality of service and reliability of actual platforms, preventing a wide adoption of the Grid paradigm. In [9] a straightforward deployment of virtual machines in a Grid infrastructure is presented. Although this strategy does not require additional middleware to be installed and it is not bounded to a virtualization technology. However, it presents attractive benefits, like increasing software robustness or saving administration efforts, so improving the quality of life in the Grid.

The work in [3] is a lean middleware that stands between the hybrid infrastructure and the application layer, enables a seamless and flexible but efficient use of any combination of heterogeneous computing resources in intensively communicating applications. The work in [14] suggests two level of check pointing such as system level and application level. The saved state of applications or system using checkpoints can also be used for job migration using job schedulers of grid.

This system level check pointing is extended to Virtual Machines and are controlled by execution manager until the job is completed.

Eucalyptus uses Greedy (First fit) and Round robin algorithm which is a random method to select adaptive physical resources for the VM requests that not considering maximum usage of physical resource. The queuing system, advanced reservation and preemption scheduling policies are not considering the utilization rate of physical resource [11].

3 Architecture

The conventional grid environment consists of computational nodes in a cluster and a local resource management system controls each cluster and schedules job within the cluster. All such cluster managers are controlled by a Metascheduler scheduling jobs across clusters within the grid. The jobs are submitted in head node and the computational nodes are bound by the grid middleware, which offers various web service based functionalities for grid job execution. The cloud environment contains the nodes with hypervisor for bring up virtualization and these nodes forms a cluster controlled by cluster controller. All these cluster controllers are controlled and managed by the cloud controller. The architecture in Figure 1 provides an overview of integration.

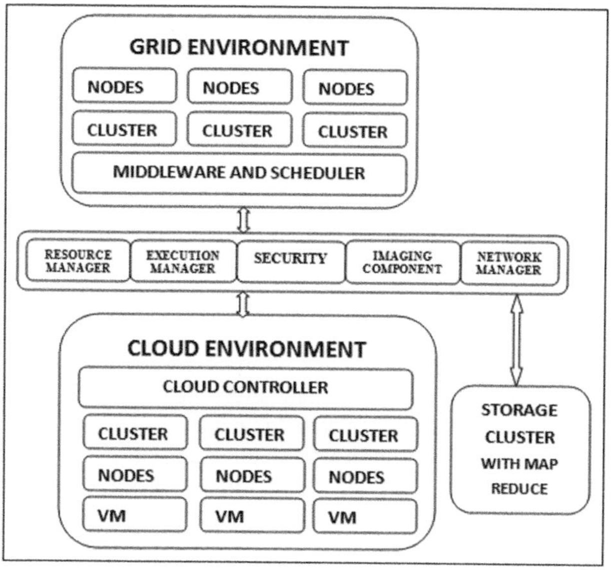

Fig. 1. Integrated Grid and Cloud with Storage Cluster

3.1 Integrator

We introduce an intermediate Integrator component responsible for integration. A storage cluster is integrated with the integrator component, accessible by both grid and cloud jobs. When cloud jobs need additional resources, they are passed to the grid through the Integrator. The Integrator diverts such cloud requests to grid. In this context, the proposed Integrator acts as an intermediary and helps in passing jobs between the two environments when the need arises. This Integrator component consists of five modules such as Resource manager, Execution manager, Security Manager, Imaging Component, Network Manager.

Resource Manager

Resource Manager (RM) is the key component of integrated environment. This component manages the grid resources when a cloud instance is running in grid environment and manages the cloud resources when the grid jobs are running in cloud environment. RM has the capability to query or coordinate with the higher layer at both the ends, and they cannot migrate beyond to lower level.

When a grid job is submitted to the metascheduler of grid, it queries for the availability of the suitable resources to execute the job, through grid middleware services. If the query returns with result stating that no resources are available, then jobs wait in queue in grid metascheduler. Such requests are passed on to the RM of Integrator, a new request to Cloud is raised by RM. The Cloud then handles the request, makes the instance with required libraries for grid on which grid job executes. On the other hand, when cloud controller returns job in a situation where there are no resources in cloud, it is passed to RM of Integrator and then to grid metascheduler. This metascheduler provisions the cloud VM in grid for execution.

Management overheads occur when scheduling the VMs over cross platform. A hybrid solution that adaptively selects the optimal transfer method depending on network capabilities and Cloud site constraints is presented in [10], which can be adopted for VM migration and execution.

The Resource manager consists of the following components: Request handler, Job pool, Storage Cluster controller, Resource monitor.

When the Integrator receives a request from the either grid or cloud stating that it cannot process the request, the job is sent to a queue called Job Pool. The Request handler fetches the request from the job pool and identifies the request domain type whether grid or cloud. It reads the cloud request and converts the request specification into grid resource specification language (RSL) such that the request can be understood by the grid schedulers and middleware. Similarly, a grid request waiting for execution resources are fetched from the queue by the Request handler and the RSL is parsed and converted to cloud specific requirement format before submitting such a request to cloud.

The Storage controller controls the storage cluster with MapReduce and distributed file system. This monitors and manages the jobs submitted to the storage cluster from both grid and cloud.

The Resource monitor registers the log of the resources when grid jobs are submitted to cloud or cloud instances are provisioned in grid. Also the cloud instances running in the grid are metered by the Resource monitor and the information is passed to the cloud for billing.

Once the request is submitted to the corresponding environment RM informs the submitted job information to the other components of the Integrator such as Execution manager, Image manager for further processing.

Execution Manager

Execution manager (EM) is responsible for managing the execution of grid jobs in cloud environment and cloud instances in grid environment.

EM is responsible for execution of jobs in integrated environment. As grid cannot contact cloud and cloud cannot contact the grid directly, EM acts as communication interface between them when cross job execution takes place.

When jobs of one environment are completed in the other alternate environment, the output data is fetched by the Execution manager and passed onto the environment from which the job has originally come. Once task is completed the EM destroys the instances deployed at the alternate site. EM connects the storage cluster with mapreduce to the jobs under execution if the jobs are in need of. This EM is also responsible for dynamic clustering and VO formation which is explained in the forthcoming section.

Imaging Component

Imaging Component (IM) acts as repository for holding the cloud images along with the application bundled, and grid jobs bundled along with required operating system, binaries, libraries.

This IM as it acts as an intermediate repository of images can reduce the bandwidth consumption, networking overheads at the cloud and at MS. This also reduces the delay in fetching the instances, images, jobs from its corresponding registry so that execution starts without delay considerably in an integrated environment.

Network Manager

Integration component integrates coordinates and controls grid and cloud operational in different networking domains and in different subnets. Within grid, dynamic virtual organization is formed for better execution of jobs. When the grid jobs are submitted to Cloud the virtual organization is to be extended to the cloud instances.

The grid and cloud be integrated through a peer to peer network for enhanced data transfer and secured communication. A completely distributed peer-to-peer network is required, immune to super-peer failure [3].

The Network Manager (NM) is responsible for maintaining the network state across the domains, and makes the ease of accessibility.

Security Manager

Cloud and Grid have their own security mechanism. Single sign-on will resolve the credentials needs and ease the security mechanism. Cross CA authentication can also provide better enhanced security to the integrated environment.

3.2 Storage Cluster

Storage cluster is integrated with the integrator component and controlled by resource manager. When the applications over instances running in grid environment need to process large volume of data, the data sets are passed onto the cluster through the execution manager.

The storage cluster with map reduce over distributed file system process the data and stores in it. On the other side, if grid jobs running over cloud need to process huge volumes the same can be processed through the cluster with the aid of execution manager. In a conventional grid, the jobs are executed on physical nodes that provide high performance compared to the grid jobs executed on cloud over virtual machines. To enhance the performance of integrated environment the storage processing is done in a dedicated cluster.

In [15], a dynamic and real-time virtual machine scheduler is presented that monitors job execution pathways and optimize job success rate for HPC workloads when ran on virtual machines in the scientific grids. This dedicated storage cluster can reduce the load processing overheads at the VMs thereby a considerable increase in performance and service quality can be obtained.

3.3 Dynamic Clustering in Integrated Grid and Cloud

The process of dynamic cluster formation is shown in Figure 2 as follows,

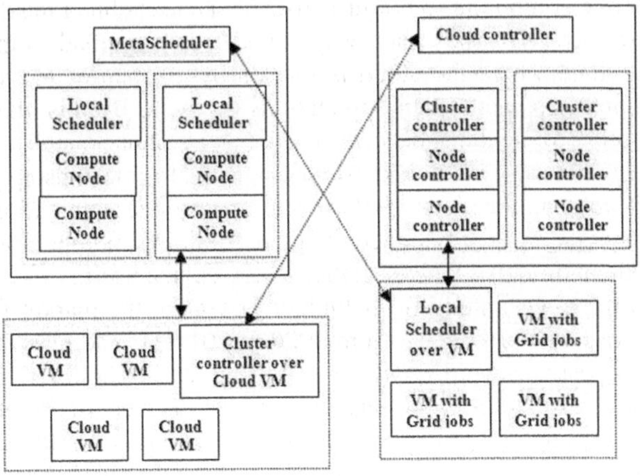

Fig. 2. Dynamic Clustering in integrated environment

The hierarchical layers of grid and cloud environment are not restructured for dynamic clustering. When Grid environment is in need of resources, it fetches from the cloud. In cloud the grid jobs are executed on virtual machines whose instances composed of grid bundle with all the runtime executables. In the execution manager of integrator component we propose a cluster manager responsible of forming a cluster of virtual machines at both the ends.

This dynamic clustering approach reduces the network overhead as the metascheduler in grid communicates only with the local scheduler over VM in cloud not with the underlying execution nodes. The latency time is reduced as an intermediate registry is maintained internally within the cluster.

On the other hand, when the private cloud is in need of resources, it is fetched from the grid. The cloud instances are deployed on to grid. These instances among themselves form a cluster dynamically which is controlled by the cluster controller in one of the cloud virtual machines under execution in Grid. This cluster controller is controlled by the Cloud controller running in the cloud site. Once the user terminates the instances, the cluster gets dissolved. A Registry is maintained by the cluster controller where the images are stored internally for quick and easy recovery in case of any crash in the instances. The registry also holds the intermediate status of the applications over cloud VMs running in Grid.

When the dynamically formed cluster is in need of the storage cluster attached to the integrator component, the cluster through integrator includes the storage cluster. Figure 3 shows the inclusion of storage cluster in the Dynamic clustering environment.

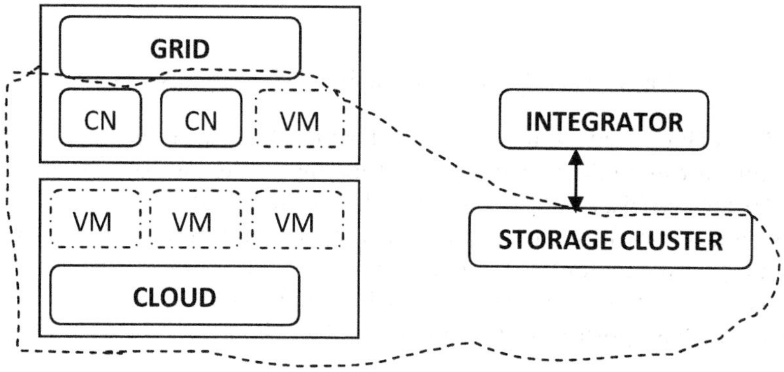

Fig. 3. Storage Cluster integration with VM Cluster

We propose the formation of virtual organization across the grid virtual machines formed in the cloud along with the grid execution nodes operational in the conventional grid as shown in Figure 4.

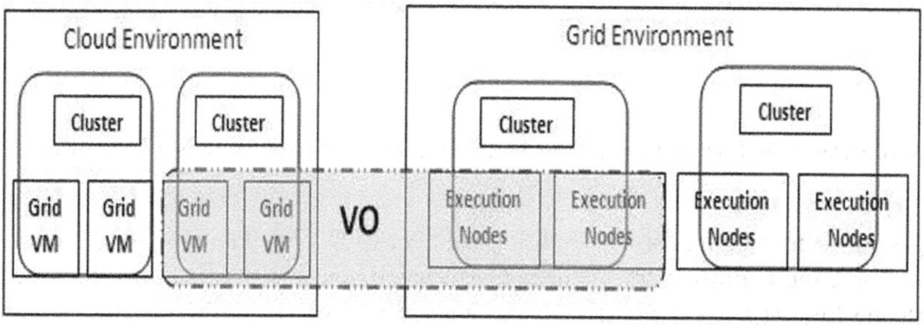

Fig. 4. Dynamic Clustering in integrated environment

The Execution manager keeps track of the instances and finds for similar execution environment. The instances with similar job nature and having similar instance ID are identified by the corresponding cluster controller and local schedulers. This information is passed on to the corresponding heads such as metascheduler or cloud controller that passes the information to the Execution manager of the Integrator. If there is more than 3 similar instances across, the information is passed on to Globus toolkit and to the Network manager of Integrator. Globus toolkit forms the VO among the nodes.

4 Implementation

Grid environment is implemented with debian Linux operating system and Torque as local scheduler, Globus toolkit[17] as middleware, and Gridway as Meta scheduler. Cloud environment is established with Eucalyptus[18] as cloud middleware, Xen as hypervisor and libvirt for hypervisor to communicate with middleware. Storage Cluster is implemented with Hadoop map-reduce[19].

When cloud jobs need additional resources, they are passed to the grid through the Integrator. The Integrator diverts such cloud requests to grid. In this context, the proposed Integrator acts as an intermediary and helps in passing jobs between the two environments when the need arises.

The Integrator component is implemented in java. In the Resource manager, the job queue and resource queue are implemented using PostgreSQL database. The Request handler queries the job records from the job pool database and passes the request information to grid metascheduler or cloud controller. When the request is processed by grid or cloud, the filed jobs identified by the job id are transferred through FTP to the execution nodes.

The storage manger is implemented with shell scripts. It queries the head node of the storage cluster for the status of the running jobs. The storage cluster head node information is passed on the grid and cloud. The Execution manager has a table in database which stores the job ID, resource ID, status and time stamp of the jobs submitted.

In our implementation, migration of cloud instances to grid, and grid jobs to cloud is done manually. The VM Image bundling, CA establishment, signing of certificates by CA is done manually. The Image manager consists of database that stores information of the images, owner of the image, image ID, license etc. The Network manager has a NATing table consisting of resource ID, job ID, actual IP address and translated IP address. The input to this table is obtained by querying scheduler and controller. We have created a directory for temporary storing of the images under Image manager, and the images are transferred to the execution environment through file transfer protocol, using passwordless SSH. The file transfer can be enhanced with GSI-FTP, a grid file transfer protocol which is more secured.

At Cloud Head node

Table 1. No of VM and Load

No of VMs	Load in %
2	62
4	69
6	76
8	85
10	96

Table 2. No of Queries, VM and Load

No of Queries	No of VMs	Load in %
1	3	65
5	3	72
10	3	79
20	3	86
40	3	95

Table 3. No of VM, Query and Delay

No of VMs in Grid	No of Queries	Delay in Access in Sec
1	2	2
5	4	2.75
10	8	4.5
15	16	8.5
20	32	13

Table 4. Load at Cloud Physical Node

No of VM	Total No. of Queries	Load
1	1	41
2	10	45
3	20	53
4	40	61
6	80	82
8	115	95

Table 5. Load in Grid VM

No of Queries	Load
0	55
1	60
5	68
10	80
15	97

It is observed from the table 1 that on the Cloud head node, the load of the head node increases gradually as the number of grid instances running on cloud increases. Table 2 provided the statistical data of load of the head node, providing various queries to grid instances over cloud. The load increases minimally when the number of queries to the grid instances increases even for constant number of VMs. From Table 3 it is observed that as the number of Cloud instances running as VMs in Grid increases along with the number of queries, the delay in accessing the VMs or applications on VM increases rapidly. The increase in load is predicted to be due to memory leakage in the cloud controller or cluster component of eucalyptus.

In Grid Head Node

Table 6. Load in Grid Head node

No of Cloud VMs	No of Queries to VM	Load
1	0	10
5	10	14
10	20	16
15	30	23
20	40	30
25	50	37

Table 7. Load at Cloud VM over Grid

No of queries	Load
1	0.15
10	0.18
20	0.22
30	0.27
40	0.34
50	0.4
60	0.52
70	0.64

However it is observed that at the grid head node or at the grid execution node, the load is not rapidly raising when the number of VMs or queries / transactions to the cloud instances running over grid increases. This does not wisely affect the overall performance of the grid environment.

A sample application is hosted on the Cloud instance running over grid environment. Table 8 shows the test report and Figure 5 shows the performance of the application over VM.

Table 8. Application and database access from grid

Test Run	User Scenario	Page Name	Error	Count	Percentage	URL
spark App and DB	spark App and DB same	request_10.1	404 Object Not Found	5	100.00%	http://192.168.100.102/spark_promotion/images/drop2.gif
spark App and DB	spark App and DB same	request_10.2	CONNECTION DROPPED BY SERVER	5	100.00%	http://192.168.100.102/spark_promotion/images/right2.gif
spark App and DB	spark App and DB same	request_21.2	REQUEST TIMED OUT	1	20.00%	http://weather.services.conduit.com/weatherrequest.ctp
spark App and DB	spark App and DB same	request_22.13	404 Object Not Found	5	100.00%	http://192.168.100.108/favicon.ico

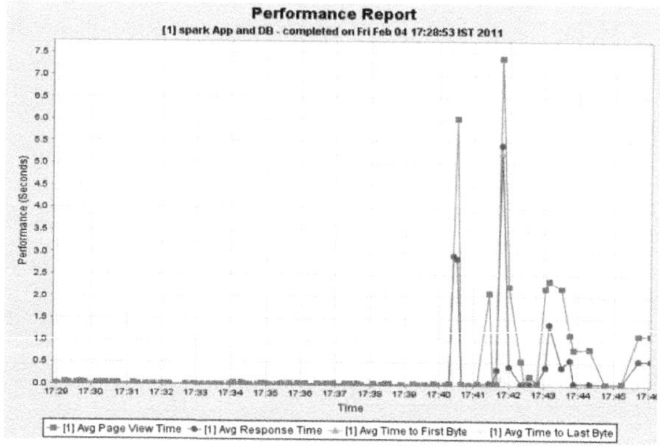

Fig. 5. Performance of application over VM on grid

Execution of data sets over Hadoop cluster from the virtual machines at both grid and cloud environment provides considerably better performance. In our implementation, considering that all the three grid, cloud and Hadoop clusters lies in the same network domain.

5 Conclusion and Future Work

We proposed an architecture that successfully integrates grid and cloud and make them work in tandem. We have addressed the problem of resource availability in both grid and cloud due to which jobs may wait for execution, at peak time by integrating grid computing environment with private cloud, thereby improving service availability of both. To improve the performance, we have integrated storage cluster with the Integrator. For better execution management, dynamic clustering and VO formation among the grid and cloud integrated environment is used. Although in the proposed architecture, the grid environment runs on a virtualized kernel that has a provision to support virtualization, the performance of jobs submitted to grid is not affected. This work helps to achieve service availability, effective utilization of resources, improved quality of service and to green ICT with minimal number of servers operational in data centres.

Our future work is on the execution management of grid jobs and cloud instances, with semantic approach, enhancing the network with peer to peer network to avoid the delay in accessing the cloud and grid and fine tuning the cloud. Fine tuning the cloud middleware would help to overcome the delay in processing the request thereby reducing virtualization overhead. Peer to peer connectivity can be established among the grid and cloud head node, and can be dynamically created between the execution nodes, thereby improving the networking problems. Cross CA Authentication between grid and cloud can be established for security in integrated environment. Finally, we can extend the proposed grid-cloud integration to cloud-cloud integration.

References

1. Wu, S., Zhu, W., Jiang, W., Jin, H.: VMGrid: A Virtual Machine Supported Grid Middleware. In: The IEEE International Conference on Granular Computing (GrC 2008), China (2008)
2. Marshall, P., Keahey, K., Freeman, T.: Elastic Site Using Clouds to Elastically Extend Site Resources. In: 10th IEEE/ACM International Conference on Cluster, Cloud and Grid Computing (CCGRID 2010), Australia (2010)
3. Mathias, E., Baude, F.: Multi-domain Grid/Cloud Computing Through a Hierarchical Component-Based Middleware. In: 8th International Workshop on Middleware for Grids, Clouds and e-Science (MGC 2010), India (2010)
4. Wentzlaff, D., Gruenwald III, C., Beckmann, N.: An Operating System for Multicore and Clouds: Mechanisms and Implementation. In: ACM Symposium on Cloud Computing (SoCC 2010), Indianapolis (2010)
5. Hoffa, C., Mehta, G., Freeman, T., Deelman, E., Keahey, K., Berriman, B., Good, J.: On the use of cloud computing for scientific workflows. In: 4th IEEE International Conference on e-Science (e-SCIENCE 2008), USA (2008)
6. Zhang, C., Sterck, H.D.: Cloudwf: A computational workflow system for clouds based on hadoop. In: The 1st International Conference on Cloud Computing (CloudCom 2009), China (2009)
7. Rajan, A., Rawat, A., Verma, R.K.: Virtual Computing Grid using Resource Pooling. In: 2008 International Conference on Information Technology, USA (2008)
8. Khalil, W., Schikuta, E.: Towards a Virtual Organization for Computational Intelligence. In: The Fourth International Conference on Digital Society (ICDS 2010), Netherlands (2010)
9. Rubio-Montero, A.J., Huedo, E., Montero, R.S., Llorente, I.M.: Management of Virtual Machines on Globus Grids Using GridWay. In: 21st IEEE International Parallel and Distributed Processing Symposium (IPDPS 2007), USA (2007)
10. Schmidt, M., Fallenbeck, N., Smith, M., Freisleben, B.: Efficient Distribution of Virtual Machines for Cloud Computing. In: The 18th Euromicro Conference on Parallel, Distributed and Network-based Processing (PDP 2010), Italy (2010)
11. Zhong, H., Tao, K., Zhang, X.: An Approach to Optimized Resource Scheduling Algorithm for Open-source Cloud Systems. In: The Fifth Annual ChinaGrid Annual Conference (Chinarid 2010), China (2010)
12. Bittencourt, L.F., Senna, C.R., Madeira, E.R.M.: Enabling Execution of Service Workflows in Grid/Cloud Hybrid Systems. In: 1st IEEE/IFIP International Workshop on Cloud Management (CLOUDMAN 2010), Japan (2010)
13. Lin, S.-J., Huang, M.-C., Kuan-Chou, Huang, K.-C.: Design and Implementation of Job Migration Policies in P2P Grid Systems. In: 2008 IEEE Asia-Pacific Services Computing Conference (APSCC), Taiwan (2008)
14. Mehta, J., Chaudhary, S.: Checkpointing and Recovery Mechanism in Grid. In: 16th International Conference on Advanced Computing & Communication (ADCOM 2008), India (2008)
15. Khalid, O.: Deadline Aware Virtual Machine Scheduler for Grid and Cloud Computing. In: 24th International Conference on Advanced Information Networking and Applications Workshops (WAINA 2010), Australia (2010)

16. Caron, E., Desprez, F., Loureiro, D.: Cloud Computing Resource Management through a Grid Middleware: A Case Study with DIET and Eucalyptus. In: IEEE 2009 International Conference on Cloud Computing (CLOUD-II 2009), India (2009)
17. Foster, I.: Globus Toolkit Version 4: Software for Service-Oriented Systems. J. Comput. Sci. & Technol. (July 2006)
18. Nurmi, D., Wolski, R., Grzegorczyk, C., Obertelli, G., Soman, S., Youseff, L., Zagorodnov, D.: The Eucalyptus Open-source Cloud-computing System. In: 9th IEEE/ACM International Symposium on Cluster Computing and the Grid (CCGRID 2009), USA (2009)
19. Attebury, G., et al.: Hadoop Distributed File System for the Grid. In: IEEE Nuclear Science Symposium and Medical Imaging Conference, USA (2009)

An Overview and Comparative Study of Segmentation Techniques for Extraction of Tongue Region for Computerized Tongue Diagnosis

Bikesh Kumar Singh, A.S. Thoke, and Keshri Verma

National Institute of Technology, Raipur (C.G), India
{bikesh_020581,asthoke}@yahoo.co.in ,
keshriverma@gmail.com

Abstract. Extraction of Tongue Contours is an important issue in development of disease diagnostic expert system [DDES] using tongue image analysis. Tongue inspection is a commonly used practice in Traditional Chinese Medicine (TCM) to monitor the health of the patient. The tongue body is an absolutely essential guide in differentiating syndromes in TCM. In early years tongue extraction method was realized manually by opening image files and removing non tongue areas manually. This gives high accuracy but consumes lot of time and energy. Computerized analysis of tongue body can provide fast and valuable diagnostic information. In early years tongue extraction method was manual giving high accuracy but consumes lot of time and energy. In developing an expert system for tongue diagnosis, the accuracy if system is highly dependent on extraction of exact tongue region. In this paper we investigate and discuss various techniques proposed for automatic extraction of tongue area and make the comparative analysis of the same.

Keywords: Tongue Extraction, TCM, Medical Imaging, Computer Aided Diagnosis.

1 Introduction

Tongue diagnosis in TCM is a commonly used approach for determining the true condition of patient. The appearance of the tongue color, texture and coating reflects the improvement or deterioration of patient's conditions. One of the major issues in computerized tongue analysis and diagnosis is capturing the tongue image followed by tongue region extraction and calibration of tongue color. The captured tongue image usually consists of background skin, teeth, lips etc. Due to weak edges of tongue low level image processing techniques such as region growing, region splitting, region merging and basic edge detection techniques etc. fails to properly segment the tongue area. In early years tongue extraction method was realized manually by opening image files and removing non areas manually. This gives high accuracy but consumes lot of time and energy. In this paper we discuss recent developments in algorithms used for extraction of exact tongue area and make a comparative analysis of the same. The rest of the paper is organized as follows:

D. Nagamalai, E. Renault, and M. Dhanushkodi (Eds.): PDCTA 2011, CCIS 203, pp. 473–483, 2011.

section 2 discusses various algorithms proposed for extraction of tongue area and recent development in the field, followed by conclusions, comparative analysis and future requirements in section 3.

2 Methods for Segmentation of Tongue Area

Before extraction of features from tongue images, it is important that the captured image must be properly segmented to separate exact tongue area. For tongue diagnosis using image processing techniques extraction of exact tongue region highly determines the accuracy of the system. A system developed for automatic extraction and tracking of tongue surface movements from ultrasound image sequences was first reported in 1999 [1]. This technique involves positioning of the ultrasound transducer under the chin as shown in figure 1 to track surface movement. However extraction of tongue counter using this technique may not be useful in tongue diagnosis as it does not captures any color or texture information of the tongue except for the tongue boundary.

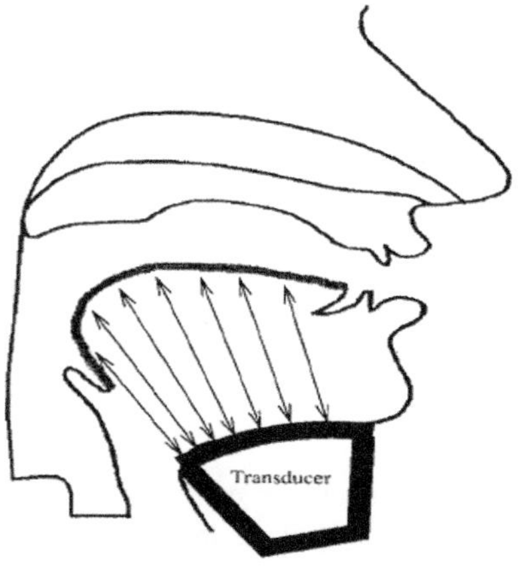

Fig. 1. Position of ultrasound transducer

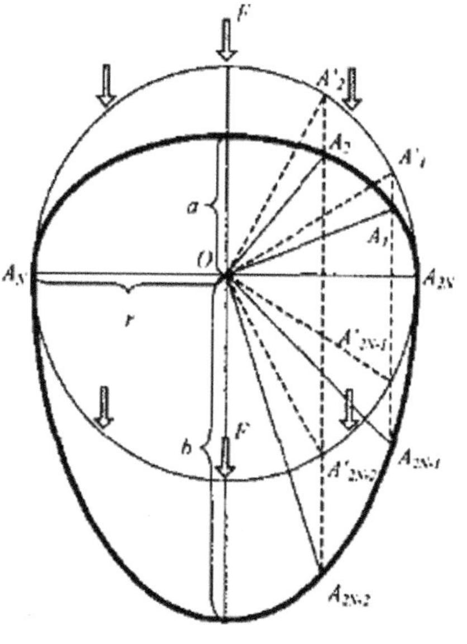

Fig. 2. A bielliptical tongue template over the chin

Tongue area extraction using Bi-elliptical deformable template for tongue extraction is reported [2] to address problems such as limited capture range, undesirable contracting and clustering effect, lack of global control with those of active contour model (ACM). A specific deformable model for tongue body composed of two elliptical segments namely upper semi-ellipse and lower semi-ellipse corresponding to upper and lower boundary of tongue body was used as shown in figure 2. Parameters like template centre, length of template radius etc. were used to describe the template.

The parameters were updated with time by minimizing energy function defined as:

$$E = \frac{1}{Length} \int_{Bi-elliptical-curve} P(\tilde{x})ds \tag{1}$$

With

$$P(\tilde{x}) = -|\nabla I(X,Y)| - |\nabla(G_\sigma * I(X,Y)| \tag{2}$$

where G_σ is a 2-D Gaussian function with standard deviation σ, ∇ is a gradient operator and p(x) is external force field, P is vector consisting of various parameters used to describe the template, I(X,Y) is a grey level image. This method was found superior over traditional DT (Deformable templates) and ACM with respect to stability. Since tongue shape is not fixed, it is not possible to model a tongue shape with sufficient accuracy. This led to developments of other techniques for tongue extraction such as those by using color information.

One such method uses difference in R (Red component) and hue values between tongue image and face image to detect tongue edges followed by boundary extraction and edge line interpolation [3]. However under different and uneven lighting conditions and R and hue may not be sufficient to separate face and tongue.

Active contours or a snake was another approach which is used by many authors for tongue extraction [4-9]. An active contour is a set of points which aims to enclose the target feature. Active contours arrange set of points so as to describe the target feature by enclosing it. An initial contour is first placed outside the target feature and then it is evolved so as to enclose it. Active contours are expressed as energy minimization process. A method for tongue segmentation combines watershed transform and active counter model [4]. The watershed transform determines watershed ridgelines between dark and light regions of the tongue image. Since tongue region is mostly light in intensity image, the watershed ridge lines are found at edges of the tongue area thus providing initial contour. Then to get exact position of contour, parametric active contours (snakes) were used. The process is illustrated in figure 3.

Another new approach for tongue extraction may be use of active shape modeling. The essence of this approach concerns a point model of the shape, the variations in these points is called point distribution model. The chosen landmark points are labeled on the training images. One such method using B-splines was introduced for tongue extraction. B-splines is considered to be most efficient curve representation due to properties such as compactness, continuity, local shape controllability and invariance to affine transformation. Tongue segmentation using B-spline [5] integrates prior knowledge and computer graphics technologies in to tongue detection. Once the tongue image is obtained then after preprocessing such as denoising and image enhancement some landmark points are laid on around the tongue area as shown in figure 4 for tongue extraction. If the land mark points are taken very close covering all edges of the tongue region, the accuracy is highly acceptable. However this may consume more time in laying landmark points on the tongue area.

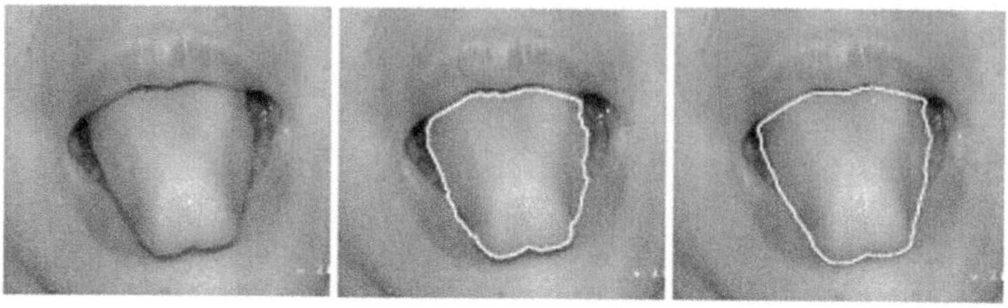

Fig. 3. The initializing procedure and segmentation result using watershed and ACM

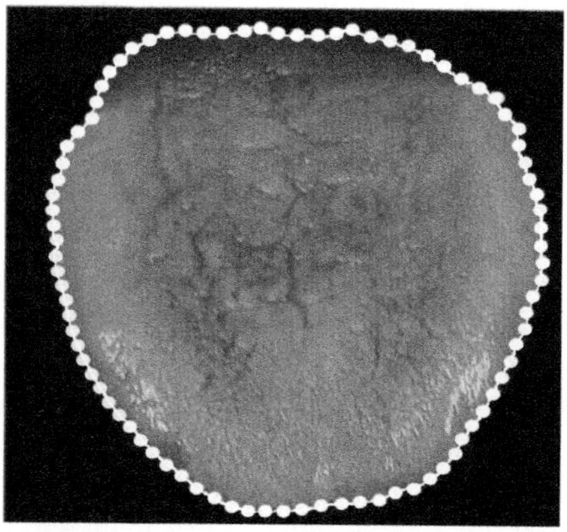

Fig. 4. Tongue image labeled with landmark points

A segmentation technique called as 'live wire method' allows user to select region of interest accurately and quickly. This method is also used for segmentation of tongue area [6]. It is based on lowest cost path algorithm. Image is first convolved with a Sobel filter to extract edges. Each pixel of the resulting image is a vertex of the graph and has edges going to the 4 pixels around it, as up, down, left, right. The edge costs are defined based on a cost function.

The method of tongue area extraction by using region merging with number of pre-processing and post processing operations is proposed [7]. The tongue image was first histogram equalized using brightness and saturation. Histogram of an image represents the relative frequency of occurrence of various grey levels in the image; apply a monotone transform resulting in an approximately uniform histogram. In general, histogram equalization stretches/compresses an image such that, pixel values that occur frequently in input image occupy a bigger dynamic range in output image, i.e., get stretched and become more visible. After histogram equalization edge enhancement was done to divide the image in to smaller regions and then region merging was performed. However some areas near the tongue boundary was not segmented due to shading caused from strobe light. Then local minimum was detected at the boundary of the tongue body which may be again difficult if boundary of the merged region is far away from real boundary. To find the real boundary, the discontinuity point with large difference between the current and next positions of the points on edge was found in each direction. Then the next point with local minima was detected at a new point moved progressing direction by one pixel from current point where direction in y direction for left and right boundaries or x direction from bottom boundary. However in case of flat tongue with small volume the shading can not appear at boundary. Hence color difference was performed. After local minimum correction and color edge detection curves are drawn in Catmul-Rom spline with sampled points of start, end and few midpoints. Finally edge smoothening using median filtering was performed. The method is illustrated in figure 5 and results are shown in figure 6.

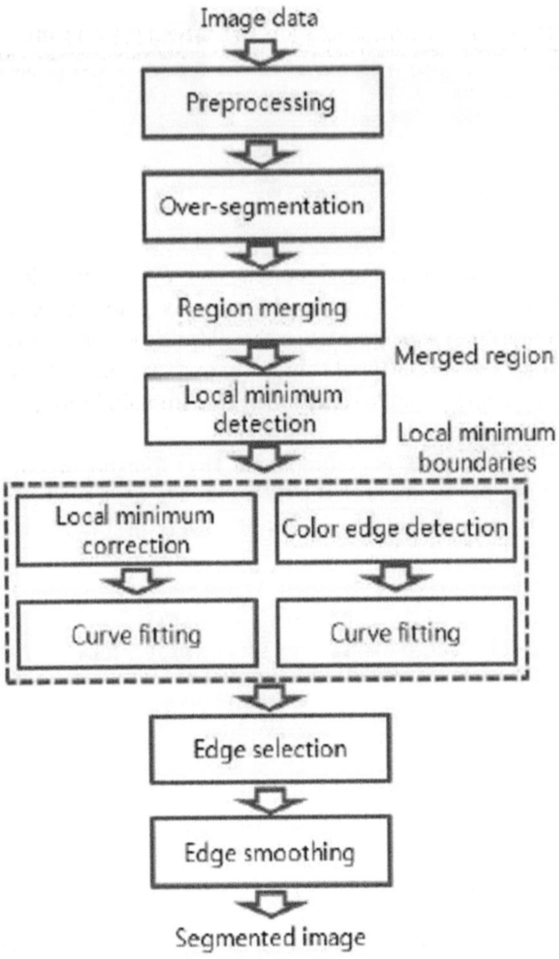

Fig. 5. Flowchart of proposed method [7]

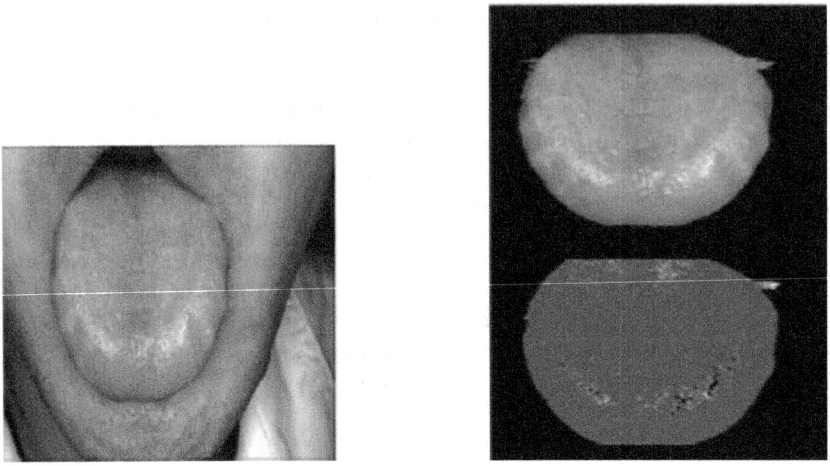

Fig. 6. Results using method illustrated in Figure 5

Tongue extraction using gradient vector flow [8] involves minimizing the energy function

$$E= \iint \mu(u_x^2 + u_y^2 + v_x^2 + u_y^2) + |\nabla f|^2 |v - \nabla f|^2 dxdy \quad (3)$$

for the gradient vector flow field to be the vector field v(x, y) = u(x,y),v(x, y)] and F is the edge map. To get good initialization contours the tongue image is transformed from RGB to HSV color space and component H is transformed in to binary image using median filtering. By combining the binary image of H-Component and contour of root part of the tongue, the GVF yield vectors that point in to boundary concavities as shown in Figure 7.

Tongue extraction accuracy can be increased by fusing more than one attribute say space information [9]. The hue and intensity values were used and experiments were conducted by assuming that characteristics of pixels in tongue area are similar and pixels are adjacent to each other in all directions. Thus aim of the proposed algorithm [9] is to minimize the function $\sum_{x_i \in s} |F(x_i) - F'|$ where $F(x_i)$ denotes the characteristics of pixel xi and F' denotes characteristics of object area and tongue. When this function is minimized an optimal homogenous tongue area can be obtained as shown in figure 8. In this method selection of appropriate initial pixel is very important to find full tongue area accurately. An initial pixel characteristic must be very similar to those of tongue area. However tongue of unhealthy person may not have completely homogenous pixel characteristics and may put limitations on this method.

Another method using double snake's model [10] was proposed to segment tongue area. Captured image was first filtered using median filtering and then transformed in to HIS color space. Two snakes were then used as shown in figure 9, one from inside and other from outside the tongue body to locate the tongue contour.

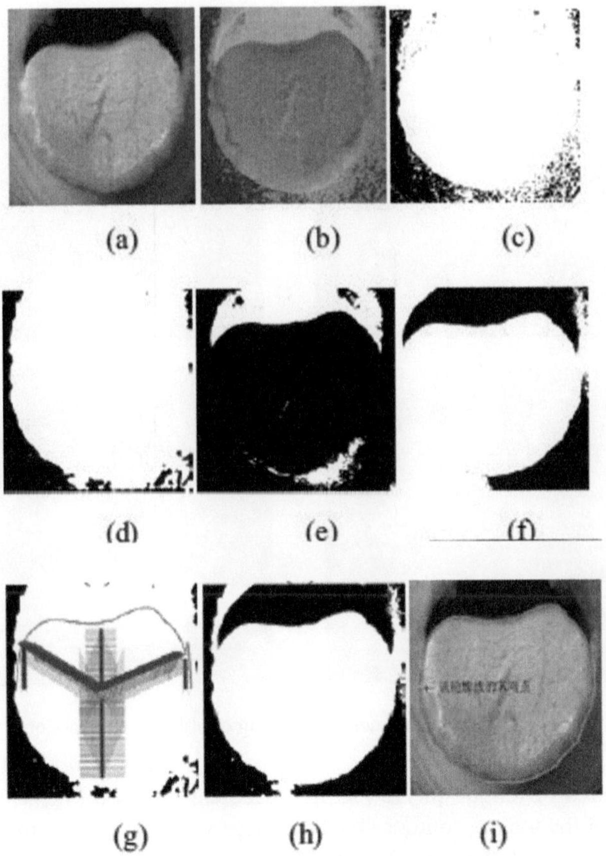

Fig. 7. Initialization of tongue contour

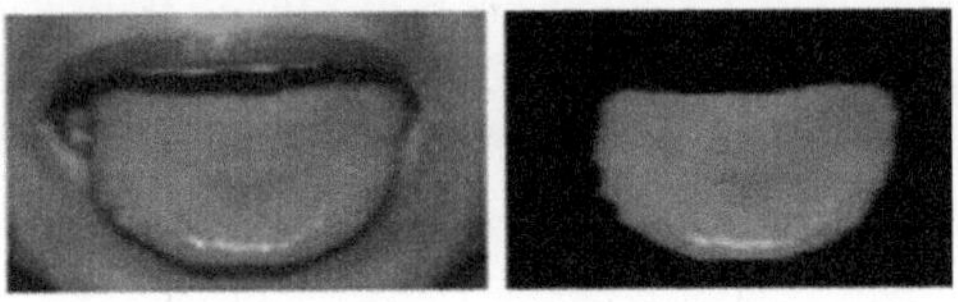

Fig. 8. Tongue extraction results

The hue statistics of skin tongue and lips are different. The value ranges between 15^0 and 60^0 for skin while that for tongue and lips are close to 0^0 and 360^0 respectively. This property can be used [11] to separate the tongue section from skin section. The centre of the tongue surface is detected and then borderline between tongue and skin was searched from outside to inside through polar co-ordinate conversion. The brightness of the pixels at intersection between the internal section of surface of the tongue and oral cavity and lower lip is used as basis of separation.

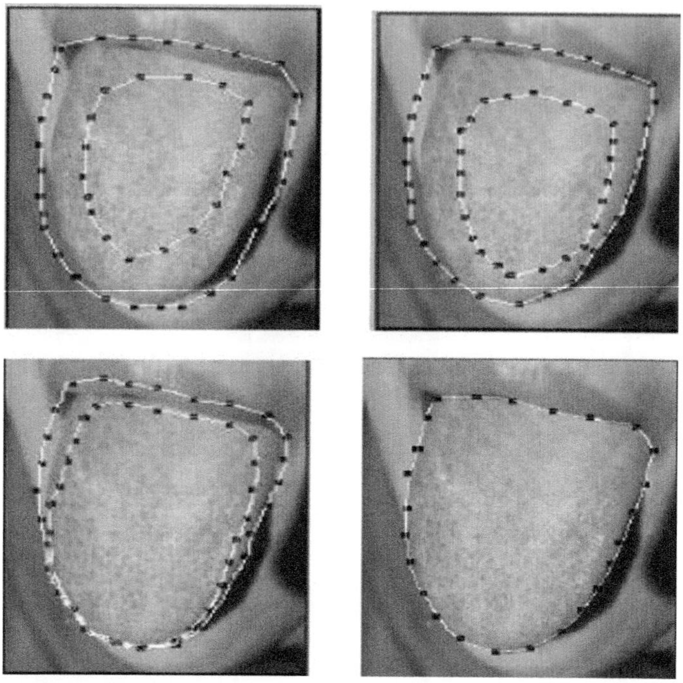

Fig. 9. Tongue segmentation using double snake's model

Color features of tongue in HSV color space can be used [12, 13] for automatic initialization of the tongue contour. Tongue image was first transformed from RGB to HSV color space and then its 'H' and 'V' components were were separated and converted in to binary image using following rule:

i. If the H or V component is more than 110 its value becomes 1.
ii. If the H or V component is less than 110 its value becomes 0.

Then these binary images representing 'H' and 'V' were fused to get initial contour of the tongue. The process is very much similar to that shown in figure 7 except for an improved level set algorithm which was used for convergence.

By using the well known Ostu's thresholding an appropriate thresholding can also be used to segment the tongue image [14,15]. The first step is to compute the histogram and probabilities of each intensity levels. Then the initializing the class probabilities w_i and class means μ_i to be updated after each iteration. Weights w_i are the probabilities of the two classes separated by threshold t. Then threshold is varied from t=1 to maximum intensity and after each iteration w_i and μ_i are updated and threshold corresponding to maximum variance or minimum intra class variance is obtained.

Recently authors [16] combined GVF, watershed segmentation and region merging to segment exact tongue area. Watershed transform was used for initial segmentation of tongue image. However since watershed segmentation is very sensitive to noise, to reduce over segmentation the image is first pre-processed by an effective edge preserving noise reduction method based on partial differential equation

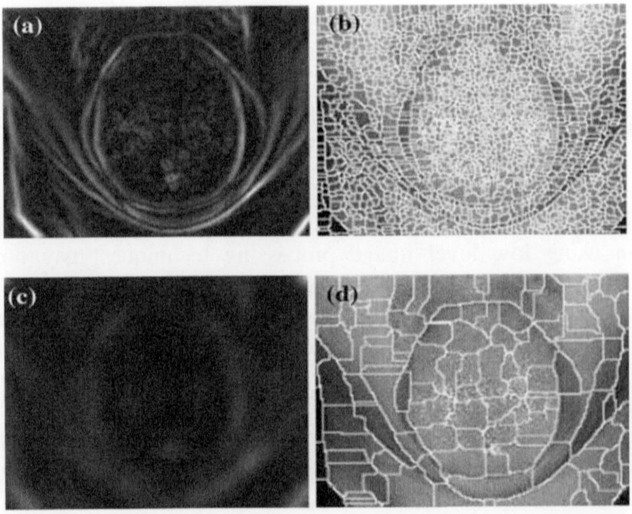

Fig. 10. (a) Gradient of tongue image. (b) Watershed segmentation of tongue in (a). (c) GVF Processing of (a). (d) Watershed segmentation of (c).

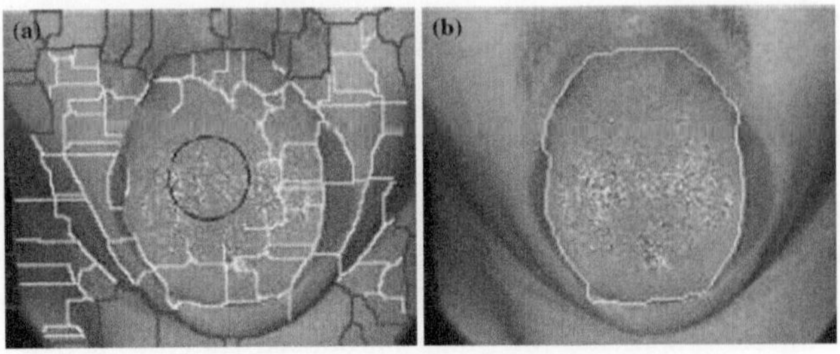

Fig. 11. (a) Markers gotten by prior knowledge. (b) Extracted Tongue contour by MSRM algorithm.

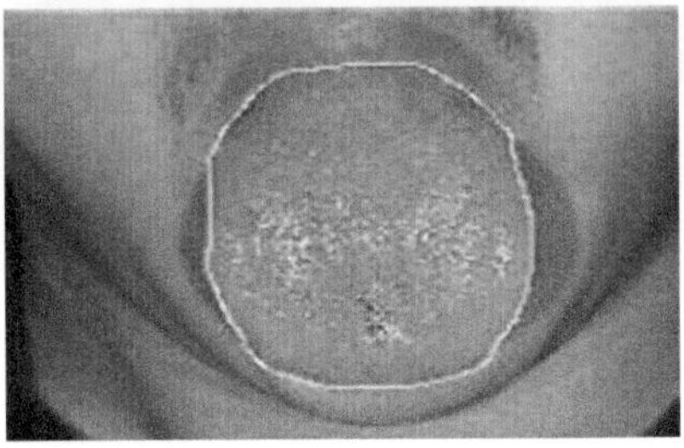

Fig. 12. Refined tongue contour by snakes algorithm

[GVF approach]. Watershed segmentation segments the image in to many small regions. Then region merging was used to extract exact tongue area. The two regions were merged if Bhattacharyya coefficient between histogram of two regions is maximally similar. This algorithm is called MSRM algorithm. After region merging snake algorithm was used to refine region merging result and thus extracting tongue region. The process is illustrated in figure 10, 11 and 12 respectively.

3 Conclusions

In this paper we reviewed and discussed various approaches used for extraction of exact tongue surface form its background consisting of lips, skin, chicks etc. Tongue segmentation using low level image processing techniques may not achieve the desired accuracy due to weak edges of tongue. Many authors proposed tongue segmentation using color features. However homogeneity of tongue color may change due to certain diseases and uneven lightning conditions. Thus segmentation of tongue using color features may give satisfactory results for homogenous tongue but may lack in accuracy if tongue color is non homogenous due to some disease or lightning conditions. Some authors also tried to find tongue surface by template matching. But such techniques require knowledge of a mathematical model or template and the shape must be fixed or should be flexible in terms of parameters that define the shape. Unfortunately the shape of the tongue is not fixed and it is really difficult to find parameters that exactly define the tongue area. Active contours or snakes proposed by some authors are flexible but its evolution is essentially controlled by local properties such as local curvature or strength of the edges which is very low in case of tongue images. The chosen range of parameters may have been learnt by extensive testing on the database of images of similar type to one used in application or selected by experience. The active contours have difficulties progressing in to boundary concavities. To solve this problem pressure forces, GVF etc. have been proposed, but they solve only one problem giving rise to new difficulties and not utilizing color information which often plays important role. Further the tongue segmentation using snakes may require large convergence number and spends too much time. A completely different approach was then introduced called as active shape modeling which involves laying down some landmark points as close as possible to cover the entire tongue surface covering all the sharp edges. This technique can give high accuracy but may consume more time in laying down the landmark points. Some authors also fused more than one technique to determine the initial contour of the tongue. Most of the present algorithms are very particular to generalize the initial contour very close to true boundary of the image otherwise the results may not converge to desired accuracy.

References

1. Akgul, Y.S., Kambhamettu, C., Stone, M.: Automatic Extraction of tongue Contours. IEEE Transactions on Medical Imaging 18(10), 1035–1045 (1999)
2. Pang, B., Wang, K., Zhang, D., Zhang, Zhang, F.: On Automated Tongue Image Segmentation in Chinese Medicine. In: Proceedings of 16th International Conference on Pattern Recognition (ICPR 2002), vol. 1, p. 10616 (2002)
3. Jang, J.H., Kim, J.E., Park, K.M., Park, S.O., Chang, Y.S., Kim, B.Y.: Development of the Digital Tongue Inspection System with Image Analysis. In: Proceedings of the Second Joint EMBSBMES Conference, Houstan, TX, USA, pp. 1033–1034 (October 2002)

4. Wu, J., Zhang, Y., Bai, J.: Tongue Area Extraction in Tongue Diagnosis of Traditional Chinese Medicine. In: Proceedings of the 2005 IEEE Engineering in Medicine and Biology 27th Annual Conference, Shanghai, China, September 1-4, pp. 4955–4957 (2005)
5. Zhi, L., Yan, J., Zhou, T., Tang, Q.: Tongue shape Detection Based on B-Spline. In: Proceedings of the Fifth International Conference on Machine Learning and Cybernetics, Dalian, August 13-16, pp. 3829–3832 (2006)
6. Ikeda, N., Fujiwara, Y., Yoshida, H.: Tongue diagnosis support system. In: Proceedings of SICE-ICASE International Joint Conference, Bexco, Busan, Korea, October 18-21, pp. 4464–4467 (2006)
7. Kim, K. H., Do, J.-H., Ryu, H., Kim, J-Y.: Tongue Diagnosis Method for Extraction of effective Region and Classification of Tongue Coating. In: Proceedings of First Workshop on Image Processing Theory, Tools and Applications, IPTA 2008, pp. 1–7 (November 23-26, 2008)
8. Li, W., Loo, J., Hu, S., Xu, J., Zhang, Z.: Towards the Objectification of Tongue Diagnosis: the Degree of Tooth marked. In: Proceedings of IEEE International Symposium on IT in Medicine and Education, pp. 592–595 (2008)
9. Ming-Feng, Z., Jian-Qiang, D., Kang, Z., Cheng-Hua, D.: A Novel Approach for Tongue Image Extraction Based on Combination of Color and Space Information. In: Proceedings of 3rd IEEE International Conference on Bioinformatics and Biomedical Engineering, ICBBE 2009, pp. 1–4 (2009)
10. Xue-ming, Z., Hang-dong, L., Li-zhong, Z.: Application of Image Segmentation Technique in Tongue Diagnosis. In: Proceedings of International Forum on Information Technology and Applications, pp. 768–771 (2009)
11. Lo, L.,Hou, M., Chen, Y., Chiang, J., Hsu, C.: Automatic Tongue Diagnosis system. In: Proceedings of 2nd International Conference on Biomedical Engineering and Informatics, BMEI 2009, pp. 1–5 (2009)
12. Li, W., Hu, S., Yao, J., Song, H.: The Separation Framework of Tongue Coating and Proper in Traditional Chinese Medicine. In: Proceedings of 7th International Conference on Information, Communications and Signal Processing, ICICS 2009 (2009)
13. Li, W., Hu, S., Wang, S., Xu, S.: Towards The Objectification of Tongue Diagnosis: Automatic Segmentation of Tongue Image. In: Proceedings of 35th Annual Conference of IEEE Industrial Electronics, IECON 2009, pp. 2121–2124 (2009)
14. Ostu, N.: A Threshold Selection Method from Gray Level Histogram. IEEE Transactions on Systems, Man and Cybernatics 9(2), 62–66 (1979)
15. Wei, C.C., Wang, C.H., Huang, S.W.: Using Threshold Method to Separate the Edge, Coating and Body of Tongue in Automatic Tongue Diagnosis. In: Proceedings of Sixth International Conference on Networked Computing and Advanced Information Management (NCM), pp. 653–656 (2010)
16. Ning, J., Zhang, D., Wu, C., Yue, F.: Automatic Tongue Image Segmentation Based on Gradient Vector Flow and Region Merging. Journal of Neural Computing and Applications (2010), doi:10.1007/s00521-010-0484-3

Efficient Broadcasting in Parallel Networks Using Network Coding

Nitin Rakesh[1] and Vipin Tyagi[2]

[1] Department of CSE, Jaypee University of Information Technology, Waknaghat, Dist. Solan, H.P., India
[2] Department of CSE, Jaypee University of Engineering and Technology, Guna, M.P., India
{nitin.rakesh,dr.vipin.tyagi}@gmail.com

Abstract. Before evolution of network coding, communication in multi-dimensional networks nominates store-and-forward approach. This approach limits information to process in an in-network manner. Furthermore, this traditional approach was unable to find efficient paths and became a bottleneck for several applications. Network coding was introduced as a remedy and offered a new way to transmit information over acyclic and cyclic networks. In this paper, we identified potential areas of network coding application in parallel architecture and specify the relevant facts and results. To diminish the issues of complexity, we have implemented Linear Network Coding (LNC) on 2D-Mesh as a parallel network. For verification of our approach, we have considered some 2D-Mesh architectures for implementing network coding approach, and we have examined our results on this network. We have developed a Parallel network coding approach, which reduces/removes information size and communication complexity exponentially with code length.

Keywords: Coding, Information Rate, Broadcasting, Routing.

1 Introduction

Network Coding evolved as an efficient approach for data communication [1-6]. It is observed that information rate from source node to sink can potentially become higher when coding scheme is wider [1]. Also it is proved constructively in [1] that by linear coding alone, that the rate at which a message reaches each node can achieve the individual max-flow bound. And provide realization of transmission scheme and practically construct linear coding approaches for both acyclic and cycled networks [1]. This approach shows that multicast of different data is possible when network coding is performed in the network. So, the coding of information does not increase the information content. The capacity of a network to transmit information from the source to destination can become higher if the coding scheme becomes wider but it is limited to max-flow for a very wide coding scheme [1].

Communication is performed on networks and networks can be acyclic or cyclic and single-source or multi-source. We are not concerned about the network topology but how much data and how fast it can be received by the destination node is an

D. Nagamalai, E. Renault, and M. Dhanushkodi (Eds.): PDCTA 2011, CCIS 203, pp. 484–494, 2011.

important issue. Let us consider two networks with single-source and multi-source data transmission (see figure 1). Figure 1 (a) shows single-source network with Þ$_1$ as a source node which transmits two bits (đ$_1$ and đ$_2$) to destination node Þ$_3$ and Þ$_7$. Similarly, figure 1 (b) shows multi-source network with Þ$_1$ and Þ$_2$ as source nodes which transmits đ$_1$ and đ$_2$ individually to destination Þ$_3$ and Þ$_4$ such that at the end Þ$_3$ and Þ$_4$ receives đ$_1$ and đ$_2$ both.

Now, this communication in figure 1 for both single-source and multi-source network is possible only using networks coding. This is the source of motivation to find the application of network coding for tribulations which can be resolved using network coding only. It is also necessary to find the areas in which network coding results more efficient and robust results. Communication means data transfer and for data transfer network coding is more prolific. In this paper we have identified such areas of applications which require network coding. We study network coding on 2D-Mesh network to substantiatethat this approach is effective and reduces the time complexity issues in parallel networks. We consider a general parallel multicast framework-multisource multicast, which is possible with correlated sources (see fig. 1).

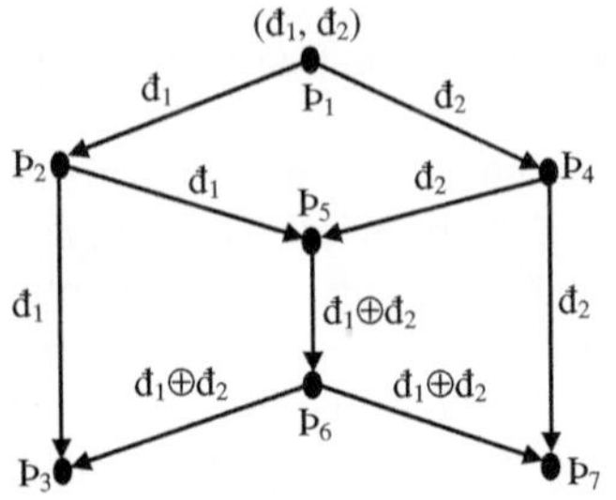

Fig. 1. Networks ($\check{N}$) used to explain LNC at different nodes to perform complete data transfer. Each link in these networks denotes data transmission.

Contemplate fig. 1, in which each ofthe incoming transmissions from source to destination nodehasawareness of complete linear combination of data set from source node (see fig. 1). This information is updated at each coding node by applying the same linear mapping to the coefficient vectors as applied to the information signals. Let the set of two bits (*đ*$_1$, *đ*$_2$) is multicast, in a parallel network, as in fig. 1, from the source *Þ*$_1$ to destination *Þ*$_3$ and *Þ*$_7$. Now, (*đ*$_1$, *đ*$_2$) is sent to node *Þ*$_2$ and *Þ*$_4$ of this network, *đ*$_1$ is received by *Þ*$_2$ and *đ*$_2$ is received by *Þ*$_4$. Then both *Þ*$_2$ and *Þ*$_4$ transfer the information further to *Þ*$_5$. Similarly, *Þ*$_5$ receives two diverse data from different sources andperform network coding (*đ*$_1$⊕*đ*$_2$) on the received data. This encoded data is sent from *Þ*$_5$ to *Þ*$_6$ and then from *Þ*$_6$ to *Þ*$_3$ and *Þ*$_7$. It is decoded to receive the data (*đ*$_1$, *đ*$_2$) at *Þ*$_3$ and *Þ*$_7$. This approach shows that multicast of diverseinformation is efficient when network coding is performed in the network.

We have implemented this approach with 2D-Mesh network and it results in efficient broadcasting manner of data by coding information. In this paper we study the behavior in 2D-Mesh and simulated results based on broadcast and computation issues. We analyzed the conditions with and without network coding. This paper shows that the problem of computation and communication at each node can either be removed or reduced. We reduce both of these problems by suggesting efficient broadcasting using network coding for parallel networks.

The remaining paper is organized in five sections. In section second, the problem is formulatedand the related work on these problems is indicated. Section third provides solution approach by providing efficient broadcasting mechanism in 2D-Mesh network. Section fourth, illustrates the benefits of network coding for 2D-Mesh and results states the proof of implementation and consolidates the results by means of simulation. In Section fifth, we are concluding this paper and future extensions to this approach are stated.

2 Problem Formulation and Related Work

2.1 Problem Formulation

A network in any of the phase of communication is said to be directed based on the flow of data with respect to the algorithm. A node without any input is said to be *source node* and nodes with one or more inputs is said to be *non-source node*. The set of non-source nodes contains the destination node. Let us reconsider the network in fig. 1 in which a single-source Þ_1 sends data through other nodes in the network to Þ_3 and Þ_7. Node Þ_5 receives multiple inputs at a unit of time. Now, either data from Þ_2 i.e. đ_1 or data from Þ_4 i.e. đ_2 can be received. This will create a setback to communication in this network. This can be resolved only by implementing network coding approach within this network. By coding nodes which receives multiple data at a unit of time will result in $\text{đ}_1 \oplus \text{đ}_2$. This XOR value will act as one data unit and can be easily received by other nodes having information of decoding scheme.

In parallel networks, the basic problem is fast receiving of complete and correct information at an optimal information rate and this communicationinvolves multiple nodes and all acting as sender as well as receiver. Moreover, the data communication in these networks is reliant on the network properties (bisection width, diameter, number of edges per nodes etc.). Subsequently, for data communication a common approach is requiredwhich is independent of network properties. As a solution, linear network coding can be used for both acyclic and cyclic directed parallel networks to provide efficient broadcasting and reduces the computation load of different nodes.

Now, let us formulate the problem by considering the 2D-Mesh network of size 4×4 (see fig. 2). The entire aim in this network is to send the information of all nodes to the destination node (node 16). This aim can be achieved by initiating the active processor [7] (node 1) and then the combination of remaining nodes (see fig. 3). In fig. 1, step 1, 2…5 denotes the participation of nodes in that step and the data size increases with the increase in the number of nodes. Let us explain the computing scenario in details. Node 1sends data to node 2 and 5, now, both 2 and 5 can either alliance the data, using network coding, received from node 1 or store either of the data and forward other to node 3. The traditional approach of data communication increases the communication time and the data storage at each node. Furthermore, at each node receiving multiple data, the computation time involved will increase and the requirements of storage at each node also increases for each transmission.

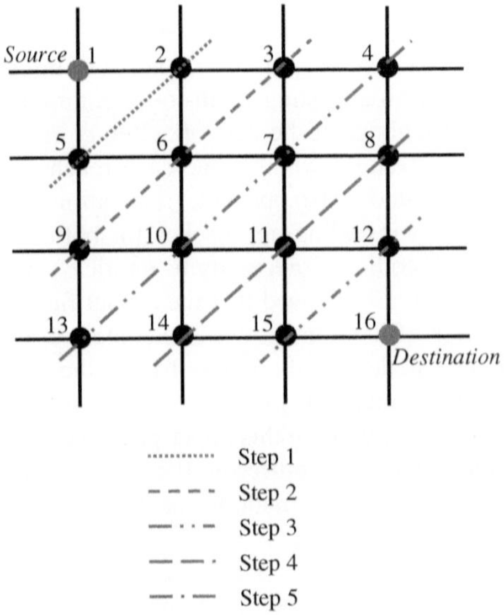

Fig. 2. 2D-Mesh Architecture

This approach of communication makes parallel architectures more complex and unfeasible in practical implementation. The energy required to perform broadcast on these networks is high as the computation and communication time at each node is increasing exponentially. These networks can become more efficient and feasible when the problem of computation and communication can either be removed or reduced. In this paper, we reduce both of these problems by suggesting energy efficient broadcasting using network coding for parallel networks.

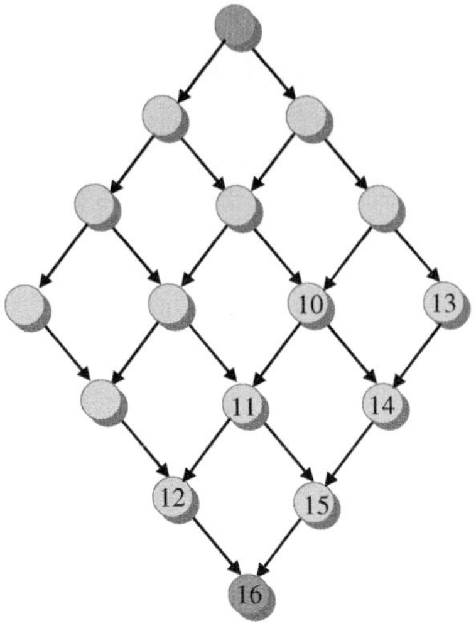

Fig. 3. Graph representation of2D-Mesh

2.2 Related Work

Shuo-Yen *et al.* [1] described an approach on network information flow and improved the performance in data broadcasting in all-to-all communication in order to increase the capacity or the throughput of the network. Yen *et al.* prove constructively that by linear coding alone, the rate at which a message reaches each node can achieve the individual max-flow bound. Also, provide realization of transmission scheme and practically construct linear coding approaches for both cyclic and acyclic networks. [1] shows that network coding is necessity to multicast two bits per unit time from a source to destinations. It also showed that the output flow at a given node is obtained as a linear combination of its input flows. The content of any information flowing out of a set of non-source nodes can be derived from the accumulated information that has flown into the set of nodes. [8] selected the linear coefficients in a finite field of opportune size in a random way. In this paper packetizing and buffering are explained in terms of encoding vector and buffering the received packets. It showed that each node sends packets obtained as a random linear combination of packets stored in its buffer and each node receives packets which are linear combinations of source packets and it stores them into a matrix. While Widmer *et al.* [9] gave an approach with energy efficient broadcasting in network coding.

Subsequent work by Fragouli *et al.* [10] gave two heuristics and stated that each node in the graph is associated with a forwarding factor. A source node transmits its source symbols (or packets) with some parameters bounded by this forwarding factor. And when a node receives an innovative symbol, it broadcast a linear combination over the span of the received coding vector. [11] deals with network coding of a single message over an acyclic network. Network coding over undirected networks was introduced by [12] and this work was followed by [13], [14] and [15]. The network codes that involve only linear mapping with a combination of global and local encoding mapping involves linear error-correction code [16], [17], [18] and [19] have also been presented.

3 Achieving Efficient Broadcasting

In this section we endeavor to reduce the problems in parallel networks as stated in above section. For this we need the requirements of network coding approach so that we can consider the above stated problem according to these requirements. Furthermore, these requirements are mapped on 2D-Mesh network to achieve the maximum network capacity and attain efficient broadcasting.

3.1 Necessities of Network Coding

To construct requirements for network coding let us consider the approaches and examples of Li *et al.* [1].Consider network as in fig. 4 in which $Þ_1$ is the source node and $Þ_2$, $Þ_4$, $Þ_5$ and $Þ_6$ are routing nodes between $Þ_1$ and $Þ_3$, $Þ_7$.The busy channels of network in fig. 1 do not form directed cycles; for example, consider the sub-network $\{Þ_1, Þ_2, Þ_5, Þ_6, Þ_3\}$ which is acyclic. For nodes except $Þ_1$ and $Þ_5$, the number of incoming busy channels is equal to outgoing busy channels andthe number of outgoing channels to $Þ_1$ is equals to number of incoming channels to $Þ_5$. Now, to minimize the number of nodes to be coded, let us consider Max-Flow Min-Cut Theorem, for every non-source node $Ᵽ_2$ (See fig.4 for explanation of Max-Flow Min-Cut), the minimum value of all cuts between $Ᵽ_1$ and $Ᵽ_2$ is equal to *maxflow*($Ᵽ_2$) [20, Ch. 4, Theorem 2.3].

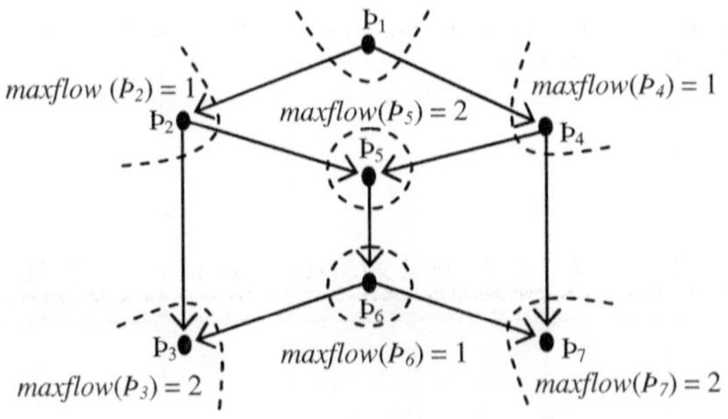

Fig. 4. Max-Flow for networkin fig. 1

Using the conventions defined by Li *et* al. [1], assume that d is the maximum *max-flow*($Ᵽ_2$) over all $Ᵽ_2$ and the symbol Ω denoted a d-dimensional vector space over large base field. Let us define *linear-code multicast* (*LCM*) ν on a communication network ($\check{N}$, $Ᵽ_1$) with vector space $\nu(Ᵽ_6)$ assigned to every node $Ᵽ_2$ and a vector $\nu(Ᵽ_6 Ᵽ_3)$ to every channel $Ᵽ_6 Ᵽ_3$ such that

1) $\nu(Ᵽ_1) = \Omega$;
2) $\nu(Ᵽ_6 Ᵽ_3) \in \nu(Ᵽ_6)$ for every channel $Ᵽ_6 Ᵽ_3$;
3) For φ, collection of non-source nodes in the network

$$\langle \nu(Ᵽ_2): Ᵽ_2 \in \varphi \rangle = \langle \{\nu(Ᵽ_6 Ᵽ_3): Ᵽ_6 \notin \varphi,\ Ᵽ_3 \in \varphi\} \rangle.$$

Example 1: Suppose in network $\check{N}$ of fig. 1, $Ᵽ_1$ multicast two bits $đ_1$ and $đ_2$ to destination nodes $Ᵽ_3$ and $Ᵽ_7$. This is achieved with the LCM ν specified by

$$\nu(Ᵽ_1 Ᵽ_2) = \nu(Ᵽ_2 Ᵽ_5) = \nu(Ᵽ_2 Ᵽ_3) = \binom{1}{0}$$

$$\nu(Ᵽ_1 Ᵽ_4) = \nu(Ᵽ_4 Ᵽ_5) = \nu(Ᵽ_4 Ᵽ_7) = \binom{0}{1}$$

$$\nu(Ᵽ_5 Ᵽ_6) = \nu(Ᵽ_6 Ᵽ_3) = \nu(Ᵽ_6 Ᵽ_7) = \binom{1}{1}$$

The data sent on a channel is the product of information vector with the assigned channel vector e.g. data set on $Ᵽ_5 Ᵽ_6$ is $đ_1 \oplus đ_2$.

3.2 Achieving Efficient Broadcasting in 2D-Mesh Network

We introduce efficient broadcasting in 2D-Mesh network with the aim to reduce the computation and communication time required to send data between different node of this network. For understandability of readers, let us consider a $n \times n$ 2D-Mesh network and all the nodes in this architecture are sources and receivers. Each node in 2D-Mesh can broadcast information to its closest connected neighboring nodes, so, communication is like square grid (see fig. 5).

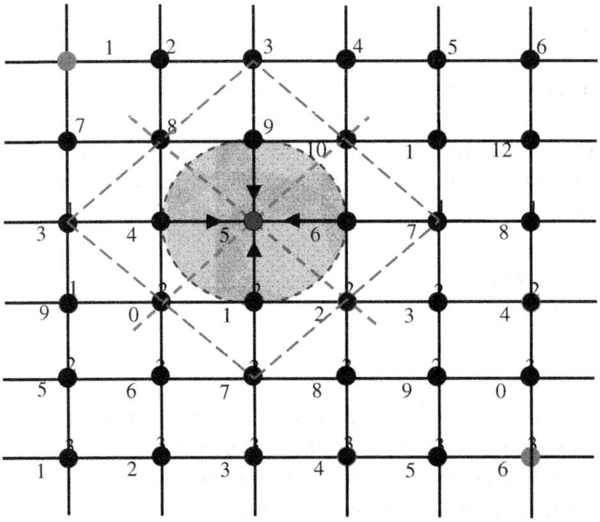

Fig. 5. Shows the data flow at node 15. The data from nodes 9, 14, 16 and 21 reaches to node 15. Node 15 performs XOR operation on this data set. After this operation node 15 will send {9⊕14⊕16⊕21} to nodes 9, 14, 16, 21.

The communication in above manner, data from node 9, 14, 16 and 21 will reach node 15. This means that in every transmission four node's data reaches to the center node. The data is the XORed to result in one data i.e. the information at the center node 15, after receiving data from 9, 14, 16 and 21 will be:

$$y_{15} = g_9 x_9 + g_{14} x_{14} + g_{16} x_{16} + g_{21} x_{21}$$

where, y is the information field and $y_{15} \in y$, and y is associated with an encoding vector g, where $\{g_9, g_{14}, g_{15}, g_{16}, g_{21}\} \in g$. Similarly, x_i is the data symbol from node i. Assuming $g_9 \rightarrow g`_1$, $g_{14} \rightarrow g`_{14}$, $g_{16} \rightarrow g`_{16}$, $g_{21} \rightarrow g`_{21}$. Similarly,$y_9 \rightarrow$ ly,$y_9 \rightarrow y`_1$, $y_{14} \rightarrow y`_{14}$, $y_{16} \rightarrow y`_{16}$, $y_{21} \rightarrow y`_{21}$ and $x_9 \rightarrow x`_1$, $x_{14} \rightarrow x`_{14}$, $x_{16} \rightarrow x`_{16}$, $x_{21} \rightarrow x`_{21}$.

Now, the matrix formed at encoding end will be as followed:

$$\begin{bmatrix} g`_1 & 0 & 0 & 0 \\ 0 & g`_2 & 0 & 0 \\ 0 & 0 & g`_3 & 0 \\ 0 & 0 & 0 & g`_4 \end{bmatrix} \begin{matrix} y`_1 \\ y`_2 \\ y`_3 \\ y`_4 \end{matrix} \rightarrow \begin{bmatrix} 1 & 0 & 0 & 0 \\ 0 & 1 & 0 & 0 \\ 0 & 0 & 1 & 0 \\ 0 & 0 & 0 & 1 \end{bmatrix} \begin{matrix} x`_1 \\ x`_2 \\ x`_3 \\ x`_4 \end{matrix}$$

Assuming that the data at $g`_1 = [1\ \ 0\ \ 0\ \ 0]$, $g`_2 = [0\ \ 1\ \ 0\ \ 0]$, $g`_3 = [0\ \ 0\ \ 1\ \ 0]$ and $g`_4 = [0\ \ 0\ \ 0\ \ 1]$. So, the data received by the destination node is the XOR of these data values.

$$\begin{array}{rcccc} & 1 & 0 & 0 & 0 \\ & 0 & 1 & 0 & 0 \\ & 0 & 0 & 1 & 0 \\ + & 0 & 0 & 0 & 1 \\ \hline & 1 & 1 & 1 & 1 \\ \hline \end{array}$$

This is data of same size which the destination node contains previously, i.e., using network coding for broadcasting information between different nodes in a parallel network reduces the issues of data size. Considering, traditional approach to communicate for same data set and between same nodes i.e. nodes 9, 14, 16 and 21 results in an array having four data values at different locations. The size of this array increases with the increase in data communication between the nodes. This increasing data size increases the storage at each node for each communication step (see fig. 6).

Array [0]	Array [1]	Array [2]	Array [3]
[1 0 0 0]	[0 1 0 0]	[0 0 1 0]	[0 0 0 1]

Fig. 6. Storage requirements for data of 9, 14, 16 and 21 nodes. This size increases with the increase in communication.

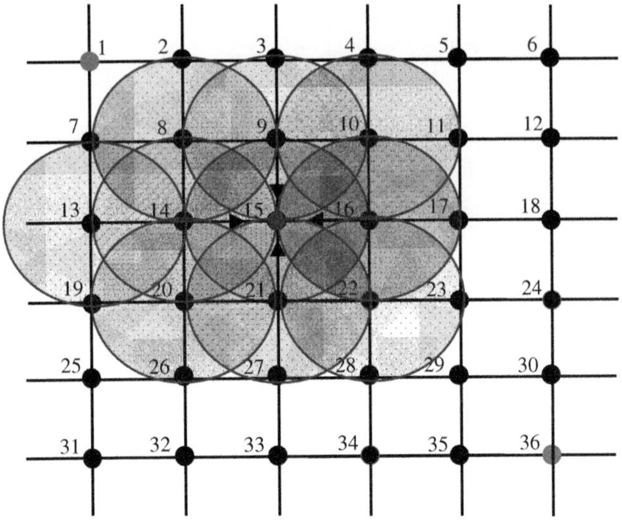

Fig. 7. The data size increases as the communication increases. The above figure shows how data size in a 2D-Mesh increases with the increase in communication using traditional store and forward approach.

According to the traditional approach of communication in parallel networks the communication and computation time depends upon the size of data (see fig. 7). The data accumulation at each node increases and it makes an increase in the size of data. The conventional approach of data communication in parallel networks do not provide efficient broadcasting possible. This is proved so that network coding not only reduces the data size but also increases the efficiency of communication in 2D-Mesh parallel network by performing XOR on the received set of data.

4 Simulations and Results

Let us consider 2D-Mesh network and study data communication without using network coding. Let us assume that in fig. 8 the source node sends data to its neighboring node. In step 1 the data size increases at receiving nodes and itturn into two bits each. During communication at step 2, two receiving node obtain data of size three bits each and otherachieve data size five. Likewise, till last step the data size will increase to thirty four bits. Finally, destination node receives data of size sixty eight from its previous node; combining both size of this node becomes sixty nine. This shows that communication without network coding in 2D-Mesh network is very incompetent. The results for this scenario is shown in fig. 9.

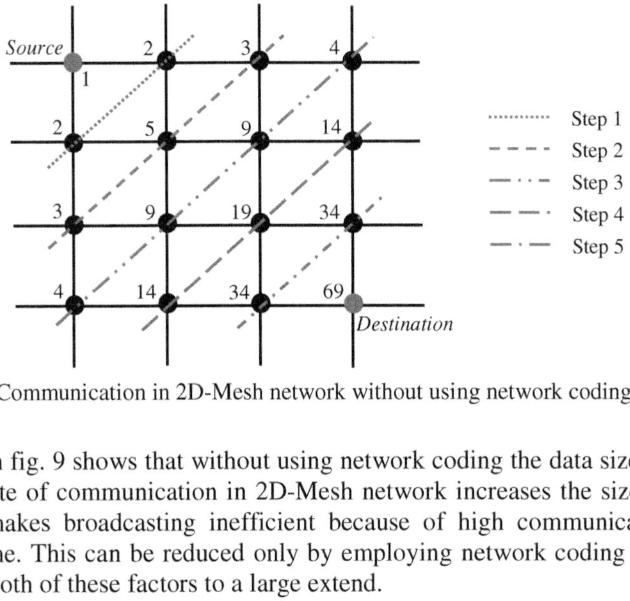

Fig. 8. Communication in 2D-Mesh network without using network coding

The results in fig. 9 shows that without using network coding the data size increases and as the rate of communication in 2D-Mesh network increases the size also increases. This makes broadcasting inefficient because of high communication and computation time. This can be reduced only by employing network coding approach which reduces both of these factors to a large extend.

Considering above assumptions for communication in 2D-Mesh network. The communication within this network using network coding decreases the data size at each step. The source node transfers data to neighboring nodes and the receiving node encodes the data received with their own data. Now this XOR data is one bit size and is further XORed to result other one bit data at respective nodes. This process is

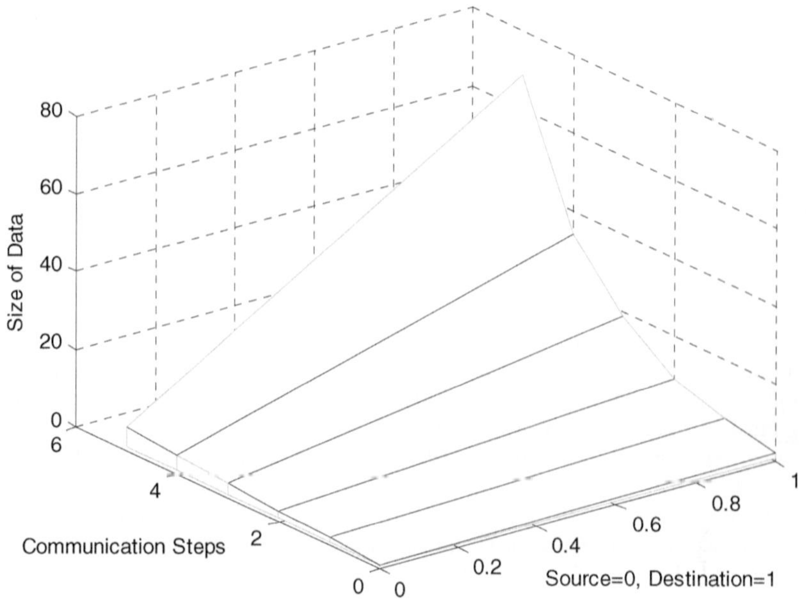

Fig. 9. Increase in data size as the data from source reaches the destination at different communication steps. The data size grows exponentially as the communication increases.

performed till the complete information is received at destination node which will finally get one bit information at destination node.The approach of network coding with this parallel network provides efficient method in communication. Also, due to decrease in data size of nodes receiving data, the complication of data communication between different nodes can also reduce.

5 Conclusion and Future Work

This paper provides an application of network coding in the field of parallel network. We have proved that network coding provides an efficient broadcasting mechanism for 2D-Mesh network by reducing the data size requirements at each node. The result shows that network coding is a innovative development in the field of parallel communication. It provides network capacity gain during data communication. We have also proved that implementation of this approach reduces the communication and computation complexity of parallel communication. As, communicational and computational complexities are the major issues in the development of network overhead, this approach resolves these major problems from 2D-Mesh network.

The extension to this approach with respect to network independent parameters is still obligatory to be researched. Factors like traffic controlling in parallel network, probability of data identification at any destination, implementation of network coding only at compulsory nodes and many such issues are still to be prepared and examined.

References

1. Li, S.-Y.R., Yeung, R.W., Cai, N.: Linear network coding. IEEE Trans. Information Theory 49, 371–381 (2003)
2. Yang, M., Yang, Y.: A Hypergraph Approach to Linear Network Coding in Multicast Networks. IEEE Transactions on Parallel and Distributed Systems 21, 968–982 (2009)
3. Cai, N.: Valuable messages and random outputs of channels in linear network coding. In: Proceedings of the 2009 IEEE International Conference on Symposium on Information Theory, vol. 1, pp. 413–417 (2009)
4. Chou, P.A., Wu, Y.: Network coding for the internet and wireless networks. IEEE Signal Processing Mag., 77–85 (2007)
5. Yeung, R.W., Li, S.-Y.R., Cai, N., Zhang, Z.: Network coding theory: A tutorial. Foundation and Trends in Communications and Information Theory 2, 241–381 (2006)
6. Lin, Y., Li, B., Liang, B.: Stochastic analysis of network coding in epidemic routing. IEEE Journal on Selected Areas Communication 26, 794–808 (2008)
7. Quinn, M.J.: Parallel Computing: Theory and Practice, Tata. Mcgraw Hill, New York (1994)
8. Chou, P.A., Wu, Y., Jain, K.: Practical Network Coding. In: Proc. 41st Annual Allerton Conference on Communication, Control and Computing (2003)
9. Widmer, J., Fragouli, C., Boudec, J.–Y.L.: Low-complexity energy-efficient broadcasting in wireless ad-hoc networks using network coding. In: Proc. Network Coding, Theory, and Applications Workshop (2005)
10. Fragouli, C., Widmer, J., Boudec, J.-Y.L.: A network coding approach to energy efficient broadcasting: from theory to practice. In: Proc. of IEEE International Conference on Computer Communications (2006)
11. Li, S.-Y.R., Yeung, R.W.: On the Theory of Linear Network Coding. Submitted to IEEE Trans. Inform. Theory
12. Li, Z., Li, B.: Network coding in undirected networks. In: Proc. 38th Annual Conference on Information Sciences and Systems, Princeton, NJ, pp. 17–19 (2004)
13. Kramer, G., Savari, S.A.: Cut sets and information flow in networks of two-way channels. In: Proc. IEEE International Symposium on Information Theory (2004)
14. Argawal, A., Charikar, M.: On the advantage of network coding for improving network throughput. In: Proc. IEEE Information Theory Workshop (2004)
15. Rasala-Lehman, A.: Network coding. Massachusetts Institute of Technology, Department of Electrical Engineering and Computer Science (2005)
16. Berlekamp, E.R.: Blockcoding for the binary symmetric channel with noise-less, delay-less, feedback in Error Correcting Codes. In: Mann, H.B. (ed.). Wiley, New York (1968)
17. Lin, S., Costello Jr., D.J.: Error control coding: Fundamentals and applications. Prentice-Hall, Englewood Cliffs (1983)
18. Blahut, R.E.: Theory and practice of error control codes. Addison-Wesley, Massachusetts (1983)
19. Wicker, S.B.: Error control systems for digital communication and storage. Prentice Hall, Englewood Cliffs (1995)
20. Lawler, E.L.: Combinatorial Optimization: Network and Matroid. Saunder College Pub., Fort Worth (1976)

A Fast Adaptive Replication Placement for Multiple Failures in Distributed System

Sanjay Bansal[1], Sanjeev Sharma[2], and Ishita Trivedi

[1] Chameli Devi School of Engineering
Rajiv Gandhi Prodhyogiki Vishwavidya
Indore, India
Sanju2.bansal@gmail.com
[2] School of Information Technology
Rajiv Gandhi Prodhyogiki Vishwavidya
Bhopal, India
sanjeev@rgtu.net

Abstract. Replicated Checkpointing is emerging as a scalable fault tolerance technique. The fault tolerance capability is severely limited by number of replicas as well as improper replica placements. Dynamic generation of more replicas for mission critical and important data and their efficient placement requires high overheads due to computation again from initial stage. The performance becomes a severe problem for larges numbers of process or data need to replicate at run time again and again. Such increase of fault tolerance capability is bottleneck by rapid degradation of performance due to high overheads. In this paper we propose an algorithm disjoint algorithm which will not place the extra replicas without recomputing from initial stage but also will place replicas at totally disjoint set of nodes. This will avoid the system to break down the system from link or switch failure. This paper proposed architecture as well as experimental result to show effectiveness of proposed approach.

Keywords: Replica Placement, Distributed System, Replica on Demand.

1 Introduction

Distributed Computing uses multiple geographically distant computers and solves computationally intensive task efficiently [1]. There are certain strong reasons that justify using distributed computing in comparison to single powerful computer like mainframes. Cluster computing is one way to perform distributed computing. Several computing nodes connected together form a cluster. Several Loosely coupled clusters of workstations are connected together by high speed networks for parallel and distributed applications. Cluster computing offers better price to performance ratio than mainframes. If one machine crashes, the system as a whole can still survive in distributed system. Computing power can be added in small increments in distributed systems. In this way incremental growth can be achieved. Cluster computing has increased in popularity due to greater cost-effectiveness and performance. Recent advancement in processors and interconnection technologies has made clusters more reliable, scalable, and affordable [2].

D. Nagamalai, E. Renault, and M. Dhanushkodi (Eds.): PDCTA 2011, CCIS 203, pp. 495–502, 2011.

Fault-tolerance is an important and critical issue in cluster computing. Due to very large size and computation complexity, the chances of fault are more. As the size of clusters increases, mean time to failure decreases. Most of time, such failures are not due to one fault but due to more than one fault. M.J. Fischer raise the issue that any protocol can be overwhelmed by faults that are too frequent or too severe, so the best that one can hope for is a protocol that is tolerant to a prescribed number of "expected" faults[3]. In such a situation, inclusion of fault tolerance is very essential. There are certain areas like air traffic control, railways signaling control, online banking and distributed disaster system high dependability and availability is essential. In absence of sufficient multiple fault tolerance, huge human lives and money could be lost. Hence there is a strong need for improved algorithms for multiple fault tolerance with performance.

John Paul Walter proposed a checkpointing based replication [4]. Replication is done on different computing nodes instead of dedicated checkpointing server in order to reduce the overheads. Number of replicas decides the number of faults it can tolerate. Replication placement is one of the crucial aspects for high dependability. Placing the different replicas on nearby nodes may prone to breakdown just due to switch failure. As the number of replicas increases fault tolerant capability increased but cost also increases drastically. Instead of uniform replicas for all data one may opt for more replicas for critical and important data or process and less for less critical and less important data. These all approaches and issues are addressed in this paper. In section two we have proposed architecture for replica on demand.

2 Related Work

Replica placement is one of the important issues for high dependable distributed system. Replica placement deal with how many different should be deployed and how to locate them. Replica placements become more crucial for dynamic distributed system. D.L McCue et. suggested a need of dynamic and adaptable replica placement[5]. A dynamic replica placement architecture is proposed by Byoung-Dai Lee for dynamic number of replicas [BL,01].These dynamic and adaptive replica placement policies must ensure performance over long period of system operation. Jaun Calos Leonardo et.al. propose an adaptable replication scheme for reliable distributed object oriented computing. He proposed an adaptable replication scheme that permits replacement of down replicas or change the number of replicas when partial failures occur and chooses the most adequate consistency protocol for the current configuration [7]. However he has not address the issue of none varying the replicas at run time for some important processes to enhance the fault tolerant capability at run time. Xueyan Tang proposed a polynomial-time algorithm is then proposed to compute the optimal replication strategy which designates where each object should be replicated and how to keep the replicas up-to-date [8].However the minimal cost replication problem under dynamic replication creation is not addressed here. Qiao Lian el.at proposed a analytical framework to reason and quantify the impact of replica placement policy to system reliability. In this framework he addressed impact of replication placement on handling multiple failures [9]. Bassam A. Alqaralleh also addresses the need of adaptive replica placement strategy [10]. Wei FU et. proposed a QOS aware replica placement[11]. Vinodh Venkatesan investigated impact of various replica placements on reliability of system [12]. The Random Node Selection algorithm originally designed by Sankaran et. al., revised by John Paul Walters and Vipin Chaudhary, aimed to place replica at some far random node rather than placing it near the critical place. The goal is to randomly generate 'r' replicas per node, subject to certain constraints [4].S.bansal el.at. proposed stair case based replication algorithm[13].We have proposed a algorithm in this paper in order to place the replicas on disjoined nodes in case new nodes join to the system or number of replicas are increased for important processes or nodes.

3 Formal Description of Architecture

Architecture of proposed adaptive disjoint replication placement is shown in fig1. It consist of following modules.

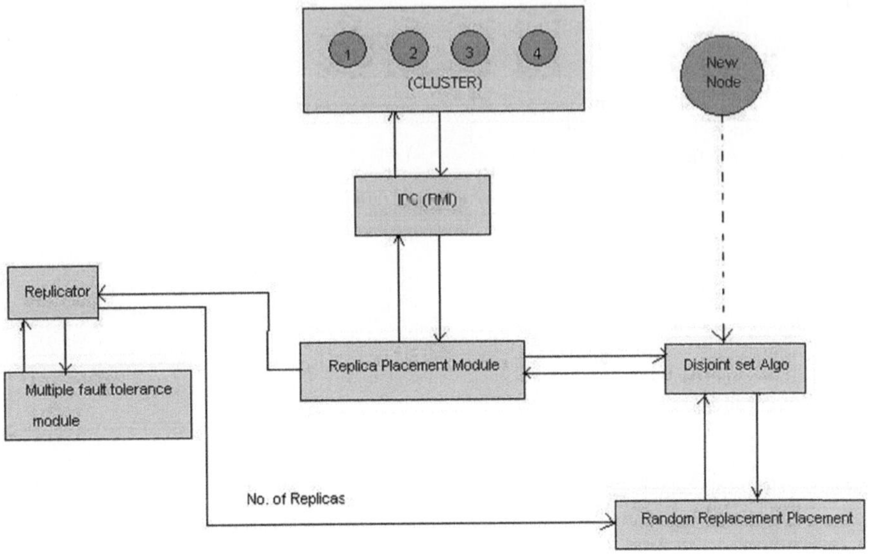

Fig. 1. Architecture of Proposed Replica Placement for Dynamic Distributed System

3.1 Distributed System

It consists of geographically distant computers or nodes with Remote Method Invocation.

3.2 Multiple Fault Tolerance Modules

It decides the fault tolerance capability of different nodes and process. Replica numbers corresponding to some nodes or processes are varied at run time. Placement of these run time replicas or replica on demand is done by the disjoint algorithm module with very minimal cost.

3.3 Replica Placement Module

We have used following algorithm 1 proposed by John Paul Walter with following assumptions.

1. A node should not replicate to itself.
2. A node should replicate to exactly r nodes, each of which may only store r replicas.
3. Each of a node's r replicas should be unique.

The algorithm proposed by John Paul Walter for replica placement is as follows

```
Algorithm 1. Compute random replica placements
Input: Integer r, the number of replicas
Input: Integer n, the number of nodes
Output: Replica array, Replicas [0...n - 1][0...r - 1]
for all i such that 0 = i < n do
Preload node i's replicas with i
end for
Circular-shift each column (j index) of Replicas
    by column index - 1
for all i such that 0 = i < n do
for all j such that 0 = j < r do
repeat
z = random node, s.t. 0 = z < n
v = Replicas[z][j]
until z  = i
if v  = i and Replicas[i][j]  = z then
valid replica = 1
for all k such that 0 = k < r do
if Replicas[i][k] == v or Replicas[i][j] == Replicas[z][k] then
valid replica = 0
end if
end for
if valid replica then
Replicas[z][j] = Replicas[i][j]
Replicas[i][j] = v
end if
end if
end for
end for
```

It has no provision for the replicas generated at run time for existing node as well as new nodes arrival. Replicas placement for new node arrival or additional replicas generated at run time is done by disjoint module.

3.4 Disjointing Module

This module only take care about placement of replica of following two cases

Case 1: When New Node needed to be inserted in an already developed distributed system.

Case 2: When number of replicas required to be increased for some important and crucial data. This module does not disturb too many already placed replicas. This only computes placement of additional replicas for either cases.The algorithm used by this module is as follows

Algorithm 2. Disjoint Algo: Compute runs time and new replica placements

```
1:-while new nodes are joined
2: for all such that 0 = i < n do
3: Preload node nn's replicas with r replica of itself(number of replicas)
4: end for
5 While (no of new nodes * replica)
6. for all k= 1 to r/2-1( number of replicas at every node)
7   Take a random node j;
8. Remove node j from list
9 If replica (j+k) exist
10 Exchange replica j+k with new node replica
11 end if
12 end while
13 if number of replicas are increase for some or all nodes
14 preload addition replicas to itself
15.   for m=1 to dr(additional replicas of r nodes)
16 choose a random node k
17   (if k==m)
18 continue
19 end if
20   if (m replica already exists ) than
21 continue;
20 else
21 transfer extra replica to m node
23 remove k from node list;
23 end for
```

4 Experimental Set Up

We have performed a experiment on 64 nodes. Distributed environment is set up by Remote Method Invocation. The simulation creates an interactive distributed environment that shows the dynamic changes as follows:

Case 1: When New Node needed to be inserted in a already developed distributed system.

Case 2: When number of replicas required to be increased in an already developed distributed system to improve its fault tolerance capability.

5 Result

We obtain following results as shown in Table 1. Result is obtained by simulating the algorithm in RMI based distributed computing. Since proposed algorithm eliminates the need of computation from initial stage, performance is improved. Once all placement of replica done and if extra replicas are generated either due to new nodes arrival or due to increase of replicas for existing node than computation is required for only extra replicas instead of all.

Table 1. Performance comparison after new nodes are added

No of nodes initially	Number of new nodes joining	Replica Placement Time in (ms)	
		Purposed Method	Simple
8	4	95	145
12	8	123	247
20	16	212	349
36	18	324	567

6 Graphical Representation

In this section a graph is plotted for results obtained in section 5. Graphical presentation is shown below in fig 2.

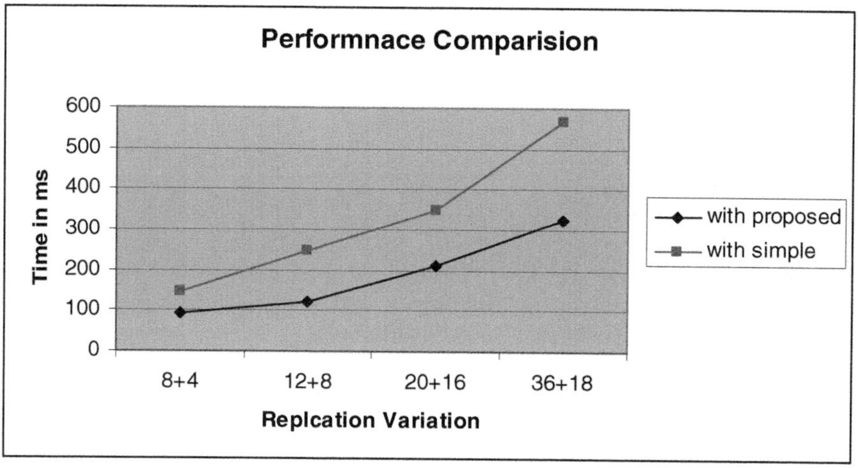

Fig. 2. Graphical Representation for Result Obtain

7 Conclusion

From the result table and graphical representation it is clear that proposed approach takes less time as compare to simple non adaptive placement approach that computes the placement from initial stage if number of replica changes rapidly or new nodes joins the distributed system. Our approach is adaptive to change in number of replicas of each process or some process. In case of new nodes arrival the disjoint module only compute placement for new nodes replicas without doing much computation for all existing replicas. It takes less bandwidth and latency since only fever number of replica or moved in distributed system in case of significant number of new nodes joins to the distributed system. Fault tolerance capability is also improved since placements of replicas are done on disjoined nodes. In case of several nodes failure of same link, disjoint replica placement increases dependability of distributed system as well.

References

1. Georgina, G.: D5.1 Summary of parallelization and control approaches and their exemplary application for selected algorithms or applications, LarKC/2008/D5.1 /v0.3, pp. 1–30
2. Buyya, R.: High Performance Cluster Computing: Architectures and Systems, vol. 1. Prentice-Hall, Englewood Cliffs (1999)
3. Fischer, M.J., Lynch, N.A., Paterson, M.S.: Impossibility of Distributed Consensus with One Faulty Process. Journal of the Assccktion for Computing Machinery 32(2), 374–382 (1985)
4. Walters, J.P., Chaudhary, V.: Replication-Based Fault Tolerance for MPI Applications. IEEE Transactions oN Parallel and Distributed Systems 20(7) (July 2009)
5. McCue, D.L., Liule, M.C.: Computing Replica Placement in Distributed Systems (1992), 0-8186-3170492 $3.00 Q 1992 IEEE
6. Lee, B.-D., Weissman, J.B.: Dynamic Replica Management in the Service Grid (2001), 0-7695-1296-8/01 $10.00 *0* 2001 IEEE
7. Leonardo, J.C., Yoshida, T.: An Adaptable Replication Scheme for Reliable Distributed Object-Oriented Computing. In: Proceedings of the17 th International Conference on Advanced Information Networking and Applications, AINA 2003 (2003), 0-7695-1906-7/03 $17.00 © 2003 IEEE
8. Tang, X., Chanson, S.T.: Minimal Cost Replication of Dynamic Web Contents under Flat Update Delivery. IEEE Transactions on Parallel and Distributed Systems 15(5) (May 2004)
9. Lian, Q., Chen, W., Zhang, Z.: On the Impact of Replica Placement to the Reliability of Distributed Brick Storage Systems. In: Proceedings of the 25th IEEE International Conference on Distributed Computing Systems, ICSCS 2005 (2005), 1063-6927/05 $20.00 © 2005 IEEE
10. Alqaralleh, B.A., Wang, C., Zhou, B.B., Zomaya, A.Y.: Effects of Replica Placement Algorithms on Performance of structured Overlay Networks, 1-4244-0910-1/07/$20.00 ©2007 IEEE

11. Fu, W., Xiao, N., Lu, X.: A Quantitative Survey on QoS-aware Replica Placement. In: 2008 Seventh International Conference on Grid and Cooperative Computing (2008), 978-0-7695-3449-7/08 $25.00 © 2008 IEEE, doi:10.1109/GCC.2008.23
12. Venkatesan, V., Iliadis, I., Hu, X.-Y., Haa, R.: Effect of Replica Placement on the Reliability of Large-Scale Data Storage Systems. In: 2010 18th Annual IEEE/ACM International Symposium on Modeling, Analysis and Simulation of Computer and Telecommunication Systems (2010) 1526-7539/10 $26.00 © 2010 IEEE
13. Bansal, S., Sharma, S., Trivedi, I.: A novel stair-case replication (SCR) based fault tolerance for MPI applications. In: Das, V.V., Thomas, G., Lumban Gaol, F. (eds.) AIM 2011. CCIS, vol. 147, pp. 445–448. Springer, Heidelberg (2011), doi:10.1007/978-3-642-20573-6_80

A Distributed Algorithm for Power-Efficient Data Gathering in Randomly-Distributed Wireless Sensor Networks

Antonella Di Stefano and Giovanni Morana*

University of Catania, Catania 95125 , Italy
{ad,gmorana}@diit.unict.it

Abstract. This article proposes a robust and power efficient technique for data gathering in randomly distributed wireless sensor networks. This solution, based on a self organized distributed algorithm, combines the benefits of the chain-based and cluster-based solutions to obtain, for each sensor, a particular arrangement of neighborhood relationship. This allows sensors to autonomously manage and balance the data flow (transmitted/received) with the other sensors obtaining, at the same time, a low power consumption and a high scalability.

Keywords: WSN, Power Consuming, Sensors, Tree organization, Distributed Algorithm.

1 Introduction

One of the most challenging issues in the field of WSN research concerns the design of a power-efficient strategy for the collection of sensed data. Currently, the most effective solutions are based on two different classes of hierarchical approach: cluster-based [2000, 2004, 2009] and chain-based solutions [2002, 2006]. This paper proposes a new hierarchical approach based on a self-organized distributed algorithm that combines the benefits of the chain-based and cluster-based solutions to obtain a tree-based arrangement of the sensors. This allows a better management of the lifetime of the network, reducing the power consumed during the operations of data transmission/reception. In particular, the solution proposed obtains great advantages in the management of data fusion and in-networking computing. It eliminate the problems of sensors clustering and cluster head election typical of the cluster-based solutions and, at the same time, chains building in the chain-based ones. The rest of the paper is organized as follows. After presenting the related work in Section 2, Section 3 discusses and compares the proposed solution with cluster-based and chain based approaches, highlighting the critical aspects that the proposed solution overcame. Section 4 explains in detail the protocol proposed to create the tree. Section 5 evaluates the performance of prosed algorithm for some simulation scenarios and discusses the obtained results. Finally, brief conclusion is given in Section 6.

* Corresponding author.

D. Nagamalai, E. Renault, and M. Dhanushkodi (Eds.): PDCTA 2011, CCIS 203, pp. 503–512, 2011.

2 Related Work

The scientific literature have proposed several techniques [2000, 2002, 2004, 2009] for managing power consumption in WSNs.

The clustering techniques are based on the fact that a limited amount of sensors with an higher energy level collects the data gathered from their neighbors and take charge of the expensive process of transmitting data to the BS (after a process of data fusion and aggregation). The sensor that takes care of transmission to base station is called cluster head (CH). Each cluster head, collects the information transmitted by a set of close sensors (avoiding, in this way, many long-distance transmissions) and transmits the summary packet to the base station, directly or via multi-hops, in order to minimize the quantity of battery consumption for all the sensors belonging to the cluster. To avoid an excessive battery consumption on cluster heads, the process of data gathering is divided in round (having a given time duration) and, for each round, a new cluster head is elected and, as a consequence, new clusters are formed. The main challenges of this approach are the rules for cluster head election and cluster creation, that should take a low amount of control messages, and the strategies to distribute uniformly the cluster heads into sensed area. In LEACH [2000], the most know solution for hierarchical approaches, each sensor, for each round, has (i) a probability to elect itself as cluster head dependent from its own desiderata percentage to become cluster head, (ii) the current round number and (iii) the amount of rounds that this sensor was not a cluster head. Although it has many limitation in real scenario, LEACH provides a very effective and distributed solution for election in that there are only a low amount of control messages wasted to create the cluster but it does not assure an uniform distribution of cluster heads into the sensed area. This drawback is overcame by a centralized version of LEACH, (LEACH-C), that however requires too many control messages causing an great overhead. Moreover, LEACH does not guarantee that the creation clusters includes all the sensors: this means that could be blind-areas. In HEED [2004], the election of cluster heads is more complex in that it takes into account not only the sensors residual battery (further improving the network lifetime) but various other information, as the degree of sensors or their proximity to their neighbors: this allows HEED to obtain a good distribution of cluster heads but, also in this case, the complete coverage of the area is not guaranteed. A different approach for cluster heads election in adopted in TDC [2009] and in its extensions (2 RTD and 3RTD [2009]). In these solutions, each sensor waits for a random amount of time (different for each sensor) before electing itself as a cluster head: when the timer expires and no neighbor has proposed itself as cluster head, the sensor becomes the cluster head and communicate this information to its neighbors. This communication among sensors introduces a little overhead but allows to reach a very good distribution of cluster head and avoid the creation of blind-areas in the networks.

PEGASIS [2002], and its extensions [2006], are hierarchical solutions based, instead, on the construction of chains of sensors. The idea behind this type of technique foresees the creation of a sensors chain in which each sensor receives data from a single source and transmits data to a single destination. These data, through the process of data-fusion, are collected in a single sensor, changing for each round, that forwards the data to the base station. This mechanism allows to overcome the problems related to clustering and strongly reduces the energy consumption. Unfortunately, although the chain-based technique permits a better power management then the cluster-based one, it introduces some new issue like the use of a greedy algorithm[1] in order to create the chain, the exchange of many control messages for the coordination of sensors, the knowledge of the position of all sensors belonging to the network. This aspects makes it very difficult to be used in a real scenario.

3 The Proposed Solution

The process of data gathering considered in this work is based on a pop-based strategy routing the sensed data towards the base station through a multi-hop path. This represents the simplest way to collect information without an a priori knowledge of network topology. The data transmitted is usually application-specific information that can be packed into small-dimension messages.

The distance between each pair of sensors (receiver and transmitter) involved in the paths has a large influence on the battery duration and, consequently, on the lifetime of each sensor and thus of the coverage maintenance of entire network. Let us consider the most adopted model in the scientific literature [[2002]] to evaluate the power consume,

$E_{Tx}(k,d) = E_c * k + \epsilon_{amp} * k * d^2$ transmitting energy consumption
$E_{Rx}(k) = E_c * k$ receiving energy consumption

where $E_c = 50nJ/bit$ is the energy needed to enable the transmitter or receiver device, $\epsilon_{amp} = 100pJ/(bit * m^2)$ is the amplification factor in transmission, k is the number of bits in the received or transmitted packet and d is the distance between the involved sensors. Making the common assumption that each sensor is multi-input single-out, it is possible to obtain transfer function below: $2 * (E_c * k) * N + \epsilon_{amp} * k * d^2$. This formula depends from three fundamental parameters: the number of inputs (N), the number of bits(k) per message and the distance d between the considered sensor and the one to be reached. Considering a constant size of 2000 bits for each received/transmitted packet, the above formula becomes: $2 * 10^{-1} * N + 2 * 10^{-4} * d^2[mJ]$. Two considerations can be done:

(1) the reception of a message has a low impact on battery life. However, if the number of connections is high, i.e. there are many sensors (N) that transmit directly to the one considered, the lifetime of battery could be strongly reduced. This consideration has been done also taking into account a process of data fusion needed to generate the summary packet to be forwarded.

[1] It is possible to use a GPS device on each sensor to simplify the chain creation process. Although this solution speeds up the initial network set up, the maintenance of an additional electronic device on sensors increase the power consuming.

(2) the distance represents the main factor that affects the energy consumption and, as a consequence, the most critical aspect to face in the design of data gathering process. For instance, due the presence of d^2 factor, the transmission of a 2000 bits packet to a sensor distant 30 meters consumes the same energy of the reception of the same packet but, transmitting the same packet to a double distance (i.e. 60 meters) required an amount of energy equals to the reception of 4 messages.

Many of the power-aware solutions for data gathering proposed in literature are based on the above considerations. The cluster based solutions, for example, derive its advantages minimizing the number of long-range transmission using CHs. The main disadvantage of this technique is the quantity of energy consumed by these CHs. Each CH has to deliver the summary packet to the BS wherever it is. Therefore, when the BS is too far, or it is difficult or even impossible for the sensor to create a efficient multi-hops path towards the BS, the energy consumption becomes very high. Moreover, since each sensor have a limited transmission/receiving range and, as a consequence, a limited amount of close sensors, it has a limited number of possible choice (many time only one) when it has to choose the cluster to join. This means that, if the CH is distant form many sensors belonging to the related cluster, the benefits of this solution can be very low. For these reasons, all the cluster based techniques have featured by an effective strategy to elect a CH, rotating this role at each round, and to create the cluster identifying the related sensors and, overall, to distribute the CHs geographically. Unfortunately, if the cluster is not well-balanced, some sensors tend to consume a great quantity of battery, creating speedy several holes in the sensed area and wasting the coverage of the network.

The techniques based on the construction of chains of sensors overcomes the performance of cluster-based solution in that they fix the number of interaction sensors to two: one in transmission and one in reception. This mechanism allows both to greatly reduce the energy consumption (each sensor receives and transmits to another neighbor sensor) but, above all, maintains a constant consumption of energy for each sensor in each round of data gathering (except for the sensor that must send data to the base station). This last represents the most important difference between above mentioned strategies. For cluster-based sensor, the power consuming model is:

- $2 * 10^{-1} * N_{cluster} + 2 * 10^{-4} * d_{BS}^2$ when working as cluster head (usually 5 times on N)
- $2 * 10^{-4} * d_{CH}^2$ when working as cluster element

For chain-based sensor, instead, the power consuming model is:

- $2 * 10^{-1} + 2 * 10^{-4} * d_S^2$
- $2 * 10^{-1} + 2 * 10^{-4} * d_{BS}^2$ when it is its turn to transmit to BS (1 times on N)

From above formulas it is possible to note how the sensors in the cluster-based solution have a more fluctuating energy consumption respect to the chain-based one. Indeed, in the chain-based solution the distance d_S from the transmitter sensor remains quite constant in that sensors consume the same energy for each data gathering round (except for that round in which it submits to BS), while a sensor in the cluster-based solution changes its energy consumption each time the related cluster changes (it changes the distant d_{CH} to CH). Unfortunately, although the chain-based technique permits a better power management respect to the cluster-based one, it has to adopt an additional greedy algorithm to create the chain and the exchange of several control messages for coordination of sensors. It is possible to use a GPS device on each sensor to simplify the chain creation process. Although this solution speeds up the initial network set up, the maintenance of an additional electronic device on sensors increases the power consuming.

Moreover, for any state changes of sensor (for instance, a sensor could become temporary unreachable), it is necessary a rearrangement of the chain that could lead to inefficient solutions (i.e. sensor having great distance between themselves) and, in the worst case, a complete restore of the chain.

Taking into account all the above considerations, the proposed solution tries to combine the advantages of both techniques to overcome the problems related to them.

The distributed algorithm here proposed builds "degenerate" sensor chains in that it releases the constraint of "single" input in favor of selecting the shortest link for a greater amount of sensors. Indeed, although each sensor has an unique "nearest neighbor"[2], a sensor could be the "nearest neighbor" for a number of more than one sensors[3].

As a consequence, the constraint that each sensor must have a single receiving sensor and a single transmitting sensor, could lead to an ineffective links configuration. Allowing the reception of data from multiples sources (as it happens for CHs), it is possible to obtain a hybrid type of links configuration that, generally, consumes a lower quantity of energy. In this sensors configuration the energy wasted in receiving from more than one sensors is balanced and overcame by the energy saved in transmitting toward those sensors that are the most close. Although the new model presents, respect to the chain-based one, an additional energy consumption factor due to number of receiving sensors, it has a lower fluctuations (in that there are not communications toward base station) and, statistically, the average distance between sensors is, for what said before, lower that the chain based-solution. Adopting this strategy the idea of chain of sensors is strongly modified: now each sensor can have multiple links for receiving data but still only one link for the transmission. The sensors configuration is built as a tree, starting from the base station, i.e. the root node that will receive all generated data, and reaching all the sensors belonging to the network, each one having a single parent and, optionally, one or more children. As it happens for the chain based solution, the creation of the minimum spanning tree could

[2] A sensor having more than a single nearest sensor represent a favorable condition and it does not represent a problem.

[3] This condition is very frequently, especially when the density of sensor is very high.

be done by the BS exploiting GPS devices, but, as said above, this approach requires additional hardware increasing the energy consumption in each sensor.

The challenge of this proposed strategy, indeed, is the design of a distributed and efficient (in terms of a low amount of control messages) algorithm to build the considered three. The next section will explain the solution here proposed.

The only assumption done in proposed approach regards the capability of each sensor to adjust its power transmission level.

3.1 The Algorithm

As said before, the considered tree has to be built starting from the base station, through a distributed strategy in which each sensor, working autonomously, has to be able to determine the best configuration of neighbors, from which it will obtain the sensed data, from here called IncomingSensors, and the unique sensor to which these data have be sent, TargetSensor, that is the neighbor through which it is possible to reach the BS. In this process, the sensor has to optimize the function $2 * 10^{-1} * N + 2 * 10^{-4} * d_{TS}^2$ where d_{TS} is the distance between the sensor and the TargetSensor.

The best solution is given by $N = 1$ e $d_{TS} = min\{d_i\}, i \in [1, N-1]$. Unfortunately, this solution is not always feasible.

The creation of a tree, in fact, imposes several constraints on the number and type of connections between the sensors thus making the considered problem as a constrained optimization one.

First, each sensor needs to know by what neighbor it can reach the base station[4]. Unfortunately, not all the neighbors permit to reach the BS: this means that the set of eligible neighbors that can become TargetSensor is a subset of the all neighbors. From the set of possible TargetSensors, the each sensor has to choose the closest one.

Even for the number of IncomingSensor, N, it has to be consider many oppose aspects. The value of N, in fact, strongly influences the type of created tree. Choosing a high value of N means creating trees having smaller paths (and hence lower propagation delays), but also means to obtaining nodes, i.e. sensors, with high traffic to manage in that there could be too many messages to collect and fuse: this entails both a great energy consumption and the creation of a possible failure point (if the node goes down many information could be loss).

On the other hand, a network with a low value of N has a low energy consumption but has long routes and, as a consequence, a greater value of transmission delay. Also, a lower value of N could create holes in coverage of the network: this happens, for example, if all the neighbors of a single sensor do not take it into account, i.e. do not choose it neither as IncomingSensor nor as TargetSensor.

Another important issue, regarding the formation of a tree, concerns the need to avoid the creation of cycles. In fact, if a sensor A transmit its sensed data to sensor B that belongs to the set of IncomingSensor of sensor A (or of one of its

[4] In this case, it is not important the number of hops but only the distance in meter from the other sensor that leads to the base station.

children), the structure created it is not a tree and, consequently, it is not an effective organization of sensors relationship.

The solution here proposed is able to overcome the above mentioned limitations and makes possible the creation, through the exchanging of only $2 * N$ messages, of a tree that permits a power-effective data gathering and a long-life networks functioning. This solution, completely distributed, foresees that each sensor executes the several steps in order to establish which is the TargetSensor and which are the IncomingSensors. All the sensors execute the same algorithm, starting from the base station that initialize the entire process. The protocol foresees three types of messages:

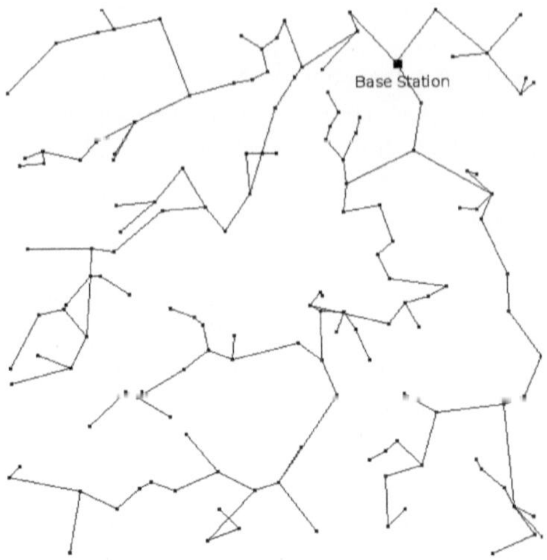

Fig. 1. An example of created tree

- EXPLORE: it is used (in transmission) to notify the presence of a certain sensor to its neighbor and, from the other hand (in reception), to understand how many sensors can become neighbors.
- DISTANCE2BS: it is a message that contains the distance in terms of number of hops of the sender from the BS. This message is used to understand the sensors trough which it is possible to reach the BS. The number of hops stored in this message is very important in that it is used to avoid the creation of loops (the details will be explained below).
- NEIGHBOR_QUERY: it is a message used from "isolated" neighbors to force the establishment of a neighbor relationship with other sensors (in order to cover the entire network).

The algorithm consists into three phases.

In the first phase, each sensor (including the BS) forwards the message EXPLORE covering the maximum area in relation to its transmission range. When a sensor is *active*, it waits for a given random time interval and then broadcasts the message EXPLORE. In this time interval, the sensor listens the messages EXPLORE arriving from the other sensors, that will be considered as potential neighbors. From each message EXPLORE received, the sensor is able to understand its distance from the sensor that has transmitted the message by exploiting the signal strength. Each sensed sensor is stored in a list (neighbors' list) ordered by distance value. After this phase, each sensor waits for the reception of message DISTANCE2BS.

The first message DISTANCE2BS is generated by the BS with hops number equals to zero and broadcast to its neighbors. Each time a sensor received the a message DISTANCE2BS, it increase by 1 the value of hops and forwards it to its neighbors. After that, the BS ends its task and begins to wait for sensed data[5].

When a sensor receives a message DISTANCE2BS, it understand that the process for the creation of the tree is started: since each sensor can reach the base station through more than one of its neighbors, it can collect a great number of messages DISTANCE2BS. The sender of each message DISTANCE2BS represents a possible candidate to be a TargetSensor: all these message can be used to build a feasible solution. The grater the number of received messages, the greater the probability to transmit to the nearest sensor.

The reception of the first DISTANCE2BS forces the sensor to stat the timer within which it will wait other messages. The duration of this time interval can influence the number of IncomingSensors of the sensor: it will be proportional to the number of neighbors of the sensor in order to guarantee that sensors having a greater number of neighbors will wait for a greater amount of time. When this timer expires, the sensor has to decide which sensor will become the related TargetSensor and, basing on an heuristic formula, the number of IncomingSensor and, as a consequence, N. In particular, N will be inversely proportional to the distance d: the closer the sensors, the grater the value of N.

This strategy has been adopted in order to maintain quite uniform the energy consumption among the sensors: in fact, if the distance from TargetSensor (d_{TS}) is little, the number of IncomingSensors can be high and vice versa. Once N has been fixed, the sensor sends its message DISTANCE2BS to the first N sensors in its neighbor's list. The distance in terms of hops of this message is very important in the construction of tree in that it is used to avoid loops. In fact, guaranteeing that no one of the IncomingSensors have a distance in hops less than that of the sensor, allows to state that no loop is in the tree.

Although the restriction in the number of N is a good strategy for reducing the power consuming, it can rise to same "isolated" sensors, i.e. sensors without neighbor. To avoid this condition, the protocol foresees a third, and last, phase. This phase starts when, after a given amount of time, a sensor that has received same messages EXPLORE but has not received any message DISTANCE2BS,

[5] There are many advanced techniques to hear the wireless channel saving energy. For the proposal of this paper it is not important to know which of those techniques it is used.

Table 1. Simulation Parameters

Sensed area	500 X 500 m^2	Wireless range	100 m
BS position	random	Dim. of Packet	2000 bits
E_c	50 nJ/bit	ϵ_{amp}	$100pJ/(bit * m^2)$

Table 2. Simulations Results Summary

Algorithm	N sensors	FND	25% ND
PEGASIS	100	424	883
TBA	100	402	1006
PEGASIS	200	454	916
TBA	200	423	1516
PEGASIS	300	468	972
TBA	300	473	1923

forwards the message NEIGHBOR_QUERY to the before sensed neighbors in order to force them to retransmit the message DISTANCE2BS (ignoring the limits imposed by the d_{TS}). This guarantees that all sensors have at least one link toward the base station. Figure 1 shows an example of the created tree.

4 Simulation Results

In order to evaluate the performance of proposed algorithm, it has been compared to PEGASIS, the most known chain-based solution. This choice has been done since the performance of PEGASIS overcomes, in terms of network lifetime, the ones of LEACH and of the other cluster-based solutions. The simulations have been done considering an area of 500X500 m^2, varying each time the number of sensor (100, 200, 300) considered. Table 1 shows the parameters characterizing the simulated scenario. Each simulation has evaluated the number of "data gathering cycles" completed before that (I) the first node dies and (II) the 25% of nodes die. The table 2 shows the results of simulations. Although PEGASIS shows better performance in terms of number of of rounds required before the first node dies, the benefits of the proposed solution (TBA - Tree Based Algorithm) is substantially better with regard to the number of rounds necessary to die the 25% of the nodes. This is a very important aspect in that TBA is able to maintain the network active for a greater number of rounds. Moreover, when the number of nodes increases, TBA overcomes PEGASIS in both considered metrics. This is explained by the fact that, increasing the nodes density, the number of sensors that takes advantage of establishing multiple incoming connections, i.e. number of IncomingSensor, increases (this parameter, in PEGASIS, remains constant and equals to 1).

5 Conclusion

In this paper the authors introduce an algorithm for power-effective data gathering in randomly distributed sensors networks. The main characteristic of this algorithm regards the way in which the sensors are organized: differently from the common hierarchical organizations (cluster or chain based), in the proposed solution the sensors have an tree based organization. In this tree, which starts from the base station and links all the sensors belonging to the network, the connections among nodes are created taking into account the amount of energy consumed by each sensor in order to maintain it constant. As shown in 4, this approach permits an increment of network lifetime respect to the PEGASIS solution for considered metrics. This solution is based on a completely distributed algorithm that, exploiting the self-organization ability of sensors, are able to build a tree using few (only 2*N) control messages. The chosen organization, furthermore, permits to maintains good performance when the number of deployed sensors increase, demonstrating good scalability (i.e. scalability). An important characteristic of this solutions, good for randomly distributed networks, is the ability to maintains its performance independently from the position of the base station respect to other sensors.

References

[2000] Heinzelman, W., Chandrakasan, A., Balakrishnan, H.: Energy-Efficient Communication Protocol for Wireless Microsensor Networks. In: Proceedings of the 33rd Hawaii International Conference on System Sciences, HICSS 2000 (January 2000)

[2002] Lindsey, S., Raghavendra, C.: PEGASIS: Power-Efficient Gathering in Sensor Information Systems. In: IEEE Aerospace Conference Proceedings, vol. 3, 9-16, pp. 1125–1130 (2002)

[2003] Ozgur Tan, H., Korpeoglu, I.: Power Efficient Data Gathering and Aggregation in Wireless Sensor Networks. SIGMOD Record 32(4), 66–71 (2003)

[2004] Younis, O., Fahmy, S.: Heed: A hybrid, energy-efficient, distributed clustering approach for ad-hoc sensor networks. IEEE Transactions on Mobile Computing 3(4), 366–379 (2004)

[2006] Yueyang, L., Hong, J., Guangxin, Y.: An Energy-Efficient PEGASIS-Based Enhanced Algorithm in Wireless Sensor Networks. China Communications, 91–97 (August 2006)

[2009] Chuang, P., Yang, S., Lin, C.: Energy-Efficient Clustering in Wireless Sensor Networks. In: Hua, A., Chang, S.-L. (eds.) ICA3PP 2009. LNCS, vol. 5574, pp. 112–120. Springer, Heidelberg (2009)

[2009] Chuang, P., Yang, S., Lin, C.: Energy-Efficient Clustering in Wireless Sensor Networks. In: Hua, A., Chang, S.-L. (eds.) ICA3PP 2009. LNCS, vol. 5574, pp. 112–120. Springer, Heidelberg (2009)

Mobile Computing with Cloud

Ishwarya Chandrasekaran

Alcatel-Lucent India Limited, Bangalore 560045, India
ishwarya.chandrasekar@alcatel-lucent.com

Abstract. Cloud computing is evolving as a new paradigm of computing in which dynamically scalable and often virtualized resources are provided as a service over the Internet. The confluence of hardware virtualization, cloud and mobile computing drives the new era of mobile cloud computing. Platforms such as android, iOS, Windows 7 erodes the power of computing platforms like Microsoft Windows and Apple Mac OS and is creating cross platform app centric environment in which end-users and in particular the consumer marketplace will drive developments in business computing. There are endless possibilities that can be brought about with the mobile cloud in the near future. This paper discusses the current state of mobile cloud computing and the services provided by cloud providers like Amazon and how easy it is to build a mobile application on top of Amazon S3 with their APIs. Open challenges in mobile cloud computing are also discussed to highlight the future research directions.

Keywords: Mobile Cloud, Amazon S3, NoSQL, HTML5, Android.

1 Introduction

Today's mobile phone users can perform a wide range of tasks by downloading applications to their handset from online stores. These applications are called native applications specific to the mobile operating system and they use the computing power and memory contained in the device to run the application. Sophisticated applications which requires more processing power and memory is not suited to run on these devices. Hence it poses a challenge for the mobile application developers to build different versions of the same application for multiple mobile operating systems and more sophisticated applications require robust computing power and memory in the handset.

Cloud computing, an evolving trend with which we can access various services over the internet, can bring unprecedented sophistication in mobile ecosystem. It can leverage the power of handsets by executing the applications on the cloud instead of locally running them on the mobile device. This give rise to the new term called mobile cloud computing. Mobile cloud applications can not only be accessed by smartphones, but they can also be accessed by low cost featured phones where the processing power and memory is restrained. The demand for resources by the mobile applications can be fulfilled by cloud platforms such as Amazon EC2 [2], Microsoft Azure [3] and Google AppEngine [4] which can provide the resources that are deficit in mobile phones.

D. Nagamalai, E. Renault, and M. Dhanushkodi (Eds.): PDCTA 2011, CCIS 203, pp. 513–522, 2011.

Several views exist on mobile cloud computing. From one perspective, mobile cloud computing can be defined as an architecture where the data processing and storage happens outside of the mobile device. Mobile cloud applications move the computing power and data storage away from mobile phones into the cloud, bringing the apps and mobile computing to not just smartphone users but a much broader range of mobile subscribers. On the other way round, mobile cloud computing can be thought of as a cloud where the cloud is formed by a group of mobile devices that share their computing power to run applications on them. By this way mobile cloud computing can bring tremendous benefits to the feature phone enabled users as equivalent to the smart phone users. Mobile computing can also mean using portable devices to run stand-alone applications and/or accessing remote applications via wireless networks [5]. This paper mainly concentrates on building mobile cloud applications and processing them directly on cloud rather on the device itself.

According to the latest study from Juniper Research, the market for cloud-based mobile applications will grow 88% from 2009 to 2014[1]. The market was just over $400 million this past year but by 2014 it will reach $9.5 billion. Driving this growth will be the adoption of the new web standard HTML5, increased mobile broadband coverage and the need for always-on collaborative services for the enterprise. ABI Research predicts that there will be nearly one billion end users accessing the "mobile cloud" by 2014. Smartphone applications will move from the handset itself to the cloud, creating an ecosystem for new kind of smartphones sometimes termed "Mobile Cloud Phones" [6].

The rest of the paper is organized as follows. Section 2 discusses the concept of mobile cloud computing and the architecture. In Section 3, recent technologies like HTML5 and NoSQL that drives mobile cloud computing are discussed. We then illustrate an example of building a mobile cloud application with Amazon S3 and its framework in Section 4. Section 5 presents some related work on mobile cloud computing applications. In Section 6 the challenges of mobile cloud applications are discussed and finally Section 7 concludes this paper and highlights the future work.

2 Mobile Cloud Computing

2.1 Concepts and Benefits

Mobile cloud computing lets user to access his information anytime anywhere with a mobile device. Businesses use mobile cloud to access company data, regardless of their employee's location, making them faster and more efficient. Fragmentation remains one of the major drawbacks of different mobile operating systems. This issue can be resolved by building mobile cloud applications which can run across various operating systems requiring only a web interface to connect to cloud and run the applications. When a mobile application is computed on cloud, essentially it means that the processing power is moved out of the handset and computing is fully taken care by the cloud. This can reduce the energy consumed by the individual handsets and significantly save battery life on the mobile devices.

2.2 Mobile Cloud Architecture

Figure 1 shows basic mobile cloud architecture. It shows how the mobile device is connected to the IP network which in turn is connected to the cloud. The mobile device first connects to the base station. The base station connects the device to IP network with any one of the technologies like GPRS, EDGE or Wi-Fi which is then connected to the cloud to access the services provided by them. Any type of computing or storage can be moved away from the mobile device into the cloud and after processing the results can be returned to the devices. This enables phones with limited resources to run sophisticated applications with the help of cloud.

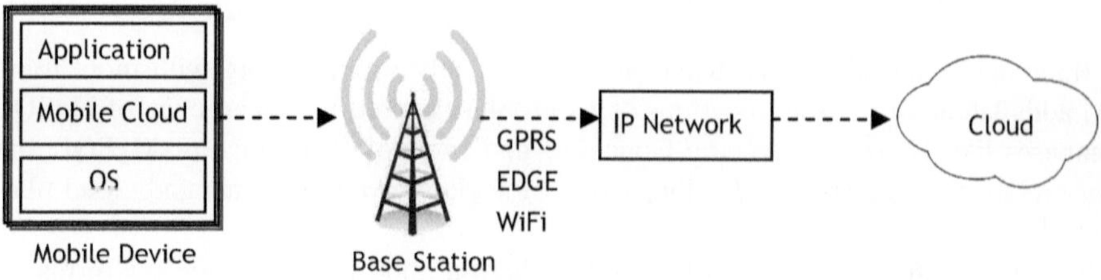

Fig. 1. General Mobile Cloud Architecture

3 Technologies Driving Mobile Cloud

3.1 HTML5

The biggest challenge in mobile cloud computing is intermittent network availability. A cloud-based application will stop working if the connection is lost. To overcome such situations, HTML5, an evolving programming language can be used to build mobile applications which can enable data caching on the handset, allowing the user to continue their work until cellular signal is restored. HTML5 basically has structural elements or tags that provide more descriptive semantics.

With the introduction of HTML5, offline application caching is supported by means of application cache which can store the resources to be used by browser when it's offline, granting partial access to the users to the web site or application. The application cache is a collection of resources obtained from a cache manifest provided by the web application. It contains a list of resources to be stored for use when there is no network connectivity. So the user can still visit the web page when he is offline and do browsing with the help of cached resources. It also enhances speed of loading the web page as the files are stored locally and reduces the load on server as the browser will only download the resources from the server that have been changed.

HTML 5 would eventually make webapps powerful and as capable as native apps. Even though the HTML5 API's are not completely implemented in all mobile operating systems yet, they are sure to revolutionize the mobile cloud industry in the near future by decreasing the time and cost of developing applications across devices.

3.2 NoSQL Databases

The relational database model (RDBMS) has been the dominant model for decades. But today NoSQL (Next Generation Databases that are non-relational, distributed, open-source, horizontal and scalable) databases are gaining momentum as an alternative model for database management. NoSQL databases are not meant for mission critical applications and they cannot replace the traditional RDBMS. These databases aim to give user a choice to select the appropriate database that is suitable for his applications. NoSQL databases are used by big players like Google, Facebook for their humongous applications that requires parallelism and huge scalability. Since they can be effectively used in a cloud environment, they are called as the "Databases for the cloud".

Relational databases don't distribute well typically when dealing with more users and adds latency to our applications. This problem caused the emergence of NoSQL databases like Hbase, Cassandra, CouchDB and MongoDB in place of MySQL and other relational databases under the covers of social networking sites and cloud platform providers.

The features of NoSQL databases make them a good fit for mobile platforms. A new mobile version of the CouchDB database system, called CouchOne Mobile, is available for Android operating system. Basically, CouchDB is the file system of HTML5 web. It solves a huge problem of building web applications that run and synchronize with mobile devices and lets developers write HTML5 applications one time, then easily run them and share data across mobile platforms and the cloud [7].

CouchOne Mobile consists of an application platform complete with geo spatial and full text indexing. CouchOne Mobile's lightweight architecture is optimized for native data store on any mobile device. It allows developers to write web applications once, scale vertically and share data and applications across any computing platform or mobile device by taking advantage of CouchDB's sophisticated replication functionality to synchronize data between desktop and mobile applications.

Inspite of the increasing bandwidth of mobile networks, they are not very reliable. Slow internet connectivity for accessing a social network is bearable but the network connectivity is important when dealing with enterprise applications. So the mobile applications need to have a local cache of data to work with when the network connectivity is slow or down and should be able to synchronize the data that has been modified during the downtime with the enterprise whenever the network becomes available again without any difficulty. CouchDB's replication and sync facilities allow developers to build web or native applications that work even if the Internet connection is slow, intermittent or completely down. The users of CouchOne Mobile benefit from more responsive applications and increased battery life.

Although NoSQL databases has gained a lot of attention by a wide range people there are certain obstacles like maturity of the databases, support provided for them and skilled administration required for these databases that needs to be addressed before taking them to the mainstream of enterprises. NoSQL databases can bring out the best when used as a solution for a right kind of problem.

4 Amazon SDK for Mobile Cloud

Mobile cloud computing is build upon the basic principles of cloud computing and provides on demand access to different services like platform, software or infrastructure by bringing those to the mobile domain. Many cloud providers like Google and Amazon support mobile cloud services with their platforms. Amazon has released its SDK for Android and iOS to simplify the development of cloud applications stored on the Amazon Web services cloud platform. This facilitates the developers with limited resources, to build and provision new mobile cloud services using the Amazon web services. The SDK includes libraries that makes it simple to handle the HTTP connections, request retries and error handling which happens to be an abstruse task previously. It enables the developers to use the AWS infrastructure in their mobile applications, including:

- *Storage*- to store and retrieve any amount of data using Amazon Simple Storage Service (Amazon S3).
- *Database*- allows developers to add a highly available, scalable, and flexible non-relational data store using Amazon SimpleDB with little or no administrative burden.
- *Messaging*- this feature makes the developers to integrate reliable, highly scalable mobile-to-mobile communication into applications using Amazon Simple Queue Service (Amazon SQS), and Amazon Simple Notifications Service (Amazon SNS).

4.1 Amazon S3 an Online Storage Solution

Amazon Simple Storage Service is an easy and inexpensive internet hard-drive from Amazon Web Services primarily meant for storing data in the cloud. There is no limit how much data we can store in S3. For instance, we can store web images or backup our entire computer hard drive on S3. It provides a scalable data storage infrastructure that aims to offer reliable, fast, infinite data durability, low data access latency and 99.9% availability with pay-as-you-go billing model [8]. The data is redundantly stored in the multiple servers across different data centers of Amazon and bandwidth used for transfer of data can be controlled.

4.2 Architecture of Amazon S3

Buckets. There are two-levels of namespaces for the data stored in S3. At the top level, bucket partitions the namespace of the objects. Data is stored as objects in Amazon S3 which is contained in bucket. Objects within the bucket can have any name but bucket name should be unique across S3. Buckets identify the account responsible for storage and data transfer charges. They play a role in access control and they serve as the unit of aggregation for usage reporting. A bucket can be created by sending a simple PUT request to a URI specifying the name of the bucket.

Objects. Amazon S3 is a key value store designed to store unlimited number of data objects. Objects consist of object data, which can be upto 5GB in size and metadata and a set of name-value pair to describe the object. Relevant permissions to create, view or delete an object within the bucket can be set to restrict their access. We can also view the access logs for a bucket and select a geographical region for Amazon S3 to store the buckets and the data contained in it.

Keys. Each object in S3 has a unique identifier called key for that particular object within the bucket. It is the name that we assign to an object with which we can retrieve it. Every object in S3 can be identified by the combination of Service endpoint, bucket name and key together.

Figure 2 gives an overview of how files from mobile devices can be stored in Amazon S3. Each file is stored as an object in S3 which has meta data associated with it that describes the object.

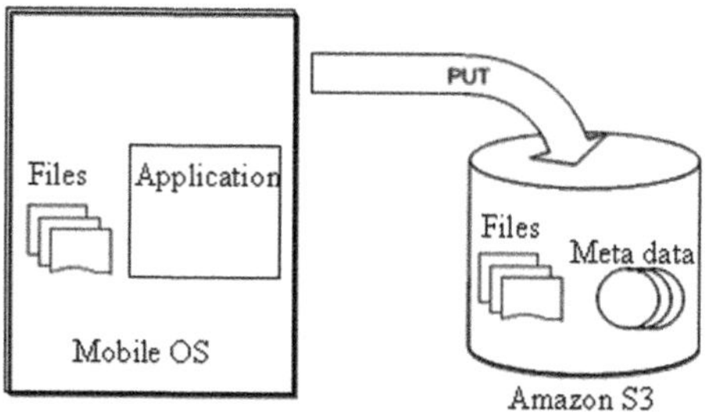

Fig. 2. Uploading Files to S3 from Mobile

4.2.1 Authentication and Access Control

When a user sign up for an Amazon Web Services account, he is assigned with a unique identity called 'AWS Access Key Id'. Amazon S3 REST API uses a custom HTTP scheme based on a keyed-HMAC (Hash Message Authentication Code) for authentication. To authenticate a client request, selected elements of the request are concatenated to form a string which is then combined with the Secret access key that is generated by Amazon during registration to form the HMAC of the string. This process is called as signing the request and output of HMAC is called signature. Finally this signature is added as a parameter to the request. At the receiving end, the system fetches the AWS Secret key and computes its own HMAC using the same mechanism. Then it matches this HMAC with the HMAC the user sent. If the request matches, the user is allowed to proceed further or else the request is dropped and an error message is sent to him.

Every resource in Amazon S3 has Access Control List (ACL) associated with it, which specifies what type of access a user has to the contents of S3. Each ACL can have maximum of 100 grants rule. A Grant rule consists of a Grantee and permission. Grantees can be classified as a Owner, who has by default all the rights to grant permissions or User by Email, who can be granted permissions to access buckets and Objects if he has an account with Amazon or User by Canonical Representation, where we can grant permissions to user using his/her Amazon Customer CanonicalUser ID.

4.2.2 Amazon S3 Application Programming Interfaces (API)

Three data access protocols namely SOAP, REST and BitTorrent can be used to interface with Amazon S3 and access their storage.

SOAP. Simple Object Access Protocol (SOAP) is a framework for exchanging structured information over transport protocols such as HTTP and SMTP. SOAP messaging format is based upon Extensible Markup Language (XML) and it consists of three parts: an envelope, which defines the message and how to process it, a set of encoding rules for expressing instances of application-defined data types, and a convention for representing procedure calls and responses [9].

REST. Representational State Transfer (REST) is an architecture style of networked systems that defines how web standards, such as HTTP and URIs, are supposed to be used. It reduces the complexity of SOAP by using a limited set of HTTP commands to access and manipulate the server side state or data records [10].

BitTorrent. BitTorrent is a peer-to-peer file sharing protocol designed to distribute huge amount of data, especially when large number of clients simultaneously attempt to download same file [11]. Bit torrent protocol can be used to retrieve any publicly accessible object in Amazon S3. Using this each client downloads some pieces of an object from one Amazon S3 client and some other pieces from other clients, while simultaneously uploading pieces of the same object to other interested peers.

4.3 Building Application with Amazon S3

We consider developing a photo sharing application for android that is built on top of Amazon S3, which uses the S3 resources extensively to share photos to other mobile devices. The application aims to share photo using Amazon S3 storage.

Amazon provides SDK for different mobile operating system to utilize its services. Amazon API for android is implemented in our application to share the photos. The advantage of using Amazon API is to seamlessly connect to S3 for storing and retrieving objects from them. Rather than using conventional http multipart upload request to a server using Apache API or so, the concept is simplified and made easier using Amazon API which abstracts the complexity of transferring the file from the mobile device to the S3 storage. This facilitates the developer to create applications in minimum time with less effort. Figure 3 depicts the photo share application architecture.

4.3.1 Application Workflow

Initially the client sends request to create a bucket in S3. REST API is used to interface with S3, so a HTTP PUT request is used to create a bucket in S3. There are many S3 storage locations available all over the world, so we can specify to which S3 location our request should be routed and accordingly the request is routed to that particular S3 storage for processing. On receiving the request from client, S3 creates a bucket. Then the client sends request to upload the photo to S3. On receiving the upload request, S3 stores the file that is transferred from the mobile device as an object inside the bucket. After storing the object, an endpoint URL that points to the photo that is stored in S3 is sent to the mobile device. This URL can then be shared among the users who want to view the photo. Permissions can be set accordingly for the users to view/edit/delete the photo in S3.

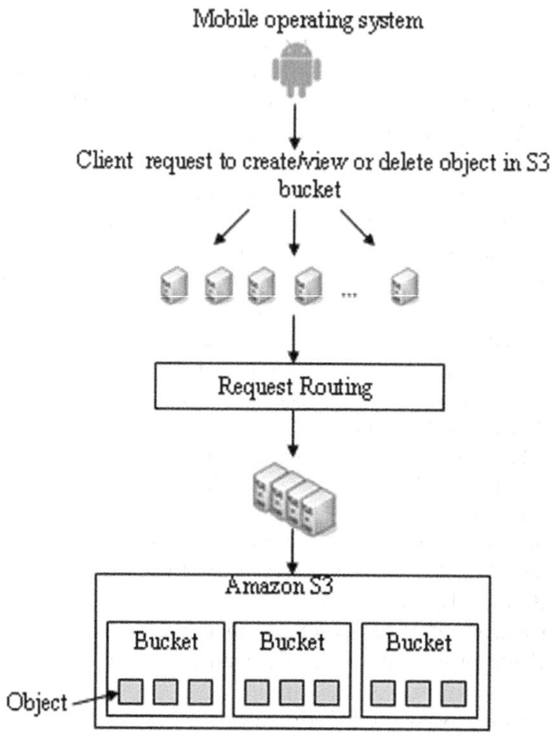

Fig. 3. PhotoShare Application Architecture

The biggest advantage of Amazon S3 is that the total volume of data and number of objects that we can store are unlimited. Individual Amazon S3 objects can range in size from 1 byte to 5 terabytes and the largest object that can be uploaded in a single PUT is 5 gigabytes. We can use the Multipart Upload capability for storing objects larger than 100 megabytes and they charge a less amount for the storage of data when the free tier exceeds. Hence it is scalable and inexpensive to store the data on Amazon S3 which facilitates the developers to build applications easily on top of it.

5 Related Work

Amazon S3 storage solution has been extensively discussed by Mayur Palankar et al. [12], where they focus on analyzing whether S3 can be suited for Science grids. Their results reveal that Amazon S3 can be best suited for data storage in science grids due to its good data availability and durability. Our work primarily focuses on building mobile cloud applications with different technologies, which leverages the power of featured phones and enables them to execute computationally intensive applications. We bring in the advantage of mobile cloud apps over native apps and how it solves the pain of developers in building different versions of the same application for different mobile operating systems. Farshad A. Saimimi et al. [13] introduce an infrastructure for rapid prototyping and deployment of Mobile Service Clouds to address the issue of dynamic services at the wireless edge of the internet. Xinwen Zhang et al. [14] propose a security framework for elastic applications on mobile devices where they discuss about secure session management and authentication between mobile device and cloud. Our paper highlights efficient ways to build mobile cloud apps and how to seamlessly access them across the devices.

6 Mobile Cloud Challenges

The major challenge of mobile cloud is to have minimum network latency and seamless internet connection to connect to the cloud from different mobile devices. The issue of network connectivity can be subsequently minimized with the power of 4G networks that has huge bandwidth and can provide the best possible connectivity. In case of poor network connectivity, HTML5 can be used to store the data in local cache and synchronize with the server when it is up and running. Apart from these NoSQL databases like Couchone can be used to synchronize the mobile data to desktop applications.

7 Conclusions and Future Work

Mobile cloud deployment seems to be logical and beneficial from a business point of view. As many businesses are in the position to determine a mobile strategy in the light of increasing complexities and fragmentation of mobile platforms and devices, the mobile cloud promises a way to overcome these limitations. It is simpler to develop for the mobile cloud rather than fragmented platforms and devices. With different technologies like HTML5 and NoSQL mobile cloud app development can be made efficient mainly addressing the issue of network latencies. Services provided by cloud providers also facilitate developers to build apps with minimum time, like Amazon S3 storage discussed in our work provides best possible way to store huge amount of data at one time. Although there are certain inherent challenges that needs to be addressed in the field of mobile cloud computing, it will become a disruptive force, with the power it has to reach a huge crowd of mobile phone users and the way it can run across various mobile devices without being tied to any carrier and depending upon only on the web to access the application. Our future research direction is towards addressing intermittent network connectivity and latency issue with mobile broadband technologies.

References

1. Juniper research on mobile cloud services, `http://juniperresearch.com/reports/mobile_cloud_applications_and_services`
2. Amazon elastic compute cloud (EC2).AWS, http://www.amazon.com/ec2/
3. Microsoft azure, http://www.microsoft.com/azure/13

4. Google app engine, http://appengine.google.com
5. Satyanarayanan, M.: Mobile computing: The next decade. In: Proc. 11th Intl. Conf. on Mobile Data Management (MDM 2010), Kansas, MO (2010)
6. ABI research on mobile cloud application, http://www.abiresearch.com/research/1003385-Mobile+Cloud+Applications
7. Couchone for mobile, http://www.couchbase.com/products-and-services/mobile-couchbase
8. Amazon Simple Storage Service, http://aws.amazon.com/s3/
9. W3C, Soap Version 1.2 (June 2003), http://www.w3.org/TR/soap/
10. Fielding, R.T.: Architectural Styles and the Design of Network-Based Software Architectures, PhD Dissertation, University of California, Irvine (2000)
11. BitTorrent, http://en.wikipedia.org/wiki/BitTorrent_(protocol)
12. Palankar, M.R., Iamnitchi, A., Ripeanu, M., Garfinkel, S.: Amazon S3 for science grids: a viable solution. In: Proc. of the 2008 International Workshop on Data-Aware Distributed Computing (2008)
13. Samimi, F.A., Mckinley, P.K., Masoud Sadjadi, S.: Mobile Service Clouds: A self-managing infrastructure for autonomic mobile computing services. In: Proc. of the Second IEEE International Workshop on Self-Managed Networks, Systems and Services (2006)
14. Zhang, X., Schiffman, J., Gibbs, S., Kunjithapatham, A., Jeong, S.: Securing elastic applications on mobile devices for cloud computing. In: Proc. of the 2009 ACM Workshop on Cloud Computing Security (November 2009)

Implementation of AAA Server for PMIPv6 in NS-2

Nitesh M. Tarbani and B.R. Chandavarkar

Dept of Computer Science and Engineering
NITK-Surathkal, India-575025
ntarbani@gmail.com, brc@nitk.com

Abstract. Proxy Mobile IPv6 is a network-based mobility protocol where the mobility management signaling is performed by a network entity on behalf of the node requiring mobility itself. Mobile IPv6 (MIPv6) enables Mobile Node (MN) to maintain its connectivity to the Internet during handover. The Mobile Access Gateway (MAG), located in the access router, retrieves the MN profile information from Authentication, Authorization, and Accounting (AAA) server and sends the customized Router Advertisements to the MN, emulating the home network behavior. Theoretically there is an inclusion of AAA server in PMIPV6 but the practical inclusion is not been attempted yet, hence this paper proposes an architecture for including the AAA server into the NS2 for PMIPV6.

Keywords: AAA server, LMA, MAG, Proxy care of address.

1 Introduction

In the current era of technology mobility gained a lot of popularity in terms of allowing the users to access the resource while roaming. The roaming facility is provided to the users using mobile IP. The challenging issue for the industry is to maintain the connectivity during the change of Point of attachment (PoA). There are two models to support the mobility, i.e Network-based and Host based. Network based mobility models allow Mobile Node (MN) to continue their IP sessions as they move from one PoA to another without the involvement of MN in the signaling or management of their movement. This makes the MN unaware of its mobility. This reduces the complexity and cost of MN. IP mobility for nodes that have mobile IP client functionality in the IPv6 stack as well as those nodes that do not, would be supported by enabling Proxy Mobile IPv6 protocol. Therefore it increases compatibility and interoperability between various systems and user equipments. In contrast, in host-based mobility model MN should support Mobile IP to continue their IP sessions as they move from one PoA to another. In this mobility model MN actively involved in the handover management, which includes detecting the new point of attachment, sending binding updates to Home Agent (HA) and correspondent Node (CN) and so on. In comparing to network based mobility model, host based model increases the complexity of Mobile node and compatibility with other network entities.

The rest of the paper is organized as follows. Section 2 describes PMIPv6.Section 3 describes Existing Architecture of PMIPv6 in ns-2. Section 4 describes Proposed

D. Nagamalai, E. Renault, and M. Dhanushkodi (Eds.): PDCTA 2011, CCIS 203, pp. 523–531, 2011.

Architecture of PMIPv6 in ns-2. Section 5 describes implementation of AAA server in NS-2 Section 6 describes Simulation setup. Section 7 describes Simulation results and analysis. Section 8 presents Conclusion.

2 PMIPv6

Brief about PMIPv6

Proxy Mobile IP (PMIP) is a network-based mobility management protocol. It achieves this by using MIPv6's signaling and the reuse of the home agent functionality through a proxy mobility agent in the network. The entire network (Proxy mobile IPv6 domain) within which the MN is authorized to roam is under the same administrative management. Thus, PMIPv6 is called as localized network based mobility management protocol. PMIPv6 relies on the proxy mobility agents in the network to detect the MN's attachments and detachments and then signal this information, in the form of binding updates without the active participation of the MN itself [2]. This scheme defines two core functional elements; Local Mobility Anchor (LMA) and the Mobile Access Gateway (MAG) [3].

Operation of Proxy MIPv6

Every MN in a proxy mobile IP domain is assigned an MN-Identifier which it (MN) presents as part of access authentication when it attaches to MAG in the domain [1]. With this identifier, both the MAG and the LMA can obtain the MN's policy profile from the AAA server. The moment an MN enters its Proxy Mobile IPv6 domain and is authenticated and assigned a home link (address), the network ensures that this home link conceptually follows the MN as it roams within the domain. Fig 1 shows operation of PMIPv6.

The MAG uses this MN-Identifier to look up the MN's policy profile from the AAA server so as to obtain the MN's LMA address. Upon obtaining this address, the MAG will generate and send a PBU message on behalf of the MN to the MN's LMA via the obtained address. This PBU message is intended to update the LMA with the current location of the MN. Obtaining the MN's policy profile also provides the MAG with parameters necessary for emulating the MN's home agent. This means making the MN believe that it's still connected to its HA. After authenticating the request, the LMA will send a PBA response message back to the MAG. If the response that the LMA sent is positive, the LMA will also set up a route for the MN over a tunnel to the MAG. The MAG on receiving the PBA would establish a bi-directional tunnel with the LMA, add a default route through the tunnel to the LMA and finally grant the MN permission to transmit data. All traffic from the MN as well as all other MNs connected to the same MAG and LMA will be routed through this tunnel to the LMA and then to their CNs. On receiving the PBA, the MAG also sends a Router Advertisement to the MN advertising the MN's home network prefix. If the MN has not obtained an IP address by this time, it will generate one using the obtained home network prefix. The method of obtaining or generating an IP address can be by either stateless or stateful auto configuration and is determined by the MN's stored policy profile. The established tunnel hides the topology and enables an MN to use an IP address that is topologically anchored at the LMA, from any attached access link in the proxy mobile IPv6 domain. An LMA also ensures that only authorized MAGs send PBUs on behalf of MNs. MAGs do not only send PBUs when they detect the presence of an MN on their ANs, they also send PBUs when they detect that an MN has left their AN or when the lifetime of the binding update for an MN that is still attached to it, expires.

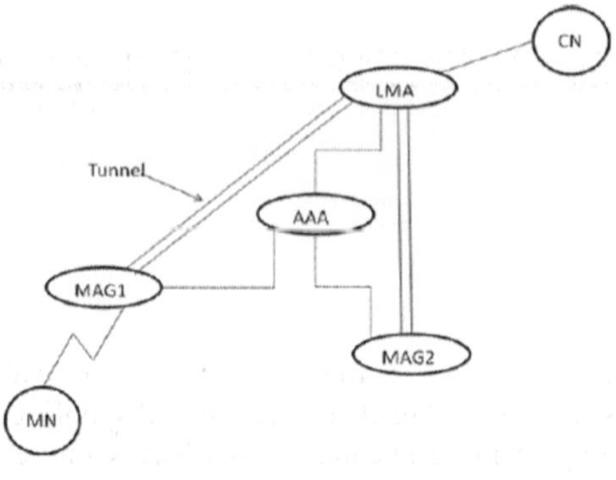

Fig. 1. Oprational diagram for PMIPv6

3 Existing Architecture

The working of existing architecture of PMIPv6 in NS-2 is as follows [6].It includes implementation of LMA and MAG [7]. The Router Solicitation message from the mobile node may arrive at any time after the mobile node's. For updating the local mobility anchor about the current location of the mobile node, the mobile access gateway sends a Proxy Binding Update message to the mobile node's local mobility anchor. Upon accepting this Proxy Binding Update message, the local mobility anchor sends a Proxy Binding Acknowledgement message including the mobile node's home network prefix. It also creates the Binding Cache entry and sets up its endpoint of the bi-directional tunnel to the mobile access gateway. The mobile access gateway on receiving the Proxy Binding Acknowledgement message sets up its endpoint of the bi-directional tunnel to the local mobility anchor and also sets up the forwarding for the mobile node's traffic. At this point, the mobile access gateway has all the required information for emulating the mobile node's home link. It sends Router Advertisement messages to the mobile node on the access link advertising the mobile node's home network prefix as the hosted on-link prefix.The mobile node, on receiving these Router Advertisement messages on the access link, attempts to configure its interface. The local mobility anchor, being the topological anchor point for the mobile node's home network prefix, receives any packets that are sent to the mobile node by any node in or outside the Proxy Mobile IPv6 domain. The local mobility anchor forwards these received packets to the mobile access gateway through the bi-directional tunnel. The mobile access gateway on other end of the tunnel, after receiving the packet, removes the outer header and forwards the packet on the access link to the mobile node. Fig 2 shows the current signaling call flow when the mobile node enters the Proxy Mobile IPv6 domain in ns-2.

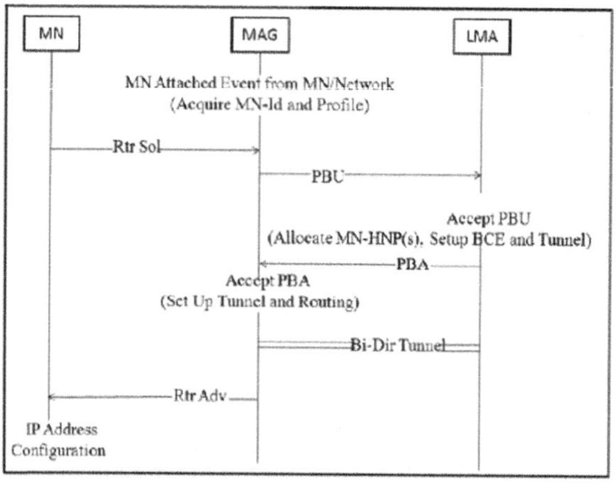

Fig. 2. Current Mobile Node Attachment - Signaling Call Flow

The mobile access gateway acts as the default router on the point-to- point link shared with the mobile node. Any packet that the mobile node sends to any correspondent node will be received by the mobile access gateway and will be sent to its local mobility anchor through the bi-directional tunnel. The local mobility anchor on the other end of the tunnel, after receiving the packet, removes the outer header and routes the packet to the destination.

4 Proposed Architecture

4.1 Simulation Environment

Fig 3 shows the proposed signaling call flow when the mobile node enters the Proxy Mobile IPv6 domain in ns-2. The Router Solicitation message from the mobile node may arrive at any time after the mobile node's. After acquiring MN ID, MAG send query packet to AAA server. At AAA server, authentication of MN is done using MN ID. AAA server search MN ID in list maintained. If AAA server finds the MN ID is present in list, it means MN is authenticated. If AAA server finds that MN is authenticated, it sends LMA address to MAG. MAG update MN's list present and send PBU message to LMA. Remaining work is similar to that of existing architecture.

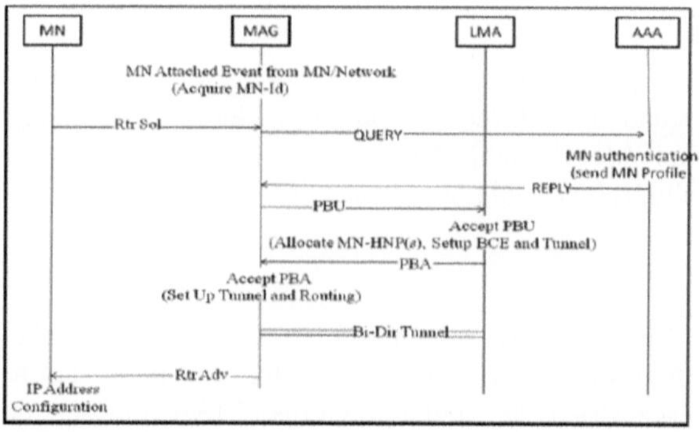

Fig. 3. Proposed Mobile Node Attachment - Signaling Call Flow

5 Implementation of AAA Server

In this section the AAA server implementation in NS2 will be described according to the architecture defined in the previous section.NS2 uses C++ as a back end language and TCL scripts can be used for generating scenarios and changing parameter of the core implementation for dynamic result. In ns-2 following functions of AAA server are implemented using C++. Fig 4 shows flow chart of working of AAA server.

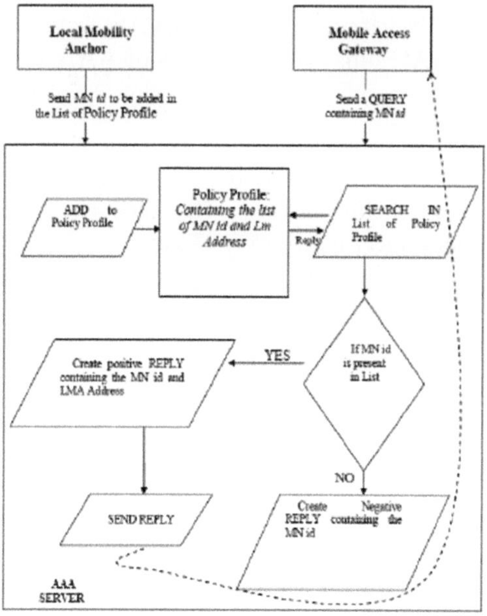

Fig. 4. Flow Chart of working of AAA server

Register new MN

This function is used to register LMA address along with the MN ID of MN. Various policies can be used along with MN ID and LMA address based on requirements but we have considered only MN ID and LMA address. We have used data structure to maintain this list having fields as lmaa and mn id. This function is called from TCL script.

Process Query

When MN will come in contact with MAG it will send query packet to AAA server. The task of handling query packet is done by this function. This function calls find function which takes MN ID as input and returns LMAA if present or returns -1. After obtaining LMAA this function calls send query function and supplies LMAA as input.

Send reply

This function is called by above function. This function calls create reply which create packet containing reply for MAG containing LMA address or -1. After creating reply packet this function sends packet to MAG.

To implement above changes in existing ns-2 there was need to add functions in existing MAG in ns-2. Those functions are explained below.

Set AAA address

This function takes AAA server address as input and save it for use in future. As whenever new MN gets attached to MAG it sends query to AAA server. For sending query MAG must know address of AAA server.

Send query

When MN gets attached to MAG, MAG sends query to AAA server to find out address of LMA to which MN belongs. This function calls create query to create query packet. After this, query is sent to AAA server.

Process reply

Reply packet sent by AAA server is handled by this function. If packet consists of LMA address then PBU is sent to proceed further. If packet does not contain LMA address then it gives error message that MN is not registered yet.

6 Simulation Setup

For simulation we have considered one corresponding node (CN), one mobile node (MN), two MAGs and different numbers of LMAs. The topology used for the simulation is same as that shown in Fig 1. CN has data that to be sent to MN. We have simulated for 1,2,3,4 and 5 numbers of LMAs and calculated hand off delay in two scenarios. Table 1 shows the configuration of other necessary parameters for the simulation:

Table 1. Results Obtained From Software Agents For Nodes 0 And 1

Simulation tool	NS-2.29
Simulation time	20sec
Number of LMAs	1,2,3,4and 5
Packet size	1000 bytes
Routing protocol	PMIPv6 without AAA, with AAA
Traffic type	CBR

7 Simulation Results and Analysis

The performance parameters considered for the study is Hand off delay. Handoff delay time defines the granularity with which the mobility infrastructure can maintain network reachability to a MN as it moves across access regions. Fig 5 and Fig 6 show hand off procedure in PMIPv6

In both cases t1 represents time at which MN gets disconnected from MAG1, t2 represents time at which MAG2 detects MN in its area and t3 represents time at which MAG2 connects MN. Therefore hand off delay can be given as

$$HOD = t3\text{-}t1,$$

Where HOD is hand off delay. Time t2-t1 is same in both cases, due to which we are concentrating only on time t3-t2. It is observed that though hand off delay for one LMA was less in case of absence of AAA server, it increases rapidly with increase in number of LMA. For more than one number of LMA, Hand off delay was observed less in case of presence of AAA server. Following Hand off delay was observed during simulation

Case I: Without AAA server

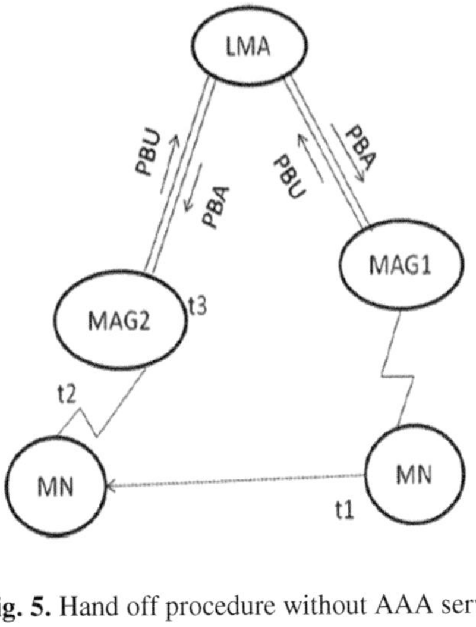

Fig. 5. Hand off procedure without AAA server

Case II: With AAA server

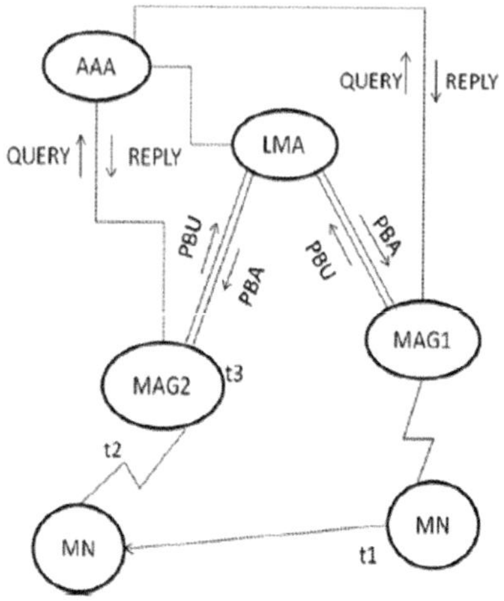

Fig. 6. Hand off procedure with AAA server

Table 2. Hand off delay for five LMAs

NO. of LMAs	Without AAA server	With AAA server
1	0.004022	0.006044
2	0.008044	0.006044
3	0.012065	0.006044
4	0.016087	0.006044
5	0.020109	0.006044

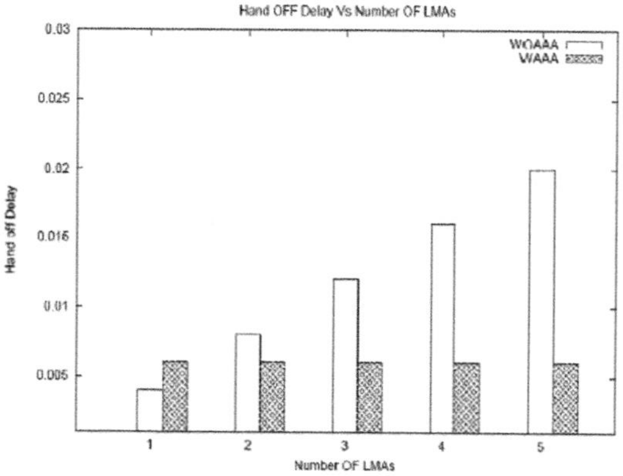

Fig. 7. Hand off delay for five LMAs

8 Conclusion

In this paper we have proposed implementation of AAA server in NS-2. The patch available for PMIPv6 does not contain implementation of AAA server. We have successfully implemented AAA server in NS-2. In presence of AAA server hand off delay remains constant and it is less then hand off delay observed in case of absence of AAA server. Future work may include detection of direction of movement of MN so that new MAG to which MN may connect, can be anticipated.

References

1. Zhou, H., Zhang, H.: An Authentication Protocol for Proxy Mobile IPv6 (2008) IEEE doi:10.1109/MSN.2008.27
2. Sun, H., Song, J., Chen, Z.: Survey of Authentication in Mobile IPv6 Network (2010), 978-1-4244 5176 0/10/26.00 © 2010 IEEE
3. Lee, J.-H., Lee, J.-H., Chung, T.-M.: Ticket-based Authentication Mechanism for Proxy Mobile IPv6 Environment. IEEEDOI 1109 / ICSNC (2008) 254; Pal, P., Schantz, R., Atighetchi, M., Loyall, J.: What Next in Intrusion Tolerance. BBN Technologies Cambridge, MA.
4. Lee, J.-C., Park, J.-S.: Fast Handover for Proxy Mobile IPv6 based on 802.1I Networks ISBN 978-89-5519-136-3
5. Magagula, L.A., Chan, H.A.: Early Discovery and Pre-authentication in Proxy MIPv6 for Reducing Handover Delay (2008) IEEEdoi:10.1109 /BROADC-OM.2008.84
6. Gundavelli, S., Leung, K., Devarapalli, V., Chowdhury, K., Patil, B.: Proxy Mobile IPv6, Internet Draft, draft-ietf-netlmm-proxymip (February 6-11, 2008).8
7. Liza, F.F., Yao, W.: Implementation Architecture of Proxy Mobile IPv6 Protocol for NS2 Simulator software (2009) IEEEdoi:10.1109/ICCSN.2009.156

Cloud Based Application Development for Mobile Devices for Accessing LBS

Keerthi S. Shetty and Sanjay Singh

Department of Information and Communication Technology
Manipal Institute of Technology, Manipal University, Manipal, India
keert.cs@gmail.com, sanjay.singh@manipal.edu

Abstract. A mobile device like a smart phone is becoming one of main information processing devices for users these days. Using it, a user not only receives and makes calls, but also performs information processing tasks such as retrieving information about nearest restaurants, ATMs etc. With the rapid improvement in technology of these mobile computing devices, Location Based Services (LBS) have been gaining a lot of attention over the years. The location service provider uses the geographical position of the user to provide services to the end users. However, a mobile device is still resource constrained, and some applications usually demand more resources than a mobile device can afford. To alleviate this, a mobile device should get resources from an external source. One of such sources is cloud computing platforms. We can predict that the mobile area will take on a boom with the advent of this new concept. The aim of this paper is to exchange messages between user and location service provider in mobile device accessing the cloud by minimizing cost, data storage and processing power. Our main goal is to provide dynamic location-based service and increase the information retrieve accuracy especially on the limited mobile screen by accessing cloud application. We have implemented our application in Android.

1 Introduction

Mobile phones are becoming pervasive. Given the advances in mobile phones, users start to consider a mobile phone a personal information processing tool. That is, a user expects to execute any application on top of a mobile device. The information retrieval in mobile devices is a tedious task due to the limited processing capability and low storage space available. Therefore ways to explore technology where offloading to mobile devices can be overcome is a research issue. Hence the advent of Cloud computing in Location-Based Services increases the user's information retrieve capability by overcoming the mobile's storage space and processing capability. A lot of development in the field of mobile computing devices can be seen during the recent years. With the rapid improvement in technology of these mobile computing devices, Cloud Computing has been gaining a lot of attention over the years. Cloud computing, a rapidly developing information technology, has aroused the concern of the whole world.

D. Nagamalai, E. Renault, and M. Dhanushkodi (Eds.): PDCTA 2011, CCIS 203, pp. 532–543, 2011.

Cloud computing is Internet-based computing, whereby shared resources, software and information, are provided to computers and devices on-demand. It is not a new concept; it is originated from the earlier large-scale distributed computing technology [9]. However, it will be a subversion technology and cloud computing will be the third revolution in the IT industry, which represent the development trend of the IT industry from hardware to software, software to services, distributed service to centralized service.

Cloud computing is also a new mode of business computing, it will be widely used in the near future. The core concept of cloud computing is reducing the processing burden on the users' terminal by constantly improving the handling ability of the "cloud", eventually simplifying the users' terminal to a simple input and output devices, and busk in the powerful computing capacity of the cloud on-demand [9]. But any form of work in the field of mobile devices accessing cloud service provider in LBS has been minimal.

Integration between mobile devices and cloud computing is presented in several previous works. Christensen [4] presents general requirements and key technologies to achieve the vision of mobile cloud computing. The author introduces an analysis on smart phones, context awareness, cloud and restful based web services, and explains how these components can interact to create a better experience for mobile phone users.

Luo [8] introduced the idea of using cloud computing to enhance the capabilities of mobile devices. The main goal of this work is to show the feasibility of such implementation, introducing a new partition scheme for tasks. The best point about this paper is the considerations about using the cloud to back mobile computing.

Giurgiu et al. [6] has used the cloud as the container for mobile applications. Applications are pre-processed based on the current context of the user, so only the bundles that can run on the local device and minimize the communication overhead with the cloud are offloaded to the mobile device from the cloud. They focus on partition policies to support the execution of application on mobile devices, and do not tackle any other issue related to mobile cloud computing.

Chun and Maniatis [5] have explored the use of cloud computing to execute mobile applications on behalf of the device. They propose the creation of clone VMs to run applications/services the same way that they will run on mobile devices in order to avoid inconsistencies produced to run part of a program in different architecture. Their work is strongly tied to distributed file systems, and assumes connectivity to the cloud.

In this paper, We present the application which has been implemented in Java for Android devices which require the Android SDK and ADT Plug-in. It was selected because it provides rich APIs for map, location functions and also there were implementations available for cloud computing providers on top of this platform. So we introduce the android operating system into our mobile information retrieve system. It can effectively interact with cloud service providers to retrieve information in Location Based Services.

The remaining paper is organized as follows. Section 2 discusses the theoretical background of LBS and the message exchange that occurs in the system and cloud computing, android operating system. Section 3 describes the architecture of the system developed. Section 4 discusses about the system functionality of the system. Section 5 gives the algorthmic description. Section 6 describes the implementation details of the system. Finally, a conclusion has been drawn in section 7.

2 Theoretical Background

2.1 Location Based Services

Location Based Service(LBS) uses the geographical position of a user to provide services such as health, work, entertainment services etc. The mobile service provider are the entities that provide these services to the user.

A distinct characteristic of LBS is its capability to provide service not just based on time and location, but also based on the user requirement at a particular location. The LBS system should be aware of the user needs and capable of mapping it to the location at which the service is required. The complexity of this system increases when the accuracy of the position and the dependency relationships between the locations need to be considered [7].

There are various devices and techniques that can be used to detect the location of the user in the system. Some of the examples are Global positioning system (GPS), RFID etc.

GPS based systems. The Global Positioning System is a navigation system that consists of 28 high-altitude satellites with highly accurate atomic clocks. These satellites are used to find the precise geographical position of a user. The GPS services are usually freely available [11].

The GPS receiver uses a triangulation method of the satellites to pinpoint the location of a user. It can be used to find the exact location to an order of a few meters. Error larger than a few meters is intolerable in these systems. GPS systems have a response time of the order of a few milliseconds making it an highly efficient system for LBS.

RFID systems. It is one of the technologies that has gained a lot of importance in the recent times. The distinct characteristics that separate it from other context aware technologies are contact-less, multi-object recognition, non-line-of-sight, long distance, large store of memory, programmability and penetrability [11]. The main advantage of RFID is its ability to map a physical object to a virtual object in its RFID network. This is achieved by assigning a physical tag to each physical object.

The entire area under the RFID system is divided into zones. These zones are then mapped into space of information tags. This mapping makes it easier to determine the accurate locations of the physical objects.

Currently, there is no system that is capable of giving the exact location information. GPS works accurately only on outdoors. It fails to provide satisfactory results when there is some kind of obstruction. Whereas on the other hand, RFID tags can be used on a request/response model to store unique RFID tags or some other form of identifier in their memory, and hence can be used to track mobile objects irrespective of their location.

2.2 Message Exchange in LBS

When a user enters into the coverage area of a Location Service Provider(LSP), various messages are exchanged. It could be the LSP sending a list of services to the client, or the user selecting among the list of services, or the messages could also include the LSP performing the authentication and authorization based on the information received from the mobile device. These messages exchanged form the backbone of the LBS system.

2.3 Cloud Computing

Cloud is a virtualized pool of computing resources. It can:

- Manage a variety of different workloads, including the batch of back-end operations and user-oriented interactive applications.
- Rapidly deploy and increase workload by speedy providing physical machines or virtual machines.
- Support for redundancy, self-healing and highly scalable programming model, so that workload can be recover from a variety of inevitable hardware/software failure.
- Real-time monitor resources usage, rebalance the allocation of resources when needed [3].

2.4 Android Operating System

The Open Handset Alliance released the Google Android SDK on November 12, 2007 [2]. The conception of the Android platform is attracting more and more programmers in mobile computing fields. Android is a package of software for mobile devices, including an operating system, middleware and core applications. The Android SDK provides powerful tools and APIs necessary to develop applications on the Android platform using the Java programming language. Android platform is of open system architecture, with versatile development and debugging environment, but also supports a variety of scalable user experience, which has optimized graphics systems, rich media support and a very powerful browser. It enables reuse and replacement of components and an efficient database support and support various wireless communication means. It uses a Dalvik virtual machine heavily optimized for mobile devices [1]. Android also supports GPS, Video Camera, compass, and 3D-accelerometer and provides rich APIs for map and location functions. Users can flexibly access, control and process the free Google map and implement location based mobile service in his mobile systems at low cost. Android platform will not only promote the technology (including the platform itself) of innovation, but also help to reduce development costs, and enable developers to form their mobile systems with unique characteristics.

3 System Architecture

The Fig.1 gives the architecture diagram of the cloud application. The application has been implemented in Java for android devices which require the Android SDK and ADT Plug-in. In this paper, we first proposed a location-based data and service middleware, which is mainly responsible for the collection and disposal of different data type and services existing in different network information platform. Based on the pretreated information, this interface module will repackage the heterogeneous data and service and republic them as web service. The details of the cloud application layer are given in [10].

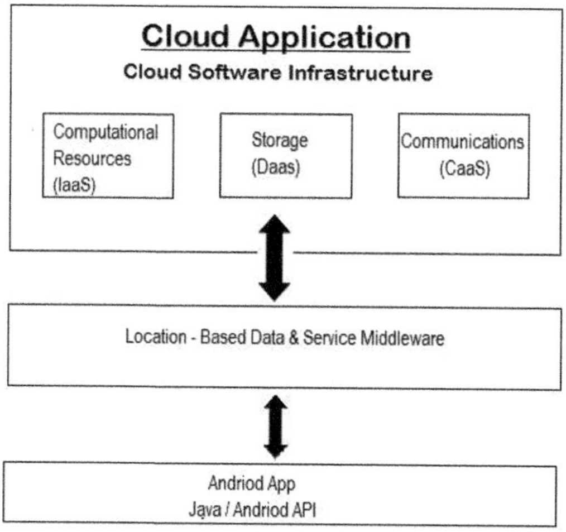

Fig. 1. Architecture of Cloud Application

4 System Functionality

Each location has several Cloud Units(CU) which acts as mobile support station to support services for mobile users in this location. Cloud units in every location are connected to Cloud Service Provider (CSP). In our system, we have considered only insurance related services. Each cloud stores insurance related information like health insurance, motor insurance, and whole life policy etc. The cloud enabled mobile application is shown in Fig.2.

4.1 Role of LSP and User

When a user enters into the coverage area of LSP, user needs to register with LSP to access the available services. LSP performs authentication by assigning user with unique ID i.e.,Phone Number. User is able to access required service by providing unique ID. Use case diagram of LSP and User is shown in Fig.3.

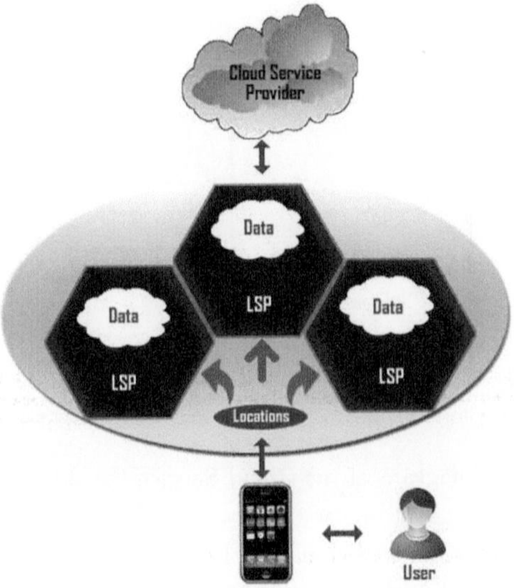

Fig. 2. Cloud Enabled Mobile Application

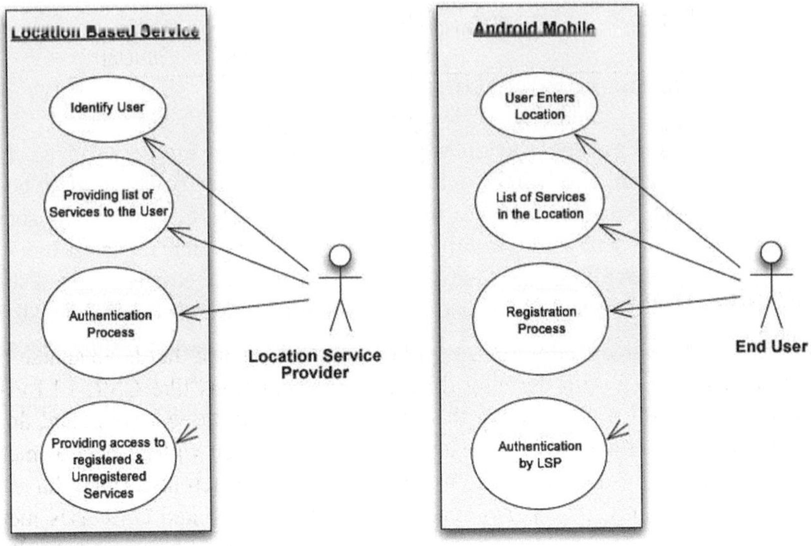

(a) (b)

Fig. 3. Usecase Diagram of (a) Location Service Provider (b) User

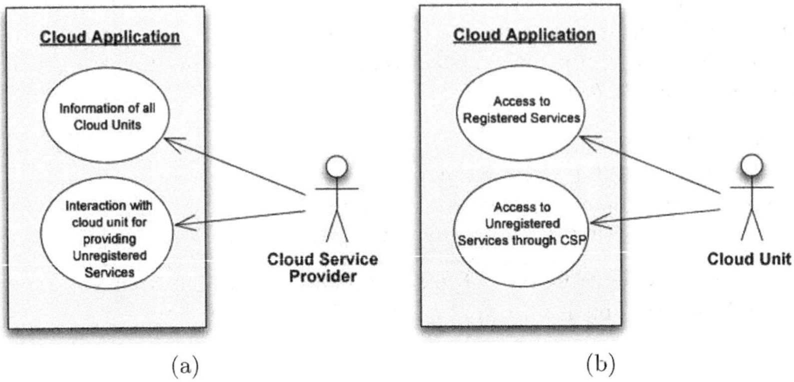

Fig. 4. Usecase Diagram of (a) Cloud Service Provider (b) Cloud Unit

In location based service, each location has several cloud units. Cloud units in every location are connected to CSP. These two have different computing ability and its main task is different. The cloud units aim at dealing the requests from users directly. The CSP is for dealing the key computing of some service. Cloud units in each location send requests to the CSP for some complex service. Use case diagram of CSP and CU is shown in Fig.4.

5 Algorithmic Description

The LSP performs authentication when a user registers for its services. If the user is authenticated, the LSP provides the list of services to the user. The user selects a service among the services in this list. This list contains all the services the user is registered to and available in that location. Each location has cloud units capable of providing services to the user. User can access registered service from cloud units directly. User needs to contact cloud units present in each location for unregistered services. CU contacts CSP to provide required services to the user. This can be explained better with the help of a pseudo code given in Algorithm 1. The Algorithm 1 depicts the overall working of the system.

In Algorithm 2, the location of the user is identified using either RFID or GPS. Once the location has been identified, the number of users has to be computed. Once this computation is done, the location co-ordinates of the particular user is sent to the LSP.

In Algorithm 3, the location co-ordinates returned by Algorithm 2 is used as a parameter to identify all the services available in that location.

In Algorithm 4, for the given list of services available in that location, the LSP checks whether the user is authorized to use the service or not. For all the services that the user is authorized, a list is created and sent to the user.

Algorithm 1. LocationBasedService()

```
RegisterUser (phoneno)
for every Registered_user do
    when user enters any of the location
    Identify_Location()
    Identify_services_in_Location (location)
    if user is authenticated then
        for every user do
            Provide_List_of_Services (services)
        end for
        for every registered service selected by user do
            user access cloud unit present in location for service
            for every unregistered service selected by user do
                Cloud Unit Present in location contacts CSP
                CSP provides the service
            end for
        end for
    end if
end for
```

Algorithm 2. Identify_Location()

```
Identify the location the user is currently present using either RFID or GPS.
Identify the number of users present in the location for whom the services have to
  be provided.
return Location co-ordinates.
```

Algorithm 3. Identify_Services (location)

```
Identify the different services that are available in the particular location.
Identify the what type of services to be provided to a specific user.
return Location co-ordinates.
```

Algorithm 4. Provide_List_of_Services (services)

```
if user is authorized for the service then
    add it to the list of available services.
end if
return List_of_Services
```

6 Implementation Details

Our main goal is to provide dynamic location-based service and increase the information retrieve accuracy especially in the limited mobile screen by accessing cloud application. The location is capable of providing multiple services. Each location has multiple cloud units. Cloud units stores information like Motor, Health, Pet and Life Insurance. We have modularized the system into different modules of the system.

- **Creating the CSP:** It stores information about all the cloud units present in each location.
- **Registration Process:** When a user enters into the coverage area of service provider, user registers with service provider to access the available services based on his preferences. User enters his credentials to get registered and the location service provider assigns him with the userID.
- **Authentication performed by the specific LSP:** The service provider performs authentication when a user registers for its services. If the user is authenticated, the service provider provides the access to the registered services. This list contains all the services the user is registered to in that location. The service provider provides the requested service to the user as long as the user is in that location.
- **User access CU for the registered services:** When a user enters into the coverage area of service provider and gets registered with the LSP for his preferable services and gain access to the registered services. Each location has multiple cloud units which provide information to the registered user based on his request.
- **User accessing CSP through the CU for unregistered services:** Registered user can directly interact with cloud units but not with cloud service provider. Cloud units in each location send requests to the cloud service provider for some complex service.

The application is developed for Insurance Domain. User can obtain the insurance related information and available agents lists for policies and agent information in that location.

The application will first obtain the user's current location and show the name of the current location as well as services under that location. User is provided with two options. Register button for new user to register with LSP for required services. Login button for already registered user. It is shown in Fig.5.

When a user enters into the coverage area of LSP, user needs to register with LSP to access the available services. User enters his credentials to get registered and LSP assigns user with unique ID. It is shown in Fig.6.

Registered user enters his login credentials to get access to the registered services. LSP performs authentication by unique ID assigned to each user, pop-up message is displayed "Authenticated User". It is shown in Fig.7.

Once the registered user login to the application the services selected by the user is displayed. He can selects the service for required information.Information about the policies and available agent list in that location is displayed. User can select the agent and agent information is provided to the user. It is shown in Fig.8.

Fig. 5. Screenshot showing services under LocationA

(a) (b)

Fig. 6. Screen Shots Showing (a) Registration Process (b) UniqueId Generation

(a) (b)

Fig. 7. Screen Shots Showing (a) Login Credentials (b) Authentication Process

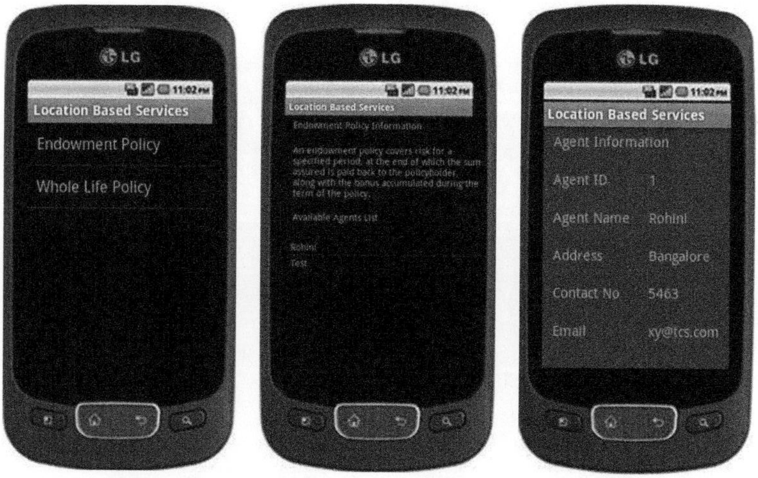

(a) (b) (c)

Fig. 8. Screen Shots Showing (a)Registered Services from User (b) Information about Services (c) Agent Information

7 Conclusion

Providing dynamic location-based service and improving the information retrieve accuracy especially in the limited mobile screen have become the important research areas in the development of LBS. Cloud computing brings us the approximately infinite computing capability, good scalability, service on-demand and so on. Cloud provides secure and dependable data storage center. In this paper, we have proposed retrieving information in mobile device accessing CSP based on the locations. Registered user can access services directly from the CU whenever he wants irrespective of the location. Processing power is faster and it is energy efficient. The application was implemented in Java for android devices. In the future, we believe that our efforts need to focus more on security issues and platform independent cloud application.

References

1. Android - an open handset alliance project (2011), http://www.code.google.com-/intl/zh-CN/android/
2. Open hanset alliance (2011), http://www.openhandsetalliance.com/
3. Boss, G., Malladi, P., Quan, D., Legregni, L., Hall, H.: Hipods, www.ibm.com/developerworks/websphere/zones/hipods/
4. Christensen, J.: Using RESTful web-services and cloud computing to create next generation mobile applications. In: Proceeding of the 24th Conference on Object Oriented Programming Systems Languages and Applications - OOPSLA 2009, p. 627. ACM Press, New York (2009)
5. Chun, B., Maniatis, P.: Augmented Smartphone Applications Through Clone Cloud Execution. In: HOTOS Workshop. USENIX (2009)
6. Giurgiu, I., Riva, O., Juric, D., Krivulev, I., Alonso, G.: Calling the cloud: enabling mobile phones as interfaces to cloud applications. In: Bacon, J.M., Cooper, B.F. (eds.) Middleware 2009. LNCS, vol. 5896, pp. 83–102. Springer, Heidelberg (2009)
7. Hoareau, C., Ichiro, S.: Query language for location-based services: A model checking approach. IEICE - Trans. Inf. Syst. E91-D(4), 976–985 (2008)
8. Luo, X.: From Augmented Reality to Augmented Computing: A Look at Cloud-Mobile Convergence. In: International Symposium on Ubiquitous Virtual Reality, pp. 29–32 (2009)
9. Maggiani, R.: Cloud computing is changing how we communicate. In: Proceeding of the IEEE International Professional Communication Conference (IPCC), Waikki, USA, pp. 1–4 (2009)
10. Youseff, L., Butrico, M., Silva, D.D.: Toward a unified ontology of cloud computing. In: Grid Computing Environment Workshop, pp. 1–10 (2008)
11. Zhang, T., Ouyang, Y., Li, C., Xiong, Z.: A scalable rfid-based system for location-aware services. In: International Conference on Wireless Communications, Networking and Mobile Computing, WiCom 2007, pp. 2117–2123 (September 2007)

B-SPECS: An Optic Based Recognition Tool for Blind

S. Cyril Naves

Department of Information Technology
Sri Sairam Institute of Technology, Anna University, Chennai, India
cyrilnaves91@gmail.com

Abstract. People with visual impairments usually know their environment using a wide range of tools and constant assistance from a peer. They are faced with problems such as an independent and a peaceful mode of aid .Even though a plethora of instruments such as canes built in with sensors can offer safety but in order to sense their surrounding there remains a void space. There exist a need for a system to offer uninterrupted and a reliable tutoring to the blind. This system: B-SPECS is one which helps solve the hassle and anxiety in the mind of a blind person offering continuous intelligence support. This paper proposes a novel spectacle model tool which assists the blind in recognizing their environment with a repository of images and intelligently identifying any new images which will trigger new learning of images achieving self directed learning. The image database is matched with a query image from the surrounding and the resultant is informed to the blind user with an audio enabled in the device. In case of a novel image, it is screened from the image sensor directed via a 3G enabled video conference requesting a help from a peer to the user. The image matching is done with a region based fuzzy feature matching in this optic based recognition. Blind can use this tool mitigating their dependency on others and freely adapt to their environment ensuring an effective learning of their place and easily carrying out their work with increased confidence.

Keywords: image classification, content based image retrieval, fuzzy feature, UMTS, segmentation, image sensor.

1 Introduction

The number of blind people in the world is estimated to be around 38 million by the World Health Organization .The three main causes with respect to blindness are glaucoma, trachoma and cataract which can be medically solved. But the losses of eyesight due to accidents, blind from birth are complex to be treated. These people are enabled with education by Braille form, by sense of touch, and narration based learning. Their mode of safety and assistance while commuting in a new environment are by canes, watch dogs or by assistance from a nearby person. But in some cases they are too dependent on their peers, even with respect to certain essentials such as accessing an atm, restroom, or a new location can be very difficult for a blind as he becomes psychologically tired. In order for an independent and less stressful form of

D. Nagamalai, E. Renault, and M. Dhanushkodi (Eds.): PDCTA 2011, CCIS 203, pp. 544–551, 2011.

life for a blind this idea was proposed in enabling them to work freely. This tool was titled **B-SPECS** in recognition to the work of Louis Braille i.e., Braille Spectacles.

2 Background

Typically this device is built in the form of a spectacle with an camera associated image sensor mounted in the mid axial of the spectacle and thereby the array of images as operate by the user transmits the surrounding image as a query to the already predefined database of images and then matched with and responds to the user with an audio description of the image. In case the processor intercepts a new image it is stored in the form of a queue data structure waiting to be either sent via video teleconferencing and later a sound description is added to this foreign image. The image matching is done with unique process of image segmentation, representation and feature matching.

3 Component Specifications

Image Sensor: The image sensor built in is a CMOS sensor which is a type of active pixel sensor. This converts the incoming light into voltage and the transfers to a memory. The technical specification of the sensor suitable will be of **Capturing speed:** 30frames per second

Width: 1600
Height: 1200
Aspect ratio: 4:3
Actual pixel count: 1,920,000
Mega pixel: 4
Night vision: Bright white light led.

Processor: Cortex-A8 processor [4] is used with enabled NEON technology based packed SIMD processing. Registers are considered as vectors of elements of same type. The processor is enabled for accelerating multimedia application. Its frequency ranges from 600MHz to 1GHz with a superscalar micro architecture.

Memory: A ROM memory is used with a faster access mode for a cache for it. "Smart" memory card architecture is used with significantly increased performance by a fast dynamic random access memory which allows up to 8byte data transfers after every 27 ns after initial access.

Power: A rechargeable Lithium-ion button cell is used with relatively 1000 mAh is implemented.

Speaker: A micro speaker is fit in with the audio description from the image database in it.

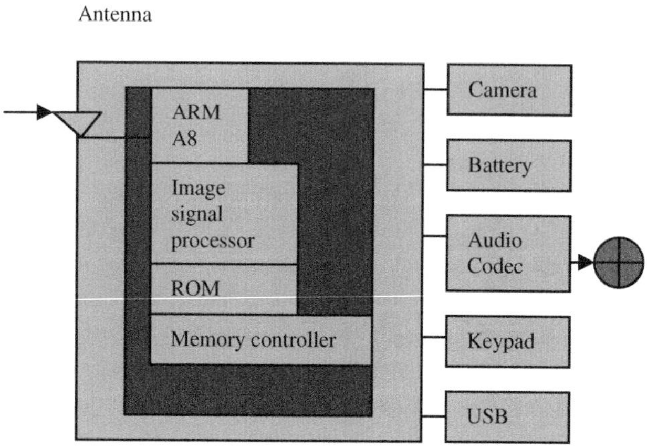

Fig. 1. Block diagram of BSPECS

4 Architecture

The device is first enabled with a camera with a sensor directing towards a memory which sources to the processor allowing segmentation of the image and then comparing and matching with the existing database repository of images, following an audio output via the speaker.

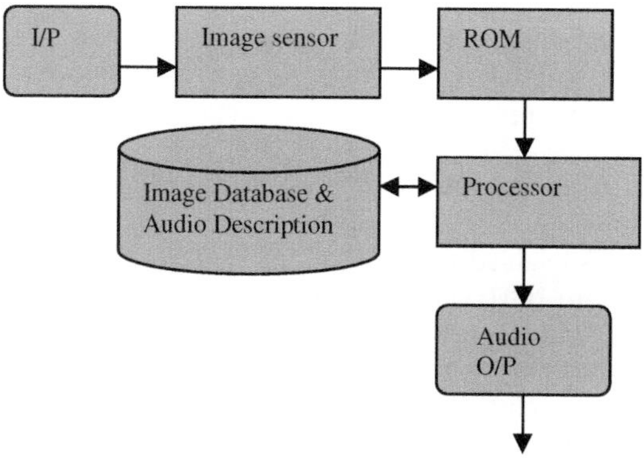

Fig. 2. Functional Block Diagram of matched query image

When a new image is detected by the system it allows for video calling with a 3g enabled network allowing the image to be seen by a peer requesting his assistance.

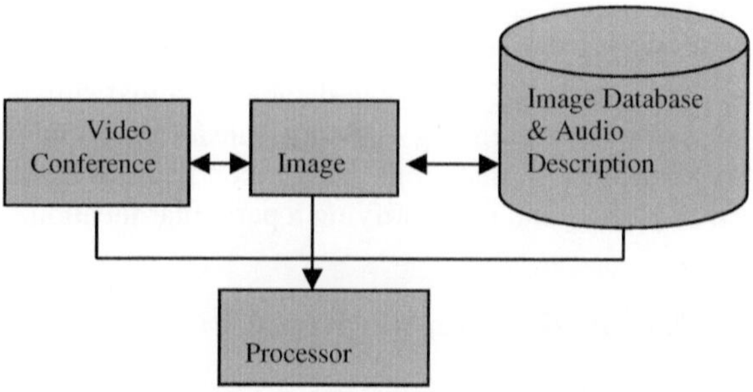

Fig. 3. Functional Block Diagram of unmatched query image

5 Implementation and Working

The device when worn by the user as a spectacle frame the camera is directly focused from user's frontal view enabling an upright capture of the image. Then the image is passed on to a memory in which the image is to be stored in as a signature enabling for a fuzzy logic[3] based approach in matching the query image [1] with the image database in getting a unified feature matching.

Case1: Query image present in database: Then on matching the image with the fuzzy feature an audio is directed to the user with the description of the identified image with reference to either an object or a being. Audio description of the form e.g.:" This is a butterfly"

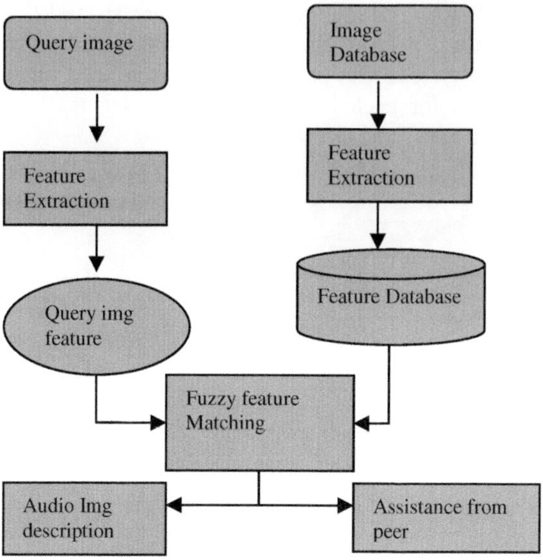

Fig. 4. Working Layout of BSPEC

Case2: Query image not present in database: In case when the compared image is not present in the database it is stored in the form of a queue as a self directed learning later on the updation of the image database. In that situation of the user the image is sent via a video conferencing enabling transfer of the image to a peer of the use requesting his assistance in that arena. This second case is also useful in directing with a live direction of the blind in identifying a particular location.

6 Algorithm Deployed in Region Based Fuzzy Feature Matching

In the image matching a fuzzy logic approach of unified feature matching is done for region based image retrieval. In this the image is represented by a set of segmented region each of which is characterized by a fuzzy feature reflecting color, texture and shape properties [2]. As a result image is associated with a family of fuzzy feature corresponding to regions. [3] Fuzzy features naturally characterize the gradual transition between regions within an image and incorporate the segmentation related uncertainties into the retrieval algorithm.

The resemblance of two images is then defined as the overall similarity between two families of fuzzy features and quantified by a similarity measure, UFM measure, which integrates properties of all the regions in the images [1]. Compared with similarity measures based on individual regions and on all regions with crisp-valued feature representations, the UFM measure greatly reduces the influence of inaccurate segmentation and provides a very intuitive quantification [7].

6.1 Preprocessing Image Database

In this all images in the database are first segmented into regions. Regions are represented by multidimensional fuzzy sets in feature space [2]. The collections of fuzzy sets for all regions of an image constitute the signature of the image. [5]To segment an image, the system first partitions the image into small blocks. A feature vector is then extracted for each block. The block size is chosen to compromise between texture effectiveness and computation time.

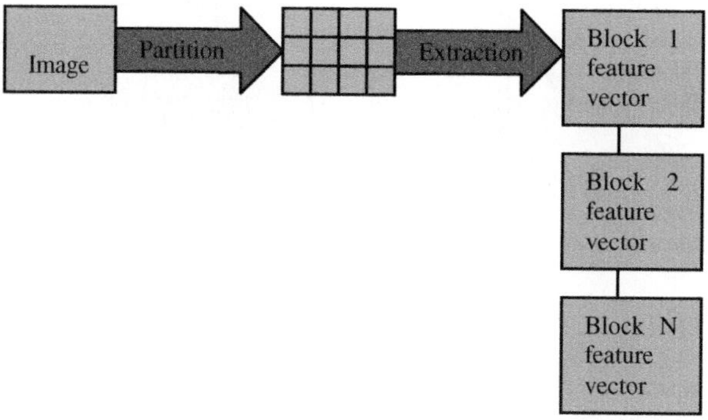

Fig. 5. Partition of query and database image into Blocks

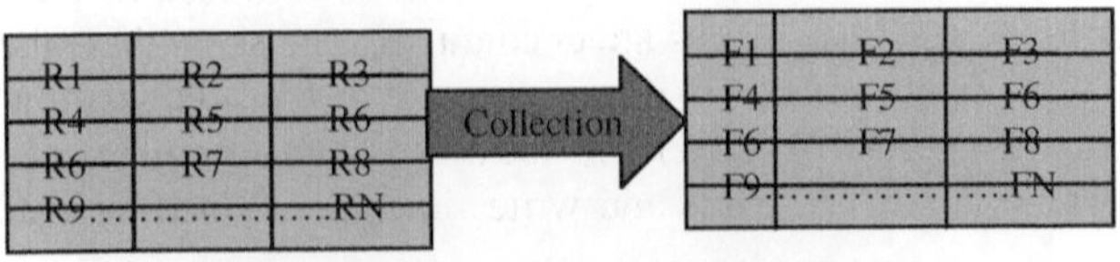

Fig. 6. Representing image region as a set of feature vector

Fig. 7. Example query image from camera

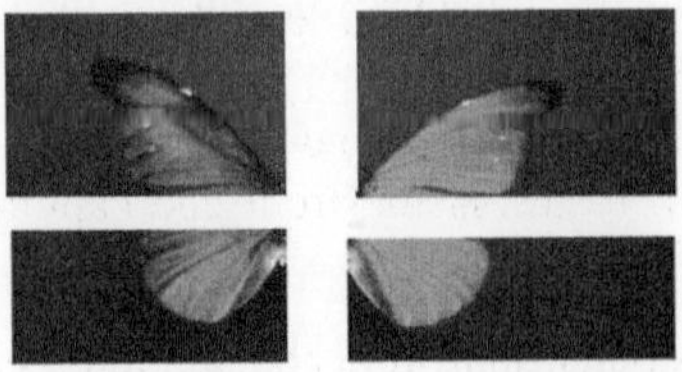

Fig. 8. Extraction of feature vector from Query image

Fig. 9. Sample image database

Fig. 10. Feature extracted Image database

6.2 Preprocessing Query Image

In this we consider two scenarios namely, inside query and outside query. For inside query, the query image is in the database. Therefore, the fuzzy features and semantic types can be directly loaded from the codebook [6].

If query image is not in the database the image then it stored in a queue data structure waiting for a description and directed via video conferencing assistance from a peer.

6.3 Computing UFM Measures

The UFM measure is the summation of all the weighted entries of similarity vectors between the query image and corresponding image database [5].

6.4 Returning Query Results

Images in database are sorted in descending order according to UFM measures obtained from previous step and the system then returns the audio description of the image to the user.

7 Conclusion

In this model we described a supporting device for the blind with a pervasive computing enabled tool for image recognition using a fuzzy logic approach in it.

The system proposed is smart in constantly evolving its database for new images and also in other case supporting the user with a help access with a video conferencing enabled in it seeking assistance from a trusted person. The system is optimized for faster access time and computation speed suitable as a guide for the blind.

References

[1] Smith, J.R., Chang, S.F.: VisualSEEK: A Fully Automated Content-Based Query System. In: Proc. ACM Multimaedia (1996)
[2] Unser, M.: Texture Classification and Segmentation Using Wavelet Frames. IEEE Trans. Iamge Processing (1995)
[3] Vertan, C., Boujemma, N.: Embedding Fuzzy logic in Content Based Image Retrieval. In: Proc.19th Intl.' Meeting North Am, Fuzzy Information Processing Soc. (July 2000)
[4] Cortex A8 ARM processor, White paper of ARM
[5] Chen, Y., Wang, J.Z.: Region Based Fuzzy Feature Matching. IEEE Transaction on Pattern Analysis and Machine Intelligence (September 2002)
[6] Shi, J., Malik, J.: Normalized Cuts and Image Segmentation. IEEE Trans. Pattern Analysis and Machine Intelligence 22(8), 888–905 (2000)
[7] Gupta, A., Jain, R.: Visual Information Retrieval. Comm. ACM 40(5), 70–79 (1997)

Parameter-Free Minimum Spanning Tree (PFMST) Based Clustering Algorithm

B.H.V.S. Ramakrishnam Raju[1] and V. Valli Kumari[2]

[1] Department of information Technology, SRKR Engineering College, Bhimavaram, Andhra Pradesh, India, 534204
rkraju_bhvs@yahoo.com
[2] Dept of Computer Science & Systems Engineering, Andhra University, Visakhapatnam, Andra Pradesh, India, 5300 03
vallikumari@gmail.com

Abstract. A number of existing clustering algorithms can solve the problem of clustering, but most of them require the setting of many input parameters. Two main problems with parameter-laden algorithms are the subsequent. First, incorrect settings may root an algorithm to fail in finding the true patterns. Second, an algorithm may account false patterns that do not really exist. This is probably to occur when the user fails to realize the role of parameters in the clustering process. In this paper, as a step towards justifying these problems, we propose a Parameter-Free Minimum Spanning Tree (PFMST) algorithm to automatically determine the number of clusters. The proposed algorithm is tested for both synthetic and real data sets based on ratio of intra-cluster and inter-cluster distances. The results show that the proposed algorithm for clustering is competitive or superior to the Standard K-Means clustering.

Keywords: Minimum Spanning Tree, validity ratio, clusters.

1 Introduction

Unsupervised learning or clustering is the process of grouping data objects into natural clusters so that data objects within the same cluster have high similarity while data objects belonging to different clusters have low similarity [1-2]. The similarity can be measured in different ways; a common practice is to use a distance measure: the smaller the distance, the greater is the similarity. Clustering has a variety of applications but is a computationally complex problem. There are basically five categories of clustering algorithms: namely partitioning algorithms, hierarchical algorithms, density-based algorithms, grid-based algorithms and graph-based algorithms [3]. Partitioning algorithms like K-means [2] divide data points into K clusters and then iteratively optimize a criterion function by re-assigning some data points. Hierarchical clustering [4] usually produces hierarchical trees instead of producing explicit clusters directly. Density-based algorithms like DENCLUE [5] and DBSCAN [6] usually consider clusters as dense regions of points separated by less dense regions. Grid based algorithms, like CLIQUE [7] and STING [8] firstly divide the data space into regular cells and then perform all clustering operations on the grid structure. Graph-based

D. Nagamalai, E. Renault, and M. Dhanushkodi (Eds.): PDCTA 2011, CCIS 203, pp. 552–560, 2011.

algorithms, usually construct a graph to model the relationship between data points. Such algorithms mainly differ in their criterion for removing inconsistent edges from the graph so as to collect the remaining connected components as clusters. Some well known algorithms in literature include Zhan's Minimum Spanning Tree (MST) based clustering [9], the new SNN clustering [10], CHAMELEON [11], and Cluster Editing method [12-13], HCS algorithm [14], etc. Although there are many effective and efficient clustering algorithms in literature, many of them still suffer from problems such as high time complexity or sensitivity to parameter setting, for example, setting the value k (no. of clusters) and tuning. To reduce the dependence of performance of clustering on parameters, a method is proposed in this paper to automatically detect clusters in the dataset. The paper is based on the approach that, an MST contains all the information for single linkage cluster analysis [15], and is thus well known for discovering arbitrary shaped clusters. There are two algorithms that are often used to find the MST: the Kruskal algorithm and the Prim algorithm.

The MST clustering algorithm is known to be capable of detecting clusters with irregular boundaries [9]. Contrasting to traditional clustering algorithms, the MST clustering algorithm does not assume a spherical shaped clustering structure of the underlying data. The Euclidean Minimum Spanning Tree (EMST) clustering algorithm [9] uses the Euclidean minimum spanning tree of a graph to produce the structure of point clusters in the n-dimensional Euclidean space. Clusters are detected to achieve some measure of optimality, like as minimum intra-cluster distance or maximum inter-cluster distance [1]. The EMST clustering algorithm has been widely used in practice. Once the MST is built for a given input, there are two different ways to produce a group of clusters. If the number of clusters k is given beforehand, the simplest way to obtain k clusters is to sort the edges of the minimum spanning tree in descending order of their weights, and remove the edges with the first k – 1 heaviest weights [1, 22]. The second approach does not require a preset cluster number. Edges, which satisfy a predefined inconsistency measure, are removed from the tree. The resulting connected components are called clusters. To reduce the dependence of clustering performance on parameters, in this paper, we propose a Parameter-Free MST (PFMST) based clustering algorithm. Our algorithm creates clusters by removing the inconsistent edges by first spiltting the MST and then merges the subtrees which are close. We use the inconsistency measure suggested by Zahn [9] for splitting the MST to create initial clusters.

2 Related Work

Clustering Algorithms based on minimum and maximum spanning tree were extensively studied. Avis [23] found an O ($n^2 \log^2 n$) algorithm for the min-max diameter-2 clustering problem. Asano, Bhattacharya, Keil, and Yao [1] later presented an optimal O(n log n) algorithm using maximum spanning trees for minimizing the maximum diameter of a bipartition. The clustering problems were considered under two different optimization criteria. One was to minimize the maximum intra-cluster distance (diameter), and the other was to maximize the minimum inter-cluster distance. The identification of inconsistent edges causes problem in the MST clustering algorithm. There exist various ways to divide clusters successively, however there is not a suitable choice for all cases.

Zahn [9] proposes to construct an MST of a point set and delete inconsistent edges — the edges, whose weights are significantly larger than the average weight of the nearby edges in the tree. Zahn proposed the following criterion to determine the inconsistent edges: an edge is inconsistent if its length is more than *f* times the average length of the edges, or more than *f* times the average of the length of nearby edges. The algorithm is able to detect clusters of various shapes and sizes. Although, Zahn's MST based clustering method works well for a two-dimensional data set, in more than two dimensions special heuristics are needed. The simplest version of Zahn's method is when the lengths of the edges are compared with the average edge length of MST. This MST clustering algorithm has been widely used in practice.

Xu , Olman and Xu [24] used an MST to represent multidimensional gene expression data. They described three objective functions and the corresponding clustering algorithms for computing a k-partition of the spanning tree for any predefined k > 0. The selection of the correct number of clusters is actually a kind of validation problem [25]. A large number of clusters provides a more complex "model" where as a small number may approximate data too much. Hence, several methods and indices have been developed for the problem of cluster validation and selection of the number of clusters [26, 27]

Grygorash, et al [28], proposed two EMST based clustering algorithms to address the issues of undesired clustering structures and an unnecessarily large number of clusters. The first algorithm, Hierarchical EMST (HEMST), assumes that the number of clusters is given. The second algorithm, Maximum Standard Deviation Reduction (MSDR) clustering algorithm partitions the point set into a group of clusters by maximizing the overall standard deviation reduction. The final number of clusters is determined by finding the local minimum of the standard deviation reduction function. MSDR algorithm automatically determines the desired number of clusters. This algorithm does not require the users to select and try various parameter combinations in order to get the desired output. Both the algorithms are tested for color image segmentation.

Xie [29] proposed an Improved MST (IMST) algorithm,. The time complexity of this algorithm is claimed to be less than the time complexity of prim's algorithm. The number of subtrees, k is to be set by the user to divide the MST into subtrees. Päivinen [30] proposed a scale-free minimum spanning tree (SFMST) clustering algorithm which constructs a scale free network and outputs clusters containing highly connected vertices and those connected to them. Three strategies were proposed for defining the inconsistent edges. The first strategy is to remove k longest edges from the spanning tree to get a clustering to k+1 cluster. In the second strategy, an edge is defined as inconsistent if it is of "considerably different" length, when comparing with its neighboring edges. For each node in the MST an average length of its edges, m, is calculated along with the standard deviation σ. If for some edge *e* satisfies $|e - m| > q\sigma$ the edge is treated as inconsistent. Here q is a positive constant. The third strategy is similar to the second except that all the edges that lie at most two steps away from the current node are taken into account when calculating mean and standard deviation. The results showed that the second and third strategies gave the better results than the first strategy. Yu [3] proposed a threshold criterion for the single linkage cluster analysis and incorporates it into the Minimum Spanning Tree

(MST) based clustering method. Since the threshold can be automatically decided according to the underlying data distributions, arbitrary shaped clusters can be discovered with little human intervention. Experiments were conducted on spatial data.

3 Proposed Algorithm

In this paper, a new approach to automatically cluster the given dataset is proposed, called as Parameter-Free Minimum Spanning Tree (PFMST) algorithm. The block diagram (Fig. 1) shows our proposed clustering process.

3.1 Minimum Spanning Tee Clustering

Usually, MST-based clustering algorithms consist of three steps:

1. Construction of a minimum spanning tree;
2. Elimination of the inconsistent edges to get a set of connected components (clusters); and
3. Repetition of step ii until some terminating condition is satisfied.

To get clustering from MST, a strategy for removing inconsistent edges is needed.

3.2 Splitting Process

Our algorithm starts by constructing a Minimum Spanning Tree (MST) from the given data set. The weight (w) of the edge in the tree is Euclidean distance between the two end points. Next, the average weight $\hat{w}$ of the edges in the entire MST and their standard deviation σ are computed; any edge with $w > \hat{w} + \sigma$ [28] is removed from the tree. This results in a set of disjoint subtrees, where each subtree is cluster. The clusters' centers are then identified.

3.3 Merging Process

The clusters identified are to be merged for good clustering based on compactness and separation metrics [4]. The distances of the points from their cluster centres are used to determine whether the clusters are compact. For this purpose, the intra-cluster distance, which is simply the distance between a point and its cluster centre, is measured and we take the average of all of those distances, defined as

$$\operatorname{int} ra = \frac{1}{N} \sum_{i=1}^{K} \sum_{x \in C_i} \|x - z_i\|^2 \tag{1}$$

Where N is the number of data items in the dataset, K is the number of clusters, and Z_i is the cluster centre of cluster C_i. We obviously want to minimize this measure. We can also measure the inter-cluster (separation) distance, or the distance between clusters, which should be as big as possible. We calculate this because the distance between cluster centres, and take the minimum of this value, defined as

$$\begin{aligned} \text{inter} &= \min\left(\left\| z_i - z_j \right\|^2\right), \\ .i &= 1,2,\dots,K-1 \\ j &= i+1,\dots,K \end{aligned} \tag{2}$$

The minimum of this value is to be considered as the smallest of this distance to be maximized. Both these metrics are combined into validity ratio [31] as

$$validity = \frac{\text{intra}}{\text{inter}} \tag{3}$$

Since we want to minimize the intra-cluster distance, we consequently want to minimize the validity measure. The inter-cluster distance measure is to be maximized and validity measure is to be minimized. Therefore, the clustering which gives a minimum value for the validity ratio gives the ideal value for number of clusters. The algorithm merges the clusters until ideal numbers of clusters are formed. The clusters whose distance between their centers is minimum are merged together in each iteration. The iteration continues as long as the validity ratio is decreasing and merging process stops when the ratio starts increasing. The number of clusters after merging is designated as optimal number of clusters for the given dataset.

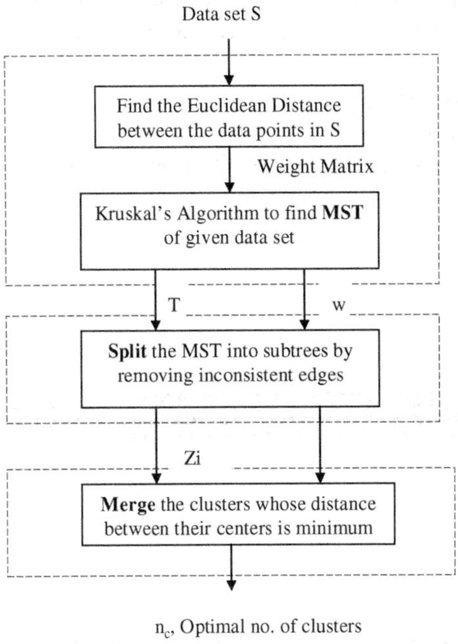

Fig. 1. Block diagram of proposed clustering process

Since the number of clusters are significantly less compared to the given, n, number of points in the data set, the complexity of this algorithm is solely depends on the number of clusters produced. For constructing MST the time complexity is $O(n^2)$ times. For removing the inconsistent edges from MST it requires $O(an)$ and for merging the clusters requires $O(bn)$. So the total complexity is $(n^2) + (an) + (bn)$.

4 Experimental Results

Experiments were conducted for both synthetic and real data sets from UCI Machine Learning Repository [32]. The reason for choosing the synthetic datasets is that they are easy to control and can be designed to contain a certain number of clusters. Three synthetic datasets were generated. The details of these datasets are shown in the Table.1. The real world data sets, which we use, are Iris, Soybean and Breast Tissue datasets. The details of real world datasets are presented in Table 2. The results are compared against standard K-Means algorithm.

We use raw data sets in the experiments, because of the accuracy of the methods to solve clustering cases. If we tend to normalize the data, although it is usual to get the better clustering results, the clustering results not only depend on clustering methods, but also depend on normalization methods. Therefore, we decide not to normalize the data in order to ensure that the clustering results absolutely depend on the accuracy of clustering methods. The results of our proposed method are compared with K-Means method. First the results for few synthetic data sets are exhibited and then for real data sets from UCI Machine learning repository.

Table 1. Synthetic datasets

Name of the data set	No. of attributes	Data Size (N)	Expected No. of clusters (k)
Dataset1	2	60	3
Dataset2	2	40	2
Dataset3	2	163	3

Table 2. Real datasets from UCI Repository

Name of the dataset	No. of attributes (d)	Data Size (N)	Expected No. of clusters (k)
Iris	4	150	3
Soybean	35	47	4
Breast Tissue	9	106	6

Table 3 shows the validity ratio for different data sets. The validity ratio is calculated for K Means clustering for value of k i.e. the number of clusters is equal to the optimal number of clusters produced by PFMST.

The MST clustering produced a number of small clusters containing one to few elements. This means that these elements are far away from the root of the tree than the other nodes. These elements might be considered as outliers. The validity ratio as shown in table 3 for Dataset1 and Dataset2 is similar to that of the K-Means Algorithm. The validity ratio based on PFMST clustering for Dataset3 is 0.1209, where as for K-Means this ratio is 0.2163. In presence of outliers, our algorithm shows better results than K-Means algorithm.

Table 3. Validity Ratio

Name of the Data Set	Validity Ratio	
	K-means	PFMST
Dataset1	0.0223	0.0223
Dataset2	0.0229	0.02289
Dataset3	0.2163	0.1209
Iris	0.4332	0.2373
Soybean	0.1903	0.1859
Breast Tissue	0.0307	0.0307

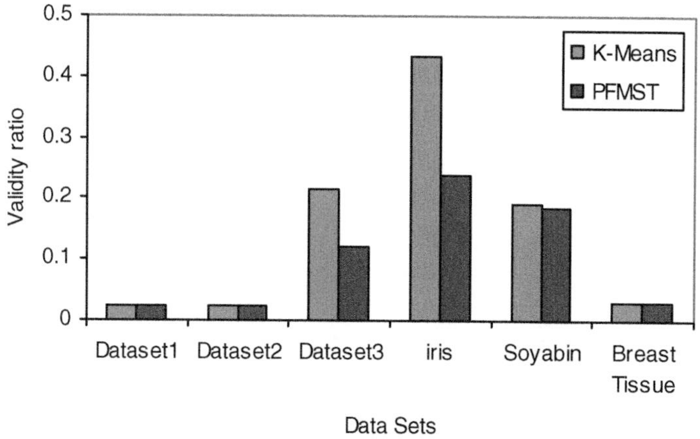

Fig. 2. Comparison of K-Means and PFMST Algorithms

In order to analyze the accuracy of our proposed method, we now demonstrate the results using some real world datasets from UCI Repository. The datasets used are Iris, Soybean and Breast Tissue. As shown in table 3 the validity ratio for real datasets is less or equal to the validity ratio determined by K-Means Algorithm. Our validity measure worked more consistently for both synthetic and real datasets. Fig. 3 shows validity ratio bar charts of synthetic and real datasets produced.

By incorporating the validity ratio based on the intra-cluster and inter-cluster distance metrics, the number of clusters present in the dataset can be determined automatically. The validity ratio used in our algorithm shows a minimum value for the number of clusters produced. The proposed algorithm does not require the users to select and try various parameters in order to get desired output.

5 Conclusions

In this work, we argue that clustering algorithms with parameters are troublesome to use and make it difficult to compare results across different methods. As a step towards justifying these problems, it was demonstrated that the proposed Parameter-Free MST algorithm can compete with or out perform parameter-laden algorithms like K-Means algorithm on a wide variety of problems. The proposed algorithm does not require the users to select and try various parameters in order to get the desired output. Since our method is based on MST it can also handle clustering boundaries of any shape. By introducing some sophisticated merging techniques, as well as selecting an appropriate threshold values, may produce more refined segmentation.

References

1. Asano, T., Bhattacharya, B., Keil, M., Yao, F.: Clustering algorithms based on minimum and maximum spanning trees. In: Proceedings of the 4th Annual Symposium on Computational Geometry, pp. 252–257 (1988)
2. Han, J., Kamber, M.: Data mining: concepts and techniques. Morgan Kaufmann, San Francisco (2001)
3. He, Y., Chen, L.: MinClue: A MST-based Clustering Method with Auto-Threshold-Detection. In: Proceedings of the 2004 IEEE Conference on Cybernetics and Intelligent Systems, Singapore, December 1-3, pp. 229–233 (2004)
4. Jain, A.K.: Algorithms for Clustering Data. Prentice Hall, Englewood Cliffs (1988)
5. Hirneburg, A., Keirn, D.A.: An efficient approach to clustering in large multimedia databases with noise. In: Proc. 4th Int. Conf. on Knowledge Discovery and Data Mining, pp. 58–65 (1998)
6. Ester, M., Kriegel, H.P., Sander, Xu, X.: A density-based algorithm for discovering clusters in large spatial databases with noise. In: Proc. 3rd Int. Con. on Knowledge Discovery and Data Mining, pp 226–231 (1996)
7. Agarwal, R., Gherke, J., Gunopulos, D., Raghavan, P.: Automatic subspace clustering of high dimensional data for data mining applications. In: Proc.1998 ACM SICMOD Int. Conf. on Management of Data, pp. 94–105 (1998)
8. Wang, W., Yang, J., Muntz, R.: Sting: a statistical information grid approach to spatial data mining. In: Proc.1997 Int. Conf. on Very Large Data Bases, pp. 186–195 (1997)
9. Zahn, C.T.: Graph-theoretical methods far detecting and describing gestalt clusters. IEEE Trans. on Computers c(20), 68–86 (1971)
10. Ertoz, L., Strinbach, M., Kumar, V.: Finding clusters of different sizes, shapes, and densities in noisy, high dimensional data. In: SIAM International Conference on Data Mining (May 2003)
11. Karypis, G., Han, E., Kumar, V.: Chameleon: A hierarchical clustering algorithm using dynamic modeling. IEEE Trans. on Computers: Special issue on Data Analysis and Mining 32(8), 68–75 (1999)

12. Gramm, J., Guo, J., Hüffner, E., Niedermier, R.: Graph-modeled data clustering: fixed-parameter algorithms for clique generation. In: Petreschi, R. (ed.) CIAC 2003, vol. 2653, pp. 108–119. Springer, Heidelberg (2003)
13. Shamir, R.R., Tsur, D.: Cluster graph modification problems. In: Kučera, L. (ed.) WG 2002. LNCS, vol. 2573, pp. 379–390. Springer, Heidelberg (2002)
14. Hartuv, E., Shamir, R.: A clustering algorithm based on graph connectivity. Information Processing Lecturers 76(4-6), 175–181 (2000)
15. Gower, C., Ross, C.J.S.: Minimum spanning frees and single linkage cluster analysis. Applied Statistics 8(1), 54–64 (1969)
16. Victor, S.P., John Peter, S.: A Novel Minimum Spanning Tree Based Clustering Algorithm for Image Mining. European Journal of Scientific Research 40(4), 540–546 (2010)
17. Zhang, J., Wang, N.: Detecting outlying subspaces for high-dimensional data: the new task. Algorithms and Performance, Knowledge and Information Systems 10(3), 333–555 (2006)
18. Loureiro, A., Torgo, L., Soares, C.: Outlier detection using Clustering methods: A data cleaning Application. In: Proceedings of KDNet Symposium on Knowledge-based Systems for the Public Sector, Bonn, Germany (2004)
19. He, Z., Xu, X., Deng, S.: Discovering cluster-based Local Outliers. Pattern Recognition Letters 24(9-10), 1641–1650 (2003)
20. Jaing, M., Tseng, S., Su, C.: Two-phase Clustering Process for Outlier Detection. Pattern Recognition Letters 22(6-7), 691–700 (2001)
21. Al-Zoubi, M.B.: An Effective Clustering-Based Approach or Outlier Detection. European Journal of Scientific Research 28(2), 310–316 (2009)
22. Chen, S.H., Hsieh, W.M.: Fast algorithm for VQ codebook design. Proc. Inst. Elect. Eng. 138, 357–362 (1991)
23. Avis, D.: Diameter Partitioning. Discrete and Computational Geometry 1, 265–276 (1986)
24. Xu, Y., Olman, V., Xu, D.: Minimum spanning trees for gene expression data clustering. Genome Informatics 12, 24–33 (2001)
25. Karthikeyan, T., John Peter, S.: Meta Similarity Noise-free Clusters Using Dynamic Minimum SpanningTree with Self-Detection of Best Number of Clusters. Journal of Emerging Trends in Computing and Information Sciences 2(4), 192–200 (2011)
26. Hardy, A.: On the Number of Clusters. Computational Statistics & Data Analysis 23(1), 83–96 (1996)
27. Still, S., Bialek, W.: How many clusters? An information-theoretic perspective. Neural Computation 16, 2483–2506 (2004)
28. Grygorash, O., Zhou, Y., Jorgensen, Z.: Minimum Spanning Tree Based Clustering Algorithms. In: Proceedings of the 18th IEEE International Conference on Tools with Artificial Intelligence, ICTAI 2006 (2006)
29. Xie, Z., Yu, L., Yang, J.: A Clustering Algorithm Based on Improved Minimum Spanning Tree. In: Fourth International Conference on Fuzzy Systems and Knowledge Discovery, FSKD 2007 (2007)
30. Paivinen, N.: Clustering with a minimum spanning tree of scale-free-like structure. Pattern Recogn. Lett. 26(7), 921–930 (2005)
31. Ray, S., Turi, R.H.: Determination of Number of Clusters in K–Means Clustering and application in color Image Segmentation. In: Proc. 4th Intl. Conf. ICAPRDT 1999, Calcutta, India, pp. 137–143 (1999)
32. `http://archive.ics.uci.edu/ml/index.html` (viewed on 10-3-2011)

State of Software Metrics to Forecast Variety of Elements in the Software Development Process

S. Arun Kumar and T. Arun Kumar

School of Computing Science and Engineering, VIT University,
Vellore, Tamil Nadu, India
vanathiarunkumar@gmail.com

Abstract. Software metrics are mainly utilized to measure and characterize the software development process. Cost, Time and Productivity are key attributes in the software development process. Predictability is the concept which leads to know prior the outcome of the system development. Predicting the various elements which relates to the software development process in advance is quite complex. The main aim of this paper is to propose a comprehensive set of software metrics for predicting the cost, time and productivity in advance with help of available inputs in the project instantiated. These metrics tends to be the horoscope of a project development. Our main objective is to resolve the complexity, enhancing the efficiency of the system development in earliest manner. This paper is mainly deals with analyzing and evaluating predictive metrics with predefined models. The implementation of the metrics to predict the outcome of the project whether the project leads to success or failure even before the project instantiated. If the project leads to success, predicting whether it attains massive or moderate profit. If the project leads to failure, check the alternative way to recover from failure i.e., to reduce the complexity and enhancement of efficiency.

Keywords: Software Predictability, Predictability Metrics, COCOMO, Time, Cost and Productivity.

1 Introduction

Metrics are the unit of measurement to characterize the software development process, with the use of the metrics to improve that process and product. Metrics concerns about enhance the efficiency and reduce the complexity of the project. Software metrics are all about measurements the way to improve and assist the software development with respect to process, project, and product. Software metrics are applicable to the whole development life cycle from initiation, when costs must be estimated; to monitoring the reliability of the end product, product changes over time with the enhancement. The predictability metrics to cover the monitoring and controlling the progress of the software development.

D. Nagamalai, E. Renault, and M. Dhanushkodi (Eds.): PDCTA 2011, CCIS 203, pp. 561–569, 2011.

2 Literature Survey

2.1 Methodology for Evaluating Predictive Metrics

Methodology for evaluating predictive metrics has been given by Jarret Rosenberg [1]. The methodology with different specification to align the metrics. Our proposed working principle of predictive metrics based on validating with help of these methodologies to measure the project success and failure.

2.2 State of Metrics in Software Industries

The state of metrics in software industries has been given by Mauricio J. Ordonez, Hisham M. Haddad [2]. Before heading to developing predictive metrics, it is essential to know the state of metrics followed in industries. Cost of Defects will lead to present a convincing argument for the benefit of using metrics. The author uses data from software metrics database and an industry profit-loss model to develop a method to compute the actual cost of software defects. Many consider these initiatives and efforts a significant contribution toward promoting the practice of software metrics. Sources of data include product comparisons, analysis of source code size and complexity, defect logging, project post mortem studies, and project schedule and resource plans. Identifying with metrics implemented in the software industries will enhance the requirements needed for the development of the predictive metrics. Collision in the data accuracy will be prevented in all such cases. Our predictive metrics is comparing with actual estimation and computed sample estimation of efforts, time, cost and productivity.

3 Metrics for Predictability

Normally metrics are applied during the project development and end of the process to enhance the efficiency and to reduce the complexity. It is possible to predict the result during the software development process. However predicting the result before the project development is quite complex. We propose a metrics that will predict the result before the project gets instantiated. We predict in all categories of metrics from product, project and process with possible aspects. Predicting happens with the manual estimation based on available input data from both client side and organization side. Approximately estimated costs and duration of the project has been given by client side. Sample size, effort, duration, developers are measured and predicted with 1/2 of the manual estimated data. If it is satisfies, the project leads to success with massive profit or else the project leads to failure. To recover from failure once again predicted with 2/3 of the manual estimated data. If it is satisfied then the project leads to success with moderate profit or else the project leads to perfect failure. The reason for taking 1/2 of the Input is to predict whether the project leads to success and on basis allocating cost for other resources, appointing staffs for other work apart from development, etc.

4 Adaptation of COCOMO

Our predictive metrics applied with help of available estimation models. The Constructive Cost estimation Model (COCOMO) model is concerned with the representation of the process to be estimated. There are many models including static single and multivariable models developed by Walston and Felix at IBM [7], Putnam resource allocation model, etc. But COCOMO model is more convenient and reliable for predictive metrics rather than other model. This model gained rapid popularity following the publication of B.W. Boehm's excellent book 'Software Engineering Economics in 1981 [3]. COCOMO is a hierarchy of software cost estimation model, which includes basic, intermediate and detailed sub models.

5 Basic COCOMO Model

We are adopting only basic COCOMO model because other models cannot be applied for prediction. The basic model aims at estimating, in a quick and rough fashion, most of the small to medium size software projects. Because the intermediate model comprises cost drivers which can be applied only during the process and the input has been taken on live. Like intermediate model, detailed sub model deals with life cycle-phases which can be implemented on live projects.

5.1 Project Identification

Three modes of software development are considered in this model: organic, semidetached and embedded. The given project by the client has been identified through these modes.

5.2 Predicting the Elements in Software Development Process

After identifying the project, the maximum Lines of Codes (in thousands-KLOC) has been taken as Size to manipulate sample effort, duration, staff scheduling and productivity. It is all been manipulated by the following formulas. Here a, b, c and d are basic COCOMO coefficients.

Effort = a(KLOC)^b Person Months (PM) Duration = c(Effort)^d Months (M) Average Staff Size (SS) = Effort/Duration Persons (P) Productivity = KLOC/Effort KLOC/Person Months (KLOC/PM)

6 Working Principle of Proposed Approach

The proposed solution for this system is to know the result even before the project gets instantiated. There are two blocks of condition which gives the profit details by where it satisfies in the blocks. Else the project leads to perfect failure. After predicting in all aspect, the outcome has been compared efficiently with the manual estimation. Report has been generated for success or failure of the system. These predictions occur approximately not in accurate. However the project has to be done for clear outcomes.

6.1 Key Identification

- $ - $ INPUT, $ PREDICT, $ OUPUT are the subsystems or phases of the project.
- *- *COST, * DURATION,* DEVELOPERS are available data given by the organization and client
- # - # DURATION, #DEVELOPERS, #PRODUCTIVITY are the sample manipulation for predicting with the given data.

6.2 System Architecture

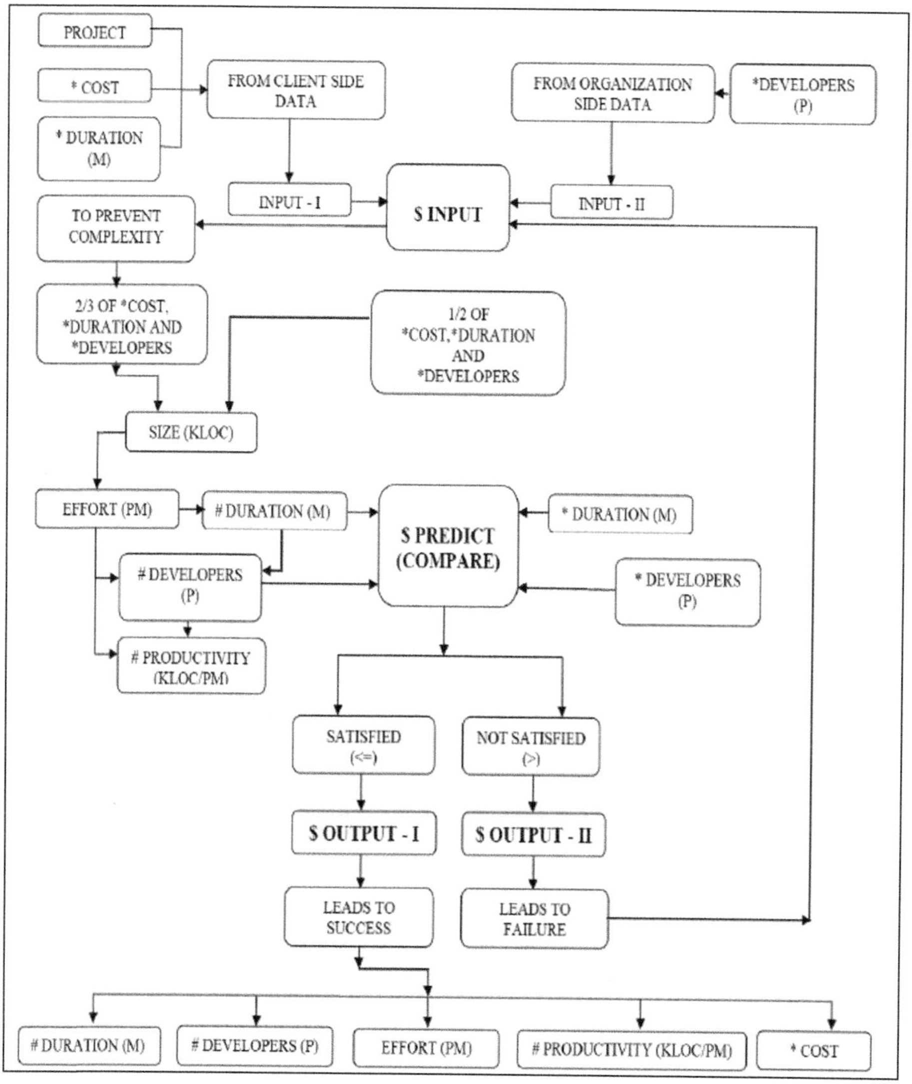

Fig. 1. Principle of Proposed System

7 System Design

Design concerns about in three stages namely input phase, prediction phase and output phase.

7.1 Process of Input Phase

Name and Nature of the project has been given by the user as a first stage input. Manually estimated cost and duration for the appropriate project has been given by the user in second stage input. An overall developer of the organization has been taken as an input in the third stage. Sequence of Process in input phase as follows:

1. Initialize the Client Side Data
2. Input the Project Name
3. Input the Cost
4. Input the Duration
5. Initialize the Organization Side Data
6. Identifies the project from Client Side
7. Input the project type
8. Input the Overall Developers
9. Input goes to prediction phase

7.2 Process of Prediction Phase

For gaining big profit in the aspect of cost and duration, only 1/2 of the given Cost, Duration and Developers have been taken for the prediction of massive profit. By the nature of the project, Maximum number of Lines of Code (LOC) or Thousand Lines of Codes (KLOC) has been assumed based on the COCOMO basic model.

Table 1. Assumptions of lines of code (LOC)

Nature of the project	Organic	Semi-Detached	Embedded
Maximum LOC	50000	300000	Above 300000 (for prediction, it is considered for 600000)

With the assumed Lines of code and with the COCOMO basic model co-efficient, the sample Effort, Duration, Developers and Productivity has been estimated. Then the sample estimation is efficiently compared with the manual estimation. If the sample estimation is not get exceeds or less than the manual estimation, then sample estimated values are given as an outcome to the user on the basis of approximation. Cost estimation predicted by the sample values of effort, duration and developers. Sample estimated value of effort, duration, developers and productivity remains unchanged for the respective projects whereas value of cost may vary according to the input and the phase of operation. If the sample estimation exceeds over the manual estimation again the process starts from the beginning with 2/3 of the given data for the prediction of moderate profit. However the condition satisfies the values of sample estimation remains unchanged. If it is not satisfies, then the project leads to failure. Sequence of Process in prediction phase as follows:

1. Manipulate 1/2 of the cost and developers
2. Input the Maximum KLOC of the project type
3. Evaluate sample size in terms KLOC
4. Evaluate sample Effort from size
5. Evaluate sample Duration from Effort
6. Evaluate sample Developers from Effort and Duration and evaluate productivity
7. Compare the sample Duration and Developers with input Duration and Developers
8. If it is satisfies
9. To output phase I
10. Else
11. To output phase II

7.3 Process of Output Phase

Predicted result given to the user whether the project leads to success of failure. If it is leads to success, then further prediction whether the project gets massive profit or moderate profit in the aspects of time and cost. Sequence of Process in output phase as follows:

1. If the control passes to output phase - I
2. Project Leads to Success
3. Result the Sample Duration, Developers, and Productivity
4. Result the Effort and Cost
5. Else
6. The control passes to output phase - II
7. Result the Project Leads to Failure
8. Result to Recover from Failure
9. Control Passes to Input Phase
10. Manipulate 2/3 of the cost and developers
11. Control Passes to Prediction Phase

8 System Construction

Our Proposed design is aimed to begin it is possible to predict the result before the software development process. We propose a metrics that will predict the result before the project gets instantiated. We predict in all categories of metrics from product, project and process with possible aspects. Predicting happens with the manual estimation as an Input Data from both client side and organization side. Estimated costs and duration of the project has been given by client side. Overall developers in the company are given, and then the company does the project identification. Prediction happens with 1/2 of the manual estimated data. If it is satisfies, the project leads to success with massive profit or else the project leads to failure. To recover from failure once again predicted with 2/3 of the manual estimated data. If it is satisfied then the project leads to success with moderate profit or else the project leads to perfect failure. The reason for taking 1/2 of the Input is to predict whether the project leads to success and on basis allocating cost for other resources, appointing staffs for other work apart from development, etc. Hence our implementation is a new type of prediction for a project. If the condition satisfies in the first or second block, then the generated sample values are given as output. Except cost, every sample values are remains unchanged. Constant values differ for each type of project namely organic, embedded and semi detached. Industry level prediction has to be done in the future in the all aspects of metrics. Quality metrics are has to be implemented in future.

8.1 Result of Sample Estimation

As we stated earlier the sample estimation is effectively compared with the manual estimation for the prediction. If any of the 1/2 or 2/3 of the given data satisfies, generated sample values reported. These sample values are remains unchanged for each respective mode. Only the cost value varies according to the input.

In each mode all the conditions are applied and expected output achieved. For understanding purpose we provide the outputs for all modes with condition it satisfies. In the organic mode, 1/2 condition has been applied. In the semi-detached mode, 2/3 condition has been applied and finally in the embedded mode, failure condition has been applied.

The sample estimated values of organic, semi-detached and embedded are listed below.

Table 2. VALUES OF SAMPLE ESTIMATION PROJECTS

(By any of the 1/2 or 2/3 of the given data)

VALUES OF SAMPLE ESTIMATION	ORGANIC	SEMI-DETACHED	EMBEDDED
DEVELOPERS(Persons)	8.78659	51.94372	176.73278
EFFORT(Persons-Months)	145.92501	1784.41990	7763.97272
DURATION(Months)	16.60769	34.35294	43.93057
PRODUCTIVITY(LOC/Person-Month)	342.64173	168.1218633	77.280024
COST(Person-Rupees)	Varies with the input	Varies with the input	Varies with the input

8.2 Organic Mode Prediction (WITH 1/2 CONDITION)

PREDICTION	INPUT(MANUAL ESTIMATION)	OUTPUT(SAMPLE ESTIMATION)
PREDICTION RESULT	Nil	SUCCESS
PROFIT OR LOSS	Nil	MASSIVE PROFIT
DURATION	35	16.60769
DEVELOPERS	25	8.78659
EFFORT	Nil	145.92501
PRODUCTIVITY	Nil	342.64173
COST	5000000	569048.8766220639

8.3 Semi Detached Mode Prediction

Table 3. SEMI-DETACHED MODE PREDICTION (WITH 2/3 CONDITION)

PREDICTION	INPUT(MANUAL ESTIMATION)	OUTPUT(SAMPLE ESTIMATION)
PREDICTION RESULT	Nil	SUCCESS
PROFIT OR LOSS	Nil	MODERATE PROFIT
DURATION	35	34.35294
DEVELOPERS	25	51.94372
EFFORT	Nil	1784.41990
PRODUCTIVITY	Nil	168.1218633
COST	20000000	385032.07989777246

8.4 Embedded Mode Prediction

Table 4. EMBEDDED MODE PREDICTIONS (WITH FAILURE CONDITION)

PREDICTION	INPUT(MANUAL ESTIMATION)	OUTPUT(SAMPLE ESTIMATION)
PREDICTION RESULT	Nil	FAILURE
PROFIT OR LOSS	Nil	LOSS
DURATION	60	Nil
DEVELOPERS	300	Nil
EFFORT	Nil	Nil
PRODUCTIVITY	Nil	Nil
COST	400000000	Nil

9 Conclusion and Future Enhancement

By predicting the time, cost and productivity t before the project instantiated, decision making is possible. After predicting in all aspect, the outcome has been compared efficiently with the manual estimation. Report has been generated for success or failure of the system. These predictions occur approximately not in accurate. Approximation reduces the complexity in decision making process. But the concept of predictability will enhance the efficiency as earlier and rectifies the complexity. So in all the aspects prediction will reduce the loss of the process. Even it may not satisfy the real time industries; definitely it will be basic fundamentals for future enhancement.

References

1. Rosenberg, J.: A Methodology for Evaluating Predictive Metrics. In: IEEE Software Metrics Symposium on Sun Microsystems (1998)
2. Ordonez, M.J., Haddad, H.M.: The State of Metrics in Software Industry, pp. 453–458. IEEE, Los Alamitos (2008)
3. Boehm, B., Abts, C., Chulani, S.: Software development cost estimation approaches - A survey. Annals of Software Engineering, 177–205 (2000)
4. MacDonell, S.G., Shepperd, M.J.: Combining techniques to optimize effort predictions in software project management. Journal of Systems and Software, 91–98 (2003)
5. Mair, C., Shepperd, M.: The Consistency of Empirical Comparisons of Regression and Analogy-based Software Project Cost Prediction. In: ISESE Proceedings (2005)
6. Boehm, B.W.: Software engineering economics. Prentice-Hall, New Jersey (1981)
7. Walson, C.E., Felix, C.P.: A method for Programming Measurement and Estimation. IBM System Journal 16(1), 54–73 (1977)
8. Roger, P.: Software Engineering. McGraw Hill Publication, New York (2000)
9. Basil, V.R.: Resource Models: Models & Metrics for Software Management and Engineering, pp. 4–9. IEEE, Los Alamitos (1980)
10. Jones, C.: Applied Software Measurement, Assuring Productivity and Quality. McGraw Hill, New York (1991)
11. Arun Kumar, S., Arun Kumar, T.: Characterization and Validation of Requirements Management Measures using Correlation and Regression Model. International Journal of Computer Science & Information Technology (IJCSIT) 3(2) (April 2011)
12. Arun Kumar, S., Arun Kumar, T., Swarnalatha, P.: Significance of Software Metrics to quantity design and code quality. International Journal of Computer Applications (IJCA) 11(6) (2010) ISSN 0975 – 8887
13. Arun Kumar, S., Senthil Kumaran, U., Swarnalatha, P.: The realization of automated testing tool for OOC. International Journal of Engineering Science and Technology (IJEST) 2(12), 6987–6998 (2010) ISSN 0975-5462
14. Carol, L.M.: Software Measurement Practical Approach. IEEE, Los Alamitos (2006)

A Recent Survey on DDoS Attacks and Defense Mechanisms

A. Srivastava[1,*] B.B. Gupta[1,2], A. Tyagi[1], Anupama Sharma[1], and Anupama Mishra[1]

[1] Department of Computer Science, Graphic Era University, Dehradun, India
gupta.brij@gmail.com
[2] Department of Electronics and Computer Engineering,
Indian Institute of Technology Roorkee, Roorkee, India

Abstract. Distributed Denial-of-service (DDoS) attack is one of the most dangerous threats that could cause devastating effects on the Internet. DDoS mainly started in 1998 but the influence of it was realized by the people only when the big organizations and corporations were hit by DDoS attacks in July 1999. Since then several DDoS attack tools such as Trinoo, Shaft, Tribe flood network (TFN), Tribe flood network 2000 (TFN2K) and Stacheldraht are identified and analyzed. All these tools could launch DDoS attacks from thousands of compromised host and take down virtually any connection, any network on the Internet by just a few command keystrokes. This survey paper deals with the introduction of DDoS attacks, DDoS attack history and incidents, DDoS attack strategy, DDoS attack tools, and classification of various attack and defense mechanisms. Finally, direction for future research work has been pointed out.

1 Introduction

Today, Distributed Denial of Service (DDoS) attacks have become a common threat to online businesses. With over 50,000 distinct attacks per week, DDoS attacks have become highly visible and costly form of cyber-crime, and are increasingly being proactively addressed by online businesses to avoid devastating costs of DDoS-related downtime [1,2,3]. Recent trends in the Internet [4, 5] show that the total amount of the DDoS attacks reached over 100 gigabit per second barrier. It also shows that the amount of DDoS attack traffic has been increasing in size year by year. A study conducted by Arbor networks [5] shows the year by year increase of the DDoS attack traffic on the Internet, from the year 2001 to 2010 as shown in Figure 1.

Denial of service attacks (DoS) deny services to legitimate users offered by the server or target machine. With time, DoS attack evolved to distributed denial of service attack where attacker compromises some other vulnerable machines on the Internet to coordinate attack at a single instant of time on the victim machine thus multiplying the effect of denial of service [6].

---

[*] Corresponding author.

D. Nagamalai, E. Renault, and M. Dhanushkodi (Eds.): PDCTA 2011, CCIS 203, pp. 570–580, 2011.

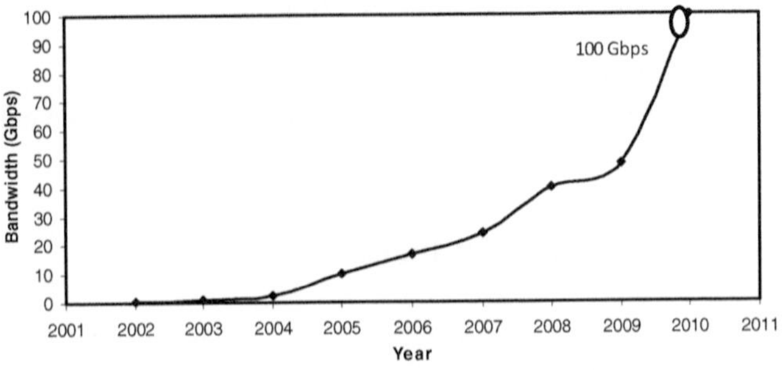

Fig. 1. Increase in DDoS attack traffic

Figure 2 shows the typical scenario under DDoS attack where legitimate users use only a bandwidth of 3 Mbps while the botnet can generate traffic of attack size ranging from 3-100Gbps. A Botnet of 20,000 [7] machines can bring down almost 90% of the Internet Websites.

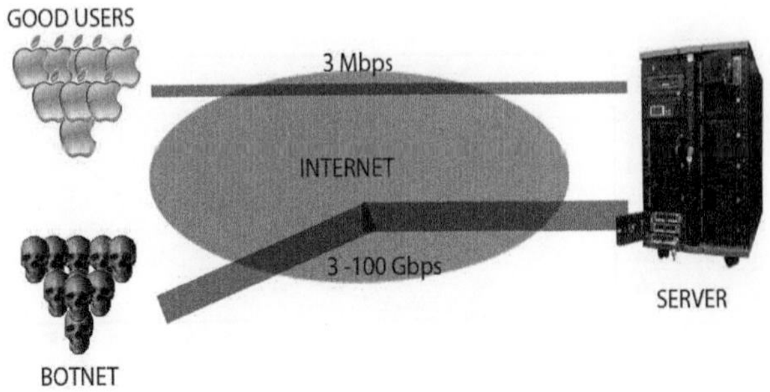

Fig. 2. Scenario under DDOS attack

Earlier, hackers used to have few machines and exploit some spoofing techniques to spoof multiple IP addresses. To the target machine, it would appear as if the attack is coming from multiple IP addresses. However now the time has changed and the hackers look for the vulnerable machines that lack security and use all those compromised machines to launch a real DDoS attack. They take the advantage of distributed system services offered by the operating systems like resource sharing, public folder sharing, accessibility, and so on. With increasing number of Internet users, DDoS attack has become the second most significant threat after virus infection to the Internet users [8].

In this paper, we will describe the DDoS problem, DDoS attack history and incidents, their classification along with the defense mechanisms to deal with them. In addition to this, paper also presents the challenges dealing with this problem and direction for further research work.

Rest of the paper is organized as follows: Second section deals with DDoS attacks history and recent incidents. Third section gives brief overview of DDoS attack.

Fourth section describes the components of DDoS attack and how it can be launched. Fifth section classifies describes the classification of DDoS attack mechanisms. Sixth section shows classification of the DDoS defense mechanisms. Seventh section describes the challenges in dealing with DDoS attacks. Finally, section eighth concludes the paper and states future scope for further research.

2 DDoS Attack History and Incidents

A revolution came into the world of computer and communication with the advent of Internet. Therefore, Internet has become increasingly important to the current society. It has changed our way of communication, business mode, and even everyday life [1]. The impact of Internet on society can be seen from figure 3 which shows exponential increase in number of hosts interconnected through Internet [9].

As, we can see from figure 3, there were only around 1 million Internet host in January 1993, which has increased to more than 775 million Internet hosts in October 2010. More and more users are connected to Internet and most of them are unaware about Internet Security. Poorly managed machines tend to be easier to compromise by attackers.

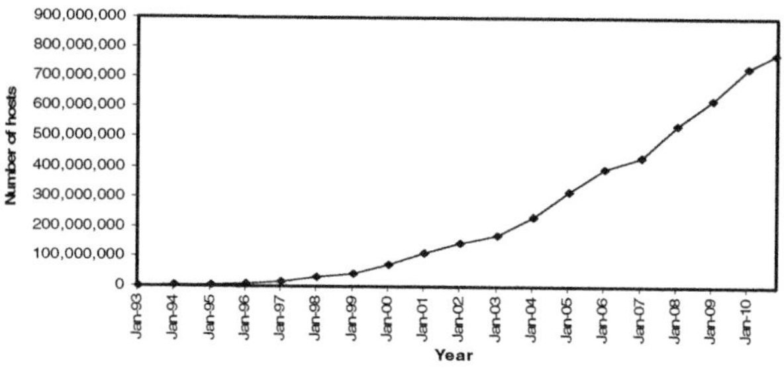

Fig. 3. Internet Domain Survey Host Count

According to this survey, the estimated Internet users are 1,966,514,816 for June 30, 2010. DDoS is one of the major threats to the Internet because of its ability to create a huge volume of unwanted traffic. The primary goal of these attacks is to prevent access to a particular resource like a Web site [11].

The first reported large-scale DDoS attack occurred in August, 1999, against the University of Minnesota. [12].This attack shut down the victim's network for more than two days. In the year 2000, a DDoS attack stopped several major commercial Web sites, including Yahoo and CNN, from performing their normal activities. Moore et al. [13] used backscatter analysis on three week-long datasets to assess the number, duration and focus of DDoS attacks, and to characterize their behavior. They found that more than 12,000 attacks had occurred against more than 5,000 distinct victim networks in February, 2001.

Initially these attacks were supposed to be a problem only with synchronous means of communication, which worked on IRC (Internet Relay chat) servers. So, these servers were initially banned from networks but, the attack on high profile websites such as Yahoo in 2000, wikileaks in 2009 and so on have proved these attacks to be a affecting whole of the Internet regardless of the means of communication [14]. Considering the attack on Yahoo in 2000, which pushed the site offline for about 3 hrs as the site received an unprecedented level of traffic of about 1GB/sec which was a huge amount to handle.

3 Overview of DDoS Attacks

As mentioned in [15], to create an effective DDoS attack, three steps are needed: Scanning, Propagation and Communication.

Scanning is the first step to exploit any system. The attacker first recruits the machines that have some vulnerability. Earlier this process was done manually by the attacker but now this process is automated. Some scanning strategies such as hit list scanning, topological scanning, permutation scanning, and local subnet scanning are popular or potential in deployment of DDoS attacks [6]. Attacker uses these techniques to continuously scan the vulnerable machines over the Internet and installs malicious scripts into them. So these machines become capable of recruiting other slaves or zombies under them too.

Propagation: While scanning deals with just looking for vulnerable machines, propagation deals with recruiting further machines with the help of already compromised machines which can be used further to generate a stream of packets towards the victim` s machine. Central source propagation model, back-chaining model and autonomous model are three main models of propagation [16].

Communication: The communication channel is important for coordinating an attack. Either Agent-Handler model or IRC model can be used to communicate with each other. In Agent-Handler Modal communication can be done by using TCP/ICMP/UDP protocol between attacker to handler, handler to agent and vice versa. In this model the communicators know each other` s identity. Internet Relay Chat (IRC) is a multi-user, on-line chatting system. In IRC (Internet Relay Chat) Model, the communicators cannot communicate directly so tracebacking is not easy that make it most widely used model by the attackers over a network.

4 DDoS Attack Strategy

Launching DDoS attack involves four components: attacker, control masters (or handlers), agents (or slaves or zombies), victim (or target machine). Attacker first scans millions of machines over the Internet for finding vulnerable machines whose security can be exploited easily. These machines are known as masters or handlers as these are directly under the control of attacker. The process of recruiting handlers is completely automated and is done through continuous scanning of remote machines looking for any security loopholes. The attacker installs malicious codes into these infected machines which then become capable of deploying further infected machines [17].

The machines deployed by handlers are directly under their control and are known as slaves or zombies. Attacker indirectly controls these machines through handlers. These handlers and zombies, on the signal of attacker are used to start a coordinated attack on target machine. This makes the target machine incapable of communicating or utilizing any of its resources. Attacker often uses IP spoofing in handlers and zombies to hide the identity of these machines. This leaves future scope for attacker of using the same machines for creating DDoS attack.

5 Classification DDoS Attack Mechanisms

We can classify DDoS attacks into two broad categories: flooding attacks and logical attacks [26]. Flooding attacks creates avalanche of transmitting packets at the victim side which makes the target machine incapable of handling request from the legitimate users.

In case of flooding attacks, the attacker keeps on sending request packets to the server at a particular rate. Due to increase in attack packets, the legitimate users decrease their flow of packets as per network Congestion control mechanism. Once the total request rate from the server becomes greater than the service rate of the server, the request packets starts getting buffered in the server and after some time the requests start dropping down. Finally, the time comes when whole of the bandwidth is exhausted by the attack packets only and the legitimate users are denied of the services, thus creating successful DDoS attack. In Logical or software attack, a small number of malformed packets are designed to exploit known software bugs on the target system. These attacks are relatively easy to counter either through the installation of software patches that eliminate the vulnerabilities or by adding specialized firewall rules to filter out malformed packets before they reach the target system [27].

A. Types of flooding attacks

i). *SYN flooding attack*: A normal TCP connection involves 3-way handshaking. In case of attack, the attacker uses spoofed IP addresses to send requests to a server. The server responds by sending the SYN/ACK signal waiting for the ACK signal from its client. But this time no reply comes since the IP is spoofed and the real client is unaware of the ACK signal that the server is expecting. This leaves the half open connections on the server side thus consuming its resources. Therefore, creating thousands and thousands of requests like this can force the server to crash or hang [28].

ii). *ICMP attack:* An attacker sends forged ICMP echo packets to broadcast addresses of vulnerable networks. All the systems on this network reply to the victim with ICMP ECHO replies. This rapidly exhausts the bandwidth available to the target, effectively denying its services to legitimate users [2, 29].

iii). *UDP Flood Attack:* A UDP flood attack is possible when an attacker sends a UDP packet to a random port on the victim system. The victim system will look for the application waiting on that port. When it realizes that there is no application that is waiting on the port, it generates an ICMP packet of destination unreachable to the forged source address. If flood of UDP packets are send to the victim machine, the system will surely go down [2].

B. Types of Logic Attack

i) *Ping of Death:* It's the use of ping command to exploit the fact that the maximum packet size that TCP/IP allows for being transmitted over the Internet is restricted to 65,536 octets. In this attack, the target system is pinged with a data packet that exceeds the maximum bytes allowed by TCP/IP. A simple command

C:\>ping 66000 hostname can force the system to hang or crash. Nowadays our host systems are safe from this type of attack because these attacks were prevalent in UNIX systems [2].

ii) *Teardrop Attack:* Whenever a packet is send over the Internet, it is broken down into fragments at the source system and reassembled at the destination system. An attacker sends two fragments that cannot be reassembled properly making use of a bug in the TCP/IP fragmentation re-assembly code of various operating systems by manipulating the offset value of packet and cause reboot or halt the victim system [2].

iii) *Land Attack*: An attacker sends a forged packet with the same source and destination IP address. Whenever victim system replies to that packet it actually sends that packet to itself, thus creating an infinite loop between the target system and target system itself thus causing the system to crash or reboot [2].

6 Classification of DDoS Defense Mechanisms

DDoS defense mechanisms can be classified as follows:
A. DDoS Attack Prevention: Attack prevention methods try to stop all well known signature based and broadcast based DDoS attacks from being launched in the first place or edge routers, keeps all the machines over Internet up to date with patches and fix security holes. Signature of the packets is matched with the existing database consisting of known attack patterns at each edge router [2]. To prevent the DDoS attack against target machine we have the following approaches:-

i) *Filtering* all packets entering and leaving the network protects the network from attacks conducted from neighboring networks, and prevents the network itself from being an unaware attacker. This measure requires installing ingress and egress packet filters on all routers. It is used to filter spoofed IP address but approaches to prevent it needs global implementation that is not practical [30, 31].

ii) *Firewall* can allow or deny protocols, ports or IP addresses but some complex attack like on port 80 cannot be handled by it because it is unable to distinguish between legitimate traffic and DDoS attack traffic. Only those attacks can be identified whose signatures are already there in the database. A slight variation from the original attack pattern can leave the attack undetected. Also new attacks cannot be detected [32].

iii) *Anti-DDoS HTTP Throttling:* Google has very cleverly devised a new mechanism that has made their new Google chrome browser to prevent DDoS attacks from being perpetrated, intentionally or accidentally, by web pages and extensions running within Chrome. It cannot stop someone from sending DDoS attacks to a server or website but, if a website is down because of DDoS or similar attacks, Chrome can stop it's users from sending requests (accessing) to that website for a while, thus reducing load on the server. The way this mechanism works is, once a few server errors (HTTP error codes 500 and greater) in a row have been detected for a given URL, Chrome assumes the server is either unavailable or overloaded due to a DDoS, and denies requests to the same URL for a short period of time. If, after this period of time, requests keep failing, this interval is again increased using an exponential factor, and so on and so forth until the maximum interval is reached. It's important to note that failures due to the throttling itself are not counted as failures that cause the back-off interval to be increased.

B. DDoS Detection: Attack detection aims to detect an ongoing attack as soon as possible without misclassifying and disrupting legitimate traffic. DDoS detection approaches can be classified as follows:

i) *Signature based detection:* Signature based approach employs a priori knowledge of attack signatures. The signatures are manually constructed by security experts analyzing previous attacks and used to match with incoming traffic to detect intrusions. SNORT [33] and Bro [34] are the two widely used signature based detection approaches. Signature based techniques are only effective in detecting traffic of known DDoS attacks whereas new attacks or even slight variations of old attacks go unnoticed.

ii) A*nomaly based detection:* Anomaly-based system uses a different philosophy. It treats any network connection violating the normal profile as an anomaly. A network anomaly is revealed if the incoming traffic pattern deviates from the normal profiles significantly [2]. Detecting DDoS attacks involves first knowing normal behavior of our system and then to find deviations from that behavior. Anomaly based techniques can detect novel attacks; however, it may result in higher false alarms.

C. DDoS Response:
After detecting an attack we must block the traffic from its source. Identification of source is difficult because their IP addresses are spoofed and thus difficult to trace back [2].

i) *Filtering* the malicious traffic can be done but it is really difficult to isolate the malicious packets and legitimate packets.
ii) *Rate throttling* is a measure which is used when there is high number of false positives in identifying the malicious packets. In this technique the rate of malicious traffic packets is reduced.
iii) *Passive traceback* [35-39] aims at tracking the real attacker causing the DDoS attack.

D. DDoS Attack Mitigation and Tolerance:
This aims at reducing the effect of the attack on victim machine during DDoS attack [2].

i) It can be done by using *load balancer* at the server side. Other methods can be implemented at routers like better queue management, traffic control scheduling.
ii) *Fault tolerance* is a well-developed research area whose designs are built-in in most critical infrastructures and applied in three levels: hardware, software and

system. The idea of fault tolerance is that by duplicating the network's services and diversifying its access points, the network can continue offering its services when flooding traffic congests one network link.

iii) *Quality of service* (QoS) describes the assurance of the ability of a network to deliver predictable results for certain types of applications or traffic. Many Intrusion tolerant QoS techniques and Intrusion tolerant QoS systems have been developed in order to mitigate DDoS attacks.

7 DDoS Defense Challenges and Discussion

In spite of numerous defense techniques and mechanism developed, the problem of DDoS is hardly tackled. As mentioned in [6, 40] there are various factors that are responsible for dealing with this problem:

i) The Internet security is highly interdependent; therefore, dealing with DDoS at victim side only doesn't solve the problem. If an attacker manages to exploit a legitimate machine which is authorized to communicate with victim machine, then that machine can be used to attack the victim because incoming traffic from the legitimate machine will be considered as normal traffic by the victim machine.

ii) Internet is not designed as a system to keep the track of incoming and outgoing traffic; it just designed to push packets from one hop to another.

iii) Need of a widespread and contiguous deployment of defense systems since Internet is widely distributed.

iv) Use of legitimate traffic models by attacker.

v) Internet service providers do not want to cooperate due to business purposes.

vi) Due to IP spoofing and encryption techniques between the attacker and agent machines, tracing the real attacker even after getting devastated by DDoS attack is not possible.

vii) The defense technique used may itself be able to slow down the request rate of legitimate users while filtering the traffic.

viii) The limited availability of resources is also one core reason.

We opt for a defense mechanism only after the attack has been launched. The work being carried out is mostly concentrated on developing defense mechanism [15] only after the attack is detected. We monitor the incoming traffic based on several performance metrics. But this defense mechanism mostly fails to detect the attack and the first signal of attack comes from the customer's report showing service unavailability. At that time, the victim is already under attack. Currently there are many challenges development effective DDoS defense mechanisms. These challenges include

(a) Large number of ignorant participants
(b) No common characteristics of DDoS streams
(c) Use of legitimate traffic models by attackers
(d) No administrative domain cooperation
(e) Use of automated tools
(f) Hidden identity of participants

(g) Persistent security holes on the Internet
(h) Lack of attack information, and
(i)Absence of standardized evaluation and testing approaches.

8 Conclusion and Future Work

DDoS attack has now become the number one threat to Internet in present scenarios. There is millions of dollars loss to the companies suffering from these attacks. The major challenge is to differentiate between the legitimate traffic and attack traffic. Since most of the attackers uses the legitimate attack models differentiating between the two becomes a trivial task. We know there is no one to govern over the Internet. The security of Internet is highly dependent on others. Internet needs to be more secure and users needs to be more aware about Internet security So to deploy a defense mechanism only at the victim's side alone is not going to solve this problem. We need to deploy defense techniques at every level, whether its edge router, core routers, ISP levels, etc. Moreover our effort should be more on dealing with these attacks before the actual damage has happened.

References

1. Leiner, B.M., Cerf, V.G.: A Brief History of the Internet, http://www.isoc.org
2. Gupta, B.B., Joshi, R.C., Misra, M.: Defending against Distributed Denial of Service Attacks: Issues and Challenges. Information Security Journal: A Global Perspective 18(5), 224–247 (2009)
3. Gupta, B.B., Misra, M., Joshi, R.C.: An ISP level Solution to Combat DDoS attacks using Combined Statistical Based Approach. International Journal of Information Assurance and Security (JIAS) 3(2), 102–110 (2008)
4. Mills, E.: Radio Free Europe DDOS attack latest by activists (May 2008), http://news.cnet.com/8301-10784_3-9933746-7.html, CNET News
5. Vamosi, R.: Study: DDoS attacks threaten ISP infrastructure (November 2008), http://news.cnet.com/8301-1009_3-10093699-83.html CNET News
6. Mirkovic, J., Reiher, P.: A taxonomy of DDoS attack and DDoS defense mechanisms. ACM SIGCOMM Computer Communications Review 34(2), 39–53 (2004)
7. Prolexic Technologies, DDOS problem, http://www.prolexic.com/index.php/the-DDoS-problem/
8. Gupta, B.B., Joshi, R.C., Misra, M.: Distributed Denial of Service Prevention Techniques. International Journal of Computer and Electrical Engineering (IJCEE) 2(2), 268–276 (2010) ISSN: 1793-8198
9. The ISC Internet Domain Survey, https://www.isc.org/solutions/survey
10. Internet World Stats, Internet User Statistics–The Big Picture: World Internet Users and Population Stats, http://www.internetworldstats.com/stats.htm
11. CERT Coordination Center, Denial of service attacks (March 2007), http://www.cert.org/techtips/denialofservice.html
12. Garber, L.: Denial-of-service attacks rip the Internet. IEEE Computer 33(4), 12–17 (2000)
13. Moore, D., Voelker, G.M., Savage, S.: Inferring Internet denial-of-service activity. In: Proceedings of the 10th USENIX Security Symposium (August 2001)

14. Sachdeva, M., Singh, G., Kumar, K., Singh, K.: DDoS Incidents and their Impact: A Review. The International Arab Journal of Information Technology 7(1), 14–20 (2010)
15. Xiang, Y., Zhou, W., Chowdhury, M.: A Survey of Active and Passive Defense Mechanisms against DDoS Attacks. Technical Report, TR C04/02, School of Information Technology, Deakin University, Australia (2004)
16. Houle, K.J., Weaver, G.M.: Trends in Denial of Service Attack Technology, CERT (October 2001), http://www.cert.org/archive/pdf/DoS_trends.pdf
17. Douligeris, C., Mitrokotsa, A.: DDoS attacks and defense mechanisms: classification and state of the art. Elsevier Science Direct Computer Networks 44, 643–666 (2004)
18. Dittrich, D.: The DoS Project's Trinoo Distributed Denial of Service attack tool, University of Washington (October 21, 1999), http://staff.washington.edu/dittrich/misc/trinoo.analysis.txt
19. Dittrich, D.: The Tribe Flood Network Distributed Denial of Service attack tool, University of Washington (October 21, 1999), http://staff.washington.edu/dittrich/misc/tfn.analysis.txt
20. Barlow, J., Thrower, W.: TFN2K- An Analysis," Axent Security Team (February 10, 2000), http://security.royans.net/info/posts/bugtraq_ddos2.shtml
21. Dittrich, D.:The Stacheldraht Distributed Denial of Service attack tool, University of Washington (December 1999), http://staff.washington.edu/dittrich/misc/stacheldraht.analysis.txt
22. Dittrich, D., Weaver, G., Dietrich, S., Long, N.: The Mstream distributed denial of service attack too (May 2000), http://staff.washington.edu/dittrich/misc/mstream.analysis.txt
23. Bysin: Knight.c sourcecode, PacketStormSecurity.nl (July 11, 2001), http://packetstormsecurity.nl/distributed/knight.c
24. Hancock, B.: "Trinity v3, a DDoS tool," hits the streets. Computers Security 19(7), 574 (2000)
25. Marchesseau, M.: Trinity-Distributed Denial of Service Attack Tool (September 11, 2000), http://www.giac.org/certified_professionals/practicals/gsec/0123.php
26. Gupta, B.B., Joshi, R.C., Misra, M.: Dynamic and Auto Responsive Solution for Distributed Denial-of-Service Attacks Detection in ISP Network. International Journal of Computer Theory and Engineering (IJCTE) 1(1), 71–80 (2009) ISSN: 1793-821X
27. Molsa, J.: Mitigating denial of service attacks: A tutorial. Journal of Computer Security 13, 807–837 (2005)
28. CERT, CERT Advisory CA-1996-21 TCP SYN Flooding and IP Spoofing Attacks (September 1996)
29. Azrina, R., Othman, R. (n.d.) Understanding the various types of denial of service attack, http://www.niser.org.my/resources/dos_attack.pdf
30. Park, K., Lee, H.: On the effectiveness of route-based packet filtering for distributed DoS attack prevention in power-law Internets. In: Proceedings of the ACM SIGCOMM 2001 Conference on Applications, Technologies, Architectures, and Protocols for Computer Communications, pp. 15–26. ACM Press, New York (2001)

31. Peng, T., Leckie, C., Ramamohanarao, K.: Protection from distributed denial of service attack using history-based IP filtering. In: Proceedings of IEEE International Conference on Communications (ICC 2003), Anchorage, AL, vol. 1, pp. 482–486 (2003)
32. McAfee (n.d.) Personal Firewall, http://www.mcafee.com/myapps/firewall/ov_firewall.asp
33. Roesch, M.: Snort-Lightweight Intrusion Detection for Networks. In: Proceedings of the USENIX Systems Administration Conference (LISA 1999), pp. 229–238 (November 1999)
34. Paxson, V.: Bro: A System for Detecting Network Intruders in Real-Time. International Journal of Computer and Telecommunication Networking 31(24), 2435–2463 (1999)
35. Stone, R.: CenterTrack: An IP Overlay Network for Tracking DoS Floods. In: 9th Usenix Security Symposium, pp. 199–212 (August 2000)
36. Burch, H., Cheswick, B.: Tracing Anonymous Packets to Their Approximate Source. In: Proceedings of the 14th Systems Administration Conference (LISA 2000), New Orleans, Louisiana, USA (December 2000)
37. Bellovin, S.M.: ICMP Traceback Messages, Internet Draft, Network Working Group (2000)
38. Mankin, A., Massey, D., Wu, C.-L., Felix Wu, S., Zhang, L.: On Design and Evaluation of Intention-Driven ICMP Traceback. In: Proceedings of Computer Communications and Networks (2001)
39. Wang, B., Schulzrinne, H.: A Denial-of-Service-Resistant IP Traceback Approach. In: 3rd New York Metro Area Networking Workshop, NYMAN 2003 (2003)
40. Kumar, K., Joshi, R.C., Singh, K.: An Integrated Approach for Defending against Distributed Denial-of- Service (DDoS) Attacks. In: Proceedings of IRISS-2006, IIT Madras (2006), http://www.cs.iitm.ernet.in/~iriss06/iitr_krishan.pdf

CSPR: *Column* Only *SPARSE* Matrix Representation for Performance Improvement on GPU Architecture

B. Neelima and Prakash S. Raghavendra

Department of Information Technology,
NITK Surathkal, Mangalore, Karnataka, India, 575 025
reddy_neelima@yahoo.com, srp@nitk.ac.in

Abstract. General purpose computation on graphics processing unit (GPU) is prominent in the high performance computing era of this time. Porting or accelerating the data parallel applications onto GPU gives the default performance improvement because of the increased computational units. Better performances can be seen if application specific fine tuning is done with respect to the architecture under consideration. One such very widely used computation intensive kernel is sparse matrix vector multiplication (SPMV) in sparse matrix based applications. Most of the existing data format representations of sparse matrix are developed with respect to the central processing unit (CPU) or multi cores. This paper gives a new format for sparse matrix representation with respect to graphics processor architecture that can give 2x to 5x performance improvement compared to CSR (compressed row format), 2x to 54x performance improvement with respect to COO (coordinate format) and 3x to 10 x improvement compared to CSR vector format for the class of application that fit for the proposed new format. It also gives 10% to 133% improvements in memory transfer (of only access information of sparse matrix) between CPU and GPU. This paper gives the details of the new format and its requirement with complete experimentation details and results of comparison.

Keywords: GPU, CPU, SPMV, CSR, COO, CSR-vector.

1 Introduction

Graphics processing unit was tricked by the programmer to do general purpose computation than doing only graphics related operations. The motivation behind the development of graphics processor evolution, to general purpose computation processor, is different than that of the CPU evolution, to multi core. Hence data formatting and optimizations designed with respect to CPU and its evolutions have to be tailored to GPU specific architectures. Even though GPU gives better performance of the accelerated applications than CPU and multi core, full utilization of the processor for much better performance is possible by tailor made data formatting and computations with respect to the architecture under consideration. Sparse matrix computations and usage is very large in most of the scientific and engineering applications. In sparse matrix, sparse vector multiplication is of singular importance in wide applications. This paper concentrates on sparse matrix vector multiplication aspect of compute intensive applications and

D. Nagamalai, E. Renault, and M. Dhanushkodi (Eds.): PDCTA 2011, CCIS 203, pp. 581–595, 2011.

through a new format shows the memory transfer and performance improvements than the existing data formats of sparse matrices. The results shown for proposed new data format are applicable to GPU in general but the results are particular to NVIDIA GPU analyzed on Geforce GT 525M.

Optimizing performance on GPU needs creation of thousands of threads, because it uses latency hiding by using thousands of threads and gives high throughput. Few of the existing methods like CSR, use row wise thread creation that cannot use global coalescing feature of GPU and GPU is underutilized if the number of non-zero elements per row is less than 32, the size of a warp. CSR vector is modified version of CSR that benefits from global coalescing by using fragmented reductions. The proposed CSPR (Column only SPaRse format) reduces the sparse matrix vector multiplication to constant time and threads can be launched continuously by parallelizing the outer loop for creating many threads. CSPR can be applied to any sparse matrix in general but better performances are seen for the matrices with large number of rows with minimum number of non-zero values per row and centrally distributed few dense rows as shown in Fig. 3. For such matrices, it can give 2x to 54x performance improvements compared to CSR, COO and CSR vector format. CSPR embeds the row information into column information and uses a single data structure; hence it can also optimize the memory transfer between CPU and GPU. CSPR format uses only one data structure to access the sparse matrix hence it is a good format for the internally bandwidth limited processors like GPU.

The paper is organized as follows. The next section gives the details of GPU architecture in general and CUDA in particular. Section III gives the sparse matrix introduction and its importance in scientific computation along with the introduction to data formats of sparse matrices. Section IV gives related work with respect to data formats and sparse matrices. Section V gives the working set up and introduction to sparse matrices considered for testing the new format. Section VI gives the experimental results and analysis. Section VII gives the conclusions and future work.

2 GPU Architecture

GPU is the co-processor on the desktop. It is connected to host environment via peripheral component interconnect (PCI Express 16E) to communicate with the CPU. The GPU used for the experimentation here is NVIDIA Geforce GT 525M, but the format proposed is in general applicable to all types of sparse matrices and all processor architectures including CPU. The proposed format is better suited and gives better performance on latency hiding based throughput oriented processors like GPU for specific class of sparse matrix structure. The third generation NVIDIA GPU has 32 CUDA cores in one SM (Streaming Multiprocessor). It supports double precision floating point operations. NVIDIA GPU has compute unified device architecture that uses the unified pipeline concept and the latest GPU supports up to 30000 co-resident threads at any point of time. GPU uses latency hiding to increase parallelism that is when active threads are running other threads will finish pending loads and become active to execute. It uses single instruction multiple threads concepts (SIMT) and executes the computation in warps that consists of 32 threads [1-3].

GPU has architectural optimizations like hardware multithreading that supports global memory access coalescing for more than half warp(16) access and memory optimizations like using texture cache for read only and reusable data like vector values in sparse computation. Global coalescing is accessing continuous memory locations for continuous threads. In CSR format each thread is assigned to a row. For a 30k row matrix 30k threads are launched in the first iteration and in the second iteration second element of each row are considered for all 30k rows and the process continues till the largest row finishes. Global coalescing is not used as every iteration accesses one element from each row. In the proposed CSPR format threads are launched per non-zero element and continuous threads access the continuous data and hence the global coalescing (16 threads (half warp) or 32 threads (one warp) access single memory segment) is used [4-5]. GPU texture cache can be used for x vector to be multiplied with the sparse matrix that can be reused from cache and hence the performance improvements. The results shown in this paper are without using the texture cache for x vector.

3 Sparse Matrix

Sparse matrix is one in which number of non zero elements are less. Hence sparse matrices are represented using different format to avoid zero multiplications. Sparse matrices will have different variety of sparsity (distribution of non-zero elements in the entire matrix) i.e. the distribution of non zero elements make sparsity based data representation to further optimize the performance of sparse based computations. Sparse based computations also consist of sparse matrix to dense matrix computations, sparse matrix to sparse matrix multiplication and sparse matrix to dense vector multiplication. This paper particularly concentrates on sparse matrix vector multiplication which is of high importance in most of the scientific and engineering applications that needs solving large linear systems (Ax=b) and Eigen value problems (Ax=Yx), where, A is a sparse matrix and x is a dense column vector. As sparse matrices are represented in a new format to remove unnecessary zero computations, accessing sparse matrix elements is not direct. Hence the sparse matrices are memory bound and any new format or new optimization that is specific for the architecture is of great importance.

There are different standard formats like DIA (diagonal), ELL, CSR and COO explained here in brief to give a comparison for the new format proposed. DIA is structure specific data format representation that is suitable for the matrices that have non-zero elements spread across the diagonals of the matrix. DIA format uses two data structures to represent the sparse matrix. One data structure is used to store the data of the size equal to the number of rows multiplied by the number of diagonals that have non-zero elements. Another data structure is to store indices of diagonals of size equal to number of diagonals. ELL or ELLPACK format that is applicable to the matrices with uniform row lengths. It uses two data structures to store data and indices of the size equal to the number of rows multiplied by max number of elements per row.

$$A = \begin{pmatrix} 0 & 4 & 5 & 0 \\ 2 & 0 & 0 & 2 \\ 0 & 0 & 1 & 0 \\ 0 & 3 & 0 & 0 \end{pmatrix}$$

CSR:

val =	[4	5	2	2	1	3]
vol =	[1	2	0	3	2	1]
ptr =	[0	2	4	5	6]	

COO:

val =	[4	5	2	2	1	3]
col =	[1	2	0	3	2	1]
ptr =	[0	0	1	1	2	3]

CSPR:

val =	[4	5	2	2	1	3]
ind =	[1	2	4	7	10	13]

Fig. 1. Sample data format representation of sparse matrix A in CSR, COO and CSPR formats

CSR (compressed row format) and COO (coordinate format) are applicable to unstructured matrices that have non uniform row lengths in specific but they are more general data format representations of the sparse matrix. CSR uses three data structures, one to represent data, second to represent column index, both of size equal to number of non-zero elements and third data structure is used to store pointer to the row of size equal to number of rows. COO also uses three data structures, same as CSR except the third one is direct row representation of size equal to number of non-zero elements. If DIA and CSR data formats are compared for more structured matrices then DIA will give better performance, because CSR is more general format and DIA is more structure specific and give better performance than the general format. Bell and Garland give a detailed analysis of the data formats with respect to GPU in [6].

Fig. 1 gives the representation of sparse matrix 'A' in CSR, COO and CSPR formats considered in this paper. The proposed data format, CSPR, concentrates on unstructured matrices with non-uniform row lengths. CSPR use two data structures, one to represent the data and the other to represent the column and row indices, both of size equal to number of non-zero elements. CSPR embeds the row information into the column information and hence the reduction in the data structure. This introduces extra computation in extracting the embedded data while performing the sparse matrix vector computation. But in a throughput oriented processor like GPU where 1000s of threads run, this computation will not affect the performance. Hence this format is suitable for computation intensive processor like GPU and hence the performance and memory benefit also. The results shown are considering the formats of unstructured sparse matrix like COO, CSR.

Fig. 2 gives the SPMV implementation algorithm of CSR and CSPR format. As CSPR is using the single data structure that embeds row and column information, it needs extra computation to extract the same in SPMV computation. These extra computations introduced into SPMV are not considered for performance evaluation as they are integer operations. But if these two integer operations are considered for only performance evaluation, then CSPR gives much better performance than that shown in this paper. CSPR needs threads to be synchronized for the row-wise computation values.

```
// Basic SPMV implementation of CSR and CSPR
// Ax = b where A is in sparse, n is size of A
// out to store row wise sum, sout single value multiplication
CSR:  for ( i = 0; i < m; i++)
      {
      for ( k = ptr [ i ]; k < ptr [ i + 1] ; ++k )
      out + = val [ k ] * x [ col [ k ] ] ;
      }
CSPR: for (i = 0; i < m; i ++)
      {
      row  =  ind [ i ] / n;
      col  =  ind [ i ] % n;
      sout  =  val [ row ] * x [ col ]
      atomicadd (out+row| out);
      }
```

Fig. 2. CSR and CSPR SPMV implementations based on the formats given in Fig. 1

The process of synchronization is hidden by the latency hiding mechanism of the GPU and gives higher performance for matrices with large number of rows. It gives comparatively equal or better performance for matrices with very less number of rows that are highly dense; because of the synchronization process takes time for the larger row. Any data format specific to one class of sparse matrix gives best performance for that class and regular performance for the other class of matrices like DIA and ELL format. Bell and Garland [6] have proposed new HYB format that improves performance for the matrices that can take best of both ELL and COO format. HYB gives high performance improvement for those sparse matrices that fit into ELL and COO combination. CSPR is not suited for the structured matrices that can be well represented using ELL and DIA and hence performance comparison cannot be done.

Table 1 represents the data structures required and their sizes for the different formats discussed above. The paper considers square matrices only. If M is the size of the matrix, total number of elements are M*M, including zeros. N is the number of non- zero elements in the given matrix. R is the structure variable representation for the structured matrices like R is number of diagonals with non-zero elements in diagonal format or R is the maximum elements in a row for uniform row lengths in ELL etc. CSPR method reduces the computation time complexity to constant time compared to CSR format, giving abundant data parallelism and memory usage is less and optimizes memory transfer from CPU to GPU than any of the existing methods.

Table 1. Data structure requirements of different data formats of SPMV

Sparse Data Format	# of Data Structures	Size of Data Structure1	Size of Data Structure2	Size of Data Structure3
DIA	2	M*R	R	--
ELL	2	M*R	M*R	--
CSR	3	N	N	M
COO	3	N	N	N
CSPR	2	N	N	--

4 Related Work

The initial work related to improving application performance that have sparse based operations has started with deriving different representations like CSR, ELLPACK, COO, DIA etc., instead of loading the entire matrix on to the memory and do zero computations [7-8]. Later these formats have been optimized with respect to memory systems and different architectures and combination of different formats have been derived to get the maximum performance. Formats like blocked CSR uses memory tiling to improve performance of the applications. Most optimization and parallelization methods are initially derived for the dense matrix and the same is automatically used for the sparse matrix also. For example, blocked or tiled access of dense matrix, when used for sparse matrix, may not be effective as the structure of sparse matrix is different from dense matrix [9-15].

Vuduc, et al. [16-18] has given list of optimizations that can be done with respect to sparse matrices. Then with the advent of multi core era, there is a need to optimize the sparse computations with these new architectures. William, s., et al. [19] show new ways of optimizations required with respect to new architectures. William, s., et al. has given new optimizations for the multi core architectures and shown huge performance improvements in the applications. Their work has not considered GPUs.

Bell and Garland [20-25] show the implementation of SPMV on GPU and give optimizations to make these computations more effective. Their work has given a new data format from the combination of existing standard formats. Their new format name HYB is a combination of ELL and COO. They did not considered restructuring of the matrix to give another new format. Their work also does not consider the memory transfer between CPU and GPU. They defense their statement by saying that the data structures can be created on the device. If we are using the true data and not creating the data on the device, entire data including the zero and non zero elements has to be transferred on to the device to create the desired data structure. CSPR is designed with respect to GPU architecture, to reduce memory transfer between CPU and GPU and also reduce the memory requirement in the internal GPU architecture. GPU computation power is abundant, so a format that can use less memory and if required with extra computation can give better performance on GPU processor. One such format is CSPR. CSPR work can be considered as the extension of the work by

Bell and Garland [6] (shows performance improvement with a new format HYB) and CSPR results show that if GPU specific formats are designed, they can give better improvements in the performance even though applicable to some class of sparse structures. CSPR can be further optimized by considering data layout at the fine grain level and computation mapping at the coarse grain level for the given class of sparse matrix structure and GPU architecture.

5 Experimental Setup

The data format algorithm implementations are tested on Intel corei7-2630QM CPU with NVIDIA Geforce GT 525M with 1GB-DDR3 memory. The sparse matrices considered here are taken from sparse matrix collection of University of Florida [26]. The matrices selected are same as used by William, s., et al. and Bell and Garland [6, 19]. These set of matrices are taken only because they represent the real data set and results will be more genuine than the synthetic matrices. Table 2 represents the general characteristics of the selected matrices. Fig. 3 to Fig. 5 shows the undirected or bipartite graph representation of the selected matrices. These figures are given to differentiate between the structures of sparse matrices and based on that performance analysis for the new format is explained. The algorithm works with any GPU in general but the implementation is done with respect to CUDA architecture v3.2. The results shown are for single precision and without using the texture cache for the x vector. CSPR can also use the texture cache for index, as every value is accessed twice depending on the optimization possible.

Table 2. Characteristics of the matrices used in the evaluation of CSPR

Matrix	Rows	Columns	NNZ	NNZ/Rows
Pdb1HYS	36,417	36,417	4,344,765	199.3
consph	83,334	83,334	6,010,480	72.1
cant	62,451	62,451	4,007,383	64.1
pwtk	217,918	217,918	11,634,424	53.3
rma10	46,835	46,835	2,374,001	50.6
shipsec1	140,874	140,874	7,813,404	55.4
mac_econ	206,500	206,500	1,273,389	6.1
mc2depi	525,825	525,825	2,100,225	3.9
cop20k	121,192	121,192	2,624,331	21.6
scircuit	170,998	170,998	958,936	5.6
webbase	1,000,005	1,000,005	3,105,536	3.1
rail2428	4,284	1,092,610	11,279,748	2632.9

Fig. 3 represents the graph structure of a sparse structure that has few rows very dense and all other rows are medium dense. CSPR needs synchronization of row values. In these types of matrices that have large row computations, synchronization overhead is overcome by latency handling mechanism and gives the best performance than CSR and COO.

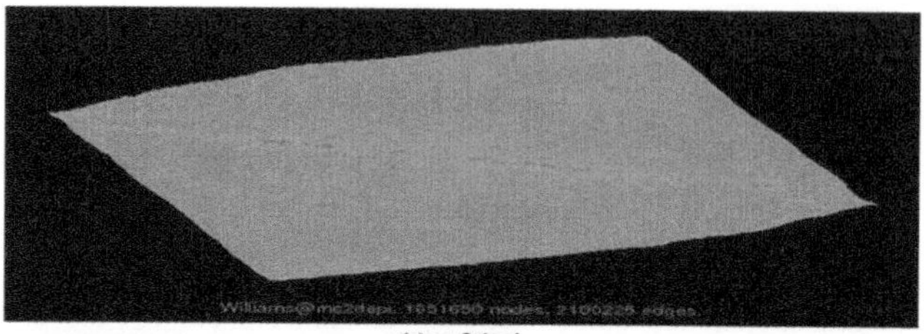

(a)mc2depi

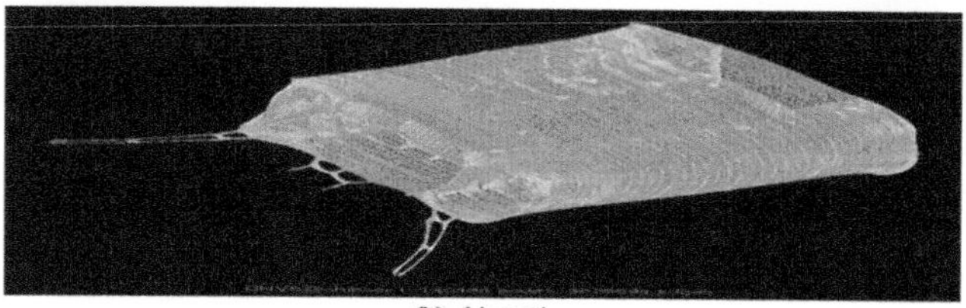

(b) shipsec1

Fig. 3. Graph representation of (a) mc2depi and (b) shipsec1-best suited sparse structure for CSPR

Fig. 4 shows the graph structure of consph and cop20k_A that have dense like matrix structure. CSPR gives good performance than CSR and COO in this case also but percentage of variation in performance is less than the Fig. 3 type graphs. Because of the little synchronization overhead involved for the last few rows when there is no computation.

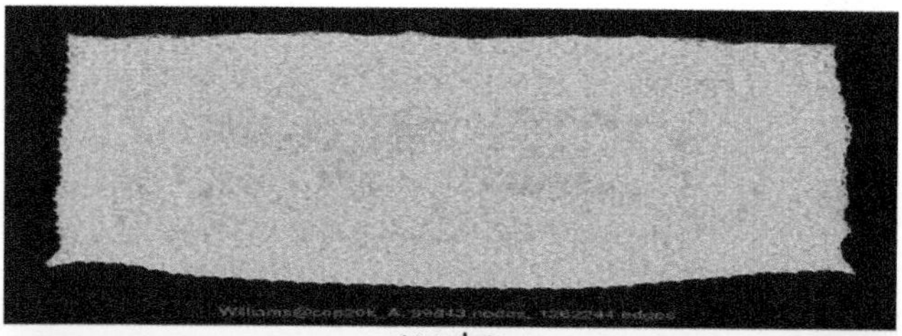

(a)consph

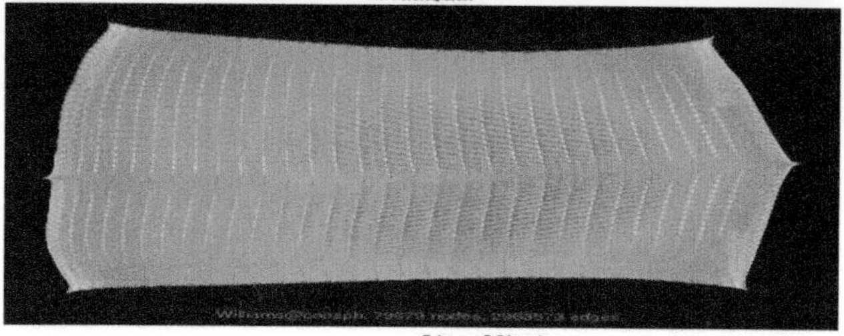

(b)cop20k_A

Fig. 4. Graph representation of (a) consph and (b)cop20k_A that have little synchronization overhead for performance lag

Fig. 5 shows the graphs of another sparse matrix structure represented by matrices pwtk and cant. These matrices have many rows with very less dense values. Here CSPR gives performance almost equal to COO or CSR (scalar) because computation time is dominated by synchronization time.

The implementations do not consider any GPU specific optimizations or global matrix transformations like transpose etc. Implementations for COO or CSPR do not use parallel reduction or segmented scan for performance improvements as suggested by Bell and Garland [6]. To create parallelization for multiple threads CSPR implementation uses an explicit parallel loop instead of the CUDA idioms. Hardware managed features like global coalescing and execution divergence are handled accordingly by the hardware. CSPR embeds additional information into the existing column indices because of which memory alignment usage is required for some large matrices. Results with memory alignment implementations are not shown in this paper and relative values are used to show the results and analysis. This paper do not use persistent or block oriented programming as used by Bell and Garland [6].

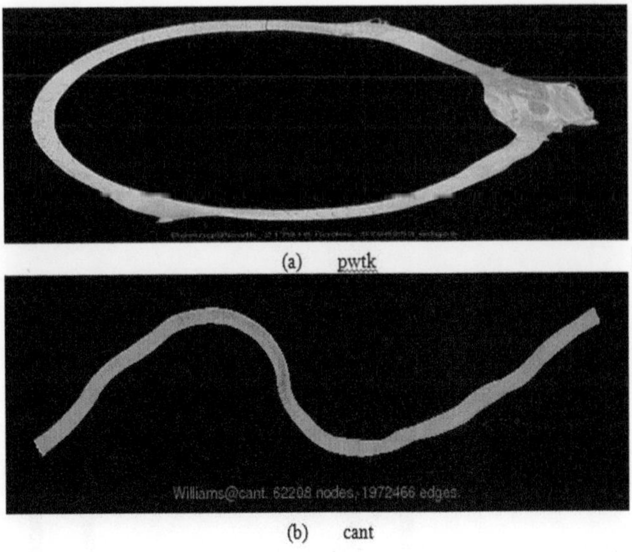

Fig. 5. Graph representation of (a) pwtk and (b) cant that have non dense rows and give high synchronization overhead

6 Results and Analysis

The results and analysis are done and comparisons are given for the proposed CSPR method to CSR (scalar), CSR (vector) and COO data formats. As CSPR is also more generalized format and gives better performance for more unstructured matrices with small dense rows and large less dense rows. Comparisons or results are not shown with respect to DIA(diagonal) or ELL format that are tailor made for more structured matrices. The results are discussed with respect to three aspects of evaluation for the four data formatting methods of sparse matrix, namely CSR (scalar), COO, CSR (vector) and the proposed method CSPR. The analysis is done with respect to number of floating point operations per second. The performance shown are not the maximum computation capability of the device as GPU specific optimizations are not used to the fullest in the current implementation. All the four algorithms implemented are compared for the performance evaluation and the analysis is valid as they use the same target platform and same programming environment. Hence most of the results are comparative. Some of the results of the matrices are not shown to avoid much deviation of the graphs and project the other prominent results.

The performance evaluation is done by taking number of non-zero elements of the matrix multiplied by two, for the two floating point operations, divided by the total average time of execution taken for 500 trials. CSPR includes extra computation in terms of extracting the access information which is embedded into single data structure. If we consider all these integer operations as single floating point operation, then the performance improvement is much higher. But as these are introduced computations but not the actual sparse computation, they are not considered in the results shown here.

In general, the performance of the COO matrix is almost constant irrespective of the matrix structure. CSR scalar gives better performance when the number of elements per row is high, i.e for matrices with highly dense rows with less number of rows. CSR (vector) gives better performance for very large number of non-zero values per row.

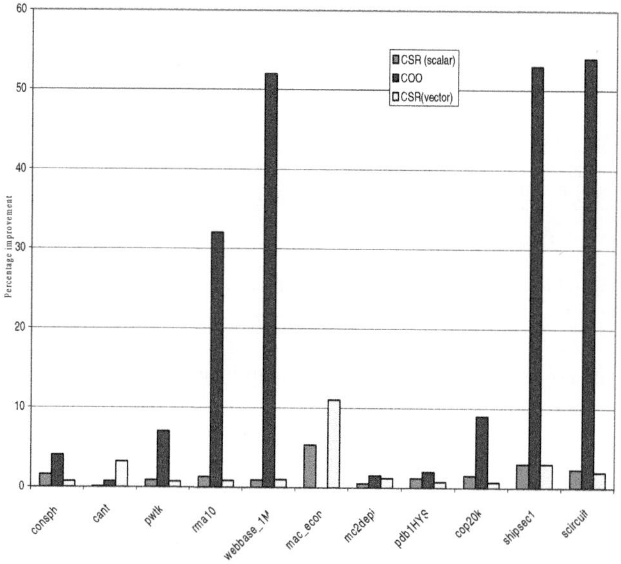

Fig. 6. Percentage improvement of performance of CSPR compared with the three formats under consideration

CSPR gives very high performance when matrices have very large number of rows with less non zero values per row and very few dense rows dominated in the center part of the matrix. When middle rows are dense, by the time dense row computation finishes the previous rows synchronization will also be done. The performance of CSPR is very high than all the other methods considered here for such matrices. If the number of non-zero values per row is medium then the performance is still good. But for highly dense large rows, the performance decreases than the best suited because of synchronization effect of last few rows. If the number of non-zero elements per row is very less, irrespective of whether number of rows is large or small, the performance decreases because computation time is dominated by synchronization time. Hence CSPR can be considered for high performance gains for matrices that are unstructured, have very large number of rows with very minimum zero values per row and very few dense rows. The details of performance variation are shown in Fig. 7.

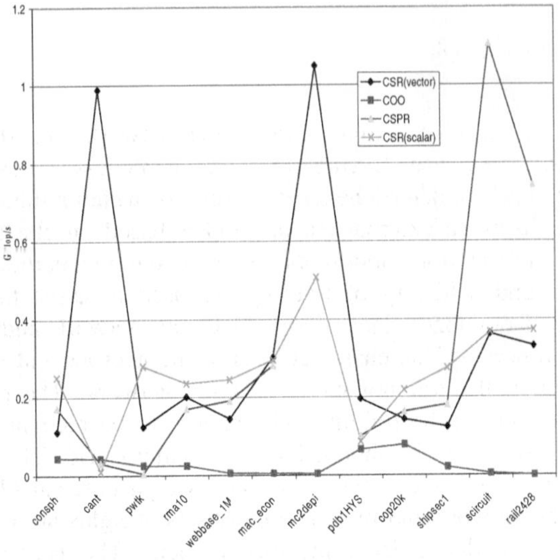

Fig. 7. Throughput comparison for the SPMV computation

12 matrices considered here are analyzed with respect to the new data format and performance analysis. The matrix mc2depi (shown in Fig. 3) which has 530K rows with an average of 3.9elements/row gives the highest performance (not shown) than any other format and any other matrix considered here. The performance improvements seen are 54x than the other methods. The overhead of synchronization is overcome by the maximum number of rows and its distribution of non-zero elements in rows. It also gives high performance than other three formats, for matrices scircuit, shipsec1 and rail2428 that have large rows with minimum distribution of elements and few rows with dense distribution. The matrices mac_econ, rma10, webbase_1m are more suited for the matrices with structure that fall in Fig. 3 and hence the performance improvement because of the same computation and synchronization behavior.

Matrices consph and cop20k_A have large number of dense rows and introduces synchronization overhead especially for the last row computations. Hence decrease in performance than CSR (vector). For the matrices cant and pwtk the performance is better than COO and CSR (scalar) but less than the CSR (vector), because there are large numbers of rows that are sparse and computation time is very less that is dominated by the synchronization time. Hence there is a decrease in performance improvement. These results are given in Fig 7. CSPR format gives 2x to 5x performance improvement compared to CSR (compressed row format), 2x to 54x performance improvement with respect to COO (coordinate format) and 3x to 10x improvement compared to CSR vector format for the class of application that fit for the proposed new format. The results of comparison are shown in Fig. 6.

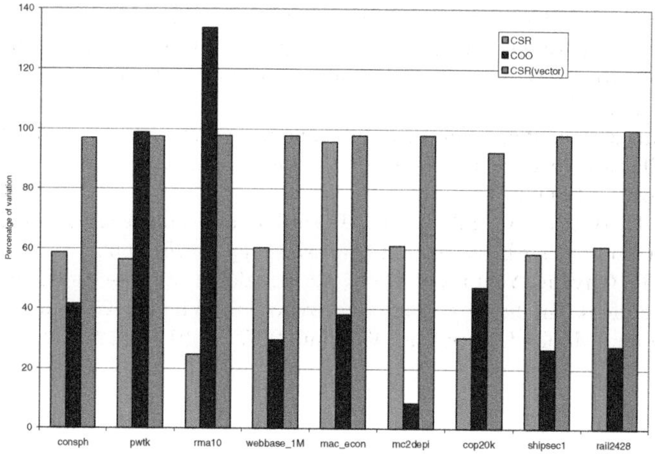

Fig. 8. Percentage variation of CPU-GPU memory transfer w.r.t. CSPR

Next evaluation criteria considered is effect of memory transfer from CPU to GPU. As the proposed method reduces the number of data structures required form two to one for the accessing information of the sparse matrix. Percentage variation of these memory transfers with respect to CSR, COO and CSR vector are given in Fig. 8. As it has reduced the data structures required it gives 10% to 133% improvement in only memory transfer time. This may be negligible if the data structure created on the device but if number of data structures required is reduced, the GPU architecture internal memory access optimization can also be made effective (not considered in this paper). This memory transfer is considered only for the access information transfer only and data value transfer time is not considered. The comparison is given in terms of percentage of variation. The memory transfer time is calculated as number of non-zero elements divided by the time taken for respective data structure transfer time and the computation time. Then these times are compared for the CSPR format against all the other three formats considered here. These results are encouraging and show that other new formats with respect to GPU can be created to improve sparse matrix computation.

Next evaluation considered is effective bandwidth utilization in terms of GBytes/s. It is computed as total number of reads and writes in bytes divided by average execution time. Number of reads and writes are taken as number of nonzero elements and the corresponding accesses from the data structure. The results are shown in Fig. 9. In most of the case CSPR is better than CSR-scalar and COO data formats.

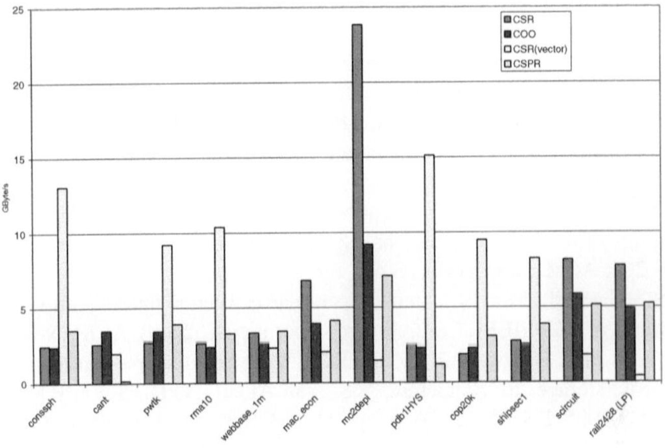

Fig. 9. Effective bandwidth comparison w.r.t CSPR

7 Conclusions and Future Work

GPU processor evolution as general purpose computation processor has given challenges and opportunities to the scientific community. It is challenging in effective and efficient way of utilizing the processor. It gives high performance opportunities to increase the application performance using massive data parallelism. The implementation of CSPR is to tackle the challenges and increase the opportunities of GPU in high performance computing. SPMV computation optimization is of utmost importance for the scientific community in any form i.e. by new data formats or new optimization techniques. Results and analysis of CSPR shows that it can give 2x to 54x performance improvement for various matrices compared to CSR, COO and CSR vector formats. It gives 10% to 133% improvement in CPU to GPU memory transfer time. Effective memory bandwidth utilization is also on par with the other methods.

CSPR results are encouraging to work towards any other possibilities of new formats specific to GPU that can give better data parallelism and also optimizes for the internal memory architecture of GPUs. CSPR needs large data type to represent the new data structure. This can be overcome by memory align. This also can be optimized by using multi kernel merge launch that can reduce this large data type requirement. Other formats like embedding the information into bits and extracting from bits can also be looked-in with respect to GPU. This work will be extended by considering optimizations for data layout optimization in internal architecture of GPU at the fine grain level and thread assignment mapping tailored to requirement of the application to give much desired performance benefits from the GPU.

References

1. Young, G.O.: Synthetic structure of industrial plastics (Book style with paper title and editor). In: Peters, J. (ed.) Plastics, 2nd edn., vol. 3, pp. 15–64. McGraw-Hill, New York (1964)
2. `http://www.drdobbs.com/supercomputingforthemasses` (July 28, 2010)
3. `http://developer.nvidia.com/` (December 2010)
4. Ryoo, S., et al.: Optimization Principles and Application Performance Evaluation of a Multithreaded GPU Using CUDA. In: Proceedings of the 13th ACM SIGPLAN Symposium on Principles and Practice of Parallel Programing (PPoPP 2008). ACM, New York (2008)
5. Ryoo, S., et al.: Program Optimization Space Pruning for a Multithreaded GPU. In: Proceedings of the 2008 International Symposium on Code Generation and Optimization, pp. 195–204. ACM, New York (2008)
6. Bell, N., Garland, M.: Efficient sparse matrix-vector multiplication on CUDA. In: Proceedings of ACM/IEEE Conf. Supercomputing (SC 2009). ACM, New York (2009)
7. D'Azevedo, E.F., Fahey, M.R., Mills, R.T.: Vectorized sparse matrix multiply for compressed row storage. In: Sunderam, V.S., van Albada, G.D., Sloot, P.M.A., Dongarra, J. (eds.) ICCS 2005. LNCS, vol. 3514, pp. 99–106. Springer, Heidelberg (2005)
8. Vuduc, R.W., Moon, H.-J.: Fast sparse matrix-vector multiplication by exploiting variable block structure. In: Yang, L.T., Rana, O.F., Di Martino, B., Dongarra, J. (eds.) HPCC 2005. LNCS, vol. 3726, pp. 807–816. Springer, Heidelberg (2005)
9. Blelloch, G.E., Heroux, M.A., Zagha, M.: Segmented operations for sparse matrix computations on vector multiprocessors. Technical Report, CMU-CS-93-173, Department of Computer Science, Carnegie Mellon University (CMU), Pittsburgh, PA, USA (1993)
10. Geus, R., Röllin, S.: Towards a fast parallel sparse matrix-vector multiplication. In: Proceedings of the International Conference on Parallel Computing, ParCo (2001)
11. Mellor-Crummey, J., Garvin, J.: Optimizing sparse matrix vector multiply using unroll-and-jam. International Journal of High Perfromance Computing Applications 18(2) (2002)
12. Nishtala, R., Vuduc, R., Demmel, J.W., Yelick, K.A.: When cache blocking sparse matrix vector multiply works and why. Journal of Applicable Algebra in Engineering, Communication, and Computing 18(3) (2007)
13. Temam, O., Jalby, W.: Characterizing the behavior of sparse algorithms on caches. In: Proceedings of the 1992 ACM/ IEEE Conference on Supercomputing (SC 1992). IEEE Computer Society Press, Los Alamitos (1992)
14. Toledo, S.: Improving memory-system performance of sparse matrix-vector multiplication. In: Proceeding of Eighth SIAM Conference on Parallel Processing for Scientific Computing (1997)
15. Vastenhouw, B., Bisseling, R.H.: A two-dimensional data distribution method for parallel sparse matrix-vector multiplication. Journal of SIAM Review 47(1), 67–95 (2005)
16. Im, E.J., Yelick, K., Vuduc, R.: Sparsity: Optimization framework for sparse matrix kernels. International Journal of High Performance Computing Applications 18(1), 135–158 (2004)
17. Vuduc, R.: Automatic performance tuning of sparse matrix kernels. Doctoral Dissertation, University of California, Berkeley, Berkeley, CA, USA (2003)
18. Vuduc, R., James, W.D., Katherine, A.Y.: OSKI: A library of automatically tuned sparse matrix kernels. In: Proceedings of SciDAC. J. Phys.: Conf. Series, vol. 16, pp. 521–530. IOP Science (2005)

19. Williams, S., et al.: Scientific computing kernels on the Cell processor. In: Proceedings of the 2007 ACM/IEEE Conference on Supercomputing (SC 2007). Kluwer Academic Publishers Norwell (2007); International Journal of Parallel Programming 35(3), 263–298 (2007)
20. Lee, B.C., Vuduc, R., Demmel, J., Yelick, K.: Performance models for evaluation and automatic tuning of symmetric sparse matrix-vector multiply. In: Proceedings of the International Conference on Parallel Processing (ICPP 2004). IEEE Computer Scoiety, Washington, DC, USA (2004)
21. Baskaran, M.M., Bordawekar, R.: Optimizing sparse matrix-vector multiplication on GPUs using compile-time and run-time strategies. Technical Report RC24704 (W0812-047), IBM T.J.Watson Research Center, Yorktown Heights, NY, USA (December 2008)
22. Bolz, J., Farmer, I., Grinspun, E., Schröder, P.: Sparse matrix solvers on the GPU: Conjugate gradients and multigrid. In: Proceedings of Special Interest Group on Graphics Conf (SIGGRAPH), San Diego, CA, USA (July 2003)
23. Christen, M., Schenk, O.: General-purpose sparse matrix building blocks using the NVIDIA CUDA technology platform. In: Proceedings of Workshop on General-Purpose Processing on Graphics Processing Units, GPGPU (2007)
24. Garland, M.: Sparse matrix computations on manycore GPUs. In: Proceeding of ACM/IEEE Design Automation Conf. (DAC), Anaheim, CA, USA, pp. 2–6 (2008)
25. Geus, R., Röllin, S.: Towards a fast sparse symmetric matrix-vector multiplication. Journal of Parallel Computing 27(7), 883–896 (2001)
26. `http://www.cise.ufl.edu/research/sparse/matrices/Williams/index.html`

Quantization of Social Data for Friend Advertisement Recommendation System

Lynne Grewe and Sushmita Pandey

California State University East Bay, Computer Science,
25800 Carlos Bee Blvd, Hayward, CA , USA 94542
lynne.grewe@csueastbay.edu

Abstract. This paper addresses the first stage of a Friend-based Advertisement Recommendation System. Our system operates in the environment of social networks like MySpace and Facebook. The goal of the system is to use social data from a user and their friends to make peer-pressure based advertisement recommendations. Gleaning this social information from the user and their pre-chosen set of friends is the focus of this paper. We discuss what this data is, how it is obtained and most importantly how we "quantize" it into numerical information that can be further processed for use in our recommendation system. Different techniques including linguistic as well as web services are explored. Results on real social data are given.

Keywords: Social Data, Quantization, Recommendation System.

1 Introduction and Previous Work

With the advent of Social Networks like MySpace and Facebook and their new and ricer set of personal user information, we explore how it can be used for the purpose of social advertising. In particular, this work discusses the capture and analysis of this social information for the purposes of advertisement recommendations. Much work has gone on in the related areas of advertisement recommendation and web personalization. However, the uniqueness of the data from social networks and the concept of friends take the possibilities to a new level.

How "taste statements" are indicated by social network profile interests are discussed in [1]. We believe that the accumulation of these "taste indicators" across friends in a social network will be highly useful in the creation of our "peer pressure based advertisement recommendation system", PPARS.

There are numerous areas of research that are related to the development of our Peer Pressure Advertisement Recommendation System, PPARS. In this section, we sample some of the related work in areas such as Social Data Mining and conclude by defining the goals of PPARS and giving its overview.

Data Mining can be generically defined as the process of sorting through possibly large amounts of data and using what is relevant. Social Data Mining could then be defined as doing this with social data or in a social setting. "Social Data" is defined generically as any data dealing with "social aspects" of a person or organization. This

D. Nagamalai, E. Renault, and M. Dhanushkodi (Eds.): PDCTA 2011, CCIS 203, pp. 596–614, 2011.

can include demographic data, records of social activities and interactions, person-generated messages and content [2].

The authors in [3] discuss the challenges of advertising in social environments of virtual realities. However, the authors discuss the concept of "peering" for people and objects as important. We agree and further hypothesize that finding these linkages will make advertising more effective and appealing in different ways than traditional advertising.

In [4], the authors look at how social user-defined groups change membership as a function of how a user relates in self-declared friendship to the existing members of the group. This work looked at the social environments of LiveJournal and co-authorship and conference publications in DBLP, which is a site giving bibliographic information on major computer science journals and proceedings. They found that friendship was important but, also the "structure" of this friendship indicated by how the user's friends are themselves connected in friendship. This indicates that examining the friendship in more detail as we propose to do in our system could be useful.

In [5] processes are described that modeled social influence as groupings of individuals in social networks coordinating their decisions. The common place term for this is "peer influence" or "peer pressure".

In [6] the authors examine some useful trends related to such friendship and found that one third of the friends where closer in terms of physical location. This could indicate that our system would work well for local advertisement. The concept of not only friends but foes is discussed in [7]

Viral Marketing, the concept of quick spreading information through a network of people, is examined in the works of [8-11] where again the idea of "influence" is important in the process.

Some research has focused on the prediction of users becoming friends. In [12], the authors look at building interest ontology to be used in prediction of potential friendship relationships in the Live Journal network (blogging). What is important in this work for us is that it points to the usefulness of the analysis of interests and implied shared interests between users. Our work looks at capturing these interests for the purpose of "peer-pressured advertisement". In [12], the authors form a concept hierarchy that clusters interests. The hierarchy is comprised of single-word concepts taken from terms which themselves have a maximum of four 15-characters terms to describe an interest. A major difference between our work and [12] is that we are working in a social networking environment where there is a richer set of social data of much greater variation. PPARS must deal with completely open ended narratives and at the same time can also be given constrained social data like that of a person's smoking status. Hence an important first part of our system is recognition of the "type" of social data.

1.1 Problem Statement and PPARS System Overview

For PPARS (Peer Pressure Advertisement Recommendation System), the definition of "Social Data" includes any information inside a person's profile on the Social Network. Our system is used in conjunction with a social network application or could be used by the social network provider. Figure 1 shows an example of the first use-case scenario. Social network applications are one of the most popular features of Social Networks like MySpace and Facebook. A typical revenue stream for these applications is advertisement. PPARS can be used for enhanced, peer-based advertising.

The following is a list of problems and requirements for PPARS that we will concentrate on in this paper featuring the front end capture and processing of social data.

- Gathering timely social data in a manner that is not obstructive but easily processed.
- Easy integration into Social Networks.
- Access to both User and Friends data.
- Selection of meaningful/useful Social Data
- Separation and parsing of social data into meaningful data pieces
- Understanding and Categorization of Social Data
- Interpretation of social data pieces into quantized computer manageable data

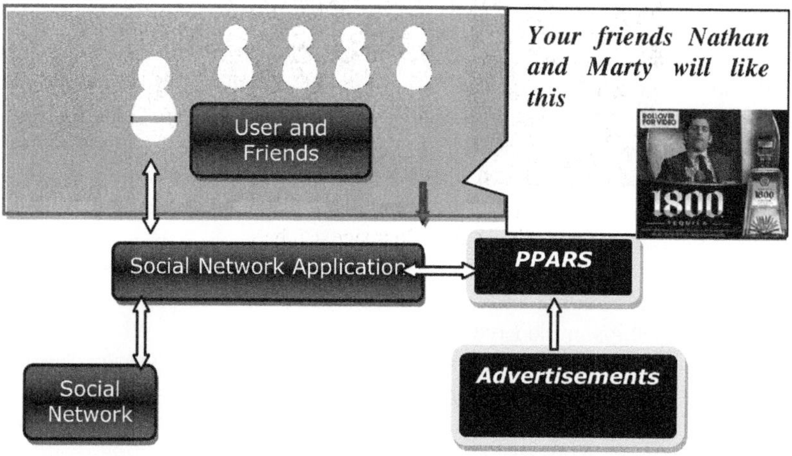

Fig. 1. PPARS Use Case Scenario providing peer-based advertisement recommendations for Social Network Applications

Figure 2 shows a diagram of PPARS major components. First data in the form of user social data and their friends social data is input into a "front-end" subsystem, the main topic of this paper, which takes this data and puts it into a quantized form that can then be reasoned about to create peer groupings. These peer groupings are then matched to Advertisements which have been similarly modeled. Social teasers are created for such pairings which then can be delivered to the user as a "peer-pressured" based advertisement.

Figure 3 shows the "front-end" subsystem that is responsible for the quantization of the raw user and friend social data. As we discuss in the next sections it consists of the two main stages of parsing and quantization.

In the remainder of this paper, we begin by discussing what social data is given to PPARS. This is followed by a section each for the two main components of the PPARS front end, parsing and quantization. Results of each step are given on real data. As a forward look into the remaining parts of PPARS, an example peer-based recommendation is shown. Finally the paper concludes with a description of possible future work.

2 Social Data

As PPARS operates in the Social Network environment, it is dependent on the network's policies and access protocols for data access. While most of the Social Networks provide third-party applications like ours, access to user and friend data there are some limitations.

First, is the fact that each social network collects different social data from its users. Fortunately, most of it is similar and taken from a user's profile. Unfortunately, the names of this "in-common" data, the format, syntax and complexity vary from user to user and network to network. A recent coalition of many networks including MySpace, LinkedIn, Hi5, Orkut and others created an in-common access protocol called OpenSocial with unified data access. For this reason, we have utilized OpenSocial for social data access. Unfortunately, this does not remove the fact that there is data that is not in common, and the format and syntax and complexity varies from network to network and also user to user.

Our use of OpenSocial as a uniforming data access protocol gives us access to a rich set of possible data items listed below:

> About Me, Activities, Addresses, Age, Body type, Books, Cars, Children, Current Location, Date of Birth, Drinker, Emails, Ethnicity, Fashion, Food, Gender, Happiest When, Has App, Heroes, Humor, ID, Interests, Job Interests, Jobs, Languages Spoken, Living Arrangements, Looking for, Movies, Music, Name, Network Presence, Nick Name, Pets, Phone number, Political views, Profile song, Profile url, Profile video, Quotes, Relationship status, Religion, Romance, Scared of, Schools Sexual Orientation, Smoker, Sports, Status, Tags, Thumbnail url, Time zone, Turn offs, Turn ons, TV shows, Urls.

Listing 2.1 shows a few real user data samples (altering for privacy reasons) to illustrate the range of user data. After looking at many user data samples, a number of patterns presented themselves. From these observations we classified each data piece into either numerical, categorical or "other" data types. The other data type indicating data that cannot be readily categorizable for this stage of our system. An example of this is the user's profile image.

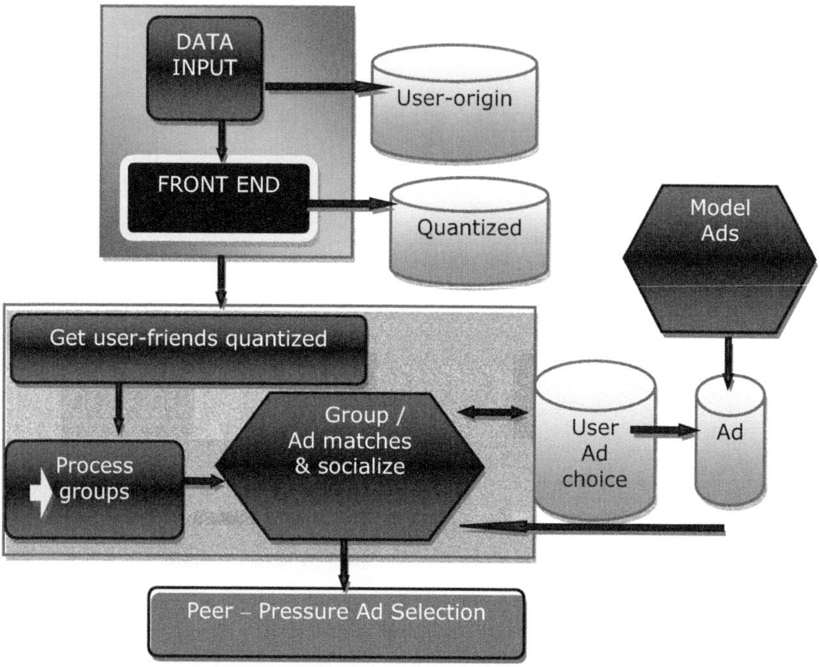

Fig. 2. PPARS global view

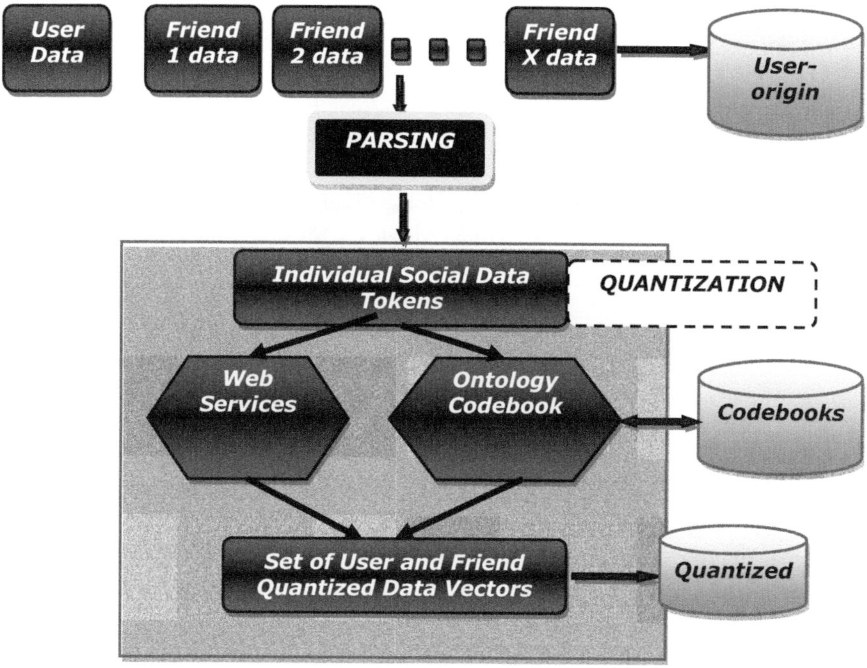

Fig. 3. PPARS front end

Social Data Field	Entry
AboutMe	Ok, so I am a graduate of Drexel University with degrees in Computer Science and Mathematics. I currently live in Portland oregeon with my wife and son. I enjoy Biking, Snowboarding/skiing, computers, race cars, and hanging out with friends.
Interests	Snowboarding/skiing, computers, race cars, and hanging out with friends.
Movies	The Departed, Jaws, Encino Man, Star Wars
Status	Married
Smoker	No
Schools	University Of Portland Portland, OR Graduated: N/A Degree: Master's Degree Major: Mathematics 2009 to Present Drexel University Pittsburg, Pennsylvania Graduated: 2003 Student status: Alumni Degree: Bachelor's Degree Major: Computer Science Minor: Math Clubs: Art Club Speech Club Greek: Theta Omega

Listing 2.1. A few of the social data entries for an anonymous user (details altered to protect privacy)

3 Parsing

The first stage of the PPARS data processing front-end is parsing. Ideally we want to take a potentially complex user data narrative that has a varied syntax and separate it into individual data elements that have contained complete meanings or semantic units. Such data elements could be then processed for meaningful quantification.

Unfortunately, parsing into data elements representing individual semantic units is not easy and can be challenging even for the human observer. For this first implementation of PPARS, we concentrate on syntax alone leaving the incorporation of semantics and expert knowledge for future study. An advantage of syntax only parsing is speed. We have two forms of syntax-only based Parsing that the system can run under. The first is very minimal only separating the user data entry into sentences. We call this Simple Parsing. The other option we can run PPARS under, which we nominally call Complex Parsing, is shown in Figure 4. The attempt with Complex Parsing is to get at the atomic, hopefully completely contained, data elements (semantic units) without over segmenting.

We have developed both to test their results in the varied kinds of user data syntax. As we will see there are cases where our Complex Parsing algorithm can sometimes result in over segmentation of data whereas Simple Parsing often results in under segmentation of data.

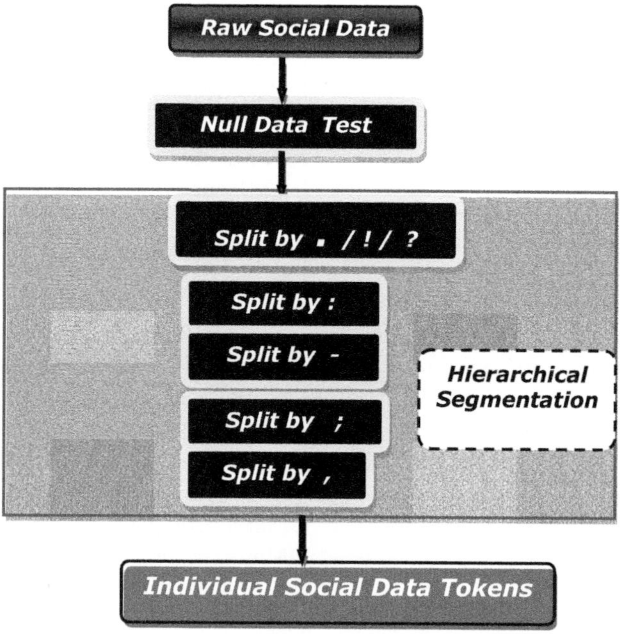

Fig. 4. "Complex" syntax only Parsing Subsystem of PPARS

We conclude this section by showing the results of our parsing subsystem on a few real user entries. We have concentrated solely on western structured languages and primarily concerned ourselves with English but, have also tested with Spanish successfully. Many of the words and personal information has been changed to protect privacy but, the essence of the grammar and kinds of information are preserved to illustrate some of the wide range of user data available.

Listing 3.1 shows sample input a user created for "ABOUT ME" which consists of well formatted multiple sentences that result in splitting into three sentences. This listing illustrates the importance of separation by ".".

Listings 3.2 shows simple lists separated by commas and the resulting data tokens. Many users create comma separated entries like this. However, there is also the use of commas to separate phrases in narrative. Partitioning into separate phrases for narratives we found in general did not lose any essential information.

Listing 3.3 shows a use of the colon ":" to separate in this case a header from the information. While in many examples we saw it may be possible to eliminate the precedent clause of the colon phrase, we feel that sometimes there can be useful information in this part of the phrase and felt that its inclusion would not be detrimental. An example of this is shown in Listing 3.4 where the user for their MUSIC entry separated their information by headers with colons into "Bands, Solo Artists, Singers, Albums".

A number of results of Listing 3.4 are interesting. One thing that happens is that the social network in this case does not deliver the data with the formatted bold that you see in the listing. Hence PPARS is not able to understand that Solo Artists is separated from the word before it "Journey" and it hence yields the social data token "Journey Solo Artist".

Another interesting thing about parsing using the "-" symbol is that in some cases it is used as a clarifier, as is the case in listing 3.4. By this we mean the user has specified and artist and an album name. PPARS separates this into two entries. This can as we will see later give more support to a user liking this artist. However, we feel this is not necessarily wrong because if a user goes to the trouble of listing an album and the artist name together that there is a significant level of user interest.

Sometimes users incorporate excessive or creative use of punctuations. Listing 3.5 shows a more excessive case of create use of punctuations.

One problem with the data delivered by many social networks is that it often delivers a string without any line returns, even when they are present in the social network's display of the user data when the user enters them. An example of this is Listing 3.6. The lack of format information like line returns created by the user can be problematic for user formatted data like that in Listing 3.6. This will be a challenging problem and is the currently greatest failure for the PPARS parsing subsystem.

"I work as an engineer at Motorola. I work in the peripherals department and do chip design. I am doing some management."

Resulting Social Data Tokens:

- I work as an engineer at Motorola
- I work in the peripherals department and do chip design
- I am doing some management

Listing 3.1. ABOUT ME user data example that consist of well formatted sentences

"Internet, Movies, Reading, Karaoke,Building alternate communities"

Resulting Social Data Tokens:

- Internet
- Movies
- Reading
- Karaoke
- Language
- Building alternative communities

Listing 3.2. INTERESTS user data sample formatted in a list

"Films: Lawrence of Arabia, Ben Hur"
Resulting Social Data Tokens:

- Films
- Lawrence of Arabia
- Ben Hur

Listing 3.3. MOVIES use data sample, formatted in a list with user provided header information

"**Bands:** Superdrag, Weezer, The Doors, The Beach Boys, Journey **Solo Artists:** Billy Joel, **Albums:** Appetite for Destruction - Guns & Roses; Blue - Weezer"
Resulting Social Data Tokens:

- Bands
- Superdrag
- The Doors
- Cheap Trick
- The Beach Boys
- Journey Solo Artists
- Billy Joel
- Albums
- Appetite for Destruction
- Guns & Roses
- Blue
- Weezer

Listing 3.4. MUSIC user data sample, showing use of colon clauses to partition information into different sub-categories

"speaking abt meh......ummm diff than u think!!!!!!!!!! high feelin but still happy.....i do wot i think is right....hate if s'one bothers....and i really dun care wat people think abt me...

Resulting Social Data Tokens:

- speaking abt meh
- ummm diff than u think
- hight feelin but still happy
- i do wot I think is right
- hate if s'one bothers
- and i really dun care wat people think abt me

Listing 3.5. ABOUT ME user data that is both creative in spelling, punctuation and content

" Purdue University West Lafayette, IN Graduated: 2010 Student status: Alumni Degree: Bachelor's Degree Major: Business/ Management 2002 to 2006 Kokomo High School

```
Kokomo,IN Graduated: 2006 Student status: Alumni Degree:
High School Diploma

  User entered data:
        Purdue Universtiy
        West Lafayette, IN
        Graduated: 2010
        Student status: Alumni
        Degree: Bachelor's Degree
        Major: Marketing/ Management

        2002 to 2006
        Kokomo High School
        Kokomo,IN
        Graduated: 2006
        Student status: Alumni
        Degree: High School Diploma
  Resulting Social Data Tokens:
```

- Purdue University West Lafayette
- IN
- Graduated
- 2010 Student status
- Alumni Degree
- Bachelor's Degree Major
- Business/ Management 2002 to 2006Kokomo High School Kokomo
- IN Graduated
- 2006 Student status
- Alumni Degree
- High School Diploma

Listing 3.6. User data entry that shows PPARS system receives unformatted string not illustrating line breaks can cause problems

4 Quantification

The next subsystem of PPARS's front-end is that of quantization, the conversion of our parsed data elements into a quantized space that can be used for peer grouping and advertisement matching. Clustering or grouping algorithms take place typically in a numeric space.

In signal process, quantization is defined as the approximation of a continuous range of values into a set of discrete values. We apply the word quantization in a different but, similar sense to what PPARS does. For example, PPARS would take the data element "Gone with the Wind" and convert it to a evidential support of MOVIE_ROMANCE = 0.2. In this sense, we are taking free formed data elements of potentially infinite (never) combinations of words and converting it to discrete numeric values.

How do we convert our parsed data elements into meaningful numeric values? First, it is important to note that the classification of an advertisement so it can be matched to peer groupings must also be performed in this same numeric space. This would indicate that we might drive how and even what we quantize by the need to deliver advertisements.

Up to this point we have not addressed the choice of what social data PPARS should use given the possible input. For this research, we used all social data that was available. However, reduction of the social data space is possible and could be directed by the advertiser needs.

Recall that we are given a set of pre-define social data (see section 2), so this starts the process of quantization – we already know that our parsed data elements come from pre-determined social indicators like Movies, About me, Music, etc. This is very helpful is the choice of techniques to quantize the data.

Also, recall that after examining all the social data delivered by our social networks to PPARS we observed that the data could be classified as either being numerical, categorical or other. We have developed different quantization schemes based on whether it is numerical or categorical. Any data deemed to be in the "other" data type, like a user's image or profile song URL, is ignored and not used in PPARS. Typically these belong to media and not textual information. While image processing is an expertise of the author, the effective and reliable extraction of user social data information from images and other media is not a solved problem and for this reason not considered for the first stage of our PPARS system.

Another example of data that falls into the "other" data type is the user's name and nickname. While PPARS uses this information in the delivery and personalization of the advertisement it is not deemed directly useful information for peer grouping and advertisement recommendation and hence not used for processing.

As noted above, users may not specify all of the possible social data in their profiles. When this is the case, we represent missing data with a -1 value. We choose this as a unique numeric value that would not be a result of any of PPARS quantization schemes.

In the next sections, we describe how both numerical and categorical social data are quantized and give real data examples.

4.1 Numerical

Some of our social data like Age is inherently numerical. In the case of Age, the value itself can be used. Users can present age in either integer or floating point formats like "33" or "33.5" respectively.

A field like Date of Birth is numerical but, not as a single value, it has three numeric values for Month, Date and Year. While this could be converted to an age metric, some information would be lost. Knowing the month and date may be useful as an advertiser may want to offer "Birthday specials" to a user or birthday focused merchandise (like birthstone jewelry) to the user.

There are other social data listed like ID and Has App that are not inherently social and in the case of ID are arbitrarily assigned to the user offering no useful social data for peer grouping or advertisement classification. These types of data are ignored by PAPRS.

4.2 Categorical

The bulk of the social data is of the categorical type. For a social data that is categorical, we must first define the categories that exist for it. Once a set of categories is selected the mapping of a raw data element into one or more categories must take place and is called categorization. We add the further restriction that this categorization must be done numerically, in essence the mapping yielding a vote or evidence for one or more categories the data element is mapped to.

While there is not a universal taxonomy for all categorical social data, there are some pre-existing taxonomies for specific data like Movies, Books and TV that can be used. For example, when considering Movies there are international services like IMDB (Internet Movie Database) and Internet Video Archive that for every movie define the genre of the movie into a set including Action, Drama, Romance, Thriller and more. Similarly, when you go to a video store (online or in person) movies are similarly grouped by genre. So using this as an indicator or preferences for movies has been used for a number of years.

Hence when parsing the social data "Movies" PPARS does so into the categories of: MOVIE_ACTIONADVENTURE, MOVIE_BIOGRAPHY, MOVIE_CHILDRENS, MOVIE_COMEDY, MOVIE_DRAMA, MOVIE_FAMILY, MOVIE_HEALTH_WORKOUT, MOVIE_HORROR, MOVIE_MUSICAL, MOVIE_MYSERYSUSPENCE, MOVIE_NONFICTION, MOVIE_SCIFICTION, MOVIE_WAR, MOVIE_WESTERN, MOVIE_HEALTH, MOVIE_DOCUMENTARY, MOVIE_THRILLER.

This brings up the interesting fact that with categorical data, unlike numerical data, PPARS is often mapping the data from a single contained phrase to a vector of possible values. In the case of movies above, the vector has 15 dimensions. If we had the social data elements of "Jaws", "Raiders of the Lost Ark" and "Mummies", each of the 3 data elements would go through the categorization process accumulating evidence in the 15 dimensional movie categories vector.

Some categorical data like About Me, Activities, Fashion, Happiest When, Heroes, Humor, Interests, Looking For and others do not have a well known taxonomy. In these cases, we looked at numerous user data samples to come up with trends that turned into categories. We also kept in mind our goal of describing and serving advertisements with the same categories and looked at Google [13] and Yahoo! [14] for a list of their advertising taxonomies. From all of this information, we choose what we thought were a good set of categories. However, it remains to be seen what might be a best selection. We suspect that it will change depending on the advertising database as well as a given set of user data

Other categorical data like Ethnicity, Languages Spoken, Religion and to a lesser extent Job Interests also do not have a predefined taxonomy but, certainly have a number of well known possibilities. It is easier than data like About Me to come up with categories for these.

There is yet another kind of categorical social data and that is of the enumerated type. In this instance, the social data's value is stipulated and constrained by the social network. Examples of this include Body type, Gender, Looking For, Drinker and Smoker. Consider Gender where the user must select between male and female. In these enumerated case, the categories are predetermined by the social container.

If a social data element is categorical, the categorization steps are the following: First if a web service exists for this social data, the data element is passed to the web service and the results are processed. If there are no results or if there is no web service for this social data then the data element is passed to a keyword matching quantization stage to generate possible results. If there are no results, all the categories are left at their initialized default values of -1, indicating no value.

4.3 Categorization: Web Service Quantization

We have employed different web services for the social data of Movies, TV, Music and Books. The web services we are using are REST based and involve making HTTP requests and filtering some form of text, typically XML, response. To understand the basics of how these web services work, we will discuss the movie web service. The Movie WebService we use is called the Internet Video Archive, IVA, [15]. The primary reason for the choice of using the Internet Video Archive over IMDB (Internet Movie Database) [16] is that unlike IMDB it is free for use, a very important feature on our academic budget. However, it would be relatively easy to convert to the use of another webservice.

For movies, IVA allows queries by a number of features of which title, actor and director are of interest to us. A whole surplus of information is retrieved in the output but, we have decided to concentrate on what in their xml output is referred to as media category or in common terms genre.

There may be more than one result given to us by a web service like IVA. Depending on what we are doing, we have chosen to handle the multiple results differently. In the case of a Director or an Actor, we process all of the results, recording the genre of each result. Then we return the most popular genre from the total results. For the data element "Meryl Streep" this results in a search by actor name yielding the most popular genre of "Drama" even though she has appeared also in comedies.

However, in the case of processing a title, we only use the first result. This is because typically the multiple results from a title search are different movies sometimes with the same title or sometimes with similar titles.

Given any social data element parsed from the user's MOVIE data, we cannot know apriori if it is a title or actor or director's name. It may even be the genre of movies a user likes. After reviewing numerous user's MOVIE data and given the specificity of Movie information, we first attempt to process the data element as a movie title and if this results in no hits then as an actor and finally as a director. If none of these provide a hit then the web service passes the data element on to the next stage, keyword matching quantization.

For reference, we use [17] as our web service to process TV data, [18] as our web service to process Book data and [19] as our web service to process Music data. These were chosen for their popularity and free usage.

An example of results on parsing Movie data with the web service is shown below. These results are correct and as would be expected.

```
Up,Forrest Gump,Rear Window,District 9,Pac-Man,WALL·E,My
Flesh and Blood, MacMusical,
```

Yields:

```
MOVIE_FAMILY=0.6, MOVIE_SCIFI=0.2,
MOVIE_DOCUMENTARY=0.4,  MOVIE_THRILLER=0.2
```

Under segmentation produced in by PPARS parsing subsystem can sometimes yield problems with getting accurate web service results. A real data element resulting from parsing Music data results is "Juggy D sohniye ni sohniye". In this example, it is relatively clear that "Jiggy D" is the name of an artist but, the following phrase of "sohniye ni sohniye" looks to an English speaker (note this user has all data in English) as something in another language. While "Jiggy D" by itself parses as an artist in IMDB the string "Juggy D sohniye ni sohniye" does not parse appropriately.

4.4 Categorical: Keyword Matching Quantization

Keyword Matching Quantization is the last stop for social data elements that have been unsuccessfully quantized via web services and is the first stop for social data like ABOUT ME or INTERESTS for which no effective web service quantization is available. Generally, these data elements do not represent proper nouns or titles but, are narrative in nature. Understanding of these narrative data elements in terms of quantizing their values into a set of pre-selected categories is what this component must achieve.

Looking at the field of Natural Language Processing and at our specific categorization goals and desire for quick processing, we choose to implement a basic technique of NLP involving the implementation of a word and phrase dictionary we refer to as Keyword Matching. The idea is for each social data (i.e. ABOUT ME, INTERESTS but, also MOVIES, etc) we create a database of common Keywords or phrases. For example, in the PPARS's keyword database for ABOUT ME, the phrase "real estate" is stored with the following evidence: ABOUT_ME_WORK = 0.2, ABOUT_ME_HOME = 0.2. This means that when the phrase "real estate" is seen as (or in) a data element from ABOUT ME it should build up support for both work and home.

Currently we limit the range of an evidence value entered in by an expert from 0.0 to 1.0. One potential problem is the relative accuracy of these weights. To reduce inaccuracies, we believe that it is important that only the same single database manager or one familiar with the bulk of current keyword database entries should be allowed to enter in values to the keyword database. As part of this work, we have experimented with using uniform evidentiary weights rather than those specified by an expert.

Thus, Keyword Matching Quantization is taking each data element and looking for matches in our Keyword database and increasing the evidence support for each category hit. For example, for data element A if there is a keyword database hit for ABOUT_ME_SOCIAL, then we would want to increase the current value of user[ABOUT_ME_SOCIAL] by the value stored in the database or alternatively we can increment by a default uniform value.

The listing below shows the results when running under both increment methods. The words "student", "work" , "love" and "cars" have entries for different ABOUT_ME_* categories. In the Keyword database they are all 0.2 except for the word "work" that has a value of 0.5 for the ABOUT_ME_WORK category. This results in evidence for ABOUT_ME_WORK being much larger, 0.7, when the Keyword database strength values are used over the 0.4 value that results from the increment of default 0.2 values (there are two hits for ABOUT_ME_WORK – one "student" and the other "work").

```
Data element: ' I am a student and I work and love cars'
```

Strength	Default (0.2)
ABOUT_ME_ENTERTAINMENT=0.2 ABOUT_ME_WORK = 0.7 ABOUT_ME_HOME = 0.2 ABOUT_ME_SOCIAL = 0.2 ABOUT_ME_FOOD = -1	ABOUT_ME_ENTERTAINMENT=0.2 ABOUT_ME_WORK = 0.4 ABOUT_ME_HOME = 0.2 ABOUT_ME_SOCIAL = 0.2 ABOUT_ME_FOOD] = -1

Listing 4.1. Quantization – accumulating evidence using Keyword database strength or using default incremental values of 0.2

When we look for matches for our data elements in our database tables, we do so in a case insensitive way. This is important to accommodate the sometimes unusual use of case in social data.

There are three methods we have implemented to perform our Keyword database matches and are called: STRICT, DB_ENTRY_CONTAINS_DATA_ELEMENT, and DB_ENTRY_PARTOF_DATA_ELEMENT.

The Strict method means that the individual data element must exist word for word including any special characters in the KeywordDB table. Hence if the data element is "I love cars" this must be an entry in the KeywordDB table for a hit/match to happen. Obviously, undersegmentation from the parsing stage would yield to a lot of failure or necessitate a ridiculously large database. So, in general, we believe running the system under the STRICT matching scheme is not realistic.

The DB_ENTRY_CONTAINS_DATA_ELEMENT means that the data element can be part of an entry in the database table. The database entry contains but, can have more than the data element. So, the data element "I love cars" would create a hit to a database entry of "I love cars a lot". This would help in situations of oversementation from parsing.

The last method, DB_ENTRY_PARTOF_DATA_ELEMENT, splits the data element into its blank space separated elements. For example the data element "I love cars" would be split into three sub-elements of "I", "love", "cars". Then we use the SQL IN clause to see if there are any database entries in this list of sub-elements. This is usually equivalent to parsing words and atomic phrases (ones with no blank spaces but, possible to have hyphenation and other non-parsed separators). This method is the longest as we are not further segmenting our data element into "atomic" words/phrases for matching but, in general with a simple and sparse Keyword database will yield the most hits.

In Listing 4.2 we show the results of Quantization Keyword matching for all three methods on a sample string. These results indicate that safest method of quantization may be DB_ENTRY_PARTOF_DATA_ELEMENT. This is because we are matching at the atomic level and realistically the creation of a Keyword database table that goes much beyond the atomic level is not feasible. A better but, more computationally expensive however easy to implement solution would be to quantize using ALL three methods. We leave this along with the exploration of the use of semantics and further syntax rules from NLP as areas of future investigation.

One limitation of our implementation of the DB_ENTRY_PARTOF_DATA_ELEMENT is that we do a database query to see if there is an entry that is in the list of "atomic" sub-elements created out of the current data element. This means, if we the data element A= "I am a student" and the data element B= "I am a student who loves being a student" both will yield the same results with regards to the word "student" in the 2 elements. Is this correct or should instead the evidence from the word student be twice as much for data element B over data element A? It is not obvious which one is correct. Regardless, it would be easy to implement a fourth algorithm that instead of a single database query using the SQL IN clause containing the N sub-elements it would have N separate database queries one for each sub-element. This would of course increase the computational complexity by N.

Recall that when we accumulate evidence for our social data categories we cap off the evidence to a maximum of 1.0. So, if each use of the word "student" added 0.2 in value to ABOUT_ME_WORK it would mean that we could only account for 5 such entries. The need for a maximum relates to the next stages of PPARS involving grouping and advertisement classification and matching. What maximum value to choose is arbitrary but, we have chosen 1.0 along with the default evidence accumulation value of 0.2 to reflect the average maximum number of entries (here 5) you might see in social data reflecting a maximum or very strong usage of a term. These heuristic values were chosen after viewing hundreds of entries for each social data and we feel reflect a good (albeit small) cross sampling of the social network population.

```
Original String: ' I am a student and I work and love
cars'

Output  STRICT:    no hits
Output DB_ENTRY_CONTAINS_DATA_ELEMENT:   no hits

Output DB_ENTRY_PARTOF_DATA_ELEMENT

        keyword = student  → ABOUT_ME_WORK =0.2
        keyword = work  → ABOUT_ME_WORK =0.5
        keyword = cars → ABOUT_ME_ENTERTAINMENT =0.2
        keyword = LOVE →  ABOUT_ME_HOME=0.2,
        ABOUT_ME_SOCIAL=0.2
```

Listing 4.2. Results of Processing a data element using 3 Quantization Keyword Matching Algorithms

5 Future Results

While this paper does not discuss the peer grouping, advertisement classification or advertisement matching and serving in PPARS, we have some preliminary results and have shown an example here. Figure 5 shows an advertisement served to a peer grouping that have strong correlation to the advertisement in the ABOUT_ME_HOME, GENDER and AGE categories. It is an advertisement from Walmart and Better Homes about a magazine typically for women and related to home.

Fig. 5. Advertisement served for peer grouping with high correlation in ABOUT_ME HOME, GENDER and AGE categories

6 Conclusion and Future Work

We have discussed the difficult task of parsing and quantization of social data for the purposes of creating a Peer Pressure Advertisement Recommendation System, PPARS. This step is critical to be able to perform the subsequent numerical clustering into peer groups and advertisement classification and matching.

We have discussed a few forms of syntax based parsing and shown with real world social data its success and failures. We have implemented two different parsing schemes both yielding different levels of under segmentation. We believe that under segmentation is in general more beneficial than over segmentation, as it is easier to break apart that to put back together information.

Next, we discussed how we quantized numerical and categorical parsed data. In the categorical case, we discussed how categories were derived and also discuss the two main forms of quantization via web services and keyword matching. Results on real data showing the system working and highlighting potential failures were given.

There are numerous areas of future work. At this point we are completing the remaining parts of our PPARS system and it is through testing these results we can better understand the efficacy of our parsing and quantization subsystems that are the topic of this paper. Future work for parsing includes trying to tackle the issue of lack of user format. Another is adding semantics and NLP techniques beyond syntax to the parsing. Dealing with parentheses is another piece of future parsing work.

With regards to quantization there are numerous areas of future research. One intriguing idea is to have a feedback loop that could suggest ways of altering categories based on goodness of results. A difficulty here is that the advertisements would need to be re-classified and this would generally involve a user in the loop. With regards specifically to web service quantization looking at techniques to combine results from multiple types of web service requests (i.e. movie title, actor and director) rather than doing them serially could yield superior results. Also, with regards to web service quantization is the addition of secondary web services when multiple exist. The difficulty introduced will be correct mapping results into the same categories.

In the area of keyword matching, increasing the size of or beginning database is a necessary piece of future work before the system could be deployed.

Finally, expanding the quantification to the "other" data type including image analysis and music/song analysis would be of interest but, involve large bodies of unsolved research.

References

1. Liu, H.: Social Network Profiles as Taste Performances. Journal of Computer-Mediated Communication, 13(1), article 13 (2007)
2. Terveen, L., Hill, W.: Beyond Recommendation Systems: Helping pWeople Each other, http://www.grouplens.org/papers/pdf/rec-sys-overview.pdf
3. Clemons, E., Barnett, S., Appadurai, A.: The Future of Advertising and the Value of Social Network Websites: Some Preliminary Examinations. In: Proceedings of the Ninth International Conference on Electronic Commerce. ACM International Conference Proceeding Series, vol. 258 (2007)
4. Backstrom, L., Huttenlocher, D., Kleinberg, J., Lan, X.: Group Formation in Large Social Networks- Membership, Growth, and Evolution. In: Proc. 12th ACM SIGKDD International Conference on Knowledge Discovery and Data Mining (2006)
5. Blume, L.: The statistical echanics of strategic Interaction. Games and Economic Behavior 5, 387–424 (1993)
6. Liben-Nowell, D., Novak, J., Kumar, R., Raghavan, P., Tomkins, A.: Geographic Routing in Social Networks. Proceedings of the National Academy of Sciences 102(33), 11623–11628 (2005)
7. Leskovec, J., Huttenlocher, D., Kleinberg, J.: Signed Networks in Social Media. In: Proc. 28th ACM SIGCHI Conference on Human Factors in Computing Systems (CHI) (2010)
8. Kemp, D., Kleinber, J., Tardos, E.: Maximizing the Spread of Influence in a Social Network. In: Proceeding 9th ACM SIGKDD International Conference on Knowledge Discovery and Data Mining, pp. 137–146 (2003)
9. Leskovec, J., Adamic, L., Huber, B.: The Dynamics of Viral Marketing. In: Proceedings 7th ACM Conference on Electronic Commerce (2006)
10. Young, H.: Individual Strategy and Social Structure: An Evolutionary Theory of Institutions. Princeton Press, Princeton (1998)
11. Domingos, P., Richardson, M.: Mining the Network Value of Customers. In: Proc. 7th ACM SIGKDD International Conference on Knowledge Discovery and Data Mining, pp. 57–66 (2001)
12. Aljandal, W., Hsu, W., Bahirwani, V., Caragea, D.: Ontology-Aware Classification and Association Rule Mining for Interest and Link prediction in Social Networks. In: Proceedings of the Association for the Advancement of Artificial Intelligence Spring Symposium on Social Semantic Web, pp. 1–8 (2009)
13. Google Ads, http://adwords.google.com
14. Yahoo! Ads, https://adcenter.microsoft.com/

15. Internet Video Archive IVA, http://api.internetvideoarchive.com/Documentation.aspx?node=Protocol
16. Internet Movie DataBase, IMDB, http://imdb.com
17. TV search on IMDB, http://www.imdb.com/search/title?title_type=tv_series&title="
18. Google Books Search, http://books.google.com/books/feeds/volumes?
19. IVA's music API, http://api.internetvideoarchive.com/Music/**

Fidelity Index Based on Demand (FBOD) Secure Routing in Mobile Ad Hoc Network

Himadri Nath Saha[1], Debika Bhattacharyya[1], and P.K. Banerjee[2]

[1] Department of Computer Science and Engineering,
Institute of Engineering and Management, West Bengal, India
[2] Department of Electronics and Communication Engineering, Jadavpur university,
West Bengal, India
him_shree_2004@yahoo.com, bdebika@yahoo.com

Abstract. Currently the mobile wireless technology is experiencing rapid growth. However the major challenge for deployment of this technology with its special characteristics is securing the existing and future vulnerabilities. The lack of static infrastructure causes several issues in mobile Ad Hoc network (MANET) environment, such as node authentication and secure routing. In this paper we propose a new approach for secure routing of data packets in MANET. This approach will reduce the computational overhead to a lot extent. The protocol is based on a specific criterion of the nodes called “fidelity Index”. We first explain what fidelity index is and give a comprehensively detailed description of the scheme. Then we exemplify and simulate the scheme with several case studies and lastly discuss the security strengthening aspects of this simple yet robust scheme under some scenarios.

Keywords: fidelity, delay, fidelity index, sequence number, hop destination, flooding attack, black hole attack, co-operative black hole attac, routing.

1 Introduction

Mobile Ad-hoc Network (MANET) is a collection of wireless mobile hosts without fixed network [1] infrastructure and centralized administration (Figure-1). Communication in MANET [2] is done via multi-hop paths. MANET contains diverse resources; Nodes operate in shared wireless medium; [3] Network topology changes unpredictably and very dynamically; Radio link [4] fidelity is necessary; connection breaks are pretty frequent. Moreover, density of nodes, number of nodes and mobility of these hosts may vary in different applications. There is no stationary infrastructure. Each node in MANET [5] acts a router that forwards data packets to other nodes. Therefore selection of effective, suitable, adaptive and robust routing scheme is of utmost importance .FBOD is a secure routing scheme based on fidelity index. FBOD is a robust, effective, suitable, adaptive and cost effective scheme.

D. Nagamalai, E. Renault, and M. Dhanushkodi (Eds.): PDCTA 2011, CCIS 203, pp. 615–627, 2011.

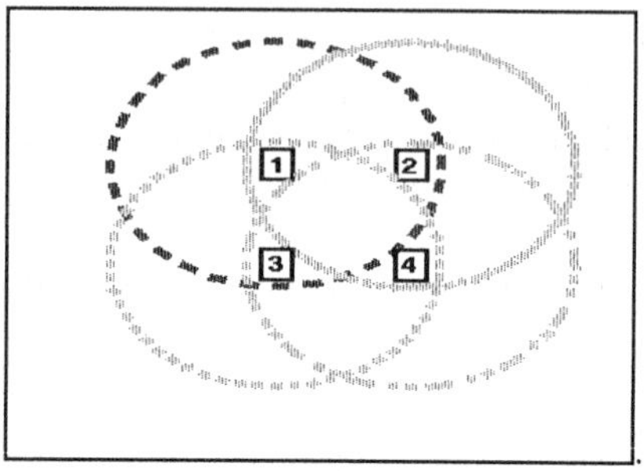

Fig. 1. An ad-hoc mobile network with four nodes

Section 2 describes some previous work in related field. Section 3 discusses fidelity. Delay matrix is discussed in section 4. Section 5 elaborates fidelity index. Section 6 presents a description of the scheme Section 7 presents FBOD algorithm Section 8 consists of simulation results. Section 9 is a treatment on security aspects. Lastly we present our conclusions in section 10.

2 Related Work

S.Matri [6], SCAN [7], Gonzalez [9] and Himadri [27,28,29], in their literatures have shown ways to mitigate attacks on different MANET networks. We have extended their work in this field.

3 Fidelity

Fidelity is the most important concept of this routing scheme. Fidelity is an integer number that is associated with each node. This fidelity of a node denotes many things about the node itself and also deciphers other information regarding the topology of the entire network. It also helps to maintain security [10] to some extent.

To make it understandable in one sentence, "fidelity is a counter that is associated with a node, which is increased whenever it forwards a data packet successfully." Whenever a node comes in a network its fidelity is zero and whenever it goes permanently off from the network its value is again refreshed to zero. Otherwise whenever a node will forward any data packet it will always increase a counter value and that counter value is its fidelity. Note whenever a source node sends a data packet to a destination node, all the intermediate nodes helping to transmit its data packet will increase their counter but the source and the destination node do not increase their fidelity value.

Fidelity is a measure of these two factors:-

A. How reliable a node is for forwarding a data packet

Whenever we observe that the fidelity value of a particular node is greater that of another node then we can conclude that the one having the greater value is a more durable node than the other from who's its value is greater. It is quite logical because a node with greater value indicates that it is an experienced node in the network and it has transmitted packets most dutifully than other nodes.

B. Network topology

If we can find some nodes with higher fidelity in a region of the network, we conclude that the network activity is higher in that region. More precisely we can also infer that the node density is also higher in that region for it is impossible to have one node having very high fidelity [11] surrounded by nodes with low fidelity because a high fidelity [12] node must send packets to someone in its vicinity which will make that other node's fidelity value also high. Thus a high fidelity value accounts for high network activity as well as high density of nodes in its surroundings.

4 Delay Matrix

Delay is one of the most important factors in this scheme. Delay signifies the time delay between two nodes. Delay matrix is basically a square matrix having dimension n*n, where n=no of nodes. Each (i, j)th entry in the matrix indicates delay between ith and jth node in a network. For example, we are taking a 2*2 matrix which is a delay matrix of a network having 2 nodes 0, 1. The delay between those two nodes is 5 units.

(i,j)	0	1
0	0	5
1	5	0

5 Fidelity Index

Fidelity Index (FI) is basically a real no associated with each node. This index is the main factor in order to choose any neighbor to forward the message to destination. Each node sorts its neighbors in decreasing order of FI. If we get the time delay for a particular node as T and the fidelity value is F, then we can calculate the fidelity index (FI) = X * F + (1-X)/T, where X<1 & its value depends on the practical behavior of the network. The value of the X can be user given input. For our simulation we are considering x=.6 to give more stress on fidelity (security issue).

6 Description of the SCheme

The term "friends of a node" used in this paper, indicates actually the nodes that fall in the physical range of a particular node. When a node is a message to send, the node will check which nodes are in its neighborhood and what are their fidelity value and the delay between those nodes. Sender will broadcast a request along with an echo message. After getting reply they will make their friend list. More precisely the friend list consists of a table that contains two attributes. The first one is the address [13] of the nodes which are within its range and other is the fidelity index of that particular node. When each node is updated then they will sort that table according to the decreasing order of the fidelity index (FI). Before we enter into the detailed discussion of our scheme (FBOD) there are some concepts that need to be understood. These are as follows-

There will be a sequence counter in every node. If a message is generated in a node then it will be increased by one. This sequence no. will be forwarded as a part of the message. Every node will maintain a buffer where (source, sequence no.) will be stored for last n no. of received messages. After getting a message a node will verify the tuple [9] (source, sequence no) of that message with those tuples in its buffer [14]. If anyone of them matches with that message then that node will reject that message silently. It will prevent flooding attack.

The timeout period of every node through which message is traversed, will be gradually decreased by a critical factor [15] i.e. if timeout period of sender node is x then timeout period of receiver node will be (x-m), where m will be critical factor. This factor [16] helps us to control the max no of hops a message can traverse to reach destination.

Now the scheme is as follows-A node can do either of three activities - message generate, message forward, message receive. If it is not doing any of the three then it is idle. Now if a message is generated in a node and it needs to be sent then the node will remain busy until an acknowledgement is received for this message. It is to be noted that a busy node can accept & process an acknowledgement and can send a fail message.

Now if destination is directly reachable from generator node then it will send message to destination node and will wait for acknowledgement, and remain busy until acknowledgement is received. If the destination node is busy it will send a fail message to generator node. After getting fail message or if timeout period exceeds, generator node will keep on sending the message after a certain time periodically until acknowledgement is received.

If destination is not directly reachable then generator node will send message to the node in its range that has highest fidelity index. If generator node get a fail message from that node or if timeout period exceeds then it will send the message to the node having second highest fidelity index and it will continue like this. If the whole list is exhausted in this way then the process will again continue from the node having highest fidelity index. Only generator node will follow this process. Other nodes will send a fail message to its predecessor if the whole list is exhausted.

When a node receives a message, if it is busy then it will send a fail message to sender, otherwise it will check whether it itself is a destination or not. If it is destination, it will accept the message and send acknowledgement to sender otherwise this node will send message to the node in its range that have highest fidelity index and that process will continue. In that acknowledgement message the sequence no. will be same as received message but source will be substituted by destination.

7 FBOD Algorithms

Update friend list

STEP 1: Send Hello packet, Echo packet and a special broadcast request to the friends for knowing the identity, delay and fidelity of the friends

STEP 2: Receive replies from friends
STEP 3: Calculate FI=0.6*F+0.4/T, where F=fidelity value of a neighbour node & T=time delay to reach that neighbour. We have taken here the value of X as 0.6.
STEP 4: Update my friend list
STEP 5: Sort friend list in a decreasing order of FI

Generated data

STEP 1: Set my status=busy
STEP 2: If destination directly reachable from here

- Send packet to destination
- Wait for ACK
- If ACK received consider success
- Else if timeout occurs or FAIL received, arrange for resending
  Else
- Send data packet to the friend having highest FI
- Wait for ACK
- If ACK received consider success and go to step 3
- Else if timeout occurs or FAIL received, arrange for resending to the friend with next highest FI
- Continue above three steps until ACK received
- If list is exhausted without getting an ACK then again start from the friend with the highest FI and try each node in friend list in the same manner as above.
- While trying to send if the list is exhausted thrice abort

STEP 3: Set my status=free

Received data

STEP 1: If my status=busy send FAIL to sender
STEP 2: Else

- Make my status=busy
- Process received data
- Make my status=free

Process received data

STEP 1: If message destination=my address

- Accept data
- Generate ACK
- Send the ACK to the node from which it directly received the message
- If the received packet is found duplicate then discard the received packet.

STEP 2: Else

- Forward data packet
- Check if forward operation is successful

- If successful increase my fidelity value by 1 and send ACK to the node from which it directly received the message
- Else send FAIL to the node from which it directly received the message

Forward data packet

STEP 1: If message destination is directly reachable from here

- Send packet to destination
- Wait for ACK
- If ACK received consider success
- Else if timeout occurs or FAIL received, arrange for resending to destination.
- If resending fails 3 times consider failure.

STEP 2: Else

- Send data packet to the friend having highest FI
- Wait for ACK
- If ACK received consider success
- Else if timeout occurs or FAIL received, arrange for resending to the friend with next highest FI
- Continue above three steps until ACK received
- If list is exhausted without getting an ACK then consider failure.

8 Simulation Result

We have simulated this scheme with JAVA. We need to know something to make out these simulations. These are

1. Small circle signifies node in the network.
2. Blue circle around node signifies range of that node.
3. Red color indicates that the node is free.
4. Black color indicates that the node is busy.
5. Yellow line between two nodes indicates sending of request & echo message to probe fidelity value & delay.
6. Pink line between two nodes indicates reply of probing with information.
7. Red line between two nodes indicates sending of message.
8. Green line between two nodes indicates sending of acknowledgement.
9. Blue line between two nodes indicates sending of fail message.
10. Any node inside the range of a node is its neighbor node.

Now we will describe one test case simulations.

This is a network having six nodes. Their corresponding fidelity values are written beside the nodes. Here we are trying to send a message from node 0 to node 5. Following figures depict the simulation results.

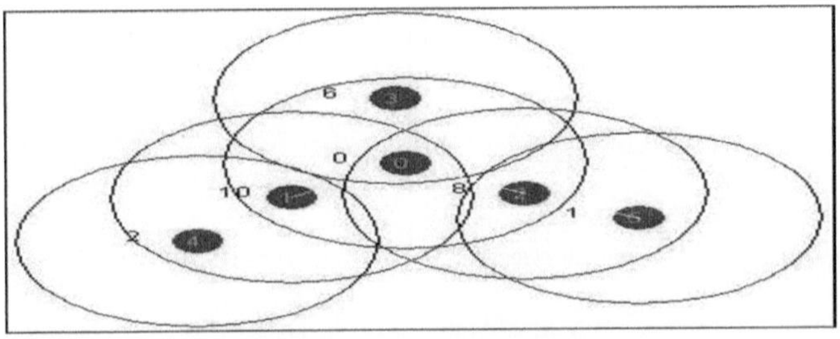

Fig. 2. Design of network

The result we get after network designing is given below-
Output of netdesign.jar:-

6<*Number of nodes*>

0	10	7	6	2	1
-1	0	0	0	-1	-1
0	-1	-1	-1	0	-1
0	-1	-1	-1	-1	0
0	-1	-1	-1	-1	-1
-1	0	-1	-1	-1	-1
-1	-1	0	-1	-1	-1

We got the adjacency list.txt as above and input **delay matrix**:-

0	3	2	1	-1	-1
3	0	-1	-1	2	-1
2	-1	0	-1	-1	4
1	-1	-1	0	-1	-1
-1	2	-1	-1	0	-1
-1	-1	4	-1	-1	0

0<*time instance-0*>
0<source> 5<destination> hello<*msg*>

Then we run the simulation and see the results.
The steps of the visual simulation are given below-

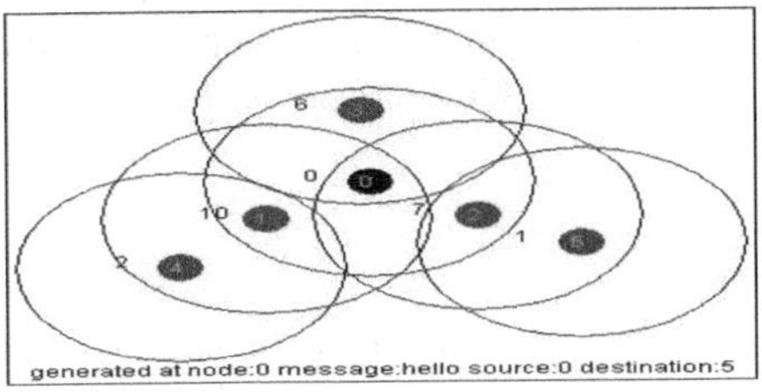

Fig. 3. Message generated at node 0

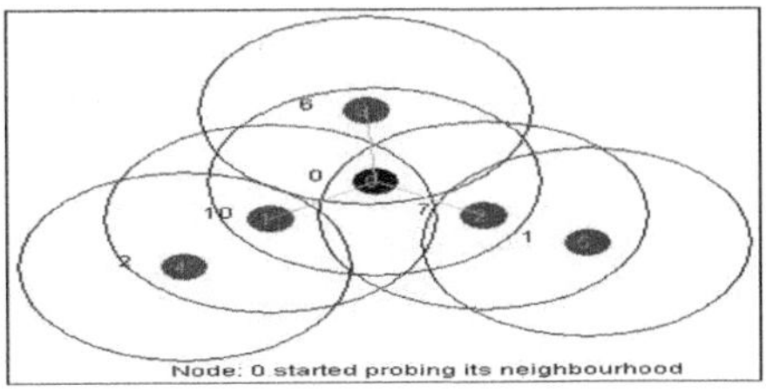

Fig. 4. Node 0 started probing

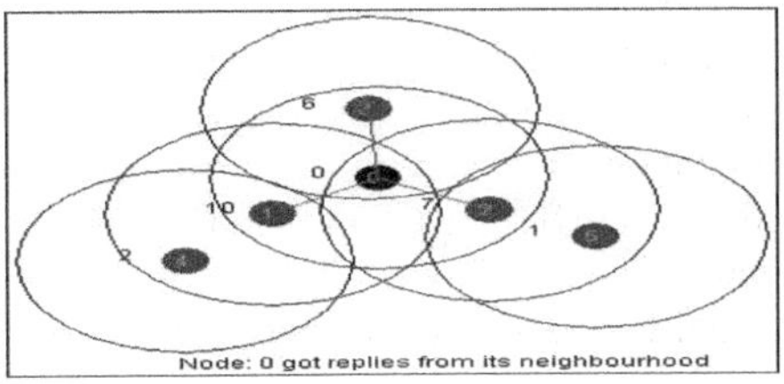

Fig. 5. Node 0 got replies from neighbour nodes

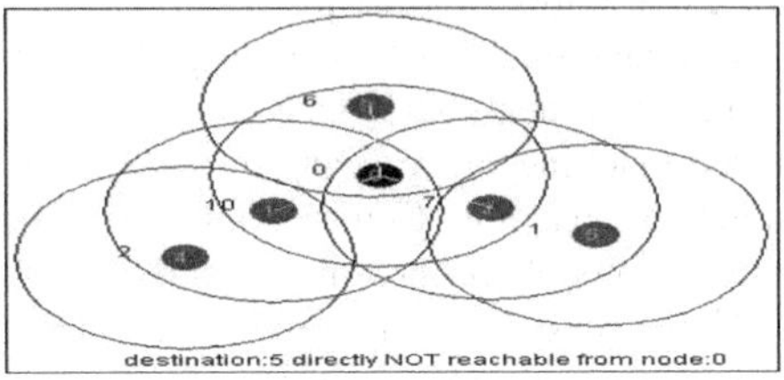

Fig. 6. Destination is not directly reachable from source node

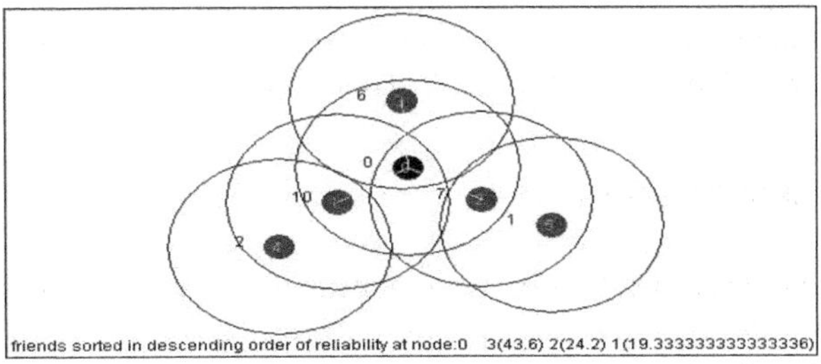

Fig. 7. Friend nodes are sorted in descending order of Fidelity Index written beside neighbour nodes in bracket

For node 1, FI=.6*10+.4*(100/3) =19.333333333
For node 2, FI=.6*7+.4*(100/2) =24.2
For node 3, FI=.6*6+.4*(100/1) =43.6
NOTE: We have taken (100/T) instead of (1/T) for the sake of calculation.

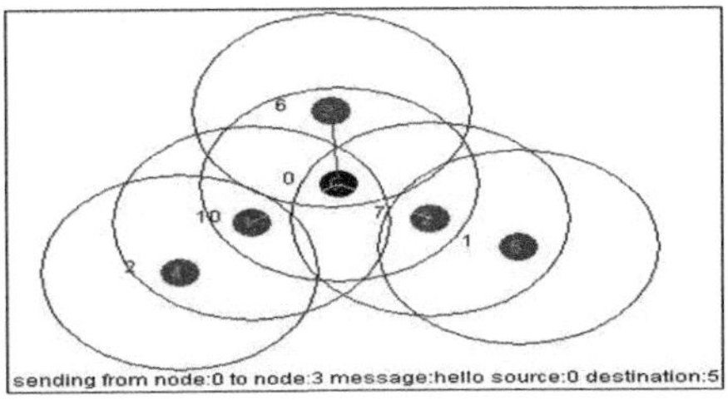

Fig. 8. Node 0 is sending message to node 3

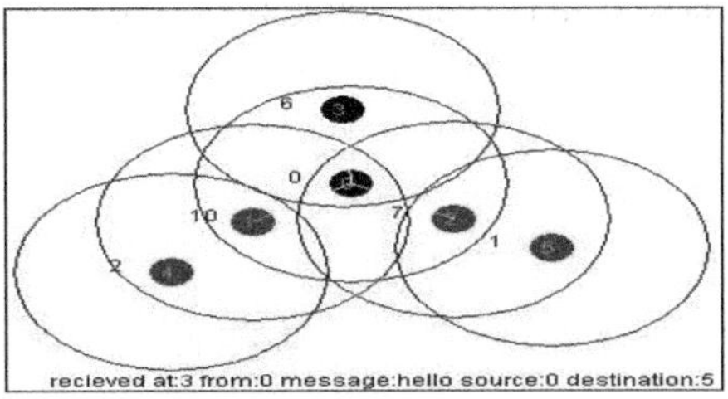

Fig. 9. Message is received at node 3

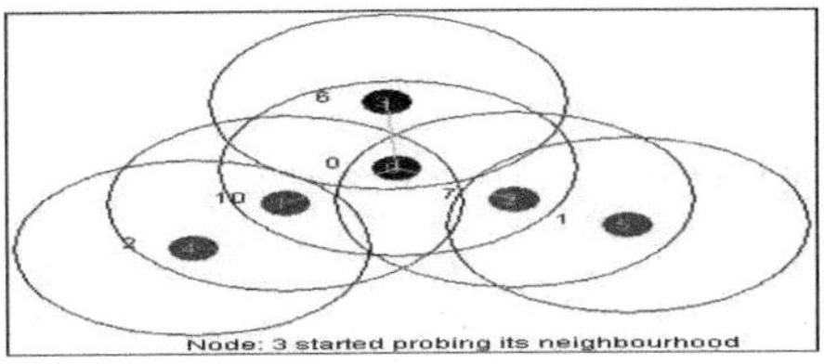

Fig. 10. Node 3 is starts probing neighbour nodes

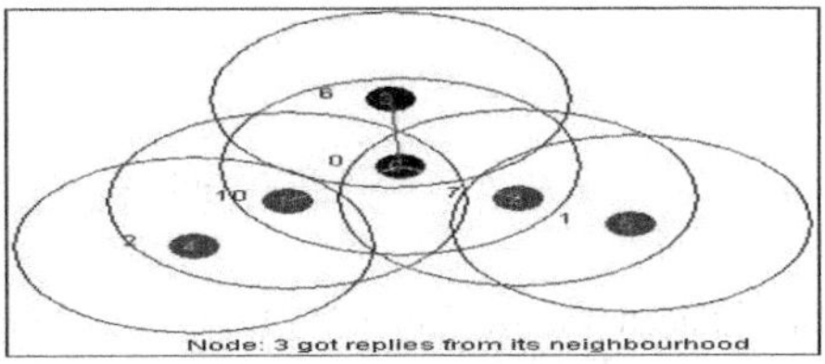

Fig. 11. ode 3 receives reply from neighbours

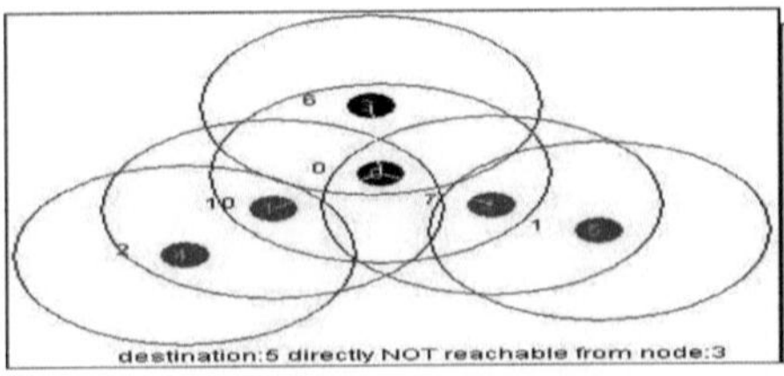

Fig. 12. Destination is not reachable from node 3

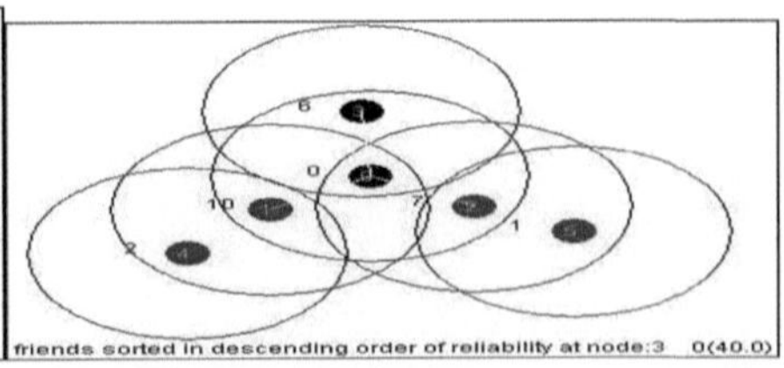

Fig. 13. Friend nodes are sorted in descending order of Fidelity Index written beside neighbor nodes in bracket

For node 0, FI=.6*0+.4*(100/1) =40.0

NOTE: We have taken (100/T) instead of (1/T) for the sake of calculation.

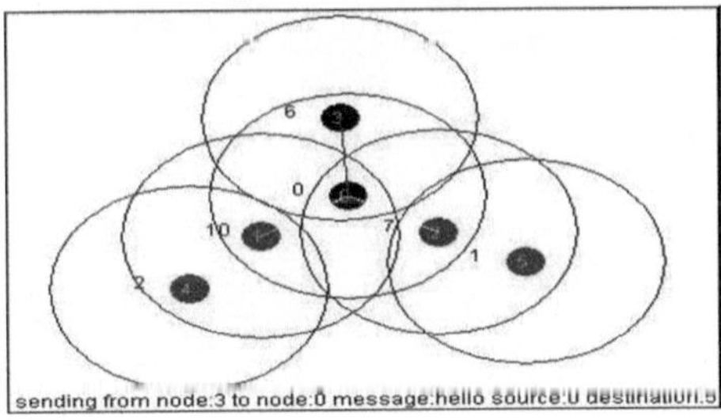

Fig. 14. Node 3 is sending message to node 0

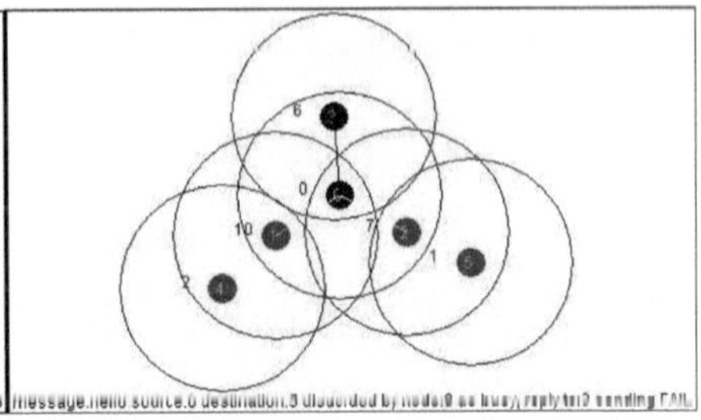

Fig. 15. Node 0 discarded the massage

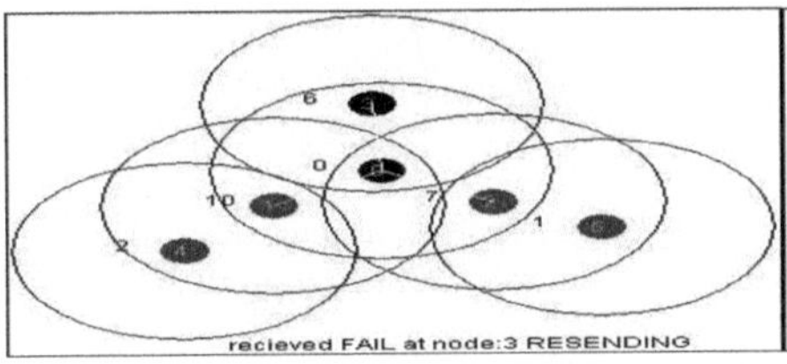

Fig. 16. Node 3 receives a FAIL message

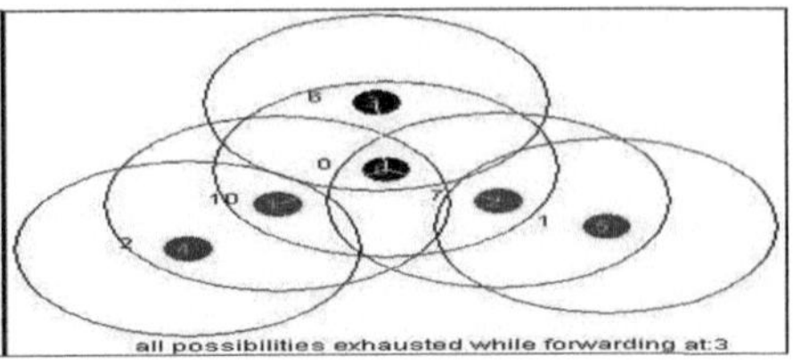

Fig. 17. Message cannot be forwarded from node 3

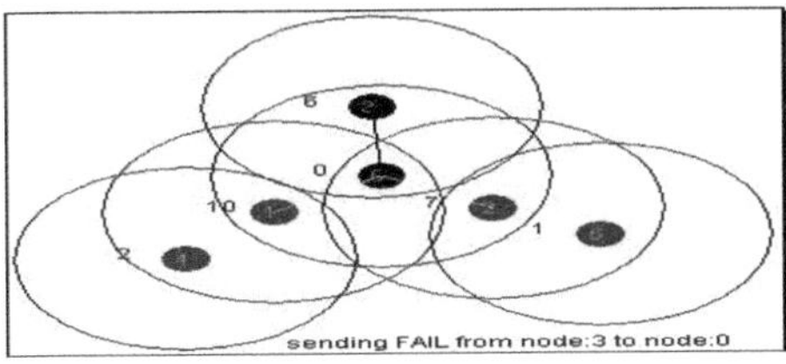

Fig. 18. Node 3 is sending FAIL message to node 0

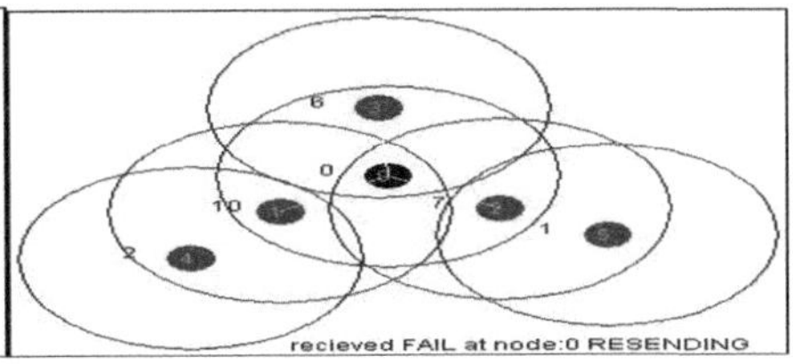

Fig. 19. Node 0 receives FAIL message

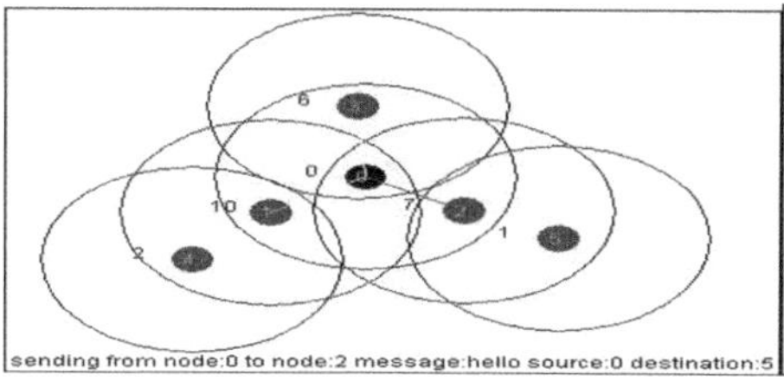

Fig. 20. Node 0 forwarding message to node 2

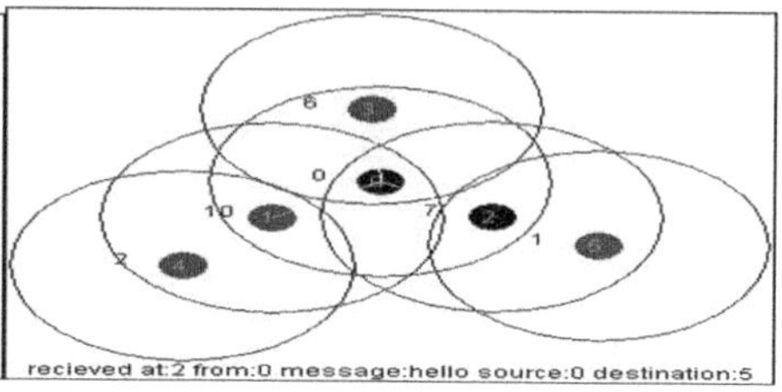

Fig. 21. Node 2 receives message

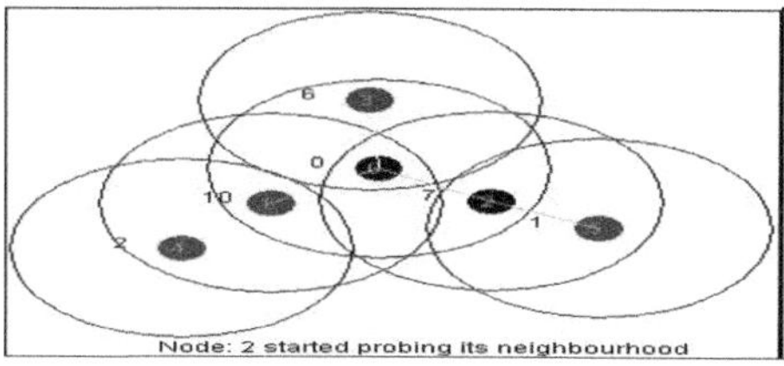

Fig. 22. Node 2 started probing neighbours

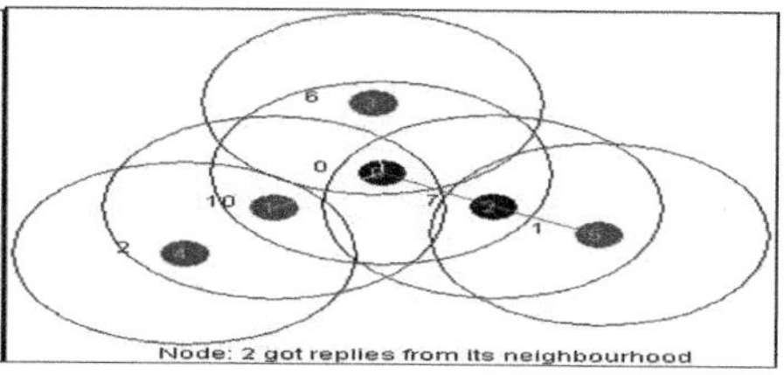

Fig. 23. Node 2 receives reply from neighbour

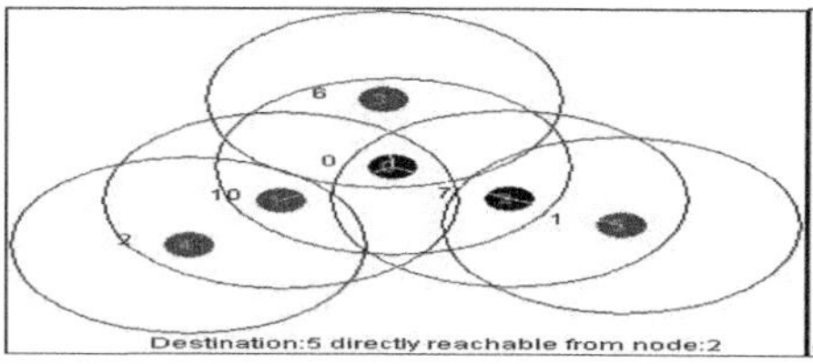

Fig. 24. Destination node 5 is reachable from node 2

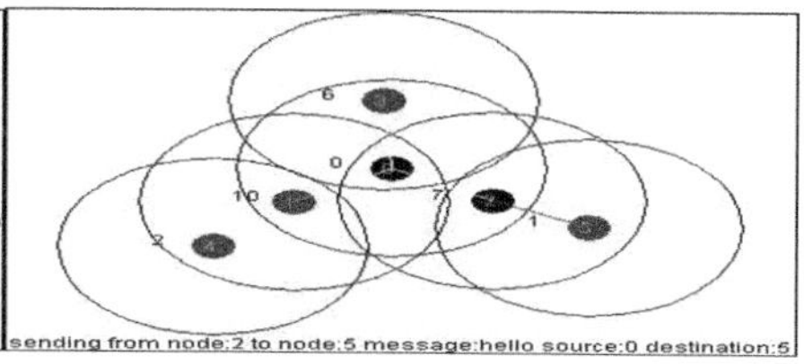

Fig. 25. Node 2 sending message to node 5

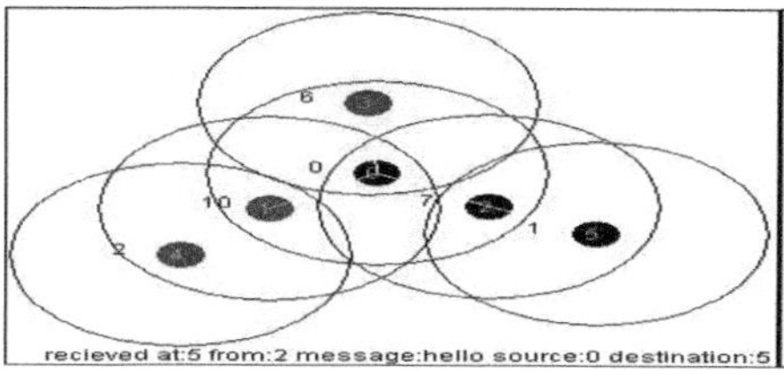

Fig. 26. Node 5 receives message from node 2

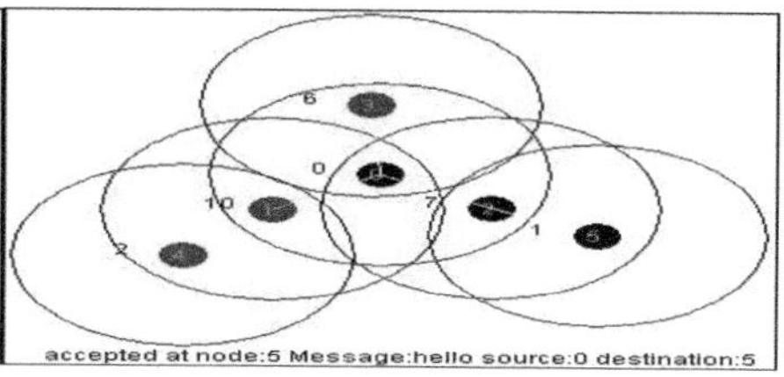

Fig. 27. Node 5 accepts the message and generates an ACK

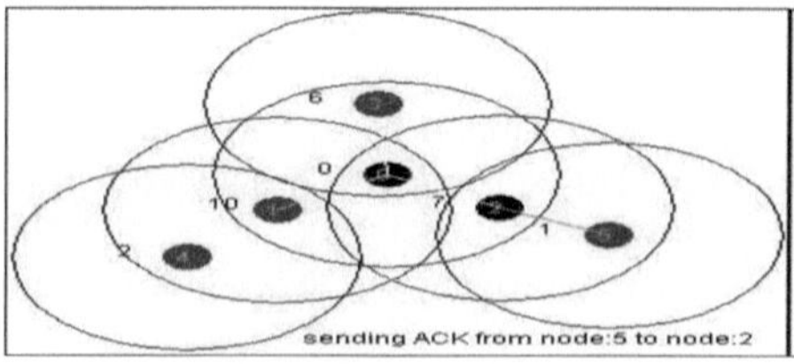

Fig. 28. Node 5 sending ACK to node 2

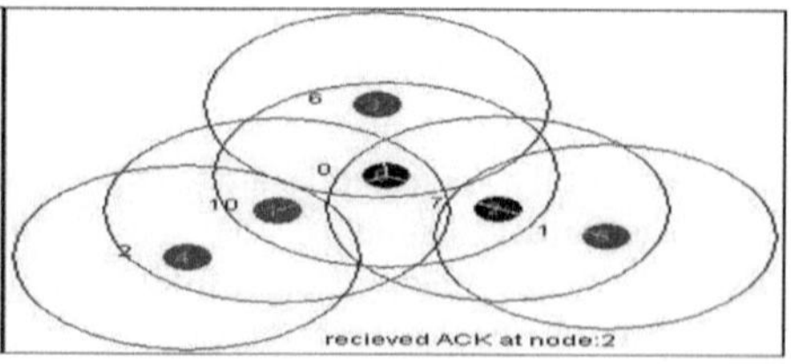

Fig. 29. Node 2 receives ACK

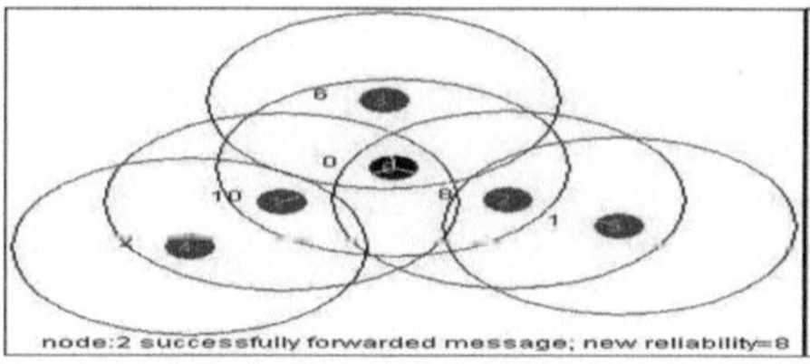

Fig. 30. Fidelity of node 2 increases

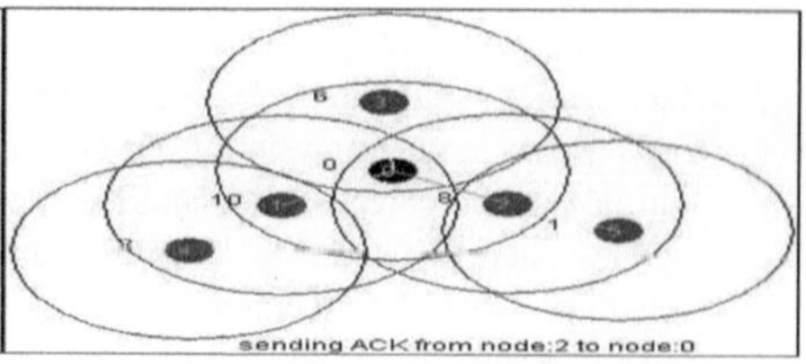

Fig. 31. Node 2 forwarding ACK to node 0

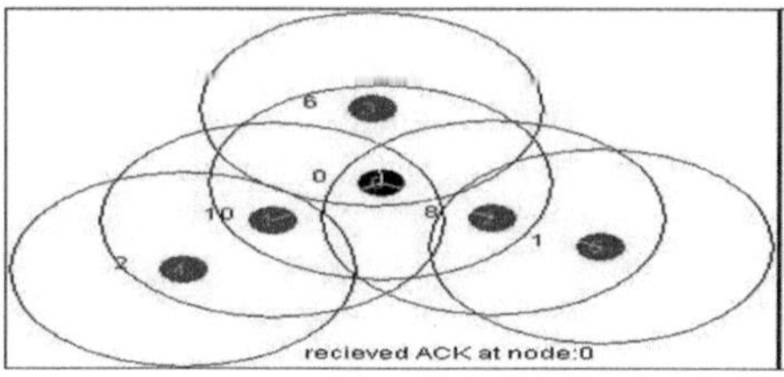

Fig. 32. Node 0 received ACK from node 2

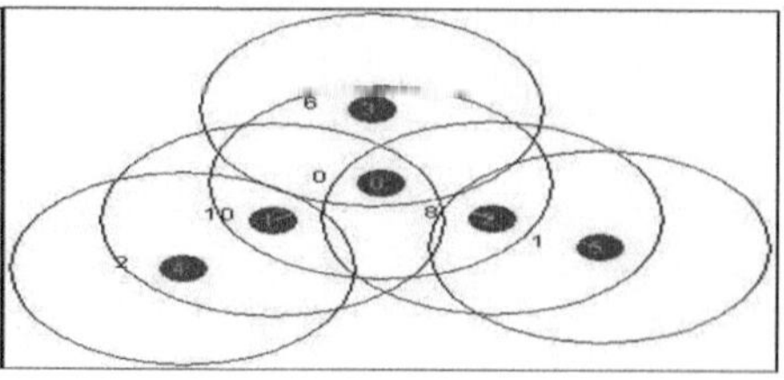

Fig. 33. Messages transferred successfully

Message transfer is completed.

9 Security Aspects

This scheme can efficiently mitigate Flooding attack [17], Black Holes [19] [20], Co-operative Black hole [19], Grey hole [17], Black mail attack [17], Rushing attack [26] and Wormhole Attack [17]. Our simulation has effectively depicted its immunity towards these attacks. This scheme is also safe from attacks to which AODV [2] [20] [23], DSDV [21] is commonly subjected.

10 Conclusion

This is a very light weight scheme with minimum computational overheads. In DSDV, we need to maintain a routing table. AODV has a lot of overhead while discovering routes, which clogs the network for sending data packets to desired destination. No such complicacies exist in our scheme instead it has some of their benefits. FBOD is an on-demand routing scheme and the physical hardware support needed to implement it is substantially low which increases its scalability. This scheme also has added features so as to nullify some of the security threats which cause faults in the MANET networks. This scheme can further be extended by improving the delay and reducing the number of packets dropped.

References

1. Deng, H., Li, W., Agrawal, D.P.: Routing Security in Wireless Ad Hoc Networks. IEEE Communications Magazine (October 2002)
2. Ramesh, V., Subbaiah, P., Koteswar Rao, N., Janardhana Raju, M.: Performance Comparison and Analysis of DSDV and AODV for MANET (IJCSE) International Journal on Computer Science and Engineering 02(02), 183–188 (2010)
3. Li, H., Chen, Z., Qin, X.: Secure Routing in Wired Networks and Wireless Ad Hoc Networks. IEEE, Los Alamitos (2004)
4. Papadimitratos, P., Haas, Z.J.: Secure message transmission in mobile ad hoc networks. Ad Hoc Networks, 193–209 (2003)
5. Liu, K., Deng, J., Varshney, P.K., Balakrishnan, K.: An Acknowledgment-Based Approach for the Detection of Routing Misbehavior in MANETs. IEEE Transaction on Mobile Computing 6(5) (May 2007)
6. Matri, S., Giuli, T.J., Lai, K., Baker, M.: Mittigating Routing misbehaviour in Mobile Ad Hoc Networks. In: Proceedings of the 6th Annual Internaional Conference on Mobile Computing and Networking (MOBICOM), Boston, Massachusetts, United States, pp. 255–265 (2000)
7. Yang, H., Shu, J., Meng, X., Lu, S.: SCAN: Self-organized network-layer security in mobile ad hoc networks. IEEE Journal on Selected Areas in Communications 24(2), 261–273 (2006)
8. Anjum, F., Ghosh, A.K., Golmie, N., Kolodzy, P., Poovendran, R., Shorey, R., Lee, D., Sac, J.: Security in Wireless Ad hoc Networks. IEEE Journal on Selected Areas in Communications 24(2) (February 2006)
9. Gonzalez, O.F., Howarth, M., Pavlou, G.: Detection of Packet Forwarding Misbehavior in Mobile Ad-Hoc Networks. In: 10th IFIP/IEEE International Symposium on Integrated Network Management, IM 2007, May 21. Center for Communications Systems Research, University of Surrey, Guildford, UK (2007)
10. Komninos, N., Vergados, D., Douligeris, C.: Layered security design for mobile ad hoc networks. Journal Computers & Security 25, 121–130 (2006)
11. Luo, H., Zerfos, P., Kong, J., Lu, S., Zhang, L.: Self-securing Ad Hoc Wireless Networks. In: 7th IEEE Symp. on Comp. and Communications (ISCC), Taormina (2002)
12. Wen, H.A., Lin, C.L., Hwang, T.: Provably Secure Authenticated Key Exchange Protocols for Low Power Computing Clients. Computers and Security 25, 106–113 (2006)
13. Patwardhan, A., Parker, J., Iorga, M., Joshi, A., Karygiannis, T.: Secure Routing and Intrusion Detection in Ad Hoc Networks. In: 3rd International Conference on Pervasive Computing and Communications (PerCom 2005), Kauai Island, Hawaii (2005)
14. Otero, A.R., Otero, C.E., Qureshi, A.: A Multi-Criteria Evaluation of Information Security Controls Using Boolean Features. International Journal of Network Security & its Application (IJNSA) 2(4) (October 2010)

15. Wua, B., Wua, J., Fernandeza, E.B., Ilyasa, M., Magliveras, S.: Secure and efficient key management in mobile ad hoc networks. Journal of Network and Computer Applications 30, 937–954 (2007)
16. Nam, J., Cho, S., Kim, S., Won, D.: Simple and Efficient Group Key Agreement Based on Factoring. In: Laganá, A., Gavrilova, M.L., Kumar, V., Mun, Y., Tan, C.J.K., Gervasi, O. (eds.) ICCSA 2004, Part I. LNCS, vol. 3043, pp. 645–654. Springer, Heidelberg (2004)
17. Khokhar, R.H., Ngadi, A., Mandala, S.: A Review of Current Routing Attacks in Mobile Ad Hoc Networks. International Journal of Computer Science and Security 2(3), 18–29
18. Lee, J.-S., Chang, C.-C.: Secure communications for cluster-based ad hoc networks using node identities. Journal of Network and Computer Applications, International Journal of Computer Science and Security 1(1), 67 (2006)
19. Avoiding Black Hole and Cooperative Black Hole Attacks in Wireless Ad hoc Networks, http://www.scribd.com/doc/26788447/Avoiding-Black-Hole-and-Cooperative-Black-Hole-Attacks-in-Wireless-Ad-hoc-Networks
20. Papadimitratos, P., Haas, Z.J.: Secure Link State Routing for Mobile Ad Hoc Networks. In: Proc. IEEE Workshop on Security and Assurance in Ad Hoc Networks, pp. 27–31. IEEE Press, Los Alamitos (2003)
21. Perkins, C.E., Bhagwat, P.: Highly Dynamic Destination-Sequenced Distance-Vector Routing (DSDV) for Mobile Computers. Comp. Comm. Rev., 234–244 (October 1994)
22. Komala, C.R., Shetty, S., Padmashree, S., Elevarasi, E.: Wireless Ad hoc Mobile Networks. In: National Conference on Computing Communication and Technology, pp. 168–174 (2010)
23. Perkins, C.E., Royer, E.M., Das, S.R.: Ad Hoc On Demand Distance Vector (AODV) Routing/ IETF Mobile Ad Hoc Networks Working Group, Internet Draft, work in progress (February 17, 2003)
24. Parker, J., Undercoffer, J.L., Pinkston, J., Joshi, A.: On Intrusion Detection in Mobile Ad Hoc Networks. In: 23rd IEEE International Performance Computing and Communications Conference Workshop on Information Assurance. IEEE, Los Alamitos (April 2004)
25. Li, H., Singha, M.: Trust Management in Distributed Systems. IEEE Computer Society, Los Alamitos (February 2007)
26. Perkins, C., Belding-Royer, E., Das, S.: Ad hoc On-Demand Distance Vector (AODV) Routing (2003)
27. Saha, H.N., Bhattacharyya, D., Banerjee, P.K.: A Priority Based Protocol for Mitigating Different Attacks in MANET. International Journal for Computer Science and Communication 1(2), 299–302 (2010)
28. Saha, H.N., Bhattacharyya, D., Banerjee, P.K.: A Distributed Administration Based Approach for Detecting and Preventing Attacks in MANET. International Journal for Scientific and Engineering Reasearch 2(3), 1–11 (2011)
29. Saha, H.N., Bhattacharyya, D., Banerjee, P.K.: Semi-Centralized Multi-Authenticated RSSI Based Solution to Sybil Attack. International Journal of Computer Science and Emerging Technologies I(4), 338–341 (2010)

Optimization of Dynamic Channel Allocation Scheme for Cellular Networks Using Genetic Algorithim

Jeshuran Pandian, Prithvin Murugiah, Narendran Rajagopalan, and C. Mala*

Computer Science and Engineering
Department, National Institute of Technology,
Tiruchirapalli, Tamil Nadu, India, 620015
{106108045,106108050,406109002,mala}@nitt.edu
http://www.nitt.edu/

Abstract. The spectrum used for wireless transmissions today is becoming overcrowded, due to the increase in the number of users and applications and the demand for the available frequency bands by the various service providers. The major factor that prevents reuse of these bands is the interference caused by neighboring cells. An efficient method to reduce interference needs to be devised. This paper presents work based on the optimization of dynamic channel allocation using genetic algorithm (GA). This attempts to allocate the channel to users such that overall congestion in the network is minimized by reusing already allocated frequencies. The working of Genetic Algorithm which is used in the optimization procedure is also explained. The optimized channel is then compared with a non-optimized channel to check the efficiency of the genetic algorithm.

Keywords: dynamic channel allocation, fixed channel allocation, cellular networks, genetic algorithm, crossover, fitness function.

1 Introduction

The tremendous growth in mobile communication makes channel allocation critical due to the limited spectra available. The amount of spectrum left and the increasing cost have led to a limited spectrum available to each operator and hence making efficient use of it is required. The reuse of channel also becomes vital in this regard. Channels can be reused when the two stations do not interfere. Each operator can hence use all the spectra available to it by dynamically allocating frequencies to each cell in real time.

Studies have shown that under low traffic Dynamic Channel Allocation (DCA) fairs better in comparison to Fixed Channel Allocation (FCA) (also known as Static Channel Allocation (SCA)) [4][5][6]. However under high traffic conditions, FCA fairs better as there is always a constant stream of calls in high traffic, hence avoiding wastage of spectrum. Optimization isn't required in this case. But when there is medium to low traffic, Dynamic Channel Allocation can be used more efficiently than Fixed Channel Allocation [2].

* Corresponding author.

D. Nagamalai, E. Renault, and M. Dhanushkodi (Eds.): PDCTA 2011, CCIS 203, pp. 628–637, 2011.

Given the limitations and wastage of spectrum in FCA, it is obvious that the currently used fixed or static allocation scheme cannot accommodate the requirements of the devices in the near future. The solution to this may be found in DCA. Using DCA, the channel is allocated dynamically depending on the need of the service demands of the end user. This makes it more efficient than FCA.

But this leads to the issue of how the allocation is to be managed and optimized. In this paper, a Genetic Algorithm (GA) [1][2][8] is used to optimize the dynamicity of the channel. Taking three of the parameters for allocation and optimizing them using GA, an optimum usage scheme for these three parameters was obtained.

Genetic algorithms belong to the larger class of evolutionary algorithms (EA), which generate solutions to optimization problems using techniques inspired by natural evolution. It is a search heuristic that mimics the process of natural evolution such as inheritance, mutation, selection and crossover.

The rest of the paper is organized as follows. Section 2 presents fundamentals of Fixed Channel Allocation (FCA) and Dynamic Channel Allocation (DCA). In section 3, a description of Genetic Algorithm (GA) is given. The result of the optimization procedure is presented in section 4. Conclusions and future work that can be derived from this are presented in section 5.

2 Fundamental Channel Allocation Schemes

Channel allocation schemes are basically used to allocate bandwidth and communication channels to base stations, access points and terminal equipments. The objective is to achieve maximum efficiency. Two types of strategies are followed –

- Fixed Channel Allocation (FCA)
- Dynamic Channel Allocation (DCA)

In FCA, each cell is given predetermined set of voice channel. A call can only connect by using an unused channel. If all the channels are occupied then the call is blocked in this system. This leads to congestion in traffic and some calls being lost when traffic gets heavy in some cells while some other cells may be idle at the same time.

A more efficient way of channel allocation would be Dynamic Channel Allocation (DCA) in which the voice channel is not allocated to cell permanently, but instead for every call request, the base station requests a channel from the Mobile Switching Center (MSC) [4][5]. The channel is then allocated following algorithms which accounts for the likelihood of future blocking within the cell. This requires the MSC to collect real time data on channel occupancy, traffic distribution, Radio Signal Strength Indications, etc.

In this paper, three major factors which affect the channel allocation are taken namely Periodicity, Number of Users and Residual Bandwidth for the purpose of optimization.

The fitness function with these three parameters is coined as –

$$\text{Max } f(x) = p + 1/n + rb \quad (1)$$

where, p is periodicity,
n is number of users, and
rb is residual bandwidth.

Periodicity is taken as the amount of time a user holds on to a certain frequency allocated to him, i.e. the time taken by a user in a certain call. This affects the allocation as knowledge of the amount of time the spectra is in use is vital for optimal allocation of the spectra to the users. The range of call times was obtained using recorded history of usage by users over a period of time to find the average range of time that users hold the channel allocated to them.

The variable n stands for the number of users requesting allocation of frequency to make a certain voice or data call at a certain time. This is proportional to the number of users active in the given cell. This is also obtained using knowledge of the recent history of traffic in each cell owned by the operator.

The third variable is the residual bandwidth. Residual bandwidth refers to the left over spectra available to be allocated in each cell. Here the advantage of DCA over FCA takes effect as in FCA each cell is allocated with a given set of frequencies while in DCA the total spectrum can be allocated to any of the cells. Therefore, the spectrum available to each cell is much wider in DCA in comparison to FCA. More spectra can be allocated to high traffic cells since low traffic cells do not need to hold any given spectrum.

With these three parameters, the fitness function given in eqn. (1) is used to optimize the dynamic channel allocation scheme using Genetic Algorithm.

3 Genetic Algorithm

Genetic Algorithms [1] are most commonly used as optimization algorithms. They are based on mechanics of natural selection (Darwin's Theory of Evolution). Natural Selection combines survival of the fittest and a randomized information exchange procedure to form a new generation from a previous generation in evolution. Genetic Algorithms follow the same procedures of using the fittest of the old generation as well as creation of new strings from previous generation through information exchange.

The mechanics of the genetic algorithm are simple involving only operations as copying of strings, swapping partial strings, etc. Initially, for applying genetic algorithm to a given problem, two things are needed namely – (i) an initial set of values which are basically strings of 0's and 1's (also known as individuals) based on the given parameters and (ii) a function known as fitness function, for evaluating how good or bad a particular individual is. This set of all the initial strings together is called as the initial population.

The initial population maybe generated in random or based on some initially assumed data for the given parameters. The string length of each individual depends on the problem at hand, the amount of optimization required and on the parameters as well. Some parameters may have many number of states while some others might not have that many. Hence, each parameter maybe allotted a certain number of bits based on the number of different states it can have. Its priority in the fitness function also matters. Priority is decided based on the effect of the parameter on the fitness function. If a small change in the state of a parameter affects the fitness of an individual drastically, then it is given a higher priority and vice versa. A parameter with higher priority maybe allotted more number of bits in order to increase the optimization of that parameter more which in turn increases the optimization of the whole procedure as such. The string length, as mentioned earlier, also depends on the amount of optimization required. If the string length is very high, i.e. a large number of states of the parameter are considered, and the population size is high, then all the variations of the states of the parameters maybe involved in the optimization procedure and hence might lead to a higher level of optimization. The population size is also decided based on the amount of optimization required for the given problem. More the population size, more is the variation in the generation, and hence more the optimization as more variations are analyzed during the optimization procedure. So as seen, the amount of optimization required decides almost all the factors involved in the initial population generation.

Once the initial population is generated, a simple set of operations is performed on it to generate successive populations which improve over time (hence, optimization). A simple genetic algorithm which does exactly that is composed of three operations – (i) Reproduction, (ii) Crossover and (iii) Mutation.

Reproduction [1][8] is the process in which individuals are copied according to their fitness, which is calculated using the fitness function. Individuals with a higher fitness function (in a maximization problem) are copied over to the next generation while those with the least fitness function are neglected or discarded. Copying an individual according to its fitness leads to a higher probability of it contributing a better offspring (having a higher fitness) in the next generation. Copying of individuals is achieved based on its percentage contribution to the sum of all the fitness functions put together.

Crossover [1][8] is the process of information exchange. After reproduction is over, the set of individuals are then paired in random and mated. Mating is the process where each pair undergoes swapping of all the characters from one string to its mate from a randomly decided position in the string. This random point is known as crossover point. This is the primary step involved in the evolutionary process of genetic algorithm. Crossover combined with reproduction leads to effective optimization through recombination of individuals.

Mutation [1][8] is the process of altering of value of an individual in random, i.e., changing the value of a random character in an individual from 0 to 1 or vice versa. It is implemented to ensure that there is no loss of optimization if by chance, all of the population contains 0's or 1's at a particular location which will just be carried forward to the next generation as such if only reproduction is used and crossover leading to incomplete optimization. The frequency of mutation is usually of the order of one mutation per thousand reproduction cycles, which is similar to the mutations rates in natural selection.

A simple example [1] to demonstrate all the functions of a genetic algorithm is given below. Assume the initial population as shown and the let the fitness function be $f(x) = x^2$.

Table 1. Example to demonstrate Genetic Algorithm [1]

Individual No.	X Values	Population (binary representation of x)	$f(x) = x^2$	Percentage Contribution to Sum(p)	Copies (p*4)
1.	13	0 1 1 0 1	169	14 %	0.56≈1
2.	24	1 1 0 0 0	576	49 %	1.96≈2
3.	8	0 1 0 0 0	64	6 %	0.24≈0
4.	19	1 0 0 1 1	361	31 %	1.24≈1

The initial population contains a population of 4 individuals. Their fitness is calculated using the fitness function as shown. After the fitness is calculated for each individual, the sum of all the fitness functions of the individuals is found (here it is 1170). Then, the percentage contribution for each individual to the sum is found. This percentage contribution multiplied by the total population size, gives the number of copies of each of the individuals present in the following generation. The result of this operation on the above set of individuals leads to 2 copies of individual 2 and individual 3 being discarded giving rise to the intermediate population of:

0 1 1 0 1
1 1 0 0 0
1 1 0 0 0
1 0 0 1 1

At this point, the procedure of crossover is implemented on this intermediate population set. Suppose, individual 1 is paired with individual 2 and individual 3 with individual 4. Assume the crossover points are 4 and 1 respectively. Then, the crossover occurs as:

0 1 1 0 | 1 ⟶ 0 1 1 0 | 0
1 1 0 0 | 0 ⟶ 1 1 0 0 | 1

1 1 | 0 0 0 ⟶ 1 1 | 0 1 1
1 0 | 0 1 1 ⟶ 1 0 | 0 0 0

Mutation then occurs at a probability of 0.0001 which is highly improbable for one reproduction cycle. But if mutation were to occur, at say individual 1, then it would be something like:

0 1 1 0 1 ⟶ 1 1 1 0 1

At this point, a new population set is generated. The procedure of Reproduction, Crossover and Mutation is carried out repeatedly till a termination condition for the optimization is reached. The termination condition maybe a highest level of fitness reached or fixed number generations reached or satisfaction of certain constraints which is decided depending on the problem. Once the termination condition is reached, the population that is generated after the last iteration is said to be optimized.

In our tests, the following procedures were performed as a part of the genetic algorithm that was implemented –

- Initial population is randomly generated.
- Each individual is evaluated as per the fitness function.
- Repeat on each generation until termination –

  (a) Best individuals are selected for reproduction.
  (b) New individuals are obtained through crossover and mutation.
  (c) New individuals are evaluated as per the fitness function.
  (d) Least-fit individuals of the population are replaced with the new individuals.

3.1 Proposed Optimization Scheme for Dynamic Channel Allocation Using Genetic Algorithm

In the proposed scheme, an initial random population of 100 is generated with a random number generator. Each of the three parameters were given equal priority and taken as 8-bit values. Hence, 100 random numbers of 24-bit string length was generated to be the initial population.

Table 2. Initially generated random population

Individual No.	Periodicity(p)	No. of Users(n)	Residual Bandwidth(rb)	f(x)=p+1/n+rb
1.	179	136	140	319.00735
2.	128	167	249	377.00598
3.	55	82	54	109.01219
4.	96	152	68	164.00658
5.	55	26	110	165.03845
6.	3	35	57	60.028572
7.	49	247	233	282.00406
8.	10	127	133	143.00787
9.	165	172	250	415.0058
10.	43	181	245	288.00552
11.	26	161	173	199.00621
12.	173	214	95	268.00467
13.	3	251	105	108.00398
14.	208	71	248	456.0141
15.	205	79	172	377.01266
16.	183	248	31	214.00403
17.	170	198	234	404.00507
18.	29	80	128	157.0125
19.	221	114	25	246.00877
20.	17	220	200	217.00455

The 8-bit representation of each of the parameters is as follows –

- A periodicity value of 15 seconds is represented by the 00000001, 30 seconds as 00000010 and so on.
- 1 user requesting a channel is represented as 00000001, 2 users as 00000010 and so on.
- Residual bandwidth is represented by percentage of bandwidth remaining, i.e. 100% bandwidth remaining is represented by 11111111 and 0% bandwidth as 00000000 and so on.

Table 2 gives a sample of the initial population that is generated which is then used for optimization.

The f(x) values were then calculated for each of the individuals of the initial population. The sum of the f(x) values was calculated and the percentage contribution of each of the individuals was calculated. The individuals with a higher contribution percentage as compared to the rest were favored and the ones with a lower percentage contribution were given lesser preference during the selection procedure for mating for the next generation. The selected individuals were paired in random with another individual and mating was carried out. Crossover with a probability of 1 and mutation with a probability of 0.001 were the operations carried out during the mating procedure. This is the point in the algorithm where optimization, or evolution as is the case here, occurs. The best of the individuals were taken and then mated to get

Table 3. Population after the final iteration

Individual No.	Periodicity(p)	No. of Users(n)	Residual Bandwidth(rb)	f(x)=p+1/n+rb
1.	181	136	140	321.00735
2.	89	167	249	338.00598
3.	219	167	249	468.00598
4.	162	152	68	230.00658
5.	12	247	233	245.00404
6.	17	247	233	250.00404
7.	2	172	250	252.00581
8.	110	172	250	360.0058
9.	237	172	250	487.0058
10.	12	181	245	257-00552
11.	170	161	173	343.00623
12.	206	71	248	454.0141
13.	208	71	248	456.0141
14.	57	71	248	305.0141
15.	205	79	172	377.01266
16.	208	79	172	380.01266
17.	237	198	234	471.00507
18.	220	198	234	454.00507
19.	134	198	234	368.00507
20.	173	80	128	301.0125

individuals with the favorable qualities of both the parent individuals. This leads to a new generation of individuals with a higher average f(x) value.

This generational process is repeated until a termination condition has been reached. In our tests, a fixed number of generations was used and the optimization procedure was terminated after 10 iterations. Table 3 gives the result of the optimization of the sample initial population taken in Table 2.

4 Performance Analysis

The performance of the proposed method of optimization is shown in below. Taking different number of users requesting a call in the system, the change in performance is seen after optimization using GA.

Table 4. Performance of Genetic Algorithm while varying number of users(n)

Sr. No.	No. of Users	Throughput without GA (%)	Throughput with GA (%)
1.	50	56.59	72.15
2.	100	53.40	69.13
3.	150	53.40	71.20
4.	200	51.97	68.95
5.	250	49.37	69.18

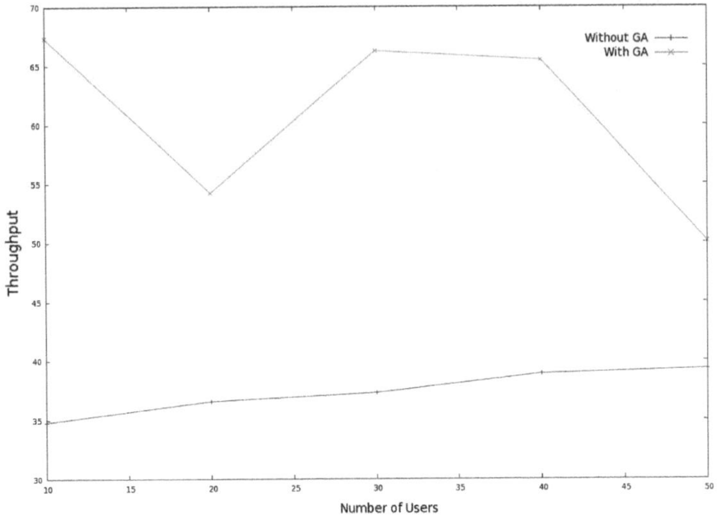

Fig. 1. Performance of Genetic Algorithm while varying number of users (n)

As the number of calls vary, i.e. varying the number of users in the system from 50 to 250, the performance of the system with and without Genetic Algorithm is found. From the results seen from the graph in Fig.1 and Table. 4, it is clear that the throughput is high while using Genetic Algorithm.

Taking different periodicity of a call in the system, i.e. different call durations, the change in performance after optimization using GA was observed.

Table 5. Performance of Genetic Algorithm while varying periodicity (p)

Sr. No.	Periodicity	Throughput without GA (%)	Throughput with GA (%)
1.	10	34.83	67.38
2.	20	36.58	54.24
3.	30	37.29	66.27
4.	40	38.89	65.11
5.	50	39.31	50.11

Varying the time taken by each call, i.e. varying periodicity, the performance of the system with and without Genetic Algorithm is found. The results are as shown in the Table. 5 and Fig. 2.

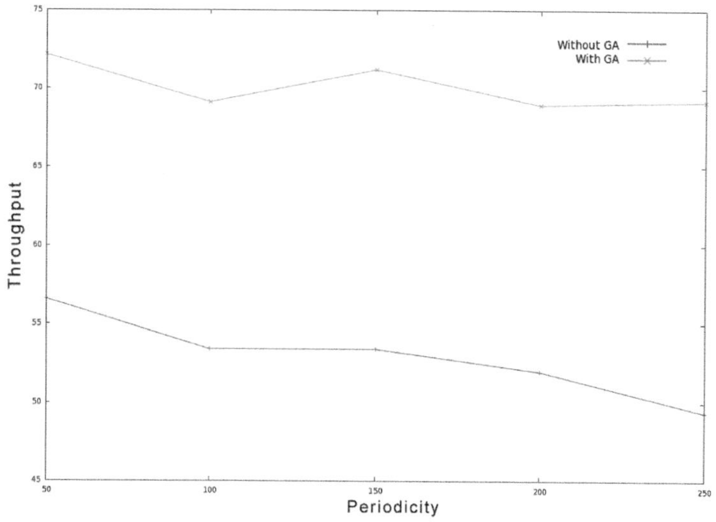

Fig. 2. Performance of Genetic Algorithm keeping periodicity(p) constant

The performance of the Genetic Algorithm can be seen in the graph shown in Fig. 2 also. Hence, GA gives a high performance throughput for the proposed optimization.

5 Conclusion

It can be observed from the results that the optimization using Genetic Algorithm fairs remarkably better. In this case, optimized Dynamic Channel Allocation uses three parameters namely Periodicity, Number of Users requesting a call and Residual Bandwidth by using GA. It is seen that with periodicity, the throughput is increased by almost 30 percent and with number of users as a parameter, it is increased by 20 percent.

References

1. Goldberg, D.E.: Genetic Algorithms in Search, Optimization, and Machine Learning. Pearson Education, India (2004)
2. Tsai, C., Lin, F., Tsai, C.: An efficient GA-based approach for fixed channel assignment in cellular radio networks. In: Proceedings of 2003 IEEE International Symposium on Computational Intelligence in Robotics and Automation, vol. 1(16-20), pp. 384–389 (July 2003)
3. Martinez, D., Andrade, A.G., Martinez, A.: Interference-Aware Dynamic Channel allocation scheme for cellular networks. IEEE Press, Los Alamitos
4. Qing, Z., Sadler, M.: A Survey of Dynamic Spectrum Access. IEEE Signal Processing Magazine 70(5), 79–89 (2007)
5. Granelli, F., Przemyslaw, P., Venkatesha, P., Hoffmeyer, J.: Standardization and Research in Cognitive and Dynamic Spectrum Acess Networks: IEEE SCC41 efforts and Other Activities. IEEE Communications Magazine 48(1), 71–79 (2010)
6. Katzela, I., Naghshineh, M.: Channel assignment schemes for cellular mobile telecommunication systems: a comprehensive survey. IEEE Personal Communications 3(3), 10–31 (1996)
7. Kaabi, F., Ghannay, S., Filali, F.: Channel allocation and routing in Wireless Mesh Networks:A Survey and qualitative comparison between schemes. International Journal of Wireless and Mobile Network 2(1), 132–151 (2010)
8. Wikipedia, http://www.wikipedia.org/

Analysis of Feature Recognition of Neural Network Method in the String Recognition

Amit Kumar Gupta[1] and Yash Pal Singh[2]

[1] MCA Department, KIET, Ghaziabad (UP), India
[2] Reader and Head, CSE Deptt. BIET, Jhansi (UP), India
amitid29@gmail.com, yash_biet@yahoo.co.in

Abstract. This paper aims that analysing neural network method in pattern recognition. A neural network is a processing device, whose design was inspired by the design and functioning of human brain and their components. The proposed solutions focus on applying Feature Recognition Neural Network model for pattern recognition. The primary function of which is to retrieve in a pattern stored in memory, when an incomplete or noisy version of that pattern is presented. An associative memory is a storehouse of associated patterns that are encoded in some form. In auto-association, an input pattern is associated with itself and the states of input and output units coincide. When the storehouse is incited with a given distorted or partial pattern, the associated pattern pair stored in its perfect form is recalled. Pattern recognition techniques are associated a symbolic identity with the image of the pattern. This problem of replication of patterns by machines (computers) involves the machine printed patterns. There is no idle memory containing data and programmed, but each neuron is programmed and continuously active.

Keywords: Neural network, machine printed string, pattern recognition.

1 Introduction

An Artificial Neural Network (ANN) is an information processing paradigm that is inspired by the biological nervous systems, such as the brain. It is composed of a large number of highly interconnected processing elements (neurons) working in unison to solve specific problems. A Neural Network is configured for pattern recognition or data classification, through a learning process. In biological systems, Learning involves adjustments to the synaptic connections that exist between the neurons. Neural networks process information in a similar way the human brain does. The network is composed of a large number of highly interconnected processing elements working in parallel to solve a specific problem. Neural networks learn by example. A neuron has many inputs and one output. The neuron has two modes of operation (i) the training mode and (ii) the using mode. In the training mode, the neuron can be trained for particular input patterns. In the using mode, when a taught input pattern is detected at the input, its associated output becomes the current output. If the input pattern does not belong in the taught list of input patterns, the training rule is used. Neural network has many applications. The most likely applications for the neural

D. Nagamalai, E. Renault, and M. Dhanushkodi (Eds.): PDCTA 2011, CCIS 203, pp. 638–647, 2011.

networks are (1) Classification (2) Association and (3) Reasoning. An important application of neural networks is pattern recognition. Pattern recognition can be implemented by using a feed-forward neural network that has been trained accordingly. During training, the network is trained to associate outputs with input patterns. When the network is used, it identifies the input pattern and tries to output the associated output pattern. Four significant approaches to PR have evolved. These are [5].

Statistical pattern recognition: Here, the problem is posed as one of composite hypothesis testing, each hypothesis pertaining to the premise, of the datum having originated from a particular class; or as one of regression from the space of measurements to the space of classes. The statistical methods for solving the same involve the computation other class conditional probability densities, which remains the main hurdle in this approach. The statistical approach is one of the oldest, and still widely used [8].

Syntactic pattern recognition: In syntactic pattern recognition, each pattern is assumed to be composed of sub-pattern or primitives strung together in accordance with the generation rules of a grammar string of the associated class. Class identifications accomplished by way of parsing operations using automata corresponding to the various grammars [15, 16]. Parser design and grammatical inference are two difficult issues associated with this approach to PR and are responsible for its somewhat limited applicability.

Knowledge-based pattern recognition: This approach to PR [17] is evolved from advances in rule-based system in artificial intelligence (AI). Each rule is in form of a clause that reflects evidence about the presence of a particular class. The sub-problems spawned by the methodology are:-

1. How the rule-based may be constructed, and
2. What mechanism might be used to integrate the evidence yielded by the invoked rules?

Neural Pattern Recognition: Artificial Neural Network (ANN) provides an emerging paradigm in pattern recognition. The field of ANN encompasses a large variety of models [18], all of which have two important string.

1. They are composed of a large number of structurally and functionally similar units called neurons usually connected various configurations by weighted links.
2. The Ann's model parameters are derived from supplied I/O paired data sets by an estimation process called training.

2 Methodology

Different neural network algorithms are used for recognizing the pattern. Various algorithms differ in their learning mechanism. Information is stored in the weight matrix of a neural network. Learning is the determination of the weights. All learning methods used for adaptive neural networks can be classified into two major categories: supervised learning and unsupervised learning. Supervised learning incorporates an external teacher. After training the network, we should get the response equal to target response. During the learning process, global information may be required. The aim is to determine a set of weights, which minimizes the error. Unsupervised learning uses no external teacher and is based on clustering of input data. There is no prior information about input's membership in a particular class. The string of the patterns and a history of training are used to assist the network in defining classes. It self-organizes data presented to the network and detects their emergent collective properties. The characteristics of the neurons and initial weights are specified based upon the training method of the network. The pattern sets is applied to the network during the training. The pattern to be recognized are in the form of vector whose elements is obtained from a pattern grid. The elements are either 0 and 1 or -1 and 1. In some of the algorithms, weights are calculated from the pattern presented to the network and in some algorithms, weights are initialized. The network acquires the knowledge from the environment. The network stores the patterns presented during the training in another way it extracts the features of pattern. As a result of this, the information can be retrieved later.

3 Problem Statement

The aim of the paper is that neural network has demonstrated its capability for solving complex pattern recognition problems. Commonly solved problems of pattern have limited scope. Single neural network architecture can recognize only few patterns. Relative performance of various neural network algorithms has not been reported in the literature. In this paper discusses on various neural network algorithms with their implementation details for solving pattern recognition problems. The relative performance evaluation of these algorithms has been carried out. The comparisons of algorithms have been performed based on following criteria:

(1) Noise in weights
(2) Noise in inputs
(3) Loss of connections
(4) Missing information and adding information.

4 Feature Recognition Neural Network

Feature recognition neural network is also used for character recognition. This network learns the patterns by remembering their different segments. It uses recognition by parts technique by remembering the different sections of the pattern. Thus noise or deformation in one section of the pattern does not affect the overall recognition process. This is the basis of the development of the feature recognition algorithm[23].

This network has two labels. The first level detects the sub patterns. The second level is responsible for detecting the patterns them selves and provides the output class. The pattern grid distributes the inputs over the first level. The neurons in the first level detect the sub patterns and feed a single neuron in level two. That fires if all the sub patterns are detected. The neurons of second level fires whenever, any one of the former neuron detects the sub pattern.

To recognize any pattern the network goes to following steps:

(1) The network learns all the training patterns and remembers their sub patterns.
(2) The new pattern (test patterns) is also divided in to sub patterns.
(3) Each of the sub patterns is compared individually against the corresponding sub patterns of training patterns and suitable match is found.
(4) Then it finds the total number of sub patterns that matched for any pattern and finds the closest overall match [23].

5 Algorithm

Step 1: A set of training vectors

$$A_P = \{\mathbf{a}_{1p}, \mathbf{a}_{2p}, \ldots\ldots\ldots\ldots, \mathbf{a}_{np}\} \qquad \text{for p=1, 2, } \ldots\ldots\ldots\text{p}$$

Is given as input where $\mathbf{a}_{ip}$ =0 or 1

n is the dimension of training vector.

Step 2: The weights are

$$W_P = \{w_{1p}, w_{2p}, \ldots\ldots\ldots\ldots, w_{pp}\}$$

Where $w_{ip} = 1$ if $\mathbf{a}_{ip} = 1$

-1 if $\mathbf{a}_{ip} = 0$

Step 3: Each pattern is divided in to s number of sub patterns which is given by

$$A_{sP} = \{\mathbf{a}_{1sp}, \mathbf{a}_{2sp}, \ldots\ldots\ldots\ldots, \mathbf{a}_{nsp}\} \quad \text{For s = 1, 2, } \ldots\ldots\text{, S}$$

p = 1, 2, ……, P

m is the dimension of vector obtained from each pattern.

Step 4: The weight matrix formed from sub patterns is

$$W_{sP} = \{w_{1sp}, w_{2sp}, \ldots\ldots\ldots\ldots, w_{ssp}\}$$

Where $W_{jsP} = 1$ if $\mathbf{a}_{jsP} = 1$

-1 if $\mathbf{a}_{jsP}$ =0

For j = 1,2,……m

Step 5: For all the sub patterns of every training patterns threshold is calculated as

$$\theta_{sP} = A_{sP}(W_{sP})^t \qquad \text{for s= 1,2,}\ldots\ldots\text{S}$$

p = 1,2,…..P

Step 6: Test pattern is presented to the network and stored as the vector

at= (at_1, at_2, ………at_n)

Step 7: Test pattern is divided into sub patterns

ats_s= (ats_1, ats_2, ………ats_m) for s= 1,2,……S

Step 8: Inner product of sub patterns of test patterns with sub patters of every stored patterns is calculated and stored in the vector **p**.

$$\mathbf{p}_{sp} = A_{sp}(\mathbf{a}ts)^t \quad \text{for } s = 1,2,\ldots\ldots S$$
$$p = 1,2,\ldots\ldots P$$

Step 9: Each threshold θ_{sP} is compared with p_{sP} and variable parfire is set accordingly.

$$\theta_{sP} = p_{sP} \text{ partial firing } \text{parfire}_{sp} = 1$$
$$\text{Otherwise } \text{parfire}_{sp} = 0$$

Step 10: overall firing of each neuron of output layer is calculated as

$$fire_p = \sum_{s=1}^{S} parfire_{sp}$$

Step 11: Maximum of all fire_p for p= 1,2,……P is selected, which gives the out class p[23].

6 Result

Three layers network configuration has been taken. The output layer has 26 neurons one corresponding to each character. 26 characters in the form of 9×9 pattern grids are given as training pattern to the network. Each pattern is divided into 9 sub patterns of size 3x3. The network correctly classifies 23 characters when they are presented individually to the network as test patter. The neuron corresponding to the character no. has maximum value of the variable fire. The network can not differentiate O and Q from C and also R from P. This has been shown in table 1.

Table 1. Given input and obtained output in FRNN

Char acter	Input Pattern	Input Sub Pattern	Output
A	o o o * * * o o o o o * o o o * o o o * o o o o o * o * o o o o o o o * * * * * * * * * * * o o o o o o o * * o o o o o o o * * o o o o o o o * * o o o o o o o *	o o o * * * o o o o o * o o o * o o o * o o o o o * o * o o o o o o o * * * * * * * o o * * o o o o o o o * * o o o o o o o * * o o o o o o o * * o o o o o o o *	Maximum fire is of neuron 1

Table 1. (*Continued*)

B	* * * * * * * * o * o o o o o o o * * o o o o o o o * * o o o o o o * o * * * * * * * o o * o o o o o o * o * o o o o o o o * * o o o o o o o * * * * * * * * * o	* * * * * * * * o * o o o o o o o * * o o o o o o o * * o o o o o o * o * * * * * * * o o * o o o o o o * o * o o o o o o o * * o o o o o o o * * * * * * * * * o	Maximum fire is of neuron 2
Character	**Input Pattern**	**Input Sub Pattern**	**Output**
C	o o * * * * * o o o o o o o o o * o * o o o o o o o * * o o o o o o o o * o o o o o o o o * o o o o o o o o * o o o o o o o * o * o o o o o * o o o * * * * * o o	o o * * * * * o o o * o o o o o * o * o o o o o o o * * o o o o o o o o * o o o o o o o o * o o o o o o o o * o o o o o o o * o * o o o o o * o o o * * * * * o o	Maximum fire is of neuron 3
O	o o * * * * * o o o o o o o o o * o * o o o o o o o * * o o o o o o o * * o o o o o o o * * o o o o o o o * * o o o o o o o * o * o o o o o * o o o * * * * * o o	o o * * * * * o o o * o o o o o * o * o o o o o o o * * o o o o o o o * * o o o o o o o * * o o o o o o o * * o o o o o o o * o * o o o o o * o o o * * * * * o o	Maximum fire is of neurons 3 and 15
Q	o o * * * * * o o o o o o o o o * o * o o o o o o o * * o o o o o o o * * o o o o o o o * * o o o o o o o * * o o o o * o o * o * o o o o * * o o o * * * * * o *	o o * * * * * o o o * o o o o * o * o o o o o o o * * o o o o o o o * * o o o o o o o * * o o o o o o o * * o o o o * o o * o * o o o o * * o o o * * * * * o *	Maximum fire is of neurons 15

Table 1. *(Continued)*

P	* * * * * * * * o * o o o o o o o * * o o o o o o o * * o o o o o o o * * * * * * * * * o * o o o o o o o o * o o o o o o o o * o o o o o o o o * o o o o o o o o	* * * * * * * * o * o o o o o o o * * o o o o o o o * * o o o o o o o * * * * * * * * * o * o o o o o o o o * o o o o o o o o * o o o o o o o o * o o o o o o o o	Maximum fire is of neuron 15
R	* * * * * * * * o * o o o o o o o * * o o o o o o o * * o o o o o o o * * * * * * * * * o * o o * o o o o o * o o o * o o o o * o o o o * o o o * o o o o o * o o	* * * * * * * * o * o o o o o o o * * o o o o o o o * * o o o o o o o * * * * * * * * * o * o o * o o o o o * o o o * o o o o * o o o o * o o o * o o o o o * o o	Maximum fire is of neurons 15 and 17

Effect of Noise in Inputs on Algorithm

The network is trained with characters without noise. Then by presenting each of the character, the network is tested. It has been observed that the no of characters recognized correctly differs for algorithms. Noise is introduced to the input vectors at the time of testing and its effect has been observed on algorithms. This has been done by adding random numbers to the test vector.

Loss of Connection

In the network, neurons are interconnected and every interconnection has some interconnecting coefficient called weight. If some of these weights are equated to zero then how it is going to effect the classification or recognition, is studied under this section. The number of connections that can be removed such that the network performance is not affected has also been found out for algorithm. If connection of input neuron's to all the output neuron is removed, and the pixel corresponding to that neuron number is off than it makes no difference. But if that pixel is on, in the output that becomes off.

Missing Information

Missing information means some of the on pixels in pattern grid are made off. For the algorithm, how many information we can miss so that the strings can be recognized correctly varies from string to string. We cannot switch off pixel from any place. Which pixel is being switched also matters. For few strings table 2 shows the number of pixels that can be switched off for all the stored strings in algorithm.

Table 2. Missing Information: No of pixels that can be made on in algorithm

Character	Algorithm
A	1
B	2
C	4
O	2
Q	3
P	6
R	3

Adding Information

Adding information means some of the off pixels in the pattern grid are made on. In this section, the classification or recognition ability of networks after adding information is studied. Table no. 3 shows detailed description about the number of pixels that can be made on for all the strings that can be stored in networks.

Table 3. Adding Information: No of pixels that can be made on in algorithm

Character	Algorithm
A	10
B	18
C	18
O	18
P	29
Q	20
R	20

7 Merits and Demerits

The network uses simple integer weights. It converges in a single iteration. It gives the results instantaneously without weighting for nay stabilization period convergence is guaranteed.

The network is complex and it involves a large no. of neurons. Although its structure is simpler when compared to Neocognitron. But the no. of neurons required is greater than as compared to other methods. But this demerit is overshadowed from the point of view of storage capacity.

8 Conclusion

The performance of Feature Recognition Neural Network algorithms has been studied under six criteria. It has been observed that a certain algorithm performs best under a particular criterion. The algorithms have also been compared based on the number of neurons and the number of unknowns to be computed.

The detailed description in table 4.

Table 4. Performance of Feature Recognition Neural Network Algorithm under different criterion

Criteria	Feature Recognition Neural Network
Number of Neurons	2366
Number of Unknowns	21294
Capacity	23
Effect of Noise in Weight (Random No. Added)	Not works
Effect of Increase of Weight	Not works
Noise in Input	Not works
Range of No. of Pixels that can made off	0-8
Range of No. of Pixels that can made on	7-32
No of Connection we can loose (wt=0)	234

References

1. Hussain, B., Kabuka, M.R.: A Novel Feature Recognition Neural Network and its Application to string Recognition. IEEE Transactions on Pattern Recognition and Machine Intelligence 16(1), 98–106 (1994)
2. Xu, Z.B., Leung, Y., He, X.W.: Asymmetrical Bidirectional Associative Memories. IEEE Transactions on Systems, Man and Cybernetics 24, 1558–1564 (1994)
3. Schalkoff, R.J.: Pattern Recognition: Statistical Structured and Neural; Approach. John Wiley and Sons, Chichester (1992)
4. Fukuanga, K.: Stastitical Pattern recognition, 2nd edn. Academic Press, London (1990)
5. Govindan, V.K., Sivaprasad, A.P.: String Recognition- A review. Pattern Recognition 23(7), 671–683 (1990)
6. Fu, K.S.: Syntactic Pattern Recognition. Prentice-Hall, Englewood Cliffs (1996)
7. Chen, Y.K., Wang, J.F.: Segmentation of single or multiple touching handwritten numeral strings using background and foreground analysis. IEEE Trans. Pattern Anal. Mach. Intell. 22, 1304–1317 (2000)
8. Zurada, J.M.: Introduction to artificial Neural Systems. Jaico Publication House, New Delhi
9. Liu, C.L., Nakashima, K., Sako, H., Fujisawa, H.: Handwritten digit recognition: benchmarking of state-of-the-art techniques. Pattern Recognition 36, 2271–2285 (2003)
10. Plamondon, R., Srihari, S.N.: On-line and o8-line handwritten recognition: a comprehensive survey. IEEE Trans. Pattern Anal. Mach. Intell. 22, 62–84 (2000)

11. Liu, C.L., Nakashima, K., Sako, H., Fujisawa, H.: Handwritten digit recognition: investigation of normalization and feature extraction techniques. Pattern Recognition 37, 265–279 (2004)
12. Oliveira, L.S., Sabourin, R., Bortolozzi, F., Suen, C.Y.: Automatic segmentation of handwritten numerical strings: a recognition and verification strategy. IEEE Trans. Pattern Anal. Mach. Intell. 24(11), 1438–1454 (2002)
13. Bhattacharya, U., Das, T.K., Datta, A., Parui, S.K., Chaudhuri, B.B.: A hybrid scheme for handprinted numeral recognition basedon a self-organizing network andMLP classiHers. Int. J. Pattern Recognition Artif. Intell. 16, 845–864 (2002)
14. Liu, C.L., Sako, H., Fujisawa, H.: Effects of classifier structure and training regimes on integrated segmentation and recognition of handwritten numeral strings. IEEE Trans. Pattern Recognition Mach.Intell. 26(11), 1395–1407 (2004)
15. Kim, K.K., Kim, J.H., Suen, C.Y.: Segmentation-based recognition of handwritten touching pairs of digits using structural features. Pattern Recognition Lett. 23, 13–24 (2002)
16. Jain, A., Duin, P., Mao, J.: Statistical pattern recognition: A review. IEEE Trans. Pattern Anal. Machine Intell. 22(1), 4–37 (2000)
17. Tax, D.M.J., van Breukelen, M., Duin, R.P.W., Kittler, J.: Combining multiple classifiers by averaging or by multiplying? Pattern Recognition 33, 1475–1485 (2000)
18. Oliveira, L.S., Sabourin, R., Bortolozzi, F., Suen, C.Y.: Impacts of verification on a numeral string recognition system. Pattern Recognition Letters 24, 1023–1031 (2003)
19. Pal, U., Chaudhuri, B.B.: Indian script character recognition: a survey. Pattern Recognition 37, 1887–1899 (2004)
20. Ye, X., Cheriet, M., Suen, C.Y.: StrCombo: combination of string recognizers. Pattern Recognition Letters 23, 381–394 (2002)
21. Haikin, S.: Neural Networks: A comprehensive Foundation. Macmillan College Publishing Company, New York (1994)
22. Sadri, J., Suen, C., Bui, T.D.: Agenetic framework using contextual knowledge for segmentation and recognition of handwritten numeral strings. Pattern Recognition 40, 898–919 (2007)
23. Bishop, C.M.: Neural Networks for Pattern Recognition. Oxford University Press, Oxford (2003)

Load Balancing in Distributed Systems Using Network Transferable Computer

Vijayakumar G. Dhas[1], Sathish Kumar Anaikkalpalayam Chinnasamy[2], Mathangi Swaminathan[3], and Lavanya Veeravagu[3]

[1] Department of Information Technology, MIT, Anna University, Chennai
vgdhas@yahoo.com
[2] Force10 Networks India (p) Ltd, Chennai
acsathishkumar@gmail.com
[3] MIT, Anna University, Chennai
mathangi_swami@yahoo.com
lavzworld@gmail.com

Abstract. Dynamic load balancing (DLB) is a method for balancing the server load, and as an offset, the network traffic, in distributed systems. The DLB method is based on Network Transferable Computer (NTC) and Mobile IP, and works using the concept of virtualization. A management system is provided to handle the entire process. It (1) analyzes packets for the server (2)calculates the fluctuation rate of the amount of packets toward the server (3)estimates the future amount of packets.(4)determines whether the server will virtually move or not and a new location of the server (5)takes care of post migration analysis. The evaluation of this method is underlined by simulations, which will show effective reduction of server load.

Keywords: Load balancing, mobile ip, virtualisation, hypervisor, xen, network transferrable computer(NTC), network traffic, server load.

1 Introduction

Load balancing is a technique to distribute workload evenly across two or more computers, network links, CPUs, hard drives, or other resources, in order to optimize resource utilization, maximize throughput, minimize response time, and avoid overload.

There are lots of potential causes of high server loads. Server load levels very much depend on what is being run on the server. Possible causes are: (1) Running one or several resource-intensive applications (2) Running a malicious script or a 'runaway script' which can continuously loop, dragging down the server's resources. (3) Running too many websites on one server resulting in high server load. (4) Too many requests from clients, resulting in high server load. (5) Running out of memory and swapping to the swap file. (6) Server backups or server updates are taking place. (7) Server comes under intermittent or continuous Internet attack, like DoS or DDoS attacks, which disrupts the normal functioning of the server by overloading it. This can be done by sending thousands of requests at a time. (8) Running mis-configured software.

D. Nagamalai, E. Renault, and M. Dhanushkodi (Eds.): PDCTA 2011, CCIS 203, pp. 648–664, 2011.

Several problems arise when the server load is very high. Some of them are: (1) If the client is accessing an overloaded web server, the pages get loaded very slowly and take an unreasonable large amount of time. (2) Processes in overloaded database servers take a very long time to search through a database. (3) When the load becomes extremely high, the server simply shuts down, leading to a server crash.

In this paper, load that is caused by too many requests from clients, which consume the server's resources extensively, is balanced.

In client server systems, reply packets are relatively larger than request packets and access to a particular server host often causes excessive traffic on a path connected to the server. Building a server of the virtual machine using the NTC system implemented with Mobile IP mechanism, the server has a capability to move to an alternate network in order that request or reply packets avoid passing through the crowded path. Because the server is a virtual machine, a new real machine is not necessary. Also because the server itself moves from one network to another, the contents of the server are the same at any time, which saves management costs.

2 Related Work

In [9], a framework called "Network Transferable Computer (NTC)" is a system which transports a running image of OS to other computers using Virtual Machine.

A load balancing method that uses NTC system associated with Mobile IP for building a server is proposed. In this method, the system analyzes the information gathered from the local network to which the target server is attached and it moves the server itself to an another network so that considerable access traffics do not pass the particular path. As soon as the local information is analyzed, the system can decide whether the server moves virtually or not, and, if it should move, where the server will move. After moving to another network, it is possible to get more information from the network and to modify the decision criteria. Thus this method realizes an adaptable load balancing on network traffic.

In[17], another dynamic load balancing (DLB) method for network traffic has been devised for client-server systems, wherein intense access to a particular server host often causes excessive traffic on a path connected to the server. Although mirror servers are used for load balancing of host performance, this may not be to sufficient to balance the load of network traffic. In the DLB method a server has the capability to move to another network, so that flows of packets toward/from the server change and a part of packets avoid going through the crowded path. This reduction of the traffic in the congested path achieves balancing of network traffic. The DLB method is based on Network Transferable Computer (NTC) and Mobile IP.

In [1], a modified version of LDMA has been devised called ELDMA (Enhanced Load balancing Decision making using Decentralized Mobile Agent), which distributes the load equally among the Web servers organized in a mesh topology, by a communication media. In LDMA, the rank is assigned to the Web server as and when it enters the cluster. The rank shows the priority of processing a request by the servers in the cluster. Each server involves in the decision making for processing the request by exchanging the message. It causes high communication overhead between the servers. In the proposed scheme, a rank is dynamically assigned to the servers based on CPU processing time and memory utilization. In addition to that the communication overhead is reduced by restricting the message exchange between the servers. The performance of the proposed scheme is evaluated using load distribution, throughput and network traffic.

In [14], the existing load balancing technology in Content Distribution Network (CDN) only emphasizes even load distribution among servers, and it doesn't make use of network topology information and file access history; hence user request cannot get timely response. To solve this problem, this paper puts forward a load balancing algorithm based on the distributed binning strategy. This algorithm can make full use of network topology information and file access history as well as server load information, analyzing the popularity of files with the access history of the cluster of clients from the server, efficiently finishing distribution and routing of the high popularity files among servers so that users can closely obtain the required contents, ease internet congestion and enhance response speed of user accessing websites.

3 Proposed Solution

A. BRIEF OUTLINE

A server of the virtual machine on the NTC system (NTC Server) is established aiming at load balancing of the network traffic. Mobile IP is implemented in order that the server can communicate with clients after moving to another network. Portable machines or terminals for wireless networks are used as Mobile Nodes. Using the server of the virtual machine as a Mobile Node saves another real machine and it means just transporting a running image of the OS saved by hibernation mechanism.

The routers with Mobile IP are required to play the role of the Home Agent or the Foreign Agent in order that the network is acceptable to Mobile Nodes. In the DLB method, because the Host OS is able to play the role of the router for the virtual machine, the Host OS takes the role of the Home Agent or the Foreign Agent. Mobile IP is installed in the Host OS and it will transfer packets addressed to the virtual machine toward the other real machine when the same virtual machine is moved.

Then the management system is constructed on the Host OS of the NTC system, which will make all the moving decisions for load balancing.

B. Detailed Explanation

NTC SYSTEM

"The Network Transferable Computer (NTC)" is a system which transports an image of running Operating System (OS) to another computer. By using Virtual Machine software, it is possible to realize the same architecture on various computers.

A hibernation process saves the OS in a storage device which is physically moved to another machine or transferred through the network.

MOBILE IP

Mobile IP is a mechanism that gives hosts capability to communicate with other host on IP based networks even if they move from one network to other. The term Mobile Node (MN) is used for a movable host. The network to which MN is originally attached is called Home Network (HN), and the network to which MN can move is named Foreign Network (FN). A server of the virtual machine using the NTC system is implemented with Mobile IP mechanism. The server is a virtual machine, a new real machine is not necessary. Also the server itself moves from one network to another, the contents of the server are the same at any time, which saves management costs.

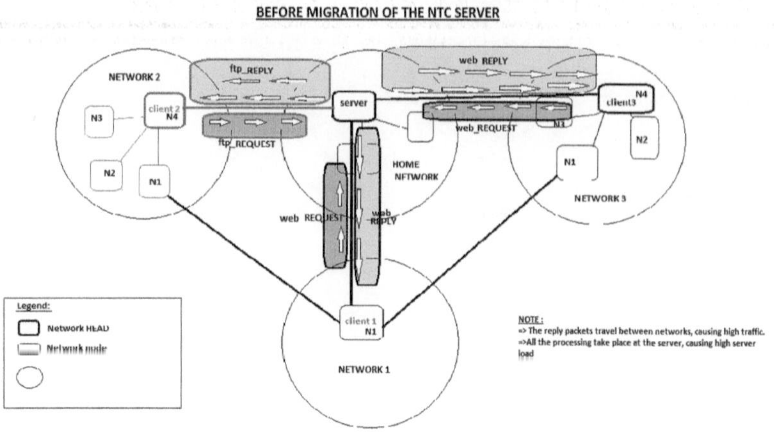

Fig. 3(a). Before virtual migration of NTC server

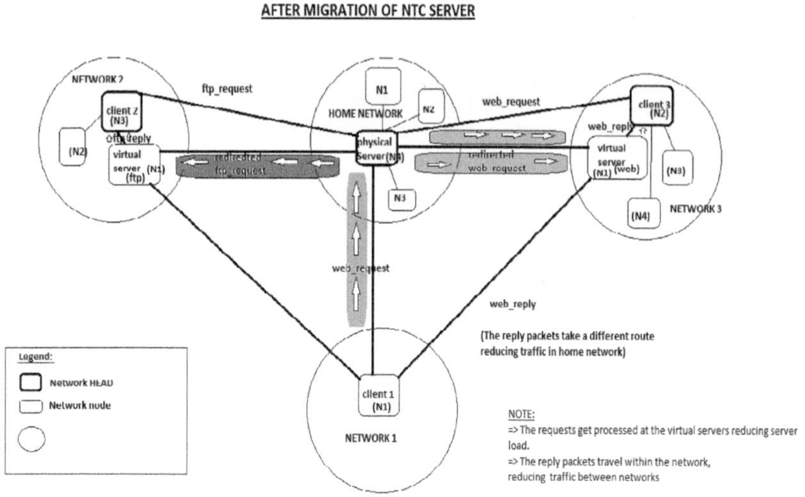

Fig. 3(b). After virtual migration of NTC server

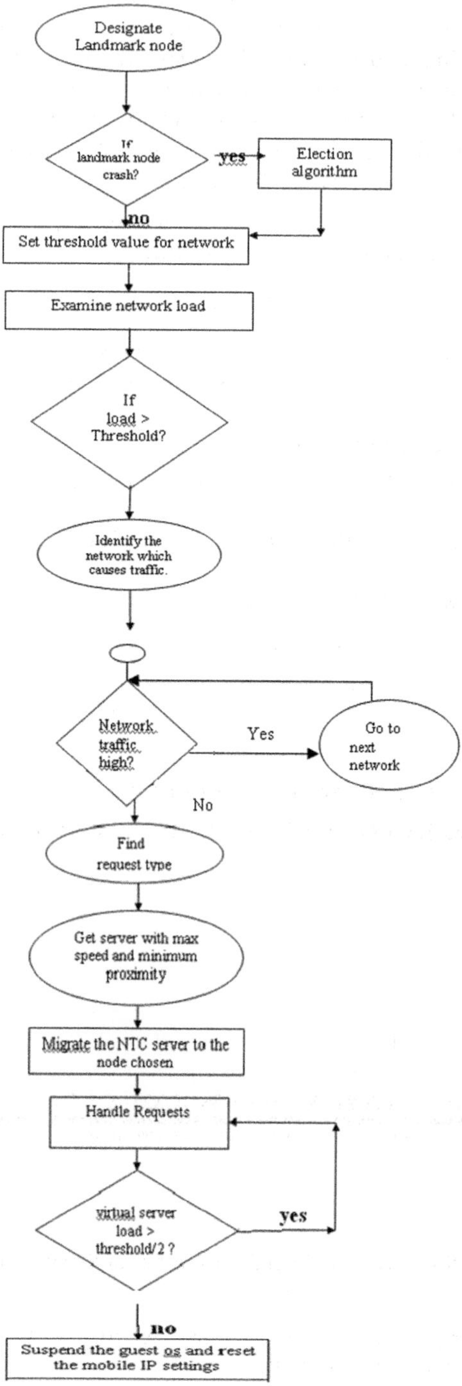

Fig. 3(c). Workflow diagram

The head node for each network is designated using election algorithm. Then it acquires all the details of other nodes in its network. If the landmark node crashes, another landmark node is elected. Threshold value is set for each server. If the load exceeds the threshold value, the network which causes the traffic is identified.

The request type is analyzed and segregation of the optimum resource required for processing the request is carried out. A server with maximum speed and minimum load and proximity is identified. The NTC server is migrated to the node chosen. The concept of load balancing using the NTC system is associated with Mobile IP. HN means the Home Network of the NTC server. FN is the Foreign network to which the NTC server is migrated. Some client nodes of each group generate requests towards the server. All the requests to the HN are diverted to the NTC server in the FN and the requests are processed. After balancing the load, the NTC server is suspended, post migration analyses is carried out followed by resetting of mobile IP.

Before virtualization, clients and servers in two different networks communicate, and this causes excessive load. This load is balanced by virtualizing the server OS in an alternate network, here the client network has been chosen. After balancing the load, the NTC server is suspended, post migration analyses is carried out followed by resetting of Mobile IP.

C. Architecture

I. System Architecture

Each system may have several Operating Systems running in it, in addition to its own OS and hardware. Each Guest OS is called a virtual machine and one or more applications run in it. Every system has a Virtual Machine Monitor that acts an interface between the Host and the Guest OSs. The hardware is shared between the all the OSs.

II. Network Topology

Each network has a head node, which is elected by the other network nodes. Election algorithm is used in case this head node crashes, to elect another node as the head node. This head node maintains all the details of the nodes in its network like type of node, IP address, node ID, server load, processing speed of server and load metric values. The ratio of the distances between the network heads is noted so that the closest network to any other network can be obtained. This is useful while finding an alternate network using the modified ant algorithm.

The overall network architecture is shown in Figure 3(d).

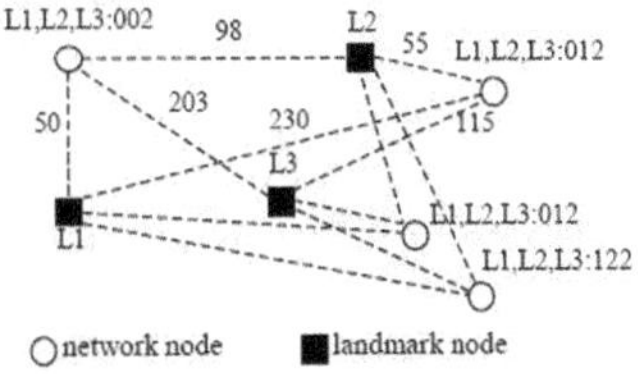

Fig. 3(d). Network Topology

Landmark node depicts the node in which the Guest OS is virtualized. Network node stands for any node in the network.

D. System Components

The major system components consist of the following:

I. Dispatcher Unit

The dispatcher table contains fields such as IP Address of server in home network, foreign network, and the load status of landmark node. This information is provided to the dispatcher table by the home agent, and is made use of by the dispatcher to redirect requests to the foreign network.

II. Mobile IP Management Unit

It is used for ensuring reliability. The home and foreign agents periodically sends an I Am Alive (IAA) signal to this unit. If the Mobile IP Management Unit does not get an IAA signal for a certain period, it detects a crash and creates the required agent. There is a back up Mobile Agent Management unit that gets to work, in case, the current active unit fails.

III. Variable Length Input Queue Unit

This has the list of networks lying in the shortest path between client and server. The traffic associated with each network is also included. This dynamic queue is used to choose the network that is at an optimal distance from both the client and server.

IV. Dynamic Lookup Unit

This has load details of the individual servers, their IP Addresses and their processing speed, and is available with the head node. This is used to choose the appropriate server for virtualization. This queue is updated whenever a node enters or leaves the network.

V. OS Transition Unit

It holds the details of the virtualized OS like its foreign network ID, new server IP Address, its state (running, suspended, or exit) and the resources virtualized. Using this, the server is made aware of the status of its OS, and the resources transferred.

E. ALGORITHMS

Description of Algorithms

In this section, the algorithms used in implementing load balancing have been discussed.

1 Election Algorithm

This is used to elect a head node both initially and whenever it node crashes. Bully method of election is used. Hence the node with the highest server ID is elected as the new head whenever the old one crashes.

2 Token Based Algorithm

A token is passed around the servers; each server enters its load into the token. This is finally sent to the head node.

Dynamic load balancing requires both a metric to determine the system load as well as a mechanism for controlling process migration. Ideally, the metric should not only be simple and fast to compute, but also effective.

- CPU load
- Request rate
- Number of idle workers
- Current hosts
- Requests being processed currently

The server status is provided by the apache server by modifying its configuration to reflect the server's activity and performance. This web page displays the server status dynamically. Hence the current cpu load is always reflected and it can be determined if the current server load is greater than the threshold or not. A machine readable version of the status file is also available.The ExtendedStatus tag keeps track of extended status for each request. Hence it is turned on in the configuration file.

Algorithm

n: number of servers in the network
i:1
***Proc** Serve-Token (token)*
    While (i<n)
Insert processor's LOAD into the token
Pass token
i->i+1
end while
end Proc

FNA ALGORITHM

The system examines the request pattern towards a server and moves the server to the Foreign Network if the traffic amount after moving to the foreign network will become smaller than that of leaving the server in the home network itself. The path through which the server is moved is decided based on the traffic through each path. The moving decision is explained using the flowchart in Figure 3(e).

3 Traffic Estimation

Moving decision is done after estimation of the next situation. The system examines whether the FNA condition is satisfied or not by using the estimated number of client nodes. It also examines whether the expected traffic caused by the server moving is small enough compared with expected traffic caused by request and reply. In each interval k , numbers of client nodes on the HN area and the FN area are counted through analyzing the server access logs. The number of client nodes on one area at current time t, at previous time t-k, at next time t +k are respectively denoted by $Q_{.}$, $Q_{.-.}$, $Q_{.+.}$. The ratio of $Q_{.}$to $Q_{.-.}$ is denoted by $r_{.}$ and the ratio of $Q_{.}$ to the number of client nodes at time t – ik is $r_{.-.}$ The number of measuring intervals is denoted by n.

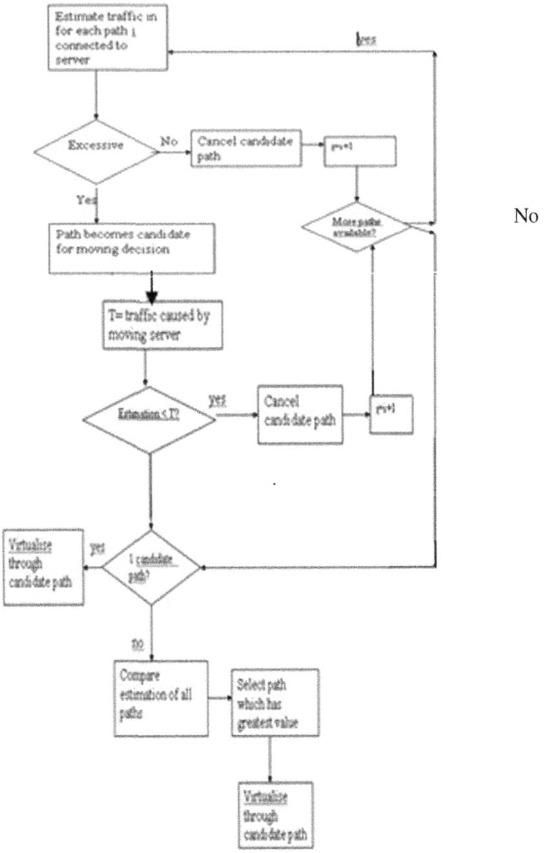

Fig. 3(e). Selection of candidate path

The average ratio R at current time is shown below. Once the system decides to virtualize the server OS, the path through which the OS should be transferred is decided based on the flowchart in Figure 3(e).

$$R = \frac{1}{n}\sum_{i=1}^{n} r_{i} \qquad (1)$$

Then, the system estimates Q_{est} as follows:

$$Q_{est} = Q_{i} \times R$$

4 Modified Ant Algorithm

Ant algorithm locates the shortest path between two networks. The modified version also finds the networks existing in the path, finds an optimal network, checks if its load is high, and interacts with the landmark node of the network if the load is less than half of the threshold value. It then locates the server which has high processing speed and least load, for virtualization. The algorithm has the following steps:

- Compute shortest distance between the two nodes.
- Maintain list of network heads of networks lying in the shortest path in a queue.
- For each network starting from that in the middle of the queue, check the traffic in the network.
- If it is too high, alternatively proceed left and right of the network chosen in the last step, checking each one's load.
- If any network load is found to be optimal, then stop at that point and check the individual server loads within that network.
- Choose the server which has minimum load metrics.
- Carry out the virtualization process.

Modified Ant Algorithm

N: Total number of networks between client and server nodes.

```
1. Find shortest path between client and server.
2. For each network i in shortest path
              Add i to dynamic queue.
3. Select intermediate network i=N/2 from the queue. Check its load.
           If load is optimum
       goto over;
4. Else
      Set j=i+1, k=i-1;
n=k;
found=0;

5.      For nth network in queue till either k=0 or j=N-1,

        a. check network load
          if(n=k)
          {  if(loadk> threshold)
        {    if(k!=i-1)
               {j=j+1;
                 n=j;
               Goto 5b.}
            Else
             {n=j;
             Goto 5.}
        }
    else  goto over;
        }

        Else if  (n=j)
```

```
        {   if(loadj>threshold))
             {k=k-1; n=k;
              Goto 5}
             else{
                goto over;}
        }
}

6. if(k=0 or j=N-1){
check load for the remaining unchecked node(ifany).
        if(load<threshold)
         goto over;
}

if (found=0)
  take n=N/2 as the network;
goto over;

over: found=1;
        nth network is chosen;
 find server in the network with optimal load.
```

5 Check_Kt_Node
To deal with the dynamism of P2P systems such as node joins and departures, each KT node (say X), where KT refers to a k-ary tree, will periodically run the routine check_KT_node. If X's responsible region is completely covered by that of X's hosting virtual server (i.e., the termination condition of the partitioning of X's region is met), then X is already a leaf node and there is no need to grow any more children.

6 Delete_Kt_Node
X may need to prune its children (if any) (e.g., due to node departures). This is done by running the subroutine delete_KT_ children.

7 Add_Kt_Node
If X's responsible region cannot be fully covered by that of X's hosting virtual server (e.g., due to node additions into the underlying DHT), X needs to grow its children by running the subroutine add_KT_children.

4 Implementation

Hypervisors are used to provide virtual servers. Server virtualization can provide benefits such as:

- consolidation
- increased utilization

- rapid provisioning
- dynamic fault tolerance against software failures (through rapid bootstrapping or rebooting)
- hardware fault tolerance (through migration of a virtual machine to different hardware) the ability to securely separate virtual operating systems,
- the ability to support legacy software as well as new OS instances on the same computer.

Xen's support for virtual machine live migration from one host to another with the avoidance of downtime.

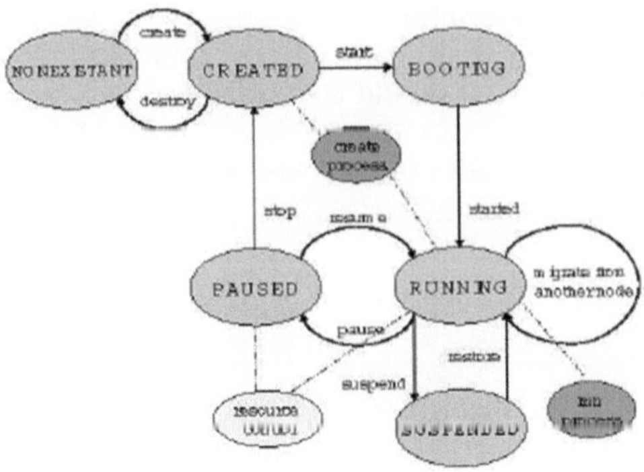

Fig. 4(a). Xen Architecture

Virtualization also has benefits when working on development (including the development of operating systems): running the new system as a guest avoids the need to reboot the physical computer whenever a bug occurs. Various pieces of software that require different operating systems can also be executed using virtualization.

Figure 4(a) shows the various stages of the Xen lifecycle model. Each of these stages is implemented while virtualizing the NTC server. Postmigration analysis is carried out after setting the state of the hypervisor to 'suspended'.

Test Environment

The developed system has been tested on a Local Area Network consisting of 60 nodes. All the 60 nodes have been divided into three subnets of 20 nodes each. One of the nodes on one network say A has been configured to be the web server and also ftp server with the needed server softwares. When there were communication between the other two subnets say B and C, there was little change in the traffic on the home network (A). Whenever there were communications involving the server on the home network, the reply messages sent by the server caused much traffic between the client and the home network. Also due to many computations to be performed by the server, the server was unable to process all the requests within the expected time. The response time for the requests kept on increasing. We defined a threshold limit for the server, considering the various parameters that are found to affect the load on the server. When this limit was crossed, a live migration of the guest OS is done on to one of the systems which was preconfigured for virtualization and is able to run this live migrated Guest OS.

Software Prerequisites
PHYSICAL SERVER : XEN3.0 should be installed for enabling support for virtualization and migratrion, jdk (version greater than 1.5) should be available.

TARGET NODE : This is the node, where the guest OS is about to be migrated. It should have support for virtualization, which is provided by XEN3.0. The Xen kernel should have been started and running.

Jdk (version greater than 1.5) should be available.

OTHER NODES: The other nodes on the network should have the ability to generate web requests and ftp requests to the server.

5 Conclusion

An effective load balancing method is proposed, which is based on server load. The basic features needed for a load balancer are taken care and implemented. As an offset to the load balancing strategy, the network traffic is also balanced. This is because once the server is known to be overloaded, it is transported to another network, and hence the bandwidth that the server replies will consume is eliminated. This reduces the network traffic. The real server buffers the incoming requests. It then checks for the load status and the status of the real server and based on the status, the buffered TCP requests are processed. Depending on the type of requests that arrive most, from a particular network, an image of the server and the resource is migrated to an alternate network. A priority is assumed to each of the virtual servers, depending on the load on the respective virtual server. This priority value is consulted while redirecting the request from the real server. A management system is provided that processes the incoming requests, analyses the traffic from a particular network, and keeps track of the dynamic network topology and takes migrating decisions. The management system receives an update from each of the virtual servers, in the event of a significant change in its load.

The main drawback is that of setting the initial threshold value. This has to be optimal. If the threshold value is too low, change of server will happen too frequently, and that is an overhead. If, on the other hand, the threshold value is too high, it is possible that most of the requests go to one server, which would result in the other servers being idle for long, and decrease the effectiveness of load balancing. The threshold, therefore, has to be optimal, so as to ensure that load is distributed evenly among the servers, and at the same time, change of current server does not happen too frequently.

6 Results

Two different analyses were done to determine the feasibility of the load balancing mechanism described in this paper. One of them was finding out if the migration policy is feasible and the other was determining if the method of load balancing produced any tangible results in terms of decrease in response time of the server.

6.1 Time of Transfer

A study was done on the time taken to transfer files of different sizes during migration.

Figure 6(a) shows that even as the file size increases drastically, the time of transfer of the file varies by a very small amount only. This shows that migration of the OS, which is equivalent to a large file transfer, does not take too much time, and hence is feasible.

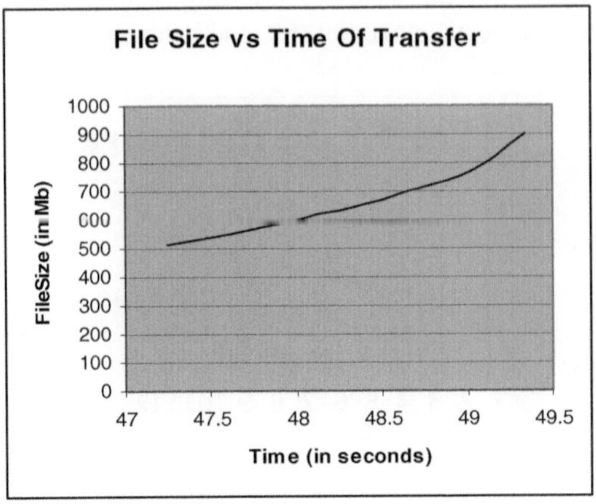

Fig. 6(a). Time of transfer

6.2 Response Time

Another analysis was done regarding the change in response time of the server before and after load balancing technique was applied.

As shown in figure 6(b), the response time of an overloaded server, before applying the load balancing technique, keeps increasing rapidly. In contrast, the response time after balancing the load, becomes very low, even as the number of requests becomes very high.

As observed in the figure, initially the server has a response time of 4seconds; this is due to the time that is taken for migration and the initial configurations. After that, even as the request size increases from 100 to 150, the response time remains constantly at a very low value of 3seconds. Only when the numbers of requests become too high does it increase slightly from 3 to 4seconds.

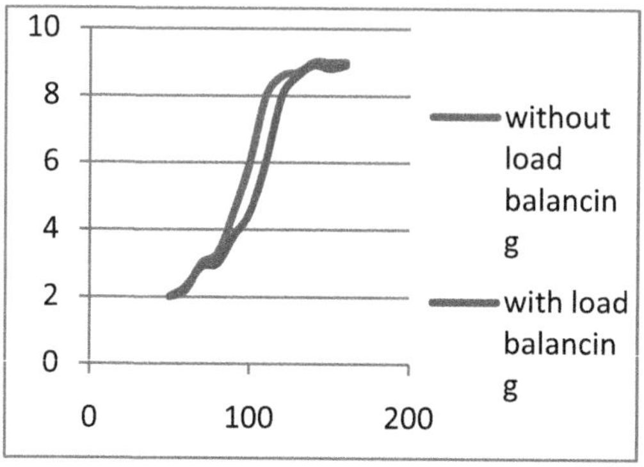

Fig. 6(b). Nof of requests vs Response time

Hence it can be inferred that the response time remains low for optimal number of requests. As the number of requests start increasing to larger values, this may increase marginally. This proves the efficiency of the load balancing mechanism.

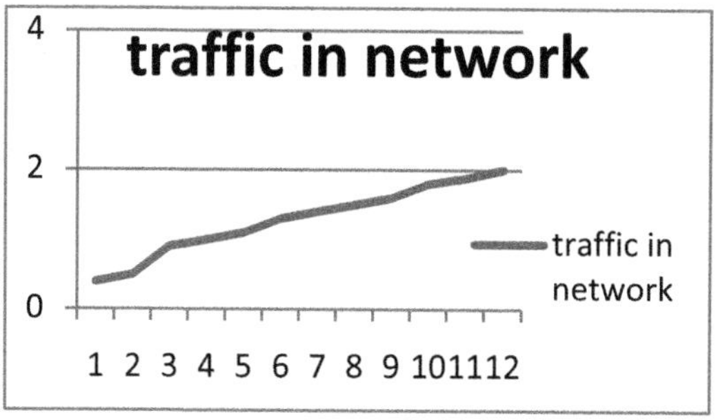

Fig. 6(c). No of requests (hundreds)vs Traffic (MB)

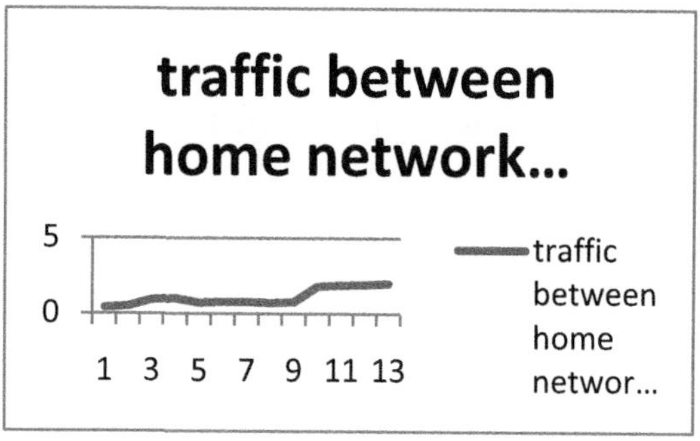

Fig. 6(d). No of requests(hundreds) vs Traffic(MB)

From Figure 6(c) we could infer that the traffic on the network keeps on increasing with increase in the number of requests.

After the load balancing system is implemented, the traffic between the networks is also found to reduce after reaching the threshold traffic. Then it remains constant until the requests are redirected towards the client network, due to the absence of reply packets from the home network. After the system is migrated back, the traffic regains its previous state.

7 Future Work

Other parameters apart from the number of requests at each server, such as the processing speed of the CPU, estimated time for each request to be processed, can be introduced. Priority can be introduced in processing the requests in the queue of every server. This will enhance the load distribution, taking into consideration the heterogeneity of requests. A mechanism can be devised to do the same.

References

1. Aramudhan, M., Karthikeyan, S., Mohan, K, Rhymend Uthaiaraj, V., et al.: ELDMA: Enhanced Load balancing Decision making using Decentralized Mobile Agent Framework. In: Proceedings of International Conference on Computer and Communication Engineering (2008)
2. Qi, B., Zhao, C.: Ant Algorithm Based Load Balancing for Network Sessions. In: Third International Conference on Natural Computation, ICNC 2007 (2007)
3. Zhao, H., Liu, X., Li, X.: DLBEM: Dynamic Load Balancing Using Expectation-Maximization, Scalable Software Systems Laboratory, Department of Computer Science, Oklahoma State University Stillwater, OK 74048, USA (2007), IEEE
4. Umenol, H., Paraynot, M.L.C., Teramotol, K., Kawanot, M., Inamasul, H., Enokil, S., Kiyamal, M., Aoyama, T., Fukunaga, T.: Performance Evaluation on Server Consolidation Using Virtual Machines. In: Proceedings of the Tenth International Conference on Parallel and Distributed Systems (2006)
5. Chen, K., Xin, J., Zheng, W.: Empirical Performance Evaluation of Message Passing Programs Running in Virtual Machines. Department of Computer Science and Technology Tsinghua University, Beijing, China (2008), IEEE
6. El-Khatib, K., Tropper, C.: On Metrics for the Dynamic Load Balancing of Optimistic Simulations. In: Proceedings of the 32nd Hawaii International Conference on System Sciences. School of Computer Science McGill University, Montreal (1999)
7. Lim, K.-S., Kim, C.-G.: Dynamic Load Balancing in Distributed Computer Systems with Star Topology (1995), IEEE
8. Steinder, M., Whalley, I., Carrerat, D., Gawedat, I., Chess, D.: Virtualization in autonomic management of Server heterogeneous workloads. IBM Thomas J. Watson Research Center (2007), IEEE
9. Hiyasuki, M., Inoue, S., Kakuda, Y., Toda, K., Suzaki, K.: Adaptable Load Balancing Using Network Transfearble Computer Associated with Mobile IP. In: Proceedings of the 25th IEEE International Conference on Distributed Computing Systems Workshops (2003)

10. Misra, Mandal, C.: Ant-aggregation: Ant Colony Algorithm for optimal data aggregation. Wireless Sensor Networks (2006), IEEE
11. Sehgal, N.K., Ganguli, M.: Applications of Virtualization for Server Management and Security (2006), IEEE
12. Zeng, P., Zang, C., Yu, H.: An Ant-Based Routing Algorithm to Achieve the Lifetime Bound for Target Tracking Sensor Networks. Shenyang Institute of Automation, Chinese Academy of Sciences
13. Zhu, Y., Hu, Y.: Efficient, Proximity-Aware Load Balancing for DHT-Based P2P Systems. IEEE Transactions ON Parallel and Distributed Systems 16(4) (April 2005)
14. Bai, Y., Jia, B., Zhang, J., Pu, Q., Mastorakis, N.: An Efficient Load Balancing Technology in CDN. International Journal of Applied Mathematics and Informatics (2007)
15. Xu, Z., Bhuyan, L.: Effective Load Balancing in P2P Systems. In: Proceedings of the Sixth IEEE International Symposium on Cluster Computing and the Grid. University of California, Riverside, Suffolk University (2008)
16. Steinder, Z., Whalley, I., Carrerat, D., Gawedat, I., Chess, D.: Server virtualization in autonomic management of heterogeneous workloads. In: ICNF (2008)
17. Hisayuki, M., Kakuda, Y., Toda, K., Suzaki, K.: Dynamic Load Balancing Using Network Transferable Computer

A Simulation of Performance of Commit Protocols in Distributed Environment

Kahkashan Tabassum[1], Fahmina Taranum[1], and Avula Damodaram[2]

[1] Muffakham Jah College of Engineering & Technology
Banjara Hills, Hyderabad -500155, India
kahkashan@mjcollege.ac.in, ftaranum@mjcollege.ac.in
[2] Jawaharlal Nehru Technological University
Kukatpally, Hyderabad - 500 085, India
adamodaram@jntuh.ac.in

Abstract. In distributed environment the transparency of transaction is the most significant feature. It helps in maintaining data consistency at more than one network and ensures whether a transaction will entirely complete or aborts. Complex mechanisms are required to manage transactions in distributed systems. If each transaction was committed locally at a specific network and could not be committed on another network then the transaction scenario results in the inconsistent data problem. Commit Protocols are magnificent sources of committing transactions and maintaining data integrity and consistency. In this paper we intend to simulate the performance of atomic commit protocols (one-phase commit protocol, two-phase commit protocol and three-phase commit protocol), their working and functionality in order to maintain the data integrity, atomicity and transaction transparency.

Keywords: Distributed system (DS), Atomic Commit Protocol (ACP), Window of Vulnerability (WoV), ACID properties.

1 Introduction

A distributed system is characterized by various communicating components that are located at different networked computers but still coordinate their activities by passing messages among themselves. Thus the characteristics of distributed systems can be outlined as concurrency of communicating components, independent failure and absence of a universally global clock. Some of the examples of distributed systems are 1) An intranet 2) The internet 3) Pervasive and Mobile computing. Sequences of activities such that either all the operations within them may succeed and all the outcomes of the activities are permanently visible or all the operations within the activities do not succeed anywhere and there are no visible outcomes that may be due to unintentional failure or an intentional failure (abort) are called Transaction. These transactions are characterized by a special point of completion or no return point called commit point The operations can be undone before this point in the transaction. All changes become permanent after commit point. Corrective action can be taken if problems occur after this point the changes can't be reversed.

D. Nagamalai, E. Renault, and M. Dhanushkodi (Eds.): PDCTA 2011, CCIS 203, pp. 665–681, 2011.

Properties of Transactions. Atomicity specifies that either all or none statements execute in the transaction. Consistency – A consistent state of data is expected before and after operation. Isolation - A transaction must operate by itself and its effect on other transaction should be invisible. Durability – The changes made during a committed transaction must be persistent and reusable if there is a power failure.

Atomic Commit If a set of distinct changes is applied and succeeded as a single operation then it is called an atomic commit. The changes made at the time of atomic commit are reversed in case of a transaction failure to ensure the consistent state for the system. Atomic operations are isolated and this ensures only one atomic commit is completed at a time. Atomic commits are commonly used in distributed systems.

Necessity for Atomic Commits. Atomic commits are required in order to update data. The entire operation is required to be completed as one atomic commit. The atomic commits require coordination between multiple systems but the computer networks do not offer such reliable services for coordination according to the Two Generals Problem [1]. The problem of coordination increase as databases become more and more distributed. The coordination is done by using the Atomic Commit Protocols:

a). One Phase Commit Protocol (1PC). In a distributed transaction, the client requests the operation possibly at more than one server. A transaction completes when the client is interested in commit or abort after processing the operation. To complete the transaction in an atomic manner the coordinator has to communicate the commit or abort request to every participant in the transaction and also keep this request repeating until every participant have acknowledged their completion. This is called one-phase atomic commit protocol.

b). Two Phase Commit Protocol (2PC). It is an algorithm that coordinates all the processes participating in an atomic transaction based on whether to commit, roll back or abort the transaction. This protocol is widely used because even if there is temporary failure of the system due to communication, any process, network node then it can overcome such problem. But it is not resilient to configuration failures and system administrator (user) intervention. To recover from failure the participants of the process use log records. The log records can withstand failures although they are slow to generate.

c). Three Phase Commit Protocol (3PC). This is a distributed algorithm in which all the participant entities agree on committing a database transaction existing in a distributed networking environment. A 3PC is a non-blocking protocol. An upper bound is fixed on the amount of time required 3PC before a transaction is allowed to either commit or abort that ensures release of the locks after the timeout if any resource holds on a given transaction when it is attempting to make a 3PC commit.

2 Literature Survey

In a distributed system components networked by a set of computers not only communicate but also coordinate by passing different messages among them. This definition leads to the following characteristics of distributed systems: concurrency of components, absence of a global clock and independent failure [1].

Transaction Management in Distributed Systems. Transactions in a distributed system can access data at more than one site. A transaction has a number of sub transactions running at a site accessing the data available. A sub transaction is similar to an agent for the transaction and can commit at local or global transaction. Due to any reason if global transaction do not commit then the sub transactions also do not commit. Similarly if any agent do not commit locally then all others should rollback the changes done so far.

a) A One-Phase Commit Protocol. In 1PC, if the coordinator decides to commit or rollback or abort a transaction then it communicates this to the participant in one request (broadcast). The participants receive this and accordingly acknowledge any of the action in the form of commit or rollback or abort. Consider a distributed transaction a system site with three participants. When 1PC protocol starts all the participants have processed locally but have not committed the transaction so far. When the transaction completes locally the participant sends a message to the coordinator ("Done"). All the participants now wait for the coordinator's decision of either commit or abort of transaction. This time duration is known as window of vulnerability (WoV) [1, 2].Within this the participant will be waiting to hear message from the coordinator and do not commit or abort the transaction unless it is communicated to the participant from the coordinator. If the coordinator fails in this window the transaction will be in a blocked state. If not Commit or Abort message is broadcasted to the participants by the coordinator. After receiving this message the participant executes the transaction and acknowledges the message from coordinator. In 1PC the coordinator should wait to receive the messages (Done) [3] from all participants before it proceeds with the transaction. In this scenario the participants finished working on the transaction early have to wait for large duration and the resources used by the transaction must be locked at a various sites. Consequently locked resources are not available to other transactions. Even the read-only transactions cannot use the locked resources. This creates a negative impact of the performance on the local system. Hence there is a deadlock and 1PC is a blocking protocol.

The critical issue with 1PC is the failure of the coordinator within the window of vulnerability due to which the participants stay blocked for very long period of time. If the coordinator does not fail the window of vulnerability of a participant will be the time it takes for all other participants to finish the transaction and the coordinator broadcasting the Commit whereas the failure of coordinator extends it to include the repair time of the coordinator also. The point of observation here is that the participants cannot decide unilaterally the commit or abort of a transaction in case of the coordinator getting failed. If the coordinator fails after giving the Commit to at least one of the participants then all participants commit the transaction whereas in case none of the participants received the Commit, then all of the participants stay blocked. The participants may be allowed to make a decision in the absence of Coordinator - any decision of the participants made collectively being similar or dissimilar to the one the coordinator had taken locally can be considered. The window of vulnerability and the blocking properties of 1PC are reduced by the use of an enhanced two-phase commit protocol.

b) A Two-Phase Commit Protocol

The advantage of 1PC is its simplicity and ease of implementation. But it suffers with serious drawback of lack of resilience. 2PC extends the 1PC by reducing the vulnerability of the servers in the transaction to some extent. In 2PC the coordinator is responsible to commit the transaction after receiving Done message from all participants. It can also Abort the transaction by sending a Global abort message to the participants. The transaction is aborted by the coordinator only after receiving Abort ACK from the participants. The different phases of this protocol – In the first phase of 2PC, Prepare message is given by coordinator to all participants. Once the decision of commit is taken by the coordinator the participants vote by giving Ready or Not Ready message depending on whether they are in favor of commit or not. If Not ready is heard by any one of the participant then the coordinator gives a Global Abort message to all and enters into second phase. The participants acknowledge this message by using Abort ACK message [3]. Similarly on hearing Ready from all participants the coordinator gives a Global Commit and enters second phase. Participants then replies by means of Commit ACK message. During this phase the transactions perform cleanup (writing log) and other recovery actions.

c) A Three-Phase Commit Protocol

Three-phase commit (3PC) protocol has been proposed by Skeen to overcome the limitation in 2PC. The 3PC is resilient and consists of two protocols that can be utilized for the events of termination and recovery. In the event of a failure the termination protocol is used. The latter protocol is used to resolve the problem of consistent state with respect to the active site after recovery from a failed state.

3PC-Coordinator Termination Protocol The 3PC uses a **preCommit** state and the rest of the steps taken to manage failure of participant by the coordinator in 3PC are similar to 2PC. If the coordinator observes the failure of the participant when it is in any of the state - Before Commit, Preparing, Aborted or Committed states [7], it handles it in a similar way as managed by 2PC.

3PC-Participant Termination Protocol. The failure of the coordinator in 3PC calls for nomination of a new coordinator and it is accomplished voting of the participants. Either they compete among themselves for the role, or predetermine the next coordinator. To protect the new coordinator against the failure, the newly elected coordinator synchronizes all the participants' termination protocols to match its own by means of giving a broadcast from the new coordinator. This forces all the participants to make a transition to the new coordinator's state. Once this happens and the new coordinator is in one of precommit or commits state then the transaction is committed, otherwise aborted.

Recovery Protocols in 3PC. The transaction's state at the instant of failure is determined by the log information in the 3PC.

3PC-Coordinator Recovery Process. A coordinator reads a log stored locally after it gets repaired to determine the state at the instant it failed.

3PC-Participant Recovery Process. A participant reads a log stored locally after it gets repaired to determine the state at the instant it failed. The participants' states in the 3PC are the same as in 2PC except the precommit state.

3 A Simulation of Performance of Commit Protocols

To ensure atomicity, we incorporate the use of atomic commit protocols. These protocols allow us to ensure whether the transaction commits or aborts or roll backs successfully. This paper simulates 3 types of atomic commit protocols and based on certain criteria they make sure that atomicity is guaranteed. An atomic commit is an operation in which a set of varied changes are applied as only one operation and if these changes are effective then it is said to be atomic commit otherwise if a failure comes before atomic commit occurs then all the changes in it are reversed. This guarantees a consistent state to the system. Another key property called isolation is required by atomic operations that ensures only one atomic commit is processed atone instant of time. Atomic commits [7] satisfies the two key **ACID** properties i.e. atomicity and consistency [6]. Consistency is achieved if each change in the atomic commit is consistent. As shown in the above example multi step operations require critical atomic commits. True atomic commits cannot exist due to hardware design of the physical disk on which the data resides. The smallest area that can be written to on disk is known as a sector. A single data entry may span several different sectors. Only one sector can be written at a time. The writing limit restricts the true atomic commits. After the data entries in memory have been modified they are queued for writing to the disk. Thus the Atomic Commit Protocols [9] are used to solve these problems of disk writes associated with atomic commits.

3.1 Process Logic

Below the working of the atomic commit protocols is given through which atomicity and consistency can be achieved.

One- phase commit protocol: A client can request the operation at more than one server in a distributed environment. A transaction completes when a client commits or aborts it. One way to atomically complete the is to allow the coordinator communicate the commit or abort request to the participants involved in the transaction and keep repeating this request until it is acknowledged by all participants. This is called one-phase atomic commit protocol. Coordinator - The coordinator is an entity that commits or abort or rollbacks a transaction. Participant - The participant handles the transaction and waits for the coordinators to commit or rollback.

Two- phase commit protocol: This protocol has two phases. First phase is Commit-request phase (Voting phase) - In this phase a coordinator attempts to prepare all participating processes called participants (workers or cohorts). Every participant can vote either Yes or No in this phase depending on whether they want to participate or not. The second phase is called Commit phase. In this phase the coordinator decides whether to commit or abort the transaction based on voting of the participants. It then notifies the result to all the participants.

Three- phase commit protocol: The 3PC is a distributed non-blocking algorithm since it places an upper bound on the amount of time required before a transaction either commits or aborts to ensure if a given transaction is attempting to commit via 3PC holds some resource locks. If so it is made to release the locks after the timeout. The steps taken by the Coordinator are as follows: 1) On receiving a transaction request the coordinator aborts it in case of a failure at this point. Otherwise, the coordinator sends a **canCommit** and enters in wait state. 2) If there is a failure, timeout, or if the coordinator receives a **No** message in the wait state, the coordinator aborts the transaction and sends an **abort** message to all participants. If the coordinator receives **Yes** messages from all participants within the time window then it sends **preCommit** message to all participants and enters in prepared state. 3) If the coordinator succeeds in the prepared state, it will move to the commit state. However if the coordinator times out while waiting for an acknowledgement from a participant, it will abort the transaction. In the case where all acknowledgements are received, the coordinator enters in commit state as well. The steps carried out by a Participant are as follows: 1). The participant receives a **canCommit** message from the coordinator. If the participant agrees it sends a **Yes** message to the coordinator and moves to the prepared state. Otherwise it sends a **No** message and aborts. If there is a failure, it enters in abort state. 2) In the prepared state, if the participant receives an **abort** message from the coordinator, fails, or times out waiting for a commit, it aborts. If the participant receives a **preCommit** message, it sends an ACK message back.

4 System Design

The above figure depicts the System Architecture of Commit Protocols. It consists of a transaction processor, data processor and local data of each processor. A transaction processor (or transaction manager or coordinator) will distribute the transaction to be executed on multiple data processors (participants) and coordinate the transaction to maintain the data consistency and atomicity. The data processor will execute the transaction by using its local data and responds to the transaction processor request. A distributed transaction allows a transaction to reference several different local or remote data processor sites. The following figures depict the design (activity and state diagrams) of the 3 PC atomic commit protocol. All the three protocols 1 PC, 2 PC and 3 PC were simulated. But the design and output screens corresponding to 3 PC are given below due to space constraints.

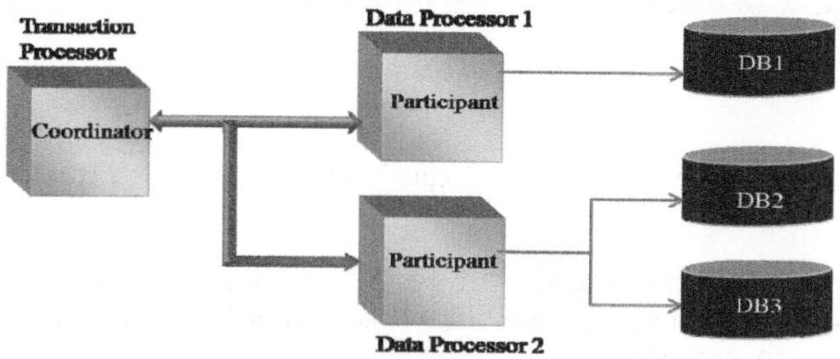

Fig. 1. System Architecture for Commit Protocol

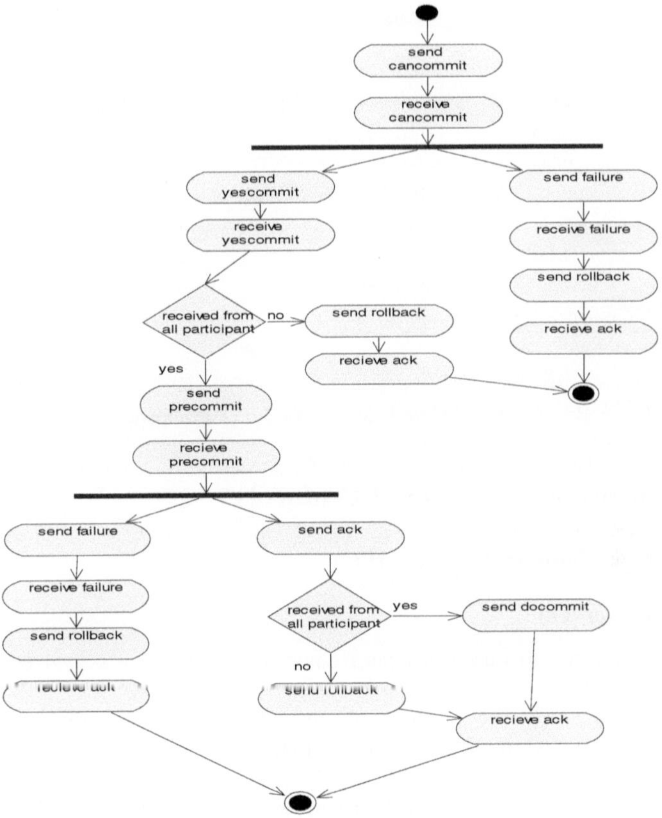

Fig. 2. Activity Diagram for 3PC

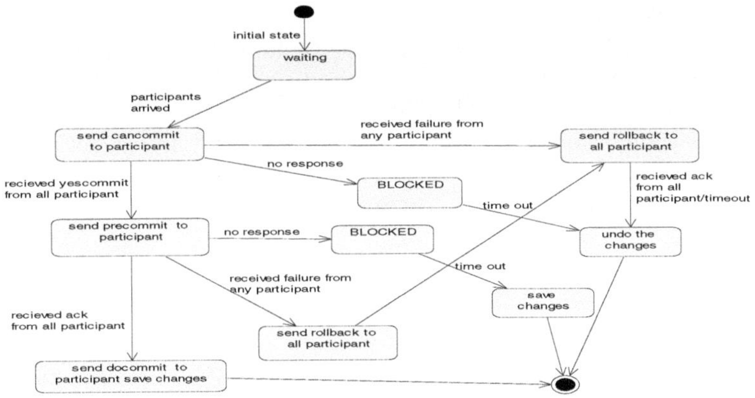

Fig. 3. State Diagram for 3PC Coordinator

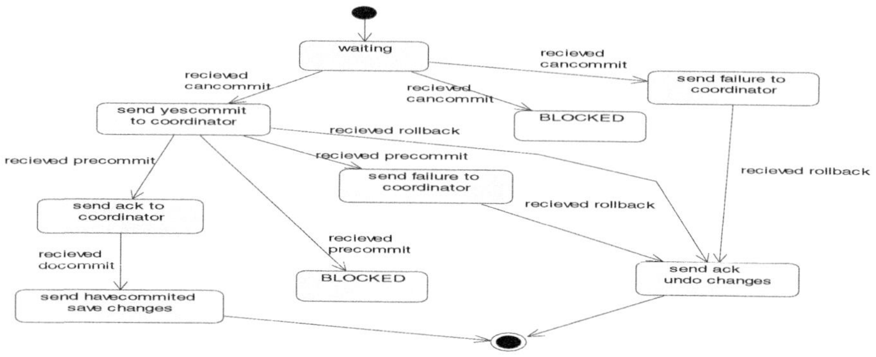

Fig. 4. State Diagram for 3PC Participant

5 Implementation of Commit Protocols

5.1 One Phase Commit Protocol (1PC)

Coordinator (Server)

1. The Coordinator first takes as input the number of participant's involved or taking part in the session.
2. Depending upon the number of participant's, the coordinator generates a variable transaction which involves modifying a variable value, by taking input from the user.
3. It then divides the task into the relative amount of participant's available and sends each of them the data.
4. The coordinator then asks the user whether the user wants to simulate the transaction as a commit or rollback, by taking input from the keyboard as "1" or "0" respectively.
5. After a certain considerable amount of time, the coordinator initiates the commit or rollback functionality by sending each of the participants's either a commit message or a rollback message.
6. The coordinator after sending the message waits for an acknowledgement from each.
7. of the participant's and it goes into a commit or rollback state and terminates.

Participant (Client)

1. The participant first takes as input the port number from the user to connect to the coordinator by using a unique id.
2. After establishing connection with the coordinator, the participant waits for a task to be given by the coordinator.
3. Upon receiving the task, it starts the execution of the transaction, by asking a variable number to be entered by the user for modification.
4. It makes changes to the variable my making a temporary copy. It performs all modifications on this shadow copy.

5. After a certain considerable amount of time, the coordinator issues either a commit or rollback message.
6. The participant checks the message, if it's a Commit, it assigns the temporary variable value to the original value and makes the changes and sends acknowledgement of the success to the coordinator.
7. If the message received is Rollback, it makes no changes to the original value and just sends an acknowledgement to the coordinator and keeps the original value as it is.
8. After sending the respective acknowledgement to the coordinator the participant moves into either the commit or rollback state and terminates.

5.2 Two Phase Commit Protocol (2PC)

Coordinator (Server)

1. The Coordinator first takes as input the number of participant's involved or taking part in the session.
2. Depending upon the number of participant's, the coordinator generates a variable transaction which involves modifying a variable value, by taking input from the user.
3. It then divides the task into the relative amount of participant's available and sends each of them the data.
4. The coordinator then asks the user whether the user wants to simulate the coordinator crashing, by taking input from the keyboard as "1" or "0".
5. If the input for simulating the coordinator crashing is "1" i.e. a "YES" then the coordinator enters a "BLOCKED" state and the protocol fails.
6. After a certain considerable amount of time, the coordinator initiates the commit or rollback functionality by sending each of the participants's a "CAN COMMIT?" message indicating the beginning of the voting phase.
7. After sending the can commit message, the coordinator waits for all the participants to vote, if the entire participant's vote a "YES COMMIT" , the coordinator moves into second phase.
8. If anyone of the participants votes a "FAILURE", then the coordinator sends the entire participant's a "Rollback" message and waits for acknowledgements. The state is changed to Roll backed and the coordinator then terminates.
9. Else if the participant's vote a yes commit, then phase 2 begins where the coordinator now sends a "Commit" message and waits for acknowledgements.
10. After the 2nd phase completes the state is changed to Commit and the coordinator terminates.

Participant (Client)

1. The participant first takes as input the port number from the user to connect to the coordinator by using a unique id.
2. The participant also asks the user whether the user wants to simulate participant crashing before the voting phase, by taking an input from the keyboard either "1" or "0".

3. If the input for simulating the participant crashing is “1” i.e. a “YES” then the participant enters a “BLOCKED” state and the protocol fails.
4. After establishing connection with the coordinator, the participant waits for a task to be given by the coordinator.
5. Upon receiving the task, it starts the execution of the transaction, by asking a variable number to be entered by the user for modification.
6. It makes changes to the variable my making a temporary copy. It performs all modifications on this shadow copy.
7. After a certain considerable amount of time, the coordinator issues a “CAN COMMIT?” message which initiates the voting phase.
8. The participant’s make use of the random function present in the math class to choose a random number. Using this random number the participant decides whether to send “YES COMMIT” or “FAILURE” to the coordinator.
9. If the participant decides based on the random value to send “YES COMMIT”, the message is sent to the coordinator and the participant waits for a reply.
10. If the If the participant decides based on the random value to send “FAILURE”, the message is sent to the coordinator and the participant waits for a reply.
11. The participant receives a message, if it’s a Commit, it assigns the temporary variable value to the original value and makes the changes and sends acknowledgement of the success to the coordinator.
12. If the message received is Rollback, it makes no changes to the original value and just sends an acknowledgement to the coordinator and keeps the original value as it is.
13. After sending the respective acknowledgement to the coordinator the participant moves into either the commit or rollback state and terminates.

5.3 Two Phase Commit Protocol (2PC with Modification)

Coordinator (Server)

1. The Coordinator first takes as input the number of participant’s involved or taking part in the session.
2. Depending upon the number of participant’s, the coordinator generates a variable transaction which involves modifying a variable value, by taking input from the user.
3. It then divides the task into the relative amount of participant’s available and sends each of them the data.
4. The coordinator then asks the user whether the user wants to simulate the coordinator crashing, by taking input from the keyboard as “1” or “0”.
5. If the input for simulating the coordinator crashing is “1” i.e. a “YES” then the coordinator enters a “BLOCKED” state and the protocol fails.
6. After a certain considerable amount of time, the coordinator initiates the commit or rollback functionality by sending each of the participants’s a “CAN COMMIT?” message indicating the beginning of the voting phase.
7. After sending the can commit message, the coordinator waits for all the participants to vote, if the entire participant’s vote a “YES COMMIT” , the coordinator moves into second phase.

8. If anyone of the participants votes a "FAILURE", then the coordinator sends the entire participant's a "Rollback" message and waits for acknowledgements. The state is changed to Roll backed and the coordinator then terminates.
9. If any of the participant's do not reply due to crashing, the coordinator has a timeout which when completes if a reply is not received by the coordinator from the participant, the coordinator assumes the participant is unresponsive and replies all other participant's to "ROLL BACK" and waits for acknowledgements and then terminates.
10. Else if the participant's vote a yes commit, then phase 2 begins where the coordinator now sends a "Commit" message and waits for acknowledgements.
11. After the 2nd phase completes the state is changed to Commit and the coordinator terminates.

Participant (Client)

1. The participant first takes as input the port number from the user to connect to the coordinator by using a unique id.
2. The participant also asks the user whether the user wants to simulate participant crashing before the voting phase, by taking an input from the keyboard either "1" or "0".
3. If the input for simulating the participant crashing is "1" i.e. a "YES" then the participant enters a "BLOCKED" state.
4. This "BLOCKED" state does not allow participant to send/receive any message or proceed further. While the coordinator maintains a timeout for this particular case, if the participant is unresponsive it sends all other participant's a "Roll back" message and upon whose arrival all other responsive participant's "Roll back", it makes no changes to the original value and just sends an acknowledgement to the coordinator and keeps the original value as it is and terminates.
5. After establishing connection with the coordinator, the participant waits for a task to be given by the coordinator.
6. Upon receiving the task, it starts the execution of the transaction, by asking a variable number to be entered by the user for modification.
7. It makes changes to the variable my making a temporary copy. It performs all modifications on this shadow copy.
8. After a certain considerable amount of time, the coordinator issues a "CAN COMMIT?" message which initiates the voting phase.
9. The participant's make use of the random function present in the math class to choose a random number. Using this random number the participant decides whether to send "YES COMMIT" or "FAILURE" to the coordinator.
10. If the participant decides based on the random value to send "YES COMMIT", the message is sent to the coordinator and the participant waits for a reply.
11. If the If the participant decides based on the random value to send "FAILURE", the message is sent to the coordinator and the participant waits for a reply.
12. The participant receives a message, if it's a Commit, it assigns the temporary variable value to the original value and makes the changes and sends acknowledgement of the success to the coordinator.

13. If the message received is Rollback, it makes no changes to the original value and just sends an acknowledgement to the coordinator and keeps the original value as it is.
14. After sending the respective acknowledgement to the coordinator the participant moves into either the commit or rollback state and terminates.

5.4 Three Phase Commit Protocol (3PC)

Coordinator (Server)

1. The Coordinator first takes as input - number of participant's involved in the session.
2. Depending upon the number of participant's, the coordinator generates a variable transaction which involves modifying a variable value, by taking input from the user.
3. It then divides the task into relative amount of participant's and sends them the data.
4. The coordinator then asks the user whether the user wants to simulate the coordinator crashing after "YES COMMIT", by taking input from the keyboard as "1" or "0".
5. The coordinator then asks the user whether the user wants to simulate the coordinator crashing after "PRE COMMIT", by taking input from the keyboard as "1" or "0".
6. After a certain considerable amount of time, the coordinator initiates the commit or rollback functionality by sending each of the participants's a "CAN COMMIT?" message indicating the beginning of the voting phase.
7. After sending the can commit message, the coordinator waits for all the participants to vote, if the entire participant's vote a "YES COMMIT" , the coordinator moves into second phase.
8. If anyone of the participants votes a "FAILURE", then the coordinator sends the entire participant's a "Rollback" message and waits for acknowledgements. The state is changed to Roll backed and the coordinator then terminates.
9. If any of the participant's do not reply due to crashing, the coordinator has a timeout which when completes if a reply is not received by the coordinator from the participant, the coordinator assumes the participant is unresponsive and replies all other participant's to "ROLL BACK" and waits for acknowledgements and then terminates.
10. Else if the participant's vote a yes commit, then phase 2 begins where the coordinator now sends a "Commit" message and waits for acknowledgements.
11. If the user asked for simulating the coordinator crashing after "YES COMMIT", then the coordinator gets "BLOCKED".
12. This "BLOCKED" state does not allow coordinator to send/receive any message or proceed further. While the participant maintains a timeout for this particular case, if the coordinator is unresponsive, all other participant's "Roll back" by default and terminate.
13. Else the 2nd phase begins the, in this phase the coordinator sends a message to the participant saying "PRE COMMIT", now the coordinator waits for the participants to send acknowledgements.

14. If the user asked for simulating the coordinator crashing after "PRE COMMIT", then the coordinator gets "BLOCKED".
15. This "BLOCKED" state does not allow coordinator to send/receive any message or proceed further. While the participant maintains a timeout for this particular case, if the coordinator is unresponsive, all other participant's "COMMIT" by default and terminate.
16. Else the 3rd phase begins where the coordinator now sends a "Commit" message and waits for acknowledgements.
17. After the 3rd phase completes the state is changed to Commit and the coordinator terminates.

Participant (Client)

1. The participant first takes as input the port number from the user to connect to the coordinator by using a unique id.
2. The participant also asks the user whether the user wants to simulate participant crashing before the voting phase i.e. "YES COMMIT", by taking an input from the keyboard either "1" or "0".
3. If the input for simulating the participant crashing is "1" i.e. a "YES" then the participant enters a "BLOCKED" state.
4. This "BLOCKED" state does not allow participant to send/receive any message or proceed further. While the coordinator maintains a timeout for this particular case, if the participant is unresponsive it sends all other participant's a "Roll back" message and upon whose arrival all other responsive participant's "Roll back", it makes no changes to the original value and just sends an acknowledgement to the coordinator and keeps the original value as it is and terminates.
5. The participant also asks the user whether the user wants to simulate participant crashing before the acknowledgement of. "PRE COMMIT", by taking an input either "1" or "0".
6. If the input for simulating the participant crashing is "1" i.e. a "YES" then the participant enters a "BLOCKED" state.
7. This "BLOCKED" state does not allow participant to send/receive any message or proceed further. While the coordinator maintains a timeout for this particular case, if the participant is unresponsive it sends all other participant's a "Roll back", it makes no changes to the original value and just sends an acknowledgement to the coordinator and keeps the original value as it is and terminates.
8. After establishing connection with the coordinator, the participant waits for a task to be given by the coordinator.
9. Upon receiving the task, it starts the execution of the transaction, by asking a variable number to be entered by the user for modification.
10. It makes changes to a temporary(shadow) copy of variable and performs all modifications.
11. After a certain considerable amount of time, the coordinator issues a "CAN COMMIT?" message which initiates the voting phase.
12. The participant's make use of the random function present in the math class to choose a random number. Using this random number the participant decides whether to send "YES COMMIT" or "FAILURE" to the coordinator.

13. If the participant decides based on the random value to send "YES COMMIT", the message is sent to the coordinator and the participant waits for a reply.
14. If after sending "YES COMMIT" the reply received is "PRE COMMIT" then the participant's make use of the random function present in the math class to choose a random number. Using this random number the participant decides whether to send "ACK" or "FAILURE" to the coordinator.
15. Else if the message received is Rollback, it makes no changes to the original value and just sends an acknowledgement to the coordinator and keeps the original value as it is.
16. If the participant received "PRE COMMIT" then it decides based on the random value to send "ACK", the message is sent to the coordinator and the participant waits for a reply.
17. If reply received is "COMMIT" then the participant commits and assigns the temporary var value to the original value making changes and sends ack of the success to the coordinator.
18. If the message received is Rollback, it makes no changes to the original value and just sends an acknowledgement to the coordinator and keeps the original value as it is.
19. After sending the respective acknowledgement to the coordinator the participant moves into either the commit or rollback state and terminates.

6 Experiments and Results

Table 6.1 shows the states of 3 PC based on inputs from the user. If none of the coordinator or participant crashes then the output state is either "COMMIT" or "ROLL BACK". If coordinator fails after yes commit then the state is "ROLLBACK" and if it fails after pre-commit then the state is "COMMIT". If the participant fails before yes commit then the state is "ROLL BACK" and if the participant fails before sending acknowledgement of pre commit then the state is "ROLL BACK". The remaining combinations are shown in the table and some combinations have no action as there combination cannot exist.

Table 1. Three phase commit protocol Test Case

	COORDINATOR FAILING(AFTER YES COMMIT)	COORDINATOR FAILING(AFTER PRE COMMIT)	PARTICIPANT FAILING(BEFORE YES COMMIT)	PARTICIPANT FAILING(BEFORE ACK OF PRE COMMIT)	STATUS OF THE TRANSACTION
3PC COMMIT PROTOCOL	NO	NO	NO	NO	COMMIT/ROLL BACK
	YES	NO	NO	NO	ROLLBACK
	NO	YES	NO	NO	COMMIT
	NO	NO	YES	NO	ROLLBACK
	NO	NO	NO	YES	ROLLBACK
	YES	NO	YES	NO	ROLLBACK
	NO	YES	NO	YES	COMMIT
	YES	YES	YES	YES	ROLLBACK

6.2 Output Screen Shots

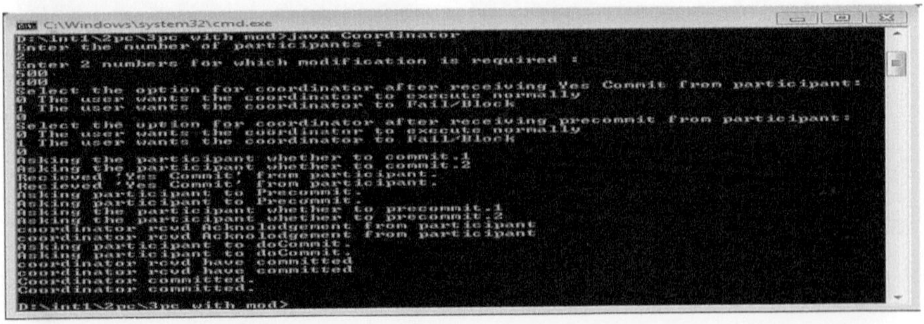

Screen 1. Three Phase Commit Protocol - 3PC Commit State (Coordinator)

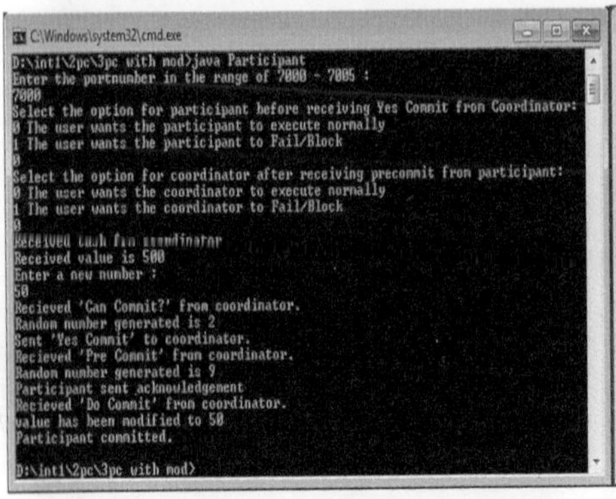

Screen 2. Participant1

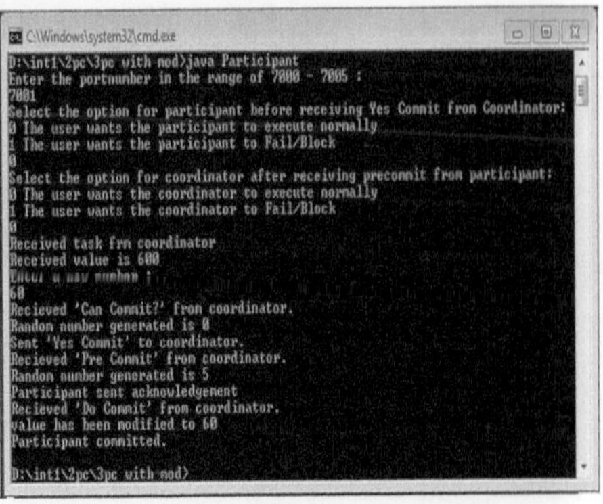

Screen 3. Participant2

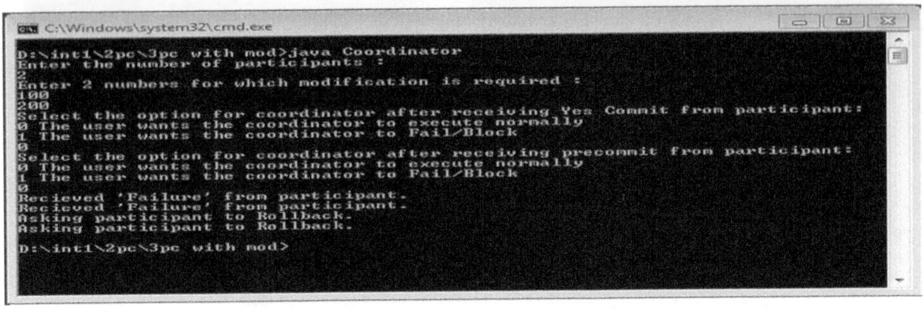

Screen 4. 3PC Rollback State after Yes Commit (Coordinator)

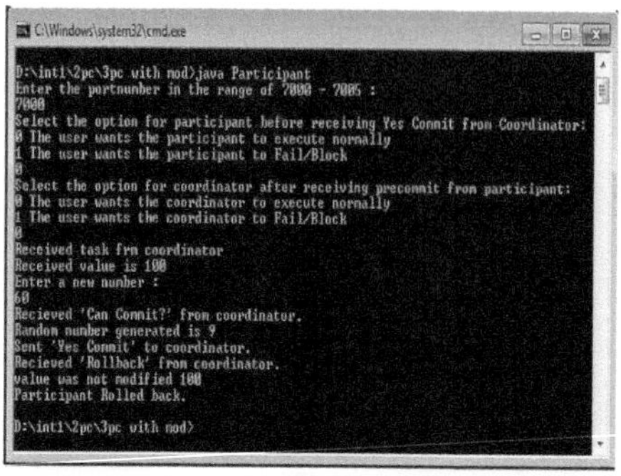

Screen 5. Participant 1

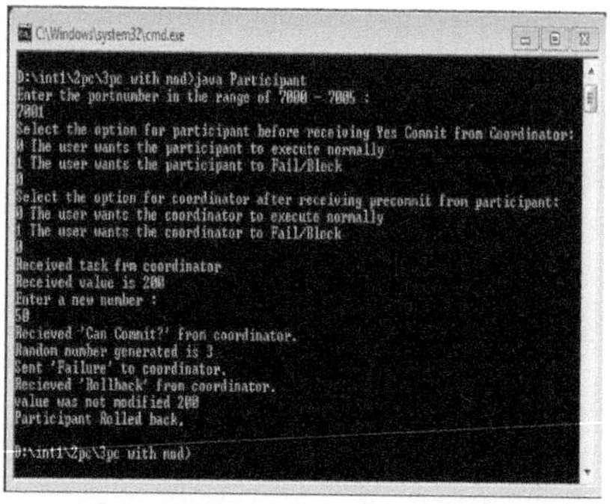

Screen 6. Patticipant 2

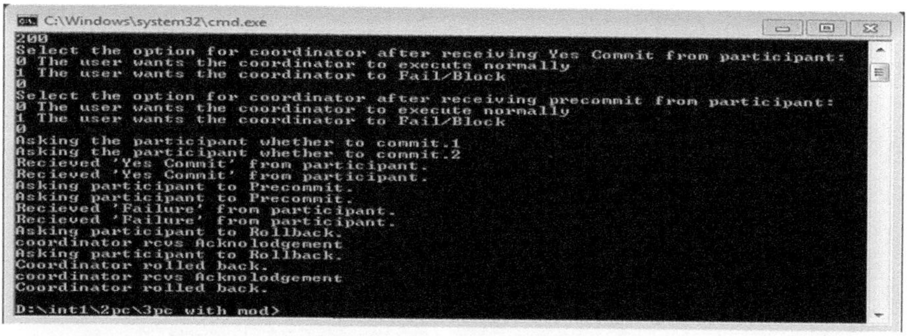

Screen 7. 3PC Rollback State after Pre Commit - Coordinator

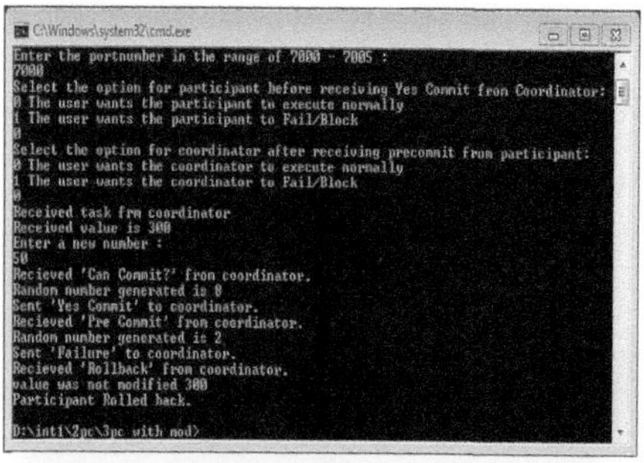

Screen 8. Participant1

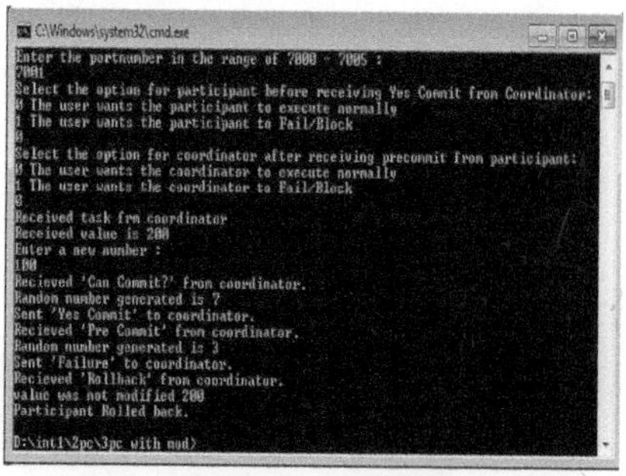

Screen 9. Participant2

7 Conclusion and Future Work

We have simulated the atomic commit protocols namely one-phase commit, two-phase commit and three-phase commit protocols which are required to maintain atomicity and consistency in a distributed environment. These protocols are used in a number of applications including Banking, Trading shares of stock, Insurance application, Inventory control to record orders, Manufacturing, Retail to record sales, Government for registration of an automobile, Online shopping, Transportation to track shipment, Telecommunications, Military Command and Control and many more. The future work includes optimizing the basic set of commit protocols simulated in this paper. The optimizations can be applied to two-phase commit protocol and three-phase commit protocol. The most famous variants for 2PC are Tree 2PC commit protocol (Nested or Recursive 2PC) and Dynamic two-phase commit (D2PC) and with regard to 3PC an enhanced three phase commit (E3PC).

References

[1] Coulouris, G., Dollimore, J., Kindberg, T.: Distributed Systems Concepts and Design, ch. 1,2,4,6,12,13. Addison Wesley Publishers, Reading ISBN 7-111-11749-2
[2] Rahimi, S.K., Haug, F.S.: Distributed Database Management Systems, ch. 8. A John Wiley & Sons, Inc., Chichester ISBN 977-0-470-40745-5
[3] Bernstein, P.A., Newcomer, E.: Principles of Transaction Processing, 2nd edn., ch. 7. Morgan Kaufmann, San Francisco ISBN 977-1-55760-623-4
[4] Bernstein, P.A., Hadzilacos, V., Goodman, N.: Concurrency Control and Recovery in Database Systems, ch. 7. Addison Wesley Publishing Company, Reading (1977) ISBN 0-201-10715-5
[5] Booch, G., Rumbaugh, J., Jacobson, I.: The Unified Modeling Language User Guide. Pearson Education, London
[6] Mohan, C., Lindsay, B., Obermarck, R.: Transaction management in the distributed database management system. ACM Trans.on Database Systems 11(4) (1986)
[7] Mohan, C., Narang, I.: Recovery and coherency.– control protocols for fast inter- system page transfer and fine-granularity locking in a shared disks transaction environment. In: Proceedings of 17th International Conference on Very Large Databases, pp. 193–207 (September 1991)
[8] Park, T., Yeom, H.Y.: A consistent group commits protocol for distributed database systems. In: Parallel and Distributed Computing Systems (August 1999)
[9] Rahm, E.: Recovery concepts for data sharing systems. In: Proceedings of the 21st International Conference on Fault-Tolerant Computing (FTCS-21), pp. 109–123 (June 1991)

Biomedical Informatics Data Modeling of the 911 Call Center at Newark, New Jersey, USA

Arif M. Rana, Syed S. Haque, and Syed V. Ahamed

Department of Health Informatics
University of Medicine and Dentistry of New Jersey
School of Health Related Professions
Newark, New Jersey, USA

Abstract. This paper discusses a Biomedical Informatics statistical data model for a 911 Call Center (911CC) patient care response times at Newark, New Jersey, USA. Study of the techniques used in collecting the patient's arrival/service times, analyzing the arrival/service time using statistical techniques, and developing Biomedical Informatics statistical distributions which has 95% goodness of fit level (confidence level $\alpha = 95\%$) is proposed. The derived statistical distributions are further used in modeling the Biomedical Informatics fast data network to further research the delay in the response time for the critical care patient serviced by the 911CC. These statistical models are also used in modeling how effectively a Biomedical Informatics network model can electronically distribute the patient condition and the associated medical data to relevant participants of the 911CC process, namely the Emergency Medical Technicians (EMT), doctors, nurses, and the appropriate hospital authorities.

Keywords: 911 Call Center, Biomedical Informatics, Critical Care Patient, Data/Network Model, K-S Test, Q-Q Plots, Response Times, and Statistical Distributions.

1 Introduction

The problems facing a 911CC in any metropolitan city are complex. The population in these cities is growing rampantly due to geo-economical situations. As a result, the traffic is rising at an alarming rate, hence congestion occurs. This in turn causes the 911CC to be less effective in transporting critical care patients from their homes to a nearby hospital/medical facility so that they can receive medical treatment.

The Emergency Medical Services (EMS) is lightly to moderately equipped to handle a 911CC patient's health situation; they have walkie-talkies, and some basic CPR equipments, oxygen tanks, etc, to mobilize the condition of the patient. This is not adequate enough to provide a good care to the critically injured patient [1].

Literature has reported that patients with severe chest pains require basic emergency health care to be provided on-site in order for them to survive [2]. For that

D. Nagamalai, E. Renault, and M. Dhanushkodi (Eds.): PDCTA 2011, CCIS 203, pp. 682–691, 2011.

to happen, a fast mode of data network communication between the ambulance, hospital, and the patient health care database has to be designed. The first part of this design is to develop a statistical model to quantify the arrival/service pattern of the 911CC patients using a statistical distribution. The results obtained should be used in conjunction with the descriptive patient information obtained as provided in [3]. The continued part of this work is to use these results in developing a fast wired/wireless network to transfer vital information about 911CC patients to the hospitals/service centers to accomplish better care.

This paper focuses on the first part of the solution, viz., the arrival/departure statistical modeling of the 911CC patients. In this paper, how statistical techniques are used in modeling the arrival/processing timing of 911CC patients as a discrete event process is proposed. Subsequently the discrete event model obtained is used in developing network simulations to further design a fast wired/wireless network so that 911CC patients can receive quick and adequate medical care.

Real time calls and their associated data, an exhaustive data collection mechanism about real calls from the 911CC patients, were collected from Newark, NJ, USA for the years 2004-2006. The collected data was massaged into a meaningful columnar data and subsequently used in developing a Biomedical Informatics statistical model.

The tools used to obtain the Biomedical Informatics statistical model in this study, involves statistical techniques such as the Kolmogorov-Smimov (K-S) test, Q-Q plot, and Chi-Square Goodness-of-Fit test [4, 5]. The paper is outlined as follows: Section 2 provides the problem statement, Section 3 details the 911CC process, Section 4 discusses Biomedical Informatics data collection, Section 5 provides the Biomedical Informatics data modeling, Section 6 provides patient arrival/service distribution model results, and Section 7 concludes the paper based on the tabulated results.

2 Problem Statement

The 911CC patients go through a very time consuming and elaborate process before they are treated at the hospital. Section 3 provides the comprehensive list of stages in this process from the time the initial call is made to a 911CC up until the time the patient is left at the hospital or in the hands of a care taker.

The problem of a 911CC is to provide prompt and adequate emergency care to its callers. The issues involved in this problem are multi-fold:

- Population in Newark is increasing at an alarming rate, causing traffic congestion, which results into transportation delays. Emergency care suffers as a result.
- Time used to transport patients from pickup site to the emergency medical care facility is too long for critically care patients. Emergency care suffers as a result.

- Detailed information about the patient's condition and/or medical history is not fully available to the doctors and nurses until the patient has been transported to the medical facility. Emergency care suffers as a result.

This paper addresses the Biomedical Informatics data modeling of 911CC patients as defined in the following stages: (i) data collection; (ii) data massaging, and; (iii) data analysis using statistical means.

Similar studies [6, 7] in the literature were conducted which focuses primarily on patients being serviced by the hospital only, and not in the context of a 911 call center set-up. Our study happens to be unique in its scope and research and primarily focuses on the general issues and problems faced by metropolitan cities in providing quality 911CC support to its residents. Hence, the general methodology presented in this paper can be applied to any metropolitan city where 911CC issues exist.

To address the aforementioned issues, the following strategy is proposed:

1. Identify the 911CC process at Newark, NJ, USA and determine the proper data columns that need to be analyzed and validated.
2. The data collection from the 911CC authority, which is confidential and governed by a Privacy Act, needs to be analyzed by developing appropriate scripts to extract and understand the meaning of the data.
3. Extracted data needs to be analyzed using statistical techniques and results to be validated by visual inspection and statistical tools.
4. Results obtained are used to further develop wired/wireless networks in conjunction with pre-existing networks in the metropolitan city. Subsequent network modeling will depend on the results from the data modeling work as presented here and network results will not be discussed in this paper.

3 The 911CC Process

This section provides details of the processes and stages a patient using the 91CC goes through before he/she is admitted to a hospital facility (Figure 1):

(i) Stage 1: The patient who needs help contacts the 911CC;
(ii) Stage 2: The 911CC upon receiving the request calls the nearest ambulance and provides detailed information about the patient;
(iii) Stage 3: The ambulance arrives at the patient location and does a preliminary assessment;
(iv) Stage 4: If further medical care is needed and/or required, the patient is loaded into the ambulance and transported to the nearest medical facility;
(v) Stage 5: While patient is in transit, the ambulance calls the medical facility relaying basic patient information and status;
(vi) Stage 6: The patient is transported to the medical facility for complete tests and evaluation.

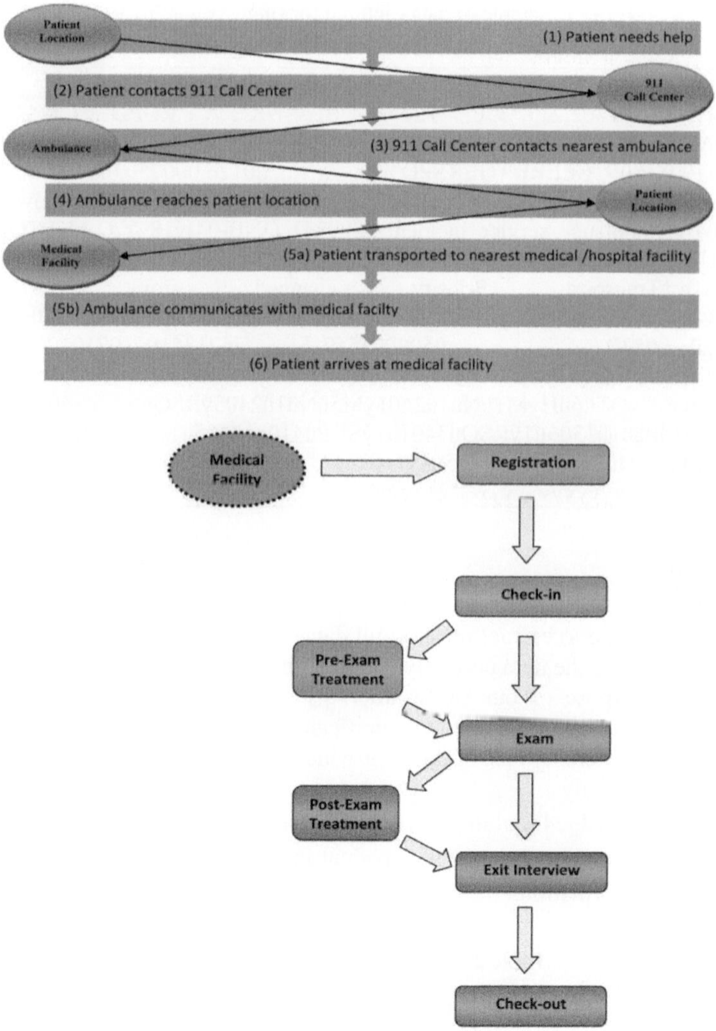

Fig. 1. 911CC patient process

4 Biomedical Informatics Data Collection

Real time data was collected for these stages from the 911CC at Newark, New Jersey for the years 2004-2006. A total of 167 columns of data for each patient was collected and stored in the Emergency Medical Services database. The raw data collected is in the form of text separated by commas as seen in Table 1. This data as seen in the table shows the complexity involved in understanding and extracting the meaningful data for further analysis.

Table 1. Sample of data captured for single patient by 911CC

Snippet of one row element of data
5009341,13542,1402,213,"350 KING BLV-NK","A","RUPD",,"CW","H107-ST MICHAELSMC","B","26B01",84561,84940,84995,85536,86369,88,,1897,379,55,54 1,833,119,0,1809,"SEERUTGERSPD",,,,,,,,,,,,1,,,,,,,0126,000750,0537,0743,0573,,4, 0743,13542,84598,,9733535582,,,,"Nature: 26B01-Sick Person/Unknown status (JNB-04)ýAmbulance service incident 5009341 (JNB-04)ý18 Y/O/M ETOH (JNB-04)ýRUTGERS POLICE ON SCENE (JNB-04)ýPROQA FAILURE-CARDS USED (JNB-04)ý*Transport Priority changed from (JTH-17)","84598ý84598ý84613ý84617ý84618ý5",,"NK",,,,1,10,9,,,,,,0,0,,,,"350 MLK",,0,,,,,0537,,,,,,,,,,,,,,,,,,,,,,,,,0500006569,,6,,,,,,,"74213510ý40710100","74176560ý40742150","74177760ý40741410",,,0,"CWü1ü1ü1402ü1ü1306ýSü2üHýNü3üHýWü4üHýEü5üHýDTü6üHýM1üNü1ü2401ýM5üNü1ü2405ýRSQüNü1ü3401ýIBüNü1üIB","CWü1402ü1ü1306ü1ýRSQü3401ü1ýSUPü410ü1ü405ü1ýýý405ü1ý2401ü1ý3401ü1ý410ü1ý1404ü2ý1306ü1ý2405ü1ý1402ü1","6ý10ýBLSý9ü0ü0ý1ü0ü0ý0ý1ý0ý1",13542,,,,,,,"ýýýýýýýýýýýýýýý","214ýýý",,,,,,,,,,,,,,,,,,,,,07103,,,

The complexity of the collected data prompted us to develop specialized scripts using Perl language to extract meaningful data. Perl is a powerful scripting language and is used to parse the data perfectly to extract the chosen columns.

For the purpose of our study, after discussing with the EMS authorities the importance of each column and their significance, we selected 24 different columns of data that was of interest to us. Table 2 provides the columns of data fields used in this study for further analysis.

The selected 24 columns are divided into two groups: Group 1 provides general information about the 911CC patient information and; Group 2 addresses the patient arrival information.

Table 2. Relevant fields extracted for study

Group 1 Field	Group 1 Field Description
ID	Patient ID
DATE.REC	Date of call received
GRID	Grid number of call placed
LOCATION	Physical address of call placed to EMS
PRIORITY	Priority of call received
INIT.BY	Initiator of call made to EMS
TRANS.TO	Facility patient transported to
TRANS.PRI	Transportation priority level
PAT.COND	Condition of patient determined by EMS
Group 2 Field	**Group 2 Field Description**
RECEIVED	T1: Time call was received
DISPATCHED	T2: Time call was dispatched to EMS
ENROUTE	T3: Time EMS started in route to patient

Table 2. (Continued)

ON.SCENE	T4: Time EMS arrived at patient location
TRANSPORT	T5: Time EMS left patient location
ARRIVAL	T6: Time EMS arrived at hospital facility
AVAIL1	T7: Time EMS became available
AVAILABLE	T8: Time EMS became available
ELAP1	T2-T1: DISPATCHED - RECEIVED
ELAP2	T3-T2: ENROUTE - DISPATCHED
ELAP3	T4-T3: ON.SCENE - ENROUTE
ELAP4	T5-T4: TRANSPORT - ON.SCENE
ELAP5	T6-T5: ARRIVAL - TRANSPORT

These two groups of data capture vital information about the issues involving the 911CC patients. This data is critical to our study. Group 1 fields provide descriptive nature of information about the 911CC patients. Group 2 fields provide important data about service/arrival timings of 911CC patients from home to a hospital facility. This is used in developing our Biomedical Informatics statistical data model.

5 Biomedical Informatics Data Modeling

In this paper, variables in Group 2 of the data collected were used to further analyze the arrival/service/patient care timing information. The data modeling of the variables in Group 2 data was addressed as follows:

1) First the data is ordered into several bins. Each bin is a representation of the amount of time that has elapsed before the next sampling time interval is used in analyzing the data. In a single day consisting of 86400 seconds (24*60*60), calls are received at different times by the 911CC. If we select the sampling interval (bin size) of 40 minutes length i.e., 2400 seconds apart and collect calls within each interval or bin, a total of 480 bins in a day is available for analysis.
2) Calls in every bin are collected and their respective frequency/uni-variate statistics computed. The frequency and the bin size provide basic information to appropriately categorize the data into a proper distribution.
3) The frequency/bin interval is further used in plotting the data in the form of a frequency histogram. A visual inspection of the data is also performed.
4) The frequency histogram data is fitted against known distributions such as Weibull/Exponential/Gamma/Exponential and others.
5) To validate the distribution with quantifiable approaches, several statistical measures are used, such as Q-Q Plot, K-S test and the Chi Square test.
6) Based on good validation, the columnar data is categorically distributed by a known distribution which was then used in the network modeling of the Biomedical Informatics data network.

Using these techniques, the arrival/departure/service timing for 911CC patients were analyzed. The following section provides details on such analysis.

6 Patient Arrival and Service Distribution Model

In this section, a sample analysis of the ([ARRIVAL] – [RECEIVED]) timing is provided. The [RECEIVED] time is the time when the 911CC receives the call from the emergency care patient. The [ARRIVAL] time is the time when the ambulance reaches the hospital. The difference between the two times gives a good idea of how long it takes for a patient to reach the appropriate medical facility. Using the concept of bins and frequency obtained, the histogram of the data is visualized in Figure 2. The Q-Q plot and distribution fit results are captured in Figure 3 and Table 3 respectively.

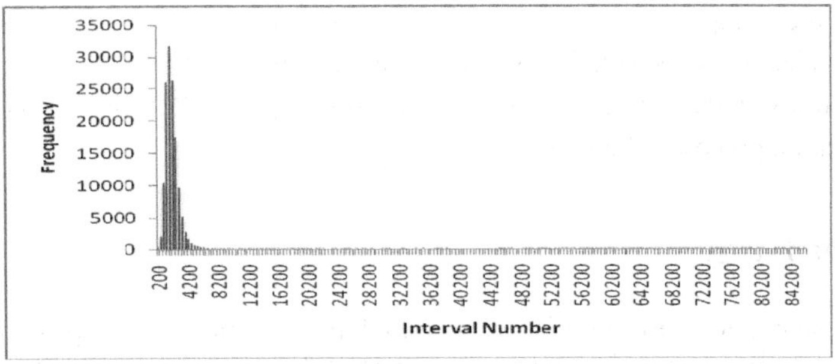

Fig. 2. ([ARRIVAL] – [RECEIVED]) frequency histogram

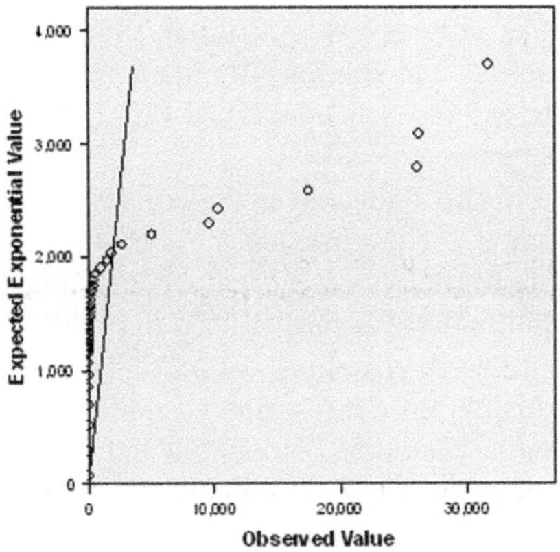

Fig. 3. ([ARRIVAL] – [RECEIVED]) QQ plot

Table 3. ([ARRIVAL] – [RECEIVED]) summary

Variable	Results
[ARRIVAL] – [RECEIVED]	Mean: 632.5231 seconds Distribution: Exponential Scale: 0.002

Based on the results provided in Table 3, it takes on average 632 seconds (10.5 minutes) for a patient to reach the hospital from the time a call is made to the Newark 91CC. This timing is critical when treating a 911CC patient who, for example suffers from acute cardio/chest pains. The chest pain patient needs to be attended to quickly; critical functionality of their health is directly correlated to delays in getting a quick response.

In comparison with the previous years of data, traffic congestion has played a big role in making this timing grow with each continuing year. Hence getting quality care to 911CC patients is at risk.

7 Results and Conclusions

Based on the analysis conducted on the chosen variables, similar results can be obtained for other variables. Table 4 provides a summarized result on some of the selected variables. This only provides the grim reality of how traffic congestion delays and the health of the patients are closely related.

Table 4. Summarized results of selected variables

Variable	Mean (seconds)	Distribution
RECEIVED	1344.6759	Weibull (1498.9, 3.6)
DISPATCHED	1255.8519	Weibull (1397.4, 3.7)
ENROUTE	1182.3889	Weibull (1314.8, 3.8)
ON.SCENE	1028.3889	Weibull (1140.5, 3.9)
TRANSPORT	632.6111	Weibull (700.7, 4.0)
ARRIVAL	632.5231	Weibull (701.2, 3.9)
AVAILABLE	1344.5602	Weibull (1500.3, 3.6)
ELAP1 (DISPATCHED – RECEIVED)	1255.5602	Exponential (.001)
ELAP2 (ENROUTE – DISPATCHED)	1182.3333	Exponential (.001)
ELAP3 (ON.SCENE - ENROUTE)	1028.3519	Exponential (.001)
ELAP4 (TRANSPORT - ON.SCENE)	632.5648	Exponential (.002)
ELAP5 (ARRIVAL - TRANSPORT)	632.4815	Exponential (.002)
ELAP8 (ARRIVAL – RECEIVED)	632.3935	Exponential (.002)
ELAP9 (AVAILABLE – RECEIVED)	1344.3519	Exponential (.001)

Hence the study and results we have obtained so far are used as parameters to simulate the real life model as a discrete event simulation of arrival/service behavior of a 911CC patient service system. This kind of analysis provides us a clear mathematical model of the data which was collected and analyzed. Subsequently, we were able to develop a Biomedical Informatics network model for the 911CC at Newark.

This study thus provided us with a mathematical model for discrete event simulation and the parameters needed for each variable. From this, we generated the arrival/service pattern of the 911CC process (the amount of time a patient undergoes from when their call is processed to when they are serviced at the hospital). Pictorially, we can represent the traffic, arrival/service behavior of all entities involved. The 911CC, hospitals, ambulance center, and patient's location are represented in Figure 4.

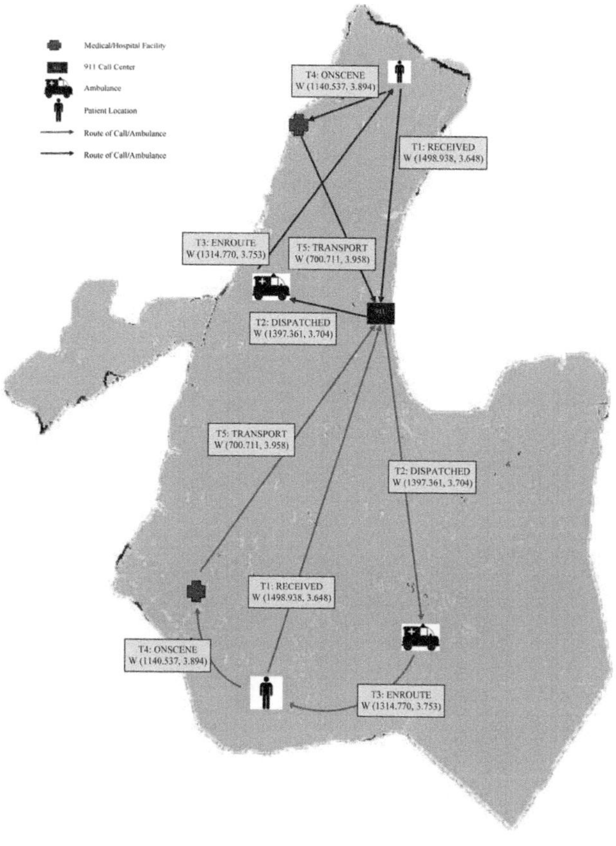

Fig. 4. Network model for the Newark 911CC

Patients suffering from different ailments are at the mercy of service times. Prompt attention and service will further aid in the patient's speedy treatment and recovery. Metropolitan congestion and the amount of time the patient has before he/she is attended by a physician stress the importance of critical care. In view of the findings, we suggest three possible ways to improve the overall response time in transporting the patient:

First, we propose that the ambulance office facility keep a dynamic look up of the routes most frequently travelled and alternate routes in a database and update by live traffic conditions such that when the location of the patient is identified, the updated route is also dispatched and suggested to the EMS drivers. In addition, GPS devices with the ambulance drivers should offer the shortest travel time rather than the short route in view of the type of emergency of the patient and the local traffic conditions.

Second, we propose that inter-operability of the technology used between all participants of the 911CC process be streamlined and data be transmitted in parallel rather than in series. This can be achieved by better understanding the current data/network model of the wired/wireless communications infrastructure and then implementing a better model through the use of optimized simulations.

Third, if the problem is perceived as a m (911 calls) line, n (medical centers) server problem, then the average waiting time ('t' with a single server) can be statistically reduced to ('t' / n) by increasing the servers. Appropriately designed medical networks will be able to compute the parameters for a quick response.

References

1. Data collected from the Newark, New Jersey UMDNJ EMS 911Call Center
2. Schull, M.J., Morrison, L.J., Vermeulen, M., Redelmeier, D.A.: Emergency department overcrowding and ambulance transport delays for patients with chest pain. Canadian Association Medical Journal 168(3), 277–283 (2003)
3. Rana, A.M.: A Generic Methodology to Design a Biomedical Informatics Data/Network Model for a 911 Call Center. University of Medicine and Dentistry of New Jersey, Doctoral Thesis (May 2011)
4. Walpole, R.E., Myers, R.H.: Probability and Statistics for Engineers. Macmillan, New York (1972)
5. Law, A.M., Kelton, W.D.: Simulation Modeling and Analysis, 2nd edn. McGraw-Hill, New York
6. Heller, M., Hogan, K.B., Appino, P.A., Cohon, J.L., Revelle, C.S.: An Emergency Medical Services Simulation Model for Baltimore City: An Overview. In: Proceedings of the 1982 Winter Simulation Conference, pp. 413–418 (1982)
7. Swisher, J.R., Jun, B., Jacobson, S.H., Balci, O.: Simulation of the Question Physician Network. In: 1997 Winter Simulation Conference Proceedings, pp. 1146–1157 (1997)

Author Index

Batch number: 10838023

Printed by Printforce, the Netherlands